'The Editors of *The Routledge Companion to Trust* should be congratulated for putting together an outstanding compendium of research and theory in the field of trust in the workplace. The contributors are leaders in the field and this work takes the field to a different league in terms of scholarship. This is a must buy for any academic, graduate student and practitioner interested in this very significant construct.'
— *Sir Cary L. Cooper, CBE, is the 50th Anniversary Professor of Organizational Psychology and Health at the University of Manchester, UK*

'This volume on trust offers an interdisciplinary review of the big insights, key studies, and critical unanswered questions. Trust me: if you're looking for a state-of-the-art guide to research in this area, you've come to the right place.'
— *Adam Grant, The Saul P. Steinberg Professor of Management and Psychology at Wharton, University of Pennsylvania, USA*

'Several decades of research has convincingly shown the role of trust as a catalyst in shaping organizational behavior and outcomes. This great volume brings together some of the latest thinking on trust and provides an excellent overview for researchers and practitioners alike.'
— *Ranjay Gulati, Unit Head, Organizational Behavior, Harvard Business School, USA*

'The topic of trust is foundational in organizational, political, and social life. This encyclopedic volume provides a comprehensive, research-based overview of what we know and what we need to know about trust in ways useful for both academics and practitioners. It is "everything you need to know about trust" in one carefully curated place.'
— *Jeffrey Pfeffer, Thomas D. Dee II Professor of Organizational Behavior, Graduate School of Business, Stanford University, USA*

'This *Routledge Companion to Trust* contains chapters reflecting the current state of thinking and research on trust. It is required reading for anyone engaged in trust theories, research, and practices. Trust me!'
— *Andrew H. Van de Ven, Professor Emeritus, University of Minnesota, USA*

THE ROUTLEDGE COMPANION
TO TRUST

In recent years, trust has enjoyed increasing interest from a wide range of parties, including organizations, policymakers, and the media. Perennially linked to turbulence and scandals, the damaging and rebuilding of trust is a contemporary concern affecting all areas of society.

Comprising six thematic sections, *The Routledge Companion to Trust* provides a comprehensive survey of trust research. With contributions from international experts, this volume examines the major topics and emerging areas within the field, including essays on the foundations, levels and theories of trust. It also examines trust repair and explores trust in settings such as healthcare, finance, food supply chains, and the internet.

The Routledge Companion to Trust is an extensive reference work which will be a vital resource to researchers and practitioners across the fields of management and organizational studies, behavioural economics, psychology, cultural anthropology, political science and sociology.

Rosalind H. Searle is Professor of Human Resource Management and Organisational Psychology at the Adam Smith Business School, University of Glasgow, UK.

Ann-Marie I. Nienaber is Professor in Human Resource Management and Organisational Behaviour and Head of the Trust and Workplace Relations research group at Coventry University, UK. She is also affiliated to the Centre for Management, University of Muenster, Germany.

Sim B. Sitkin is Michael W. Krzyzewski University Professor, Professor of Management, Professor of Public Policy, Faculty Director of the Fuqua/Coach K Center on Leadership and Ethics, and Director of the Behavioral Science and Policy Center at Duke University, USA.

Routledge Companions in Business, Management and Accounting

Routledge Companions in Business, Management and Accounting are prestige reference works providing an overview of a whole subject area or sub-discipline. These books survey the state of the discipline including emerging and cutting edge areas. Providing a comprehensive, up to date, definitive work of reference, Routledge Companions can be cited as an authoritative source on the subject.

A key aspect of these Routledge Companions is their international scope and relevance. Edited by an array of highly regarded scholars, these volumes also benefit from teams of contributors which reflect an international range of perspectives.

Individually, Routledge Companions in Business, Management and Accounting provide an impactful one-stop-shop resource for each theme covered. Collectively, they represent a comprehensive learning and research resource for researchers, postgraduate students and practitioners.

For a full list of Routledge Companions in Business, Management and Accounting, please visit https://routledge.com/series/RCBMA. Recently published titles include:

The Routledge Companion to the Makers of Modern Entrepreneurship
Edited by David B. Audretsch and Erik E. Lehmann

The Routledge Companion to Business History
Edited by Abe de Jong, Steven Toms, John Wilson and Emily Buchnea

The Routledge Companion to Qualitative Accounting Research
Edited by Zahirul Hoque, Lee D. Parker, Mark A. Covaleski and Kathryn Haynes

The Routledge Companion to Accounting and Risk
Edited by Margaret Woods and Philip Linsley

The Routledge Companion to Wellbeing at Work
Edited by Sir Cary L. Cooper and Michael P. Leiter

The Routledge Companion to Performance Management and Control
Edited by Elaine Harris

The Routledge Companion to Management Information Systems
Edited by Robert D. Galliers and Mari-Klara Stein

The Routledge Companion to Critical Accounting
Edited by Robin Roslender

The Routledge Companion to Trust
Edited by Rosalind H. Searle, Ann-Marie I. Nienaber and Sim B. Sitkin

The Routledge Companion to Tax Avoidance Research
Edited by Nigar Hashimzade and Yuliya Epifantseva

THE ROUTLEDGE
COMPANION TO TRUST

Edited by
Rosalind H. Searle, Ann-Marie I. Nienaber
and Sim B. Sitkin

LONDON AND NEW YORK

First published 2018
by Routledge
4 Park Square, Milton Park, Abingdon, Oxon OX14 4RN
605 Third Avenue, New York, NY 10017

First issued in paperback 2022

Routledge is an imprint of the Taylor & Francis Group, an informa business

Publisher's Note
The publisher has gone to great lengths to ensure the quality of this reprint
but points out that some imperfections in the original copies may be
apparent.

British Library Cataloguing-in-Publication Data
A catalogue record for this book is available from the British Library

Library of Congress Cataloging-in-Publication Data
Names: Searle, Rosalind H., editor. | Nienaber, Ann-Marie I.,
1980– editor. | Sitkin, Sim B., editor.
Title: The Routledge companion to trust / edited by Rosalind H. Searle,
Ann-Marie I. Nienaber and Sim B. Sitkin.
Description: New York : Routledge, 2017. |
Series: Routledge companions in business, management and accounting |
Includes bibliographical references and index.
Identifiers: LCCN 2017004364| ISBN 9781138817593 (hardback) |
ISBN 9781315745572 (ebook)
Subjects: LCSH: Trusts and trustees—United States. |
Trusts and trustees—Great Britain.
Classification: LCC HG4352 .R68 2017 | DDC 158.2—dc23
LC record available at https://lccn.loc.gov/2017004364

Typeset in Bembo and Minion Pro
by Florence Production Ltd, Stoodleigh, Devon, UK

ISBN 13: 978-1-03-247630-8 (pbk)
ISBN 13: 978-1-138-81759-3 (hbk)

DOI: 10.4324/9781315745572

This book is dedicated to the memory of Graham Dietz, a great scholar who died tragically young on 20 December 2014 with so much still to contribute. He was a strong and critical scholar, a great and impassioned teacher, a fun and enlivening presence in any gathering, and a dear and oft-missed friend.

CONTENTS

Contents

FIGURES

TABLES

CONTRIBUTORS

Reinhard Bachmann is Professor of International Management, Director of the Centre for Trust Research and Head of the School of Finance and Management at SOAS (formally known as the School of Oriental and African Studies), University of London. He has published widely on inter-organisational and institutional trust. His articles have appeared in journals such as *Organization Studies*, *Cambridge Journal of Economics*, *British Journal of Sociology*, *Journal of Trust Research* etc. He has also edited (together with Akbar Zaheer) the *Handbook of Trust Research* (2008) and the *Handbook of Advances in Trust Research* (2013). Among his previous academic employers are the University of Groningen, ETH Zurich and the University of Cambridge.

Michael Baer is an assistant professor at Arizona State University's W. P. Carey School of Business, Department of Management and Entrepreneurship. He received his PhD from the University of Georgia's Terry College of Business. He earned an MBA and a BA from Brigham Young University. His research focuses on trust (of course), fairness and impression management.

Laurie J. Barclay is an associate professor in the Lazaridis School of Business and Economics at Wilfrid Laurier University in Waterloo, Ontario, Canada. Dr. Barclay's research interests include organisational justice, emotions and workplace aggression. Her most recent work focuses on the role of emotions in justice and how individuals can effectively recover from unfair workplace experiences, including how to facilitate forgiveness in organisations. Her research has been published in leading journals (e.g. *The Academy of Management Annals*, the *Journal of Applied Psychology*, the *Journal of Management*, *Organizational Behavior and Human Decision Processes*) and she has received numerous research awards including the Ontario Early Researcher Award.

Robert J. Bies is Professor of Management and Founder of the Executive Master's in Leadership Program at the McDonough School of Business at Georgetown University. He is a faculty fellow of the Center for Social Justice Research, Teaching, & Service at Georgetown University. Professor Bies's current research focuses on leadership, the delivery of bad news, organisational justice, trust and distrust dynamics and revenge, forgiveness and mercy in the workplace. His research has been published in leading journals (e.g. *The Academy of Management Annals*, *Academy of Management Journal*, *Academy of Management Review*, *Journal of Applied Psychology*, *Journal of Management*, *Organizational Behavior and Human Decision Processes*). He is also co-author of the book, *Getting Even: The Truth About Workplace Revenge—and How to Stop It*.

Katinka M. Bijlsma-Frankema retired as Associate Professor of Organization Theory at VU University, Amsterdam and Professor of Organization Sciences at the European Institute for Advanced Studies in Management. She is now Senior Researcher at the University of Groningen, The Netherlands. Her research interests include trust, distrust, control, team learning and performance of teams. She is Founder and past Chair of the First International Network on Trust (FINT). She co-edited special issues on trust (and control), including *Group and Organization Management* (2007) and edited volumes on trust (Edward Elgar, 2005) and organizational control (Cambridge University Press, 2010).

Douglas Bilton is the Assistant Director of Standards and Policy at the Professional Standards Authority for Health and Social Care, where he has worked since 2006. Prior to this, he read English Literature at Emmanuel College, Cambridge, then worked at the British Medical Association on the negotiation of senior hospital doctors' terms and conditions, a London teaching hospital implementing a new NHS consultant contract and a London strategic health authority in medical human resources. He holds a Master's in Public Administration from Warwick Business School. He is the co-author of various publications on health professional regulation policy including 'Asymmetry of Influence: The Role of Regulators in Patient Safety' (The Health Foundation, 2013); 'Rethinking Regulation' (Professional Standards Authority, 2015); and 'Regulation Rethought' (Professional Standards Authority, 2016).

Kirsimarja Blomqvist is a professor for knowledge management at the School of Business and Management at Lappeenranta University of Technology (LUT), Finland. Her research focuses on trust, knowledge, innovation and digitalisation in new forms of organising. Her research articles have been published, for example, in *California Management Review*, *Scandinavian Journal of Management*, *Creativity and Innovation Management*, *Research Policy*, *R&D Management*, *Technovation* and *Industrial Marketing Management*. She also serves as Assistant Editor for the *Journal of Trust Research* and an editorial review board member for *Industrial Marketing Management*, the *Journal of Organization Design* and the *Journal of Co-operative Organization and Management*.

Anna Brattström is an assistant professor at Lund University, School of Economics and Management, Sweden. Her research focuses on innovation, entrepreneurship and collaboration. Her work has been published, for example, in *Entrepreneurship Theory and Practice*, *Research Policy* and the *Journal of Product Innovation Management* and *Small Business Economics*. In 2015, she was a finalist for the ISPIM and Wiley Innovation Management Dissertation Award and she received the Swedish Forum of Entrepreneurship Young Scholar Award.

Zheng Cheng (PhD, The University of Kansas, 2016) is an assistant professor of management at Lubar School of Business, at the University of Wisconsin–Milwaukee. Applying both the behavioural and economic perspectives, his research focus is on the role of intangible assets in shaping firm strategies in the context of international expansion, inter-firm collaboration and top management. His works have been published in the *Journal of Business Ethics* and presented at various academic conferences. In October 2015, he received the Best Conference Paper Award at the Strategic Management Society Denver Conference.

Jason A. Colquitt is the William Harry Willson Distinguished Chair and Professor in the University of Georgia's Terry College of Business, Department of Management. He received his PhD from Michigan State University's Eli Broad Graduate School of Management and earned his BS in Psychology from Indiana University. His research interests include justice, trust and personality influences on task and learning performance.

Karen S. Cook is the Ray Lyman Wilbur Professor of Sociology and Vice Provost for Faculty Development and Diversity at Stanford University. She is also the Director of the Institute for Research in the Social Sciences (IRiSS) at Stanford and a trustee of the Russell Sage Foundation. Professor Cook has a long-standing interest in social exchange, social networks, social justice and trust in social relations. She has edited a number of books in the Russell Sage Foundation Trust Series, including *Trust in Society* (2001), *Trust and Distrust in Organizations: Emerging Perspectives* (with R. Kramer, 2004), *eTrust: Forming Relations in the Online World* (with C. Snijders, V. Buskens and Coye Cheshire, 2009) and *Whom Can We Trust?* (with M. Levi and R. Hardin, 2009). She is co-author of *Cooperation Without Trust?* (with R. Hardin and M. Levi, 2005). In 1996, she was elected to the American Academy of Arts and Sciences and in 2007 to the National Academy of Sciences. In 2004, she received the ASA Social Psychology Section Cooley Mead Award for Career Contributions to Social Psychology.

Jacqueline A-M. Coyle-Shapiro is Professor in Organizational Behaviour in the Department of Management at the London School of Economics and Political Science and is a visiting research professor at the Centre for Workplace Excellence, University of South Australia Business School. Her research interests include employment relationship, psychological contracts, social exchange theory and organisational citizenship behaviour.

Deanne N. Den Hartog is Full Professor of Organizational Behaviour and Head of the Leadership and Management Section of the Amsterdam Business School at the University of Amsterdam, The Netherlands. Her research interests include leadership, trust, employee proactivity and HRM. She has published widely on these topics and serves on several editorial boards.

Marjo-Riitta (Maikki) Diehl is a professor of organisational behaviour and HRM in the Management and Economics Department at EBS Business School in Germany. She received her PhD from the London School of Economics and Political Science. Her research interests include organisational justice, social exchange theory, trust and psychological contracts. Her work has appeared in outlets including the *Journal of Management, Human Relations* and the *Journal of Managerial Psychology*. She currently serves on the editorial boards of the *Journal of Organizational Behaviour* and the *International Journal of Human Resource Management*.

Laliv Egozi is a doctoral candidate in the Department of Business Administration at the University of Haifa. She earned her MA in Social Psychology (2009) from the University of Haifa and MBA (2000) from Derby College. Previously, she managed the Haifa Center for Victims of Rape and Sexual Assault. Currently, she lectures at the Faculty of Industry and Management at Affeka College.

Guy Enosh, PhD is Associate Professor at the School of Social Work at the University of Haifa, Israel. He serves as Head of the Committee for Ethical Research with Human Beings of the Faculty of Welfare and Health Sciences. His research areas focus on causes and effects of conflict and aggression, encompassing contexts such as intimate violence, provider–client conflicts and researcher–participant power relations. In addition, he studies biases in professional decision-making.

Donald L. Ferrin is Professor of Organisational Behaviour and Human Resources at the Lee Kong Chian School of Business, Singapore Management University. He received his PhD from the University of Minnesota's Carlson School of Management in 2000. Don's research focuses entirely on trust, including determinants and consequences of interpersonal trust, trust in leadership, trust development processes, trust in the context of networks, trust violations and trust repair strategies, effects of culture on trust, trust in the context of negotiation, trust in ecommerce and group- and organisation-level trust repair. Don currently serves as the Deputy Editor-in-Chief of the *Journal of Trust Research*.

C. Ashley Fulmer is a visiting assistant professor at Tippie College of Business, Department of Management and Organizations. She received her PhD in Organizational Psychology from the University of Maryland, College Park and served on the faculty of National University of Singapore. Her research centres on trust in organisations, negotiation and conflict management, cross-cultural organisational behaviour and levels of analysis theory and research. Her work has been published in journals such as the *Academy of Management Review*, the *Journal of Applied Psychology* and the *Journal of Management*.

Nicole Gillespie is Associate Professor of Management at UQ Business School, University of Queensland and International Research Fellow at the Centre for Corporate Reputation at Oxford University. Her research focuses on organisational and stakeholder trust, particularly in challenging contexts such as after-trust failures and scandals, during organisational change, in mega-projects and virtual service delivery. Her research appears in leading journals including *Academy of Management Review*, the *Journal of Management*, the *Journal of Applied Psychology*, *Organization Studies*, *Business Ethics Quarterly* and *Human Resource Management*, as well as commissioned reports and policy notes on building and repairing trust for the Institute of Business Ethics and the UK Parliament. Nicole currently serves as the Deputy Editor-in-Chief of the *Journal of Trust Research*.

Brian C. Gunia (PhD in Management, Northwestern University) is an associate professor at the Johns Hopkins Carey Business School. His research, which focuses on the ways that people can help themselves act more ethically and/or negotiate more effectively, has been published in several management and psychology journals including the *Academy of Management Journal*, the *Journal of Applied Psychology* and *Psychological Science*. Brian teaches classes in negotiation and organisational behaviour and he previously worked as a consultant at Deloitte.

Maximilian Holtgrave is a postdoctoral researcher at Muenster School of Business and Economics, Germany. His research interests include issues of trust, control and identity management in the workplace. He has published his work in a number of academic journals including the *European Management Journal* and *Human Resource Management* and lectures on international management and organisational theory.

Robert F. Hurley is the Director of the Consortium for Trustworthy Organizations and a professor at Fordham University. He has published over 30 articles or book chapters. His book *The Decision to Trust* (Jossey-Bass) was named one of the best leadership books of 2013 by the *Washington Post* and won the Alpha Sigma Nu book award in 2013.

Adam A. Kay is a lecturer in management at the University of Queensland. He is a former biotech manager, business coach and international arbitration lawyer. His research interests include mindfulness, ethical and pro-social behaviour in the workplace and corporate social responsibility. To date, Adam's work has been published in chapters of the *Atlas of Moral Psychology* and *Oxford Bibliographies in Management*, as well as in peer-reviewed journal articles with *Academy of Management Perspectives* and the *Journal of Personality and Social Psychology*.

Peter H. Kim is a professor of management and organization at the University of Southern California's Marshall School of Business. His research interests concern the dynamics of interpersonal perceptions and their implications for negotiations, work groups and dispute resolution, with particular attention to matters of trust and its repair after alleged transgressions. His research has been published in many leading management and psychology journals, has received ten national/international awards and has been reported in a wide range of media outlets.

Sharon H. Kim (PhD in Organizational Behaviour, Cornell University) is an assistant professor at the Johns Hopkins Carey Business School. Her research focuses on individual and group creativity in organisations. Her recent work examines the complexities of creative problem solving in healthcare contexts.

M. Audrey Korsgaard (PhD New York University) is Professor of Management and Organizational Behavior at the University of South Carolina. Her research addresses the topics of prosocial orientation motivation and trust and their relationship to interpersonal and intragroup cooperation. She has studied these issues in a variety of work settings, including supervisor–subordinate relationships, investor–entrepreneur relations, work teams and joint ventures.

Roy J. Lewicki is the Irving Abramowitz Professor of Business Ethics and Professor of Management and Human Resources Emeritus at the Max M. Fisher College of Business, The Ohio State University. He maintains research and teaching interests in the fields of negotiation, conflict management, trust development and repair, leadership and ethical decision-making. His research has appeared in leading journals such as *Academy of Management Review*, *The Academy of Management Annals*, the *Journal of Management* and the *Journal of Applied Psychology*, and numerous edited handbooks. He is the author of the market-leading textbooks on negotiation including *Negotiation* (Lewicki, Barry and Saunders, 2014) and *Essentials of Negotiation* (Lewicki, Saunders, Barry, 2015). He has been named a fellow of the Academy of Management, where he has won their Distinguished Teaching Award, and also named a fellow of the International Association of Conflict Management, where he has served as President and won their Lifetime Achievement Award.

E. Allan Lind is a professor of management and leadership at Duke University's Fuqua School of Business. He received his PhD in 1974 from the University of North Carolina at Chapel Hill and, in the years since, he has studied the psychology of fairness in a variety of academic, organisational and government contexts.

Chris P. Long is an associate professor of Management and the Paul Naughton Research Fellow at the Tobin College of Business, St. John's University. In his research, he examines the actions that leaders take within complex and dynamic business environments to accomplish a variety of key performance objectives. Much of his current work focuses on how authorities integrate and balance their efforts to promote control, trust and fairness as well as how these actions influence subordinates' perceptions, motivations and behaviours. He holds a PhD in Management from Duke University.

Theodore G. Lynn is Professor of Digital Business at Dublin City University Business School, where he lectures at a postgraduate level on digital marketing and strategic thinking. He is the Principal Investigator of the Irish Centre for Cloud Computing and Commerce, an industry-led multidisciplinary applied research centre. Professor Lynn has founded a number of technology companies and is an advisor to a number of domestic and international companies.

Fergus Lyon is Professor of Enterprise and Organisation at Middlesex University and is the editor of the Edward Elgar *Handbook of Research Methods on Trust*. He has published in a range of entrepreneurship, management and environmental science journals on trust, alternative organisational forms and sustainability. He is leading a research program on enterprise and investment for the Centre for the Understanding of Sustainable Prosperity (CUSP). He has a background in international development and is actively involved in conservation and farming activities in the UK.

Serena C. Lyu is an assistant professor in human resources at the School of International Business Administration, Shanghai University of Finance and Economics. Serena's research focuses on interpersonal trust, organisational socialisation, emotions and moods, and negotiations.

Kim Mather is a senior lecturer in HRM at Keele University, Staffordshire, UK and she is also the course director of the postgraduate part-time Industrial Relations and HRM courses. Her current research interests include public-sector employment relations, developments in the labour management and labour processes of UK public-sector workers and the changing nature of professional and managerial work.

Lovisa Näslund is Assistant Professor at Stockholm Business School at Stockholm University and a researcher at the Stockholm Centre for Organizational Research (Score). She received her PhD in Business Administration in 2012 from Stockholm School of Economics. In her research, she has studied the creation of trust: in systems and interpersonal relations in markets; across organisational boundaries in professional services; and in the food sector. In particular, she has studied eco-labelling and the drivers of consumer trust in organic food. Her research has been published in journals such as *Human Relations*.

Ann-Marie I. Nienaber is Professor in Human Resource Management and Organisational Behaviour at the Centre for Trust, Peace and Social Relations (CTPSR) at Coventry University and the Head of the research group 'Trust and Workplace Relations'. She is also affiliated to the Centre for Management, University of Munster, Germany. Her research interests focus on trust in and between international organisations, trust in innovation management and entrepreneurship and ethical management. Her research has been awarded several times, for example by the British Academy of Management, the International Association for Management of Technology and Emerald Group Publishing Limited.

Samantha Peters is a management practitioner with some twenty years' experience in the health sector, most recently as Chief Executive and Registrar of the General Optical Council (the UK's regulator for optical professionals and businesses) where she worked from 2011 to 2017. Samantha has an Executive Master's in Business Administration from Cass Business School, where she received a Tallow Chandlers Award for her research on the subject trust and organisational failure. Samantha is current studying at the School of Management at the University of Bath. Her research is focused on the role that organisations play in promoting or inhibiting kindness, compassion and altruism by their users, employees and other stakeholders.

Laura Poppo is the Donald and Shirley Clifton Chair in Leadership at the University of Nebraska–Lincoln. She received her PhD from The Wharton School, University of Pennsylvania and has been on the faculty of Washington University, Virginia Tech and the University of

Kansas. She is known globally as a thought leader for her research in strategy, which has influenced scholars in many disciplines, including economics, law, marketing, supply chain management and strategic management. Her research interests include outsourcing, alliances, vertical integration, contracting and trust, encompassing the context of doing business in China. Her current research examines problem solving, creativity, innovation, identity and trust repair.

Nadine Raaphorst is an assistant professor at the Institute of Public Administration, Leiden University, The Netherlands. Her work focuses on street-level bureaucrats' uncertainty experiences in daily work and how they categorise citizen-clients in terms of trustworthiness.

Colette Real is a PhD research scholar at Dublin City University Business School, supported by the Dublin City University Daniel O'Hare Research Scholarship Scheme. Her research examines how trust can be a source of value for organisations by contributing to effective workplace relationships. She lectures in organisational psychology and human resource management at undergraduate and Master's level. Colette also worked for several years on a wide variety of organisational change programmes in the financial services industry in Ireland.

Philipp D. Romeike is currently working as a consultant, focusing on strategy implementation in financial institutions. He also is a management researcher with a focus on leadership and trust research. His work has been published in various international peer-reviewed journals, including the *Journal of Managerial Psychology*, *Personnel Review*, *Human Performance* and the *European Journal of Management*. His MSc and PhD thesis on managing virtual work relationships has been awarded prizes from the London School of Economics and the University of Muenster.

Maria Francisca Saldanha is a PhD candidate in the Lazaridis School of Business and Economics at Wilfrid Laurier University in Waterloo, Ontario, Canada. Her research interests include justice and forgiveness in the workplace. She is currently developing victim-centred interventions to facilitate recovery from injustice and examining the role of third parties in forgiveness processes. Her previous work related to forgiveness and recovery has been published in the *Journal of Business Ethics* and *The Oxford Handbook of Justice in Work Organizations*.

Rosalind H. Searle is Professor of Human Resource Management and Organisational Psychology at the Adam Smith Business School, University of Glasgow, UK and a chartered occupational psychologist. She earned a Bachelor's degree in Psychology with Occupational Psychology at the University of Hull and an MBA from Liverpool John Moores University. She also received a PhD degree on innovation and teams from Aston University. Her primary research interests include organisational trust, and HRM and trust. She also studies counterproductive work behaviour in organisations, working with regulators and organisations to understand the role of trust and ameliorate professional misconduct. She has published in *Human Resource Management*, the *Journal of Organizational Behaviour* and the *Journal of Human Resource Management and Long Range Planning*. She serves as Assistant Editor for the *Journal of Trust Research* and an editorial board member for the *Journal of Management*.

Dean A. Shepherd is the Ray and Milann Siegfried Professor of Entrepreneurship at the Mendoza College of Business, Notre Dame University. Dean received his doctorate and MBA from Bond University, Australia. His research and teaching is in the field of entrepreneurship; he investigates both the decision-making involved in leveraging cognitive and other resources to act on opportunities and the processes of learning from experimentation (including failure), in ways that ultimately lead to high levels of individual and organisational performance. Dean has published papers primarily in the top entrepreneurship, general management, strategic management, operations management and psychology journals and has written (or edited) over 20 books.

Sabina Siebert is Professor of Management in the Adam Smith Business School, University of Glasgow. Her research focuses on organisational change, organisational trust and the study of professions, including lawyers and doctors. She has recently researched trust and distrust in secret organisations, trust in science and differentiation in elite professions. She has published in the *Academy of Management Journal*, *Organization Studies*, the *Human Resource Management Journal*, *Sociology* and *Work Employment and Society*.

Sim B. Sitkin is Michael W. Krzyzewski University Professor, Professor of Management, Professor of Public Policy, Director of the Behavioral Science & Policy Center and Faculty Director of the Fuqua/Coach K Center on Leadership and Ethics at Duke University. He is co-founder and Co-President of the Behavioral Science & Policy Association. His research focuses on the effect of formal and informal organisational control systems and leadership on risk taking, accountability, trust, learning, change and innovation. Sim is Founding Editor of *Behavioural Science and Policy* and past Editor of *The Academy of Management Annals*. He is a fellow of the Academy of Management, the International Network for Trust Research and the Society for Organizational Behavior. His most recent books are *Organizational Control* (with Laura Cardinal and Katinka Bijlsma-Frankema) and *The Six Domains of Leadership* (with E. Allan Lind).

Frédérique Six is Associate Professor of Public Governance at Vrije Universiteit Amsterdam. Her research focuses on public governance issues and in particular the relationship between trust and control; applying this to how (public) professionals are governed and to regulation. She has published in journals such as *Public Management Review*, the *Journal of Management Studies* and the *International Journal of Human Resource Management*; and co-edited *The Trust Process* (2003) and *Trust in Regulatory Regimes* (2017).

Kathleen M. Sutcliffe (PhD University of Texas at Austin) is a Bloomberg Distinguished Professor at the Johns Hopkins University with appointments in the Carey Business School, the School of Medicine and the Armstrong Institute for Patient Safety. Her research focuses on high-reliability organising and resilience. She is currently studying these matters in wildland firefighting, oil and gas exploration and healthcare.

Edward C. Tomlinson is Professor of Management at West Virginia University. He earned a Bachelor's degree in Economics and Business at Virginia Military Institute and an MBA from Lynchburg College. He also received Master's and PhD degrees in Labor and Human Resources from the Fisher College of Business at The Ohio State University. His primary research interests deal with how attributions affect the development and repair of interpersonal trust.

Thomas M. Tripp is a professor of management at Washington State University. Dr. Tripp has published on topics that include workplace revenge and forgiveness, consumer retaliation against firms and organisational justice in leading journals (e.g. *The Academy of Management Annals*, the *Journal of Applied Psychology*, the *Journal of Marketing*, the *Journal of the Academy of Marketing*

Sciences, Organizational Behaviour and Human Decision Processes, the *Journal of Occupational Health Psychology* and *Leadership Quarterly*). He is also co-author of the book, *Getting Even: The Truth About Workplace Revenge—and How to Stop It.* Dr. Tripp earned a PhD in Organizational Behaviour from the Kellogg School of Management at Northwestern University and a BS in Psychology from the University of Washington.

Shay S. Tzafrir is an associate professor and Head of the Department of Business Administration at the University of Haifa. He received his PhD and MSc in behavioral science from the Technion – Israel institute of Technology. He also earned a BA and MA in political science, as well as an LLB, all from the University of Haifa. He serves as an associate editor for special issues in the *Journal of Management, Spirituality & Religion.* His current research interest includes the role trust plays in various organisational factors, such as strategic human resource management, and organisational performance. His articles have been published in journals such as *Human Resource Management, Human Resources Management Review,* the *International Journal of Human Resource Management, Industrial Relations,* the *Journal of Organizational and Occupational Psychology,* the *Journal of Business Ethics, Organizational Studies* and others.

Steven Van de Walle is Research Professor of Public Management at the Public Governance Institute, KU Leuven, Belgium. His work focuses on public sector reform and the interaction between citizens and public services.

Lisa van der Werff is an assistant professor in Organisational Psychology at Dublin City University Business School. Her research interests include trust, motivation and workplace transitions. Her work has been published in leading journals in the management and information systems disciplines, including the *Academy of Management Journal,* the *Journal of Management,* the *Journal of Computer Information Systems* and *IEEE Transactions on Services Computing.*

Daan van Knippenberg is Joseph F. Rocereto Chair of Leadership at LeBow College of Business, Drexel University. His main research interests are in leadership, diversity, teams and creativity. Daan is Co-Editor-in-Chief of *The Academy of Management Annals* and was Founding Editor of *Organizational Psychology Review* and Associate Editor of the *Academy of Management Journal, Organizational Behavior and Human Decision Processes* and the *Journal of Organizational Behavior.* He is a fellow of the Academy of Management, a fellow of the Society for Industrial and Organizational Psychology and a fellow of the American Psychological Association.

Antoinette Weibel is Full Professor in Human Resource Management at the University of St. Gallen, Switzerland and Director of the Institute for Work and Employment Research HSG. In her research, she specialises in organisational trust and how institutional sources, such as formal controls and incentives systems, relate to employee trust and engagement. Professor Weibel has previously held academic positions at the University of Konstanz and the University of Liechtenstein. She holds a PhD and a Habilitation in Management from the University of Zurich.

Michele Williams is Assistant Professor and John L. Miclot Faculty Fellow in Entrepreneurship, Tippie College of Business, University of Iowa, and a faculty fellow at the Scheinman Institute on Conflict Resolution, Cornell University. Her research focuses on the development of cooperative, high-performance interpersonal relationships. Michele examines (1) trust and other relational foundations of collaboration and early-stage entrepreneurship, as well as (2) the impact of gender and social categorisation on these processes. Michele has been published in leading journals (e.g., *Academy of Management Review, Organizational Science*, the *Journal of Business Venturing, Leadership Quarterly* and the *Journal of Organizational Behavior*). She serves on editorial boards and as an Associated Editor for the *Journal of Trust Research*.

Trenton A. Williams is an assistant professor at the Kelley School of Business at Indiana University. Prior to joining the Kelley School, he earned his PhD in Entrepreneurship and Strategic Management at Indiana University and was an assistant professor at the Syracuse University's Whitman School of Management. His research focuses on resource-constrained entrepreneurship, resilience and decision-making.

PREFACE

Roy J. Lewicki

Billions and billions and billions of years ago – when I was a doctoral student working with the eminent Prof. Morton Deutsch – the obligatory reading on trust was three of Deutsch's articles: 'Trust and Suspicion' (1958); 'The Effects of Motivational Orientation on Trust and Suspicion' (1960); and 'Cooperation and Trust: Some Theoretical Notes' (1962). The articles began to introduce some very important concepts about trust: definitions of trust and its distinctiveness from other psychological constructs; the distinction between trust and trustworthiness; and the linkages between trust and cooperative or competitive behaviours. A rereading of these articles today indicates that they set the groundwork for the richness and complexity of the construct. Yet most remarkably, with some very limited exceptions – e.g. gaming studies in which trusting choices were operationalized as the dependent variable (Kee & Knox, 1970) or trust as an enduring component of personality (e.g. Rotter, 1971) – researchers fundamentally neglected the construct for the next 30 years! Only a handful of articles (e.g. Lewis & Weigert, 1985) addressed the construct in some meaningful way.

As sharply as academic interest in the construct of trust disappeared through the seventies and eighties, there was an equally dramatic re-emergence of research on trust in the mid 1990s, largely in the field of organizational behaviour. No single source or author can be easily credited for originating this rebirth. Instead, both academic and 'practice' traditions seemed to lead scholars back to recognizing the centrality of trust as foundational to interpersonal and organizational relationships, but also recognizing how little was known about it. Among organizational theorists, perspectives on optimal strategies for organizational governance were changing from a heavy reliance on organizational structure and hierarchy to a focus on the importance of transactional relationships within and between individuals, groups, organizations and networks (e.g. Ashkenas, Ulrich, Jick & Kerr, 2002). Formal structure and legalistic agreements were being replaced by informal social contracts and trust as the 'glue' that bound those relationships together (e.g. Putnam, 1995). A similar movement was occurring in the law, as attorneys and legal educators recognized the limitations of formal legal mechanisms for resolving all varieties of disputes, and began to stress the importance of alternative dispute resolution processes such as mediation to provide more long term solutions to marital and business disputes. On the academic side, a number of seminal contributions on the multifaceted nature of trust appeared within a short time period, almost all compilations of works from a variety of theoretical perspectives and levels of analysis. These included:

- Kramer and Tyler's *Trust in Organizations* (1996), a book that resulted from a conference of multidisciplinary scholars focusing on trust dynamics;
- a special issue of *Academy of Management Review*, hosted by Rousseau, Sitkin, Burt and Camerer (1998), which offered a now-broadly accepted definition of the trust construct and a number of theoretical contributions that are still viewed as seminal today;
- important papers that moved beyond the then-dominant cognitive, economics-driven, rational-choice perspective on trust to the incorporation of emotions (e.g. McAllister, 1995);
- initiation of an important distinction to be drawn between the dynamics of trust and the dynamics of distrust (Sitkin & Roth, 1993; Lewicki, McAllister & Bies, 1998);
- the role of intuitive judgment processes in trust development (Kramer, 1994); and an understanding of trust as a bilateral process, including key elements of the other party's trustworthiness (Mayer, Davis and Schoorman, 1995) as instrumental to a broader understanding of trust dynamics.

The last twenty years have witnessed a virtual explosion of trust research. The key role of trust has been incorporated into research in almost every social science discipline, and permeated all types of organizational research. Trust has been extensively studied in multiple research studies as an independent, moderator, mediator and dependent variable. It has been examined at multiple levels of analysis, from the intrapsychic processes of trust formation, to the interpersonal dynamics in negotiation and conflict management, to the key role of trust in understanding leadership, to the importance of trust in the formation and management of strategic alliances, to the key role of trust in knitting together the fabric of our daily social interaction. Its cross-cultural variations and embodiments have also been extensively explored. And all of this work for a phenomenon which cannot be directly seen or grasped or materially measured, but must be inferred through a variety of indirect measures of cognition, affect, motivation, intention and behaviour.

The essays in the current volume significantly advance the multiple perspectives, theories and dynamics of trust, and the contexts in which they emerge and operate. They offer a strong balance of theoretical insights, reviews of research and exploration of the dynamics of trust in contexts such as health-care, labour relations and entrepreneurship. I am confident that this volume will significantly integrate and advance research on specific important and emergent themes trust in general and on specific important and emergent themes such as trust dynamics and trust repair. It will quickly become a required resource on the bookshelf of trust researchers and practitioners alike.

Bibliography

Ashkenas, R., Ulrich, D., Jick, T. & Kerr, S. (2002) *The Boundaryless Organization: Breaking the Chains of Organizational Structure*. San Francisco, CA: Jossey Bass.

Deutsch, M. (1958) Trust and suspicion. *Journal of Conflict Resolution*, 2, 4, 265–279.

Deutsch, M. (1960) The effects of motivation on trust and suspicion. *Human Relations*, 13, 10, 123–139.

Deutsch, M. (1962) Cooperation and trust: Some theoretical notes. In M. R. Jones, *Nebraska Symposium on Motivation*. Lincoln, NE: University of Nebraska Press, 275–320.

Kee, H. W. & Knox, R. E. (1970) Conceptual and methodological considerations in the study of trust and suspicion. *Journal of Conflict Resolution*, 14, 3, 357–366.

Kramer, R. (1994) The sinister attribution error: Paranoid cognition and collective distrust in organizations. *Motivation and Emotion*, 18, 2, 199–230.

Kramer, R. D. & Tyler, T. R. (1996) *Trust in Organizations: Frontiers of Theory and Research*. Thousand Oaks, CA: Sage Publications.

Lewicki, R., McAllister, D. & Bies, R. (1998) Trust and distrust: New relationships and realities. *Academy of Management Review*, 23, 3, 438–458.

Lewis, J. D. & Weigert, A. (1985) Trust as a social reality. *Social Forces*, 63, 4, 967–985.

Mayer, R. C., Davis, J. H. & Schoorman, F. D. (1995) An integrative model of organizational trust. *Academy of Management Review*, 20, 709–734.

McAllister, D. (1995) Affect and cognition-based trust as foundations for interpersonal cooperation in organizations. *Academy of Management Journal*, 38, 1, 24–59.

Putnam, R. (1995) Tuning in, tuning out: The strange disappearance of social capital in America. *Political Science & Politics*, 28, 4, 664–683.

Rotter, J. (1971) Generalized expectancies for interpersonal trust. *American Psychologist*, 26, 5, 443–452.

Rousseau, D., Sitkin, S., Burt, R. & Camerer, C. (1998) Not so different after all: A cross-discipline view of trust. *Academy of Management Review*, 23, 3, 393–404.

Sitkin, S. & Roth, N. L. (1993) Explaining the limited effectiveness of legalistic remedies for trust/distrust. *Organization Science*, 4, 3, 367–392.

INTRODUCTION

Rosalind H. Searle, Ann-Marie I. Nienaber and Sim B. Sitkin

Why read this book?

Trust matters. Over the last 20 years there has been a cumulative increase in trust as a topic of interest not only to scholars, but also for the public. Turning on a TV news programme or opening a newspaper reveals the salience of trust, be it the news concerning its violation or the aftermath. Trust is an area that is of interest far beyond academia, extending to a broad array of groups from corporations and practitioners, to governments and policy makers, and to media and public. Periods of turbulence and scandal seem to be endemic since the start of the twenty-first century, and have been accompanied by profound questions about trust and the growing issue of distrust, and so whether and how we can restore or repair trust is a germane matter. Indeed, trust and its decline is very much a zeitgeist.

Trust has important impact across levels and across sectors. It emerges as a matter of importance in sectors critical for our economies, with the public's trust jeopardized by the actions of institutions, leaders, organizational members and officials. Recent scandals in sectors such as government, religion, banking, energy, food and manufacturing show how the actions of a single organization or even a single individual may have a huge impact across a sector, and are able to raise deep challenges for government and regulators faced with trying to prevent their repetition. This demonstrates trust is of great relevance on three levels: the *individual level, the organizational level* and *the wider system-level*.

Trust on the individual level can be placed in jeopardy due to the emergence of particular labour practices such as zero-hours contracts or the rise of self-employment, or from inappropriate use of company pension provisions, all of which shift risk from the firm to the employee. At an organizational level, trust breaches, such as that identified in the emissions scandal of Volkswagen, can taint an entire brand, with consequences for both their products and employees. Viewed at the system level, such scandals can challenge practices for an entire sector. Further, the public and third sectors are not immune from trust issues, with widespread failures of these sectors to detect and handle effectively trust breaches. This is evident in the UK's BBC problems, including inappropriate fixing of competition winners and sexual abuse by paedophilic presenters, or in a number of police forces in countries including India, USA and UK with differences in their treatment of citizens on ethnicity and gender lines.

Trust is even more visible and impactful nowadays. While, sadly, the examples of trust challenges are not new, it is the speed with which social media can draw attention to events that can more rapidly ignite large-scale social unrest and demonstrations. The reputation loss to such organizations can have damaging long-term consequences, including raising concerns about the competence and integrity of their staff, while also fostering higher levels of ongoing scrutiny and distrust by politicians and the public. Concerns about trust and distrust can become a more prominent feature for political leaders and parties during elections, but also during periods of crisis, such as the UK's Brexit, or in the handling of various countries' financial crises. The trustworthiness of political actors, especially their integrity, are legitimate questions for those seeking or holding public office. The media play an important role in drawing and fanning public concerns, but also in their potential to incite further trust violations.

Who should read this book?

The goal of this book is to provide a comprehensive reference that offers students, researchers and practitioners an introduction to current scholarship in the expanding discipline of trust. We want to make convenient to our readers access either to a new area – trust – or insight into a previously unfamiliar specialized area of trust research for more knowledgeable readers. Thus, we aim our collection at readers in behavioural economics, cultural anthropology, organizational behaviour, management studies, political science, psychology and sociology. It is designed to create the opportunity to reflect and consider trust in all its guises. To achieve this, we have assembled contributions from key and emergent authors that highlight the current state of their part of this field. Our contributors include established and up-and-coming contributors from research and practice, enabling us to develop a single repository on the current state of knowledge, the existing debates and emergent concerns, which in turn can better inform and extend the field of trust.

Authors were asked to do two things – to provide a review of their domain for those new to the area, to identify the important new and emerging challenges and also the omissions to our current theoretical and conceptual understandings of that aspect of trust. By doing this, they have served the community well by reflecting on the distinct earlier works Lewicki mentioned in his Preface. They show that, while much has been done in the domain of trust, there is both more to develop and also a need to return to important neglected or partially answered questions. This collection is specifically designed to open debate between more OB- and micro-based fields of trust research typical of behavioural economics and psychology and those approaching trust from more meso- and macro-based perspectives such as sociological, organization theory, strategic, anthropological, political science and culture researcher perspectives. Through the gathering of these diverse perspectives, fresh insight into old issues might be generated, as well as more novel knowledge devised.

How is the book structured?

As editors, we offer some structure to the field by organizing the contributions into six key sections. Within the sections and across the book, the editors and authors have attempted to highlight dialogues and connections to other chapters. Key conferences have created useful places for authors themselves to discuss and identify synergies, most notably the European Group of Organization Studies' (EGOS) standing working group on organizational trust, events of the First International Network Trust Research (FINT) and the Academy of Management (AOM). We asked authors to provide a balanced overview of current knowledge in their key topic, to identify pertinent issues and debates and to offer a fresh and critical perspective on where that area needs to be developed. Thus each chapter is simultaneously past, current and future oriented.

The book is organized in six *thematic parts*, comprising 31 chapters in total. The first three are foundations and conceived as essentially *intradisciplinary* in character, designed to explore the development of key theories and perspectives which have been used to examine trust. The last three parts deal with the application of trust and current topics.

Part I: The first section, entitled **'Foundations of trust'**, includes four chapters focusing on key concerns, or underpinnings for trust scholarship. We begin with the sometimes neglected topic of affect-based trust. Here, Daan van Knippenberg draws attention to the social and emotional processes, arguing for the importance of affect, emotion and mood in trust. He identifies the role of emotional contagion. M. Audrey Korsgaard reviews research on the interpersonal concept of reciprocal trust, a complex, bidirectional phenomenon which involves a self-reinforcing dynamic process. Kirsimarja Blomqvist and Karen S. Cook turn our attention towards swift trust, identified by Meyerson, Weick and Kramer; they examine specifically swift trust and the role of technology and virtual interactions. The distinction between trust and distrust is discussed by Sim B. Sitkin and Katinka M. Bijlsma-Frankema in the last chapter of this section.

Part II: The next section **'Levels of analysis'** includes four chapters specifically considering the distinct levels of analysis used in the study of trust, from micro to more multi-foci approaches. Donald L. Ferrin and Serena C. Lyu provide an exploration of the field pertaining to an interpersonal level of analysis. They review 20 years of work, identifying the significant antecedents, functions and consequences of interpersonal trust within organizations. Ann-Marie I. Nienaber, Maximilian Holtgrave and Philipp D. Romeike explore the team level of analysis and separate further two important distinctions – trust within and trust between teams. They also consider the determinants and outcomes of trust at each of these team levels, noting the similarities and differences between intra- and inter-team trust. They raise important considerations for the development of theory and measurements in this area. Anna Brattström and Reinhard Bachmann then consider inter-organizational trust from four theoretical perspectives, distinguishing between attention in each perspective on the various misalignments in each of incentives (cooperation concerns) and activities (coordination concerns). Finally, C. Ashley Fulmer discusses the use of more complex cross- and multi-level analysis for trust. She reflects on the value of this approach highlighting where this perspective has real value to the field. She advocates further development of both theory and methods to extend this more sophisticated approach to the study of trust.

Part III: The third section, **'Theories of trust'**, looks at some of the main theoretical perspectives used to study trust, contrasting the application of psychological, sociological and economics-based theories. The section begins with Michael Baer and Jason A. Colquitt's exploration of the psychological antecedents of trust, including dispositions to trust and trustworthiness, which dominate approaches to the field, and two neglected antecedents (i.e. the roles of affect and heuristics). E. Allan Lind examines the intersection of fairness and trust to review some of the main studies from organizational justice research. He provides insight into the theory and methods used to study trust and trusting behaviour. Using empirical evidence, he outlines situations where impressions of fair treatment may be a substitute, or replacement, for judgments of trust. Our attention then shifts to the study of trust through the lens of social exchange theory. Jacqueline A-M. Coyle-Shapiro and Marjo-Riitta Diehl look at trust and its role in social exchange relationships within the context of the employee–organization relationship (EOR). They revisit the origins of this concept before bringing their review up to date with the current work that is based on such perspectives. Reinhard Bachmann takes a contrasting sociological perspective in reviewing an institutional theory perspective on trust, highlighting scenarios in which institutions might be more critical for trust, and considers the importance of regulation for trust. Laura Poppo and Zheng Cheng build on the importance of regulation by reviewing research on trust and contracts using perspectives of transaction cost economics and social embeddedness. They consider the specific role of contracts and trust and whether they are complements or substitutes in business-to-business exchanges. In the final chapter of this section, we return to a more socio-psychological perspective with Edward C. Tomlinson's review of attribution analysis. He explores the role of attributions in the development, decline and repair of trust and argues that attribution deserves more attention in future trust studies because of its centrality to trust dynamics.

Part IV: The topic of **'Trust repair'** has been gaining a lot of attention and we have therefore created a section concerned specifically with trust breach and repair. Peter H. Kim reviews the topic of interpersonal trust repair, and then Nicole Gillespie and Sabina Siebert reflect on organizational repair. We conclude this section with a chapter that takes a distinct view on trust repair by focusing on the issue of forgiveness. Robert J. Bies, Laurie J. Barclay, Maria F. Saldanha, Adam A. Kay and Thomas M. Tripp consider trust and distrust and their role in forgiveness. They also offer alternatives for situations where the nature of the breach makes forgiveness impossible.

Part V 'Applications': One of the key questions we have wanted to explore in this book is whether trust is different in distinct contexts. In the penultimate section, we examine the issue of trust in eight different applied settings to consider more explicitly the salience of trust and what matters in various contexts. These include health (Samantha Peters and Douglas Bilton), finance (Robert F. Hurley), professionals (Frédérique Six), employee relations (Kim Mather), the internet (Lisa Van der Werff, Colette Real and Theodore G. Lynn), entrepreneurship (Trenton A. Williams and Dean A. Shepherd), safety-critical contexts (Brian C. Gunia, Sharon H. Kim and Kathleen Sutcliffe), and food (Lovisa Näslund and Fergus Lyon). In each, the significance of trust for and to different stakeholders can vary, but the salience of trust and the consequences of its breach makes it an important topic for each applied area – both because the inclusion of trust adds substantially to the depth of understanding of researchers on each application and also because these varied applications provide additional forums and insights upon which future trust researchers can build. More specifically, subtle distinctions emerge in reading across these contributions about the distinctions between trust and distrust, and the roles of distinct actors. The chapters illuminate issues of power, regulation and control and clearly identify not only the key differences for each distinct area, but also fruitful avenues for further research. Our introduction to this section includes more details on the key issues each raises, as well as highlighting links to other chapters where synergies arise.

Part VI: In the final section of the book, we consider **'Future directions'** by identifying some of the important emergent topics and concerns for the field. These chapters highlight topics that are fresh and those where there are important resurgences of interest. Deanne N. Den Hartog explores the central topic of trust in leadership and trust fostered by leadership. Then, Nadine Raaphorst and Steven Van de Walle examine trust in and by the public sector. They consider the trust issue in and for citizens. Rosalind H. Searle outlines the importance of trust for and in Human Resource Management, a currently underdeveloped area with great potential for future work. This has strong links to the subsequent chapter of Chris P. Long and Antoinette Weibel; which discusses the differences and relationship between trust and control. Finally, Shay S. Tzafrir, Guy Enosh and Laliv Egozi bring us full circle by looking more closely at the question of affect, specifically trust and anger.

We complete our book with some **concluding thoughts** to offer some synthesis and signal potential future topics and concerns, but also to identify emergent approaches that might profitably be adopted in this field. A postscript from Michele Williams considers developments in the curriculum for trust and discusses how it might be used in teaching.

PART I

Foundations of trust

The foundations part includes four chapters which examine six key topics that are important for the field. In the first of our foundation chapters, Daan van Knippenberg examines affect-based trust, a topic which is neglected in many studies, leading to it having an underestimated role in trust. He makes the case for it being distinct from cognition-based trust, considering its unique antecedents and consequences. Important here, and why we deliberately position this as our first foundation chapter, is the contention that affect-based trust has a stronger influence on trust than cognitive-based trust. This chapter is concerned not merely with emotions but with relationships.

Then in Chapter 2 M. Audrey Korsgaard reviews the interpersonal concept of reciprocal trust, a complex, bidirectional phenomenon which involves a self-reinforcing dynamic process. Korsgaard develops further the importance of relationships, which van Knippenberg puts central as a foundation, to consider three key facets of reciprocal trust: trust spirals and their directions, the dynamics of relationships and the shapes of the trust trajectory.

This is followed by Kirsimarja Blomqvist and Karen S. Cook who focus on swift trust, updating a concept which Meyerson, Weick and Kramer (1996) introduced. In their chapter, as well as testing some of the founding propositions, they look at new organizational phenomena and specifically at the role of technology and virtual interactions to explore knowledge-creation activities, in which trust might be required to form rapidly and has to deliver immediate benefits.

Sim B. Sitkin and Katinka M. Bijlsma-Frankema in Chapter 4 take us to the debate of trust versus distrust. Their chapter considers two distinct ways that distrust has been approached: as a subset of trust and in its own right as a distinct phenomenon. They review the evidence to identify further directions that arise from these different perspectives for the field.

1

RECONSIDERING AFFECT-BASED TRUST

A new research agenda

Daan van Knippenberg

It is hard to envision social relationships that would not require some level of trust between parties to function effectively. Regardless of whether these are relationships between individuals, group members, organizations or linkages across those levels (e.g. individual–employing organization), regardless of whether these are work or non-work relationship, regardless of whether these are short-term or longer-term relationships, arguably all relationships build on trust between parties to be effective (cf. Fulmer & Gelfand, 2012). Not surprisingly then, trust is a concept studied widely in the social and behavioural sciences (Rousseau, Sitkin, Burt & Camerer, 1998). The jumping off point for the current discussion of trust is that in this impressive body of work there is such an emphasis on trust as a cognitive phenomenon that the role of affective processes in trust is under-investigated and, I would contend, underestimated. The idea that one would trust, or distrust, someone because one has "a good feeling" about the person, or a "bad feeling" about the person seems completely natural; yet, this idea is essentially absent from the empirical work on trust.

Following the widely used definition by Rousseau et al. (1998) I understand trust to be the willingness to accept vulnerability based upon positive expectations about another's behaviour (key here is that vulnerability entails risk, and trust thus captures the willingness to expose one-self to that risk). Expectations are cognitions, and it is therefore probably not surprising that trust research has been strongly dominated by a cognitive approach to trust in which trust is understood as the outcome of a subjectively rational cognitive process. This is illustrated in influential conceptual treatments of trust (e.g. Mayer, Davis & Schoorman, 1995) and in the observation that most empirical work tends to focus on cognition-based trust (e.g. Dirks & Ferrin, 2002). Even so, affect – moods and emotions – may play a role in trust. In trust research, this is captured first and foremost by the concept of affect-based trust, trust based on the personal bond between two people (McAllister, 1995; Webber, 2008). Despite the fact that affect-based trust is in a sense a "minority perspective" in trust research, there is enough work on affect-based trust to take stock of its contribution to the trust literature. The aim of this chapter is to do exactly that, and to review what we know from empirical research on affect-based trust to assess the case for a unique role of affect within the greater body of trust research – is there evidence of unique antecedents? Of unique consequences? The review aims to not merely "sum up" the evidence, but to arrive at both integrative conclusions and identify a way forward for research in affect-based trust – a research agenda.

Presaging things to come, the first-blush conclusion would be that affect-based trust and cognition-based trust are moderately to strongly correlated, but do represent different constructs with unique antecedents and consequences. Moreover, there is evidence that affect-based trust tends to be the stronger influence and that cognition-based trust can be seen as a precursor to affect-based trust. On closer consideration, however, one may spot the elephant in the room: affect-based trust does not so much invoke affect as it invokes relationship; it is relationship-based trust much more than affect-based trust. From its definition as trust based on the personal bond between two people, onwards it is arguably better labelled relationship-based trust than affect-based trust in that the relationship is definitional but affect is not. In that sense the label affect-based trust is something of a misnomer, and the primary driver of the difference between affect-based and cognition-based trust may not be so much the contrast between affect and cognition but the extent to which the trust is relationship-based or reflects an assessment of the other party's trustworthiness that is relatively independent of the relationship between parties. Recognizing this important alternative understanding of the affect-based–cognition-based trust distinction, I propose that research in affect-based trust does not, or at the very least not unequivocally, address the role of affect in trust. The key conclusion I would advance, therefore, concerns the need for research on the one hand to clarify the relationship basis versus affective basis of affect-based trust, and on the other hand to unambiguously study the role of affect in trust.

Affect-based trust: state of the science

As outlined by Lewis and Weigart (1985) and Mayer et al. (1995), our assessment of the extent to which some other party (person, group, organization) can be trusted has a strong component of subjective rationality. Trust follows from what one sees as good reasons – indicators of a party's trustworthiness. Schoorman et al. (1995) for instance argue that the key indicators of trustworthiness concern the other party's competence, integrity and benevolence. As noted by Lewis and Weigart (1985) and McAllister (1995), however, the quality of the relationship between parties and its emotional connotations can also be a basis for trust, and this has led to the rise of the concept of affect-based trust (as I will argue below, a misnomer for what conceptually and empirically is relationship-based trust). In research in management, McAllister (1995) captured this probably in the most influential way by explicitly distinguishing and operationalizing cognition-based trust and affect-based trust. In this understanding of trust, the key antecedent of affect-based trust is the quality of the relationships between parties. Indeed, operationally McAllister's measure of affect-based trust reflects judgment of relationship quality as much as the willingness to be vulnerable in the relationship (i.e. only the latter matches the more common definition of trust) and does not have the notion of affect as a basis for trust as a main theme underlying the items. Cognition-based trust, in contrast, would be based primarily on more factual indicators of a party's competence, integrity and benevolence (i.e. feeding into expectations of what the party is able and motivated to do; cf. Mayer et al., 1995).

Affect is clearly implied by the quality of a relationship, but I argue that this is a limited and limiting view of the role affect may play in trust, and moreover one that does not unambiguously speak to the role of affect but rather puts the quality of the relationship and not affect centre-stage. Before we get to that argument, however, I first provide a concise review of research on affect-based trust. The review aims to be representative, not exhaustive. To reflect my misgivings about the construct naming, I will refer to the construct as "affect-based trust", that is, within quotation marks to indicate I am quoting the label used but not sharing the conclusion that the label is correct.

"Affect-based trust": empirical evidence

"Affect-based trust" is conceptualized as rooted in the quality of the relationship between parties. By implication, cognition-based trust would not be, or to a lesser degree, rooted in this relationship. When cognition-based trust is understood as rooted in assessment of the other party's competence, integrity and benevolence (Mayer et al., 1995), it seems reasonable to conclude that these are assessments that need not be based on the quality of the relationship with the other party (even when a relationship might give one access to relevant information pertaining to competence and integrity). For instance, we may assess someone's competence on the basis of their CV, or judge a person's integrity based on information available through others without any relationship with that person. In that sense, cognition-based trust could be said to be person-based – in contrast to the relationship-based nature of the concept known as "affect-based trust". Cognition-based trust can thus be a precursor to "affect-based trust" to the extent that cognitive judgments of the other party's trustworthiness may set the stage for the development of a high-quality relationship or for the absence of such a development.

Consistent with this logic, McAllister (1995) found support for a model in which relationship quality was a unique antecedent of "affect-based trust" in peers, and cognition-based trust too was an antecedent of "affect-based trust" (and "affect-based trust" predicted performance). Other studies also report such evidence of cognition-based trust as an antecedent of "affect-based trust". Schaubroeck, Peng and Hannah (2013) for instance found that cognition-based trust in leader and peers predicted "affect-based trust", which in turn predicted identification and performance. Newman, Kiazad, Miao and Cooper (2014) observed that ethical leadership predicted cognition-based trust, which in turn predicted "affect-based trust", which predicted organizational citizenship behaviour. Other research shows that such findings generalize beyond interpersonal relationships at work, such as for consumer trust (Johnson & Grayson, 2005), inter-organizational trust (Robson, Katsikeas & Bello, 2008; see also Dowell, Morrison & Heffernan, 2015) and trust in virtual communities (open source software development; Stewart & Gosain, 2006).

Research also corroborates McAllister's (1995) argument and findings that "affect-based trust" and cognition-based trust have unique antecedents and consequences. Chua, Ingram and Morris (2008) for instance found that "affect-based trust" and cognition-based trust have different types of social network ties as precursors, and Dunn, Ruedy and Schweitzer (2012) show that "affect-based trust" suffers from upward comparison to the other party (i.e. because it puts one in an unfavourable light) whereas downward comparison is bad for cognition-based trust (i.e. because it implies lower competence).

Other research shows that "affect-based trust" and cognition-based trust have (partially) different consequences. Ergeneli, Ari and Metin (2007) found for instance that cognition-based trust predicted the competence and meaning aspects of psychological empowerment, whereas "affect-based trust" predicted the impact aspect of empowerment. Ng and Chua (2006) found that "affect-based trust" was positively related to cooperation whereas cognition-based trust was not. Ha, Park and Cho (2011) found that "affect-based trust" was related to information sharing and benefit/risk sharing, whereas cognition-based trust was related to joint decision making and benefit/risk sharing. Chua, Morris and Mor (2012) found that cultural meta-cognition was positively related to "affect-based trust" (but not cognition-based trust) in cross-cultural relationships. Taking a moderator perspective Parayitam and Dooley (2009) studied conflict and trust in strategic decision-making teams and found that cognition-based trust was a moderator in the relationship between conflict and outcomes whereas "affect-based trust" did not moderate the relationship.

A series of studies also speaks to different roles for "affect-based trust" and cognition-based trust in leadership. Yang, Mossholder and Peng (2009) observed that cognition-based trust mediated the relationship of supervisory procedural justice with performance and job satisfaction, whereas "affect-based trust" mediated the relationship between supervisory procedural justice and helping behaviour at work. In a different spin on the mediating role of these two types of trust for justice effects, Colquitt, LePine, Piccolo, Zapata and Rich (2012) showed that "affect-based trust" mediated the social exchange-based (i.e. relationship-based) effects of organizational justice, whereas cognition-based trust mediated the uncertainty-reducing effects of justice. Miao, Newman, Schwarz and Xu (2013) reported that "affect-based trust" mediated the relationship between participative leadership and organizational commitment whereas cognition-based trust did not have a mediating role. Schaubroeck, Lam and Peng (2011) found that servant leadership influenced team performance through "affect-based trust" and team psychological safety. Transformational leadership (a concept that has been invalidated by conceptual and empirical problems; van Knippenberg & Sitkin, 2013) influenced team performance through cognitive trust. Zhu, Newman, Miao and Hooke (2013) found that "affect-based trust" mediated the relationship between transformational leadership and commitment, performance and organizational citizenship behaviour, whereas cognition-based trust negatively mediated the transformational leadership-performance relationship (one may wonder whether the negative role of cognition-based trust is due to the high correlation between the two elements of trust; i.e. controlling for the overlap with "affect-based trust", what does the residual variance in cognitive trust mean?). Yang and Mossholder (2010) observed that "affect-based trust" in a supervisor predicted in-role and extra-role behaviours, commitment and job satisfaction. Affect-based trust in management predicted commitment. Cognition-based trust in management predicted job satisfaction.

There is also some evidence that there may be cross-cultural differences in the role of "affect-based trust". Hu (2007) reported that Taiwanese managers respond more with "affect-based trust" than US managers to information that is relevant to "affect-based trust", whereas there are no country differences in responses to information relevant to cognitive trust. This finding is consistent with the greater cultural orientation on relationships (not affect) in Taiwan.

Some studies also suggest that "affect-based trust" may be the stronger influence on outcomes than cognition-based trust. Webber (2008) for example showed that "affect-based trust" has a stronger positive relationship with team performance than cognition-based trust. Carter and Mossholder (2015) found that supervisor–group trust congruence was positively related to group performance and organizational citizenship behaviour for both "affect-based trust" and cognition-based trust, but stronger for "affect-based trust". Such findings are consistent with the notion that "affect-based trust" is relationship-based more than cognition-based trust, and thus more proximal to outcomes that are contingent on the quality of the relationship.

Other work suggests a less differentiated picture, but at least one in which "affect-based trust" and cognition-based trust make independent contributions to predicting outcomes. Hansen, Morrow and Batista (2002) found that "affect-based trust" and cognition-based trust both predicted cohesion, performance and satisfaction. Chowdhury (2005) observed that both "affect-based trust" and cognition-based trust were positively related to knowledge sharing.

Conclusions to draw: unique roles of affect-based and cognition-based trust

All this work points to different roles of "affect-based trust" and cognition-based trust. "Affect-based trust" and cognition-based trust may have unique antecedents and consequences, and "affect-based trust" may be the stronger, more proximal influence on outcomes, where cognition-based trust may be seen as a basis of "affect-based trust". Other work shows that "affect-based trust" and cognition-based trust are independent predictors of outcomes. There thus is converging evidence of separate roles of "affect-based trust" and cognition-based trust.

A first-blush conclusion then would be that there are good grounds for the study of "affect-based trust" in addition to the dominant focus on cognition-based trust, especially also in view of the arguments that "affect-based trust" may be the stronger, more proximal influence on outcomes of interest. Closer consideration suggests two important caveats to that conclusion, however, that would ultimately suggest great caution in embracing the concept of "affect-based trust" and to focus on alternative ways forward in the study of affect and trust. These two caveats are addressed next.

Conclusions to draw: "affect-based trust" and cognition-based trust highly correlated

A rough inventory of the correlations observed between "affect-based trust" and cognition-based trust shows that these are most often high. Several studies report correlations above $r = .60$ or $r = .70$ (e.g. Carter & Mossholder, 2015; Chowdhury, 2005; Dowell et al., 2015; McAllister, 1995; Miao et al., 2013; Schaubroeck et al., 2013) or at least in the $r = .45$–60 range (Johnson & Grayson, 2005; Robson et al., 2008; Stewart & Gosain, 2006). Correlations of such magnitude suggest nontrivial overlap between constructs (i.e. trust as the end result likely is an important element of both, regardless of its base). Empirically, this means that not controlling for cognition-based trust in the study of "affect-based trust" may lead to attributions of influence to "affect-based trust" that may reside in the shared variance with cognition-based trust – and vice versa, but given trust's definition rooted in cognition, the former issues seems to be more worrying than the latter.

This observation is relevant in judging evidence from studies focusing on "affect-based trust" without including a measure of cognition-based trust. Chen, Eberly, Chiang, Farh and Cheng (2014) for instance found that "affect-based trust" mediated the relationship between paternalistic leadership and job performance, and Lapointe, Vandenberghe and Boudrias (2014) found that "affect-based trust" mediated the relationship between socialization tactics and organizational commitment. Taking a moderator perspective, Kim, Lee and Wong (2015) reported that supervisor humour reduced social distance with higher "affect-based trust". Reiche et al. (2014) found that subordinate organizational citizenship behaviour predicted manager trustworthy behaviour mediated by "affect-based trust", but that this mediation only held in individualistic and not in collectivistic countries. While these findings are interesting, they also raise the question of to what extent they might be attributable to the overlap between "affect-based trust" and cognition-based trust.

A first critical note thus is that the study of "affect-based trust" would benefit from taking as standard practice the inclusion of a measure of cognition-based trust. Even then, however, given the high correlations observed in several studies, future research would benefit, and arguably require, more developed measures that more clearly distinguish between the two types of trust empirically. Arguably, however, there is a more fundamental issue that would need to be addressed first – the issue I turn to next.

Conclusions to draw: "affect-based trust" confounds relationship and affect

The elephant in the room in the study of "affect-based trust" is that in definition and operationalization the concept of "affect-based trust" de facto equates relationship basis with affective basis. Whereas no one will dispute that a high-quality interpersonal relationship has affective implications, there is no theory anywhere in the social sciences that allows us to equate relationship basis with affective basis (and I do not see any scope to develop such theory). It is reasonable to assume that relationship quality is positively related to positive affect, but this thus means that the concept of "affect-based trust" confounds affective basis with relationship basis. Moreover, given that it may be argued that affect is an inseparable *aspect* of relationship quality, but not that positive affect towards another person by necessity implies good relationship quality, it seems more reasonable to treat the conceptualization and operationalization of "affect-based trust" as in effect concerning relationship-based trust rather than "affect-based trust" – all the more so because at face value the "affect-based trust" items tap into relationship quality much more than into affective basis (e.g. "We have a sharing relationship. We can both freely share our ideas, feelings and hopes." "I can talk freely to this individual about difficulties I am having at work and know that (s)he will want to listen.").

Such a reconceptualization would be consistent with the available evidence. There is not a single finding in the previous review that requires that "affect-based trust" is understood as affect-based rather than relationship-based for its interpretation; there are findings that are decidedly more parsimoniously explained from the perspective of relationship-based trust (e.g. McAllister's, (1995), antecedents findings; Colquitt et al.'s (2012) social exchange mediation finding). It would also be consistent with a positioning of relationship-based trust as distinct from person-based trust (a.k.a. cognition-based trust): trust may be based on relatively direct indicators of a person's competence and integrity, but relationship quality may also lead individuals to attribute such qualities to others, in a sense substituting for, or complementing, such more direct indicators.

Importantly, I see the notions of relationship-based trust (trust based on the quality of the relationship between parties) and person-based trust (trust based on perceptions of the other party's competence, integrity and benevolence independent of one's relationship with the other party) as helpful in clarifying how these conceptualizations and measurements are better understood than the "affect-based trust"–cognition-based trust distinction. I do not see a strong basis, however, to move forward with the notions of relationship-based and person-based trust, and complement these with a new, reconceptualized notion of affect-based trust. The reason for this is twofold. First, a basis for trust can be conceptualized and measured as an antecedent of trust and need not be reflected in a separate type (measure) of trust itself; from the notion that trust can have different bases does not logically follow that we should distinguish different types of trust. Second, and more important probably, I believe the focus should lie on the role affect plays in trust. This role can be expressed in multiple ways, from trust based on one's own affective state (the most likely definition of what would be called affect-based trust) to trust based on one's cognitive interpretation of the other party's affect. Grouping this all together as one "type" of trust makes less sense, but reducing the focus simply so we can have a well-defined third type of trust to complement relationship-based trust and person-based trust makes little sense either. The issue here, ultimately then, is not to talk about types of trust but to establish that (a) "affect-based trust" does not capture affect-based trust, and (b) that there is a good case to study the role of affect in trust.

Thus, it would be important to recognize that what is known as "affect-based trust" – but is better seen as relationship-based trust – only indirectly and in a confounded way captures a potential influence of affect (and not all potential influences of affect). This implies that a focus on this conceptualization and operationalization is not a particularly fruitful way of studying the role of affect in trust. Probably the most important conclusion from this review and conceptual analysis, then, is that to understand the role of affect in trust we would do well to break free of the concept of "affect-based trust" as it is currently understood and operationalized. With this conclusion in mind, we may ask anew what the role of affect in trust is – a question I consider in the next section.

Affect and emotions as basis for trust

The attention to the role of affect in trust is consistent with a larger movement towards the study of affect to complement a dominant focus on cognitive perspectives in research in organizational behaviour (cf. Elfenbein, 2007). Affect is understood to refer to both emotions and moods, and in relationship to trust questions regarding the role of affect can be summarized as concerning how own emotions or mood influence trust in another party, and how the other party's emotions or mood influence trust in the first party. These are questions of obvious interest in view of the evidence that own affect may influence judgment (Forgas, 1995; Schwarz & Clore, 1983) and that other's affect may both inspire own affect (Hatfield, Cacioppo & Rapson, 1994; Sy, Côté & Saavedra, 2005) and function as social information (Keltner & Haidt, 1999; Van Kleef, 2009).

The notion of affect as information (Schwarz & Clore, 1983) essentially reflects the fact that how we feel about something is informative. Our affect may influence our judgment with or without our conscious awareness. Forgas (1995) even argues that the influence of affect on judgment typically is stronger the less we are aware of the influence (i.e. because this stops us from consciously "correcting" for the influence of affect). Affect may also influence our judgment when we consciously consider it, being positive about something that "feels right" or conversely passing negative judgment on something that "does not feel right". The most obvious influence of affect is affect-congruent judgment (Forgas, 1995); positive affect (i.e. feelings that are subjectively pleasant; Watson & Tellegen, 1985) invites positive judgments, negative affect invites negative judgments.

Affect and trust: affect as information and more

Our feelings may thus also influence the degree to which we trust another party. This has been noted in conceptual analyses by Jones and George (1998) and Williams (2001) (see also Lewicki, McAllister & Bies, 1998; Saunders, Dietz & Thornhill, 2014, for the notion that trust and distrust are associated with specific emotions). Despite the general notion of affect as an influence on judgment, and these trust-specific conceptual statements, there has to date been surprisingly little empirical follow up – but empirical work does underscore the notion of affect colouring judgment. Dunn and Schweitzer (2005) found in a series of experiments that happiness and gratitude were associated with higher trust, whereas anger was associated with lower trust. Ballinger, Schoorman and Lehman (2009) found that affective reactions to leadership change predicted trust in the new leader; the more people experienced positive affect because the old leader was leaving, the more they trusted the new leader. Both studies can be seen as reflecting affect-congruent judgment in trust. Research by Lount (2010) showed experimentally that the influence of affect need not result in what could be called affect-based trust, however. Lount focused on the notion that positive mood can also invite a greater reliance on schemata, and found that the relationship between positive mood and trust was influenced by the presence of cues that indicated whether the other party was trustworthy or untrustworthy. When available cues about the other party promoted trust, people in a positive mood increased their trust; when cues promoted distrust, people in a positive mood decreased their trust. The role of affect in trust may thus be broader than as an influence infusing trust judgments.

Affect and trust: emotional contagion

Exposure to other's affect may also influence us. Moods and emotions are observable through a range of nonverbal behaviours such as facial expressions and body posture. They may also be conveyed by paraverbal aspects of communication (i.e. how we say it rather than what we say) and by verbally communicating feelings. A first way in which other's affect may influence is through emotional contagion (Elfenbein, 2014; Hatfield et al., 1994). Exposure to other's affect may invite the same affective state in an individual, for instance through mimicry of the non-verbal expression of the affect that subsequently invites the same affect in oneself. The affective state can then influence judgment and behaviour along the lines outlined in the previous paragraphs. For trust, the notion of emotional contagion would for instance imply that individuals displaying positive affect may invite more trust through a process of emotional contagion and affect-congruent judgment. I am not aware of trust research to this effect, but research in leadership and affect does show that leader affective displays may invite emotional contagion and affect-congruent judgment of leadership (e.g. Visser, van Knippenberg, Van Kleef & Wisse, 2013; for a review, see van Knippenberg & Van Kleef, 2016), and it does not seem too far-fetched to see this as circumstantial evidence that similar processes may influence trust judgments.

Affect and trust: affect as social information

Other's affect may also be processed as social information (Keltner & Haidt, 1999; Van Kleef, 2009). The notion here is not that of emotional contagion – other's affect need not influence own affect – but of cognitive interpretation (van Knippenberg & Van Kleef, 2016). Observing another party's affective state is informative. In work settings, it may for instance give indications of other's assessment of task performance (e.g. disappointment may signal performance below expectations; happiness may signal success) or of the other's assessment of us (e.g. a happy smile vs. an annoyed look in greeting). Such cognitive interpretations may feed into judgment and behaviour, as for instance illustrated by the finding that leader anger may result in the perception that the leader believes the team is performing poorly and thus invite better performance (Van Kleef, Homan, Beersma, van Knippenberg, van Knippenberg & Damen, 2009).

Others' displays of affect thus also have the potential to influence trust through a process of cognitive interpretation. I am not aware of empirical research showing exactly this, but research in leadership and affect holds some indications that can be seen as circumstantial evidence for this. Melwani, Mueller and Overbeck (2012) for instance found in experimental research that leader display of contempt or compassion resulted in more positive judgments of the leader because the affective display was interpreted as a sign of intelligence (i.e. both contempt and compassion suggest superiority to the target of the emotion, and thus competence/intelligence). From the perspective of competence as one of the key indicators of trustworthiness (Mayer et al., 1995) – and intelligence as a sign of competence – it does not seem too bold a prediction that such a cognitive interpretation could also invite trust in the leader. In a related vein, Tiedens (2001) showed experimentally that anger displays resulted in attributions of a higher status to a leader than displays of sadness; this too may be understood in terms of competence and thus as a precursor to trust. Affective displays may likewise speak to the other key indicators of trustworthiness – integrity and benevolence (Mayer et al., 1995). Arguably, for instance, the display of warm interpersonal emotions may suggest benevolence.

Conclusions to draw: a research agenda to really study affect-based trust

In sum then, there is a good case that affect – own affective state and observation of other's affective state – may influence trust. There is also initial and circumstantial evidence corroborating these notions. What is currently missing, however, is programmatic research systematically exploring these issues. From my critique on the "affect-based trust" concept as better seen as capturing relationship-based trust, I propose that the real study of affect-based trust has yet to take off. Research in moods and emotions offers a good conceptual and empirical basis to develop research on the processes through which own and other's affect may influence trust (i.e. affect-congruent judgment, emotional contagion, cognitive interpretation; e.g. van Knippenberg & Van Kleef, 2016). Given the evidence for the important role affect may play in judgment and behaviour (e.g. Elfenbein, 2007), there thus seems to be a strong case to complement the current streams of research on trust with a focus on the role of affect in trust.

References

Ballinger, G. A., Schoorman, F. D., & Lehman, D. W. 2009. Will you trust your new boss? The role of affective reactions to leadership succession. *Leadership Quarterly*, 20: 219–232.

Carter, M. Z., & Mossholder, K. W. 2015. Are we on the same page? The performance effects of congruence between supervisor and group trust. *Journal of Applied Psychology*, 100(5): 1349–1363. Advance online publication. http://dx.doi.org/10.1037/a0038798

Chen, X. P., Eberly, M. B., Chiang, T. J., Farh, J. L., & Cheng, B. S. 2014. Affective trust in Chinese leaders: Linking paternalistic leadership to employee performance. *Journal of Management*, 40: 796–819.

Chowdhury, S. 2005. The role of affect- and cognition-based trust in complex knowledge sharing. *Journal of Managerial Issues*, 17: 310–326.

Chua, R. Y. J., Ingram, P., & Morris, M. W. 2008. From the head and the heart: Locating cognition- and affect-based trust in managers' professional networks. *Academy of Management Journal*, 51: 436–452.

Chua, R. Y. J., Morris, M. W., & Mor, S. 2012. Collaborating across cultures: Cultural metacognition and affect-based trust in creative collaboration. *Organizational Behavior and Human Decision Processes*, 118: 116–131.

Colquitt, J. A., LePine, J. A., Piccolo, R. F., Zapata, C. P., & Rich, B. L. 2012. Explaining the justice–performance relationship: Trust as exchange deepener or trust as uncertainty reducer? *Journal of Applied Psychology*, 97: 1–15.

Dirks, K. T., & Ferrin, D. L. 2002. Trust in leadership: Meta-analytic findings and implications for research and practice. *Journal of Applied Psychology*, 87: 611–628.

Dowell, D., Morrison, M., & Heffernan, T. 2015. The changing importance of affective trust and cognitive trust across the relationship lifecycle: A study of business-to-business relationships. *Industrial Marketing Management*, 44: 119–130.

Dunn, J. R., Ruedy, N. E., & Schweitzer, M. E. 2012. It hurts both ways: How social comparisons harm affective and cognitive trust. *Organizational Behavior and Human Decision Processes*, 117: 2–14.

Dunn, J. R., & Schweitzer, M. E. 2005. Feeling and believing: The influence of emotion on trust. *Journal of Personality and Social Psychology*, 88: 736–748.

Elfenbein, H. A. 2007. Emotions in organizations: A review and theoretical integration. *Academy of Management Annals*, 1: 315–386.

Elfenbein, H. A. 2014. The many faces of emotional contagion: An affective process theory of affective linkage. *Organizational Psychology Review*, 4: 326–362.

Ergeneli, A., Arı, G. S., & Metin, S. 2007. Psychological empowerment and its relationship to trust in immediate managers. *Journal of Business Research*, 60: 41–49.

Forgas, J. P. 1995. Mood and judgment: The affect infusion model (AIM). *Psychological Bulletin*, 117: 39–66.

Fulmer, C. A., & Gelfand, M. J. 2012. At what level (and in whom) we trust: Trust across multiple organizational levels. *Journal of Management*, 38: 1167–1230.

Ha, B.-C., Park, Y.-K., & Cho, S. 2011. Suppliers' affective trust and trust in competency in buyers: Its effect on collaboration and logistics efficiency. *International Journal of Operations & Production Management*, 31: 56–77.

Hansen, M. H., Morrow, J. L., & Batista, J. C. 2002. The impact of trust on cooperative membership retention, performance, and satisfaction: An exploratory study. *International Food and Agribusiness Management Review*, 5: 41–59.

Hatfield, E., Cacioppo, J. T., & Rapson, R. L. 1994. *Emotional contagion*. New York, NY: Cambridge University Press.

Hu, H.-H. 2007. A comparative study of the effects of Taiwan-United States employee categorization on supervisor trust. *Social Behavior and Personality*, 35: 229–242.

Johnson, D., & Grayson, K. 2005. Cognitive and affective trust in service relationships. *Journal of Business Research*, 58: 500–507.

Jones, G. R., & George, J. M. 1998. The experience and evolution of trust: Implications for cooperation and teamwork. *Academy of Management Review*, 23: 531–546.

Keltner, D., & Haidt, J. 1999. Social function of emotions at four levels of analysis. *Cognition and Emotion*, 13: 505–521.

Kim, T.-Y., Lee, D.-R., & Wong, N. Y. S. 2015. Supervisor humor and employee outcomes: The role of social distance and affective trust in supervisor. *Journal of Business and Psychology*, 31(1): 125–139

Lapointe, E., Vandenberghe, C., & Boudrias, J.-S. 2014. Organizational socialization tactics and newcomer adjustment: The mediating role of role clarity and affect-based trust relationships. *Journal of Occupational and Organizational Psychology*, 87: 599–624.

Lewicki, R. J., McAllister, D. J., & Bies, R. J. (1998). Trust and distrust: New relationships and realities. *Academy of Management Review*, 23: 438–458.

Lewis, J. D., & Weigert, A. 1985. Trust as a social reality. *Social Forces*, 63: 967–985.

Lount, R. B. 2010. The impact of positive mood on trust in interpersonal and intergroup interactions. *Journal of Personality and Social Psychology*, 98: 420–433.

Mayer, R. C., Davis, J. H., & Schoorman, F. D. 1995. An integrative model of organizational trust. *Academy of Management Review*, 20: 709–734.

McAllister, D. J. 1995. Affect- and cognition-based trust as foundations for interpersonal cooperation in organizations. *Academy of Management Journal*, 38: 24–59.

Melwani, S., Mueller, J. S., & Overbeck, J. R. 2012. Looking down: The influence of contempt and compassion on emergent leadership categorizations. *Journal of Applied Psychology*, 97: 1171–1185.

Miao, Q., Newman, A., Schwarz, G., & Xu, L. 2013. Participative leadership and the organizational commitment of civil servants in China: The mediating effects of trust in supervisor. *British Journal of Management*, 24: S76–S92.

Newman, A., Kiazad, K., Miao, Q., & Cooper, B. 2014. Examining the cognitive and affective trust-based mechanisms underlying the relationship between ethical leadership and organisational citizenship: A case of the head leading the heart? *Journal of Business Ethics*, 123: 113–123.

Ng, K. Y., & Chua, R. Y. J. 2006. Do I contribute more when I trust more? Differential effects of cognition- and affect-based trust. *Management and Organization Review*, 2: 43–66.

Parayitam, S., & Dooley, R. S. 2009. The interplay between cognitive- and affective conflict and cognition- and affect-based trust in influencing decision outcomes. *Journal of Business Research*, 62: 789–796.

Reiche, B. S., et al. 2014. Why do managers engage in trustworthy behavior? A multilevel cross-cultural study in 18 countries. *Personnel Psychology*, 67: 61–98.

Robson, M. J., Katsikeas, C. S., & Bello, D. C. 2008. Drivers and performance outcomes of trust in international strategic alliances: The role of organizational complexity. *Organization Science*, 19: 647–665.

Rousseau, D., Sitkin, S., Burt, R., & Camerer, C. 1998. Not so different after all: A cross-discipline view of trust. *Academy of Management Review*, 23: 393–404.

Saunders, M. N. K., Dietz, G., & Thornhill, A. 2014. Trust and distrust: Polar opposites, or independent but co-existing? *Human Relations*, 67: 639–665.

Schaubroeck, J., Lam, S. S. K., & Peng, A. C. 2011. Cognition-based and affect-based trust as mediators of leader behavior influences on team performance. *Journal of Applied Psychology*, 96: 863–871.

Schaubroeck, J., Peng, A. C., & Hannah, S. T. 2013. Developing trust with peers and leaders: Impacts on organizational identification and performance during entry. *Academy of Management Journal*, 56: 1148–1168.

Schwarz, N., & Clore, G. L. 1983. Mood, misattribution, and judgment of well being: Informative and directive functions of affective states. *Journal of Personality and Social Psychology*, 45: 513–523.

Stewart, K. J., & Gosain, S. 2006. The impact of ideology on effectiveness in open source software development teams. *MIS Quarterly*, 30: 291–314.

Sy, T., Côté, S., & Saavedra, R. 2005. The contagious leader: Impact of the leader's mood on the mood of group members, group affective tone, and group processes. *Journal of Applied Psychology*, 90: 295–305.

Tiedens, L. Z. 2001. Anger and advancement versus sadness and subjugation: The effect of negative emotion expressions on social status conferral. *Journal of Personality and Social Psychology*, 80: 86–94.

Van Kleef, G. A. 2009. How emotions regulate social life: The emotions as social information (EASI) model. *Current Directions in Psychological Science*, 18: 184–188.

Van Kleef, G. A., Homan, A. C., Beersma, B., van Knippenberg, D., van Knippenberg, B., & Damen, F. 2009. Searing sentiment or cold calculation? The effects of leader emotional displays on team performance depend on follower epistemic motivation. *Academy of Management Journal*, 52: 562–580.

van Knippenberg, D., & Sitkin, S. B. 2013. A critical assessment of charismatic-transformational leadership research: Back to the drawing board? *Academy of Management Annals*, 7: 1–60.

van Knippenberg, D., & Van Kleef, G. A. 2016. Leadership and affect: Moving the hearts and minds of followers. *Academy of Management Annals*, 10: 799–840.

Visser, V., van Knippenberg, D., Van Kleef, G. A., & Wisse, B. 2013. How leader displays of happiness and sadness influence follower performance: Emotional contagion and creative versus analytical performance. *Leadership Quarterly*, 24: 172–188.

Watson, D., & Tellegen, A. 1985. Toward a consensual structure of mood. *Psychological Bulletin*, 98: 219–235.

Webber, S. 2008. Development of cognitive and affective trust in teams. *Small Group Research*, 39: 746–769.

Williams, M. 2001. In whom we trust: Group membership as an affective context for trust development. *Academy of Management Review*, 26: 377–396.

Yang, J., & Mossholder, K. W. 2010. Examining the effects of trust in leaders: A bases-and-foci approach. *Leadership Quarterly*, 21: 50–63.

Yang, J., Mossholder, K. W., & Peng, T. K. 2009. Supervisory procedural justice effects: The mediating roles of cognitive and affective trust. *Leadership Quarterly*, 20: 143–154.

Zhu, W., Newman, A., Miao, Q., & Hooke, A. 2013. Revisiting the mediating role of trust on transformational leadership effects: Do different types of trust make a difference? *Leadership Quarterly*, 24: 94–105.

2

RECIPROCAL TRUST

A self-reinforcing dynamic process

M. Audrey Korsgaard

Introduction

Interpersonal trust is commonly defined as an individual's willingness to be vulnerable to another party based on positive expectations of the actions of the other party (e.g. Mayer, Davis & Schoorman, 1995; Rousseau, Sitkin, Burt & Camerer, 1998). This definition of trust is unidirectional, underscoring the point that trust is a psychological state that originates within the individual. Yet, interpersonal trust occurs within a dyadic context, wherein parties voluntarily interact in ways that mutually benefit each other. Such relationships are characterized as social exchange relationships that extend beyond formal economic exchanges. Social exchange relationships often emerge in long-term work relationships, for example between leaders and followers (Mitchell, Cropanzano & Quisenberry, 2012) or buyers and suppliers (Poppo, Zhou & Ryo 2008), enriching the flow of resources between parties to the benefit of each party.

Both parties in an exchange relationship are at once actors – gauging the degree to which they can trust the other party to take risks in the relationship – and partners – demonstrating their trustworthiness by being a reliable and beneficent partner. Trust in this context is a complex, bidirectional phenomenon wherein each party is mutually influenced by the other's cooperation and trust. This view of trust, referred to in this chapter as *reciprocal trust*, treats trust as a dynamic process between exchange partners, providing a more complete picture of the nature and impact of trust (Krasikova & LeBreton, 2012). Adopting this view has important implications for understanding how trust is built, lost and recovered.

Context, individual differences and the flow of resources can also conspire against the relationship to breed distrust, which is qualitatively different from low trust. Whereas low trust involves a lack of confidence or positive expectations, distrust involves negative expectations of the target's conduct, a belief that such conduct involves a malicious intent (Lewicki, McAllister & Blies, 1998). Whereas trust motivates approach behaviour – a willingness to engage with a partner and take risks – distrust motivates avoidant behaviour. While it is distinct from trust (Dimoka, 2010), the same dynamics that occur with reciprocal trust are likely to influence the evolution and escalation of distrust.

This chapter explores the concept of reciprocal trust as a self-reinforcing dynamic process. Using this conceptualization, three key facets of reciprocal trust come to the fore: the direction of trust spirals, the dynamic nature of the relationships over time and the shape of the trust trajectory. Current literature is reviewed from the perspective of these three issues and areas of inquiry are identified.

Reciprocal trust as a self-reinforcing process

Reciprocal trust is not a state or characteristic of a relationship but, rather, a dynamic process that describes the evolution of trust between two parties (Korsgaard et al., 2015; Serva, Fulmer & Mayer, 2005). This process is represented by repeated cycles of trust and cooperative exchanges wherein trust emerges and builds from the balanced, voluntary exchange of resources. Reciprocal trust is predicated on the influence of trust on cooperation *and* the influence of cooperation on trust. The actor's cooperation indirectly affects the partner's cooperation through partner trust. That is, an actor's cooperative behaviour – actions that benefit the partner – is a sign of the actor's trustworthiness. The partner accordingly trusts the actor and is therefore willing to cooperate in return. The reciprocal relationship also reflects the principle that trust, by motivating cooperative behaviour, begets trust (Ferrin, Bligh & Kohles, 2008). This principle implies that the actor's trust indirectly affects the partner's trust through cooperative behaviour. Seppälä, Lipponen, Pirttila-Backman and Lipsanen (2011) supported these links, finding that supervisor's trust in the subordinate predicted subordinate trust in supervisor and was partially mediated by the extent to which the supervisor granted the subordinate autonomy (a benefit in the exchange relationship).

This process is illustrated in Figure 2.1 which describes the cycles of trust and cooperation between two exchange partners, X and Y. Note that this figure also allows that one party's cooperation may have a direct impact on the other party's cooperation ($c_x \rightarrow c_y$ and $c_y \rightarrow c_x$), and that one party's trust may have a direct impact on the other party's trust ($t_x \rightarrow t_y$ and $t_y \rightarrow t_x$)

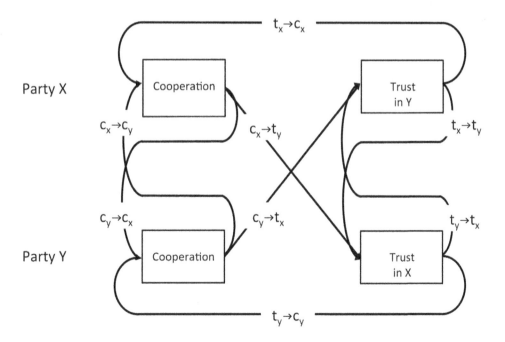

Figure 2.1 The trust–cooperation cycle

These potential direct relationships depend on the stage of the relationship and are discussed later in this chapter. At the heart of reciprocal trust is the cycle of relationships between trust and cooperation, represented by paths from trust to cooperation within persons ($t_x \rightarrow c_x$, $t_y \rightarrow c_y$) and from cooperation to trust between persons ($c_x \rightarrow t_y$, $c_y \rightarrow t_x$). Note that cycles portrayed in these figures are bidirectional in that each party is both giving and receiving benefits and thus is both a trustor and a trustee; thus, the paths of influence from Party X to Party Y and from Party Y to Party X are mirror images of one another. Further, as implied by the feedback loops, the trust-cooperation cycles involve repeated interactions over time.

The feedback loops in the reciprocal trust process suggests a self-reinforcing causal sequence wherein one party's trust, by motivating cooperation, influences the other party's trust ($t_x \rightarrow c_x \rightarrow t_y$, $t_y \rightarrow c_y \rightarrow t_{xz}$). The reciprocal trust process unfolds over time as each party alternately acts as trustor and trustee, giver and recipient. As partners cycle through this process, trust is built or dissolved as cooperation escalates or de-escalates. Thus, reciprocal trust is best conceptualized as a dynamic, self-reinforcing cycle between parties (Zand, 1972).

Evidence of the reciprocal trust cycle

Empirically examining the relationships suggested by the reciprocal trust is challenging, as it requires a bidirectional assessment of trust and cooperation in a dyadic, longitudinal framework, design features that have been put to limited use (Korsgaard et al., 2015). That said, there is a small but growing body of evidence supporting the reciprocal trust cycle. Serva et al. (2005) examined dynamics between teams of project managers and developers. They focused on risk-taking behaviours which, like cooperative behaviour, are beneficial to the other party but expose the actor to exploitation or malfeasance. They found that the managing teams' risk-taking behaviour led the teams to trust more and as a result engage in risk-taking behaviour as well. These linkages were tested over four cycles of exchanges between parties, with each party being the trustee and the trustor. Ferrin et al. (2008) also found evidence of a reciprocal trust spiral using a repeated prisoner's dilemma paradigm over five cycles of exchanges in which parties were simultaneously trustor and trustee. They found that actor cooperation predicted partner trust and, similarly, partner trust predicted partner cooperation such that both trust and cooperation increased over time. Further, they found that partner trust mediated the relationship between actor cooperation and partner cooperation. While not directly tested, their findings exhibited a growth trend in cooperation and trust over time, suggesting that participants, who were relative strangers, were liable to build trust over time through cooperative exchanges.

Another study involving strangers illustrated the power of direct experience on building reciprocal trust. Juvina, Martin, Gonzalez & Lebiere (2013) had participants play 200 rounds of a two-person dilemma game and then assessed their trust. Participants thus had ample opportunity to learn the value of cooperating (and hence acting in a trustworthy manner) and to form assessments of their partner's trustworthiness. They found that the degree of joint cooperation in the first 200 rounds predicted subsequent trust. Participants again played 200 rounds of a dilemma game and reported their trust. Cooperation rates in the second game were predicted by trust resulting from the preceding game, and cooperation in the second game predicted subsequent trust. They also found evidence that the relationship between cooperation across the two games was mediated by trust.

Halbesleben and Wheeler (2015) examined the growth in helping and trust between co-workers in established relationships. The authors argued that because coworker help is a valued resource, employees invest in relationships with coworkers who provide help by providing help to the coworker. However, employees must believe that that such investment will produce returns in the future; they must therefore trust their coworkers to provide further help and resources. This sequence reflects a cycle of cooperative exchanges and trust between employees that should increase over time. Consistent with predictions, they found that changes in coworker helping was associated with changes in employees' perceived support, Support, in turn, was associated with an increase in employees' trust in the coworker, which subsequently led to increased helping directed at the coworker. This cycle reflected growth in both trust and helping over time.

These findings provide support for a self-reinforcing dynamic cycle, but understanding of the dynamics is far from conclusive. Self-reinforcing dynamic processes imply a trajectory of growth or decline, but that trajectory can vary in direction, strength and pattern. For example, while the findings of Ferrin et al. (2008) and Habesleben and Wheeler (2015) point to an upward spiral, the incidence of trust violations (Elangovan & Shapiro, 1998) and the prevalence of distrust and cynicism (Stavrova & Ehlebracht, 2016) belie the robustness of a virtual cycle. Indeed, there are many varieties of trajectories that trust may follow (Fulmer & Gelfand, 2013). The section that follows examines what the current literature reveals about the nature of reciprocal trust viewed as a self-reinforcing dynamic process and what questions remain to be answered.

Important characteristics of reciprocal trust dynamics

Self-reinforcing dynamic processes vary on three important characteristics. First, self-reinforcing dynamic processes imply a *direction* of trajectory on the core variables. Reciprocal trust implies that cycles of relations between trust and cooperation result in changes in trust in a consistent direction, leading to growth or decay in trust over time. Second, dynamic systems not only involve changes in the levels of variables but in the *strength of the relationships over time* (Mitchell & James, 2001). Variables that may have been critical to the evolution of trust in early stages become less relevant over time, whereas other variables become highly relevant to the growth and maintenance of trust at later stages. Third, dynamic systems should specify a certain *shape* of the trajectory that indicates the rate of change and the direction of change in trust and cooperation. For example, as suggested by social exchange theory, trust may increase in an incremental, linear fashion as a function of repeated favourable exchanges. On the other hand, game theory (Axelrod, 1981) would suggest that the growth function trust may be asymptotic, wherein there is deceleration in the rate of change as the parties move to equilibrium. Conversely, the notion of optimum trust implies an inverted U function (Wicks, Berman & Jones, 1999).

The direction of trust spirals, the change in strength of reinforcing relationships and the shape of trajectories represent three key areas of inquiry in the study of reciprocal trust. To specify the direction of trust spirals, it is necessary to understand what triggers or inhibits reciprocal trust spirals in the first place and what determines whether those spirals are virtuous or vicious. The dynamic quality of the relationships underpinning reciprocal trust suggests that strength of self-reinforcing relationships between cooperation and trust change over time. The dynamics of relationship strength raises questions regarding the factors that grow versus maintain trust over longer term relationships. This aspect of reciprocal trust dynamics is central to stage models of trust (e.g. Lewicki & Bunker, 1996). To understand the shape of trust spirals, it is important to understand the factors may alter or qualify the trajectory and the nature of these shifts. For example, the points of inflection in a growth function may reflect a steady accrual of some factor that has reached some threshold (Morgeson et al., 2015) or they may reflect discontinuous shifts associated with particular events or 'shocks' (Ballinger & Rockmann, 2010). Each of these features of reciprocal trust trajectories are reviewed below.

The direction of reciprocal trust

Theory and research would suggest that the reciprocal trust cycle trust is likely to be virtuous as opposed to vicious. Early stages in a relationship are apt to begin with trusting behaviour as people are generally biased toward trusting (Wicks, Berman & Jones, 1999). A recent meta-analysis (Johnson & Mislin, 2011) of trust games (Berg, Dickhaut & McCabe, 1995) indicated that roughly 50 percent of participants will trust a stranger with a sum of money without a guarantee of any return. Further, theory on swift or presumptive trust (McKnight, Cummings & Chervany, 1998; Meyerson, Weick & Kramer 1996) posits that initial trust may exist among strangers based on predisposition and on context cues such as role constraints, group reputation and social categorization. Thus, in early interactions, individual differences and cues that predispose the individual to trust are likely to be important initiators of a virtuous trust cycle (Van der Werff & Buckley, in press). The tendency toward a virtuous cycle is also supported by empirical evidence. As noted earlier, Ferrin et al. (2008) and Halbesleben & Wheeler (2015) both found evidence of an upward spiral in the linkages between trust and cooperation over time. A recent meta-analysis (Vanneste, Puranam & Kretschmer, 2014) found a modest positive correlation between the duration of a relationship and trust, suggesting that the longer parties were in a relationship, the more they trusted one another.

However, anecdotal evidence suggests that not all relationships follow an upward trajectory (Anderson & Jap, 2005), and less is known about why this might be the case. Thus, an important question is what *initiates* a positive versus negative trajectory. Research suggests that if individuals enter into the relationship with low trust, they are likely to experience a downward spiral of low cooperation and trust (Zand, 1972). Research on the neurological underpinnings of trustworthiness judgments provides insight. This literature suggests that individuals rapidly and subconsciously infer trustworthiness based limited cues, such as facial features (Holz, 2013). Given the impact of initial impressions of trust on subsequent inferences and behaviour (McKnight et al., 1998; Holz, 2013), these swift judgments are liable to lead to very different trajectories associated with distrust or trust. These inferences can occur outside the conscious awareness of the actor and may be prompted by irrelevant cues. Individuals are more apt to rely on automatic processing and thus be subject to biasing cues when individuals are fatigued, distracted and lacking in motivation (Kruglanski, 2012). Thus, the course of trust or distrust may be set by the mindset of individual at the initiation of the relationship.

The degree to which the parties in an exchange relationship are different on individual characteristics associated with trusting may also determine whether reciprocal trust spirals are virtuous or vicious. Propensity to trust and other related individual differences predict trust and trusting behaviour (Colquitt et al., 2007), whereas individual differences such as cynicism and hostility are associated with distrust (Vranceanu, Gallo & Bogart, 2006) and self-protective or avoidant behaviour (Stavrova & Ehlebracht, 2016). Attempts to build trust on the part of the actor disposed to trust are likely to be spurned by the partner disposed to distrust, resulting in in a loss of trust on the part of the actor. Ferguson and Peterson (2015) found support for this pattern within groups, finding that diversity on propensity to trust was associated with a downward spiral in intragroup trust and performance.

Similarly, individual differences in suspicion may lead to a downward spiral of distrust. In a series of studies, Marr, Thau, Aquino & Barclay (2012) found that individuals who are prone to seek information that threatens the relationship (e.g. that their partner is cheating) are more likely to make sinister attributions about their partner; that is, they are likely to infer malicious intent to their partner, which is a hallmark of distrust (Lewicki et al., 1998). These authors also found that suspicious individuals are more likely to be socially rejected by others, thus their distrust breeds avoidant behaviour – another hallmark of distrust – on the part of their partner.

The direction of trust spirals is also shaped by direct experience. Given the fragility of trust, particularly in early stages of a relationship, the escalation of trust and cooperation is contingent on subsequent direct experience (Holtz, 2013). Insight into this contingency can be drawn from a study involving a repeated trust game (Delgado-Márquezto, Aragon-Correa Hurtado-Torres & Aguilera-Caracuel, 2015). In this study, the authors examined the relationship between changes in the amount given by the trustor on the degree of reciprocation from the trustee. They found that *increases* in the amount trustors gave were associated with *increases* in the amount returned. Thus, actors in early stages of trust tend to reciprocate proportionately, whether they are the recipient of a favour or experience a violation of an expectation. As trust is affirmed, actors may increase or expand the benefits they provide, thereby increasing their partner's trust in them.

Conversely, as trust is undermined, actors may decrease the benefits they provide, thereby decreasing their partner's trust. Early experiences, when trust is fragile, may trigger a trajectory that ultimately leads to distrust. Drawing on a qualitative study of distrust and conflict, Bijlsma,-Frankema, Sitkin & Werbel (2015) concluded that early violations can trigger a process of sense-making in which the offended party seeks to determine motives and intentions of the other party that may ultimately lead to distrust. Similarly, Tomlinson and Lewicki (2006) have argued that violations of exchanges that are persistent or very large in magnitude are liable to lead to distrust.

The strength of relationships over time

As noted above, the dynamic relationships underpinning reciprocal trust may not only involve changes in the level of the constructs – that is, growth or decline in trust – but changes in the strength of relationships as well – that is, the strength of links between cooperation and trust. That the strength of certain relationships in the reciprocal trust process will change over time is implied in stage models of trust (Lewicki & Bunker, 1996; Rousseau, Sitkin & Camerer, 1998; Shapiro, Sheppard & Cheraskin, 1992). These models suggest three stages of trust. The first, *deterrence-based* (Shapiro et al., 1992) or *calculus-based* (Lewicki & Bunker, 1996), refers to early stage relationships that are relatively transactional. Trust is conditional on the potential costs and benefits to each party of trusting and being trustworthy. In the second stage, *knowledge-based trust* is based on the accumulated knowledge of the partner's trustworthiness over repeated interactions. The third and most robust stage of trust is *identification-based* trust wherein the actor's values and interests are aligned with the partner. As the basis of trust shifts, the paths of influence between cooperation and trust change over time.

In the initial stages of the relationship, there should be a relatively strong direct causal relationship of the actor's cooperation on partner cooperation ($c_x \rightarrow c_y$, $c_y \rightarrow c_c$). The receipt of a benefit from a potential exchange partner triggers the norm of reciprocity (Gouldner, 1960). Because this is a widely held and internalized societal norm, individuals are likely to reciprocate merely out of compliance with the norm, not because they necessarily trust the benefactor. Reinforcement learning also plays a role: research suggest initial cooperative behaviour is not predicated on trust levels but merely on the experience of receiving rewards or punishments (Couchard, Van & Willinger, 2004).

Further, calculus-based trust suggests that the influence of cooperation on trust is apt to be relatively weak ($c_x \rightarrow t_y$, $c_y \rightarrow t_c$). Trust in this stage is based not on the behaviour of the other party but, rather, the incentive and disincentives for trusting and being trustworthy that are inherent in the situation. At the same time, individuals in the calculus-based stage are likely to be vigilant with regard to each other's actions. Biele, Rieskamp & Czienskowski (2006) conducted a repeated prisoner's dilemma in which participants could play with up to three different partners in each round. They also gave participants opportunity to seek information on the choices of their partner and the outcomes they received as a result of joint choices. They found that participants tended to mutually gravitate toward the same partner to the exclusion of the other two potential partners. Moreover, participants paid more attention to their partner's choices than to the outcomes they received. These findings suggest that, when individuals are forming exchange relationships, they are more concerned with learning about their partner than the actual outcome of the exchanges. This suggests that the influence of cooperative behaviour on the trust should increase as partners progress through this stage.

The impact of direct experience in early stages is likely to depend on whether the experience affirms or violates trust and the magnitude of the experience. Accepted wisdom suggests that trust is built slowly and lost quickly. This is consistent with the general psychological principle that individuals tend to be more sensitive to negative, as opposed to positive, information and experiences (Baumeister, Bratslavsky, Finkenauer & Vohs, 2001). Thus, violations of trust are apt to more strongly influence subsequent trust than affirmations. Further, partners in a downward spiral are more likely to focus on cues regarding untrustworthiness and more likely to experience negative outcomes. Thus, during early stages, experiences should exert a stronger influence on trust levels in a downward spiral than an upward spiral. Finally, if violations are high in frequency or magnitude in early stages, the costs of trust become too great and distrust is likely to be triggered (Tomlinson & Lewicki, 2006).

As the relationship progresses to knowledge-based trust, partners form more fixed impressions of one another, resulting in a more stable trusting stance that guides each party's level of cooperation. Because individuals are likely to interpret events in ways that are consistent with their expectations, trust is likely to colour interpretations of the actor's behaviour (Holz, 2013; Delgado-Marquez et al., 2015). Hence, minor deviations from the expected level of cooperation are likely tolerated or discounted. The direct relationship between actor and partner cooperation ($c_x \to c_y, c_y \to c_x$) should thus grow weaker as the partners rely more on their enduring judgments of each other in lieu of their immediate experience. Instead, the relationship between actor and partner cooperation should be mediated by trust ($c_x \to t_y \to c_y, c_y \to t_x \to c_x$). Consistent with this supposition, Ferrin et al. (2008) found that the direct relationship between actor and partner cooperation was no longer significant in later stages of interaction.

When trust progresses to the identification-based stage, changes in trust are even less contingent on patterns of cooperation. Partners at this stage are less likely to be actively assessing trustworthiness and more likely to focus on addressing the needs of their partner and the relationship. An important outgrowth of identification is that the relationship itself holds value such that individuals place a greater value on being trusted by their partner. Being trusted by the partner affirms and reinforces the actor's trust; thus there should be a direct relationship between actor and partner trust ($t_x \to t_y, t_y \to t_x$). In this way, identification-based trust motivates greater investments in the relationship and benevolent demonstrations of trust. Thus, while the impact of cooperative behaviour on trust ($c_x \to t_y, c_y \to t_x$) may be weaker at this stage, the impact of trust on cooperation ($t_y \to c_y, t_x \to c_x$) should become stronger or more expansive (Lewicki, Tomlinson & Gillespie, 2006).

The shift in paths of influence described above was supported in a recent study of teams by Jones and Shah (2016). The authors tracked the trust of team members over time, finding a general positive trajectory. The authors identified three loci of influence in the growth in trust. The first is the trustor, which encompasses the characteristics of trustor that lead them to trust. The second locus is the trustee, which encompasses the effect of the actions of the trustee in building the trustor's trust. The third locus is the dyad, which pertains to the cycle of reciprocal exchanges and the factors in the dyadic context that contribute to a relational identity (e.g. social identity). The authors estimated the variance in trustworthiness perceptions attributable to each locus over the course of the group's life. They found the trustor was most important early in the relationship and became less relevant over time. In contrast, the relevance of trustee and the dyad grew over time. These findings generally support the waxing and waning of different paths of influence in reciprocal trust as the relationship progresses through stages.

Another recent study, however, provided evidence to the contrary. In a three-month study of newcomers, Van der Werff and Buckley (in press) also found evidence of a positive trust trajectory. Consistent with theory (Holz, 2013), they found that trust propensity predicted initial levels of trust but did not predict changes in trust. However, there were no changes in the impact of presumptive cues, which theory suggests should be relevant in initial stages (e.g. McKnight et al., 1998). That is, individual differences that predispose a certain level of trust become less relevant over time, but contextual cues that predispose a certain level of trust continue to impact trust levels. Further the impact of trustworthiness cues, which were relevant as quickly as the first week of employment, did not significantly change over time. The conflicting implications of the findings of these two studies underscore the need for further work on stage models of trust.

Progression through these stages in the shifts in paths of influence that accompany stage shifts are likely to be contingent on the direction of the trust spiral. Progression to identification-based trust necessarily requires positive growth in trust. If trust is following a negative trajectory, it is likely that vigilance will remain high. Therefore, a strong causal impact of cooperation on trust is likely to persist. Such relationships are apt to stall at a low level of trust or even shift to distrust. On the other hand, Tomlinson and Lewicki (2006) have argued that individuals can develop identification-based *dis*trust. This form of distrust is based on the fact that the parties have conflicting core values. In a qualitative study of the evolution of distrust, Bijlsma-Frankema, et al. (2015) observed that distrust prevented individuals from observing positive cues Thus, like identification-based trust, identification-based distrust is thought to be robust to countervailing behaviours and cues.

Moderators of the strength of reciprocal trust

The dynamic nature of reciprocal trust addresses within-person changes in the strength of reciprocal trust. A related issue is within-dyad differences. Reciprocal trust spirals presume that partners possess or eventually develop comparable levels of trust over time (Zand, 1972). Over the course of repeated interactions, each party's trust will indirectly determine the other party's trust, leading to mutual levels of trust. Consistent with the prediction, Ferrin et al. (2008) observed correlation between partners' trust that increased over time, suggesting that the more experience exchange partners had with one another, the more likely their trust correlated. However, studies of trust between partners in various personal and work relationships suggest only modest correlations between each partner's trust in the other (Korsgaard et al., 2015) suggesting that trust between parties often fails to cohere. Given that convergence in trust is a logical outflow of the self-reinforcing effect of reciprocal trust, when trust between partners is asymmetric, it suggests a weak feedback loop that underpins the trajectory of reciprocal trust. Thus, understanding the nature of trust asymmetry provides important insights into the moderators of the strength of the reciprocal trust.

One reason why trust asymmetries occur is dyadic differences in information and power (Korsgaard et al., 2015). Because information reduces uncertainty, partners with more information may have greater trust. Similarly, partners with greater power and hence greater ability to sanction and reward exchanges, may have greater trust in their partner than their counterpart has in them. In a study of mergers and acquisitions, Graebner (2009) found trust differences between buyers and sellers that were attributable to information and power asymmetries. Further, these differences are also likely to lead to divergent interpretations of the same event. For example, persons with greater power tend to feel entitled to greater benefits (De Cremer & Van Dijk, 2005) and as a result may perceive exchanges to be fair when the less empowered party may feel the exchange was unfair. Thus, the reinforcing effect of reciprocal trust may be undermined by within-dyad differences in the sense-making process.

An important question associated with moderators of the trust trajectory is the degree to which the resulting asymmetry persists or whether asymmetry inhibits the progression of trust. Information and power asymmetry are apt to weaken feedback loops such that each party's trust may develop at different rates and stabilize at different levels. As relationships mature, partners are less vigilant about particular exchanges and more prone to hold fast to their existing impressions of one another (Lewicki et al., 2006). As a result, reciprocal trust may evolve to a state of chronic trust asymmetry. It is noteworthy that asymmetries in trust have been observed in relatively long-term personal (Cross & Simpson, 2012) and professional relationships (Brower et al., 2009) and can have negative consequences for the performance of individuals and groups (De Jong & Dirks, 2012; Carter & Mossholder, 2015).

The pattern of trust trajectories

Initial tests of reciprocal trust (e.g. Ferrin et al., 2008; Serva et al., 2005) imply or assume a linear and incremental dynamic process. This is consistent with social exchange theory, which suggests that trust levels are likely to gradually increase or decrease over time as a function of the pattern of exchanges (Blau, 1964). However, other theoretical perspectives, including game theory and stage models of trust, suggest a less linear progression in the evolution of trust. Indeed, there may be numerous nonlinear trajectories of reciprocal trust that reflect qualitatively different relationships (Fulmer & Gelfand, 2013). These trajectories are likely to reflect changes in the rate of growth as well as changes in the direction of the trajectory. Further, nonlinear trajectories may include discontinuities wherein levels of trust and cooperation shift abruptly.

Changes in the rate of change

A variety of theoretical perspectives suggest that the rate of change in trust is neither linear nor continuous. For example, game theory would suggest an asymptotic function wherein cooperation levels increase or decrease until they reach some stable point. Game theory posits that exchange partners eventually achieve an equilibrium in their exchange behaviour, meaning that each partner comes to a fixed strategy given what the other party is doing (Axelrod, 1981). Over repeated interactions, exchange partners come to understand what the best possible outcome is, given the more or less cooperative behaviour of their partner, and effectively 'lock in' to a pattern of cooperation and, hence, trust.

Similarly, once parties enter into the identification-based stage of trust and distrust, the rate of change in trust or distrust are likely to accelerate and then stabilize. A longitudinal study of newcomers to an accounting firm by Van der Werff and Buckley (in press) found the growth in trusting behaviour was nonlinear, with a deceleration after about the first month of employment, reflecting a relatively stable level of trusting behaviour. Similarly, Bijlsma-Frankema et al., (2015) observed that individuals 'lock in' to a particular level of distrust, after which perceptions and judgment are unlikely to change. Because value-based distrust contributes intractable conflict, the behaviours associated with high levels of distrust may continue to escalate.

An alternative to establishing a stable level of trust may be to continue to grow trust to an excessive degree. Trust could be considered excessive if it leads to complacency and a lack of appropriate oversight (Kramer, 1999; McEvily, Perrone & Zaheer, 2003), thus allowing for exploitation or malfeasance (Anderson & Jap, 2005). For example, Langfred (2007) found that, when individuals are working autonomously, very high levels of trust within teams were associated with lower team performance. This finding was mediated by monitoring; that is, highly trusting teams did not monitor individual behaviour closely, which is necessary to prevent process loss in teams (e.g. free riding and coordination problems). A similar phenomenon has been observed at the organizational level. Molina-Morales and Martineze-Fernadez (2006) found a curvilinear relationship between trust and innovation, indicating that very high levels of trust were associated with lower levels of innovation. While neither of these studies examined changes in trust over time, the findings indicate that there may be a point at which the trajectory for trust changes direction.

Discontinuities and thresholds

Another aspect of nonlinear change is the potential for discontinuous growth. Discontinuous growth refers to discontinuities or transitions in a phenomenon such that the phenomenon can be divided into distinct periods or phases, each with its own growth trend (Bliese, Ployhart & Chan, 2007). As noted above, stage models of trust specify distinct phases of trust. As parties transition from one phase to another, there may be shifts in trust levels. Research and theory on discontinuous change in trust is limited, but insights from theory on change and self-reinforcing systems suggest that trust spirals may exhibit discontinuous change for two main reasons: discrete events (Morgeson et al., 2015; Ballinger & Rockmann, 2010) or the accumulation of experiences that reach a threshold (Perlowa & Repenning, 2009).

Events are discrete happenings which involve some departure from the current state of the environment (Morgeson et al., 2015). Events may prompt a behavioural reaction from one or both of the parties which could trigger an abrupt increase or decrease in trust. One type of event relevant to trust is what Ballinger and Rockmann (2010) describe as anchoring events, exchanges in which the partner's behaviour deviates from expectations and is attributable to the actor. These events are effectively 'game-changers', leading individuals to apply new rules to exchanges and to reformulate new goals for the relationships. For example, a negative anchoring event may prompt revenge or competition whereas a positive event may prompt altruism. Events may also be external to the dyad, but somehow affect the rules of engagement and risks associated with the relationship. Events that are novel, critical and disruptive are more likely to prompt a revision in trust and subsequent behaviour (Morgeson et al., 2015), resulting in a shift in trust spirals.

Thresholds, in contrast, involve the accumulation of experiences or events that eventually lead to an abrupt or qualitative change. This sort of phenomenon might reflect the process of maturation or reinforcement learning implied in early stages of trust (Couchard et al., 2004) which suggests that experiential knowledge of the other party leads to a higher, more robust level of trust (Lewicki et al., 2006). An interesting implication of a threshold effect is that it would predict a period of stability while experience builds, followed by dramatic change in trust. Consistent with this prediction, Van der Werff and Buckley (in press) observed three distinct periods in the development of newcomer trust: a period of rapid growth, followed by a period of stability and trust, followed again by a period of growth in trust. This finding points to the need to understand what underlies the apparent tipping points in trust.

In the case of distrust, research (Bisjlma-Frankema et al., 2015) suggests an unfolding process that begins with cues or violations that lead one party to to question the other's motivations and values. Initially, these events may appear isolated and associated with a single domain. As these observations accumulate, they reach a threshold level wherein the partner infers a more pervasive and fundamental conflict of values, shifting from low trust to distrust. This tipping point is thought to lead to a high and robust level of distrust.

Reversals in the trust spiral

An important subset of discontinuous changes is that which involves a reversal in the direction of the spiral. Reversals may stem from the 'game-changing' events described by Ballenger and Rockman (2010) that cause individuals to revise their assessment of their partner's trustworthiness in the opposite direction to the previous trend. Once the reversal takes hold, the self-reinforcing nature of the trust spiral is likely to perpetuate the new direction of the spiral. Another important factor in reversals is the direction of the deviation. As noted earlier, individuals are apt to react more strongly to negative cues and experiences (Baumeister et al., 2001). Thus, the magnitude of an event necessary to reverse the trend in trust is likely to be lower in the case where a negative event occurs in an upward trust spiral as compared to the case where a positive event occurs in a downward spiral.

Tipping points may also play an important role. Insight into this dynamic can be drawn from Perlowa and Repenning's (2009) research on tipping points among competing processes in new product development. They examined two competing self-reinforcing processes – addressing problems to achieve goals and silencing of problems to preserve relationships. They found that, initially, silencing was intermittently used, but the accumulation of silencing compounded the performance problems that had motivated silence in the first place. Silencing reached a tipping point whereby the emphasis decisively shifted from performance goals to silencing for its own sake. The same dynamic may explain how the trajectory of trust abruptly reverses. The frequency of deviations required to reach a tipping point is likely to differ depending on the direction of the deviation, as the process that leads to a shift from negative to positive trust spiral is apt to be more challenging. Research on trust recovery suggests that consistent, positive acts are necessary to rebuild trust (Schweitzer, Hershey & Bradlow, 2006). Further, reversing a downward spiral is apt to be especially challenging if the prior untrustworthy behaviour is believed to be a result of character as opposed to ability (Kim, Ferrin, Cooper & Dirks, 2004) or to immutable as opposed to malleable qualities (Haselhuhn, Schweitzer & Wood, 2010).

The timing of the event is also relevant to shifts in the direction of spirals. In later stages of relationships, actors are apt to give greater latitude to their partner's behaviour. Thus, the quality and history of the relationship also influence reactions to behavioural deviations (Fulmer & Gelfand, 2013). Finally, individual differences may also play a role in whether a partner's behavioural deviation will result in a shift in the direction of the spiral. For example, persons high in self-esteem and those having a secure attachment style are more likely to tolerate a violation of trust, whereas those high in cynicism and equity sensitivity are likely to be more vigilant and less tolerant of trust violations (Fulmer & Gelfand, 2013).

Another factor in the reversal of trust spirals is the shadow of the future, that is, the knowledge that a relationship may soon end. Couchard et al. (2004) compared individuals playing a one-shot trust game to those playing a repeated game. Not surprisingly, players gave and returned more when they were playing repeated rounds as compared to a one-shot round. Players in the repeated condition knew how many rounds they were playing and, in the last round, shared and returned significantly less than in previous rounds. More troubling, trustees gave significantly less in the last round of the repeated game than did trustees in the one-shot condition. This finding suggests that the anticipation of the termination of a relationship can unleash a degree of selfish behaviour that is greater than what would be observed in the absence of a long-term relationship. A similar pattern was found in a study of trust between suppliers and buyers. Poppo, et al. (2008) found the length of the relationship was positively related to trust. However, this relationship was moderated by expectations of continuity. When expectations were low – that is, the shadow of the future loomed closer – trust was lower in relationships with a longer history.

Taking stock of reciprocal trust

Reciprocal trust understood as a self-reinforcing dynamic process, offers a parsimonious and compelling basis for understanding how trust develops between partners. Trust builds or degrades through repeated exchanges between partners, and the level of cooperation both drives and is driven by trust. Recent research has supported this basic process and thus provides validation of the role of reciprocal trust in the evolution of trust. But, as a dynamic self-reinforcing process, reciprocal trust involves complexities beyond simple positive linear relationships between cooperation and trust. This chapter sought to identify the aspects of this process that are not fully specified.

Several key opportunities and unresolved issues emerge from applying the reciprocal trust framework. With regard to the direction of trust spirals, our current understanding of the potential triggers of virtuous and vicious trust spirals is limited. With regard to the strength of trust spirals over time, theory provides strong logic for certain shifts in the relevance of disposition, context and behaviour over time, but the limited evidence is not entirely consistent with theory. Further, more research is needed on the moderators of growth and decline. Greater understanding of curvilinear patterns of trust and the notion of optimum trust may provide insight into how to avoid the sort of complacency that often precedes ethical scandals (Schafer and Fleming, 2014).

Perhaps the least chartered territory is the nature of discontinuous change, triggers and thresholds in trust spirals. Delineating these features of reciprocal trust promises to provide greater understanding of the evolution and devolution of trust. The study of discontinuous change – and in particularly tipping points – may foster a better understanding of the distinction between trust and distrust. While theory and research (e.g. Dimoka, 2010) strongly suggest a distinction between trust and distrust, research also suggests that they are unlikely to co-occur within the same domain (Biljsma-Frankema, Weible & Sitkin, 2015). A tipping point effect in which there is a discontinuous shift from trust to distrust would explain why trust and distrust do not co-occur. The investigation of discontinuous change offers practical value as well. For example, there are many circumstances such as employee onboarding and joint venture start-ups, in which organizations would benefit from accelerating the growth in trust.

These directions for further research point to the need to place time and time-based con-structs at the forefront of theory. As a developmental process, time has substantive meaning to reciprocal trust, particularly in the light of reinforcement learning early in relationships (Cochard et al., 2004) and threshold or tipping point effects in later relationships (Perlowa & Repenning, 2009). Conceptualizing time in terms of maturation or tipping points requires more extensive theoretical specification than currently exists. Testing relationships in a self-reinforcing dynamic model poses many challenges to quantitative and qualitative research methods. Given the complexity of these questions, scholars might benefit from exploring mixed method approaches (Turner, Cardinal, Burton, in press).

Viewing reciprocal trust as a self-reinforcing dynamic process challenges implicit thinking about trust and cooperation. There is no shortage of evidence and theorizing on the influence of cooperation on trust and of trust on cooperation. The thinking and data, while implying a self-reinforcing process, have largely developed from a static perspective on the phenomenon.

Many questions regarding the boundaries of the self-reinforcing process remain to be answered. Pursuit of answers to these questions holds promise for the theory and practice of building and maintaining trust.

References

Anderson, E., & Jap, S. D. (2005). The dark side of close relationships. *MIT Sloan Management Review*, 46(3), 75–82.

Axlerod, R., & Hamilton, W. D. (1981). The evolution of cooperation. *Science, 211*, 1390–1396.

Ballinger, G. A., & Rockmann, K. W. (2010). Chutes versus ladders: anchoring events and a punctuated-equilibrium perspective on social exchange relationships. *Academy of Management Review, 35*(3), 373–391.

Baumeister, R.F., Bratslavsky, E., Finkenauer, C., & Vohs, K.D. (2001). Bad is stronger than good. *Review of General Psychology, 5*(4), 323–370.

Berg, J., Dickhaut, J., & McCabe, K. (1995). Trust, reciprocity, and social-history. *Games and Economic Behavior, 10*(1), 122–142.

Bijlsma-Frankema, K., Sitkin, S. B., & Weibel, A. (2015). Distrust in the balance: The emergence and development of intergroup distrust in a court of law. *Organization Science, 26*(4), 1018–1039.

Blau, P.M. (1964). *Exchange and power in social life*. New Brunswick, NJ: Transaction Publishers.

Bliese, P. D., Chan, D., & Ployhart, R. E. (2007). Multilevel methods: Future directions in measurement, longitudinal analyses, and, nonnormal outcomes. *Organizational Research Methods, 10*(4), 551–563.

Brower, H. H., Lester, S. W., Korsgaard, M. A., & Dineen, B. R. (2009). A closer look at trust between managers and subordinates: Understanding the effects of both trusting and being trusted on subordinate outcomes. *Journal of Management, 35*(2), 327–347.

Carter, M. Z., & Mossholder, K. W. (2015). Are we on the same page? The performance effects of congruence between supervisor and group trust. *Journal of Applied Psychology, 100*(5), 1349–1363.

Cochard, F., Van, P. N., & Willinger, M. (2004). Trusting behavior in a repeated investment game. *Journal of Economic Behavior & Organization, 55*(1), 31–44.

De Cremer, D., & Van Dijk, E. (2005). When and why leaders put themselves first: Leader behaviour in resource allocations as a function of feeling entitled. *European Journal of Social Psychology, 35*(4), 553–563.

De Jong, B. A., & Dirks, K. T. (2012). Beyond shared perceptions of trust and monitoring in teams: implications of asymmetry and dissensus. *Journal of Applied Psychology, 97*(2), 391–406.

Delgado-Márquez, B. L., Aragón-Correa, J. A., Hurtado-Torres, N. E., & Aguilera-Caracuel, J. (2015). Does knowledge explain trust behaviors and outcomes? The different influences of initial knowledge and experiential knowledge on personal trust interactions. *International Journal of Human Resource Management, 26*(11), 1498–1513.

Dimoka, A. (2010). What does the brain tell us about trust and distrust? Evidence from a functional neuroimaging study. *MIS Quarterly, 34*(3), 373–396.

Elangovan, A. R., & Shapiro, D. L. (1998). Betrayal of trust in organizations. *The Academy of Management Review, 23*(3), 547–566.

Ferguson, A. J., & Peterson, R. S. (2015). Sinking slowly: Diversity in propensity to trust predicts downward trust spirals in small groups. *Journal of Applied Psychology, 100*(4), 1012–1024.

Ferrin, D. L., Bligh, M. C., & Kohles, J. C. (2008). It takes two to tango: An interdependence analysis of the spiraling of perceived trustworthiness and cooperation in interpersonal and intergroup relationships. *Organizational Behavior & Human Decision Processes, 107*(2), 161–178.

Fulmer, C. A., & Gelfand, M. J. (2013). How do I trust thee? Dynamic trust patterns and their individual and social contextual determinants. In *Models for intercultural collaboration and negotiation*, eds. K. Sycara, M. Gelfand, A. Abbe, pp. 97–131. New York, NY, US: Springer Science + Business Media.

Gouldner, A. W. (1960). The norm of reciprocity: A preliminary statement. *American Sociological Review, 25*(2), 161–178.

Graebner, M. E. (2009). Caveat venditor: Trust asymmetries in acquisitions of entrepreneurial firms. *Academy of Management Journal, 52*(3), 435–472.

Halbesleben, J. B., & Wheeler, A. R. (2015). To invest or, not? The role of coworker support and trust in daily reciprocal gain spirals of helping behavior. *Journal of Management, 41*(6), 1628–1650.

Haselhuhn, M. P., Schweitzer, M. E., & Wood, A. M. (2010). How implicit beliefs influence trust recovery. *Psychological Science, 21*(5), 645–648.

Holtz, B. C. (2013). Trust primacy: A model of the reciprocal relations between trust and perceived justice. *Journal of Management, 39*(7), 1891–1923.

Johnson, N. D., & Mislin, A. A. (2011). Trust games: A meta-analysis. *Journal of Economic Psychology, 32*(5), 865–889.

Juvina, I., Saleem, M., Martin, J. M., Gonzalez, C., & Lebiere, C. (2013). Reciprocal trust mediates deep transfer of learning between games of strategic interaction. *Organizational Behavior & Human Decision Processes, 120*(2), 206–215.

Kim, P. H., Ferrin, D. L., Cooper, C. D., & Dirks, K. T. (2004). Removing the shadow of suspicion: The effects of apology versus denial for repairing competence- versus integrity-based trust violations. *Journal of Applied Psychology, 89*(1), 104–118.

Korsgaard, M. A., Brower, H. H., & Lester, S. W. (2015). It isn't always mutual: A critical review of dyadic trust. *Journal of Management, 41*(1), 47–70.

Kramer, R. M. (1999). Trust and distrust in organizations: Emerging perspectives, enduring questions. *Annual Review of Psychology, 50*(1), 569.

Krasikova, D. V., & LeBreton, J. M. (2012). Just the two of us: Misalignment of theory and methods in examining dyadic phenomena. *Journal of Applied Psychology, 97*(4), 739–757.

Kruglanski, A. W. (2012). Lay epistemic theory. In *Handbook of theories of social psychology*, eds. P. M. Van Lange, A. W. Kruglanski, E. T. Higgins, pp. 201–223. Thousand Oaks, CA: Sage Publications.

Langfred, C. W. (2007). The downside of self-management: A longitudinal study of the effects of conflict on trust, autonomy, and task interdependence in self-managing teams. *Academy of Management Journal, 50*(4), 885–900.

Lewicki, R. J., & Bunker, B. B. (1996). Developing and maintaining trust in work relationships. In *Trust in organizations: Frontiers of theory and research*, eds. R. Kramer & T. R. Tyler, pp. 114–139. Thousand Oaks, CA: Sage.

Lewicki, R. J., Tomlinson, E. C., & Gillespie, N. (2006). Models of interpersonal trust development: Theoretical approaches, empirical evidence, and future directions. *Journal of Management, 32*(6), 991–1022.

Lewicki, R. J., & Robinson, R. J. (1998). Ethical and unethical bargaining tactics: An empirical study. *Journal of Business Ethics, 17*(6), 665–682.

Marr, J. C., Thau, S., Aquino, K., & Bartclay, L. J. (2012). Do I want to know? How the motivation to acquire relationship-threatening information in groups contributes to paranoid thought, suspicion behavior, and social rejection. *Organizational Behavior and Human Decision Processes, 117*(2), 285–291.

Mayer, R. C., Davis, J. H., & Schoorman, F. D. (1995). An integrative model of organizational trust. *The Academy of Management Review, 20*(3), 709–734.

McEvily, B., Perrone, V., & Zaheer, A. (2003). Introduction to the special issue on trust in an organizational context. *Organization Science, 14*(1), 1–4.

McKnight, D. H., Cummings, L. L., & Chervany, N. L. (1998). Initial trust formation in new organizational relationships. *Academy of Management Review, 23*, 473–490.

Meyerson, D., Weick, K. E., & Kramer, R. M. (1996). Swift trust and temporary groups. In *Trust in organizations: Frontiers of theory and research*, eds. R. M. Kramer & T. R. Tyler, pp. 166–195. Thousand Oaks, CA: Sage.

Mitchell, M. S., Cropanzano, R. S., & Quisenberry, D. M. (2012). Social exchange theory, exchange resources, and interpersonal relationships: A modest resolution of theoretical difficulties. In *Handbook of social resource theory: Theoretical extensions, empirical insights, and social applications*, eds. K. Törnblom, & A. Kazemi, pp. 99–118. New York, NY, US: Springer Science + Business Media.

Mitchell, T. R., & James, L. R. (2001). Building better theory: time and the specification of when things happen. *Academy of Management Review, 26*(4), 530–547.

Molina-Morales, F. X., & Martínez-Fernández, M. T. (2009). Too much love in the neighborhood can hurt: How an excess of intensity and trust in relationships may produce negative effects on firms. *Strategic Management Journal, 30*(9), 1013–1023.

Morgeson, F. P., Mitchell, T. R., & Dong, L. (2015). Event system theory: An event-oriented approach to the organizational sciences. *Academy of Management Review, 40*(4), 515–537.

Perlowa, L. A., & Repenning, N. P. (2009). The dynamics of silencing conflict. *Research in Organizational Behavior, 29*, 195–223.

Poppo, L., Zhou, K. Z., & Ryu, S. (2008). Alternative origins to interorganizational trust: An interdependence perspective on the shadow of the past and the shadow of the future. *Organization Science, 19*(1), 39–55.

Rousseau, D. M., Sitkin, S. B., Burt, R. S., & Camerer, C. (1998). Not so different after all: A cross-discipline view of trust. *Academy of Management Review, 23*(3), 393–404.

Schafer, D., & Fleming, S. (2014). BoE accused of complacency over forex rate rigging claims. *Financial Times*, Available from: www.ft.com [11 March 2014].

Schweitzer, M. E., Hershey, J. C., & Bradlow, E. T. (2006). Promises and lies: Restoring violated trust. *Organizational Behavior and Human Decision Processes, 101*(1), 1–19.

Seppälä, T., Lipponen, J., Pirttila-Backman, A., & Lipsanen, J. (2011). Reciprocity of trust in the supervisor–subordinate relationship: The mediating role of autonomy and the sense of power. *European Journal of Work & Organizational Psychology, 20*(6), 755–778.

Serva, M. A., Fuller, M. A., & Mayer, R. C. (2005). The reciprocal nature of trust: A longitudinal study of interacting teams. *Journal of Organizational Behavior, 26*(6), 625–648.

Shapiro, D. L., Sheppard, B. H., & Cheraskin, L. (1992). Business on a handshake. *Negotiation Journal, 8*(4), 365–377.

Stavrova, O., & Ehlebracht, D. (2016). Cynical Beliefs About Human Nature and income: Longitudinal and Cross-Cultural Analyses. *Journal of Personality & Social Psychology, 110*(1), 116–132.

Tomlinson, E., & Lewicki, R. J. (2006). Managing distrust in intractable conflicts. *Conflict Resolution Quarterly, 24*(2), 219–228.

Turner, S. F., Cardinal, L. B., & Burton, R. M. (in press). Research design for mixed methods: A triangulation-based framework and roadmap. *Organizational Research Methods*.

van der Werff, L., & Buckley, F. (in press). Getting to know you: A longitudinal examination of trust cues and trust development during socialization. *Journal of Management*.

Vanneste, B. S., Puranam, P., & Kretschmer, T. (2014). Trust over time in exchange relationships: Meta-analysis and theory. *Strategic Management Journal, 35*(12), 1891–1902.

Vranceanu, A., Gallo, L. C., & Bogart, L. M. (2006). Hostility and perceptions of support in ambiguous social interactions. *Journal of Individual Differences, 27*(2), 108–115.

Wicks, A. C., Berman, S. L., & Jones, T. M. (1999). The structure of optimal trust: Moral and strategic implications. *Academy of Management Review, 24*(1), 99–116.

Zand, D. E. (1972). Trust and managerial problem solving. *Administrative Science Quarterly, 17*(2), 229–239.

3

SWIFT TRUST

State-of-the-art and future research directions

Kirsimarja Blomqvist and Karen S. Cook

Introduction

In 1996, the year after Fukuyama (1995) published his major work on the role of social trust in the economic development of various societies, Kramer and Tyler edited an important collection of articles in the book, *Trust in Organizations*. In this volume Meyerson, Weick and Kramer introduced the concept '*swift trust*', which they argued applied to the rapid emergence of trust in temporary groups or what they referred to colloquially as 'organizational one-night stands', during which important, but finite, tasks are accomplished often by relative strangers with varying degrees of success. They list the significant characteristics of such groups and indicate how traditional conceptions of the development of trust generally fail to capture the ways trust functions in these more temporary forms of organizing.

In this chapter we review briefly the nature of swift trust as conceptualized by Meyerson et al. (1996) and the empirical work that has attempted to test some of the propositions they laid out. In addition, we comment on the limitations of this conceptualization and how new organizational phenomena require us to extend their work to capture innovative efforts in many domains that also exhibit rapidly forming or 'swift' trust among those who engage in these enterprises. We discuss whether this conceptualization applies to knowledge creation activities, among other types of activities, in various settings (referred to as 'fast trust', see Blomqvist, 2002 and 2005; Blomqvist & Cook, 2014).

The influential article written by Meyerson et al. (1996) twenty years ago describes swift trust as 'a unique form of collective perception and relating that is capable of managing issues of vulnerability, uncertainty, risks, and expectations' required in temporary systems where 'familiarity, shared experience, reciprocal disclosure, threats and deterrents, fulfilled promises, and demonstrations of non-exploitation of vulnerability' are not typically available (Meyerson et al., 1996, 167). The focus on temporary systems is significant because since the mid-nineties there has been a steady increase in the range and extent of activities and tasks handled by teams of people (often strangers) brought together, both within and between organizations, for brief periods to accomplish their goals. There has also been rapid growth in the connections between those within and between organizations as networks increase the potential for creative linkages between individuals and groups to work together across boundaries – virtual, physical and cultural in nature.

Trust is generally most likely to have the greatest effect in situations in which weak organizational structures exist and where risk, uncertainty and complexity are prevalent (Dirks & Ferrin, 2001). Trust enhances coordination among team members and strengthens their commitment to the accomplishment of shared goals (Dirks, 1999; De Jong & Elfring, 2010). Trust is clearly important for coordination and cohesion in ad hoc temporary organizing activities, but as Meyerson et al. (1996) suggest, its bases may be different from those in more traditional organizational settings where relationships are more structured and conditions more stable or static.

Temporary organizing efforts usually lack the characteristics of more established social systems with traditional sources of trust such as familiarity, shared experience, reciprocal disclosure, threats and deterrents, fulfilled promises and demonstrations of non-exploitation of vulnerability (see Meyerson et al., 1996, 167). They typically consist of individuals who come together to address a specific need or solve a problem. These individuals are selected for the team due to their specific expertise and skills, do not necessarily know each other on the basis of past encounters, and may not work together again in the future. Often they have a short time frame in which to accomplish the task and they need to begin action immediately as demonstrated in swift starting action teams, referred to as 'SWAT' (Meyerson et al., 1996; Wildman et al., 2012; Bakker, 2013).

Temporary teams have actually been a common mode of organizing for some time in many project-based industries such as those involving construction and film (Goodman & Goodman, 1976; Bechky, 2006), advertising, consulting and software development (e.g. Scarbrough et al., 2004), research and development (R&D), and in flight crews, combat groups and emergency response teams (Weick, 1993; Grabher, 2002, Wildman et al., 2012; Bakker, 2010 and 2013). These modes of production have often involved the emergence of 'swift' trust among those engaged in the activity, since the individuals brought together to accomplish the task at hand may be new to one another and are typically reassigned on the basis of needs or roles and may not interact again.

In the current environment, the development of digital and social technologies make temporary organizing an increasingly lucrative option for firms interested in tapping into dispersed and specialized knowledge across organizational borders. The knowledge intensification of products and services, together with global competition, has led to widespread interest in new forms of organizing knowledge-based production such as open innovation (Chesbrough, 2003; Boudreau & Lakhani, 2013), online communities (Faraj et al., 2011) and crowdsourcing (Afuah & Tucci, 2012). Thus, the rapid formation of teams to accomplish specific tasks clearly extends beyond emergency efforts to respond to critical events and other activities that support the rapid deployment of expertise to accomplish an important task, often outside of standard organizational structures.

Even if technology plays a crucial role in efficiently connecting and facilitating the work of individuals and teams with dispersed knowledge and expertise, the human element is still the key differentiating factor determining success in knowledge-based, highly competitive environments. Ad hoc forms of organizing expertise and the use of digitalization to facilitate it are very challenging for firms, as well as for individuals, because of the lack of organizational structures, processes and cultures, not to mention 'standard operating procedures'. Increasingly, complex tasks require interdependence, a willingness to be vulnerable and an ability to rely on each other, especially under tight time constraints. The role of trust is further accentuated in knowledge-intensive contexts where trust is required for individuals to even begin to disclose their knowledge and to rely on one another's expertise (Gillespie & Mann, 2004; Holste &

Fields, 2010). While trust is essential under these conditions, its evolution is not guaranteed. On the contrary, the lack of interpersonal familiarity and the existence of very tight time limits, as well as the technological mediation of communication, make the evolution of trust challenging.

Despite its popularity, it is not clear how applicable the current conceptualization of 'swift trust' is to relatively new business environments characterized by globalization, rapid technological change, and the necessity of continuous innovation. In our conclusion we discuss whether the original conceptualization of 'swift trust' should be broadened to encompass these new forms of organizing, or whether a new concept should be developed that is more appropriate for explaining rapidly evolving trust and cooperation in the domain of knowledge-intensive enterprises. We first analyse some of the past empirical research on swift trust at the team level. Then we discuss recent conceptual and qualitative research on trust to help us evaluate the boundaries of swift trust and its applicability to new domains of temporary organizing in the innovation context, and we conclude with suggestions for further research.

Swift trust: a review and commentary

Conceptualization of swift trust

Meyerson et al. (1996, 191) defined swift trust as a unique form of collective perception and relating that is capable of managing issues of vulnerability, uncertainty, risk and expectations. Swift trust, they argue, is 'more a cognitive and depersonalized action form of trust than interpersonal and there is less emphasis on feeling, commitment, and exchange' (Meyerson et al., 1996, 191). According to them, 'groups that have more time for their tasks also have more time to develop complex relations that may become problematic'. They suggest that behavioural expectations should be defined more in terms of tasks and specialties than personalities and that relationships in a temporary system are among role occupants as much as between individuals with distinct personalities (Meyerson et al., 1996, 173). The bounded nature of the temporary group focuses the mind on the task at hand thereby keeping interpersonal relations less complex (Meyerson, 1996, 190).

The term, 'swift trust', was coined to apply to temporary systems defined as 'a set of *organizational actors* working together on a complex task over a limited period of time' (Meyerson et al., 1996, 168; originally used in Goodman & Goodman, 1976, 494). The characteristics of temporary systems relevant to swift trust formation include the existence of participants' clear roles, diverse skills, limited history and prospects of working together, as well as being part of a small pool of talent often from overlapping networks, working on non-routine (unique) and complex interdependent tasks that require continuous interaction, clear deadlines and explicit goals (Meyerson et al., 1996, 169, 173, 181).

In such contexts the inherent vulnerability, uncertainty and risks involved must be managed together with the mutual expectations of the participants. The authors suggest that: '*trust must be conferred presumptively ex ante*' (Meyerson et al., 1996, 170). The temporary system characteristics required for the emergence of swift trust are viewed simultaneously as potential sources for building trust. Given vulnerability, individuals may cultivate alternative partners, projects and networks. They may also cultivate their adaptability and feeling of mastery, being able to handle anything; or they may presume that others are trustworthy, possibly initiating a positive trust-building cycle. In addition, individual reputation and the prospect of future interaction (if it exists) enhance their willingness to build trust and to be trustworthy. Role clarity also facilitates trust building in such time-constrained situations in which strangers come together relatively quickly to jointly accomplish a task.

The Meyerson et al. (1996) article is in many respects surprisingly timely despite being published twenty years ago. These authors clearly identified the changing nature of temporary systems characterized by intensified competition requiring immediate adaptability, the rise of network-based organizations, an increase in the number of temporary workers, and time compression (Meyerson et al., 1996, 169). In the following section we discuss some of the most notable empirical research on swift trust.[1]

Empirical studies of swift trust

In one of the early empirical papers on swift trust, Iacono and Weisband (1997) studied fourteen student teams in three universities carrying out interdependent tasks. Their findings indicate the importance of *initiating interaction, responding to one another,* and the *frequency of interaction.* They also found that a focus on *work content* and sufficient *social penetration* during the early phases of the project increased the teams' work effectiveness. In a subsequent study of global virtual student teams, Jarvenpaa et al. (1998) were the first to show that the perceptions of other team members' *integrity and ability* were more important than assessments of their *benevolence* in building team trust. They also discovered that members' *own propensity to trust* had a significant positive effect on trust. In a related study, Jarvenpaa and Leidner (1998) emphasize the fragile and temporal nature of swift trust, indicating that better *communication about the project and the relevant tasks* clearly helped create and maintain trust.

Following Jarvenpaa et al. (1998), Kawanattachai and Yoo (2002) subsequently investigated international MBA students' business simulations of cross-functional teams, revealing that virtual teams developed a higher degree of *cognition-based trust* than affect-based trust. They also found that the cognitive dimension of swift trust was positively related to team performance and that high-performing teams that established trust quickly were better at developing and maintaining high levels of trust throughout the project. Extending this work, Robert et al. (2009) conducted a vignette study of distributed student teams and showed that *category-based processing* of team-member characteristics and an individual's own *disposition to trust* dominated the initial formation of swift trust. They also found that once individuals obtained sufficient information to assess a team member's trustworthiness, the effects of swift trust declined and trust based on knowledge of their team members' behaviours dominated.

The more recent Crisp and Jarvenpaa (2013) study of global, virtual, ad hoc student teams enhances our understanding of the normative action components of these situations, such as *standard setting and monitoring* that helps to maintain the more fragile, early trust beliefs that form. They also discovered significant paths from early trust beliefs to normative actions, and from normative actions to later trusting beliefs, indicating the important mediating role of actions that establish and enforce norms, which then sustain trust.

Most of the existing empirical research on swift trust is carried out with student teams in experimental settings, however, there are some interesting field studies. Chuboda and Maznevski (2000), for example, study three global, virtual teams including those from a large U.S. manufacturing firm and its strategic partners. They show that effective teams fit their communication patterns to the task and generated a deep rhythm of face-to-face communication interspersed with periods of remote communication. A related ethnographic field study by Kotlarsky and Oshri (2005) of two globally distributed software-development projects emphasizes *collaboration as renewing the set of relations* between globally distributed project members through continuous participation and engagement. Later Sarker et al. (2011) studied two distributed hybrid student teams engaged in developing information systems applications for real clients. They discovered that *communication and trust work together* to influence performance, supporting previous empirical work on swift trust.

Based on a conceptual study of swift trust in a humanitarian aid supply network, Tatham and Kovacs (2010) argue that the antecedent conditions influencing the formation of trust include *third party information, dispositional trust, rules (including contracts, processes and structures), categories, and roles*. Wildman et al. (2012) integrate research on trust into a theoretical framework to describe how individual team members' trust towards their team builds based on cognitive, affective, behavioural and contextual perspectives. They suggest that trust-related schemas and emotional reactions together mediate the relationship between surface-level cues and individual-level trust in the team. Individual team members' propensities to trust have a direct effect, and imported information moderates the relationship between these surface-level cues and the mediators (Wildman et al., 2012, 4). Later Bakker et al. (2013) found in their experiment on creative teams that short-term project teams used more heuristics in their decision-making. They suggest that time pressure may lead to category-driven information processing and confirmation, rather than accuracy, and in the limited time available evaluation seems to be based on surface-level cues such as group membership (Williams, 2001) or third-party trust (Wildman et al., 2012).

Swift trust has been studied conceptually, qualitatively and quantitatively through the use of surveys and experiments. In the virtual context, researchers have primarily used surveys, complemented with participant observation and qualitative interviews (Jarvenpaa et al., 1998; Wilson et al., 2006), but they have also employed trust games and other experimental settings to investigate trust in teams (Piccoli & Ives, 2003).

The bulk of the empirical research on swift trust, however, has involved students solving relatively complex tasks requiring interdependence. Using students as the primary research population has allowed stable conditions for comparable research designs and experiments. However, the composition of student teams often lacks certain types of diversity, a limitation of the existing work on swift trust for its applicability to newer forms of organizing. Diversity is an important condition especially for knowledge creation and innovation, yet it is challenging to study with research designs that use groups of students as the main source of data. Longitudinal empirical research is helpful since it employs research designs in which trust is measured before and after various experimental interventions (e.g. exercises in which students can familiarize themselves with each other and/or evaluate each other's trustworthiness based on a pilot task they engage in prior to the experimental manipulation).

The studies we have cited have provided some valuable information concerning how trust can be intentionally built over time in virtual teams. However, Piccoli and Ives' (2003) longitudinal experimental study on virtual student teams demonstrates that behaviour control mechanisms such as reneging and incongruent behaviour revealing a failure to meet obligations had negative effects on trust in virtual teams by increasing vigilance that makes trust failures more salient. These authors point to a significant managerial dilemma: any managerial intervention that increases salience and vigilance may actually weaken virtual team trust.

What do we know in general about swift trust based on past research? First, the existing empirical research on swift trust confirms the proposition that the *trustor's disposition to trust* has an impact on swift trust. The important role of the trustor's generalized trust can be understood in light of the trustor's limited information concerning the trustee's behaviour in the early phases of collaboration.

Second, empirical research supports the Meyerson et al. (1996) idea that *swift trust is founded primarily on cognition* instead of affect. Of the trustee's attributes that reveal their trustworthiness, empirical research confirms that the *ability and integrity* dimensions have an effect on swift trust, whereas benevolence does not. It has been proposed that ability and integrity are more general and somewhat easier to evaluate with less information and time, whereas benevolence is relationship specific and requires more information, interaction and experience to assess (Wildman et al., 2012). This reasoning is in line with the collective and role-based nature of swift trust as portrayed by Meyerson et al. (1996). Further, the technology-mediated virtual team research setting, as well as the tasks examined, may be more conducive to acquiring cognitive rather than affect-based information.

Third, in line with Meyerson et al.'s (1996) original characterization of swift trust, empirical research strongly supports the role of *communication* as an important antecedent of swift trust. Researchers emphasize, especially, early, frequent and proactive communication, e.g. *initiating and responding behaviour*, and factual communication about the *project, work content and the tasks involved* as means to increase the effectiveness of teams.

Fourth, for strong team performance it has been found important that trust needs to be established quickly. Fifth, because of its fragile and temporal nature, trust also has to be maintained actively throughout the project. Building *norms for communication and behaviour*, such as *standard setting*, has been found to maintain swift trust.

Sixth, despite the emphasis on role-based trust and task-based communication, the existing qualitative research indicates that *relational communication* could strengthen emerging swift, yet fragile, trust, and have a positive effect on knowledge sharing (Kotlarsky & Oshri, 2011) and task performance (Adams et al., 2007). For example, Iacono & Weisband (1997, 412) report that teams with a high level of trust actively engaged in *socialization* and that *both cognitive and affective-based trust* were present in such teams. Based on their qualitative data, Jarvenpaa et al. (1998) suggest that *positive tone* and *empathetic task communication* reinforce trust. The Adams et al. (2007) study on swift trust in military simulations reveals that individuating information and the sharing of identity had positive effects on the rate of trust formation, as well as on task performance. In a similar vein, Jarvenpaa & Leidner (1998) found that *sharing personal information* at the beginning of the project was related to high initial team trust.

Finally, based on longitudinal studies of virtual teams it was also discovered that once individuals obtained sufficient information to assess a team member's trustworthiness, the effects of swift trust declined and trust based on knowledge of their team members' behaviours became dominant.

More recent conceptual studies of swift trust emphasize the role of *third party trust* and rules, such as contracts, processes and structures. This theorizing includes more complex models including mediating and moderating relationships. In addition, team members' emotions, not addressed much in empirical studies in virtual team contexts, are emphasized in theory development.

Studies carried out in various contexts reveal different aspects of swift trust providing a richer view of the phenomenon. It is interesting to note how the Meyerson et al. (1996) original definition of swift trust tended to dismiss consideration of the feelings, commitment and exchange so central to human social interaction by noting that swift trust is 'more a cognitive and depersonalized action form of trust than it is interpersonal' (Meyerson et al 1996, 191).

Twenty years ago the idea of rapidly evolving trust was highly novel and it may be that the de-emphasis of the more relational aspects of trust building can be partially explained by the specific time constraints and task conditions they focused on, as well as by the dominant understanding at the time that trust evolves mainly through gradual risk-taking and learning. The original theory of swift trust partly draws its novelty from showing that in time-constrained contexts trust evolves without relational investments, which were viewed as costly and as potential sources of friction. As noted by the authors: 'Moreover, there isn't time to engage in the usual forms of confidence-building activities that contribute to the development and maintenance of trust in more traditional, enduring forms of organization' (Meyerson et al., 1996, 167). Instead, 'in temporal organizations members manage their vulnerability by cultivating adaptability, feelings of mastery, alternative partners, and by presuming that others are trustworthy' (Meyerson et al., 1994, 172).

The authors do not discuss knowledge-intensive collaboration, accentuated more recently in contemporary contexts, yet they do pay attention to context by noting that the nature of the task interdependence and the vulnerability involved may be enough to trigger the rapid development of trust (Meyerson et al., 1996, 175). This discussion reflects their specific notion of swift trust. In the past few decades there has been less research on the role of emotions and trust in organizational contexts (with some exceptions, e.g. Williams, 2001) and only relatively recently has there been a call for more research on the relationship between emotions and trust in the organizational context (Schoorman et al., 2007).

The role of trust depends on the nature of the tasks involved as well as the situation. Much of the research on trust is carried out in virtual contexts where the computer-mediated nature of the communication tends to depersonalize the interactions. Knowledge-intensive creative tasks may require more or different types of trust than other types of tasks. Some situations provide more information concerning trustworthiness than others do.

We expect that the depersonalizing effect of computer-mediated communication, as well as the changing nature of the tasks and the participants involved, will affect the emergence of swift trust and its impact (for more on the contextual nature of trust, see Lewis & Weigert, 1985; Rousseau & Fried, 2001; for trust in the Internet see van der Werff et al., this volume). Next, we discuss these changing contexts involving new types of organizing efforts as well as the applicability of the notion of swift trust.

Extending swift trust to new domains of organizational activity

In this section we identify some potential directions for future research based on the nature of current business environments and an increasing focus on knowledge-intensive products and services. To illustrate the changing nature of trust and its application at both the dyadic and community levels, we briefly outline ongoing research on rapidly evolving trust in encounters between Silicon Valley investors and start-up founders (e.g. Blomqvist & Cook, 2014), as well as research on experts solving complex problems on a digital platform (Blomqvist et al., 2015). We reflect on the implications of changes in the contemporary business context for rapidly evolving trust and whether such phenomena require a broader conceptualization of swift trust. In the process, we identify some of the weaknesses or limitations of the existing conceptualization.

From interpersonal relationships to interpersonal relationships

Meyerson et al (1996) focused on temporary systems defined as 'a set of *organizational actors* working together on a complex task over a limited period of time' (Bakker, 2010, 468; Meyerson et al., 1996). Goodman & Goodman (1976, 492) emphasized the diverse set of individuals involved in the theatre context identified as: 'a set of *diversely skilled people* working together on a complex task over a limited period of time'. A focus on the interpersonal context is relevant in the current environment in which the rapid development of IT-based and social technologies has made it possible and increasingly common for individual agents (often not affiliated with specific organizations) to engage in temporary groups to solve ad hoc tasks on digital platforms (e.g. Yoo et al., 2012).

From cognitive to affective based trust

As discussed earlier, rapidly evolving 'swift' trust is conceptualized as being based on cognitive processes, not on affect. However, the increasing knowledge intensiveness of team tasks calls for affect-based trust that enables individuals to share ideas and discuss personal insights derived from their tacit knowledge. Affect-based trust provides the relational space often required for such creative interactions and the generation of new knowledge essential to the production of innovative outcomes. Interestingly, it is not only the intensification of knowledge, but also the rapid development of complex mediating technologies, that requires an emphasis on the role of emotions in heuristic decision-making regarding trustworthiness, as argued in the van der Werff et al. chapter on trust in the Internet in this volume. Current research on trust and fairness (see Chapter 10 by Lind, this volume; also Chapter 14 by Tomlinson, this volume re: causal attributions of trustworthiness) indicates that early assessments of the fairness and integrity of the actors involved is also key to whether trust develops. Lind (this volume), in reviewing the relevant evidence, notes that fairness heuristics are typically used as early clues to the potential trustworthiness of others, especially of those in authority relations. Clearly, future research should focus more on affect and the emotional components of swift trust, de-emphasized in earlier work (with a few exceptions, e.g. Wildman et al., 2012).

To support this line of inquiry we note that Jarvenpaa & Leidner (1998), based on qualitative data, find that empathetic task communication and the adoption of a positive tone had a positive impact on team processes and outcomes. In addition, some of the early research on temporary forms of organizing indicates that interpersonal liking is an important factor in team leadership (see Bakker, 2010). The role of emotions and positive affect is accentuated especially in the case of relatively demanding, creative tasks and contexts that focus on innovation (Blomqvist & Cook, 2014).

From pre-specified contributions to creative collaboration requiring tacit knowledge

Empirical research on swift trust, as noted above, has mainly dealt with student teams working on interdependent tasks such as the development of business plans. These teams tend to lack the full range of characteristics that define collaborative, creative teams. Creative teamwork involves building synergy across domain specific knowledge, the continuous generation of ideas, and very few pre-specified contributions (Malhotra et al., 2001), as might be involved in more routine role-based tasks. In line with Malhotra et al. (2001) we argue that the continuous pursuit of innovation and the need to focus on solving complex problems in the current environment requires new ways of working given the open-ended nature of the tasks at hand, instead of the enactment of pre-planned modes of operation (and/or role based performances) that tend to assume the existence of more predictable tasks.

From clear to more ambiguous expectations

Meyerson et al.'s (1996) definition of swift trust in temporary teams involves clear tasks and explicit deadlines. Wildman et al. (2012: 2) describe the immediate and urgent nature of task performance as the defining characteristic of swift starting action teams as they perform the relevant task 'almost immediately' upon team formation. Meyerson et al. (1996, 175) suggest that trust in temporary systems can develop swiftly because the expectations that are invoked tend to be general, task based, plausible, easy to confirm, and stable.

In contemporary business environments, in contrast, ad hoc teams may start to collaborate without a clear task. In expert communities, such as those involved with *Ideo* and *Solved* that apply design-thinking methods, complex problem solving may begin with a 'define' phase during which participants make sense of the task before actually attempting to solve the problem. Sometimes experts start interacting even earlier, discussing the possible problem or opportunity before moving to the task definition phase. The unclear and more ambiguous nature of the task changes the focus and the temporal rhythm that is characteristic of the evolution of swift trust. Individuals' expectations may be more ambiguous and dynamic when they are not easy to confirm and not based on clear tasks or divisions of labour. This type of situation involves greater uncertainty and risks that make us question whether swift trust, if it occurs, is sufficient in these contexts for efficient team collaboration.

More fluid than stable team composition

Digital technologies and platforms provide opportunities for the generation of fast product and service pilot projects that benefit not only the focal firms, but also their complementary ecosystem partners. The ambiguous nature of the complex problem to be solved and the technology involved leads to the formation of increasingly fluid temporary teams, where experts join and exit the innovation process along the way (Brandon & Hollingshead, 2004). The fluidity of these teams provides a challenge for the existing conceptualization of swift trust because it requires ongoing efforts on the part of team members to build reciprocal trust with new individuals who join the team, as well as a focus on maintaining team-level trust when the composition of the team changes. Roles and norms have to be continuously renegotiated and re-enforced. In addition, new member socialization has to be fast paced and effective.

From a limited to an unlimited pool of talent and less common ground

Meyerson et al (1996, 173, 181) explicitly list the characteristics of temporary systems that have an impact on the emergence of swift trust. One such characteristic is that the 'participants are part of a limited pool of talent in overlapping networks'. This fact creates fertile ground for trust in part because overlapping networks reinforce reputations and norms of trustworthiness. Globalization, together with the rise of the digital talent platforms, has changed the situation so that in the current business environment there is an almost unlimited pool of talent and many of those willing to be engaged do not come from networks that overlap. As a result, over time there may be more unfamiliar members joining the ongoing enterprise, much less third party 'guaranteed' trust, and fewer social control mechanisms readily available as antecedents of swift trust.

The increasingly unfamiliar and heterogeneous nature of the actors joining these innovation efforts implies a need for different social, economic and legal relationships (Purvis et al., 2001; Yoo et al., 2012, see also Chapter 22 by van der Werff et al., this volume). In many current business environments, digitalization and the distributed innovation process increase the heterogeneity of the knowledge resources available through connecting distinct industries and previously unrelated bodies of knowledge. Such efforts require an understanding of how to integrate these heterogeneous knowledge resources derived from highly specialized professions and industries (Yoo et al., 2012, 1401). The complexity involved necessitates trust, even trust that emerges quickly, but it is not based on clear roles, standardized expectations, existing normative frameworks or network-based reputations.

Based on our review of the concept *swift trust* and the subsequent empirical research on this topic, we have learned that swift trust is first and foremost about cognitive trust. This rapidly evolving type of trust is based on predispositions, heuristics, social categorization, active communication and actions supporting the heuristics or providing trust as a byproduct of action. Benevolence and affect have not been viewed as part of swift trust, even if the complementary qualitative data (Jarvenpaa et al., 1998; Iacono & Weisband, 1997; Kotlarsky & Oshri, 2011; Adams, 2007) and conceptual research (Williams, 2001; Wildman et al., 2012) indicate that affect-based trust may support high-performance teams. In addition, our qualitative data from past and ongoing research in knowledge-intensive contexts such as R&D collaborations in small and large technology firms (Blomqvist, 2002 and 2005), first encounters between start-up founders and investors (Blomqvist & Cook, 2014) and expert teams solving complex problems on digital platforms (Blomqvist & Cook, 2015) support the importance of affect in rapidly evolving trust between diverse and unfamiliar parties engaged in knowledge-intensive collaborations.

In qualitative research on a virtually operating expert community Blomqvist et al. (2015) find that experts have expectations beyond those that derive from cognitive trust concerning other experts as individuals and not just as occupants of particular roles. A more extensive form of trust based on affect, as well as cognition, enables them to share valuable tacit knowledge and to understand how to communicate in ways that enhance mutual understanding. While role-based trust and task-based communications may suffice for relatively tangible tasks, they do not suffice for intangible, creative and open-ended tasks in which participants need to engage as individuals, without the restrictions often produced by formal roles. These factors result in an increase in vulnerability and require stronger trust than that associated with role or task-based collaboration. Exchanging personal views, ideas and intuitions under these conditions makes it possible to co-create or innovate based on participants' shared tacit knowledge.

In first encounters between start-up founders and investors, founders are very attentive to multiple cues and they analyse the *behavioural, cognitive and affect-based cues* given off by potential investors. Investors prefer to spend time only with founders they like and find coachable. Thus, *interpersonal affect* plays a key role in investor decision-making, which is, not characteristic of interactions that tend to be based on 'swift trust' (Blomqvist & Cook, 2014).

We argue that the cognitive view of swift trust is too narrow, especially for contemporary knowledge-intensive contexts in which knowledge sharing, co-creation and innovation have become the raison d'être for collaboration. Findings from recent research indicate that affect *complements but does not substitute for* the cognitive basis of rapidly evolving trust. The importance of affect is accentuated in time-constrained situations since warmth and liking are often processed intuitively even *before* cognitive evaluations occur (Fiske et al., 2007). Analytical evaluations of the competence dimension of trustworthiness becomes more difficult the greater the diversity of the parties involved. Positive affect may also be interpreted as a signal of goodwill trust providing a type of heuristic or set of cues concerning the perceived trustworthiness of the parties involved in the task at hand (Dunn & Schweitzer, 2005; Izard, 2009). In general, we view the findings concerning the bases of swift trust and its impact to be dependent on the research context.

More field research in various contexts could provide a richer view of the wide range of settings in which trust emerges rapidly and is central to task success.

Conclusions

The rapid pace of technological change and the increasingly dispersed nature of valuable knowledge makes it ever more important for individuals and organizations to make new connections, for which the ability to build trust quickly is a significant element of potential success. We expect that the time currently needed to develop trust through technology-mediated communication is likely to decrease due to the existence of media-rich communication platforms and applications that enhance virtual communication across space and time. The ongoing technological developments together with social media tools and the changing culture of communication provide opportunities for media-rich, multiplex communication that produces information concerning different bases of trust including personality and identity.

Further research is needed on the relational perspective and how parties learn of each other's personal identities. Meyerson et al. (1996, 173) note that: 'people who enact roles in an innovative and idiosyncratic manner could incur distrust'. Roles provide predictability, yet the contemporary need for continuous innovation calls for synergies through the creative combination of diverse and idiosyncratic thinking from agents acting as individual personalities, not only as role occupants. The focus on role-based trust is thus a limitation of the concept of *swift trust*, especially in the relatively new era of knowledge-based innovation, since task-relevant roles are rarely fully explicitly defined a priori in such uncharted territory.

There is a great deal of practical interest in rapidly evolving trust, not only among knowledge-intensive firms and knowledge workers, but also among those who develop digitalized business models such as those represented by TaskRabbit, Uber and Airbnb. Research on rapidly evolving trust has practical relevance in many types of online social interactions and transactions (e.g. among peers or P2P, consumers or C2C, businesses to consumers or B2C, and business to business or B2B) ranging from dating to the renting, selling and even the sharing of goods and services (Sundararajan, 2016; Parker et. al., 2016).

Automation, cloud technologies and artificial intelligence are predicted to replace up to 49 percent of the current jobs in Europe and the United States (Frey & Osborne, 2013, see also McAfee & Brynjolfsson, 2014). During this shift, complex human abilities such as those involving interpersonal social skills and an ability to rapidly build interpersonal trust in face-to-face or online interactions are essential for a variety of human tasks. Studying individual mechanisms for coping with the management of vulnerability, risk, uncertainty and personal expectations in temporary freelance groups, could be highly relevant for those not only investigating, but also implementing digital talent platforms.

Furthermore, we expect that understanding the dynamics of rapidly evolving trust is essential for the continued development of social technologies, enabling efficient and effective interdependent online collaborations. The more there is need for the interdependency, task complexity, and need for creativity, the more important is the ability to build trust rapidly. Finally, we expect that the most interesting and valuable applications come from combining trust-enabling social technologies with the high-level expertise of those equipped with the skills, values and norms to quickly build trust.

At its best, rapidly evolving interpersonal trust makes cooperation more efficient and often personally satisfying. At its worst, if manipulated, it can also lead to opportunism and even distrust. The fast-changing context for work- and business-related social interactions requires revisiting our theories of trust and our assumptions about the evolution of trust. More fluid structures require quick assessments of trustworthiness and rapid trust building. Understanding these processes is likely to be increasingly useful and potentially very significant in an ever-changing global economy in which interactions and transactions are primarily digitally mediated. The work on swift trust opened the door to studying such phenomena. Now we need to extend that work and develop a broader conceptualization that will inform us about the terms of trust and its evolution in more complex, rapidly changing social and economic environments.

Note

1   In selecting the articles for review (included in Table A4.1 in Appendix 4.1) we searched for articles published after 1996 in which swift trust was one of the key concepts or mentioned in the abstract. This yielded over three hundred article abstracts, which we reviewed to find empirical work on swift trust, preferably in which there were propositions about swift trust. In line with Meyerson et al. (1996) our primary interest was swift trust in teams. Given this focus we excluded literature from the e-commerce context. Because the number of empirical studies about swift trust in teams was scarce, we added selected conceptual and/or qualitative articles not specifically including propositions on swift trust, but enhancing our understanding of the nature of rapidly evolving trust.

References

Adams, B., Waldherr, S., Sartori, J., & Thomson, M. (2007). Swift trust in distributed ad hoc teams. Retrieved from http://oai.dtic.mil/oai/oai?verb=getRecord&metadataPrefix=html&identifier=ADA47 7148

Afuah, A., & Tucci, C. L. (2012). Crowdsourcing as a solution to distant search. *Academy of Management Review*, *37*(3), 355–375.

Bakker, R. M. (2010). Taking stock of temporary organizational forms: A systematic review and research agenda. *International Journal of Management Reviews*, *12*(4), 466–486.

Bakker, R. M., Boroş, S., Kenis, P., & Oerlemans, L. A. (2013). It's only temporary: time frame and the dynamics of creative project teams. *British Journal of Management*, *24*(3), 383–397.

Bechky, B. A. (2006). Gaffers, gofers, and grips: Role-based coordination in temporary organizations. *Organization Science*, *17*(1), 3–21.

Blomqvist K. (2002). Partnering in the Dynamic Environment: The Role of Trust in Asymmetric Technology Partnership Formation. PhD thesis. Acta Universitatis Lappeenrantaensis 122.

Blomqvist K. (2005) Trust in a dynamic environment – Fast trust as a threshold condition for asymmetric technology partnership formation in the ICT sector. In *Trust in Pressure, Investigations of Trust and Trust Building in Uncertain Circumstances*, K. Bijlsma-Frankema & R. Woothuis (eds), Cheltenham, UK, pp. 127–147.

Blomqvist K., & Cook, K. (2014). It's like falling in love! Fast trust in first knowledge encounters between socio-cognitively diverse individuals. A paper presented at EGOS conference, July 3–5, Rotterdam.

Blomqvist, K., Cook, K., & Kemppinen, K. (2015). Fast evolving trust in virtually operating global problem solving teams, a presentation at Academy of Management 2015 Symposium on Team-based organizations in a global new world org. by Lena Zander, Gundula Lücke and Audr I. Mockaitis.

Boudreau, K. J., & Lakhani, K. R. (2013). Using the crowd as an innovation partner. *Harvard Business Review*, *91*(4), 60–69.

Brandon, D. P., & Hollingshead, A. B. (2004). Transactive memory systems in organizations: Matching tasks, expertise, and people. *Organization Science*, *15*(6), 633–644.

Brynjolfsson, E., & McAfee, A. (2014). *The Second Machine Age: Work, Progress, and Prosperity in a Time of Brilliant Technologies*. Norton.

Chesbrough, H. (2003). The era of open innovation. *MIT Sloan Management Review*, *44*(3), 35–41.

Crisp, C. B., & Jarvenpaa, S. L. (2013). Swift trust in global virtual teams. *Journal of Personnel Psychology*, *12*(1), 45–56.

De Jong, B. A., & Elfring, T. (2010). How does trust affect the performance of ongoing teams? The mediating role of reflexivity, monitoring, and effort. *Academy of Management Journal*, *53*(3), 535–549.

Dirks, K. T. (1999). The effects of interpersonal trust on work group performance. *Journal of Applied Psychology*, *84*(3), 445.

Dirks, K. T., & Ferrin, D. L. (2001). The role of trust in organizational settings. *Organization Science*, *12*(4), 450–467.

Dunn J. R., & Schweitzer M. E. (2005). Feeling and believing. The influence of emotion on trust. In *Journal of Personality and Social Psychology*, *88*(5), 736–748.

Faraj, S., Jarvenpaa, S. L., & Majchrzak, A. (2011). Knowledge collaboration in online communities. *Organization Science*, *22*(5), 1224–1239.

Fiske, S. T., Cuddy A. J. C., & Glick P. (2007). Universal dimensions of social cognition: warmth and competence. In *Trends in Cognitive Sciences* 11(2), 77–83.

Frey, C. B., & Osborne, M. A. (2013). *The Future of Employment. How Susceptible Are Jobs to Computerisation.* Working paper. Oxford Martin School, Oxford University.

Gillespie, N. A., & Mann, L. (2004). Transformational leadership and shared values: The building blocks of trust. *Journal of Managerial Psychology*, *19*(6), 588–607.

Goodman, R. A., & Goodman, L. P. (1976). Some management issues in temporary systems: A study of professional development and manpower: The theater case. *Administrative Science Quarterly*, 21, 494–501.

Grabher, G. (2002). Cool projects, boring institutions: temporary collaboration in social context. *Regional Studies*, *36*(3), 205–214.

Holste, J. S., & Fields, D. (2010). Trust and tacit knowledge sharing and use. *Journal of Knowledge Management*, *14*(1), 128–140.

Iacono, C. S., & Weisband, S. (1997, January). Developing trust in virtual teams. In *Proceedings of the Thirtieth Hawaii International Conference on System Sciences*, (Vol. 2, pp. 412–420).

Izard, C. E. (2009). Emotion theory and research: Highlights, unanswered questions, and emerging issues. *Annual review of Psychology*, 60, 1-25.

Jarvenpaa, S. L., & Leidner, D. E. (1998). Communication and trust in global virtual teams. *Journal of Computer-Mediated Communication*, *3*(4), 791–815.

Jarvenpaa, S. L., Knoll, K., & Leidner, D. E. (1998). Is anybody out there? Antecedents of trust in global virtual teams. *Journal of Management Information Systems*, *14*(4), 29–64.

Kotlarsky, J., & Oshri, I. (2005). Social ties, knowledge sharing and successful collaboration in globally distributed system development projects. *European Journal of Information Systems*, *14*(1), 37–48.

Lewis, J. D., & Weigert, A. (1985). Trust as a social reality. *Social Forces*, *63*(4), 967–985.

Malhotra, A., Majchrzak, A., Carman, R., & Lott, V. (2001). Radical innovation without collocation: A case study at Boeing-Rocketdyne. *MIS Quarterly*, *25*(2), 229–249.

Meyerson, D., Weick, K. E., & Kramer, R. M. (1996). Swift trust and temporary groups. In *Trust Organizations: Frontiers of Theory and Research*, 166–195.

Parker, G., Van Alstyne, M., & Choudary, S. (2016). *Platform Revolution*. New York: Norton.

Piccoli, G., & Ives, B. (2003). Trust and the unintended effects of behavior control in virtual teams. *MIS Quarterly*, R. M. Kramer & T. R. Tyler (eds), Thousand Oaks, CA: Sage, pp. 365–395.

Purvis, R. L., Sambamurthy, V., & Zmud, R. W. (2001). The assimilation of knowledge platforms in organizations: An empirical investigation. *Organization Science*, *12*(2), 117–135.

Robert, L. P., Denis, A. R., & Hung, Y. T. C. (2009). Individual swift trust and knowledge-based trust in face-to-face and virtual team members. *Journal of Management Information Systems*, *26*(2), 241–279.

Rousseau, D. M., & Fried, Y. (2001). Location, location, location: contextualizing organizational research. *Journal of Organizational Behavior*, *22*(1), 1–13

Sarker, S., Ahuja, M., Sarker, S., & Kirkeby, S. (2011). The role of communication and trust in global virtual teams: a social network perspective. *Journal of Management Information Systems*, *28*(1), 273–310.

Schoorman, F. D., Mayer, R. C., & Davis, J. H. (2007). An integrative model of organizational trust: Past, present, and future. *Academy of Management Review*, *32*(2), 344–354.

Sundararajan, A. (2016). *The Sharing Economy: The End of Employment and the Rise of Crowd-Based Capitalism.* MIT Press.

Tatham, P., & Kovács, G. (2010). The application of 'swift trust' to humanitarian logistics. *International Journal of Production Economics*, *126*(1), 35–45.

Wildman, J. L., Shuffler, M. L., Lazzara, E. H., Fiore, S. M., Burke, C. S., Salas, E., & Garven, S. (2012). Trust development in swift starting action teams: A multilevel framework. *Group & Organization Management*, *37*(2), 137–170.

Williams, M. (2001). In whom we trust: Group membership as an affective context for trust development. *Academy of Management Review, 26*(3), 377–396.

Wilson, J. M., Straus, S. G., & McEvily, B. (2006). All in due time: The development of trust in computer-mediated and face-to-face teams. *Organizational Behavior and Human Decision Processes, 99*(1), 16–33.

Yoo, Y., Boland Jr, R. J., Lyytinen, K., & Majchrzak, A. (2012). Organizing for innovation in the digitized world. *Organization Science, 23*(5), 1398–1408.

Appendix 3.1

Table A3.1 Selected research articles on swift trust

Reference	Conceptualization	Theoretical background	Research context	Method & data	Task	Findings
Meyerson, D., Weick, K.E. & Kramer, R.M. (1996). Swift trust and temporary groups. In *Trust in Organizations: Frontiers of Theory and Research*, 166–195.	'A unique form of collective perception and relating that is capable of managing issues of vulnerability, uncertainty, risk and expectations'. It is more a cognitive and depersonalized action form of trust than interpersonal, and there is less emphasis on feeling, commitment, and exchange' (Meyerson et al. (1996, 191)	N/A	Temporary teams, mainly focus in F2F teams, illustrations from theatre and film industry	Conceptual study with illustrations from practice and other studies	Complex, non-routine (unique) tasks requiring interdependency and continuous relating	Paper is theoretical with illustrations from various contexts
Iacono, C. S., & Weisband, S. (1997, January). Developing trust in virtual teams. In *Proceedings of the Thirtieth Hawaii International Conference on System Sciences* (Vol. 2, pp. 412–420).	A temporary, distributed work group as a group of people who must work closely together for a short period of time, learn from each other and accomplish specific goals, but for whom face-to-face contact is too costly or simply not possible most of the time	N/A. Focus on naturally occurring communication in context. Communication is conceptualized as a social activity requiring the attention and interaction of two or more people	Student teams from three US universities	A survey and discussion of analysis of 14 teams of students from three different universities	Interdependent work: research, write and present a five page policy paper	They did not provide clear propositions but analysed team communication through discourse analysis as *initiations* and *responses* in communication interaction. They found that high levels of trust were maintained in teams that engaged in

continued . . . .

Table A3.1 Continued

Reference	Conceptualization	Theoretical background	Research context	Method & data	Task	Findings
						continuous and frequent interaction, were more efficient in moving through the phases of the project, focused on the work content of their projects, and achieved sufficient amount of social penetration during first part of the project (Iacono & Weisband 1997, p. 412)
Jarvenpaa, S-L; Knoll, K. & Leidner, D.E. (1998). Is anybody out there? Antecedents of trust in global virtual teams. *Journal of Management Information Systems*, 14(4), 29–64	Swift trust is based on broad categorical social structures and clear roles and later on action	Meyerson et al. (1996) Swift trust	Global temporary virtual teams	8-week study where 3 virtual exercises given to 350 students forming 75 teams	First two voluntary tasks to provide information of ability, goodwill and integrity, then to propose and present a www service or offering to global IS practitioners	At first team trust was predicted more by predictions of other team members' integrity, and least by their benevolence. The salience of other members' perceived ability on trust decreases over time. Members' own propensity to trust has a significant effect on trust. High trust teams exhibit swift trust from the outset

Citation	Definition	Theory basis	Team type	Study	Findings
Jarvenpaa, S.L. & Leidner, D.E. (1998). Communication and trust in global virtual teams. *Organization Science*, 3(4,) 791–815	Swift trust is based on broad categorical social structures and clear roles and later on (depersonalized) action. Trust as the willingness of a party to be vulnerable to the actions of another party based on the expectation the other will perform a particular action important to the trustor, irrespective of the ability to monitor or control that other party. (Meyerson et al., 1996)	Meyerson et al. (1996); McGrath (1991) Time, Interaction, and Performance (TIP) theory; Walther (1997) Social Identification/ Deindividuation theory (SIDE)	Global temporary virtual teams	8-week study with 3 virtual exercises given to 350 students forming 75 teams (same as Jarvenpaa et al, 1999)	The results suggest that global virtual teams may experience a form of 'swift' trust, but such trust appears to be very fragile and temporal. Communication about project and task appears to be necessary for maintaining trust. Social communication complementing task communication may strengthen trust
Kawanattachai, P. & Yoo, Y. (2002). Dynamic nature of trust in virtual teams. *Journal of Strategic Information Systems*, 11, 186–213	Trusting other members from the beginning of the project, not on the basis of past experiences, but rather on the basis of their background, professional credentials and affiliations	Meyerson et al. (1996); McAllister (1995) on Cognitive and affect-based trust	Global temporary virtual teams	Web-based business simulation game with 146 MBA students of 10 nationalities forming 36 four-person virtual teams	Kawanattachai & Yoo's findings supported the role of cognition-based trust in virtual teams. They found first that virtual teams developed a higher degree of *cognition-based trust* than affect-based trust (H1). They also found that the swift trust in cognitive dimension was related to team

continued . . . .

Table A3.1 Continued

Reference	Conceptualization	Theoretical background	Research context	Method & data	Task	Findings
						performance (H2) and that the high-performing teams establishing trust quickly were better at developing and maintaining high-level trust throughout the project.
Kotlarsky, J., & Oshri, I. (2005). Social ties, knowledge sharing and successful collaboration in globally distributed system development projects. *European Journal of Information Systems*, 14(1), 37–48	Key concepts are transactive memory and rapport	N/A	Distributed system development teams at SAP and LeCroy	An in-depth ethnographic study of globally distributed software development projects. A case study with 10 interviews from both companies	Distributed system development projects, no more information available on the tasks	Based on their study of two distributed system development projects Kotlarsky & Oshri (2005, 45) argue that collaboration is about renewing the set of relations between globally distributed project members through continuous participation and engagement. They suggest creating social space between team members and introducing a variety of communication tools as well as clear communication procedures

Robert Jr., L. P., Dennis, A. R., & Hung, Y-T. C. (2009). Individual swift trust and knowledge–based trust in face–to–face and virtual team members, *Journal of Management Information Systems*, 26(2), 241–2	Category-matching process based on team member characteristics, not on their behaviors	Meyerson et al. (1996); McKnight et al. (1998); Kramer (1999); Mayer et al. (1995)	Geographically and temporally distributed teams	Vignettes given to 203 undergraduate business students. Communication environment manipulated by describing the communication as occurring either F-to-F or through e-mail messages among geographically and temporally distributed team members	Vignette scenarios on used to simulate teaming events related to swift vs. knowledge–based trust	Category-based processing of team member characteristics and an individual's own disposition to trust dominated the initial formation of swift trust. Once individuals got sufficient information to assess a team member's trustworthiness, the effects of swift trust declined and knowledge–based trust formed using team members' behaviors became dominant
Sarker, S., Ahuja, M., Sarker, S., & Kirkeby, S. (2011). The role of communication and trust in global virtual teams: a social network perspective. *Journal of Management Information Systems*, 28(1), 273–310	Trust as 'the willingness of a party to be vulnerable to the actions of another party, based on the expectation that the other will perform a particular action important to the trustor, irrespective of the ability to monitor or control the other	Authors call it networked individualism paradigm, a social network perspective	Distributed work teams	Two sets of distributed hybrid virtual teams engaged in systems development projects where teams worked on developing (analyse, design, develop and test) IS application projects for real clients	Student systems development projects for real clients	Sarker et al. (2011) test three proposed models (additive, interaction, and mediation) describing the role of trust in its relationship with communication to explain performance. They find that the concepts of communication and trust are inherently relational and not properties of

continued . . .

Table A3.1 Continued

Reference	Conceptualization	Theoretical background	Research context	Method & data	Task	Findings
	party' (Mayer et al., 1995, 712)					individuals. They further argue that a social network approach is potentially more appropriate than attribute-based approaches that have been utilized in prior research, and suggest that the 'mediating' model best explains how communication and trust work together to influence performance
Crisp, C. B., & Jarvenpaa, S. L. (2013). Swift trust in global virtual teams: Trusting	Swift trust as a cognitive and action form of trust	Meyerson et al., (1996); Tajfel (1978), Social identity and self-categorization theories	Global virtual ad-hoc teams	8-week longitudinal quasi-experimental study of 68 ad hoc global virtual teams with 280 under–	Writing a business plan for a new company related to b2b e-commerce	Crisp and Jarvenpaa (2013) show that early trusting beliefs have direct and mediated effects on late trusting

beliefs and normative actions. *Journal of Personnel Psychology*, 12(1), 45

graduate students from four continents performing a virtual business plan exercise

beliefs. They found significant paths from early trust beliefs to normative actions, and from normative actions to late trusting beliefs. They further found out that late trusting beliefs had a positive effect on team performance, and that the relationship of team performance and late trusting beliefs was mediated by normative actions. High early trusting beliefs gave team members the necessary confidence to engage in normative actions, which became a sustainable basis of late trusting beliefs and performance

4

DISTRUST

Sim B. Sitkin and Katinka M. Bijlsma-Frankema

Introduction

Trust has long been recognized as having important societal effects (Fox, 1974; Lewis & Weigert, 1985, Mayer, Davis, & Schoorman, 1995; Sitkin & Roth, 1993; Zucker, 1986). Over the years, organizational scholars have studied trust at the interpersonal, organizational, and inter-organizational levels (for reviews see Colquitt, Scott, & LePine, 2007; Dirks & Ferrin, 2002; Fulmer & Gelfand, 2012; Rousseau, Sitkin, Burt, & Camerer, 1998; Schoorman, Mayer, & Davis, 2007). For trust researchers, core definitions, constructs, variables, and operationalizations have begun to converge.

In contrast, distrust research has been much slower to emerge, especially as a distinct area of study (Kramer, 1999; Rousseau, et al., 1998). Yet work on distrust has grown steadily and has more recently shown a dramatic increase in attention (for recent overviews, see Bijlsma-Frankema, Sitkin, & Weibel, 2015; Guo, Lumineau, & Lewicki, 2016; Saunders, Dietz, & Thornhill, 2014). In this chapter, we provide an overview of the ways in which distrust has been conceptualized and studied – both as a subset of trust and as a distinct phenomenon.

Conceptualizing distrust

Distrust is generally defined in terms of negative expectations towards people's intentions or behaviours (Van de Walle & Six, 2014). A well-known distrust description is offered by Lewicki and Tomlinson (2003: 5) when they characterize distrust (as contrasted with trust) in this way: "low trust signals low confidence in things hoped for, whereas distrust signals a sense of assurance regarding things feared." Lewicki and his colleagues have used this framing to offer a widely used definition (Lewicki, McAllister, & Bies, 1998: 439; Lewicki, Tomlinson, & Gillespie, 2006): "Confident negative expectations and perception about the intentions and beliefs of another." More recently Bijlsma-Frankema and her colleagues (Bijlsma-Frankema, et al, 2015; Bijlsma-Frankema, Wisse, Täuber, Sitkin, Sanders, & van de Brake, 2016) have built upon the widely cited Rousseau, et al. (1998) definition of trust to distinguish distrust as "A psychological state, comprising the unwillingness to accept vulnerability, based on pervasive negative perceptions and expectations of . . . motives, intentions, or behaviours."

Distinct conceptualizations of distrust

Distrust has been conceptualized in the literature as equivalent to low trust and, alternatively, as distinct from trust. Within the distrust-as-distinct camp, there have been two fundamentally different ways of theorizing about that distinction: distrust as a precluding precondition for trust, and distrust as orthogonal to trust.

Distrust as low trust

Trust researchers for many years largely ignored distrust as a serious construct. Despite some early qualitative and quantitative studies of distrust (e.g., Constantinople, 1969; Fox, 1974; Wrightsman, 1974), nearly all trust research until quite recently simply did not call out distrust as meriting special consideration. As a result, terms like distrust, mistrust, and low trust were not distinguished in any systematic way. To the contrary, the terms distrust or mistrust were used interchangeably with references to low trust. More specifically, when it did explicitly reference distrust, this research typically conceptualized distrust as equivalent to very low trust or the absence of trust (Hardin 2004; Luhmann, 1979; Mayer, et al., 1995; Robinson, 1996; Rotter, 1980). Thus, distrust essentially was conceptualized as anchoring the low end of a single continuum and thus did not merit separate consideration (Schoorman, Mayer, & Davis, 2007).

To some extent, this approach has been reflected in more recent work on trust repair (Kim, Dirks, & Cooper, 2009; see also Bies, Tripp, Barclay, Kay, & Francisca Saldanha, this volume, on forgiveness). Trust repair studies (e.g., Dirks & Ferrin, et al., 2009) have focused on repairing problematic trust situations, where actions that increase expectations of trustworthiness in one domain can enhance trust in other domains and the ability to address other problems (e.g., Ferrin, Kim, Cooper, & Dirks, 2007). As we will note, this approach does not fully reflect the distinct literatures.

Distrust as distinct from trust

In the early 1990s, distrust began to be conceptualized as distinct from trust (e.g., Sitkin & Roth, 1993; Sitkin & Stickel, 1996); in terms of determinants, effects, and process models. As a result, a distinct cluster of research has emerged focusing on distrust.

Empirical research, including measurement construction and validation studies (Clark & Payne, 1997; Constantinople, 1969; Wrightsman, 1974), has supported differentiating trust and distrust as two distinct constructs. Specific contexts and methods in which the distinction has been found are as diverse as quantitative studies of electronic commerce customers (Benamati, Serva, & Fuller, 2006; Chang & Fang, 2013; Cho, 2006; Komiak & Benbasat, 2008; Ou & Sia, 2010), qualitative studies of judicial employees (Bijlsma-Frankema, et al., 2015), and neuro-imaging research (showing that trust and distrust activate different areas of the brain) (Dimoka, 2010; Patent & Searle, 2012; Patent, 2014).

As noted above, there are two quite different conceptualizations of distrust as distinct or "mutually exclusive" (Bigley & Pearce, 1998: 414) from distrust. In the first, distrust was conceptualized as pervasive and, once evoked, obviating the possibility of trust (Sitkin & Roth, 1993). In the second, trust and distrust are distinct but can co-exist such that both trust and distrust can be simultaneously high or low (Lewicki, et al., 1998). We will discuss each conceptualization below.

Distrust as a precluding precondition to trust

Building on Mayer, et al. (1995), most trust research has approached the relationship between trustworthiness and trust as linear, and most empirical studies (e.g., Dirks & Ferrin 2001, 2002) have found significant linear relations consistent with the distrust-as-low-trust conception. In addition, much of this work has viewed trust as domain specific (Mayer, et al., 1995) – where high trust in one domain, say financial acumen and advice, is unrelated to a willingness to trust in another domain, say how I might develop a better working relationship with my boss – and most empirical findings have been consistent with this view (Ferrin, Kim, Cooper, & Dirks, 2007) as well, indicating a lack of pervasiveness of trust (i.e., that it is unusual for trust to be equally strong across all domains).

In contrast with the domain-specificity reported in trust research, some have called for a different theoretical approach for distrust (Kramer, 1994, 1996; Mayer, et al., 1995; Sitkin & Roth, 1993; Zand, 1972). From this perspective, distrust is theorized as a self-reinforcing cyclical process that pervades across domains (Bijlsma-Frankema, et al., 2015; Korsgaard, this volume; Sitkin & Roth, 1993). From this view, distrust is a negative psychological state regarding distrusted others, an all-encompassing negative lens through which distrusted others are perceived.

In this approach, distrust is conceptualized as involving a punctuated shift, a fundamental distinction from trust. Through this lens, once distrust has been evoked, the trustee shifts to a distrust frame such that it may be impossible to return to even considering a degree of trust (Robinson & Morrison, 2000; see also Bies, et al., this volume). Once a pervasive negative distrust lens is in place, it is argued, there are no domains of action that are distrust-free, thus blocking the capacity to gain a foothold to build trust in any domain so long as distrust remains present.

Once the distrust tipping point has been reached, there is a fundamental shift from loose to tight coupling among contextual conditions (domains, attributes, etc.). Under these conditions, a perceived violation in one domain negatively affects perceptions of other domains (Anderson & Pearson, 1999; Coleman, et al., 2007; Friedman & Currall, 2003; Perlow & Repenning, 2009), creating an integrated "lock-in" (Friedman & Currall, 2003) system with feedback loops that reinforce only the negative, and do not credit any effort at compensatory action (Bijlsma-Frankema, et al., 2015; Coleman et al., 2007). What this implies is that, once distrusted, every action is suspect and its motivation and value base questioned, no matter how well-intended it may be. In other words, once distrust is fully developed, otherwise highly trustworthy behaviour in one domain (e.g., financial advice) can have no implications for the level of trust in another domain (e.g., workplace politics). In other words, while trust and distrust have distinct antecedents, consequences, and processes, the pursuit of trust is not independent of the amelioration of distrust concerns. Unless distrust has been eliminated there is "no room for trust" because the presence of distrust leads the foundations of trustworthiness (shared values, integrity, benevolence, etc.) to be implicitly or explicitly undermined.

Distrust as orthogonal to trust

An alternative distrust theory proposed by Lewicki, et al., (1998) has been quite influential and posits a distinctive view of the trust/distrust relationship. Specifically, they posit that trust and distrust are not only distinct variables but are independent (orthogonal). They capture this idea in a 2x2 table in which they depict 4 cells (high/high, low/low, low/high, and high/low) to suggest that trust and distrust are independent and distinct, and thus can coexist. Their model is based on several key notions. First, that trust and distrust relations vary in the degree of interdependence between the parties. Second, that joint trust/distrust conditions are characterized as "highly segmented and bounded" (p. 445). Thus, this model of why distrust is distinct from trust is quite different in its assumptions (e.g., pervasiveness), key variables (e.g., value congruence), and basic conception of distrust (e.g., synoptic vs incremental) when compared with the "distrust as a precluding precondition" model. The orthogonal conception of distrust not only rejects (by definition) distrust as a precondition for trust, but also excludes, at least in the current model, pervasiveness as an essential feature of distrust (since pervasiveness would preclude the co-presence of trust). This has the advantage of facilitating the incorporation of ambivalence (e.g., when both trust and distrust are simultaneously present) and multiplex relationships (i.e., trust in some domains in a relationship and distrust in others). The key for our purpose is to recognize that while these two approaches share an important feature in conceptualizing trust and distrust as distinct, they are also fundamentally different in the other fundamental respects outlined here.

Models of distrust

To review the models of distrust in the literature and how they have been studied, we will draw upon Mohr's (1982) framework for characterizing basic theoretical models. Specifically, Mohr (1982) distinguished variance and process models as a useful way to understand what theories are being proposed and tested with respect to a given phenomenon.

Variance models

In the case of distrust, variance models focus on how distrust varies across different determinants and effects.

Determinants of distrust

Felt vulnerability is an antecedent common to both trust and distrust models. Two key and distinctive determinants of distrust have been identified in the literature: perceived value incongruence and negative attributions of motives (see Bijlsma-Frankema, et al., 2015).

Perceived value incongruence has been defined as "the belief that others adhere to values that are perceived as incompatible with the actor's core values" (Bijlsma-Frankema et al., 2015: 1020). It signifies an interpersonal break based on a perceived incompatibility between the values of the trustor and the trustee. Sitkin and Roth (1993) proposed value incongruence as the signature and distinctive determinant of distrust, tainting trustor perceptions of the current and future motives and actions of the trustee (e.g., Martinko, Harvey, Sikora, & Douglas, 2011) a framing that has been studied and supported in qualitative and quantitative studies (e.g., Bijlsma-Frankema, et al., 2015; Bijlsma-Frankema, et al., 2016; Sitkin & Stickel, 1996).

It has been theorized (Sitkin & Roth, 1993; Sitkin & Stickel, 1996; Tomlinson & Lewicki, 2006) and observed (Chambers & Melnyk, 2006) that distrust is fostered by perceived value incongruence. Distrust arises as others come to be characterized as unpredictable and threatening, thus fostering a sense of uncertainty and vulnerability (Sitkin & Roth, 1993). As Tomlinson and Lewicki (2006, 222) note: "We expect that we have little in common with the other and that the other is a committed adversary who is out to harm us." Under such conditions, these models suggest, distrust – the unwillingness to be vulnerable – arises.

The attribution of negative motives or incongruent values (Kelley, 1967; Tomlinson, this volume) can be a determinant of distrust when the motives or values in question are fundamental ones, and thus are pervasively relevant. In other words, when motives or values are seen as central to a person or organization's motives, character, or worldview, they are likely to engender a distrust response (Sitkin & Roth, 1993).

Yet another approach to a variance model of distrust determinants is the contingency model proposed Lewicki, et al. (1998) in which trust and distrust are posited in a 2x2 table and later tested by Saunders, Dietz, and Thornhill (2014). In this frame, the key causal variables are degree of indifference, and level of positive versus negative prior experience. Saunders, et al. (2014) found mixed support with a small sample. So more robust and definitive direct tests of variables are still needed.

Effects of distrust

Variance models have also examined the effects of distrust, and one could argue that distrust has emerged as an important social phenomenon for researchers, in large part because of its significant negative consequences (Sitkin & Roth, 1993; Tomlinson & Lewicki, 2006). Studies have highlighted a wide range of severe distrust-related consequences for individuals, groups and organizations, such as problematic interpersonal (Chan, 2003; Cho, 2006), intergroup (Bijlsma-Frankema, et al., 2015; Glynn, 2000; Kramer, 2004; Sitkin & Stickel, 1996) and organizational relations (Connelly, Miller, & Devers, 2012; Fox, 1974). More specific effects include avoidance of influence (Sheppard & Tuchinsky, 1996), avoidance of interaction (Bies & Tripp, 1996; Bijlsma-Frankema, et al., 2015; March & Olsen, 1975), lack of cooperation (Cho, 2006), conflict (Sitkin & Stickel, 1996; Fiol, Pratt, & O'Connor, 2009; Tomlinson & Lewicki, 2006), unwillingness to share views and preferences (Bijlsma-Frankema, 2004; March & Olsen, 1975), information distortion and disbelief (Kramer, 1994), stigmatization (Sitkin & Roth, 1993), paranoia (Kramer, 2004), and strong negative emotions, such as hostility toward distrusted others (Chambers & Melnyk, 2006).

Several interesting effects of distrust that have been examined over a number of decades of research and merit highlighting: seeking revenge for negative consequences, diminished co-operation, and reduction of negative consequences through shielding or avoidance (see Bies, et al., this volume). Revenge refers to negative reciprocity (Fox, 1974; Gouldner, 1960; Serva, et al., 2005), or "getting even" (McKnight & Choudhury, 2006; Tripp & Bies, 2010). Theories of both trust and distrust have recognized cooperation as a key consequence (Deutsch, 1971; Fox, 1974). The rationale for reduced willingness to cooperate as an effect of distrust is that it results from an accumulating and reciprocal diminished willingness to act fairly on the part of the other party as well as self-exhibited accumulating routines of uncooperative behaviour (see Lind, this volume). Avoidance is another documented effect of distrust (Bies & Tripp, 1996; Bijlsma-Frankema, 2004; Bijlsma-Frankema, et al., 2015; March & Olsen, 1975) and refers to attempts to reduce or prevent future harm (Bies & Tripp, 1996; Tripp & Bies, 2010; Bijlsma-Frankema, 2004; Bijlsma-Frankema, et al., 2015; Deutsch, 1958; Lewicki, et al., 1998; Sitkin & Stickel, 1996). These studies consistently support the effect of distrust on avoidance behaviours.

Finally, affective responses to distrust have received attention, though much work is left to be done (see van Knippenberg, this volume). More specifically, trust and distrust have been depicted as engendering quite different emotional reactions (see Lewicki, et al., 1998 for a summary; see also van Knippenberg, this volume). Whereas low trust is portrayed as simply dampening positive feelings (such as feeling calm, secure, accepting, ambivalent, or confident) distrust is portrayed as engendering strong negative feelings of fear, betrayal, anxiety, wariness, even hostility, anger, or hate (e.g., Bies & Tripp, 1996, 2015; Kramer, 1996; Lewicki, et al., 1998; McKnight & Choudhury, 2006; Sitkin & Stickel, 1996; Tripp & Bies, 2010).

Process models

There is a long history of modeling distrust as a recursive, cyclical process sometimes referred to as "the spiral of distrust" (Fox, 1974; Sherif, Harvey, White, Hood, & Sherif, 1961; Sitkin & Roth, 1993; Sitkin & Stickel, 1996; Zand, 1972). Building on and extending this history, Bijlsma-Frankema and her colleagues (Bijlsma-Frankema, et al., 2015; Bijlsma-Frankema, et al., 2016) developed and tested several process models of distrust in which key variables serve as both determinants and effects of distrust. They posited and found evidence for specific process characteristics of previously hypothesized (but not previously empirically examined) self-amplifying cycles. In doing so, they built on, elaborated, and formalized previously published ideas about escalating cycles of distrust (Korsgaard, this volume; Serva, Fuller, & Mayer, 2005) by examining self-amplifying cycles in which distrust intensifies and spreads across domains of the relationship. Central elements of their models include pervasiveness (Sitkin & Roth, 1993) and the intensification of negative perceptions and behaviours (e.g., Sherif, et al., 1961). Their depiction of the role of pervasive negative perceptions and expectations extended prior work by developing and testing a more precise and explicit conceptual description of how pervasiveness and self-amplification, the two commonly agreed-upon characteristics of distrust and its development (Cho, 2006; Dimoka, 2010; Fox, 1974; Kramer, 1994, 1996; Lewicki, et al., 1998; Sherif, et al., 1961; Sitkin & Roth, 1993; Sitkin & Stickel, 1996; Zand, 1972) manifest as steps in a distrust development process model. More specifically, they explored the cycle of negative reciprocity, amplifying attributions, and perceived value incongruence (Bijlsma-Frankema, et al., 2015; Bijlsma-Frankema, et al., 2016).

Drawing on commitment, learning conflict research (e.g., Meyer & Allen, 1991; Weick, 1995), Bijlsma-Frankema, et al.'s (2015) intergroup distrust process model was derived from a qualitative study of distrust development between judges and court administrators, highlighting the mutual reinforcing cycles of negative behaviours and perceptions which can result in distrust development and escalation (Becker & Geer, 1961; Blumer, 1969). In the Bijlsma-Frankema, et al. model of the distrust escalation process, negative perceptions foster negative behaviours, and once displayed these negative behaviours in turn foster matching negative perceptions and behaviours.

One interesting area of focus is the role of avoidance of interaction (Bies & Tripp, 1996; Bies, et al., this volume; Bijlsma-Frankema, 2004; March & Olsen, 1975; Meyer & Allen, 1991), and negative attributions of motives and value incongruence (Chambers & Melnick, 2006; McKnight, Kacmar, and Choudhury, 2004; Sitkin & Roth, 1993; Sitkin & Stickel, 1996; Tomlinson & Lewicki, 2006) as both determinants and effects of distrust. Overall, their model identifies four process "amplifying mechanisms": pervasiveness, overmatching of negative behaviours, intensification of negative perceptions through negative reciprocity, and intensification of negative perceptions through within-group convergence (Bijlsma-Frankema et al., 2015).

Punctuated threshhold models

In addition to tracing roots to early discussions of trust and distrust self-amplifying cycles (e.g. Fox, 1974), distrust researchers have proposed a punctuated threshold model of distrust (Roth, Sitkin, & House, 1994; Sitkin & Roth, 1993; Sitkin & Stickel, 1996) that goes beyond describing the variables or the processes involved in explaining the emergence and evolution of distrust and theorizes that the absence of distrust serves as a threshold that permits trust to be built. In other words, if distrust is present, factors that typically help to build trust will have no effect. But once distrust-related issues have been fully addressed, then trust-building processes can begin to engage. Thus, this punctuated threshold is not a matter of degree. Instead, it posits that on one side of the threshold the process works one way (distrust may strengthen but it remains pervasive and self-reinforcing), and on the other side of the threshold high and low trust can occur in pockets and can begin to accumulate both in depth and breadth.

Some recent empirical studies of this model by Bijlsma-Frankema and colleagues (2015, 2016) have drawn upon and elaborated these punctuated threshold models. More specifically, these studies have modelled distrust establishment and escalation from the conflict escalation/intractability literature to propose a two-stage escalation model (Anderson & Pearson, 1999; Coleman, et al., 2007; Coyle-Shapiro & Diehl, this volume; Friedman & Currall, 2003; Perlow & Repenning, 2009) with a threshold switch from the first to the second stage. These models suggest that "low trust processes differ fundamentally from distrust processes and that the switch from low trust to distrust is punctuated" (Bijlsma-Frankema, et al., 2015) and that this trigger feature is the key that distinguishes this approach from conceptualizations of distrust as equivalent to low trust and also from orthogonal models of distrust. In these models, the mere presence of distrust obviates the possibility of trust (Sitkin & Roth, 1993; Bijlsma-Frankema, 2015), thus challenging the notion that trust and distrust, although distinct, can co-exist (Lewicki, et al., 1998; Lewicki & Tomlinson, 2003).

Future directions in distrust research

Distrust versus trust

Despite a long history of treating distrust as an isolated subset of trust that did not require independent consideration, there is an accumulating body of theoretical and empirical evidence that supports the notion of two distinct constructs, with distinct determinants, effects, and processes. These tests include measurement construction and validation studies (Clark & Payne, 1997; Constantinople, 1969; Wrightsman, 1974) and, more recently, advanced construct discrimination tests (Benamati, Serva, & Fuller, 2006; Chang & Fang, 2013; Cho, 2006; Komiak & Benbasat, 2008; Ou & Sia, 2010), including one study that used neuro-imaging to show that trust and distrust activate different brain areas (Dimoka, 2010). One might suggest in a prescriptive way that this should be considered a settled scientific issue, though such a suggestion would probably be descriptively inaccurate and thus will be left to future work to settle.

Pervasiveness

The issue of domain- and context-specificity versus pervasiveness remains an area about which a consensus has not yet been achieved. While the historical focus on trust as domain- and context-specific (Ferrin, Kim, Cooper, & Dirks, 2007; Mayer, et al., 1995) is not under dispute, the concomitant assumption of a lack of pervasiveness has been disputed with respect to distrust (Bijlsma-Frankema, 2015; Lewicki, et al., 1998; Sitkin & Roth, 1993; Sitkin & Stickel, 1996).

Four key opportunities arise with respect to future studies of the pervasiveness issue. First is the question of whether pervasiveness does in fact distinguish trust from distrust. While some results appear to be supportive of this conclusion, the findings are still preliminary and require more examination. Second, we need a better understanding of the process by which pervasiveness is triggered, grows, stabilizes, and recedes. Third, when pervasiveness is part of our theories, what exactly do we mean by pervasiveness in terms of what domains are being subsumed? For example, is the issue that distrust crosses cognitive, affective, and behavioural boundaries for the trustor? Or does it refer to implicating the full range of contexts for which the trustee might be relied upon? Or does it involve the various aspects of the trustee's trustworthiness? (For example, different competencies or benevolence in one area of competing interests and not another) (Six, Skinner, Searle, Weibel, Gillespie, & Den Hartog, 2016; see also Baer & Colquittt, this volume; Lyu & Ferrin, this volume; Lind, this volume.) Fourth, in comparing the two distrust-is-distinctive models, does pervasiveness preclude the building of trust, or can high trust and high distrust co-exist? Answers to such questions can help us narrow down the range of distrust theories, or can help us see that the descriptive value of different theories is contingent on specifiable situational factors. For each of these issues, there is some research that provides a springboard, but much work is yet to be done.

In addition, if distrust researchers can sort out these kinds of pervasiveness questions, it can provide an opportunity for distrust research to influence other areas of study that are not primarily about distrust, but do involve an element of distrust. For example, studies of conflicts between professionals and their organizations (e.g., Sorensen & Sorensen, 1974), peace and reconciliation, and intractable conflicts (Fiol, et al., 2009) have not yet explained why some conflicts become intractable and others do not. But as Coleman, et al. (2007) and Fiol, et al. (2009) have noted, pervasive distrust may characterize the intractable, whereas domain-specific low trust may make other conflicts more tractable. One explanation for this difference, which remains to be explored, is whether distrust and low trust elicit fundamentally different emotional responses (see van Knippenberg, this volume) and that these emotions may require quite distinct attention to achieve positive resolution. These questions may best be answered by distrust researchers to the benefit of those who study conflict and reconciliation (e.g., see Bies, et al., this volume; Lind, this volume).

Intergroup distrust

As discussed earlier in this chapter, the volume of distrust research has grown at the interpersonal level. Yet, with few exceptions (e.g., Bjilsma-Frankema, et al., 2015; Glynn, 2000; Kramer, 2004; Sitkin & Stickel, 1996), little work has examined distrust at the inter group level. Thus, this area of focus offers ripe opportunities for future research. For example, research on peace and reconciliation efforts, and intractable intergroup conflicts (Fiol, Pratt, & O'Connor, 2009; Tomlinson & Lewicki, 2006) has discussed the potentially important role of distrust, but has not been subjected to close examination. Yet this phenomenon might well lend itself to comparing different models of distrust noted here to determine their relative explanatory power.

Another potential opportunity for distrust research concerns the role of distrust in ingroup/outgroup relations and issues of intergroup cognitive separation and negative perceptions (Brewer, 1999; Friedman & Currall, 2003; Gaertner & Dovidio, 2000; Labianca, et al., 1998; Pruitt & Kim, 2004). Recent populist and nationalist movements around the world, including anti-immigration initiatives, often provide examples of this phenomenon.

Methodological issues in the study of distrust

Future distrust research should employ more multi-method approaches as well as more longitudinal approaches. While experiments and in-depth case studies have begun to emerge, along with physiological studies of distrust, it would be useful to add several methodological features to the mix. First, comparative and multiple case studies (Eisenhardt, 1989) and surveys would be helpful as we continue to expand our understanding of the best ways to model distrust and to assess the generalizability of our findings. Second, the use of multiple methodologies with our research papers would be helpful in triangulating results and nailing down distrust–

related mechanisms more precisely. Finally, recent work has suggested the benefits of longi-tudinal studies of distrust to better understand the trajectories by which distrust is triggered, evolves (or doesn't), and resolves (or persists) (Bijlsma-Frankema, et al, 2015; Solinger, Hofmans, Bal, & Jansen, 2016; Solinger, van Olffen, Roe, & Hofmans, 2013)

Applications

Distrust research has many opportunities for important current organizational applications. For example, the recent financial crisis provided one such context (e.g., Gillespie & Hurley, 2013) and will surely continue to provide many future opportunities, as will the apparent fracturing of democratic political coalitions across the world. The more general level of distrust in societal institutions across the globe (Edelman, 2016) suggests that similar issues can be found with disappointing ease, and with mounting evidence of detrimental consequences. The energy, health, and food sectors, and political organizations are obvious examples. Across the globe, refugee and immigration crises, tribal and religious conflicts, scandals within religious organizations, and even questions being raised about the fundamental values and practices of basic science itself can be informed by using a distrust lens.

Conclusion

Though slower to emerge than trust research, distrust research has taken on a distinct and rapidly growing profile. It is a robust area of study with new theoretical contributions, qualitative and quantitative empirical studies, and research syntheses. New methodologies (e.g., physiological) and new field contexts provide technological and logistical bases for potentially important new developments that can not only advance our understanding of distrust in organizations and society, but also can feed back and inform our more voluminous extant research on trust.

References

Anderson, L.M., & C.M. Pearson. (1999). Tit for tat? The spiraling effect of incivility in the workplace. *Academy of Management Review*, 24(3), 452–471.

Becker, H.S., & Geer, B. (1961). *Boys in white: Student culture in medical school*. Chicago, IL: University of Chicago Press.

Benamati, J., Serva, M.A., & Fuller, M.A. (2006). Are trust and distrust distinct constructs? An empirical study of the effects of trust and distrust among online bank users. *Proceedings of the 39th Hawaiian International Conference on System Sciences*. Los Alamitos, CA: IEEE Society Press.

Bies, R.J., & Tripp, T.M. (1996). Beyond distrust: "Getting even" and the need for revenge. In R. Kramer, T. Tyler, (Eds.), *Trust in organizations: Frontiers of theory and Research*. Thousand Oaks, CA: Sage, 246–260.

Bigley, G.A., & Pearce, J.L. (1998). Straining for shared meaning in organizational science: Problems of trust and distrust, *Academy of Management Review*, 23(3), 405–421.

Bijlsma-Frankema, K.M., Sitkin, S.B., & Weibel, A. (2015). Distrust in the balance: The emergence and development of intergroup distrust in a court of law. *Organization Science*, 26(4), 1018–1039.

Bijlsma-Frankema, K., Wisse, B., Täuber, S., Sitkin, S., Sanders, S., & van de Brake, J. (2016). Distrust of supervisors: Towards a dynamic approach. Under review.

Blumer, H. (1969). *Symbolic interactionism: Perspectives and method*. Englewood Cliffs: Prentice-Hall.

Brewer, M.B. (1999). The psychology of prejudice: Ingroup love or outgroup hate? *Journal of Social Issues*, 55(3), 429–444.

Chambers, J.R., & Melnyk, D. (2006). Why do I hate thee? Conflict misperceptions and intergroup mistrust. *Personality and Social Psychology Bulletin*, 32(10), 1295–1311.

Chang, Y.S., & Fang, S.R. (2013). Antecedents and distinctions between online trust and distrust: Predicting high- and low risk internet behaviors. *Journal of Electronic Commerce Research*, 14(2), 149–166.

Cho, J. (2006). The mechanism of trust and distrust formation and their relational outcomes. *Journal of Retailing*, 82(1), 25–35.

Clark, M.C., & Payne, R.L. (1997). The nature and structure of worker's trust in management. *Journal of Organizational Behavior*, 18, 205–224.

Coleman, P.T., Vallacher, R.R., Nowak, A., & Bui-Wrzosinska, L. (2007). Intractable conflicts as attractor: A dynamical systems approach to conflict escalation and intractability. *American Behavioral Scientist*, 50, 1454–1475.

Colquitt, J.A., Scott, B.A., & LePine, J.A. (2007). Trust, trustworthiness, and trust propensity: A meta-analytic test of their unique relationships with risk taking and job performance, *Journal of Applied Psychology*, 92(4), 909–927.

Connelly, B.L., Miller, T., & Devers, C.E. (2012). Under a cloud of suspicion: Trust, distrust, and their interactive effect in interorganizational contracting, *Strategic Management Journal*, 33, 820–833.

Constantinople, A. (1969). An Eriksonian measure of personality development in college students, *Developmental Psychology*, 1, 357–372

Deutsch, M. (1958). Trust and suspicion. *Journal of Conflict Resolution*, 2(4), 265–279.

Dimoka, A. (2010). What does the brain tell us about trust and distrust? Evidence from a functional neuroimaging study. *MIS Quarterly*, 34(3), 373–396.

Dirks, K., & Ferrin, D.L. (2001). The role of trust in organizational settings. *Organization Science*, 12(4), 450–467

Dirks, K., & Ferrin, D.L. (2002). Trust in leadership: Meta-analytical findings and implications for research and practice. *Journal of Applied Psychology*, 87(4), 611–628.

Dirks, K., & Ferrin, D.L. (2009). Repairing relationships within and between organizations: Building a conceptual foundation. *Academy of Management Review*, 34, 68–84.

Edelman, R. (2016). Beyond the grand illusion, accessed 28/01/2016 www.edelman.com/p/6-a-m/beyond-grand-illusion/

Eisenhardt, K.M. (1989). Building theory from case study research. *Academy of Management Review*, 14, 532–550.

Ferrin, D.L., Kim, P.H, Cooper, C.D., & Dirks, K.T. (2007). Silence speaks volumes: The effectiveness of reticence in comparison to apology and denial for responding to integrity- and competence-based trust violations. *Journal of Applied Psychology*, 92, 893–908.

Fiol, C.M., Pratt, M.G., & O' Connor, E.J. (2009). Managing intractable identity conflicts. *Acadademy of Management Review*, 34(1), 32–55.

Fox, A. (1974). *Beyond contract: Work, power and trust relations*. London: Faber and Faber.

Friedman, R.A., & Currall, S.C. (2003). Conflict escalation: Dispute exacerbating elements of e-mail communication. *Human Relations*, 56(11), 1325–1347.

Fulmer, C.A., & Gelfand, M.J. (2012). At what level (and in whom) we trust: Trust across multiple organizational levels, *Journal of Management*, 38(4), 1167–1230.

Gaertner, S.L., & Dovidio, J.F. (2000). From superordinate goals to decategorization, recategorization and mutual differentiation. *International Journal of Psychology*, 35(3–4), 193.

Gillespie, N., & Hurley, R. (2013). Trust and the global financial crisis. In R. Bachmann & A. Zaheer, (Eds.), *Handbook of Advances in Trust Research*, 177–203. Cheltenham, UK: Edward Elgar.

Glynn, M.A. (2000). When cymbals become symbols: Conflict over organizational identity within a symphony orchestra. *Organization Science*, 11(3), 285–298.

Gouldner, A.W. (1960). The norm of reciprocity: A preliminary statement. *American Sociological Review*, 25, 161–178.

Guo, S-L., Lumineau, F., & Lewicki, R.J. (2016). Revisiting the foundations of organizational distrust, *Foundations and Trends in Strategic Management*, 1(1), 1–88.

Hardin, R. (2004). Distrust: Manifestations and management. In R. Hardin, (Ed.), *Distrust*. New York: Sage, 3–34.

Kelley, H.H. (1967). Attribution theory in social psychology. In D. Levine (Ed.) *Nebraska Symposium on Motivation*. Lincoln, NE: University of Nebraska Press.

Kim, P.H., Dirks, K.T., & Cooper, C.D. (2009). The repair of trust: A dynamic bilateral perspective and multilevel conceptualization. *Academy of Management Review*, 34(3), 401–423.

Komiak, S.Y.X., & I. Benbasat. (2008). A two-process view of trust and distrust building in recommendation agents: A process-tracing study. *Journal of the Association for Information Systems*, 9(12), 727–747.

Kramer, R.M. (1994). The sinister attribution error – Paranoid cognition and collective distrust in organizations. *Motivation and Emotion*, 18(2), 199–230.

Kramer, R.M. (1996). Divergent realities and convergent disappointments in the hierarchic relation: Trust and the intuitive auditor at work. In R.M. Kramer and T.R. Tyler, (Eds.), *Trust in organizations: Frontiers of theory and research.* Thousand Oaks, CA: Sage, 216–245.

Kramer, R.M. (1999). Trust and distrust in organizations: Emerging perspectives, enduring questions. *Annual Review of Psychology,* 50, 569–598.

Kramer, R.M. (2004). Collective paranoia: Distrust between social groups. In R. Hardin, (Ed.), *Distrust.* New York: Russell, 136–167.

Labianca, G., Brass, D.J., & Gray, B. (1998). Social networks and perceptions of intergroup conflict: The role of negative relationships and third parties. *Academy of Management Journal,* 41(1), 55–67.

Lewicki, R.J., McAllister, D.J., & Bies, R.J. (1998). Trust and distrust: New relationships and realities. *Academy of Management Review,* 23(3), 438–458.

Lewicki, R.J., & Tomlinson, E.C. (2003). The effects of reputation and post violation communication on trust and distrust. *16th Annual Conference of the International Association of Conflict Management.* Melbourne, Australia.

Lewis, J.D., & Weigert, A. (1985). Trust as a social reality. *Social Forces,* 63(4), 967–985.

Luhmann, N. (1979). *Trust and power: Two works.* New York: Wiley.

March, J.G., & Olsen, J.P. (1975). Uncertainty of past – Organizational learning under ambiguity. *European Journal of Political Research,* 3(2), 147–171.

Martinko, M.J., Harvey, P., Sikora, D., & Douglas, S.C. (2011). Perceptions of abusive supervison: The role of subordinates' attribution styles. *The Leadership Quarterly,* 22(4), 751–764.

Mayer, R.C., Davis, J.H., & Schoorman, F.D. (1995). An integrative model of organizational trust. *Academy of Management Review,* 20(3), 709–734.

McKnight, D.H., Kacmar, C.J., & Choudhury, V. (2004). Dispositional trust and distrust distinctions in predicting high and low-risk internet expert advice sites perceptions. *e-service journal,* 3(2), 35–58.

McKnight, D.H., & Choudhury, V. (2006). Distrust and trust in e-commerce: Do they differ? *Proceedings of the 8th International Conference on Electronic Commerce,* 482–491.

Mohr, L.B. (1982). *Explaining organizational behavior.* San Francisco: Jossey-Bass.

Ou, C.X., & Sia, C.L. (2010). Consumer trust and distrust: An issue of website design. *International Journal of Human-Computer Studies,* 68(12), 913–934.

Patent, V., & Searle, R. (2012). Measuring trust propensity. *First International Network on Trust Workshop, 13th–15th June 2012, Milan.* Conference Paper, Milan.

Patent, V., (2014). *The role of trust perceptions and propensity to trust in applicants' experience of recruitment and selection* (PhD Thesis). *Psychology.* Milton Keynes, UK: The Open University.

Perlow, L.A., & Repenning, N.P. (2009). The dynamic of silencing conflict. *Research in Organizational Behavior,* 29, 195–223.

Pruitt, D.G., & Kim, S.H. (2004). *Social conflict: Escalation, stalemate, settlement.* Boston, MA: McGraw Hill.

Robinson, S.L. (1996.) Trust and the breach of the psychological contract. *Administrative Science Quarterly,* 41(4), 574–599.

Robinson, S.L., & Morrison, E. (2000). The development of psychological contract breach and violation: A longitudinal study, *Journal of Organizational Behavior,* 21(5), 525–546

Roth, N., Sitkin, S., & House, A. (1993). Stigma as a determinant of legalization. In S. Sitkin & R. Bies, (Eds.), *The legalistic organization.* Newbury Park, CA: Sage, 137–168.

Rotter, J.B. (1980). Interpersonal trust, trustworthiness and gullibility. *American Psychologist,* 35(1), 1–7.

Rousseau, D.M., Sitkin, S.B., Burt, R.S., & Camerer, C.F. (1998). Introduction to special topic forum: Not so different after all: A cross-discipline view of trust. *Academy of Management Review,* 23(3), 393–404.

Saunders, M.N.K., Dietz, G., & Thornhill, A. (2014) Trust and distrust: Polar opposites, or independent but co-existing? *Human Relations,* 67(6), 639–665.

Schoorman, F.D., Mayer, R.C., & Davis, J.H. (2007). An integrative model of organizational trust: Past, present, and future. *Academy of Management Review,* 32(2), 344–354.

Serva, M.A., Fuller, M.A., & Mayer, R.C. (2005). The reciprocal nature of trust: A longitudinal study of interacting teams. *Journal of Organizational Behavior,* 26(6), 625–648.

Sheppard, B.H., & Tuchinsky, M. (1996). Interfirm relationships: A grammar of pairs. In B.M. Staw, L.L. Cummings, (Eds.) *Research in organizational behavior.* Greenwich, CN: JAI Press, 331–373.

Sherif, M., Harvey, O.J., White, B.J., Hood, W.R., & Sherif, C.W. (1961). *Intergroup conflict and cooperation: The robbers cave experiment.* Norman, OK: University of Oklahoma.

Sitkin, S.B., & Roth, N.L. (1993). Explaining the limited effectiveness of legalistic "remedies" for trust/distrust. *Organization Science,* 4(3), 367–392.

Sitkin, S.B., & Stickel, D. (1996). The road to hell: The dynamics of distrust in an era of quality. In R.M. Kramer, T.R. Tyler, (Eds.), *Trust in Organizations*. Thousand Oaks, CA: Sage Publications, 196–215.

Six, F., Skinner, D., Searle, R., Weibel, A., Gillespie, N., & Den Hartog, D. (2016). *Trusting your organization: the role of respectful behaviours*. Under review.

Solinger, O.N., Hofmans, J., Bal, P.M., & Jansen, P.G.W. (2016). Bouncing back from psychological contract breach: How commitment recovers over time. *Journal of Organizational Behavior*, 37(4), 494–514.

Solinger, O.N., van Olffen, W., Roe, R.A., & Hofmans, J. (2013). On becoming (un)committed: a taxonomy and test of newcomer onboarding scenarios. *Organization Science*, 24(6), 1640–1661.

Sorensen, J.E., & Sorensen, T.L. (1974). The conflict of professionals in bureaucratic organizations. *Administrative Science Quarterly*, 19, 98–106.

Tomlinson, E., & Lewicki, R.J. (2006). Managing distrust in intractable conflicts. *Conflict Resolution Quarterly*, 24(2), 219–228.

Tripp, T.M., & Bies, R.J. (2010). "Righteous" anger and revenge in the workplace: The fantasies, the feuds, the forgiveness. In M. Potegal et al. (Eds.), *International Handbook of Anger*. Berlin: Springer Science, 413–431.

Van de Walle S., & Six, F.E. (2014). Active trust and active distrust as distinct concepts: A comparative approach to why studying distrust is important. *Journal of Comparative Policy Analysis*, 16(2), 158–174.

Weick, K.E. (1995). *Sensemaking in organizations*. London: Sage.

Wrightsman, L.S. (1974). *Assumptions about human nature: A social-psychological analysis*. Monterey, CA: Brooks/Cole.

Zand, D.E. (1972). Trust and managerial problem solving. *Administrative Science Quarterly*, 17(2), 229–239.

Zucker, L.G. (1986). Production of trust: Institutional sources of economic structure, 1840–1920. *Research in Organizational Behavior*, 8, 53–111.

PART II

Levels of analysis

This part includes four chapters which examine the distinct levels of analysis used to study trust, from micro through to recent more multi-foci approaches. It begins with Serena C. Lyu and Donald L. Ferrin's exploration of the interpersonal-level of analysis, reviewing the empirical evidence obtained over the last twenty years regarding the antecedents, functions and consequences of interpersonal trust within organizations. Their review is of value to researchers and practitioners as it outlines the key findings and implications which may inform the actions of senior management. They consider which empirical relationships are also mediated or moderated by trust. This chapter has clear links to Chapter 2 by Korsgaard, on the dynamics and raising the importance of cultural metacognitions, as well as Chapter 26 by Den Hartog, on leaders.

Then in Chapter 6 Ann-Marie I. Nienaber, Maximilian Holtgrave and Philipp D. Romeike explore the team level of analysis, and distinguish between trust at the intra- and inter-team levels. Like Lyu and Ferrin, they identify the determinants and outcomes of trust at each level, noting the similarities and differences between intra- and inter-team trust. They highlight both areas for theory development and areas more concerned with improvements to the measurement of trust in teams.

Next, Anna Brattström and Reinhard Bachmann focus on the interorganizational level of analysis. They explore two distinct concepts of cooperation and coordination for interorganizational relationships. They compare interorganizational trust research from four theoretical perspectives (rational choice, transaction cost, social exchange and neo-institutional theories), by exploring whether and how these concerns of cooperation/coordination are explicitly or implicitly examined. This separation of coordination and cooperation is used to identify important further research questions for interorganizational relationships.

In Chapter 8, C. Ashley Fulmer builds on her earlier work with Gelfand (2012) to outline the use of more complex models for trust that include a cross- and multi-level focus. She reflects on such models and where trust and its antecedents and consequences are at different levels of analysis. She considers studies using this approach including attention on generalized and political trust, trust in co-workers, teams, management/organizations and inter-organizational relationships. She also reviews studies undertaken to examine trust conflicts. She emphasizes how further studies using a cross- or multi-level approach might offer significant and productive avenues for future trust research, developing an agenda for further theory and methods developments.

5

DETERMINANTS, CONSEQUENCES AND FUNCTIONS OF INTERPERSONAL TRUST WITHIN ORGANIZATIONS

What is the empirical evidence?

Serena C. Lyu* and Donald L. Ferrin*

Introduction and objectives

In a 1999 review article, trust luminary Roderick Kramer observed that "Trust has . . . moved from bit player to center stage in contemporary organizational theory and research" (1999, p. 594). However, *since* 1999 the annual number of peer-reviewed articles published on trust has demonstrated a rapid upward trajectory (Ferrin, 2013). If trust research had reached "center stage" by 1999, we would have to conclude that, by 2017, trust research – probably as much as any other construct in the organizational sciences – had truly captured the attention of scholars and practitioners worldwide. Trust has moved from bit player, to center stage, and now to celebrity status.

This widespread recognition of the importance of trust has attracted a critical mass of scholars who have produced (and continue to expand) a scientific literature that provides extensive insights into the nature, determinants, consequences, and functions of trust. However, this literature is now so expansive that it is difficult for any single scholar to comprehend it. Fortunately, trust scholars have also focused on making sense of the literature in the form of systematic reviews, including both narrative (Burke et al., 2007; Costa et al., 2015; Dirks & Ferrin, 2001; Ferrin & Gillespie, 2010; Fulmer & Gelfand, 2012; Kramer & Lewicki, 2010; Lewicki et al., 2006; Searle et al., 2011) and meta-analytic (Colquitt et al., 2007; Dirks & Ferrin 2002; Kong et al., 2014; Lu et al., 2017) reviews.

Each of these reviews has had a specific focus, and aimed to address a specific set of questions, that has advanced our understanding of trust. In most of these reviews, the central aim was to provide conceptual understanding of what trust is, and how and why trust operates the way it does. To do so, these reviews assessed, analyzed, and qualitatively or quantitatively summarized the findings and insights from a range of primary studies. The large majority of these primary studies, in turn, had typically attempted to assess a theoretically interesting question by operationalizing theoretical concepts into measurable variables, measuring those constructs empirically, assessing empirical relations among the constructs, and then drawing inferences from those empirical relationships to generate theoretical insights. Thus, the review articles reflect inferences, and in many cases inferences about inferences, ultimately drawn from concrete data in a great mass of primary studies on empirical relationships between trust and related variables. From these inferential processes, scholars have generated many valuable theoretical insights that comprise important advances in understanding the nature and operation of trust within organizational settings.

The current review aims to supplement the existing reviews by taking a different tack. Rather than attempting to draw theoretical insights from the expanse of empirical studies, we aim to focus only on the concrete and empirical, answering the question, "*What has been demonstrated, empirically, regarding the determinants, consequences, and functions of interpersonal trust within organizations?*" We believe that answering this question is valuable for at least three reasons. First, given that the field's theoretical inferences are ultimately drawn from or justified based on primary data, it is valuable for researchers to have access to a summary of actual empirical findings. This will enable researchers to reconsider the appropriateness of existing frameworks, and also consider whether alternative theoretical framings might be suitable for making sense of the empirical literature. Second, future research will benefit from knowing what effects have already been demonstrated so that unnecessary replication can be avoided, and also to provide researchers with insight into what empirical findings can be expected or should be extended in future studies. Third, practitioners (and also scholars who aim to provide advice to practitioners) navigate a world of the literal and concrete. While we would hope that many practitioners will appreciate trust frameworks that operate at higher levels of abstraction, we contend that practitioners are more likely to be interested in specific insights (with references to the primary studies that generated those insights) into *what* constructs have been found to predict trust, *what* constructs have been found to be outcomes of trust, and *what* empirical relationships are mediated or moderated by trust. Such insights are relatively more likely to provide clear implications for action that can be better justified to senior management.

As mentioned above, practitioners navigate a world of the literal and concrete. When practitioners face a need or opportunity to build trust, or when they are asked to justify a proposed trust intervention, practitioners are likely to yearn for answers to questions such as the following: "What, specifically, predicts trust?" "What, specifically, does trust predict?" "How large are those effects?" "How much research has been conducted?" "And in what contexts has the research been conducted?" Accordingly, we expect that practitioners will find the present review to be extremely useful when designing and implementing trust-related interventions in their own organizations. That said, we also strongly encourage practitioners to read the primary studies, and to consider the limitations in internal and external validity of those studies, when planning their organizational interventions.

Accordingly, the objectives of this review are to systematically review and succinctly summarize the empirical evidence concerning determinants, outcomes, and functions of interpersonal trust within organizational settings. Our review aims to provide a distinct contribution in that it (1) focuses only on what has been found empirically (rather than summarizing theoretical perspectives); (2) is focused only on interpersonal trust within organizational settings; and (3) has a clearly defined empirical base (clearly delineated body of past research to be reviewed). We begin by describing our review methodology, starting with the definition of interpersonal trust that guided our review.

Review methodology

Interpersonal trust

The present review is focused specifically on interpersonal trust. We define "interpersonal" narrowly, but "trust" more broadly. Specifically, by "interpersonal" we refer to the trust that one individual has toward another specific individual. Therefore, we include studies that measured "trust in manager" or "trust in coworker," but we exclude studies that measured "trust in managers," "trust in fellow group members," and "trust in coworkers" (e.g., Grant & Sumanth, 2009). Similarly, we exclude studies that measured "trust in employer" or "trust in management" (e.g., Robinson, 1996) because these do not refer to a specific individual. We also exclude studies that measured or manipulated interpersonal trust, but then aggregated these measures to a higher level such as the group level (e.g., Crossley et al., 2013; Dirks, 1999). And we also exclude studies that focused on propensity to trust given that the referent of trust propensity is not a specific individual, but "people" or "others" (Frazier et al., 2013).

Recently, scholars have focused increasing attention on interpersonal trust as a dyadic phenomenon (Korsgaard et al., 2015). According to Korsgaard and colleagues, mutual trust is an emergent attribute of the dyad wherein both parties come to share a given level of trust (e.g., Anderson & Thompson, 2004) whereas trust asymmetry captures the degree to which each party's trust in the other converges (Tomlinson et al., 2009); accordingly, both are dyad-level constructs. In contrast, reciprocal trust is a process rather than a construct, in which each party is both trustor and trustee and one party's trust may influence the other's and vice versa (e.g., Ferrin et al., 2008). Given our definition of interpersonal trust as one individual's trust in another specific individual, we include studies of reciprocal trust (such studies examine how one individual's trust in another individual at a specific time point influences the second individual's trust in the first at a later time point, and therefore both trust measures are consistent with our definition of "interpersonal") but exclude studies of mutual trust and trust asymmetry (such studies combine two individuals' trust toward each other into a single measure that conveys the average level or deviation in trust between the two individuals, and therefore these measures do not fit our definition of "interpersonal").

By "trust" we refer to conceptual definitions, and their operationalizations, consistent with Mayer, Davis, and Schoorman's (1995) perceived ability, perceived benevolence, perceived integrity, and trust (defined as willingness to accept vulnerability) constructs, McAllister's (1995) affect- and cognition-based trust constructs (based on confident positive expectations), and variations thereon. Studies defining trust as a behavior (e.g., trust game studies), and felt trust (e.g., Lau et al., 2014) were excluded. We also exclude studies of interpersonal "distrust" and "mistrust" given emerging evidence that interpersonal distrust may be distinct from interpersonal trust (e.g., Saunders et al., 2014). Additionally, because the dynamics of interpersonal trust violations and repair are arguably distinct from those of interpersonal trust development and maintenance (Kim et al., 2004), we have excluded studies of trust violations and repair from our review.

Search methodology

We began by identifying 15 scientific journals that we believe are likely to have published high-quality, double-blind peer-reviewed empirical studies of interpersonal trust in the period from the early 1990s to present: *Academy of Management Journal, Administrative Science Quarterly, Group and Organization Studies, Human Relations, Journal of Applied Psychology, Journal of International*

Business Studies, Journal of Management, Journal of Management Studies, Journal of Organizational Behavior, Journal of Trust Research, Leadership Quarterly, Organizational Behavior and Human Decision Processes, Organization Science, Organisation Studies, and *Personnel Psychology.* Then, within each journal, we performed a Web of Science search, using the search term "trust," for the period from the early 1990s to September 2015, to identify articles to be considered for our review. Our next step was to review the abstracts for all such articles to identify any studies that were likely to have examined interpersonal trust as defined above. For any abstracts so identified, we then reviewed the article to assess whether it had in fact examined interpersonal trust as defined, and also whether it had provided empirical evidence (i.e., statistically significant findings) of determinants of trust, outcomes of trust, or evidence that trust functioned as a mediator or moderator. All studies that met those conditions were included in our review.

Our focus is on studies that provide insight into interpersonal trust within organizational settings. The majority of studies identified in our review analyzed survey and/or other data on employees in the workplace. Some studies (particularly laboratory studies) were not specifically situated within an organizational context, but nevertheless were conducted with the intent to provide insights relevant to work organizations, and are therefore included in our review.

Outline of the review

In the following sections, we first review the empirical evidence on the determinants and consequences of interpersonal trust. These are followed by a review of empirical evidence of the mediating role and moderating role of interpersonal trust. Because a mediating role implies, by definition, that interpersonal trust is also functioning as a determinant and consequence of other constructs, the findings in the Mediation section could arguably also be repeated in the Determinants and Consequences sections. However, in the interest of brevity and clarity, we only report these studies in the Mediation section. We conclude with a discussion of the implications and limitations of our review, and directions for future research.

Determinants of interpersonal trust

An interpersonal trust relationship can be considered to comprise the trustor, the trustee, the relationship between the trustor and the trustee, and the context within which they are embedded. Accordingly, the determinants of interpersonal trust can be categorized into these same four categories: trustor factors, trustee factors, relationship factors, and contextual factors. In the organizational context, the referents in interpersonal trust relationships include individuals such as a leader, a coworker, a fellow negotiator, etc. Depending on the referent, scholars have investigated different sets of determinants. Because of the large number of studies, we have organized the review by discussing each category of determinants and related trust referent in turn. Table 5.1 summarizes the specific empirical findings by study. Categories of determinants are listed in the top row. The studies are presently in chronological order so that readers can observe how the empirical research has evolved from the early 1990s to the present. We do not include the integrative reviews and quantitative meta-analyses in the table.

Trustor factors

Trustor's propensity to trust or generalized trust has been found to facilitate interpersonal trust directly (Colquitt et al., 2007, Mayer et al., 1995), probably because individuals with high trust propensity are more willing to form new relationships prior to gaining information about the

Table 5.1 Determinants of trust by referent and category

Authors	Conceptual-ization[1]	Measure[2]	Referent[3]	Trustor factors	Trustee factors	Shared relation factors	Communi-cation processes	Structural/network factors	Organiza-tional factors	External factors
Thomas and Ravlin (1995)	Trust (Willingness to accept vulnerability "WTAV")	Bond (1983)	Foreign manager		Cultural adaptation					
Korsgaard and Roberson (1995)	General trust	Cook and Wall (1980)	Manager	Non-instrumental voice						
De Dreu et al. (1998)	General trust		Negotiation partner	Social motive; punitive capability						
Farh et al. (1998)	General trust/loyalty	Podsakoff et al. (1990)	Supervisor; the Guanxi connection			Guanxi; relational demography				
Korsgaard et al. (1998)	General trust	Roberts and O'Reilly (1974)	Manager	Assertiveness; self-appraisal						
Elsbach and Elofson (2000)	Perceived competency	McCroskey (1966)	Decision maker		Easy-to-understand language; a legitimating decision process label					
Lee et al. (2000)	General trust	Roberts and O'Reilly (1974)	Supervisor	Power distance orientation	Procedural justice					

continued . . .

Table 5.1 Continued

Authors	Conceptual-ization[1]	Measure[2]	Referent[3]	Trustor factors	Trustee factors	Shared relation factors	Communi-cation processes	Structural/network factors	Organiza-tional factors	External factors
Young and Perrewe (2000)	General trust	Butler (1991)	Mentor; protégé		Social support; openness to advisement and coaching; having accomplished required work					
Chattopad-hyay and George (2001)	Cognition-based trust; affect-based trust	McAllister (1995)	Peer			Work-status dissimilarity			Temporary worker-dominated groups	
Korsgaard et al. (2002)	General trust	Butler (1991)	Manager		Open com-munication; demonstrating concern for employee					
Malhotra and Murnighan (2002)	General trust		Partner			Binding vs. non-binding contract				
Ambrose and Schminke (2003)	Cognition-based trust; affect-based trust	McAllister (1995)	Supervisor		Interactional justice				Organic organization	

Becerra and Gupta (2003)	Perceived trustworthiness (ability, benevolence, and integrity)	Mayer and Davis (1999)	Manager	Trust propensity		Frequency of communication	Trustor's and trustee's positions within organization	Cooperative, competitive, mixed rewards
Ferrin and Dirks (2003)	General trust	Cummings and Bromiley (1996)	Peer					
Naquin and Paulson (2003)	General trust	Cummings and Bromiley (1996)	Negotiation partner			Online negotiation		
Perrone et al. (2003)	General trust	Rempel et al. (1985)	Purchasing manager	Role autonomy				
Brown et al. (2005)	Affect-based trust	McAllister (1995)	Supervisor	Ethical leadership				
Rao et al. (2005)	General trust	One item from Xin and Pearce (1996)	Business associate					Facilitative governments
Ferrin et al. (2006)	Perceived integrity	One item from Mayer and Davis (1999)	Coworker	Organizational citizenship behaviors			Trust transferability; structural equivalence	
Levin et al. (2006)	Perceived benevolence	Johnson et al. (1996)	Supervisor and subordinate	Trustworthy behavior	Relationship length; demographic similarity; shared perspective			
de Jong et al. (2007)	Cognition-based trust; affect-based trust	McAllister (1995)	Team member	Perceived help	Task dependence			

continued . . .

Table 5.1 Continued

Authors	Conceptual-ization[1]	Measure[2]	Referent[3]	Trustor factors	Trustee factors	Shared relation factors	Communi-cation processes	Structural/network factors	Organiza-tional factors	External factors
Choi (2008)	Trust (WTAV)	Roberts and O'Reilly (1974)	Supervisor		Perceived justice					
Chua et al. (2008)	Cognition-based trust; affect-based trust	McAllister (1995)	Managerial peer					Economic resource, task advice, and career guidance ties; friendship and career guidance ties		
Gino and Schweitzer (2008)	General trust	Johnson-George and Swap (1982)	Student advisor/participant	Incidental gratitude; neutral emotional state; incidental anger						
Lau and Liden (2008)	Trust (WTAV; disclosure intentions)	One item from Gillespie (2003)	Coworker					Leader's trust in coworker		
Ballinger et al. (2009)	Trust (WTAV)	Mayer and Davis (1999)	Supervisor	Affective reaction to the departure of prior leader	Perceived ability	Student participant				

continued . . . .

Hill et al. (2009)	General trust	Cummings and Bromiley (1996)			Face-to-face communication	Competitive vs. cooperative context
Johnson and Lord (2010)	Trust (WTAV)	Mayer and Gavin (2005)	Experimenter	Interdependent and independent/individual self-identities; Justice		
Norman et al. (2010)	Trust (WTAV)	Mayer and Gavin (2005)	Leader	Leader positivity; leader transparency		
Sy (2010)	Perceived integrity	Gabarro and Athos (1976)	Leader	Implicit followership theories		
Vignovic and Thompson (2010)	Cognition-based trust; affect-based trust	McAllister (1995)	Student participant/the e-mail sender	Technical language violations; etiquette violations; cultural background of email sender		
Wong and Boh (2010)	Perceived trustworthiness		Managerial peer			Network heterogeneity, non-overlapping contacts; network density

Table 5.1 Continued

Authors	Conceptual-ization[1]	Measure[2]	Referent[3]	Trustor factors	Trustee factors	Shared relation factors	Communi-cation processes	Structural/network factors	Organiza-tional factors	External factors
Yakovleva et al. (2010)	Perceived trustworthi-ness (ability, benevolence, and integrity)	Jarvenpaa et al. (1998)	Coworker (reciprocal trust)	Propensity to trust	Perceived trustworthi-ness				Co-located vs. virtual work	
Cameron and Webster (2011)	Affect-based trust	McAllister (1995)	Commun-ication partner (reciprocal trust)		Incivility					
Kalshoven et al. (2011)	General trust	Cook and Wall (1980)	Supervisor		Ethical leader behaviors					
Jiang et al. (2011)	Cognition-based trust; affect-based trust	McAllister (1995)	Executive of overseas partner			The same cultural ethnicity				Relative firm size; firm age
Mayer et al. (2011)	Trust (WTAV) and per-ceived trustworthi-ness (ability, benevolence, and integrity)	Mayer and Davis (1999)	Supervisor		Power; influence tactics					
Chua et al. (2012)	Affect-based trust	McAllister (1995)	Managerial peer	Cultural metacognition						

Study	Trust type	Measure	Referent			
Dunn et al. (2012)	Cognition-based trust; affect-based trust	McAllister (1995) and Johnson-George and Swap (1982)	Student participant			Upwards comparison; downward comparison
Lount and Pettit (2012)	General trust; perceived benevolence	Johnson-George and Swap (1982) and Mayer and Davis (1999)	Student participant	Status		Interpersonal affect regulation
Niven et al. (2012)	General trust	One item from Levin and Cross (2004)	Coworker			
Frazier et al. (2013)	Trust (WTAV)	Mayer and Gavin (2005)	Supervisor	Propensity to trust; optimism	Perceived ability, benevolence, and integrity	
Saunders et al. (2014)	Trust (WTAV)	Card sort method	Manager		Managerial actions and policies relating to quality of communication and job security	
Halbesleben and Wheeler (2015)	General trust	Cook and Wall (1980)	Coworker (reciprocal trust)		Social support; OCBs	
Kwan et al. (2015)	Affect-based trust	McAllister (1995)	The target employee			Assumed familiarity to others

continued . . .

Table 5.1 Continued

Authors	Conceptual-ization[1]	Measure[2]	Referent[3]	Trustor factors	Trustee factors	Shared relation factors	Communi-cation processes	Structural/ network factors	Organiza-tional factors	External factors
Levine and Schweitzer (2015)	General trust; perceived benevolence and integrity		Game partner		Prosocial lies					
Vogel et al. (2015)	Perceived benevolence	Tepper & Henle (2011)	Supervisor		Abusive supervision					Anglo vs. Confucian culture

Notes

1 In general, if fewer than 75 percent of the items in a trust scale tap into perceived trustworthiness (i.e., ability, benevolence, and integrity), cognition-based trust, affect-based trust, or trust (willingness to accept vulnerability), we classify the scale as general trust.

2 Indicates the scale used or adapted from. If the authors did not state the source of the measure, we leave the cell blank, indicating that the authors created the scale themselves.

3 We indicate in parentheses those studies that investigated reciprocal based trust on the definition by Korsgaard et al. (2014).

trustee (Mayer et al., 1995). Propensity to trust is considered to be a dispositional, stable within-person factor. People vary in their propensity to trust due to their different developmental experiences, personalities, and cultural backgrounds (Mayer et al., 1995). Colquitt and colleagues (2007) meta-analyzed the relationships among trust, propensity to trust, and trustworthiness and found that propensity to trust is positively correlated with perceptions of trustee's trustworthiness and trust itself. The effect of propensity to trust on trust in coworker has been found to be stronger when people work virtually than co-located, and trustworthiness fully mediated the influence of trust propensity on trust (Yakovleva et al., 2010). In developing and validating their propensity to trust scale, Frazier, Johnson, and Fainshmidt (2013) found that propensity to trust was significantly related to, yet distinct from, trait optimism, and that trustworthiness perceptions are the cognitive evaluations that translate one's propensity to trust to one's willingness to be vulnerable to another (i.e., trust).

In addition to trust propensity, a number of other trustor characteristics have been examined. In negotiation contexts, De Dreu, Giebels, and Van de Vliert (1998) manipulated negotiators' social motive and punitive capability and found that trust is low when cooperative negotiators have high punitive capability. Focusing on incidental emotions, Gino and Schweitzer (2008) found that people who feel incidental gratitude are more trusting than are people in a neutral emotional state, and people in a neutral state are more trusting than are people who feel incidental anger. A recent meta-analysis by Lu et al. (2017) found that trustor attributes (positive affect, negative affect, and social motives) all have significant and relatively strong relationships with interpersonal trust in dyadic negotiations. In workplace trust judgments, positive affective reactions to the departure of a prior leader had a significant positive effect on trust toward the successive leader (Ballinger et al., 2009). In a series of lab experiments, Lount and Pettit (2012) found that people with high status tended to judge others as more benevolent and thus place more trust in others. In the context of performance appraisal decisions, Korsgaard and Roberson (1995) found that non-instrumental voice of a subordinate had an impact on the subordinate's trust toward the manager. Korsgaard, Roberson, and Rymph (1998) found that subordinates who were trained to communicate assertively in an appraisal review reacted more favourably to their managers with higher levels of trust toward the manager. Leaders' implicit followership theories predicted followers' trust in leaders because these perceptions may influence the extent to which leaders exhibit more or less trusting behaviors and the extent to which followers reciprocate in kind to leaders' display of trust (Sy, 2010). In an Executive MBA student sample, Chua, Morris, and Mor (2012) found that managers with lower cultural metacognition were less likely to have developed affect-based trust in their intercultural relationships.

Trustee factors

Consistent evidence, including meta-analytic evidence (Colquitt et al., 2007), has supported the proposition advanced by Mayer et al. (1995) that trust (defined as willingness to accept vulnerability toward a referent based on confident positive expectations) is predicted by perceptions of the referent's ability, benevolence, and integrity. In the workplace, trustworthiness behaviors such as being open, discrete, receptive, and available (Korsgaard et al., 2002; Levin et al., 2006), and organizational citizenship behaviors (OCBs) including voluntary help and individualized support (Ferrin et al., 2006; Young & Perrewe 2000), have been shown to influence a trustee's perceived trustworthiness and improve interpersonal trust. In the context of buyer–supplier relations, more-autonomous purchasing managers elicit higher levels of trust because they are better able to meet the positive expectations of their external counterparts by being more integrative, responsive, and competent (Perrone et al. 2003). Cameron and Webster (2011) found that individuals' incivility behaviors in a dyad could influence their interpersonal trust in each other. Trustees' behaviors can also have mixed effects on trust. Levine and Schweitzer (2015) found that prosocial lies, and false statements told with the intention of benefitting others, increase benevolence-based trust but harm integrity-based trust.

In terms of trust in leaders, Dirks and Ferrin's (2002) meta-analytic review reported that leadership behaviors (i.e., transformational and transactional leadership) had strong effects on subordinates' trust in supervisors. Meanwhile, other types of leadership behaviors have also been shown to impact trust in leaders such as ethical leadership (Brown et al., 2005; Kalshoven et al., 2011), participative leadership (Huang et al., 2010), servant leadership (van Dierendonck, 2011), and authentic leadership (Norman et al., 2010). In addition to leadership behaviors, various other managerial behaviors have been shown to impact employees' trust. For example, Korsgaard, Brodt, and Whitener (2002) demonstrated that managers' use of open communications and demonstrating concern for employees could increase trust. In a five-month longitudinal field study of the use of influence tactics and power on the development of employee trust, Mayer, Bobko, Davis, and Gavin (2011) found that changes in trust levels were substantially related to increases in specific types of power use and influence attempts. Participative decision making also increased trust between partners in collaboration simulations (Dirks & Ferrin, 2002). Elsbach and Elofson (2000) demonstrated that easy-to-understand language and a legitimating decision-making label could increase perceptions of competence-based trustworthiness. With a constrained card sort method and an associated in-depth interview method, Saunders, Dietz, and Thornhill (2014) found that managerial actions and policies that are related to consideration, inspiration, and quality of communication and job security have significant effects on trust. Scholars have also investigated leadership behaviors that can decrease trust. One study found that the negative effects of perceived abusive supervision on trust were stronger for subordinates within the Anglo versus the Confucian Asian culture (Vogel et al., 2015).

In addition to leadership behaviors, researchers have consistently found positive relationships between organizational justice, ethical behaviors, and trust (Dirks & Ferrin, 2002, Colquitt & Rodell, 2011). Beyond the main effects of organizational justice (i.e., distributive, procedural, and interactional justice) on interpersonal trust (Dirks & Ferrin, 2002), several contingency models have recently been tested. In a sample of Hong Kong employees, researchers found that the relationship between procedural justice and trust in supervisor was higher for those with low power-distance orientations (Lee et al., 2000). Ambrose and Schminke (2003) found that that the relationship between interactional justice and supervisory trust was stronger in organic organizations as compared to mechanistic organizations. Choi (2008) found that employees' perceptions of the fairness of their supervisor moderated the relationship between the perceived justice of a particular event and their trust in managers. Other researchers have investigated the mechanisms underlying the relationship between justice and trust. By manipulating justice in a laboratory experiment, Johnson and Lord (2010) found that the effects of justice on trust were mediated by the activation of interdependent and independent/individual self-identities.

Scholars have also studied how culture influences employees' trust in leaders and partners. Responses from employees in the US subsidiaries of Japanese manufacturing firms confirmed that cultural adaptation by a foreign manager was negatively related to internal causal attributions for the manager's behavior, and those attributions were directly related to participants' intentions to trust (Thomas & Ravlin, 1995).

To conclude, trustee factors in terms of perceived ability, benevolence, and integrity play critical roles in determining interpersonal trust levels. Work behaviors that indicate an individual's trustworthiness also promote trust. Specifically, for trust in supervisors, leadership behaviors, leaders' decision-making behaviors, organizational justice, and cultural adaptation behaviors have been demonstrated to increase trust.

Relationship factors

Relationship factors are elements shared between trustor and trustee. They can be categorized into the relationship itself, shared similarity, relationship interdependence, exchange processes, and communication processes between trustor and trustee. First, several studies have considered the effects of relationship length on trust. A recent meta-analysis found that the correlation between trust and relationship duration is on average positive but small, suggesting the presence of unobserved moderators (Vanneste et al., 2014). Using relationship length as the moderator, Levin, Whitener, and Cross (2006) found that trustworthiness perceptions were related to demographic similarity in newer relationships, to trustworthiness behaviors in more established relationships, and to shared perspective in more mature relationships.

Second, the degree of similarity between trustor and trustee is also likely to impact trust (Fulmer & Gelfand, 2012). For example, interpersonal trust was found to be higher when individuals perceived guanxi and relational demography (i.e., similarities between individuals) (Farh et al., 1998), and when the trustor and trustee shared cultural-ethnic similarity (Jiang et al., 2011). Trust in peers (internal workers) was lower when individuals perceived work-status dissimilarity in temporary-worker-dominated groups (Chattopadhyay & George, 2001). In addition, Kwan et al. (2015) studied the mere exposure effect – objects, ideas or people more frequently encountered in the physical or social environment are usually more positively evaluated. They found this effect altered individuals' assumed familiarity to others and influenced affect-based trust when participants had the motivation to be connected to their peers (Kwan et al., 2015).

Third, different interdependent relationships between trustor and trustee also influence the trust between them. For example, Malhotra and Murnighan (2002) found that non-binding contracts lead to personal attributions for cooperation and thus may provide an optimal basis for building interpersonal trust. Considering different task-interdependent relations, de Jong, Van der Vegt, and Molleman (2007) found that when both team members are highly dependent on each other, an increase in task dependence was associated with higher levels of perceived help from and interpersonal trust in the team member.

Fourth, scholars have recognized that trust development may spiral between trustor and trustee in that trust promotes cooperative behaviors, which in turn promotes trust between individuals in a relationship. Several empirical studies have modeled such spiraling between two parties. With a dyadic design, Ferrin, Bligh, and Kohles (2008) found strong support in a laboratory setting for a trust-cooperation spiral between individuals in which an individual's cooperative behavior influenced the partner's trust perceptions which in turn influenced the partner's cooperative behaviors. Similarly, Halbesleben and Wheeler (2015) modeled and empirically demonstrated a reciprocal resource gain spiral between pairs of coworkers and found support that a coworker's organizational citizenship behaviors towards individuals (OCBIs) leads to an individual's perceived social support, which in turn leads to trust and OCBIs toward that coworker, and vice versa.

The communication processes between the trustor and trustee also influences trust. Relative to face-to-face (FTF) negotiations, online negotiations were found to be related to lower levels of trust (Naquin & Paulson, 2003; Lu et al., 2017). Meanwhile, researchers have found that in online communications, participants formed negative trustworthiness perceptions of the sender of an e-mail containing technical language violations and etiquette violations (Vignovic & Thompson, 2010). Yet, scholars have also found that communication medium interacts with organizational context and time to influence trust because individuals gather additional information from others over time, and consequently the difference in trust between FTF and online communications decreases (Hill et al., 2009). Beyond the medium itself, communication processes also moderate the effects of other predictors on trust. As communication frequency increases, the trustor's general attitudinal predisposition towards peers becomes less important and the trustor's and trustee's positions within the organization become more important as determinants of perceived trustworthiness (Becerra & Gupta, 2003). Meanwhile, communications that regulate interpersonal affect by improving others' affect have been found to be associated with individuals' perceptions of friendship and trust (Niven et al., 2012). The relationship between positive affect and trust was stronger in online versus FTF negotiations (Lu et al., 2017).

Contextual factors

Contextual factors reflect a broad set of potential determinants of trust. This category of factors is based on the understanding that the interpersonal trust relationship is embedded in a larger context including other relationships around the focal relationship (i.e., the network), the organizational context, and the environment that is external to organizations.

Social network analysis studies have found that different network characteristics impact interpersonal trust. Network characteristics such as trust transferability (i.e., the extent to which trustor and trustee share a common trusted third party) and structural equivalence (i.e., the similarity in the relationships the trustee and trustor have and do not have with others in a network) have been found to promote interpersonal trust (Ferrin et al., 2006). Trust in a coworker was found to be affected by the extent to which the coworker is trusted by the leader (Lau & Liden, 2008). Different ties between trustor and trustee have different implications for trust: task advice and career guidance ties have been found to lead to cognition-based trust while friendship and career guidance ties lead to affect-based trust (Chua et al., 2008). And, managers whose advocates (i.e., third parties) have many non-overlapping contacts, high network density, and high network heterogeneity have higher peer reputations for trustworthiness (Wong & Boh, 2010).

Organizational context has also been found to impact interpersonal trust, primarily through reward structures. A cooperative reward structure has been found to encourage teamwork and promote trust, while a competitive reward structure encourages individual efforts (Hill et al., 2009). Ferrin and Dirks (2003) found that the presence of cooperative reward structures fostered higher levels of interpersonal trust than did competitive reward structures via the effects of goal structures on participants' actual behaviors, perceived motives, and perceived performance. Reward structures of many organizations routinely compare employees with each other by ranking employees or publicly recognizing an employee for special achievement (Dunn et al., 2012). Given the frequency of such comparisons, Dunn, Ruedy, and Schweitzer (2012) investigated how comparisons with someone whose performance is superior to one's own (upward comparisons) and comparisons with someone whose performance is inferior to one's own (downward comparisons) influence trust. They found that upward comparisons harm affective trust and downward comparisons harm cognitive trust (Dunn et al., 2012).

Factors external to the organizations can also exert an impact on interpersonal trust. Negotiators from the loose culture trust one another more than negotiators from the tight culture (Lu et al., 2017). Considering firm size and age in shaping intra-cultural and intercultural trust, Jiang et al. (2011) found that firm age was positively associated with Chinese senior executives' affect-based trust for the senior executive of the same cultural ethnicity at overseas partner firms. Rao et al. (2005) conducted structured interviews with managers from China, Hong Kong, Thailand, and the United States and asked them to identify three business associates and rate each relationship. They assigned country-specific facilitative government index scores to each respondent and found that a facilitative government that provides structures to facilitate business transactions can lead to higher levels of interpersonal trust in business associates (Rao et al., 2005).

In sum, it is clear that trustee factors, trustor factors, relationship factors, and contextual factors do impact interpersonal trust. Mayer et al.'s (1995) conceptual model provided a crucial road-map for how trustor's propensity to trust and the perceived trustworthiness of the trustee were expected to impact trust. However, their model provided relatively less insight into trustor factors other than trust propensity, relationship factors or contextual factors, or upstream variables that might influence trust via perceived ability, benevolence, or integrity. The research reviewed in this section has provided extensive insight into other trustor factors, and upstream, relationship, and contextual factors. These empirical findings highlight a need for conceptual frameworks that can model how interpersonal trust is influenced by the broad range of trustor, upstream, relationship, and contextual factors that have been uncovered in empirical research.

Consequences of interpersonal trust

Interpersonal trust has been found to have generally positive effects on a wide range of attitudinal and behavioral workplace outcomes. The behavioral outcomes can be categorized into knowledge sharing, cooperation, communication, attachment (e.g., commitment; intention to quit or stay) and performance (e.g., job performance; OCBs) (Fulmer & Gelfand, 2012). Most studies on the relationship between trust in interpersonal referents and individual outcomes have focused on trust in leader. Table 5.2 summarizes the specific empirical findings by study, again presenting them in chronological order so that readers can observe how research has evolved over time. Categories of consequence are listed in the top row. We again do not include integrative reviews and quantitative meta-analyses in the table.

Several empirical studies have confirmed that trust in leader or manager influences attitudinal outcomes such as job satisfaction and work engagement (Cunningham & MacGregor, 2000; Moorman et al., 2013; Yang & Mossholder, 2010), satisfaction with the leader and ratings of leader justice (Holtz, 2015; Holtz & Harold, 2009). Quantitative meta-analyses have also confirmed that trust in leader increases belief in the information from the leader and commitment to decisions (Dirks & Ferrin, 2002). Both trust in leader and trust in coworker can increase risk-taking preferences (Colquitt et al., 2007). In addition, Zapata, Olsen, and Martins (2013) suggested and found that leaders' perceptions of employee trustworthiness (benevolence and integrity) positively affected interpersonal and informational justice that the employee received from the leader through the social exchange mechanisms of felt obligation and trust.

Interpersonal trust in peers (e.g., a coworker, a peer manager) has also been found to promote knowledge exchange and knowledge creation (Chung & Jackson, 2011). In the mentor-protégé relationship, mentor's trust is related to career-related support, psychosocial support, and role modeling received by the protégé (Wang et al., 2010). And in a study of dormant ties, Levin, Walter, and Murnighan (2011) found that the perceived benevolence of dormant tie contacts is related to receipt of useful information.

Trust also plays an important role in conflict resolution within the workplace. Research has found that when mediating a dispute between two peers, participants sent more rapport-building messages when the trust exhibited between two disputants was low (Ross & Wieland, 1996). Interpersonal trust is also related to smoother negotiation and reduced conflict in buyer–supplier relationships (Zaheer et al., 1998). In two experiments and two field studies, De Cremer and Tyler (2007) consistently found that trust in an authority increases people's willingness to cooperate with the authority across a wide range of social situations.

In terms of attachment, trust in leader is likewise positively related to organizational commitment and negatively related to intention to quit (Brower et al., 2008; Costigan et al., 2013; Cunningham & MacGregor, 2000; Dirks & Ferrin, 2002; Moorman et al., 2013; Harris et al., 2014; Thau et al., 2007; Yang & Mossholder, 2010).

Table 5.2 Consequences of trust by referent and category

Authors	Conceptual-ization[1]	Measure[2]	Referent	Attitudes and preferences	Knowledge sharing and organizational learning	Communication, cooperation, and conflict	Attachment (commitment and turnover)	Performance
McAllister (1995)	Cognition-based trust; affect-based trust		Peer					Need-based monitoring; affiliative citizenship behavior; assistance citizenship behavior; performance
Ross and Wieland (1996)	General trust	Experimental manipulation	Peer			Rapport-building messages sent by mediator		
Zaheer et al. (1998)	General trust	Rempel and Holmes (1986)	Contact person of supplier			Eased negotiation and reduced conflict		
Cunningham and MacGregor (2000)	Predictability, perceived benevolence and fairness		Supervisor	Job satisfaction			Absence, intention to quit	
Premeaux and Bedeian (2003)	General trust		Supervisor					Speaking up
Mayer and Gavin (2005)	Perceived trustworthiness (ability, benevolence, and integrity); Trust (WTAV)	Mayer and Davis (1999)	Plant manager					In-role performance; OCBs

Study	Trust type	Trust measure	Referent	Mediator	Intermediate outcome	Outcome
De Cremer and Tyler (2007)	General trust	Manipulated (in two experiments); Tyler and Huo (2002) (in two field studies)	An authority	Willingness to cooperate with the authority		
George and Zhou (2007)	Cognition-based trust	McAllister (1995)	Supervisor			Creativity
Thau et al. (2007)	General trust	Cook and Wall (1980) and Robinson and Rousseau (1994) (in study 2)	Supervisor		Intention to stay	Antisocial work behavior
Brower et al. (2008)	Trust (WTAV)	Mayer and Davis (1999)	Manager; subordinate		Intention to quit	Individual-directed OCBs; organization-directed OCBs; in-role performance
Holtz and Harold (2009)	General trust	Robinson and Rousseau (1994)	Supervisor	Overall justice perception		
Wang et al. (2010)	Cognition-based trust; affect-based trust	McAllister (1995)	The protégé	Mentoring functions received by the protégé		
Yang and Mossholder (2010)	Cognition-based trust; affect-based trust		Supervisor	Job satisfaction	Affective organizational commitment	
Chung and Jackson (2011)	General trust	Burt (1992) and Sparrowe et al. (2001)	Coworker	Knowledge creation		In-role and extra-role performance

continued . . .

Table 5.2 Continued

Authors	Conceptual-ization[(1)]	Measure[(2)]	Referent	Attitudes and preferences	Knowledge sharing and organizational learning	Communication, cooperation, and conflict	Attachment (commitment and turnover)	Performance
Gao et al. (2011)	General trust	Robinson and Rousseau (1994)	Leader					Employee voice
Levin et al. (2011)	Perceived benevolence	Levin and Cross (2004) and Levin et al. (2006)	Dormant tie contact		Receipt of useful knowledge			
Palanski and Yammarino (2011)	Perceived integrity (behavioral integrity)	Simons et al. (2007)	Leader					Follower job performance
Costigan et al. (2013)	Cognition-based trust; affect-based trust	McAllister (1995)	Supervisor				Turnover intentions	
Li and Tan (2013)	Cognition-based trust; affect-based trust	McAllister (1995)	Supervisor					Job performance

Study	Trust construct	Scale source	Referent			
Zapata et al. (2013)	Perceived trustworthiness (benevolence, and integrity); trust (WTAV)	Mayer and Davis (1999)	Employee			Leader interactional justice rule adherence
Moorman et al. (2013)	Perceived integrity; general trust	Roberts and O'Reilly (1974) (in study 2)	Leader	Job satisfaction; work engagement	Intention to quit	Leader effectiveness
Harris et al. (2014)	Trust (WTAV)	Robinson and Rousseau (1994)	Leader		Turnover intentions	Newcomer creativity; task performance
Holtz (2015)	Initial trustworthiness perception	Huang and Murnighan (2010)	Individual in scenario	Perception of justice		

Notes.

1 In general, if fewer than 75 percent of the items in a trust scale tap into perceived trustworthiness (i.e., ability, benevolence, and integrity), cognition-based trust, affect-based trust, or trust (willingness to accept vulnerability), we classify the scale as general trust.

2 Indicates the scale used or adapted from. If the authors did not state the source of the measure, we leave the cell blank, indicating that the authors created the scale themselves.

Trust has also been empirically associated with a range of performance outcomes: job performance, OCBs, creativity, and proactive behaviors. For example, manager's perceived trustworthiness and resultant trust in manager have been shown to increase employee in-role performance and OCBs (Mayer & Gavin, 2005). Yang and Mossholder (2010) distinguished trust in supervisor from trust in management and found affect-based trust in supervisor was a significant predictor of in-role and extra-role work behaviors. Perceived leader behavioral integrity has been confirmed to promote follower job performance (Palanski & Yammarino, 2011). Moorman et al. (2013) also found that perceived leader behavioral integrity and resultant trust in leaders lead to leader effectiveness, and subordinates' lower intentions to quit, higher job satisfaction and work engagement. Li and Tan (2013) provided evidence that trust in supervisor affected subordinates' performance via promoting psychological availability and psychological safety.

When developing the cognition-based and affect-based trust scale, McAllister (1995) found that cognition-based trust led to affect-based trust in peers, which in turn impacted manager need-based monitoring, affiliative citizenship behavior, and assistance citizenship behavior. Meanwhile, an employee's level of trust in supervisor was found to be negatively related to antisocial work behaviors via attachment to the organization (Thau et al., 2007). Brower et al. (2008) investigated the role of trust from both manager and subordinate perspectives and found strong support for the effect of the manager's trust in subordinate on subordinates' behavior and intentions, beyond the effect of trust in the manager. They further found a significant joint effect of trust in the manager and trust in the subordinate on individual-directed OCBs (Brower et al., 2008).

Trust has also been linked with creativity. Employee creativity has been found to be higher when supervisors provide a supportive environment in which trust in the supervisor is high (George & Zhou, 2007). Similarly, newcomer creativity is high when a newcomer's trust in the leader is high because increased levels of trust likely result in more receptive newcomers and contribute to an overall context that is conducive to creativity (Harris et al., 2014).

Research has also demonstrated that trust in supervisor can promote voice or speaking-up behaviors (Gao et al., 2011; Premeaux & Bedeian, 2003). Gao et al. (2011) further demonstrated that the relationship between leader trust and employee voice became more positive when empowering leadership was higher rather than lower.

In addition to the consequences mentioned above, a recent meta-analysis on trust in negotiations found that interpersonal trust predicts higher joint outcomes and outcome satisfaction (Kong et al., 2014). Results also found that trust had a positive relationship with integrative behaviors, which had a negative relationship with the trustor's outcome; in contrast, trust had a negative relationship with distributive behaviors, which had a positive relationship with the trustor's outcome.

Overall, research on interpersonal trust has documented a number of valuable benefits of trust. Interpersonal trust in various referents including the leader, coworker, and negotiation partner has been demonstrated to promote a wide range of desirable work and other outcomes. The literature on consequences of interpersonal trust is extensive and includes a number of narrative and meta-analytic reviews (Dirks & Ferrin, 2001; Dirks & Ferrin, 2002; Fulmer & Gelfand, 2012; Burke et al., 2007; Searle et al., 2011; Costa et al., 2015).

One key component of the Mayer et al. (1995) model of organizational trust is the moderating factor of perceived risk: the effect of an individual's trust in another (defined as willingness to accept vulnerability) on the individual's risk-taking in the relationship is posited to interact with perceived risk. Specifically, when the individual perceives risk to be high, even a very high level of trust may not predict risk-taking in the relationship, whereas when the individual perceives risk to be low, even a low level of trust may predict risk-taking in the relationship. Considering how elemental this moderation proposition is to the Mayer et al. model, we were surprised that our review failed to identify any studies that had empirically validated the moderation effect. This absence of research is particularly surprising when contrasted with the extensive research supporting the other elements of the model, which were validated meta-analytically by Colquitt et al. (2007). Thus, one important direction for future research is to empirically validate the moderating effect of perceived risk.

The mediating role of interpersonal trust

In this section, we review studies that have hypothesized and found support for predictions that interpersonal trust will mediate the effect of some predictors on some outcomes. The support is typically established using empirical tests such as those provided by Baron and Kenny (1986) or Sobel (1982), or bootstrapping (Preacher & Hayes, 2008), path modeling, or latent variable structural equation modeling. We only report significant or marginally significant effects. As will be seen in this review, a relatively large number of studies have hypothesized and found mediation. By reviewing them, we can gain insight into the question, "In what empirical relationships does interpersonal trust provide a valuable mediating role?"

It is important to note that the seminal model of organizational trust advanced by Mayer and colleagues (Mayer et al., 1995) posits a mediation effect: The effects of the trustor's perceptions of the trustee's ability, benevolence and integrity on the trustor's risk-taking in a relationship are mediated by the trustor's trust, defined as willingness to accept vulnerability. Strong and robust support for this mediation effect has been provided in meta-analytic form (Colquitt et al., 2007). We do note, however, that the first step of the mediation effect posited and validated by these researchers is a path from trust perceptions to trust intentions, both of which are trust-related cognitive states existing within the trustor. In the remainder of this section, we would like to expand beyond this particular mediated effect to inquire into how trust (whether a perception, expectation, or intention as defined earlier in this paper) may mediate other empirical relations.

Stream 1: Mediating role of trust in relationships between leaders' behaviors and followers' work-related attitudes and behaviors. Our review highlighted two broad streams of mediation effects (Table 5.3). The first stream reflects what can now be considered a critical mass of studies that have hypothesized and supported the fundamental prediction that a leader's behaviors influence a range of followers' work-related attitudinal and behavioral outcomes via the follower's trust in the leader. A first set of these studies found support for the effects of transformational and transactional leadership. In two independent samples of US-based employees and their supervisors, Pillai, Schriesheim, and Williams (1999) found that the effect of supervisors' transformational leadership behaviors on subordinates' OCBs was mediated by subordinates' trust in the supervisor; they further found support for a three-step mediation effect in which the effects of transformational leadership influenced trust via subordinates' perceptions of organizational procedural justice, with trust then ultimately influencing OCBs. In a US-based lab study, Jung and Avolio (2000) found that confederates' transformational and transactional leadership behaviors influenced followers' performance quality and satisfaction with the leader via trust in the leader. In a sample of American employees and their supervisors, Rubin, Bommer, and Bachrach (2010) found that supervisors' operant behaviors (contingent reward, non-contingent reward, and noncontingent punishment, but not contingent punishment), predicted

Table 5.3 Interpersonal trust as a mediator

Authors	Conceptualization[1]	Measure[2]	Referent	Predictors	Attitudinal outcomes	Behavioral outcomes
STREAM 1: MEDIATION OF THE EFFECTS OF LEADER BEHAVIORS ON SUBORDINATES' ATTITUDINAL AND BEHAVIORAL OUTCOMES						
Pillai et al. (1999)	Perceived ability	Nyhan & Marlowe Jr. (1997)	Supervisor	Transformational leadership; transactional leadership; procedural justice		OCBs
Jung and Avolio (2000)	General trust	Podsakoff et al. (1990)	Supervisor	Transformational leadership; transactional leadership	Satisfaction with the leader	Performance quality
Yang et al. (2009)	Affect-based trust; cognition-based trust		Supervisor	Procedural justice	Job satisfaction	Task performance; helping behavior
Rubin et al. (2010)	General trust	Podsakoff et al. (1990, 1996)		Operant leadership (contingent reward; noncontingent reward; noncontingent punishment)		OCBs
Van Dijke et al. (2010)	General trust	Scott (1983)	Fellow organizational participant (Study 2); supervisor (Study 3)	Procedural justice	Perceived charisma (Study 2); perceived legitimacy (Study 2)	OCBs (Study 3)
Khazanchi and Masterson (2011)	Perceived integrity	Robinson (1996)	Supervisor	Interpersonal justice; informational justice		LMX; information sharing, creativity
Colquitt et al. (2012)	Affect-based trust; cognition-based trust	McAllister (1995)	Supervisor	Distributive justice; procedural justice; interpersonal justice	Normative commitment; uncertainty	Job performance
W. Zhu et al. (2013)	Affect-based trust; cognition-based trust	McAllister (1995)	Supervisor	Transformational leadership	Affective organizational commitment	OCBs; job performance
Chen et al. (2014)	Affect-based trust	McAllister (1995)	Supervisor	Paternalistic leadership (benevolence; morality)		In-role performance; OCBs
Y. Zhu and Akhtar (2014)	Affect-based trust; cognition-based trust	McAllister (1995)	Supervisor	Transformational leadership		Helping behavior

STREAM 2: OTHER MEDIATED EFFECTS

Study	Trust measure	Scale source	Trustee			
Simons et al. (2007)	Perceived integrity (behavioral integrity)		Manager	Employee race (black vs. non-black)	Employees' trust in manager; interpersonal justice perceptions; satisfaction; organizational commitment; intent to stay	Actor's cooperation
Ferrin et al. (2008)	Perceived integrity	Cummings and Bromiley (1996)	Partner in a lab simulation	Partner's cooperation		
Rafaeli et al. (2008)	General trust		Stranger	Recognizability of an organizational logo		Initial compliance with a request made by a stranger
Hofmann et al. (2009)	Affect-based trust		Co-worker	Formally-designated role (helping role)	Employees' intent to seek help	
Mislin et al. (2011)	Perceived benevolence and perceived integrity (combined into a single factor)	Mayer and Davis (1999)	Negotiation counterpart	Negotiator's mood (positive vs. neutral); contract incentives from counterpart		Negotiators' contract implementation
Sonenshein et al. (2011)	Perceived ability and integrity (combined into a single factor)	Mayer and Davis (1999)	Borrower	Borrowers' verbal accounts		Lending decisions
Kacmar et al. (2012)	General trust	Treadway et al. (2004)	Supervisor	Relationship conflict between supervisor and employee		Subordinates' OCBs
Ladegard and Gjerde (2014)	General trust	Dietz and Den Hertog (2006); Mayer and Davis (1999); Mayer and Gavin (2005)	Subordinate	Leadership coaching intervention	Subordinates' perceived empowerment; turnover intent	
Reiche et al. (2014)	Affect-based trust	McAllister (1995)	Subordinate	Subordinates' OCBs		Managers' trustworthy behavior

Notes.

1 In general, if fewer than 75 percent of the items in a trust scale tap into perceived trustworthiness (i.e., ability, benevolence, and integrity), cognition-based trust, affect-based trust, or trust (willingness to accept vulnerability), we classify the scale as general trust.

2 Indicates the scale used or adapted from. If the authors did not state the source of the measure, we leave the cell blank, indicating that the authors created the scale themselves.

trust in the supervisor, which in turn influenced employees' OCBs. In a study of employees and their supervisors in Mainland China, W. Zhu, Newman, Miao, and Hooke (2013) found that affect-based trust in the leader mediated the positive effects of supervisors' transformational leadership behaviors on subordinates' affective organizational commitment, OCBs, and job performance, whereas cognition-based trust in the leader mediated a negative effect of transformational leadership on job performance. And in a sample of employees and their supervisors in Mainland China, Y. Zhu and Akhtar (2014) found that both affect- and cognition-based trust toward the leader mediated the effect of supervisors' transformational leadership behaviors on subordinates' helping behaviors; a moderated mediation analysis further indicated that the effects of affect- and cognition-based trust on helping behavior differed according to the level of subordinates' prosocial motivation.

A second set of studies found support for the mediated effects of leaders' justice behaviors. In a sample of Taiwan-based employees and their supervisors, Yang, Mossholder, and Peng (2009) found that the effect of supervisors' procedural justice behaviors on subordinates' helping behaviors was mediated by subordinates' affect-based trust in the supervisor, whereas the effects of supervisors' procedural justice behaviors on subordinates' job satisfaction and task performance were mediated by subordinates' cognition-based trust in the supervisor. In a laboratory experiment conducted to replicate field findings of Netherlands-based employees and their supervisors, and uncover mediating mechanisms, van Dijke, De Cremer, and Mayer (2010) found that trust in a fellow organizational member mediated the effect of the member's procedural justice behaviors on the trustor's perceptions of the member's charisma and legitimacy; however, this effect held only for high-power members, not low-power members; in a follow-up field study of US employees and their supervisors, employees' trust in their supervisors mediated the effects of supervisors' procedural justice behaviors on subordinates' OCBs. Analyzing data from a sample of Indian employees and their supervisors, Khazanchi and Masterson (2011) presented a structural equation model indicating multiple stages of mediation in which supervisors' informational and interpersonal justice behaviors influenced employees' trust in their supervisors, which in turn influenced leader-member exchange, then employee information sharing, and then employee creativity. And in a study of US-based employees, Colquitt et al. (2012) found that both affect- and cognition-based trust (ABT and CBT) mediated the effects of three forms of justice (distributive, procedural, and interpersonal) on job performance. The authors presented a three-step mediation model in which justice behaviors influenced ABT and CBT; ABT then influenced normative commitment while CBT influenced uncertainty, and then normative commitment and uncertainty influenced job performance.

Finally, one study examined the role of trust in mediating the effect of yet another leadership behavior – paternalistic leadership – on employee outcomes. In a study aimed at studying leadership behaviors in the Confucian Chinese context, using a sample of employees and their supervisors in Taiwan, Chen et al. (2014) found that subordinates' affect-based trust toward their supervisors mediated the effects of supervisors' benevolence and morality behaviors (but not authoritarianism behaviors) on subordinates' in-role performance and OCBs.

In sum, we see a sizeable number of empirical studies demonstrating that employees' trust in the leader mediates the effects of leadership behaviors on employees' work-related attitudes and behaviors. We further note that these studies have been situated in a variety of research settings (field and lab), in very distinct cultures (Western, Chinese, Indian), using different data sources (employee report, supervisor report, archival). This consistency of findings over the diversity of research settings, country/cultural contexts, and methods, lends considerable weight to the notion that the effects are robust.

Stream 2: Other mediating effects. The 'second stream' of studies is probably better characterized as multiple rivulets rather than a single stream. Extending the theme from above which focused on the effects of trustees' behaviors (specifically, leadership behaviors), a first group of studies has examined the mediated effects of a much broader range of trustee factors, including employees' OCBs, partners' cooperative behaviors, borrowers' verbal accounts in a lending context, counterparts' contract terms in a negotiation context, formal roles granted to a fellow employee, and the subtle symbols of credibility (logos on t-shirts) accompanying a compliance request.

In an 18-country field study of managers and their subordinates, Reich et al. (2014) found that the effects of subordinates' OCBOs (OCBs directed toward the organization) and OCBs (OCBs directed toward peers) on managers' trustworthy behavior was mediated by managers' trust in the subordinates. As mentioned above, in a lab study, Ferrin, Bligh, and Kohles (2008) found that an actor's trust in a partner mediated the effect of the partner's cooperative behavior on the actor's cooperative behavior, and these dynamics spiraled back and forth between actor and partner over time. Following a field study that indicated that borrowers' verbal accounts (e.g., explanations, acknowledgments, denial) influenced lenders' decisions on whether or not to loan funds, Sonenshein, Herzenstein, and Dholaki (2011) conducted a laboratory experiment to explore the psychological mechanisms that might explain the effect; they found that verbal accounts influence lenders' perceptions of borrowers' trustworthiness, which in turn influence lending decisions. In a laboratory study exploring the factors that would influence negotiators to accept risky terms in the implementation of a negotiated agreement, Mislin, Campagna, and Bottom (2011) found that individuals' trust toward their counterpart mediated the effects of contract form (incentives for implementation). In a study of US-based employees, Hofmann, Lei and Grant (2009) found that employees' decisions to seek help from a particular coworker were predicted by the coworker having a formally-designated helping role, and the effect was mediated by the employee's affect-based trust toward the coworker. And in a laboratory setting, Rafaeli, Sagy, and Derfler-Rozin (2008) found in two separate studies (Studies 2 and 4) that individuals were more likely to comply with a request (e.g., to taste some food; make a monetary donation) made by a stranger if the stranger was wearing a shirt with a familiar logo (vs. no logo); the effect was mediated by individuals' trust toward the stranger.

Yet another set of mediation studies has focused not on trustee factors, but on a range of trustor factors that can influence downstream variables via trust: the trustor's race, the trustor's mood, and training received by the trustor. In a sample of America- and Canada-based employees rating their managers, Simons et al. (2007) found that black employees (as compared to non-black employees) reported lower levels of trust in their manager, interpersonal justice perceptions, satisfaction, organizational commitment, and intent to stay with the organization, and the effect of race on these outcomes was mediated by behavioral integrity, i.e., employees' perception of the alignment of their manager's words with his or her deeds. Mislin and colleagues' study (cited above) further found that the negotiator's mood (positive vs. neutral) impacted contract implementation via the negotiator's trust in the counterpart. And in a field quasi-experimental study of the effects of a leadership coaching intervention in a Norway-based sample of leaders and their subordinates, Ladegard and Gjerde (2014) found that the coaching intervention increased leaders' trust in their subordinates, which in turn increased subordinates' perceived empowerment and decreased their turnover intentions.

Finally, one mediation study has considered how trust may mediate the effect of a dyadic factor on downstream outcomes. Specifically, in a study of US-based employees and their supervisors, Kacmar, Bachrach, Harris and Noble (2012) found that the effect of supervisor-employee conflict on employees' task-focused OCBs was mediated by employees' trust in supervisors.

Thus, in contrast to the first stream of studies examining how trust mediates the effect of leadership behaviors, this second stream reflects a much broader line of inquiry. Although there certainly is not a critical mass of studies in any one area, the evidence provides enticing hints that trust may mediate the effects arising from a very broad range of trustor, trustee, and dyad factors. These effects may occur with trust in strangers as well as known parties, in reaction to trustee symbols in addition to behaviors, and as a result of trustors' individual race, mood, and training. The studies have been situated in a broad range of contexts, and have examined a broad range of outcomes. Clearly this is an area of inquiry that is likely to burgeon in the years ahead.

In conclusion, scholars have devoted considerable attention to understanding the mediating role of trust. Ample evidence now exists that leadership behaviors influence work-related outcomes via subordinate trust. And numerous studies point to exciting new possibilities, and suggest important new directions for future research into how trust may mediate other important effects.

The moderating role of interpersonal trust

In this section, we review studies that have hypothesized and provided empirical evidence that interpersonal trust moderates the effect of a predictor variable on an outcome variable. Note that in this section we are interested only in those studies in which interpersonal trust interacted with another predictor variable, *and* the authors hypothesized that trust was acting as the moderator, not the independent variable. Studies in which trust was hypothesized to be the predictor, not the moderator, have already been reported in the Consequences section, above.

The distinctions between trust as a main effect, versus trust as a moderator, were articulated by Dirks and Ferrin (2001), who made the case that in "strong situations" (where there are strong norms, guidelines, incentives, etc. for behavior), trust was relatively more likely to moderate the effects of other predictors, whereas in "weak situations" trust was relatively more likely to function as a main effect predictor. Dirks and Ferrin provided a broad review of empirical studies on trust (with a focus including but not limited to interpersonal trust) that found somewhat inconsistent and relatively weak support for trust as a main effect, and more consistent support (though with a much smaller number of studies) for moderation effects.

Our review identified only a small number of studies in which interpersonal trust was both hypothesized and found to have had a moderation effect (Table 5.4). In a laboratory study of a dyadic decision-making simulation involving knowledge sharing between partners, Quigley, Tesluk, Locke, and Bartol (2007) found that the positive effect of an individual's task self-efficacy on his or her setting of higher goals was stronger when the individual trusted his or her partner. In a study of US-based employees and their supervisors (previously discussed above regarding its mediation findings), Kacmar and colleagues (2012) separately found that the negative effect of conflict among employees on employees' task-focused OCBs was weaker for employees who had higher trust in their supervisor. In a study of Mainland China-based employees and their supervisors, Zhang and Zhou (2014) found support for a three-way interaction in which the effect of supervisors' empowering leadership behaviors on employees' creative self-efficacy and creativity were stronger for employees who reported higher levels of trust in their leader and higher uncertainty avoidance. This effect was replicated in a second sample (from different occupational groups and a different industry) of Mainland China-based employees and their supervisors. Finally, in a sample of US- and Taiwan-based employees and their supervisors, Cheng

Table 5.4 Interpersonal trust as a moderator

Authors	Conceptualization[1]	Measure[2]	Referent	Predictors	Attitudinal outcomes	Behavioral outcomes	Description
Quigley et al. (2007)	Perceived trust-worthiness (ability, benevolence, integrity)		Partner in a dyadic decision-making simulation	Self-efficacy on the task		Goal setting	Interpersonal trust strengthened the positive effect of task self-efficacy on setting of higher goals
Kacmar et al. (2012)	General trust	Treadway et al. (2004)	Supervisor	Relationship conflict among employees		Employee's OCBs	Trust in the leader weakened the negative effect of relationship conflict on employee OCBs
Zhang and Zhou (2014)	Affect-based trust	McAllister (1995)	Supervisor	Empowering leadership	Creative self-efficacy	Creativity	The effect of empowering leadership behaviors on employees' creative self-efficacy and creativity was strengthened for employees with high trust in the leader and high uncertainty avoidance
Cheng et al. (2015)	Perceived integrity	Craig and Gustafson (1998)	Supervisor	Perceived supervisor support	Commitment to the supervisor		For US- (Taiwan-)based employees, high (low) trust in the leader strengthened the effect of perceived supervisor support on commitment to the supervisor

Notes.

1 In general, if fewer than 75 percent of the items in a trust scale tap into perceived trustworthiness (i.e. ability, benevolence, and integrity), cognition-based trust, affect-based trust, or trust (willingness to accept vulnerability), we classify the scale as general trust.

2 Indicates the scale used or adapted from. If the authors did not state the source of the measure, we leave the cell blank, indicating that the authors created the scale themselves.

et al. (2015) found support for a three-way interaction in which trust in the leader moderated the positive effect of supervisor support on employee commitment to the supervisor. In the US sample, trust in the leader strengthened the relationship, whereas in the Taiwan sample trust in the leader weakened the relationship. In all of the studies reviewed in this paragraph, a variable other than trust was hypothesized to be the exogenous variable, and the authors hypothesized and found that that exogenous variable interacted with trust to impact downstream variables, thus providing evidence of the moderating effect of trust.

In sum, the empirical evidence suggests that interpersonal trust moderates the effects of a range of predictors, specifically trustors' attitudes (self-efficacy), group factors (conflict among coworkers) and trustee behaviors (empowering leadership and supervisor support). What is per-haps most surprising about the review findings is that such a relatively small number of studies has expressly hypothesized and found moderation effects for interpersonal trust. In fact, a consider-ably larger number of studies has provided empirical evidence that interpersonal trust interacts with other factors; however, most of those studies have positioned trust as a predictor rather than a moderator. We speculate that the tendency of researchers to position trust as a main effect rather than a moderator is due to the strong recognition of the importance of trust, and the groundswell of research on trust over the last two decades. Because of the prominence of trust, researchers may have demonstrated a greater interest in studying the direct consequences (benefits) of trust (and how they might differ depending on contextual or other factors) than on the indirect effects of how trust might influence the impact of other predictors. This being the case, we would like to make the observation that most organizational contexts are in fact "strong situations" in which trust is probably already playing a moderating role by facilitating or hindering the effects of countless other organizational factors. Consequently, trust may play a much broader role in organizations than is currently recognized. Thus, the role of interpersonal trust as a moderator represents an important and promising avenue for future research.

Discussion

Objectives and limitations of the review

Our aim has been to address the question, *"What has been demonstrated, empirically, regarding the determinants, consequences, and functions of interpersonal trust within organizations?"* To address this question, we conducted a systematic review of empirical research conducted on interpersonal trust since the early 1990s, published in 15 of the most prominent journals in the organization sciences.

Before discussing the general findings and implications, it is worthwhile to consider the limitations of our review. First, as stated at the outset, this review is intentionally atheoretical; it aims to describe only what has been demonstrated empirically, and therefore does not develop or inform any higher-level conceptual understanding of the operation of trust. We view this as a unique strength as well as a limitation of our review, as we hope our focus on the empirical evidence will help scholars keep sight of, and better access, the raw material from which our theoretical understandings have been built; we also hope it will help practitioners identify the specific ways in which trust is likely to impact organizational outcomes and the specific ways in which trust may be built.

Second, we limited our review to 15 journals that we identified as being likely to publish high-quality empirical studies on interpersonal trust within organizational settings. The selection of these 15 journals was a subjective judgment. One disadvantage of this approach is that we are certain to have omitted studies that were published in other journals, some of which were reviewed elsewhere (e.g., in Fulmer & Gelfand, 2012). One advantage is that the bounds of our search are clearly delineated, and therefore we were better able to avoid researcher judgment (and potential bias) in inclusion/exclusion decisions. A second advantage is that our review entirely comprises double-blind peer reviewed articles of moderate to very high standard.

Third, we have included only those studies that reported a statistically significant (or marginally significant) empirical effect. We did not systematically search for articles that reported null effects. Therefore, it is likely that null effects are under-represented in our review due to the file drawer problem (Rosenthal, 1979). Typically, meta-analytic reviews include search procedures to identify and include studies more likely to have null effects (such as contacting authors for unpublished work and including doctoral dissertations) and statistical procedures to reduce the effect of publication bias; however, these are recognized as imperfect responses to the file drawer problem. Narrative reviews typically do not utilize such procedures. Therefore, our review is similar to other narrative reviews, and less similar to meta-analyses, in its potential under-representation of null effects. Finally, by including only those articles that reported statistically significant effects, we omitted empirical studies that were qualitative, inductive, or otherwise took empirical approaches that did not involve quantitative hypothesis testing.

Fourth, for ease of explication, in discussing the articles we often used causal language that would not be justified based on the degree of internal validity of the studies reviewed. (This is particularly the case in our discussion of the findings of field studies). Our causal language expresses the likely direction of causality as discussed by the original authors and/or implicit in the nature of the empirical relationship studied, not our conclusion about whether causality has been demonstrated empirically.

Review findings and future research directions

What has been empirically demonstrated regarding determinants of interpersonal trust? As can be seen in the above review, a wide range of antecedents has been investigated across different referents. First, some common antecedents have been examined across different referents such as trustees' demonstration of concern or helping behaviors (Ferrin et al., 2006; Korsgaard et al., 2002) and shared similarity between trustor and trustee (Jiang et al., 2011; Farh et al., 1998). There is also a potential that antecedents applied to one referent can be examined with another referent. For example, Niven et al. (2012) found that communications that regulate interpersonal affect by improving others' affect have been found to be associated with individuals' perceptions of friendship and trust in specific coworker. Whether interpersonal affect regulation influences trust levels in the leader-member relationship is worthy of future research. Table 5.1 also illustrates that there is substantial potential that antecedents applied to trustor can be examined with trustee. For example, the cultural metacognition of managers has been found to impact their trust in partners in intercultural collaboration tasks (Chua et al., 2012). Whether the trustee's cultural metacognition impacts trust or not is worthy of investigation. In addition, we were able to identify some empirical papers that investigated the spiral development of trust between trustor and trustee (Ferrin et al., 2008; Halbesleben & Wheeler, 2015). Understanding the reciprocity between trustor and trustee is important to understand the self-reinforcing cycle of trust development. We recommend and look forward to much more research identifying how trust develops and cycles between individuals.

What has been empirically demonstrated regarding outcomes of interpersonal trust? Research on consequences of interpersonal trust has focused on a range of valuable work outcomes including job satisfaction, knowledge sharing and creation, cooperation, commitment, attachment, and performance. Indeed, interpersonal trust has positive effects on these desirable work behaviors and outcomes. In general, we observed that a number of frequently-studied outcomes of trust have been examined across different referents. For example, the effect of trust on citizenship behavior has been studied in the context of trust toward supervisors (Brower et al., 2008) and peers (McAllister, 1995). This research is useful for exploring and extending the generalizability of existing knowledge. We recommend that future research also examine the effect of trust on outcomes that may be unique to a specific referent or context. For example, Wong et al. (2010) focused on the role of trust in the organizational socialization process by exploring how trust impacts specific mentoring functions received by the protégé. We also observed that in studying the consequences of interpersonal trust, a number of empirical studies had operationalized interpersonal trust as trust in multiple individuals (e.g., trust in coworkers) rather than trust in a single individual (trust in a coworker). Consistent with our inclusion/exclusion criteria set out above, we excluded such papers from our review because they cannot be considered to study interpersonal trust. We would like to further emphasize our view that trust in multiple individuals is a fundamentally different construct from trust in a single individual, and these two constructs are likely to have different outcomes and different developmental processes. Researchers should use caution when applying "interpersonal trust" theories to constructs that are not interpersonal in nature, or, instead, appropriately tailor the interpersonal trust theories for application to situations in which the trustee is multiple individuals rather than a single individual.

What has been empirically demonstrated regarding the mediating role of interpersonal trust? First, a critical mass of studies has provided what we consider to be robust evidence that trust in a leader mediates the effects of leadership behaviors (particularly transformational, transactional, and justice behaviors) on a range of work-related follower outcomes (performance, OCBs, satisfaction, commitment, turnover intent, etc.). Thus, trust should be considered an important mechanism through which leadership behaviors influence desired employee-level outcomes. Second, authors have branched out in a number of different directions, providing initial evidence that interpersonal trust mediates a wide range of other effects. As just a few examples, interpersonal trust transmits one party's cooperation to another's cooperation (Ferrin et al., 2008), transforms employees' OCBs into managerial trustworthy behavior (Reiche et al., 2014), converts a leadership coaching intervention into followers' perceived empowerment and reduced turnover intent (Ladegard & Gjerde, 2014), and transmits the effects of employees' race on their job satisfaction, commitment, and turnover intent (Simons et al., 2007). Based on these findings, we recommend and look forward to much more research identifying how and where trust plays an important mediating role.

Finally, what has been empirically demonstrated regarding the moderating role of interpersonal trust? A relatively large number of studies in our review reported that interpersonal trust had interacted with other variables to predict downstream outcomes. However, these findings more often reflect a hypothesized main effect of trust rather than a hypothesized moderated effect. That said, a handful of studies reported trust's moderating effect. For instance, trust in supervisor suppressed the negative effect of employee relationship conflict on OCBs (Kacmar et al., 2012), enhanced the effect of empowering leadership behaviors on creativity (Zhang & Zhou, 2014), and both enhanced and suppressed (depending on culture) the effect of supervisor support on employees' commitment to the supervisor (Cheng et al., 2015). We believe that scholars have perhaps focused insufficient research attention on how trust may moderate the effects of other predictor variables in the organizational context. An exploration of the moderating effects of trust is likely to reveal that trust has much more widespread effects within organizational settings, most likely enhancing or hindering the effects of many other motivators, leadership behaviors, and other organizational factors, on valued employee and organizational outcomes. We strongly encourage such future research.

Although we did not specifically set out to assess the measurement of trust, we did document the measures used. The trust literature is fortunate to have a good range of well-validated measures (see McEvily & Tortoriello, 2011 for a review of the best-validated trust measures). Consequently, we were dismayed to see that so many studies in our review used operationalizations of trust that were outdated and/or poorly validated. Future research should use the measures identified by McEvily and Tortoriello. Researchers should use a different measure only if they can make the case that the different measure is conceptually distinct from the measures identified by McEvily and Tortoriello, or has superior psychometric properties. Peer reviewers should hold authors to these standards.

We were also curious to identify studies that had focused on trust development processes. We expected that trust development studies could take at least two forms. First, studies might examine how an individual's trust in another person changes in level or nature over time (e.g., as proposed by Lewicki & Bunker, 1996). Supporting this model, Levin, Whitener, and Cross (2006) found that trustworthiness perceptions were related to demographic similarity in newer relationships, to trustworthiness behaviors in more established relationships, and to shared perspective in more mature relationships. Second, studies might examine how trust is transmitted from one person to another over time. Supporting this model, Ferrin, Bligh, and Kohles (2008) found a positive spiral between individuals in a lab setting in that one individual's trust promotes cooperation, which increases the other person's trust, in a self-reinforcing cycle. And in a field setting, Halbesleben and Wheeler (2015) found support for a reciprocal resource gain spiral in which a coworker's OCBs lead to an individual's perceived social support, which in turn leads to trust and OCBs toward that coworker (Halbesleben & Wheeler 2015). In sum, our review uncovered some initial evidence supporting two core models of trust development, but research on trust development remains in its infancy. Further research is sorely needed.

It is well recognized that laboratory experimental studies offer high levels of internal validity but very limited external validity, whereas field survey studies offer some external validity but minimal internal validity (Stone-Romero, 2011). Our review revealed a reasonable balance of field surveys and laboratory experiments. Assuming the strengths of one compensate for the weaknesses of the other, we can derive some comfort that the scientific literature as a whole provides findings that meet some minimal level of internal and external validity. However, the literature is sorely lacking in field experiments and quasi-experiments, which are unique in their ability to simultaneously deliver relatively high levels of internal and external validity *within a single study* (Stone-Romero, 2011). And from a practical perspective, field experiments and quasi-experiments provide much more direct insights into the effectiveness of trust-related interventions in work organizations. Our review uncovered only one field quasi-experiment (Ladegard & Gjerde, 2014). Given the obvious scientific and practical advantages of field experiments and quasi-experiments, we strongly encourage trust researchers to increase their use of field experimental research.

Practical implications

As mentioned above, practitioners navigate a world of the literal and concrete. When practitioners face a need or opportunity to build trust, or when they are asked to justify a proposed trust intervention, practitioners are likely to yearn for answers to questions such as the following: "What, specifically, predicts trust?" "What, specifically, does trust predict?" "How large are those effects?" "How much research has been conducted?" "And in what contexts has the research been conducted?" Accordingly, we expect that practitioners will find the present review to be extremely useful when designing and implementing trust-related interventions in their own organizations. That said, we also strongly encourage practitioners to read the primary studies, and to consider the limitations in internal and external validity of those studies, when planning their organizational interventions.

Conclusion

Concluding this review, we would like to express a degree of awe at the sheer number of double-blind peer-reviewed studies published on interpersonal trust since the early 1990s. The fact that trust research has now moved from bit player to center stage to celebrity status reflects an enormous investment of time, effort, and passion on the part of researchers, an enormous investment of time and effort from research participants, and an impressive financial investment on the part of universities. The fact that these investments have been made reflects a broad recognition of both the importance of trust and the trust challenges that we face in organizations and in society. Having generated this body of scientific knowledge, it is equally important that the knowledge be put into practice. We hope that this review, focused as it is on the operational level, will be useful to those putting research into practice as well as those further advancing the science of trust.

Note

* Both authors contributed equally to this review.

References

Ambrose, M. L., & Schminke, M. (2003). Organization structure as a moderator of the relationship between procedural justice, interactional justice, perceived organizational support, and supervisory trust. *Journal of Applied Psychology*, 88(2), 295–305.

Anderson, C., & Thompson, L. L. (2004). Affect from the top down: How powerful individuals' positive affect shapes negotiations. *Organizational Behavior & Human Decision Processes*, 95(2), 125–139.

Ballinger, G. A., Schoorman, F. D. & Lehman, D. W. (2009). Will you trust your new boss? The role of affective reactions to leadership succession. *The Leadership Quarterly*, 20(2), 219–232.

Baron, R. M., & Kenny, D. A. (1986). The moderator-mediator variable distinction in social psychological research: Conceptual, strategic, and statistical considerations. *Journal of Personality and Social Psychology*, 51(6), 1173–1182.

Becerra, M., & Gupta, A. K. (2003). Perceived trustworthiness within the organization: The moderating impact of communication frequency on trustor and trustee effects. *Organization Science*, 14(1), 32–44.

Bond, M. H. (1983). Linking person perception dimensions to behavioral intention dimensions: The Chinese connection. *Journal of Cross-Cultural Psychology*, 14(1), 41–63.

Brower, H. H., Lester, S. W., Korsgaard, M. A., & Dineen, B. R. (2008). A closer look at trust between managers and subordinates: Understanding the effects of both trusting and being trusted on subordinate outcomes. *Journal of Management*, 35(2), 327–347.

Brown, M. E., Treviño, L. K. & Harrison, D. A. (2005). Ethical leadership: A social learning perspective for construct development and testing. *Organizational Behavior and Human Decision Processes*, 97(2), 117–134.

Burke, C. S., Sims, D. E., Lazzara, E. H., & Salas, E. (2007). Trust in leadership: A multi-level review and integration. *The Leadership Quarterly*, 18(6), 606–632.

Burt, R. S., (1992). *Structural holes: The social structure of competition*. Cambridge, MA: Harvard Business School Press.

Butler, J. K. (1991). Toward understanding and measuring conditions of trust: Evolution of a conditions of trust inventory. *Journal of Management*, 17(3), 643–663.

Cameron, A.-F., & Webster, J. (2011). Relational outcomes of multicommunicating: Integrating incivility and social exchange perspectives. *Organization Science*, 22(3), 754–771.

Chattopadhyay, P., & George, E. (2001). Examining the effects of work externalization through the lens of social identity theory. *Journal of Applied Psychology*, 86(4), 781–788.

Chen, X. P., Eberly, M. B., Chiang, T. J., Farh, J. L., & Cheng, B. S. (2014). Affective trust in Chinese leaders: Linking paternalistic leadership to employee performance. *Journal of Management*, 40(3), 796–819.

Cheng, C. Y., Jiang, D. Y., Cheng, B. S., Riley, J. H., & Jen, C. K. (2015). When do subordinates commit to their supervisors? Different effects of perceived supervisor integrity and support on Chinese and American employees. *The Leadership Quarterly*, 26(1), 81–97.

Choi, J. (2008). Event justice perceptions and employees' reactions: Perceptions of social entity justice as a moderator. *Journal of Applied Psychology*, 93(3), 513–528.

Chua, R. Y. J., Ingram, P., & Morris, M. W. (2008). From the head and the heart: Locating cognition- and affect-based trust in managers' professional networks. *Academy of Management Journal*, 51(3), 436–452.

Chua, R. Y. J., Morris, M. W., & Mor, S. (2012). Collaborating across cultures: Cultural metacognition and affect-based trust in creative collaboration. *Organizational Behavior and Human Decision Processes*, 118(2), 116–131.

Chung, Y., & Jackson, S. E. (2011). Co-worker trust and knowledge creation: A multilevel analysis. *Journal of Trust Research*, 1(1), 65–83.

Colquitt, J. A., Scott, B. A., & LePine, J. A. (2007). Trust, trustworthiness, and trust propensity: A meta-analytic test of their unique relationships with risk taking and job performance. *Journal of Applied Psychology*, 92(4), 909–927.

Colquitt, J. A., & Rodell, J. B. (2011). Justice, trust, and trustworthiness: A longitudinal analysis integrating three theoretical perspectives. *Academy of Management Journal*, 54(6), 1183–1206.

Colquitt, J. A., LePine, J. A., Piccolo, R. F., Zapata, C. P., & Rich, B. L. (2012). Explaining the justice–performance relationship: Trust as exchange deepener or trust as uncertainty reducer? *Journal of Applied Psychology*, 97(1), 1–15.

Cook, J., & Wall, T. (1980). New work attitude measures of trust, organizational commitment and personal need non-fulfilment. *Journal of Occupational Psychology*, 53(1), 39–52.

Costa, A. C., Ferrin, D. L. & Fulmer, C. A., (forthcoming). Trust at work. In: N. Anderson, D. S. Ones, H. K. Sinangil, & C. Viswesvaran (eds.), *Handbook of industrial, work, and organizational psychology*. 2nd ed. London: Sage.

Costigan, R. D., Insinga, R., Berman, J. J., Kranas, G., & Kureshov, V. A. (2013). The significance of direct-leader and co-worker trust on turnover intentions: A cross-cultural study. *Journal of Trust Research*, 3(2), 98–124.

Craig, S. B., & Gustafson, S. B. (1998). Perceived leader integrity scale: An instrument for assessing employee perceptions of leader. *The Leadership Quarterly*, 9(2), 127–145.

Crossley, C. D., Cooper, C. D., & Wernsing, T. S. (2013). Making things happen through challenging goals: Leader proactivity, trust, and business-unit performance. *Journal of Applied Psychology*, 98(3), 540–549.

Cummings, L. L., & Bromiley, P., (1996). The Organizational Trust Inventory (OTI): Development and validation. In: R. M. Kramer, and T. R. Tyler (eds.), *Trust in organizations: Frontiers of theory and research*. (pp. 302–330). Thousand Oaks, CA: Sage.

Cunningham, J. B., & MacGregor, J. (2000). Trust and the design of work: Complementary constructs in satisfaction and performance. *Human Relations*, 53(12), 1575–1591.

De Cremer, D., & Tyler, T. R. (2007). The effects of trust in authority and procedural fairness on cooperation. *Journal of Applied Psychology*, 92(3), 639–649.

De Dreu, C. K. W., Giebels, E., & Van de Vliert, E. (1998). Social motives and thrust in integrative negotiation: The disruptive effects of punitive capability. *Journal of Applied Psychology*, 83(3), 407–422.

de Jong, S. B., Van der Vegt, G. S., & Molleman, E. (2007). The relationships among asymmetry in task dependence, perceived helping behavior, and trust. *Journal of Applied Psychology*, 92(6), 1625–1637.

Dietz, G., & Den Hartog, D. N. (2006). Measuring trust inside organisations. *Personnel Review*, 35(5), 557–588.

Dirks, K. T. (1999). The effects of interpersonal trust on work group performance. *Journal of Applied Psychology*, 84(3), 445–455.

Dirks, K. T., & Ferrin, D. L. (2001). The role of trust in organizational settings. *Organization Science*, 12(4), 450–467.

Dirks, K. T., & Ferrin, D. L. (2002). Trust in leadership: Meta-analytic findings and implications for research and practice. *Journal of Applied Psychology*, 87(4), 611–628.

Dunn, J., Ruedy, N. E., & Schweitzer, M. E. (2012). It hurts both ways: How social comparisons harm affective and cognitive trust. *Organizational Behavior and Human Decision Processes*, 117(1), 2–14.

Elsbach, K. D., & Elofson, G. (2000). How the packaging of decision explanations affects perceptions of trustworthiness. *Academy of Management Journal*, 43(1), 80–89.

Farh, J.-L., Tsui, A. S., Xin, K., & Cheng, B. S. (1998). The influence of relational demography and Guanxi: The Chinese case. *Organization Science*, 9(4), 471–488.

Ferrin, D. L., & Dirks, K. T. (2003). The use of rewards to increase and decrease trust: Mediating processes and differential effects. *Organization Science*, 14(1), 18–31.

Ferrin, D. L., Dirks, K. T., & Shah, P. P. (2006). Direct and indirect effects of third-party relationships on interpersonal trust. *Journal of Applied Psychology*, 91(4), 870–883.

Ferrin, D. L., Bligh, M. C., & Kohles, J. C. (2008). It takes two to tango: An interdependence analysis of the spiraling of perceived trustworthiness and cooperation in interpersonal and intergroup relationships. *Organizational Behavior and Human Decision Processes*, 107(2), 161–178.

Ferrin, D. L., & Gillespie, N., (2010). Trust differences across national-societal cultures: Much to do, or much ado about nothing? In: M. N. K. Saunders, D. Skinner, G. Dietz, N. Gillespie, & R. J. Lewicki (eds.), *Organizational trust: A cultural perspective.* (pp. 42–86). Cambridge, UK: Cambridge University Press.

Ferrin, D. L. (2013). On the institutionalisation of trust research and practice: Heaven awaits! *Journal of Trust Research*, 3(2), 146–154.

Frazier, M. L., Johnson, P. D., & Fainshmidt, S. (2013). Development and validation of a propensity to trust scale. *Journal of Trust Research*, 3(2), 76–97.

Fulmer, C. A., & Gelfand, M. J. (2012). At what level (and in whom) we trust: Trust across multiple organizational levels. *Journal of Management*, 38(4), 1167–1230.

Gabarro, J. J., & Athos, J., (1976). *Interpersonal relations and communications.* Englewood Cliffs, NJ: Prentice Hall.

Gao, L., Janssen, O., & Shi, K. (2011). Leader trust and employee voice: The moderating role of empowering leader behaviors. *The Leadership Quarterly*, 22(4), 787–798.

George, J. M., & Zhou, J. (2007). Dual tuning in a supportive context: Joint contributions of positive mood, negative mood, and supervisory behaviors to employee creativity. *Academy of Management Journal*, 50(3), 605–622.

Gillespie, N. (2003). Measuring interpersonal trust in work relationships. *Australian Journal of Psychology*, 55, 124–124.

Gino, F., & Schweitzer, M. E. (2008). Blinded by anger or feeling the love: How emotions influence advice taking. *Journal of Applied Psychology*, 93(5), 1165–1173.

Grant, A. M., & Sumanth, J. J. (2009). Mission possible? The performance of prosocially motivated employees depends on manager trustworthiness. *Journal of Applied Psychology*, 94(4), 927–944.

Halbesleben, J. R. B., & Wheeler, A. R. (2015). To invest or not? The role of coworker support and trust in daily reciprocal gain spirals of helping behavior. *Journal of Management*, 41(6), 1628–1650.

Harris, T. B., Li, N., Boswell, W. R., Zhang, X. A., & Xie, Z. (2014). Getting what's new from newcomers: Empowering leadership, creativity, and adjustment in the socialization context. *Personnel Psychology*, 67(3), 567–604.

Hill, N. S., Bartol, K. M., Tesluk, P. E., & Langa, G. A. (2009). Organizational context and face-to-face interaction: Influences on the development of trust and collaborative behaviors in computer-mediated groups. *Organizational Behavior and Human Decision Processes*, 108(2), 187–201.

Hofmann, D. A., Lei, Z. K., & Grant, A. M. (2009). Seeking help in the shadow of doubt: The sensemaking processes underlying how nurses decide whom to ask for advice. *Journal of Applied Psychology*, 94(5), 1261–1274.

Holtz, B. C. (2015). From first impression to fairness perception: Investigating the impact of initial trustworthiness beliefs. *Personnel Psychology*, 68(3), 499–546.

Holtz, B. C., & Harold, C. M. (2009). Fair today, fair tomorrow? A longitudinal investigation of overall justice perceptions. *Journal of Applied Psychology*, 94(5), 1185–1199.

Huang, L., & Murnighan, J. K. (2010). What's in a name? Subliminally activating trusting behavior. *Organizational Behavior and Human Decision Processes*, 111(1), 62–70.

Huang, X., Iun, J., Liu, A., & Gong, Y. (2010). Does participative leadership enhance work performance by inducing empowerment or trust? The differential effects on managerial and non-managerial subordinates. *Journal of Organizational Behavior*, 31(1), 122–143.

Jarvenpaa, S. L., Knoll, K., & Leidner, D. E. (1998). Is anybody out there? Antecedents of trust in global virtual teams. *Journal of Management Information Systems*, 14(4), 29–64.

Jiang, C. X., Chua, R. Y., Kotabe, M., & Murray, J. Y. (2011). Effects of cultural ethnicity, firm size, and firm age on senior executives' trust in their overseas business partners: Evidence from China. *Journal of International Business Studies*, 42(9), 1150–1173.

Johnson-George, C., & Swap, W. C. (1982). Measurement of specific interpersonal trust: Construction and validation of a scale to assess trust in a specific other. *Journal of Personality and Social Psychology*, 43(6), 1306–1317.

Johnson, J. L., Cullen, J. B., Sakano, T., & Takenouchi, H. (1996). Setting the stage for trust and strategic integration in Japanese-U.S. cooperative alliances. *Journal of International Business Studies*, 27(5), 981–1004.

Johnson, R. E., & Lord, R. G. (2010). Implicit effects of justice on self-identity. *Journal of Applied Psychology*, 95(4), 681–695.

Jung, D. I., & Avolio, B. J. (2000). Opening the black box: An experimental investigation of the mediating effects of trust and value congruence on transformational and transactional leadership. *Journal of Organizational Behavior*, 21(8), 949–964.

Kacmar, K. M., Bachrach, D. G., Harris, K. J., & Noble, D. (2012). Exploring the role of supervisor trust in the associations between multiple sources of relationship conflict and organizational citizenship behavior. *The Leadership Quarterly*, 23(1), 43–54.

Kalshoven, K., Den Hartog, D. N., & De Hoogh, A. H. B. (2011). Ethical Leadership at Work questionnaire (ELW): Development and validation of a multidimensional measure. *The Leadership Quarterly*, 22(1), 51–69.

Khazanchi, S., & Masterson, S. S. (2011). Who and what is fair matters: A multi-foci social exchange model of creativity. *Journal of Organizational Behavior*, 32(1), 86–106.

Kim, P. H., Ferrin, D. L., Cooper, C. D., & Dirks, K. T. (2004). Removing the shadow of suspicion: The effects of apology versus denial for repairing competence- versus integrity-based trust violations. *Journal of Applied Psychology*, 89(1), 104–118.

Kong, D. T., Dirks, K. T., & Ferrin, D. L. (2014). Interpersonal trust within negotiations: Meta-analytic evidence, critical contingencies, and directions for future research. *Academy of Management Journal*, 57(5), 1235–1255.

Korsgaard, M. A., & Roberson, L. (1995). Procedural justice in performance evaluation: The role of instrumental and non-instrumental voice in performance appraisal discussions. *Journal of Management*, 21(4), 657–669.

Korsgaard, M. A., Roberson, L., & Rymph, R. D. (1998). What motivates fairness? The role of subordinate assertive behavior on manager's interactional fairness. *Journal of Applied Psychology*, 83(5), 731–744.

Korsgaard, M. A., Brodt, S. E., & Whitener, E. M. (2002). Trust in the face of conflict: The role of managerial trustworthy behavior and organizational context. *Journal of Applied Psychology*, 87(2), 312–319.

Korsgaard, M. A., Brower, H. H., & Lester, S. W. (2015). It isn't always mutual: A critical review of dyadic trust. *Journal of Management*, 41(1), 47–70.

Kramer, R. M. (1999). Trust and distrust in organizations: Emerging perspectives, enduring questions. *Annual Review of Psychology*, 50, 569–598.

Kramer, R. M., & Lewicki, R. J. (2010). Repairing and enhancing trust: Approaches to reducing organizational trust deficits. *Academy of Management Annals*, 4, 245–277.

Kwan, L. Y. Y., Yap, S., & Chiu, C. -Y. (2015). Mere exposure affects perceived descriptive norms: Implications for personal preferences and trust. *Organizational Behavior and Human Decision Processes*, 129(1), 48–58.

Ladegard, G., & Gjerde, S. (2014). Leadership coaching, leader role-efficacy, and trust in subordinates. A mixed methods study assessing leadership coaching as a leadership development tool. *The Leadership Quarterly*, 25(4), 631–646.

Lau, D. C., Lam, L. W., & Wen, S. S. (2014). Examining the effects of feeling trusted by supervisors in the workplace: A self-evaluative perspective. *Journal of Organizational Behavior*, 35(1), 112–127.

Lau, D. C., & Liden, R. C. (2008). Antecedents of coworker trust: Leaders' blessings. *Journal of Applied Psychology*, 93(5), 1130–1138.

Lee, C., Pillutla, M., & Law, K. S. (2000). Power-distance, gender and organizational justice. *Journal of Management*, 26(4), 685–704.

Levin, D. Z., & Cross, R. (2004). The strength of weak ties you can trust: the mediating role of trust in effective knowledge transfer. *Management Science*, 50(11), 1477–1490.

Levin, D. Z., Whitener, E. M., & Cross, R. (2006). Perceived trustworthiness of knowledge sources: The moderating impact of relationship length. *Journal of Applied Psychology*, 91(5), 1163–1171.

Levin, D. Z., Walter, J., & Murnighan, J. K. (2011). Dormant ties: The value of reconnecting. *Organization Science*, 22(4), 923–939.

Levine, E. E., & Schweitzer, M. E. (2015). Prosocial lies: When deception breeds trust. *Organizational Behavior and Human Decision Processes*, 126(1), 88–106.

Lewicki, R. J., & Bunker, B. B., (1996). Developing and maintaining trust in work relationships. In R. M. Kramer, & T. R. Tyler (eds.), *Trust in organizations: Frontiers of theory and research.* (pp. 114–139). Thousand Oaks, CA, US: Sage Publications.

Lewicki, R. J., Tomlinson, E. C., & Gillespie, N. (2006). Models of interpersonal trust development: Theoretical approaches, empirical evidence, and future directions. *Journal of Management*, 32(6), 991–1022.

Li, A. N., & Tan, H. H. (2013). What happens when you trust your supervisor? Mediators of individual performance in trust relationships. *Journal of Organizational Behavior*, 34(3), 407–425.

Lount, R. B., Jr., & Pettit, N. C. (2012). The social context of trust: The role of status. *Organizational Behavior and Human Decision Processes*, 117(1), 15–23.

Lu, C., Kong, D. T., Ferrin, D. L., & Dirks, K. T. (2017). What are the determinants of interpersonal trust in dyadic negotiations? Meta-analytic evidence and implications for future research. *Journal of Trust Research*, 7(1), 22–50.

Malhotra, D., & Murnighan, J. K. (2002). The effects of contracts on interpersonal trust. *Administrative Science Quarterly*, 47(3), 534–559.

Mayer, R. C., Bobko, P., Davis, J. H., & Gavin, M. B. (2011). The effects of changing power and influence tactics on trust in the supervisor: A longitudinal field study. *Journal of Trust Research*, 1(2), 177–201.

Mayer, R. C., & Davis, J. H. (1999). The effect of the performance appraisal system on trust for management: A field quasi-experiment. *Journal of Applied Psychology*, 84, 123–136.

Mayer, R. C., Davis, J. H., & Schoorman, F. D. (1995). An integrative model of organizational trust. *Academy of Management Review*, 20(3), 709–734.

Mayer, R. C., & Gavin, M. B. (2005). Trust in management and performance: Who minds the shop while the employees watch the boss? *Academy of Management Journal*, 48(5), 874–888.

McAllister, D. J. (1995). Affect- and cognition-based trust as foundations for interpersonal cooperation in organizations. *Academy of Management Journal*, 38(1), 24–59.

McCroskey, J. C. (1966). Scales for the measurement of ethos. *Speech Monographs*, 33(1), 65–72.

McEvily, B., & Tortoriello, M. (2011). Measuring trust in organisational research: Review and recommendations. *Journal of Trust Research*, 1(1), 23–63.

Mislin, A. A., Campagna, R. L., & Bottom, W. P. (2011). After the deal: Talk, trust building and the implementation of negotiated agreements. *Organizational Behavior and Human Decision Processes*, 115(1), 55–68.

Moorman, R. H., Darnold, T. C., & Priesemuth, M. (2013). Perceived leader integrity: Supporting the construct validity and utility of a multi-dimensional measure in two samples. *The Leadership Quarterly*, 24(3), 427–444.

Naquin, C. E., & Paulson, G. D. (2003). Online bargaining and interpersonal trust. *Journal of Applied Psychology*, 88(1), 113–120.

Niven, K., Holman, D., & Totterdell, P. (2012). How to win friendship and trust by influencing people's feelings: An investigation of interpersonal affect regulation and the quality of relationships. *Human Relations*, 65(6), 777–805.

Norman, S. M., Avolio, B. J., & Luthans, F. (2010). The impact of positivity and transparency on trust in leaders and their perceived effectiveness. *The Leadership Quarterly*, 21(3), 350–364.

Nyhan, R. C., & Marlowe, H. A. (1997). Development and psychometric properties of the Organizational Trust Inventory. *Evaluation Review*, 21(5), 614–635.

Palanski, M. E., & Yammarino, F. J. (2011). Impact of behavioral integrity on follower job performance: A three-study examination. *The Leadership Quarterly*, 22(4), 765–786.

Perrone, V., Zaheer, A., & McEvily, B. (2003). Free to be trusted? Organizational constraints on trust in boundary spanners. *Organization Science*, 14(4), 422–439.

Pillai, R., Schriesheim, C. A., & Williams, E. S. (1999). Fairness perceptions and trust as mediators for transformational and transactional leadership: A two-sample study. *Journal of Management*, 25(6), 897–933.

Podsakoff, P. M., MacKenzie, S., & Bommer, W. (1996). Transformational leader behaviors and substitutes for leadership as determinants of employee satisfaction, commitment, trust and organizational citizenship behaviors. *Journal of Management*, 22(2), 259–298.

Podsakoff, P. M., MacKenzie, S. B., Moorman, R. H., & Fetter, R. (1990). Transformational leader behaviors and their effects on followers' trust in leader, satisfaction, and organizational citizenship behaviors. *The Leadership Quarterly*, 1(2), 107–142.

Preacher, K., & Hayes, A. (2008). Asymptotic and resampling strategies for assessing and comparing indirect effects in multiple mediator models. *Behavior Research Methods*, 40(3), 879–891.

Premeaux, S. F., & Bedeian, A. G. (2003). Breaking the silence: The moderating effects of self-monitoring in predicting speaking up in the workplace. *Journal of Management Studies*, 40(6), 1537–1562.

Quigley, N. R., Tesluk, P. E., Locke, E. A., & Bartol, K. M. (2007). A multilevel investigation of the motivational mechanisms underlying knowledge sharing and performance. *Organization Science*, 18(1), 71–88.

Rafaeli, A., Sagy, Y., & Derfler-Rozin, R. (2008). Logos and initial compliance: A strong case of mindless trust. *Organization Science*, 19(6), 845–859.

Rao, A. N., Pearce, J. L., & Xin, K. (2005). Governments, reciprocal exchange and trust among business associates. *Journal of International Business Studies*, 36(1), 104–118.

Reiche, B. S., Cardona, P., Lee, Y.T., Canela, M.Á., Akinnukawe, E., Briscoe, J.P., . . . & Grenness, T. (2014). Why do managers engage in trustworthy behavior? A multilevel cross-cultural study in 18 countries. *Personnel Psychology*, 67(1), 61–98.

Rempel, J. K., Holmes, J. G., & Zanna, M. P. (1985). Trust in close relationships. *Journal of Personality and Social Psychology*, 49(1), 95–112.

Rempel, J. K., & Holmes, J. G. (1986). How do I trust thee? *Psychology Today*, 20(2), 28–34.

Roberts, K. H., & O'Reilly, C. A. (1974). Measuring organizational communication. *Journal of Applied Psychology*, 59(3), 321–326.

Robinson, S. L. (1996). Trust and breach of the psychological contract. *Administrative Science Quarterly*, 41(4), 574–599.

Robinson, S. L., & Rousseau, D. M. (1994). Violating the psychological contract: Not the exception but the norm. *Journal of Organizational Behavior*, 15(3), 245–259.

Rosenthal, R. (1979). The file drawer problem and tolerance for null results. *Psychological Bulletin*, 86(3), 638–641.

Ross, W. H., & Wieland, C. (1996). Effects of interpersonal trust and time pressure on managerial mediation strategy in a simulated organizational dispute. *Journal of Applied Psychology*, 81(3), 228–248.

Rubin, R. S., Bommer, W. H., & Bachrach, D. G. (2010). Operant leadership and employee citizenship: A question of trust? *The Leadership Quarterly*, 21(3), 400–408.

Saunders, M. N. K., Dietz, G., & Thornhill, A. (2014). Trust and distrust: Polar opposites, or independent but co-existing? *Human Relations*, 67(6), 639–665.

Scott, D. (1983). Trust differences between men and women in superior-subordinate relationships. *Group and Organization Studies*, 8(3), 319–336.

Searle, R., Weibel, A., & Den Hartog, D. N., (2011). Employee trust in organizational contexts. In: G. P. Hodgkinson & J. K. Ford (eds.), *International review of industrial and organizational psychology 2011* (Vol. 26, pp. 143–191). Chichester, UK: John Wiley & Sons.

Simons, T., Friedman, R., Liu, L. A., & McLean Parks, J. (2007). Racial differences in sensitivity to behavioral integrity: Attitudinal consequences, in-group effects, and "trickle down" among Black and non-Black employees. *Journal of Applied Psychology*, 92(3), 650–665.

Sobel, M. E., (1982). Asymptotic confidence intervals for indirect effects on structural models. *Sociological Methodology*, 13, 290–312.

Sonenshein, S., Herzenstein, M., & Dholakia, U. M. (2011). How accounts shape lending decisions through fostering perceived trustworthiness. *Organizational Behavior and Human Decision Processes*, 115(1), 69–84.

Sparrowe, R. T., Liden, R. C., Wayne, S. J., & Kraimer, M. L. (2001). Social networks and the performance of individuals and groups. *Academy of Management Journal*, 44(2), 316–325.

Stone-Romero, E. F. (2011). Research strategies in industrial and organizational psychology: Non-experimental, quasi-experimental, and randomized experimental research in special purpose and nonspecial purpose settings. In S. Zedeck (ed.), *APA handbook of industrial and organizational psychology: Building and developing the organization* (Vol. 1, pp. 37–72). Washington, DC: American Psychological Association.

Sy, T. (2010). What do you think of followers? Examining the content, structure, and consequences of implicit followership theories. *Organizational Behavior and Human Decision Processes*, 113(2), 73–84.

Tepper, B. J., & Henle, C. A. (2011). A case for recognizing distinctions among constructs that capture interpersonal mistreatment in work organizations. *Journal of Organizational Behavior*, 32(3), 487–498.

Thau, S., Crossley, C., Bennett, R. J., & Sczesny, S. (2007). The relationship between trust, attachment, and antisocial work behaviors. *Human Relations*, 60(8), 1155–1179.

Thomas, D. C., & Ravlin, E. C. (1995). Responses of employees to cultural adaptation by a foreign manager. *Journal of Applied Psychology*, 80(1), 133–146.

Treadway, D. C., Hochwarter, W. A., Ferris, G. R., Kacmar, C. J., Douglas, C., Ammeter, A. P., & Buckley, M. R. (2004). Leader political skill and employee reactions. *The Leadership Quarterly*, 15(4), 493–513.

Tyler, T. R., & Huo, Y. J., (2002). *Trust in the law: Encouraging public cooperation with the police and courts*. New York, NY: Russell Sage Foundation.

van Dierendonck, D. (2011). Servant leadership: A review and synthesis. *Journal of Management*, 37(4), 1228–1261.

van Dijke, M., De Cremer, D., & Mayer, D. M. (2010). The role of authority power in explaining procedural fairness effects. *Journal of Applied Psychology*, 95(3), 488–502.

Vanneste, B. S., Puranam, P., & Kretschmer, T. (2014). Trust over time in exchange relationships: Meta-analysis and theory. *Strategic Management Journal*, 35(12), 1891–1902.

Vignovic, J. A., & Thompson, L. F. (2010). Computer-mediated cross-cultural collaboration: Attributing communication errors to the person versus the situation. *Journal of Applied Psychology*, 95(2), 265–276.

Vogel, R. M., Mitchell, M. S., Tepper, B. J., Restubog, S. L., Hu, C., Hua, W., & Huang, J. C. (2015). A cross-cultural examination of subordinates' perceptions of and reactions to abusive supervision. *Journal of Organizational Behavior*, 36(5), 720–745.

Wang, S., Tomlinson, E. C., & Noe, R. A. (2010). The role of mentor trust and protégé internal locus of control in formal mentoring relationships. *Journal of Applied Psychology*, 95(2), 358–367.

Wong, S. -S., & Boh, W. F. (2010). Leveraging the ties of others to build a reputation for trustworthiness among peers. *Academy of Management Journal*, 53(1), 129–148.

Xin, K. R., & Pearce, J. L. (1996). Guanxi: Connections as substitutes for formal institutional support. *Academy of Management Journal*, 39(6), 1641–1658.

Yakovleva, M., Reilly, R. R., & Werko, R. (2010). Why do we trust? Moving beyond individual to dyadic perceptions. *Journal of Applied Psychology*, 95(1), 79–91.

Yang, J., & Mossholder, K. W. (2010). Examining the effects of trust in leaders: A bases-and-foci approach. *The Leadership Quarterly*, 21(1), 50–63.

Yang, J., Mossholder, K. W., & Peng, T. K. (2009). Supervisory procedural justice effects: The mediating roles of cognitive and affective trust. *The Leadership Quarterly*, 20(2), 143–154.

Young, A. M., & Perrewe, P. L. (2000). What did you expect? An examination of career-related support and social support among mentors and protégés. *Journal of Management*, 26(4), 611–632.

Zaheer, A., McEvily, B., & Perrone, V. (1998). Does trust matter? Exploring the effects of inter-organizational and interpersonal trust on performance. *Organization Science*, 9(2), 141–159.

Zapata, C. P., Olsen, J. E., & Martins, L. L. (2013). Social exchange from the supervisor's perspective: Employee trustworthiness as a predictor of interpersonal and informational justice. *Organizational Behavior and Human Decision Processes*, 121(1), 1–12.

Zhang, X., & Zhou, J. (2014). Empowering leadership, uncertainty avoidance, trust, and employee creativity: Interaction effects and a mediating mechanism. *Organizational Behavior and Human Decision Processes*, 124(2), 150–164.

Zhu, W., Newman, A., Miao, Q., & Hooke, A. (2013). Revisiting the mediating role of trust in trans-formational leadership effects: Do different types of trust make a difference? *The Leadership Quarterly*, 24(1), 94–105.

Zhu, Y., & Akhtar, S. (2014). How transformational leadership influences follower helping behavior: The role of trust and prosocial motivation. *Journal of Organizational Behavior*, 35(3), 373–392.

6

TRUST IN TEAMS

A review across levels

*Ann-Marie I. Nienaber, Maximilian Holtgrave
and Philipp D. Romeike*

Introduction

When Research in Motion (RIM), the maker of Blackberry, was founded above a bagel store in a small Canadian city, not many people would have guessed the remarkable rise of the company. By 2009, RIM controlled half of the smartphone market, making it one of the fastest-growing and most valuable companies in the world. Today the company has less than a one-percent share of the market and its management is seriously considering quitting the smartphone business. How could a company that once ousted global giants such as Microsoft or Motorola from the market and took on the most powerful wireless carriers fall so quickly and to such depths? While many regard the fall of RIM as yet another example of how the ferocious competitive forces of Silicon Valley have overturned traditional industries, there is much more to this riveting story. As McNish and Silcoff (2015) reveal in their outstanding account of the company's rise and fall, key to both RIM's success and failure was a top management team that at its heart consisted of the two founders: Mike Lazaridis, a remarkable engineer who oversaw technical functions, and Jim Balsillie, an aggressive entrepreneur who headed marketing and sales. These men's trust in their shared vision and the trust of the technical, and marketing and sales teams in their leadership brought RIM to the top of the world. But just as quickly as it promoted RIM's rise, a fallout between Lazaridis and Balsillie over falsely backdated stock options and disagreements regarding RIM's future strategy destroyed the trust between the two founders and opened fault lines within the top management team and between technical and marketing and sales departments. The internal feuds that ensued crippled RIM so badly that it had not much with which to counter Apple's and Google's entry into the smartphone market.

Anyone who has ever been part of a team where team members did not trust each other, or who has tried to manage a team where trust was not present, will undoubtedly be able to relate to the fate of RIM. A team without trust is not really a team but merely a group of individuals who work side by side and often make disappointing progress. Likewise, an organization in which teams do not trust each other is bound to fail, as the fall of RIM illustrates. Departments will not share information, battle over rights and responsibilities, and fail to cooperate with one another. Broadly speaking, neither single divisions nor organizations will be able to reach their full potential if there is no trust within and between teams.

Scholars usually underline the huge number of benefits of teams compared to more bureaucratic forms of organizing (Guzzo & Dickson, 1996) including a higher quantity and quality of generated ideas, improved problem solving, and increased commitment to decisions (Anderson & West, 1996). These benefits may result in enhanced organizational productivity and performance (Applebaum & Blatt, 1994; Levine & D'Andrea Tyson, 1990). Not surprisingly then, team work is a long-lasting and dominant trend within organizations (Romeike, Nienaber & Schewe, 2016). In 1992, 88 percent of Fortune 1,000 firms relied on teams (Lawler, Mohrman, & Ledford, 1992) and with globalization and technology advancing at impressive speeds, in 2012, 66 percent of multinational companies relied on virtual teams and 80 percent expected a further increase in the near future (Gilson, Maynard, Jones Young, Vartiainen, & Hakonen, 2014). Moreover, research has demonstrated that when trust is in place, individual team members become part of an effective, cohesive group that is stronger than the sum of its individual parts (e.g. Colquitt, LePine, Zapata, & Wild, 2011; De Jong & Elfring, 2014). The same applies to trust between teams, which has been found to be a crucial determinant of information exchange among departments and thus for the organization's innovative and competitive capabilities (Howorth, Westhead, & Wright, 2004; Tsai & Ghoshal, 1998). Hence, a better understanding of what facilitates trust in teams and how the presence or lack of trust manifests itself is crucial. Yet, even though the large body of research on trust in teams has uncovered an abundance of findings, so far there has been no systematic review of trust within and between teams.

In reviewing research on trust in teams, we believe this chapter offers three important benefits. First, in distinguishing between trust at the intra- and inter-team level, we offer a novel conceptualization of trust in teams with which to organize and review previous studies and findings. Second, we discuss the antecedents and consequences of trust at each level. In doing so we highlight similarities and differences between intra- and inter-team trust. Finally, we review efforts to integrate trust research across the intra- and inter-team levels and articulate an agenda for future research, discussing possible advancement of theory and measures regarding trust in teams. Given that organizations depend on the functioning of intra- and inter-team relations, we believe this review of trust in teams to be of particular interest to research and practice alike.

We proceed as follows: In the next section, we will define and discuss the key terms 'teams' and 'trust in teams'. Then, we look in detail at intra- and inter-team trust and outline the different antecedents and consequences of trust in teams at different levels. Lastly, we integrate the extant findings across levels, highlighting so-called spill-over effects and discussing theories and measures of trust across levels which offer promising avenues for future research.

Key distinctions regarding teams and trust in teams

Trust has become one of the most frequently studied constructs in organizational research (Fulmer & Gelfand, 2012). Historically, scholars have primarily emphasized interpersonal and organizational trust while paying little attention to team trust (Clarke & Payne, 1997; Nienaber, Romeike, Searle, & Schewe, 2015). However, with organizational hierarchies having become flatter and operations being now more team-centered than ever (De Jong, Dirks, & Gillespie, 2016), there has recently been a rise in scholarly attention to trust in teams.

Numerous definitions of groups, teams, and other forms of collectives have been offered by the scientific literature, all with subtle differences (Mathieu, Maynard, Rapp, & Gilson, 2008). As a shared characteristic, teams are commonly regarded as groups of individuals, usually with hierarchical configurations (supervisors and subordinates) (Alderfer, 1987; Edmondson, 1999; Hackman, 1987). As organizational subunits, teams have clearly defined membership, whereby the members of a single team share common task objectives, carry out interdependent tasks, and produce collective outcomes (Kozlowski & Ilgen, 2006).

Within organizations, teams may have many different configurations and perform a wide set of functions. For many organizations today, co-located work and service teams deliver the core tasks, while organizationally or geographically dispersed teams may be used for more complex tasks (Kirkman & Mathieu, 2005; Townsend, DeMarie, & Hendrickson, 1998). In the face of continued globalization, hyper-competition, and rapid technology change, and in line with the transition from a manufacturing to a knowledge-based economy, the existence of virtual and global teams creates a strong need for inter-team collaboration (Scott & Einstein, 2001; Chapter 22 by Van der Werff et al., this volume).

Several taxonomies have been offered in the literature (e.g. Cohen & Bailey, 1997; Devine, 2002; Hackman, 1990; Sundstrom, 1999). Whereas taxonomies highlight the fact that teams can differ, we agree with Mathieu and colleagues (2008), who state that the categories these taxonomies offer 'are simply proxies for more substantive issues' (p. 412). For example, teams may be distinguished based on the time their members have been working together or the fluctuation in their membership. Hence, different types of teams operate under different conditions and face different demands. As a result, they also differ in their capabilities to develop trust and their qualifications for and reliance on such development.

Although there is no universally accepted definition of trust, scholars agree that positive expectations and a willingness to accept vulnerability are two central elements of this concept (Mayer, Davis, & Schoorman, 1995; Rousseau, Sitkin, Burt, & Camerer, 1998). On the team level, positive expectations refer to the belief that the actions of one or more individuals within a team or of a team in total will be beneficial or at least not detrimental (Gambetta, 1988; Luhmann, 1988). This state of positive expectations builds on a perception of the team's or team members' trustworthiness and ultimately promotes acceptance of vulnerability and fosters a suspension of uncertainty regarding the team's or team members' actions. In sum, trust in teams transforms uncertainty into momentary 'certainty', which enables a leap toward positive expectations and acceptance of vulnerability beyond a level which good reasons alone would warrant (Möllering, 2001).

As such, one would expect research on trust in teams to have arrived at clear and precise insights. Unfortunately however, studies on this topic have yielded mixed and contradictory results that lack coherence and remain widely spread across levels of analysis (De Jong, Dirks, & Gillespie, 2016). When analyzing trust in teams, research commonly distinguishes between teams as a referent and as a level of analysis. As a referent, the team is the trustee regardless of whether the trustor is an individual, another team, or an organization. As a level of analysis, the team is the trustor and trust refers to a collectively shared perception among team members, regardless of who the trustee is (Fulmer & Gelfand, 2012). Due to the numerous perspectives, conceptualizations, and understandings that go along with this distinction, we propose a separate distinction of two levels at which trust in teams operates, in order to systematically review and integrate research in this field: Whereas (1) intra-team trust refers to shared generalized perceptions of trust *within a team*, (2) inter-team trust refers to a team's shared generalized perception of trust *towards another team*. Figure 6.1 depicts our conceptualization of these two distinct levels of trust in teams.

For intra-team trust, we additionally need to distinguish the separate relationships that exist within a team, i.e. (1) the horizontal relationships between team members who operate at the same hierarchical level, (2) the vertical relationships across hierarchical levels between team members and their team leader, and (3) vice versa.

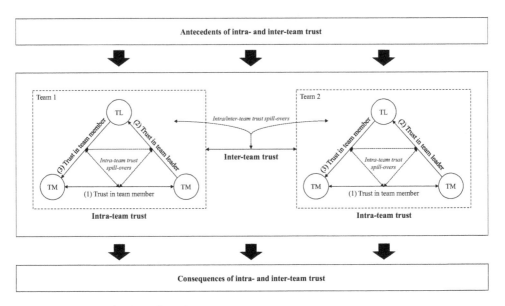

Figure 6.1 Conceptualization of trust in teams

Intra-team trust

Intra-team trust is defined as the shared generalized perceptions of trust that team members have in their team, including their fellow teammates and their team leader. Intra-team trust thus refers to an aggregate level of trust (Langfred, 2004), comprising all individual team members' perceptions of trust. Considering the superior–subordinates configuration of teams, intra-team trust comprises shared perceptions of trust with two principal referents – trust in team members and trust in team leader – and across three lines of relationships: (1) horizontal team members' trust in fellow team members, (2) vertical team members' trust in the team leader, and (3) vertical team leader's trust in team members. All three relationships are shown in Figure 6.1. The aggregate trust across these three relationships determines the level of intra-team trust. It is important to note that the three relationships described above may not be mutual, meaning that if one team member (A) holds a certain level of trust towards a fellow team member (B) this does not necessarily mean that B holds the exact same level of trust towards A. Although Ferrin, Bligh, and Kohles (2008) demonstrated that the level of trust between individuals increasingly correlates over time, most studies found evidence for asymmetric trust relationships between two parties (e.g. Brower, Lester, Korsgaard, & Dineen 2009; Korsgaard, Brower, & Lester, 2015). As intra-team trust is essentially an aggregate of the individual team members' perceptions of trust, it combines possibly asymmetric perceptions between team members. Yet, most conceptualizations and measures of intra-team trust have a tendency to overlook such possible disparities in team members' levels of trust. Following Tomlinson, Dineen, and Lewicki (2009), we note that it is important for research on intra-team trust relationships to pay greater attention to the individual level of trust on both sides of a relationship.

In general, shared perceptions of trust within the team have been argued to emerge from three different sources: (1) from team membership and, thus, through a social categorization process (Williams, 2001), (2) from team members' collective 'sense-making' about shared experiences (Shamir & Lapidot, 2003), and (3) from contextual factors that reassure team members and constrain their interactions (McKnight, Cummings, & Chervany, 1998). Combined, these three sources lead to similar levels of trust among team members and team leader (Schoorman, Mayer, & Davis, 2007). In fact, most studies that follow a team-level conceptualization of intra-team trust refer to generalized expectations for all team members (e.g. Langfred, 2004; Simons & Peterson, 2000). Having in mind the possible imbalance of trust levels and the dynamic development of trust among team members over time, an identification of the patterns of intra-team trust might be more useful. In this respect, different theoretical paradigms concerning trust are prominent across the three relationships within teams.

Taking a **team member-view**, many studies build on *social exchange theory* (Axelrod, 1984; Blau, 1964; Deutsch, 1958) to explain how team members develop trust based on repeated interaction with their fellow team members or team leader. Balanced exchanges and experience of fairness and satisfaction have been shown to increase team members' trust (Ambrose & Schminke, 2003; Aryee, Budhwar, & Chen 2002; Fulmer & Gelfand, 2012; Khazanchi & Masterson, 2011). In particular, studies that investigate the effects of perceived support (Rhoades & Eisenberger, 2002; Whitener, 2001) and psychological contracts (Montes & Irving, 2008; Restubog, Hornsey, Bordia, & Esposo, 2008; Robinson, 1996; Zhao, Wayne, Glibkowski, & Bravo, 2007) on teams draw heavily on this theory. Regarding the specifics of vertical intra-team relationships, *attribution theory* (Heider, 1958; Weiner, 1992) has been used to explain how team members perceive the trustworthiness of their supervisor (Tomlinson & Mayer, 2009). This perspective has been particularly influential in the exploration of the effects of leadership behaviour (Gillespie & Mann, 2004; Korsgaard, Brodt, & Whitener, 2002), monitoring, and contracts (Ferrin, Bligh, & Kohles, 2007; Malhotra & Murnighan, 2002) on team member trust in team leaders.

From the **team leader's perspective**, in turn, research has frequently drawn on *leader-member exchange theory* to reflect on the quality of the reciprocal exchanges between team leaders and their subordinates (Graen & Uhl-Bien, 1995). The basic notion of this perspective is that leaders tend to develop unique relationships with individual team members, affecting several dimensions of work relationships such as obligation, respect, and trust (Ferris et al., 2009). In this sense, team leader's trust is largely contingent on its perception of subordinates' characteristics and behaviour (Fulmer & Gelfand, 2012). Similarly, research on mentoring has focused on the value of frequent positive interaction across hierarchical levels and has suggested that interpersonal comfort and trust are central to effective relationships between mentors and protégés (Ferris et al., 2009; Nienaber, Romeike, Searle, & Schewe, 2015; Young & Perrewé, 2000).

Antecedents of intra-team trust

Research on intra-team trust has historically received only scant attention, but is becoming more and more frequently the object of scientific studies (De Jong, Dirks, & Gillespie, 2016; Fulmer & Gelfand, 2012). Following the conceptualization, intra-team trust refers to a shared perception of trust across the horizontal and vertical intra-team relationships between team members and team leaders. In their seminal review of trust, Fulmer & Gelfand (2012) highlight how intra-team trust depends on the unique and shared characteristics of the trustor and trustee. For horizontal, intra-team relationships between fellow team members, research has identified numerous factors that aid or hinder the development of interpersonal trust, among which we highlight selected examples. Regarding the trustor, a general propensity to trust has been shown to enhance a team member's willingness to form high-quality relationships with fellow team members and thus ease the development of trust (Dirks & Ferrin, 2002; Rotter, 1980). This is largely because a team member's propensity to trust positively correlates with its perceptions of fellow team members' trustworthiness (Colquitt, Scott, & LePine, 2007). Trustworthiness has been argued to be rated along three principal dimensions: ability, benevolence, and integrity (Mayer et al., 1995). Hence a team member's perception of his/her fellow team members' trustworthiness fosters trust in horizontal intra-team relationships. Moreover, research has highlighted the value of shared characteristics between team members in terms of building trust. Jiang and colleagues, for example, demonstrated that trust is higher when the trustor and trustee share a common ethnic background (Jiang, Chua, Kotabe, & Murray, 2011). Lastly, team members have been shown to have more trust in those fellow team members who are trusted by the team leader (Lau & Liden, 2008).

For vertical intra-team relationships between team members and team leaders, a team member's high propensity to trust has been linked to high trust in leaders, even when perceptions of the leader's trustworthiness were low (Grant & Sumanth, 2009). Further, team members' secure attachment style demonstrably led to higher trust in team leaders (Simmons, Gooty, Nelson, & Little, 2009). As in horizontal relationships, the trustee's trustworthiness dimensions have been shown to affect levels of trust (Colquitt et al., 2007). Regarding team leaders' trust in team members, analyses of mentor-protégé relationships have revealed team members' support behaviours, meeting of expectations (Young & Perrewé, 2000), voluntary help (De Jong, Van der Vegt, & Molleman, 2007), and expectations of loyalty (Rosanas & Velilla, 2003) increase levels of trust. Further, a team leader's trust in a team member is higher when perceiving the team member as able to uphold commitments, particularly when the team member has high autonomy (Perrone, Zaheer, & McEvily, 2003). Interestingly however, Sniezek and Van Swol (2001) found that trust from individuals with higher power, such as team leaders, in those with lesser power, such as team members, was lower than vice versa.

Regarding team members' trust in team leaders, perceptions of team leader competence, benevolence, and integrity have been found to increase levels of trust (Dirks & Ferrin, 2002). These may be based on specific leader behaviours such as communicating a collective vision (Gillespie & Mann, 2004), demonstrating individualized support (Hernandez, 2008; Korsgaard et al., 2002; Roussin, 2008), and perceptions of leader fairness (Choi, 2008) as well as distributive, procedural, and interactional justice (Cohen-Charash & Spector, 2001; Colquitt, LePine, Piccolo, Zapata, & Rich, 2012; Li & Cropanzano, 2009; Yang, Mossholder, & Peng, 2009). However, this is always seen from a team member's point of view which does not automatically mean that the level of trust at both sides of the relationship is the same (e.g. Korsgaard et al., 2014; De Jong & Dirks, 2012). For example, even though a team's members may have a high level of trust in their team leader, the team leader may not place an equal level of trust in the team members. In this regard, scholars such as De Jong and Dirks (2012) have repeatedly stressed that it is important for research to consider the dispersion of trust that may exist within a team.

In reviewing the literature about leader behaviours that influence team trust to enhance team performance (e.g. Schaubroeck, Lam, & Peng, 2011), scholars have used either a functional approach that deals with specific leadership styles and may influence team behaviours (e.g. Hackman, 2002) or take into account different dimensions of leader behaviour that are mentioned in the broader leadership literature (e.g. Pillai, Schriesheim, & Williams, 1999). Over the years, a vast number of leadership styles have been investigated in terms of how different leadership styles influence assessments of team leaders' trustworthiness. Among many others, positive effects have been ascribed to ethical leadership (Brown, Treviño, & Harrison, 2005; Kalshoven, Den Hartog, & De Hoogh, 2011), transformational leadership (Jung & Avolio, 2000; Jung, Yammarino, & Lee, 2009), transactional leadership (Jung & Avolio, 2000), empowering leadership (Caldwell & Dixon, 2010), and participative and consultative decision making (Dirks

& Ferrin, 2002; Gillespie & Mann, 2004; Huang, Iun, Liu, & Gong, 2010). Regarding the relationship between leader behaviour and intra-team trust, very little research can be found. Studies in this field usually focus on either the specifics of team leadership (e.g. Hackman and Walton, 1986; Morgeson, DeRue, & Karam, 2010; Zaccaro, Rittman, & Marks, 2002) or on broader team dynamics (e.g. Mathieu et al., 2008; Ilgen, Hollenbeck, Johnson, & Jundt, 2005). Taking the findings of the more general leadership literature into account, some of the findings in this field might be attributable to trust research. For example, the team leadership literature suggests that different individuals might be necessary to effectively manage a team (e.g. Carson, Tesluk, & Marrone, 2007), which would mean considering multiple vertical relationships of team members' trust in more than one team leader (for more details on trust and leadership, see also Chapter 26 by Den Hartog, this volume).

Feelings of psychological intimacy emerge from high trust across horizontal and vertical intra-team relationships (Mohammed, Ferzandi, & Hamilton, 2010). The existence of trusting relationships between team members across intra-team relationships has been found to allow team members and leaders to anticipate repayment of favours they extend to others, and that this, in return, increases feelings of obligation to repay others' favours (Chung & Jackson, 2013; Coleman, 1988). In this light it has been argued that perceived inclusion, that is, the degree to which an individual perceives that he or she is a valued member of the team, facilitates feelings of obligation and trust (Shore et al., 2011). As Putnam (1995) put it, team membership may broaden the individual sense of self, developing the 'I' into the 'we'. Through this process, teams develop shared mental models or a 'group mind', which produces similarity and commonality within the team (Klimonski & Modammed, 1994). This in turn provides the basis for a team-wide shared perception of trust to emerge. However, the shared level of intra-team trust has been argued to depend strongly on the team's context (Fulmer & Gelfand, 2012). Similarity of outlook among team members, for example, has been demonstrated to affect intra-group behaviour in that individuals with deviating (e.g. very high or low) levels of dominating behaviour were reportedly more likely to become the targets of abusive behaviour (Aquino & Byron, 2002). A high level of shared values among team members and leaders has been found to increase intra-team trust by aiding social identification (Jehn & Mannix, 2001). In a similar vein, but in the context of the index of gender dissimilarity, identification with the team has been reported to depend on the degree of gender dissimilarity (as measured by the index of dissimilarity) within that team. Women show a lesser degree of identification with the team the greater the gender dissimilarity that exists (Chattopadhyay, George & Shulman, 2008; see also Chapter 28 by Searle, this volume). That is, the smaller the proportion of women in a team, the less likely are those women to identify with the team. It has also been suggested demographic (race and sex) dissimilarity may affect intra-team trust positively, particularly for those employees with low levels of dogmatism (Chattopadhyay, 2003). Additionally, intra-team trust has been shown to depend on each team member's level of vulnerability (Lapidot, Kark, & Shamir, 2007) as well as the unpredictability and danger of the team's task context (Colquitt et al., 2011).

Regarding the contextual characteristics of the team, a large body of research has recently begun to study the role of trust in virtual and globally dispersed teams (see also Chapter 22 by Van der Werff and colleagues, this volume). Scholarly attention on these types of teams centres on the paradox that while 'trust needs touch' (Handy, 1995; p. 46), only trust can prevent geographical distances from becoming psychological distances (Jarvenpaa & Leidner, 1999; O'Hara-Devereaux & Johansen, 1994). Accordingly, studies have found geographic dispersion negatively affects communication within the team and lowers members' attachment to the team (e.g. Romeike, Nienaber, & Schewe, 2016; Haas, 2006; Maznevski & Chudoba, 2000) and have revealed that trust in virtual teams is fragile and fractures rapidly (Hinds & Bailey, 2003; Jarvenpaa & Leidner, 1999). Not surprisingly then, the effect of team members' propensity to trust has been found to be higher in virtual than collocated teams (Yakovleva, Reilly, & Werko, 2010) and the benefit of team familiarity stronger for teams that are geographically dispersed (Espinosa, Slaughter, Kraut, & Herbsleb, 2007).

Consequences of intra-team trust

As with its antecedents, we need to distinguish between the consequences of trust in horizontal and vertical intra-team relationships and the consequences of the corresponding shared perceptions of intra-team trust. For horizontal intra-team relationships, research has identified a wide range of behavioural consequences (Fulmer & Gelfand, 2012). For example, trust between fellow team members has been linked to increased knowledge exchange (Andrews & Delahaye, 2000; Golden & Raghuram, 2010; Levin & Cross, 2004; Mäkelä & Brewster, 2009; Nonaka, 1994), facilitation of future cooperation (Rosanas, 2008), decreases in counterproductive behaviour (Colquitt et al., 2007), and teamwork and continuous improvement (Coyle-Shapiro & Morrow, 2003). For vertical intra-team relationships between team members and leaders, most research has focussed on the effects of trust on team member attitudes and behaviours, while little attention has been paid to its effects on team leaders. Regarding the latter, research on mentor-protégé relationships has revealed mentors' trust in protégés promotes mentoring functions such as role modelling or career and psycho-social support (Wang, Tomlinson, & Noe, 2010). Regarding the effects on team members, trust in team leaders has been found to increase job satisfaction while reducing uncertainty at work and intention to quit (Colquitt et al., 2012; Dirks & Ferrin, 2002), to raise team member support for the team leader (Brockner, Siegel, Daly, Tyler, & Martin, 1997), and to lead to stronger commitment to decisions made by the team leader (Dirks & Ferrin, 2002), to name just a few. Moreover, trust in leaders has been shown to facilitate feedback-seeking behaviour among team members (Hays & Williams, 2011) and raise their willingness to risk speaking up (Premeaux & Bedeian, 2003). Acknowledging that that the levels of trust across a team's members may differ, a recent experiment by Korsgaard and colleagues (2014) revealed that in dyadic intra-team relationships, the benefit of one team member's trust is lost if the fellow team member does not share the same level of trust.

On the aggregate level, a shared team-wide perception of trust increases satisfaction with the team (Chou, Wang, Wang, Huang, & Cheng, 2008), proactive idea implementation, and problem solving (Parker, Williams, & Turner, 2006). Additionally, Nonaka (1994) states that the building of intra-team trust may have the potential to accelerate the creation of an implicit perspective shared by team members, thus aiding in organizational knowledge creation. In their seminal review of team mental models, Mohammed and colleagues (2010) further highlighted several outcomes of shared cognition, such as increases in viability, collective efficacy, and team performance. In sum, however, research investigating the relationship between intra-team trust and team performance has produced mixed and often controversial findings (De Jong, Dirks, & Gillespie, 2016). While some studies found support for a positive effect of trust on performance (De Jong & Elfring, 2010), others failed to demonstrate a significant effect (Aubert & Kelsey, 2003) or even found evidence for a negative relationship (Langfred, 2004). Reflecting on these findings, De Jong and colleagues (2016) note that the fragmentation of the field has triggered two reactions: skepticism as to whether intra-team trust has a main effect on team performance at all and an extensive search for moderators of the trust-performance relationship. Both have so far delivered promising results, demonstrating that intra-team trust may be distal and may affect performance indirectly (Dirks, 1999; Dirks & Ferrin, 2001) or be limited to affect only selected performance dimensions (Aubert & Kelsey, 2003; Jarvenpaa, Shaw, & Staples, 2004), and identifying effective moderators such as task interdependence (Beal, Cohen, Burke, & McLendon, 2003; DeChurch & Mesmer-Magnus, 2010) and routineness (Chung & Jackson, 2013). The notion that trust in other referents (i.e. the team leader) may be a more effective driver of team performance, however, was recently ruled out by a meta-analysis conducted by De Jong and colleagues (2016). As an alternative explanation for the mixed findings, Chung and Jackson (2013) found empirical evidence for an inverted-U shape relationship between intra-team trust and team performance.

Aside from the trust-performance debate, research has indicated certain consequences of intra-team trust to be of particular relevance to teams operating under specific conditions and demands. For the context of virtual teams, Hinds and Bailey (2003) showed how task conflict can translate into affective conflict when intra-team trust is low, because 'team members are more likely to question others' intentions and make attributions that do not adequately account for situational factors' (p. 618). Concordantly, Mannix, Griffith, and Neale (2002) argued a lack of common social identity is one of the most important barriers virtual and globally dispersed teams must overcome to be able to effectively deal with conflict. Here, shared perceptions of trust were found to aid in bridging the physical and contextual gaps that separate members of geographically dispersed teams by creating psychological ties (Hinds & Mortensen, 2005).

Future research on intra-team trust

As demonstrated, research on intra-team trust has heavily focussed on the horizontal and vertical intra-team relationships, whereas research that explores the shared perceptions of intra-team trust is much less common. Hence, we know a great deal about the antecedents and consequences on the relationship level, but comparatively little about how trust develops and manifests itself on the team level. This leads us to conclude that more research is necessary to understand how shared perceptions of trust emerge and to identify patterns (dynamics) of trust in teams rather than focussing on a mean, aggregate level of team trust. Bliese (2000) suggested that trust may be contagious, such that one team member's perception of trust is affected by but also influences other team members' perceptions of trust. Still, insights on how trust may spread across team members are rather limited. Research has hinted that team leaders may play a key role in influencing intra-team values and climate (Dansereau & Alutto, 1990; Naumann & Bennett, 2000) and setting expectations for team members. Likewise, team members' characteristics should affect the emergence of intra-team trust. Here, incorporating general leadership theory's consideration of multiple leaders in a single team at the same time might require the attention of trust scholars in the future, as such team configuration would enhance the complexity of intra-team trust relations.

De Jong and Dirks (2012) showed that the existence of asymmetric levels of trust in dyadic intra-team relationships moderates the effect of the aggregate, mean level of intra-team trust on team performance. This means that those teams that perform better have a less asymmetric dispersion of trust, which we believe is worth taking into consideration in future research. In this light, Fulmer and Gelfand (2012) suggested trust research incorporate theories from the fit literature, as fit between the trustor and the trustee on dimensions such as norms, values, and perspectives seems to be crucial for trust to develop (Chattopadhyay & George, 2001; Edwards & Cable, 2009; Gillespie & Mann, 2004; Jehn & Mannix, 2001). However, different dimensions may be relevant for different teams or at different times. For example, shared backgrounds may be beneficial to trust development in collocated or newly formed teams whereas task-oriented fit may be more important for virtual and globally dispersed teams or those that have been working together for a long period of time.

Considering further promising avenues for future research, we believe it worthwhile to transfer established antecedents and consequences from horizontal and vertical intra-team relationships to the shared-team domain and test their applicability at this level. Regarding the horizontal and vertical intra-team relationships, we note a significant imbalance towards studies favouring research that focusses on team members' perceptions of trust; with considerably less attention paid towards team leaders' trust in team members (Fulmer & Gelfand, 2012). This is striking, because evidence has found team members who feel trusted exhibit higher levels of commitment and innovation (Ruppel & Harrington, 2000), report higher perceptions of justice (Kickul, Gundry, & Posig, 2005), and have higher performance (Dirks & Skarlicki, 2009). Little is known, however, about what drives trust or perceptions of being trusted along vertical intra-team relationships. We thus recommend future research explore this area in greater depth to add to our knowledge about the antecedents and consequences of team leader trust in team members.

Inter-team trust

Even though trust research is still very much dominated by the individual level of analysis, the number of studies conducted at the inter-team level has grown steadily over the past years (Fulmer & Gelfand, 2012). Like intra-team trust, inter-team trust refers to an aggregate level of trust. In contrast, however, the referent for inter-team trust is not one's own but another team. Hence, we define inter-team trust as a team's shared generalized perceptions of trust towards another team. This distinction is crucial due to important differences between the intra- and inter-team levels – one of which is significantly lower levels of trust between teams than within them (Song, 2009). Just like trust within a team, however, trust between teams has been found to be essential for the functioning and success of organizations (Tsai & Ghoshal, 1998).

Research on inter-team trust has built on several theoretical perspectives, many of which have been adopted from the individual or organizational levels (Fulmer & Gelfand, 2012). One of the most prominent theories is *social exchange theory* (Serva, Fuller, & Mayer, 2005) and the related principles of equity and reciprocity that have been applied to explain inter-team trust (Gainey & Klaas, 2003). Further, research on this level has drawn heavily on the *social identity approach*, which consists of two distinct, but closely related theories: *social identity theory* (Tajfel & Turner, 1986) and *self-categorization theory* (Turner, Hogg, Oakes, Reicher, & Wetherell, 1987). Social identity theory suggests that individuals conceptualize their social environment as a series of in-groups (us) and out-groups (them) (Hogg & Terry, 2000), based on which an individual defines and categorizes his/her 'place in society' (Tajfel, 1978, p. 63). Implicit in *self-categorization theory* is the idea that social groups emerge whenever individuals perceive themselves to be members of a single social category (Turner, 1982). Research has shown that the categorization into in-group and out-group involves a perception of other groups as less competent, honest, trustworthy, and cooperative than one's own group (Barrett, 2010; Brewer, 1979; Williams, 2001), establishing barriers to trust at the inter-team level (Newell, David, & Chand, 2007; Polzer, Crisp, Jarvenpaa, & Kim, 2006; Tsai & Ghoshal, 1998). Similarly, scholars have relied on *social information processing theory* and the related *media richness theory* to investigate the pitfalls of inter-team communication and to understand how teams develop trust towards one another (Daft & Lengel, 1986; Walumbwa, Luthans, Avey, & Oke, 2011), usually in the context of virtual teams (Wilson, Straus, & McEvily, 2006). Furthermore, studies on inter-team trust have taken a network perspective, examining how a team's network position and intra-organizational embeddedness affects its relationship to other teams (Tsai, 2001). Additionally, a growing body of research focusses on the social interdependence of teams and the conflicts and trust violations which may occur, frequently drawing on *attribution theory* to explain how teams make sense of negative incidents (Janowicz-Panjaitan & Krishnan, 2009) and *conflict management theory* (Hempel, Zhang, & Tjosvold, 2009). Lastly, research has recently begun to investigate inter-team distrust, taking also the conflict literature into account (e.g. Bijlsma-Frankema, Sitkin, & Weibel, 2015).

Antecedents of inter-team trust

As research on inter-team trust has adopted many of its theoretical and methodological approaches and its research aims from findings related to trust from the individual and organizational levels, several of the same factors, but also additional ones, that foster the development of trust between teams have been identified. Of these, we highlight selected examples. Generally, inter-team trust has been found to be weaker than intra-team trust, and trust among two teams has been found to be lower than among three or more teams (Polzer et al., 2006; Song, 2009). Following *social exchange theory*, inter-team trust depends on the trustor's perception of equity and reciprocity in the relationship with the other team. In this light, high-risk-taking behaviour by a team has been demonstrated to signal its willingness to be vulnerable and encourage the partner team to respond with trust (Serva et al., 2005). Similarly, knowledge about the partner team is of importance for the development of inter-team trust, which is why scholars have pointed out the value of frequent interaction and a shared vision among teams (Tsai & Ghoshal, 1998). However, other studies have highlighted how cognitive flexibility can raise levels of inter-team trust, particularly between top-management and middle-management teams (Raes, Heijltjes, Glunk, & Roe, 2011). Building on *social identity* and *self-categorization theories*, studies have revealed actual demographic similarity, as well as perceived similarity between teams, fosters inter-team trust (Fulmer & Gelfand, 2012). Priem and Nystrom (2014) captured this relationship in their seminal discussion of common ground as a source of trust. Such common ground between teams, which is the entirety of mutual ideas, values, and information jointly held by two or more individuals (Stalnaker, 2002), can be derived from two sources. Whereas personal common ground is built over the course of shared experiences between the teams, communal common ground stems from a common cultural and ethnic background (Clark, 1996)

Unique to this level of analysis, a large body of research has investigated the interrelationship between inter-team conflicts and trust. Not surprisingly, there seems to be wide consensus among scholars that conflicts are detrimental to inter-team trust (Fulmer & Gelfand, 2012). For example, Bijlsma-Frankema and colleagues (2015) revealed in their case study of groups of judges and administrators in a court of law how value incongruence can trigger conflict, which then may lead to a self-amplifying cycle of inter-group distrust. However, as a study by Langfred (2007) demonstrated, different types of conflict may have different effects on trust, with relationship conflicts possibly decreasing trust and task conflicts having no or lesser effect. Moreover, research has hinted at the possibility of a positive effect on inter-team relations and trust in cases in which the conflict is successfully overcome. In particular, cooperative approaches, in which teams focus on their mutual goals and aim to resolve conflicts for mutual benefit, have been linked to increased inter-team trust, whereas competitive approaches that result in one-sided, imposed resolutions have been found to lead to fragmented relations and loss of trust (Hempel et al., 2009; Wong & Tjosvold, 2010).

Similarly to research at the intra-team level, research on trust between teams is paying increasing attention to organizational changes in team configuration, particularly the virtualization of teamwork. In general, studies have demonstrated inter-team communication is key for the development and sustainability of trust (Fulmer & Gelfand, 2012). However, the use of information and communication technologies has been found to further decrease the already low levels of trust among geographically dispersed teams (Polzer et al., 2006; Wilson et al., 2006). On the upside, other studies indicate that the drawbacks of this team co-location in terms of trust may decrease as team members become more adept at relying on virtual communication (Alge, Wiethoff, & Klein, 2003; DeRosa, Hantula, Kock, & D'Arcy, 2004). Teams can strengthen inter-team trust by committing to timely communication of substantive information, data transparency, and more task-focussed enthusiastic exchanges (Jarvenpaa & Leidner, 1999; Palanski, Kahai, & Yammarino, 2011).

Consequences of inter-team trust

Notably, the value of trust between teams in terms of predicting their performance seems to be considerably lower compared to the value of trust within teams (Dirks, 2000). For example, De Jong and Elfring (2010) indicated that the effect of inter-team trust on performance might be mediated by other factors such as adaptability and effort of the partnering teams. Moreover, inter-team trust seems to be of value for organizations as it has been associated with a multitude of positive consequences. For example, a trusting relationship between teams has been shown to foster the exchange of information, knowledge and resources (Howorth, Westhead, & Wright, 2004; Tsai & Ghoshal, 1998) and team learning (Bogenrieder & Nooteboom, 2004), all of which in turn are likely to enhance the innovation capabilities of the partnering teams and of the organization as a whole. Further, trust between teams has been linked to improvements in the teams' decision-making effectiveness (Alge et al., 2003), team affective commitment (Costa, 2003), team organizational citizenship behaviour (OCB), and performance (Hempel et al., 2009; Joshi, Lazarova, & Liao, 2009; Langfred, 2004; Walumbwa et al., 2011). Lastly, team-level satisfaction has been found to be higher when inter-team trust is present (Costa, 2003). In turn, studies on distrust have revealed diminished cooperation and avoidance of interaction with the other group as behavioural consequences of a lack of inter-group trust or distrust (Bijlsma-Frankema et al., 2015).

As Fulmer and Gelfand (2012) show, inter-team trust has also been demonstrated to have beneficial moderating effects. On that note, trust between teams was found to alleviate the link between receiving negative feedback and subsequent relationship conflict between teams (Peterson & Behfar, 2003), or the inflation of inter-team task conflicts to relationship conflicts (Simons & Peterson, 2000).

Future research on inter-team trust

Though relatively young, the field of inter-team trust research has already produced a number of significant findings and has developed distinct topical and theoretical features, as found in studies on inter-team conflicts and trust (e.g. Hempel et al., 2009; Bijlsma-Frankema et al., 2015). Nevertheless, knowledge about the antecedents and consequences of inter-team trust is still relatively limited and warrants further research. As far as we know, no studies have yet examined factors such as team characteristics or teams' propensity to trust as antecedents of inter-team trust. Additionally, we encourage future research to investigate additional consequences of inter-team trust. In this light, Fulmer and Gelfand (2012) suggested studies could compare the impact of trust across different levels, as understanding the (dis-)similarities of trust at the intra- and inter-team level has important implications for theory and practice alike. Consequently, researchers should examine the impact of inter-team trust on creativity, for which a positive effect has been shown on the individual level (e.g. Ford & Gioia, 2000). Further, we believe that the relationship between inter-team trust and performance is in particular need of clarification, as this link has been found to be weaker than expected (Dirks, 2000) and several factors have been suggested to act as mediators (De Jong & Elfring, 2010).

In order to better capture the organizational consequences of inter-team trust, we encourage future research to take a broader stance and to look beyond dyadic inter-team relationships. Here, the field of inter-team trust research could capitalize on the method of social network analysis, which has been successfully utilized at the intra-team or organizational levels. Future studies could explore the effects of network characteristics such as network position, network density, or subnetworks on inter-team cooperation and trust development (Coleman, 1988; Millar & Choi, 2009). Moreover, we consider it highly interesting to investigate potential links between intra- and inter-team networks, such as how information and knowledge is exchanged between members of different teams and how perceptions of trust are developed.

Integration across levels

Building on our conceptual framework of intra- and inter-team trust, we now discuss the value of research that integrates both levels. As organizations rely on the functioning of teams as much as inter-team relations, and as our review has indicated certain links between these levels, we deem it important to analyse the current state of research that considers trust in teams across levels and highlight a pathway for further integration in the future. Hence, we look at established and potential links between the relationships within teams as well as intra- and inter-team levels and also discuss the possibilities and merits of integrating theories and measures of trust across the different levels at which trusting relationships exist.

Spill-overs of trust across levels

Although not new, the idea that trust at one level might be dependent on or might spill over to affect trust at another level has in the past not received much attention. However, it seems that recently more and more scholars have started investigating this exciting area of research. Generally, the notion of potential spill-overs of trust follows the idea of structuration theory (DeSanctis & Poole, 1994; Giddens, 1984) that intra- and inter-team relations are embedded in the greater organizational structure and in turn shape this structure. In this light, Cappelli and Sherer (1991) and Mowday and Sutton (1993) have noted already that context usually operates as a cross-level effect in which conditions at one level affect interactions at another level. Concordantly, Fulmer & Gelfand note that 'trust within any one level does not occur in a vacuum' (p. 1204) and hence needs to be put in the context of related levels (Johns, 2006). Although by nature a two-way street where both bottom-up and top-down effects are possible, most cross-level research has investigated top-down conceptions, often labelled trickle-down effects (Wo, Ambrose, & Schminke, 2015). In fact, several studies have demonstrated that the external and organizational environment provides context for trust between and within teams (Fulmer & Gelfand, 2012) and research has also found evidence for spill-overs across several trust-related factors, including perceptions of justice (Ambrose, Schminke, & Mayer, 2013), behavioural integrity (Simons, Friedman, Liu, & Parks, 2007), and ethical leadership (Mayer, Kuenzi, Greenbaum, Bardes, & Salvador, 2009). However, as relationships within and between teams can be understood as mutually constraining, we need to consider the possibility of bidirectional interrelations and distinguish between bottom-up and top-down spill-overs of trust across the intra-team relationship and also between the intra- and inter-team level.

Most research in this area has focussed on top-down spill-overs of trust within teams. For example, Chou and colleagues (2008) found that the level of trust in horizontal intra-team relationships was higher the greater the degree of shared values within the team. Similarly, Shamir and Lapidot (2003) found that team members' trust is contingent on values at the higher level. Hence, it seems likely that the level of trust in vertical intra-team relationships may influence trust at the horizontal relationships among teammates. Scholars have drawn on several theoretical perspectives to explain such spill-over effects (for an empirical review see Wo et al., 2015). Referring to *social exchange theory*, research has proposed that trust may spill over from the team leader to team members because team members reciprocate their superiors' behaviours (Mayer et al., 2009; Tepper & Taylor, 2003). Similarly, *social learning theory* has been used to suggest team members may study and emulate their team leaders' conduct (Mawritz, Mayer, Hoobler, Wayne, & Marinova, 2012; Mayer et al., 2009). Emphasizing negative behaviour, theoretical reflections on *displaced aggression* have led scholars to propose that team members may mirror poor treatment they receive from their team leaders within their horizontal relationships with teammates (Marcus-Newhall, Pedersen, Carlson, & Miller, 2000; Tedeschi & Norman, 1985). Regarding bottom-up spill-overs of trust, little research has been done to investigate how trust in vertical intra-team relationships may be affected by trust among team-members (Fulmer & Gelfand, 2012). Social exchange and social learning theory seem to suggest, however, that high shared levels of trust between team members may provide a climate that is conducive to team members having trust in the team leader and vice versa, and we consider this to be a promising area for future research.

Considerably less research has focussed on trust spill-overs between the intra- and inter-team levels. In one of the few studies to tackle this interesting issue, Keenan and Carnevale (1989) investigated the effects of simulated intra-team disputes on inter-team cooperation. Their results demonstrate that intra-team cooperation enhances the degree of inter-team cooperation whereas, to a lesser extent, intra-team conflicts spill over to produce greater inter-team competitiveness. In sum, these findings provide evidence for possible bottom-up spill-overs of trust from the intra- to the inter-team level. However, additional research on this matter seems necessary. To the best of our knowledge, no scientific study so far has considered potential top-down spill-overs whereby trust at the inter-team level affects trust within the teams. A promising theoretical background for this proposed effect comes from the psychological effect of priming. Priming describes how individuals' actions and emotions are influenced by subconscious events the individual is not aware of (Chartrand & Bargh, 1996; Tversky & Kahneman, 1986). As Staw, Sutton, and Peled (1994) argue, people with positive feelings are likely to react more favourably to others. As such, factors such as affection and perceptions of safety or belonging related to the organizational environment might influence the level of trust among an organization's members. Translated to the team setting, the priming effect indicates that inter-team trust may create an environment that is conducive to the development of trust between members of a single team (Johnson & Grayson, 2005). Hence, we believe this is a promising area of future research.

In addition to direct spill-overs of trust, research has indicated the possibility of antecedents and consequences across relationships and levels (Klein, Dansereau, & Hall, 1994). For example, intra- and inter-team trust may be driven by factors on different levels, such as organizational climate or interorganizational competition. Likewise, Dirks and Ferrin (2001) proposed that trust may amplify or suppress the effects of other factors, indicating that trust within and between teams may determine consequences on different levels. In this light, investigating the effect of inter- or intra-team trust on organizational performance seems just one of many intriguing avenues for future research.

Theory across levels

Reviewing studies on intra- and inter-team trust reveals a multitude of theories research draws on to explain cause-effect relationships, which Fulmer & Gelfand (2012) in their review describe as a great strength of trust research. We deem it important to stress that several of the antecedents and consequences of trust in teams may possibly be understood through multiple theoretical perspectives. For example, studies have relied on both social exchange theory and social identity theory to explain the positive relationship between inter-team trust and information sharing (Fulmer & Gelfand, 2012; Howorth et al., 2004). Hence, we advocate the theoretical diversity of the field and encourage researchers to continue exploring the applicability of additional theoretical explanations.

However, we believe that, in particular, the promising field of cross-level research, which investigates spill-overs of trust, would benefit from a more diverse application of theories, as the theoretical foundations of studies in this field appear to be somewhat limited. As most theories are not confined by their nature to the particular level that most heavily draws on them, we consider a theoretical transfer between levels would be most valuable. For example, attribution theory, which has frequently been used to describe how team members perceive the trust-worthiness of their supervisor (Tomlinson & Mayer, 2009), could help to explain bottom-up trust spill-overs from the intra- to the inter-team level. Similarly, the social identity approach, which describes processes of categorization of in-groups (us) versus out-groups (them) (Hogg & Terry, 2000) and which has been used to analyse inter-team trust, might also be useful to better understand trust spill-overs between vertical and horizontal intra-team relationships. In sum, freeing theories from their own 'intellectual silos' (Fulmer & Gelfand, 2012, p. 1206) and testing theoretical principles across levels should have great potential to move trust research forward.

Measures across levels

Even though some scales such as those of McAllister (1995) or Mayer and Davis (1999) have seen wide use among trust scholars, the state of trust measurement is somewhat fragmented today. Highlighting this issue, McEvily and Tortoriello (2011) noted that 'different researchers use different measurement instruments to meet the idiosyncratic purposes of a particular study' (p. 24). Hence, we deem it important to reflect on and contrast measures used in research on trust in teams across the two levels.

As our review and conceptual framework suggest, intra-team trust, and with it trust in inter-team relationships, emerges from the shared perceptions of trust across the horizontal and vertical intra-team relationships. As such, the challenge for research on intra-team trust seems to lie in adequately capturing the shared team level perceptions of trust. Researchers often rely on selected representatives of a team as key informants to inform them about levels of intra-team trust (Fulmer & Gelfand, 2012). However, whether this approach is capable of capturing shared perceptions is highly questionable, particularly considering Song's (2009) finding that representatives rated levels of intra-team trust lower than teams as a whole did based on a group decision. In order to better capture shared perceptions of trust, three modes of measurement have been suggested: (1) the direct consensus composition model and (2) the referent-shift consensus composition model, both described by Chan (1998), as well as (3) the dispersion model. For both the direct consensus composition model and the referent-shift consensus composition model, intra-team trust is conceived as the aggregated level of trust among all team members and leaders, and measurement is possible only when there is sufficient consensus regarding levels of trust among all respondents. The difference between both composition models lies in the style of the individual ratings. Whereas the direct consensus model aggregates ratings of trust across the horizontal and vertical intra-team relationships (e.g. 'I trust my team leader.'), the referent-shift consensus model aggregates individual perceptions of intra-team trust (e.g. 'Within this team, we trust our team leader.'). As Fulmer and Gelfand (2012) note, measures across both models may vary because individuals' perceptions of intra-team trust may deviate from their own levels of trust. Dispersion models, as a third alternative, differ from composition models in that they do not aggregate but instead aim to assess the level of agreement among respondents concerning their shared perception of trust.

Additionally, aligning definitions and measures of trust sometimes imposes a challenge to studies on trust in teams. For example, the study of Serva and colleagues (2005) effectively examined intra-team trust but deployed a measure that assessed a team's trust in another team (i.e. inter-team trust), not the level of trust within a team. As a second example, the study by Dirks (1999) adopted a multidimensional conceptualization of intra-team trust and consistently adopted McAllister's (1995) multidimensional measure. However, flaws in the data collection process (i.e. a laboratory setting which used tower building with wooden blocks) failed to confirm the multidimensional nature of the construct.

In sum, research needs to pay greater attention to using measures that are aligned with a study's underlying definitions and theories of trust in teams. Moreover, we encourage future researchers to report the modes and measures used to assess trust in teams more transparently in order to reduce the risk of having their results misinterpreted.

Conclusion

Within this chapter, we have offered a comprehensive review of the current state of research on trust in teams. We have organized our review along a novel conceptualization of trust on the intra- and inter-team level. For both levels, we discussed the antecedents and consequences of trust thoroughly, revealing similarities and differences and highlighting avenues for future research. To complement this review, we have analysed current efforts to integrate trust research across the intra- and inter-team levels and examined promising prospects for the advancement of theory and measures of trust in teams. In sum, we believe this review aids researchers and practitioners alike in understanding what facilitates trust in teams and how the presence or lack of trust in teams manifests itself.

References

Alderfer, C. P. (1987). An intergroup perspective on organizational behavior. In J. W. Lorsch (ed.), *Handbook of organizational behavior*. Englewood Cliffs, NJ: Prentice-Hall.

Alge, B. J., Wiethoff, C., & Klein, H. J. (2003). When does the medium matter? Knowledge-building experiences and opportunities in decision-making teams. *Organizational Behavior and Human Decision Processes, 91*(1), 26–37.

Ambrose, M. L., & Schminke, M. (2003). Organization structure as a moderator of the relationship between procedural justice, interactional justice, perceived organizational support, and supervisory trust. *Journal of Applied Psychology, 88*(2), 295–305.

Ambrose, M. L., Schminke, M., & Mayer, D. M. (2013). Trickle-down effects of supervisor perceptions of interactional justice: A moderated mediation approach. *Journal of Applied Psychology, 98*(4), 678–689.

Anderson, N., & West, M. A. (1996). The Team Climate Inventory: Development of the TCI and its applications in teambuilding for innovativeness. *European Journal of Work and Organizational Psychology, 5*(1), 53–66.

Andrews, K. M., & Delahaye, B. L. (2000). Influences on knowledge processes in organizational learning: The psychosocial filter. *Journal of Management Studies, 37*(6), 797–810.

Applebaum, E., & Blatt, R. (1994). *The new American workplace*. Ithaca, NY: ILR.

Aquino, K., & Byron, K. (2002). Dominating interpersonal behavior and perceived victimization in groups: Evidence for a curvilinear relationship. *Journal of Management, 28*(1), 69–87.

Aryee, S., Budhwar, P. S., & Chen, Z. X. (2002). Trust as a mediator of the relationship between organizational justice and work outcomes: Test of a social exchange model. *Journal of Organizational Behavior, 23*(3), 267–285.

Aubert, B. A., & Kelsey, B. L. (2003). Further understanding of trust and performance in virtual teams. *Small Group Research, 34*(5), 575–618.

Axelrod, R. (1984). *The evolution of cooperation*. New York, NY: Basic Books.

Barrett, M. (2010). Boundary object use in cross-cultural software development teams. *Human Relations, 63*(8), 1199–1221.

Beal, D. J., Cohen, R. R., Burke, M. J., & McLendon, C. L. (2003). Cohesion and performance in groups: A meta-analytic clarification of construct relations. *Journal of Applied Psychology, 88*(6), 989.

Bijlsma-Frankema, K., Sitkin, S. B., & Weibel, A. (2015). Distrust in the balance: The emergence and development of intergroup distrust in a court of law. *Organization Science, 26*(4), 1018–1039.

Blau, P. (1964). *Exchange and power in social life*. New York, NY: John Wiley.

Bliese, P. D. (2000). Within-group agreement, non-independence, and reliability: Implications for data aggregation and analysis. In K. J. Klein & S. J. Kozlowski (eds.), *Multilevel theory, research, and methods in organizations: Foundations, extensions, and new directions* (pp. 349–381). San Francisco, CA: Jossey-Bass.

Bogenrieder, I., & Nooteboom, B. (2004). Learning groups: What types are there? A theoretical analysis and an empirical study in a consultancy firm. *Organization Studies, 25*(2), 287–313.

Brewer, M. (1979). In-group bias in the minimal intergroup situation: A cognitive-motivational analysis. *Psychological Bulletin, 86*(2), 307–324.

Brockner, J., Siegel, P. A., Daly, J. P., Tyler, T., & Martin, C. (1997). When trust matters: The moderating effect of outcome favorability. *Administrative Science Quarterly, 42*(3), 558–583.

Brower, H., Lester, S., Korsgaard, A., & Dineen, B. (2009). A closer look at trust between managers and subordinates: Understanding the effects of both trusting and being trusted on subordinate outcomes. *Journal of Management, 35*, 327–347.

Brown, M. E., Treviño, L. K., & Harrison, D. A. (2005). Ethical leadership: A social learning perspective for construct development and testing. *Organizational Behavior and Human Decision Processes, 97*(2), 117–134.

Caldwell, C., & Dixon, R. D. (2010). Love, forgiveness, and trust: Critical values of the modern leader. *Journal of Business Ethics, 93*(1), 91–101.

Cappelli, P., & Sherer, P. D. (1991). The missing role of context in OB: The need for a meso-level approach. *Research in Organizational Behavior, 13*, 55–110.

Carson, J. B., Tesluk, P. E., & Marrone, J. A. (2007). Shared leadership in teams: An investigation of antecedent conditions and performance. *Academy of Management Journal, 50*(5), 1217–1234.

Chan, D. (1998). Functional relations among constructs in the same content domain at different levels of analysis: A typology of composition models. *Journal of Applied Psychology, 83*(2), 234–246.

Chartrand, T. L., & Bargh, J. A. (1996). Automatic activation of social information processing goals: Nonconscious priming reproduces effects of explicit conscious instructions. *Journal of Personality and Social Psychology, 71*(3), 464–478.

Chattopadhyay, P., & George, E. (2001). Examining the effects of work externalization through the lens of social identity theory. *Journal of Applied Psychology, 86*(4), 781–788.

Chattopadhyay, P. (2003). Can dissimilarity lead to positive outcomes? The influence of open versus closed minds. *Journal of Organizational Behavior, 24*(3), 295–312.

Chattopadhyay, P., George, E., & Shulman, A. D. (2008). The asymmetrical influence of sex dissimilarity in distributive vs. colocated work groups. *Organization Science, 19*(4), 581–593.

Choi, J. (2008). Event justice perceptions and employees' reactions: Perceptions of social entity justice as a moderator. *Journal of Applied Psychology, 93*(3), 513–528.

Chou, L., Wang, A., Wang, T., Huang, M., & Cheng, B. (2008). Shared work values and team member effectiveness: The mediation of trustfulness and trustworthiness. *Human Relations, 61*(12), 1713–1742.

Chung, Y., & Jackson, S. E. (2013). The internal and external networks of knowledge-intensive teams: The role of task routineness. *Journal of Management, 39*(2), 442–468.

Clark, H. H. (1996). *Using language*. Cambridge, UK: Cambridge University Press.

Clark, M. C., & Payne, R. L. (1997). The nature and structure of workers' trust in management. *Journal of Organizational Behavior, 18*(3), 205–224.

Cohen-Charash, Y., & Spector, P. E. (2001). The role of justice in organizations: A meta-analysis. *Organizational Behavior and Human Decision Processes, 86*(2), 278–321.

Cohen, S. G., & Bailey, D. E. (1997). What makes teams work: Group effectiveness research from the shop floor to the executive suite. *Journal of Management, 23*(3), 239–290.

Coleman, J. S. (1988). Social capital in the creation of human capital. *American Journal of Sociology, 94*, 95–120.

Colquitt, J. A., Lepine, J. A., Piccolo, R. F., Zapata, C. P., & Rich, B. L. (2012). Explaining the justice-performance relationship: Trust as exchange deepener or trust as uncertainty reducer? *The Journal of Applied Psychology, 97*(1), 1–15.

Colquitt, J. A., LePine, J. A., Zapata, C. P., & Wild, R. (2011). Trust in typical and high-reliability contexts: Building and reacting to trust among firefighters. *Academy of Management Journal, 54*(5), 999–1015.

Colquitt, J. A., Scott, B. A., & LePine, J. A. (2007). Trust, trustworthiness, and trust propensity: A meta-analytic test of their unique relationships with risk taking and job performance. *Journal of Applied Psychology, 92*(4), 909–927.

Costa, A. (2003). Work team trust and effectiveness. *Personnel Review, 32*(5), 605–622.

Coyle-Shapiro, J. A., & Morrow, P. C. (2003). The role of individual differences in employee adoption of TQM orientation. *Journal of Vocational Behavior, 62*(2), 320–340.

Daft, R. L., & Lengel, R. H. (1986). Organizational information requirements, media richness and structural design. *Management Science, 32*(5), 554–571.

Dansereau, F., & Alutto, J. A. (1990). Level-of-analysis issues in climate and culture research. In B. Schneider (ed.), *Organizational climate and culture*: 193–236. San Francisco, CA: Jossey-Bass.

De Jong, B. A., & Dirks, K. T. (2012). Beyond shared perceptions of trust and monitoring in teams: Implications of asymmetry and dissensus, *Journal of Applied Psychology, 97*(2), 391–406.

De Jong, B. A., Dirks, K. T., & Gillespie, N. (2016). Trust and team performance: A meta-analysis of main effects, moderators, and covariates. *Journal of Applied Psychology, 101*(8), 1134–1150.

De Jong, B. A., & Elfring, T. (2010). How does trust affect the performance of ongoing teams? The mediating role of reflexivity, monitoring, and effort. *Academy of Management Journal, 53*(3), 535–549.

De Jong, S. B., Van der Vegt, G. S., & Molleman, E. (2007). The relationships among asymmetry in task dependence, perceived helping behavior, and trust. *Journal of Applied Psychology, 92*(6), 1625–1637.

DeChurch, L. A., & Mesmer-Magnus, J. R. (2010). The cognitive underpinnings of effective teamwork: A meta-analysis. *Journal of Applied Psychology, 95*(1), 32–53.

DeRosa, D. M., Hantula, D. A., Kock, N., & D'Arcy, J. (2004). Trust and leadership in virtual teamwork: A media naturalness perspective. *Human Resource Management, 43*(2–3), 219–232.

DeSanctis, G., & Poole, M. S. (1994). Capturing the complexity in advanced technology use: Adaptive structuration theory. *Organization Science, 5*(2), 121–147.

Deutsch, M. (1958). Trust and suspicion. *Journal of Conflict Resolution, 2*(4), 265–279.

Devine, D. J. (2002). A review and integration of classification systems relevant to teams in organizations. *Group Dynamics-Theory Research and Practice, 6*(4), 291–310.

Dirks, K. T. (1999). The effects of interpersonal trust on work group performance. *Journal of Applied Psychology, 84*(3), 445–455.

Dirks, K. T. (2000). Trust in leadership and team performance: Evidence from NCAA basketball. *Journal of Applied Psychology, 85*(6), 1004–1012.

Dirks, K. T., & Ferrin, D. L. (2001). The role of trust in organizational settings. *Organization Science, 12*(4), 450–467.

Dirks, K. T., & Ferrin, D. L. (2002). Trust in leadership: Meta-analytic findings and implications for research and practice. *Journal of Applied Psychology, 87*(4), 611–628.

Dirks, K. T., & Skarlicki, D. P. (2009). The relationship between being perceived as trustworthy by coworkers and individual performance. *Journal of Management, 35*, 136–157.

Edmondson, A. (1999). Psychological safety and learning behavior in work teams. *Administrative Science Quarterly, 44*(2), 350–383.

Edwards, J. R., & Cable, D. M. (2009). The value of value congruence. *Journal of Applied Psychology, 94*(3), 654–677.

Espinosa, J. A., Slaughter, S. A., Kraut, R. E., & Herbsleb, J. D. (2007). Familiarity, complexity, and team performance in geographically distributed software development. *Organization Science, 18*(4), 613–630.

Ferrin, D. L., Bligh, M. C., & Kohles, J. C. (2007). Can I trust you to trust me? A theory of trust, monitoring, and cooperation in interpersonal and intergroup relationships. *Group & Organization Management, 32*(4), 465–499.

Ferrin, D. L., Bligh, M. C., & Kohles, J. C. (2008). It takes two to tango: An interdependence analysis of the spiraling of perceived trustworthiness and cooperation in interpersonal and intergroup relationships. *Organizational Behavior and Human Decision Processes, 107*, 161–178.

Ferris, G. R., Liden, R. C., Munyon, T. P., Summers, J. K., Basik, K. J., & Buckley, M. R. (2009). Relationships at work: Toward a multidimensional conceptualization of dyadic work relationships. *Journal of Management, 35*(6), 1379–1403.

Ford, C. M., & Gioia, D. A. (2000). Factors influencing creativity in the domain of managerial decision making. *Journal of Management, 26*(4), 705–732.

Fulmer, C. A., & Gelfand, M. J. (2012). At what level (and in whom) we trust trust across multiple organizational levels. *Journal of Management, 38*(4), 1167–1230.

Gainey, T. W., & Klaas, B. S. (2003). The outsourcing of training and development: Factors impacting client satisfaction. *Journal of Management, 29*(2), 207–229.

Gambetta, D. (1988). Can we trust trust? In D. Gambetta (ed.), *Trust: Making and breaking cooperative relations* (pp. 213–237). Cambridge, MA: Basil Blackwell.

Giddens, A. (1984). *The constitution of society: Outline of the theory of structuration.* Berkeley, CA: University of California Press.

Gillespie, N. A., & Mann, L. (2004). Transformational leadership and shared values: The building blocks of trust. *Journal of Managerial Psychology, 19*(6), 588–607.

Gilson, L. L., Maynard, M. T., Young, N. C. J., Vartiainen, M., & Hakonen, M. (2015). Virtual teams research 10 years, 10 themes, and 10 opportunities. *Journal of Management, 41*(5), 1313–1337.

Golden, T. D., & Raghuram, S. (2010). Teleworker knowledge sharing and the role of altered relational and technological interactions. *Journal of Organizational Behavior, 31*(8), 1061–1085.

Graen, G. B., & Uhl-Bien, M. (1995). Relationship-based approach to leadership: Development of leader-member exchange (LMX) theory of leadership over 25 years: Applying a multi-level multi-domain perspective. *Leadership Quarterly, 6*(2), 219–247.

Grant, A. M., & Sumanth, J. J. (2009). Mission possible? The performance of prosocially motivated employees depends on manager trustworthiness. *Journal of Applied Psychology, 94*(4), 927–944.

Guzzo, R. A., & Dickson, M. W. (1996). Teams in organizations: Recent research on performance and effectiveness. *Annual Review of Psychology, 47*(1), 307–338.

Haas, M. R. (2006). Acquiring and applying knowledge in transnational teams: The roles of cosmopolitans and locals. *Organization Science, 17*(3), 367–384.

Hackman, J. R. (1987). The design of work teams. In J. Lorsch (ed.), *Handbook of organizational behavior* (pp. 315–342). Englewood Cliffs, NJ: Prentice-Hall.

Hackman, J. R. (1990). *Groups that work (and those that don't).* San Francisco, CA: Jossey-Bass.

Hackman, J. R. (2002). *Leading teams: Setting the stage for great performances.* Boston, MA: Harvard Business School Press.

Hackman, J. R., & Walton, R. E. (1986). Leading groups in organizations. In: P. S. Goodman, et al. (eds), *Designing effective work groups* (pp. 72–119). San Francisco: Jossey-Bass.

Handy, C. (1995). Trust and the virtual organization. *Harvard Business Review, 73*(3), 40–50.

Hays, J. C., & Williams, J. R. (2011). Testing multiple motives in feedback seeking: The interaction of instrumentality and self protection motives. *Journal of Vocational Behavior, 79*(2), 496–504.

Heider, F. (1958). *The psychology of interpersonal relations.* New York, NY: John Wiley.

Hempel, P. S., Zhang, Z. X., & Tjosvold, D. (2009). Conflict management between and within teams for trusting relationships and performance in China. *Journal of Organizational Behavior, 30*(1), 41–65.

Hernandez, M. (2008). Promoting stewardship behavior in organizations: A leadership model. *Journal of Business Ethics, 80*(1), 121–128.

Hinds, P. J., & Bailey, D. E. (2003). Out of sight, out of sync: Understanding conflict in distributed teams. *Organization Science, 14*(6), 615–632.

Hinds, P. J., & Mortensen, M. (2005). Understanding conflict in geographically distributed teams: The moderating effects of shared identity, shared context, and spontaneous communication. *Organization Science, 16*(3), 290–307.

Hogg, M. A., & Terry, D. J. (2000). Social identity and self-categorisation processes in organizational contexts. *Academy of Management Review. 25*(1), 121–140.

Howorth, C., Westhead, P., & Wright, M. (2004). Buyouts, information asymmetry and the family management dyad. *Journal of Business Venturing, 19*(4), 509–534.

Huang, X., Iun, J., Liu, A., & Gong, Y. (2010). Does participative leadership enhance work performance by inducing empowerment or trust? The differential effects on managerial and non-managerial subordinates. *Journal of Organizational Behavior, 31*(1), 122–143.

Ilgen, D. R., Hollenbeck, J. R., Johnson, M., & Jundt, D. (2005). Teams in organizations: From input-process-output models to IMOI models. *Annual Review Psychology, 56*, 517–543.

Janowicz-Panjaitan, M., & Krishnan, R. (2009). Measures for dealing with competence and integrity violations of interorganizational trust at the corporate and operating levels of organizational hierarchy. *Journal of Management Studies, 46*(2), 245–268.

Jarvenpaa, S. L., & Leidner, D. E. (1999). Communication and trust in global virtual teams. *Organization Science, 10*, 791–815.

Jarvenpaa, S. L., Shaw, T. R., & Staples, D. S. (2004). Toward contextualized theories of trust: The role of trust in global virtual teams. *Information Systems Research, 15*(3), 250–267.

Jehn, K. A., & Mannix, E. A. (2001). The dynamic nature of conflict: A longitudinal study of intragroup conflict and group performance. *Academy of Management Journal, 44*(2), 238–251.

Jiang, C. X., Chua, R. Y., Kotabe, M., & Murray, J. Y. (2011). Effects of cultural ethnicity, firm size, and firm age on senior executives' trust in their overseas business partners: Evidence from China. *Journal of International Business Studies, 42*(9), 1150–1173.

Johns, G. (2006). The essential impact of context on organizational behavior. *Academy of Management Review, 31*(2), 386–408.

Johnson, D., & Grayson, K. (2005). Cognitive and affective trust in service relationships. *Journal of Business research, 58*(4), 500–507.

Joshi, A., Lazarova, M. B., & Liao, H. (2009). Getting everyone on board: The role of inspirational leadership in geographically dispersed teams. *Organization Science, 20*(1), 240–252.

Jung, D. I., & Avolio, B. J. (2000). Opening the black box: An experimental investigation of the mediating effects of trust and value congruence on transformational and transactional leadership. *Journal of Organizational Behavior, 21*(8), 949–964.

Jung, D., Yammarino, F. J., & Lee, J. K. (2009). Moderating role of subordinates' attitudes on transformational leadership and effectiveness: A multi-cultural and multi-level perspective. *Leadership Quarterly, 20*(4), 586–603.

Kalshoven, K., Den Hartog, D. N., & De Hoogh, A. H. (2011). Ethical leadership at work questionnaire: Development and validation of a multidimensional measure. *Leadership Quarterly, 22*(1), 51–69.

Keenan, P. A., & Carnevale, P. J. (1989). Positive effects of within-group cooperation on between-group negotiation. *Journal of Applied Social Psychology, 19*(12), 977–992.

Khazanchi, S., & Masterson, S. S. (2011). Who and what is fair matters: A multi-foci social exchange model of creativity. *Journal of Organizational Behavior, 32*(1), 86–106.

Kickul, J., Gundry, L. K., & Posig, M. (2005). Does trust matter? The relationship between equity sensitivity and perceived organizational justice. *Journal of Business Ethics, 56*(3), 205–218.

Kirkman, B. L., & Mathieu, J. E. (2005). The dimensions and antecedents of team virtuality. *Journal of Management, 31*(5), 700–718.

Klein, K., Dansereau, F., & Hall, R. (1994). Levels issues in theory development, data collection, and analysis. *Academy of Management Review, 19*(2), 195–229.

Klimoski, R., & Mohammed, S. (1994). Team mental model: Construct or metaphor? *Journal of Management, 20*(2), 403–437.

Korsgaard, M., Brodt, S. E., & Whitener, E. M. (2002). Trust in the face of conflict: The role of managerial trustworthy behavior and organizational context. *Journal of Applied Psychology, 87*(2), 312–319.

Korsgaard, M. A., Brower, H., & Lester, S. (2015). It isn't always mutual: a critical review of dyadic trust, *Journal of Management, 41*(1), 47–70.

Kozlowski, S. W., & Ilgen, D. R. (2006). Enhancing the Effectiveness of Work Groups and Teams. *Psychological Science in the Public Interest, 7*(3), 77–124.

Langfred, C. (2004). Too much of a good thing? Negative effects of high trust and individual autonomy in self-managing teams. *Academy of Management Journal, 47*(3), 385–399.

Langfred, C. (2007). The downside of self-management: A longitudinal study of the effects of conflict on trust, autonomy, and task interdependence in self-managing teams. *Academy of Management Journal, 50*(4), 885–900.

Lapidot, Y., Kark, R., & Shamir, B. (2007). The impact of situational vulnerability on the development and erosion of followers' trust in their leader. *Leadership Quarterly, 18*(1), 16–34.

Lau, D. C., & Liden, R. C. (2008). Antecedents of coworker trust: Leaders' blessings. *Journal of Applied Psychology, 93*(5), 1130–1138.

Lawler, E. E., Mohrman, S. A., & Ledford, G. E. (1992). *Employee involvement and total quality management: Practices and results in Fortune 1000 companies* (1st edn). The Jossey-Bass management series. San Francisco, CA: Jossey-Bass.

Levin, D. Z., & Cross, R. (2004). The strength of weak ties you can trust: The mediating role of trust in effective knowledge transfer. *Management Science, 50*(11), 1477–1490.

Levine, D., & D'Andrea Tyson, L. (1990). Participation, productivity, and the firm's environment. In A. S. Blinder (ed.), *Paying for productivity* (pp. 183–237). Washington, DC: Brookings Inst.

Li, A., & Cropanzano, R. (2009). Do East Asians respond more/less strongly to organizational justice than North Americans? A meta-analysis. *Journal of Management Studies, 46*(5), 787–805.

Luhmann, N. (1988). Familiarity, Confidence, Trust: Problems and Perspectives. In D. Gambetta (ed.), *Trust: Making and breaking cooperative relations* (pp. 94–107). New York, NY: Blackwell.

Mäkelä, K., & Brewster, C. (2009). Interunit interaction contexts, interpersonal social capital, and the differing levels of knowledge sharing. *Human Resource Management, 48*(4), 591–613.

Malhotra, D., & Murnighan, J. K. (2002). The effects of contracts on interpersonal trust. *Administrative Science Quarterly, 47*(3), 534–559.

Mannix, E. A., Griffith, T., & Neale, M. A. (2002). The phenomenology of conflict in distributed work teams. In P. Hinds & S. Kiesler (eds), *Distributed Work* (pp. 213–233). Cambridge, MA: The MIT Press.

Marcus-Newhall, A., Pedersen, W. C., Carlson, M., & Miller, N. (2000). Displaced aggression is alive and well: A meta-analytic review. *Journal of Personality and Social Psychology, 78*(4), 670–689.

Mathieu, J., Maynard, M. T., Rapp, T., & Gilson, L. (2008). Team effectiveness 1997–2007: A review of recent advancements and a glimpse into the future. *Journal of Management, 34*(3), 410–476.

Mawritz, M. B., Mayer, D. M., Hoobler, J. M., Wayne, S. J., & Marinova, S. V. (2012). A trickle-down model of abusive supervision. *Personnel Psychology, 65*(2), 325–357.

Mayer, D. M., Kuenzi, M., Greenbaum, R. L., Bardes, M., & Salvador, R. (2009). How does ethical leadership flow? Test of a trickle-down model. *Organizational Behavior and Human Decision Processes, 108*(1), 1–13.

Mayer, R. C., & Davis, J. H. (1999). The effect of the performance appraisal system on trust for management: A field quasi-experiment. *Journal of Applied Psychology, 84*(1), 123–136.

Mayer, R. C., Davis, J. H., & Schoorman, F. D. (1995). An integrative model of organizational trust. *Academy of Management Review, 20*(3), 709–734.

Maznevski, M. L., & Chudoba, K. M. (2000). Bridging space over time: Global virtual team dynamics and effectiveness. *Organization Science, 11*(5), 473–492.

McAllister, D. J. (1995). Affect-and cognition-based trust as foundations for interpersonal cooperation in organizations. *Academy of Management Journal, 38*(1), 24–59.

McEvily, B., & Tortoriello, M. (2011). Measuring trust in organisational research: Review and recommendations. *Journal of Trust Research, 1*(1), 23–63.

McKnight, D. H., Cummings, L. L., & Chervany, N. L. (1998). Initial trust formation in new organizational relationships. *Academy of Management Review, 23*(3), 473–490.

McNish, J., & Silcoff, S. (2015). *Losing the signal: The untold story behind the extraordinary rise and spectacular fall of Blackberry*. New York, NY: Flatiron Books

Millar, C., & Choi, C. (2009). Networks, social norms and knowledge sub-networks. *Journal of Business Ethics, 90*(4), 565–574.

Mohammed, S., Ferzandi, L., & Hamilton, K. (2010). Metaphor no more: A 15-year review of the team mental model construct. *Journal of Management* (online first).

Möllering, G. (2001). The nature of trust: from Georg Simmel to a theory of expectation, interpretation and suspension. *Sociology, 35*(2), 403–420.

Montes, S. D., & Irving, P. G. (2008). Disentangling the effects of promised and delivered inducements: Relational and transactional contract elements and the mediating role of trust. *Journal of Applied Psychology, 93*(6), 1367–1381.

Morgeson, F. P., DeRue, D. S., & Karam, E. P. (2010). Leadership in teams: A functional approach to understanding leadership structures and processes. *Journal of Management, 36*, 5–39.

Mowday, R. T., & Sutton, R. I. (1993). Organizational behavior: Linking individuals and groups to organizational contexts. *Annual Review of Psychology, 44*(1), 195–229.

Naumann, S. E., & Bennett, N. (2000). A case for procedural justice climate: Development and test of a multilevel model. *Academy of Management Journal, 43*(5), 881–889.

Newell, S., David, G., & Chand, D. (2007). An analysis of trust among globally distributed work teams in an organizational setting. *Knowledge and Process Management, 14*(3), 158–168.

Nienaber, A-M., Romeike, P. D., Searle, R., & Schewe, G. (2015). A qualitative meta-analysis of trust in supervisor-subordinate relationships. *Journal of Managerial Psychology, 30*(5), 507–534.

Nonaka, I. (1994). A dynamic theory of organizational knowledge creation. *Organization Science, 5*(1), 14–37.

O'Hara-Devereaux, M., & Johansen, R. (1994). *Globalwork: Bridging distance, culture, and time*. San Francisco, CA: Jossey-Bass Publishers.

Palanski, M. E., Kahai, S. S., & Yammarino, F. J. (2011). Team virtues and performance: An examination of transparency, behavioral integrity, and trust. *Journal of Business Ethics, 99*(2), 201–216.

Parker, S. K., Williams, H. M., & Turner, N. (2006). Modeling the antecedents of proactive behavior at work. *Journal of Applied Psychology, 91*(3), 636–652.

Perrone, V., Zaheer, A., & McEvily, B. (2003). Free to be trusted? Organizational constraints on trust in boundary spanners. *Organization Science, 14*(4), 422–439.

Peterson, R. S., & Behfar, K. J. (2003). The dynamic relationship between performance feedback, trust, and conflict in groups: A longitudinal study. *Organizational Behavior and Human Decision Processes, 92*(1), 102–112.

Pillai, R., Schriesheim, C., & Williams, E. (1999). Fairness perceptions and trust as mediators for transformational and transactional leadership: A two sample study. *Journal of Management, 25*, 897–933.

Polzer, J., Crisp, C., Jarvenpaa, S., & Kim, J. (2006). Extending the faultline model to geographically dispersed teams: How colocated subgroups can impair group functioning. *Academy of Management Journal, 49*(4), 679–692.

Premeaux, S., & Bedeian, A. G. (2003). Breaking the silence: The moderating effects of self-monitoring in predicting speaking up in the workplace. *Journal of Management Studies, 40*(6), 1537–1562.

Priem, R. L., & Nystrom, P. C. (2014). Exploring the dynamics of workgroup fracture common ground, trust-with-trepidation, and warranted distrust. *Journal of Management, 40*(3), 764–795.

Putnam, R. D. (1995). Bowling alone: America's declining social capital. *Journal of Democracy, 6*(1), 65–78.

Raes, A. M., Heijltjes, M. G., Glunk, U., & Roe, R. A. (2011). The interface of the top management team and middle managers: A process model. *Academy of Management Review, 36*(1), 102–126.

Restubog, S. L. D., Hornsey, M. J., Bordia, P., & Esposo, S. R. (2008). Effects of psychological contract breach on organizational citizenship behaviour: Insights from the group value model. *Journal of Management Studies, 45*(8), 1377–1400.

Rhoades, L., & Eisenberger, R. (2002). Perceived organizational support: A review of the literature. *Journal of Applied Psychology, 87*(4), 698–714.

Robinson, S. (1996). Trust and breach of the psychological contract. *Administrative Science Quarterly, 41*(4), 574–599.

Romeike, P., Nienaber, A.-M., & Schewe, G. (2016). How differences in perceptions of own and team performance impact trust and job satisfaction in virtual teams. *Human Performance, 29*, 291–309.

Rosanas, J. (2008). Beyond economic criteria: A humanistic approach to organizational survival. *Journal of Business Ethics, 78*(3), 447–462.

Rosanas, J. M., & Velilla, M. (2003). Loyalty and trust as the ethical bases of organizations. *Journal of Business Ethics, 44*(1), 49–59.

Rotter, J. B. (1980). Interpersonal trust, trustworthiness, and gullibility. *American Psychologist, 35*(1), 1–7.

Rousseau, D. M., Sitkin, S. B., Burt, R. S., & Camerer, C. (1998). Not so different after all: A cross-discipline view of trust. *Academy of Management Review, 23*(3), 393–404.

Roussin, C. (2008). Increasing trust, psychological safety, and team performance through dyadic leadership discovery. *Small Group Research, 39*(2), 224–248.

Ruppel, C. P., & Harrington, S. J. (2000). The relationship of communication, ethical work climate, and trust to commitment and innovation. *Journal of Business Ethics, 25*(4), 313–328.

Schaubroeck, J., Lam, S. S., & Peng, A. C. (2011). Cognition-based and affect-based trust as mediators of leader behavior influences on team performance. *Journal of Applied Psychology, 96*(4), 863.

Schoorman, F. D., Mayer, R. C., & Davis, J. H. (2007). An integrative model of organizational trust: Past, present, and future. *Academy of Management Review, 32*(2), 344–354.

Scott, S. G., & Einstein, W. O. (2001). Strategic performance appraisal in team-based organizations: One size does not fit all. *Academy of Management Executive, 15*(2), 107–116.

Serva, M. A., Fuller, M. A., & Mayer, R. C. (2005). The reciprocal nature of trust: A longitudinal study of interacting teams. *Journal of Organizational Behavior, 26*(6), 625–648.

Shamir, B., & Lapidot, Y. (2003). Trust in organizational superiors: Systemic and collective considerations. *Organization Studies, 24*(3), 463–491.

Shore, L. M., Randel, A. E., Chung, B. G., Dean, M. A., Ehrhart, K. H., & Singh, G. (2011). Inclusion and diversity in work groups: A review and model for future research. *Journal of Management, 37*(4), 1262–1289.

Simmons, B. L., Gooty, J., Nelson, D. L., & Little, L. M. (2009). Secure attachment: Implications for hope, trust, burnout, and performance. *Journal of Organizational Behavior, 30*(2), 233–247.

Simons, T., Friedman, R., Liu, L. A., & Parks, J. M. (2007). Racial differences in sensitivity to behavioral integrity: Attitudinal consequences, in-group effects, and "trickle-down" among black and non-black employees. *Journal of Applied Psychology, 92*(3), 650–665.

Simons, T. L., & Peterson, R. S. (2000). Task conflict and relationship conflict in top management teams: The pivotal role of intragroup trust. *Journal of Applied Psychology, 85*(1), 102–111.

Sniezek, J. A., & Van Swol, L. M. (2001). Trust, confidence, and expertise in a judge-advisor system. *Organizational Behavior and Human Decision Processes, 84*(2), 288–307.

Song, F. (2009). Intergroup trust and reciprocity in strategic interactions: Effects of group decision-making mechanism. *Organizational Behavior and Human Decision Processes, 108*(1), 164–173.

Stalnaker, R. (2002). Common ground. *Linguistics and Philosophy, 25*(5), 701–721.

Staw, B. M., Sutton, R. I., & Pelled, L. H. (1994). Employee positive emotion and favorable outcomes at the workplace. *Organization Science, 5*(1), 51–71.

Sundstrom, E. (1999). *Supporting work team effectiveness: Best management practices for fostering high performance.* San Francisco, CA: Jossey-Bass.

Tajfel, H. (1978). Social categorisation, social identity and social comparison. In H. Tajfel (ed.), *Differentiation between social groups: Studies in the social psychology of inter-group relations* (pp. 61–76). London, UK: Academic Press.

Tajfel, H., & Turner, J. C. (1986). An integrative theory of intergroup conflict. In S. Worchel & W. Austin (eds), *Psychology of intergroup relations* (pp. 2–24). Chicago, IL: Nelson-Hall.

Tedeschi, J. T., & Norman, N. M. (1985). A social psychological interpretation of displaced aggression. *Advances in Group Processes, 2*, 29–56.

Tepper, B. J., & Taylor, E. C. (2003). Relationships among supervisors' and subordinates' procedural justice perceptions and organizational citizenship behaviors. *Academy of Management Journal, 46*(1), 97–105.

Tomlinson, E., & Mayer, R. (2009). The role of casual attribution dimensions in trust repair. *Academy of Management Review, 34*(1), 85–104.

Tomlinson, E. C., Dineen, B. R., & Lewicki, R. J. (2009). Trust congruence among integrative negotiators as a predictor of joint-behavior outcomes. *International Journal of Conflict Management, 20*, 173–187.

Townsend, A. M., DeMarie, S. M., & Hendrickson, A. R. (1998). Virtual teams: Technology and the workplace of the future. *Academy of Management Executive, 12*(3), 17–29.

Tsai, W. (2001). Knowledge transfer in intraorganizational networks: Effects of network position and absorptive capacity on business unit innovation and performance. *Academy of Management Journal, 44*(5), 996–1004.

Tsai, W., & Ghoshal, S. (1998). Social capital and value creation: The role of intrafirm networks. *Academy of Management Journal, 41*(4), 464–476.

Turner, J. C. (1982). Towards a cognitive redefinition of the social group. In H. Tajfel (ed.), *Social Identity and Intergroup Relations* (pp. 15–40). New York, NY: Cambridge University Press.

Turner, J. C., Hogg, M. A., Oakes, P. J., Reicher, S. D., & Wetherell, M. S. (1987). *Rediscovering the social group. A self-categorization theory.* Oxford, UK: Basil Blackwell.

Tversky, A., & Kahneman, D. (1986). Rational choice and the framing of decisions. *Journal of Business, 59*(4), 251–278.

Van der Werff, L., Real, C., & Lynn, T. (forthcoming). Individual trust and the internet. In R. Searle, A. Nienaber, & S. Sitkin (eds.), *Trust*. Oxford, UK: Routledge.

Walumbwa, F. O., Luthans, F., Avey, J. B., & Oke, A. (2011). Authentically leading groups: The mediating role of collective psychological capital and trust. *Journal of Organizational Behavior, 32*(1), 4–24.

Wang, S., Tomlinson, E. C., & Noe, R. A. (2010). The role of mentor trust and protégé internal locus of control in formal mentoring relationships. *Journal of Applied Psychology, 95*(2), 358–367.

Weiner, B. (1992). *Human motivation: Metaphors, theories, and research.* Thousand Oaks, CA: Sage.

Whitener, E. (2001). Do "high commitment" human resource practices affect employee commitment? A cross-level analysis using hierarchical linear modeling. *Journal of Management, 27*(5), 515–535.

Williams, M. (2001). In whom we trust: Group membership as an affective context for trust development. *Academy of Management Review, 26*(3), 377–396.

Wilson, J. M., Straus, S. G., & McEvily, B. (2006). All in due time: The development of trust in computer-mediated and face-to-face teams. *Organizational Behavior and Human Decision Processes, 99*(1), 16–33.

Wo, D. X., Ambrose, M. L., & Schminke, M. (2015). What drives trickle-down effects? A test of multiple mediation processes. *Academy of Management Journal, 58*(6), 1848–1868.

Wong, A., & Tjosvold, D. (2010). Guanxi and conflict management for effective partnering with competitors in China. *British Journal of Management, 21*(3), 772–788.

Yakovleva, M., Reilly, R. R., & Werko, R. (2010). Why do we trust? Moving beyond individual to dyadic perceptions. *Journal of Applied Psychology, 95*(1), 79–91.

Yang, J., Mossholder, K. W., & Peng, T. K. (2009). Supervisory procedural justice effects: The mediating roles of cognitive and affective trust. *Leadership Quarterly, 20*(2), 143–154.

Young, A. M., & Perrewé, P. L. (2000). What did you expect? An examination of career related support and social support among mentors and protégés. *Journal of Management, 26*(4), 611–632.

Zaccaro, S. J., Rittman, A. L., & Marks, M. A. (2002). Team leadership. *The Leadership Quarterly, 12*(4), 451–483.

Zhao, H., Wayne, S., Glibkowski, B., & Bravo, J. (2007). The impact of psychological contract breach on work-related outcomes: A meta-analysis. *Personnel Psychology, 60*(3), 647–680.

7

COOPERATION AND COORDINATION

The role of trust in inter-organizational relationships

Anna Brattström and Reinhard Bachmann

Introduction

How should we understand the role of trust in inter-organizational relationships? Trust refers to the 'willingness of one party to be vulnerable to the actions of another party based on the expectations that the other will perform a particular action important to the trustor, irrespectively of the ability to monitor or control that other party' (Mayer, Davis, & Schoorman, 1995: 712). The prevailing view in inter-organizational trust research is of trust as a mechanism, which entails a mutual willingness to accept vulnerability in the inter-organizational relationship (Mayer et al., 1995). Hence, inter-organizational trust research has suggested that trust makes partners willing to rely on each other, even though the other is potentially opportunistic, goals may be misaligned and the ability to monitor or control the other party is limited (Dyer & Singh, 1998; Zaheer & Venkatraman, 1995). In short, trust has been understood as a mechanism that eases concerns of opportunism and thereby enables cooperation.

Yet, within the broader stream of research on inter-organizational governance, it is increasingly acknowledged that cooperation is only one facet of inter-organizational collaboration (e.g. Faems, Janssens, Madhok, & Van Looy, 2008; Gulati, Wohlgezogen, & Zhelyazkov, 2012; Lumineau, 2015). In this research stream, scholars have emphasized that set aside cooperation – inter-organizational relationships can also fail, merely because partners are unable to effectively *coordinate* their joint activities (Gulati et al., 2012). Inter-organizational governance scholars therefore have started to make a conceptual distinction between *cooperation concerns*, stemming from misaligned incentives, and *coordination concerns*, stemming from misaligned activities, in inter-organizational relationships (e.g. Dekker, 2004; Faems et al., 2008; Gulati & Singh, 1998; Gulati et al., 2012; Lumineau, 2017; Malhotra & Lumineau, 2011). Because coordination can be challenging, independent of whether cooperation concerns are present or not (and vice versa), inter-organizational governance research increasingly sees cooperation and coordination as distinct facets of inter-organizational relationships, which are not necessarily related.

The conceptual distinction between cooperation and coordination has enabled a more complete understanding of inter-organizational governance. Gulati and Singh (1998), for example, relied on this distinction to theorize a more complete view of contracts, suggesting that contracts have both cooperative and coordinative clauses, each having distinct implications for inter-organizational governance. Lumineau and Verbeke (2016) even propose that inter-organizational governance theory has too much focused on cooperation and opportunism, suggesting that coordination should be assigned a more prominent role in theorizing inter-organizational relationships. Yet, inter-organizational trust research has tended to one-handedly see trust as a mechanism that facilitates cooperation, while not making explicit if and how trust can also play a coordinative role in inter-organizational relationships (see Zhong et al., 2017 for a meta-analysis and review). In other literature (e.g. Bachmann, 2001), the latter has been suggested to be fundamental in boundary-transcending relationships, but here cooperation is not systematically taken into account. In this chapter, we therefore unpack this conceptual distinction, with the purpose of developing a comprehensive and, at the same time, nuanced understanding of the role of trust in inter-organizational relationships.

In so doing, we discuss and compare four theoretical perspectives on inter-organizational trust: (1) rational choice theory, (2) transaction cost theory, (3) social exchange theory and (4) neo-institutional theory. We discuss how the role of trust for cooperation and coordination is explicitly or implicitly conceptualized within each of these perspectives. Building on these insights, we also discuss how the underlying assumptions of these different theoretical perspectives yield divergent perspectives on the role of trust in inter-organizational relationships. Finally, we rely on the distinction between coordination and cooperation to outline important questions for future research.

Cooperation and coordination – conceptual distinctions

Inter-organizational relationships, or 'repeated, contract-based transactions of idiosyncratic assets between the same organizations' (Ring & van de Ven, 1992: 483) encompass diverse forms, ranging from joint ventures, alliances and buyer–supplier relationships to informal collaborations and R&D consortia. They allow an organization to focus on its core activities and develop its own, distinct resource base, while at the same time, relying on their partnering organizations to supplement or complement their own resources (Doz & Hamel, 1998).

Cooperation concerns

A common challenge in inter-organizational relationships is the difficulty of sustaining cooperation when objectives are misaligned. Gulati et al. (2012: 3) define this challenge as *cooperation concerns*, referring to the 'joint pursuit of agreed-on goal(s) in a manner corresponding to a shared understanding about contributions and payoffs'. To some extent, each firm in an inter-organizational relationship has its own, distinct objectives. Therefore, each party may also have incentives to maximize the own firm's gains at the partner's expense. Such misalignment of goals gives rise to cooperation concerns.

Consider, for example, an R&D alliance between two firms. In this type of inter-organizational relationships, each firm makes investments in knowledge and other intangible resources, which are difficult to measure, monitor and follow up. Consequently, there is a risk of opportunistic behaviour. This includes, for example, one party freeriding on the other. One firm may also decide to leak knowledge or in other ways use the R&D output that is created within the relationship for its own benefit outside the alliance. In short, cooperation concerns arise when there is a risk that one partner behaves in a way that benefits the own firm, but which is a disadvantage for the partner organization. Such misalignment of goals can lead to a gradual deterioration of engagement in the relationship. In an instructive case study, Doz (1996) shows that failure to align incentives triggers a vicious circle where learning and understanding are hampered and frustration increasing. This, consequently, increases the likelihood of inter-organizational failure.

Coordination concerns

Another challenge in inter-organizational relationships is the coordination of activities (e.g. Dekker, 2004; Faems et al., 2008; Gulati et al., 2012; Lumineau, 2017; Thompson, 1967). We refer to this challenge as *coordination concerns*, or the 'deliberate and orderly alignment or adjustment of partners' actions to achieve jointly determined goals' (Gulati et al., 2012: 7). Different from cooperation concerns, coordination concerns do not arise because partners are opportunistic or unwilling to work together for the benefit of their own firms. Instead, coordination concerns arise because partners are unable to effectively align interdependent activities. Coordination concerns can therefore arise independently of whether cooperation concerns are present or not (and vice versa).

There are many reasons why coordination concerns arise in inter-organizational relation-ships. Collaborating partners may, for example, lack shared systems and routines, which makes coordination difficult. Or, the collaboration may involve multiple individuals at multiple hierarchical levels, which also makes coordination of inter-organizational more complex and difficult. As another example, consider an inter-organizational relationship that crosses cultural and institutional boundaries. This is a setting where partners – independent of whether *incentives* are aligned or not – can find it challenging to effectively coordinate work, especially when the collaborating firms operate under different cultural practices.

The relationship between cooperation and coordination

Both coordination concerns and cooperation concerns exist in inter-organizational relationships, but they do not necessarily co-vary (Gulati et al., 2012). Cooperation concerns are resolved by aligning incentives and preventing stealing, knowledge leakage or lying, or in other ways sus-taining commitment to the inter-organizational relationships. Coordination concern requires a different set of mechanisms, related to finding practices and routines for coordinating work tasks and transferring knowledge. Therefore, the resolving of cooperation concerns does not auto-matically mean that partners will also be able to coordinate their joint activities and interactions. Partners may be unable to align their activities; focus their efforts; or accomplish joint tasks, not because they do not intend to do so, but because they are unable to coordinate their (tacit) assumptions and behaviours (Gulati et al., 2012). In a similar vein, the resolving of coordination concerns does not necessarily mean that partners cannot be concerned about the possibility of opportunism and misaligned cooperation incentives. In a case study, Faems et al. (2008) demonstrate how a contract with strong coordinative clauses enabled the continuation of an inter-organizational relationship, even though partners did not have positive expectations about the other party's intention to perform according to the agreement, i.e. to cooperate. In other words, they were able to coordinate their expectations, in spite of cooperation concerns being present. Thus we conclude that cooperation and coordination are two distinct facets of inter-organizational collaboration (Gulati et al., 2012).

Perspectives on the role of trust in inter-organizational relationships

In this chapter, we aim to more carefully specify the coordinative and cooperative roles of trust in inter-organizational relationships. Extant research, in contrast, has tended to focus primarily on the role of trust to resolve cooperation concerns, but remains relatively silent on the role of trust with regard to the coordination of expectations in inter-organizational relations (Zhong et al., 2017). Within research on trust and control, for example, trust is seen as a mechanism that resolves cooperation concerns, whereas control is discussed both in cooperative and coordinative dimensions (e.g. Brattström & Richtnér, 2014; Dekker, 2004; Faems et al., 2008; Lumineau, 2017; Long & Sitkin, 2006; Malhotra & Lumineau, 2011). By distinguishing the coordinative dimension from the cooperative dimension of *control*, this literature has moved beyond a simplistic dichotomy being assumed between these two mechanisms (e.g. Faems et al., 2008). At the same time, this literature remained more silent on the role of trust for coordination.

In other literatures (e.g. Bachmann, 2001), the coordinative role of trust is much more explicit. Within this literature, trust is assumed to increase stability and predictability in inter-organizational relationships, thereby facilitating coordination of tasks. At the same time, this line of research remains more silent on the relationship between trust and cooperation.

In this chapter, we build on and extend prior research by discussing the extent to which trust can also be seen as a mechanism that resolves both cooperation and coordination in inter-organizational relationships. To fulfil this purpose, we scrutinize four fundamental theoretical perspectives that are often applied to theorize the role of trust in inter-organizational relationships: (1) rational choice theory, (2) transaction cost theory, (3) social exchange theory and (4) neo-institutional theory. In order to allow for comparison and to identify underlying assumptions, we first discuss how each of these theoretical perspectives conceptualizes trust and its development. Second, we discuss how scholars have relied on each theory to understand the role of trust for resolving cooperation and coordination concerns in inter-organizational relationships. Table 7.1 provides an overview of this analysis.

Rational choice theory and trust

Conceptual background

In this theoretical perspective it is assumed that the behaviour of actors (i.e. individuals or organizations) is best explained by reference to the idea that actors are calculative, opportunistic and profit-maximizing. Basically all economic theories, including transaction cost economics, build on this notion, but also in sociological theory this premise can be found. For example, Coleman (1990) is a prominent sociological scholar who represents the rational choice approach. Rational choice theory tends to see each actor in relative isolation. It can take environmental arrangements into consideration when social actors make their decisions, but this approach would only treat these as external variables rather than as constitutive parts of social processes and relationships within which social actors' decisions are embedded. Such external factors are seen as having a very specific and clearly defined influence on actors' calculations rather than just shaping the ideas that actors develop in specific environments. Rational choice would thus claim to be able to make predictions about social actors' behaviour. Calculation, after all, is a formal process based on clearly defined principles. The fact that actors may deal with vague knowledge in an intuitive manner, as well as behaving differently across different cultural backgrounds, is not seen as a useful premise when the behaviour of social actors, let them be individuals or organizations, is to be explained.

Table 7.1 Trust, cooperation and coordination in inter-organizational settings

	Rational choice theory	Transaction cost economics	Social exchange theory	Neo-institutional theory
Conceptual background	Trust is seen as an outcome of rational calculations – actors trust when they consider it rational to do so.	In extended versions of the transaction cost framework, trust is seen as a 'shift parameter' that enables less formal governance, or a more flexible use of formal governance.	Trust is seen as a taken-for-granted outcome of favourable social exchange.	Trust is seen as a fact of life, present in all kinds of interaction.
Mechanisms through which trust resolves cooperation concerns in inter-organizational relationships	Trust enables risk taking in inter-organizational relationships since violation of trust would be irrational.	Trust eases concerns of opportunism since it enables risk taking *as if* opportunism was not a problem.	Trust eases concerns of opportunism since violations of trust would violate relation-specific norms that are established in the dyadic relationship.	The issue of cooperation failure is not seen as a key aspect of trust.
Mechanisms through which trust resolves coordination concerns in inter-organizational relationships	The issue of coordination failure is not seen as a key aspect of trust.	Trust allows for a more flexible application of formal governance and resolving of conflict, thus facilitating coordination.	Indirectly, trust facilitates coordination by enabling a more flexible coordination of tasks.	Institutionalized trust induces stability and predictability in relationships and thereby facilitates coordination.
Representative references	Coleman (1990) Buskens (2002) Hardin (2002)	Gulati and Nickerson (2008) Williamson (1991) Williamson (1993) Vanneste et al. (2014)	Das & Teng (2002) Blau (1968) McEvily et al. (2003) Lioukas & Reuer (2015)	Zucker (1986) Bachmann (2001) Bachmann and Inkpen (2011)

The rational choice and the role of trust in inter-organizational relationships

From a rational choice perspective, a potential trustor considers what it can possibly gain from investing trust in a social relationship (Hardin 2002). An organization that has decided to trust another organization has done this because members within that organization believe that the risk of being betrayed by the partner does not weigh as much as what they can benefit if the trustee reciprocates the favours. For example, if a powerful buyer firm helps out a temporarily struggling supplier with a short-term loan, the favour that this firm might get back in the future from the trusted supplier in an equally difficult situation is expected to count more than the risk that the trustee will never return anything. Coleman (1990) suggests viewing a trustor like someone who places a bet. If a trusting organization decides whether or not it will risk losing money, reputation, social contacts etc. or refrain from so doing, the behaviour of that organization will follow a simple mathematical equation: $p/1-p$ is greater, smaller or equal to L/G. In this formula, p is probability that the trusting organization's engagement will turn out to be worthwhile; L is the potential loss if it is disappointed by the trustee; and G is the potential gain if the trusted partner organization behaves trustworthily.

Rational choice theorists are interested in cooperation and not so much in the coordination of activities. The view is that acting organizations will in most cases have conflicting interests as each of them seeks to maximize organizational profits. Often the latter will only be achieved at the expense of the other. Each acting organization is assumed to have significant incentives to cheat. However, and as game theory – a stream of literature derived from rational choice premises – argues, there can be situations where actors need to cooperate in order to collectively reap potential gains, which might otherwise not be accessible for anyone without accepting unreasonable amounts of risk (Axelrod, 1984). Many alliances in the corporate world are perfect examples for this. The coordination aspect of trust plays no great role in this theoretical perspective as the 'common good' is indeed difficult to conceptualize if only rational and self-interested individual and collective actors are assumed (Hardin, 2002).

Transaction cost theory and trust

Conceptual background

At its central premise, transaction cost economics assumes that firms will choose the governance structure – make, ally or buy – which minimizes costs of transactions (e.g. Williamson, 1979; 1985; 1991). Transaction cost economics predicts that firms will vertically integrate transactions (make), rather than rely on the market (buy), when exchange hazard is high and transactions occur frequently. In other words, when contracting, negotiation or administration of a task is costly, then it is more efficient to do the task in-house than, for example, outsource to a third party or buy a product 'off-the-shelf'. Conversely, when exchange hazard and costs of transactions are low, then it is more efficient to outsource the task, rather than doing it within the firm. Inter-organizational relationships ('ally' in Williamson's parlance) lie in-between these two extreme forms of governance (Williamson, 1991). Hence, the formation of inter-organizational relationships, in Williamson's framework, is determined by the costs of transaction.

Trust does not play a major a role in the transaction cost framework. Quite the contrary, Williamson (1993) firmly makes the case that trust is an absent, or even impossible, aspect of economic exchange. Instead, Williamson assumes that economic agents are always opportunistic and calculative (Williamson, 1993). Trust cannot be formed in the presence of calculativeness, and calculativeness also devalues pre-existing trust. Trust, therefore, is 'reserved for very special relations between family, friends, and lovers. Such trust is also the stuff of which tragedy is made. It goes to the essence of the human condition' (Williamson, 1993: 484).

Williamson's claim against trust has been heavily debated, questioned and criticized (e.g. Bachmann & Zaheer, 2008; Cohen, 2014; James, 2014; McEvily, 2011; Möllering, 2014; Nooteboom, Berger, & Noorderhaven, 1997). One of the most common critiques targets Williamson's separation between trust and calculativeness (Möllering, 2014). McEvily (2011: 1266) envisages that trust is to be conceptualized as a 'family of hybrid form concepts', where trust and risk co-occur and overlap. Cohen (2014) proposes that one can trust genuinely – but for calculative reasons – in so far as trust is based on the understanding of risk and reward. With this conceptualization, genuine trust can both exist and play an important role in inter-organizational collaborations. James (2014) proposes a slightly different argument, namely that trust is calculative for as long as risk can be estimated, but that trust cannot be calculative under genuine uncertainty (cf. Knight, 1916).

Transaction cost theory extensions and the role of trust in inter-organizational relationships

Even though trust is not part of the transaction cost framework, several scholars (e.g. Chiles & McMackin, 1996; Gulati & Nickerson, 2008; Poppo, Zhou, & Li, 2015; Vanneste, Puranam, & Kretschmer, 2014) have sought to extend the transaction cost framework to theorize the role of trust in inter-organizational relationships. Within these theoretical extensions, the assumption of opportunism is relaxed and trust is conceptualized as a 'shift parameter' (Gulati & Nickerson, 2008), enabling collaborating partners to use less extensive safeguards. Trust, in these extensions of the transaction cost framework, has both a cooperative and coordinative role to play.

Assigning trust a cooperative role, Gulati and Nickerson (2008) propose that in a situation where exchange hazard is high, trust can enable a less formal mode of governance (ally) instead of a more formal one (buy). This is because, when trust is present, transacting partners are assumed to be less concerned with opportunism stemming from misaligned goals. Whereas Williamson (1993) would reject the notion that trust, within the realms of economic transactions, can ever be strong-enough to enable such a substitution effect, Gulati and Nickerson (2008) do find empirical support for their argument. By surveying exchange relationships geared to sourcing components in the U.S. auto industry, they find that relationships with a high degree of trust are more likely to rely on less formal governance modes. In other words, they propose that there is a substitutive effect between prior trust and formal governance.

In addition to resolving cooperation concerns, Gulati and Nickerson (2008) also assign trust a coordinative role, arguing that trust enables a more flexible division of tasks – hence better coordination. Trust enables collaborating organizations to resolve conflicts more effectively, without having to seek explicit agreements or involve third parties (Gulati & Nickerson, 2008). Moreover, because trust enables commitment of resources, such as information exchange and joint systems for planning and coordination, trust also allows more flexible interaction, which in turn puts collaborators in a better position to adapt to unforeseen events. Viewing trust as a coordinative mechanism, trust is assumed to have a complementary effect on formal governance during the course of inter-organizational relationships (Gulati & Nickerson, 2008). Subsequent studies (e.g. Poppo et al., 2016; Vanneste et al., 2014) have continued to build on this insight, finding that these substitutive and complementary effects are stronger for relational trust than for calculative trust.

Social exchange theory and trust

Conceptual background

Social exchange theory (e.g. Blau, 1964; Homans, 1958; Thibaut & Kelley, 1959) explains how series of interactions between social actors (e.g. individuals, groups, organizations) generate commitments (Emerson, 1976). Social exchange refers to 'voluntary actions of individuals that are motivated by the returns they are expected to bring and typically in fact bring from others' (Blau, 1964: 6). Social exchange creates norms of reciprocity (Gouldner, 1960), meaning that exchange partners feel morally obliged to behave in a manner that is considered fair among those involved (Cropanzano & Mitchell, 2005). Hence, one of the basic principles of this theory is that relationships, under certain conditions, develop over time into feelings of personal obligation and gratitude (Cropanzano & Mitchell, 2005). Social exchange theorists do not explicitly define trust, but rather take it for granted (Möllering, 2007) and see it as an outcome of favourable social exchange (Cropanzano & Mitchell, 2005). Even so, inter-organizational trust scholars often rely on social exchange theory and assume that trust exists in repeated exchange relationships between organizations (e.g. Das & Teng, 2002; Elfenbein & Zenger, 2014; Gulati, 1995; Gulati & Singh, 1998; Lioukas & Reuer, 2015; Zaheer et al., 1998).

Social exchange theory and the role of trust in inter-organizational relationship

Within social exchange theory, trust is primarily understood as an *outcome* of repeated interaction, while the *role* of trust in inter-organizational relationships is not directly addressed. Yet, in a broader sense, social exchange theory has been used to argue that trust enables the resolving of cooperation concerns in inter-organizational relationships (e.g. Cropanzano & Mitchell, 2005; Das & Teng, 2002). When norms of reciprocity and feelings of friendship are established, partners become confident that the other side will not behave opportunistically, since such behaviour would violate the established norms of reciprocity, feelings of friendship and emotional attachment (e.g. Das & Teng, 2002).

Scholars have relied on social exchange theory to suggest that trust can, indirectly, also have a coordinative role. McEvily, Perrone and Zaheer (2003) argue that trust enables serial equity in repeated exchanges, which in turn facilitates the coordination of mutual expectations. Serial equity enables the coordination of tasks to be extended over time and 'through a variety of different currencies, e.g. exchange in kind (Ouchi, 1980)' (McEvily et al., 2003: 96). Hence, when trust is present, organizations can maintain a higher degree of flexibility in the coordination of tasks, without re-negotiating or changing basic structures. Such flexibility can be valuable when organizations need to coordinate independent and joint activities in response to unforeseen events (McEvily et al., 2003). In a similar vein, Liu, Luo and Liu (2009) build on social exchange theory, arguing that after partners have established norms of trust through repeated exchange they are more able to articulate and understand one another's expectations. This facilitates adaptation and problem solving in inter-organizational relationships. Trust, they argue, also induces stability and predictability in inter-organizational relationships. This motivates partners to make relationship-specific investments, such as promoting one another's production technology or investing in joint activities. Nooteboom et al. (1997) also rely on social exchange theory, when suggesting that on the basis of repeated exchanges the establishment of trust becomes perceived as valuable in itself. Trust, thereby, can function as a superordinate goal, which resolves conflict and helps align subordinate objectives. Also in this perspective, trust is given both a cooperative and coordinative role to play in inter-organizational relationships.

Neo-institutional theory and trust

Conceptual background

This theoretical approach is based on the idea that the behaviour of social actors (e.g. individuals, groups or organizations) is oriented towards certain patterns and rules that exist in the environment in which they interact. Actors are conceived of as social rather than rational or even calculative. It is not ruled out that actors behave according to explicit and rational reasoning but this is not the norm in everyday conduct where actors semi-consciously follow more or less successful routines (Powell & DiMaggio, 1991; Scott, 1995).

The established patterns, rules and norms of social behaviour constitute the institutional framework, which this approach sees as fundamental in explaining the actual behaviour of actors. This is not a deterministic one-way process where behaviour is a direct outcome of the institutional arrangements. Rather, it is assumed that (1) institutions shape or channel the behaviour of actors instead of determining it, and that (2) institutions would not exist if they were not continuously reproduced by actors' affirmative behaviour. The latter also means that actors can change the meaning, importance and legitimacy of social rules and norms. This, however, is more the exception, whereas in general, a stable and reliable order is assumed to guide actors' behaviour. Some critics of the neo-institutional approach have pointed out that this theoretical framework focuses more on the influences of institutions than on the creative potential of action. In this context it has been noticed that the process of creating and reproducing institutions is placed emphasis on by structuration theory (Giddens, 1984), which can thus be seen as a useful complement to neo-institutional theory (Barley & Tolbert, 1997; Kroeger, 2012).

The neo-institutionalist approach does not normally see actors as calculative and profit-maximizing; in their usual day-to-day practice actors are assumed to follow rules in a semi-conscious way. Trust is thus simply seen as a deep-seated characteristic of human behaviour, present in all kinds of interaction. Strong institutional frameworks can facilitate trust, i.e. 'institutional-based trust' among actors (Zucker, 1986; Lane & Bachmann, 1996); trust itself can be institutionalized (Kroeger, 2012; Schilke & Cook, 2013); and trust – like power, meaning or legitimacy – can be seen as an element of the structuration process in which institutions and actions are embedded (Sydow, 1998).

Similar to social exchange theory, neo-institutional theory also emphasizes that social interaction occurs in a relatively stable social framework in which trustees are assumed to benefit from being trustworthy. The two perspectives, however, are different in how they theorize the origin of that social framework. Social exchange theory emphasizes the repeated exchange occurring between the same actors and the establishment of cooperative norms that follow from such repeated exchange. Social exchange theory, thereby, provides insights about the development of trust over time in a specific relationship. Neo-institutional theory, in contrast, acknowledges the role of systemic structures that exist outside the specific boundaries of a relationship. In complement to social exchange theory, neo-institutional theory provides insights into how initial trust is established in an inter-organizational relationship. Thus, the two theoretical perspectives are seen to be combinable in a useful way.

Neo-institutional theory and the role of trust in inter-organizational relationships

Because neo-institutionalist theory views actors as more driven by routines than by calculation, the coordination aspect of trust is deemed most important (Bachmann & Inkpen, 2011).

Bachmann (2001) suggests that trust leads to predictability and stability in inter-organizational exchange. Stable inter-organizational interaction, in turn, enables the establishment of standardized and shared rules, norms and routines, which have a positive influence on the coordination of actors' expectations (see also Bachmann & Inkpen, 2011; Jones, Hesterly, & Borgatti, 1997). The issue of cooperation is not assumed to be the key aspect of trust. If an individual or organization turns out to be untrustworthy, this may well be of interest for those individuals or organizations involved in a specific situation, but the reproduction of the social order is not put in question through such events. As human actors have a free will, there will always be some actors who will prefer to cheat to maximize their interests. Generally, however, a social actor's behaviour is channelled into a certain direction by way of the institutional environment in which the actor's interaction with others is placed. This alone is enough to reduce the risk of betrayal and to encourage individual and organizations to invest trust in many relationships.

There can never be any guarantees that actors will behave trustworthily. However, neo-institutionalists tend to see a reliable institutional order as enabling coordination by reducing the inherent risk of trust. On the whole, neo-institutionalists do not believe that the cooperation concerns are irrelevant, but they emphasize the alignment of interests through effective coordination processes. Only where this is achieved in the first place, can conflicting interests and potential cooperation be meaningfully articulated.

Agenda for future research

In the previous section, we have discussed how the role of trust for aligning goals (cooperation) and for aligning tasks (coordination) in inter-organizational relationships is conceptualized within four fundamental theoretical perspectives: rational choice theory, transaction cost theory, social exchange theory and neo-institutional theory. Against that backdrop, we outline below three important areas for future research.

Towards a processual view of trust and inter-organizational coordination

As our review illuminates, inter-organizational trust research in general has remained much more explicit about the role for trust in resolving cooperation concerns, but more implicit about the role of trust for coordination purposes. We therefore see promise in further investigating the coordinative role of trust. In particular, we encourage longitudinal studies in how coordinative processes and trust development co-evolve in inter-organizational exchanges. Too much of the existing literature has taken a static view on trust and coordination. As discussed, social exchange theory (e.g. McEvily et al., 2003) and transaction cost theory (e.g. Gulati & Nickerson, 2008) have been applied to frame coordination as a favourable *outcome* of inter-organizational trust. A process perspective, by contrast, would focus more on how coordination and trust building co-evolve during the life-cycle of an inter-organizational relationship. This type of process-oriented research could help uncover novel mechanisms underlying trust and the coordination of mutual expectations, thereby providing insights into how trust facilitates coordination, how effective coordination contributes to building trust, and to what extent the process of inter-organizational trust development and the process of coordinating expectations and interaction are independent on one another.

We expect a processual perspective to be particularly relevant in contexts where coordination issues are challenging. This could include contexts characterized by high uncertainty, unpredictability and volatility, such as in innovative or entrepreneurial settings. This could also include contexts where the concept of coordination becomes particularly complex, for example when inter-organizational collaboration spans multiple sites, task domains or partners. In these types of contexts, coordination mechanisms can hardly be specified ex ante. Instead, a processual perspective that focuses on the sequence and pace at which trust and coordination emerge over time could contribute to a realistic and useful theory about the role of trust in inter-organizational relationships.

Towards an integrative perspective on trust, cooperation and coordination

Firms increasingly engage in cooperative relationships with competitors (e.g. Gnyawali & Park, 2011). This is especially relevant in industries characterized by rapid technological change, shortened product life-cycles or requirements for heavy investments into research and development (Ritala et al., 2009). Not least in such contexts, research on trust, cooperation and coordination processes is pivotal in understanding the dynamics and the factors contributing to the success of inter-organizational relationships.

However, as our analysis shows, there is a considerable scarcity of research that can explain inter-organizational trust development on the basis of cooperation *and* coordination processes. Within a rational choice perspective, coordination is not recognized as an issue, while within the transaction cost and social exchange frameworks, coordination is identified as relevant, but primarily seen as an indirect outcome of favourable cooperation. In a neo-institutionalist view, by contrast, coordination has been the primary focus of analysis, while cooperation is conceptualized as a secondary phenomenon, derived from the successful coordination of expectations.

Given the nascent state of theory development on trust, coordination and cooperation, we encourage future research to look into processes of trust development, cooperation and coordination through inductive and longitudinal empirical analyses, without making a priori assumptions about the causality or temporal order between these processes. We expect such an effort to generate novel insights, not only into the role of trust, but also more generally related to collaborative processes in inter-organizational relationships. Important research questions could include if/how successful cooperation enhances coordination processes and vice versa, or if/how trust mediates or moderates the relationship between cooperation and coordination in inter-organizational relationships.

Towards conceptual tightening

Theoretical advances occur when concepts are refined; while being specified, they can be applied across a variety of contextual settings (Chimezie & Osigweh, 1989). By specifying the role of trust in resolving coordination and cooperation issues separately, our review illuminates important boundary conditions of the four theories we discuss. We show, for instance, how neo-institutional theory is not very useful for theorizing cooperation in inter-organizational relationships, but may be very suitable for understanding how collaborating firms overcome the challenge of coordination. The rational choice approach, on the other hand, provides one possible explanation for how firms come to accept their vulnerability in an inter-organizational collaboration. At the same time, we have also identified the limits of the rational choice approach, specifically where the question of how collaborating parties achieve successful coordination processes is concerned.

By drawing attention to boundary conditions, our review also points to promising complementarities between the different theoretical perspectives that we have discussed. We encourage future research to explore under which conditions a neo-institutional approach can be combined with other theoretical perspectives to understand trust, cooperation *and* coordination in inter-organizational relationships. We also suggest future research to more carefully differentiate trust from alternative outcomes of inter-organizational interaction. Lioukas & Reuer (2015) set a promising example by disentangling trust from learning outcomes of social exchange processes. Following this line of inquiry, it should be possible to distinguish cooperative from coordinative outcomes of calculative, rational, social or institutional processes.

Another approach to digging deeper into the issues related to trust, cooperation and coordination could build on a more careful distinction of the unit of analysis. Inter-organizational relationships are multi-level phenomena, where trust simultaneously exists on the individual, organizational and institutional levels of analysis. We therefore find it important to investigate if/how trust 'in institutions' brings about cooperative and coordinative processes which are different from 'trust in individuals' or 'trust in organizations'. It would also be useful to know the mechanisms that connect trust, cooperation and coordination across levels of analysis. Taken together, we encourage inter-organizational trust research to build on a multi-level approach. This would include research that focuses on how trust, coordination and cooperation are simultaneously manifested at the inter-personal, inter-organizational and institutional levels of inter-organizational relationships.

Conclusion

In this chapter, we have discussed four theories that are commonly applied to conceptualize the role of trust in inter-organizational relationships. In so doing, we have drawn attention to the cooperative and coordinative facets of inter-organizational relationships and we have discussed how different theoretical perspectives are more or less apt for understanding the role of trust in inter-organizational relationships. We also hope that our chapter can persuade trust scholars to study the role of inter-organizational trust through multiple theoretical lenses, letting different theoretical perspectives complement one another and, thus, provide a more comprehensive view of trust in inter-organizational relationships.

References

Bachmann, R. (2001). Trust, power and control in trans-organizational relations. *Organization Studies*, 22(2), 337.

Bachmann, R., & Zaheer, A. (2008). Trust in interorganizational relations. In S. Cropper, M. Ebers, C. Huxman, & P. Smith Ring (eds), *The Oxford handbook of inter-organizational relations* (pp. 533–554). Oxford, UK: Oxford University Press.

Bachmann, R., & Inkpen, A. C. (2011). Understanding institutional-based trust building processes in inter-organizational relationships. *Organization Studies*, 32(2), 281–301.

Blau, P. (1964). *Exchange and power in social life*. London: John Wiley.

Brattström, A., & Richtnér, A. (2014). Good cop – bad cop: Trust, control and the lure of integration. *Journal of Product Innovation Management*, 31(3), 584–598.

Buskens, V. (2002). *Social networks and trust*. London: Kluwer Academic Publishers.

Chiles, T. H., & McMackin, J. F. (1996). Integrating variable risk preferences, trust, and transaction cost economics. *Academy of Management Review*, 21(1), 73–99.

Chimezie, Y., & Osigweh, A. B. (1989). Concept fallibility in organizational science. *Academy of Management Review*, 14(4), 579–594.

Cohen, M. A. (2014). Genuine, non-calculative trust with calculative antecedents: Reconsidering Williamson on trust. *Journal of Trust Research*, 4(1), 44–56.

Cropanzano, R., & Mitchell, M. S. (2005). Social exchange theory: An interdisciplinary review. *Journal of Management*, 31(6), 874–900.

Das, T. K., & Teng, B.-S. (2002). Alliance constellations: A social exchange perspective. *Academy of Management Review*, 27(3), 445–456.

Dekker, H. C. (2004). Control of inter-organizational relationships: Evidence on appropriation concerns and coordination requirements. *Accounting, Organizations and Society*, 29(1), 27–49.

Doz, Y., & Hamel, G. (1998). *Alliance advantage: The art of creating value through partnering*. Boston: Harvard Business School Press.

Doz, Y. L. (1996). The evolution of cooperation in strategic alliances: Initial conditions or learning processes? *Strategic Management Journal*, 17(Summer special issue), 55–84.

Dyer, J. H., & Singh, H. (1998). The relational view: Cooperative strategy and sources of interorganizational competitive advantage. *The Academy of Management Review*, 23(4), 660–679.

Elfenbein, D. W., & Zenger, T. R. (2014). What is a relationship worth? Repeated exchange and the development and deployment of relational capital. *Organization Science*, 25(1), 222–244.

Emerson, R. M. (1976). Social exchange theory. *Annual review of sociology*, 2, 335–362.

Faems, D., Janssens, M., Madhok, A., & Van Looy, B. (2008). Toward an integrative perspective on alliance governance: Connecting contract design, trust dynamics, and contract application. *Academy of Management Journal*, 51(6), 1053–1078.

Giddens, A. 1984. *The Constitution of Society. Outline of the Theory of Structuration*. Cambridge, UK: Polity Press.

Gnyawali, D. R., & Park, B.J. (2011). Co-opetition between giants: Collaboration with competitors for technological innovation. *Research Policy*, 40(5), 650–663.

Gulati, R. (1995). Does familiarity breed trust? The implications of repeated ties for contractual choice in alliances. *Academy of Management Journal*, 38(1), 85–112.

Gulati, R., & Singh, H. (1998). The architecture of cooperation: Managing coordination costs and appropriation concerns in strategic alliances. *Administrative Science Quarterly*, 43(4), 781–814.

Gulati, R., & Nickerson, J. A. (2008). Interorganizational trust, governance choice, and exchange performance. *Organization Science*, 19(5), 688–708.

Gulati, R., Wohlgezogen, F., & Zhelyazkov, P. (2012). The two facets of collaboration: Cooperation and coordination in strategic alliances. *The Academy of Management Annals*, 6, 531–583.

Hardin, R. (2002). *Trust and Trustworthiness*. New York: Russell Sage Foundation.

Homans, G. C. (1958). Social behavior as exchange. *American Journal of Sociology*, 52, 597–606.

James, H. S. (2014). You can have your trust and calculativeness, too: Uncertainty, trustworthiness and the Williamson thesis. *Journal of Trust Research*, 4(1), 57–65.

Jones, C., Hesterly, W. S., & Borgatti, S. P. (1997). A general theory of network governance: Exchange conditions and social mechanisms. *Academy of Management Review*, 22(4), 911–945.

Knight, F. H. (1916). *Risk, uncertainty and profit*. New York: Houghton Mifflin.

Lioukas, C., & Reuer, J. (2015). Isolating trust outcomes from exchange relationships: Social exchange and learning benefits of prior ties in alliances. *Academy of Management Journal*, 58(6), 1826–1847.

Liu, Y., Luo, Y., & Liu, T. (2009). Governing buyer-supplier relationships through transactional and relational mechanisms: Evidence from China. *Journal of Operations Management*, 27(4), 294–309.

Long, C. P., & Sitkin, S. B. (2006). Trust in the balance: How managers integrate trust-building and task control. In R. Bachmann and A. Zaheer (eds), *Handbook of trust research*, (87–106). Cheltenham, UK: Edward Elgar.

Lumineau, F. (2017). How contracts influence trust and distrust. *Journal of Management*, 43(5), 1553–1577.

Lumineau, F., & Verbeke, A. (2016). Let's give opportunism the proper back seat. *Academy of Management Review*, 41(4), 739–741.

Madhok, A. (1995). Revisiting multinational firms' tolerance for joint ventures: A trust-based approach. *Journal of International Business Studies*, 26(1), 117–137.

Malhotra, D. K., & Lumineau, F. (2011). Trust and collaboration in the aftermath of conflict: The effects of contract structure. *Academy of Management Journal*, 54(5), 981–998

Mayer, R. C., Davis, J. H., & Schoorman, F. D. (1995). An integration model of organizational trust. *The Academy of Management Review*, 20(3), 709–734.

McEvily, B. (2011). Reorganizing the boundaries of trust: From discrete alternatives to hybrid forms. *Organization Science*, 22(5), 1266–1276.

McEvily, B., Perrone, V., & Zaheer, A. (2003). Trust as an organizing principle. *Organization Science*, 14(1), 91–103.

Möllering, G. (2007). *Trust: Reason, routine, reflexivity*. Bingley, UK: Emerald Group Publishing.

Möllering, G. (2014). Trust, calculativeness, and relationships: A special issue 20 years after Williamson's warning. *Journal of Trust Research*, 4(1), 1–21.

Nooteboom, B., Berger, H., & Noorderhaven, N. G. (1997). Effects of trust and governance on relational risk. *The Academy of Management Journal*, 40(2), 308–338.

Ouchi, W. G. (1980). Markets, bureaucracies, and clans. *Administrative Science Quarterly*, 25(1), 129–141.

Poppo, L., Zhou, K. Z., & Li, J. J. (2016). When can you trust "trust"? Calculative trust, relational trust, and supplier performance. *Strategic Management Journal*, 37(4), 724–741

Ritala, P., Hurmelinna-Laukkanen, P., Blomqvist, K. (2009). Tug of war in innovation – coopetitive service development. *International Journal of Services Technology and Management*, 12(3), 255–272

Thibaut, J. W., & Kelley, H. H. (1959). *The social psychology of groups*. New York: Wiley.

Thompson, J. D. (1967). *Organizations in action*. New York: McGraw Hill.

Vanneste, B. S., Puranam, P., & Kretschmer, T. (2014). Trust over time in exchange relationships: Meta-analysis and theory. *Strategic Management Journal*, 35(12), 1891–1902.

Williamson, O. E. (1979). Transaction-cost economics: The governance of contractual relations. *Journal of Law and Economics*, 22(2), 233–261.

Williamson, O. E. (1985). *Economic institutions of capitalism*. New York: Free Press.

Williamson, O. E. (1991). Comparative economic organization: The analysis of discrete structural alternatives. *Administrative Science Quarterly*, 36(2), 269–296.

Williamson, O. E. (1993). Calculativeness, trust, and economic organization. *Journal of Law and Economics*, 36(1), 453–486.

Zaheer, A., McEvily, B., & Perrone, V. (1998). Does trust matter? Exploring the effects of interorganizational and interpersonal trust on performance. *Organization Science*, 9(2), 141–159.

Zaheer, A., & Venkatraman, N. (1995). Relational governance as an interorganizational strategy: An empirical test of the role of trust in economic exchange. *Strategic Management Journal*, 16(5), 373–392.

Zhong, W., Su, C., Peng, J., & Yang, Z. (2017). Trust in interorganizational relationships: A meta-analytic integration. *Journal of Management*, 43(4), 1050–1075.

8

MULTILEVEL TRUST

Antecedents and outcomes of trust at different levels

C. Ashley Fulmer*

Introduction

Diverse disciplines have examined trust and demonstrated its positive effects on a wide range of outcomes, including employee job satisfaction and performance (Colquitt, Scott, & LePine, 2007; Dirks & Ferrin, 2002), teacher professionalism and school effectiveness (Forsyth, Adams, & Hoy, 2011), consumer purchases and brand loyalty (Geyskens, Steenkamp, & Kumar, 1998), medical treatment adherence and patient outcomes (Lee & Lin, 2009), business alliance performance (Cullen, Johnson, & Sakano, 2000), international conflict de-escalation (Axelrod, 1984), national democracy (Putnam, 1993) and economic well-being (Fukuyama, 1995). Together, the body of research underscores the critical role of trust whether in everyday life or in extraordinary times, in historical events or in the fast-changing present, in the privacy of our home or in international political arenas.

Despite this, there remains a critical gap in our knowledge of trust that has begun to gain attention only recently – that trust is an inherently multilevel phenomenon. Trust, which arises from interpersonal relationships between parties, is without exception embedded within larger circles of relationships beyond the parties involved and in the broader contexts, structures and systems. For example, trust between a trustor and a coworker may be influenced by the characteristics of the trustor and the behaviour of the coworker. However, it can also be influenced by the trustor's relationship with other coworkers within the same unit, the trustor's and coworker's relationships with a common supervisor, the organizational climate of the firm, the norms of the industry and the cultural values and practices of the society. Accordingly, while trust research thus far has predominantly focused on the level of analysis in which the main construct of interest resides, research that involves multiple levels of analysis is growing.

The focus on levels of analysis and the broader context is consistent with the emphasis on contextualizing research in social sciences (McLaughlin, 1998; Rousseau & Fried, 2001). Context has been defined as 'situational opportunities and constraints that affect the occurrence and meaning of organizational behaviour as well as functional relationships between variables' (Johns, 2006, p. 386). Examples of a context can include relationship history, team climate and organizational structure, among others. The notion is related to the concept of situational strength

(Mischel, 1977; Weick, 1996), where strong situations dictated by norms and pressures limit individual variations and responses. Increasingly, we recognize that organizations, teams and individuals are all nested in broader contexts and systems that vary in occupations (Colquitt, LePine, Zapata, & Wild, 2011), market conditions (Bacharach & Bamberger, 2004), temporal events (Lieb, 2003) and national cultures (Hofstede, 1980).

Contexts are integral to multilevel trust research because they can exert direct downward effects or moderate the lower-level relationships (Johns, 2006). Accordingly, I highlight in this review the cross-level factors influencing a trust relationship. I also examine trust as a context that affords or constrains the outcome at another level. Table 8.1 shows a summary of the review, indicating the categories of the cross-level predictors and outcomes that have been examined in the literature. Such a multilevel framework better situates our knowledge of trust in a larger, complex system that approximates reality. As a result, it 'makes our models more accurate and our interpretation of results more robust' (Rousseau & Fried, 2001, p. 2). Before the review, I first briefly discuss relevant levels of analysis concepts, providing trust definitions at different levels and highlighting model differences.

Table 8.1 Categories of cross-level predictors and outcomes

	Cross-level factors for individual level trust	Unit level trust for cross-level outcomes
Generalized trust and political trust	National-level economics, political systems, religion and social capital Municipality-level size and political system Community-level generalized trust and civic participation	Individual-level anti-immigrant attitudes, outgroup trust, happiness, physical and mental health, and angel investment Firm-level tax compliance
Trust in coworkers	National-level cultures Organizational-level contexts and reward structure Similarity between trustor and trustee	Individual-level helping behaviour
Trust in teams	Team-level diversity, processes, performance	Individual-level job satisfaction, territorial behaviour and perceptions of team member contributions
Trust in leaders	Organizational-level climate and structure Team-level psychological safety and judgments Type of relationship Type of followers	Individual-level job satisfaction, perceptions of leader fairness, organizational commitment, organizational citizenship and creativity Team-level performance
Trust in management and organization	National-level cultures External market conditions Organizational-level control systems and human resource practices Team-level climate	Individual-level employee commitment, and in-role and extra-role performance
Interfirm trust	National-level cultures, generalized trust and institutions External environment uncertainty Type of relationship Trust between boundary spanners	

What are levels of analysis?

The level of analysis concerns the appropriate level for analysing a given research question, which can be at the individual, dyadic, team, organizational and national/cultural levels. Explicit consideration of the level of analysis is critical to ensure that the theory, measurement, analysis and implications are at the level appropriate to the research question and are aligned. It also avoids a fallacy of the wrong level (Galtung, 1967; Rousseau, 1985), where one incorrectly assumes that a relationship or process that occurs in one level would similarly apply at a different level. Any extrapolation to a different level needs to be empirically tested. For example, whereas the relationship between job attitudes and employee performance at the individual level is inconsistent, Ostroff (1992) found a positive relationship between the two at the organizational level. As another example, while self-efficacy and performance exhibit a positive relationship at the between-individual level, the relationship has been found to be negative in within-individual research (Lord, Diefendorff, Schmidt, & Hall, 2010).

Likewise, the definition of trust should reflect the level of analysis. Trust at the individual level refers to an individual's psychological state of being willing to be vulnerable based on positive expectations (Mayer, Davis, & Schoorman, 1995; Rousseau, Sitkin, Burt, & Camerer, 1998). Trust at higher levels of analysis refers to trust consensus, or a shared psychological state among unit members of being willing to be vulnerable based on positive expectations (Fulmer & Gelfand, 2012). Without sufficient agreement in the levels of trust, higher-level trust does not exist and only individual-level trust should be examined.

When a research question concerns trust at one level and its antecedents and consequences at different levels, the research can take the form of a cross-level or multilevel model. While the two models are closely related and share similarities, the majority of empirical research centres on cross-level models. Cross-level models concern specifically how a construct or relationship at one level can be affected by or has an impact on another construct at a different level. An example is that the strength of the individual-level relationship between interactional justice and trust in supervisors depends on the form of the organization at the organizational level (Ambrose & Schminke, 2003). Multilevel models are more complex than cross-level models and thus less frequently examined. They refer to models in which a construct or relationship at one level is affected by or affects constructs at multiple levels of analysis (Klein, Dansereau, & Hall, 1994). An example is that individuals' trust in leaders is influenced by both team-level and organizational-level climates (Burke, Sims, Lazzara, & Salas, 2007).

Cross-level and multilevel trust review

The review of the trust literature on cross-level and multilevel models proceeds first by the trust referent, including generalized and political trust, coworkers, teams, leadership, management and organization, and another organization (interfirm relationships). Each section then contains a review of cross-level predictors and cross-level outcomes. An additional section focuses on cross-level and multilevel trust during conflicts and after trust violations. Where applicable, I identify the theoretical framework for each paper. Table 8.1 shows a summary of the current state of the literature, highlighting the categories of cross-level predictors and outcomes that have been considered thus far.

Generalized trust and political trust

A host of country and regional factors have been found to influence individuals' generalized trust. For example, national-level GDP is positively related to generalized trust at the individual level (Hooghe, Reeskens, Stolle, & Trappers, 2009), while national-level income inequality (Borgonovi, 2012; Elgar & Aitken, 2011; Fairbrother & Martin, 2013; Freitag & Bühlmann, 2009; Hooghe et al., 2009), corruption (Freitag & Bühlmann, 2009) and religious diversity (Borgonovi, 2012) are negatively related. Regions with a protestant tradition have also been found to have higher individuals' generalized trust, supporting social capital theory which considers social networks as a type of social good (Traunmüller, 2011). Country- and regional-level factors likewise influence individuals' political trust in their national parliament and local government: national-level corruption, past communism and size of municipality are related to lower political trust, whereas proportional electoral systems are related to higher political trust (Denters, 2002; Van de Meer, 2010).

Research has also considered contexts moderating the effects of individual differences on generalized and political trust. Using the World Values Survey from 31 countries, in a multilevel model, Paxton (2007) predicted based on social identity theory and found a positive relationship between citizens' membership in associations that are connected to other associations and their generalized trust both at the individual and country levels. Further, the positive relationship between education and generalized trust is stronger in countries high on income inequality and religious diversity (Borgonovi, 2012). The relationship between individuals' race and their political trust is moderated by systems of political representation at the city level such that cities with mayor-council systems have lower levels of trust than cities with council-manager or commission forms of government (Rahn & Rudolph, 2005).

Both generalized trust and political trust, in turn, have been related to a host of individual attitudinal outcomes. In a multilevel model, across 15 European countries, both individual level and regional level generalized trust is negatively related to individuals' anti-immigrant attitudes (Rustenbach, 2010). Research has also examined moderation by higher-level contextual factors. Based on cognitive dissonance theory, the negative relationship between individuals' trust in institutions such as justice systems and unions and endorsement of private ownership of business was found to be stronger in countries with a larger government sector (Jakobsen, 2010). In addition, the relationship between generalized trust and support for democracy at the individual level varies across countries depending on the existing country-level democracy (Jamal & Nooruddin, 2010).

Importantly, generalized trust has also been linked to subjective well-being and health, and the relationships are contingent upon the national or regional context. Both generalized trust at the individual and country levels are associated with happiness at the individual level (Tokuda, Fujii, & Inoguchi, 2010). Higher average generalized trust at the country level was associated with better self-rated health at the individual level (Kim, Baum, Ganz, Subramanian, & Kawachi, 2011). In rural Chinese villages, the negative relationship between mistrust in the village and mental health at the individual-level is stronger when the village-level mistrust is high. Further, the village-level trust in the village has a stronger relationship to individuals' physical and mental health than the individual level trust in the village (Wang, Schlesinger, Wang, & Hsiao, 2009). Similarly, in the United States, Kim and Kawachi (2006) found that community-level generalized trust strengthens the relationship between individual-level generalized trust and self-rated health. Further, individuals with higher levels of generalized trust and civic participation enjoy better health in countries with high levels of social capital than their counterparts, but the individual-level relationship is weaker in countries with lower levels of social capital (Poortinga, 2006).

Finally, research has considered the moderating effects of country-level generalized trust on individual-level and firm-level outcomes. Examining different forms of trust, Muethel and Bond (2013) found that in societies high on dispositional and rule-based trust, employees have higher outgroup trust than those in societies high on categorization-based trust. In the area of entrepreneurship, individuals in countries high on generalized trust are more likely to act as an angel investor and invest in entrepreneurship (Ding, Au, & Chiang, 2015). Country-level trust also strengthens the relationship between perceived entrepreneurial skills and angel investment, but weakens the relationship between new business opportunities and angel investment (Ding et al., 2015). Further, the relationship between legal protections in society and entrepreneurship is weaker in emerging economies but the relationship is mitigated when the society has high generalized trust (Kim & Li, 2014). For firm outcomes, research shows that country-level general trust weakens the negative relationship between a firm's corruption and the firm's tax compliance (Alon & Hageman, 2013).

Coworkers

Research on trust in coworkers has examined cross-level influences including organizational contexts and structures, demographic and cultural differences, and network attributes. For example, reward structures have a strong influence on interpersonal trust, with cooperative reward structures increasing trust and competitive reward structures decreasing trust (Ferrin & Dirks, 2003). Higher-level contextual moderators also influence individual-level trust relationships. In contexts where high reliability is important, individuals' trust in members is more strongly related to ability and integrity as compared to in typical contexts where individuals' trust in members is more strongly related to benevolence and identification. Trust in the typical context is related to withdrawal, whereas trust in the high-reliability context is related to physical symptoms (Colquitt et al., 2011). Further, when the organizational context is competitive, electronic introduction of dyadic partners decreases trust more than face-to-face introduction (Hill, Bartol, Tesluk, & Langa, 2009).

Other studies have examined how demography can exert contextual influences on trust. One recent study focuses on differences in age between the trustor and trustee. Age diversity in client's team is negatively related to client–consultant trust when the client and consultant are of similar age but positively related to client–consultant trust when the client and consultant are of different ages (Williams, 2016). Other research in this area focuses on national cultural values as a context. Doney, Cannon, and Mullen (1998) proposed that national cultures influence individuals' trust in coworkers through the effects of norms, values and behavioural assumptions on trust-building processes. Empirical research has largely examined trust in the Chinese context. For Chinese managers, economic exchanges and ties with third parties have a positive effect on trust, while for American managers, friendship ties have a positive effect (Chua, Morris, & Ingram, 2009). When there lacks long-term interactions, the Chinese exhibit less spontaneous trust than Americans (Özer, Zheng, & Ren, 2014). Further, cultural similarity with overseas partners promotes affective trust among the Chinese (Jiang, Chua, Kotabe, & Murray, 2011).

Other studies have utilized network analysis to understand how the larger network influences trust in coworkers at the individual level. For example, similar shared ties with all other third parties in a network influence one's trust in another (Ferrin, Dirks, & Shah, 2006). Similarly, Howorth and Moro (2006) examined the relationships between bank managers and entrepreneurs in close-knit communities in Italy and found that third-party ties influence the trust development. Drawing on social exchange and social influence theories, Wong and Boh (2010) predicted and found that other managers' trust in a focal manager is influenced by the network attributes of the focal manager's advocates – peers who have received social support or advice from the focal manager and who can thus convey positive information about the focal manager.

They found that network attributes such as network density and non-overlapping ties exerted a positive effect on trust in the focal manager.

Research has also examined the effects of trust in coworkers at the unit level. Choi (2006) found that it exerts a direct effect on employees' helping behaviour at the individual level and moderates the effects of perceived organizational support and perceived unit fairness on their helping behaviour at the individual level.

Teams

Theoretical work has explored factors at the team level in influencing trust in teams at the individual level. Based on social identity and social information processing theories, Wildman and colleagues (2012) proposed a theoretical framework and posited that some team processes such as backup and coordination behaviours would increase individuals' trust in teams, while other team processes such as monitoring and conflict behaviours would decrease individuals' trust in teams. These authors also suggest that current team performance would influence individuals' future trust in the similar type of teams and that the individual-level relationship between generalized trust and trust in teams would be stronger when teams are in a context of high task uncertainty. Looking at team geographical diversity as a higher-level contextual moderator, in an empirical study, Joshi, Lazarova and Liao (2009) drew on social identity theory and found that the individual-level relationship between perceptions of inspirational leadership and trust in teams is stronger when the team is more geographically dispersed across different cities and countries and a high proportion of members are telecommuters.

Trust in teams at the individual level has also been examined as a mediator in cross-level relationships. Using network analysis and drawing on the similarity attraction paradigm, Chou, Wang, Wang, Huang, and Cheng (2008) found that trust in teams at the individual level mediates the relationship between shared work values at the team level and individuals' satisfaction with the organization. Interestingly, these authors also found that being trusted by team members mediates the relationship between shared work values at the team level and individuals' performance. At a higher level of analysis, Braun, Peus, Weisweiler, and Frey (2013) found that team trust at the team level mediates the relationship between team-level perceptions of supervisor transformational leadership and individual-level employee job satisfaction. One recent study examined the moderating effect of team-level trust in teams. Team trust reduces individual territorial behaviours for those who feel psychological ownership. However, team trust also makes coworkers judge individuals who do exhibit territorial behaviours as contributing less to the team (Brown, Crossley, & Robinson, 2014).

Leadership

Theoretical and empirical research on trust in leaders has examined factors at multiple levels of analysis. Drawing on social exchange theory, Burke and colleagues (2007) posited that team psychological safety and organizational climate can both exert downward influences on individuals' trust in their leaders. Focusing on organizational form as a contextual moderator, Ambrose and Schminke (2003) found that the relationship between interactional justice and trust in supervisors at the individual level, based on social exchange theory, is stronger with an organic organizational structure than a mechanistic organizational structure. Examining team-level factors, Shamir and Lapidot (2003) found that employees' trust in leaders is influenced by their teams' judgments and evaluations of leader trustworthiness, consistent with social information processing theory. Antecedents of trust in leaders may also differ as the relationship with the leader matures. In a new relationship between the employee and supervisor, leader ability and integrity lead to trust in the supervisor, whereas in an established relationship, in addition to leader integrity, trust in the supervisor is also high when the employee is high on generalized trust and perceives the supervisor to be high on benevolence (Frazier, Tupper, & Fainshmidt, 2016).

Cross-level and multilevel research has also examined outcomes of trust in leaders. In a multi-level model, trust in leaders has been proposed to have effects across levels including employee attitudes, team learning and organizational performance (Burke et al., 2007). After accounting for individual-level leader-member exchange (LMX), group-level trust in leaders was found to predict individual-level organizational citizenship behaviour (OCB), perceptions of leader fairness and job satisfaction (Wech, 2002). These findings are consistent with social exchange and social information processing theories. Interestingly, the effects of trust in leaders can vary in different groups of employees. While trust in the leader mediates the relationship between leader-participative leadership and task performance and organizational citizenship toward the organization for non-managerial subordinates, for managerial subordinates, empowerment mediates the relationship (Huang, Iun, Liu, & Gong, 2010).

Finally, research has also examined team-level trust in leaders as a moderator on individual-level outcomes. It has been found to strengthen the positive relationship between team learning goal orientation and individual creativity through team information exchange (Gong, Kim, Lee, & Zhu, 2013). Unit-level trust in senior management strengthens the relationship between employee perceptions of manager justice in performance appraisal and organizational commitment (Farndale & Kelliher, 2013). A recent study looked at both a team's and the leader's trust in one another and examined the influences of congruence in these two forms of trust. To the extent that the workgroup and leader share affective trust congruence, the group performance was higher (Carter & Mossholder, 2015).

Management and organization

Research on trust in management and organizations has examined contextual influences at the organizational and societal levels, focusing on HR practices, organizational systems, conditions external to the organization and national cultures. Searle (2013) identified that HR practices which aim to foster high involvement work systems that facilitate communication and employee empowerment and participation as well as work systems that aim to improve performance management processes and address employee concerns can increase trust in the organization and top management (Appelbaum, Bailey, Berg, & Kalleberg, 2001; Mayer & Davis, 1999; Searle et al., 2011). Drawing on social exchange theory, Whitener (2001) predicted and found that human resource (HR) practices related to developmental appraisals and equitable reward systems strengthen the relationship between perceived organizational support and trust in management at the individual level.

In addition to HR practices, well-implemented organizational control systems that are consistent and flexible, and that value trustworthiness increase employees' trust in the organization (Weibel et al., 2015). Focusing on voice in particular, different voice arrangements have different effects on employees' trust in management: direct voice has a positive effect, whereas voice through union representation has a negative effect (Holland, Cooper, Pyman, & Teicher, 2012). Looking beyond the organization, Hodson (2004) found that external market conditions, including diversity in labour force and instability of product market, reduce perceptions of organizational trustworthiness at the individual level. Outside of the organization, national cultures can exert contextual moderating influences on the effect of trust in management. Specifically, job formalization is negatively related to individuals' trust in management, particularly in individualistic cultures (Huang & Van de Vliert, 2006).

With regard to outcomes, based on social exchange theory, individuals' trust in the organization was predicted and found to mediate the link between group safety climate and individuals' outcomes including safety motivation, job satisfaction and turnover intention (Kath, Magley, & Marmet, 2010). Individual-level trust in management also moderates the effect of HR practices on employee attitudes. It strengthens the relationship when HR practices are oriented to increase motivation as compared to when HR practices are oriented to increase ability or opportunity to participate (Innocenti, Pilati, & Peluso, 2011).

At the higher unit level, Farndale and Kelliher (2013) found that the unit climate of trust in management is directly related to higher employee commitment, and at the same time strengthens the relationship between perceptions of line-manager fairness in performance appraisal and commitment at the individual level. At the organizational level, Li, Bai and Xi (2012) found that collective trust in the organization mediates the effects of organizational mechanistic structure, ethical values and top management teams transformational leadership on individuals' in-role and extra-role performance, supporting their predictions based on social exchange theory.

Interfirm

Across various trust referents, interfirm trust has received the most theoretical attention, with a particular focus on the relationship between interpersonal and interfirm trust. Currall and Inkpen (2002) proposed that trust in an international joint venture can be conceptualized at three levels of analysis: individual (e.g. operations managers), group (e.g. groups of managers) and organizational. Thus, boundary spanners of a firm can deal with their counterparts as individuals, a group, or with the partner firm directly. In a similar vein, Mouzas, Henneberg and Naudé (2007) suggested that both interpersonal and interorganizational trust and reliance should be considered in interfirm relationships. For example, they viewed high interpersonal trust and low interorganizational reliance as representing a personal relationship, and low interpersonal trust and high interorganizational reliance as representing an expedient relationship.

In the context of interorganizational negotiations, Jeffries and Reed (2000) proposed that interorganizational trust moderates the relationship between interpersonal trust between the negotiators and the Pareto efficiency of the negotiation solution. Specifically, when interorganizational trust is high, Pareto efficiency would be higher when interpersonal trust is low. In an empirical study, Fang, Palmatier, Scheer and Li (2008) found that interorganizational trust amplifies not only the positive effect of trust between boundary spanners on interfirm coordination, but also its negative effect on responsiveness due to routinized rigidity.

Recently, Schilke and Cook (2013) drew on institutional theory, social identity theory and process theory of trust to propose a cross-level process of interorganizational trust. The development of interorganizational trust includes four stages. Stage 1 (Initiation) begins when a focal boundary spanner develops initial trust in the partner firm based on prior interactions or reputation of the partner firm. Stage 2 (Negotiation) follows when trust between boundary spanners of partner firms develops. Stage 3 (Formation) occurs when the focal boundary spanner transfers the trust in the partner boundary spanner to the partner firm, and finally, in Stage 4 (Operation), the trust in the partner firm becomes shared among members in a focal firm and thus operates at the organizational level between firms.

Research has also considered higher-level factors for interorganizational trust. Institutions such as legal protection and community norms are conducive to building trust, particularly in the early stage of interfirm relationship or when the relationship needs to be built quickly

(Bachmann & Inkpen, 2011). Other research explores contextual moderators in the relation-ship between interorganizational trust and outcomes, focusing on environmental uncertainty. In buyer and supplier relationships, when market uncertainty is high, relational trust that the buyer has in the supplier is strongly related to supplier performance (Poppo, Zhou, & Li, 2015). Further, the effect of interorganizational trust on firm performance is strengthened when external uncertainty is high (Gaur, Mukherjee, Gaur, & Schmid, 2011).

Research on interfirm trust has also examined national differences. Generalized trust of the country where a firm is located influences the firm's perceived trustworthiness of their international joint venture partner (Ertug, Cuypers, Noorderhaven, & Bensaou, 2013). National differences also moderate the types of factors that influence interfirm trust. Dutch auto dealers decrease trust in both positive and negative inequality in their relationships with suppliers, whereas US auto dealers only decrease trust in negative inequality (Scheer, Kumar, & Steenkamp, 2003).

Conflicts and trust violations

Limited research has examined cross-level and multilevel models of trust post-violation or during conflicts. Elangovan and Shapiro (1998) proposed that organizational culture (e.g. self-interest oriented) and organizational norms can moderate how individuals evaluate and respond to interpersonal trust betrayal. Drawing on attribution theory, Janowicz-Panjaitan and Krishnan (2009) discussed that the nature of trust violations may vary at the corporate and operating levels and their effects can spillover from one level to another. Gillespie and Dietz (2009) drew on the system and multilevel theories and proposed a multilevel model in relation to organizational failure and individual employees' perceptions of organizational trustworthiness. Specifically, organizational implementation of interventions that constrain untrustworthy behaviour and demonstrate the organization's ability, integrity and benevolence should improve employees' perceptions of trustworthiness. Research on multilevel trust after violations is largely theoretical.

Empirically, recent research shows that trust repair is more difficult with groups than with individuals, but the difference decreases if violators can match their responses to the type of violations, such as apologizing for competence-based violation and denying integrity-based vio-lation (Kim, Cooper, Dirks, & Ferrin, 2013). In the area of conflict management, an empirical study has been conducted. Currall and Judge (1995) found that a history of failed conflict management between two groups is negatively related to the mean level of interpersonal trust that the groups' boundary spanners have in each other.

Discussion

In this chapter, I review the literature on trust in cross-level and multilevel models. Together, the body of research clearly demonstrates that trust is a highly embedded construct. As can be seen in Table 8.1, research has considered many categories of cross-level predictors and out-comes across the different trust referents. Specifically, for generalized and political trust, research has linked an array of national, municipality and community factors to individual-level trust. However, as research on generalized trust has largely developed separately from research on the other referents, it would be interesting to explore whether organizational factors, such as climate and leaders, can change individuals' generalized trust. It is worthy to note that, in addition to individual outcomes, research on national-level generalized trust has examined its impact on firm outcomes. Additional research such as on within- and between-community and team can broaden the range of outcomes for generalized and political trust.

For trust in coworkers, while research has examined national-level and organizational-level predictors, it would be worthwhile to understand the influences of team factors and leadership. For example, how do different leadership styles affect unit-level trust in coworkers? Likewise, more outcomes can be explored for unit-level trust in coworkers, such as the impact of organizational-level trust in coworkers (trust climate) on team processes and outcomes. With regard to trust in teams, research needs to move beyond a focus on team-based influences. Leadership, HR practices and organizational cultures are just a few possible predictors for individual- and team-level trust in teams.

Moving on to trust in leaders, in addition to the organizational and team cross-level factors that have been examined, a fruitful avenue for research is in national-level influences on individual- and team-level trust in leaders. For trust in management and organization, research has examined factors at the national, organizational and team levels. However, research can examine the effects of unit-level trust on outcomes beyond the individual level, such as within-team and between-team outcomes. Research on interfirm trust has examined factors at the national and dyadic levels. Again, more outcomes at different levels can be explored. For example, interfirm trust may exert cross-level influences on interteam exchanges or employee performance within a firm.

Looking more broadly across referents, research has largely been limited to examining the influences of cross-level predictors on individual-level trust and the influence of unit trust on individual-level outcomes. Consequently, we know very little about cross-level contextual influences on trust at higher-levels, such as team trust and interfirm trust. For example, it is possible that industry norms and organizational structures lead to different team trust across organizations. We also know little about cross-level effects of trust on higher-level outcomes, such as organizational trust on coordination among different units in an organization and on conflicts among team members.

The review also shows the various theoretical perspectives adopted across referent areas in predicting and explaining trust relationships and patterns. However, a small set of theories has received the majority of attention. Chief among these are social exchange theory (Blau, 1964), social information processing theory (Salancik & Pfeffer, 1978) and social identity theory (Tajfel & Turner, 1979). By contrast, theories such as process theory of trust (Lewicki & Bunker, 1996) and system theory (Burke, 2002) have been infrequently adopted. To better predict and understand trust in cross-level and multilevel models, researchers need to more explicitly incorporate trust theories and multilevel theories in their work. Levels theories such as sensemaking (Weick, 1995), event cycle (Morgeson & Hofmann, 1999) and compilation (Kozlowski & Klein, 2000) should help build and expand the current multilevel research on trust.

Beyond these empirical and theoretical gaps, the field needs additional research and methodological advances to better understand the role of trust across levels. Below, I highlight theoretical implications of this review before turning attention to future research directions and methodological considerations.

Theoretical implications

The rich findings from cross-level and multilevel models of trust underscore the importance to move beyond the predominant focus on trust at a single level of analysis. Clearly, trust does not only exert effects on outcomes and is subject to factors that are at the same level of analysis. Without considering antecedents, consequences, moderators and mediators at other levels, research at a single level presents an incomplete picture of trust that risks oversimplifying relationships and even drawing erroneous conclusions. These findings also highlight the critical role that context plays in influencing trust. Trust research has been criticized to be largely decontextualized (Li, 2012). The review demonstrates that trust can involve different processes and exhibit different patterns across groups, organizations, industries, time and locations.

Due to the relatively small number of current studies, a comparison of trust relationships across levels of analysis is difficult. As cross-level and multilevel research continues to accumulate, it would be interesting to examine questions such as whether trust in leaders at the individual, team and organization levels has similar relationships with performance outcomes. Further, for trust relationships at higher levels, research so far has largely relied on theories at the individual level. An important consideration for future research is whether theories at the individual level are sufficient to examine relationships at a higher level or cross-level. From the levels perspective, theories need to be adapted at higher levels to ensure alignment of the level.

In addition to semi-isomorphism in theories and relationships, there remains an empirical question whether trust at higher levels of analysis is conceptually equivalent to trust at the individual level. Definitions of trust at higher levels so far have been based on the definition at the individual level. Future research should examine this assumption of construct quasi-isomorphism (see Tay, Woo, & Vermunt, 2014, for procedures). For example, shared trust in teams and trust climate in organizations may or may not consist of the same elements of positive expectations and willingness to be vulnerable (cf. Fulmer & Gelfand, 2012). It is possible that trust at the higher levels comprises different components than trust at the individual level.

Future directions

Based on the review of the literature, I also identify a number of broader areas that require future research investigation, including using the multilevel approach to understand trust dynamics after violation, a focus on the dyadic level, and examining the emergence of unit-level trust and trust compilation. Following these, I highlight three methodological consider-ations, including an explication of the level of analysis and trust referent, challenges associated with studying dispersion and emergence, and drawing causal inferences.

The act of trust entails inherent risks that put the trustor in a position vulnerable to violations (Yamagishi, Cook, & Watabe, 1998). Unfortunately, violations have been found to be common occurrences rather than exceptions in organizations (Robinson & Rousseau, 1994). Workplace conflicts are likewise prevalent (Bendersky, 2003). Given this, it is alarming that limited research has examined trust during conflicts or after violations, particular across levels of analysis as reflected in this review. As with trust at a single level (Schoorman, Mayer, & Davis, 2007), the preponderance of extant cross-level and multilevel research has focused on trust development. Much more research is needed on trust during conflicts and post-violation in relation to factors at different levels within a system. Further, scholars have long acknowledged that trust is dynamic and fluctuates over time (Rousseau et al., 1998). Cross-level and multilevel research is thus also needed to examine trust changes as it forms, once it is established and when violations have occurred. To understand these temporal dynamics, levels theory and methodology (e.g. Goldstein, Healy, & Rasbash, 1994) should be incorporated.

As can be seen in the review, research has examined trust across individual, team, organ-izational, community and societal levels. In contrast, trust at the dyadic level has been largely overlooked. Tse and Ashkanasy (2015) highlight the dyadic level as a missing link in multilevel research. The dyadic level is particularly suitable for examining the notions of trust symmetry and asymmetry, which has only recently received attention. Research on the single level has shown the benefits of trust symmetry, including resource exchanges (Bouty, 2000) and OCB (Brower, Lester, Korsgaard, & Dineen, 2009). In interfirm relations, competitive external environments and cultural and institutional differences have been found to reduce trust symmetry (Graebner, 2009; Zaheer & Zaheer, 2006). The dyadic perspective can also be examined at the team level. De Jong and Dirks (2012) found that trust asymmetry among pairs of members in a team weakens the relationship between trust at the team level and team performance.

Additionally, future research can examine the concept of trust dispersion – the extent to which members in a unit agree or disagree on their levels of trust, and trust emergence – the dynamic process through which individual-level trust coalesces to form collective trust at a higher level (Fulmer & Ostroff, 2016). Shared trust in a unit forms when members are under similar sets of external influences, experiences and interaction patterns (cf. Kozlowski & Klein, 2000). Shared trust can be considered as a type of social context that reflects more than a mere aggregation of individual trust within a unit, but also unique unit-level processes and system pressures (cf. Ferris et al., 1998). Considering the level of consensus in trust within a unit (trust dispersion) and changes in the degree of consensus over time (trust emergence) would help clarify how collective trust comes about and functions at a higher level of analysis.

A focus on dispersion also affords additional and noteworthy ways to understand trust at the unit level. While the typical consensus model focuses on the composition form of aggregation (Koslowski & Klein, 2000), dispersion focuses on the compilation form of aggregation. Compilation can take various meaningful patterns. For example, the most trusting member or the least trusting member in a unit may exert the most influence on certain outcomes, rather than the average level of trust or the degree of dispersion in a unit. As another example, trust in a unit may show a pattern similar to a fault line where two subgroups can be differentiated based on their levels of trust. Other compilation patterns in a unit may follow meaningful patterns based on network linkages among members or divergent relationships with the unit leader (i.e. differentiated leader–member exchanges; see Henderson, Liden, Glibkowski, & Chaudhry, 2009 for a review). These are promising directions awaiting future investigation.

Methodological considerations

To facilitate future comparison and integration of studies across levels, researchers need to be explicit about both the level of analysis and the trust referent of their work. This review, along with the broader literature on levels (e.g. Klein et al., 1994), points to the importance to align the levels for theory, measurement, analysis, and interpretation in a study. Similarly, in theory, measurement and interpretation, studies sometimes include multiple trust referents. As highlighted in research on interfirm trust (Currall & Inkpen, 2002; Schilke & Cook, 2013), a boundary spanner's trust in his or her counterpart, a partner firm and other firms in general can be expected to differ, and a boundary spanner's trust in a partner firm may differ from an organization's or the management's trust in the same referent. Therefore, the level and referent in trust research should be identified and kept consistent in a study. Moreover, careful considerations are needed to decide between a referent shift and a direct consensus model in theory, measurement and interpretation (Chan, 1998). When trust originates from individuals (e.g. interpersonal trust or team trust in members), a direct consensus model is appropriate. When the trust construct concerns perceptions of others or a unit in general (e.g. third-party perspective and trust climate), a referent shift model should be adopted.

Although trust emergence and dispersion present interesting avenues for future research, it is not always clear how researchers can study them. In the dispersion model, the variable of interest is the extent to which unit members share their levels of trust in a referent, or the degree of agreement among members. In contrast, emergence study requires a demonstration of a change in consensus/dispersion over time. For example, as a team works and socializes together over time, trust consensus should increase and thus emergence can be observed. When there are significant changes in team membership, the level of trust consensus may decrease during the period. So far, little theoretical work has explicated the unfolding processes and patterns of emergence across time (Fulmer & Ostroff, 2016) and quantitative research remains lacking (Kozlowski & Chao, 2012). To truly examine trust emergence, longitudinal studies are needed to document changes in trust consensus. When consensus is measured only in one or two time points, researchers can examine the state of dispersion without inference to dynamic emergence.

Given the inherent challenges of conducting multilevel research, it is not surprising that extant research heavily relies on the concurrent survey method. Future research on cross-level and multilevel models of trust needs to expand the methodological repertoire to afford inferences of causality. Some researchers have already raised questions regarding causality in cross-level trust models. For example, Jamal and Nooruddin (2010) questioned whether it is individuals' generalized trust that promotes national democracy, or existing democracy that leads to higher individual-level generalized trust. While causal inferences at the community and societal levels will be difficult to make, research at the individual, team and organizational levels should be able to discern causality by utilizing laboratory and field experiments.

Conclusion

In this review chapter, I focus on the recent developments in cross-level and multilevel models of trust. The body of research demonstrates that, in addition to the behaviours and characteristics of the parties that are directly involved in a trust relationship, trust is influenced by social context and broader organizational and cultural systems in which the parties are embedded. In addition, the research also shows that trust can exert impact beyond the parties involved to influence others who share overlapping social networks and ultimately the same system where the trust relationship is embedded. By considering trust in a multilevel system, we gain a more nuanced and realistic understanding of this important phenomenon and have potential to improve our theoretical precision and practical recommendations.

Note

* This chapter is based upon research funded by the National University of Singapore Start-Up Grant to the author. The author thanks Yu Tse Heng and Jia Hui Lim for their assistance in preparation of this work.

References

Alon, A., & Hageman, A. M. (2013). The impact of corruption on firm tax compliance in transition economies: Whom do you trust? *Journal of Business Ethics, 116(3),* 479–494.

Ambrose, M., & Schminke, M. (2003). Organization structure as a moderator of the relationship between procedural justice, interactional justice, perceived organizational support, and supervisory trust. *Journal of Applied Psychology, 88,* 295–305.

Appelbaum, E., Bailey, T., Berg, P., & Kalleberg, A. L. (2001). Do high performance work systems pay off? In S. Vallas (ed.), *The transformation of work* (pp. 85–107). Bingley, UK: Emerald Group Publishing.

Axelrod, R. (1984). *The evolution of cooperation.* New York, NY: Basic Books.

Bacharach, S., & Bamberger, P. (2004). The power of labor to grieve: The impact of the workplace, labor market, and power-dependence on employee grievance filing. *Industrial & Labor Relations Review, 57,* 518–539.

Bachmann, R., & Inkpen, A. C. (2011). Understanding institutional-based trust building processes in inter-organizational relationships. *Organization Studies, 32,* 281–301.

Bendersky, C. (2003). Organizational dispute resolution systems: A complementarities model. *Academy of Management Review, 28,* 643–656.

Blau, P. M. (1964). *Exchange and power in social life.* New Brunswick, NJ: Transaction Publishers.

Borgonovi, F. (2012). The relationship between education and levels of trust and tolerance in Europe. *The British Journal of Sociology, 63,* 146–167.

Bouty, I. (2000). Interpersonal and interaction influences on informal resource exchanges between R&D researchers across organizational boundaries. *Academy of Management Journal, 43,* 50–65.

Braun, S., Peus, C., Weisweiler, S., & Frey, D. (2013). Transformational leadership, job satisfaction, and team performance: A multilevel mediation model of trust. *The Leadership Quarterly, 24,* 270–283.

Brower, H. H., Lester, S. W., Korsgaard, M. A., & Dineen, B. R. (2009). A closer look at trust between managers and subordinates: Understanding the effects of both trusting and being trusted on subordinate outcomes. *Journal of Management, 35,* 327–347.

Brown, G., Crossley, C., & Robinson, S. L. (2014). Psychological ownership, territorial behavior, and being perceived as a team contributor: The critical role of trust in the work environment. *Personnel Psychology, 67,* 463–485.

Burke, W. W. (2002). *Organization change: Theory and practice.* London: Sage Publications.

Burke, C. S., Sims, D. E., Lazzara, E. H., & Salas, E. (2007). Trust in leadership: A multi-level review and integration. *The Leadership Quarterly, 18,* 606–632.

Carter, M. Z., & Mossholder, K. W. (2015). Are we on the same page? The performance effects of congruence between supervisor and group trust. *Journal of Applied Psychology, 100,* 1349–1363.

Chan, D. (1998). Functional relations among constructs in the same content domain at different levels of analysis: A typology of composition models. *Journal of Applied Psychology, 83,* 234–246.

Choi, J. N. (2006). Multilevel and cross-level effects of workplace attitudes and group member relations on interpersonal helping behavior. *Human Performance, 19,* 383–402.

Chou, L. F., Wang, A. C., Wang, T. Y., Huang, M. P., & Cheng, B. S. (2008). Shared work values and team member effectiveness: The mediation of trustfulness and trustworthiness. *Human Relations, 61,* 1713–1742.

Chua, R. Y., Morris, M. W., & Ingram, P. (2009). Guanxi vs networking: Distinctive configurations of affect-and cognition-based trust in the networks of Chinese vs American managers. *Journal of International Business Studies, 40,* 490–509.

Colquitt, J. A., Scott, B. A., & LePine, J. A. (2007). Trust, trustworthiness, and trust propensity: A meta-analytic test of their unique relationships with risk taking and job performance. *Journal of Applied Psychology, 92,* 909–927.

Colquitt, J. A., LePine, J. A., Zapata, C. P., & Wild, R. E. (2011). Trust in typical and high-reliability contexts: Building and reacting to trust among firefighters. *Academy of Management Journal, 54,* 999–1015.

Cullen, J. B., Johnson, J. L., & Sakano, T. (2000). Success through commitment and trust: The soft side of strategic alliance management. *Journal of World Business, 35,* 223–240.

Currall, S. C., & Inkpen, A. C. (2002). A multilevel approach to trust in joint ventures. *Journal of International Business Studies, 33,* 479–495.

Currall, S. C., & Judge, T. A. (1995). Measuring trust between organizational boundary role persons. *Organizational Behavior and Human Decision Processes, 64,* 151–170.

De Jong, B. A., & Dirks, K. T. (2012). Beyond shared perceptions of trust and monitoring in teams: Implications of asymmetry and dissensus. *Journal of Applied Psychology, 97,* 391–406.

Denters, B. (2002). Size and political trust: evidence from Denmark, the Netherlands, Norway, and the United Kingdom. *Environment and Planning C: Government and Policy, 20,* 793–812.

Ding, Z., Au, K., & Chiang, F. (2015). Social trust and angel investors' decisions: A multilevel analysis across nations. *Journal of Business Venturing, 30,* 307–321.

Dirks, K. T., & Ferrin, D. L. (2002). Trust in leadership: Meta-analytic findings and implications for research and practice. *Journal of Applied Psychology, 87,* 611–628.

Doney, P. M., Cannon, J. P., & Mullen, M. R. (1998). Understanding the influence of national culture on the development of trust. *Academy of Management Review, 23,* 601–620.

Elangovan, A. R., & Shapiro, D. L. (1998). Betrayal of trust in organizations. *Academy of Management Review, 23,* 547–566.

Elgar, F. J., & Aitken, N. (2011). Income inequality, trust and homicide in 33 countries. *European Journal of Public Health, 21,* 241–246.

Ertug, G., Cuypers, I. R., Noorderhaven, N. G., & Bensaou, B. M. (2013). Trust between international joint venture partners: Effects of home countries. *Journal of International Business Studies, 44*, 263–282.

Fairbrother, M., & Martin, I. W. (2013). Does inequality erode social trust? Results from multilevel models of US states and counties. *Social Science Research, 42*, 347–360.

Fang, E., Palmatier, R. W., Scheer, L. K., & Li, N. (2008). Trust at different organizational levels. *Journal of Marketing, 72*, 80–98.

Farndale, E., & Kelliher, C. (2013). Implementing performance appraisal: Exploring the employee experience. *Human Resource Management, 52*, 879–897.

Ferrin, D. L., & Dirks, K. T. (2003). The use of rewards to increase and decrease trust: Mediating processes and differential effects. *Organization Science, 14*, 18–31.

Ferrin, D. L., Dirks, K. T., & Shah, P. P. (2006). Direct and indirect effects of third-party relationships on interpersonal trust. *Journal of Applied Psychology, 91*, 870–883.

Ferris, G. R., Arthur, M. M., Berkson, H. M., Kaplan, D. M., Harrell-Cook, G., & Frink, D. D. (1998). Toward a social context theory of the human resource management-organization effectiveness relationship. *Human Resource Management Review, 8*, 235–264.

Forsyth, P. B., Adams, C. M., & Hoy, W. K. (2011). *Collective trust: Why schools can't improve without it.* New York, NY: Teachers College Press.

Frazier, M. L., Tupper, C., & Fainshmidt, S. (2016). The path(s) to employee trust in direct supervisor in nascent and established relationships: A fuzzy set analysis. *Journal of Organizational Behavior, 37*(7), 1023–1043.

Freitag, M., & Bühlmann, M. (2009). Crafting trust the role of political institutions in a comparative perspective. *Comparative Political Studies, 42*, 1537–1566.

Fukuyama, F. (1995). Trust: The social virtues and the creation of prosperity. *World and I, 10*, 264–268.

Fulmer, C. A., & Gelfand, M. J. (2012). At what level (and in whom) we trust: Trust across multiple organizational levels. *Journal of Management, 38*, 1167–1230.

Fulmer, C. A., & Ostroff, C. (2016). Convergence and emergence in organizations: An integrative framework and review. *Journal of Organizational Behavior, 37*, S122–S145.

Galtung, J. (1967). *Theory and methods of social research.* New York, NY: Columbia University Press.

Gaur, A. S., Mukherjee, D., Gaur, S. S., & Schmid, F. (2011). Environmental and firm level influences on inter-organizational trust and SME performance. *Journal of Management Studies, 48*, 1752–1781.

Geyskens, I., Steenkamp, J. B. E., & Kumar, N. (1998). Generalizations about trust in marketing channel relationships using meta-analysis. *International Journal of Research in Marketing, 15*, 223–248.

Gillespie, N., & Dietz, G. (2009). Trust repair after an organization-level failure. *Academy of Management Review, 34*, 127–145.

Goldstein, H., Healy, M. J., & Rasbash, J. (1994). Multilevel time series models with applications to repeated measures data. *Statistics in Medicine, 13*, 1643–1655.

Gong, Y., Kim, T. Y., Lee, D. R., & Zhu, J. (2013). A multilevel model of team goal orientation, information exchange, and creativity. *Academy of Management Journal, 56*, 827–851.

Graebner, M. E. (2009). Caveat venditor: Trust asymmetries in acquisitions of entrepreneurial firms. *Academy of Management Journal, 52*, 435–472.

Henderson, D. J., Liden, R. C., Glibkowski, B. C., & Chaudhry, A. (2009). LMX differentiation: A multilevel review and examination of its antecedents and outcomes. *The Leadership Quarterly, 20*, 517–534.

Hill, N. S., Bartol, K. M., Tesluk, P. E., & Langa, G. A. (2009). Organizational context and face-to-face interaction: Influences on the development of trust and collaborative behaviors in computer-mediated groups. *Organizational Behavior and Human Decision Processes, 108*, 187–201.

Hodson, R. (2004). Organizational trustworthiness: Findings from the population of organizational ethnographies. *Organization Science, 15*, 432–445.

Hofstede, G. (1980). Motivation, leadership, and organization: Do American theories apply abroad?. *Organizational Dynamics, 9*, 42–63.

Holland, P., Cooper, B. K., Pyman, A., & Teicher, J. (2012). Trust in management: The role of employee voice arrangements and perceived managerial opposition to unions. *Human Resource Management Journal, 22*, 377–391.

Hooghe, M., Reeskens, T., Stolle, D., & Trappers, A. (2009). Ethnic diversity and generalized trust in Europe: A cross-national multilevel study. *Comparative Political Studies, 42*, 198–223.

Howorth, C., & Moro, A. (2006). Trust within entrepreneur bank relationships: Insights from Italy. *Entrepreneurship Theory and Practice, 30*, 495–517.

Huang, X., Iun, J., Liu, A., & Gong, Y. (2010). Does participative leadership enhance work performance by inducing empowerment or trust? The differential effects on managerial and non-managerial subordinates. *Journal of Organizational Behavior, 31*, 122–143.

Huang, X., & Van de Vliert, E. (2006). Job formalization and cultural individualism as barriers to trust in management. *International Journal of Cross Cultural Management, 6*, 221–242.

Innocenti, L., Pilati, M., & Peluso, A. M. (2011). Trust as moderator in the relationship between HRM practices and employee attitudes. *Human Resource Management Journal, 21*, 303–317.

Jakobsen, T. G. (2010). Public versus private: The conditional effect of state policy and institutional trust on mass opinion. *European Sociological Review, 26*, 307–318.

Jamal, A., & Nooruddin, I. (2010). The democratic utility of trust: A cross-national analysis. *The Journal of Politics, 72*, 45–59.

Janowicz-Panjaitan, M., & Krishnan, R. (2009). Measures for dealing with competence and integrity violations of interorganizational trust at the corporate and operating levels of organizational hierarchy. *Journal of Management Studies, 46*, 245–268.

Jeffries, F. L., & Reed, R. (2000). Trust and adaptation in relational contracting. *Academy of Management Review, 25*, 873–882.

Jiang, C. X., Chua, R. Y., Kotabe, M., & Murray, J. Y. (2011). Effects of cultural ethnicity, firm size, and firm age on senior executives' trust in their overseas business partners: Evidence from China. *Journal of International Business Studies, 42*, 1150–1173.

Johns, G. (2006). The essential impact of context on organizational behavior. *Academy of Management Review, 31*, 386–408.

Joshi, A., Lazarova, M. B., & Liao, H. (2009). Getting everyone on board: The role of inspirational leadership in geographically dispersed teams. *Organization Science, 20*, 240–252.

Kath, L. M., Magley, V. J., & Marmet, M. (2010). The role of organizational trust in safety climate's influence on organizational outcomes. *Accident Analysis & Prevention, 42*, 1488–1497.

Kim, D., Baum, C. F., Ganz, M. L., Subramanian, S. V., & Kawachi, I. (2011). The contextual effects of social capital on health: A cross-national instrumental variable analysis. *Social Science & Medicine, 73*, 1689–1697.

Kim, P. H., Cooper, C. D., Dirks, K. T., & Ferrin, D. L. (2013). Repairing trust with individuals vs. groups. *Organizational Behavior and Human Decision Processes, 120*, 1–14.

Kim, D., & Kawachi, I. (2006). A multilevel analysis of key forms of community-and individual-level social capital as predictors of self-rated health in the United States. *Journal of Urban Health, 83*, 813–826.

Kim, P. H., & Li, M. (2014). Seeking assurances when taking action: Legal systems, social trust, and starting businesses in emerging economies. *Organization Studies, 35*, 359–391.

Klein, K. J., Dansereau, F., & Hall, R. J. (1994). Levels issues in theory development, data collection, and analysis. *Academy of Management Review, 19*, 195–229.

Kozlowski, S. W. J., & Chao, G. T. (2012). The dynamics of emergence: Cognition and cohesion in work teams. *Managerial and Decision Economics, 33*, 335–354.

Kozlowski, S. W. J., & Klein, K. J. (2000). A multilevel approach to theory and research in organizations: Contextual, temporal, and emergent processes. In K. J. Klein & S. W. J. Kozlowski (eds), *Multilevel theory, research, and methods in organizations: Foundations, extensions, and new directions* (pp. 3–90). San Francisco, CA: Jossey-Bass.

Lee, Y. Y., & Lin, J. L. (2009). The effects of trust in physician on self-efficacy, adherence and diabetes outcomes. *Social Science & Medicine, 68*, 1060–1068.

Lewicki, R. J., & Bunker, B. (1996). Developing and maintaining trust in work relationships. In R. M. Kramer & T. R. Tyler (eds), *Trust in organizations: Frontiers of theory and research* (pp. 114–139). Thousand Oaks, CA: Sage.

Li, P. P. (2012). When trust matters the most: The imperatives for contextualising trust research. *Journal of Trust Research, 2*, 101–106.

Li, P. P., Bai, Y., & Xi, Y. (2012). The contextual antecedents of organizational trust: A multidimensional cross-level analysis. *Management and Organization Review, 8*, 371–396.

Lieb, P. S. 2003. The effects of September 11th on job attribute preferences and recruitment. *Journal of Business and Psychology, 18*, 175–190.

Lord, R. G., Diefendorff, J. M., Schmidt, A. M., & Hall, R. J. (2010). Self-regulation at work. *Annual Review of Psychology, 61*, 543–568.

Mayer, R. C., & Davis, J. H. (1999). The effect of the performance appraisal system on trust for management: A field quasi-experiment. *Journal of Applied Psychology, 84*, 123–136.

Mayer, R. C., Davis, J. H., & Schoorman, F. D. (1995). An integrative model of organizational trust. *Academy of Management Review, 20,* 709–734.

McLaughlin, M. (1998). Listening and learning from the field: Tales of policy implementation and situated practice. In A. Hargreaves, A. Lieberman, M. Fullan, & D. Hopkins (eds), *International handbook of educational change* (pp. 70–84). Dordrecht, the Netherlands: Kluwer.

Mischel, W. (1977). The interaction of person and situation. In D. Magnusson & N. S. Endler (eds), *Personality at the crossroads: Current issues in interactional psychology* (pp. 333–352). Hillsdale, NJ: Lawrence Erlbaum.

Morgeson, F. P., & Hofmann, D. A. (1999). The structure and function of collective constructs: Implications for multilevel research and theory development. *Academy of Management Review, 24,* 249–265.

Mouzas, S., Henneberg, S., & Naudé, P. (2007). Trust and reliance in business relationships. *European Journal of Marketing, 41,* 1016–1032.

Muethel, M., & Bond, M. H. (2013). National context and individual employees' trust of the out-group: The role of societal trust. *Journal of International Business Studies, 44,* 312–333.

Ostroff, C. (1992). The relationship between satisfaction, attitudes, and performance: An organizational level analysis. *Journal of Applied Psychology, 77,* 963–974.

Özer, Ö., Zheng, Y., & Ren, Y. (2014). Trust, trustworthiness, and information sharing in supply chains bridging China and the United States. *Management Science, 60,* 2435–2460.

Paxton, P. (2007). Association memberships and generalized trust: A multilevel model across 31 countries. *Social Forces, 86,* 47–76.

Poortinga, W. (2006). Social capital: An individual or collective resource for health? *Social Science & Medicine, 62,* 292–302.

Poppo, L., Zhou, K. Z., & Li, J. J. (2015). When can you trust "trust"? Calculative trust, relational trust, and supplier performance. *Strategic Management Journal, 37,* 724–741.

Putnam, R. D. (1993). The prosperous community: Social capital and public life. *American Prospect, 13,* 35–42.

Rahn, W. M., & Rudolph, T. J. (2005). A tale of political trust in American cities. *Public Opinion Quarterly, 69,* 530–560.

Robinson, S. L., & Rousseau, D. M. (1994). Violating the psychological contract: Not the exception but the norm. *Journal of Organizational Behavior, 15,* 245–259.

Rousseau, D. M. (1985). Issues of level in organizational research: Multi-level and cross-level perspectives. *Research in Organizational Behavior, 7,* 1–37.

Rousseau, D. M., & Fried, Y. (2001). Location, location, location: Contextualizing organizational research. *Journal of Organizational Behavior, 22,* 1–13.

Rousseau, D. M., Sitkin, S. B., Burt, R. S., & Camerer, C. (1998). Not so different after all: A cross-discipline view of trust. *Academy of Management Review, 23,* 393–404.

Rustenbach, E. (2010). Sources of negative attitudes toward immigrants in Europe: A multi-level analysis. *International Migration Review, 44,* 53–77.

Salancik, G. R., & Pfeffer, J. (1978). A social information processing approach to job attitudes and task design. *Administrative Science Quarterly, 23,* 224–253.

Scheer, L. K., Kumar, N., & Steenkamp, J. B. E. (2003). Reactions to perceived inequity in US and Dutch interorganizational relationships. *Academy of Management Journal, 46,* 303–316.

Schilke, O., & Cook, K. S. (2013). A cross-level process theory of trust development in interorganizational relationships. *Strategic Organization, 11,* 281–303.

Schoorman, F. D., Mayer, R. C., & Davis, J. H. (2007). An integrative model of organizational trust: Past, present, and future. *Academy of Management Review, 32,* 344–354.

Searle, R. H. (2013). Recruitment, retention and role slumping in child protection: The evaluation of in-service training initiatives. *British Journal of Social Work, 43,* 1111–1129.

Searle, R., Den Hartog, D. N., Weibel, A., Gillespie, N., Six, F., Hatzakis, T., & Skinner, D. (2011). Trust in the employer: The role of high-involvement work practices and procedural justice in European organizations. *The International Journal of Human Resource Management, 22,* 1069–1092.

Shamir, B., & Lapidot, Y. (2003). Trust in organizational superior: Systemic and collective considerations. *Organization Studies, 24,* 463–491.

Tajfel, H., & Turner, J. C. (1979). An integrative theory of intergroup conflict. In W. Austin & S. Worchel (eds), *The social psychology of intergroup relations* (pp. 33–47). Monterey, CA: Brooks/Cole.

Tay, L., Woo, S. E., & Vermunt, J. K. (2014). A conceptual and methodological framework for psychometric isomorphism validation of multilevel construct measures. *Organizational Research Methods, 17,* 77–106.

Tokuda, Y., Fujii, S., & Inoguchi, T. (2010). Individual and country-level effects of social trust on happiness: The Asia barometer survey. *Journal of Applied Social Psychology, 40,* 2574–2593.

Traunmüller, R. (2011). Moral communities? Religion as a source of social trust in a multilevel analysis of 97 German regions. *European Sociological Review, 27,* 346–363.

Tse, H. H., & Ashkanasy, N. M. (2015). The dyadic level of conceptualization and analysis: A missing link in multilevel OB research?. *Journal of Organizational Behavior, 36,* 1176–1180.

Van der Meer, T. (2010). In what we trust? A multi-level study into trust in parliament as an evaluation of state characteristics. *International Review of Administrative Sciences, 76,* 517–536.

Wang, H., Schlesinger, M., Wang, H., & Hsiao, W. C. (2009). The flip-side of social capital: The distinctive influences of trust and mistrust on health in rural China. *Social Science & Medicine, 68,* 133–142.

Wech, B. A. (2002). Trust context: Effect on organizational citizenship behavior, supervisory fairness, and job satisfaction beyond the influence of leader-member exchange. *Business and Society, 41,* 353–360.

Weibel, A., Den Hartog, D. N., Gillespie, N., Searle, R., Six, F., & Skinner, D. (2015). How do controls impact employee trust in the employer? *Human Resource Management, 55*(3), 437–462.

Weick, K. E. (1995). *Sensemaking in organizations.* Thousand Oaks, CA: Sage.

Weick, K.E. (1996). Enactment and the boundaryless career: Organizing as we work. In M. B. Arthur, D. M. Rousseau (eds), *The boundaryless career: A new employment principle for a new organizational era* (pp. 40–57). New York, NY: Oxford University Press.

Whitener, E. M. (2001). Do "high commitment" human resource practices affect employee commitment? A cross-level analysis using hierarchical linear modeling. *Journal of Management, 27,* 515–535.

Wildman, J. L., Shuffler, M. L., Lazzara, E. H., Fiore, S. M., Burke, C. S., Salas, E., & Garven, S. (2012). Trust development in swift starting action teams: A multilevel framework. *Group & Organization Management, 37,* 137–170.

Williams, M. (2016). Being trusted: How team generational age diversity promotes and undermines trust in cross-boundary relationships. *Journal of Organizational Behavior, 37,* 346–373.

Wong, S. S., & Boh, W. F. (2010). Leveraging the ties of others to build a reputation for trustworthiness among peers. *Academy of Management Journal, 53,* 129–148.

Yamagishi, T., Cook, K. S., & Watabe, M. (1998). Uncertainty, trust, and commitment formation in the United States and Japan. *American Journal of Sociology, 104,* 165–194.

Zaheer, S., & Zaheer, A. (2006). Trust across borders. *Journal of International Business Studies, 37,* 21–29.

PART III

Theories of trust

In Part III we consider the key antecedents and approaches to trust research through seven chapters. Michael Baer and Jason A. Colquitt commence this part with their exploration of some of the more psychologically focused approaches to the study of trust, by reflecting on the antecedents of trust. They start with the question 'Why do people trust?', before embarking on a review of key concepts related to disposition-based trust, highlighting how propensity and other individual differences might affect trust. They then unpack trustworthiness, looking at various models – including dominant sub-facets such as Mayer et al.'s (1995) ability, benevolence and integrity dimensions – to reflect on the boundary conditions and circumstances in which some facets might come to the fore. This chapter links to Chapter 2 by Korsgaard, emphasizing the dearth of work on dynamics. Next they link to Chapter 1 by van Knippenberg, to make the case for more emphasis on the study of affect in trust research. Finally, they identify the hitherto under-explored role of heuristics as a significant antecedent of trust.

E. Allan Lind turns attention to the important perspective of organizational justice research and theory, and trust and trusting behaviour. Through reviewing fairness he identifies, from a psychological perspective, how and why justice is so entwined with trust. He examines empirical evidence that reveals situations where impressions of fair treatment may be a substitute or replacement for judgments of trust. Thus he reveals how fairness not only enhances trust, but can usurp it. Drawing from work undertaken by social, organizational and political psychology, and also organizational behaviour, law and society studies, he reveals how the study of fair treatment, especially fair processes rather than outcomes, provides insight into group and organizational inclusion. His chapter also links with others that consider some of the dynamic aspects of relationships (Chapter 2 by Korsgaard, Chapter 11 by Coyle-Shaprio & Diehl) by showing how fairness and trust concerns shift over the course of a relationship.

Our attention then shifts to perhaps the most dominant perspective in the study of trust, that of social exchange theory, with Jacqueline A-M. Coyle-Shapiro and Marjo-Riitta Diehl looking at trust and its role in social exchange relationships within the context of employee-organization relationship. They return to the origins of this concept before considering current work that draws on the theory, including that on psychological contracts, idiosyncratic deals (i-deals), perceived organizational support and employment relationships. This chapter has strong links to many of the subsequent chapters in the context and applications part (see Chapters 18–25), as well as to Searle's review of trust and Human Resource Management in Chapter 28, where this perspective dominates.

In Chapter 12 Reinhard Bachmann makes the case value of institutional theory focus for trust. He outlines three reasons why institutional perspective is often not included. In response, he argues for the importance of being clear regarding whether the focus on trust concerns how the institution arranges itself, or how the institution shapes the behaviours of social actors. He goes onto reflect on where an institutional-perspective can be particularly important.

The sociological and economic approach is retained in Laura Poppo and Zheng Cheng's review of trust and contracts. They consider the important role of contracts and trust in business-to-business exchanges through the perspectives of transaction cost economics and social embeddedness. They consider evidence supporting the impact of trust, contracts and/or performance and how they relate to each other as complements and substitutes. The chapter has strong links to Chapter 29 by Long and Weibel, on control and trust.

In the final chapter of this section, we return to a more social-psychological perspective and a theory that has been identified as critical for the further development of the field, with Edward C. Tomlinson's review of attribution analysis. This is an approach that is central to understanding trust dynamics and therefore has resonance with other chapters, including Chapter 2 by Korsgaard, on reciprocal trust. In this chapter the founding work of Kelley from the late 1960s is reviewed and the psychological basis of understanding why attributions are central to trust dynamics is outlined. The chapter explores the role of attributions in the development, decline and repair of trust.

References

Kelley, H. H. (1967). Attribution theory in social psychology. In D. Levine (Ed.) *Nebraska Symposium on Motivation*. Lincoln, NE: University of Nebraska Press.

Mayer, R. C., Davis, J. H., & Schoorman, F. D. (1995). An integrative model of organizational trust. *Academy of Management Review*, 20, 709–734.

9

WHY DO PEOPLE TRUST?

Moving toward a more comprehensive consideration of the antecedents of trust

Michael D. Baer and Jason A. Colquitt

Introduction

Why do people trust? Considering the substantial literature on trust, one might initially expect that a single chapter would be unable to adequately review the answers to this question. On closer inspection, however, the answers provided by the literature comprise a very narrow set of answers. Indeed, narrative and meta-analytic reviews of trust have observed that empirical research has been almost entirely limited to exploring just two broad answers to this question – because people have trusting dispositions and because others are trustworthy (Colquitt, Scott, & LePine, 2007; Dirks & Ferrin, 2002; Möllering, 2006). In other words, the literature has reached a consensus that people trust as a result of their dispositional tendencies to rely on the words and deeds of others, and because others demonstrate, in a variety of ways, that they can be relied upon (Mayer, Davis, & Schoorman, 1995).

This narrow focus in the literature can be at least partially attributed to early conceptual models of trust, most notably the 'integrative model of trust' presented by Mayer, Davis, and Schoorman (1995). Mayer and colleagues defined *trust* as the willingness to be vulnerable to another party based on the expectation that the party will perform a desired action, regardless of the trustor's ability to monitor that party. Previous scholars had defined trust as an aspect of the trustor's personality (Rotter, 1967; Webb & Worchel, 1986; Wrightsman, 1964) and as synonymous with the positive expectations arising from the characteristics of a trustee (e.g. Butler & Cantrell, 1984; Sitkin & Roth, 1993). Mayer et al. (1995), however, argued that these constructs were more appropriately modeled as antecedents of trust. In their model, the disposition to trust was labelled *trust propensity* – a stable individual difference that reflects a generalized tendency to rely on the words and deeds of others (see also Rotter, 1967; Stack, 1978; Wrightsman, 1964). Characteristics of the trustee were labelled *trustworthiness* – a multidimensional construct reflecting perceptions of the trustee's task-specific skills (*ability*), concern for the trustor (*benevolence*) and values (*integrity*). Although a broad range of trustee characteristics have been examined within the literature, Mayer and colleagues proposed that ability, benevolence and integrity are a parsimonious yet inclusive set.

Notwithstanding the strides that have been made in understanding these antecedents of trust, several key areas remain unexplored. First, the concept of trust propensity has dominated treatments of disposition-based trust. Yet, is trust propensity the only individual difference that affects trust, or are there other traits that contribute to a disposition to trust? Second, although trustworthiness has been conceptually and empirically divided into the sub-facets of ability, benevolence and integrity (Mayer & Davis, 1999; Mayer et al., 1995), little has been done to determine the boundary conditions for the importance of each facet (Colquitt et al., 2007). For example, does ability matter more than integrity in some jobs? Is this pattern reversed in other jobs? Similarly, despite theoretical suggestions that the impact of trustworthiness on trust may depend on the personality of the trustor (Mayer et al., 1995), these dynamics have not yet been explored.

Although two decades of empirical and conceptual research have provided considerable support for Mayer et al.'s set of antecedents, some scholars have suggested that a comprehensive model of trust should necessarily include an affective component (e.g. Jones & George, 1998; Lewicki & Bunker, 1996; Lewis & Weigert, 1985; McAllister, 1995; Williams, 2001). Trustworthiness and, to a lesser extent, the disposition to trust, form a calculative, cognitive foundation of trust (Lewicki & Bunker, 1996; Lewis & Weigert, 1985). In a departure from this cognitive approach, many scholars have proposed that trust also stems from the emotional bonds between trustor and trustee (Johnson-George & Swap, 1982; Lewicki & Bunker, 1996; Lewis & Weigert, 1985; McAllister, 1995; Rempel, Holmes, & Zanna, 1985). This base of trust has received a number of different labels, including emotional trust (Johnson-George & Swap, 1982; Lewis & Weigert, 1985), affect-based trust (McAllister, 1995), faith (Rempel et al., 1985) and relational trust (Rousseau et al., 1998). There are some differences between these conceptualizations, but they converge on the notion that care and concern are an important base of trust.

Even though these conceptualizations seem to suggest affect is a widely-accepted 'third' base of trust, many scholars have noted that Mayer et al.'s concept of benevolence encompasses the care and concern that characterizes conceptual and empirical treatments of affective bases of trust (Colquitt, LePine, Zapata, & Wild, 2011; Colquitt et al., 2007; Dietz & Den Hartog, 2006; McEvily & Tortoriello, 2011). Indeed, Mayer et al. defined benevolence as 'the extent to which a trustee is believed to want to do good to the trustor . . . [it] suggests that the trustee has some specific attachment to the trustor' (1995: 718). Adding to this conceptual and empirical confusion, whereas some scholars have conceptualized affect as a characteristic of the dyadic relationship between trustor and trustee (e.g. McAllister, 1995), others have conceptualized affect in terms of the emotions and sentiments of the trustor (e.g. Dunn & Schweitzer, 2005; Jones & George, 1998). Still other scholars have adopted an approach that includes both conceptualizations (Williams, 2001). In sum, the literature has yet to reach a conceptual or empirical consensus on the role of affect as an antecedent of trust.

Although a model of trust that includes both emotional and rational bases may appear comprehensive, there are phenomena that this model cannot adequately explain. For example, consider the experience of employees who join a new organization. During the initial stage of employment, employees will have had little time to gather 'data' on the trustworthiness of their coworkers or supervisors. Likewise, they will not have had the opportunity to form emotional bonds with their new colleagues. Yet, scholars have observed that individuals in new situations still trust – at levels not fully explained by dispositional trust (for a review, see Balliet & Van Lange, 2013). If this trust is not based on disposition, rational reasons, or emotions, what explains why these employees trust? In a departure from the conscious, cognitive approach that has dominated empirical investigations of trust, scholars have begun to suggest that trust is also influenced by less-conscious, heuristic predictors. For example, McKnight and colleagues (1998)

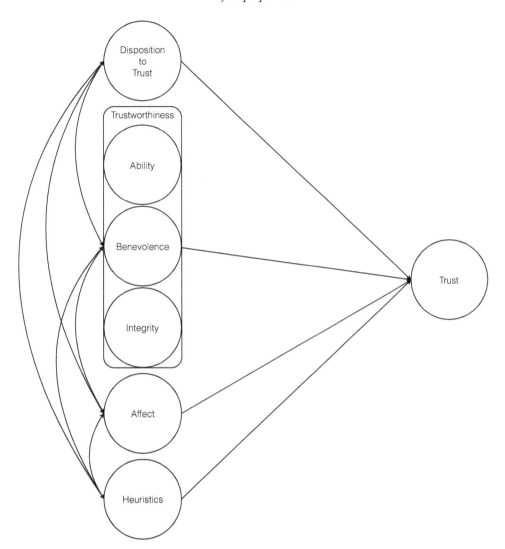

Figure 9.1 Antecedents of trust

proposed that trust in the organization may be influenced by the extent to which the organizational setting seems normal, customary and in the proper order. Although this stream of research is in its nascent stage, we argue that heuristics provide insight into trust dynamics that are unexplained by current models.

In this chapter, we first review the research addressing the disposition to trust and trustworthiness. Next, we review the conceptual and empirical research on the role of affect as a base of trust. Finally, we propose that heuristics are an important (yet relatively unexplored) antecedent of trust. In each section we highlight areas with unanswered questions and make recommendations for future research. Thus, this chapter reviews the current answers to 'Why do people trust?' while also suggesting new answers. Our expanded approach to the antecedents of trust is represented in Figure 9.1. This figure is intended as a broad overview of several categories of antecedents rather than as a graphical representation of specific hypotheses regarding these antecedents. By more closely examining the role of the disposition to trust, trustworthiness and affect, and expanding the focus to additional antecedents of trust, this chapter should aid scholars and organizations in taking a more holistic approach to understanding and increasing trust.

The disposition to trust

Consider the following scenario. Two friends – Chris and Pat – are separately approached in a mall parking lot by a stranger who claims to need a couple of dollars for bus fare so he can pick up his kids from school. Chris gives the man the benefit of the doubt and hands over the two dollars. Pat assumes it is a scam and politely tells the guy to take a hike. This scenario illustrates the idea of a trusting (or distrusting, in Pat's case) disposition. Some of the earliest research on the disposition to trust was conducted by Rotter (1967, 1971, 1980), who argued that trust was based on an individual's generalized expectancies of others. He proposed that the characteristics of a trusting personality could be distilled to a single trait, defining *interpersonal trust* as an individual's generalized expectancy that others can be relied on. Rotter's (1967, 1971, 1980) conceptualization of trust as a relatively stable personality characteristic is illustrated by a sample item from his Interpersonal Trust Scale (Rotter, 1967): 'Most people can be counted on to do what they say they will do.' This generalized expectancy that others can be relied upon has been referred to by other scholars as *dispositional trust* (Kramer, 1999), *generalized trust* (Stack, 1978) and *trust propensity* (Mayer et al., 1995; McKnight, Cummings, & Chervany, 1998).

Research suggests that the disposition to trust may begin to take shape in children as early as 6 to 18 months of age (Deutsch & Krauss, 1965; Rotter, 1971), with development likely occurring through at least two mechanisms: reinforcement and modelling (Webb & Worchel, 1986). With respect to reinforcement, the extent to which needs are met during this developmental period may provide a baseline for the extent to which others in life can be expected to meet one's needs (Erikson, 1963; Webb & Worchel, 1986). As needs are met in the infant–parent relationship, the infant may extend positive expectancies to others, both within and outside the family (Sakai, 2010). Although these expectancies are likely not the only determinant of a general willingness to trust others, they may be a 'necessary precursor' (Webb & Worchel, 1986: 217).

Scholars have proposed that the general willingness to trust is also influenced by the extent to which a trusting orientation is modelled by the parents (Katz & Rotter, 1969; Stolle & Nishikawa, 2011). Although trust propensity is heavily influenced by primary caregivers, it may also continue to be refined through experiences with peers, teachers and other close sources (Flanagan & Stout, 2010; Katz & Rotter, 1969; Rotter, 1967; Webb & Worchel, 1986; for a review, see Sakai, 2010). In support of this proposal, studies of twins' trust propensity suggests that non-shared environmental influences in childhood have an even greater impact on trust propensity than shared environmental influences (Hiraishi, Yamagata, Shikishima, & Ando, 2008; Sturgis et al., 2010).

In management research, many of the hypothesized effects of the disposition to trust are grounded in social learning theory (Rotter, 1954; Rotter, Chance, & Phares, 1972). According to social learning theory, expectancies in each situation are determined not only by experiences in that situation but also by experiences in similar situations. The theory also specifies that the influence of generalized expectancies is relative to the amount of experience the person has in that particular situation (Rotter, 1980). For example, a person's expectations of a used-car dealer are likely influenced by experiences with that particular dealer as well as experiences with previous dealers. If previous dealers were dishonest, the person will likely expect the current dealer to also be dishonest. Through interactions with the current dealer, however, the person gains situation-specific 'data', thereby decreasing the impact of generalized expectancies. Research supports these proposals, finding that the impact of trust propensity decreases over time as individuals gather information on trustworthiness (Gill, Boies, Finegan, & McNally, 2005; van der Werff & Buckley, in press).

It follows that the disposition to trust should be particularly relevant in novel situations. When actors are unfamiliar with one another, they have little to no situation-specific data on which to base trust. Accordingly, the generalized expectancy resulting from past experiences likely plays a pivotal role (Bigley & Pearce, 1998). McKnight and colleagues (1998) argued that dispositional trust is becoming increasingly important in the current work environment as increased turnover, corporate restructuring and temporary work teams are resulting in a higher frequency of new work relationships. Despite the proposed importance of dispositional trust, it has received far less empirical attention than trustworthiness (Colquitt et al., 2007; Kramer, 1999). Some of this lack of attention may be due to a general consensus that the relationship between dispositional trust and trust will decrease as familiarity with the trustee increases (Bigley & Pearce, 1998; Mayer et al., 1995; Rotter, 1967). Yet, Mayer et al. (1995) suggested that even in familiar relationships trust propensity is likely to exhibit an effect on trust. Colquitt et al. (2007) tested this proposal in a meta-analysis, finding that trust propensity continued to have a significant relationship with trust when controlling for trustworthiness.

Despite the clear consensus that the disposition to trust is an important antecedent of trust, questions remain. In contrast with Rotter's view of a trusting disposition as a fixed, enduring trait, Hardin (1992) proposed that the inclination to trust (or distrust) is reinforced by the trustor's own behaviour. People with low dispositional trust are less likely to engage in cooperative behaviour, making it unlikely that they will encounter information that alters their generalized perceptions of others. Reflecting on this notion, Bigley and Pearce (1998) questioned whether organizational interventions might be able to modify the disposition to trust. At first glance, the proposal to modify a trait seems counter to the nature of traits as fixed and enduring (McCrae & Costa, 1994). Recent research, however, has been moving toward perspectives that acknowledge the stability of personality while also allowing for change and variation across situations and one's life span (Fleeson & Jolley, 2006; Judge, Simon, Hurst, & Kelley, 2014). Sitkin and colleagues (Sitkin & Pablo, 1992; Sitkin & Weingart, 1995) made similar arguments with respect to risk propensity – a concept that shares considerable overlap with trust propensity (Mayer et al., 1995). They suggested that risk propensity is a stable, cumulative tendency that can nonetheless change over time as a result of experience (Sitkin & Weingart, 1995).

To date, recommendations for increasing trust have focused almost entirely on what the trustee can do to be more trustworthy (e.g. Korsgaard, Brodt, & Whitener, 2002; Whitener, Brodt, Korsgaard, & Werner, 1998; for a review see Fulmer & Gelfand, 2012). This is not surprising, given that the disposition to trust has been treated as a stable trait. If, however, this disposition is malleable, organizations may also be able to foster trust through a trustor-focused approach. Empirical research has not yet addressed the variability of the disposition to trust, but some inferences can be drawn from recent work on the variability of the Big Five personality traits (Judge et al., 2014). Judge and colleagues found that daily work experiences (i.e. citizenship behaviour, motivation and interpersonal conflict) predicted short-term variations in personality – resulting in what they referred to as 'personality states'. Similarly, workplace experiences that prime positive emotions and cognitions may have positive effects on the disposition to trust. We suggest that explorations of the state-like nature of dispositional trust adopt the methodological approach followed by Judge et al. (2014), wherein they examined the deviations from baseline tendencies using an experience sampling design and hierarchical linear modeling. This approach allows researchers to account for both between- and within-person variance in traits. From this perspective, participants are asked how trusting or suspicious they are 'today', as opposed to in general.

Moving beyond trust propensity, are there other individual differences that can predict unique variance in trust? One potential answer to this question is found in a return to Sitkin and Pablo's (1992) theorizing about the role of individual differences in risk behaviour (see also Sitkin & Weingart, 1995). Sitkin and colleagues proposed that individuals have a relatively stable risk propensity – the tendency to either take or avoid risks. This pattern of risk taking or risk aversion influences both how risks are evaluated and what risks are deemed acceptable. Although there are some clear similarities between trust propensity and risk propensity, the constructs differ in at least one important way. Unlike trust propensity, risk propensity does not involve an evaluation of the trustee.

The importance of this distinction is illustrated in the following scenario, in which a supervisor has two employees who have similar perceptions of the supervisor's trustworthiness and levels of trust propensity, but differing levels of risk propensity. Both employees have presented the supervisor with ideas for improving unit performance, and the supervisor has suggested to both employees that she can present their ideas to upper management. It is an inherently risky proposition, as the supervisor may botch the presentation or fail to give the employees credit for their ideas. Both employees may, based on a low general tendency to trust others, be less inclined to entrust this critical task to their supervisor. Yet, while the employee with low risk propensity may determine that the risks do not outweigh the benefits in this particular situation, an employee with high risk propensity may decide to 'roll the dice' and trust the supervisor. In this example, risk propensity acts as a trait with independent effects on trust, above and beyond trust propensity.

In sum, there are substantial unanswered questions about the disposition to trust and its effects on trust. We highlighted a couple of these questions: First, is the disposition to trust fixed? Second, are there dispositional predictors of trust that lie outside of trust propensity? In addition to providing theoretical insights, the answers to these questions also have practical utility. In most conceptual and empirical approaches to trust, the disposition to trust is treated as a single exogenous variable – trust propensity. From an organizational perspective, this model suggests that apart from selecting employees with high trust propensity, efforts to build trust should be focused on increasing the trustworthiness of the trustees, such as supervisors and organizations (Korsgaard et al., 2002; Whitener et al., 1998; for a review see Fulmer & Gelfand, 2012). If, however, trust propensity can be shaped by interventions (Bigley & Pearce, 1998), organizations may be able to take both trustor- and trustee-focused approaches to fostering trust. Relatedly, if there are additional traits that contribute to a trusting disposition, organizations may benefit from selecting employees who possess these traits.

Trustworthiness

The disposition to trust has a limited ability to explain trust. Research, experience and common sense suggest that individuals – despite having a relatively stable disposition to trust – do not trust everyone equally in every situation. Similarly, an individual may trust a particular person in one area but not in another area (Barber, 1983; Hardin, 2002). Addressing these points, Lewis and Weigert (1985) argued trust is not simply based on a trusting personality, but also on the characteristics of the trustee. To illustrate, consider a new employee who is just getting acquainted with a coworker. In the first days of employment, the employee's willingness to be vulnerable to the coworker on critical tasks is likely dependent on the employee's generalized expectancies. After all, the employee has little 'hard data' on which to base the decision. Over time, however, the employee will start to gather data on the coworker's characteristics, such as task-specific capabilities, goodwill and dependability, thereby decreasing the impact of general-ized expectancies. In light of these dynamics, scholars have argued that the characteristics of the trustee – generally referred to as *trustworthiness* – are the primary determinant of trust (Gabarro, 1978; Lewis & Weigert, 1985; Mayer et al., 1995; Mishra, 1996; Pirson & Malhotra, 2011; Sitkin & Roth, 1993). Although the characteristics that comprise trustworthiness have received a number of different labels in the literature, current treatments generally conform to Mayer et al.'s (1995) proposal that trustworthiness is encapsulated by ability, benevolence and integrity.

Ability

Ability is the knowledge, skills and competencies required to perform effectively in some specific domain (Mayer et al., 1995). This definition highlights the notion that ability, and its relation-ship with trust, are task specific. For example, a skilled auto mechanic might be trusted to replace a transmission, but not to perform a medical procedure. Ability matters because of the interdependent nature of trust (Kee & Knox, 1970; Sitkin & Roth, 1993). Consider a supervisor who has been given a project from upper management. To efficiently complete the project, the supervisor contemplates delegating an important part of the project to a subordinate. Given that the supervisor is ultimately responsible for the outcome of the project, it is unlikely that the subordinate will be chosen at random. Rather, the supervisor is likely to select and trust a subordinate who has the ability to effectively accomplish the assigned task. In support of this proposal, Sitkin and Roth (1993) theorized ability is the primary indicator of trust within organizations.

Various scholars have used the term *competence* to refer to a construct that is conceptually similar to ability (e.g. Butler, 1991; Butler & Cantrell, 1984; Gabarro, 1978; Hardin, 2002; Kee & Knox, 1970). Barber (1983: 14) proposed trust is the expectation of 'technically competent role performance'. Of the nine bases of trust inductively identified by Gabarro (1978), four of them – *functional competence, interpersonal competence, general business sense* and *good judgment* – are representative of ability. Sitkin and Roth (1993) referred to a similar concept – an employee's ability to reliably complete assignments – as *task reliability*. Likewise, Cook and Wall (1980) focused on the capability and reliability aspects of ability as predictors of trust. *Expertness* – the degree to which an individual is a source of valid assertions – is another construct that is similar to ability (Hovland, Janis, & Kelley, 1953). Concepts coded as ability in Colquitt et al.'s (2007) meta-analysis of trust included competence, expertise, knowledge and talent.

Benevolence

Benevolence is the extent to which the trustor believes the trustee is concerned about the trustor's well-being, apart from any self-interested motives (Mayer et al., 1995). Larzelere and Huston (1980) proposed a trustor is likely to question whether a potential partner is genuinely interested in the trustor's welfare or is motivated by individualistic goals. To the extent that a trustee is seen as benevolent, the trustor is more likely to predict positive outcomes in the relationship. As a consequence, the trustor's willingness to be vulnerable increases. For example, a supervisor would likely rely on attributions of benevolence when deciding whether or not to share sensitive information with an employee. An employee with low benevolence would be expected to disclose that information if it provided a personal benefit. Conversely, an employee who was concerned about the supervisor's welfare would be less likely to breach confidence.

Other scholars have discussed concepts that overlap with benevolence. Gabarro (1978) suggested favourable perceptions of a trustee's motives were a base of trust. Barber (1983) similarly argued that trust was based on an expectation that others would demonstrate a concern for interests above their own. Along these lines, Rempel et al. (1985) noted trust is dependent on a belief that the trustee will be responsive and caring. Other scholars have suggested trust is based on expectancies of altruism (Frost, Stimpson, & Maughan, 1978; Lindskold & Bennett, 1973). Several researchers (Butler, 1991; Butler & Cantrell, 1984; Jennings, 1971) have used the term *loyalty* – wanting to protect and make the trustor look good – to refer to benevolence. Concepts coded as benevolence in Colquitt et al.'s (2007) meta-analysis included openness, loyalty, concern and perceived support.

Integrity

Integrity is the trustor's perception that the trustee adheres to a set of values that the trustor finds acceptable (Mayer et al., 1995). To a large extent, perceptions of integrity are based on consistency between the trustee's words and deeds (Larzelere & Huston, 1980; Rempel et al., 1985; Schlenker, Helm, & Tedeschi, 1973; Simons, 2002). Speaking to this issue, Simons' (2002) definition and treatment of behavioural integrity focused on word–deed alignment. In contrast, Mayer et al. (1995) argued that adhering to a set of values or having high word–deed consistency is not sufficient for perceptions of integrity. This proposal was based, in part, on theorizing from Sitkin and Roth (1993), who suggested a base of trust was the compatibility of values and beliefs between trustor and trustee. They proposed a lack of value congruence would decrease trust. To illustrate the necessity of integrating the idea of word–deed consistency and values congruence into a definition of integrity, consider an employee who values and single-mindedly pursues personal gain. Although the employee's actions have high integrity – they are internally consistent, after all – a supervisor is unlikely to perceive the employee as having integrity unless the supervisor shares similar values (Mayer et al., 1995). At first glance, the integration of value congruence and word–deed consistency into a definition of integrity seems a bit inconsistent with the definition proposed by Simons (2002). Further scrutiny reveals, however, that his model of behavioural integrity includes a concept that overlaps with value congruence. He proposed that the more a trustor cares about the issue related to word–deed consistency – i.e. an alignment or misalignment on values held by the trustor – the more the event will affect integrity perceptions.

Other scholars have also addressed the nature of integrity and its importance to trust. Larzelere and Huston (1980) proposed attributions of honesty allow a trustor to take the trustee's word at face value. Accordingly, the trustor has more positive expectations of the outcome and a greater willingness to be vulnerable in the relationship. The critical nature of integrity perceptions were shown empirically by Butler and Cantrell (1984), who found that integrity was one of the most important bases of trust. In an extension of this research, Butler (1991) examined several antecedents of trust that fit beneath the umbrella of integrity: integrity, promise fulfillment, consistency and fairness. Cook and Wall (1980) proposed *trustworthy intentions* were a key predictor of trust. Although this construct overlaps with benevolence, some of their scale items are reflective of integrity. Concepts coded as integrity in Colquitt et al.'s (2007) meta-analysis included procedural justice, promise keeping and credibility.

Summarizing the state of the literature, Möllering (2006: 13) proposed that a consensus has been reached: trust is 'primarily and essentially' a function of perceived trustworthiness. Supporting this claim, a meta-analysis revealed that all three facets of trustworthiness were strongly correlated with trust, while trust propensity was modestly correlated with trust (Colquitt et al.,

2007). Importantly, all three facets exhibited unique relationships with trust in meta-analytic structural equation modeling. Given the strong support for Mayer et al.'s conceptualization of trustworthiness, where should research on this critical antecedent look next? Before providing new directions, we first provide a word of caution. It is tempting to infuse novelty into a study on trust by adding a 'new' trustee characteristic that predicts trust. For example, consider a study that shows that a certification (e.g. an MBA or PhD) is associated with trust. On the one hand, that sort of certification could be argued to trigger affect- or heuristic-based forms of trust, of the type reviewed in the following sections. On the other hand, that certification could simply be a proxy for ability. In that sense, the *predictor* would not be new, merely the *operationalization* of the predictor would be new. We would therefore caution scholars to control for ability, benevolence and integrity when introducing new predictors of trust so that incremental validity can be examined.

Returning to ability, benevolence and integrity themselves, one question concerns how often they hold a unique relevance to trust. In their theorizing, Mayer et al. (1995: 729) noted that 'the question "Do you trust them?" must be qualified: "trust them to do what?"' To illustrate the importance of this question, consider an employee who may need to rely on a supervisor to handle a critical aspect of a project. In this case the primary consideration may be whether the supervisor has the requisite task-specific skills to effectively contribute. Now contemplate an employee who may be considering whether or not to disclose the commission of a costly error. In this case, the primary consideration may be whether the supervisor is concerned about the employee's well-being. Both situations involve an element of risk and action depends on the employee's willingness to be vulnerable, but the most important facet of trustworthiness is likely different in the two cases. Research has not provided much insight into these dynamics. Even though trustworthiness has been examined in a substantial amount of trust research, almost no work has examined moderators of the trustworthiness − trust relationship. In an exception to this trend, Colquitt and colleagues' (2011) research with a group of firefighters showed that in high-reliability task contexts trust was based on integrity, whereas in typical task contexts trust was also based on benevolence. Accordingly, we suggest that future research strive to unpack the situational dynamics of trustworthiness. Researchers who pursue this path might find it fruitful to examine Sitkin and colleagues' (Sitkin & Roth, 1993; Sitkin & Weingart, 1995) work on risk propensity, as they address the notion that the role of trustworthiness as an antecedent of trust may be situationally dependent.

Following the question of which facets are important in which situations, we add the question 'For whom are those facets important?'. Mayer et al.'s (1995) model of trust suggests that trust propensity moderates the effects of trustworthiness on trust. We are unaware of this suggestion receiving attention in management research, but some information systems research on trust in Internet shopping found that trust propensity magnified the effects of integrity yet did not impact the effects of ability (Lee & Turban, 2001). The lack of research on this issue is somewhat surprising. The assumption in the literature is that trust propensity matters at the initial stages of a relationship, but that its importance wanes over time. If, however, trust propensity continues to impact trust through interactive effects with trustworthiness, researchers may have underestimated its importance. There are likely other personality traits that similarly moderate the relationships between the trustworthiness facets and trust. Consider, for example, the need for affiliation − a personality attribute reflecting individuals' desire for emotional support and their tendency to react positively to that support (Hill, 1987, 1991). Hill (1991) found that need for affiliation amplified the effects of partner warmth on the desire to interact with that partner. That same dynamic could occur for the relationship between benevolence and trust. Research investigating the moderating influences of these, and other, personality variables on the relationships between the facets of trustworthiness and trust would certainly provide insight into for whom these facets matter.

Affect

In the same year that Mayer et al. (1995) gave scholars a new way of thinking about the cognitive drivers of trust, another paper increased the salience of affect. McAllister (1995: 26) described affect-based trust as growing out of the 'emotional bonds' and 'emotional ties' between people. Affect-based trust was contrasted with cognition-based trust, or trust rooted in ability and integrity sorts of concepts. In a sample of managers and professionals across industries, McAllister (1995) showed that affect-based trust grew out of instances of citizenship – with helpful behaviours presumably deepening emotional bonds. His results also showed that affect-based trust grew out of repeated interactions – with more time presumably allowing connections to deepen. Importantly, affect-based trust was strongly correlated with cognition-based trust, but not so strongly as to suggest the two were redundant. Did other trust scholars take note of McAllister's (1995) concepts? Citation counts would certainly suggest they did, with over 5,000 citations in Google Scholar – a level eclipsed only by Mayer et al.'s (1995) own 10,000 for trust articles in that time period.

McAllister's (1995) theorizing was rooted in earlier treatments of the affective-cognitive duality of trust (Lewis & Wiegert, 1985; Johnson-George & Swap, 1982; Rempel et al., 1985). For example, Johnson-George and Swap (1982) described how trust operates in close personal relationships. They argued that a sense of emotional safety was important, even aside from a sense of reliability. A similar duality was shown in Rempel et al.'s (1985) examination, with trust in close relationships depending not just on predictability or consistency, but also on emotional comfort. What McAllister (1995: 37) did, in part, was apply such ideas to relationships between employees. In that context, affect-based trust was characterized by strong agreement with beliefs like 'we have a sharing relationship', 'we would both feel a sense of loss if one of us was transferred' and 'we have both made considerable emotional investments in our working relationship'.

The content of McAllister's (1995) affect-based trust scale is similar in many respects to conceptualizations of leader-member exchange – especially those that include affect. For example, Liden and Masyln (1998) argued that the depth and quality of a leader-subordinate dyad could be described by the degree of mutual contribution, mutual loyalty, mutual respect and mutual affect. From this affect-based perspective, deeper, more high quality relationships are marked by both members liking one another and considering themselves friends as much as colleagues. Given that similarity, it is not surprising that affect-based trust itself serves as a valid indicator of the depth and quality of dyadic relationships (Colquitt, Baer, Long, & Halvorsen-Ganepola, 2014).

As noted above, McAllister's (1995) affect-based trust conceptualization also winds up being quite similar to Mayer et al.'s (1995) benevolence facet of trustworthiness. In their measure of benevolence, Mayer and Davis (1999: 136) asked trustors whether trustees were 'concerned about my welfare', would 'go out of their way to help me' and look out for 'what is important to me'. Those sorts of behaviours seem like the building blocks of a 'sharing relationship', to use one of McAllister's (1995) phrases. Put differently, those sorts of behaviours seem like the 'considerable emotional investments' that McAllister (1995) describes – the kind that wind up creating a 'sense of loss' if one member of the trustor–trustee dyad is taken away. Indeed, affect-based trust can be viewed as a form of 'mutual benevolence' – as the consequence of both members of a dyad engaging in caring and concerned behaviour.

The similarities between McAllister's (1995) affect-based trust conceptualization and Mayer and Davis's (1999) benevolence conceptualization are helpful, insofar as they allow scholars to picture how results from one model would likely look if examined through the lens of the other model. For example, if affect-based trust was more predictive of some outcome than cognition-based trust in some context, scholars could likely assume that benevolence would be more predictive than either ability or integrity. That said, the fact that McAllister's (1995) conceptualization incorporates both dyadic behaviours and the feelings that result from those behaviours means that scholars cannot isolate the unique role played by affect. That observation begs the question of what affect-based trust would look like if the 'affect' term was taken more literally.

Affect can be described as an umbrella term for the feelings that individuals experience, including in-the-moment states and more cross-situational states (Barsade & Gibson, 2007). One kind of in-the-moment state is mood, a diffuse and low-intensity state that is somewhat unfocused, with no clear cause or target. Moods tend to be classified according to pleasantness (i.e. good or bad) and activation (i.e. high energy or low energy). From this perspective, employees can be in enthusiastic moods (high pleasantness, high activation), relaxed moods (high pleasantness, low activation), depressed moods (low pleasantness, low activation), or nervous moods (low pleasantness, high activation). Another kind of in-the-moment state is emotions, more intense states that have a clear cause and target. Although emotions could be classified in the same way as moods, they tend to be more differentiated, with specific labels, antecedents and consequences. Those include joy, pride, affection, nostalgia, anger, sadness, fear, resentment and disgust (Barsade & Gibson, 2007; Elfenbein, 2007).

Such feeling states point to an alternative means of conceptualizing affect-based trust, other than mutual benevolence: the covariation of affect and a willingness to be vulnerable. Consider the case of an employee who has been working on an engaging project for most of the day. The employee finds herself in an enthusiastic state – a feeling that could be labelled an emotion if the project was a conscious cause or a mood if the root of the feeling was less salient. Regardless, now presume that some part of the project needs to be delegated to a coworker, creating an opportunity for accepting vulnerability. If that positive mood triggers an intention to delegate, that would be an example of affect-based trust. One could conceive of this affect-based trust occurring directly, with the enthusiasm predicting the willingness to be vulnerable independent of ability, benevolence and integrity. Alternatively, one could conceive of an indirect influence, with enthusiasm shaping perceptions of ability, benevolence and integrity, which would go on to predict the delegation intentions. Of course, negative states could engender affect-based distrust in the same way, with negative moods and emotions reducing intentions to accept vulnerability, either directly or indirectly.

More cross-situational feeling states provide an additional means of conceptualizing affect-based trust. Sentiments are defined as tendencies to respond effectively to a particular person or object (Frijda, 1994; Stets, 2003). If a given person triggers the same emotions again and again, the affect can wind up getting 'stuck' to the person, creating a sentiment. Indeed, once created, the sentiment can itself wind up re-triggering the original emotions. Take the example of an employee who winds up working with an old friend from high school. Being around the old friend triggers nostalgia, first at lunch, then at a meeting, then at a sales conference, and so forth. Eventually, the nostalgia transfers from an emotion to a sentiment. If that nostalgia winds up predicting the intention to delegate something to the coworker, it would become one nuanced form of affect-based trust.

Indeed, sentiments could complement another type of trust that has not yet been mentioned in our review: 'identification-based trust' (Lewicki & Bunker, 1996; Shapiro, Sheppard, & Cheraskin, 1992). This type of trust occurs when the trustor believes that the trustee shares some common group membership – that he or she is 'one of us'. As described by Lewicki and Bunker (1996), identification-based trust is even deeper than the trust engendered by ability, benevolence and integrity – a form of trust that they label 'knowledge-based trust'. Lewicki and Bunker (1996) argued that a sense of shared group membership creates a mutual understanding and an assumption that relevant desires, values and intentions are shared. From an affective perspective, however, it is just as likely that shared group membership engenders pride and affection. Those sentiments may be the 'active ingredients' in triggering a willingness to accept vulnerability; not mutual understanding. Alternatively, it may be that the shared group membership removes fear or resentment, preventing the sorts of sentiments that could undermine a willingness to accept vulnerability.

Of course, the value in this more literal conceptualization of affect-based trust rests on this question: can these in-the-moment or more cross-situational feeling states actually predict a willingness to be vulnerable? Fortunately, theories in the affect domain suggest that the answer to that question is 'yes'. For example, affective events theory suggests that feeling states can shape both evaluative judgments and information processing strategies (Weiss & Cropanzano, 1996). Thus, positive states could make it more likely that trustors will exhibit trusting intentions. Similarly, the affect infusion model argues that affect can 'fill in the gaps' for decisions where relevant information is lacking (Forgas, 1995). Thus, if information on a trustee's ability, benevolence or integrity is missing, a positive feeling state could substitute for that information, thereby engendering a willingness to be vulnerable. Such feeling states could even prime the trustor to more vividly recall positive ability, benevolence or integrity data when weighing whether to trust. Of course, it remains to be seen how powerful such influences would be when controlling for both trust propensity and trustworthiness.

Heuristics

Thus far, our review of the antecedents of trust has reflected the notion that trust has both a cognitive base and an affective base (e.g. Johnson-George & Swap, 1982; Lewicki & Bunker, 1996; Lewis & Weigert, 1985; McAllister, 1995; Rempel et al., 1985). This approach is concisely illustrated by Lewis and Weigert's (1985) assertion that trust is based on 'strong positive affect for the object of trust (emotional trust) or on "good rational reasons" why the object of trust merits trust (cognitive trust), or, more usually, some combination of both' (p. 972). One element that is critical to the creation of both bases is time. In the case of the cognitive base, the trustor must have had time to gather data on the trustee. In the case of the affective base, the trustor must have had time to develop emotional ties with the trustee. If time is critical to the creation of trust, what explains why people trust in new situations?

It is tempting to rely on the disposition to trust to explain this phenomenon, but recent research indicates that trust propensity is only weakly correlated with organizational newcomers' initial trust levels (van der Werff & Buckley, in press; see also Berg, Dickhaut, & McCable, 1995; Kramer, 1994). Further, suggesting that trust propensity does not provide an adequate answer to this question, a recent meta-analysis found that the disposition to trust was only weakly to moderately correlated with trusting behaviours in one-shot encounters with strangers (Balliet & Van Lange, 2013). Similarly, people's participation in trust games has been shown to far exceed their generalized expectations (for a review, see Dunning, Anderson, Schlosser, Ehlebracht, & Fetchenhauer, 2014). In sum, the disposition to trust provides only a partial answer to why people trust in new situations.

A promising answer to this question is provided by a trend in cognitive and social psychology. Scholars in these disciplines have reached a general consensus that reasoning operates through two parallel processes – one that is conscious, deliberate and rational, and one that is less conscious, rapid and heuristic (for a review, see Evans, 2008). Although a number of different terms and theories have been applied to these two processes, they generally fit the labels and characterization provided by Chaiken and colleagues (Chen & Chaiken, 1999: 74; see also Chaiken, 1980; Chaiken, Liberman, & Eagly, 1989): '*Systematic processing* entails a relatively analytic and comprehensive treatment of judgment-relevant information' whereas '*heuristic processing*, entails the activation and application of judgmental rules or "heuristics" that, like other knowledge structures, are presumed to be learned and stored in memory' (emphasis in original). To illustrate the two types of processing, consider a professor who is grading an essay. That professor may pore over the essay evaluating the logic and comprehensiveness of the arguments. This analytic evaluation illustrates systematic processing. That professor may also be unknowingly impacted, however, by the length of the essay. Indeed, research indicates that longer arguments activate a 'length implies strength' heuristic which has a positive impact on the perceived quality of the arguments (Wood, Kallgren, & Preisler, 1985). This less-conscious evaluation illustrates heuristic processing.

At first glance, the 'new' idea of a heuristic base of trust appears to overlap with the not-so-new concept of swift trust (Meyerson, Weick, & Kramer, 1996) and, more recently, the concept of presumptive trust (Kramer & Lewicki, 2010). Both of these concepts bear some similarity to the notion of a heuristic base of trust in that they are formed early in a relationship, before the trustor has had an opportunity to gather specific knowledge about the trustee. Like heuristic-based trust, swift trust – as the label suggests – does not necessarily require much time to form. At this point, however, the concepts diverge. Swift trust is hypothesized to stem from situational cues – e.g. interdependence, fail-safe mechanisms, group membership – that indicate the other group members are unlikely to violate trust. Meyerson et al. (1996) emphasize that this is a calculative, cognitive process. Likewise, Kramer and Lewicki (2010) defined presumptive trust as a positive expectation of an individual stemming from knowledge of that individual's shared membership in an organization, and what that membership signals. In both cases, these scholars emphasize that rapidly-formed trust stems from a conscious, rule-based, cognitive process – a clear departure from the less-conscious, associative process that characterizes heuristic processing.

Some trust scholars have begun to incorporate the idea of heuristic processing into their research. One of the earliest instances was McKnight et al.'s (1998) theorizing on initial trust formation. Exploring what they referred to as the 'paradox of high initial trust levels', McKnight and colleagues proposed that initial trust was based on dispositional trust, structural assurances that trust won't be violated, and 'hidden factors' that signal future endeavours will be successful. With respect to those hidden factors, they introduced the concept of situational normality beliefs – the belief that things are normal, customary and in their proper order. To illustrate the process through which situational normality beliefs should affect trust, they noted that a person who enters a bank expects a setting conducive to safe, professional service. If nothing seems out of the ordinary, the person can rapidly, and with little conscious thought, infer that interactions with that bank will follow established guidelines. It follows that in organizations that exhibit situational normality, the resulting rapid, associative connection between normal and dependable may contribute to the formation of initial trust.

Research on situational normality has been sparse and largely limited to the field of information systems, although the notion of normality acting as a heuristic predictor of trust is supported by empirical research which indicates that 'normal' mobile banking technologies and websites increase the likelihood that people will trust (Gefen, Karahanna, & Straub, 2003; Gu, Lee, & Suh, 2009). At the interpersonal level, some additional support comes from recent research that indicates people with typical (i.e. normal) faces are more likely to be trusted (Sofer, Dotsch, Wigboldus, & Todorov, 2015). Scholars have determined that people can form impressions of another's trustworthiness after as little as 100 milliseconds of exposure to that person's face, and that additional exposure only serves to increase confidence in those impressions (for a review, see Todorov, Olivola, Dotsch, & Mende-Siedlecki, 2015). When considered through a dual-process lens, these findings provide support for the proposal that trust may also be based on heuristic predictors.

Management researchers have only recently begun to empirically investigate heuristic predictors of trust. One of these investigations was conducted by Rafaeli and colleagues (2008), who found that the presence of an organizational logo increased initial compliance with a request made by a stranger; this relationship was mediated by trust. They argued that this process occurs in an unconscious fashion, with logos activating a heuristic that signals because everything is in proper order, trust is appropriate. Lending support to their argument that initial trust can form without conscious awareness, they found these relationships even when the logo represented a fictitious company. Accordingly, trust could not have been based on prior experience with the company. In related research, Huang and Murnighan (2010) found that subliminally priming participants with the names of trusted people led to greater trust in strangers. Across three experiments, none of the participants recognized the subliminal primes, lending support to the idea that trust can form through automatic, heuristic processing.

We suggest that research into heuristics as a base of trust start by examining the question that is not fully answered by current approaches to trust: Why do employees who are new – either to the group, unit or organization – trust? Research at the interpersonal level clearly shows that physical appearances have a significant impact on people's initial and lasting impressions of others' characteristics (for reviews, see Eagly, Ashmore, Makhijani, & Longo, 1991; Langlois, Kalakanis, Rubenstein, Larson, Hallam, & Smoot, 2000; Todorov et al., 2015). Many of these inferred traits are particularly relevant to trust. For example, facial appearance has been found to influence perceptions of warmth and honesty (Berry, 1990), as well as competence (Todorov, Mandisodza, Goren, & Hall, 2005). Much of the research in this vein has explored facial attractiveness, relying on the 'what is beautiful is good' heuristic to explain the positive effects (Eagly et al., 1991; Langlois et al., 2000). Other research has investigated the effects of having a baby-faced appearance, with the effects explained by heuristics associated with honesty and naivety (e.g. Zebrowitz & McDonald, 1991). Specifically, baby-faced individuals are seen as more honest yet less competent (Montepare & Zebrowitz, 1998). Other research suggests that men with wider faces cue heuristics associated with aggression, leading to decreased perceptions of trustworthiness and trusting behaviour (Stirrat & Perrett, 2010).

People are largely limited on the extent to which they can alter their appearance to inspire trust. After all, aside from resorting to cosmetic surgery, facial features are relatively fixed. So, when it comes to actionable recommendations for organizations looking to increase employee trust in supervisors, does the bottom line become 'Hire attractive, trustworthy-looking managers?' Putting aside the ethical implications, this suggestion has dubious practical utility, as the validity of facial inferences has received very little support (Alley, 1988; Cohen, 1973; Hassin & Trope, 2000; Zebrowitz et al., 1996; for exceptions, see Berry, 1990, 1991; Bond, Berry, & Omar, 1994). In other words, selecting trustworthy-looking people doesn't ensure that trustworthy people have been hired. Accordingly, we suggest that research look to identifying heuristic cues that can be altered rather than selected for, as this approach will provide more actionable recommendations to organizations. One potential direction lies in the 'power of a smile'. Adding to a robust literature that has demonstrated smiling people are considered more sincere, altruistic and competent (e.g. Brown & Moore, 2002; Reis et al., 1990), scholars have more specifically shown that smiling can increase perceptions of trustworthiness (LaFrance & Hecht, 1995) and trusting behaviour (Krumhuber, Manstead, Cosker, Marshall, Rosin, & Kappas, 2007). In short, there may be considerable benefits to trust for people who 'turn that frown upside down'.

Other 'alterable' heuristic predictors of trust that have received some attention in literatures outside of management include professional dress for physicians (Rehman, Nietert, Cope, & Kilpatrick, 2005), the presence/absence of facial hair in dating relationships (Barber, 2001), and the speed of speech (Miller, Maruyama, Beaber, & Valone, 1976). Whether these and other heuristic predictors predict important systematic variance in trust above and beyond the disposition to trust, trustworthiness and affect is an unanswered question. We suggest that the importance of these heuristic predictors will depend on the research question and stage of trust development. On the one hand, these predictors are more likely to be consequential factors in new relationships. On the other hand, these initial impressions may act as anchors that have lasting effects on trust. Exploration of these issues would contribute to a more complete understanding of the antecedents of trust in individuals.

With respect to individuals' perceptions of the organization itself, we are unaware of research that has specifically examined trust or trustworthiness as outcomes of appearances. Indeed, despite the growing consensus that the physical environment has a pervasive effect on organizational life (for reviews, see Davis, Leach, & Clegg, 2011; Elsbach & Pratt, 2007; Zhong & House, 2012), organizations often fail to give environmental factors their due attention (Elsbach & Bechky, 2007; Vilnai-Yavetz & Rafaeli, 2006). In contrast with the lack of attention in management research, the field of environmental psychology has long suggested that the physical environment can promote a sense of belonging or 'place attachment' (for a review, see Lewicka, 2011a). Recent research indicates that place-attached people tend to place more trust in others in the same environment and to be more benevolent themselves (Lewicka, 2011b). In sum, this research suggests that the physical workplace might have real effects on employee trust. Whether these effects are heuristic or conscious is an unanswered empirical question, although organizational scholars have theorized that they most often occur without conscious awareness (Gagliardi, 2006; Strati, 1999).

In contrast with individuals, organizations seemingly have more – and considerably less invasive – options for altering their appearances in ways that are conducive to trust. After all, it is easier to paint a room and rearrange the office furniture than to alter the width of one's face. If the environment is supplying heuristic cues that have a meaningful impact on trust, organizations would be wise to give more thoughtful attention to logistical decisions such as where new employees will be trained and located. Yet, what are the specific aspects of the physical environment that might have a heuristic effect on trust? One potential answer is the extent to which the environment is aesthetically pleasing. Although research is silent on this issue, just as attractive people cue a 'what is beautiful is good' heuristic (Eagly et al., 1991; Langlois et al., 2000), aesthetically-pleasing workplaces may signal that the organization is 'good' and, therefore, worthy of trust. Given the wide range of aesthetic preferences, crafting a universally pleasing and trust-inducing appearance may seem like an impossible venture. Fortunately, research indicates that some design elements are generally widely appreciated, including the presence of windows, a uniform color palette and high ceilings (Gifford, Hine, Muller-Clemm, D'Arcy, & Shaw, 2000).

Conclusion

Despite the many important strides that have been made in identifying and exploring the antecedents of trust, many unanswered questions remain. We have suggested that the more deeply explored antecedents of trust – trust propensity and trustworthiness – still hold questions that bear addressing. Answers to these questions may provide organizations with greater ability to increase trust with the organization through various means, such as selection and training. Although not a 'new' conceptual direction for trust research, affect is a relatively unexplored direction for empirical trust research. Attending to the issues raised in this chapter may provide additional avenues for increasing trust. Indeed, the traditionally cognitive approach may have been ignoring a substantial opportunity to improve trust within organizations. Likewise, an inattention to less-conscious, heuristic predictors has left our understanding of initial trust formation in the dark. By exploring the rapid, heuristic judgments that characterize initial impressions, organizations may be able to affect initial trust levels, which in turn may have lasting implications. In sum, a more conscious acknowledgement of all the bases of trust should provide organizations with the ability to take a holistic approach to forming and maintaining trust among employees, coworkers, supervisors and the organization.

References

Alley, T. R. 1988. Physiognomy and social perception. In T. R. Alley (Ed.), *Social and applied aspects of perceiving faces*: 167–186. Hillsdale, NJ: Erlbaum.

Balliet, D., & Van Lange, P. A. M. 2013. Trust, conflict, and cooperation: A meta-analysis. *Psychological Bulletin*, 139: 1090–1112.

Barber, B. 1983. *The logic and limits of trust*. New Brunswick, NJ: Rutgers University Press.

Barber, N. 2001. Mustache fashion covaries with a good marriage market for women. *Journal of Nonverbal Behavior*, 25: 261–272.

Barsade, S. G., & Gibson, D. E. 2007. Why does affect matter in organizations? *Academy of Management Perspectives*, 21: 36–59.

Berg, J., Dickhaut, J., & McCabe, K. 1995. Trust, reciprocity, and social history. *Games and Economic Behavior*, 10: 122–142.

Berry, D. S. 1990. Taking people at face value: Evidence for the kernel of truth hypothesis. *Social Cognition*, 8: 343–361.

Berry, D. S. 1991. Accuracy in social perception: Contributions of facial and vocal information. *Journal of Personality and Social Psychology*, 61: 298–307.

Bigley, G. A., & Pearce, J. L. 1998. Straining for shared meaning in organization science: Problems of trust and distrust. *Academy of Management Review*, 23: 405–421.

Bond, C. F., Berry, D. S., & Omar, A. 1994. The kernel of truth in judgments of deceptiveness. *Basic and Applied Social Psychology*, 15: 523–534.

Brown, W. M., & Moore, C. 2002. Smile asymmetries and reputation as reliable indicators of likelihood to cooperate: An evolutionary analysis. *Advances in Psychology Research*, 11: 59–78.

Butler, J. K., Jr. 1991. Toward understanding and measuring conditions of trust: Evolution of a conditions of trust inventory. *Journal of Management*, 17: 643–663.

Butler, J. K., Jr., & Cantrell, R. S. 1984. A behavioral decision theory approach to modeling dyadic trust in superiors and subordinates. *Psychological Reports*, 55: 19–28.

Chaiken, S. 1980. Heuristic versus systematic information processing and the use of source versus message cues in persuasion. *Journal of Personality and Social Psychology*, 39: 752–766.

Chaiken, S., Liberman, A., & Eagly, A. H. 1989. Heuristic and systematic processing within and beyond the persuasion context. In J. S. Uleman & J. A. Bargh (Eds.), *Unintended thought*: 212–252. New York: Guilford Press.

Chen, S., & Chaiken, S. 1999. The heuristic-systematic model in its broader context. In S. Chaiken & Y. Trope (Eds.), *Dual-process theories in social psychology*: 73–96. New York: Guilford Press.

Cohen, R. 1973. *Patterns of personality judgments*. New York: Academic Press.

Colquitt, J. A., Baer, M. D., Long, D. M., & Halvorsen-Ganepola, M. D. K. 2014. Scale indicators of social exchange relationships: A comparison of relative content validity. *Journal of Applied Psychology*, 99: 599–618.

Colquitt, J. A., LePine, J. A., Zapata, C. P., & Wild, R. E. 2011. Trust in typical and high-reliability contexts: Building and reacting to trust among firefighters. *Academy of Management Journal*, 54: 999–1015.

Colquitt, J. A., Scott, B. A., & LePine, J. A. 2007. Trust, trustworthiness, and trust propensity: A meta-analytic test of their unique relationships with risk taking and job performance. *Journal of Applied Psychology*, 92: 902–927.

Cook, J., & Wall, T. 1980. New work attitude measures of trust, organizational commitment and personal need non-fulfillment. *Journal of Occupational Psychology*, 53: 39–52.

Davis, M. C., Leach, D. J., & Clegg, C. W. 2010. The physical environment of the office: Contemporary and emerging issues. *International Review of Industrial and Organizational Psychology*, 26: 193–237.

Deutsch, M., & Krauss, R. M. 1965. *Theories in social psychology*. New York: Basic Books.

Dietz, G., & Den Hartog, D. N. 2006. Measuring trust inside organisations. *Personnel Review*, 35: 557–588.

Dirks, K. T., & Ferrin, D. L. 2002. Trust in leadership: Meta-analytic findings and implications for research and practice. *Journal of Applied Psychology*, 87: 611–628.

Dunn, J. R., & Schweitzer, M. E. 2005. Feeling and believing: The influence of emotion on trust. *Journal of Personality and Social Psychology*, 88: 736–748.

Dunning, D., Anderson, J. E., Schlösser, T., Ehlebracht, D., & Fetchenhauer, D. 2014. Trust at zero acquaintance: More a matter of respect than expectation of reward. *Journal of Personality and Social Psychology*, 107: 122–141.

Eagly, A. H., Ashmore, R. D., Makhijani, M. G., & Longo, L. C. 1991. What is beautiful is good, but . . .: A meta-analytic review of research on the physical attractiveness stereotype. *Psychological Bulletin*, 110: 109–128.

Elfenbein, H. A. 2007. Emotion in organizations: A review and theoretical integration. *Academy of Management Annals*, 1: 371–457.

Elsbach, K. D., & Bechky, B. A. 2007. It's more than a desk: Working smarter through leveraged office design. *California Management Review*, 49: 80–101.

Elsbach, K. D., & Pratt, M. G. 2007. The physical environment in organizations. *Academy of Management Annals*, 4: 181–224.

Erikson, E. H. 1963. *Childhood and society*. New York: Norton.

Evans, J. S. B. T. 2008. Dual-processing accounts of reasoning, judgment, and social cognition. *Annual Review of Psychology*, 59: 255–278.

Flanagan, C. A., & Stout, M. 2010. Developmental patterns of social trust between early and late adolescence: Age and school climate effects. *Journal of Research on Adolescence*, 20: 748–773.

Fleeson, W., & Jolley, S. 2006. A proposed theory of the adult development of intraindividual variability in trait-manifesting behavior. In D. K. Mroczek & T. D. Little (Eds.), *Handbook of personality development*: 41–59. Mahwah, NJ: Erlbaum.

Forgas, J. P. 1995. Mood and judgment: The affect infusion model (AIM). *Psychological Bulletin*, 117: 39–66.

Frijda, N. H. 1994. Varieties of affect: Emotions and episodes, moods, and sentiments. In P. Ekman & R. J. Davidson (Eds.), *The nature of emotion*: 59–67. New York: Oxford University Press.

Frost, T., Stimpson, D. V., & Maughan, M. R. C. 1978. Some correlates of trust. *Journal of Psychology*, 99: 103–108.

Fulmer, C. A., & Gelfand, M. J. 2012. At what level (and in whom) we trust: Trust across multiple organizational levels. *Journal of Management*, 38: 1167–1230.

Gabarro, J. J. 1978. The development of trust, influence, and expectations. In A. G. Athos & J. J. Gabarro (Eds.), *Interpersonal behaviors: Communication and understanding in relationships*: 290–303. Englewood Cliffs, NJ: Prentice Hall.

Gagliardi, P. 2006. Exploring the aesthetic side of organizational life. In S. R. Clegg, C. Hardy, T. B. Lawrence, & W. R. Nord (Eds.), *The SAGE handbook of organizations studies*: 701–724. London: SAGE.

Gefen, D., Karahanna, E., & Straub, D. W. 2003. Trust and TAM in online shopping: An integrated model. *MIS Quarterly*, 27: 51–90.

Gifford, R., Hine, D. W., Muller-Clemm, W., D'Arcy, J. R., & Shaw, K. T. 2000. Decoding modern architecture: A lens model approach for understanding the aesthetic differences of architects and laypersons. *Environment and Behavior*, 32: 163–187.

Gill, H., Boies, K., Finegan, J. E., & McNally, J. 2005. Antecedents of trust: Establishing a boundary condition for the relation between propensity to trust and intention to trust. *Journal of Business and Psychology*, 19: 287–302.

Gu, J.-C., Lee, S.-C., & Suh, Y.-H. 2009. Determinants of behavioral intention to mobile banking. *Expert Systems with Applications*, 36: 11605–11616.

Hardin, R. 1992. The street-level epistemology of trust. *Analyse & Kritik*, 14: 152–176.

Hardin, R. 2002. *Trust and trustworthiness*. New York: Russell Sage Foundation.

Hassin, R., & Trope, Y. 2000. Facing faces: Studies on the cognitive aspects of physiognomy. *Journal of Personality and Social Psychology*, 78: 837–852.

Hill, C. A. 1987. Affiliation motivation: People who need people . . . but in different ways. *Journal of Personality and Social Psychology*, 52: 1008–1018.

Hill, C. A. 1991. Seeking emotional support: The influence of affiliative need and partner warmth. *Journal of Personality and Social Psychology*, 60: 112–121.

Hiraishi, K., Yamagata, S., Shikishima, C., & Ando, J. 2008. Maintenance of genetic variation in personality through control of mental mechanisms: A test of trust extraversion, and agreeableness. *Evolution and Human Behavior*, 29: 79–85.

Hovland, C. I., Janis, I. L., & Kelley, H. H. 1953. *Communication and persuasion*. New Haven: Yale University Press.

Huang, L., & Murnighan, J. K. 2010. What's in a name? Subliminally activating trusting behavior. *Organizational Behavior and Human Decision Processes*, 111: 62–70.

Jennings, E. E. 1971. *Routes to the executive suite*. New York: McGraw-Hill.

Johnson-George, C., & Swap, W. 1982. Measurement of specific interpersonal trust: Construction and validation of a scale to assess trust in a specific other. *Journal of Personality and Social Psychology*, 43: 1306–1317.

Jones, G. R., & George, J. M. 1998. The experience and evolution of trust: Implications for cooperation and teamwork. *Academy of Management Review*, 23: 531–546.

Judge, T. A., Simon, L. S., Hurst, C., & Kelley, K. 2014. What I experienced yesterday is who I am today: Relationship of work motivations and behaviors to within-individual variation in the Five-Factor model of personality. *Journal of Applied Psychology*, 99: 199–221.

Katz, H. A., & Rotter, J. B. 1969. Interpersonal trust scores of college students and their parents. *Child Development*, 40: 657–661.

Kee, H. W., & Knox, R. E. 1970. Conceptual and methodological considerations in the study of trust and suspicion. *Journal of Conflict Resolution*, 14: 357–366.

Korsgaard, M. A., Brodt, S. E., & Whitener, E. M. 2002. Trust in the face of conflict: The role of managerial trustworthy behavior and organizational context. *Journal of Applied Psychology*, 87: 312–319.

Kramer, R. M. 1994. The sinister attribution error: Paranoid cognition and collective distrust in organizations. *Motivation and Emotion*, 18: 199–230.

Kramer, R. M. 1999. Trust and distrust in organizations: Emerging perspectives, enduring questions. *Annual Review of Psychology*, 50: 569–598.

Kramer, R. M., & Lewicki, R. J. 2010. Repairing and enhancing trust: Approaches to reducing organizational trust deficits. *Academy of Management Annals*, 4: 245–277.

Krumhuber, E., Manstead, A. S. R., Cosker, D., Marshall, D., Rosin, P. L., & Kappas, A. 2007. Facial dynamics and indicators of trustworthiness and cooperative behavior. *Emotion*, 7: 730–735.

LaFrance, M., & Hecht, M. A. 1995. Why smiles generate leniency. *Personality and Social Psychology Bulletin*, 21: 207–214.

Langlois, J. H., Kalakanis, L., Rubenstein, A. J., Larson, A., Hallam, M., & Smoot, M. 2000. Maxims or myths of beauty? A meta-analytic and theoretical review. *Psychological Bulletin*, 126: 390–423.

Larzelere, R., & Huston, T. 1980. The dyadic trust scale: Toward understanding interpersonal trust in close relationships. *Journal of Marriage and the Family*, 42: 595–604.

Lee, M. K. O., & Turban, E. 2001. A trust model for consumer Internet shopping. *International Journal of Electronic Commerce*, 6: 75–91.

Lewicka, M. 2011a. Place attachment: How far have we come in the last 40 years? *Journal of Environmental Psychology*, 31: 207–230.

Lewicka, M. 2011b. On the varieties of people's relationships with places: Hummon's typology revisited. *Environment and Behavior*, 43: 676–709.

Lewicki, R. J., & Bunker, B. B. 1996. Developing and maintaining trust in work relationships. In R. M. Kramer & T. R. Tyler (Eds.), *Trust in organizations: Frontiers of theory and research*: 114–139. Thousand Oaks, CA: SAGE.

Lewis, J. D., & Weigert, A. 1985. Trust as a social reality. *Social Forces*, 63: 967–985.

Liden, R. C., & Maslyn, J. M. 1998. Multidimensionality of leader-member exchange: An empirical assessment through scale development. *Journal of Management*, 24: 43–72.

Lindskold, S., & Bennett, R. 1973. Attributing trust and conciliatory intent from coercive power capability. *Journal of Personality and Social Psychology*, 28: 180–186.

Mayer, R. C., & Davis, J. H. 1999. The effect of the performance appraisal system on trust for management: A field quasi-experiment. *Journal of Applied Psychology*, 84: 123–136.

Mayer, R. C., Davis, J. H., & Schoorman, F. D. 1995. An integrative model of organizational trust. *Academy of Management Review*, 20: 709–734.

McAllister, D. J. 1995. Affect and cognition-based trust as foundations for interpersonal cooperation in organizations. *Academy of Management Journal*, 38: 24–59.

McCrae, R. R., & Costa, P. T. 1994. The stability of personality: Observations and evaluations. *Current Directions in Psychological Science*, 3: 173–175.

McEvily, B., & Tortoriello, M. 2011. Measuring trust in organisational research: Review and recommendations. *Journal of Trust Research*, 1: 23–63.

McKnight, D. H., Cummings, L. L., & Chervany, N. L. 1998. Initial trust formation in new organizational relationships. *Academy of Management Review*, 23: 473–490.

Meyerson, D., Weick, K. E., & Kramer, R. M. 1996. Swift trust and temporary groups. In R. M. Kramer & T. R. Tyler (Eds.), *Trust in organizations: Frontiers of theory and research*: 166–195. Thousand Oaks, CA: SAGE.

Miller, N., Maruyama, G., Beaber, R. J., Valone, K. 1976. Speed of speech and persuasion. *Journal of Personality and Social Psychology*, 34: 615–624.

Mishra, A. K. 1996. Organizational responses to crisis: The centrality of trust. In R. M. Kramer & T. R. Tyler (Eds.), *Trust in organizations: Frontiers of theory and research*: 261–287. Thousand Oaks, CA: SAGE.

Möllering, G. 2006. *Trust: Reason, routine, reflexivity*. Amsterdam, the Netherlands: Elsevier.

Montepare, J. M., & Zebrowitz, L. A. 1998. Person perception comes of age: The salience and significance of age in social judgments. In M. P. Zanna (Ed.), *Advances in experimental social psychology* (vol. 30): 93–161. San Diego, CA: Academic Press.

Pirson, M., & Malhotra, D. 2011. Foundations of organizational trust: What matters to different stakeholders? *Organization Science*, 22: 1087–1104.

Rafaeli, A., Sagy, Y., & Derfler-Rozin, R. 2008. Logos and initial compliance: A strong case of mindless trust. *Organization Science*, 19: 845–859.

Rehman, S. U., Nietert, P. J., Cope, D. W., & Kilpatrick, A. O. 2005. What to wear today? Effect of doctor's attire on the trust and confidence of patients. *The American Journal of Medicine*, 118: 1279–1286.

Reis, H. T., Wilson, I., Monestere, C., Bernstein, S., Clark, K., Seidl, E., Franco, M., Gioioso, E., Freeman, L., & Radoane, K. 1990. What is smiling is beautiful and good. *European Journal of Social Psychology*, 20: 259–267.

Rempel, J. K., Holmes, J. G., & Zanna, M. P. 1985. Trust in close relationships. *Journal of Personality and Social Psychology*, 49: 95–112.

Rotter, J. B. 1967. A new scale for the measurement of interpersonal trust. *Journal of Personality*, 35: 651–665.

Rotter, J. B. 1971. Generalized expectancies for interpersonal trust. *American Psychologist*, 26: 443–452.

Rotter, J. B. 1980. Interpersonal trust, trustworthiness, and gullibility. *American Psychologist*, 35: 1–7.

Rotter, J. B., Chance, J., & Phares, E. J. 1972. *Applications of a social learning theory of personality*. New York: Holt, Rinehart, & Winston.

Rousseau, D. M., Sitkin, S. B., Burt, R. S., & Camerer, C. 1998. Not so different after all: A cross-discipline view of trust. *Academy of Management Review*, 23: 393–404.

Sakai, A. 2010. Children's sense of trust in significant others: Genetic versus environmental contributions and buffer to life stressors. In K. J. Rotenberg (Ed.), *Interpersonal trust during childhood and adolescence*: 56–84. Cambridge, UK: Cambridge University Press.

Schlenker, B. R., Helm, B., & Tedeschi, J. T. 1973. The effects of personality and situational variables on behavioral trust. *Journal of Personality and Social Psychology*, 25: 419–427.

Shapiro, D., Sheppard, B. H., & Cheraskin, L. 1992. Business on a handshake. *The Negotiation Journal*, 8: 365–378.

Simons, T. 2002. Behavioral integrity: The perceived alignment between manager's words and deeds as a research focus. *Organization Science*, 13: 18–35.

Sitkin, S. B., & Pablo, A. L. 1992. Reconceptualizing the determinants of risk behavior. *Academy of Management Review*, 17: 9–38.

Sitkin, S. B., & Roth, N. L. 1993. Explaining the limited effectiveness of legalistic "remedies" for trust/distrust. *Organization Science*, 4: 367–392.

Sitkin, S. B., & Weingart, L. R. 1995. Determinants of risky decision-making behavior: A test of the mediating role of risk perceptions and propensity. *Academy of Management Journal*, 38: 1573–1592.

Sofer, C., Dotsch, R., Wigboldus, D. H. J., & Todorov, A. 2015. What is typical is good: The influence of face typicality on perceived trustworthiness. *Psychological Science*, 26: 39–47.

Stack, L. C. 1978. Trust. In H. London & J. E. Exner, Jr. (Eds.), *Dimensionality of personality*: 561–599. New York: Wiley.

Stets, J. E. 2003. Emotions and sentiments. In J. DeLamater (Ed.), *Handbook of social psychology*: 309–335. New York: Kluwer Academic/Plenum Publishers.

Stirrat, M., & Perrett, D. I. 2010. Valid facial cues to cooperation and trust: Male facial width and trustworthiness. *Psychological Science*, 21: 349–354.

Stolle, D., & Nishikawa, L. 2011. Trusting others—How parents shape the generalized trust of their children. *Comparative Sociology*, 10: 281–314.

Strati, A. 1999. *Organization and aesthetics*. London: SAGE.

Sturgis, P., Read, S., Hatemi, P. K., Zhu, G., Trull, T., Wright, M. J., & Martin, N. G. 2010. A genetic basis for social trust. *Political Behavior*, 32: 205–230.

Todorov, A., Mandisodza, A. N., Goren, A., & Hall, C. C. 2005. Inferences of competence from faces predict election outcomes. *Science*, 308: 1623–1626.

Todorov, A., Olivola, C. Y., Dotsch, R., & Mende-Siedlecki, P. 2015. Social attributions from faces: Determinants, consequences, accuracy, and functional significance. *Annual Review of Psychology*, 66: 519–545.

van der Werff, L., & Buckley, F. 2017. Getting to know you: A longitudinal examination of trust cues and trust development during socialization. *Journal of Management*, 43: 742–770.

Vilnai-Yavetz, I., & Rafaeli, A. 2006. Managing organizational artifacts to avoid artifact myopia. In A. Rafaeli & M. G. Pratt (Eds.), *Artifacts and organizations: Beyond mere symbolism*: 9–21. Mahwah, NJ: Erlbaum.

Webb, W. M., & Worchel, P. 1986. Trust and distrust. In S. Worchel & W. G. Austin (Eds.), *Psychology of intergroup relations*: 213–228. Chicago: Nelson-Hall.

Weiss, H. M., & Cropanzano, R. 1996. Affective events theory: A theoretical discussion of the structure, causes and consequences of affective experiences at work. *Research in Organizational Behavior*, 18: 1–74.

Whitener, E. M., Brodt, S. E., Korsgaard, M. A., & Werner, J. M. 1998. Managers as initiators of trust: An exchange relationship framework for understanding managerial trustworthy behavior. *Academy of Management Review*, 23: 513–530.

Williams, M. 2001. In whom we trust: Group membership as an affective context for trust development. *Academy of Management Review*, 26: 377–396.

Wood, W., Kallgren, C. A., & Preisler, R. M. 1985. Access to attitude-relevant information in memory as a determinant of persuasion: The role of message attributes. *Journal of Experimental Social Psychology*, 21: 73–85.

Wrightsman, L. S. 1964. Measurement of philosophies of human nature. *Psychological Reports*, 14: 743–751.

Zebrowitz, L. A., & McDonald, S. M. 1991. The impact of litigants' babyfaceness and attractiveness on adjudications in small claims courts. *Law and Behavior*, 15: 603–623.

Zhong, C.-B., & House, J. 2012. Hawthorne revisited: Organizational implications of the physical work environment. *Research in Organizational Behavior*, 32: 3–22.

10

TRUST AND FAIRNESS

E. Allan Lind

Introduction

We have known for a long time that trust is linked to perceptions of fairness, especially perceptions of procedural fairness. The very first study of procedural justice (Walker, LaTour, Lind, & Thibaut, 1974) showed that disputants in a laboratory conflict resolution process trusted the judge more when fair procedures were used – specifically, when the procedure allowed the disputants themselves more control over the presentation of evidence. In another early study, Tyler, Rasinski, and McGraw (1985) found citizen perceptions of procedural fairness to be an exceptionally strong predictor of overall trust in government. In the years since, Tyler and others have demonstrated repeatedly the close relationship between perceived fairness and trust in authorities (see e.g. Tyler, 1984, 1987, 1990, 1997; Tyler & Caine, 1981; Tyler & Degoey, 1996; Tyler, Goff, & MacCoun, 2015; Tyler & Lind, 1992; Tyler, Rasinski, & Spodick, 1985). The link is seen not only in the political and citizen-state encounter contexts that Tyler, Rasinski, & McGraw (1985) studied, but also in studies conducted in organizational contexts, in the laboratory and in other social settings. In this chapter, I will explore some organizational justice research and theory that involve particularly close links to trust and trusting behaviour.[1]

The idea that perceptions of fair process generally enhance ratings of trust in authorities and improve acceptance of decisions is now well-accepted in social, organizational and political psychology, as well as in organizational behaviour and law and society studies. When they were first discovered, though, these relationships were viewed as quite surprising, especially because the typical finding is that the strongest correlations between fairness and trust involve *procedural* or *process* fairness measures. It is generally the fairness of treatment, not the fairness of outcomes, that is most closely linked to trust. Several commentators pointed out that this sort of fairness could conceivably be simulated by leaders and authority structures to create what is termed in Marxist analysis a 'false consciousness' of justice (see, e.g. Cohen, 1985). Since impressions of fair treatment might or might not reflect true trustworthiness, the argument goes, why should people rely on these impressions to judge whether they will trust an authority figure or an organization? The major thrust of theories and research on the psychology of fairness argues that the answer to this question is that fair treatment is seen as a sign of inclusion in the group or organization (or a good relationship with the person) that is behaving fairly.

As research and theory developed through the 1980s, it became apparent that fairness judgments were driven as much by what fair treatment says about group membership as by the

183

material outcomes that result from fair or unfair treatment. That is, at least part of the reason that fair treatment enhances trust is that fair process is interpreted as showing inclusion and respect for the person within the group. Lind and Tyler (1988) reviewed the research literature on procedural justice through the mid-1980s and proposed Group Value Theory, which explained the effects of procedural justice by linking the perception of fair treatment to feelings of inclusion and status within the group that employs fair processes. According to Group Value Theory, the sting of treatment that is perceived as unfair derives, at least in part, from the implication that one is or might be excluded from the group or that one has low status. Later, Tyler and Lind (1992) presented a Relational Model of Authority, which explored further the links between perceptions of fair treatment and such things as trust in authorities and acceptance of authorities' decisions. Tyler and Lind explained the by-then widely observed correlations and experimental links between fairness and trust by arguing that such elements of fair treatment as dignity, concern and voice carry messages of a sound and secure relationship with the authority and the group, and it is this perception that is the key factor that makes fairness produce greater trust and more trusting behaviour.

The 'direct effect' enhancement of trust by perceptions of fair treatment, as evidenced by ubiquitous positive correlations between fairness and trust and explained by Group Value Theory and the Relational Model of Authority, has continued to be supported by research in organizational, political and social contexts. The idea that fairness has many of its downstream effects through its enhancement of trust does not seem to be the whole story, though. Over the past two decades, new theory and the accumulation of more empirical evidence have come together to suggest that there are situations in which impressions of fair treatment may substitute or stand in for judgments of trust. Fairness not only enhances trust, it seems, it sometimes serves as a replacement for trust.

Fairness Heuristic Theory

A return to the question of why fairness matters so much in reactions to authorities, organizations and institutions was the impetus for development of a new theory of the psychology of perceived fairness that emerged in the late 1990s and that has been tested and refined in the years since. Lind (1995, 2001, 2011; Lind, Kulik, Ambrose, & Park, 1993; Van den Bos, Lind, & Wilke, 2001; see also Proudfoot and Lind, 2014, Tost & Lind, 2010; see Tyler & Blader, 2003, for another line of theoretical and empirical work on this topic) proposed that fairness judgments matter in part because fairness perceptions are sometimes used as 'heuristics,' psychological surrogates, for firm attributions of trustworthiness in many situations. Fairness Heuristic Theory was designed to be a more nuanced theory of how people generate and use fairness judgments, a theory that would take into account work in social and cognitive psychology done after the creation of Group Value Theory and the Relational Model of Authority.

Fairness Heuristic Theory devotes considerable attention to how and when people use impressions of the fairness of their treatment by others to decide whether to act *as though* they trust the person or organization in question. To give the material below a personal tone, let us consider a hypothetical employee – Beth – who has recently accepted a job at a pharmaceutical company. Beth is excited at the prospect of the new job, her new boss, and the new organization. She accepted the job because it promises her a chance to do exciting work and to advance her career, but whether it rises to the level of conscious concern or not she may be worried about whether her skills will be used well, whether her work preferences respected, and whether her individual career aspirations fulfilled. In other words, there is reason for her to be concerned about whether her new coworkers, supervisor and the organization itself will welcome her as a valuable addition to the corporate team or whether they will simply use her work and give her little recognition and security in return for her investment of time and her own identity in the company.

Fairness Heuristic Theory takes as its starting point this area of concern in all relationships, which the theory terms the 'fundamental social dilemma' (Lind, 2001). Social dilemmas, of course, are decisions in which options that are good for the long-term benefit or survival of a social group are pitted against the possibility that some in the group might exploit others for their immediate, individual benefits. In the prototypic social dilemma – the 'tragedy of the commons' – a pasture held in common by the farmers in a village is healthy and productive as long as each farmer limits his or her use of the pasture (Hardin, 1968). It is in each farmer's individual self-interest to put as many of his or her animals as possible on the commons, though, and if too many farmers put too many animals grazing on the commons the pasture will become depleted and the village as a whole will suffer. The dilemma for each farmer is whether to act in a restrained way that advances the social good or to act in a selfish way that benefits him or her individually while harming others in the group.

Fairness Heuristic Theory points out that a more general type of social dilemma is a ubiquitous feature of social, organizational, and political life: We must all decide, at least implicitly, how much of our independence, effort, and identity we will give to every social or organizational relationship to which we belong. To invest psychologically in our personal relationships, organizations, and social institutions helps the general good and often allows us to gain more than we would by ourselves, but investing our identity and efforts in these social entities also brings risks of exploitation or exclusion. This is the 'fundamental social dilemma.' The theory points out that resolving this basic dilemma would not be difficult if the person could be sure that he or she will not be excluded from or exploited by others in the relationship. If trust in the others involved in the social entity were perfect, it would just be a question of calculating whether there is more to be gained, in terms of identity or outcomes, from being in the relationship than from going it alone. But the world is not perfect, and we all know of people who have trusted and been used or cast off – indeed, most people have experienced that themselves. Often, too, the very relationships that can provide the greatest satisfaction and social identity are those where exclusion or exploitation would be most devastating. Our relationships with those we love, with the organizations we work for, and with our government are precisely those where the fundamental social dilemma is most severe (because we can gain so much *and* lose so much). And sometimes we simply do not have enough information or experience to make solid judgments about the trustworthiness of others in these important relationships. Of course, the ideas behind the concept of a fundamental social dilemma also drive much of the academic and practical attention devoted to trust in organizations – it is vulnerability to exclusion and exploitation that makes us care about trust (Mayer, Davis, & Schoorman, 1995).

The idea of ubiquitous and important fundamental social dilemmas is one of the key insights of Fairness Heuristic Theory; another is the proposition that in fact we seldom have sufficient real 'data' to really judge the trustworthiness of others. Classic work in Social Exchange Theory and in the psychology of interdependence (e.g. Thibaut & Kelley, 1959; see also Kelley & Thibaut, 1978) viewed trust as something that is accumulated across time when trust-related risks, minor at first and then more serious, are taken and found to be safe. According to this view of trust, in our example Beth would gradually invest more and more of her time and effort in the organization, above and beyond what is required by the minimum requirements of her job, and her trust in her coworkers, boss, and the company, would increase if (and only if) these actions were met with approval and greater inclusion, or decrease if the organization showed signs of exploiting or excluding her. This way of thinking about trust certainly has merits in some situations – note, for example, work on 'calculative trust' (Lewicki & Bunker, 1995) – but in many instances there is simply not enough time (and probably not enough mental 'slack') to arrive at firm trust estimates before one must act in a trusting or cautious manner.

The problem with this view of how people come to form and use trust is that the process it posits takes too long and demands too much in terms of attention and mental resources. Fairness Heuristic Theory points out that people need some way to know very early in social and organizational relationships whether it is safe to act as though authorities are trustworthy. In addition, the theory notes that the idea that people are constantly testing, observing and revising the trustworthiness of others implies a level of attention and thought that is at odds with discoveries over the past several decades in social and cognitive psychology. A great deal of research and theory in these disciplines suggests that people are cognitive misers (Fiske & Taylor, 1991); that we often use heuristics and cognitive 'short-cuts' to form attributions and judgments that then form the basis of actions (see also Chapter 14 by Tomlinson, this volume). We simply do not have the mental resources to constantly evaluate and re-evaluate each relationship each time we need to take a social risk. There is a substantial and growing literature on 'swift trust' (see, e.g. Chapter 3 by Blomqvist and Cook, this volume; Meyerson, Weick, & Kramer, 1996; Wildman et al., 2012)

Fairness Heuristic Theory proposes that, especially early in relationships, fairness judgments – which can be formed quickly and on the basis of limited experience – are used in place of judgments of trustworthiness. We know from research on fairness judgments in general, and procedural fairness judgments in particular, that people are able to use nuances of their personal treatment and the formal and informal procedures they encounter to generate quite quickly an impression of the fairness of their relationships with the people and organizations with whom they come in contact (see, generally, Lind & Tyler, 1988). If people use their impressions of fairness to guide their actions in either trusting or distrusting directions (as dictated by whether the impression is one of fair or unfair treatment), then the theoretical problems with traditional accounts of trust would be solved. Because the impressions can be generated very quickly, the issues with the timing and cognitive load problems that plague the traditional model would be resolved.

Thus, according to the Fairness Heuristic Theory account, Beth would be particularly vigilant about how fairly she was being treated in the process of being hired and during her first days on the job. If she was given a voice in decisions that affected her work, if she was treated with fairness and respect, if she was given adequate explanations for why decisions were made, and if those in authority seemed to be acting in an unbiased way – all elements of procedural justice – her overall impressions of fairness would be positive. But if one or more of these early indicators of fairness was lacking, her fairness impressions would be less positive, perhaps even negative. Fairness Heuristic Theory goes on to posit that her overall fairness impressions, positive or negative, would guide Beth as she resolved the fundamental social dilemma on a day-to-day basis at work. Positive fairness judgments would lead her to greater emotional investment and cooperation with her team, her boss, and her new company. Negative fairness judgments would lead her to less cooperation, less emotional investment, and a quid-pro-quo approach to expending extra effort in service of the company.[2]

There is empirical support for these predictions in some data on how people use trust to decide whether to be loyal to organizational leaders (see also Chapter 26 by Den Hartog, this volume). In an analysis of ratings from a 360-degree leadership survey,[3] Lind (2016) found that ratings of the loyalty that direct reports felt for their immediate supervisors could be predicted very well from their ratings of the supervisors' fairness and their ratings of trust in the supervisor (overall R^2 = .646). Ratings of loyalty to the supervisor seemed a good measure of willingness to invest effort and identity in what the team leader was seeking, since this scale consisted of items asking for ratings of team members' loyalty, emotional connection, and personal support for the supervisor. The theory predicts that the relative impact of fairness and trust ratings on loyalty would vary depending on how long the rater had been working with this supervisor – in early relationship ratings fairness would be a stronger driver of loyalty than trust, while in relationships of some duration trust would be the stronger driver of loyalty. As seen in Figure 10.1, when the employee had worked with the supervisor for less than a month, perceptions of fairness were very strong predictors of loyalty. For these new work relationships, trust did not make any real contribution to explaining loyalty over and above perceived fairness. For those with longer work relationships, the relative contribution of trust in explaining loyalty variations increased, so that for those who had worked with their supervisor for 1–12 months fairness and trust were about equally important, and for those who had worked with their supervisor for more than a year trust begins to predominate in explaining loyalty. Of course, this is precisely the pattern of correlations that one would expect if people use their fairness judgments to decide emotional investment early in their relationships with an authority and then rely on their trust judgments later in the relationship. (It is interesting to note, with an eye to future work on the timing of fairness and trust as antecedents of loyalty and leadership, that the impact of fairness increases again in those who have worked with their leader for 4–12 months. Perhaps anticiaption of a first annual review makes fairness a stronger consideration in this time period.)

An earlier laboratory study confirms the theory's prediction that there is a substitution of fairness for trust in driving acceptance of decisions when trust judgments are not available. Van den Bos, Wilke, and Lind (1998)[4] manipulated perceptions of fairness and trust in a laboratory experience in which experimental participants worked on a task and then received remuneration supposedly decided by another participant in their work group. Because the experimenters had

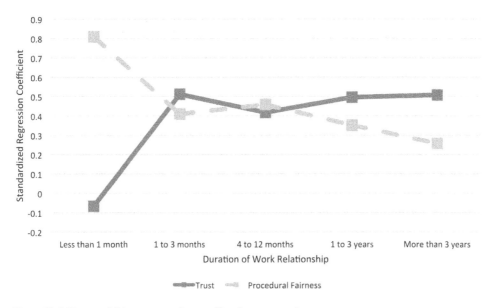

Figure 10.1 Trust and fairness as predictors of loyalty to supervisor

control over the information supplied to the real participants, they could manipulate both trust information and fairness information. The real participants were told that the allocator had participated in a previous study, and they were given what were said to be ratings of trust for the allocator in that earlier study. The ratings either averaged 6.9 on a seven-point trust scale (high trust) or 1.1 (low trust) on that scale. In an additional, trust unknown, condition no trust ratings were given to the participants. Fairness information was manipulated for all participants by having the supposed allocator either give the real participants an opportunity to express them- selves about what they thought they deserved in terms of payment or not giving any such oppor- tunity. (This 'voice' manipulation is a standard and very powerful way of affecting perceived fairness.) Fairness Heuristic Theory predicts that the fairness manipulation would have a strong effect on acceptance of the outcome (i.e. on ratings of satisfaction with and perceived fairness of the ultimate allocation) only when there was no information available about trust – that is, only in the 'trust unknown' condition.

As can be seen from Figure 10.2, this is precisely what was seen in the data. When the par- ticipants had trust information about the person who decided their remuneration, they used that information rather than the fairness of the process to decide how acceptable their payment was. On the other hand, when participants did not have trust information, the fairness of the process was the primary determinant of acceptance of the payment decision.[5]

The psychological processes involved in the transition from fairness-based to trust-based responses, according to Fairness Heuristic Theory, involve moving from one way of using information on fairness to another. According to the theory (Lind, 2001),[6] there are two distinct ways that people process and use fairness information. The theory describes differences in the processing of fairness information during a 'judgmental phase' and processing of fairness information during a 'use phase.' During the judgmental phase, a person is attentive to any in- formation that might give information about process or outcome fairness. Factors that increase

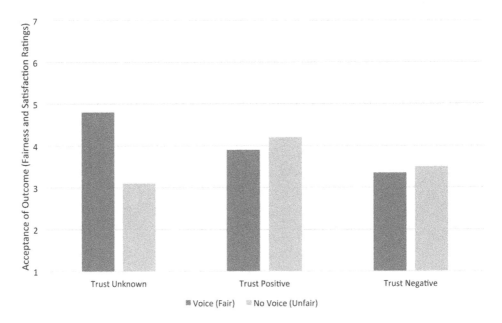

Figure 10.2 Reactions to remuneration decisions

(or in their absence decrease) perceived fairness – things like voice, respect, explanations, bias, or inequitable outcomes – will attract attention and will push fairness perceptions up or down accordingly. The judgmental phase is relatively brief, however, and once a coherent fairness perception is formed, that judgment is put to use guiding actions and moving other judgments and attitudes.

Once a fairness judgment becomes coherent, fairness judgments are processed differently, according to the theory. Instead of constantly looking for, evaluating, and integrating fairness information into a global fairness judgment, the person in question will 'solidify' his or her overall fairness judgment, and fairness perceptions will be used rather than revised. The now-solidified generalized fairness judgment, among other factors, is used to generate and guide trust judgments; and fairness judgments, along with trust judgments, will exert an influence on co-operation, identification with the group, and reactions to authorities. According to the theory, in this phase, new incoming fairness-relevant information is likely to be assimilated to, rather than actively integrated with, existing fairness judgments.

Fairness Heuristic Theory posits these two distinct ways of processing and using fairness information based on the argument that if people were constantly processing fairness-relevant information, there would no cognitive advantage to fairness heuristics relative to Exchange Theory trust processes. One of the major psychological advantages of fairness heuristics, according to the theory, is that they are readily available guides to attitudes and behaviour in the early stages of relationships, allowing meaningful actions to be undertaken in the presence of incomplete trust. This advantage would be lost if the fairness judgments were constantly being re-processed. Instead of constantly re-evaluating the social situation, a fairly stable fairness judgment is formed, which becomes resistant to change and shapes subsequent fairness and trust judgments.

In terms of the organizational example described above, we would expect Beth to move from her early focus on finding and processing fairness information to a different way of reacting to her team, her supervisor and her new organization. The early-days sensitivity to issues like voice and respectful treatment would leave her with either a positive or a negative impression of the overall fairness of her new situation, and as this overall fairness judgment solidified she would begin to use it to interpret new experiences. If her overall impression was that things were fair, she would begin to trust more and more, and she would use her impressions of fairness and her growing trust to explain what was happening. A later lapse in her supervisor's consideration of Beth's views, for example, might be explained away as being due to time pressures on the job, and what would have been an early 'ding' to Beth's overall fairness judgment would now be seen as just something that happens in all jobs. Of course, if Beth's overall fairness judgment coming out of her early experiences was negative, later fairness enhancing actions would be less likely to turn that judgment around. If a rude or seemingly biased supervisor later came to Beth seeking her views on important job decisions, she would be likely to be suspicious of the supervisor's motives rather than feeling pleased that she was finally being treated fairly.

Research has supported this Fairness Heuristic Theory prediction that early fairness information is especially powerful simply because it is early. In the terminology of social and cognitive psychology, this is termed a 'primacy effect.' Lind, Kray, and Thompson (2001) exposed participants in a laboratory work group to unfair treatment (denial of voice) in the first, second, or third of three work sessions. (In the remaining sessions, the participants experienced a fair, voice-present experience.) In a control group, the participants received fair treatment in all three work sessions. Fairness Heuristic Theory predicts that unfair treatment will have a stronger impact on perceived fairness if it is experienced early, rather than later, in the work interaction. Figure 10.3 shows the mean ratings of the fairness of the supervisor and mean ratings (at the end of all three work sessions) of the participant's acceptance of the supervisor's authority.[7]

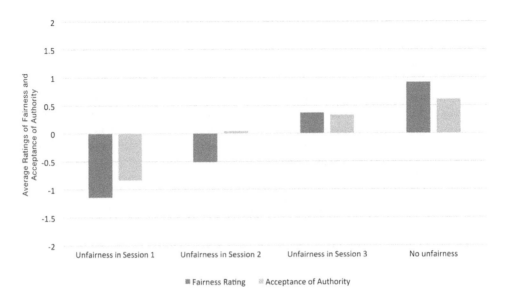

Figure 10.3 Fairness information has stronger impact early in relationship

As can be seen, the unfair treatment had a stronger impact when it came on the first round of work than on the third round, just as the theory would predict. In a conceptually similar theory, Van den Bos, Lind, Vermunt, and Wilke (1997) found evidence that early information on one type of justice drives later reactions to other types of justice. Thus, if one learns first that the outcome of a decision is equitable, this will make one more likely later to interpret the process as fairness, and if one learns first that the process is fair, that will make it more likely that the outcome will be seen as fair. The theory suggests that this pattern of assimilating later fairness information to early fairness judgments occurs because people need to generate quickly a stable fairness judgment to guide their behaviour.

The studies described above provide some good empirical support for the Fairness Heuristic Theory propositions that fairness judgments are used as substitutes for trust early in relationships and that once formed these early fairness judgments influence subsequent judgments and behaviour. Given that our focus in this volume is trust, it is especially intriguing to see that what justice researchers would call a fair process effect is functioning as a 'trust-like' phenomenon in the context of new relationships. Remembering that the logic of Fairness Heuristic Theory begins with the idea that people need some sort of judgment to guide them through the fundamental social dilemma and allow them to act before they have any solid basis for trusting, it is interesting to ask whether there are other judgments that might also be used in this way.

Other trust heuristics

A set of studies by Janson, Levy, Sitkin, and Lind (2008) looked for evidence of social heuristics in judgments about leaders, and found support not only for a fairness heuristic but also for heuristics involving leader self-sacrifice and leader prototypicality. Janson and her colleagues reasoned that just as people can use fairness as a temporary guide to solving the fundamental social dilemma, in work contexts they might also use impressions of a leader's dedication (his or her willingness to make sacrifices for the team's goals) or prototypicality (beliefs that the leader shares core values with the team) as shortcuts to accepting the leader. Their analyses of ratings of leaders in organizations in North America, Europe, India, and New Zealand suggested that both of these potential heuristics sometimes substitute for fairness judgments in driving early leader evaluations.

Janson et al. (2008) did not compare the impact of these other potential heuristics to the impact of trust judgments, though, so some additional work is needed to prove the case that they work as substitutes for trust. Some new analyses using the data used to generate Figure 10.1 (Lind, 2016) look at the relative contributions of trust and dedication at various points in the work relationship.[8] In regression equations predicting loyalty to one's supervisor from dedication and trust showed the same changes across time as did the regressions using process fairness: as seen in Figure 10.4, during the first 3 months working with a new supervisor, the direct-report raters seemed to place much more emphasis on evidence that the supervisor was dedicated to the team's success than on their personal trust impressions, while after this initial period they placed more emphasis on trust.

These findings, along with the Janson et al. (2008) study, provide evidence for the use of nonfairness social heuristics as a substitute for trust early in a hierarchical relationship. As was the case with fairness, these heuristics are constructs that can be generated rather quickly from observance of the person in question. Just as was the case with the process fairness judgments whose effects were presented in Figure 10.1, the dedication judgments shown in Figure 10.4 showed much stronger direct links to loyalty than did trust judgments early in the relationship, then they settled back to having a moderate direct link, but one that was somewhat less than the direct link for trust judgments. Additional research is needed to see in what other ways the psychology of perceived dedication might show the sort of changing influence seen in the operation of the fairness heuristic. Might it be the case, for example, that perceived dedication shows the same sort of primacy effects that have been demonstrated for fairness judgments?

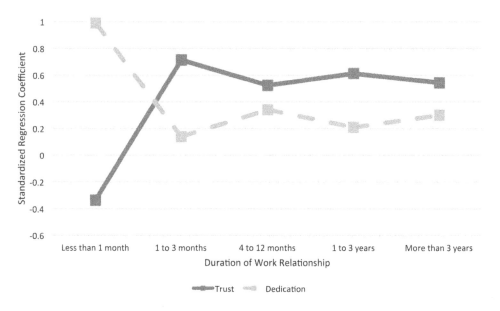

Figure 10.4 Trust and dedication as predictors of loyalty to supervisor

Do perceptions of dedication 'solidify' and dictate how new self-sacrifice information is interpreted? Whether perceptions of dedication show these same heuristic-linked effects or not, the findings presented here and those described in the Janson et al. (2008) article provide a good motivation to consider how and why trust-like heuristics work in social and organizational relationships.

Trust-like heuristics and the fundamental social dilemma

The ideas that led to the development of Fairness Heuristic Theory, and the empirical work on the functioning and dynamics of the fairness and dedication heuristics, provide an interesting picture of the antecedents of early and later trust-like behaviour. The basic concept of the fundamental social dilemma coupled with the observation that in modern life people must routinely find some quick but effective way to resolve the dilemma motivated the search for heuristics that might guide personal investment early in social and organizational relationships. The essential question was 'What readily observable actions or processes might commonly be thought to show safety from exclusion or exploitation?'. In the case of fairness, there was a long history of research and theory linking the impact of fair treatment to feelings of greater inclusion and greater safety from exploitation. It made sense that individuals looking for a way to decide if they could safely cooperate or invest their identities would look to process fairness for guidance.

Note, Fairness Heuristic Theory and the extension of ideas about trust heuristics make no assertion that people are aware they are looking for signs of fairness (or dedication etc.) to use in place of trust. Indeed, some recent work on the neuroscience of reactions fairness and inclusion supports the idea that there are deeply engrained processes that feed the phenomena described above. Naomi Eisenberger and Matthew Lieberman, both social neuroscientists, have studied how the human brain responds to fair treatment and to exclusion by conducting fMRI scans of experimental participants exposed (during the scan) to fair treatment or to social exclusion (Eisenberger, 2011; Eisenberger, Lieberman, & Williams, 2003; Lieberman, 2014; Lieberman & Eisenberger, 2012; Tabibnia, Satpute, & Lieberman, 2008). Their findings show that the parts of the human brain that are most activated by fair treatment are the same areas that activate in the presence of physically pleasing stimuli. And the areas of the brain that 'light up' in fMRI scans of people experiencing social exclusion are the areas that are activated by physical pain and that make decisions about how to respond to pain. It is not much of a stretch at all to say that this work shows that our brains respond to fairness with feelings of pleasure and to signs of exclusion with real pain reactions. These findings suggest that what we are describing as heuristics might well be, at least in the case of fairness judgments, emotional reactions to various types of treatment that guide trust-like behaviour. Perhaps we just distrust those who exclude us early in relationships simply because they hurt us, and trust those who treat us fairly because they make us feel good.

Lieberman (2014) suggests that these pleasure and pain responses to social fairness and exclusion are the result of evolutionary processes that 'piggyback' important social attractions and aversions on pre-existing brain mechanisms for seeking benefit and avoiding harm. To see how this would work, let us begin by considering that in nature the fundamental social dilemma has very high stakes indeed. Many social animals face an implicit decision between cooperation and self-protection, between making sacrifices for the good of the pack or the herd or acting alone. Social animals are social because the group gets better resources for its members, but in most mammals and birds there are also situations that can benefit one individual over another. Going it alone can prove very dangerous, though. For most social mammals and birds (and for us humans as well, through much of our evolutionary history), exclusion from the primary social group means a much reduced chance of survival. It is therefore a matter of life-and-death to know if one is about to be excluded. Similarly, evolutionary biologists have been very much concerned over the years with why social animals behave cooperatively to distant relatives and to unrelated members of social units. Their conclusion is that cooperation makes evolutionary sense if members of a community can perceive who will exploit their cooperation. Thus both individual survival and continued success as a member of a cooperative community depend on resolving the fundamental social dilemma.

The finding from the exclusion studies, which shows that the pain reaction seems to be moderated by a context-judgment area of the brain, might give a neurological account of why heuristics fall away as relationships deepen and solidified perceptions of fairness and trust develop which can override the immediate pain of exclusion. Once fairness and trust judgments solidify, they can override the pain of temporary exclusion or the pleasure of transient fairness.

Whether this line of thought is correct or not – whether we do indeed have built-in, 'hard-wired,' heuristics that guide human behaviour in the absence of strong trust judgments or not – the empirical studies described above give us a strong reason to think that there are some fundamental differences between how we decide to do trusting things early versus later in relationships. This chapter has focused on the use of fairness as one heuristic that produces trust-like behaviour, because there is far and away more empirical work on the fairness heuristic than on, for example, a dedication heuristic. The data we do have on the dedication heuristic suggests that there are heuristics other than fairness, and it would be interesting for future researchers and theorists to look for these short-cuts to cooperation and identity investment. As suggested earlier, the best candidates for such heuristics would be perceptions that are based on readily observable and relatively unambiguous behaviour of others and that seem to be diagnostic of whether one is likely to be exploited or excluded. There seems little doubt that if other social heuristics do exist, knowing what they are and how they work will help us to advance our understanding of how people come to cooperate, what drives their psychological investment in social and work relationships, and how trust ultimately develops.

Future directions

This chapter has dealt for the most part with fairness theories that suggest new ways of looking at the origins of trusting behaviour, especially Fairness Heuristic Theory and the idea that people sometimes use fairness judgments as substitutes for trust as they decide how much to cooperate and invest their identity in teams and organizations. There are at least two lines of work on practical implications of these ideas that suggest future directions for research and application. First, the idea of primacy effects in the generation of fairness judgments and the associated findings showing early use of perceived fairness as a substitute for full-fledged trust provide guidance to new leaders as they work to gain acceptance and loyalty. Second, the concept of phase-shifting – the idea that fairness judgments are sometimes more and other times less susceptible to change – suggests applications to organizational change processes and invites research on those applications.

Caza, Caza, and Lind (2016) provide an analysis of how new leaders can deal with the thorny problems that arise when they take over from a previous abusive leader. Caza and her colleagues note that teams with a history of abusive leadership are likely to have developed strong distrust for the organization and any new leader it assigns. How then, they ask, can a new leader break the cycle of perceived abuse, distrust, and poor performance? The analysis that Caza et al. present relies heavily on Fairness Heuristic Theory (and other ideas about heuristics) to lay out some behaviours and situations that would make the team more or less likely to see the new leader as fair, and they offer suggestions on how the organization and the new leader can promote fairness judgments and start a cycle of increasing, rather than deteriorating, trust. The Caza et al. analysis invites more research on these issues, especially research that looks at early-tenure effects on reactions to leaders and teams.

One of the least investigated predictions of Fairness Heuristic Theory is the idea that fairness judgment processing and use are episodic phenomena – that people shift from generating and revising fairness judgment to simply using the judgments to guide other attitudes and behaviour. Some years ago, Tost and Lind (2010) pointed out that one application of such phase-shifting would be in organizational change initiatives. If people can be shifted back into fairness judgment mode *and* if they can be shown that the process and outcome of proposed change is fair (see also Lind & Arndt, 2016; Proudfoot & Lind, 2014), then one would expect that changes would be more readily accepted. The problem, until recently, was that there was not much research that showed phase-shifting effects. A very recent study by Soenen, Melkonian, and Ambrose (in press) looked at phase-shifting perceptions in the context of organizational changes. They found that when people experiencing organizational change perceived the change to be making changes in their relationship with the organization, their post-change fairness judgments were less similar to their pre-change fairness judgments. This suggests that, as predicted by Fairness Heuristic Theory, perceived fundamental changes in a relationship prompt a new round of fairness judgment processing. In addition, Soenen et al. identified four factors – magnitude of the change, managerial exemplarity, coworker support, and dispositional resistance to change – that account for much of the variation in phase-shifting. Just as the Caza et al. analysis invites research attention on the interplay of fairness and trust in early-tenure leadership contexts, the work of Soenen et al. (in press) and Tost and Lind (2010) invite similar exploration of how these two constructs play out, and play out against each other, in organizational change.

Notes

1   Most of the theoretical work considered in this chapter involves ideas set forth by four scholars: Lind, Tyler, Van den Bos, and Blader. There are certainly other theories that address the psychology of fairness – Folger and Cropanzano's Fairness Theory (2001) and Jost and Kay's work on System Justification Theory are two relatively recent examples. Fairness Theory and System Justification Theory are not addressed here because the phenomena and constructs they focus on are not closely aligned with trust and trust phenomena.

2   It is worth noting that there is no assertion in Fairness Heuristic Theory that people think actively about the fundamental social dilemma and the use of fairness judgments to resolve it. In the last section of this chapter, the case will be made that there are elements of this social behaviour that are 'hardwired' into our brains. The working of the heuristics we consider here may well be simply a question of deeply engrained responses to perceptions that in turn trigger or inhibit trust-like behaviour.

3   The survey used was the 'Six Domains Leadership Survey' (Sitkin and Lind, 2009; Lind and Sitkin, 2015). The survey database consisted of ratings of executives who had participated in open-enrollment executive education programs at Duke University over a number of years. The data used in the analyses described were ratings by direct reports only. (The survey typically also collects ratings from peers and supervisors.) The procedural fairness measure used in the analyses combined items from the scales on the leaders' concern and respect and their attention to fairness.

4   The data presented here are averaged ratings across both of the outcome measures reported in the article; these data are from Van den Bos et al., Experiment 2.

5   The only significant effect was the interaction between fairness and trust information, and this interaction was caused by the substantial simple effect of process when trust was unknown. There were no significant simple effects for fairness of the process when trust was known to be either positive or negative.

6   The names and number of phases described here is that used by Lind (2001); in other accounts of the theory, especially the Van den Bos et al. (2001) chapter, the description is a bit different. The major difference is that the Van den Bos et al. parse the process more finely by including a pre-formation phase that exists before any attention is given to fairness.

7 The means are taken from the high group identification conditions. A separate prediction from Fairness Heuristic Theory was that the primacy effect would be stronger for high than for low group identification, and this was indeed the case. Both variables were rated on a 7-point scale from -3 to +3

8 Prototypicality ratings were not available in the dataset. The dedication measure was composed of three items asking the rater whether he or she thought the supervisor made personal sacrifices for the team, was a good fit for the team, and was courageous. The overall multiple R for prediction of loyalty from dedication and trust across all time periods was .799. When fairness, dedication, and trust were all entered into the multiple regression equation, both fairness and dedication showed substantially larger beta values for raters who were in the first three months of working with a supervisor and trust showed larger beta values than the other two variables for raters who had worked with their supervisor for four months or more.

References

Caza, B. B., Caza, A., & Lind, E. A. (2016). Breaking the cycle: How new leaders establish positive relationships in the aftermath of abusive supervision. Unpublished manuscript, University of Manitoba.

Cohen, R. L. (1985). Procedural justice and participation. *Human Relations*, 38, 643–663.

Eisenberger, N. I. (2011). Social pain: Experiential, neurocognitive, and genetic correlates. In A. Todorov, S. T. Fiske, & D. A. Prentice (Eds.), *Social neuroscience: Toward understanding the underpinnings of the social mind*. Oxford: Oxford University Press.

Eisenberger, N. I., Lieberman, M. D., & Williams, K. D. (2003). Does rejection hurt? An fMRI study of social exclusion. *Science*, 302, 290–292.

Fiske, S.T., & Taylor, S.E. (1991). *Social Cognition* (2nd ed.). New York: McGraw-Hill.

Hardin, G. (1968). The Tragedy of the Commons. *Science*, 162, 1243–1248.

Janson, A., Levy, L., Sitkin, S. B., & Lind, E. A. (2008). Fairness and other leadership heuristics: A four nation study. *European Journal of Work and Organizational Psychology*, 17, 251–272.

Kelley, H. H., & Thibaut, J. (1978). *The psychology of interdependence*. New York: Wiley.

Lewicki, R. J. & Bunker, B. B. (1995). Trust in relationships: A model of trust development and decline. In B. B. Bunker & J. Z. Rubin (Eds.), *Conflict, cooperation, and justice*. San Francisco: Jossey Bass.

Lieberman, M. D. (2011). Why symbolic processing of affect can disrupt negative affect: Social cognitive and affective neuroscience investigations. In A. Todorov, S. T. Fiske, & D. A. Prentice (Eds.), *Social neuroscience: Toward understanding the underpinnings of the social mind*. Oxford: Oxford University Press.

Lieberman, M. D. (2014). *Social: Why our brains are wired to connect*. New York: Broadway Books.

Lieberman, M. D., & Eisenberger, N. I. (2012). A pain by any other name (rejection, exclusion, ostracism) still hurts the same: The role of dorsal anterior cingulate cortex in social and physical pain. In J. T. Cacioppo, P. S. Visser, & C. L. Pickett (Eds.), *Social neuroscience: People thinking about thinking People*. Cambridge, MA: MIT Press.

Lind, E. A. (1995). *Social conflict and social justice: Some lessons from the social psychology of justice*. Leiden, the Netherlands: Leiden University Press.

Lind, E. A. (2001). Fairness heuristic theory: Justice judgments as pivotal cognitions in organizational relations. In J. Greenberg & R. Cropanzano (Eds.), *Advances in organizational justice*. Palo Alto, CA: Stanford University Press.

Lind, E. A. (2011). Culture and Fairness: Some possible dynamics of cultural variation in the psychology of fairness. In K. Ohbuchi & N. Asai (Eds.) *Inequality, discrimination, and conflict in Japan: Ways to social justice and cooperation*. Victoria, AU: Transpacific Press.

Lind. E. A. (2016). Unpublished data. Duke University.

Lind, E. A. & Arndt, C. (2016). Perceived fairness and regulatory policy. Unpublished manuscript, Duke University.

Lind, E. A., Kray, L. J., & Thompson, L. (2001). Primacy effects in justice judgments: Testing predictions from fairness heuristic theory. *Organizational Behavior and Human Decision Processes*, 85, 189–210.

Lind, E. A., Kulik, C., Ambrose, M., & Park, M. (1993). Individual and corporate dispute resolution: Using procedural fairness as a decision heuristic. *Administrative Science Quarterly*, 38, 224–251.

Lind, E. A., & Sitkin, S. (2015). *The six domains of leadership*. Columbia, SC: Learning with Leaders.

Lind, E. A., & Tyler, T. R. (1988). *The social psychology of procedural justice*. New York: Plenum Press.

Mayer, R. C., Davis, J., & Schoorman, F. D. (1995). An integrative model of organizational trust. *Academy of Management Review*, 20, 709–734.

Meyerson, D., Weick, K. E., & Kramer, R. M. (1996). Swift trust and temporary groups. In R. M. Kramer & T. Tyler (Eds.), *Trust in organizations: Frontiers of Theory and Research*. London: Sage Publications.

Proudfoot, D., & Lind, E. A. (2014). Fairness heuristic theory, the uncertainty management model, and fairness at work. In M. Ambrose & R. Cropanzano (Eds.), *Oxford handbook of justice in the workplace*. New York: Oxford University Press.

Sitkin, S., & Lind, E. A. (2009). *Six domains of leadership survey*. Durham, NC: Delta Leadership, Inc.

Soenen, G., Melkonian, T., & Ambrose, M. (In press). To shift or not to shift? Determinants and consequences of phase-shifting on justice judgments. *Academy of Management Journal*.

Tabibnia, G., Satpute, A. B., & Lieberman, M. D. (2008). The sunny side of fairness: Preference fairness activates reward circuitry (and disregarding unfairness activates self-control circuitry). *Psychological Science*, 19, 339–347.

Thibaut, J., & Kelley, H. H. (1959). *The social psychology of groups*. New York: Wiley.

Tost, L. P, & Lind, E. A. (2010). Sounding the alarm: Moving from system justification to system condemnation in the justice judgment process. In E. A. Mannix, M. A. Neale, & E. Mullen (Eds.), *Research on managing groups and teams* (Vol. 13). Greenwich, CT: Elsevier Science Press.

Tyler, T. R. (1984). The role of perceived injustice in defendants' evaluations of their courtroom experience. *Law & Society Review*, 18, 51–74.

Tyler, T. R. (1987). Conditions leading to value expression effects in judgments of procedural justice: A test of four models. *Journal of Personality and Social Psychology*, 52, 333–344.

Tyler, T. R. (1990). *Why people obey the law: Procedural justice, legitimacy, and compliance*. New Haven, CT: Yale University Press.

Tyler, T. R. (1997). The psychology of legitimacy: A relational perspective on voluntary deference to authorities. *Personality and Social Psychology Review*, 1, 323–345.

Tyler, T. R., & Blader, S. (2003). Procedural justice, social identity, and cooperative behavior. *Personality and Social Psychology Review*, 7, 349–361.

Tyler, T. R., & Caine, A. (1981). The influence of outcomes and procedures on satisfaction with formal leaders. *Journal of Personality and Social Psychology*, 41, 642–655.

Tyler, T. R., & Degoey, P. (1996). Trust in organizational authorities: The influence of motive attributions on willingness to accept decisions. In R. Kramer and T. R. Tyler (Eds.), *Trust in organizations*. Thousand Oaks, CA: Sage.

Tyler, T. R., Goff, P. A., & MacCoun, R. J. (2015). The impact of psychological science on policing in the United States: Procedural justice, legitimacy, and effective law enforcement. *Psychological Science in the Public Interest*, 16, 75–109.

Tyler, T. R., & Lind, E. A. (1992). A relational model of authority in groups. In M. Zanna (Ed.), *Advances in experimental social psychology* (Vol. 25). New York: Academic Press.

Tyler, T. R., Rasinski, K., & McGraw, K. (1985). The influence of perceived injustice on support for political authorities. *Journal of Applied Social Psychology*, 15, 700–725.

Tyler, T. R., Rasinski, K., & Spodick, N. (1985). The influence of voice on satisfaction with leaders: Exploring the meaning of process control. Journal of Personality and Social Psychology, 48, 72–81.

Van den Bos, K., Lind, E. A., Vermunt, R., & Wilke, H. (1997). How do I judge my outcome when I don't know the outcomes of others: The psychology of the fair process effect. *Journal of Personality and Social Psychology*, 72, 1034–1046.

Van den Bos, K., Lind, E. A., & Wilke, H. (2001). The psychology of procedural justice and distributive justice viewed from the perspective of fairness heuristic theory. In R. Cropanzano (Ed.), *Justice in the workplace: Volume II—From theory to practice*. Mahwah, NJ: Lawrence Erlbaum & Associates.

Van den Bos, K., Wilke, H. A. M., & Lind, E. A. (1998). When do we need procedural fairness? The role of trust in authority. *Journal of Personality and Social Psychology*, 75, 1449–1458.

Walker, L., LaTour, S., Lind, E. A., & Thibaut, J. (1974). Reactions of participants and observers to modes of adjudication. *Journal of Applied Social Psychology*, 4, 295–310.

Wildman, J. L., Shuffler, M. L., Lazzara, E. H., Fiore, S. M., Burke, C. S., Salas, E., & Garven, S. (2012). Trust development in swift starting action teams: A multilevel framework. *Group & Organization Management*, 37, 137–170.

11

SOCIAL EXCHANGE THEORY

Where is trust?

Jacqueline A-M. Coyle-Shapiro and Marjo-Riitta Diehl

Introduction

Social exchange theory is one of the most influential conceptual frameworks for understanding behaviour in organizations (Cropanzano & Mitchell, 2005) and a dominant theoretical framework to understanding the employee-organization relationship (Coyle-Shapiro & Conway, 2004). The versatility of its explanatory power reaches beyond the employee-organization relationship to include leadership (Liden, Sparrowe & Wayne, 1997), organizational justice (Colquitt, Scott, Rodell, Long, Zapata, Conlon & Wesson, 2013; Rupp, Shao, Jones & Liao, 2014), workplace exclusion (Scott, Restubog & Zagenczyk, 2013) and the impact of the Dark Triad (machiavellianism, narcissism and psychopathy) on work behaviour (O'Boyle, Forsyth, Banks & McDaniel, 2012). A common although not exclusive focus of social exchange theory is to understand relationships, underpinning mechanisms and associated outcomes. In this chapter, we highlight the role of trust in social exchange relationships as it applies to the employee-organization relationship (EOR).

Our chapter is organized as follows. First, we review the historical development of social exchange theory starting with its roots in the work of Malinowski (1922) and Mauss (1954) and ending with contemporary developments highlighting the implications of a social exchange perspective to understanding trust. Then, we examine current EOR frameworks that draw on social exchange theory: psychological contracts (PC), idiosyncratic deals (i-deals), perceived organizational support (POS) and employment relationships (ER) and review the empirical evidence on the role of trust in these EOR frameworks. Finally, we discuss the theoretical implications for our understanding of trust in the EOR.

Although there is an agreement that trust is an important aspect of organizational life, a number of definitions have been put forward to capture the meaning of trust such as 'confident positive expectations' (Lewicki et al., 1998) or a 'willingness to rely' (Doney, Cannon & Mullen, 1998). Mayer, Davis and Schoorman (1995) define trust as 'the willingness of a party to be vulnerable to the actions of another party based on the expectations that the party will perform a particular action important to the trustor, irrespective of the ability to monitor or control that other party' (p. 712). Trust, in social exchange terms occurs when the donor trusts the recipient to reciprocate a benefit – it is trust that allows the donor to be vulnerable to non reciprocation and herein lies the risk. Rousseau, Sitkin, Burt and Camerer (1998) note that for trust to arise, risk and interdependence are needed. The source of the risk is the uncertainty of the other's intentions and actions, and the interdependence arises from the fact that interests of one party cannot be achieved without relying on the other (Rousseau et al., 1998).

Historical development of social exchange theory

As this historical review will reveal, the development of social exchange theory and its use weaves its way through a number of disciplines, starting with anthropology and ending within the mainstream management field as reflected in its prominence in *Academy of Management Journal* as a micro theory (Colquitt & Zapata-Phelan, 2007) and one of the most often evoked theories in the *Journal of Applied Psychology* (Colquitt, Baer, Long & Halvorsen-Ganepola, 2014).

Origins of social exchange theory

The roots of social exchange theory can be traced back to the early anthropological work by Malinowski (1922) in his classical study of exchange ('Kula') among the natives of the Trobriand Islands. Malinowski (1922) outlined the key principles of 'Kula' (exchange): (a) it is ongoing 'once in the Kula, always in the Kula' (p. 83), (b) it requires mutual trust; (c) the bestowing of a gift needs to be repaid with 'an equivalent counter-gift after a lapse of time, be it a few hours or even minutes though sometimes as much as a year or more may lapse between payments' (p. 95); (d) the equivalence of the returning gift is at the discretion of the giver and it cannot be enforced by coercion. Although, the opening gift is given spontaneously, the counter-gift is given under pressure of fulfilling an obligation. Two features of Malinowski's work on exchange are noteworthy. First, the idea of equivalence in exchange is critical to exchange relationships as when two equivalent gifts are exchanged 'these two have married' (p. 356). The emphasis given to equivalence is exemplified by the idea of intermediary gifts – when an equivalent gift cannot be exchanged, a gift of lesser value is given to 'fill the gap' until such time as an equivalent gift can be returned. Second, this exchange of gifts (if one is in the Kula) lasts a lifetime and there is a symbolic significance to the giving of gifts which remain in the transitory possession of the receiver – gifts are given and taken in an ongoing and never-ending manner.

In the seminal book *The Gift* by Mauss (1954), he argues that there is no such thing as a free gift. Rather, he outlines the system of gift exchange called 'potlatch' that is governed by three obligations: to give presents, to receive presents and to reciprocate presents received. All three obligations carry constraints and burdens – 'a gift is received "with a burden attached"' (Mauss, 1954, p. 41) and the essence of potlatch is the obligation to reciprocate. So important is this to 'potlatch' that Mauss (1954) in his study of tribes notes 'the punishment for failure to reciprocate is slavery for debt' (p. 42), while reciprocation of a gift needs to be given with interest. Consistent with Malinowski (1922), Mauss emphasizes the role of reciprocal action, drawing upon a Mauri proverb 'give as much as you take, all will be very well' (p. 71).

This early anthropological work on tribes examining economy of exchange through gift giving highlights several aspects of the role of trust. First, the gift giver is trusting that a counter gift will be returned; second, trust is lost if this does not occur. As Mauss (1954) notes, 'one loses face for ever if one does not reciprocate' (p. 42); and, third, when a counter gift of equivalent value is return, it facilitates the development of trust. Although these gifts do not necessarily have economic value but are symbolic, the signals sent by the gift reflect the gift giver's trustworthiness. Trust is generated with an ongoing cycle of giving and receiving of at least equivalent gifts within a system where sanctions such as loss of rank and status within the tribe are imposed for trust violations.

Seminal contributions to social exchange theory

Although Homans (1958) used the term social exchange, it was Blau's (1964) work that spearheaded the conceptual development of social exchange theory. He was the first to precisely differentiate different types of exchange relationships and explicitly discuss trust. Prior to this, Homans (1958), Thibaut & Kelly (1959) and March and Simon (1958) provided seminal contributions.

Homans (1958) drew attention to social behaviour as exchange in the context of individual interactions in groups. He defined social behaviour as 'an exchange of goods, material goods but also non-material ones, such as the symbols of approval or prestige' (p. 606). Individuals strive for balance in their exchange relationships and seek to maximize profit (rewards less cost) compared to others in their group. As Homans (p. 606) notes, 'persons that give much to others try to get much from them, and persons that get much from others are under pressure to give much to them'. Thibaut and Kelley (1959) also examine individual interactions in a small-group context making predictions about the consequences for the individual in terms of costs and rewards. An individual will be more likely to remain in a dyadic relationship when his/her rewards/costs combination is more favourable than the comparison level of alternatives. The higher the outcomes (compared to the alternatives), the more dependent the individual is on the relationship. If an individual's outcomes fall above the comparison level (i.e. what he/she believes they deserve), an individual will judge the outcome to be attractive and satisfying; if the outcomes fall below, the outcomes will be judged as unattractive and unsatisfying. Further, an individual will leave the relationship when his/her outcomes drop below the comparison level of alternatives.

March and Simon (1958) were the first to examine exchange relationships in the context of employee-organization in which the organization offers inducements in return for employee contributions. In explaining why organizational members continue their participation in the organization, March and Simon (1958) argue that the organization needs to provide inducements that are greater in value compared to the contributions members are required to make. These contributions, in turn, provide the basis and affect the extent to which the organization can offer those inducements. Therefore, the organization can continue as long as the contributions of members are sufficient to provide the inducements that are large 'enough' to elicit those contributions. The contingent interplay between the inducements offered by the organization and contributions elicited from employees is made explicit.

Neither Homans (1958) nor March and Simon (1958) explicitly discussed reciprocity, but it is implicit in their description of exchange. Gouldner (1960) in his seminal work on the norm of reciprocity was the first to define the concept although it had been used prior to this. He suggests that the norm of reciprocity is universal and makes two demands of individuals: '(1) people should help those who have helped them, and (2) people should not injure those who have helped them' (Gouldner, 1960 p. 171). The obligation to reciprocate is contingent upon the value of the benefit received such that the 'debt is in proportion to and varies with – among other things – the intensity of the recipient's need at the time the benefit was bestowed ('a friend in need . . .'), the resources of the donor ('he gave although he could ill afford it'), the motives imputed to the donor ('without thought of gain') and the nature of the constraints which are perceived to exist or be absent 'he gave of his own free will') (Gouldner, 1960, p. 171). According to Gouldner (1960), when one party gives a benefit, an obligation is created and the recipient is indebted to the donor until such point as he/she repays the benefit. Echoing the sentiment of Mauss (1954), Gouldner (1960) states 'it is morally improper, under the norm of reciprocity, to break off relations or to launch hostilities against those to whom you are still indebted' (p. 175).

Malinowski (1922) discussed equivalence in gifts and this idea was more precisely addressed by Gouldner (1960) who differentiated between heteromorphic and homeomorphic reciprocity – the former captures the exchange of different things that are equal in value as defined by the exchange partners while the latter captures exchanges that are identical with regard to what is exchanged or the circumstances under which the exchange occurs. The function of the norm of reciprocity is twofold: first, it acts as a starting mechanism to allow an exchange relationship to develop if the recipient of a benefit reciprocates; second, once the norm of reciprocity has been established between the two parties, it provides the basis for each party's confidence that benefits will indeed be reciprocated. Thus, the norm of reciprocity acts as a starting mechanism to develop trust and a stabilizing mechanism to maintain or enhance trust.

While Gouldner's (1960) work elaborates and details what remained undefined in prior work concerning reciprocity, Blau (1964) did the same when it comes to exchange relationships, where he distinguished between social and economic exchange. Blau (1964) describes economic exchange, as one where the exchange is specified and the method used to assure that each party fulfils its specific obligations is the formal agreement upon which the exchange is based, eliminating the need for trust. In contrast, social exchange involves unspecified obligations – 'favors that create diffuse future obligations, not precisely specified ones, and the nature of the return cannot be bargained about but must be left to the discretion of the one who makes it' (p. 93). These relationships take time to develop as the nature of the benefits exchanged start off small and expand to include socioemotional resources – this allows for trust to develop over time. As Blau (1964) notes, '. . . doing a favour demonstrates trust in another; the other's reciprocation validates this trust as justified' (p. 107). Trust is created and trustworthiness developed through the adherence of the exchange partners to the norm of reciprocity as the benefits exchanged expand in nature and value over time. According to Blau (1964), the timing of reciprocation is important – 'posthaste reciprocation of favors, which implies a refusal to stay indebted for a while and hence an insistence on a more businesslike relationship is condemned as improper' (p. 99) as this would demonstrate ingratitude. Thus, remaining obligated to another party for an appropriate time facilitates the development of trust as it signals a long-term view of the relationship.

These seminal works build upon and extend the early anthropological work regarding the role of trust in social exchange relationships. First, reciprocity is the key to the development of trusting relationships – the donor takes a risk that the beneficiary will not reciprocate while concurrently signalling their trust in the beneficiary to reciprocate. Second, the reciprocation of a benefit helps the beneficiary demonstrate their trustworthiness. Third, the role of time between exchanges highlighted by Malinowski (1992) was further developed by Blau (1964) who argued that remaining obligated to another facilitates the establishment of trust. Finally, analogous to climbing a ladder one rung at a time, trust evolves slowly as the value of the resources exchanged increases and the parties demonstrate their trustworthiness in terms of reciprocation. Trust, therefore, is predicated on the actions and reactions of the parties in an exchange relationship.

Subsequent developments in social exchange theory

Emerson (1962) introduced the idea of power dependence in social relations and argues that 'power resides implicitly in the other's dependence' (p. 32). His approach to social exchange accentuates the role of power and dependence aptly titled as power-dependence theory. Emerson (1972a and b) argues that exchanges involve mutual dependence where the parties are dependent upon each other for valued outcomes; benefits obtained are contingent upon benefits received in the exchange. In essence, Emerson (1972a) states that the extent to which B is dependent upon A is contingent upon the value of the benefits A provides and B's access to alternatives, such that the greater the value attached to the benefits A provides and the fewer alternatives available to B, the greater B's dependency on A. The less the dependency of one party on another, the greater the power structural advantage. Emerson (1972a) also argued that the initiation of the exchange varies directly with dependence – a party is more likely to initiate exchange with another with whom they are more (rather than less) dependent upon.

Emerson (1976, 1981) distinguished between four forms of social exchange: productive, negotiated, reciprocal and generalized. Productive exchange involves the coordination of efforts or combining of resources to generate a joint good – all parties contribute to and benefit from this collective endeavour. Lawler, Thye and Yoon (2000) give an example of a group of unions coming together on a common approach to negotiate with the city government. Negotiated exchange involves two parties directly and jointly agreeing the terms constituting a discrete transaction. In reciprocal exchanges, each party's contribution to the exchange is separately performed and non-negotiated, governed by direct reciprocation. Generalized exchanges are indirect in that the giving and receiving of benefits among members of a group as the recipient of a benefit may not reciprocate the source – A provides a benefit to B who reciprocates C and D reciprocates A. In this type of exchange, repayment of a benefit is stipulated but the target of the reciprocal act can be any member of the group. Here, we limit our attention to negotiated and reciprocal exchange as these two types of exchange have contrasting implications for the role of trust.

Molm (1994) outlined the key differences between negotiated and reciprocal exchanges along two dimensions: (a) the contingency of each party's outcomes on the joint action or the other party's actions and (b) the party's information about the other's reciprocity. In negotiated exchanges, each party's outcomes depend on the joint actions of them and the other party for bilateral benefits, and both parties know what they are getting and giving, having negotiated an agreement. In contrast, in reciprocal exchanges, each party's outcomes depend exclusively upon the other party and benefits can flow unilaterally (benefits given may not be reciprocated) without knowledge as to whether reciprocity will occur and if it does, when it will occur. Molm (2003) subsequently highlighted timing of inequality as another key difference. In negotiated exchanges, each transaction provides equal or unequal outcomes for the parties but in reciprocal exchange, the extent of equality or inequality is only known over the course of time by the frequency and value of reciprocity. Finally, Molm (2003) noted that uncertainty in reciprocity varies between negotiated and reciprocal exchange. She argues that reciprocal acts can be compared in terms of equivalence on the following dimensions: function (good or harm), magnitude of value and probability/frequency of occurrence. In negotiated exchanges, the only uncertainty pertains to the magnitude of value that each party receives as it is unlikely that a party would negotiate good for harm, and the probability of reciprocity is not an issue in a bilateral negotiation of exchange. In reciprocal exchanges, there is uncertainty in two dimensions: the probability of reciprocity happening and the magnitude of its value. Finally, although both forms of exchange involve risk, the nature of this risk is different. In reciprocal exchange, there is the risk of non-reciprocation – the giving of a benefit without receiving any benefit in return (Molm, 2003). In negotiated exchange, the risk is what Molm (2003) terms 'risk of exclusion' which reflects the failure to reach an agreement.

Molm and her colleagues have undertaken a substantial body of experimental research to examine the differences between negotiated and reciprocal exchange, and, here, we focus on a few that are germane to our review of social exchange. Molm, Takahashi and Peterson (2000) using an experimental design find that trust and affective commitment are stronger under reciprocal exchanges than negotiated exchanges. The authors argue that risk is a necessary condition for the development of trust – the vulnerability to exploitation provides fertile ground for the growth of trust. It also provides the opportunity for the receiving party to demonstrate their trustworthiness in terms of whether they reciprocate or not. Molm (2003) argues that the act of reciprocation is in and of itself more important than the magnitude of its value and this may be explained by consistent reciprocity being a mechanism to reduce uncertainty and make risky reciprocal exchanges more predictable. Further, Molm (2003) argues that reciprocation may provide expressive benefits (i.e. feeling valued) that may substitute for reduced value of the benefits. Molm, Takahashi and Peterson (2003) find that although negotiated exchange appears fairer as it gives parties greater control over their outcomes and greater voice, experimental findings support the contrary – negotiated exchange partners were deemed less fair than reciprocal exchange partners and this held true across equal and unequal exchanges. The authors argue that the sheer act of negotiating an exchange accentuates the salience of the conflict of interests that in turn triggers self-serving attributions (ascribing unfavourable motives and traits to the other party) that increase perceived unfairness.

From a social exchange lens, trust is conceptualized as an expectation that an exchange partner will behave benignly and not exploitatively based on inferences about the partner's traits and intentions. In economic exchange (Blau, 1964) or negotiated exchange (Emerson, 1972a), the agreement reached provides assurance that both parties will fulfil the terms and therefore 'as long as an "assurance" structure is present, there is little opportunity for trust to develop' (Molm et al., 2000) as uncertainty and risk have been minimized. As the early contributors to social exchange highlight, the initial offer of a favour carries the greatest risk and uncertainty as the donor risks exploitation (i.e. the favour will not be reciprocated) and the risk of exclusion (the beneficiary rejects the offer to enter into a relationship). Therefore, the party who initiates the exchange is willing to be vulnerable to the other party and in providing a benefit is demonstrating trust in the other party that they will indeed reciprocate. In the absence of assurance, social exchange relationships require trust that benefits will be reciprocated and obligations discharged.

Molm et al. (2000) note that because of the greater risk for exploitation in reciprocal exchanges as a result of the absence of assurances, there is a greater opportunity for the exchange partners to demonstrate trustworthiness. Therefore, vulnerability to risk where the opportunity to exploit is turned down provides fertile ground for trust to develop; reciprocity turns on the development of trust, which should escalate with frequent and stable exchange interactions. Consequently, a social exchange relationship engenders trust, obligation and gratitude, and over time leads to a relationship characterized by interdependency, mutual trust and bonding (Blau, 1964).

Contemporary developments

In tracing the development of social exchange theory up to this point, two observations can be made in terms of trust. First, trust is situationally derived based on the exchange interactions between the parties. This view downplays the role of personality-based, institution-based and cognition-based trust (McKnight, Cummings & Chervany, 1998) to argue that trust results from the adherence to the norm of reciprocity in exchange relationships. Second, trust develops gradually over time, beginning with low-value benefits and escalating to high-value benefits as the parties demonstrate their trustworthiness through reciprocity. A recent development complements this view by exploring the role of anchoring events in quickly altering the nature of the relationship with implications for trust and distrust.

Ballinger and Rockmann (2010) examine how 'anchoring events' can fundamentally alter social exchange relationships and challenge the assumption that social exchange relationships develop slowly. These anchoring events can trigger 'quick trust' if positive or distrust if negative. The authors examine the role of highly memorable exchanges in setting the basis for the subsequent relationship which contrasts with the tenets of social exchange theory that 'relationship development is not a matter of a single stimulus-response. It is more analogous to climbing a ladder' (Cropanzano & Mitchell, 2005, p. 890). Rather, as Ballinger and Rockmann (2010) state, 'relationships can reach different forms via a "chute" – a punctuated process where the rules for future exchange are quickly, dramatically and durably changed by the outcome of a single event' (p. 374). An anchoring event is one where an individual is highly dependent upon another for a resource needed to achieve a central goal, the outcome positively or negatively deviates from an expectation that is based on past relationship exchanges and the donor is judged to have intended and controlled this outcome (Ballinger & Rockmann, 2010). Such an event triggers an affective response (anger, gratitude), and the magnitude and direction of the affective reaction is encoded in memory that an individual remembers and interprets the target's future behaviour so as to support the remembered event.

When an anchoring event occurs in the context of a reciprocity-based relationship, an individual will update their preferred rules for future exchanges and adjust their expectations from their exchange partner (Ballinger & Rockmann, 2010) such that a negative anchoring event will trigger distrust and lead an individual to select a rule that provides them with greater protection – to maximize their own outcomes or revenge. Because these have negative implications for the other party, Ballinger and Rockmann (2010) view these as negative nonreciprocal states. After a positive anchoring event, the trust created will facilitate an individual selecting a rule that favours the other party, such as altruism, and this is termed a positive nonreciprocal state. The authors propose that anchoring events are more likely to occur early in reciprocal relationships and as the relationship becomes more positive (or negative), an anchoring event that is positive (negative) is more likely to occur. In a positive relationship, the individual sees the target as responsible for good actions which makes it less likely that any negative behaviour will be attributed internally to the target. This in turn makes the occurrence of a negative anchoring event less likely in a positive relationship. On the contrary, in a negative relationship, any disappointing outcome will be attributed internally to the target and as the individual is more vigilant, it is likely that further negative anchoring events will occur (i.e. the straw that breaks the camel's back) and trigger the relationship into a negative nonreciprocal state.

When a negative nonreciprocal relationship develops as a consequence of an anchoring event (in contrast to a gradual process), the potency of the anchoring event, the defining memory, will bias actions and interpretations, and the difficulty facing the target to demonstrate their trustworthiness will make it less likely that a positive anchoring event will revert the relationship to a reciprocal one (Ballinger & Rockmann, 2010). A negative anchoring event is more likely to shift a positive nonreciprocal relationship to a different rule if the positive state was reached through a prior anchoring event (a positive one) because a gradual development of a positive nonreciprocal relationship is more immune to transgressions as a result of the accumulation of investment in that relationship.

This view extends prior work on the implications of social exchange relationships for the role of trust. First, Ballinger and Rockmann (2010) complement the traditional social exchange view of trust (develops gradually and slowly over time) by considering the impact of an 'anchoring event' on the development of 'quick trust' whereby the effect of the anchoring event is so memorable that it jump starts the creation of trust. These intense events or high-stake exchanges, when positive, are likely to lead to high levels of trust in some part triggered by the recipient's gratitude towards the beneficiary. Thus, trust can develop quickly or slowly in social exchange relationships contingent upon the nature of the initial exchanges (significant or small). It is the nature of the exchanges that determine trust levels and small initial exchanges will result in the gradual development of trust whereas highly significant initial exchanges will result in express levels of trust.

Second, Ballinger and Rockmann (2010) implicitly point to the difference in the fragility/ robustness of trust generated by the two different social exchange pathways. The authors argue that the way the relationship develops (gradual versus anchoring event), and implicitly the basis of trust, determines whether the relationship is more or less immune from transgressions. A gradual development and building of trust is likely to withstand a negative anchoring event but the relationship built upon a positive anchoring event is more likely to change as a result of a subsequent negative anchoring event. Therefore, relationships where trust develops based on positive anchoring events are likely to be based on fragile trust whereas relationships based on the gradual development of trust are likely to be more robust, all things equal.

Finally, although distrust is rarely discussed in the context of social exchange relationships, negative events happen even in the most positive of relationships (Dulac, Coyle-Shapiro, Henderson & Wayne, 2008). Ballinger and Rockmann (2010) explain how negative social exchange relationships can develop through repeated negative anchoring events in which the focal individual develops distrust in their exchange partner as a way of protecting their own interests, and the relationship shifts to a non-reciprocal negative one. The authors argue that it will be difficult to move this relationship to a reciprocal one and the best that can be hoped for is 'an "uneasy peace" where the individual acts solely to maximise and protect his or her own interests without any concern for the outcomes (benefits or damages) to the target' (p. 383). This is likely to lead to a relationship based on distrust defined as 'confident negative expectations regarding another's conduct' (Lewicki, McAllister & Bies, 1998). Given its negative deviation from prior expectations, a negative anchoring event is likely to lead to perceptions of betrayal (as demonstrated by the empirical evidence on psychological contracts) which as Lewicki et al. (1998) argue is likely to provide not only the foundation for distrust but also a negative framing through which subsequent actions are evaluated, culminating in paranoid cognitions. Should the exchange partner attempt to act benevolently, this is likely to be interpreted by the focal individual through a negative frame of reference and hence dismissed as manipulation, thereby making the reparation of distrust unrealistic. This fits in with what Bijlsma-Frankema, Sitkin and Weibel (2015) label amplification in the development of distrust.

In summary, social exchange theory provides two pathways through which exchanges may elicit trust – the traditional view that trust develops gradually over time as the exchanges increase in value and a contemporary view whereby an unexpected positive deviation from expectations in terms of the exchange can create a memorable anchoring event leading to the quick establishment of trust. These pathways are likely to affect the degree to which trust is fragile or robust in terms of stability. Finally, negative anchoring events can trigger a path of distrust as this event shapes how an individual interprets subsequent events/exchanges in that relationship.

Current EOR frameworks

Having cursorily traced the historical development of social exchange theory and the role of trust in social exchange theory, we now turn to examining current employee-organization relationship (EOR) frameworks that draw upon social exchange theory. We confine our review here to psychological contracts, idiosyncratic deals, perceived organizational support and employment relationships and exclude leader-member exchange (LMX) as it focuses on the relationship an employee has with their immediate supervisor rather than the organization. We also exclude organizational justice but recognize that Homans (1958) discussed distributive justice in his early work, and in the last decade, social exchange theory has risen in prominence to explain justice effects (Colquitt et al., 2013). As Rupp and colleagues (2014, p. 162) posit, 'a key aspect of social exchange theory (as applied to justice theory) is that fairness drives social exchange'. However, we exclude it here because unlike the other EOR frameworks, it does not explicitly capture the relationship that may develop between employees and their employer even if it facilitates the development of high-quality social exchange relationships (Colquitt et al., 2013). In short, our inclusion/exclusion principle rests upon capturing the employee-organization relationship, drawing on social exchange theory with implications for trust in that relationship.

Psychological contracts

Although Argyris (1960) was the first to coin the term 'psychological contract', it was Rousseau's (1989) seminal article that is credited with reinvigorating interest in psychological contracts and stimulating a body of research that shows no signs of slowing down. Rousseau (1989) defined the psychological contract as 'an individual's beliefs regarding the terms and conditions of a reciprocal exchange agreement between that focal person and another party. Key issues here include the belief that a promise has been made and a consideration offered in exchange for it, binding the parties to some set of reciprocal obligations' (p. 123). MacNeil (1974) distinguished transactional and relational contracts and this distinction was incorporated into psychological contract theory. Transactional contracts involve highly specific exchanges that are narrow in scope; economic in focus, explicit and time bound (Robinson, Kraatz & Rousseau, 1994). In contrast, relational contracts are broader in focus, opened ended, involve the exchange of socio-emotional as well as economic resources, are characterized by trust and are implicitly managed (Rousseau, 1990).

A key aspect of psychological contract theory that has been heavily researched is the consequences of psychological contract breach and violation (and to a lesser extent fulfilment). Psychological contract breach, 'the cognition that one's organization has failed to meet one or more obligations within one's psychological contract in a manner commensurate with one's contributions' (Morrison & Robinson, 1997), that can lead to feelings of violation, 'an intense reaction of outrage, shock, resentment, and anger' (Rousseau, 1989, p. 129). In contrast, psycho-logical contract fulfilment, 'the extent to which one party to the contract deems the other has met its obligations' (Lee et al., 2011, p. 204), describes how well the organization fulfils the employee's psychological contract. The underlying explanation for the consequences of psychological contract breach/violation and fulfilment, is the norm of reciprocity whereby employees positively/negatively reciprocate psychological contract fulfilment/breach. The perceived fulfilment of the psychological contract by the employer is likely to generate a perception among employees of employer trustworthiness while breach/violation is likely to trigger distrust in the employer.

Idiosyncratic deals

'I-deals refer to voluntary, personalized agreements of a nonstandard nature negotiated between individual employees and their employers regarding terms that benefit each party' (Rousseau,

Ho & Greenberg, 2006, p. 978). The principal characteristics of i-deals are that they are individually negotiated by either the employer or the employee, heterogeneous in that some of the terms are differentiated from what other comparable employees receive (i.e. especially provided), mutually beneficial so that both the interests of the employee and employer are served, and that they vary in scope from a single idiosyncratic element to an entirely different deal (Rousseau, 2005; Rousseau et al., 2006). Researchers argue that organizations use i-deals to recruit, retain and reward high performers; for employees, i-deals can signal their market value or the value an employer places on the individual employee (Rousseau et al., 2005, 2006; Rosen, Slater, Change & Johnson, 2013). Social exchange is used to explain the effects of i-deals on employee attitudes and behaviour because of their beneficial effect, and this should create an obligation to reciprocate (Anand et al., 2010; Liu et al., 2013; Ng & Feldman, 2012). For the focal employee, the receipt of an i-deal may generate trust although the implications, as discussed later, for co-workers may lead to the development of distrust.

Perceived organizational support

Perceived organizational support (POS) captures an individual's perception concerning the degree to which an organization values their contributions and cares about their well-being (Eisenberger, Huntington, Hutchison & Sowa, 1986). Organizational support theory (OST) posits that perceived organizational support triggers a social exchange process in which employees feel obligated to reciprocate the support that they have received (Kurtessis, Eisenberger, Ford, Buffardi, Stewart & Adis, 2017). As Rhoades and Eisenberger (2002, p. 698) note, 'to the extent that both the employee and the employer apply the reciprocity norm to their relationship, favourable treatment received by either party is reciprocated, leading to beneficial outcomes for both'. As such, POS generates employee trust in the organization.

Employment relationships

Building on the inducement-contribution model and exchange theory (Blau, 1964; March & Simon, 1958), Tsui et al. (1997) describe four approaches to the employee-organization relationship from the employer's perspective. These four approaches capture different employer expectations about employee contributions and the inducements offered in return along two dimensions: the degree of balance/imbalance in each party's contributions/inducements and whether the focus of these contributions/inducements is economic or social exchange. The quasi-spot contract (also called job-focused) is a balanced economic exchange that is specified – the employer offers short-term purely economic inducements in return for highly specified outcomes. Mutual investment (also called organization-focused) is a balanced social exchange that arises when both the employee and employer have an open ended and long-term investment in each other. The underinvestment approach occurs when the employer expects broad and open-ended obligations from employees in return for short-term economic inducements without any commitment to a long term relationship. The overinvestment approach is provided when the employer offers long-term investment and open ended rewards in return for highly specified employee outcomes. In their original empirical study of US employees, Tsui et al. (1997) found that a mutual investment employment relationship was most positively associated with employee attitudes and performance. These four approaches are likely to have a differential effect on trust generation.

The role of trust in current EOR frameworks – empirical evidence

Trust and psychological contracts

A key premise of the psychological contract theory is that employee perceptions of their employer's failure to fulfil its part of the deal damages the exchange relationship and leads to negative adjustments in employee emotions, attitudes and behaviours, including anger, withdrawal of trust and commitment; and reduced performance and organizational citizenship behaviour. Overall, a wealth of empirical evidence supports this assertion, including two meta-analyses (Bal, De Lange, Jansen & Van der Velde, 2008; Zhao, Wayne, Glibkowski & Bravo, 2007). In terms of Ballinger and Rockmann's (2010) notion of anchoring events in social exchange relationships, contract breach can be conceptualized as a negative anchoring event that is likely to have multiple effects and potentially trigger a negative spin in the exchange relationship. Looking specifically at the implications of psychological contract breach for trust, a number of studies have shown that breach perceptions are associated with decreased levels of trust in the organization (e.g. Clinton & Guest, 2014; Grimmer & Oddy, 2007; Deery, Iverson &Walsh, 2006; Robinson, 1996). Interestingly, in their meta-analysis, Zhao and colleagues (2007) observed a stronger correlation between breach and mistrust (.53) than between breach and violation (.43), although feelings of violation and emotional outrage are often positioned to accompany breach perceptions (Bordia, Restubog & Tang, 2008) and play a role in negative anchoring events (Ballinger & Rockmann, 2010). The negative effects of psychological contract breach on trust appear to be long-lasting, lending support to Ballinger and Rockmann's (2010) idea that negative anchoring events provide a frame of reference through which future events are interpreted. Empirical evidence suggests that breach in the previous employment generates mistrust that is carried over to the subsequent employer (Pugh, Skarlicki & Passell, 2003; Parzefall, 2012).

Reflecting the risk and vulnerability inherent in a social exchange relationship, researchers have suggested that trust may provide a key mechanism to explaining the negative effects of breach on employee attitudes and behaviours (Robinson, Kraatz & Rousseau, 1994). A number of studies have shown that trust mediates the relationship between breach and number of central employee attitudes and behaviours such as turnover intentions (Clinton & Guest, 2014; Lo & Aryee, 2004), organizational identification (Restubog, Hornsey, Bordia, & Esposo, 2008), and OCB and performance (Robinson, 1996; Restubog et al., 2008). Interestingly, Zagenczyk et al. (2014) observed this mediating role of trust especially in the case of relational breach. By undermining trust in the employer and its intentions, breach thus negatively influences an employee's willingness to engage in any further reciprocal actions. As Restubog and colleagues (2008) conclude, employees can confidently expect that the employer will reciprocate their contributions only when trust exists.

Trust and i-deals

To date, empirical research focusing explicitly on the role of trust in idiosyncratic deals remains scarce. Literature on i-deals, however, points to at least three possible roles that trust may play in deals, and even to a possible trust paradox inherent in i-deals. First, flexibility and personalized negotiations that i-deals imply may build on trust or facilitate the development of dyadic trust. Second, i-deals may compensate for trust in low-quality exchange relationships or in the case of psychological contract breach. Third, individualized deals and the resulting special treatment may generate mistrust among fellow employees at the workplace. We discuss all these options below.

By individualizing employment conditions according to employee needs, employers provide special contributions that are likely to involve symbolic and socio-emotional elements, such as trust, that employees will reciprocate (Hornung, Rousseau & Glaser, 2009). For example, Ng and Feldman (2012) found that i-deals relating to flexibility fostered trust which in turn positively influenced employee willingness to engage in OCBs. Alluding to Blau's (1964) notion of social exchange developing slowly and starting with small gestures, some degree of initial trust between the employer and the employee may be needed before they can strike an i-deal (Ng & Feldman, 2012). For example, employees might need to trust in their employer before feeling confident to ask for a personalized arrangement. Similarly, the employer may need some security in the form of trust that the employee will uphold his or her part of the specialized deal.

Existing evidence also indicates that i-deals can compensate for low-quality employment relationships, which typically imply low degrees of trust, or be used to fix problems involving mistrust in the exchange partner (Guerrero, Bentein & Lapalme, 2014; Anand, et al., 2010; Hornung et al., 2009). Hornung and colleagues were the first to observe that supervisors may try to repair relationships that involve unfulfilled expectations with i-deals, especially in the absence of any formal means or resources to address the unbalance. Guerrero and colleagues (2014) in turn show that i-deals can buffer for the negative impact of breach by maintaining the bond between the employees and their organization. In other words, i-deals appear to substitute for trust, as they reduce uncertainty and increase the feeling of control. Further, the specialized treatment may increase employees' experience of self-value in the organization.

While i-deals seem to have positive implications for trust in the exchange relationship between the employee and employer, co-workers may perceive them in a negative light – hence the trust paradox. Traditionally, consistency in treatment and standardization of benefits have been considered as a means for creating trust at the workplace (Pearce, 2001). Consequently, organizations implementing i-deals need to ensure open and transparent procedures for determining individualized employment conditions and guard their justice climate in order to prevent the development of mistrust. In line with this assertion, Lai and colleagues (2009) found that the acceptance of others' i-deals is higher when employees can trust in comparable future opportunities for themselves and others. Furthermore, recent research indicates that the effective implementation of clear rules regarding how employees should work and what they should produce can enable trust in the organization directly by signalling predictability and reliability (Weibel, Den Hartog, Gillespie, Searle, Skinner, & Six, 2016). Indirectly, they may facilitate perceptions of fairness and foster the organization's reputation. Thus, consistent and open procedures to negotiate and implement i-deals can, in the best case, have positive consequences not only for the individuals involved but also for the employer brand of the organization on the whole.

Trust and perceived organizational support

Because perceived organizational support incorporates the belief that the organization is concerned with one's well-being and values one's contributions, it appears to contribute to conditions favourable for the development and maintenance of trust in the employee-organization relationship. Empirical evidence supports this assertion. For example, Dirks and Ferrin (2002) have shown that POS positively impacts trust in leaders of the organizations, positioning POS as antecedent to trust. Similar conclusions were recently drawn by Kurtessis and colleagues (2017) who in their meta-analysis found that high POS was positively associated with trust in the organization. Other studies have in turn looked at POS as a moderating, contextual variable that enhances the effects of trust. For example, Neves and Eisenberger (2014) show that employees with high POS are more likely to trust their organization to understand the uncertainties in the context in which risk-taking is needed, and especially when the likelihood of failure is high. In other words, employees are more prone to take risks and trust their organization to accept potential failures when POS is high. In similar vein, the emergent research on trust repair has pointed to the potential of POS to act as a remedy to breaches of trust (Webber, Bishop & O'Neill 2012). Consistent with this line of research, researchers have also shown that employees in supportive relationships allow for flexibility in the delivery of their employer's contributions and are more inclined to trust in their employer to eventually fulfil their part of the employment relationship, for example in the case of psychological contract breach (Dulac et al., 2008). As Tekleab, Takeuchi and Taylor (2005, p. 154) conclude, 'POS is a foundational belief structure about the overall quality of employees' exchange relationships with their organizations that, depending on its quality, either protects employees from or makes them more susceptible to intermediate perceptions of violations by the organizations'.

In conclusion, high degrees of POS protect social exchange relationships at the workplace and trust emerges as the lubricant that enhances trust and its positive effects.

Trust and the employment relationship

The employment relationship (ER) model developed by Tsui and colleagues (1997) captures *employer* expectations about employee contributions and the inducements offered. Of the four possible ERs, mutual investment relationship appears to induce and create conditions favourable for trust. In their conceptual work, Tsui and Wu (2005) argue that organizations are best served by employing a mutual investment employment relationship, compared to the other types of ERs, positioning trust in an explanatory role. Through the mutual investment approach, employers demonstrate their trustworthiness by initiating the reciprocity process. These initial inducements offered by employers put them in a vulnerable position yet signal trust in their employees and in their continued performance and commitment (Aryee et al., 2002).

Although empirical evidence on the relationship between ER and trust is scarce, it confirms the above-mentioned theoretical assertions. In their study of US managers, Tsui et al. (1997) found that a mutual investment employment relationship relative to the other three ERs was most positively associated with perceived favourable employee attitudes, such as affective commitment and trust in coworkers and performance, including task performance and organizational citizenship behaviour. Zhang, Tsui, Song, Li and Jia (2008) in turn studied how ER and supervisory support influence trust in the organization in a sample of Chinese middle managers. They found a reinforcing effect, so that when supervisor support was high, a mutual investment ER enhanced trust in the organization. However, when supervisor support was low, the ER did not encourage trust. This finding points to the complementary effect of the organization's and supervisor's actions for the development of trust.

Theoretical implications

We discuss the theoretical implications of a social exchange lens for the role of trustworthiness in signalling the development of social exchange, the role of individual exchange-related dispositions, the development of trust and distrust and, finally, trust repair.

Role of trustworthiness in signalling the development of social exchange relationships

To this point, the emphasis has been on the beneficiary taking the risk and demonstrating a willingness to be vulnerable to the actions of the recipient in terms of reciprocating the benefit received – trusting the other party. Is the beneficiary trustworthy? Mayer, Davis and Schoorman (1995) outline a number of characteristics of the trustee that are trust enhancing: (a) ability (b) benevolence – having a positive orientation towards the trustor and (c) integrity – the trustor's perception that the trustee adheres to a set of principles that are deemed acceptable by the trustor. Social exchange theory specifically focuses on the willingness to be vulnerable (Colquitt & Rodell, 2011) and has little to say about trustworthiness and its role in the development of social exchange relationships. Specifically, the trustworthiness of the beneficiary is downplayed in the theorizing, but extrapolating from empirical evidence supports its importance. Kurtessis et al. (2017) in their meta-analysis found that high POS was positively associated with trust in the organization. While this supports the tenets of trust development in social exchange, it also suggests that an attribution of the motives of the beneficiary is important as POS captures attributions concerning the benevolent or malevolent intent of the organization (Eisenberger, Armeli, Rexwinkel, Lynch & Rhoades, 2001) which in turn heightens the felt obligation to reciprocate. This suggests that benevolence, one characteristic of trustworthiness is important to developing social exchange relationships.

So, how can trustworthiness be demonstrated? The trust literature suggests that organizational, and relational, as well as individual factors, determine the degree to which managers are deemed trustworthy (Whitener, Brodt, Korsgaard & Werner, 1998). On the one hand, the authors suggest that organizations that are decentralized, less formal and hierarchical are more likely to generate trustworthy perceptions; human resource management systems that incorporate procedural justice are more likely to signal trustworthiness and organization cultures that characterize inclusiveness, open communication and place a value on people are more likely to generate trustworthy perceptions. On the hand other, as discussed earlier, well-implemented control mechanisms can also enable trust in the organization (Weibel et al., 2016). This suggests that context is important, and in particular, the organizational context in which managers are engaging in social exchange relationships with their employees. At the same time, it suggests that particular types of organizations will be in a better position to demonstrate trustworthiness in their relationships with employees.

Individual dispositions

As mentioned earlier in this chapter, social exchange views trust as situationally determined, based on the exchanges between two parties and hence downplays the role of an individual's disposition to trust. Rotter (1967, p. 651) defined interpersonal trust 'as an expectancy held by an individual or a group that the word, promise, verbal or written statement of another individual or group can be relied upon' and trust researchers have used this to capture a propensity to trust (Conlon & Mayer, 1994). McKnight et al. (1998) argue that propensity to trust is likely to have a significant effect in *new* organizational relationships but not in ongoing relationships as other factors will swamp this effect. Mayer et al. (1995) echo this and argue that the higher the trustor's propensity to trust, the higher the trust for a trustee prior to information about the trustee becoming available. Putting this together with Ballinger and Rockmann's (2010) work on anchoring events, this suggests that a positive anchoring event coupled with a higher propensity to trust may accelerate the development of a social exchange relationship particularly when it occurs early in the relationship due to its memorable impact.

Reciprocation wariness is a 'generalised cautiousness in reciprocating aid stemming from a fear of exploitation in interpersonal relationships' (Lynch, Eisenberger & Armeli, 1999, p. 468). Wary individuals are fearful that others will use the norm of reciprocity to exploit them and hence adopt self-protective behaviours such as minimal reciprocity (Cotterell, Eisenberger & Speicher, 1992; Lynch et al., 1999). Kamdar, McAllister & Turban (2006) conclude that 'wary individuals have lower baseline expectations for exchange relationships – including not only what they can expect to receive from others but also what they are obligated to contribute to them – than less wary individuals' (p. 843). Shore et al. (2009) found that reciprocation wariness moderated the relationship between social exchange and trust in the employer such that the relationship was more positive for low wary individuals than highly wary individuals. Thus, highly wary individuals may see social exchange relationship as entailing greater personal risk due to the fear of exploitation and not adhere to the norm of reciprocity (compared to low wary individuals). Building trust through supportive actions is less likely to be effective with highly wary individuals.

These individual dispositions can hamper the development of trust in exchange relationships and suggest a number of avenues for future research. How are propensity to trust and reciprocation wariness related? If one is high on reciprocation wariness and fears exploitation, does this translate into a low propensity to trust? Is the common basis for both dispositional tendencies the fear of exploitation? What strategies can be used to counteract or diminish the effects of these dispositional tendencies when the context does not allow for the gradual development of trust?

Development of trust and distrust: climbing a ladder or chute?

Social exchange theory and the EOR frameworks reviewed here offer insights into how trust develops and what organizations can do to facilitate this in terms of fulfilling psychological contracts (e.g. Robinson, 1996; Restubog et al., 2008; Zagenczyk et al., 2014), granting i-deals (Ng & Feldman, 2012), providing organizational support (Kurtessis et al., 2017) and, a mutual investment ER (Tsui et al. 1997). Less visible in the empirical studies is the role of time in the development of trust. Researchers drawing on social exchange theory assume that the provision of support or the fulfilment of psychological contracts needs to be ongoing and continuous in order to facilitate the development of trust in the EOR. However, an event such as psychological contract breach can undermine trust and, if left unrepaired, can lead to the development of more negative EORs based on distrust. The general thrust of this strand of literature points to the gradual development of trust and the potential for its quick erosion as a consequence of negative events (e.g. psychological contract breach) in that relationship. To this end, psychological contract breach offers an explanation for the erosion of trust in employee-organization exchange relationships.

Until recently, the literature on social exchange has been rather silent on more negative (and presumably distrustful) EORs. Gouldner's (1960) seminal work on the norm of reciprocity and, in particular, the negative norm of reciprocity, dictates that individuals harm the source of the harm (an eye for an eye etc.). Gibney, Zagenczyk and Masters (2009) introduce perceived organizational obstruction which they define as 'an employee's belief that the organization obstructs, hinders or interferes with the accomplishment of his or her goals and is a detriment to his or her well-being' (p. 667). Although the authors did not capture distrust in their study, one would expect that organizational obstruction would be positively associated with distrust. Shore and Coyle-Shapiro (2012) define perceived organizational cruelty as 'the employee's perception that the organization holds him or her in contempt, has no respect for him or her personally, and treats him or her in a manner that is intentionally inhumane' (p. 141).

Continuing in a negative vein, Livne-Ofer and Coyle-Shapiro (2016) define perceived exploitative employee-organization relationships (PERs) as 'employees' perceptions that they have been purposefully and repeatedly taken advantage of by the organization, to the benefit of the organization itself, with the anticipation of continued harm in the future' (p. 3). Research and theorizing on negative EORs is very much in its infancy, and how distrust and negative EORs are related is in need of investigation. One could speculate that distrust is a consequence of these negative EORs, yet at the same time trust (or its erosion) may in part explain how positive (or neutral EORs) shift to negative ones. Trust researchers (Bijlsma et al., 2015; Lewicki et al., 1998; Sitkin, 1995) see trust and distrust as distinct phenomena that co-exist, which raises interesting possibilities in terms of how these map onto positive and negative EORs.

Trust repair and social exchange theory-based EOR concepts

Unfortunately, it is not uncommon for trust to get broken in the employee-organization relationship. Existing evidence suggests that it may even be the norm for employees to experience a violation of trust by their leaders and organizations (Conway & Briner, 2002). It is therefore not surprising that scholars are becoming increasingly interested in the concept of trust repair, which concerns improving an individual's trusting beliefs and trusting intentions that have been lowered by a trust violation (Kim, Dirks & Cooper, 2009). The relatively fresh but rapidly growing literature on trust repair has suggested various means to address mistrust in the employer (Gillespie, Dietz & Lockey, 2014; Gillespie & Dietz, 2009; Pfarrer, DeCelles, Smith & Taylor, 2008). Such means include, for example, verbal measures such as apologies, justifications and denials (Tomlinson, Dineen, & Lewicki, 2004); legalistic remedies (Sitkin, 1995); and not doing anything at all (Ferrin, Kim, Cooper & Dirks, 2007). The good news is that that broken trust can be repaired (Mishra, 1996), largely, however, contingent upon the transgressor's response (Korsgaard, Brodt and Whitener, 2002; Schweitzer, Hershey & Bradley, 2006). At the organizational level, Gillespie and Dietz (2009) developed a model for trust repair after an organization-level failure, defined as an incident, or series of incidents, that threatens the legitimacy of the organization and undermines its perceived trustworthiness. The authors propose that organizational trustworthiness is generated and enacted primarily through leadership and management practices; culture and climate; strategy; as well as systems, policies and processes, and that it is through these four systems that trust can be repaired, too.

Despite these micro- and macro-level approaches to the topic, trust repair explicitly in the context of the EOR frameworks has received relatively little attention. Kim and colleagues (2009) note that psychological contract breach and violation can offer insights into understanding the experience of trust violation. Towards this end, the EOR frameworks that specifically draw on social exchange theory can be useful in extending the present work on trust repair. Similarly, the perspective of trust repair may provide new directions for the social exchange theory-based frameworks to study the employment relationship. We elaborate on these mutually enriching possibilities and consider how they can help further develop how we theorize and research the EOR. Specifically, POS and mutual investment employment relationship and their potential role in the prevention of trust failures and in trust repair deserve further attention. If an organization cares about the wellbeing of its employees and commits to a mutual investment relationship, it is essentially engaging in *distrust regulation* (Gillespie and Dietz, 2009), i.e. preventing trust violation from occurring in the first place. This may occur, for example, through the norms and standards that underlie appropriate forms of support and contribution in the employee-employer relationship. In other words, a well-functioning social exchange relationship as operationalized by the EOR frameworks can signal trust in the employee-employer relationship. Similarly, they may also facilitate the implementation of i-deals. Employer contributions, for example, in terms of psychological contract obligations, individualized benefits within the framework of an idiosyncratic deal or transparent communication may in turn be framed to *demonstrate trustworthiness*. In case of breach of trust, they may also act to repair trust, both in terms of regulating distrust and demonstrating trustworthiness. Empirically, Dulac and colleagues (2008), for example, demonstrate that the quality of relationship an individual has, as captured by POS, influences cognitions of breach and moderates how individuals respond to contract breach. In other words, the quality of the relationship influences how an individual interprets an event implying breach of trust and also how he/she responds to that event, thereby presenting POS as a potential remedy for mistrust generated by contract violation – or by a negative anchoring event (Ballinger & Rockmann, 2010).

Finally, literature on trust repair has elaborated on the role of attribution in repair efforts and forgiveness (Kim et al., 2009; Tomlinson et al., 2004; Schweitzer et al., 2006). Similarly, attributional processes influence employee reactions to psychological contract breach (Parzefall & Coyle-Shapiro, 2011). For example, trust repair literature has discussed the role of attribution errors and external versus internal attribution in trust repair (Kim et al., 2009; Tomlinson et al., 2004) whereas the literature on psychological contract breach notes the difference between *reneging*, i.e. situations in which the organization is either unwilling or incapable of keeping what it has promised, and *incongruence*, which refers to a misunderstanding (Morrison & Robinson, 1997). Theorizing and empirical work suggests that employees are likely to experience more intense negative emotions when they attribute the initial breach to reneging (Morrison & Robinson, 1997; Robinson & Morrison, 2000). Furthermore, the empirical work of Lester and colleagues (2002) suggests that employees are more likely to attribute breach to the organization's intentional reneging, while managers tend to blame factors beyond the control of their organization. A closer integration of these literatures could improve our understanding of the mechanisms of both fixing psychological contracts and repairing trust.

Conclusions

The norm of reciprocity acts as a starting mechanism to develop trust and as a stabilizing mechanism to maintain or enhance trust – without which social exchange relationships, given their inherent risk and uncertainty would not develop. Empirical evidence from the EOR suggests that fulfilling promises, granting i-deals, developing supportive and balanced relationships with employees facilitates the development of trust by demonstrating employer trustworthiness. That said, negative events can occur and whether these events undermine trust (and create distrust) depends upon the severity of the event and also the buffering effect of the social exchange relationship in which it occurred. Recently, the EOR has begun to take into account more negative forms of the employee-organization relationship and this is likely to spotlight the role of distrust in shifting EORs from positive (or neutral) to negative.

References

Anand, S., Vidyarthi, P.R., Liden, R.C., & Rousseau, D.M. (2010). Good citizens in poor-quality relationships: idiosyncratic deals as a substitute for relationship quality. *Academy of Management Journal*, 53(5), 970–988.

Argyris, C. (1960). *Understanding Organizational Behavior*. Homewood, IL: Dorsey Press.

Aryee, S., Budhwar, P.S., & Chen, Z.X. (2002). Trust as a mediator of the relationship between organizational justice and work outcomes: test of a social exchange model. *Journal of Organizational Behavior*, 23(3), 267–285.

Bal, P.M., De Lange, A.H., Jansen, P.G.W., & Van der Velde, M.E.G. (2008). Psychological contract breach and job attitudes: A meta-analysis of age as a moderator. *Journal of Vocational Behavior*, 72(1), 143–158.

Ballinger, G.A., & Rockmann, K.W. (2010). Chutes versus ladders: Anchoring events and a punctuated-equilibrium perspective on social exchange relationships, *Academy of Management Review*, 35(3), 373–391.

Bijlsma-Frankema, K., Sitkin, S.B., & Weibel, A. (2015). Distrust in the balance: The emergence and development of intergroup distrust in a court of law. *Organization Science*, 26(4), 1018–1039.

Blau, P.M. (1964). *Exchange and Power in Social Life*. New Brunswick, NJ: Transaction Publishers.

Bordia, P., Restubog, S., & Tang, R. (2008). When employees strike back: Investigating mediating mechanisms between psychological contract breach and workplace deviance. *Journal of Applied Psychology*, 93(5), 1104–1117.

Brewer, M.B., & Gardner, W. (1996). Who is this "we"?: Levels of collective identity and self-representations. *Journal of Personality and Social Psychology*, 71(1) 83–93.

Clinton, M.E., & Guest, D.E. (2014). Psychological contract breach and voluntary turnover: Testing a multiple mediation model. *Journal of Occupational and Organizational Psychology*, 87(1), 200–207.

Colquitt, J.A., Baer, M.D., Long, D.M., & Halvorsen-Ganepola, M.D.K. (2014). Scale indicators of social exchange relationships: A comparison of relative content validity. *Journal of Applied Psychology*, 99(4), 599–618.

Colquitt, J.A., & Rodell, J.B. (2011). Justice, trust and trustworthiness: A longitudinal analysis integrating three theoretical perspectives. *Academy of Management Journal*, 54(6), 1183–1206.

Colquitt, J.A., Scott, B.A., Rodell, J.B., Long, D.M., Zapata, C.P., Conlon, D.E., & Wesson, M.J. (2013). Justice at the Millennium, a decade later: A meta-analytic test of social exchange and affect-based perspectives. *Journal of Applied Psychology*, 98(2), 199–236.

Colquitt, J.A., & Zapata-Phelan, C.P. (2007). Trends in theory building and theory testing: A five-decade study of the "Academy of Management Journal", *Academy of Management Journal*, 50(6), 1281–1303.

Conlon, E.J., & Mayer, R.C. (1994). *The effect of trust on principal-agent dyads: An empirical investigation of stewardship and agency*. Paper presented at the annual meeting of the Academy of Management, Dallas, TX.

Conway, N., & Briner, R.B. (2002). A daily diary study of affective responses to psychological contract breach and exceeded promises. *Journal of Organizational Behavior*, 23(3), 287–302.

Cotterell, N., Eisenberger, R., & Speicher, H. (1992). Inhibiting effects of reciprocation wariness on interpersonal relationships, *Journal of Personality and Social Psychology*, 62(4), 658–668.

Coyle-Shapiro, J.A-M., & Conway, N (2004). The employment relationship through the lens of social exchange. In J.A-M. Coyle-Shapiro, L. Shore, M.S. Taylor & L. Tetrick (Eds.) *The Employment Relationship: Examining Psychological and Contextual Perspectives*. Oxford: Oxford University Press.

Cropanzano, R., & Mitchell, M.S. (2005). Social exchange theory: An interdisciplinary review, *Journal of Management*, 31(6), 874–900.

Deery, S., Iverson, R., & Walsh, J. (2006). Towards a better understanding of psychological breach: A study of customer service employees. *Journal of Applied Psychology*, 91(1), 166–175.

Dirks, K. T., & Ferrin, D. L. (2002). Trust in leadership: Meta-analytic findings and implications for organizational research. *Journal of Applied Psychology*, 87(4), 611–628.

Doney, P.M., Cannon, J.P., & Mullen, M.R. (1998). Understanding the influence of national culture on the development of trust. *Academy of Management Review*, 23(3), 601–620.

Dulac, T., Coyle-Shapiro, J. A-M., Henderson, D. J., & Wayne, S. J. (2008). Not all responses to breach are the same: The interconnection of social exchange and psychological contract processes in organizations. *Academy of Management Journal*, 51(6), 1079–1098.

Eisenberger, R., Armeli, S., Rexwinkel, B., Lynch, P.D., & Rhoades, L. (2001). Reciprocation of perceived organizational support. *Journal of Applied Psychology*, 86(1), 42–51.

Eisenberger, R., Huntington, R. H., & Sowa, S. (1986). Perceived organizational support. *Journal of Applied Psychology*, 71(3) 500–517.

Emerson, R.M. (1962). Power-dependence relations. *American Sociological Review*, 27(1), 31–40.

Emerson, R.M. (1972a). Exchange theory, part I: A psychological basis for social exchange. In J. Berger, M. Zelditch & B. Anderson (Eds.) *Sociological Theories in Progress* (Vol 2). Boston, MA: Houghton-Mifflin.

Emerson, R.M. (1972b). Exchange theory, part II: Exchange relations and networks. In J. Berger, M. Zelditch & B. Anderson (Eds.) *Sociological Theories in Progress* (Vol 2). Boston, MA: Houghton-Mifflin.

Emerson, R.M. (1976). Social exchange theory. *Annual Review of Sociology*, 2(1), 335–362.

Emerson, R.M. (1981). Social exchange theory. In M. Rosenberg & R.H. Turner (Eds.) *Social Psychology: Sociological Perspectives*. New York: Basic Books.

Ferrin, D.L., Kim, P.H., Cooper, C.D., & Dirks, K.T. (2007). Silence speaks volumes: The effectiveness of reticence in comparison to apology and denial for responding to integrity- and competence-based trust violations. *Journal of Applied Psychology*, 92(4), 893–908.

Gibney, R., Zagenczyk, T.J., & Masters, M.F. (2009). The negative aspects of social exchange: An introduction to perceived organization obstruction. *Group & Organization Management*, 34(6), 665–697.

Gillespie, N., & Dietz, G. (2009). Trust repair after an organization-level failure. *Academy of Management Review*, 34(1), 127–145.

Gillespie, N., Dietz, G., & Lockey, S. (2014). Organizational reintegration and trust repair after an integrity violation: A case study. *Business Ethics Quarterly*, 24(3), 371–410.

Gouldner, A.W. (1960). The norm of reciprocity: A preliminary statement. *American Sociological Review*, 25(2), 161–178.

Grimmer, M. & Oddy, M. (2007). Violation of the psychological contract: The mediating effect of relational versus transactional beliefs. *Australian Journal of Management*, 32(1), 153–175.

Guerrero, S., Bentein, K., & Lapalme, M-E. (2014). Idiosyncratic deals and high performers' organizational commitment. *Journal of Business and Psychology*, 29(2), 323–334.

Homans, G.C. (1958). Social behavior as exchange. *American Journal of Sociology*, 63(6), 597–606.

Hornung, S., Rousseau, D. M., & Glaser, J. (2009). Why supervisors make idiosyncratic deals: Antecedents and outcomes of i-deals from a managerial perspective. *Journal of Managerial Psychology*, 24(8), 738–764.

Kamdar, D., McAllister, D.J., & Turban, D.B. (2006). "All in a day's work": How follower individual differences and justice perceptions predict OCB role definitions and behavior, *Journal of Applied Psychology*, 91(4), 277–297.

Kim, P.H., Dirks, K.T., and Cooper, C.D. (2009). The repair of trust: A dynamic bi-lateral perspective and multi-level conceptualization. *Academy of Management Review*, 34(3), 401–422.

Korsgaard, M.A., Brodt, S.E., & Whitener, E.M. (2002). Trust in the face of conflict: The role of managerial trustworthy behavior and organizational context. *Journal of Applied Psychology*, 87(2), 312–319.

Kurtessis, J.N., Eisenberger, R., Ford, M.T., Buffardi, L.C., Stewart, K.A., & Adis, C.S. (2017). Perceived organizational support: A meta-analytic evaluation of organizational support theory, *Journal of Management*, 43(6), 1854–1884.

Lai, L., Rousseau, D.M., & Chang T.T. (2009). Idiosyncratic deals: Coworkers as interested third parties. *Journal of Applied Psychology*, 94(2), 547–556.

Lawler, E., Thye, S., & Yoon, J. (2000). Emotion and group cohesion in productive exchange. *American Journal of Sociology*, 106(3) 616–657.

Lee, C., Liu, J., Rousseau, D.M., Hui, C., & Chen, Z.X. (2011). Inducement, contributions, and fulfillment in new employee psychological contracts. *Human Resource Management*, 50(2), 201–226.

Lester, S.W., Turnley, W.H., Bloodgood, J.M., & Bolino, M.C. (2002). Not seeing the eye to eye: Differences in supervisor and subordinate perceptions of and attributions for psychological contract breach. *Journal of Organizational Behavior*, 23(1), 39–56.

Lewicki, R.J., McAllister, D.J., & Bies, R.J. (1998). Trust and distrust: new relationships and realities, *Academy of Management Review*, 23(4), 438–458.

Liden, R.C., Sparrowe, R., & Wayne, SJ. (1997). Leader-member exchange theory: The past and potential for the future. In G.R. Ferris (Ed.) *Research in Personnel and Human Resources Management* (Vol 15). Greenwich, CT: JAI Press.

Liu, J., Lee, C., Hui, C, Kwan, H.K., & Wu, L-Z (2013). Idiosyncratic deals and employee outcomes: The mediating roles of social exchange and self-enhancement and the moderating role of individualism. *Journal of Applied Psychology*, 98(5), 832–840.

Livne-Ofer, E., & Coyle-Shapiro, J.A-M. (2016). Perceived Exploitative Employee-Organization Relationships: Development of a New Scale. Paper presented at the Annual Meeting of the Academy of Management 5–9 August, Anaheim, CA.

Lo, S., & Aryee, S. (2003). Psychological contract breach in a Chinese context: An integrative approach. *Journal of Management Studies*, 40(4), 1005–1020.

Lynch, P.D., Eisenberger, R., & Armeli, S. (1999). Perceived organizational support: Inferior-versus-superior performance by wary employees. *Journal of Applied Psychology*, 84(4), 467–483.

MacNeil, I.R. (1974). The many futures of contract. *Southern California Law Review*, 47, 691–816.

Malinowski, B. (1922). *Argonauts of the Western Pacific.* Prospect Heights, IL: Waveland Press Inc.

March. J. & Simon, H. (1958). *Organizations.* New York: Wiley.

Mauss, M. (1950) *The Gift: The Form and Reason for Exchange in Archaic Societies.* New York: W.W. Norton & Co, Inc.

Mayer, R.C., David, J.H., & Schoorman, F.D. (1995). An integrative model of organizational trust, *Academy of Management Review,* 20(3), 709–734.

McKnight, D.H., Cummings, L.L., & Chervany, N.L. (1998). Initial trust formation in new organizational relationships, *Academy of Management Review,* 23(3), 473–490.

Mishra, A.K. (1996). Organizational responses to crisis: The centrality of trust. In R.M. Kramer & T.R. Tyler (Eds.) *Trust in Organizations: Frontiers of Theory and Research.* Thousand Oaks, CA: Sage.

Molm, L.D. (1994). Dependence and risk: Transforming the structure of social exchange. *Social Psychology Quarterly,* 57(3), 163–176.

Molm, L.D. (2003). Theoretical comparisons of forms of exchange. *Sociological Theory,* 21(1), 1–17

Molm, L.D., Takahashi, N., & Peterson, G. (2000). Risk and trust in social exchange: An experimental test of a classical proposition. *American Journal of Sociology,* 105(5), 1396–1427.

Molm, L.D., Takahashi, N., & Peterson, G. (2003). In the eye of the beholder: Procedural justice and social exchange. *American Sociological Review,* 68(1), 128–152.

Morrison, E.W., & Robinson, S.L. (1997). When employees feel betrayed: A model of how psychological contract violation develops. *Academy of Management Review,* 22(1), 226–256.

Neves, P., & Eisenberger, R. (2014). Perceived organizational support and risk taking. *Journal of Managerial Psychology,* 29(2), 187 – 205.

Ng, T.W.H., & Feldman, D.C. (2012). Idiosyncratic deals and voice behaviour. *Journal of Management,* 41(3), 893–928.

O'Boyle, E.H., Forsyth, D.R., Banks, G.C., & McDaniel, M.A. (2012). A meta-analysis of the dark triad and work behaviour: A social exchange perspective. *Journal of Applied Psychology,* 97(3) 557–579.

Parzefall, M-R. (2012). A close call: Perceptions of alternative HR arrangements to layoffs. *Journal of Managerial Psychology,* 27(8), 799–813.

Parzefall, M-R. & Coyle-Shapiro, J.M-A. (2011). Making sense of psychological contract breach. *Journal of Managerial Psychology,* 26(1), 12–27.

Pearce, J.L. (2001). *Organization and Management in the Embrace of Government.* Mahwah, NJ: Elrbaum.

Pfarrer, M.D., Decelles, K.A., Smith, K.G., & Taylor, M.S. (2008). After the fall: Reintegrating the corrupt organization. *Academy of Management Review,* 33(3), 730–749.

Pugh, S.D., Skarlicki, D.P., & Passell, B.S. (2003). After the fall: Layoff victims' trust and cynicism in re-employment. *Journal of Organizational and Occupational Psychology,* 76(2), 201–212.

Restubog, S.L.D., Hornsey, M.J., Bordia, P., & Esposo, S. (2008). Effects of psychological contract breach on organizational citizenship behaviors: Insights from the group value model. *Journal of Management Studies,* 45(8), 1377–1400.

Rhoades, L., & Eisenberger, R. (2002). Perceived organizational support: A review of the literature. *Journal of Applied Psychology,* 87(4), 698–714

Robinson, S.L. (1996). Trust and breach of the psychological contract. *Administrative Science Quarterly,* 41(4), 574–599.

Robinson, S.L., Kraatz, M.S., & Rousseau, D.M. (1994). Changing obligations and the psychological contract: A longitudinal study. *Academy of Management Journal,* 37(1), 137–152.

Robinson, S. L. & Morrison, E. W. (2000). The development of psychological contract breach and violation: A longitudinal study. *Journal of Organizational Behaviour,* 21(5), 525–546.

Rosen, C.C., Slater, D.J., Chang, C-H., & Johnson, R.E (2013). Let's make a deal: Development and validation of the ex post i-deals scale. *Journal of Management,* 39(3), 709–742

Rotter, J.B. (1967). A new scale for the measurement of interpersonal trust. *Journal of Personality,* 35(4), 651–665.

Rousseau, D.M. (1989). Psychological and implied contracts in organizations. *Employee Responsibilities and Rights Journal,* 2(2), 121–139.

Rousseau, D.M. (1990) New hire perceptions of their own and their employer's obligations: A study of psychological contracts, *Journal of Organizational Behavior,* 11(5), 389–400.

Rousseau, D.M. (1995). *Psychological Contracts in Organizations: Understanding Written and Unwritten Agreements.* Thousand Oaks, CA: SAGE.

Rousseau, D.M. (2005). *I-deals: Idiosyncratic deals employees bargain for themselves.* New York: M.E. Sharpe.

Rousseau, D.M., Ho, V.T., & Greenberg, J. (2006). I-deals: Idiosyncratic terms in employment relationships. *Academy of Management Review*, 31(4), 977– 994.

Rousseau, D.M., Sitkin, S.B., Burt, R.S., & Camerer, C. (1998). Not so different after all: A cross discipline view of trust. *Academy of Management Review*, 23(3), 393–404.

Rupp, D.E., Shao, R., Jones, K.S., & Liao, H. (2014). The utility of a multifoci approach to the study of organizational justice: A meta-analytic investigation into the consideration of normative rules, moral accountability, bandwidth-fidelity, and social exchange. *Organizational Behavior and Human Decision Processes*, 123(2), 159–185.

Schweitzer, M.E., Hershey, J.C., & Bradley, E.T. (2006). Promises and lies: Restoring violated trust. *Organizational Behavior and Human Decision Processes*, 101(1), 1–19.

Scott, K.L., Restubog, S.L.D., & Zagenczyk, T.J. (2013). A social exchange-based model of the antecedents of workplace exclusion. *Journal of Applied Psychology*, 98(1), 37–48.

Shore, L.M., Bommer, W.H., Rao, A.N., & Seo, J. (2009). Social and economic exchange in the employee-organization relationship: the moderating role of reciprocation wariness, *Journal of Managerial Psychology*, 24(8), 701–721.

Shore, L.M., & Coyle-Shapiro, J. (2012). Perceived organizational cruelty: An expansion of the negative employee-organization relationship domain. In L.M. Shore, J.A-M. Coyle-Shapiro, & L. Tetrick, (Eds.) *The Employee-Organization Relationship: Applications for the 21st Century*. New York: Taylor & Francis.

Sitkin, S.B. (1995). On the positive effect of legalization on trust. In R.J. Bies, R.J. Lewicki, & B.H. Sheppard (Eds.), *Research on Negotiations in Organizations.* Greenwich, CT: JAI Press.

Tekleab, A.G., Takeuchi, R., & Taylor, M.S. (2005). Extending the chain of relationships among organizational justice, social exchange, and employee reactions: the role of contract violations. *Academy of Management Journal*, 48(1), 146–157.

Thibaut, J.W., & Kelley, H.H. (1959). *The Social Psychology of Groups*. NY: John Wiley & Sons.

Tomlinson, E.C., Dineen, B.R., & Lewicki, R.J. (2004). The road to reconciliation: Antecedents of victim willingness to reconcile following a broken promise. *Journal of Management*, 30(2), 165–187.

Tsui, A.S., Pearce, J.L., Porter, L.W., & Tripoli, A.M. (1997). Alternative approaches to the employee-organization relationship: Does investment in employees pay off? *Academy of Management Journal*, 40(5): 1089–1121.

Tsui, A.S., & Wu, J.B. (2005). The new employment relationship versus the mutual investment approach: Implications for human resource management. *Human Resource Management*, 44(2), 115–121.

Webber, S.S., Bishop, K., & O'Neill, R. (2012). Trust repair: The impact of perceived organisational support and issue-selling. *Journal of Management Development*, 31(7), 724–737.

Weibel, A., Den Hartog, D.N., Gillespie, N., Searle, R.H., Skinner D. & Six F. (2016). The role of control in organizational trust and trustworthiness. *Human Resource Management*, 55(3), 437–462.

Whitener, E.M., Brodt, S.E., Korsgaard, M.A., & Werner, J.M. (1998). Managers as initiators of trust: An exchange relationship framework for understanding managerial trustworthy behavior. *Academy of Management Review*, 23(3), 513–530.

Zagenczyk, T., Restubog, S., Kiewitz, C., Kiazad, K., & Tang. R. (2014). Psychological contracts as a mediator between Machiavellianism and employee citizenship and deviant behaviors. *Journal of Management*, 40(4), 11098–1122.

Zhang, A.Y., Tsui, A.S., Song, L.J., Li, C., & Jia, L. (2008). How do I trust thee? The employee–organization relationship, supervisory support, and middle manager trust in the organization. *Human Resource Management*, 47(1), 111–132.

Zhao, H., Wayne, S.J., Glibkowski, B.C., & Bravo, J. (2007). The impact of psychological contract breach on work-related outcomes: A meta-analysis. *Personnel Psychology*, 60(3), 647–680.

12

INSTITUTIONS AND TRUST

Reinhard Bachmann

Introduction

Considerable parts of trust research have not shown too much interest in the role of institutions when analysing the development, maintenance or repair of trust. One of the reasons is that, from a psychological perspective, which is applied by many trust researchers, institutions are – if at all – merely conceptualized as external factors which may or may not have "some" effect on the quality of social relationships. In this disciplinary perspective, institutions are usually neither viewed as objects of trust nor as constitutive parts of a relationship between two actors.

Another reason for trust researchers' relative negligence of institutions is that these are – even from a sociological perspective which puts institutions right in the centre of its interest – difficult to come to grips with because the elements of, for example, a country's institutional framework are numerous and tend to be overlapping and fuzzy. Thus, significant methodological problems emerge when empirical research is supposed to include a given institutional order as the object of trust or systematically account for the various institutional influences that can deeply affect trust processes in social relationships. The question usually asked in this context is: How can we measure institutions? Although not everything in the social world may be "measurable" in the strict sense, this question, nonetheless, alerts us to the fact that there are frequently validity problems occurring when institutional arrangements are empirically researched. The latter seems due to their complexity and is largely independent of which epistemological approach one might favour.

A third reason can perhaps be seen in the existence of various meanings of the term "institution". It is often not at all clear what we actually mean when we talk about institutions. Even within sociology, the term can refer to two quite different phenomena: abstract patterns of collective behaviour, for example marriage or paid labour, on the one hand, or concrete systems of established organizational forms, such as trade organizations, systems of higher education, etc. on the other. And to make it even more complicated, economists and political scientists use terminologies which suggest yet other denotations and connotations of the term "institution".

Despite all these difficulties, trust research has managed to provide at least some important insights which are conducive to understanding the role of institutions in the context of trust processes. Simmel (1950), Luhmann (1979), Zucker (1986) and Shapiro (1987) are major points of reference in this literature. Bachmann (2001), Bachmann and Inkpen (2011), Kroeger (2012) or Fuglsang and Jagd (2015) are newer contributions which try to bring light into issues related to the phenomenon of institutional(-based) trust. In the following, we will focus on major issues in the current debate on institutional trust and try to give an overview of the state of the art in this research area, even though a large number of issues are, and perhaps will remain, controversial in this research field.

The object of trust

Bachmann and Inkpen (2011: 284) have defined institutional(-based) trust as "a form of individual or collective action that is constitutively embedded in the institutional environment in which a relationship is placed, building on favourable assumptions about the trustee's future behaviour vis-à-vis such conditions". This definition suggests to use this term not for trust that people might have in institutions but for trust that people might have in each other against the background of institutional safeguards influencing their decision making and actions.

In principle it is useful to analytically be clear about what the target of trust is, namely an institutional arrangement itself or another social actor's behaviour which is constitutively shaped by these institutional arrangements, but in reality it is often difficult to make this distinction. Even the trustor him-/herself may not be able to tell whether he or she trusts a trained expert, for example a physician, or the medical system including its educational traditions and training curricula which medical experts have gone through before they meet patients (Bachmann, 1998). In one case, institutions are a reliable framework for a relationship between two actors, one of them (i.e., the trustee) being the object of trust. In the other case, the target of trust is an abstract system of institutional arrangements or organizationally structured entities which have gained the status of institutions, for example government, trade unions or universities.

Related but different to the concept of "institutional(-based) trust" is the term "generalized trust" (Uslaner, 2014) which is usually seen as social capital that has roots in cultural traditions as well as specific institutional arrangements. Fukuyama (1995) and many other other scholars (e.g. Zak & Knack, 2001; Dearmon & Grier, 2011; Bjørnskov, 2012) see this form of trust as very important with regard to the economic growth potential of countries in Asia and the West. Similar to "institutional(-based) trust" the concept of "generalized trust" does not (directly) refer to inter-personal relationships as such but the difference is that it is more open to all kinds of sources of trust and not specifically focussing on institutions as the concept of institutional (-based) trust does.

Institutional(-based) trust as trust *in institutions*

What does it actually mean when people say they trust in institutions? It means that a specific individual who represents the police, the national education system, the law courts, etc. is not seen as the object of trust and can thus fail to do his or her job properly or be replaced by another individual without too many consequences from the trustor's point of view. What is more important is that a potential trustor has general, often diffuse, confidence in the functioning of social systems, irrespective of whether these are seen as a highly abstract set of rules or more concrete organizational structures.

Similar to trust at the inter-personal level, trust in institutions can build on a potential trustor's experiences but it is also deeply cushioned into political and ideological worldviews which lack any experiential basis. This is why, for example, foreign countries' institutions are usually trusted less than the domestic ones, and people prefer to take serious conflicts within international business relationships to a law court in their home country. In other words, the psychic distance people have to relevant institutions is in fact more often determined by cultural traditions, collective beliefs, etc. than by empirically verifiable observations.

Individual representatives of abstract social systems, however, do have a function with regard to creating and reproducing trust in institutions insofar as once in a while human faces need to appear to assure trustors that there are well-trained and responsible real actors in control of the social processes by which they are affected. Giddens' (1990) calls this "face-work" and argues that all subsystems of modern societies, which build on highly abstract expert knowledge, e.g. public health care systems, engineering departments of large automobile manufacturers, the federal reserve bank, etc. depend on human faces which at least occasionally have to become visible. Only where this is the case potential trustors can re-embed expert systems into their sense-making and interactions at the very concrete and practical level of social conduct.

In this perspective, the term "institutional(-based) trust" refers to the trustworthiness of systemic patterns of collective action or organizational structures, such as for example the legal system (Tyler, 2006), or the system of higher education and academic research (Gibbs, 2004). Trust in institutions is often studied by way of large-scale surveys, among which are the World Value Survey (2005–2008) and the Edelman Barometer (2016). All these surveys look into how the public's trust in media, law courts, government and many other institutions develops over time in various parts of the world.

Institutional(-based) trust as trust between actors in the face of strong and reliable institutions

If "institutional(-based) trust" is to be understood as trust between two actors whose interaction is constitutively and deeply embedded into the institutional arrangements that surround them, we refer to the idea of actors having trust in each other in the face of a specific quality of an institutional order. In this case, one of the key questions is how institutions can actually do their job and help develop, maintain or repair trust in concrete relationships. How, for example, can the existence of reliable legal norms, industrial relations practices or professional training systems systematically lead social actors to build their relationships on trust rather than another coordination mechanism such as power or monetary incentives?

In order to unravel the functional role of institutions for trust development, it may be useful to compare it to a situation where inter-personal trust, i.e. a dyadic constellation between a potential trustor and a potential trustee, is to be created on the basis of both parties being initially unknown to each other. What is usually suggested in such circumstances is that trust can emerge if both parties establish some common ground. If there is no shared knowledge between them it is difficult to assume that trust can develop. However, if the two actors discover common characteristics or learn about each other by experiences in repeated interaction then "characteristic-based" trust or "process-based trust" – to use Zucker's (1986) terminology – can emerge. In other words, it is some form of a "common world" which is necessary in order to build trust between two actors because this allows the trustor as well as the trustee to make realistic assumptions about the other party's intentions and future behaviour.

With regard to institutional trust, we may analogously say that institutional arrangements can be seen as functional equivalents to experiential processes and the awareness of shared characteristics between two actors. In other words, institutions do essentially the same job as a shared cultural background or positive experiences in dealing with one another over some time. If, for example, a potential trustor and a potential trustee know that their sense-making is embedded in the same commonly known institutional environment – legal norms, educational and training standards, social rules about what is acceptable and what is not acceptable business behaviour, etc. – then institutions will tacitly align the actors' expectations of each other's future behaviour. Institutions can thus provide the common ground that is a vital precondition for trust, just as a shared cultural background or repeated experiences would do in the case of interpersonal trust.

Legal norms and technical or quality certification systems are examples of institutional arrangements which can facilitate business relationships and assure actors that they are sharing an understanding of what is "common practice" and what is "right" or "wrong" behaviour in specific situations. If institutions are seen as conducive to allowing specific mutual expectations between two actors, then we can also view this as a way to reduce risk. Commonalities reduce risk and the reduction of risk – or risk perception, to be precise – can be achieved by establishing a shared understanding of the social world in which relationships between actors are embedded (Granovetter, 1985). This, undoubtedly, helps to encourage a potential trustor to actually invest trust in a relationship to a potential trustee.

In this context, it is important to note that any potential trustor is confronted with the problem that he or she needs to accept "some" level of risk. This is indeed unavoidable because where there is no risk, trust is not needed. Thus, a potential trustor seeks to at least roughly assess and, where possible, reduce the risk emerging from his or her decision to trust, i.e. the risk of being betrayed by the trustee. And here is where personal experiences, personal characteristics and institutions appear to be very similar to one another, at least in functional terms. They reduce risk to a level where the trustor will actually feel encouraged to perform the "leap of faith" (Simmel, 1950; Möllering, 2006) which would often not be the case if the inherent risk of trust was not effectively reduced. This is how institutions work and why they play such an important role in trust creation processes.

In principle, there are two ways conceivable as to how, for example, legal norms can exert their risk-reducing influence. First, actors make a rational decision and possible sanctions feature as a variable in their calculation. If this variable increases over a certain threshold, this may lead to the prediction that trust will be invested by the trustor as the trustee is assumed to behave trustworthily due to his or her fear of legal sanctions being potentially mobilized against him or her. This perspective follows assumptions deeply engrained in Rational Choice (Coleman, 1990) and Game Theory (Axelrod, 1984). However, it is questionable whether such a conceptualization has actually much to do with trust. Coleman (1990) suggests to see the trustor as if he or she was a better, for example on a race track for horses or greyhounds. However, in such situations, actors do not deal with fuzzy knowledge which seems precisely what a trustor is confronted with. If all possible knowledge is available, which should be the case for a bettor, one can indeed do a risk assessment in a purely calculative manner. But, where this is a viable approach to come to a decision of what to do or not to do, there is no need for trust. It is exactly where rational risk assessments are not possible due to the prevalence of fuzzy – rather than just incomplete – knowledge where trust has its place.

The other conceivable and indeed more realistic way to conceptualize the influence of institutions on individual behaviour follows phenomenological premises, such as those present in New Institutionalist Theory (Powell & DiMaggio, 1991; Scott, 1995), Structuration Theory (Giddens, 1984), Systems Theory (Luhmann, 1996) and Practice Theory (Bourdieu, 1977). In this perspective institutional arrangements are forces that only roughly – yet effectively – shape the behaviour of actors. They are not seen as exerting their influence in a deterministic manner; they rather "channel" the minds of relevant actors into specific directions. With regard to legal norms we would – on the basis of this approach – not assume that rational actors interact in the face of fear of sanctions; rather we would suggest that a large number of semi-conscious individuals' behaviours are drawn in the same direction. If this is how institutions work, then legal norms would not need to enter individuals' highly rational calculations before they become influential. In fact, they are in most cases expected to remain latent and would actually need to be only implicitly referred to in order to be effective in encouraging trust among social actors (Luhmann, 1979). Under these circumstances, which seem much closer to empirically observable human behaviour than the Rational Choice approach, legal norms – among other social norms – are institutional forces which can significantly support high levels of trust (building) within, for example, a business community. Legal norms do their job best if no sanctions need to be mobilized against anybody. Conflict and coercion are surely a sign of legal norms having failed to function effectively, and much the same can be said about other forms of social norms and standards which are embodied in the institutional settings of a regional or national business system, or society as a whole.

Where do institutions matter the most?

Institutional(-based) trust, as trust created between two actors in the face of strong and reliable institutional arrangements, is a form of trust which differs from inter-personal trust in that institutions play a constitutive role in the trust process. It may well be true that inter-personal trust is often more intensive and thus in some situations most desirable, but it also requires a lot of effort at the level of individual conduct. If strong and reliable institutions are in place, actors can draw on their trust-encouraging effects without any effort being made by an individual on the spot. This is the advantage of institutional(-based) trust. Institutions are created collectively and are relatively stable over longer periods of time. In this sense, they can be seen as an economically efficient way to reduce risk and encourage trust. Even though this form of trust may not be as strong as inter-personal trust developed in an intimate relationship between two social actors, it is widely available and easy to draw upon where strong and reliable institutions exist. In business relationships, in particular, institutional forms of trust are often very useful and – with regard to their intensity – often completely sufficient. By contrast, the absence of institutional(-based) trust may result in high immediate costs for the relevant individuals when trust needs to be built at face-to-face level, i.e. in the form of inter-personal trust. As this option might in this situation sometimes not be seen as feasible or attractive, a potential trustor might well decide to forgo the chance to engage in any transaction or consider power or purely money-based incentive systems as the primary social coordination mechanism in a specific relationship.

Following Bachmann and Inkpen (2001), four scenarios can be identified where institutional(-based) trust matters the most in business contexts: (a) at the early stages of relationship building; (b) where swift trust is needed; (c) where the level of asset specificity is low; and (d) where relatively mature industries are concerned. Ad (a): Institutional(-based) trust matters in the early stages of relationship building because it is often the perfect first step in establishing some common ground between two actors if this only requires both parties considering that alter knows the same behavioural rules emanating from institutional arrangements as ego does. This entails minimal individual costs and can be highly effective in the initial phases of a relationship. Many social interactions would not be viable if trust could only be built at the inter-personal level at this stage of the relationship because the latter usually requires significant time and effort which is not always possible or economical for potentially transacting individuals. Ad (b): Somewhat overlapping with the function of institutional(-based) trust in the early stages of relationships, and yet different, is the importance of institutional(-based) trust in situations where "swift trust" (Meyerson et al., 1996) is required. The speed of trust building is often more important than the intensity of trust. For example, there are situations where the quality of a product offered by a seller is relatively easy to assess by a potential buyer: the price may seem attractive to him or her, and the product may lose its value if it is not bought and consumed quickly. Then it can be very useful to draw on institutional arrangements which may provide a sufficient level of trust between the buyer and seller and – most important – do so instantly. Ad (c) Not every product is highly customized. Rather, most products which we use on a daily basis are fairly standardized and mass-produced. In these cases, it is not very advisable to establish an intensive form of trust, i.e. inter-personal trust, before transactions can take place. The mere existence of strong and reliable institutions can be completely sufficient and have the desired effect. Institutions may, under these circumstances, be good enough to reduce risk to a tolerable level and thus encourage a potential trustor to actually build a relationship on trust. Ad (d) An analysis of different types of industry and their affinity to specific forms of trust can also be insightful. In the high-tech sector, for example the biotech industry, it is not uncommon that firms are small start-ups, and personal bonds between a handful experts may be of the essence to develop very profitable businesses. Thus, inter-personal trust is important here, whereas institutional(-based) trust is often most useful in relatively mature industries which are characterized by large and capital-intensive operations. The automobile or chemical industries can be seen as examples. Countries in which these industries are most developed, i.e. Germany or Japan, tend to have more room for strong and reliable institutions promoting institutional-trust in business relationships rather than inter-personal trust which generally features more strongly in countries such as the UK or the US.

Country-specific institutional frameworks and their effects on trust (building)

As indicated above, institutional arrangements can be complex and varied in terms of consistency and reliability. Any cross-country comparative research will confirm this, and much of the institutional influences on trust development, maintenance and repair can only be assessed fully in a comparative perspective (e.g. Lane, 1995; Hall & Soskice, 2001; Whitley, 2002).

In a multi-country comparative view, certain patterns tend to arise so that countries may be grouped and specific institutional arrangements which have a typical influence on trust and trust building can be identified. Liberal market economies (e.g. the UK or Australia) generally build on a low level of socio-economic regulation, i.e. institutional arrangements tend to be relatively weak and not too reliable; whereas coordinated market economies (e.g. Germany, France, etc.) tend to have a considerably stronger institutional framework. Just to pick law again as one element of the latter, the differences between the Anglo-Saxon common law tradition and the civil law tradition, which prevails in mainland Europe, are quite significant in terms of their potential to control individuals' behaviour. Civil law is based on a commonly accessible written code which leaves very little room for interpretation. Common law, by contrast, essentially rests on precedent cases, which lay people have little chance to identify and transfer to their specific circumstances. Or take the professional education and training systems, where also significant differences exist. In Germany, for example, standards of education and training are high and apply nationwide. In the UK, professional education and training can take on various forms and it is sometimes difficult to judge the skills of a professional merely on the basis of a certificate or degree which has been awarded to him or her. At least it is vital to know where a vocational training certificate or a university degree comes from. In Germany, by contrast, there is in daily practice hardly ever any reference made to the degree-awarding organization, and it would even seem a bit odd if somebody did emphasize it without being explicitly asked. German universities, for example, are considered to be all at an equal level and any university degree has thus the same value in the labour market as long as the grades are the same. This certainly is quite different in the English-speaking part of the world.

If forms and levels of trust are compared between countries representing the liberal market economy, on the one hand, and countries that draw on the coordinated market economy model, on the other, a robust correlation between the specific business system and the prevalent form of trust (development) appears to exist. Countries of the coordinated market economy type have strong institutions, and actors' behaviour is deeply embedded in specific sets of institutional rules. Thus, institutional(-based) trust is in its natural habitat in these circumstances. Liberal market economies, by contrast, have comparatively loose and variable institutional arrangements and institutional(-based) trust (building) is thus not much supported. Consequently, inter-personal trust will feature more strongly in this system and actors will indeed frequently resort to other coordination mechanisms, such as power and monetary incentives, especially where inter-personal trust creation may seem not worth the effort, for example, if it is only very cheap and simple products or services that are exchanged between a seller and a buyer. Unsurprisingly, in this environment, trust is generally less present as a coordination mechanism in business relationships than in the coordinated market economy.

Each model of socio-economic order has a place for trust. However, due to the characteristics of their specific institutional arrangements, different types of trust, i.e. inter-personal vs. institutional(-based) trust, are dominant, and the availability as well as the intensity of trust differs accordingly. Institutional(-based) trust is less intense but usually widely and effortlessly available. Building inter-personal trust, by contrast, requires more individual efforts and is thus relative scarce in business and society.

Trust and regulation: an odd couple?

It should not be ignored that some trust scholars suggest a divergent view and in fact argue that regulation is not conducive to creating trust. Their view is that the institutional guardians of trust need to be trusted themselves and thus exacerbate the problem rather than solving it (Shapiro, 1987), or they indeed go as far as to claim that strong forms of regulation are a functional equivalent to trust and will thus make trust superfluous. This is a position which is challenged by most of the "trust and/or control" literature (Arrighetti et al., 1997; Bijlsma-Frankema & Costa, 2005; Möllering, 2005) but is consistent with older strands of the socio-legal literature (Macaulay, 1963; Beale & Dugdale, 1975). What essentially follows from the latter view is that if trust is to be saved or (re-)established, for example in the financial services industry, strong forms of regulation are to be avoided and principles of business ethics should be referred to and insisted on instead (Harris et al., 2014).

On closer inspection, this view is based on an understanding of regulation which is slightly different from the concept of institutional arrangements put forward in our perspective. If regulation refers to a comprehensive set of rules that imply sanctions, which are explicitly threatened to be mobilized in the case of non-compliance, then it may be true that there is little space left for trust (Sitkin & Roth, 1993). However, if regulatory systems are embedded in cultural traditions and implicit knowledge, i.e. institutional arrangements "channel" individual actors' behaviour, rather than appearing as a formal parameter in an individual's calculation of the potential consequences of different behavioural options, then these institutional rules can do a very effective job in facilitating trust between social actors. In this case, it will not be necessary to simply rely on ethical claims if trust is to be encouraged in business relationships.

For a variety of historic reasons, the ditch between the advocates of ethics and regulation is largely congruent with the boundary between the liberal market economies and the coordinated market economies. The ethical approach seems attractive to many scholars in the English-speaking parts of the world while continental European scholars, for example, tend to have more confidence in regulatory policies. However, it is important to note that in continental Europe institutions and rules are always rooted in complex contexts in which they are interpreted and utilized. Where context matters less and explicit guidelines and check lists prevail as tends to be the case in the liberal market economy where cheap semi-skilled labour is used more frequently, strict rules and regulation may indeed not be very conducive to trust building, and ethical approaches appear more useful to this end. Of course, on both sides, ethics and rules can in some situations, go hand in hand and reinforce each other (Bachmann, Gillespie & Priem, 2015).

Future research agenda

While we may have reached some understanding of the importance of institutional arrangements in the context of trust creation, we still need to invest considerably more effort into elaborating how institutionally created trust can transform behavioural practices in organizations. How, for example, can country-specific institutional arrangements such as education and training systems, systems of financing investments or legal systems translate into meso-level behavioural systems, i.e. organizational practices, in such a way that organizations are more likely to be (seen as) trustworthy? How can macro-level financial regulation policies contribute to trustworthy practices within financial services organizations? While we can explain how individuals get motivated to behave trustworthily in the face of institutional arrangements, we have not yet developed a clear understanding of how behavioural patterns and routines, as elements of organizational structure and culture, can be shaped by way of macro-level institutional frameworks.

Also, we need to invest more effort into refining our methodologies in trust research. We currently have very few ideas as to how we can capture institutions in our empirical research. Of course, we have produced many interesting case studies and some classifications of different types of institutions within business systems. But when it comes to systematically gathering empirical data on institutional frameworks our efforts tend to produce very patchy descriptions. As mentioned in the introduction to this chapter, institutional frameworks are varied and complex and thus pose a major challenge to empirical research. Thus, it is not surprising that conventional means to collect data, such as questionnaire-based interviews, are insufficient to come to grips with institutional arrangements and their impact on social behaviour. What seems to be needed to get to the essence of institutional systems is a combination of different methods which include powerful qualitative tools, such as focus groups or repertory grids. The methods mostly used in trust research (Lyon et al., 2015) are still oriented to measuring behaviour at the micro level. However, we have to go beyond this methodological approach in order to better understand the meso and macro contexts in which trust features as a highly embedded phenomenon.

Conclusion

Institutions are apparently very important where trust building, maintenance and repair are concerned. All advanced economies either draw on strong institutional arrangements to encourage institutional(-based) trust, or indeed switch to other coordination mechanisms, such as power or monetary incentive systems, when sufficient institutional(-based) trust is difficult to produce and inter-personal trust creation is too costly to establish. Admittedly, trust is not always the best coordination mechanism. There are certainly also dark sides of trust. However, on the whole, institutional(-based) trust is surely a valuable resource which socio-economic systems need to utilize if they want to be successful (Zaheer et al., 1998).

Institutional(-based) trust is specifically relevant when the quality of inter-organizational relationships in specific business systems is under review. Even in those regions and countries where institutions are relatively weak and trust is primarily of an inter-personal trust nature, institutional(-based) trust will not be completely absent and add to the production of common ground without which no developed economy or society is able to exist. The latter provides more than a good reason to further invest in the study of institutional(-based) trust.

References

Arrighetti, A., Bachmann, R. and Deakin, S. (1997), Contract Law, Social Norms and Interfirm Cooperation. *Cambridge Journal of Economics* 21(2): 171–195.

Axelrod, R. (1984), *The Evolution of Cooperation*. New York: Basic Books.

Bachmann, R. (1998), Trust – Conceptual Aspects of a Complex Phenomenon. In: Lane, C. and Bachmann, R. (Eds.) *Trust Within and Between Organizations*. Oxford, UK: Oxford University Press, pp.298–322.

Bachmann, R. (2001), Trust, Power and Control in Trans-Organizational Relations. *Organization Studies* 22(2): 337–365.

Bachmann, R., Gillespie, N. and Priem, R. (2015), Repairing Trust in Organizations and Institutions: Toward a Conceptual Framework. *Organization Studies* 36(9): 1123–1142.

Bachmann, R. and Inkpen, A. (2011), Understanding Institutional-Based Trust Building Processes in Inter-Organizational Relationships. *Organization Studies* 32(2): 281–301.

Beale, H. and Dugdale, T. (1975), Contracts Between Businessmen: Planning and the Use of Contractual Remedies. *British Journal of Law and Society* 2(1): 45–60.

Bijlsma-Frankema, K. and Costa, A.C. (2005), Understanding the Trust-Control Nexus. *International Sociology* 20(3): 259–282.

Bjørnskov, C. (2012), How does Social Trust Affect Economic Growth? *Southern Economic Journal* 78(4): 1346–1368.

Bourdieu, P. (1977), *Outline of a Theory of Practice*. New York: Cambridge University Press.

Coleman, J. (1990), *Foundations of Social Theory*. Cambridge, MA: Harvard University Press.

Dearmon, J. and Grier, R. (2011), Trust and the Accumulation of Physical and Human Capital. *European Journal of Political Economy* 27(3): 507–519.

Edelman Trust Barometer (2016), Available at: www.edelman.com/insights/intellectual-property/2016-edelman-trust-barometer/.

Fuglsang, L. and Jagd, S. (2015), Making Sense of Institutional Trust in Organizations: Bridging Institutional Context and Trust. *Organization* 22(1): 23–39.

Fukuyama, F. (1995), *Trust: The Social Virtues and the Creation of Prosperity*. New York: Free Press.

Gibbs, P. (2004), *Trusting in the University: The Contribution of Temporality and Trust to a Praxis of Higher Learning*. London: Kluwer.

Giddens, A. (1984), *The Constitution of Society: Outline of the Theory of Structuration*. Berkley, CA: University of California Press.

Giddens, A. (1990), *The Consequences of Modernity*. Stanford, CA: Stanford University Press.

Granovetter, M. (1985), Economic Action and Social Structure: The Problem of Embeddedness. *American Journal of Sociology* 91(3): 481–510.

Hall, P.A. and Soskice, D.W. (Eds.) (2001), *Varieties of Capitalism: The Institutional Foundations of Comparative Advantage*. Oxford, UK: Oxford University Press.

Harris, D., Moriarty, B. and Wicks, A. (Eds.) (2014), *Public Trust in Business*. Cambridge, UK: Cambridge University Press.

Kroeger, F. (2012), Trusting Organizations: The Institutionalization of Trust in Inter-Organizational Relationships. *Organization* 19(6): 743–763.

Lane, C. (1995), *Industry and Society in Europe: Stability and Change in Britain, Germany and France*. Aldershot, UK: Edward Elgar.

Luhmann, N. (1979), *Trust and Power*. Chichester: Wiley.

Luhmann, N. (1996), *Social Systems*. Stanford, CA: Stanford University Press.

Lyon, F., Möllering G. and Saunders, M.N.K. (2015), *Handbook of Research Methods on Trust*. 2nd Edition. Cheltenham, UK: Edward Elgar Publishing.

Macaulay, S. (1963), Non-Contractual Relations in Business: A Preliminary Study. *American Sociological Review* 28(1): 55–69.

Meyerson, D., Weick K.E. and Kramer R.M. (1996), Swift Trust and Temporary Groups. In: Kramer R.M. and Tyler, T.R. (Eds.), Trust in Organizations: Frontiers of Theory and Research. Thousand Oaks, CA: Sage, pp.266–195.

Möllering, G. (2005), The Trust/Control Duality: An Integrative Perspective on Positive Expectations of Others. *International Sociology* 20(3): 283–305.

Möllering, G. (2006), *Trust, Reason, Routine, Reflexivity*. Amsterdam, the Netherlands: Elsevier.

Powell, W. and DiMaggio, P. (Eds.) (1991), *The New Institutionalism in Organizational Analysis*. Chicago, IL: University of Chicago Press.

Scott, W.R. (1995), *Institutions and Organizations*. Thousand Oaks, CA: SAGE.

Shapiro, S.P. (1987), The Social Control of Impersonal Trust. *American Journal of Sociology* 93(1): 623–658.

Simmel, G. (1950), *The Sociology of Georg Simmel. Translated, edited, and with an introduction by Kurt H. Wolff*. London and New York: Collier-Macmillan, Free Press.

Sitkin, S.B. and Roth, N.L. (1993), Explaining the Limited Effectiveness of Legalistic "Remedies" for Trust/Distrust. *Organization Science* 4(3): 367–392.

Tyler, T.R. (2006), *Why People Obey the Law*. Princeton, NJ: Princeton University Press.

Uslaner, E. (2014), The Economic Crisis of 2008, Trust in Government, and Generalized Trust. In: Harris, D., Moriarty, B. and Wicks, A. (Eds.), *Public Trust in Business*. Cambridge, UK: Cambridge University Press, pp.19–50.

Whitley, R. (2002), *Competing Capitalisms: Institutions and Economies*. Cheltenham, UK: Edward Elgar Publishing.

World Value Survey, Wave 5, 2005–2008, Official aggregate v.20140429. World Values Survey Association (www.worldvaluessurvey.org). Aggregate File Producer: Asep/JDS, Madrid, Spain.

Zaheer, A., McEvily, B. and Perrone, V. (1998), Does Trust Matter? Exploring the Effects of Inter-organizational and Interpersonal Trust on Performance. *Organization Science* 9(2): 141–159.

Zak, P. and Knack, S. (2001), Trust and Growth. *Economic Journal* 111(470): 295–321.

Zucker, L. (1986) Production of Trust: Institutional Sources of Economic Structure, 1840–1920. *Research in Organizational Behavior* 8: 53–111.

13

TRUST AND CONTRACTS

Complements versus substitutes in business-to-business exchanges

Laura Poppo and Zheng Cheng*

Introduction

Across companies, large and small, managers often rely on other companies to do work for them. For example, companies that focus on their core, value-added activities typically out-source support functions such as payroll, maintenance, staffing, benefits and IT support. When expanding to new products or geographic markets, managers often form alliances to access skills, knowledge and/or resources that they lack. Geographic distances can also complicate the management of such alliances as supply chains often take on a global footprint. The optimal outcome of such business-to-business (i.e. B2B) transactions is cooperation: having the trans-action executed in a manner that meets or exceeds managerial expectations. Yet, how to achieve this is a central debate in strategy research. Should managers rely exclusively on contracts, their trust of another, or both?

Two theoretical perspectives emerged to shape the debate surrounding trust and contracts, transaction cost economics (i.e. TCE) and social embeddedness. In the 1980s, TCE advanced the notion that contracts are necessary to safeguard exchanges from economic self-interest that is routed in opportunistic behaviour – if opportunities exist for one party to take advantage of another for self-gain, then it will (Williamson, 1996). Transaction cost economics assumes that people are self-interested, and if opportunities exist, they will betray one's trust (Williamson, 1996). Thus, Williamson denies the possibility of positive value derived through knowing the "identity" of parties involved in the B2B exchange.

This TCE position contrasts with that of social embeddedness in which B2B exchanges often take place in a context in which the personal identity of parties matters (Granovetter, 1985. Because economic exchange is embedded in a social structure, the quality of the relationships among economic actors must be considered. If parties "trust" one another to do what is expected or fair, then contracts are not necessary to remedy economic self-interest. Williamson (1996) counters that this type of trust exists only when it is an economically-efficient choice: "A will trust B because it is in A's interests to do so" (Ring, 1996: 151).

To examine this debate, scholars began to contrast the use of formal control systems to that of relying on relational quality. A substitution perspective advances, if trust exists, then formal controls are simply not necessary. B2B exchanges armed with strong social relationships can rely simply on their trust of the other (Granovetter, 1985; Uzzi, 1997). Others advance an extreme position: the existence of controls will undermine the use or development of trust (Ghosal & Moran, 1996; Inkpen & Currall, 2004). As a result, contracts relate negatively to trust, which implies that trust can function as a substitute for contracts (Sitkin & Roth, 1993): simply put, a substitution perspective means that if trust exists, contracts are not necessary. The primary form of coordination should be trust or contracts, not both.

An alternative to substitutes is a complementary relationship of trust and formal controls: the joint use of formal controls and trust enables greater management of risk, and thus assurance of expected outcomes. Relatedly, the interplay (or interaction) of trust and formal controls reinforces each other such that the delivery of the expected outcomes is greater than that which exists in the absence of their interaction (Sitkin, 1995; Das & Teng, 1998; Poppo & Zenger, 2002; see also Chapter 29 by Long & Weibel, this volume). The dominant logic is that their joint use of both trust and contracts offsets the limits of each one used in isolation. For example, trust allows parties to move forward in situations in which the contract is not well specified; whereas contracts set boundaries which enable a reliance on trust. While the logic underlying substitutes and complements presents alternative predictions, both perspectives share a common agenda: that an exclusive focus on formal controls to deter opportunism is not sufficient to understand governance and the performance of B2B exchanges.

The purpose of this chapter is to review the empirical literature that examines the substitutes-versus-complements debate through the lenses of transaction cost economics and social embeddedness. Because of this theoretical positioning, we limit our conceptual study of trust to that of inter-organizational trust and relational governance, acknowledging that other forms of trust also function as substitutes or complements, and trust and control occur at different levels of analysis (Zucker, 1986; Verburg, Searle, Nienaber, Hartog, Weibel, and Rupp, forthcoming). Second, we limit our review to examining one common form of formal control, complete and neoclassical contracts, while acknowledging that other forms of control exist, such as market power, direct supervision and monitoring. Third, consistent with recent meta-analytical reviews regarding the association of trust, contracts and performance (Cao & Lumineau, 2015; Krishnan, Geyskens & Steenkamp, 2015), we examine the overall level of support for three alternative ways in which trust, contracts and/or performance may relate to each other as complements and substitutes. Yet unlike the above review papers, for our review each empirical study must include measures of governance choices, contracts and trust, and ideally include additional factors that increase the likelihood in which self-interest is likely to surface (Schepker, Oh, Martynov & Poppo, 2014). The reason for this requirement is that every business exchange varies in terms of its social and economic characteristics, thus in order to assess the relationship (as substitutes or complements) between trust and contracts, both factors must be considered.

The pattern of results based on our review of this empirical literature suggests that whether trust and contracts function as complements or substitutes depends on the type of contract employed to govern the B2B relationship. For neoclassical contracts, trust supports the development of contracts (as complements) – suggesting that trusted parties appear to see the value of institutionalizing their learning in a contract, so that adaptation and conflict can be more easily and perhaps more fairly addressed in the future. Relatedly, neoclassical contracts support the development of trust, suggesting that working together over time provides a basis for trusting the other party. As a pair or interaction, our analysis further suggests that neoclassical contracts and trust positively relate to performance, a finding consistent with recent meta-analytical reviews (Cao & Lumineau, 2015; Krishnan et al., 2015).

For studies that only measure complete contracts and trust, the results are not as cohesive and are less consistent. Equivocal findings include (1) trust may promote more classical contracts or may undermine their development, and (2) classical contracts may promote or undermine the development of trust, or the two may not influence each other. Yet, contrary to this equivocality, our review shows that their combination generally results in greater performance. Interpreting this set of findings is problematic for the precise rationale (or mechanism) underlying the positive impact of trust on performance (controlling or in interaction with classical contracts) remains unclear. We address this topic in our section on future research opportunities.

Conceptualization and measurement of trust and contracts

The best way to examine the validity of these alternative positions is to take stock of the empirical literature that examines both contracts and trust in B2B exchanges, and then code and classify each study on whether their findings support complements or substitutes. Our sample of papers is fine grained and restrictive, for both the search terms of 'trust' and 'contract' must appear in the abstract. After carefully reading the abstract of an initial sample of 312 peer-reviewed papers, we identified 33 published papers that empirically examine the relationship between trust and contracts in various contexts. Because there is variation in the measurement of contracts and trust, the set of relationships examined relating trust and contracts, and the type of industry that represents the sample, these sources of heterogeneity in each paper are summarized in Appendix 13.1.

Classical versus neoclassical contracts

An important boundary condition that informs our review of complements versus substitutes is the conceptual distinction that economic risk varies and governance choices become increasingly consequential when risk exists. This assertion is based on prior literature that clearly showcases trust *as a willingness to accept vulnerability when risk exists* (Rousseau et al., 1998; Bradach & Eccles, 1989): this means parties are willing to rely or depend on another even though there is a chance that the other party may take advantage of them. Risk and vulnerability are also very important concepts in the TCE literature. Williamson (1996) explains that self-interest is more likely to threaten the bilateral execution of a transaction when transaction-specific characteristics exist, and this logic has tremendous empirical validation (see Schepker et al., 2014; Macher & Richman, 2008).

The transaction cost literature clearly specifies the characteristics of transactions that increase the level of risk associated with more complex transactions: volatility in the external environment that can impact demand or supply; difficulty in measuring or observing the actions of the other; and transaction-specific investments and assets (Williamson, 1996). In order to "safeguard" against these risk factors, contracts contain more complex contingencies, specify processes to work out conflict and/or promote adaptation, and may involve shared equity (Schepker et al., 2014; Macher & Richman, 2008). Such highly customized agreements arising from attempts to safeguard or minimize negative outcomes associated with risk factors require significant legal work.

While it is beyond the scope of this review chapter to detail all of this logic, the implication is that classical contracts, which are used as a basis for control in a low-risk environment, are fundamentally different from neo-classical contracts which are used as a basis for control in more high-risk environments. Based on classical contract law, "sharp" transactions require clear agreement and clear performance (Macneil, 1974: 738). Should disputes occur, contract law interprets the contract in a very legalistic way: more formal terms supercede less formal terms should disputes arise between formal and less formal features (e.g. written agreements versus oral amendments), and hard bargaining, to which the rules of contract law are strictly applied, characterizes these transactions.

Contracts that are more complete represent cases in which classical contract law applies: all of the relevant terms and clauses that safeguard parties from risk and set the terms and expectations of trade are easily specified (Williamson, 1996). These contracts are simpler and easier to write, they take up fewer pages, and they are likely to contain relatively standard clauses or boilerplate. Prior work shows that the predominate use of such contracts is for low-risk transactions that can also be considered as standard, common or routine (see Schepeker et al., 2014 for a recent review). In our sample of empirical studies, the survey items that measure such contracts are generally quite consistent and include items that measure the degree to which the roles, responsibilities, performance obligations and sanctions are well specified in the contract.

Neoclassical contracts, in contrast, relieve parties from strict legal enforcement when disputes arise. Perceptive parties reject classical contract law and move into a neoclassical contracting regime because this better facilitates continuity and promotes efficient adaptation (Williamson, 1991: 271–272). Thus, while identity of the parties is known, it is only useful to the extent that bilateral coordination is required to adjust to unexpected changes and disturbances. Thus, neoclassical contracts represent more complex and customized agreements due to heightened risk (Macneil, 1977; Williamson, 1996). When the transaction is more complex and it proves more difficult to specify easily through classical clauses the terms of trade, contracts become nuanced, containing contingencies as well as processes as parties attempt to foresee possible future states, guard against unknown risks and define processes that will be used to resolve conflict and promote adaptation.

Based on contract law, trust *represents a qualitatively different governance choice when neoclassical contracts exist (e.g. when risk exists) than when classical contracts exist.* As a result, we interpret evidence of substitutes or complements as a function of the contract type, and measure empirical support.

A simple example may help describe this qualitative difference: if trust substitutes for a classical contract, it means a manager is willing to rely on trust when there is relatively little economic risk of your "harming" me by failing to deliver the agreed-upon deal. That is, should a supplier betray the buyer, the buyer incurs the cost of one bad deal. After incurring this transaction cost, the manager will replace this supplier with another supplier: the logic for easy replacement is that classical contracts (i.e. "sharp in-sharp out") characterize competitive markets. Given reputation effects, this supplier will be weeded out of the market (Williamson, 1996; Hill, 1990)

Yet, if trust substitutes for neoclassical contracts, it means that you are willing to rely on trust when there is significant economic risk should one party "harm" the other by failing to deliver the agreed-upon deal. Neoclassical contracts by definition represent transactions in which there is significant bilateral dependency between the two parties (Williamson, 1996). Should one party default prematurely from the agreement, losses accrue in the form of sunk costs, specific investments in labour, equipment or brand-name. Losses further accrue in the form of switching costs because bilateral dependency by definition means that one party cannot easily replace the existing partner in a timely manner (Poppo & Zenger, 1998; Macher & Richman, 2008). In other words, a competitive supply of buyers and sellers does not exist for this type of transaction. Thus, if trust substitutes for a neoclassical contract, it means that parties forgo crafting a more complex contract that puts in place processes to resolve adjustments and disputes (such as coordination and adjustment provisions) as well as legal adjudication. Thus, for trust to substitute for neoclassical contracts, it means that the two parties can readily rely on their trust of each other to adapt as well as resolve disputes, even though risk and economic losses are significant. Thus, substitution implies trust is inherently scalable in terms of the problems it can solve in an ex post manner, and it can produce outcomes that are mutually satisfactory.

What does trust mean? Reliability, integrity, benevolence and/or cooperation

Trust implies that managers can rely on the social structure and quality of relationships to promote confidence that the other party will behave as expected (Zucker, 1986): it is "a positive expectation of the intentions or behaviour of another" (Rousseau, Sitkin, Burt & Camerer, 1998: 395). Consistent with this logic, empirical studies validate this focus: trust and its related normative conventions are associated with lower transaction costs (Artz & Brush, 2000; Larson, 1992), greater knowledge transfer (Li, Poppo, & Zhou, 2010; Szulanski, Cappetta, & Jensen, 2004) and better exchange performance in B2B exchanges (Poppo & Zenger, 2002; Zaheer, McEvily, & Perrone, 1998).

In this literature, scholars do not generally distinguish trust, which is being worthy of, from trustworthiness (Weibel, 2007), in which three dimensions figure prominently: ability, benevolence and integrity (Mayer et al., 1995). Trust is defined as "a positive expectation of the intentions or behaviour of another" (Rousseau et al., 1998: 395) and measures qualities that imply the opposite of opportunistic beliefs or self-interested behaviour: (1) positive expectations (i.e. reliability, dependability, predictability, credibility and confidence), (2) integrity (i.e. honesty, fairness, truth), (3) benevolence (i.e. goodwill, genuine concern for the others) (see also Seppanen, Blomqvist & Sundqvist, 2007) and (4) other antecedents/outcomes of trust, such as prior experience, cooperation or activities that require cooperation.

Empirical roots of trust and contracts

The formative empirical papers

The first empirical paper to examine substitution, Gulati (1995), finds that the number of prior repeated ties weakens the probability that partners rely on shared equity contracts (a.k.a. joint ventures). This result is meaningful because it contrasts with the transaction cost logic that managers are more likely to choose equity-based agreements when there is significant economic risk associated with the exchange (Schepker et al., 2014). While Gulati does not measure trust, he reasons that prior repeated ties act as a proxy for trust, and thus interprets the results as showing that trust can substitute for contracts. Additional early support for substitution comes from Uzzi (1997), who, building on his dissertation advisor's conceptualization of embeddedness (Granovetter, 1985), finds that a network of apparel firms and their suppliers in New York City did not draft formal contracts to address probable risk factors, but instead relied on their strong personal bonds with one another.

While substitution is one alternative to describe how trust relates to contracts, other alternatives are also possible. In the landmark empirical paper, Poppo and Zenger (2002) examine how contracts and trust function as complements, as an alternative view to substitution. To empirically specify these concepts, they draw upon Macneil's (1977) observation that for many complex business deals, relational norms are necessary to support the use of contracts. Since complex contracts contain processes for continuance, adjustment and conflict, they represent "incomplete" terms and specifications for conduct that has yet to transpire. This type of contract contrasts with classical contract law in which classical clauses and terms can readily assure that the transaction will be executed as expected. Macneil argues that relational norms enable the effective use and application of customized contracts to foster the execution of the business deal. Poppo and Zenger (2002) measure relational governance as a composite of trust and cooperation, and measure contracts as the degree of customization, representing the conceptual continuum from standard to neoclassical (e.g. neoclassical) contracts. Their results overwhelmingly support the complementary nature of contracts and relational governance – not substitutes. Contracts and relational governance not only function as governance companions, enabling the performance of B2B exchanges, but also support the effective use or development of each other.

Building on Poppo and Zenger (2002), Luo (2002) also examines the complementarity versus substitution of contracts and trust. Yet, Lou uses different constructs and a different set of causal relationships. He advances that prior experience, a proxy for both trust and learning with a partner, not only leads to greater specification of contingencies in joint venture contracts, but in turn, this greater specification of contractual contingencies also leads to greater levels of cooperation. He also finds that the interaction of cooperation and contracts positively strengthens joint venture performance. Overall, his work endorses complementarity of contracts and trust.

As an aggregate, the results of this first set of papers conflict with one another as they provide support consistent with the logic of both complements and substitutes. In the next section, we review empirical work since these landmark papers.

Taking stock of the empirical evidence for complements versus substitutes

In this section, we review the empirical evidence on complements versus substitutes since the publication of the landmark papers and use a quantitative count of support as a basis for our inferences. While a numerical count measure is crude, we believe it is an appropriate metric given that the sample of papers included in this study represents the highest quality papers available at this time. Also note that because there are different ways in which trust, contracts and/or performance outcomes can relate to each other, we partition our review of complements and substitutes into three sections.

#1: As a complement, does trust enable better contracting practices or does it substitute for contracts?

As a temporal process, scholars posit that trusting beliefs form by accumulating experiences and then forming expectations of what to expect from the other (e.g. Blau, 1964; Gulati, 1995; Larson, 1992; Ring & Van De Ven, 1994). Over time, relationships deepen such that a set of values and normative conventions characterize beliefs for how each party will work with the other. Scholars, however, debate how a positive track history of the relationship impacts contracts: (1) as complements in which trust relates positively to the development of contracts, or (2) as substitutes in which trust undermines or substitutes for the use of contracts.

The complement perspective argues that as parties work together they find ways to better specify or work through challenges associated with the optimal execution of the transaction. This conceptualization is consistent with the idea that trust develops through social interaction and task interdependence. Contracts are inherently incomplete and trust facilitates learning as trusted partners work through unexpected challenges. Poppo and Zenger (2002) explain:

> as a close relationship is developed and sustained, lessons from the prior period are
> reflected in revisions of the contract. Exchange experience, patterns of information

sharing, and evolving performance measurement and monitoring may all enable greater specificity (and complexity) in contractual provisions

(p. 713).

As parties develop better knowledge of how to execute the transaction, such knowledge becomes formalized and institutionalized in the contract. Consistent with this, empirical work finds that parties over time adjust the formal contract to better specify classical terms and/or procedures that enhance task execution (Mayer & Argyres, 2004). Similar findings from Luo (2002) show that repetitive exchanges breed trust and result in a higher level of specificity and contingency adaptability in their contracts.

The substitution perspective is that trust substitutes for contracts. Gulati (1995: 86) explains: "experience can engender trust among partners, and trust can limit the transaction costs associated with their future alliances. . ." because "interfirm trust . . . obliges partners to behave loyally" (p. 92). This predictability, according to Gulati, is functionally equivalent to the predictability created from contractual terms, and forms the basis for which trust substitutes for contracts. He reasons that in order to economize on the transaction costs required from drafting specific contracts managers are more likely to rely on trust, rather than contracts, when forming repeated transactions with the same partner (see Mellewigt, Madhok & Weibel, 2007).

Next we present the empirical evidence based on the following relationships between contracts (two types: classical and neoclassical) and trust (see Table 13.1), and the two alternative relationships. To be included in this table, the paper must empirically specify the main effect of trust on either classical or neoclassical contracts. Note, that in this table we are not measuring the relationship between contracts, trust and outcomes – only whether the authors empirically specify how trust impacts contracts, or how contracts impact trust.

This table indicates that 11 empirical papers examine how trust relates to contracts, and all of these inferences are based on cross-sectional data. Thus, further research is still needed to validate the following remarks.

Our summary based on a numerical count of the results follows:

1   There appears to be greater overall support for complements (8 papers), trust supports the development of contracts, than for substitutes, trust undermines the development of contracts (3 papers).

Table 13.1 Does trust enable better contracts (complements) or does it substitute for contracts?

Contract type	Empirical support	
	# of papers (references)	
	Complements	Substitutes
Classical	3 (Liu, Tao, Li & El-Ansary, 2008; Zhang & Hu, 2011; Bastl, Johnson, Lightfoot & Evans, 2012)	1 (Woolthius, Hillebrand & Nooteboom, 2005)
Neoclassical	5 (Poppo & Zenger, 2002; Luo, 2002; Blomqvist, Hurmelinna & Seppanen, 2005; Brown, Potoski & Van Slyke, 2007; Mellewigt et al., 2007)	2 (Gulati, 1995; Mellewigt et al., 2007)
Total	8	3

2 For neoclassical contracts, more results indicate that trust supports the development of contracts (complements, 5 papers) rather than undermines their development (substitutes, 2 papers). Presumably, trusted parties appear to see the value of institutionalizing this learning in a contract, so that adaptation and conflict can be more easily and perhaps more fairly addressed in the future.

3 For classical contracts, trust both supports (complements, 3 papers) and undermines the development of classical contracts (substitutes, 1 paper).

#2: As complements, do contracts foster the development of trust, or do contracts, as substitutes, undermine its development?

The next alternative examines the effect of contracts on the development of trust. Two relationships are possible: as complements, contracts relate positively to the development of trust; as substitutes, contracts undermine the development of trust. The alternative focuses on factors that influence how managers develop their initial assessment of whether they can "trust" the other party. The substitution view is that classical contracts, as a control mechanism, erode a foundation of trust – controls signal a lack of trust and erode positive social relationships (see Poppo & Zenger, 2002: 711). The alternative is that neoclassical contracts are more likely to ensure success and promote long-term business, providing a structure that promotes cooperation, and thus positive social relationships and trust (Poppo & Zenger, 2002). Luo (2002: 907) further endorses this view as contracts represent clear expectations of what the other party needs to achieve. By setting in place a framework that clearly defines each party's rights, duties and the principles and procedures of cooperation, trust will naturally develop as parties deliver the expected or promised outcomes.

Next we present the empirical evidence.

Based on Table 13.2 we offer the following summary:

1 There is greater overall support for complements, that contracts foster the development of trust (8 papers), than the alternative, contracts undermine the development of trust (4 papers).

Table 13.2 Do contracts foster (complement) or undermine (substitute) the development of trust?

Contract type	*Empirical support*		
	# of papers (references)		
	Complements	*Substitutes*	*Not significant*
Classical	2 (Woolthius et al., 2005; Ren, Oh & Noh, 2010)	3 (Malhotra & Murnighan, 2002; Faems, Janssens, Madhok & Van Looy, 2008; Malhotra & Lumineau, 2011)	1 (Handfield & Bechtel, 2002)
Neoclassical	6 (Poppo & Zenger, 2002; Luo, 2002; Malhotra & Murnighan, 2002; Faems et al., 2008; Malhotra & Lumineau, 2011; Stratling, Wijbenga & Dietz, 2012)	1 (Stratling et al., 2012)	0
Total	8	4	1

2   For neoclassical contracts, there is greater support for complements (6 papers) than substitutes (1 paper).
3   For classical contracts, the results are less consistent (2 papers support complements; 3 papers support substitutes; 1 paper is not significant).

This pattern of results suggests a possible, more nuanced interpretation for how contracts relate to trust. *Perceptions* of rigid/inflexible/controlling (classical) contracts undermine the development of trust (substitution) while perceptions of flexible (neoclassical) contracts promote the development of trust (complements). This is of theoretical significance given Ghoshal and Moran's (1996) view that perceptions can undermine trust and/or escalate opportunism.

We illustrate this interpretation with representative studies. Ren et al. (2010) find that classical contracting helps build a fair relationship between retailers and powerful suppliers, thus improving retailers' trust of suppliers. Yet, when the contract is perceived as controlling, trust is less likely. Malhotra and Murnighan (2002) find that when contracts are not binding, exchange partners might attribute cooperation to personal commitments that result in the development of trust, but when contracts are perceived as binding, trust does not develop. In their case study, Woolthius et al. (2005) also show that when contracts are not interpreted as strict legal safeguards, they promote the development of trust between partners. Faems and colleagues (2008) similarly describe in their case study research that an excessive focus on contracts, specifically the rigid application of controls, can undermine trust, and thus R&D performance; yet when the R&D contract is oriented to be more flexible, partners are more trusting and performance improves.

#3: As complements, the joint use of both contracts and trust positively impact exchange performance

A third way to assess the complementarity vs. substitution is by investigating the performance effects of trust and contracts. Two alternatives exist. As complements, contracts and trust relate positively to performance. As substitutes, several variants are possible. If trust and contracts are functionally equivalent, their joint use can cancel out the effects of the other (as independent factors) or result in a not significant interaction term. Or if their combined use undermines performance, then a negative interaction effect will be observed. A positive pairing of trust is that trust completes the limitations of contracts due to bounded rationality (Simon, 1957) and minimizes the transaction costs incurred by drafting more complete contracts (Williamson, 1996). Poppo and Zenger (2002) further suggest that contracts and trust offer different functionalities: contracts specify contingencies, processes and controls while the existence of trust fosters mutuality, bilateralism, and continuance (see also, Sitkin, 1995; Das & Teng, 2001). Consistent with this, Blomqvist et al. (2005) document the difficulties in using detailed written contracts to manage inter-organizational collaboration in a dynamic environment. They find that formal contracts, at best, can define ground rules and that trust-based governance guides specific actions for collaboration.

This form of complementarity represents the most common view of trust: it is associated with increased cooperative effort, and as such acts as a "social lubricant". There are numerous examples of how trust can further cooperation. Because I trust you, I can rely on you to do what you promised, to be fair and/or to take account of my interests when doing work. Because we trust each other, we are willing to share tacit or private knowledge that improves joint performance. Also, when trust exists, parties can act as though the future is more certain, thereby fostering perceptions of stability, bilateral coordination, and limiting performance losses that might otherwise occur when future interaction is less certain. Thus, a central logic underlying complementarity is that trust and contracts address the limitations of each other.

A related form of complementarity examines the interactive effects of trust and contracts, testing whether trust enhances the effects of contracts on performance and vice versa. Specifically, as trust narrows down the scope and severity of exchange hazards, exchange partners are more willing to be flexible and responsive in implementing contractual clauses, which are essential to capture business opportunities in a constantly changing environment. In addition, trust, serving as a social contract, might enhance the enforceability of formal contracts, especially in weak legal systems, both of which increase performance outcomes.

The substitution perspective contends that a joint use of contracts and trust might be redundant, negative or cancel each other out (in terms of an interaction effect) all of which impact the independent effects or interactive effects on performance. Existing empirical studies that develop this logic focus on goodwill trust, a form of relational trust that captures emotional bonds between the two parties. For example, Lui and Ngo (2004) argue that the existence of goodwill trust indicates lower relational risks and thus undermines the effects of contracts to safeguard against opportunism. On the other hand, extensive contracts, as a sign of distrust, might reduce the trust between partners, creating greater motivation for opportunism. Consistent with this logic, Jiang, Li, Gao, Bao and Jiang (2013) find positive interaction effects of goodwill trust and contracts on knowledge leakage.

Next, we present the empirical evidence based on the following relationships between contracts and trust (see Table 13.3), and the two alternative relationships.

Table 13.3 Do contracts and trust function as complements or substitutes in relationship to performance outcomes?

Contract type	Empirical support		
	# of papers (references)		
	Complements		Substitutes
	Independent (main effects of trust and contracts)	Interaction (trust x contracts)	
Classical	9 (Cavusgil, Delignonul & Zhang, 2004; Woolthius et al., 2005; Wu, Sinkovics, Cavusgil & Roath, 2007; Lui, 2009; Li et al., 2010; Caniëls, Gelderman & Vermeulen, 2012; Zhao & Wang, 2011; De Reuver & Bouwman, 2012; Jiang et al., 2013)	5 (Bennett & Robson, 2004; Lui & Ngo, 2004; Wu et al., 2007; Chen, Zhu, Ao & Cai, 2013; Zhang & Zhou, 2013)	4 (Lui & Ngo, 2004; Jiang et al. 2013; Zhang & Zhou, 2013; Woolthius et al., 2005)
Neoclassical	5 (Poppo & Zenger, 2002; Luo, 2002; Blomqvist et al., 2005; Judge & Dooley, 2006; Zhou & Poppo, 2010)	1 (Judge & Dooley, 2006)	0
Total	13	6	4

Based on this table we summarize:

1   There is greater overall support for complements (20 papers), that contracts and trust promote performance, rather than for substitutes in which their combination weakens or destroys performance (4 papers).
2   For neoclassical contracts, there is more support for complements (6 papers, 100 percent of the results)
3   For classical contracts, there is more support for complements (14 papers) than substitutes (4 papers).

Concluding remarks

In this review we examine how the form of contracting, classical versus neoclassical, relates to trust. This focus enriches the results of two recent review papers: (1) Cao and Lumineau's (2015) meta-analytical analysis of 149 empirical papers, which finds that as complements trust and contracts effectively offset opportunism and improve performance, and (2) Krishnan and her colleagues' (2015) review of 82 studies, which shows the positive effects of trust and contracts on performance outcomes. We explain how the interpretation of substitution (or complements) is categorically different for each type of contract. For neoclassical contracts, the value of trusting perceptions appears linked to the limits and advantages of neoclassical contracts. Trust fosters better contractual specifications of neoclassical contracts; neoclassical contracts convey expectations that help foster trust; and trust complements neoclassical contracts by promoting adaption, continuance and commitment, which result in greater performance. This summary shows limited support for substitution – that managers will rely exclusively on trust when risk exists.

For classical contracts, the story is not as cohesive. Based on our number count of results, classical contracts do not relate to trust in a consistent fashion. Yet, the joint use of classical contracts and trust results in better performance. The lack of consistent findings make interpreting the mechanism through which trust and classical contracts enable greater performance difficult. Is it because of a social bond? Is it through greater commitment to execution because trusted parties are rewarded with repeat business? Relatedly, is trust simply a perception of reliability – a trusted party – that is capable of better workmanship? More work is clearly needed to clarify this area, which we discuss as a future research opportunity.

Future research opportunities

Identifying and distinguishing underlying mechanisms: what does trust mean?

In this body of empirical papers (see Appendix 13.1) the items that measure trust relate to perceptions or behaviours that demonstrate a lack of opportunism, or the presence of integrity or benevolence, two dimensions of trustworthiness. These measures, however, do not tease out the precise mechanism that fosters cooperation or positive outcomes. That is, they do not rule out the possibility that opportunism or economic self-interest exists and accounts for trust. This is an important point because if economic incentives, not social bonds, account for trust, then trust is inherently a fragile concept, for if incentives do not exist to act trustworthily, then parties will renege on their agreement. This is an important gap since the bulk of the evidence suggests that relying on trust should be a best business practice (Cao & Lumineau, 2015; Krishnan et al., 2015). Yet one primary obstacle is that the measurement of trust in this body of literature has not partitioned trust that stems from relational bonds from that of economic self-interest (i.e. it pays to act trustworthily).

Let us give an example. Suppose an empirical study seeks to relate trust to an outcome, such as performance, to demonstrate the positive value of trust in economic exchange. In order to assess this relationship, the research must first identify whether a reliance on trust is risky. Following Rousseau and colleagues (1998: 395): "trust is a psychological state comprising *the intention to accept vulnerability* based upon positive expectation of the intentions or behaviour of another". This means that there must be some inherent risk to relying on trust. Rousseau and her colleagues explain: trust "would not be needed if actions could be undertaken with complete certainty and no risk . . . Uncertainty regarding whether the other intends to and will act appropriately is the source of risk" (1998: 395). Relatedly, the substitution perspective initially assumes that trust is only valuable if there is a lack of information such that if total knowledge of the other partner's capability and intent is available, trust is not necessary at all (Simmel & Wolff, 1964; McAllister, 1995). Thus, to understand the value of trust in economic exchange, research must specify factors that make it vulnerable to rely on trust. It is the interpretation of trust in a vulnerable context that tests its value in offsetting opportunistic behaviour (see for example Krishnan, Martin & Noorderhaven, 2006; Poppo, Zhou & Zenger, 2008; Krishnan et al., 2015), which the empirical work we viewed does not classically consider.

A second factor that limits the interpretive value of trust is whether the empirical design considers other motivations that influence the decision to trust or the decision to act in a trustworthy fashion. While critically important, this is often lacking in empirical work because incentives or the formal contract may account for the existence of trust. For example, if the contract contains specific performance clauses with strong penalties for non-compliance or incentives for repeat business, then a supplier is motivated to act trustworthily – this conclusion implies that the presence of trust is based on calculation. More formally, a calculation such as the "relentless application of calculative economic reasoning" may underlie a trusting belief or behaviour as parties consider the costs of a breach in trust against the rewards from cooperation (Williamson, 1993: 453). To measure the value of trust that is not based on a motivation for economic gain, the empirical study needs to measure the calculative influences as well as these non-calculative motives (see for example Poppo, Zhou & Li, 2016). According to this conceptual literature, social needs, specifically belonging and identifying with others, endorses a moral integrity or goodwill to realize both organizational and individual goals (Granovetter, 1985; Ring, 1996; Turner, 1987). If this is true, how does this relate to trust? This is clearly a non-calculative origin of trust, but one that current work needs to more carefully measure and examine empirically.

In closing, we suggest the following recommendations for future research:

1   In order to truly understand the value of trust as a complement or substitute for contracts in economic exchange or the value of trust as a main effect, the empirical design must determine and measure the factors that make it vulnerable to rely on trust.
2   Any interpretation of the true effects of integrity or benevolence, or a composite of trust as evidence against self-interest or opportunistic motives, must rule out the alternative explanation of calculation (i.e. it makes economic sense for me to act with integrity, benevolence or cooperation).
3   Classical contracts are categorically different from neoclassical contracts. Research needs to customize the measure of contract to reflect the types of risk present in the exchange.

Note

*   We would like to thank the editors, Rosalind H. Searle, Sim B. Sitkin and Ann-Marie I. Nienaber as well as Dave Wangrow, Rekha Krishnan and Fabrice Lumineau for this for their constructive feedback. We also appreciate editorial assistance from Suzanna Emelio.

References

Artz, K. W. and Brush, T. H. 2000. Asset specificity, uncertainty and relational norms: An examination of coordination costs in collaborative strategic alliances. *Journal of Economic Behavior & Organization* 41(4), 337–362.

Bastl, M., Johnson, M., Lightfoot, H. and Evans, S., 2012. Buyer-supplier relationships in a servitized environment: An examination with Cannon and Perreault's framework. *International Journal of Operations & Production Management* 32(6): 650–675.

Bennett, R. J. and Robson, P. J., 2004. The role of trust and contract in the supply of business advice. *Cambridge Journal of Economics* 28(4): 471–488.

Blau, P. M. 1964. *Exchange and Power in Social Life*. New York: John Wiley & Sons.

Blomqvist, K., Hurmelinna, P. and Seppanen R. 2005. Playing the collaboration game right – balancing trust and contracting. *Technovation* 25(5): 497–504.

Bradach, J. L. and Eccles, R. G. 1989. Price, authority, and trust: From ideal types to plural forms. *Annual Review of Sociology* 15(1): 97–118.

Brown, T. L., Potoski, M. and Van Slyke, D. M., 2007. Trust and contract completeness in the public sector. *Local Government Studies* 33(4): 607–623.

Caniëls, M. C., Gelderman, C. J. and Vermeulen, N. P. 2012. The interplay of governance mechanisms in complex procurement projects. *Journal of Purchasing and Supply Management* 18(2): 113–121.

Cao, Z. and Lumineau, F. 2015. Revisiting the interplay between contractual and relational governance: A qualitative and meta-analytic investigation. *Journal of Operations Management* 33: 15–42.

Cavusgil, S. T., Deligonul, S. and Zhang, C. 2004. Curbing foreign distributor opportunism: An examination of trust, contracts, and the legal environment in international channel relationships. *Journal of International Marketing* 12(2): 7–27.

Charterina, J. and Landeta, J. 2010. The pool effect of dyad-based capabilities on seller firms' innovativeness. *European Journal of Innovation Management* 13(2): 172–196.

Chen, C., Zhu, X., Ao, J. and Cai, L. 2013. Governance mechanisms and new venture performance in China. *Systems Research and Behavioral Science* 30(3): 383–397.

Das, T. K. and Teng, B. S. 1998. Between trust and control: Developing confidence in partner cooperation in alliances. *Academy of Management Review* 23(3), 491–512.

Das, T. K. and Teng, B. S. 2001. Trust, control, and risk in strategic alliances: An integrated framework. *Organizational Studies* 22(2): 251–283.

De Reuver, M. and Bouwman, H. 2012. Governance mechanisms for mobile service innovation in value networks. *Journal of Business Research* 65(3): 347–354.

Faems, D., Janssens, M., Madhok, A. and Van Looy, B. 2008. Toward an integrative perspective on alliance governance: Connecting contract design, trust dynamics, and contract application. *The Academy of Management Journal* 51(6): 1053–1078.

Ghoshal, S. and Moran, P. 1996. Bad for practice: A critique of the transaction cost theory. *Academy of Management Review* 21(1): 13–47.

Granovetter, M. 1985. Economic action and social structure: The problem of embeddedness. *American Journal of Sociology* 91(3): 481–510.

Gulati, R. 1995. Does familiarity breed trust? The implications of repeated ties for contractual choice in alliances. *Academy of Management Journal* 38(1): 85–112.

Handfield, R. B. and Bechtel, C., 2002. The role of trust and relationship structure in improving supply chain responsiveness. *Industrial Marketing Management* 31(4): 367–382.

Hill, C. W., 1990. Cooperation, opportunism, and the invisible hand: Implications for transaction cost theory. *Academy of Management Review* 15(3): 500–513.

Inkpen, A. C., Currall, S. C. 2004. The coevolution of trust, control, and learning in joint ventures. *Organization Science* 15(5): 586–599.

Jiang, X., Li, M., Gao, S., Bao, Y. and Jiang, F. 2013. Managing knowledge leakage in strategic alliances: The effects of trust and formal contracts. *Industrial Marketing Management* 42(6): 983–991.

Judge, W. Q. and Dooley, R. 2006. Strategic alliance outcomes: A transaction-cost economics perspective. *British Journal of Management* 17(1): 23–37.

Krishnan, R., Geyskens, I. and Steenkamp, J. 2015. The effectiveness of contractual and trust-based governance in strategic alliances under behavioral and environmental uncertainty. *Strategic Management Journal*. 37(12): 2521–2542.

Krishnan, R., Martin, X. and Noorderhaven, N. 2006. When does trust matter to alliance performance? *The Academy of Management Journal* 49(5): 894–917.

Larson, A. 1992. Network dyads in entrepreneurial settings: A study of the governance of exchange relationships. *Administrative Science Quarterly* 37(1): 76–104.

Li, J., Poppo, L. and Zhou, Z. 2010. Relational mechanisms, formal contracts, and local knowledge acquisition by international subsidiaries. *Strategic Management Journal* 31(4): 349–370.

Liu, Y., Tao, L., Li, Y. and El-Ansary, A. I. (2008). The impact of a distributor's trust in a supplier and use of control mechanisms on relational value creation in marketing channels. *Journal of Business & Industrial Marketing* 23(1): 12–22.

Lui, S. S. and Ngo, H. Y. 2004. The role of trust and contractual safeguards on cooperation in non-equity alliances. *Journal of Management* 30(4): 471–485.

Lui, S.S. 2009. The roles of competence trust, formal contract, and time horizon in interorganizational learning. *Organization Studies* 30(4): 333–353.

Luo, Y. 2002. Contract, cooperation, and performance in international joint ventures. *Strategic Management Journal* 23(10): 903–919.

Macher, J. T. and Richman, B. D. 2008. Transaction cost economics: An assessment of empirical research in the social sciences. *Business and Politics* 10(1): 1–63.

Macneil, I.R. 1974. The many futures of contracts. *Southern California Law Review* 47: 691–816.

Macneil, I. R. 1977. Contracts: Adjustment of long-term economic relations under classical, neoclassical and relational contract law. *Northwestern University Law Review* 72(6): 854–905.

Malhotra, D. and Lumineau, F. 2011. Trust and collaboration in the aftermath of conflict: The effects of contract structure. *Academy of Management Journal* 54(5): 981–998.

Malhotra, D. and Murnighan, J. K. 2002. The effects of contracts on interpersonal trust. *Administrative Science Quarterly* 47(3): 534–559.

Mayer, K. J. and Argyres, N. S. 2004. Learning to contract: Evidence from the personal computer industry. *Organization Science* 15(4): 394–410.

Mayer, R. C., Davis, J. H. and Schoorman, F. D. 1995. An integrative model of organizational trust. *Academy of Management Review* 20(3), 709–734.

McAllister, D. J. 1995. Affect- and cognition-based trust as foundations for interpersonal cooperation in organizations. *The Academy of Management Journal* 38(1): 24–59.

Mellewigt, T., Madhok, A. and Weibel, A. 2007. Trust and formal contracts in interorganizational relationships – substitutes and complements. *Managerial and Decision Economics* 28(8): 833–847.

Poppo, L. and Zenger, T. 1998. Testing alternative theories of the firm: Transaction cost, knowledge-based, and measurement explanations for make-or-buy decisions in information services. *Strategic Management Journal* 19(9), 853–877.

Poppo, L. and Zenger, T. 2002. Do formal contracts and relational governance function as substitutes or complements? *Strategic Management Journal* 23(8): 707–725.

Poppo, L., Zhou, K. and Li, J. 2016. When can you trust "trust"? Calculative trust, relational trust, and supplier performance. *Strategic Management Journal* 37(4): 724–741.

Poppo, L., Zhou, K. and Zenger, T. 2008. Examining the conditional limits of relational governance: Specialized assets, performance ambiguity, and long-standing ties. *Journal of Management Studies* 45(7): 1195–1216.

Ren, X., Oh, S. and Noh, J. 2010. Managing supplier-retailer relationships: From institutional and task environment perspectives. *Industrial Marketing Management* 39(4): 593–604.

Ring, P. 1996. Fragile and resilient trust and their roles in economic exchange. *Business and Society* 35(2): 148–175.

Ring, P. and Van De Ven, A. 1994. Developmental processes of cooperative interorganizational relationships. *Academy of Management Review* 19(1): 90–118.

Rousseau, D. M., Sitkin, S. B., Burt, R. B. and Camerer, C. 1998. Not so different after all: A cross-discipline view of trust. *Academy of Management Review* 23(3): 393–404.

Schepker, D., Oh, W., Martynov, A. and Poppo, L. 2014. The many futures of contracts. *Journal of Management* 40(1): 193–225.

Seppanen, R., Blomqvist, K. and Sundqvist, S. 2007. Measuring inter-organizational trust – a critical review of the empirical research in 1990–2003. *Industrial Marketing Management* 36(2): 249–265.

Simmel, G. and Wolff, K. H. 1964. *The Sociology of Georg Simmel. Translated, edited, and with an introduction by Kurt H. Wolff*. London and New York: Collier-Macmillan, Free Press.

Simon, H. A. 1957. *Models of Man: Social and Rational*. New York: John Wiley & Sons.

Sitkin, S. B. 1995. On the positive effects of legalization on trust. *Research on Negotiation in Organizations* 5(2): 185–218.

Sitkin, S. B. and Roth, N. L. 1993. Explaining the limited effectiveness of legalistic "remedies" for trust/distrust. *Organization Science* 4(3): 367–392.

Strätling, R., Wijbenga, F. H. and Dietz, G. 2012. The impact of contracts on trust in entrepreneur–venture capitalist relationships. *International Small Business Journal* 30(8): 811–831.

Szulanski, G., Cappetta, R. and Jensen, R. J. 2004. When and how trustworthiness matters: Knowledge transfer and the moderating effect of causal ambiguity. *Organization Science* 15(5): 600–613.

Turner, J. H. 1987. Toward a sociological theory of motivation. *American Sociological Review* 52(1): 15–27.

Uzzi, B. 1997. Social structure and competition in interfirm networks: The paradox of embeddedness. *Administrative Science Quarterly* 42(1): 35–67.

Verburg, R. M., Searle, R. H., Nienaber, A., Den Hartog, D., Weibel, A. and Rupp, D. Forthcoming. The role of organizational control systems in employee trust in the organization and performance outcomes. *Group & Organization Management*.

Wang, L., Yeung, J. H. Y. and Zhang, M. 2011. The impact of trust and contract on innovation performance: The moderating role of environmental uncertainty. *International Journal of Production Economics* 134(1): 114–122.

Weibel, A. 2007. Formal Control and Trustworthiness: "Shall the Twain Never Meet?". *Group & Organization Management* 32(4): 500–517.

Williamson, O. E. 1991. Comparative economic organization: The analysis of discrete structural alternatives. *Administrative Science Quarterly* 36(2), 269–296.

Williamson, O. E. 1993. Calculativeness, trust and economic organization. *Journal of Law and Economics* 36(1): 453–486.

Williamson, O. E. 1996. *The Mechanisms of Governance*. New York: Oxford University Press.

Woolthius, R., Hillebrand, B. and Nooteboom, B. 2005. Trust, contract and relationship development. *Organization Studies* 26(6): 813–840.

Wu, F., Sinkovics, R. R., Cavusgil, S. T. and Roath, A. S. 2007. Overcoming export manufacturers' dilemma in international expansion. *Journal of International Business Studies* 38(2): 283–302.

Zaheer, A., McEvily, B. and Perrone, V. 1998. Does trust matter? Exploring the effects of inter-organizational and interpersonal trust on performance. *Organizational Science* 9(2): 141–159.

Zhang, Q. and Zhou, K. Z. 2013. Governing interfirm knowledge transfer in the Chinese market: The interplay of formal and informal mechanisms. *Industrial Marketing Management* 42(5): 783–791.

Zhang, X. and Hu, D. 2011. Farmer-buyer relationships in China: The effects of contracts, trust and market environment. *China Agricultural Economic Review* 3(1): 42–53.

Zhao, Y. and Wang, G. 2011. The impact of relation-specific investment on channel relationship performance: Evidence from China. *Journal of Strategic Marketing* 19(1): 57–71.

Zhou, Z. and Poppo, L. 2010. Exchange hazards, relational reliability, and contracts in China: The contingent role of legal enforceability. *Journal of International Business Studies* 41(5): 861–881.

Zucker, L. G. 1986. Production of trust: Institutional sources of economic structure, 1840–1920. *Research in Organizational Behavior* 8: 53–111.

Appendix 13.1: Empirical review of trust and contracts: substitute versus complements

Author(s)	Year	Measurement of trust	Measurement of contracts	Complement			Substitute		
				Trust → contracts ≠	Contracts → trust ≠	(Trust +/× contracts) — outcome ≠	Trust → contracts ↘	Contracts → trust ↘	(Trust +/× contracts) — outcome ↘
Bastl et al.	2012	Relationship	Classical	✓					
Bennett and Robson	2004	Relationship	Classical			✓★			
Blomqvist et al.	2005	Composite	Neoclassical	✓		✓			
Brown et al.	2007	Benevolence	Neoclassical	✓	✓				
Caniels et al.	2012	Relationship	Classical			✓			
Cavusgil et al.	2004	Benevolence	Classical			✓			
Charterina and Landeta	2010	Benevolence	Classical		✓				
Chen et al.	2013	Cooperation	Classical			✓★			
De Reuver and Bouwman	2012	Integrity	Classical			✓			
Faems et al.	2008	Benevolence	Classical		✓		✓		
Gulati	1995	Prior Experience	Neoclassical					✓	
Handfield and Bechtel	2002	Composite	Classical			✓			✓
Jiang et al.	2013	Competence & Benevolence	Classical			✓			✓
Judge and Dooley	2006	Integrity	Neoclassical			✓★			
Li et al.	2010	Integrity & Benevolence	Neoclassical			✓			
Liu et al.	2008	Benevolence & Integrity	Classical	✓					

continued . . . .

Continued

Author(s)	Year	Measurement of trust	Measurement of contracts	Complement			Substitute		
				Trust → contracts ≠	Contracts → trust ≠	(Trust +/× contracts) — outcome ≠	Trust → contracts ↓	Contracts → trust ↓	(Trust +/× contracts) — outcome ↓
Lui	2009	Competence & Benevolence	Classical			✓			
Lui and Ngo	2004	Competence & Benevolence	Classical			✓*			✓
Luo	2002	Cooperation	Neoclassical	✓		✓			
Malhotra and Lumineau	2011	Benevolence	Classical		✓			✓	
Malhotra and Murnighan	2002	Composite	Classical		✓			✓	
Mellewigt et al.	2007	Prior experience	Neoclassical	✓			✓		
Poppo and Zenger	2002	Composite	Neoclassical	✓	✓	✓			
Ren et al.	2010	Integrity & Benevolence	Classical		✓	✓			
Stratling et al.	2012	Integrity & Benevolence	Neoclassical		✓			✓	
Wang, Yeung, and Zhang	2011	Competence	Classical				✓		
Woolthius et al.	2005	Composite	Classical		✓	✓	✓		✓
Wu et al.	2007	Competence & Benevolence	Classical			✓*			
Zhang and Hu	2011	Composite	Classical	✓		✓*			
Zhang and Zhou	2013	Relationship	Classical			✓			✓
Zhao and Wang	2011	Benevolence	Classical			✓			
Zhou and Poppo	2010	Integrity	Neoclassical			✓			

14

THE CONTRIBUTIONS OF ATTRIBUTION THEORIES TO TRUST RESEARCH

Edward C. Tomlinson

Introduction

The term *attribution* refers to an individual's suspected or inferred cause of a behaviour or event (Fiske & Taylor, 2013). Social psychologists have developed a variety of attribution theories that seek to explain the cognitive process individuals use to explain why events occur in their social environment. This chapter highlights the social-psychological basis for understanding why attributions are central to trust dynamics. Specifically, I provide an overview of attribution theories that have been invoked in trust research and review the trust literature in terms of how these theories have provided a framework for understanding trust development, decline and repair. I conclude with a brief summary and proposed agenda for future research based on current gaps in this literature.

In one of the seminal accounts of attribution theories, Kelley (1967) asserted their obvious relevance to trust research. Indeed, the nexus is compelling. As Kramer (1999) asserted, the 'interaction histories [between actor and observer] give decision makers information that is useful in assessing others' dispositions, intentions and motives. This information, in turn, provides a basis for drawing inferences regarding their trustworthiness and for making predictions about their future behaviour' (p. 575). Molm, Takahashi and Peterson (2000) view trust itself as 'expectations that an exchange partner will behave benignly, based on the attribution of positive dispositions and intentions to the partner in a situation of uncertainty and risk' (p. 1402). An attributional approach can be useful in explaining where interpersonal trust begins in a relationship and what causes it to change over time (Lewicki et al., 2006; Fulmer & Gelfand, 2012).

For this chapter, I considered several criteria for inclusion. First, I confined my review to research that deals with interpersonal trust, as opposed to trust in a collective (e.g. group: Kramer, 1994), entity (e.g. organization: Vlachos et al., 2009), or object (e.g. technological tools: Wang & Benbasat, 2008). Second, I only review research situated in an organizational (e.g. workplace) context, as opposed to other contexts (e.g. romantic relationships: Rempel et al., 1985).

Finally, during the course of preparing this chapter, I became aware of several instances where researchers (1) did not use the term 'attribution' correctly, (2) only grounded their analysis by referring to 'attribution theory' in a generic sense (ostensibly unaware that there are actually a variety of specific attribution theories), or (3) referred to a specific attribution theory, but appeared to misunderstand and hence misapply that theory to trust dynamics. I only included work that refers to the attribution construct as it has been defined by attribution theorists, and is grounded in a specific attribution theory. I now proceed to review trust research that has invoked a specific attribution theory as a key framework; I organize this trust research according to whether it focuses on trust development, decline, or repair.

Attribution theories as a framework in trust research

Throughout the course of everyday life, we encounter many effects that prompt us to determine their respective causes, especially when encountering an event that is both unexpected and negative (Wong & Weiner, 1981). This fundamental urge is ultimately goal-driven: to better predict and control or adapt to future events, we must understand what caused similar events in the past (Heider, 1958; Jones & Davis, 1965; Kelley, 1967). Social psychologists have developed several theories that attempt to model how individuals interpret causal information to yield attributions, treating this as a generally rational information processing endeavour. They have also developed theories that describe how certain biases can interfere with this process (Kelley & Michela, 1980). In both cases, theoretical attention has been devoted to understanding how individuals use information to draw causal attributions, and how they will subsequently react (e.g. emotionally, behaviourally) based upon the conclusions they reach (Kelley & Michela, 1980). I begin with attribution theories using the rational information processing approach, and review their inclusion in research on trust development, decline and repair.

Heider's attribution theory

Fritz Heider initially proposed (Heider, 1944) and subsequently developed (Heider, 1958) the earliest articulation of an attribution theory, and asserted that the actions of others can be attributed to factors within the actor (e.g. ability) or to factors operating outside of the actor (e.g. another individual, or some environmental cause). This dichotomy has come to be known as locus of causality (Weiner, 1979). The conceptual distinction between internal and external locus of causality formed the key foundation for subsequent attribution theories.

Trust development

The earliest empirical study to apply attribution theory to trust was conducted by Strickland (1958). Based on Heider's (1944) theory, Strickland posited that when an observer views an actor's trustworthy behaviour as internal (i.e. indicative of the actor's true motives), this will lead to the observer's trust in the actor. However, the same behaviour – if seen as the product of external forces influencing the actor – will lead to greater distrust and monitoring (cf. Ferrin et al., 2007a; De Jong and Dirks, 2012). A clear example of this dynamic is evident in supervisor-subordinate dyads, where the supervisor faces a dilemma: while the supervisor would like to know the extent to which a subordinate will behave in a trustworthy fashion (to work diligently without supervision), the supervisor's act of monitoring actually inhibits the collection of necessary information. As Strickland explains, 'a supervisor (or any superordinate) cannot know first-hand the nature of the loyalty of his subordinates until he perceives that they have had an opportunity to be disloyal' (p. 213). The findings generally supported the notion that more highly monitored subordinates received less trust than less monitored subordinates (despite identical work performance). This finding was replicated in two subsequent experiments (Kruglanski, 1970; Strickland et al., 1976).

Thomas and Ravlin (1995) were also interested in the supervisor-subordinate dyad, but relied on Heider's (1958) locus of causality distinction to examine subordinates' intention to trust a foreign manager in a multinational subsidiary. Their results indicated that subordinates were more likely to report trusting intentions toward a foreign manager when that manager's adaptation to the subordinates' culture was attributed to the manager's internal disposition. In a twist, however, they also predicted and found that the foreign manager's adaptation was less likely to generate an internal attribution (presumably because such frame-breaking behaviour is viewed as contrary to stereotypic expectations, and hence viewed as less diagnostic of the manager's true disposition).

Six (2007) developed a theory of interpersonal trust development that relies in part on attributional processes. Based on relational signalling theory, she argues that trust development depends in part on the trustor's perceptions of the degree to which the trustee intends to honour and maintain trust in the relationship. Such a positive signal derives from the perception that the trustee has made some personal sacrifice in order to contribute to the trustor's well-being. Specifically, when this signal is attributed to the trustee's stable dispositional tendencies (Heider, 1958), the trustor will confer greater trust (see also Six et al., 2010).

Ferrin, Bligh, and Kohles (2008) developed the perceived trustworthiness-cooperation spiral model of trust development. In this model, they posited that 'the actor's perceptions of the partner's trustworthiness cause the actor to behave cooperatively toward the partner; the partner then observes the actor's cooperation, and consequently perceives the actor as more trustworthy. Simultaneously or sequentially to this effect, the partner's perceptions of the actor's trustworthiness cause the partner to behave cooperatively toward the actor, which in turn leads the actor to perceive the partner as more trustworthy' (p. 164). They invoked Heider's (1958) theory to explain why one party's cooperation would influence the other party's trust perceptions. Recognizing that interpersonal relationships provide a mixed-motive context (i.e. both parties are simultaneously motivated to cooperate with each other to reap benefits unavailable when acting independently, yet pressured to defect in order for one to obtain a personal gain at the other's expense) suggesting an external cause of cooperation, this is also liable to be seen as a more ambiguous (due to *mixed* motives) and less likely cause. In this case, the other's cooperative behaviour is more likely to be attributed to an internal cause (i.e. indicative of the other party's trustworthiness). Ferrin and colleagues tested this trustworthiness-cooperation spiral model in interpersonal dyads and found results consistent with their predictions.

Trust decline

I did not find any trust decline research that invoked Heider's attribution theory.

Trust repair

Dirks et al. (2011) have examined the efficacy of both substantive and non-substantive (i.e. verbal apology) efforts to repair trust after a violation. Based on Heider's (1958) theory, their hypothesis development initially focused on organizing plausible substantive efforts into the degree to which they are directed at dispositional or situational causes of the trust violation. To illustrate, offering penance (i.e. financial reparation) to the trustor for the harm inflicted should demonstrate repentance (i.e. that the trustee has reformed his formerly untrustworthy disposition).

In contrast, submitting to regulation of his behaviour should indicate prevention via new rules and monitoring that works to prevent situational causes of violations in the future.

Continuing the theme of repentance, Desmet, De Cremer and van Dijk (2011a) drew from Heider's theory to argue that it is not financial reparation per se that affects perceived repentance, but the offender's voluntary (as opposed to compelled) offer of compensation. In other words, only acts seen as freely chosen can represent one's actual intentions.

Summary

Taken together, the results suggest that trust develops when trustworthy behaviour is regarded as due to factors that are internal to the trustee. Trust development is attenuated to the extent that attributions are made to an external cause. Furthermore, Heider's distinction between internal and external locus of causality has provided important conceptual tools in trust repair research with implications for what factors might contribute to an internal (versus external) attribution for behaviour, and for what these attributions suggest for how trust repair can be optimized.

Jones and Davis's correspondent inference theory

Jones and Davis (1965) theorized that observers attempt to discern the intentions motivating how actors behave to determine the stable dispositional tendencies of those actors. That is, when we see what an individual does, we may make a *correspondent inference* regarding that individual's chronic traits (i.e. an internal locus of causality). Jones and Davis posited several diagnostic cues that individuals use when determining if an individual's action implicates internal (dispositional) or external (situational) factors. To illustrate, they describe the choice an actor makes between two alternatives as more indicative of his/her disposition when the chosen alternative has a unique effect (referred to as a non-common effect) that the unchosen alternative does not. In addition, behaviour that is low in social desirability, inconsistent with social role expectations, and unconstrained by the situation is more likely to result in a dispositional attribution.

Trust development

Tillman, Lawrence and Daspit (2014) examined how the perceived motive for performing organizational citizenship behaviours (OCBs) affected various indicators of interpersonal relationship quality with a co-worker, including trust. They invoked Jones and Davis's (1965) theory to justify the relevance of the actor's perceived intent when engaging in OCBs, and posited that the positive relationship between OCBs and an observer's trust in the actor would be stronger when the attributed intent of the actor is selfless as opposed to selfish.

Trust decline

Malhotra and Murnighan (2002) considered trust decline. Specifically, they examined the impact of contracts being removed, either because the trustee did not choose a contract or because one was no longer allowed. Trust declined significantly when binding contracts were removed (regardless of the reason). However, the removal of nonbinding contracts only led to a decline in trust when the trustee chose not to use the contract; there was no decline when the contract was no longer allowed due to the experimental procedure. This corresponds to the causal attribution rationale used by Blount (1995), who asserted that unfavourable outcomes are more likely to be accepted when attributed to an environmental as opposed to a social source; the social source (i.e. a human interaction partner) can be seen as acting with intent to pursue his/her own self-interest (Buss, 1978, 1979; Jones & Davis, 1965), whereas an environmental cause cannot.

Trust repair

Basford, Offermann and Behrend (2014) studied the use of apologies by supervisors to repair damaged trust with their subordinates. They hypothesized that the degree to which supervisors were seen as trustworthy and caring before the violation predicted the perceived sincerity of an apology after the violation. They invoked correspondent inference theory (Jones & Davis, 1965) to predict that sincere apologies (as opposed to insincere and no apology conditions) would facilitate post-violation trust via two routes: (1) sincere apologies indicate the supervisor's humility, which subsequently enhances perceived transformational leadership, and (2) sincere apologies lead the subordinate to forgive the supervisor. In either case, a sincere apology is posited to influence the degree to which subordinates infer that the violation reflects the supervisor's underlying disposition. That is, by offering a sincere apology, the supervisor may portray the cause as less internal to him/herself (because an apology shows that the offence was caused by a person split into two halves: one who has committed a terrible act, but also one who has learned from this mistake: cf. Goffman (1971)), that the harm inflicted was unintentional, and that the supervisor is also suffering as a result (via the expression of remorse). Their results supported these predictions.

Summary

Jones and Davis highlighted the role of an actor's perceived intent when observing a behaviour and attributing it to either internal or external factors. Trust research has demonstrated that perceived intent matters in developing trust, weakening trust and repairing trust. This research has also identified circumstances that ostensibly signal one's intentions (i.e. choice behaviour to not renew a contract, to provide a sincere apology).

Kelley's covariation theory

Kelley's (1967) *covariation theory* advanced a series of factors that prescribe how individuals should validate tentative causal attributions regarding locus of causality. Essentially, one experiences an effect which may vary in terms of (1) how the effect is experienced by his Person compared to other persons who may be exposed to the effect, (2) how the effect might vary due to the Entity (i.e. the object or person giving rise to the effect) and (3) how dependent the effect is on Time period or Modality (or simply, the particular circumstances).

Thus, in this analysis, an attribution can be made to oneself, to the entity, or to the particular circumstances surrounding the effect. Kelley argues that causal information is analysed along three specific informational factors that accompany an effect to determine the locus of causality attribution: consensus, distinctiveness and consistency. One becomes more confident in an Entity attribution (i.e. the cause is internal to the entity) when consensus, distinctiveness and consistency are all high. Other combinations of these factors may point to an external attribution, and/or a joint attribution of causality (e.g. more than one person is responsible for causing the effect). Note that Kelley's covariation theory requires multiple observations of an actor, whereas Jones and Davis's correspondent inference theory is relevant for situations involving a single observation (Kelley, 1973; Ross, 1977).

Trust development

Malhotra and Murnighan (2002) invoked Kelley's (1967) covariation theory. Although their study was situated in the type of contractual agreement (binding or nonbinding) between parties, the core idea mirrored earlier work on supervisors and their subordinates (which were predicated on Heider's theory) insofar as trustworthy behaviour cannot be attributed to the other party unless that party's actions are seen as freely chosen instead of situationally constrained. Therefore, these authors reasoned that binding contracts generate situational (or external) attributions for a partner's compliant behaviour and actually inhibit the development of trust. Because binding contracts are legally enforceable, most individuals who enter into such a contractual agreement would be expected to comply with their obligation (i.e. high consensus). In contrast, nonbinding contracts allow compliant behaviour to be attributed to the partner's trustworthy disposition (an internal attribution).

Trust decline

Elangovan and colleagues (2007) were concerned with trust erosion in predicting the likelihood of recurring trust violations. They employed Kelley's (1967) constructs of consistency and distinctiveness to inform how trustors would develop attributions regarding the stability (from Weiner's (1986) theory, reviewed subsequently) of the violation's cause. Specifically, trust erosion is posited to be greater when the trustor attributes the cause of the violation as stable (e.g. the trustee has repeatedly committed the same violation against the trustor, has committed this violation against others, etc.). Empirical support was presented in support of these predictions.

Trust repair

Lindskold (1978) analysed Osgood's (1962) graduated and reciprocated initiatives in tension reduction (GRIT) proposal in terms of trust repair. Osgood developed the GRIT proposal during the Cold War between the United States and the Soviet Union on the premise that it could facilitate a reverse arms race to de-escalate conflict between these nations. Briefly, the GRIT proposal is initiated when one of the conflicting parties issues a general statement to the other indicating a desire to de-escalate conflict and repair trust. In this context, this party announces specific, unilateral and unconditional initiatives to serve that general objective; these initiatives are then carried out in a verifiable manner. Reciprocation by the other party is invited yet not demanded; in fact, unilateral initiatives should continue regardless of the other's reciprocation (unless the other party engages in an escalatory move, in which case the initiating party should match that escalation level precisely and then restart the GRIT process). When reciprocation occurs, the initiating party should continue with new, iteratively larger conciliatory initiatives. Lindskold (1978) reviewed the experimental research on interpersonal cooperation in mixed-motive conflicts to test the social psychological principles embedded in the GRIT proposal, and invoked Kelley's covariation theory as a theoretical framework to illustrate how trustworthiness attributions can be enhanced in the wake of a conflict.

For example, making a general statement on the desire for reconciliation, articulating specific conciliatory initiatives, and engaging in behaviours that match these statements affects the other party's sense of consistency. When these statements and behaviours (and their alignment with each other) occur in the presence of other parties, this should also give rise to consensus. Because reactions to conflict do not normally evoke conciliatory speech and actions, and because the initiating party invites verification to demonstrate extraordinary truthfulness, the initiating party may also be seen as behaving in a distinctive manner.

Summary

There appears to be a tendency in trust research to employ covariation theory incompletely or inaccurately. Covariation theory states that locus of causality is determined by more than consensus alone (cf. Malhotra & Murnighan, 2002). It should also be noted that covariation theory uses consistency and distinctiveness to determine locus of causality, not stability (cf. Elangovan et al., 2007). Finally, caution is warranted in accepting Lindskold's (1978) interpretations, as the studies he reviewed actually measured cooperative versus competitive choices in Prisoner's Dilemma and similar games, rather than trust per se. It should also be noted that this review largely entails a post hoc set of rationales for the findings (i.e. the primary studies he reviewed did not set out to test attribution theory as a means of trust repair). He also appears to have mis-applied the theory's conceptualization of consistency and consensus. Consistency in this context would involve persistent efforts to unilaterally initiate conflict de-escalation, not alignment between words and actions per se. Similarly, consensus would involve the initiating party demonstrating de-escalating behaviour to others with whom he was in conflict as well.

Kelley's discounting/augmentation principles

Kelley is also credited with two other major attribution concepts. The first relates to how individuals are posited to weight causal information (Kelley, 1971a). The *discounting principle* states that individuals will give less weight to one perceived cause when other, more plausible causes are recognized possibilities. The *augmentation principle* relies on the distinction between facilitating and inhibiting causes (i.e. the former is a cause that encourages the effect, and the latter is a cause that suppresses the effect), and states that individuals will give more importance to the diagnostic value of a facilitating cause when other plausible, inhibiting causes are acknowledged.

Trust development

Korsgaard, Brodt, and Whitener (2002) examined how employees regard the trustworthiness of their managers and they invoked Kelley's augmentation and discounting principles to posit that the relationship between managerial trustworthy behaviour and blame attributions is moderated by the perceived fairness of HR policies, such that when HR policies are viewed as fair, there is ambiguity in explaining the manager's trustworthy behaviour (it could be due to the manager's actual trustworthy intent, or to conformity with the policies). However, when HR policies are viewed as relatively unfair, managerial trustworthy behaviour will be attributed as actually reflecting the manager's internal disposition. Thus, the negative relationship between managerial trustworthiness behaviour and blame attributions should be the strongest when HR policies are deemed to be unfair, because this situation creates the context in which the manager's trustworthy intent can be unambiguously assessed. Their results supported these predictions.

Choi (2014) invoked Kelley's (1973) discounting principle to predict how the use of a signing bonus from the employer would predict subsequent trust from employees. Specifically, when the employer grants a signing bonus to a new employee, that employee is more likely to reciprocate with higher trust (and actual work effort) when there is an excess supply of workers. This argument rests on the premise that there are a greater number of plausible attributions available when there is an excess demand for workers compared to when there is an excess supply of workers: 'while workers may attribute a signing bonus offer to the employer's trust in them in both labour market conditions, when there is an excess demand for labour, workers may also attribute the signing bonus offer to the employer's desire to avoid getting shut out of the market' (p. 550). Choi presented evidence to support this prediction.

Trust decline

I did not find any trust decline research that invoked Kelley's discounting/augmentation principles.

Trust repair

The review by Lindskold (1978) discussed earlier also included logic related to the discounting principle. A dispositional attribution is augmented when the initiating party invites (as opposed to demands) reciprocation due to the inherent vulnerability that is assumed. The voluntary willingness to submit to verification avoids the initiating party's dispositional trustworthiness from being discounted by the sense that verification has been compelled by some external source.

Kim et al. (2006) focused on comparing two types of apologies in predicting trust repair: one with an internal attribution that admitted responsibility, and one with an external attribution that deflected personal culpability. Based on the discounting principle, they posited that in the case of an integrity violation an admission of guilt should outweigh a signal of redemption (thus calling for an external attribution apology that discounts (Kelley, 1973) the trustor's internal factors by pointing to the influence of external factors).

Summary

Research on this attribution approach echoes conclusions from work reviewed earlier: an observer cannot truly evaluate an actor's dispositional qualities when situational factors/constraints loom large.

Kelley's causal schema theory

Kelley also posited that individuals develop and rely on *causal schemas* (1971b). He defines a causal schema as 'a general conception the person has about how certain kinds of causes interact to produce a specific kind of effect' (p. 151). In other words, these schemata reflect individual lay theories on how certain effects likely result from certain combinations of causal factors, and allow individuals to generate causal inferences in the face of limited information. This attribution process stands in stark contrast to his earlier covariation theory. The latter is a full-scale, in-depth causal analysis undertaken when observers have sufficient ability and motivation to perform it; the former is more likely in more common, everyday situations where the event is not as important to understand and the time to undertake a thorough causal investigation is not available. Thus, causal schemas allow observers to achieve an 'economical and fast attributional analysis, by providing a framework within which bits and pieces of relevant information can be fitted in order to draw reasonably good causal inferences' (p. 152).[1] For example, Kelley articulated the multiple necessary causal schema, in which multiple causes are responsible for an effect (e.g. winning a race against other adults requires both ability and effort), and the multiple sufficient causal schema, in which at least one of multiple causes is responsible for an effect (e.g. winning a race against a child requires either some ability or some effort).

Trust development

Ferrin and Dirks (2003) drew from multiple attribution concepts to predict how reward system structures lead to trust development among workers. Briefly, reward systems can be cooperative (where payments are based on joint performance, such that workers have an incentive to cooperate with each other), competitive (where payments are only administered to the highest performing worker), or a hybrid that mixes these two approaches. They relied upon Kelley's (1973) causal schema theory to predict that the reward structure would influence individuals' perceptions of team performance, such that cooperative rewards should be mentally associated with the perception of higher dyad performance; viewing the dyad as a high-performing team, in turn, should lead to the sense that the partners trust each other. Their study found that reward structures did influence trust development via causal schemas.

Six (2007) also points to Kelley's (1973) causal schemata, noting that the trustor's a priori causal beliefs affect how he/she will interpret the trustor's behaviour. That is, she suggests the trustor's causal schema will 'determine her initial attitude which in turn will influence action. The individual's initial beliefs will or will not be confirmed through the impact of her actions on the other person' (p. 291).

Trust decline

I did not find any trust decline research that invoked Kelley's causal schema theory.

Trust repair

I did not find any trust repair research that invoked Kelley's causal schema theory.

Summary

The causal schema theory has rarely been invoked in trust research. When it has been employed, researchers have not applied the specific schemas identified in the original formulation of the theory.

Reeder and Brewer's schematic model of dispositional attribution

Reeder and Brewer (1979) further extended the study of causal schemas. Specifically, they criticized the Jones and Davis (1965) and Kelley (1967) theories for assuming that the attribution process is the same regardless of the attribute being inferred. In response, they presented a theory specifying how different dispositional qualities of an actor are grounded in an observer's schemas. As opposed to Kelley's causal schema theory which focused on assumed patterns of causal factors necessary to produce a given effect, Reeder and Brewer's *schematic model of dispositional attribution* deals with observers' preconceptions regarding 'the categories of behaviour that are believed likely to occur given each of the various dispositional levels' (p. 64). Simply stated, observers form prior expectations (i.e. schemas) for how a range of dispositions are associated with a range of potential behaviours by an actor. Once an actor is observed engaging in a specific behaviour, social perceivers work backwards to determine the dispositional influence and its implications. For example, hierarchically restrictive schemas predict that the most extreme behaviour an actor demonstrates will determine his/her disposition on that attribute, according to the nature of the given attribute. So actors with high ability are capable of behaviour across this attribute continuum based on motivation or other situational factors, whereas those with low ability are confined to the lower end of the performance distribution. The result is that '[e]xceptionally good performance is always informative of a correspondent disposition, but poor or mediocre performance can lead to correspondent inference only under circumstances that provide both motivation and opportunity for high-level performance' (p. 68). On the other hand, actors with a low degree of honesty are capable of behaviour spanning this entire attribute continuum based on contextual factors (like monitoring, incentives, etc.), whereas those with high honesty will refrain from dishonesty in any situation. The result is that a 'single dishonest behaviour is sufficient to produce a confident attribution that the actor is dishonest. Honest behaviour, on the other hand, will be informative in some situations but not others' (p. 68).

Trust development

I did not find any trust development research that invoked the schematic model of dispositional attribution.

Trust decline

I did not find any trust decline research that invoked the schematic model of dispositional attribution.

Trust repair

Kim, Ferrin, Cooper and Dirks (2004) developed their hypotheses on the schematic model of dispositional attribution. Drawing on Reeder and Brewer's (1979) work on hierarchically restricted schemas, they noted the discrepancy in how observers perceive and react to actors' competence versus integrity (which are both key aspects of trustworthiness: Mayer et al., 1995). Specifically, Reeder and Brewer argued that attributions of competence and integrity are a product of hierarchically restrictive schemas. Those who possess a high degree of competence might actually manifest behaviour anywhere along the performance continuum (e.g. even high performers can have a bad day), yet those with a low degree of competence are not perceived to be capable of high performance. In contrast, those with a high degree of integrity will behave honestly in all situations, yet those with a low degree of integrity will occasionally behave honestly (e.g. if they are subjected to surveillance). As Kim and colleagues summarize, 'hitting a home run once makes us home run hitters in the eyes of others even if we strike out afterward' yet 'embezzling from a company once makes us an embezzler even if we do not engage in additional thefts.' They predicted that this distinction in how a trust violation is perceived would lead to differential responses to two common strategies used by offenders to repair trust: apology and denial. Because a single competence violation is insufficient to establish the trustee's future intent, an apology (which signals remorse and a commitment to do better) should be associated with greater trust repair than a denial (which fails to communicate redemption). In comparison, because a single integrity violation may indeed be viewed as an ominous forecast of the trustee's future intent, a denial (which denies guilt) should be associated with greater trust repair than an apology (which admits guilt). The results supported their hypotheses.

A follow-up study added reticence as another potential response (Ferrin et al., 2007b). In addition to replicating the original study findings grounded in the schematic model of dispositional attribution, the authors found that reticence is suboptimal for an integrity violation because of its failure to acknowledge guilt, and also suboptimal for a competence violation because it fails to signal redemption.

As mentioned above, these authors conducted a separate study (Kim et al., 2006) that focused on comparing two types of apologies: one with an internal attribution that admitted responsibility, and one with an external attribution that deflected personal culpability (cf. Tomlinson et al., 2004). Once again, these authors primarily grounded their hypotheses in the schematic model of dispositional attribution. Their findings revealed that trust was repaired to a greater extent when apologies with an internal attribution were given for competence violations, and when apologies with an external attribution were given for integrity violations. Their results are consistent with the argument that in the case of a competence violation the signal of redemption should outweigh the admission of guilt (calling for an internal attribution apology), and in the case of an integrity violation an admission of guilt should outweigh a signal of redemption (calling for an external attribution apology).

The Dirks et al. (2011) study mentioned above also referred to the schematic model of dispositional attribution in order to posit that penance and regulation should repair trust for competence violations, but not for integrity violations. They also added a condition to compare the response to an apology, which is a non-substantive effort that may also convey repentance. Taken together, their findings indicated that penance, regulation and apologies can all facilitate trust repair for competence violations to the extent that they are perceived by the trustor as an expression of repentance.

A separate study by Desmet, De Cremer and van Dijk (2011b) examined the degree of financial reparation offered by an offender in the wake of a violation. While one might simply expect that more reparation leads to greater trust repair, these authors drew from the schematic model of dispositional attribution to posit that this effect would be qualified by perceptions of the offender's intent. That is, 'when a violation can be clearly attributed to bad intent, victims will discount this negative information more strongly [citation omitted] and hence will be less sensitive to the financial compensation and the goodwill that its size conveys' (p. 77). Their results across four studies supported this hypothesis.

Summary

The schematic model of dispositional attribution has been extensively (and fruitfully) applied to the issue of trust repair. Whether a trust violation is understood as a result of competence or integrity carries significant implications for an appropriate reparative effort.

Weiner's attribution theory

Weiner's attribution theory (Weiner, 1985; Weiner, 1986) makes several key contributions that go beyond the aforementioned approaches. First, he proposes two additional causal attribution dimensions beyond the locus of causality dimension that dominates prior work. These dimensions refer to how individuals evaluate information to assess how *controllable* and how *stable* an inferred cause is deemed to be. In terms of controllability, for example, a car accident might be caused by a driver who is using his cell phone (controllable) or who experiences a heart attack (uncontrollable). Similarly, the driver may have experienced a routine seizure (stable) or a very unusual and atypical distraction from a passenger (unstable). Second, this causal analysis, in turn, is predicted to generate specific emotions (that vary based on locus, controllability, stability), future expectations (based largely on stability) and subsequent behavioural reactions.

Even though the original theory was situated in an achievement (i.e. intrapersonal) context, it has been fruitfully extended to interpersonal situations as well (e.g. Takaku, 2001; Takaku, 2006).

Trust development

I did not find any trust development research that invoked Weiner's attribution theory.

Trust decline

Brockner and Siegel (1996) argued that a trust violation due to a lack of effort to honour trust should be regarded as more detrimental to trust than a trust violation due to an inability to honour trust. This is because a lack of effort is regarded as more controllable than a lack of ability (Weiner, 1986).

Tomlinson and Mayer (2009) focused predominantly on trust repair (and will be more extensively reviewed in the next section). However, their point of departure was the argument that in order to repair trust, it is first necessary to fully understand the reasons for its decline. Accordingly, they presented a causal attribution analysis of negative outcomes in trusting relationships based on Weiner (1986). Tomlinson and Mayer argued that not every negative outcome in a trusting relationship will be seen as a trust violation. Instead, they presented a parsimonious set of potential attributions for a negative outcome: the trustee's ability, benevolence or integrity (Mayer et al., 1995), or some other factor that is not connected with the trustee. They proceeded to explain how these various attributions are evaluated in terms of locus of causality, controllability and stability, with implications for the decline of trust. In short, if the cause of the negative outcome is regarded as external to the trustee (e.g. due to some other actor or the situation), then the trustee's ability, benevolence and integrity are not impugned and trust will not decline.

Trust repair

Tomlinson and Mayer (2009) applied Weiner's (1986) causal attribution theory to the problem of trust repair, and argued that only negative outcomes attributed as internal to the trustee would be viewed as trust violations (and thus invoke a need for repair). Tomlinson and Mayer went on to explain how if the cause is deemed to be internal to the trustee, this would impugn either the trustee's ability, benevolence or integrity; the ascribed trustworthiness dimension would then be analysed in terms of controllability (the extent to which the trustee is judged to have volitional control) and stability (the extent to which the trustworthiness dimension is regarded as malleable or unchanging). However, Tomlinson and Mayer argued that the same attribution diagnosis indicating a need to repair trust is relevant to the repair itself. Initial attributions by the trustor can be modified on the basis of new information (Krull, 1993). Stage models of the attribution process depict a sequence whereby observers initially categorize actors' behaviour, infer the actors' corresponding disposition, and then revise that inference based on situational factors (e.g. Gilbert et al., 1988). Thus, initial attributions (and the negative, specific emotions that accompany them) can be altered based on reparative efforts by the trustee. To the extent that the trustee can convey that the cause of the negative outcome is indeed external, uncontrollable and/or unstable (via social accounts and/or substantive actions), initial attributions can be revised in a way that facilitates trust repair. Because Weiner emphasized that stability attributions are the key driver of future expectancies, Tomlinson and Mayer argued that it should be the most central attribution dimension with regard to trust repair.

Summary

It is interesting to consider that the focal construct of repentance used by Dirks and his colleagues (2011) and Desmet and his colleagues (2011a) seems strikingly similar to the stability dimension that is situated squarely in Weiner's theory. A negative outcome due to an unstable cause is highly compatible with repentance, which Merriam-Webster defines as the turning away from sin and dedicating oneself to the amendment of one's life. The Tomlinson and Mayer model has been extended to account for how specific contextual factors (relationship dependence and offense severity) affect causal attributions for negative outcomes (Tomlinson, 2011). Overall, Weiner's model presents a more comprehensive portrayal of the attribution process than earlier theories, and appears to offer significant promise for trust research. However, empirical tests to date are lacking.

Fein and Hilton's suspicion theory

Fein and Hilton (1994) describe the *suspicion effect*: observers engage in more careful attributional processing when they become aware that an actor potentially has situationally grounded ulterior motives. In the absence of suspicion, an observer might construe the actor's behaviour as a reflection of his/her true disposition (Jones & Davis, 1965). However, Fein and Hilton describe several studies showing that observers make fewer dispositional inferences when they become aware of the possibility of an actor's ulterior motives. This effect is apparently because such attributional ambiguity regarding locus of causality prompts more thorough attributional effort and reduces the certainty with which a causal inference is reached (Fein, 1996). Nonetheless, the suspicion effect has the tendency to lead an observer to view the actor *more* negatively, especially when the actor's behaviour has personal implications for them. Fein and Hilton suggested that this is because 'the attributional thinking triggered by suspicion appears to cause perceivers to focus on the plausibility' of ulterior motives, and hence 'colour their perceptions of the actors' (p. 171).

Trust development

As reviewed earlier, Ferrin and Dirks (2003) drew from multiple attribution concepts to predict how reward system structures lead to trust development among workers. Recall that reward systems can be cooperative, competitive or a hybrid that mixes these two approaches. When under a competitive reward system, workers have an incentive to withhold and distort information. As one hypothesis, Ferrin and Dirks invoked the suspicion effect to predict that a partner's competitive behaviour would invoke suspicion that would lead to more thorough attributions, such that the fundamental attribution error (reviewed below) would be reduced (Fein, 1996). Yet, Ferrin and Dirks predicted that trust in the partner would nonetheless be inhibited, in this case as a direct result of the observer's suspicion of the partner's motives independently of the partner's behaviour. Their results indicated that reward structures did influence trust development via the suspicion effect.

Trust decline

I did not find any trust decline research that invoked Fein and Hilton's suspicion theory.

Trust repair

I did not find any trust repair research that invoked Fein and Hilton's suspicion theory.

Summary

This theory seems to have clear implications for trust decline and repair research, but has yet to be invoked in these research streams.

Bem's self-perception theory

Whereas the foregoing theories generally treat social perceivers as objective, rational information processors who systematically investigate the cause(s) of events like a detective attempting to solve a crime, another major stream of attribution research deals with predictable deviations from rationality. In other words, individuals may rely on judgemental heuristics that bias causal attributions, with implications for subsequent reactions. Bem's (1967) *self-perception theory* represents a unique attribution approach insofar as it predicts that individuals consider *their own* behaviour toward an entity and subsequently infer that *their* attitudes and beliefs toward the entity are consistent with that behaviour. That is, this theory seeks to explain how individuals explain the cause of their own behaviour. Also unlike prior approaches that primarily seek to attribute causes to either internal or external factors (e.g. Heider, 1958), Bem's theory attributes causes only to distinct types of external factors: the entity itself or the circumstances extrinsic to the entity. The theory predicts that individuals will 'infer their beliefs from their behaviour only when they have good reason to believe that their behaviour toward a stimulus [entity] is produced primarily by their feelings about the stimulus [entity]. When [they have] reason to believe that their behaviour was produced in large part by circumstantial factors extrinsic to the stimulus . . . a belief inference [does] not take place' (Nisbett & Valins, 1971, p. 66). Especially in relation to circumstances where pre-existing attitudes and internal cues are weak, this theory highlights the complex cognitive requirements of drawing attributions and individuals' willingness to employ mental shortcuts that hasten causal conclusions (Fiske & Taylor, 2013).

Trust development

In Ferrin and Dirks' (2003) study on reward system structures cited earlier, they drew from Bem's self-perception theory to predict that individuals would consider their own information sharing behaviours with their partner (elicited by the reward structure) to infer how much they trust their partner. They found that reward structures did influence trust development via self-perception. De Jong and Dirks (2012) drew from self-perception theory to argue that the monitoring of team members may lead one to conclude that those members are not trusted.

Trust decline

I did not find any trust decline research that invoked Bem's self-perception theory.

Trust repair

I did not find any trust repair research that invoked Bem's self-perception theory.

Summary

Self-perception theory has failed to play a prominent role in trust research to date.

Fundamental attribution error

The *fundamental attribution error* (Heider, 1958; Ross, 1977) refers to the tendency to over-estimate the influence of internal factors and under-estimate the influence of external factors when attributing the cause of others' behaviours. Jones and Davis (1965) label this phenomenon a *correspondence bias*, because observers tend to generate a correspondent inference that an actor's behaviour reflects his/her disposition, even when external forces are a more likely explanation. There is robust evidence of this bias in the attribution literature.

Trust development

Brockner and Siegel (1996) sought to explain the robust finding that distributive and procedural justice interact when predicting individuals' reactions to resource allocation decisions. That is, many studies have found that when procedural justice is low, individuals respond more positively when distributive justice is high; however, when procedural justice is high, the level of distributive justice is much less important in determining reactions. Stated differently, high procedural justice can mitigate otherwise negative reactions to low distributive justice. Brockner and Siegel argue that this moderated effect is not due to procedural justice per se, but rather '*the degree of trust engendered by procedural fairness*' [emphasis original] (p. 398) that interacts with distributive justice perceptions. Specifically, they contend that when individuals perceive high procedural fairness from a decision maker (i.e. the decision maker voluntarily enacts fair procedures), it leads to the attribution that the decision maker is trustworthy. This is because according to the fundamental attribution error, recipients of fair procedures are likely to attribute such treatment to the internal disposition of the decision maker. This, combined with structural elements that contribute to procedural fairness, creates a sense of stability: individuals view their experience of procedural justice 'as indicative of how they are likely to be treated in the future' (p. 403).

Returning to Ferrin and Dirks' (2003) study on reward system structures cited earlier, these researchers argued that when under a competitive reward system, workers have an incentive to withhold and distort information. Because of the fundamental attribution error, they predicted that individuals would attribute the cause of a partner's withholding and distortion of information as internal to the partner (and hence, trust the partner less), ignoring the more strongly implicated external cause (i.e. the competitive reward system structure). Their results did not support this prediction.

Six (2007) contends that when relationship partners are careful to avoid potential attribution errors (e.g. the fundamental attribution error), they can maximize trust development (see also Six et al., 2010). This would presumably apply to negative outcomes in the relationship.

Trust decline

I did not find any trust decline research that invoked the fundamental attribution error.

Trust repair

I did not find any trust repair research that invoked the fundamental attribution error.

Summary

Despite a large body of research on the fundamental attribution error, it has not been extensively explored in trust research. It seems that it would be particularly relevant to trust decline.

Actor-observer effect

A somewhat similar phenomenon is referred to as the *actor-observer effect* (Jones & Nisbett, 1971), whereby individuals tend to attribute others' behaviour to internal factors and their own behaviour to situational (external) factors. This tendency may be due to actors' more detailed knowledge of the circumstances surrounding their behaviour, and/or the differential salience of information available to actor versus observer (i.e. observers pay closer attention to the actor's behaviour and actors pay closer attention to the situation). The actor-observer effect appears to be more likely to emerge when attributing a negative (as opposed to positive) event (Malle, 2006).

Trust development

Sonenshein, Herzenstein, and Dholakia (2011) used an attribution theory lens to investigate how lenders form trustworthiness perceptions when making lending decisions regarding potential borrowers. That is, they considered how social accounts from borrowers may offer information that lenders use to assess borrower trustworthiness; they posited that certain combinations of social accounts (explanation-acknowledgement and explanation-denial) result in more favourable loan funding decisions due to how these accounts shape attributions, and hence, borrower trustworthiness. Based on the actor-observer effect, the authors noted that any negative information about the borrower (such as a low credit score) is likely to result in a negative dispositional attribution of that borrower, because the lender is less likely to have detailed situational information that may have contributed to the borrower's predicament. Combinations of social accounts provide the means for lenders to obtain this information, and allow for more positive attributions. In an acknowledgement, the borrower admits contributing to his prior financial difficulties (which should contribute to an internal attribution related to the borrower's integrity), and adding an explanation provides additional situational details that make lenders less likely to attribute the borrower's prior financial difficulties to his/her competence. A denial could either harm perceptions of trustworthiness (with the borrower seen as attempting to escape her culpability) or enhance them (i.e. contributing to one's integrity by disaffirming information that would impugn one's reputation). In this case, adding an explanation adds information that may imbue the denial with more credibility. Thus, the explanation-acknowledgement and explanation-denial account combinations are argued to positively affect borrower trustworthiness and ultimately, loan funding decisions. The authors found empirical support for these predictions.

Trust decline

I did not find any trust decline research that invoked the actor-observer effect.

Trust repair

I did not find any trust repair research that invoked the actor-observer effect.

Summary

Technically, the actor-observer effect involves a comparison in how attributions are reached for oneself in comparison to others. While Sonenshein et al. (2011) invoked the actor-observer effect, one wonders if the fundamental attribution error is more suitable for understanding their predictions and results.

Self-serving bias

The *self-serving bias* (Mezulis et al., 2004) refers to a tendency for individuals to take more responsibility for success than failure, such that their successes are attributed as more internal, stable and global than their failures. Meta-analytic investigations have verified this tendency and shown it to be robust and pervasive (e.g. Mezulis et al., 2004; Mullen & Riordan, 1988). It has been argued that this tendency is functional because it can protect one's ego and have motivational benefit (Fiske & Taylor, 2013). In fact, it has been shown to be positively related to a variety of mental and physical health outcomes (for a review, see Mezulis et al., 2004).

Trust development

I did not find any trust development research that invoked the self-serving bias.

Trust decline

Lee and Tiedens (2001) examined the self-serving bias, which prior research has often shown to be advantageous for those who convey external attributions when they are implicated in a negative event. However, because such social accounts for failure events connote the actor's lack of power in the situation, observers are likely to reject such explanations for actors in high-status roles. That is, when observers believe that actors do (or should) have the power to bring about a certain effect in their environment, and this effect fails to materialize, the actor's account offering a social account pointing to an external cause will lead observers to see him as more powerless and less credible. Supporting this prediction, the authors found that social accounts pointing to external causes were more negatively related to believability (i.e. perceived truthfulness, adequacy and trustworthiness) when actors had high (as opposed to low) status roles.

Trust repair

I did not find any trust repair research that invoked the self-serving bias.

Summary

Thus far, the self-serving bias has rarely been used in trust research. In the wake of a trust violation, it appears to point to a disconnect between how an offending trustee and a trustor will view and react to the same event.

Attribution style theory

Finally, *attribution style theory* explains the attribution process in terms of individual differences. Thus, the term *attributional style* refers to 'a tendency to make particular kinds of causal inference, rather than others, across different situations and across time' (Metalsky & Abramson, 1981, p. 38). For example, a pessimistic attribution style is reflected by attributing a negative event to internal, stable and global causes. Prior research has suggested that individual attribution style may vary across different situations.

Trust development

Hatzakis (2009) argues that '[i]n order to foster trust, it is first necessary to accurately *diagnose* [emphasis original] the current state of trust' (p. 448), and that attribution style theory can elucidate how this diagnosis occurs. Specifically, this theory suggests that individuals have a tendency to derive causal inferences in predictable patterns, with direct implications for trust. She asserts that spirals of trust (distrust) result from a tendency to frame trust-relevant events in a way that produces positive (negative) momentum. She drew from the trust/distrust literature to identify six states that reflect either trust or distrust, and then posited an attribution style corresponding to each state. For example, she identifies confidence as a state of trust based on positive evidence of trustworthiness. In the wake of a positive event, the attribution style tending to produce confidence would view the cause as (1) dispositional to the trustee (reflecting personal intentions) or situational (i.e. role-driven), (2) controllable, (3) stable and (4) global.

Trust decline

I did not find any trust decline research that invoked attribution style theory.

Trust repair

I did not find any trust repair research that invoked attribution style theory.

Summary

Attribution style research has not played a prominent role in trust research. Future trust research should empirically test Hatzakis's (2009) model of trust development, as well as explore the implications of attributional style for trust decline and repair.

Closing literature gaps in future research

Attribution theories have been used in trust research as early as 1958, yet studies integrating these two literatures have been few and far between (see also Ferrin & Dirks, 2003). Yet from the studies that have been reviewed here, it is obvious that attribution theories have provided an extremely appropriate and useful framework for trust research. Indeed, several concluding points can be made based on this review. First, there are some instances where we now appear to have a plethora of evidence on a particular attribution phenomenon (e.g. that trust for a trustee is more likely to develop when trustworthiness cannot be discounted due to a plausible external cause). Second, there are interesting patterns in extant trust research that should be explored. Specifically, are certain attribution theories more suitable for one aspect of trust research than others? Or is it possible that attribution theories that have dominated one part of the trust literature might be useful in others? For example, note that the schematic model of dispositional attribution has only been invoked in relation to trust repair, and that no trust repair research has invoked any theories pertaining to attribution biases. A third, and somewhat related observation is that there are many instances where specific attribution theories are conspicuously absent in trust development, decline or repair research streams. Hopefully this chapter provides a useful synopsis of attribution theories for researchers to use in developing and conducting future trust research.

During the process of preparing this chapter, I became aware of other issues that are worthwhile to note. First, as I mentioned at the outset, I found a number of studies that either did not use the term 'attribution' in the same way it is used in attribution research, did not invoke a specific attribution theory in their work, or simply referred to 'attribution theory' as a generic term (which is of course a misnomer, as there are multiple attribution theories). As a general rule in these cases, I believe those authors intuitively grasped the relevance of the attribution process to trust research, and that their work would have been enriched by a more systematic consideration of specific attribution theories. A second observation concerns the nature of the research that was incorporated into this chapter. Some of this cited work appeared in conceptual papers, and the key propositions still await empirical testing. But most of this research consists of empirical studies that primarily relied either on field surveys or laboratory experiments. And in most of these cases, the point of departure was in a brand-new relationship (e.g. an experimental game with an anonymous counterpart). Real-life trusting relationships often involve an established relationship history with a specific trustee, and interactions are situated in a particular context. This reminded me of an assertion made by Dirks, Lewicki and Zaheer (2009) that attribution theories are inadequate when dealing with the relationships between individuals and the context in which trust-relevant events occur. I have argued elsewhere (Tomlinson, 2011) that attribution theory can indeed be fruitfully extended in this manner, but a full resolution of this issue awaits empirical testing. Furthermore, it may be that the best way to address these matters is via qualitative research, as opposed to the more quantitative methods that have dominated past efforts to link attribution theories and trust dynamics.

Note

1   Because causal schemas appear to rely on 'satisficing', some may argue that this attributional approach should be classified with the attributional biases theories instead of with the rational information processing theories. In this chapter, my classification of causal schemas follows Kelley (1973).

References

Basford TE, Offermann LR and Behrend TS. (2014) Please accept my sincerest apologies: Examining follower reactions to leader apology. *Journal of Business Ethics* 119: 99–117.

Bem DJ. (1967) Self-perception: An alternative interpretation of cognitive dissonance phenomena. *Psychological Review* 74: 183–200.

Blount S. (1995) When social outcomes aren't fair: The effect of causal attributions on preferences. *Organizational Behavior and Human Decision Processes* 63: 131–144.

Brockner J and Siegel PA. (1996) Understanding the interaction between procedural and distributive justice: The role of trust. In: Kramer RM and Tyler TR (eds) *Trust in organizations: Frontiers of theory and research.* Thousand Oaks, CA: Sage, pp. 390–413.

Buss A. R. (1978) Causes and reasons in attribution theory: A conceptual critique. *Journal of Personality and Social Psychology* 36: 1311–1321.

Buss A. R. (1979) On the relationship between causes and reasons. *Journal of Personality and Social Psychology* 37: 1458–1464.

Choi J. (2014) Can offering a signing bonus motivate effort? Experimental evidence of the moderating effects of labor market competition. *The Accounting Review* 89: 545–570.

De Jong BA and Dirks KT. (2012) Beyond shared perceptions of trust and monitoring in teams: Implications of asymmetry and dissensus. *Journal of Applied Psychology* 97: 391–406.

Desmet PT, De Cremer D and Van Dijk E. (2011a) Trust recovery following voluntary or forced financial compensations in the trust game: The role of trait forgiveness. *Organizational Behavior and Human Decision Processes* 51: 267–273.

Desmet PT, De Cremer DE and van Dijk E. (2011b) In money we trust? The use of financial compensations to repair trust in the aftermath of a distributive harm. *Organizational Behavior and Human Decision Processes* 114: 75–86.

Dirks KT, Kim PH, Ferrin DL, et al. (2011) Understanding the effects of substantive responses on trust following a transgression. *Organizational Behavior and Human Decision Processes* 114: 87–103.

Elangovan AR, Auer-Rizzi W and Szabo E. (2007) Why don't I trust you now? An attributional approach to erosion of trust. *Journal of Managerial Psychology* 22: 4–24.

Fein S. (1996) Effects of suspicion on attributional thinking and the correspondence bias. *Journal of Personality and Social Psychology* 70: 1164–1184.

Fein S and Hilton JL. (1994) Judging others in the shadow of suspicion. *Motivation and Emotion* 18: 167–198.

Ferrin DL, Bligh MC and Kohles JC. (2007a) Can I trust you to trust me? A theory of trust, monitoring, and cooperation in interpersonal and intergroup relationships. *Group & Organization Management* 32: 465–499.

Ferrin DL, Bligh MC and Kohles JC. (2008) It takes two to tango: An interdependence analysis of the spiraling of perceived trustworthiness and cooperation in interpersonal and intergroup relationships. *Organizational Behavior and Human Decision Processes* 107: 161–178.

Ferrin DL and Dirks KT. (2003) The use of rewards to increase and decrease trust: Mediating processes and differential effects. *Organization Science* 14: 18–31.

Ferrin DL, Kim PH, Cooper CD, et al. (2007b) Silence speaks volumes: The effectiveness of reticence in comparison to apology and denial for repairing integrity- and competence-based trust violations. *Journal of Applied Psychology* 92(4): 893–908.

Fiske ST and Taylor SE. (2013) *Social cognition: From brains to culture.* Los Angeles, CA: Sage.

Fulmer CA and Gelfand MJ. (2012) At what level (and in whom) we trust: Trust across multiple organizational levels. *Journal of Management* 38: 1167–1230.

Gilbert DT, Pelham BW and Krull DS. (1988) On cognitive busyness: When person perceivers meet persons perceived. *Journal of Personality and Social Psychology* 54: 733–740.

Goffman E. (1971) *Relations in public: Microstudies of the public order.* New York: Basic Books.

Hatzakis T. (2009) Towards a framework of trust attribution styles. *British Journal of Management* 20: 448–460.

Heider F. (1944) Social perception and phenomenal causality. *Psychological Review* 51: 358–374.

Heider F. (1958) *The psychology of interpersonal relations.* New York: John Wiley.

Jones EE and Davis KE. (1965) From acts to dispositions: The attribution process in person perception. In: *Berkowitz L* (ed.) *Advances in experimental social psychology.* New York: Academic Press, 219–266.

Jones EE and Nisbett RE. (1971) The actor and the observer: Divergent perceptions of the causes of behavior. In: Jones EE, Kanouse EE, Kelley HH, et al. (eds) *Attribution: Perceiving the causes of behavior.* Morristown, NJ: General Learning Press, 79–94.

Kelley HH. (1967) Attribution theory in social psychology. In: Levine D (ed.) *Nebraska Symposium on Motivation 1967.* Lincoln: University of Nebraska Press, 192–238.

Kelley HH. (1971a) Attribution in social interaction. In: Jones EE, Kanouse EE, Kelley HH, et al. (eds) *Attribution: Perceiving the causes of behavior.* New York: General Learning Press, 1–26.

Kelley HH. (1971b) Causal schemata and the attribution process. In: Jones EE, Kanouse EE, Kelley HH, et al. (eds) *Attribution: Perceiving the causes of behavior.* Morristown, NJ: General Learning Press, 151–174.

Kelley HH. (1973) The processes of causal attribution. *American Psychologist* 28: 107–128.

Kelley HH and Michela JL. (1980) Attribution theory and research. *Annual Review of Psychology* 31: 457–501.

Kim PH, Dirks KT, Cooper CD, et al. (2006) When more blame is better than less: The implications of internal vs. external attributions for the repair of trust after a competence- v. integrity-based trust violation. *Organizational Behavior and Human Decision Processes* 99(1): 49–65.

Kim PH, Ferrin DL, Cooper CD, et al. (2004) Removing the shadow of suspicion: The effects of apology versus denial for repairing competence- versus integrity-based trust violations. *Journal of Applied Psychology* 89(1): 104.

Korsgaard MA, Brodt SE and Whitener EM. (2002) Trust in the face of conflict: The role of managerial trustworthy behavior and organizational context. *Journal of Applied Psychology* 87: 312–319.

Kramer RM. (1994) The sinister attribution error: Paranoid cognition and collective distrust in organizations. *Motivation and Emotion* 18: 199–230.

Kramer RM. (1999) Trust and distrust in organizations: Emerging perspectives, enduring questions. *Annual Review of Psychology* 50: 569–598.

Kruglanski AW. (1970) Attributing trustworthiness in supervisor-worker relations. *Journal of Experimental Social Psychology* 6: 214–232.

Krull DS. (1993) Does the grist change the mill? The effect of a perceiver's inferential goal on the process of social inferences. *Personality and Social Psychology Bulletin* 19: 340–348.

Lee F and Tiedens LZ. (2001) Who's being served? "Self-serving" attributions in social hierarchies. *Organizational Behavior and Human Decision Processes* 84: 254–287.

Lewicki RJ, Tomlinson EC and Gillespie N. (2006) Models of interpersonal trust development: Theoretical approaches, empirical evidence, and future directions. *Journal of Management* 32: 991–1022.

Lindskold S. (1978) Trust development, the GRIT proposal, and the effects of conciliatory acts on conflict and cooperation. *Psychological Bulletin* 85: 772–793.

Malhotra D and Murnighan JK. (2002) The effects of contracts on interpersonal trust. *Administrative Science Quarterly* 47: 534–559.

Malle BF. (2006) The actor-observer asymmetry in attribution: A (surprising) meta-analysis. *Psychological Bulletin* 132: 895–919.

Mayer RC, Davis JH and Schoorman FD. (1995) An integrative model of organizational trust. *Academy of Management Review* 20: 709–734.

Metalsky G and Abramson L. (1981) Attributional style: Toward a framework for conceptualization and assessment. In: Kendall P and Hollon S (eds) *Assessment strategies for cognitive-behavioral interventions*. New York: Academic Press, 13–58.

Mezulis AH, Abramson LY, Hyde JS, et al. (2004) Is there a universal positivity bias in attributions? A meta-analytic review of individual, developmental, and cultural differences in the self-serving attributional bias. *Psychological Bulletin* 130: 711–747.

Molm LD, Takahashi N and Peterson G. (2000) Risk and trust in social exchange: An experimental test of a classical proposition. *American Journal of Sociology* 105: 1396–1427.

Mullen B and Riordan CA. (1988) Self-serving attributions for performance in naturalistic settings: A meta-analytic review. *Journal of Applied Social Psychology* 18: 3–22.

Nisbett RE and Valins S. (1971) Perceiving the causes of one's own behavior. In: Jones EE, Kanouse EE, Kelley HH, et al. (eds) *Attribution: Perceiving the causes of behavior*. Morristown, NJ: General Learning Press, 63–78.

Osgood CE. (1962) *An alternative to war or surrender*. Urbana: University of Illinois Press.

Reeder GD and Brewer MB. (1979) A schematic model of dispositional attribution in interpersonal perception. *Psychological Review* 86: 61–79.

Rempel JK, Holmes JG and Zanna MP. (1985) Trust in close relationships. *Journal of Personality and Social Psychology* 49: 95–112.

Ross L. (1977) The intuitive psychologist and his shortcomings. In: Berkowitz L (ed.) *Advances in experimental social psychology*. New York: Academic Press, 173–220.

Six FE. (2007) Building interpersonal trust within organizations: A relational signalling perspective. *Journal of Management & Governance* 11: 285–309.

Six F, Nooteboom B and Hoogendoorn A. (2010) Actions that build interpersonal trust: A relational signalling perspective. *Review of Social Economy* 68: 285–315.

Sonenshein S, Herzenstein M and Dholakia UM. (2011) How accounts shape lending decisions through fostering perceived trustworthiness. *Organizational Behavior and Human Decision Processes* 115: 69–84.

Strickland LH. (1958) Surveillance and trust. *Journal of Personality* 26: 200–215.

Strickland LH, Barefoot JC and Hockenstein P. (1976) Monitoring behavior in the surveillance and trust paradigm. Representative *Research in Social Psychology* 7: 51–57.

Takaku S. (2001) The effects of apology and perspective taking on interpersonal forgiveness: A dissonance-attribution model of interpersonal forgiveness. *The Journal of Social Psychology* 141: 494–508.

Takaku S. (2006) Reducing road rage: An application of the dissonance-attribution model of interpersonal forgiveness. *Journal of Applied Social Psychology* 36: 2362–2378.

Thomas DC and Ravlin EC. (1995) Responses of employees to cultural adaptation by a foreign manager. *Journal of Applied Psychology* 80: 133–146.

Tillman CJ, Lawrence ER and Daspit JJ. (2014) A tale of perception: The role of perceived intent on OCBs and interpersonal relationships. *Journal of Behavioral and Applied Management* 15: 168–189.

Tomlinson EC. (2011) The context of trust repair efforts: Exploring the role of relationship dependence and outcome severity. *Journal of Trust Research* 1: 139–157.

Tomlinson EC, Dineen BR and Lewicki RJ. (2004) The road to reconciliation: Antecedents of victim willingness to reconcile following a broken promise. *Journal of Management* 30: 165–187.

Tomlinson EC and Mayer RC. (2009) The role of causal attribution dimensions in trust repair. *Academy of Management Review* 34: 85–104.

Vlachos PA, Tsamakos A, Vrechopoulos AP, et al. (2009) Corporate social responsibility: Attributions, loyalty, and the mediating role of trust. *Journal of the Academy of Marketing Science* 37: 170–180.

Wang W and Benbasat I. (2008) Attributions of trust in decision support technologies: A study of recommendation agents for e-commerce. *Journal of Management Information Systems* 24: 249–273.

Weiner B. (1979) A theory of motivation for some classroom experiences. *Journal of Educational Psychology* 71: 3–25.

Weiner B. (1985) An attributional theory of achievement motivation and emotion. *Psychological Review* 92: 548–573.

Weiner B. (1986) *An attributional model of motivation and emotion.* New York: Springer-Verlag.

Wong PTP and Weiner B. (1981) When people ask "why" questions, and the heuristics of an attributional search. *Journal of Personality and Social Psychology* 40: 650–663.

PART IV

Trust repair

In this part we specifically focus on the topic of trust breach and its repair to draw attention to work on this particular aspect of trust. These three chapters are designed to have resonance in terms of the concerns and issues raised through the violation of trust and thus the potential for its repair. We begin this part with Peter H. Kim's review of interpersonal trust repair. His approach identifies the major advances in the literature on trust and its repair, looking at the twin concerns of conceptualizations and influences, and then considering implications. The dynamic approach to this study is a critical matter with the importance of considering perspectives of both perpetrator and victim. He also considers the role of situational factors in transgressions before outlining an agenda for further work. This chapter links to many others, including Chapter 5 by Lyu and Ferrin, and Chapter 17 by Bies and colleagues' is also of relevance. Some of the foundation chapters, most notably Chapter 1 by van Knippenberg, Chapter 2 by Korsgaard and Chapter 4 by Sitkin and Bijlsma-Frankema would also be of use to those interested in this aspect of trust. Readers might also like to consider it alongside much of the levels of analysis and theories section, including Chapter 8 by Fulmer, Chapter 9 by Baer and Colquitt, Chapter 10 by Lind, Chapter 11 by Coyle-Shapiro and Diehl and Chapter 14 by Tomlinson. Key contexts might also emerge as significant, and so Part V in this book might be of use, too.

Nicole Gillespie and Sabina Siebert reflect on trust repair but from the organizational level of analysis. They look at problem specificity for this level of analysis and then distinguish between trust failures and trust repair considering the distinct nature and processes for interpersonal and organizational level repair. They consider different conceptual frameworks and models pertaining to organizational trust repair, and review selected relevant empirical studies. This chapter identifies and discusses the ontological and epistemological approaches that dominate the literature, and makes a case for more critical and radical perspectives that can deepen and extend our understanding.

We conclude this part with a chapter that takes a distinct view on trust repair by focusing on the issue of forgiveness in organizational settings. Robert J. Bies, Laurie J. Barclay, Maria F. Saldanha, Adam A. Kay and Thomas M. Tripp explore both trust and distrust to consider their distinct roles in enabling and shaping the possibility of forgiveness. They identify contexts in which the levels of distrust might not make this possible. This is a topic that Cherry (2012) has also considered in his book, which is critical of formal processes of forgiveness. It is would be valuable for those interested in this matter to ensure they also read Chapter 4 by Sitkin and

Bijlsma-Frankema, along with Chapter 1 by van Knippenberg and Chapter 2 by Korsgaard. Bies and colleagues examine whether forgiveness can serve as a contextual factor that might promote the restoration of trust, drawing on literature from a wider array of areas, including peace and reconciliation, and divinity. Importantly this chapter considers alternatives to forgiveness that draw on the more extensive conflict management literature.

Reference

Cherry, S. (2012). *Healing agony: Re-imagining forgiveness*. London: Continuum.

15

AN INTERACTIVE PERSPECTIVE ON TRUST REPAIR

Peter H. Kim

Introduction

Although trust has been widely recognized to be critical for many aspects of organizational life, it is also clear that trust can quite often be violated. Scholars have observed that a range of questionable practices has resulted in significant declines in organizational trustworthiness in the eyes of their employees and members of other organizations (Tyler & Kramer, 1996). The popular press has likewise raised concerns about how 'a seemingly endless stream of bad news alleging widespread management negligence and malfeasance has been chipping away at the trust vital to a free-market system' (Byrne, 2002). And these observations have been underscored by a recent survey by the American Psychological Association's Center for Organizational Excellence, which found that nearly 1 in 4 workers don't trust their employer (APA, 2014).

Such concerns have spurred a dramatic wave of interest in how trust might be repaired. Research on the repair of trust has not only surged over the past fifteen years, but also grown in nuance and sophistication. This development has occurred through a shift from a focus on lay theories and simple effects, such as whether a basic response such as an apology repairs trust, to more rigorous conceptualizations and a greater appreciation of this phenomenon's complexity. The breadth of this work has, furthermore, resulted in a wide range of case studies, theoretical frameworks, systematic empirical studies and literature reviews, each of which have helped advance our understanding of trust repair in meaningful ways.

Nevertheless, this body of research has also raised quite a number of issues that warrant further empirical attention. In fact, the number of conceptual ideas proposed in this literature still seems to outweigh efforts to investigate them, and the empirical investigations that do exist typically raise questions that warrant further empirical attention as well. To spur such efforts, I will focus this chapter on the major advances that have been made in the trust repair literature, regarding its conceptualization and influences, with the ultimate goal of considering its interactive implications (see Table 15.1). The latter, in particular, encompasses the field's growing recognition, not only of the inherently dyadic nature of the trust repair process (i.e. the need to consider this phenomenon from both the transgressor and victim perspectives), but also of the range of situational factors that might affect this outcome. This overview will then be used to highlight a number of ways in which such interactive influences on trust repair might be explored in future research.

Table 15.1 Overview

Prior investigations			Future directions
Conceptualization	Effects	Contingencies	
Definitions	**Trustees**	Violation type	**Bi-lateral implications**
Trust violations	Apologies	(competence vs.	Trustors vs. Trustees
Trust repair	Accounts (excuses &	integrity, procedural	
	justifications)	vs. interactional	**Elaboration/categor-**
Scope/relevance	Other verbal responses	injustice, severity,	**ization**
Relationship length	(promises, denials,	self vs. other,	Situational contingencies
(with or without a	no response)	documented vs.	
history of interaction)	Substantive responses	undocumented)	**Framing/**
Relationship strength	(penance, hostage	Volition (voluntary	**interpretation**
(strong or weak)	posting)	vs. involuntary)	Type of violation
Antecedents (e.g.		Reference points	
distrustful behaviour,	**Trustors**	(gains vs. losses,	
unmet expectations,	Characteristics (self-	undercompensation	
subpar outcomes,	construals, implicit	vs. overcompensa-	
true or false	theories, responses	tion)	
allegations)	to uncertainty,	Level of analysis	
	gender)	(individual vs.	
Differences	Actions (self-	group vs. organiza-	
Trust building	regulation, sense-	tion, hierarchical	
Forgiveness	making, legalistic	level, centrality	
Cooperation	remedies)	& power)	
		Context (online vs.	
		face-to-face,	
		outgroup	
		competition,	
		culture)	

The nature of trust violations and repair

As summarized in the first column of Table 15.1, some of the most fundamental advances in the trust repair literature have involved greater clarification regarding what trust violations and trust repair actually entail. Of particular significance, in this regard, has been a shift from the presumption that trust can only exist at levels that are sufficient to be violated between parties who have had significant long-term relationships to the view that trust is a much more pervasive phenomenon that can be meaningful even between parties who have had no history of inter-action (McKnight, Cummings, & Chervany, 1998; Meyerson, Weick, & Kramer, 1996). This shift is in large part due to a growing recognition that trust quite often does not start at zero and build slowly over time, but can rather be relatively high at the start of a relationship.

McKnight, Cummings and Chervany (1998), for example, observed that this high initial trust can arise for a variety of reasons, including: (1) an individual's disposition to trust, (2) a belief that regulations and laws or other institutional structures would support one's likelihood of success in a given situation and (3) rapid cognitive cues arising from group membership, reputations and stereotypes. Bacharach and Gambetta (2001) have described how this high initial trust is based on the 'trust-warranting properties' of social actors and situations, which they categorize as (1) observable personal attributes of prospective trustees (e.g. age, race, gender and attire), (2) social or relational ties between the parties (e.g. network or group membership) and (3) the situational context in which the trust-related interaction is embedded (e.g. a cooperative endeavour to avoid an outside threat). Moreover, Kramer and Lewicki (2010) have described how what they refer to as 'presumptive trust' can arise from (1) identity-based expectations (i.e. the extent to which one feels psychologically identified, or has a shared identity, with others), (2) role-based expectations (i.e. expectations that are predicated on knowledge that individuals occupy particular roles in the organization, rather than specific knowledge about the individual) and (3) rule-based expectations (i.e. an organization's codified rules for conduct). Other researchers have also delved more specifically into these different sources of high initial trust to clarify their implications, for example, by evaluating the trust-related effects of relational demographics (Lau, Lam, & Salamon, 2008), trustworthy faces (Yu, Saleem, & Gonzalez, 2014), status (Lount & Pettit, 2012) and different institutional arrangements (Bachmann & Inkpen, 2011).

These observations do not entail that the kinds of trust that might be violated in initial and longer-term relations are identical. Some data suggest, for example, that the bases of trust can differ as a relationship lengthens and deepens (Levin, Whitener, & Cross, 2006; Pirson & Malhotra, 2011). However, the aforementioned observations along with direct evidence from a number of empirical studies make clear that trust can indeed be high enough to be violated in the initial stages of a relationship (e.g. Dirks, Kim, Ferrin, & Cooper, 2011; Ferrin, Kim, Cooper, & Dirks, 2007; Kim, Ferrin, Cooper, & Dirks, 2004). This is both notable and important for the study of trust repair, given that network researchers have underscored how the vast majority of our relationships involve interpersonal connections that are relatively weak (Granovetter, 1995). These notions also help broaden the scope of the trust repair literature beyond the handful of parties with which we might have the most close-knit and long-lasting relationships (e.g. with our friends and family members) to encompass a wider array of trust-relevant targets, such as job candidates, coworkers, supervisors, CEOs, public figures, brands and institutions (e.g. Gillespie, Dietz, & Lockey, 2014; Hargie, Stapleton, & Tourish, 2010; Puzakova, Kwak, & Rocereto, 2013; Wiesenfeld, Wurthmann, & Hambrick, 2008). This potential for trust to be violated across a broad array of interactions is, furthermore, underscored by the recognition that such violations can occur quite easily. Indeed, past findings reveal that trust violations can occur for a host of reasons, including disrespectful behaviours, communication problems, unmet expectations, subpar or negative outcomes, or even unsubstantiated and/or erroneous allegations (Kim et al., 2004; Kramer & Lewicki, 2010).

Definitions and conceptual distinctions

Consistent with the notion that trust is a multi-faceted construct that is comprised of both trusting intentions (i.e. a willingness to make oneself vulnerable to another in the presence of risk) and trusting beliefs (i.e. the perceived trust-relevant qualities of the trustee, such as competence, integrity, or benevolence, upon which trusting intentions are based) (McKnight et al., 1998), trust violations have been defined as any incident that lowers these trusting beliefs in and trusting intentions toward a trustee (Kim, Dirks, & Cooper, 2009). Accordingly, trust repair has been defined as a matter of improving the trusting beliefs and trusting intentions that have been lowered by the trust violation (Kim et al., 2009).

As such, the repair of trust can be distinguished from related concepts such as forgiveness and restored cooperation. Whereas forgiveness involves the relinquishment of anger, resentment and the desire to seek revenge against an offender, and this may ultimately help restore the relationship (Aquino, Tripp, & Bies, 2006), it does not imply that the perceiver's beliefs about the offender's trustworthiness have been improved at all. Likewise, the restoration of cooperation after an offence may certainly provide a signal that trust has been repaired, and efforts to understand how to restore cooperation may shed light on how trust repair might occur (Bottom, Gibson, Daniels, & Murnighan, 2002). However, cooperation may also arise for reasons that have little to do with the perceiver's beliefs about the trustee at all, such as when new policies, procedures, or monitoring systems ultimately serve to lower the risks of cooperation (Sitkin & Roth, 1993). As such, the concept of trust repair is related to, but more specific than these related constructs, given that it entails that perceivers exhibit a greater willingness to make themselves vulnerable to a violator precisely because the perceiver's belief in that party's trustworthiness has been improved.

Moreover, in contrast to the ease with which trust violations can occur, it appears that the repair of trust is far more difficult. Although some researchers have observed that there may be occasions when a transgression can lead to restorative efforts that can enhance perceivers' perceptions of a target to an even more positive level than if the transgression had not occurred (Schminke, Caldwell, Ambrose, & McMahon, 2014), most trust repair studies have found that the level of trust after a repair effort tends to fall short of its pre-violation level (e.g. Kim et al., 2004). Additionally, the challenge of trust repair is even greater when parties lack relational closeness, such as is typical in the vast majority of organizational relationships, given that parties may be less motivated to preserve the relationship when it is weak (Finkel, Rusbult, Kumashiro, & Hannon, 2002; Tomlinson, Dineen, & Lewicki, 2004). These observations have, thus, prompted a wide range of efforts by trust repair researchers to understand how this challenge of trust repair might be approached and ultimately overcome. For simplicity when reviewing this work, the following sections of this chapter will use the term 'trustee' to refer to the mistrusted party and the term 'trustor' to refer to those whose trust has been violated.

Trustee and trustor responses

Efforts to understand how trust might be repaired have traditionally focused on the potential implications of a variety of responses a trustee might use. However, as this literature has developed, there has been growing attention to the role that trustors might play in the trust repair process as well. More specifically, there has been growing recognition of the notion that trustors are not simply passive recipients of a trustee's repair attempts, but can instead actively influence the trust repair process in ways that can meaningfully influence whether the repair of trust will occur (Kim et al., 2009; Petriglieri, 2015). The following section will, therefore, begin with a review of the types of trust responses a trustee might employ, then review a variety of ways in which trustors have been found to affect this process, and finally end by discussing a number of additional considerations that arise when the roles of both trustees and trustors are simultaneously considered (see Table 15.1, column 2).

Trustees

Research on trust repair has focused much of its attention on the types of responses a trustee might use. These include verbal responses such as apologies and accounts, as well as a number of more substantive efforts to address the incident.

Apologies

Of all the trustee responses that this literature has considered, apologies appear to have received the most attention. This is due not only to the frequency with which apologies are both expected by trustors and used by trustees after a violation, but also to the complex nature of the response itself. Researchers have observed, for example, that apologies represent a double-edged sword (Kim et al., 2004). They defined an apology as a statement that acknowledges responsibility and regret for a trust violation, and observed that this response can have a beneficial effect on trust by taking ownership for the violation and, by doing so, conveying the intent to avoid such violations in the future. Yet they also observed that this potential benefit could be counterbalanced by the fact that this response also admits culpability and, thus, theorized that the ultimate implications of an apology depend on the extent to which its positive effects on trust outweigh the negative.

This attempt to unpack the nature of apologies, on a theoretical level, has been accompanied by evidence verifying that apologies do convey signals of both responsibility and regret (Kim, Cooper, Dirks, & Ferrin, 2013), along with a number of other conceptual and empirical efforts to examine the nature of apologies in greater detail (e.g. Lewicki & Polin, 2012). Scher and Darley (1997), for example, developed a five-component model of apologies, although they too underscored how two of their components in particular are essential – an acknowledgement of responsibility and an expression of regret. Moreover, others have distinguished apologies into as many as seven different components (revelation, recognition, responsiveness, responsibility, remorse, restitution and reform) (Boyd, 2011). These theoretical analyses ultimately call for systematic empirical evaluation to gauge not only the significance of such distinctions, but also the importance of each component for trust repair. Yet despite the potential benefits of such additional elaboration, the empirical research to date provides support for the notion that the use of apologies, in general, quite often can work (e.g. Kim et al., 2004; Robbennolt, 2013; Tucker, Turner, Barling, Reid, & Elving, 2006).

Accounts

Research on the implications of accounts for trust repair encompasses two broad types of explanations, excuses and justifications. Whereas excuses seek to explain that the violation was at least partly caused by external forces, justifications seek to convince trustors to reassess the magnitude or nature of the violation itself (see Kim et al., 2009, for a review). Evidence from several studies suggests that excuses can often prove beneficial for trust repair because they can reduce the perceived responsibility of the transgressor (Crant & Bateman, 1993; Riordan, Marlin, & Kellogg, 1983; Snyder & Higgins, 1988; Wood & Mitchell, 1981). In contrast, justifications can facilitate trust repair by pointing out that the violation may actually be more appropriate than trustors might have believed due to the situation (Kim & Harmon, 2014). Typically, this involves a reference to a norm, principle and/or socially endorsed practice that the trustor may not have recognized but can foster a more favourable view of the transgressor when taken into account (Elsbach, 1994; Nesdale, Rule, & McAra, 1975). This recognition that both excuses and justifications can prove beneficial for trust repair has, furthermore, prompted efforts to understand the nature of these responses in greater detail, by examining how different characteristics of these responses, such as their perceived adequacy (Shapiro, 1991), credibility (Kim, Dirks, Cooper, & Ferrin, 2006), specificity (Frey & Cobb, 2010), type of principle to which a justification refers (Kim & Harmon, 2014) and counterfactual (if only . . .) comparisons (Bertolotti, Catellani, Douglas, & Sutton, 2013; Catellani & Bertolotti, 2014) might affect the extent to which trust repair is ultimately achieved.

Other verbal responses

This literature has, furthermore, considered the potential implications of an array of other verbal responses a trustee might use. Researchers have observed that trustees can convey not only apologies, but also explicit promises regarding their future behaviour and found that such promises can help restore trusting behaviours in laboratory simulations (Schniter, Sheremeta, & Sznycer, 2013; Schweitzer, Hershey, & Bradlow, 2006). Other studies have compared the effectiveness of apologies with the implications of denials and found that the latter can also help restore trust after a violation in some cases (Kim et al., 2013; Kim et al., 2004). However, evidence suggests that an alternative option of offering no response may be a particularly ineffective trust repair strategy (Ferrin et al., 2007), despite the fact that transgressors quite often have legitimate reasons to remain silent.

Substantive responses

Finally, other studies have sought to move beyond the effects of different verbal responses a trustee might use to investigate the implications of more substantive trust repair efforts. Such efforts are based on the notion that verbal responses alone may be discounted as 'cheap talk' and the recognition that more substantive responses could offer a way for trustees to demonstrate their repentance and intended redemption more meaningfully. Consistent with this notion, evidence suggests that voluntary acts of penance by a transgressor can help restore cooperation after a transgression (Bottom et al., 2002), as can the voluntary posting of hostages by the trustee that can give the trustor the ability to influence the trustee's outcomes (Nakayachi & Watabe, 2005). Moreover, of the various types of penance a trustee might offer, researchers have paid particular attention to the implications of financial compensation and found that such compensation can provide an important signal of repentance and thereby repair trust in some cases (Desmet, De Cremer, & Van Dijk, 2011; Dirks et al., 2011).

Trustors

Despite the importance of investigating the effectiveness of these trustee responses for trust repair, there has been growing recognition of the need to consider the role trustors might play in the repair process as well. Indeed, trustors have been theorized to play as important a role in whether the repair of trust occurs as their trustees by engaging in a variety of efforts to facilitate or impede this process (Kim et al., 2009), and this has led researchers to call for much greater attention to be paid to those implications (Barclay & Skarlicki, 2009). Part of this influence may not even be under the trustors' deliberate control, but rather a function of trustors' underlying characteristics. Researchers have observed, for example, that apologies are more effective when they align with victim's self construals (Fehr & Gelfand, 2010), when trustors believe that moral character can change over time than when they believe that moral character is fixed (Haselhuhn, Schweitzer, & Wood, 2010), and when trustors have a tendency to respond to uncertainty with high stress (van Dijke & De Cremer, 2011). Moreover, evidence suggests that trust repair may be more successful with women than men after a transgression, because the former may care more about maintaining relationships (Haselhuhn, Kennedy, Kray, Van Zant, & Schweitzer, 2015).

However, other research has begun to examine the potentially active role trustors can play in the repair process. Scholars have described how victims can engage in a self-regulation process that can lead to an array of post-violation outcomes, including the reactivation of pre-violation psychological contracts, the formation of a new contract that may be more or less attractive than the original, or the failure to form a functional psychological contract with the violator (Tomprou, Rousseau, & Hansen, 2015). A qualitative study has described how the repair of a damaged relationship between an organization and its members can require a process of active 'co-creation' that can allow members to re-identify with the organization's positive attributes (Petriglieri, 2015). Others have observed that trust repair can depend on a sense-making process through which trustors may seek to rationalize the negative event in a way that allows the relationship to be maintained (Bhattacharjee, Berman, & Reed II, 2013). Evidence also suggests that trustors' reactions to trust repair efforts can depend on whether they choose to respond to such efforts as individuals or in the context of groups, with the latter leading to particularly harsh reactions to the violator when that trustee offers an inadequate response for the incident (Kim et al., 2013). Even further, scholars have discussed the double-edged implications when trustors choose to rely on legalistic remedies (such as laws and regulations) to address trust violations by noting that, although this may help encourage post-violation cooperative behaviours (i.e. by lowering risk), they can also lead trustors to attribute trustees' future actions to those legalistic solutions, rather than trust-relevant qualities of the trustee, and thereby keep trust from improving in the future (Dirks et al., 2011; Sitkin & Roth, 1993).

Bi-lateral considerations

Finally, the potential for both trustors and trustees to affect the trust repair process has led researchers to begin considering their interactive implications. For example, researchers have sought to explain why a given trust repair effort may not always work, by conceptualizing the trust repair process as a negotiation of identity, in which both trustors and trustees seek to advance their views about the trustee on the other (i.e. with trustors upholding the belief that trust is not warranted and trustees seeking to convince trustors that further trust in the trustee is deserved) (Kim et al., 2009). This view underscores the notion that both trustors and trustees can actively influence the likelihood of trust repair (as opposed to the three broad alternatives that these researchers raised – forceful confrontation, avoidance or mistrust confirmation). Such notions have, in turn, encouraged researchers to begin considering how the relative power of trustors and trustees might affect their ability to affect this identity negotiation, along with their reactions to the trust violation and the likelihood of trust repair (Fragale, Rosen, Xu, & Merideth, 2009; Kim et al., 2009).

Researchers have, furthermore, begun to consider how trustors and trustees might differ in their evaluations of the exact same trust repair response and how this may lead to suboptimal choices regarding the type of response that is used. For example, some evidence suggests that trustees tend to overestimate the potentially negative effects of apologizing while simultaneously underestimating the potentially positive effects of doing so (Leunissen, De Cremer, Van Dijke, & Folmer, 2014). Moreover, other evidence suggests that the times in which trustors have a greater desire for an apology are precisely the times when trustees are less willing to provide one (Leunissen, De Cremer, Folmer, & Van Dijke, 2013). These kinds of inquiries into how trustors and trustees can jointly influence how the trust repair process may unfold are ultimately at the very early stages, however, and warrant more concerted attention in the future.

Contingencies

Beyond considering how trustors and trustees may affect the trust repair process, the literature has also paid increasing attention to the implications of the trust violation itself and the situation in which both the violation and the repair effort have taken place. As summarized in the third column of Table 15.1, this work has helped researchers move beyond questions related to whether a given trust repair effort might work to gain deeper insight into when and why such efforts may sometimes prove more or less effective than others.

Violation type

Researchers in this domain have paid particular attention to how the effectiveness of various trust repair efforts can depend on the type of violation that has occurred. One of the most robust findings in this regard has been the observation that whereas apologies (Ferrin et al., 2007; Kim et al., 2004), efforts to assume more blame with an internal attribution (Kim et al., 2006; Tomlinson et al., 2004) and substantive acts such as penance, regulation and compensation (Desmet et al., 2011; Dirks et al., 2011) are relatively beneficial for trust when the violation concerns matters of competence, they are far less effective when the violation concerns matters of integrity. This work is based on the notion that perceivers weigh information about competence and integrity quite differently (see Kim et al., 2009, for a review). More specifically, although people tend to weigh positive information about competence more heavily than negative information about competence, they tend to weigh negative information about integrity more heavily than positive information about integrity (Reeder & Brewer, 1979). Hence, an apology and other efforts to assume blame and signal one's intent to address the violation can be helpful for repairing competence-related violations, given that the negative information such responses would convey about guilt/blame is likely to be outweighed by their positive signals of intended redemption. However, for integrity-based violations, the negative information about guilt/blame from such responses is likely to be weighed more heavily than any positive signals of intended redemption they might offer and hence make them far less effective for trust repair.

Such notions have encouraged the use of attribution theories and frameworks to encompass the ways in which people's inferences about a violation can affect the likely success of various trust repair efforts (Chan, 2009; Tomlinson & Mayer, 2009). They have also fostered attempts to investigate how other characteristics of a trust violation can affect the success of subsequent trust repair efforts. For example, some have differentiated between whether a trust violation concerns procedural or interactional injustice (i.e. the fairness of the process through which outcomes are determined or fairness of the treatment that the individual receives, respectively) and observed that whereas procedural injustice is associated with a preference for instrumental remedies that address the need for control, interactional injustice is associated with a preference for punitive remedies that address the need for meaning (Reb, Goldman, Kray, & Cropanzano, 2006). Others have reported that the severity of the transgression can moderate the relationship between a leader's apology and trustors' positive emotions, psychological health and pride (Byrne, Barling, & Dupré, 2014). Moreover, research suggests that trustors' need for social accounts is highest when the intentions of the trustee are uncertain (De Cremer, van Dijk, & Pillutla, 2009). Further evidence suggests that whereas justifications can help repair trust when the violation had been intended to benefit another, such responses are either ineffective or harmful (relative to an apology) when the violation had been intended to benefit the self (Kim & Harmon, 2014). Finally, recent studies have begun to examine how the likelihood of trust repair can depend on the type of, or provisions within the, contract that have been violated (Harmon, Kim, & Mayer, 2015; Malhotra & Lumineau, 2011), such that the violation of documented expectations is considered more intentional than the violation of undocumented expectations, for example, and is thus more difficult to repair with an apology.

Volition

Other work in this literature has considered the implications of whether the trustee's repair attempt was made voluntarily or whether it was somehow induced by the situation. Researchers have observed that repair efforts by the trustee such as substantive forms of penance, financial compensation and the implementation of monitoring systems offer stronger signals of repentance (and hence a more meaningful signal that past violations would not be repeated in the future) when they are made voluntarily rather than when they are imposed (Desmet, De Cremer, & van Dijk, 2010; Dirks et al., 2011). This tendency to consider reparative actions more meaningful when they are voluntary than involuntary may also help explain why the self-disclosure of negative information by organizations has been suggested to lessen the damage to trustor sentiments (Fennis & Stroebe, 2014).

Nevertheless, the nature and implications of volitions may also need to be examined in greater detail. Research on the effects of apologies in civil legal disputes, for example, suggests that apologies that are given in response to a request by the victim or at the suggestion of a mediator are viewed in ways that are similar to the same apology given spontaneously; only apologies offered by attorneys on behalf of the violator were somewhat less effective (although still helpful to some degree) (Robbennolt, 2013). These kinds of observations, ultimately, raise the notion that additional features of the situation may affect both the perceptions of a violation and its implications for trust repair in ways that remain largely unexplored.

Reference points

A number of studies have also begun to suggest that the effectiveness of trust repair efforts may depend on perceptions of the violation and/or repair attempt's outcome implications. Some initial evidence suggests that whereas financial compensation may be more effective at repairing trust than an apology when the trust violation arose from the unfair allocation of losses, an apology may be more effective than financial compensation when the trust violation arose from the unfair allocation of gains (De Cremer, 2010). Additionally, research on the effectiveness of financial compensation for trust repair has observed that its implications can depend on whether the amount is sufficient to redress the harm suffered by the victim or not. In particular, financial compensation that fails to redress the harm (i.e. under-compensation) was found to be less effective than financial compensation that does redress it, and that under-compensation may require additional repair strategies (such as an apology) to maintain the relationship after a violation (Haesevoets, Folmer, De Cremer, & Van Hiel, 2013). However, the evidence thus far suggests that there may be relatively little additional benefit, with respect to trust repair, from financial compensation that would offer more than the amount required to redress the harm (i.e. over-compensation) relative to an amount sufficient to redress it (Haesevoets, Folmer, & Van Hiel, 2014).

Level of analysis

Research has, furthermore, started investigating how the repair of trust may differ depending on the level of analysis, specifically whether such efforts involve dyads, groups or organizations. This research has raised the notion that, as one moves beyond the traditional dyadic level of analysis to situations involving more than an individual trustee, one may need to consider a range of additional complications that can affect how the trustee is viewed (Fulmer & Gelfand, 2012; Gillespie & Dietz, 2009). For example, research has observed that the repair of trust can sometimes be more difficult with groups than with individuals, given that groups can share their opinions in ways that can strengthen negative sentiments, particularly when the trustee offers a suboptimal repair response (Keck, 2014; Kim et al., 2013). Additionally, scholars have considered the repair of trust from a coalitional perspective, by considering how members' motives to maintain balanced relationships in their groups can affect how and when trust repair may occur, and thus raise a motivational basis for why the repair of trust may differ between individuals and groups (Brodt & Neville, 2013).

Moreover, when the trust violation occurs in the context of a group or organization, this raises additional questions about the nature of the transgressor as well as the potential for additional types of trust repair responses to be used. Researchers have begun to speculate, for example, about how the effectiveness of trust repair efforts may depend on the hierarchical level at which the violation occurs, as well as how efforts to address trust violations at one level might affect trust at other levels (Janowicz-Panjaitan & Krishnan, 2009). Moreover, other research has examined how transgressions by a group member may be more or less damaging to the group depending on the perceived typicality of the deviant group member (van Leeuwen, van den Bosch, Castano, & Hopman, 2010), how a supervisor's attempt to repair trust after committing an injustice towards a group member can depend on the victim's strategic importance within the group (Christian, Christian, Garza, & Ellis, 2012), and how organizations may attempt to shift blame to a single individual within the organization through scapegoating and how this process may depend on the relative power of the organizational members (e.g. Boeker, 1992).

Context

Finally, a handful of studies have begun to consider how the repair of trust may differ based on the surrounding context. Some initial efforts to consider the repair of trust in online contexts, for example, suggests that customers tend to be suspicious of online sellers and that this can make denials generally ineffective (relative to apologies) for repairing trust (Matzat & Snijders, 2012). Other evidence suggests that trustors' reactions to repair attempts can be more effective in contexts where there is outgroup competition (Lei, Masclet, & Vesely, 2014). Additionally, researchers have begun to consider how the repair of trust may differ across cultures, by affecting (a) the types of rituals that might be expected or (b) the assumptions trustors make about the extent to which individuals (or the situation) exert control over what occurs (Maddux, Kim, Okumura, & Brett, 2011; Ren & Gray, 2009).

Future directions

One thing that may be gathered from this review is that although important progress has been made in our understanding of trust repair, much of the literature is still in a nascent state, with many conceptual frameworks, ideas and initial insights that still warrant further development and empirical evaluation. With this in mind, this chapter will conclude by outlining three broad ways in which the current inquiries within this literature might grow, with particular emphasis placed on moving beyond simpler main-effect type findings to delve more deeply into the kinds of interactions that can affect the course of trust repair efforts (see Table 15.1, column 4).

Bilateral implications

Thus far, the trust repair literature has focused the bulk of its attention on the kinds of repair efforts a trustee might use, with far less attention to the role trustors might play, and rather minimal attention to their dyadic influences on this phenomenon. However, if the repair of trust ultimately depends on both trustees and trustors, it seems worthwhile to pay more attention to how this phenomenon depends on their interaction, given that this may help explain why even the exact same trust repair effort may work in some cases but not others and also help illuminate the consequences when trust repair does not occur (Kim et al., 2009). In this regard, one important step researchers may take is to move beyond a focus on trustors' fixed characteristics (e.g. dispositions, implicit beliefs and demographics) to pay more attention to how trustors might actively influence the trust repair process (e.g. by granting or withholding opportunities for the trustee to address the violation, or by influencing the motivations of the trustor to engage in the trust repair effort) and by accounting for the relative influence of such trustor efforts vis-à-vis that of the repair efforts trustees might use.

Elaboration/categorization

Likewise, although the literature has begun to identify a range of contingencies that can affect the likelihood of trust repair, most of the contingencies that have been identified require much further research attention. Indeed, beyond the seemingly robust evidence substantiating the importance of the type of violation for the efficacy of subsequent trust repair efforts, many of the contingencies this chapter has outlined are based on just a handful of disparate papers whose claims require additional validation, replication and elaboration. Research on contextual contingencies, for example, seems particularly underexplored in light of the many types of settings in which trust violations and subsequent repair efforts can occur. There may, furthermore, be other contingencies underlying the trust repair process that the literature has yet to reveal. In fact, given that the current set of contingencies represents little more than a preliminary laundry list of possibilities, efforts to organize the contingencies that have so far been discovered into a more comprehensive theoretical framework/typology may prove particularly helpful for illuminating new areas for future investigation.

Framing/interpretation

Finally, the potential for such contingencies to influence the bilateral process through which trust repair may occur also raises the possibility that these contingencies may themselves also be influenced by trustors and trustees in meaningful ways. Prior research on how the relative efficacy of different trust repair efforts can depend on the type of trust violation (i.e. whether it concerns a matter of competence or integrity) has often raised this possibility by keeping the actual violation constant and simply framing the incident as a competence- or integrity-based trust violation (e.g. Ferrin et al., 2007; Kim et al., 2004). Thus, a frequent message from this work has been that efforts to shape how the violation is viewed may be as important as the trust repair effort that is used. Yet this opportunity to frame the situation differently not only seems to remain largely overlooked in practice, but also continues to escape meaningful empirical investigation.[1] More specifically, although the literature has raised the potential to frame violations differently, few studies have explored how that may be achieved. This lack of attention is particularly glaring in light of the fact that trustors and trustees may be inclined to frame the situation differently, and this may raise yet another way in which these parties may contest their views. Thus, systematic attention to how trustees may be able to frame the violation as a matter of competence, for example, despite trustors' inclinations to believe otherwise seems warranted. Likewise, it would be worthwhile to consider how many of the other kinds of contingencies this chapter has identified may be subject to framing efforts as well. In essence, to the extent that this largely unexamined arena represents a critical additional dimension that may affect the likelihood of trust repair, much more systematic empirical attention to how trustees and trustors may interact to affect this framing seems deserved.

Conclusion

In the short span of years since the repair of trust began to garner concerted research attention, this literature has developed from conveying speculative propositions and reporting simple effects to providing deeper insights into the complex interactions underlying this phenomenon. This has entailed moving beyond a focus just on the trustee to include the potentially active role played by the trustor and the additional implications of the surrounding situation. It also highlights the notion that these three elements are not static, but rather are involved in a dynamic interplay that can shape whether, how and the extent to which trust violations may ultimately be repaired. Yet this more interactive view of trust repair has only begun to emerge, and much more research is needed to investigate its implications. In this light, the trust repair literature is only at the beginning, with the potential for many important insights ahead.

Note

1   Please refer to Robert J. Bies et al.'s chapter on forgiveness in this volume for further discussion.

References

APA. (2014). Employee distrust is pervasive in U.S. workforce. Retrieved January 2017, from http://www.apa.org/news/press/releases/2014/04/employee-distrust.aspx

Aquino, K., Tripp, T. M., & Bies, R. J. (2006). Getting even or moving on? Power, procedural justice, and types of offense as predictors of revenge, forgiveness, reconciliation, and avoidance in organizations. *Journal of Applied Psychology, 91*(3), 653–668.

Bacharach, M., & Gambetta, D. (2001). Trust in signs. *Trust in Society, 2,* 148–184.

Bachmann, R., & Inkpen, A. C. (2011). Understanding institutional-based trust building processes in inter-organizational relationships. *Organization Studies, 32*(2), 281–301.

Barclay, L. J., & Skarlicki, D. P. (2009). Healing the wounds of organizational injustice: Examining the benefits of expressive writing. *Journal of Applied Psychology, 94*(2), 511.

Bertolotti, M., Catellani, P., Douglas, K. M., & Sutton, R. M. (2013). The "Big Two" in political communication: The effects of attacking and defending politicians' leadership or morality. *Social Psychology, 44*(2), 117.

Bhattacharjee, A., Berman, J. Z., & Reed II, A. (2013). Tip of the hat, wag of the finger: How moral decoupling enables consumers to admire and admonish. *Journal of Consumer Research, 39*(6), 1167–1184.

Boeker, W. (1992). Power and managerial dismissal: Scapegoating at the top. *Administrative Science Quarterly,* 400–421.

Bottom, W. P., Gibson, K., Daniels, S., & Murnighan, J. K. (2002). When talk is not cheap: Substantive penance and expressions of intent in rebuilding cooperation. *Organization Science, 13*(5), 497–513.

Boyd, D. P. (2011). Art and artifice in public apologies. *Journal of Business Ethics, 104*(3), 299–309.

Brodt, S. E., & Neville, L. (2013). Repairing trust to preserve balance: A balance–theoretic approach to trust breach and repair in groups. *Negotiation and Conflict Management Research, 6*(1), 49–65.

Byrne, A., Barling, J., & Dupré, K. E. (2014). Leader apologies and employee and leader well-being. *Journal of Business Ethics, 121*(1), 91–106.

Byrne, J. A. (2002). Restoring trust in corporate America: Business must lead the way to real reform. *Business Week, June 24,* 30–35.

Catellani, P., & Bertolotti, M. (2014). The effects of counterfactual defences on social judgements. *European Journal of Social Psychology, 44*(1), 82–92.

Chan, M. E. (2009). "Why did you hurt me?" Victim's interpersonal betrayal attribution and trust implications. *Review of General Psychology, 13*(3), 262.

Christian, J. S., Christian, M. S., Garza, A. S., & Ellis, A. P. (2012). Examining retaliatory responses to justice violations and recovery attempts in teams. *Journal of Applied Psychology, 97*(6), 1218.

Crant, J. M., & Bateman, T. S. (1993). Assignment of credit and blame for performance outcomes. *Academy of Management Journal, 36*(1), 7–27.

De Cremer, D. (2010). To pay or to apologize? On the psychology of dealing with unfair offers in a dictator game. *Journal of Economic Psychology, 31*(6), 843–848.

De Cremer, D., van Dijk, E., & Pillutla, M. M. (2009). Explaining unfair offers in ultimatum games and their effects on trust. *Business Ethics Quarterly, 20*(1), 107–126.

Desmet, P. T., De Cremer, D., & van Dijk, E. (2010). On the psychology of financial compensations to restore fairness transgressions: When intentions determine value. *Journal of Business Ethics, 95*(1), 105–115.

Desmet, P. T., De Cremer, D., & Van Dijk, E. (2011). In money we trust? The use of financial compensations to repair trust in the aftermath of distributive harm. *Organizational Behavior and Human Decision Processes, 114*, 75–86.

Dirks, K. T., Kim, P. H., Ferrin, D. L., & Cooper, C. D. (2011). Understanding the effects of substantive responses on trust following a transgression. *Organizational Behavior and Human Decision Processes, 114*, 87–103.

Elsbach, K. D. (1994). Managing organizational legitimacy in the California cattle industry: The construction and effectiveness of verbal accounts. *Administrative Science Quarterly, 39*, 57–88.

Fehr, R., & Gelfand, M. J. (2010). When apologies work: How matching apology components to victims' self-construals facilitates forgiveness. *Organizational Behavior and Human Decision Processes, 113*(1), 37–50.

Fennis, B. M., & Stroebe, W. (2014). Softening the blow: Company self-disclosure of negative information lessens damaging effects on consumer judgment and decision making. *Journal of Business Ethics, 120*(1), 109–120.

Ferrin, D. L., Kim, P. H., Cooper, C. D., & Dirks, K. T. (2007). Silence speaks volumes: The effectiveness of reticence in comparison to apology and denial for responding to integrity- and competence-based trust violations. *Journal of Applied Psychology, 92*(4), 893–908.

Finkel, E. J., Rusbult, C. E., Kumashiro, M., & Hannon, P. A. (2002). Dealing with betrayal in close relationships: Does commitment promote forgiveness? *Journal of Personality and Social Psychology, 82*(6), 956–974.

Fragale, A. R., Rosen, B., Xu, C., & Merideth, I. (2009). The higher they are, the harder they fall: The effects of wrongdoer status on observer punishment recommendations and intentionality attributions. *Organizational Behavior and Human Decision Processes, 108*(1), 53–65.

Frey, F. M., & Cobb, A. T. (2010). What matters in social accounts? The roles of account specificity, source expertise, and outcome loss on acceptance. *Journal of Applied Social Psychology, 40*(5), 1203–1234.

Fulmer, C. A., & Gelfand, M. J. (2012). At what level (and in whom) we trust trust across multiple organizational levels. *Journal of Management, 38*(4), 1167–1230.

Gillespie, N., & Dietz, G. (2009). Trust repair after an organization-level failure. *Academy of Management Review, 34*(1), 127–145.

Gillespie, N., Dietz, G., & Lockey, S. (2014). Organizational reintegration and trust repair after an integrity violation. *Business Ethics Quarterly, 24*(3), 371–410.

Granovetter, M. (1995). *Getting a job: A study in contacts and careers* (2nd ed.). Chicago: University of Chicago Press.

Haesevoets, T., Folmer, C. R., De Cremer, D., & Van Hiel, A. (2013). Money isn't all that matters: The use of financial compensation and apologies to preserve relationships in the aftermath of distributive harm. *Journal of Economic Psychology, 35*, 95–107.

Haesevoets, T., Folmer, C. R., & Van Hiel, A. (2014). More money, more trust? Target and observer differences in the effectiveness of financial overcompensation to restore trust. *Psychologica Belgica, 54*(4), 389–394.

Hargie, O., Stapleton, K., & Tourish, D. (2010). Interpretations of CEO public apologies for the banking crisis: Attributions of blame and avoidance of responsibility. *Organization, 17*(6), 721–742.

Harmon, D. H., Kim, P. H., & Mayer, K. J. (2015). Breaking the letter versus spirit of the law: How the interpretation of contract violations affects trust and the management of relationships. *Strategic Management Journal*, in press.

Haselhuhn, M. P., Kennedy, J. A., Kray, L. J., Van Zant, A. B., & Schweitzer, M. E. (2015). Gender differences in trust dynamics: Women trust more than men following a trust violation. *Journal of Experimental Social Psychology, 56*, 104–109.

Haselhuhn, M. P., Schweitzer, M. E., & Wood, A. M. (2010). How implicit beliefs influence trust recovery. *Psychological Science, 21*(5), 645–648.

Janowicz-Panjaitan, M., & Krishnan, R. (2009). Measures for dealing with competence and integrity violations of interorganizational trust at the corporate and operating levels of organizational hierarchy. *Journal of Management Studies, 46*(2), 245–268.

Keck, S. (2014). Group reactions to dishonesty. *Organizational Behavior and Human Decision Processes, 124*(1), 1–10.

Kim, P. H., Cooper, C. D., Dirks, K. T., & Ferrin, D. L. (2013). Repairing trust with individuals vs. groups. *Organizational Behavior and Human Decision Processes, 120*(1), 1–14.

Kim, P. H., Dirks, K. T., & Cooper, C. D. (2009). The repair of trust: A dynamic bilateral perspective and multilevel conceptualization. *Academy of Management Review, 34*(3), 401–422.

Kim, P. H., Dirks, K. T., Cooper, C. D., & Ferrin, D. L. (2006). When more blame is better than less: The implications of internal vs. external attributions for the repair of trust after a competence- vs. integrity-based trust violation. *Organizational Behavior and Human Decision Processes, 99*, 49–65.

Kim, P. H., Ferrin, D. L., Cooper, C. D., & Dirks, K. T. (2004). Removing the shadow of suspicion: The effects of apology vs. denial for repairing ability- vs. integrity-based trust violations. *Journal of Applied Psychology, 89*(1), 104–118.

Kim, P. H., & Harmon, D. H. (2014). Justifying one's transgressions: How rationalizations based on equity, equality, and need affect trust after its violation. *Journal of Experimental Psychology: Applied, 20*(4), 365–379.

Kramer, R. M., & Lewicki, R. J. (2010). Repairing and enhancing trust: Approaches to reducing organizational trust deficits. *Academy of Management Annals, 4*(1), 245–277.

Lau, D. C., Lam, L. W., & Salamon, S. D. (2008). The impact of relational demographics on perceived managerial trustworthiness: Similarity or norms? *The Journal of Social Psychology, 148*(2), 187–209.

Lei, V., Masclet, D., & Vesely, F. (2014). Competition vs. communication: An experimental study on restoring trust. *Journal of Economic Behavior & Organization, 108*, 94–107.

Leunissen, J. M., De Cremer, D., Folmer, C. P. R., & Van Dijke, M. (2013). The apology mismatch: Asymmetries between victim's need for apologies and perpetrator's willingness to apologize. *Journal of Experimental Social Psychology, 49*(3), 315–324.

Leunissen, J. M., De Cremer, D., Van Dijke, M., & Folmer, C. P. R. (2014). Forecasting errors in the averseness of apologizing. *Social Justice Research, 27*(3), 322–339.

Levin, D. Z., Whitener, E. M., & Cross, R. (2006). Perceived trustworthiness of knowledge sources: The moderating impact of relationship length. *Journal of Applied Psychology, 91*(5), 1163.

Lewicki, R., & Polin, B. (2012). The art of the apology: The structure and effectiveness of apologies in trust repair. In R. M. Kramer & T. Ptinksy (Eds), *Restoring trust: Challenges and prospects*, (95–128). Oxford, UK: Oxford University Press

Lount, R. B., Jr., & Pettit, N. C. (2012). The social context of trust: The role of status. *Organizational Behavior and Human Decision Processes, 117*, 15–23.

Maddux, W. W., Kim, P. H., Okumura, T., & Brett, J. M. (2011). Cultural differences in the function and meaning of apologies. *International Negotiation, 16*, 405–425.

Malhotra, D., & Lumineau, F. (2011). Trust and collaboration in the aftermath of conflict: The effects of contract structure. *Academy of Management Journal, 54*(5), 981–998.

Matzat, U., & Snijders, C. (2012). Rebuilding trust in online shops on consumer review sites: Sellers' responses to user-generated complaints. *Journal of Computer-Mediated Communication, 18*(1), 62–79.

McKnight, D. H., Cummings, L. L., & Chervany, N. L. (1998). Initial trust formation in new organizational relationships. *Academy of Management Review, 23*(3), 473–490.

Meyerson, D., Weick, K. E., & Kramer, R. M. (1996). Swift trust and temporary groups. In R. M. Kramer & T. R. Tyler (Eds.), *Trust in organizations: Frontiers of theory and research* (pp. 166–195). Thousand Oaks, CA: Sage.

Nakayachi, K., & Watabe, M. (2005). Restoring trustworthiness after adverse events: The signaling effects of voluntary 'Hostage Posting' on trust. *Organizational Behavior and Human Decision Processes, 97*, 1–17.

Nesdale, A. R., Rule, B. G., & McAra, M. (1975). Moral judgments of aggression: Personal and situational determinants. *European Journal of Social Psychology, 5*, 339–349.

Petriglieri, J. L. (2015). Co-creating relationship repair pathways to reconstructing destabilized organizational identification. *Administrative Science Quarterly, 60*(3), 518–557.

Pirson, M., & Malhotra, D. (2011). Foundations of organizational trust: What matters to different stakeholders? *Organization Science, 22*(4), 1087–1104.

Puzakova, M., Kwak, H., & Rocereto, J. F. (2013). When humanizing brands goes wrong: The detrimental effect of brand anthropomorphization amid product wrongdoings. *Journal of Marketing, 77*(3), 81–100.

Reb, J., Goldman, B. M., Kray, L. J., & Cropanzano, R. (2006). Different wrongs, different remedies? Reactions to organizational remedies after procedural and interactional injustice. *Personnel Psychology, 59*(1), 31–64.

Reeder, G. D., & Brewer, M. B. (1979). A schematic model of dispositional attribution in interpersonal perception. *Psychological Review, 86*(1), 61–79.

Ren, H., & Gray, B. (2009). Repairing relationship conflict: How violation types and culture influence the effectiveness of restoration rituals. *Academy of Management Review, 34*(1), 105–126.

Riordan, C. A., Marlin, N. A., & Kellogg, R. T. (1983). The effectiveness of accounts following transgression. *Social Psychology Quarterly, 46*, 213–219.

Robbennolt, J. K. (2013). The effects of negotiated and delegated apologies in settlement negotiation. *Law and Human Behavior, 37*(2), 128.

Scher, S. J., & Darley, J. M. (1997). How effective are the things people say to apologize? Effects of the realization of the apology speech act. *Journal of Psycholinguistic Research, 26*(1), 127–140.

Schminke, M., Caldwell, J., Ambrose, M. L., & McMahon, S. R. (2014). Better than ever? Employee reactions to ethical failures in organizations, and the ethical recovery paradox. *Organizational Behavior and Human Decision Processes, 123*(2), 206–219.

Schniter, E., Sheremeta, R. M., & Sznycer, D. (2013). Building and rebuilding trust with promises and apologies. *Journal of Economic Behavior & Organization, 94*, 242–256.

Schweitzer, M. E., Hershey, J. C., & Bradlow, E. T. (2006). Promises and lies: Restoring violated trust. *Organizational Behavior and Human Decision Processes, 101*(1), 1–19.

Shapiro, D. L. (1991). The effects of explanations on negative reactions to deceit. *Administrative Science Quarterly, 36*, 614–630.

Sitkin, S. B., & Roth, N. L. (1993). Explaining the limited effectiveness of legalistic "remedies" for trust/distrust. *Organization Science, 4*(3), 367–392.

Snyder, C. R., & Higgins, R. L. (1988). Excuses: Their effective role in the negotiation of reality. *Psychological Bulletin, 104*(1), 23–35.

Tomlinson, E. C., Dineen, B. R., & Lewicki, R. J. (2004). The road to reconciliation: Antecedents of victim willingness to reconcile following a broken promise. *Journal of Management, 30*(2), 165–187.

Tomlinson, E. C., & Mayer, R. C. (2009). The role of causal attribution dimensions in trust repair. *Academy of Management Review, 34*, 85–104.

Tomprou, M., Rousseau, D. M., & Hansen, S. D. (2015). The psychological contracts of violation victims: A Post-Violation Model. *Journal of Organizational Behavior, 36*(4).

Tucker, S., Turner, N., Barling, J., Reid, E. M., & Elving, C. (2006). Apologies and transformational leadership. *Journal of Business Ethics, 63*(2), 195–207.

Tyler, T. R., & Kramer, R. M. (1996). Wither trust? In R. M. Kramer & T. R. Tyler (Eds.), *Trust in organizations: Frontiers of theory and research* (pp. 1–15). Thousand Oaks, CA: Sage.

van Dijke, M., & De Cremer, D. (2011). When social accounts promote acceptance of unfair ultimatum offers: The role of the victim's stress responses to uncertainty and power position. *Journal of Economic Psychology, 32*(3), 468–479.

van Leeuwen, E., van den Bosch, M., Castano, E., & Hopman, P. (2010). Dealing with deviants: The effectiveness of rejection, denial, and apologies on protecting the public image of a group. *European Journal of Social Psychology, 40*(2), 282–299.

Wiesenfeld, B. M., Wurthmann, K. A., & Hambrick, D. C. (2008). The stigmatization and devaluation of elites associated with corporate failures: A process model. *Academy of Management Review, 33*(1), 231–251.

Wood, R. E., & Mitchell, T. R. (1981). Manager behavior in a social context: The impact of impression management on attributions and disciplinary actions. *Organizational Behavior and Human Decision Processes, 28*, 356–378.

Yu, M., Saleem, M., & Gonzalez, C. (2014). Developing trust: First impressions and experience. *Journal of Economic Psychology, 43*, 16–29.

16

ORGANIZATIONAL TRUST REPAIR

Nicole Gillespie and Sabina Siebert

Introduction

Organizational trust is a fundamental building block of organizations. However, as the recent corporate governance crises demonstrate, trust is often very difficult to restore once broken (Kramer & Lewicki, 2009). Understanding how organizational trust can be repaired has become an important topic for researchers in organization studies, as well as for practitioners (Bachmann, Gillespie & Priem, 2015; Kramer & Lewicki, 2010). A recent example that highlights the practical focus of this work is the emissions scandal at Volkswagen. The Volkswagen Group built their reputation on manufacturing environmentally friendly cars pledging that by 2018 the company would be the world's most environmentally friendly car manufacturer. Yet in May 2015, it was revealed that Volkswagen vehicles were producing emissions up to 40 times higher than the US legal limit. The report prompted regulatory investigations and, in September 2015, Volkswagen admitted to installing 'defeat devices' in their vehicles that sensed test situations and put the vehicle into a 'test mode' running the engine below normal power and performance. On the road, however, the test mode was switched off, and the car emitted much higher pollutants. The revelation sent a shockwave across Volkswagen's stakeholders, undermining trust, casting a crippling blow to the company's reputation and exposing the company to billions in recall costs, fines and potential criminal charges.

In this chapter, we review the emerging literature on organizational trust repair and the insights it offers on the challenging process of restoring trust, such as that faced by Volkswagen. Our focus is squarely on trust repair in the referent of the organization and institution (for a review of the literature on trust repair in interpersonal contexts, see Kim, this volume). We start by outlining the problem domain, defining trust failures and trust repair as it pertains to organizations and how the nature and processes of trust repair are different at the organizational and interpersonal levels. We then review conceptual frameworks and models on organizational trust repair, and examine select relevant empirical work. From this review, we identify and discuss the ontological and epistemological approaches that dominate the literature. We argue that while these paradigms have provided a solid foundation to the field, there is benefit in complementing this work with critical and radical perspectives to deepen and extend understanding. We conclude the chapter by identifying promising opportunities for future research.

The problem domain

Defining trust repair

Most definitions of trust repair are concerned with what Dirks and colleagues (2011: 88) describe as a process in which a trustee is 'attempting to increase trust following a situation in which a transgression (i.e. untrustworthy behaviour) is perceived to have occurred'. In other words the 'relationship repair occurs when a transgression causes the positive state(s) that constitute(s) the relationship to disappear and/or negative states to arise, as perceived by one or both parties, and activities by one or both parties to substantively return the relationship to a positive state' (Dirks et al., 2009: 69). In essence, trust repair is predominantly concerned with restoring cooperation and more specifically with re-establishing the trustor's positive expectations of the other party and in turn the 'willingness to be vulnerable' (see also Desmet, De Cremer & Van Dijk, 2011a, 2011b; Kramer & Lewicki, 2010).

Understanding trust repair at the organizational level

Our focus is on the repair of trust in the referent of an organization. This may include trust in a particular corporation, hospital, university, association or union (e.g. Volkswagen, the Royal Bank of Scotland, FIFA), an industry (e.g. banking, mining, football) or an institution (e.g. the UK Parliament, the Catholic Church, the Police). Studies into organizational and institutional trust have historically been embedded in the sociological literature on trust (e.g. Barber, 1983; Fox, 1974; Luhmann, 1979; Misztal, 1996; Shapiro, 1987; Sitkin & Roth, 1993; Sztompka, 1999; Zucker, 1986). However, most studies directly examining trust repair have been conducted at the interpersonal level. Organizational and institutional trust repair has some parallels with interpersonal trust repair, but also several significant differences that limit the ability to translate research findings across levels (Gillespie & Dietz, 2009: 128; see also Fulmer & Gelfand, 2012).

Unlike interpersonal trust, in which the focus is on an individual person or leader, trust in organizational and institutional referents is considerably more complex. This is partly because a range of organizational actors and components operating at multiple levels can influence and inform the judgements of potential trustors (Gillespie & Dietz, 2009). When one trusts an organization (e.g. a university), does one trust in the interpersonal relationships one has with organizational agents and groups (e.g. departmental colleagues, university management)? Or does one trust more in the impersonal set of systems, structures and processes that typically govern the behaviour of organizational actors (e.g. systems of accountability, control and HRM practices, etc; Bachmann, 2001; Bachmann, this volume; Luhmann, 1979; Möllering, 2001, 2006; Weibel et al., 2016)? Or perhaps one gives more precedence to the dominant cultural values and principles to which organization members and its leaders (appear to) adhere? Or the reputation of the organization (e.g. university rankings) and the quality of its goods and services (e.g. quality of research and teaching)? Or the external regulation and controls that constrains the organization's conduct? We come from the perspective that stakeholders' trust in an organization is informed by, and can be based on, a combination of all of these elements (Barber, 1983; Gillespie & Dietz, 2009). As Bachmann and Inkpen (2011: 284) point out, institutional-based trust 'is constitutively embedded in the institutional environment in which a relationship is placed'.

The complexity of organizational trust repair also reflects that the 'trustors' of organizations and institutions represent a diversity of stakeholders, including employees, suppliers, customers, shareholders, regulators, governments and the general public. These stakeholders have different interests, vulnerabilities, power and expectations in relation to organizations and institutions (see Pfarrer et al., 2008), and may develop trust in different ways due to varying levels of access, exposure and hence insight into the organization's conduct and institutional arrangement's functionality. Indeed, repairing trust at the macro level is much more complex than at the interpersonal level because stakeholders may differ in their interpretations of the nature and causes of the breach, and therefore what constitutes credible ways to restore the relationship (see Bachmann et al., 2015; Lamin & Zaheer, 2012).

Organizational trust failures

Trust failures can take on many forms. However, there are several generic, defining features that need to be present for a trust failure to be attributed to the organizational level. An organizational trust failure has been defined as 'a single major incident, or cumulative series of incidents, resulting from the action (or inaction) of organizational agents that threatens the legitimacy of the organization and has the potential to harm the well-being of one or more of the organization's stakeholders' (Gillespie & Dietz, 2009: 128).

For a trust breach to be at the organizational or institutional rather than the individual or group level, it needs to call into question the organization's or institution's legitimacy i.e. its capacity to fulfil its essential responsibilities or adhere to commonly endorsed values and standards. The trustor must attribute at least some responsibility for the breach to the organization or institution, perceiving it as having occurred (at least partially) as a consequence of actions, or negligent inaction, by actors authorized or otherwise facilitated by the organization or the relevant institutional arrangements. Put simply, the 'confident positive expectations' about an organization or an institution's capacity to meet reasonable standards of ability, benevolence and/or integrity in its conduct towards stakeholders, are replaced with negative expectations. Trust failures in organizations take many forms including accounting frauds, managerial deceit and incompetence, fatal avoidable incidents, exploitation of vulnerable people, large-scale compulsory job losses, bankruptcies and catastrophic collapses in organizational finance. Furthermore, for a trust failure to manifest at the broader institutional level, trustors need to perceive that the failure is occurring across multiple organizations within the institutional field (e.g. a large number of banks failing during the global financial crisis; child abuse identified in multiple religious organizations) or, alternatively, that the failure is occurring in institutional bodies themselves (e.g. trade associations or financial industry regulators).

At one extreme, a breakdown of trust may result from a single catastrophic incident (e.g. the Deepwater Horizon oil spill) or scandal (e.g. Volkswagen). At the other extreme, breakdown may occur based on an accumulation of trust breaches that erode trust over time (e.g. the Greek government's financial policies within the EU). In this latter case a 'tipping point' ultimately is reached where the trustor loses confidence in the organization's or institution's trustworthiness (Bachmann et al., 2015; Kramer, 2010).

It is against this background that our central question arises: 'What does it mean to repair trust in an organization or institution?' Fundamentally, repair at these macro levels requires restoring the positive expectations of the organization's or institution's trustworthiness that were damaged by the trust violation, so that trustors are again willing to make themselves vulnerable (Kramer & Lewicki, 2010; Lewicki & Bunker, 1996). Dirks and colleagues (2009: 69) further suggest relationship repair involves 'activities by one or both parties that substantively return the relationship to a positive state', highlighting that trust repair can be enacted and influenced not only by the trust violator (e.g. the organization) but also the trustor (e.g. organizational stakeholders, see also Kim, Dirks & Cooper, 2009). However, as highlighted later in this review, third parties (e.g. investigative and regulatory bodies, media, etc.) can also play an influential role in the repair of organizational trust.

Conceptual models of organizational trust repair

Various scholars have advanced conceptual models that propose and/or integrate approaches to organizational trust repair. Here we outline and evaluate prominent contributions in the organization and management literatures. We first review the conceptual frameworks that identify the underlying theoretical mechanisms by which trust is repaired. We discuss each of these theoretical mechanisms in turn, together with recent empirical investigations of their role in organizational trust repair. We then turn to a review of the stage-based models of trust repair that identify the various stages of actions required to restore organizational trust. We describe and compare these models and review empirical studies that have examined their key propositions.

Theoretical mechanisms underlying trust repair

We first examine the theoretical mechanisms underlying trust repair. Dirks et al. (2009) identify three theoretical processes for understanding trust repair – attributional, social equilibrium and structural. Recently, Bachmann, Gillespie and Priem (2015) proposed an integrative model of six complementary mechanisms for organizational trust repair that incorporates the three mechanisms proposed by Dirks and colleagues. We use this latter framework to organize our review of the theorized mechanisms of organizational trust repair, informed with insights from select recent empirical work on trust repair at the organizational and institutional level.[1]

The sense-making approach

This approach focuses on cognitive and social influence processes and is based on the premise that a shared understanding or accepted account of the trust violation, including an explanation of what went wrong and why, is required for effective trust repair (Bachmann et al., 2015: 1126). This mechanism incorporates (but is broader than) *attributional processes* that involve 'targets shaping "perceivers" attributions about whether they committed a transgression, whether it reflects on their true nature, or whether they experienced redemption' (see Dirks et al., 2009: 72). Strategies include investigations and inquiries to establish an 'official' account of 'what happened and why', as well as explanations, denials, apologies, substantive actions and offers of penance aimed at shifting attributions (Elsbach, 1994; Kim, Dirks, Cooper & Ferrin 2006; Rhee & Valdez, 2009).

Kim and colleagues' (2009) bilateral model of trust repair, while focused on interpersonal relationships, also illuminates some aspects of organizational trust repair. Their model presumes that trustors' and trustees' disagreement about whether the trustees should be trusted following a violation can be resolved through a logically derived sequence of questions: (1) 'Is the trustee innocent or guilty of committing the transgression? (2) If the trustee is guilty of the transgression, should this be attributed to the situation or to the person (in our case, the transgressing organization)? (3) If the transgression is attributed at least in part to the person (i.e. organization), is the shortcoming fix-able or is it an enduring characteristic of the trustee?' (Kim et al, 2009: 405–406). By examining the processes through which people make attributions about others, these scholars help explain why certain repair efforts may work in some contexts but not others. This work also highlights that both the trustor and the 'transgressing party' play active roles in the recovery of trust.

Relatedly, Tomlinson and Mayer (2009) developed an influential attribution theory of trust repair. This theory is based on *causal ascription* – whether trustors ascribe the cause of negative outcomes to a lack of trustee's integrity, competence and/or benevolence, and *causal attribution* – whether the negative outcome is perceived to be due to factors which are external vs. internal, controllable vs. uncontrollable and temporary/unstable vs. enduring/unchanging characteristics of the trustee. Tomlinson and Mayer (2009) propose that social accounts, such as denials, excuses, apologies and justifications, can each repair damaged perceptions of trustworthiness through attributional processes. Thus, for example, trustors' perceptions of a lack of competence or ability among senior managers can be repaired by senior managers showing that the cause of the negative outcome was due to an external factor (such as the international 'credit crunch' of 2007–8 or the sovereign debt crisis of 2011–12), an uncontrollable ability (such as an inability by non-mathematically trained bankers to predict the failure of models), and/or a more unstable form of ability (for example, lack of knowledge by bankers of the risks associated with complex mortgage-backed securities). A review of prominent cases of trust failures reveals that this type of framing of accounts is clearly used by organizations in an attempt to influence the attributions and sense-making of stakeholders (Dietz & Gillespie, 2012; see also Elsbach, 1994).

A prominent example of the sense-making approach in action is the 2010 UK Parliamentary Select Committee's inquiry into the 'Big Four' accounting firms' failures in relation to the global financial crisis. Mueller and colleagues (2015) recently analysed this case to examine the role of inquiries for restoring the public's trust in institutions. Their analysis of testimony revealed stark differences in the way the firm's managing partners and the inquiry committee interpreted and made sense of the organizational failings, and highlighted the notable avoidance of apologies and admissions of responsibility by the Big Four firms in an attempt to avoid attributions of 'fault, liability and blame'. They found that these testimonial accounts were largely discredited and dismissed by the committee who concluded that the audit market could not be trusted and required reform. Importantly, they found that the inquiry served as an important 'field-configuring event' that helped to re-legitimize the institution of auditing in Great Britain.

The relational approach

The relational approach focuses on the role of emotions and social rituals during the repair process. This approach is based on work suggesting that social rituals and symbolic acts are needed to resolve negative emotions caused by the violation and re-establish the social order and norms in the relationship (e.g. Ohbouchi, Kameda & Agarie, 1989; Ren & Gray, 2009; see also Knippernberg, this volume, for a review of affect and trust). This approach builds on and incorporates *social equilibrium processes* of trust repair (see Dirks et al., 2009). Strategies include apologies, penance (e.g. punishment, compensation, 'paying a price'), redistribution of power and resetting expectations that collectively 'settle the accounts', 'rebalance the scales' and re-establish the expectations in the damaged relationship (Dirks et al., 2009; Lewicki & Polin, 2012; Shapiro, 1991).

Most research on the relational approach has been experimental and interpersonally focused. This research suggests that after a significant trust breach, using a combination of relational repair tactics (e.g. apologies and compensation) is likely to be more effective than relying solely on one (Bottom, Gibson, Daniels & Murnighan, 2002). Other experimental research suggests that apologies and compensation work by signalling repentance (Dirks, Kim, Ferrin & Cooper, 2011), that the size of the compensation can influence repair (Desmet et al., 2011a) and that the perceived intentions behind the use of repair tactics are crucial (Schweitzer et al., 2006). Such research also suggests that the nature of the violation can influence the effectiveness of various trust repair strategies (e.g. Kim et al., 2004, 2006; Dirks et al., 2011; Reb, Goldman, Kray & Cropanzano, 2006). At the organizational level, case study research suggests that relational repair tactics are an important component of restoring stakeholder trust in an organization (e.g. Eberl, Geiger & Aßländer, 2015; Dietz & Gillespie, 2011, 2012; Gillespie et al., 2014).

Drawing on both the relational and sense-making mechanisms of trust repair, Stevens, MacDuffie and Helper (2015) take a process perspective to argue that organizations must strive to keep trust close to an optimal level within a 'control band' i.e. neither too low *nor* too high. Through the analysis of longitudinal case study data from supplier-buyer trust at Honda and Nissan, the authors introduce two concepts – recalibration and reorientation of trust – and discuss how these can be used to manage the dynamics of trust maintenance and repair in inter-organizational relationships. An organization, for example, can take smaller-scale, more cost effective recalibration actions when trust is moving towards either the high or low limit of the control band, and thereby anticipate and prevent trust failures. However, if trust is allowed to move out of the acceptable band, more expensive and time consuming reorientation actions aimed at full-blown trust repair are necessary.

Regulation and formal control

Regulation, formal rules and controls are theorized to facilitate trust repair after a breach by constraining untrustworthy behaviour and thereby preventing future organizational trust violations (i.e. 'distrust regulation', see Gillespie & Dietz, 2009). This involves organizations implementing structures 'to provide credible assurance of positive exchange and prevent future transgressions' (Dirks et al., 2009: 72) and relies on rules, structures, laws, policies, codes of conduct, sanctions and incentives to repair trust. These regulatory systems have been shown to repair organizational trust, particularly when introduced voluntarily rather than externally imposed (Dirks et al., 2011; Nakayachi & Watabe, 2005).

The inter-relationship between trust and control has a long history in the sociological literature. Institutional arrangements like contracts, role and authority structures have been referred to by Granovetter (1985: 491) as the under-socialized approaches. Drawing on these under-socialized approaches, Shapiro (1987) argues that 'impersonal trust' – founded in norms, rules and structures that procedural constrain agency, as well as selection and policing mechanisms (e.g. licensing, certification, accreditation, compliance checks), and insurance like arrangements – may provide an alternative to personalized or embedded trust relationships, particularly when trustors do not have viable means to monitor or control agents (e.g. due to lack of expertise or power). In line with Zucker (1986), Shapiro (1987) argues that these 'guardians of impersonal trust' represent institutional mechanisms that produce trust (rather than being a functional substitute for trust). However, paradoxically, these sources of impersonal trust also provide the opportunity and means for its abuse ('who guards the guardians of trust?'; see Shapiro, 1987: 645; see also Barber, 1983). Other sociological work drawing on neo-institutional theory, for example by Zucker (1986) and Lane and Bachmann (1996), emphasizes the role of the broader institutional context, including institutional norms and safeguards for the creation, maintenance and repair of trust. This focus on societal structures and norms also resonates with Luhmann's (1979) concept of system trust, which supports trust relations in organizations (Child and Möllering, 2003).

In their important theoretical and empirical contribution, Sitkin and Roth (1993) explain why legalistic remedies to damaged trust might have limited effectiveness. Their explanation draws on two aspects of trust: first, trust as expectations about an employee's ability to complete task assignments reliably (task reliability), and second, distrust which happens when the compatibility of an employee's values with the organization's cultural values is called into question (generalized value incongruence). They conclude that formal controls are effective only for restoring breaches of task reliability, not value incongruence.

A recent case study of the Siemens bribery scandal by Eberl and colleagues (2015) found that although the imposition of more rigourous internal rules restored trust with external stakeholders, at the same time it reduced flexibility in dealing with customers and suppliers, thereby demotivating employees. Their study points to the value of structural mechanisms for trust repair while also highlighting the limitations of an overly rule-based approach. Similarly, the role and limitations of structural mechanisms for trust repair are evident in Spicer and Okhmatovskiy's (2015) recent study of trust repair in the Russian bank deposit market. The authors distinguished between trust recovery due to increased regulation by the state from trust recovery due to the state's full ownership of a particular bank. They conclude that state ownership is an important independent predictor of trust repair, to a much greater degree than any other efforts by the state to regulate banks. The authors claim that regulations and their implementation are perceived by potential customers as more ephemeral than is ownership. Finally, in their meta-analysis of trust in the financial services sector, Nienaber, Hofeditz & Searle (2014) conclude that regulation is an important, but by itself insufficient, strategy for restoring trust in financial services firms.

Informal cultural controls

Organizational culture and informal controls represents another mechanism for constraining untrustworthy behaviour and promoting trustworthy behaviour in organizations (McKendall & Wagner, 1997). A corrupt, unethical or lax organizational culture is frequently implicated in trust betrayals (e.g. Seimens, FIFA, Enron, etc). Repair tactics involve implementing cultural reforms that identify and challenge the values, norms and beliefs that enabled the trust breach, as well as HR processes (e.g. induction, socialization, training, mentoring and performance management), symbolic messaging and principled leadership that reinforce desired values and behaviour, and make unethical behaviour salient and counter-cultural.

This is an important mechanism for trust repair, given work suggesting that, through identity compartmentalization, unethical organizational cultures can thrive even in the context of and in defiance of ethical norms held by employees and society (Ashforth & Mael, 1989). Sztompka (1999) identifies a breakdown in professionalism as a major contributor to organizational trust problems, as trust in the way professionals conduct their roles is a foundation to presumptive forms of trust (i.e. role-based trust, see Kramer, 1999).

Valuable insights into the role of organizational culture in trust repair can also be found in case study and practitioner reports that document case studies of successful trust preservation and repair. One such example is the CIPD report by Hope-Hailey, Searle and Dietz (2012) that draws on empirical data from UK organizations such as John Lewis Partnership, Sunderland City Council, Royal Mail and Day Lewis Pharmacy to examine the role of HR in rebuilding trust. The report demonstrates that re-establishing and preserving a culture of trust within an organization is closely tied to HR policies and practices, and how they are implemented by managers, as each area of HR policy signals the organization's competence, but also its integrity and genuine interest in the well-being of its employees.

Gillespie, Dietz and Lockey (2014) recently proposed that, in the context of an organizational integrity violation, reforms to the organizational culture *will be required* to robustly restore stakeholders' trust: structural and procedural reforms alone will not be sufficient. This aligns with the work of Michael (2006) who laments that the dominant response to corporate scandals is to address the problem through rule-based mechanisms, and points out that rules cannot substitute for an ethical culture and decision-making. The need to complement formal controls with informal cultural controls for trust repair is also a theme in Eberl et al.'s (2015) case study analysis of the Seimens case (see also Sitkin & George, 2005). Gillespie et al. (2014) also offer two other culturally related propositions, namely that in the context of an integrity violation: (a) the replacement of senior managers implicated in the trust failure (i.e. 'changing of the guard') and (b) (re-)establishing a positive organizational identity among employees (i.e. honouring and holding onto what is 'good'), will speed up and increase the likelihood that the organization will restore stakeholders' trust. In their case study analysis, they describe the cultural reforms and identity work that the organizational underwent as part of the trust repair process.

Other empirical work reinforces the central relevance and importance of the last of these strategies – identity work – for trust repair with employees. Maguire and Phillips (2008) demonstrate empirically that institutional trust, like interpersonal trust, can be identity-based. Based on a case study of Citibank in a post-merger context, the authors propose an identity-based framework for understanding employee trust in an organization, demonstrating how institutional trust is initially undermined by the ambiguity of the new organization's identity, and how, later, institutional trust can continue to be undermined by a lack of employees' identification with the new organization.

More recently, in a case study of BP during the 2010 Gulf of Mexico oil rig explosion and spill, Petriglieri (2015) found that the incident destabilized executives' organizational identification, leading to doubts about their alignment with the organization and their role within it. As a result of the trust breach, executives either re-identified and repaired their relationship with the organization, or severed the relationship. Re-identification occurred when BP executives were directly involved in the organization's response to the incident, highlighting the importance of co-creation in trust repair. In contrast, being excluded from the organization's trust repair efforts further alienated executives and hindered their re-identification.

Transparency and accountability

The focus here is on organizational reporting and monitoring based on the view that 'transparently sharing relevant information about organizational decision processes and functioning with stakeholders helps restore trust' (Bachmann et al., 2015: 1126). This mechanism is prevalent in the literature on corporate governance and public management, which suggests that principles of accountability, transparency and disclosure lay the foundation for trust (see also Child & Rodrigues, 2004).

In support of this mechanism, recent research using an experimental paradigm found that self-disclosure of negative information lessens the damaging impact of this information on consumer trust and judgements towards the company, compared to third party disclosure of the same information (Fennis & Stroebe, 2014). This relationship was found to hold for companies that had a poor reputation at the outset, whereas for companies that enjoyed a positive reputation, type of disclosure (self vs. third party) did not affect consumer trust.

Although there is much emphasis on the importance of transparent government for citizen trust, empirical evidence of a relationship between transparency and trust in government is equivocal and qualified. For example, Grimmelikhuijsen and colleagues (2013) found that transparency has a subdued and sometimes negative effect on trust in government. Furthermore, Grimmelikhuijsen and colleagues (2014) find that a positive relationship between transparency and citizens' perceptions of trust in government only occurs for the minority of citizens who have low prior knowledge of the policy topic and a low predisposition to trust the government. These experimental findings suggest that the relationship between transparency and trust in institutional and organizational contexts is far from simple or evident, and requires further empirical evaluation, as well as how these effects translate to the unique setting of trust repair.

Trust transference

This mechanism draws on the role of third parties in trust repair, based on the premise that trust can be transferred from a credible party to a discredited party through the use of certifications, memberships, affiliations and endorsements. Third parties have been found to act as the 'go-betweens' in new relationships that enable new parties to 'roll over' their expectations from the well-established relationship to the newly formed relationship where there is little knowledge or history (Shapiro, 1987; Uzzi, 1997). They do this by transferring expectations and opportunities in existing relationships to newly formed ones. In interpersonal contexts, the influence of third-party endorsements has even been shown to be equivalent to that of direct experience with the other party (Ferrin, Dirks & Shah, 2006). McEvily, Perrone & Zaheer (2003) identify that transferability is one important mechanism through which trust acts as an organizing mechanism, creating density and closure of a network.

An organizational example of trust transference comes from the previously described case study of the UK inquiry into the 'Big Four' accounting failures. In this study, Mueller and colleagues (2015) identify that a key component of the trust repair was the transfer of trustworthiness from the impartial parliamentary committee leading the inquiry to the damaged audit firms. Compared to the other trust repair mechanisms, limited work has directly examined the potentially influential role of the transference of trust for organizational trust repair; however, there is a healthy related literature on legitimacy spill-over effects in the institutional literature (e.g. see Haack, Pfarrer & Scherer, 2014; Zavyalova, Pfarrer, Reger & Shapiro, 2012).

Stage models of trust repair

Notable in the organizational trust repair literature are 'stage' models of trust repair that identify the steps and strategies that can be undertaken by a transgressor organization to restore trust. In so doing, these models typically incorporate several of the underlying trust repair mechanisms reviewed above. These include models by Lewicki and Bunker (1996), Gillespie and Dietz (2009) and Pfarrer and colleagues (2008).

The first stage model was proposed by Lewicki and Bunker (1996) and involved: (1) recognizing and acknowledging that a violation has occurred, (2) determining the nature of the violation (establishing what/who caused the violation), (3) admitting the destructive impact of the event on trust, and finally (4) willingness to accept responsibility for the violation. Hence, this model incorporates both the sense-making and relational mechanisms of trust repair.

Gillespie and Dietz (2009) proposed a model of restoring trust following an organization-level failure. They drew on the literature on trust, crisis management, strategic change, and systems and multilevel theory to propose that perceptions of an organization's trustworthiness are influenced by signals sent from four internal organizational components (leadership and management practice, structure and processes, culture and climate, and strategy) and two external components (external governance and public reputation). Based on this foundation, they propose a four-stage process of repairing trust, which integrates most of the trust repair mechanisms previously reviewed. The four stages are outlined below, together with the underlying repair mechanisms focused on at each stage:

1 *immediate response* (within the first few days of the scandal), such as verbal acknowledgement, announcement of internal investigation, and early intervention against known causes. (sense-making and relational mechanisms);

2 *diagnosis* of the causes of the failure, in a timely, accurate and transparent manner (sense-making and transparency mechanisms);

3 *reforming interventions* to the organizational system to prevent future transgressions and demonstrate renewed trustworthiness. This includes achieving integrated structural and procedural, cultural, strategic and leadership practice reforms (as derived from the diagnosis), coupled with apologies, reparations and penance, where appropriate (structural, cultural and relational mechanisms);

4 *evaluation* of the effectiveness of repair actions, to monitor and inform the need for ongoing interventions and reforms (structural, cultural and sense-making mechanisms).

Pfarrer and colleagues (2008) offer a different conceptualization of reintegration post crisis. The authors outline a process of 'reintegration' with stakeholders after a corporate transgression (i.e. a corrupt or unethical act). Drawing on the literature on stakeholder theory, image management, organizational justice and crisis management, they define reintegration as the process of rebuilding legitimacy in stakeholder relationships damaged by the organization's wrongdoing. The authors propose the following stages that are designed to address changing stakeholder questions and concerns across the reintegration process: (1) discovery 'What happened?' incorporating voluntary disclosure, internal investigation and public cooperation; (2) explanation 'How did it happen?' involving acknowledging wrongdoing, expressing regret, accepting responsibility and apologies; (3) penance 'How will the organization be punished?' including accepting the verdict, accepting punishment without resistance; and (4) rehabilitation 'What changes have been made?' including introducing internal or external changes. A key proposition underlying the model is that reintegration is more likely if the organization responds to the demands of the most salient stakeholder groups (i.e. those that have the 'most power, legitimacy and urgency of claims', noting that stakeholder salience can change over time) and achieves 'concurrence' at each stage of reintegration, that is 'a generally shared opinion among stakeholders regarding the transgression and appropriateness of the organization's actions', (Pfarrer et al., 2008: 733)

There are some parallels between these latter two frameworks: they both focus on the closely linked concepts of legitimacy and organizational trustworthiness, are deliberately normative, outlining a staged process with complementary actions, and imply that by making appropriate internal organizational reforms coupled with external governance, trust can be restored in organizations (for a summary table comparing these models, see Gillespie et al., 2014). However, these models each emphasize different aspects of the process and make unique propositions.

What is striking about all three models is that they are underpinned by an emphasis on rational action that needs to be 'timely' and 'accurate'. If a transgression has occurred, the organization's leaders (and/or those with a governance responsibility) are expected to determine the nature of the transgression, find the cause, apologize, offer reparations, launch investigations, and introduce internal and external changes. Thus, one of the core assumptions is a belief in managerial agency to address the trust breach: that is, managers are credited with the ability and authority to influence stakeholders' perceptions of the organization's trustworthiness and the legitimacy of its actions, post-violation. Hence when faced with damaged trust, managers are normally expected to take the initiative of rebuilding trust and are attributed with the power and authority to do so (Mayer & Gavin, 2005).

Two research reports published by the Institute of Business Ethics (Dietz & Gillespie, 2011; 2012) use case studies of organizations that have attempted to repair trust in practice (e.g. Mattel,

Toyota, BP, Siemens, BAE Systems and the BBC), to illustrate, support and extend the stage models of trust repair and the propositions that underlie them. In doing so, these reports explicitly highlighted a central tension often apparent in organizational trust repair: the choice between a legalistic versus relationship-based approach. The *legalistic route* aims to minimize financial risk to the company and avoids media exposure by closely containing information about the failure, for example, through reticence, denial, a lack of transparency, super-injunctions or disciplinary action against allegations. Poppo and Schepker (2010) suggest this approach is the most appropriate when organizations are embroiled in a scandal. The *relationship approach*, on the other hand, is based on the alternative premise that the best way to protect the organization's reputation is by effective management of the organization's relationships with its stakeholders, for example through transparency, candid communication, demonstrating concern for the impact of the failure on stakeholders and making reparations. In most cases these two approaches are incompatible, and yield very different long-term results.

More recently, Gillespie and colleagues (2014) conducted a longitudinal, case study examining how a UK water utility repaired trust with its stakeholders after a major integrity violation. Their results generally supported the view that thorough responses in each of the four stages proposed by Pfarrer et al. (2008) and Gillespie and Dietz (2009) facilitate effective organizational reintegration and trust repair. Their analysis of the two diametrically opposed approaches successively taken by the company's senior management team support the view that open, cooperative and conciliatory responses akin to the *relational approach* (e.g. transparency, acknowledging wrongdoing, accepting responsibility, expressing remorse) facilitate effective trust repair, whereas defensive approaches akin to the *legalistic approach* (e.g. denial, obfuscation) can undermine repair and create further distrust. Hence, these findings challenge the view proposed by some scholars (e.g. Kim et al., 2004; Poppo & Schepker, 2010; Mueller et al., 2015) that denying an integrity violation is more effective than apologizing. The case further supported the proposition by Pfarrer and colleagues (2008) that stakeholder salience and status shift across the reintegration process, and underlined the importance of attending to the most salient stakeholder at each stage.

Future research into organizational trust repair

The ontology and epistemology of trust repair

Much (but not all) of the foundational trust repair literature is based on functionalist assumptions of trust in organizations, i.e. a belief that trust can be managed through a set of relatively simple prescriptions (Möllering, 2006). These studies have adopted the language of variance theory (Langley, 1999; Van de Ven, 2007), which involves identification of antecedents and outcomes of trust repair and explanations of causal relationships between dependent and independent variables. The focus of these studies is on evaluations of trust repair interventions and on delineating those independent variables (i.e. trust repair responses) that shape recovery. The independent variables most commonly used in this research are apology and denial (e.g. Tomlinson, Dineen & Lewicki, 2004; Ferrin et al., 2007; Kim & colleagues, 2004, 2006, 2009), reticence (e.g. Ferrin et al., 2007), excuse, penance, financial compensation and justification (e.g. Bottom et al., 2002; Desmet et al. 2011a, b; Dirks & colleagues, 2006, 2011).

These normative studies of trust repair are based on a mechanical metaphor – when trust is broken, it needs to be rebuilt. Though such studies are very insightful and practically useful (particularly for interpersonal trust repair), they fail to reflect the complex reality of organizational trust repair. Some studies on trust critique the underpinning assumptions behind the majority of research that trust can be achieved in all types of relationships in an organization and that managers have the ability to shape trust relations in the interests of all. It is these two core assumptions – the extent of common goals and managerial agency – that most disturb radical theorists as they ignore the conflicting agendas that are at the heart of managing industrial relations. Some notable exceptions include Child and Rodrigues (2004) who argued that employees have too much trust in organizations that have progressively failed them, Thompson (2011) and Delbridge and Keenoy (2011) who rejected the notion of managerial agency in favour of an argument that supports the effects of strong institutional forces on employee engagement and trust, and Bijlsma-Frankema, Sitkin and Weibel (2015) who question the idea that trust can be repaired once distrust is engendered.

Our review of the extant literature indicates that there is little interpretive research on organizational trust repair. Moreover, what little exists is underpinned by interpretive thinking rather than being truly interpretive in nature. Radical perspectives are under-represented in intra-organizational trust research (Siebert, Martin, Bozic & Docherty, 2015), and this under-representation is also noticeable in organizational trust repair research. The study by Child and Rodrigues (2004) mentioned earlier suggested that breach of trust in many contemporary organizations was caused by an increase of hostile takeovers resulting in job losses, as well as by hierarchical structures in the workplace that promoted distinction and introduced divides through vast pay differentials and unequal levels of reward for performance. The authors also argued that neo-liberal thinking encouraged free allocation of resources and justified less favourable treatment of people under the guise of flexible employment practices. Despite an increasing awareness of the importance of employee trust to organizational performance, evident in the functionalist literature, there appeared to be an increase of employee fear, organizational cynicism and disengagement.

The work of Alan Fox is relevant and influential on this point. Fox (1966, 1974) is credited with making two major contributions to sociological accounts of trust within organizations. The first is a macro-sociological account of unitarist, pluralist and radical frames of reference in British industrial relations during the 1960s and 1970s. The second is a micro-sociological account of how trust dynamics in the workplace are shaped by social relations, specifically relations involving power and the division of labour in bureaucratic organizations in capitalist societies. Fox's conception of trust is often used to explain the relationship between work organization, contract and power relations between managers and employees (Starkey, 1989; Provis, 1996). Fox's (1974) analysis points to an institutionalized withholding of trust by employees made evident by suspicion, jealousy, misreading of people's motives and a lack of cooperation. Such approaches are beginning to emerge in contemporary studies of organizational trust repair (for example, Mueller et al.'s 2015 paper), but more work is needed to explore these issues further.

Siebert et al. (2015) argue that one of the limitations of trust and trust repair research is that it is often limited to what happens inside organizations while ignoring the external influences. Arguably, by focusing on the organization as the unit of analysis, researchers fail to deal with problems such as recessions, global trends in employment, civil unrests, decline of trust in institutions, politics and ideology. Many important contextual variables such as the impact of power, regimes of governance and the influence of the wider political economy should be taken into consideration while investigating how organizations can secure organizational trust among employees. A more critical perspective on trust repair may enable us to challenge or problematize underlying assumptions and ask more interesting questions that break existing paradigmatic boundaries, as well as generating novel theoretical and practical insights.

Such critical perspectives on trust repair are not the only way forward, and we conclude this chapter by suggesting other alternative theoretical perspectives on trust repair: structure agency debates, process theory and institutional theory. We also point the reader to recent reviews by Bachmann et al. (2015), Dirks et al. (2009) and Kramer and Lewicki (2010) for further suggestions on the future of trust repair research.

Structure-agency debate and trust repair

The majority of trust repair studies place undue faith in managers' ability to *manage* trust relations, and ignore the role of external factors that might affect organizational reintegration (Möllering, 2006). Shifting emphasis away from an organization as a unit of analysis to a broader focus on trust in institutions and social structures might throw some light on why some organizations cannot repair trust despite their genuine efforts to do so (Child & Rodrigues, 2004). Hence considering both the 'structure' (i.e. the broader institutional context for organizations) and 'agency' (i.e. management actions inside the organization) might enrich theoretical insights on trust repair and have practical implications for organizations. Such a rebalancing that acknowledges the structure-agency debate (Giddens, 1984), and takes cognizance of unintended consequences of managerial action (MacKay and Chia, 2013) in trust repair, may allow trust researchers to recognize the limitations of the current prescriptions and avoid raising unrealistic expectations of repair. For example, Gillespie, Hurley, Dietz and Bachmann (2012) apply this dual perspective in their analysis of strategies for repairing trust in banks following the global financial crisis: focusing trust repair efforts only internally within banks might not yield any results if we fail to acknowledge that more fundamental or radical changes are required in the institution of banking in general – its governance and state regulation (see also Nienaber, Hofeditz & Searle, 2014).

Institutional perspectives

Given the a-contextual and a-historical nature of much of the trust repair literature, a focus on how organizations are embedded in and conditioned by higher levels of institutions would seem relevant in providing a more nuanced explanation of how trust is restored.

Early institutionalists argued that by their 'embeddedness' in a broader institutional context organizations ensured structural isomorphism and ended up pursuing similar courses of action. In contrast to the early institutionalism, which predicts that organizations do not possess the necessary degree of agency because they are firmly embedded in the institutional fields, more recent institutional theory has begun to question the determinism of neo-institutionalism by promoting the role of agency among organizational actors (Lawrence & Suddaby, 2006). One such aspect of institutional theorizing is institutional work, defined as 'intelligent, situated institutional action' (Lawrence & Suddaby, 2006: 219). Institutional work provides a nuanced view of the relationship between actors and institutions (Dacin, Munir & Tracey, 2010; Lok & De Rond, 2013) and broadly identifies three institutional processes: creating, maintaining and disrupting institutions. However, in recent years, scholars have begun to discuss another aspect of institutional work – institutional repair in the face of practice breakdowns. These studies usually focus on institutions in moments of vulnerability and in situations in which the institution is being challenged (because of new entrants, practice breakdowns, breaches or external jolts) and thus the effortful work of maintaining the institution can be clearly seen (Lok & De Rond, 2013; Micelotta & Washington, 2013; Heapy, 2013). There are some parallels between investigations into trust breaches and practice breakdowns, and institutional literature might illuminate new ways of theorizing trust repair. An institutional perspective on trust repair may also open doors to the consideration of wider institutions such as the legal system, religion or political systems in shaping trust relations in organizations and institutions.

Process theory of trust repair

Although there is some recognition in the literature that trust in itself is a process (Khodyakov 2007; Möllering, 2006), the processual nature of trust repair remains underdeveloped. There have been recent calls for adopting a process theory approach to produce more complex accounts of trust repair and its attendant problems (Bachmann et al., 2015; Nooteboom, 1996; Möllering, 2013). Such approaches, which incorporate process rather than variance theorizing, have much to commend them because they deal explicitly with the longitudinal nature of trust repair. Recently, Bjilsma-Frankema and colleagues (2015) proposed a dynamic process model of distrust development that explains how and why distrust becomes entrenched in a 'self-ampli-fying cycle'. As organizational trust failures not only diminish trust, but typically trigger active distrust, this work provides important insights for trust repair. In particular, it highlights the central need to overcome perceptions of value incongruence for distrust to be overcome, and trust to be rebuilt.

Some trust repair research can be characterized by imputing a relatively unconstrained agency to senior managers' capabilities to restore trust through a set of relatively simple prescriptions, such as the symbolic and material trust repair strategies and practices discussed previously. Challenging the notion of inflated managerial agency, Siebert and Martin (2014) have suggested that 'leaving things alone' might in some cases be an effective strategy. This counter-intuitive strategy of inaction represents a threat to managerial identities and is inconsistent with the current dominant association between leadership and change. This approach, however, might suggest that leaving the process of trust repair, for example, to the influence of fading memory con-nected with the passage of time or distracting the attention of organizational stakeholders might work equally well in some circumstances, but empirical investigations are needed.

Concluding remarks

In this chapter we have provided a selective review of the extant conceptual and empirical work on repairing trust in organizations and institutions. In so doing, we identified the dominant epistemological and ontological paradigms taken in the literature to date, which largely takes a normative functionalist perspective based on variance language. We argue that while these dominant paradigms have provided a necessary and helpful foundation to this nascent field, there is a need to complement this work with critical and radical perspectives to deepen under-standing of the constraints to, and macro-level influences on, organizational trust repair. To this end, we encourage future scholarship to integrate structure-agency and institutional perspectives, as well as focus on the processual and dynamic nature of organizational trust repair.

Note

1. We point the reader to the original article for a discussion of the limitations and paradoxes of each trust repair mechanism.

References

Ashforth, B. E., & Mael, F. (1989). Social identity theory and the organization. *Academy of Management Review*, 14: 20–39.
Bachmann, R. (2001). Trust, power and control in trans-organizational relations. *Organization Studies*, 22(2): 337–65.
Bachmann, R., Gillespie, N., & Priem, R. (2015). Repairing trust in organizations and institutions: Towards a conceptual framework. *Organization Studies*, 36(9): 1123–1142.

Bachmann, R., & Inkpen, A. (2011). Understanding institutional-based trust building processes in inter-organizational relationships. *Organization Studies*, 32(2): 281–3011.

Barber, B. 1983. *The logic and limits of trust*. New Brunswick, NJ: Rutgers University Press.

Bijlsma-Frankema, K. M., Sitkin, S. B., & Weibel, A. (2015). Distrust in the balance: The emergence and development of intergroup distrust in a court of law. *Organization Science*, 26(4): 1018–1139.

Bottom, W. P., Gibson, K., Daniels, S. E., & Murnighan, J. K. (2002). When talk is not cheap: Substantive penance and expressions of intent in rebuilding cooperation. *Organization Science*, 13: 497–513.

Child, J. and Möllering, G. (2003). Contextual confidence and active trust development in the chinese business, environment. *Organization Science*, 14(1): 69–80.

Child, J., & Rodrigues, S. (2004). Repairing the breach of trust in corporate governance. *Corporate Governance*, 12(2): 143–152.

Dacin, M.T., Munir, K., & Tracey, P. (2010). Formal dining at Cambridge Colleges: Linking ritual performance and institutional maintenance. *Academy of Management Journal*, 53(6): 1393–1418.

Delbridge, R., & Keenoy, T. (2011). Beyond managerialism. *The International Journal of Human Resource Management*, 21: 799–817.

Desmet, P. T. M., De Cremer, D., & Van Dijk, E. (2011a). In money we trust? Financial compensations as a means to repair trust in the aftermath of distributive harm. *Organizational Behavior and Human Decision Processes*, 114: 75–86.

Desmet, P. T. M., De Cremer, D., & Van Dijk, E. (2011b). Trust recovery following voluntary or forced financial compensations in the trust game: The role of trait forgiveness: Personality and Economics English. *Personality and individual differences*, 51: 267–273.

Dietz, G., & Gillespie, N. (2011). *Building and restoring organizational trust*. London: Institute of Business Ethics.

Dietz, G., & Gillespie, N. (2012). *The recovery of trust: case studies of organizational failures and trust repair*. London: Institute of Business Ethics.

Dirks, K. T., Cooper, C., Ferrin, D., & Kim, P. (2006). When more blame is better than less: The implications of internal vs. external attributions for the repair of trust after a competence- vs. integrity-based trust violation. *Organizational Behavior and Human Decision Processes*, 99(4): 49–65.

Dirks, K. T., Kim, P. H., Ferrin, D. L., & Cooper, C. D. (2011). Understanding the effects of substantive responses on trust following a transgression. *Organizational Behavior and Human Decision Processes*, 114(2): 87–103.

Dirks, K., Lewicki, R., & Zaheer, A. (2009). Repairing relationships within and between organizations: Building a conceptual foundation. *Academy Of Management Review*, 34(1): 68–84.

Eberl, P., Geiger, D., & Aßländer, M. (2015). Repairing trust in an organization after integrity violations: The ambivalence of organizational rule adjustments. *Organization Studies*, 36: 1205–1235.

Elsbach, K. D. (1994). Managing organizational legitimacy in the California cattle industry: The construction and effectiveness of verbal accounts. *Administrative Science Quarterly*, 39(1): 57–88.

Fennis, B. M., & Stroebe, W. (2014). Softening the blow: Company self-disclosure of negative information lessens damaging effects on consumer judgment and decision making. *Journal of Business Ethics*, 120(1): 109–120.

Ferrin, D. L., Kim, P. H., Cooper, C. D., & Dirks, K. T. (2007). Silence speaks volumes: The effectiveness of reticence in comparison to apology and denial for responding to integrity– and competence–based trust violations. *Journal of Applied Psychology*, 92: 893–908.

Ferrin, D. L., Dirks, K. T., & Shah, P. P. (2006). Direct and indirect effects of third-party relationships on interpersonal trust. *Journal of Applied Psychology*, 91(4): 870–883.

Fox, A. (1966). *Research papers 3: Industrial sociology and industrial relations*. London, UK: Her Majesty's Stationery Office.

Fox, A. (1974). *Beyond contract: Work, power and trust relations*. London, UK: Faber and Faber.

Fulmer, C. A., & Gelfand, M. J. (2012). At what level (and in whom) we trust: Trust across multiple organizational levels. *Journal of Management*, 38(4): 1167–1230.

Giddens, A. (1984). *The constitution of society: Outline of the theory of structuration*. Cambridge, UK: Polity Press.

Gillespie, N., & Dietz, G. (2009). Trust repair after an organization-level failure. *Academy of Management Review*, 34(1): 127–145.

Gillespie, N., Dietz, G., & Lockey, S. (2014). Organizational reintegration and trust repair after an integrity violation: A case study. *Business Ethics Quarterly*, 24(3): 371–410.

Gillespie, N., Hurley, R., Dietz, G., & Bachmann, R. (2012). Restoring institutional trust after the global financial crisis. In Roderick M. Kramer and Todd L. Pittinsky (eds), *Restoring trust in organizations and leaders: Enduring challenges and emerging answers*. New York: Oxford University Press, 186–216.

Granovetter, M. (1985). Economic action and social structure: The problem of embeddedness. *American Journal of Sociology*, 91: 481–510.

Grimmelikhuijsen, S. J., & Meijer, A. J. (2014). The effects of transparency on the perceived trustworthiness of government organization: Evidence from an online experiment. *Journal of Public Administration Theory and Research*, 24(1): 137–157.

Grimmelikhuijsen, S. G., Porumbescu, G., Hong, B., and Im, T. (2013). The effect of transparency on trust in government: A cross-national comparative experiment. *Public Administration Review*, 73(4): 575–586.

Haack, P., Pfaffer, M. D., & Scherer, A. G. (2014). Legitimacy-as-feeling: How affect leads to vertical legitimacy spillovers in transnational governance. *Journal of Management Studies*, 51(4): 634–666.

Heapy, E. D. (2013). Repairing breaches with rules: Maintaining institutions in the face of everyday disruptions. *Organization Science*, 24(5): 1291–1315.

Hope-Hailey, V., Searle, R., & Dietz, G. (2012). *Where has all the trust gone?* London: Chartered Institute of Personnel and Development.

Khodyakov, D. (2007). Trust as a process: A three-dimensional approach. *Sociology*, 41(1): 115–132.

Kim, P. H., Dirks, K. T., & Cooper, C.D. (2009). The repair of trust: A dynamic bilateral perspective and multilevel conceptualization. *Academy of Management Review*, 34: 410–422.

Kim, P. H., Ferrin, D. L., Cooper, C. D., & Dirks, K. T. (2004). Removing the shadow of suspicion: The effects of apology versus denial for repairing competence versus integrity based trust violations. *Journal of Applied Psychology*, 89: 104–118.

Kim, P. H., Dirks, K. T., Cooper, C. D., & Ferrin, D. L. (2006). When more blame is better than less: The implications of internal vs. external attributions for the repair of trust after a competence- vs. integrity-based trust violation. *Organizational Behavior and Human Decision Processes*, 99: 49–65.

Kramer, R. M. (1999). Trust and distrust in organizations: Emerging perspectives, enduring questions. *Annual Review of Psychology*, 50: 569–598.

Kramer, R. M. (2010). Collective trust within organizations: Conceptual foundations and empirical insights. *Corporate Reputation Review*, 13: 82–97.

Kramer, R. M., & Lewicki, R. J. (2010). Repairing and enhancing trust: Approaches to reducing organizational trust deficits. *Academy of Management Annals*, 4(1): 245–277.

Lamin, A., & Zaheer, S. (2012). Wall street versus main street: Firm strategies for defending legitimacy and their impact on different stakeholders. *Organization Science*, 23(1): 47–66.

Lane, C., & Bachmann, R. (1996). The social constitution of trust: Supplier relations in Britain and Germany. *Organization Studies*, 17(3): 365–395.

Langley, A. (1999). Strategies for theorizing from process data. *The Academy of Management Review*, 24: 691–710.

Lawrence, T., & Suddaby, R. (2006). 'Institutional work'. In *Handbook of organization studies*, 2nd edition. S. Clegg, C. Hardy, and T. Lawrence (eds), London: Sage, 215–254.

Lewicki, R. J., & Bunker, B. (1996). Developing and maintaining trust in work relationships. In R. M. Kramer & T. R. Tyler (eds), *Trust in organizations: frontiers of theory and research* (pp. 114–139). Thousand Oaks, CA: SAGE Publications.

Lewicki, R. J., & Polin, B. (2012). The Art of the Apology: The structure and effectiveness of apologies in trust repair. In R. M. Kramer, & T. Pittinsky, (eds), *Restoring Trust in Organizations and Leaders: Enduring Challenges and Emerging Answers*. Oxford, UK: Oxford University Press.

Lok, J., & de Rond, M. (2013). On the plasticity of institutions: Containing and restoring practice breakdowns at the Cambridge University Boat Club. *Academy of Management Journal*, 56(1): 85–207.

Luhmann, N. (1979). *Trust and Power*. Chichester: Wiley.

MacKay, R. B., & Chia, R. (2013). Choice, chance, and unintended consequences in strategic change: A process of understanding of the rise and fall of Northco Automotive. *Academy of Management Journal*, 56(1): 208–230.

Maguire, S., & Phillips, N. (2008). 'Citibankers' at Citigroup: A study of the loss of institutional trust after a merger. *Journal of Management Studies*, 45(2): 372–401.

Mayer, R. C., & Gavin, M. B. (2005). Trust in management and performance: Who minds the shop while the employees watch the boss? *Academy of Management Journal*, 48(5): 874–888.

McEvily, B., Perrone, V., & Zaheer, A. (2003). Trust as an organizing principle. *Organization Science*, 14(1): 91–103.

McKendall, M. A., & Wagner, J. A. (1997). Motive, opportunity, choice, and corporate illegality. *Organization Science*, 8(6): 624–1647.

Micelotta, E. R., & Washington, M. (2013). Institutions and maintenance: The repair work of Italian professions. *Organization Studies*, 34(8): 1137–1170.

Michael, M. L. (2006). Business ethics: The law of rules. *Business Ethics Quarterly*, 16(4): 475–504.

Misztal, B. A. (1996). *Trust in modern societies*. Cambridge, UK: Polity Press.

Möllering, G. (2001). The nature of trust: From Georg Simmel to a theory of expectation, interpretation and suspension. *Sociology*, 35: 403–420.

Möllering, G. (2006). *Trust: Reason, routine, reflexivity*. Amsterdam, the Netherlands: Elsevier Science.

Möllering, G. (2013). Process view of trusting and crisis. In Bachmann, R. and Zaheer, A. (eds), *Handbook of Advances in Trust Research*, Cheltenham, UK: Edward Elgar Publishing, 285–306.

Mueller, F., Carter, C., & Whittle, A. (2015). Can audit (still) be trusted? *Organization Studies*, 36: 1171–1203.

Nakayachi, K., & Watabe, M. (2005). Restoring trustworthiness after adverse events: The signaling effects of voluntary "Hostage Posting" on trust. *Organizational Behavior and Human Decision Processes*, 97(1): 1–17.

Nienaber, A. M., Hofeditz, M., & Searle, R. (2014). Do we bank on regulation or reputation? A meta-analysis and meta-regression of organizational trust in the financial services sector. *International Journal of Bank Marketing*, 32(5): 367–407.

Nooteboom, B. (1996). Trust, opportunism and governance: A process and control model. *Organization Studies*, 17(6): 985–1010.

Ohbuchi, K., Kameda, M., & Agarie, N. (1989). Apology as aggression control: Its role in mediating appraisal of and response to harm. *Journal of Personality and Social Psychology*, 56: 219–227.

Petriglieri, J. L. (2015). Co-creating relationship repair: Pathways to reconstructing destabilized organizational identification. *Administrative Science Quarterly*, DOI: 10.1177/0001839215579234

Pfarrer M., DeCelles, K., Smith, K., & Taylor, M. (2008). After the fall: Reintegrating the corrupt organization. *Academy of Management Review*, 33(3): 730–749.

Poppo, L., & Schepker, D.J. (2010). Repairing public trust in organizations. *Corporate Reputation Review*, 13(2): 124–141.

Provis, C. (1996). Unitarism, pluralism, interests and values. *British Journal of Industrial Relations*, 34(4): 473–495.

Reb, J., Goldman, B. M., Kray, L. J., & Cropanzano, R. (2006). Different wrongs, different remedies? Reactions to organizational remedies after procedural and interactional injustice. *Personnel Psychology*, 59: 31–64.

Ren, H., & Gray, B. (2009). Repairing relationship conflict: How violation types and culture influence the effectiveness of restoration rituals. *Academy of Management Review*, 34: 105–126.

Rhee, M. & Valdez, M. (2009). Contextual factors surrounding reputation damage with potential implications for reputation repair. *Academy of Management Review*, 34(1): 146–168.

Schweitzer, M. E., Hershey, J. C., & Bradlow, E. T. (2006). Promises and lies: Restoring violated trust. *Organizational Behavior and Human Decision Processes*, 101(1): 1–19.

Shapiro, S. P. (1987). The social control of impersonal trust. *American Journal of Sociology*, 93(3): 623–658.

Shapiro, D. L. (1991). The effects of explanations on negative reactions to deceit. *Administrative Science Quarterly*, 36(4): 614–630.

Siebert, S., Martin, G., Bozic, B., & Docherty, I. (2015). Looking 'beyond the factory gates': Towards more pluralist and radical approaches to intraorganizational trust research. *Organization Studies*, 36: 1033–1062.

Siebert, S., & Martin, G. (2014). People management rationales and organizational effectiveness: The case of trust repair. *Journal of Organizational Effectiveness: People and Performance*, 1(2): 177–190.

Sitkin, S. B., & George, E. (2005). Managerial trust-building through the use of legitimating formal and informal control mechanisms. *International Sociology*, 20(3): 307–338.

Sitkin, S. B., & Roth, N. (1993). Explaining the limited effectiveness of legalistic 'remedies' for trust/distrust. *Organization Science*, 4(3): 67–392.

Spicer, A., & Okhmatovskiy, I. (2015). Multiple paths to institutional-based trust production and repair: Lessons from the Russian bank deposit market. *Organization Studies*, 36: 1143–1170.

Starkey, K. (1989). Time and professionalism: disputes concerning the nature of contract. *British Journal of Industrial Relations*, 27(3): 375–395.

Stevens, M., MacDuffie, J., & Helper, S. (2015). Reorienting and recalibrating inter-organizational relationships: Strategies for achieving optimal trust. *Organization Studies*, 36: 1237–1264.

Sztompka, P. (1999). *Trust: A sociological theory*. Cambridge, UK: Cambridge University Press.

Thompson, P. (2011). The trouble with HRM. *Human Resource Management Journal*, 21: 355–367.

Tomlinson, E. C., Dineen, B. R., & Lewicki, R. J. (2004). The road to reconciliation: Antecedents of victim willingness to reconcile following a broken promise. *Journal of Management*, 30: 165–187.

Tomlinson, E. C., & Mayer, R. C. (2009). The role of causal attribution dimensions in trust repair. *Academy of Management Review*, 34: 85–104.

Uzzi, B. (1997). Social structure and competition in interfirm networks: The paradox of embeddedness. *Administrative Science Quarterly*, 42: 35–67.

Van de Ven, A. H. (2007). *Engaged scholarship: A guide for organizational and social research*. New York: Oxford University Press.

Weibel, A., Den Hartog, D., Gillespie, N., Searle, R., Six, F., & Skinner, D. (2016). How do controls impact employee trust in the employer? *Human Resource Management*, 55(3): 437–462.

Zavyalova, A., Pfarrer, M., Reger, R., & Shapiro, D. (2012). Managing the message: The effects of firm actions and industry spillovers on media coverage following wrongdoing. *Academy of Management Journal*, 55(1): 1079–1101.

Zucker, L. G. (1986). Production of trust: Institutional sources of economic structure, 1840–1920. In B. M. Staw and L. L. Cummings, (eds), *Research in Organizational Behavior*, vol. 8. JAI Press, Inc., Greenwich, CT, 53–111.

17

TRUST AND DISTRUST

Their interplay with forgiveness in organizations

Robert J. Bies, Laurie J. Barclay, Maria Francisca Saldanha,
Adam A. Kay and Thomas M. Tripp

Introduction

> There's a world of difference ... a night and day kind of difference between forgiveness and trust. Forgiveness is about the past ... what has happened. Trust is about the future. What the relationship will be like from here on out.
>
> (Pastor Jeff Conrad)

Decades of research have established the vital importance of trust, not only to interpersonal relationships but also to any well-functioning society at large. Trust facilitates cooperation (Barnard, 1938) and enhances the stability of social institutions and markets (Williamson, 1975; Zucker, 1986). As stabilizing a force as it may be, trust is also a fragile commodity that can be easily broken (Kim, Dirks, & Cooper, 2009). Given its tenuous nature, it is perhaps not surprising that a substantial literature has emerged examining how to restore trust in the aftermath of a transgression (for a detailed discussion of trust and distrust repair, see Kim, this volume). Although much of this research focuses on how transgressors can rebuild trust through reparative actions (e.g. apologies, compensation; Kim, Ferrin, Cooper, & Dirks, 2004) or through legitimating formal and informal control mechanisms (e.g. Long & Sitkin, 2006; Sitkin & George, 2005), studies have also indicated that those who are aggrieved can play an important role in the trust-rebuilding process (e.g. Goodstein & Aquino, 2010). Of particular concern has been the role of forgiveness. Specifically, scholars have argued that violations of trust can create the opportunity for forgiveness, which can have beneficial consequences for trust restoration (e.g. Aquino, Grover, Goldman, & Folger, 2003; Kramer & Lewicki, 2010; Waldron & Kelley, 2008).

Despite the significance of trust and trust repair for forgiveness, and vice-versa, the trust and forgiveness literatures have developed relatively independently of each other. However, there is increasing recognition that our theoretical understanding and ability to effectively manage trust can be substantially enhanced through the integration of these literatures. In their review of the trust literature, for example, Schoorman, Mayer, and Davis (2007, p. 349) argued that forgiveness is 'an evolving area that holds promise for understanding trust repair' and called for empirical research on foundational questions, such as the conditions under which forgiveness is likely to occur and the role of forgiveness in trust restoration.

In this chapter, we explore these foundational questions in three ways. First, there is increasing recognition of the importance of context for forgiveness – forgiveness does not occur within a vacuum but rather in a multi-layered contextual environment. However, research has only just begun to identify the contextual factors that can impact this important phenomenon. By reviewing the literature, we highlight the roles of trust and distrust as two contextual factors that can shape forgiveness processes, with trust enabling and distrust disabling forgiveness. Second, although forgiveness is often assumed to be a positive and functional outcome, individuals can be reluctant to forgive and may even find that forgiveness can have negative consequences. For example, individuals do not always feel ready to forgive (McCullough, Fincham, & Tsang, 2003), they may not believe that forgiveness is appropriate or valued in workplace contexts (Chusmir & Parker, 1991; Palanski, 2012), or they may find that the offense has created so much distrust that forgiveness is not even considered as a possibility. We examine when forgiveness may be unlikely and explore its alternatives, especially those that can emerge when individuals have varying degrees of trust or distrust in the offender. Third, we discuss how forgiveness can shape the restoration of trust in organizational settings, as forgiveness is typically viewed as an important stepping-stone on the path to restoring trust (e.g. Kramer & Lewicki, 2010). Finally, we conclude with a call for further research into the reciprocal and dynamic nature of trust, distrust, and forgiveness.

Forgiveness in the workplace: a systems perspective

From anthropology to zoology, the study of forgiveness has intrigued researchers from a diversity of disciplines. Although forgiveness is often treated as a decision and measured at a single point in time (McCullough et al., 2003), numerous researchers have argued that it is most effectively conceptualized as a psychological process that unfolds in a series of stages over time (e.g. Baskin & Enright, 2004; McCullough et al., 2003; Wohl & McGrath, 2007). In a recent multi-disciplinary and integrative review, Bies, Barclay, Tripp, and Aquino (2016) provided a unified definition of forgiveness, describing it as 'the internal act of relinquishing anger, resentment, and the desire to seek revenge against someone who has caused harm as well as the enhancement of positive emotions and thoughts towards the harm-doer.' This definition highlights the pro-social psychological changes underlying forgiveness, in which individuals move from a focus on the past (i.e. the negative emotions one feels about the transgression) towards prosocial and positive emotions, cognitions, and behavioral intentions (McCullough et al., 2003). Further, this definition emphasizes the importance of time in forgiveness processes, with many of the conditions that facilitate forgiveness evolving over time, such as the development of empathy, the creation of distance between the victim and the negative event (Wohl & McGrath, 2007), and the re-establishment of closeness after a violation (e.g. Tsang, McCullough, & Fincham, 2006).

Although forgiveness is often considered at the individual level of analysis, it is also important to examine forgiveness from a 'systems' perspective (Bies et al., 2016). From the dyad, to the group and organization, to the broader cultural forces that surround the individual – forgiveness is enveloped by contextual layers, which can exert powerful influences over employees by creating enablers (i.e. gateways or bridges) and barriers to forgiveness. For example, cultural values can guide how employees interpret and handle conflict (Schein, 1990). Consequently, forgiveness is facilitated in cultures that support values of compassion, collective mercy, and hope (Bazemore, 1998; Walker, 2006), whereas it is hindered in cultures that view forgiveness as a sign of weakness

(Tripp & Bies, 2009), value individualism (Hook, Worthington, & Utsey, 2009), or adopt 'cultures of honor' (i.e. endorse the use of aggression to defend against personal insults or challenges to one's reputation/status; Cohen & Nisbett, 1994).

Building on the systems foundation, we argue that it is critical to examine how trust and distrust can create a context for forgiveness and explore the role of forgiveness for the restoration of trust. Specifically, we propose that trust and distrust are key factors that can influence forgiveness, with trust enabling and distrust disabling forgiveness. Further, trust and distrust can influence forgiveness by impacting the various contextual factors that envelop the individual. We begin our discussion by acknowledging the distinction between trust and distrust. Next, we highlight the important role of these constructs for forgiveness.

Trust versus distrust

Traditionally, trust and distrust were conceptualized as mutually exclusive conditions that existed at opposite ends of a single continuum (with trust being viewed as 'good' and distrust as 'bad'; cf. Lewicki, McAllister, & Bies, 1998). As the field developed, however, trust and distrust came to be defined as related but distinct constructs that serve different functions. Briefly, trust reflects positive expectations and the willingness to be vulnerable to another (Rousseau, Sitkin, Burt, & Camerer, 1998), whereas distrust involves pervasive negative expectations and perceptions about the intentions or behavior of another (Lewicki et al., 1998; for further discussion, see Lewicki, Tomlinson, & Gillespie, 2006). Thus, trust and distrust are similar in that both entail expectations – with trust reflecting 'confident positive expectations' and distrust indicating 'confident negative expectations' on the part of one party about another (McAllister, 1995). Trust and distrust also allow individuals to manage uncertainty and complexity by focusing on the likelihood of being the target of (un)desirable conduct or harmful actions (Luhmann, 1979). However, these constructs are distinct in that both have different antecedents. Sitkin and Roth (1993, p. 271), for example, argued that 'trust is violated to the extent that expectations about context-specific task reliability are not met . . . distrust is engendered when an individual or group is perceived as not sharing key cultural values.' Trust and distrust can also have different underlying processes and outcomes (cf. Kramer, 1999).

In an influential article, Lewicki et al. (1998) highlighted that trust and distrust are embedded in a dynamic system of multiplex social relations. In this view, it becomes possible for one person to both trust and distrust another person simultaneously, at different times, and in different contexts. The authors suggested a 2x2 typology in which relationships can be broadly categorized as being: (i) low trust and low distrust; (ii) high trust and low distrust; (iii) low trust and high distrust; and (iv) high trust and high distrust. When situated within the context of forgiveness, this typology suggests that the interplay between trust (an enabler of forgiveness) and distrust (a barrier to forgiveness) may create tension that can influence the emergence of forgiveness. For example, under conditions of high trust and high distrust, individuals have both shared and separate objectives with another, which can give them grounds to feel assured by and extend confidence towards others but also have grounds to be dubious about or suspicious of them. Further, under conditions of high trust and high distrust, the relationship can be characterized by 'ambivalence', with the parties assuming a default operating philosophy of 'trust but verify' (Bies, 2014; Lewicki et al., 1998).

While some may be tempted to disparage ambivalence for the uncertainty it engenders, it can also serve a functional and stabilizing role by giving rise to 'a productive tension of confidences' (Lewicki et al., 1998, p. 450). This is due to the fact that if people trust too little they get nothing done, while if they trust too much they become easy candidates for harm and betrayal.

Additionally, as Sitkin and Roth (1993) point out, organizational environments characterized by low levels of trust tend to adopt legalistic remedies to stabilize relations (e.g. policies, contracts, and dispute resolution mechanisms). While such remedies bring a measure of stability, they come at the cost of flexibility and speed. Moreover, they constrain the possibility of reconciliation and forgiveness when trust has been tested or broken. In other words, nurturing an optimal balance of trust and distrust – or ambivalent trust – that allows people to be as productive as possible without rendering them unduly vulnerable to exploitation can be an important source of competitive advantage for contemporary organizations.

Building on the above, we propose that high trust may enable forgiveness, whereas high distrust can make it more difficult to facilitate forgiveness. Specifically, forgiveness involves prosocial psychological changes (McCullough et al., 2003). When considering how to facilitate change, Lewin (1951) argued that it is important to consider the driving and restraining forces that can facilitate versus hinder change, respectively. When high trust is combined with high distrust, we argue that the drivers that facilitate forgiveness may be constrained by barriers to forgiveness. In contrast, forgiveness may be facilitated more easily in relationships that are characterized by high trust and low distrust because the enablers ('driving forces') towards forgiveness are not bound by the constraints ('restraining forces') of distrust. Taken together, it is important to examine how both *trust* and *distrust* can shape the emergence of forgiveness. In the next section, we explore how trust can facilitate and distrust can create obstacles for forgiveness in organizational contexts.

Trust as an enabler and distrust as a barrier to forgiveness

Although research examining the inter-relationships between trust, distrust, and forgiveness is in its infancy, there is evidence suggesting that trust can serve as an enabler and distrust as a barrier to forgiveness. As we argue in detail below, there are at least three ways that trust and distrust serve these functions. First, trust and distrust can create a context that influences whether violations are even perceived (e.g. Lind, 2001). For example, trust and distrust can frame the way that individuals experience and interpret violations, which can ultimately impact whether individuals choose to and/or are able to forgive (i.e. trust/distrust can serve as antecedents and/or moderating variables in the relationship between violations and reactions). Second, violations can create distrust (i.e. distrust can be an outcome of a violation), which can disable one's desire or ability to engage in forgiveness (e.g. Dirks, Kim, Ferrin, & Cooper, 2011). Third, trust and distrust can influence other contextual factors (e.g. at the levels of the dyad, group, organization, and even external environment) as well as emerge at multiple contextual levels, which can subsequently influence forgiveness.

Trust and distrust as a context for forgiveness

Within relationships, individuals often use trust to interpret and react to others' behavior (Lind, 2001). When individuals feel trust towards another, they tend to respond in a cooperative manner. By contrast, when they experience distrust, they may scrutinize requests and engage in protective behaviors. This happens because it is cognitively inefficient for individuals to deeply process every interaction, and thus they often form heuristics that guide their evaluations and inter-actions. These evaluations can create a context in which incoming events and information are interpreted. Choi (2008), for example, found that social entity judgments moderate the rela-tionship between events and reactions, such that holding positive evaluations of one's supervisor can lessen the impact of an unfair event on attitudinal and behavioral reactions towards that supervisor. In other words, individuals do not encounter events as a 'blank slate'; instead, they hold evaluations and expectations that can influence the way that they perceive, experience, and respond to events.

Within the context of forgiveness, trust and distrust can influence the way that individuals interpret the event, thereby impacting one of the key factors predicting whether individuals will forgive (Fehr, Gelfand, & Nag, 2010). Specifically, when individuals experience a violation, they are motivated to determine 'what happened' and engage in sensemaking to understand the offense, why it happened, and how they should react. However, their pre-existing judgments can influence the way that they interpret incoming information, with individuals often being motivated to maintain their current judgments (Lind, 2001). For example, individuals who believe that their supervisor is a trustworthy person are more likely to give their supervisor the benefit of the doubt and/or discount negative information whereas individuals who distrust their supervisor are more likely to give more weight to negative information. This can also influence their expectations for treatment. Skarlicki, Barclay, and Pugh (2008), for example, found that individuals who had low prior trust in their employer were more likely to retaliate when they were treated *fairly* during a layoff. Although one would expect that fair treatment would be desired, individuals with low prior trust interpreted this fairness as lacking sincerity and being 'too little, too late.'

Although forgiveness is beneficial for maintaining critical social relationships, it can be dysfunctional if it makes one vulnerable to further exploitation (Fitness & Peterson, 2008). As such, individuals must weigh the costs and benefits of forgiveness (McCullough, Kurzban, & Tabak, 2010, 2013). When individuals distrust the perpetrator or perceive that they have other attributes that make further victimization likely (e.g. the perpetrator lacks integrity), they are less likely to consider forgiveness as a viable strategy (Kim, Dirks, Cooper, & Ferrin, 2006; Kim et al., 2004), particularly when they perceive that these characteristics cannot be changed (Kim et al., 2006, 2009; Tomlinson & Mayer, 2009). In contrast, when individuals perceive that the transgressor has positive attributes, they can experience empathy thereby facilitating forgiveness (McCullough, Worthington, & Rachal, 1997). That is, people take into account their pre-existing evaluations and expectations when deciding whether to forgive an offender (Eaton, Struthers, & Santelli, 2006; Guerrero & Bachmann, 2010; McCullough, 2008).

Although trust can provide a 'buffer' for incoming negative information and/or events, it is not a panacea. In some cases, high trust can actually enhance the perceived negativity and/or felt violation. Brockner, Tyler, and Cooper-Schneider (1992), for example, found that highly committed employees showed the steepest decline in commitment in response to highly unfair treatment. The large discrepancy between one's expectations and treatment may be particularly disconcerting to these individuals. Indeed, individuals tend to re-evaluate their judgments when they experience 'phase-shifting events' that either call the relationship into question or involve an event or information that is sufficiently discordant from the current judgment that individuals must re-evaluate their judgment (Lind, 2001). In these cases, individuals who were quite trusting may revise their evaluation to either lower their level of trust or even become distrusting.

Distrust as a constraint for forgiveness

Distrust can not only serve as a frame guiding the interpretation of offenses, it can also emerge and/or intensify as a result of a violation. Some events, for example, can create uncertainty and/or negative expectations about the transgressor's future behavior (Dirks et al., 2011; Kim et al., 2009). This is particularly likely when transgressors engage in repeated or severe violations (e.g. Bradfield & Aquino, 1999; Gunderson & Ferrari, 2008), intentionally cause harm (e.g. Boon

& Sulsky, 1997), and/or deceive the individual (e.g. Desmet, De Cremer, & Van Dijk, 2011; Schweitzer, Hershey, & Bradlow, 2006). By creating distrust, these situations can be particularly challenging to forgive (Tomlinson & Lewicki, 2006).

How transgressors respond to violations can also impact one's ability to forgive. Research has shown that offenses create an 'injustice gap' – a situation where a discrepancy exists between what the victim perceives should have happened and the actual outcomes of a transgression (Exline, Worthington, Hill, & McCullough, 2003). The wider the gap, the more difficult it is to forgive. Although this gap can be reduced by the transgressor, the effectiveness of attempts to address the gap depend on factors such as whether the remedy addresses the concerns raised by the violation (e.g. Reb, Goldman, Kray, & Cropanzano, 2006) and aligns with the needs of the victim (e.g. Fehr & Gelfand, 2010). It also depends on the type of violation that has occurred (e.g. Kim et al., 2004, 2006). In their study of competence- versus integrity-based violations, for example, Kim et al. (2004) found that the effectiveness of a repair depended on the type of violation. Whereas apologizing was more effective in restoring trust for competence-based violations, denying culpability was more effective for integrity-based violations. In the case of integrity-based violations (i.e. violations involving wrongdoing that is attributable to the transgressor), apologizing can be potentially harmful because through this action, the transgressor accepts blame and may acknowledge negative intentions, which can validate the victim's concerns that this person can be untrustworthy (Kim et al., 2006).

Attempts to close the gap can also backfire, such as when the transgressor offers insincere reparations (Skarlicki et al., 2008) or fails to engage in behaviors that are consistent with the apology (i.e. post-apology behavioral consistency; Hui, Lau, Tsang, & Pak, 2011). The injustice gap can also increase when transgressors do not realize that a violation has occurred (and therefore do not take action) or refuse to acknowledge the violation (Ferrin, Kim, Cooper, & Dirks, 2007; Kim et al., 2009). When transgressors refuse to engage in reparative attempts, the gap can also widen (Okimoto, Wenzel, & Hedrick, 2013). For example, transgressors may not apologize because the organization's policies prohibit this type of action (Bies et al., 2016) or because they find apologizing to be self-threatening (McLaughlin, Cody, & O'Hair, 1983). Additionally, some transgressors are not motivated to apologize, particularly when refusing to apologize can enhance their feelings of power, control, and self-esteem (Okimoto et al., 2013). Thus, transgressors are not always able or motivated to reduce the injustice gap. As a result, their actions in the wake of a violation may even increase the gap, thereby making forgiveness not only more challenging but also more risky.

A systems perspective on trust, distrust, and forgiveness

Although forgiveness is an intrapersonal process, the systems perspective highlights how it can be influenced and shaped by the contextual layers that envelop the individual (Bies et al., 2016). We argue that trust and distrust can influence forgiveness by impacting factors within these contextual layers. For example, forgiveness can be influenced by leadership factors. Having trusted and fair leaders may enhance forgiveness, as employees may be more deferent to such leaders and more likely to follow their decisions and interests (Tyler, 1990). Thus, if organizational leaders are interested in forgiveness and reconciliation, then individuals may be more likely to forgive and reconcile when these leaders ask or inspire them to do so.

The structure of the organization and the group context may also create conditions that are ripe for distrust and increased conflict. For instance, in multi-divisional and geographically dispersed organizations, teams rely more heavily on media-lean communication (e.g. email; Hinds

& Bailey, 2003). This can result in greater misunderstandings and poorer negotiation than with media-rich communication (e.g. face to face) because less information is successfully transferred (Bies & Tripp, 2012; Daft & Lengel, 1986; Kahai & Cooper, 2003). Distance can also deprive dispersed teams of familiarity and friendship, because they spend less time together and have greater cultural differences. Additionally, individuals derive their identity from the groups to which they belong (Tajfel & Turner, 1986) and these identities can influence their affective, cognitive, and behavioral reactions (e.g. Smith 1993; Tajfel, 1981). By creating in-groups and out-groups, social identity can increase competition among groups, which can hinder forgiveness (e.g. Collier, Ryckman, Thornton, & Gold, 2010; De Dreu, Carsten, & Van Knippenberg, 2005). In other words, these structures can enhance distrust between groups, thereby making it harder for a victim from one group to forgive a perpetrator from another group (Bies et al., 2016). Further, trust can play a mediating role in this relationship. Voci (2006), for instance, found that identity threats that amplify intergroup differentiation also can cause in-group members to distrust out-group members.

In-group/out-group distinctions can also lead in-group members to believe that out-group members have hostile motives and that the in-group needs protective action. For instance, Waytz, Young, and Ginges (2014) found that people tend to attribute their own aggression more to in-group 'love' motives (e.g. protect one's own community) than to out-group 'hate' motives (e.g. destroy and cause misery to the out-group). Groups can also compare who has suffered more in a conflict by engaging in competitive victimhood (i.e. believing that one's group has suffered more than the other group with whom conflict exists or has existed), which can undermine trust and hinder forgiveness (Noor, Brown, Gonzalez, Manzi, & Lewis, 2008; Noor, Brown, & Prentice, 2008). Because calculative trust is undermined by perceptions of hostile motives (Mayer, Davis, & Schoorman, 1995), it follows that in-group/out-group distinctions may negatively impact trust, which can decrease forgiveness. Supporting this line of reasoning, Crossley (2009) showed that victims who attribute hostile motives are more likely to seek revenge than victims who attribute non-hostile motives, and revenge typically is negatively correlated with forgiveness (Tripp & Bies, 2009).

Belonging to a group also has the potential to make trust and forgiveness more likely, especially when the victim and perpetrator belong to the same group or when the group is led by individuals who behave fairly. Tyler (2001) argues that trust in the group increases group members' willingness to defer to the group authorities (e.g. company CEOs, organizational ombudspersons, union stewards), especially when these authorities use fair procedures. The use of fair procedures also affects the tendency to forgive. Aquino, Tripp, and Bies (2006) found that when victims perceived a fair procedural justice climate, it moderated the effect of power such that victims were more likely to forgive and reconcile and less likely to seek revenge. The role of procedural justice in this relationship is not that of a trigger (i.e. low procedural justice is the offense that triggers the desire for revenge), but rather the victim trusts that the organizational systems will fairly prosecute grievances, thus making revenge less necessary to ensure that justice is served (Tripp, Bies, & Aquino, 2007).

Finally, while our analysis focused on trust, distrust, and forgiveness at the individual level, these constructs can also exist within and between groups. Studies examining the intersection of trust and forgiveness at the group-level often focus on 'deep-rooted conflicts' between ethnic or religious groups (e.g. Cehajic, Brown, & Castano, 2008; Noor, Brown, Gonzalez, Manzi, & Lewis, 2008; Noor, Brown, & Prentice, 2008). In general, these studies have shown that trust can promote inter-group forgiveness, even in such difficult situations.

Taken together, empirical evidence indicates the importance of trust and distrust for forgiveness, with trust serving as an enabler and distrust as a disabler of forgiveness. Although trust and distrust can exist simultaneously, in the next section, we explore what happens when distrust takes over and makes some offenses seem 'unforgiveable.'

Hindrance or insurmountable obstacle? When distrust makes an offense unforgiveable

Some offenses create so much distrust that forgiveness is not an immediate outcome, or even a possibility. That is, distrust not only poses a barrier to forgiveness but can actually make some offenses seem too grave to be 'forgivable' (Tripp & Bies, 2009). In these cases, individuals may experience 'unforgiveness' – a 'cold' emotion that typically centers on resentment, bitterness, and even hatred, which can also include negative motivations towards the transgressor (e.g. retaliation, avoidance; Worthington & Wade, 1999). Although it is often assumed that forgiveness is merely the reduction of unforgiveness (see Worthington & Wade, 1999 for a discussion), research has shown that reducing unforgiveness does not imply that victims have forgiven their offenders (Wade & Worthington, 2003, 2005; Worthington & Wade, 1999). Similar to the distinction between trust and distrust, research suggests that it is important to differentiate between forgiveness and unforgiveness.

Unforgivable offenses are relatively common – 25 percent of people report having experienced an unforgivable offense (Zechmeister & Romero, 2002). However, harboring unforgivingness can have significant implications for the individual, including more negative and less positive affect (e.g. Kluwer & Karremans, 2009), decreased feelings of relatedness (e.g. Karremans, Van Lange, & Holland, 2005), higher stress (e.g. Worthington & Scherer, 2004), and even perceived physical burden (e.g. Zheng, Fehr, Tai, Narayanan, & Gelfand, 2015). Unforgiven offenses are also less likely to be perceived as resolved, and transgressors of these types of offenses are often depicted as immoral, cruel, and/or harmful (Zechmeister & Romero, 2002).

Unforgiveness can emerge for a variety of reasons related to the victim, perpetrator, and offense. Victims with certain personality traits (e.g. narcissistic entitlement; Exline, Baumeister, Bushman, Campbell, & Finkel, 2004) or ways of processing information (e.g. using narrow vs. broad construals; Mok & De Cremer, 2015) may be particularly prone to unforgiveness. Perpetrators who display humility can mitigate unforgiveness (Davis et al., 2013; Van Tongeren, Davis, & Hook, 2014) whereas perpetrators who have been demonized (i.e. who are viewed as evil and unredeemable) are likely to remain unforgiven (Exline et al., 2003).

Research has also examined what makes some offenses unforgiveable. Some research has focused on perceptions of the offense, with offenses that are seen as disgusting or morally condemnable being associated with unforgiveness (e.g. Cohen, Malka, Rozin, & Cherfas, 2006). Other research has focused on the nature of the event. Rapske, Boon, Alibhai, and Kheong (2010), for example, categorized 'unforgiveable' offenses according to whether they involved betrayal, violence or abuse, inappropriate communication, harm to others, relational devaluation, and reputation defamation, among others. Others have suggested that unforgiveable offenses have common underlying characteristics. In a qualitative study of unforgivable injuries, Flanigan (1992) suggested that unforgivable offenses are characterized by shattered assumptions about personal control, justice, self-worth, and the goodness of others. Bies (2007) also examined the characteristics of unforgiveable offenses within organizational contexts. We provide a detailed overview of this study below.

Unforgivable offenses in organizational contexts

In a qualitative study, Bies (2007) asked a sample of working professionals to recount an incident in which they were harmed by another person in the workplace and had decided not to forgive.

Using a grounded theory approach, three different categories for why people decide not to forgive others in the workplace emerged: shattered assumptions, damaged identity, and interpersonal indignities. We discuss each of these categories in turn.

Shattered Assumptions occur when people believe they have been betrayed and their fundamental beliefs about the sanctity of their relationship with the offender are brought into question. Common betrayals include betrayals of confidence (e.g. disclosing sensitive personal information or invading one's privacy; Bies, 1993, 1996) and betrayals of trust (e.g. violating one's fundamental expectations in a way that threatens the well-being of the trustor; Elangovan & Shapiro, 1998). Regardless of the type, betrayals can cast into doubt one's basic assumptions about the relationship and are often viewed as unforgiveable 'cardinal sins.'

Damaged Identity occurs when offenses bring into question or tarnish the victim's self-concept or reputation. Bies and Tripp (1993, 1996) indicate that identities may be damaged as a result of (a) unfair characterizations of a person or their performance (e.g. when one party unjustifiably lays responsibility for a performance failure on another party or exaggerates claims about the other party for political ends); (b) wrongful accusations (e.g. when one party falsely accuses the other of wrongdoing); (c) insults and abuse (e.g. when one party 'bad mouths' another to create an unfavourable image of that person); and (d) public criticism and beratement (e.g. when an employee is disciplined by a manager in front of colleagues). Damaging one's identity often results in intense negative emotions, including feelings of 'losing face,' being 'belittled' or 'degraded,' and even 'emotionally scarred.' In many cases, the harm done to a relationship as a result of a damaged identity is irreparable.

Interpersonal Indignities describe relational violations in which the victim feels that the offender has disregarded a sacred aspect of the victim's basic humanity. At least three types of behaviors fall within this category: (a) deceit (i.e. intentionally lying or misrepresenting the truth to another party); (b) disrespect (i.e. actions that demean or otherwise devalue the intrinsic value or worth of an individual); and (c) exposure to personal danger (i.e. a violation of one's psychological and/or physical safety; Kahn, 1990). When people experience an interpersonal indignity, it can strike a deep emotional chord in which victims can feel unfairly treated, angry, outraged, and resentful (Bies, 2001; Bies & Tripp, 1996). Further, it can create intense feelings of distrust (Lewicki et al., 1998), and even make people feel that they have been treated in a 'subhuman manner' that violates their sense of human dignity.

In summary, unforgiveable offenses can shatter assumptions, damage identities, and inflict interpersonal indignities. By creating so much distrust, these types of offenses not only create barriers to forgiveness but, in some cases, the distrust they create can become an insurmountable obstacle (Tripp & Bies, 2009). Further, similar to the way that trust and distrust can create enablers and barriers to forgiveness, we propose that the combination of forgiveness and unforgiveness can also influence trust and distrust. For example, individuals may be more willing to rebuild trusting relationships when forgiveness is high and unforgiveness is low. By contrast, distrust may be more likely to linger when unforgiveness is high. If the restoration of trust relies on individuals moving beyond the past (i.e. forgiving) to re-establish and rebuild their relationships, this begs the question of what happens when forgiveness is not a possibility. We turn to this issue next.

Beyond (un)forgiveness: other alternatives for dealing with broken trust

> It is one of the things about forgiveness you have to remember.
> It is not spiritual. It is part of real politics.
>
> (Bishop Desmond Tutu)

Forgiveness is not always a desirable or an attainable option. In some cases, the damage can only be contained, mitigated, or otherwise 'managed' (Lewicki et al., 1998; Sitkin & Roth, 1993), but never fully repaired. Given that forgiveness is often considered a 'stepping-stone' on the road to trust restoration, it is important to explore other approaches that individuals can choose, particularly when they will not or cannot forgive. Whereas some approaches (e.g. reconciliation), can allow the emergence of positive emotions and even some relationship repair, other approaches (e.g. continued conflict, withdrawal) often allow the conflict to fester, thereby making the situation worse (for the focal individual, conflicting parties, and/or even third parties). However, individuals may also resort to strategies that leave some or most of the conflict unresolved yet constrain the hostilities. Such strategies may help the parties tolerate each other and/or work together without open conflict. Further, individuals are likely to select their preferred approaches based on the level of trust and distrust that they have in the offender (Bies & Tripp, 2012). We explore approaches that range from little or no engagement with the offender (e.g. withdrawal, exit, separation), to potentially antagonistic approaches (e.g. revenge, continued conflict), to cautious engagement (e.g. détente, peaceful coexistence), to high engagement (e.g. reconciliation).

Withdrawal and exit

In some cases, individuals may choose to voluntarily withdraw or exit from the situation. Whereas withdrawal involves the individual remaining in the situation (e.g. stays in the organization but is less engaged), exit typically involves departure from the situation (e.g. by leaving the organization). Individuals may choose withdrawal when they need the time, space, and resources to process the situation or do not feel that they are able to cope (Thau & Mitchell, 2010). Withdrawal tendencies may be particularly strong when the offense is severe (i.e. unforgiveable), the costs of forgiveness are high, and/or the level of distrust is simply too high to continue in the relationship (e.g. Lee, Mitchell, Holtom, McDaniel, & Hill, 1999).

Withdrawal can be relatively minor or temporary. For instance, individuals may be less likely to engage in prosocial behaviors towards the offender and/or organization (Kamdar, McAllister, & Turban, 2006; Moorman, 1991), particularly when they do not feel supported by the organization (e.g. in a low procedural justice climate; Aquino et al., 2006). In contrast, exit is a more permanent choice that may be reserved for the most severe violations and is likely to depend on other factors, such as the presence of other attractive job opportunities as well as the embeddedness of the employee (e.g. employees are less likely to leave when they are deeply tied to the community; Lee et al., 1999; Turnley & Feldman, 1999).

Separation

Whereas withdrawal involves a feeling of giving up and a passive avoidance of the offender, separation consists of a cessation of contact between the parties (at least for a given period of time) that is either imposed by a third party or actively decided upon by the conflicting parties. Separation can assume multiple forms and have a variety of objectives. Research from law suggests that separation imposed by a third party may be used with the aim of taking control of the conflict, imposing order, reducing disruptions in the work context, and/or minimizing the chances of reoccurrence of open conflict (Bayley & Bittner, 1984). Separation may be physical (e.g. assigning different workspaces for one or both of the disputants) or symbolic (e.g. limiting lines of communication). Separation may be temporary or permanent (Davis, 1983); and it may be followed up with actions from the third party, such as when the third party further investigates the nature of the conflict, listens to the disputants, offers advice, or gives warnings (Bayley & Bittner, 1984). Although separation can also be voluntary, this option can be precluded in organizational settings where parties need to interact to fulfill their responsibilities.

The consequences of separation are somewhat unclear, with different trajectories existing for post-separation conflict. In some cases, separation can reduce the frequency and intensity of the conflict, while in others it can increase conflict over time (e.g. Drapeau, Gagné, Saint-Jacques, Lépine, & Ivers, 2009; Graham, 1997). Why are there such divergent outcomes for separation? We propose that these differences may relate to the underlying conditions that prompted the separation in the first place and also the interactions that occurred between the parties. For example, as noted above, distrust may be more difficult to overcome than low trust (Lewicki et al., 1998). When individuals have low trust, separation may allow them to ease tensions with the other party by giving them time to process their negative emotions and cognitions and rebuild their coping resources (Billings & Moos, 1981). In contrast, when individuals have high distrust, they may perceive that their values are incompatible or even fundamentally divergent with the other party (Bijlsma-Frankema, Sitkin, & Weibel, 2015). This can create uncertainty, perceived threat, and vulnerability, as well as negative expectations and perceptions towards the other party (Riek, Mania, & Gaertner, 2006). Further, if the parties have interactions or the opportunity to see the other party interacting with others, they are likely to interpret the other party's behavior through a distrust frame, which can reinforce negative evaluations and expectations, thereby enhancing the conflict. Regardless of the outcome, separation can involve adjustment to the new situation, changes in the structure of the support network of each of the parties (Walker, Logan, Jordan, & Campbell, 2004), and, in some situations, a 'process of dehumanization' of the other party (Northrup, 1989).

Revenge and continued conflict

Another possible response to an offense is to approach it aggressively; for example, by engaging in revenge. The intent of revenge is to restore justice, even the score, and/or resolve conflict by teaching the offender a lesson (Gollwitzer, Meder, & Schmidt, 2011; Tripp & Bies, 1997). Given that revenge can entail risks for the person who engages in revenge and can have negative consequences for the recipient, it is often conceptualized as a dysfunctional response. However, revenge can also be functional for groups because it can help re-establish social norms and show the offender that such behavior will not be tolerated in the future (Tripp & Bies, 1997). Engaging in revenge, however, can often have unintended consequences and can escalate the conflict rather than resolve it (Axelrod, 1997).

Continued (and even escalated) conflict can also emerge, with organizations and employees (un)intentionally promoting conflict. Bijlsma-Frankema et al. (2015), for example, outlined a self-amplifying cycle of distrust, in which one party communicates distrust to another through its behaviors. In turn, these behaviors prompt the other group to reciprocate by engaging in negative behaviors. This not only amplifies distrust through negative reciprocity, but it can also encourage 'overmatching' (i.e. negative behaviors are reacted to with more extreme negative behaviors), more negative attributions, and within-group convergence (i.e. when members of a group share their negative perceptions encouraging shared negative perceptions to arise). These conditions can result in diminished cooperation for formal relations, with individuals being less willing to act in a prosocial, helpful, and/or compliant manner. Further, individuals are also more likely to avoid contact, where possible. Specifically, groups may meet when required (e.g. to work together) but they are likely to avoid informal interactions. We propose that this amplification of distrust can make forgiveness even more difficult and may also enhance unforgiveness, particularly when negative attributions are intensified (e.g. the accumulation of negative perceptions can make specific harms seem more intentional and severe when placed in this cumulative context; Bijlsma-Frankema et al., 2015).

Organizations may also promote conflict unintentionally. Organizations can create barriers to conflict resolution through procedures, culture, and climate, as well as formalized systems (Bies et al., 2016). For example, organizations can develop formalized dispute-resolution procedures to manage conflict in the hopes that these procedures will help de-escalate and ideally resolve conflict. However, employees can feel forced into these procedures and find that these systems intensify their anger and tendency to hold a grudge. That is, these well-intentioned procedures can backfire thereby prolonging and intensifying the conflict.

Employees can also (un)intentionally sustain conflict. For example, some employees may embrace low-grade conflict and refuse to address it because it establishes a 'known' pattern for interacting. That is, they don't avoid each other or seek out confrontations, but when they do interact, it typically involves a set of patterned behavior, in which they often let their irritations and animosities surface. Further, sometimes employees just don't know how to resolve conflict and simply 'act out' whatever heated emotions and impulses they feel.

Finally, organizations can also intentionally create competition and conflict. For example, some organizations operate on the assumption that employees will work harder if they must compete with each other (i.e. they believe that competition can motivate greater productivity). For instance, General Electric was known for its 'rank and yank' performance appraisal system that ranked all employees against each other and then terminated the lowest 10 percent of employees each year. Some organizations use profit-centered divisions where each unit is directed to look after itself instead of looking after the collective organization. Although it is assumed that the organization will benefit if units are given goals that align with the organization's interests, in reality, this structure can put units in competition with each other for resources (Pfeffer & Salancik, 1974). Sometimes competition can create destructive conflict, such as when employees steal credit for others' sales. Other times, such competition can create constructive conflict. For instance, Data General famously let one group of engineers feel inferior and passed over to motivate them to prove themselves by working harder (Kidder, 1981). Indeed, they worked so hard that they created a product that saved the company.

Détente

Détente involves an abandonment of belligerent intentions and a relaxation of tension between conflicting parties (Oelsner, 2007; Pedaliu, 2009; Romano, 2009). An expression frequently used to describe détente is 'living with' (Aksu, 2010; Bardes & Olendik, 1978), indicating the need to coexist with one's enemies without necessarily resolving the issues underlying the conflict (Pedaliu, 2009). Détente emerges from the recognition of the potentially negative consequences of conflict (Romano, 2009; Suri, 2008) and the benefits that can be gained if open hostilities are terminated (Bardes & Olendik, 1978; Oelsner, 2007; Romano, 2009). Détentes can open lines of communication, thereby facilitating negotiation and dialogue (Pedaliu, 2009; Romano, 2009) and allowing the parties to achieve stability, mutual control, and deterrence (Romano, 2009; Suri, 2008). Given its characteristics, détente is not sufficient to fully resolve the problem or develop positive relationships between the parties (Aksu, 2010) and can therefore be short-lived (Oelsner, 2007).

Within an organizational context, we define détente as the actions taken by conflicting parties (or by others with the authority to do so) to terminate open hostilities against each other. Although a relatively passive strategy, détente can facilitate the emergence of a peace process by opening communication lines and easing tensions between the conflicting parties (Oelsner, 2007). Thus, we propose that détente may be more likely to emerge in ambivalent relationships – that is, when parties have some trust in each other (thereby eliciting their desire to terminate open conflict and possibly initiate a process of peace building) but also a relatively high level of distrust (thereby creating the need for the implementation of controls and deterrence).

Although there is a dearth of empirical research on détente in organizational contexts, research in international relations and political science can offer some suggestions about strategies that can facilitate its emergence. First, rules can be established governing each party's behavior (sometimes coupled with penalties for agreement breach; Aksu, 2010; Oelsner, 2007; Romano, 2009; Schlotter, 1983). Direct contact between the parties can also be promoted, either with the general aim of fostering dialogue or with the more specific aim of creating an agreement as described above (Aksu, 2010; Romano, 2009). However, these interactions may bring more benefits if they focus on concrete concerns (Romano, 2009), solutions that benefit both parties (Brands, 2006), and cooperation (Aksu, 2010; Romano, 2009; Schlotter, 1983), while avoiding sensitive issues (Aksu, 2010). Détente is likely to fail, however, when there is a superficial adherence to established policies (Pedaliu, 2009), when the pressure for consensus creates vague rules that can be interpreted and applied as desired (Romano, 2009), or when unexpected crises emerge (Aksu, 2010).

Peaceful coexistence

Peaceful coexistence implies not only 'living peacefully side by side' but also involves 'some degree of communication, interaction, and even some degree of cooperation' (Chayes, 2003, pp. 152–153). In practice, peaceful coexistence involves the recognition of each party's humanity and similarities; the acceptance of differences; the acknowledgement of the other's suffering; and the establishment of a relationship involving recognition, respect, and solidarity (Haider, 2011; Kymlicka, 2001). Such attributes are achieved through the reduction of social distance (often through direct contact between the parties), which allows for the rehumanization of the other party and the attenuation of perceived differences (Haider, 2011; Zembylas, 2011).

Despite striving for positive outcomes, peaceful coexistence does not directly address profound psychological wounds nor does it attempt to resolve deeply ingrained conflicts or inequalities (Haider, 2011). As such, many people may prefer peaceful coexistence, particularly in the aftermath of severe offenses, because it can appear less intrusive and demanding than forgiveness (Chayes & Minow, 2003). Further, peaceful coexistence can be an important first step towards reconciliation and forgiveness, given the reduction in social distance and increase in positive social interactions that is frequently involved in peace processes (Haider, 2011).

Peaceful coexistence is distinct from détente in that it involves more than a general easing of tensions; it is a more active and process-oriented strategy that involves increased contact between the conflicting parties. Within organizational contexts, we define peaceful coexistence as the actions taken by conflicting parties to not only decrease open conflict but also to increase positive interactions. This can include the reduction of social distance as well as re-humanization of the other party. However, problem solving measures aimed at addressing psychological hurts are still relatively limited. Given the dynamic between trust and distrust, we propose that peaceful coexistence is likely to emerge when trust is present and when some of the distrust has already been processed or is beginning to lessen.

Research from international relations and political science can shed light on how peaceful coexistence can be implemented in organizational contexts. For example, such strategies can involve conflict management measures (e.g. activities aimed at attenuating conflict, such as training, joint problem solving activities, and dialogue facilitation), collaborative activities (e.g.

activities aimed at facilitating direct social contact, including joint projects, establishment of shared goals, and the development of cross-cutting identities), and education (e.g. providing information and opportunities for interaction that humanize the other party) (Haider, 2009, 2011). However, these strategies may fail if there is a lack of support from organizational authorities (Haider, 2011), if key values of any of the parties are blatantly disregarded (Kubálková & Cruickshank, 1978), if there is a strong insistence on the maintenance of separate and even opposite identities between the parties (Zembylas, 2011), or if there is a failure to acknowledge the effects that the conflict may have had on the collectives to which each of the parties belong (Haider, 2011).

Reconciliation

Reconciliation involves efforts aimed at restoring a damaged relationship (Aquino, Tripp, & Bies, 2001; Aquino et al., 2006), and occurs when a mutually acceptable balance of the parties' respective welfares is achieved (McCullough et al., 2013). Unlike forgiveness (an intrapersonal process that occurs within individuals), reconciliation is a behavioral response to conflict that occurs between individuals (Palanski, 2012) or groups (Bijlsma-Frankema et al., 2015). That is, reconciliation occurs at the level of the relationship. Although forgiveness can facilitate reconciliation (e.g. Goodstein & Aquino, 2010; Hall & Fincham, 2006), reconciliation does not require forgiveness and can be attempted even when the victim still harbors negative feelings towards the offender (Aquino et al., 2006). Further, while forgiveness is a victim-centered process, reconciliation can be initiated by the victim (e.g. Aquino et al., 2001, 2006), the offender (e.g. Balkin, Harris, Freeman, & Huntington, 2009), or both (e.g. Andiappan & Treviño, 2010; McCullough et al., 2013).

Reconciliation often emerges for instrumental reasons, with this strategy being likely in relationships that are highly valued (Karremans et al., 2011; McCullough, Luna, Berry, Tabak, & Bono, 2010), when there are material interests to be preserved (Aquino et al., 2001, 2006), when victims fear repercussions if they engage in destructive responses (e.g. revenge; Aquino et al., 2001), and when the victim wishes to appear compassionate, moral, and fair (Andiappan & Treviño, 2010; Aquino et al., 2001). Further, reconciliation can involve a cessation of conflict (Rusbult, Verette, Whitney, Slovik, & Lipkus, 1991; Van Lange et al., 1997) and restored trust between the parties (Andiappan & Treviño, 2010), which can be especially helpful when two conflicting employees have to work together (Aquino et al., 2001). Despite its positive outcomes, reconciliation may not be warranted and/or functional when offenders do not show remorse (Balkin, Harris, Freeman, & Huntington, 2014), do not want to participate in the reconciliation efforts (Bradfield & Aquino, 1999), or are motivated to further exploit the victim (Exline et al., 2003). Thus, reconciliation is likely when individuals have some trust in the offender and relatively low levels of distrust.

Summary

Although it is often assumed that forgiveness is the first step in a path towards rebuilding trust, forgiveness is not always desirable or possible. Following Lewicki et al. (1998), we suggest that individuals may have to use other approaches, which vary not only in their contact with the offender but also in the degree to which they can constructively manage the conflict. Further, an individual's willingness to consider these approaches is likely dependent on the level of trust or distrust that one feels towards the offender. We propose that withdrawal, exit, and separation are more likely when trust is low and/or distrust is high whereas détente, peaceful coexistence, and reconciliation are more likely to emerge when levels of trust are relatively high. In some cases, engaging in these alternatives can facilitate forgiveness, such as when peaceful coexistence or reconciliation allows for positive interactions that can lay the foundation for later forgiveness.

Further, it is important to note that trust and distrust may initiate other behaviors that can influence how these processes unfold. For example, distrust can impact individuals' perceptions of value incongruence and vulnerability as well as heighten negative attributions, which can diminish cooperation and enhance avoidance. In a case study of distrust development, Bijlsma-Frankema et al. (2015) found that distrust was associated with diminished cooperation, which was reflected by behaviors such as contesting decisions, failing to comply with procedures, reversing decisions, spreading rumours, engaging in obstructing actions, and reinforcing decision-making authority. Distrust also enhanced avoidance, which was associated with behaviors such as retreating from 'battle zones', closing ranks, conferring with like-minded others (e.g. to validate opinions and share outrage), and decreasing communication with the other party. These behaviors can further escalate conflict and reinforce distrust, thereby hindering forgiveness and/or creating unforgiveness.

Finally, forgiveness is a process that unfolds over time as individuals experience changes in their psychological and emotional states. Thus, it is also important to note that the above-mentioned outcomes may be more likely, appropriate, and/or effective at some phases of the forgiveness process than others. For example, in the initial aftermath of a transgression, individuals may need to withdraw or separate to facilitate processing of the transgression and/or to build coping resources. Thus, they may not be able to engage in other more active alternatives (e.g. reconciliation, peaceful coexistence) until they have undergone these earlier stages in the process. Further, trust and distrust are also dynamic phenomena – building and declining as well as resurfacing in long-standing relationships (Rousseau et al., 1998). Given this possibility, managers dealing with conflicts should recognize the needs of the conflicting parties and where they are in the processes of forgiveness, rebuilding trust, and managing distrust. Otherwise, intervening with some strategies may further escalate the conflict or result in dysfunctional outcomes if the employees are not ready or able to cope with that particular alternative. Clearly, it is important to explore when these approaches are most effective as well as how these approaches impact the restoration of trust and the effective management of conflict.

Setting the stage for rebuilding trust: the role of motives and alternative outcomes

> People believe that it's hard to forgive. Well I say, to forgive is easier than learning to trust again.
>
> (Abhishek Tiwari)

Although there are numerous alternative outcomes to forgiveness, little is known about how these alternatives influence the rebuilding of trust. For example, agreeing to a détente may facilitate peace, but does peace eventually lead to forgiveness? Does engaging in continued conflict change the process for restoring and rebuilding trust? Further, it is possible that the process for rebuilding of trust is not only influenced by *what* strategies are chosen but also by *why* these strategies were selected and/or *how* the strategy is implemented.

We use the strategy of forgiveness to demonstrate. For example, some people want to forgive but find that the offender refuses to address the 'injustice gap.' To facilitate forgiveness, victims can address the gap on their own (e.g. through victim-centred interventions; Barclay & Saldanha, 2015). However, this may not provide the necessary foundation for trusting the offender, especially when the offender has not acknowledged the violation or when there are no reassurances that the offender will not further exploit them.

Further, not all forgiveness is the same. Forgiveness can vary in the degree to which it is genuine and authentic. Whereas genuine forgiveness is a voluntary process involving the release of negativity and enhancement of positive emotions and thoughts towards the offender (Enright & Coyle, 1998), individuals can also experience pseudo-forgiveness (i.e. using forgiveness for manipulative intent; cf. Enright, 2001) or hollow forgiveness (i.e. expressing forgiveness without having experienced intra-psychic changes; Baumeister, Exline, & Sommer, 1998). Although genuine forgiveness may provide a foundation for restoring trust, other forms of forgiveness may not allow for effective trust restoration.

Similarly, individuals can have different motivations for forgiving. Cox, Bennett, Tripp, and Aquino (2012) identified five motives for forgiveness: moral (i.e. forgiving because it is the morally correct thing to do), relationship (i.e. forgiving because the relationship is highly valued), apology (i.e. forgiving because the offender atoned), religious (i.e. forgiving to fulfill religious expectations), and lack of alternatives (i.e. forgiving out of fear that future offenses will occur if forgiveness is not granted). Further, the authors found that these motives were differentially related to outcomes. For example, individuals who forgave due to a lack of alternatives or for religious reasons were more likely to report stress and poorer health than those who forgave for other reasons (Cox et al., 2012).

Although trust and distrust may influence the conditions under which individuals are willing to forgive, trust, and/or distrust may not always form the foundation or even be central in forgiveness processes. For example, individuals may choose to forgive because it is in their best interests to do so (e.g. it can decrease psychological and physical stress, allow them to move on from the transgression). We term this 'functional forgiveness.' Importantly, forgiving does not entail forgetting nor does it mean that individuals need to reconcile with the transgressor. Rather, forgiveness is an intrapersonal process that occurs within the individual and it does not always necessitate interpersonal or intergroup consequences, particularly when individuals chose not to share with others that they have forgiven. In some cases, individuals may forgive but still retain low trust or even distrust in the relationship, especially if they are worried about potential future exploitation (e.g. Fitness & Peterson, 2008).

These different motives for forgiveness may also translate into other outcomes. For instance, forgiving due to lack of alternatives may result in a lower commitment to forgiveness whereas forgiving for moral reasons may result in a deeper and longer-term commitment to forgiveness. Given that forgiveness can help form the foundation for restoring trust, the more stable the foundation, the easier it will be to rebuild trust. For example, individuals who forgive because they fear what will happen if forgiveness is not granted are likely to hold some distrust, which may infuse attempts to rebuild trust and make the process more difficult.

These issues and questions are also likely to extend to the alternative outcomes discussed above. For instance, individuals who feel forced into a separation process may feel that resolution of the conflict is no longer under their control. This may make them less receptive to attempts to restore trust or even feel that they have been absolved from having an active role in the restoration process. Thus, similar to the way that trust and distrust can influence forgiveness, we suggest that what, why, and how strategies are undertaken can influence the rebuilding of trust by providing a foundation (or lack thereof) for these restoration processes.

Moving forward: methodological implications

Our analysis has not only highlighted the reciprocal and dynamic relationships between trust, distrust, and forgiveness but also the importance of exploring forgiveness and the rebuilding of trust as *processes* that occur over time and that are shaped by the context in which they occur. To better tap into these questions, we argue that it is necessary to expand beyond the cross-sectional designs that are heavily favored in the trust and forgiveness literatures. Methodologies that may be particularly useful include qualitative research, longitudinal studies, and multi-level investigations. Specifically, qualitative research can provide theoretical richness and depth, high-light theoretical processes, and draw attention to the importance of the contexts in which these processes are embedded (e.g. Bamberger, 2008; Johns, 2006; Mowday & Sutton, 1993). Longitudinal studies are important to better understand how temporal dynamics can influence these processes (including the role of subsequent events) whereas multi-level approaches can highlight the role of context. Given the process-oriented nature of these relationships, researchers may also find it helpful to leverage person-centric approaches, which highlight individuals' subjective experiences and within-person processes as they navigate daily life (Guo, Rupp, Weiss, & Trougakos, 2011; Weiss & Rupp, 2011). Expanding our methodological toolset is likely to not only yield additional theoretical and practical insights but can also open new and important research questions.

Conclusion

> Let us forgive each other – only then will we live in peace.
>
> (Leo Tolstoy)

Life in organizations is punctuated with acts of harm and wrongdoing. Repairing and rebuilding trust in these fractured, if not broken, relationships can be critically important, yet extremely difficult to accomplish. In this chapter, we examined trust and distrust as an enabler and a barrier, respectively, to forgiveness as well as how forgiveness can serve as a stepping-stone on the path to rebuilding trust. However, forgiveness is not always possible – the costs of forgiveness can sometimes outweigh the benefits, some offenses are simply unforgiveable, and some barriers to forgiveness are simply too strong to overcome. In these cases, forgiveness may not be the 'right' outcome for the individual or the organization. Instead, other approaches (e.g. reconciliation, revenge, peaceful coexistence, or exit) may be the only possible alternatives.

Given the importance of forgiveness and trust repair to effective conflict management and organizational functioning, we strongly encourage researchers to devote more scholarly attention to integrating these literatures. In addition to better understanding the roles of trust, distrust, and forgiveness in organizational settings, it is also critical to expand our focus to examining the interplay between these processes. Further, it is important to examine when alternative approaches to forgiveness are likely to be most effective and how they can influence the emergence of forgiveness and rebuilding of trust.

Addressing these research questions will require the field to leverage methodologies beyond cross-sectional studies. In addition, we must embrace new ways of thinking about these constructs, including a consideration of the role of context, person-centric experiences, and time. By integrating these literatures, we can not only deepen our theoretical insights but also facilitate the development of actionable theory and practical insights that can help managers and organizations effectively manage conflict.

Our analysis also suggests another important aspect of forgiveness and conflict management: the healing of wounds from the harms and wrongdoing of others. This focus on healing is reflected in the efforts of Nelson Mandela when he was elected president of the Republic of South Africa. As illustrated in the movie *Invictus* President Mandela focused on healing the wounds experienced during apartheid by blacks in South Africa by finding a common goal with white South Africans in supporting the national rugby team. Such leadership efforts are part of the healing process that is often overlooked in organizations – and the world. As Marianne Williamson noted, '*The practice of forgiveness is our most important contribution to the healing of the world.*' Given that offenses and violations are a part of the social fabric of organizations, the time has come to recognize the powerful roles of trust, distrust, and forgiveness in managing these issues in organizations.

References

Aksu, F. (2010). Turkish-Greek relations and the Cyprus question: Quo vadis? *UNISCI Discussion Papers*, *23*, 207–223.

Andiappan, M., & Treviño, L. K. (2010). Beyond righting the wrong: Supervisor–subordinate reconciliation after an injustice. *Human Relations*, *64*, 359–386.

Aquino, K., Grover, S. L., Goldman, B., & Folger, R. (2003). When push doesn't come to shove: Interpersonal forgiveness in workplace relationships. *Journal of Management Inquiry*, *12*, 209–216.

Aquino, K., Tripp, T. M., & Bies, R. J. (2001). How employees respond to personal offense: The effects of blame attribution, victim status, and offender status on revenge and reconciliation in the workplace. *Journal of Applied Psychology*, *86*, 52–59.

Aquino, K., Tripp, T. M., & Bies, R. J. (2006). Getting even or moving on? Power, procedural justice, and types of offense as predictor of revenge, forgiveness, reconciliation, and avoidance in organizations. *Journal of Applied Psychology*, *91*, 653–668.

Axelrod, R. M. (1997). *The complexity of cooperation: Agent-based models of competition and collaboration*. Princeton, NJ: Princeton University Press.

Balkin, R. S., Harris, N. A., Freeman, S. J., & Huntington, S. (2009). Forgiveness, reconciliation, and mechila: Integrating the Jewish concept of forgiveness into clinical practice. *Counseling and Values*, *53*, 153–160.

Balkin, R. S., Harris, N. A., Freeman, S. J., & Huntington, S. (2014). The forgiveness reconciliation inventory: An instrument to process through issues of forgiveness and conflict. *Measurement and Evaluation in Counseling and Development*, *47*, 3–13.

Bamberger, P. (2008). Beyond contextualization: Using context theories to narrow the micro-macro gap in management research. *Academy of Management Journal*, *51*, 839–846.

Barclay, L. J., & Saldanha, M. F. (2015). Recovering from organizational injustice: New directions in theory and research. In M. Ambrose & R. Cropanzano (eds), *The Oxford handbook of justice in work organizations* (pp. 497–522). Oxford, UK: Oxford University Press.

Barclay, L. J., & Saldanha, M. F. (2016). Facilitating forgiveness in organizational contexts: Exploring the injustice gap, emotions, and expressive writing interventions. *Journal of Business Ethics*. Advance online publication. DOI: 10.1007/s10551-015-2750-x

Bardes, B., & Olendik, R. (1978). Beyond internationalism: A case for multiple dimensions in the structure of foreign policy attitudes. *Social Science Quarterly*, *59*, 496–508.

Barnard, C. I. (1938). *The functions of the executive*. Cambridge, MA: Harvard University Press.

Baskin, T. W., & Enright, R. D. (2004). Intervention studies on forgiveness: A meta-analysis. *Journal of Counseling and Development*, *82*, 79–90.

Baumeister, R. F., Exline, J. J., & Sommer, K. L. (1998). The victim role, grudge theory, and two dimensions of forgiveness. In E. L. Jr. Worthington (ed.), *Dimensions of forgiveness: Psychological research and theological perspectives* (pp. 79–104). Radnor, PA: Templeton Foundation Press.

Bayley, D. H., & Bittner, E. (1984). Learning the skills of policing. *Law and Contemporary Problems*, *47*, 35–59.

Bazemore, G. (1998). Restorative justice and earned redemption: Communities, victims, and offender reintegration. *American Behavioral Scientist*, *41*, 768–813.

Bies, R. J. (1993). Privacy and procedural justice in organizations. *Social Justice Research*, *6*, 69–86.

Bies, R. J. (1996). Beyond the hidden self: Psychological and ethical aspects of privacy in organizations. In D. Messick & A. Tenbrunsel (eds), *Codes of conduct: Behavioral research into business ethics* (pp. 104–116). New York, NY: Russell Sage Foundation.

Bies, R. J. (2001). Interactional (in)justice: The sacred and the profane. In J. Greenberg & R. Cropanzano (eds), *Advances in organizational justice* (pp. 89–118). Stanford, CA: Stanford University Press.

Bies, R. J. (2007). Unforgiven: When the consequences of interactional injustice are irreversible. In M. A. Cronin, K. B. Elder, & W. E. Botsford (Co-Chairs), *R-E-S-P-E-C-T, find out what it means to OB*. Symposium conducted at the 67th meeting of the Academy of Management, Philadelphia, PA.

Bies, R. J. (2014). Reducing criminal wrongdoing within business organizations: The practical and political skills of integrity. *American Criminal Law Review, 51*, 225–243.

Bies, R. J., Barclay, L. J., Tripp, T. M., & Aquino, K. (2016). A systems perspective on forgiveness in organizations. *Academy of Management Annals, 10*, 245–318.

Bies, R. J., & Tripp, T. M. (1993). Employee-initiated defamation lawsuits: Organizational responses and dilemmas. *Employee Responsibilities and Rights Journal, 6*, 313–324.

Bies, R. J., & Tripp, T. M. (1996). Beyond distrust: "Getting even" and the need for revenge. In R. M. Kramer & T. R. Tyler (eds), *Trust in organizations: Frontiers of theory and research* (pp. 246–260). Thousand Oaks, CA: Sage Publications.

Bies, R. J., & Tripp, T. M. (2012). Negotiating the peace in the face of modern distrust: Dealing with anger and revenge in the 21st century workplace. In B. M. Goldman & D. L. Shapiro (eds), *The psychology of negotiations in the 21st century workplace* (pp. 181–210). New York, NY: Routledge.

Bijlsma-Frankema, K., Sitkin, S. B., & Weibel, A. (2015). Distrust in the balance: The emergence and development of intergroup distrust in a court of law. *Organization Science, 26*, 1018–1039.

Billings, A. G., & Moos, R. H. (1981). The role of coping responses and social resources in attenuating the impact of stressful life events. *Journal of Behavioral Medicine, 4*, 139–157.

Boon, S. D., & Sulsky, L. M. (1997). Attributions of blame and forgiveness in romantic relationships: A policy-capturing study. *Journal of Social Behavior & Personality, 12*, 19–44.

Bradfield, M., & Aquino, K. (1999). The effects of blame attributions and offender likableness on forgiveness and revenge in the workplace. *Journal of Management, 25*, 607–631.

Brands, H. (2006). Progress unseen: U.S. arms control policy and the origins of détente, 1963–1968. *Diplomatic History, 30*, 253–285.

Brockner, J., Tyler, T. R., & Cooper-Schneider, R. (1992). The influence of prior commitment to an institution on reactions to perceived unfairness: The higher they are, the harder they fall. *Administrative Science Quarterly, 37*, 241–261.

Cehajic, S., Brown, R., & Castano, E. (2008). Forgive and forget? Antecedents and consequences of intergroup forgiveness in Bosnia and Herzegovina. *Political Psychology, 29*, 351–367.

Chayes, A. (2003). Bureaucratic obstacles to imagining coexistence. In A. Chayes & M. L. Minow (eds), *Imagine coexistence: Restoring humanity after violent ethnic conflict* (pp. 152–190). San Francisco, CA: Jossey-Bass.

Chayes, A., & Minow, M. L. (2003). Imagining coexistence in conflict communities. In A. Chayes & M. L. Minow (eds), *Imagine coexistence: Restoring humanity after violent ethnic conflict* (pp. xvii–xxiii). San Francisco, CA: Jossey-Bass.

Choi, J. (2008). Event justice perceptions and employees' reactions: Perceptions of social entity justice as a moderator. *Journal of Applied Psychology, 93*, 513–528.

Chusmir, L. H., & Parker, B. (1991). Gender and situational differences in managers' values: A look at work and home lives. *Journal of Business Research, 23*, 325–335.

Cohen, A. B., Malka, A., Rozin, P., & Cherfas, L. (2006). Religion and unforgivable offenses. *Journal of Personality, 74*, 85–118.

Cohen, D., & Nisbett, R. E. (1994). Self-protection and the culture of honor: Explaining southern violence. *Personality and Social Psychology Bulletin, 20*, 551–567.

Collier, S. A., Ryckman, R. M., Thornton, B., & Gold, J. A. (2010). Competitive personality attitudes and forgiveness of others. *Journal of Psychology, 144*, 535–543.

Cox, S. S., Bennett, R. J., Tripp, T. M., & Aquino, K. (2012). An empirical test of forgiveness motives' effects on employees' health and well-being. *Journal of Occupational Health Psychology, 17*, 330–340.

Crossley, C. D. (2009). Emotional and behavioral reactions to social undermining: A closer look at perceived offender motives. *Organizational Behavior and Human Decision Processes, 108*, 14–24.

Daft, R. L., & Lengel, R. H. (1986). Organizational information requirements, media richness, and structural design. *Management Science, 32*, 554–571.

Davis, P. W. (1983). Restoring the semblance of order: Police strategies in the domestic disturbance. *Symbolic Interaction, 6*, 261–278.

Davis, D. E., Worthington, E. L., Hook, J. N., Emmons, R. A., Hill, P. C., Bollinger, R. A., & Van Tongeren, D. R. (2013). Humility and the development and repair of social bonds: Two longitudinal studies. *Self and Identity, 12*, 58–77.

De Dreu, C. K., Carsten, K. W., & Van Knippenberg, D. (2005). The possessive self as a barrier to conflict resolution: Effects of mere ownership, process accountability, and self-concept clarity on competitive cognitions and behavior. *Journal of Personality and Social Psychology, 89,* 345–357.

Desmet, P. T. M., De Cremer, D., & Van Dijk, E. (2011). In money we trust? The use of financial compensations to repair trust in the aftermath of distributive harm. *Organizational Behavior and Human Decision Processes, 114,* 75–86.

Dirks, K. T., Kim, P. H., Ferrin, D. L., & Cooper, C. D. (2011). Understanding the effects of substantive responses on trust following a transgression. *Organizational Behavior and Human Decision Processes, 114,* 87–103.

Drapeau, S., Gagné, M.-H., Saint-Jacques, M.-C., Lépine, R., & Ivers, H. (2009). Post-separation conflict trajectories: A longitudinal study. *Marriage & Family Review, 45,* 353–373.

Eaton, J., Struthers, C. W., & Santelli, A. G. (2006). The mediating role of perceptual validation in the repentance-forgiveness process. *Personality and Social Psychology Bulletin, 32,* 1389–1401.

Elangovan, A. R., & Shapiro, D. L. (1998). Betrayal of trust in organizations. *Academy of Management Review, 23,* 547–566.

Enright, R. D. (2001). *Forgiveness is a choice: A step-by-step process for resolving anger and restoring hope.* Washington, DC: APA.

Enright, R. D., & Coyle, C. T. (1998). Researching the process model of forgiveness within psychological interventions. In E. L. Jr. Worthington (ed.), *Dimensions of forgiveness: Psychological research and theological perspectives* (pp. 139–161). Philadelphia, PA: Templeton Foundation Press.

Exline, J. J., Baumeister, R. F., Bushman, B. J., Campbell, W. K., & Finkel, E. J. (2004). Too proud to let go: Narcissistic entitlement as a barrier to forgiveness. *Journal of Personality and Social Psychology, 87,* 894–912.

Exline, J. J., Worthington, E. L. Jr., Hill, P., & McCullough, M. E. (2003). Forgiveness and justice: A research agenda for social and personality psychology. *Personality and Social Psychology Review, 7,* 337–348.

Fehr, R., & Gelfand, M. J. (2010). When apologies work: How matching apology components to victims' self-construals facilitates forgiveness. *Organizational Behavior and Human Decision Processes, 113,* 37–50.

Fehr, R., Gelfand, M. J., & Nag, M. (2010). The road to forgiveness: A meta-analytic synthesis of its situational and dispositional correlates. *Psychological Bulletin, 136,* 894–914.

Ferrin, D. L., Kim, P. H., Cooper, C. D., & Dirks, K. T. (2007). Silence speaks volumes: The effectiveness of reticence in comparison to apology and denial for responding to integrity-and competence-based trust violations. *Journal of Applied Psychology, 92,* 893–908.

Fitness, J., & Peterson, J. (2008). Punishment and forgiveness in close relationships: An evolutionary, social-psychological perspective. In J. P. Forgas & J. Fitness (eds), *Social relationships: Cognitive, affective, and motivational perspectives* (pp. 255–269). New York, NY: Psychology Press.

Flanigan, B. (1992). *Forgiving the unforgivable.* New York, NY: Macmillan.

Gollwitzer, M., Meder, M., & Schmitt, M. (2011). What gives victims satisfaction when they seek revenge? *European Journal of Social Psychology, 41,* 364–374.

Goodstein, J., & Aquino, K. (2010). And restorative justice for all: Redemption, forgiveness, and reintegration in organizations. *Journal of Organizational Behavior, 31,* 624–628.

Graham, E. E. (1997). Turning points and commitment in post-divorce relationships. *Communication Monographs, 64,* 350–368.

Guerrero, L. K., & Bachmann, G. F. (2010). Forgiveness and forgiving communication in dating relationships: An expectancy-investment explanation. *Journal of Social and Personal Relationships, 27,* 801–823.

Gunderson, P. R., & Ferrari, J. R. (2008). Forgiveness of sexual cheating in romantic relationships: Effects of discovery method, frequency of offense, and presence of apology. *North American Journal of Psychology, 10,* 1–14.

Guo, J., Rupp, D. E., Weiss, H. W., & Trougakos, J. P. (2011). Justice in organizations: A person-centric perspective. In S. W. Gilliland, D. D. Steiner, & D. P. Skarlicki (eds), *Research in social issues in management: Emerging perspectives on organizational justice and ethics* (Vol. 7, pp. 3–32). Greenwich, CT: Information Age Publishing.

Johns, G. (2006). The essential impact of context on organizational behavior. *Academy of Management Review, 31,* 386–408.

Haider, H. (2009). (Re)imagining coexistence: Striving for sustainable return, reintegration and reconciliation in Bosnia and Herzegovina. *International Journal of Transitional Justice, 3,* 91–113.

Haider, H. (2011). Social repair in divided societies: Integrating a coexistence lens into transitional justice. *Conflict, Security & Development, 11,* 175–203.

Hall, J. H., & Fincham, F. D. (2006). Relationship dissolution following infidelity: The roles of attributions and forgiveness. *Journal of Social and Clinical Psychology, 25,* 508–522.

Hinds, P. J., & Bailey, D. E. (2003). Out of sight, out of sync: Understanding conflict in distributed teams. *Organization Science, 14,* 615–632.

Hook, J. N., Worthington, E. L. Jr., & Utsey, S. O. (2009). Collectivism, forgiveness, and social harmony. *Counselling Psychologist, 37,* 821–847.

Hui, C. H., Lau, F. L., Tsang, K. L., & Pak, S. (2011). The impact of post-apology behavioral consistency on victim's forgiveness intention: A study of trust violation among coworkers. *Journal of Applied Social Psychology, 41,* 1214–1236.

Kahai, S. S., & Cooper, R. B. (2003). Exploring the core concepts of media richness theory: The impact of cue multiplicity and feedback immediacy on decision quality. *Journal of Management Information Systems, 20,* 263–299.

Kahn, W. A. (1990). Psychological conditions of personal engagement and disengagement at work. *Academy of Management Journal, 33,* 692–724.

Kamdar, D., McAllister, D. J., & Turban, D. B. (2006). "All in a day's work": How follower individual differences and justice perceptions predict OCB role definitions and behavior. *Journal of Applied Psychology, 91,* 841–855.

Karremans, J. C., Regalia, C., Paleari, F. G., Fincham, F. D., Cui, M., Takada, N., Ohbuchi, K., Terzino, K., Cross, S. E., & Uskul, A. K. (2011). Maintaining harmony across the globe: The cross-cultural association between closeness and interpersonal forgiveness. *Social Psychological and Personality Science, 2,* 443–451.

Karremans, J. C., Van Lange, P. A. M., & Holland, R. W. (2005). Forgiveness and its associations with prosocial thinking, feeling, and doing beyond the relationship with the offender. *Personality and Social Psychology Bulletin, 31,* 1315–1326.

Kidder, T. (1981). *The soul of a new machine.* Boston, MA: Little Brown.

Kim, P. H., Dirks, K. T., & Cooper, C. D. (2009). The repair of trust: A dynamic bilateral perspective and multilevel conceptualization. *Academy of Management Review, 34,* 401–422.

Kim, P. H., Dirks, K. T., Cooper, C. D., & Ferrin, D. L. (2006). When more blame is better than less: The implications of internal vs. external attributions for the repair of trust after a competence-vs. integrity-based trust violation. *Organizational Behavior and Human Decision Processes, 99,* 49–65.

Kim, P., Ferrin, D., Cooper, C., & Dirks, K. (2004). Removing the shadow of suspicion: The effects of apology versus denial for repairing competence- versus integrity-based trust violations. *Journal of Applied Psychology, 89,* 104–118.

Kluwer, E. S., & Karremans, J. (2009). Unforgiving motivations following infidelity: Should we make peace with our past? *Journal of Social and Clinical Psychology, 28,* 1298–1325.

Kramer, R. M. (1999). Trust and distrust in organizations: Emerging perspectives, enduring questions. *Annual Review of Psychology, 50,* 569–598.

Kramer, R. M., & Lewicki, R. J. (2010). Repairing and enhancing trust: Approaches to reducing organizational trust deficits. *Academy of Management Annals, 4,* 245–277.

Kubálková, V., & Cruickshank, A. A. (1978). The Soviet concept of peaceful coexistence: Some theoretical and semantic problems. *Australian Journal of Politics & History, 24,* 184–198.

Kymlicka, W. (2001). *Politics in the vernacular: Nationalism, multiculturalism, and citizenship.* Oxford: Oxford University Press.

Lee, T. W., Mitchell, T. R., Holtom, B. C., McDaniel, L. S., & Hill, J. W. (1999). The unfolding model of voluntary turnover: A replication and extension. *Academy of Management Journal, 42,* 450–462.

Lewicki, R. J., McAllister, D. M., & Bies, R. J. (1998). Trust and distrust: New relationships and realities. *Academy of Management Journal, 23,* 438–458.

Lewicki, R. J., Tomlinson, E. C., & Gillespie, N. (2006). Models of interpersonal trust development: Theoretical approaches, empirical evidence, and future directions. *Journal of Management, 32,* 991–1022.

Lewin, K. (1951). *Field theory in social science.* New York, NY: Harper.

Lind, E. A. (2001). Fairness heuristic theory: Justice judgments in pivotal cognitions in organizational relations. In J. Greenberg & R. Cropanzano (eds), *Advances in organizational justice* (pp. 56–88). Stanford, CA: Stanford University Press.

Long, C. P., & Sitkin, S. B. (2006). Trust in the balance: How managers integrate trust-building and task control. In R. Bachmann & A. Zaheer (eds), *Handbook of trust research* (pp. 87–106). Cheltenham: Edward Elgar.

Luhmann, N. (1979). *Trust and power.* Chichester, UK: Wiley.

Mayer, R. C., Davis, J. H., & Schoorman, F. D. (1995). An integrative model of organizational trust. *Academy of Management Review, 20,* 709–734.

McAllister, D. J. (1995). Affect- and cognition-based trust as foundations for interpersonal cooperation in organizations. *Academy of Management Journal, 38,* 24–59.

McCullough, M. E. (2008). *Beyond revenge: The evolution of the forgiveness instinct.* San Francisco, CA: Jossey-Bass.

McCullough, M. E., Fincham, F. D., & Tsang, J. (2003). Forgiveness, forbearance, and time: The temporal unfolding of transgression-related interpersonal motivations. *Journal of Personality and Social Psychology, 84,* 540–557.

McCullough, M. E., Kurzban, R., & Tabak, B. A. (2010). Evolved mechanisms for revenge and forgiveness. In M. Mikulincer & P. R. Shaver (eds), *Human aggression and violence: Causes, manifestations, and consequences* (pp. 221–239). Washington, DC: APA.

McCullough, M. E., Kurzban, R., & Tabak, B. A. (2013). Cognitive systems for revenge and forgiveness. *Behavioral and Brain Sciences, 36,* 1–15.

McCullough, M. E., Luna, L. R., Berry, J. W., Tabak, B. A., & Bono, G. (2010). On the form and function of forgiving: Modeling the time-forgiveness relationship and testing the valuable relationships hypothesis. *Emotion, 10,* 358–376.

McCullough, M. E., Worthington, E. L. Jr., & Rachal, K. C. (1997). Interpersonal forgiving in close relationships. *Journal of Personality and Social Psychology, 73,* 321–336.

McLaughlin, M. L., Cody, M. J., & O'Hair, H. D. (1983). The management of failure events: Some contextual determinants of accounting behavior. *Human Communication Research, 9,* 208–224.

Mok, A., & De Cremer, D. (2015). Overlooking interpersonal hurt: A global processing style influences forgiveness in work relationships. *European Journal of Work and Organizational Psychology, 24,* 267–278.

Moorman, R. H. (1991). Relationship between organizational justice and organizational citizenship behaviors: Do fairness perceptions influence employee citizenship? *Journal of Applied Psychology, 76,* 845–855.

Mowday, R. T., & Sutton, R. I. (1993). Organizational behavior: Linking individuals and groups to organizational contexts. *Annual Review of Psychology, 44,* 195–229.

Noor, M., Brown, R., Gonzalez, R., Manzi, J., & Lewis, C. A. (2008). On positive psychological outcomes: What helps groups with a history of conflict to forgive and reconcile with each other? *Personality and Social Psychology Bulletin, 34,* 819–832.

Noor, M., Brown, R., & Prentice, G. (2008). Prospects for intergroup reconciliation: Social-psychological predictors of intergroup forgiveness and reparation in Northern Ireland and Chile. In A. Nadler, T. E. Malloy, & J. D. Fisher (eds), *The social psychology of intergroup reconciliation* (pp. 97–114). Oxford: Oxford University Press.

Northrup, T. A. (1989). The dynamic of identity in personal and social conflict. In L. Kriesberg, T. A. Northrup, & S. J. Thorson (eds), *Intractable conflicts and their transformation* (pp. 55–82). Syracuse, NY: Syracuse University Press.

Oelsner, A. (2007). Friendship, mutual trust and the evolution of regional peace in the international system. *Critical Review of International Social and Political Philosophy, 10,* 257–279.

Okimoto, T. G., Wenzel, M., & Hedrick, K. (2013). Refusing to apologize can have psychological benefits (and we issue no mea culpa for this research finding). *European Journal of Social Psychology, 43,* 22–31.

Palanski, M. E. (2012). Forgiveness and reconciliation in the workplace: A multilevel perspective and research agenda. *Journal of Business Ethics, 190,* 275–287.

Pedaliu, E. G. H. (2009). "A sea of confusion": The Mediterranean and détente, 1969–1974. *Diplomatic History, 33,* 735–750.

Pfeffer, J., & Salancik, G. R. (1974). Organizational decision making as a political process: The case of a university budget. *Administrative Science Quarterly, 19,* 135–151.

Rapske, D. L., Boon, S. D., Alibhai, A. M., & Kheong, M. J. (2010). Not forgiven, not forgotten: An investigation of unforgiven interpersonal offenses. *Journal of Social and Clinical Psychology, 29,* 1100–1130.

Reb, J., Goldman, B. M., Kray, L. J., & Cropanzano, R. (2006). Different wrongs, different remedies? Reactions to organizational remedies after procedural and interactional injustice. *Personnel Psychology, 59,* 31–64.

Riek, B. M., Mania, E. W., & Gaertner, S. L. (2006). Intergroup threat and outgroup attitudes: A meta-analytic review. *Personality and Social Psychology Review, 10,* 336–353.

Romano, A. (2009). Détente, entente, or linkage? The Helsinki Conference on Security and Cooperation in Europe in U.S. relations with the Soviet Union. *Diplomatic History, 33,* 703–722.

Rousseau, D. M., Sitkin, S. B., Burt, R. S., & Camerer, C. (1998). Not so different after all: A cross-discipline view of trust. *Academy of Management Review, 23*, 393–404.

Rusbult, C. E., Verette, J., Whitney, G. A., Slovik, L. F., & Lipkus, I. (1991). Accommodation processes in close relationships: Theory and preliminary empirical evidence. *Journal of Personality and Social Psychology, 60*, 53–78.

Schein, E. (1990). Organizational culture. *American Psychologist, 45*, 109–119.

Schlotter, P. (1983). Détente: Models and strategies. *Journal of Peace Research, 20*, 213–220.

Schoorman, F. D., Mayer, R. C., & Davis, J. H. (2007). An integrative model of organizational trust: Past, present, and future. *Academy of Management Review, 32*, 344–354.

Schweitzer, M. E., Hershey, J. C., & Bradlow, E. T. (2006). Promises and lies: Restoring violated trust. *Organizational Behavior and Human Decision Processes, 101*, 1–19.

Sitkin, S., & George, E. (2005). Managerial trust-building through the use of legitimating formal and informal control mechanisms. *International Sociology, 20*, 307–338.

Sitkin, S. B., & Roth, N. L. (1993). Explaining the limited effectiveness of legalistic remedies for trust/distrust. *Organization Science, 4*, 367–392.

Skarlicki, D. P., Barclay, L. J., & Pugh, S. D. (2008). When explanations for layoffs are not enough: Employer's integrity as a moderator of the relationship between informational justice and retaliation. *Journal of Occupational and Organizational Psychology, 81*, 123–146.

Smith, E. R. (1993). Social identity and social emotions: Toward new conceptualizations of prejudice. In D. M. Mackie & D. L. Hamilton (eds), *Affect, cognition and stereotyping: Interactive processes in group perception* (pp. 297–316). San Diego, CA: Academic Press.

Suri, J. (2008). Détente and human rights: American and West European perspectives on international change. *Cold War History, 8*, 527–545.

Tajfel, H. (1981). Social stereotypes and social groups. In J. Turner & H. Giles (eds), *Intergroup behavior* (pp. 144–167). Chicago, IL: University of Chicago Press.

Tajfel, H., & Turner, J. C. (1986). The social identity theory of intergroup behavior. In S. Worchel & W. G. Austin (eds), *Psychology of intergroup relations* (pp. 7–24). Chicago, IL: Nelson Hall.

Thau, S., & Mitchell, M. S. (2010). Self-gain or self-regulation impairment? Tests of competing explanations of the supervisor abuse and employee deviance relationship through perceptions of distributive justice. *Journal of Applied Psychology, 95*, 1009–1031.

Tomlinson, E. C., & Lewicki, R. J. (2006). Managing distrust in intractable conflicts. *Conflict Resolution Quarterly, 24*, 219–228.

Tomlinson, E., & Mayer, R. C. (2009). The role of causal attribution dimensions in trust repair. *Academy of Management Review, 34*, 85–104.

Tripp, T. M., & Bies, R. J. (1997). What's good about revenge? The avenger's perspective. In R. J. Lewicki, R. J. Bies, & B. H. Sheppard (eds), *Research on negotiation in organizations* (Vol. 6, pp. 145–160). Greenwich, CT: JAI Press.

Tripp, T. M., & Bies, R. J. (2009). *Getting even: The truth about workplace revenge – and how to stop it.* San Francisco, CA: John Wiley & Sons.

Tripp, T. M., Bies, R. J., & Aquino, K. (2007). A vigilante model of justice: Revenge, reconciliation, forgiveness, and avoidance. *Social Justice Research, 20*, 10–34.

Tsang, J., McCullough, M. E., & Fincham, F. D. (2006). The longitudinal association between forgiveness and relationship closeness and commitment. *Journal of Social and Clinical Psychology, 25*, 448–472.

Turnley, W. H., & Feldman, D. C. (1999). The impact of psychological contract violations on exit, voice, loyalty, and neglect. *Human Relations, 52*, 895–922.

Tyler, T. R. (1990). *Why people obey the law: Procedural justice, legitimacy, and compliance.* New Haven, CT: Yale University Press.

Tyler, T. R. (2001). Why do people rely on others? Social identity and social aspects of trust. In K. S. Cook (ed.), *Trust in society. Russell Sage Foundation series on trust* (Vol. 2, pp. 285–306). New York, NY: Russell Sage Foundation.

Van Lange, P. A. M., Rusbult, C. E., Drigotas, S. M., Arriaga, X. B., Witcher, B. S., & Cox, C. L. (1997). Willingness to sacrifice in close relationships. *Journal of Personality and Social Psychology, 72*, 1373–1395.

Van Tongeren, D. R., Davis, D. E., & Hook, J. N. (2014). Social benefits of humility: Initiating and maintaining romantic relationships. *The Journal of Positive Psychology, 9*, 313–321.

Voci, A. (2006). The link between identification and in-group favouritism: Effects of threat to social identity and trust-related emotions. *British Journal of Social Psychology, 45*, 265–284.

Wade, N. G., & Worthington, E. L., Jr. (2003). Overcoming interpersonal offenses: Is forgiveness the only way to deal with unforgiveness? *Journal of Counseling and Development, 81*, 343–353.

Wade, N. G., & Worthington, E. L., Jr. (2005). In search of a common core: A content analysis of interventions to promote forgiveness. *Psychotherapy: Theory, Research, Practice, Training, 42*, 160–177.

Waldron, V. R., & Kelley, D. L. (2008). *Communicating forgiveness*. Los Angeles, CA: Sage.

Walker, M. U. (2006). *Moral repair: Reconstructing moral relations after wrongdoing*. Cambridge, UK: Cambridge University Press.

Walker, R., Logan, T., Jordan, C. E., & Campbell, J. C. (2004). An integrative review of separation in the context of victimization: Consequences and implications for women. *Trauma, Violence, & Abuse, 5*, 143–193.

Waytz, A., Young, L. L., & Ginges, J. (2014). Motive attribution asymmetry for love vs. hate drives intractable conflict. *Proceedings of the National Academy of Sciences, 111*, 15687–15692.

Weiss, H. M., & Rupp, D. E. (2011). Experiencing work: An essay on a person-centric work psychology. *Industrial and Organizational Psychology, 4*, 83–97.

Williamson, O. E. (1975). *Markets and hierarchies: Analysis and antitrust implications*. New York, NY: Free Press.

Wohl, M. J., & McGrath, A. L. (2007). The perception of time heals all wounds: Temporal distance affects willingness to forgive following an interpersonal transgression. *Personality and Social Psychology Bulletin, 33*, 1023–1035.

Worthington, E. L. Jr., & Scherer, M. (2004). Forgiveness is an emotion-focused coping strategy that can reduce health risks and promote health resilience: Theory, review, and hypotheses. *Psychology and Health, 19*, 385–405.

Worthington, E. L., Jr., & Wade, N. G. (1999). The social psychology of unforgiveness and forgiveness and implications for clinical practice. *Journal of Social and Clinical Psychology, 18*, 385–418.

Zechmeister, J. S., & Romero, C. (2002). Victim and offender accounts of interpersonal conflict: Autobiographical narratives of forgiveness and unforgiveness. *Journal of Personality and Social Psychology, 82*, 675–686.

Zembylas, M. (2011). Ethnic division in Cyprus and a policy initiative on promoting peaceful coexistence: Toward an agonistic democracy for citizenship education. *Education, Citizenship and Social Justice, 6*, 53–67.

Zheng, X., Fehr, R., Tai, K., Narayanan, J., & Gelfand, M. J. (2015). The unburdening effects of forgiveness: Effects on slant perception and jumping height. *Social Psychological and Personality Science, 6*, 431–438.

Zucker, L. G. (1986). Production of trust: Institutional sources of economic structure, 1840–1920. In B. M. Staw & L. L. Cummings (eds), *Research in organizational behavior* (Vol. 8, pp. 53–111). Greenwich, CT: JAI Press.

PART V

Applications

One of the key questions we wanted to explore in this book is whether trust is different in distinct contexts. Here we examine the issue of trust in eight different applied settings to consider more explicitly the salience of trust and the different aspects that matter. We have tried to select contexts that have been hit by dramatic changes or scandals that have changed and to some degree eroded public trust. We indicate in our short review of each chapter their synergies with other chapters, but it is evident that all of the chapters in the preceding part on trust and its repair would be of interest to readers.

We start the part with a context in which trust is a germane issue both at interpersonal but also institutional levels – that of health. The insights offered are further enhanced as it is written by regulators for whom the consequences of trust and its breach are particularly salient. Samantha Peters, CEO of the UK's General Optical Council, and Douglas Bilton, from the UK's Professional Standards Authority, consider the significance of trust in the health context. They outline how, in healthcare, trust is a very germane concern due to the high stakes for all the individuals involved (patients, professionals and organizations), the distinct imbalances of power among the actors, and the elevated levels of risks that can be involved. These risks often have to be weighed up in situations where there are few alternatives. Reviewing the literature on trust in this context, they also bring to life the breadth of concerns through two cases, one concerning the dangerous and harmful practices of an Australian physician, Dr Harry Bailey, and his use of deep sleep therapy, and the second, Dr Harold Shipman, a UK General Practitioner who murdered fifteen patients, a case which resulted in a national public inquiry, extensive changes to regulation and had a profound impact on British health policy. The two cases demonstrate the fluidity of transfer of trust between the personal and the impersonal, and how unscrupulous and poorly monitored practitioners can secure misplaced and unwarranted trust. A trust frame is used to examine these two cases and draws attention to the importance of trust to and for this context.

The second chapter in this part examines trust within a very different but not less important context – finance. Robert F. Hurley looks at the events of the Global Financial Crisis and examines the loss of trust in banks. He considers the types of violation by universal banks and argues that it was the culmination of an ongoing erosion of organizational trust as banks have sought to adapt to challenges in their competitive environments. He puts the ongoing breach of trust of these organizations into the context of wider organizational dynamics which have seen subtle, more potentially nefarious changes to behaviours for those employed in this sector. Through this chapter he argues for changes in our understanding of trust in banks, and makes suggestions for how trustworthiness might be improved in this critical sector going forward.

Frédérique Six explores the issue of the role of trust in professions. This is a pertinent context in which to look at those who are trusted due to their unique expert knowledge, but also their perceived commitment to public service and societal values. Increasingly we have seen politicians in many countries downplaying the importance and influence of expertise and fact-based arguments, instead offering a fact-light political rhetoric. These professionals are often employed in organizations that has undergone radical austerity-focused change and so the nature of their work, and its value for and to society, has dramatically shifted and in many cases reduced. Six explores the challenges to trust in public professionals and their professions to identify two distinct patterns in the evolution of change to the relationships between professionals and their employers and regulators over the past decades: one is the adversarial struggle between professionals' desire for autonomy and managerial control; and the second, a more collaborative pattern which retains autonomy for professionals alongside managerial control. There are synergies between this chapter and Chapter 27 by Raaphorst and Van de Walle, on trust in and by the public sector and to Chapter 29 by Long and Weibel, a review of trust and control.

In Chapter 21, Kim Mather looks at employment relations, a context which is regarded by some as having inherently low trust due to the ways work is contractually and practically organized. Using the UK context, she considers trust matters in the interactions between employers, workers, trade unions and state policy. She discusses the role of distinct employment contracts in terms of the growth of casualized employment, either zero-hours or self-employment, and the impact on organizational trust. Her chapter draws attention to concepts of power, control and job regulation as a means of showing how and why employee-employer trust might be low and still declining. This chapter links to later chapters including Chapter 28 by Searle, on Human Resource Management and trust, and Chapter 29 by Long and Weibel, on control and trust.

Lisa van der Werff, Colette Real and Theodore G. Lynn turn our attention in Chapter 22 to the question of trust in the online world and consider individual trust and the internet by highlighting salient concerns at three distinct levels: interpersonal, organizational and system trust. Setting the stage for how technology is increasingly mediating both our personal and our professional relationships, they review the literature to identify similarities and differences of trust in this virtual context. There are obvious connections with Chapter 3 by Blomqvist and Cook, on swift trust.

Attention then focuses on Trust in the entrepreneurial process in Trenton A. Williams and Dean A. Shepherd's chapter, which offers both a distinct topic and a distinct perspective – considering trust at specific stages of an organization's life cycle. Through their specific lens, they illuminate the start of an organization and discuss the changes to the importance and types of trust during the defined stages of the entrepreneurial processes. This chapter also has synergies with Chapter 3 by Blomqvist and Cook, on swift trust.

Our penultimate context discusses trust in safety-critical contexts, with Brian C. Gunia, Sharon H. Kim and Kathleen M. Sutcliffe reviewing concerns of trust and distrust. Beginning with the German Wings disaster, this chapter highlights the impacts of low trust and distrust. Interestingly they note how, in this safety-critical domain, trust and distrust are not positioned as separate dimensions; instead, terms denoting low trust and distrust tend to be used interchangeably. Through their review of the literature, they identify both the positive and the negative roles that trust and these conceptually opposite factors play. They outline the key mechanism underlying these roles. This chapter has links to others including Chapter 12 by Bachmann, on trust in institutions, and Chapter 4 by Sitkin and Bijlsma-Frankema, on distrust and Chapter 16 by Gillespie and Siebert, on organizational-level trust repair.

The last chapter in this applied part considers trust in the food context, with Lovisa Näslund and Fergus Lyon outlining the importance of trust in the distinct roles and relationships for consumers, producers but also retailers. Given the recent scandals within this sector, they show the range of ways that trust matters in and for this context. Their chapter also has important synergies with others, such as Chapter 13 by Poppo and Cheng, on contracts and Chapter 29 by Long and Weibel, on control and trust. They further highlight the often critical role of interpersonal trust (see Chapter 5 by Lyu and Ferrin).

18

'RIGHT-TOUCH' TRUST

Thoughts on trust in healthcare

Samantha Peters and Douglas Bilton

Introduction

Trust is contextually charged. Like a play, it has 'sets' or 'stages' as well as 'scripts' and 'actors'. It is predicated on the arena or conditions under which it takes place (Nooteboom 2002, Nooteboom 2006). The hazards of trusting vary not only in relation to the transactions involved, but also in relation to the environment within which they take place (Williamson 1993, 2006). In certain settings one is forced to trust blindly simply because the alternatives are worse (Gambetta 2000). In healthcare, the stakes are high, the power imbalances are substantial, and the risks are elevated, but alternatives are in short supply. Patients must take risks because other options are non-existent and the consequences of going without treatment are worse. Patients may exercise some influence over this but their ability to monitor or control professionals is substantially constrained by the trusting environment. The structure of care itself is imbued with a substantial power differential inherent in professionals' body of clinical knowledge, experience in applying that knowledge, and position inside organizations, where the patient is but temporary. In such settings, risk is inevitable and vulnerability is inescapable.

Dimensions of trust in healthcare

Most definitions of trust identify two integral and inter-related dimensions: a trustor's acceptance of their own vulnerability as well as their positive expectations of another's intention towards them (Colquitt et al. 2007, Fulmer and Gelfand 2012). Typically, trust is 'the willingness of a party to be vulnerable to the actions of another party based on the expectation that the other will perform a particular action important to the trustor, irrespective of the ability to monitor or control that party' (Mayer et al. 1995, p. 712). Both dimensions, willing vulnerability and positive expectation, are visible in healthcare. The terms of risk and uncertainty under which medical decisions are taken put patients in a particularly vulnerable position (Goold 2001). Power imbalances between patients and professionals make those seeking treatment vulnerable and dependent (Dinc and Gastmans 2012). Healthcare professionals must be trusted neither to increase patients' vulnerability (e.g. by perpetuating dependency) nor to exploit it for their own ends and, moreover, to reduce the vulnerability created by ill-health (e.g. by supporting patients' self-determination) (Barnard 2016, p. 294). Such disparities not only expose patients to risk but also disempower them; in effect, they are compelled to trust professionals not to exploit them (Frowe 2005). In this context, patients' trust remains a relational phenomenon, involving risk and vulnerability and founded on expectations of how others, pre-supposed to be concerned about your interests, will behave (Gilson 2006). Thus it appears to exhibit that particular combination of risk to the trustor and inter-dependence between trustor and trustee which qualifies it as a psychological state (Rousseau et al. 1998).

Patients must consent to treatment regardless of whether their vulnerability is a state they willingly accept or have forced upon them and irrespective of their means to monitor or control others. Information asymmetries particularly constrain their ability to verify professionals' trustworthiness. The relationship can be conceptualized as an unusual form of principal agent problem: patients have limited information (about their illness or treatments); they delegate responsibility for making decisions about their care to professionals; they rely in turn on professionals' 'professionalism' to ensure that the treatment they receive is appropriate; and in this way their trust addresses the inherent uncertainty underlying medical care and acts as a substitute for information (Dwyer et al. 2012, p. 505). Patient choice is also a constraining factor. Patients who believe that they have enough choice in regards to their physician are more likely to trust them (Kao et al. 1998). Patients who lack agency to choose their physician, and in effect whether to trust (or distrust) them, may experience a form of 'forced or resigned' trust (Ward et al. 2015, p. 10). In spite of these constraints, patients generally demonstrate an acceptance of their own vulnerability together with positive expectations of healthcare agents or agencies' intentions towards them. Thus, drawing on Mayer et al. (1995), patient trust may be characterized as patients' willing acceptance of their vulnerability to treatment, founded in positive expectations of those responsible for treating them, irrespective of their ability to monitor, control or choose the treating agency.

Trust has suffered from a positive bias; however, evidence is accumulating that it has a dark side, that distrust (the victim of a negative bias) has a bright side, and that both can have positive or negative consequences (Lumineau 2014). Trust can be blind, misplaced, or excessive, leading trustors to take more risk, trust erroneously, or overlook exploitation (Langfred 2004, Goel et al. 2005, Gargiulo and Ertug 2006, Skinner et al. 2013). Healthcare failures tend to be well-known and longstanding despite considerable harm (Walshe and Shortell 2004). Patients willingly continue trusting professionals even when there is substantial evidence of systematic abuse (Sellman 2007). The trust which makes it possible for them to be treated can increase risk, exacerbate vulnerability, and enable mistreatment. For these reasons, trust in healthcare cannot be considered uniformly good, but neither can distrust be considered uniformly bad. While trust involves willing vulnerability and positive expectations, distrust encompasses an unwillingness to be vulnerable and negative expectations of others, incorporating the need to protect oneself from their conduct (Lewicki et al. 1998). In medical settings, trust and distrust can both be unfounded; for example, disclosing a medical error might diminish trust as a consequence of a trustworthy act, whereas not disclosing it might have the opposite effect (Goold 2002). Both, if misplaced, can undermine clinical relationships (Hawley 2015). However, it is not always clear when trust in a trustee is genuinely misplaced, particularly when they have an extensive array of discretionary powers (Baier 1986). This is especially problematic in healthcare settings where professionals' discretionary powers are extensive.

Healthcare is a dramatic setting with many stages on which the trusting process can unfold, and many players on them. In this environment, trust is visible at both micro and macro levels,

Table 18.1 Patient trust across healthcare levels

Trust level	Patient as trustor	Patient as trustee
Individual level	Individual patients trust in individual professionals.	Individual patients are trusted by individual professionals.
Team, group or type	Individual patients, or patients more generally, trust in professionals as a group.	Patients as a group are trusted by individual professionals, or professionals more generally.
Organizational level	Individual patients, or patients more generally, trust in specific healthcare organizations.	Patients as a group are trusted by specific healthcare organizations.
Institutional level	Individual patients, or patients more generally, trust in systems of expertise (medicine, professionalism, etc.). Individual patients or patients more generally, trust in healthcare systems (and related institutions such as insurers, regulators).	Patients as a group are trusted by the healthcare system, regulators or others.

functioning through personal (or interpersonal) and impersonal (or institutional) means. In their framework, Calnan and Rowe, for example, identify trust relations at both levels; at the micro level they argue they involve interpersonal trust between individual patients, clinicians, and managers, while at the macro level they involve institutional trust between patients, clinicians, and managers more generally, as well as in specific establishments, or healthcare systems (and related institutions) as a whole (Calnan and Rowe 2006, Rowe and Calnan 2006). Similarly, Gilson identifies trust in healthcare as either an individual, voluntary activity or a more general, impersonal one; with the former incorporating trust in known individuals, and the latter incorporating trust in strangers (Gilson 2003). Fulmer and Gelfand (2012) stress the importance of distinguishing between trust levels and targets. In healthcare, trust can be mapped onto individual professionals or specific organizations; onto teams, groups or types of individuals or organizations (e.g. nurses or hospitals); as well as onto wider institutions, including health systems as a whole (Hall et al. 2001, Rose et al. 2004). In this chapter, we focus on trust from the patient's perspective. Drawing on Fulmer and Gelfand's conceptual framework, the main levels and referents for patients are set out in Table 18.1.

Introducing trust in healthcare at an individual level

At the individual level, trust in healthcare is dominated by the personal relationship between patients and the professionals treating them, the most compelling and immediate relationship experienced by a patient undergoing care. In this setting, a range of factors nurture trust that is personal, intimate, and unquestioning. Professionals are perceived to have both legal and moral legitimacy (Downie 1990, cited in Frowe 2005). They bring a system of expertise from which non-professionals are excluded (Abbott 1988). They have an ethical provenance. Their codes and systems inculcate the features from which trust is derived (Goold 2001). The Hippocratic Oath, for example, exhorts and instils a protocol of aiding the sick without injury or harm. Professionals also hold specific roles, titles, credentials, or positions. These might reasonably create an expectation that the individuals occupying or holding them will (or are incentivized to) fulfil a trust (Hardin, 2006). In effect, we trust doctors because of their roles and expertise (Dawes 1994, cited in Meyerson et al. 1996). Patients may also believe in certain prevailing archetypes such as the caring doctor or angel of mercy. However, these are unlikely to generate unwavering trust on their own. In theory, roles can signal expectations and archetypes can suggest how they will be met, but trust which is founded in patient expectations is likely to be tested (and validated) in reality through individual ongoing relationships. In practice, all these factors could generate patient trust in the professional treating them at the individual level.

Trust is shaped by trustors' perceptions of trustees' ability, benevolence or integrity (Mayer et al. 1995, Schoorman et al. 2007). All three factors correlate highly with the creation of trust (Colquitt et al., 2007). In healthcare, trust is generally derived from clinicians' technical ability, skill, or competence, as well as their interpersonal skills, competences, and relationships with patients (Mechanic and Meyer 2000, Hall et al. 2001). Empirical data indicate that trust is created by providers demonstrating their vigilance and moral comportment (i.e. respect and caring) as well as their competence (Murray and McCrone 2015). Patients with cancer, for example, derive their trust in oncologists from perceptions of honesty and patient-centred behaviour (i.e. caring, listening and showing concern) as well as competence (Hillen et al., 2011). Benevolence is notably important. "Humaneness" is a highly rated aspect of care for patients (Wensing et al. 1998). Patients' trust comes from believing professionals will act or advocate in their best interests, as well as from finding them concerned and compassionate, comforting, and caring (Mechanic and Meyer 2000, Thom 2001, Hall et al. 2001, Calnan and Rowe 2004, Rowe and Calnan 2006). More open mandates of trust are shown to develop through physicians showing early interest in patients, being sensitive to their emotions, giving them time, and establishing common ground (Skirbekk et al. 2011). Individuals' propensity to trust will, of course, vary (Mayer et al. 1995). In theory, the importance of a professional's ability, benevolence, or integrity will resonate differently with patients depending on the intervention concerned and the characteristics of the clinicians involved, as well as their own personal propensity to trust.

Patients' trust in individual physicians remains strong (Kao et al. 1998, Hall et al. 2001, Calnan and Sanford 2004, Calnan and Rowe 2004, Zhao et al. 2016). Individual studies show patients demonstrate high levels of trust in general practitioners, hospital doctors, and specialists (Tarrant et al. 2003, Keating et al. 2004, Lord et al. 2012). The nature of that trust may, however, be shifting. In England and Wales, for example, only a minority of patients trust unconditionally or solely on the basis of professional status; instead, trust is becoming more conditional, giving way to a form which is increasingly earned through professionals' competence, patients' experience of care and the interaction between them (Calnan and Rowe 2008). Trust in professionals is progressively challenged in a world where knowledge is increasingly distributed, information asymmetries are reducing, and the internet offers quasi-trustworthy alternatives to expert opinion (Susskind and Susskind 2015). Patients' may be influenced by more general levels of trust. In Europe, for example, their trust in healthcare professionals appears to vary in line with trust at a societal level (van der Schee et al. 2007). Patients' trust might also shift in line with debates about healthcare policy or delivery, particularly where confidence has been undermined by perceptions that individuals or organizations have acted incompetently, behaved without integrity, or lacked benevolence towards patients. In Uganda, for example, patients' loss of trust in professionals' legitimacy or expertise and (government-run) healthcare institutions has been associated with the widespread transfer of injections out from the institutional sphere and into domestic settings, with the public assuming responsibility for this themselves (Birungi 1998).

Introducing trust in healthcare at an institutional level

Health systems are intricate social institutions with a complex array of relationships influenced by trust (Gilson, 2003). In this setting, a range of factors nurture trust that is impersonal, assumed and routine. Institutions are trust-generating agencies, capable of being the object of trust, the foundation for trust between parties, or of nurturing and carrying trust between those without prior interaction (Mollering 2006). Institutions can create trust by providing situational normality or structural assurances (McKnight et al. 2006, McKnight and Chervany 2006). Certain groups or systems also act as if trust is present, leading to swifter or more rapid trusting (Meyerson et al. 1996, Meyerson et al. 2006) (see Chapter 3 by Blomqvist and Cook, on swift trust). In healthcare, the institutional landscape includes medicine as a scheme of expertise, the organizations which provide care, the diverse agencies that direct or control healthcare professionals and organizations (e.g. government, regulators), as well as the system as a whole. The relationship between patients and professionals is rooted in this landscape, a backdrop which automatically promulgates trusting behaviour through institutional mechanisms and the structural assurances they provide. Healthcare organizations themselves, for example, express values, set norms, and create expectations of roles which have moral substance (Goold 2001). Inside them, relations can be codified into models or practices which support trust. The doctor-patient relationship, for example, engenders swift trust in professionals, with clinicians using shared experiences and agreement to develop trust rapidly (Dibben and Lean 2003). Consequently, not only do healthcare professionals' roles, titles, or expertise communicate their trustworthiness but the context within which they practise conveys it as well (see Chapter 9 by Baer and Colquitt).

Just as beliefs about professionals may be influenced by perceptions of ability, benevolence and integrity, so might trust or distrust in organizations or institutions. For a healthcare system to be trusted, more than competence is required; its institutions must also have an ethical basis (Gilson 2006). Once a healthcare organization accepts its role as a care provider, it is effectually entrusted with patients' well-being, and expectations concerning its competence, beneficence or confidentiality will flow from that (Goold 2001, p. 32). In South Africa, for example, patients' trust in primary care providers has been shown to be influenced by their desire for institutions to act fairly (i.e. with integrity and benevolence) as well as having competent and respectful employees (Gilson et al. 2005). In America, perceived lack of benevolence (i.e. that the system cares more about cost than health), incompetence (i.e. patients dying because of mistakes), or failings of integrity (i.e. medicines' content is not revealed) are associated with distrust in healthcare systems (Rose et al. 2004). It has been suggested that competence is likely to be of greater importance at the institutional level, with benevolence potentially weaker, replaced by the demand for fairness (Goold 2001). However, benevolence appears to be a source of significant distrust when perceived to be absent. Patients' suspicions about for-profit motives, for example, are shown to significantly erode trust in healthcare. In low- and middle-income countries, payment mechanisms are perceived to encourage providers to operate against patients' interests (Gilson 2006). In high-income countries, rationed or managed care has negatively affected trust in healthcare organizations or systems (Mechanic 1996, Mechanic 1998, Abelson et al. 2009, Maarse et al. 2016). This supports arguments that benevolence is not simply the belief that a party is well intentioned but also that any egocentric motives, such as profit, must be set aside for trust to emerge (Mayer et al. 1995).

Trusting collective situations is hard because of the scale and complexity of the institutions involved, and because the usual social mechanisms (which help manage the trusting process) have less power and influence within them (Kramer et al. 1996). Where profit motives exist, semi-strong trust can emerge if parties are protected through mechanisms (such as regulation) that punish opportunistic behaviour; however, strong trust only emerges if both parties have internalized values which clearly demarcate such opportunism as unacceptable (Barney and Hansen 1994). Drawing from this, we would expect trust to be more prevalent at the personal level in healthcare (with patients finding it easier to anticipate integrity or benevolence from individuals) than at the impersonal level, where organizations' constraints are possibly more observable. There is less research into patient trust and distrust at institutional or system level and fewer instruments to measure it (Ozawa and Sripad 2013). There is, however, evidence that trust is higher and more evident at the micro level, fuelled by features of the doctor-patient relationship (e.g. whether patients are listened too) and that distrust is higher and more evident at the macro level, fuelled by features concerning how care is organized or provided, for example, waiting times or cost cutting (Calnan and Sanford 2004). Individual studies show that healthcare systems are particularly exposed to distrust, with high levels evident in countries as diverse as America (Armstrong et al. 2006), and Sierra Leone (Pieterse and Lodge, 2015). Patients also show distrusting attitudes towards other institutions such as medicine demonstrated, for example, by hesitant, ambivalent, and distrusting attitudes towards vaccination (Yaqub et al. 2014).

Shifting trust between personal and impersonal dimensions

Patients' trust or distrust in one sphere might not automatically affect trust or distrust in another. Patients have, for example, displayed high levels of trust in practitioners while simultaneously mistrusting healthcare systems (Benkert et al. 2009). A patient can trust a professional but distrust the system, or trust the system but distrust a particular professional (Ward et al. 2015). Trust can, however, be transferred between groups or individuals on the basis of perceived similarities, group membership, or third party interaction (McEvily et al. 2003). Trust in individuals can flow from the organization they are part of, while trust in an organization can flow from the people who comprise it (Nooteboom 2006). Potential forms of patients' trust transfer are mapped out in Table 18.2. In theory, it is possible for the personal trust (or distrust) a patient has in their own healthcare practitioner or provider to be transferred to the impersonal dimension,

Table 18.2 Conceptual framework for analysing patient trust transfer

Types of patient trust	Where it can be transferred
Trust or distrust in individual professionals	Trust or distrust in professionals generally
	Trust or distrust in a specific healthcare organization (the professionals' employer)
	Trust or distrust in the health service more generally
Trust or distrust in healthcare professionals generally (as a group)	Trust or distrust in specific healthcare professional
Trust or distrust in individual healthcare organizations	Trust or distrust in its healthcare professionals (its employees)
	Trust or distrust the health service more generally
Trust or distrust in healthcare systems or institutions	Trust or distrust in healthcare professionals (individually or as a group)
	Trust or distrust in a healthcare organizations (specifically or more generally)

generating trust or distrust in the healthcare system as a whole. Individual studies support this. In Taiwan, for example, patients' interaction with professionals is shown to influence their trust in a specific hospital, as well as in allied hospitals, in turn (Lien et al. 2014). Working the other way, patients' impersonal trust (or distrust) in macro-level organizations or institutions might generate trust or distrust in practitioners at the micro level. Again, individual studies support this. In China, for example, patients' attitudes towards health policy and trust in medical services have been shown to influence satisfaction with a range of micro-level features including interaction with doctors (Tang 2011). More broadly, a comparison of 22 countries shows that generalized trust in physicians as a group is influenced by healthcare system structures (Saarinen et al. 2016).

In summary, trust in the healthcare context has a number of important features and dimensions. In this setting, trust can be personal or impersonal, operating at both micro and macro levels, vested in healthcare professionals or organizations both individually or as teams, groups or types, as well as in wider healthcare systems, and related institutions such as medicine or regulation. Patients' trust is characterized by their willing acceptance of vulnerability to treatment, founded in positive expectations of those responsible for treating them, irrespective of their ability to monitor, control, or choose the treating agency. Patients' trust may be influenced by their perceptions of trustees' ability, benevolence, and integrity. Their trust can also feasibly be transferred between different levels or targets; with a patient's trust (or distrust) in an entity at one level, in theory, capable of influencing, or being transferred to trust in another entity at another level.

Implications of trust and distrust in healthcare

Theoretically, a patient's trust will support the clinical relationship by driving satisfaction, increasing the likelihood of adherence to treatments and decreasing the likelihood of care being discontinued (Pearson and Raeke 2000). There is extensive evidence that trust mediates therapeutic processes but evidence of a direct benefit on health outcomes is lacking (Calnan and Rowe 2004). Individual studies show trust to be strongly associated with patients' satisfaction, continuity with a physician, retention in care, and intended or self-reported adherence to medication (Thom et al. 1999, Mainous et al. 2001, Baker et al. 2003, Whetten et al. 2006, Graham et al. 2010). In America, for example, the trust which patients with cancer have in their physician is shown to precipitate early detection (Mainous et al. 2004b). In Taiwan, the trust which patients with diabetes have in physicians is shown to generate enhanced self-efficacy and expectation of health outcomes, leading (in turn) to treatment adherence and improved health outcomes (Lee and Lin 2009). Conversely, distrust can have a negative impact on patients' satisfaction, relationship with professionals, and acceptance of, or adherence to, treatment (Rose et al. 2004). Distrust, mistrust and low levels of trust have been shown to reduce patient access or use of health services, deter them from following treatments and undermine continuity of care, as well as correlate with poor reported health (Thom et al. 2002, Balkrishnan et al. 2003, Whetten et al. 2006, Howerton et al. 2007, LaVeist et al., 2009, Thrasher et al. 2008). In Sweden, for example, low trust in the healthcare system as an institution is correlated with poor self-rated health (Mohensi and Lindstrom 2007), while in America, distrust in the healthcare system is shown to be associated with worse self-reported health (Armstrong et al. 2006).

In theory, much of this may be relationally or behaviourally driven; since a high level of trust in healthcare settings can encourage patients to willingly take risks or accept advice without question, while a lower level can encourage risk aversion, the pursuit of second opinions, or search for alternative agents or treatments (Rowe and Calnan 2006). Clearly, patients' behavioural interaction with those involved in giving, receiving, or organizing care is important. Trust can generate openness, encourage knowledge sharing or collective problem solving, and reduce monitoring costs, or, less helpfully, reduce constructive engagement and undermine due diligence or monitoring; whereas distrust can encourage monitoring and vigilance, or, less helpfully, increase monitoring costs (Lumineau 2014). Trust can foster the sharing, disclosing, or volunteering of knowledge or information (Dirks and Ferrin 2001). Taken too far, however, it can prompt people to reduce or suspend those actions which would safeguard them, suppress or discount evidence of un-trustworthiness or negate the need for distrust altogether (Kramer et al. 1996, Flores and Solomon 1998, McEvily et al. 2003). In the healthcare environment, a high level of trust is likely to encourage patients to share information and reduce their checking, whereas those with lower levels of trust are likely to withhold information and increase their monitoring (Rowe and Calnan 2006). In these ways, trust can increase the efficiency of care, by, for example, increasing the disclosure of sensitive information leading to appropriate treatment, and reducing the costs of verification, such as additional tests, referrals, and so on (Thom et al. 2004). Thus, if a patient trusts a professional's benevolence or integrity, they are more likely to share personal or sensitive information about their illness. If they trust a professional's knowledge, they are probably more likely to accept the diagnosis and treatment. Conversely, if a professional trusts a patient (or their knowledge of their condition), they may factor that patient's views or perspective into diagnosis and treatment.

Trust might also improve patients' affective engagement and personal or emotional efficacy. Trust can be a form of faith that mentally or emotionally removes the presence of negative consequences (Deutsch 1973), a feature which may be of real value to patients in a context which is high in emotional uncertainty. Trust can generate confidence, support a climate of psychological safety, and reduce uncertainty, while distrust can encourage productive suspicion or scepticism or alternatively foster fear, paranoia, and beliefs that others' motives are harmful (Lumineau 2014). A high level of trust in healthcare settings will foster patients' beliefs that others are not going to harm them, create the sense that it is acceptable for them to be without knowledge or control, reduce their anxiety, suspicion or scepticism, and help them to draw comfort from their relationships; whereas, lower levels of trust will foster beliefs that others may act harmfully, create the sense that it is a problem to be without knowledge or control, increase anxiety, suspicion or scepticism, and make patients anxious about relationships (Rowe and Calnan 2006). Trust in this sense may be a form of comfort which reduces patients' anxieties, thereby improving interaction. Take cancer patients for example; trust plays an important role in reducing their fears, worries, and perceived risks, with those who are more trusting worrying less and more likely to adhere to treatment and advice (Hillen et al. 2011).

Critically, for healthcare settings, trust is not a static phenomenon. It can begin with a calculated assessment of deterrents, build on the basis of knowledge, and develop into a form of identification founded in common goals and values (Lewicki and Bunker 1996). Trust in physicians increases over the duration of a relationship (Thom et al. 1999). The value of continuity builds over time as patients share experiences with their physician (Mainous et al. 2004a). Thus, continuity of care created by trust may in turn enable stronger forms of trust to develop, potentially starting with a calculation grounded in the nature of healthcare professionals' roles and anticipated value congruence, and deepening over time as that congruence is confirmed. This is likely to operate in both directions. Patients knowing they are trusted may also bring benefits in turn. Those with chronic illnesses, for example, identify trust which their physicians demonstrate in them as a factor which shapes their own sense of self-esteem and competence (Thorne and

Table 18.3 How patient trust and distrust aids care

	Trust	Distrust
Helps care	Patients access healthcare services (and continue with care). Patients accept diagnosis and adhere to treatments. Patients develop effective relationships with professionals (confidence increased, suspicion reduced, information shared). Patients' personal efficacy is enhanced (anxiety reduced, engagement increased).	Patients undertake monitoring of healthcare agents, agencies, and treatments. Patients adopt a position of healthy scepticism, and engage in questioning or verification. Patients take account of evidence of untrustworthiness. Patients perceive exploitation or malfeasance more quickly.
Hinders care	Patients do not undertake monitoring of healthcare agents, agencies or treatments. Patients adopt a position of unconstructive passivity or acceptance, and fail to question or verify. Patients negate or discount evidence of untrustworthiness. Patients perceive exploitation or malfeasance more slowly.	Patients do not access healthcare services (and/or continue with care). Patients do not accept diagnosis and/or adhere to treatments. Patients' relationships with professionals are less effective (confidence decreased, suspicion increased information withheld). Patients' personal efficacy is impaired (anxiety increased, engagement reduced).

Robinson 1988). Without trust, the affective aspects of patients' relations with professionals could be undermined, and interaction could become an inefficient and un-efficacious process, lacking the engagement necessary for diagnosis and treatment and capable of creating checks or barriers to good care. Moreover, the relationship itself could become psychologically onerous. In Norway, for example, a study of trust in an acute seclusion unit setting showed that distrusting (as opposed to trusting) can place a considerable strain on both patients and professionals (Hem et al. 2008).

Deep sleep – the danger of too much trust

A case which powerfully illuminates the dangers of too much trust and too little distrust between patients and professionals is that of Australian physician Dr Harry Bailey who practised a dangerous and harmful form of deep sleep therapy. The case also demonstrates the fluidity of transfer of trust between the personal and the impersonal, and how this can be manipulated by an unscrupulous practitioner to secure trust which is misplaced and unwarranted. Between 1965 and 1979, 1,416 deep sleep treatments were administered at the Chelmsford Private Hospital, Pennant Hills, Sydney, Australia. In total, 87 patients died but many more suffered serious physical or psychiatric consequences as a result of the treatment (Kaplan 2009, p. 167).

Bailey's perceived status and his personal charm clearly had an impact on patients' propensity; 'the charisma of the doctor or his or her status may influence patients to agree to treatments even when provided with information about side effects and potentially dangerous risks'

(Walton 2013, p. 208). Some patients entered a sexual relationship with him, having been convinced by Bailey that to do so was part of their treatment. Bailey also worked hard to create an impression of integrity and benevolence. In 1957, he persuaded the government to establish the Cerebral Surgery Unit (CSU), promising a world-class psychosurgery centre. In the wake of the failure of this unit to do anything other than routine operations, Bailey sought to bolster his own standing by traducing the reputation and motivations of others. However, it was in convincing others of his ability that it seems Bailey was most persuasive. He claimed to be a world authority, invoking the transfer of trust in the global medical and scientific establishment onto himself. His academic credentials were ideally calculated to generate credibility and induce trust, including periods in military hospitals, posts in globally renowned centres, and World Health Authority scholarships.

The ease of transfer that we describe between the macro and micro level applies not just to trust itself, but also to the transfer of data that contribute to an assessment of whether to trust; that is, whether ability, benevolence, and integrity are present. In this case, a skilful manipulator was able to lubricate this transfer such that patients would have been at the receiving end of a barrage of trust-inducing data, while at the same time having their faculty for distrust skilfully lulled into a state of ready compliance. We observed earlier in the paper that while personal trust in healthcare professionals may be high, distrust is probably both low and under-considered as distinct from trust. Patients contribute their own part to managing the risks that arise in healthcare settings,[1] particularly so in private practice where their role as a consumer is more prominent. Active distrust might be expected to be crucial to this risk management, prompting patients to ask questions and seek assurances at every stage of their treatment.

In summary, while Bailey was greatly skilled at creating a pretence of all three of the trust factors, it was in the area of his ability where he was most persuasive and skilful. At the same time, he could disable his patients' distrustful instincts, such as they were by that stage. We also see in this case evidence of skilfully but malevolently nurtured trust transfer, in particular from the impersonal to the personal, both in terms of Bailey's links to global medicine as described but also in the way that he created salubrious and luxurious physical environments in which to receive patients, in some cases quite literally seducing them into believing he was someone they could trust. Above all, this case shows that trust is a judgement based on evidence, and how, in the hands of an expert, that evidence and those judgements can be manipulated and controlled with disturbing ease.

A trusted family doctor: the case of Harold Shipman

Another case which shows how patient perceptions can be manipulated to foster high levels of trust, create misplaced trust or discourage balancing levels of distrust is that of British doctor Dr Harold Shipman. Though convicted of murdering 15 patients, Shipman was believed to have killed nearly 250 people between 1970 and 1998 (Shipman Inquiry 2002, 2005). The case generated a national public inquiry, extensive regulation, and profound reflection in British health policy (Horton 2001, Baker 2004, Field and Scotland 2004, Checkland et al. 2004, Soothill and Wilson 2005, Baker and Hurwitz 2009). Shipman was skilled in building trust interpersonally and convincing others of his ability, benevolence, and integrity. Though patients, professionals, and other associates exhibited differing propensities to trust, most considered Shipman hard working and well-intentioned, speaking of him as an able, old-fashioned, family doctor who liked to treat patients at home (Shipman Inquiry 2002, 2003, 2004). Patients felt he was on their side, described him as 'caring' and 'compassionate' and took extreme measures to stay in his care (Whittle and Ritchie 2005). Shipman signalled his benevolence by giving them extra time, listening to them, making them feel special, and doing far more than necessary (Peters 2010). He disarmed people with symbolic acts of integrity or benevolence by visibly providing expensive drugs. For example, he demonstrated putting patients' interests before profit motives. His reputation, especially for benevolence, effectively signalled his trustworthiness and was enthusiastically spread by others to promote trust in him.

Trust transfer between micro and macro levels is identifiable in this case. At the macro level, the settings Shipman worked within would have helped create a sense of normality, encouraging those around him to take the situation on trust. A panoply of local organizations (other practices, care homes, and funeral parlours, etc.) reinforced trust in him, operated as barriers to distrusting him and created a sense of normalcy. However, in this case, trust transfer is more visible at the micro level. The trust or confidence people perceived others to have in Shipman led them to trust him in turn. Shipman's staff, for example, drew trust from his being well regarded by patients and respected by his professional colleagues (Shipman Inquiry 2004). His employees, fellow professionals, and so on all reinforced personal trust in him by promulgating beliefs in his ability, benevolence, and integrity. This is evident in the police investigations, or when concerns were raised about cremations. Dr MacGillivray, for example, a doctor at the practice where Shipman had cremation forms countersigned, actively reassured the funeral directors with the explanation he had a large number of elderly patients who he liked to keep at home (Shipman Inquiry 2003).

Shipman's reputation was vigorously used to discount evidence of untrustworthiness. When concerns were raised, it was employed by those who trusted him to discount suspicions, negate distrust, or disable distrusting behaviour. There are examples of his trusted reputation being used to indicate his trustworthiness or negate suspicion when concerns were raised by fellow practitioners and funeral directors, or investigated by medical examiners or the police (Shipman Inquiry 2002, 2003, 2004, 2005). A medical advisor engaged to review cases in the first police investigation, for example, reassuringly described Shipman to the investigating inspector as an 'old fashioned doctor who often visited his patients at home and liked to keep his elderly patients at home rather than send them to the hospital,' (Shipman Inquiry 2003, p. 69). While trust in Shipman appears to have been passed from one party to another, distrust in him does not. Shipman did not generally seek to undermine distrust in him by creating mistrust in those who sought to challenge his trustworthiness in the same way Bailey did. Instead, he benefitted from others challenging distrust in him on his behalf. There are numerous examples of those who trusted him influentially sharing their trust with others, but few examples of those who distrusted him effectively doing the same. Thus, trust was transferred from one party to another but distrust, rather than being transferred, was blocked or suppressed.

Conclusions and further research

We concluded our discussion of trust in healthcare with two extreme cases of trust being abused by professionals. Cases such as these are extraordinarily rare, and the harm they cause is incalculable. However, they do put trust issues in healthcare contexts into stark relief and show that Mayer et al.'s model provides a stimulating lens for analysing trust, not only how it can be created through ability, benevolence, and integrity, and the importance of propensity to trust, but also how balancing levels of distrust might be stifled to the detriment of the patient. In our two short case studies, both perpetrators were highly skilled in manipulating their patients' propensity to trust through their claims to ability, benevolence, and integrity. In Bailey, the emphasis was on his ability and competence; for Shipman, benevolence was a more prominent feature of his self-presentation. In both cases, trust was transferred between the doctor and the settings, systems, and institutions in which they worked. As well as demonstrating the importance of trust in this context, these cases also highlight the strengths and weaknesses of knowledge in this area. The literature and the cases demonstrate the importance of the central inter-personal relationship between the treating professional and the patient in securing the patient's trust. Here, knowledge of how trust is established and lost is most advanced, and this is reflected in our earlier discussion. However, we know less in three other crucial and very closely related areas, and these are where we believe that further research should be focussed: how is trust established between a patient and the more abstract realm of systems and organizations; how does trust transfer between systems and people; and why is distrust seemingly so amenable to being suppressed in the face of evidence to the contrary?

From each of these questions, further possible research questions cascade. Taking, for example the first, our discussion of the literature and the case studies imply that trust in systems and organizations, as opposed to people, is derived from data which are tested against the same criteria of ability, integrity, and benevolence. We have also discussed how trust in systems and organizations can be transferred from trust in the people working within them. Additionally, patients will receive data about organizations through the media, through social networks and through their previous experience. Yet how do they assess and evaluate data from these different sources? Turning to the second question, it is clear that as patients experience treatment in a socially complex healthcare organization, they will have only fleeting contact with some professionals, yet their contribution may involve the highest levels of risk. What role does the organization, setting, or situation play in establishing trust in people in rapidly moving situations? Our third proposed question applies both to patients and professionals, and to seek to answer it would contribute to the ongoing pursuit of a better understanding of why people do not take action or raise concerns even when they are aware of evidence that indicates something is wrong.

Our cases indicate that healthcare contexts inspire high (rather than low) levels of trust, coupled with conversely low (rather than high) levels of distrust. In such situations, the suppression of distrust is to the detriment of patients and the public. Constructive distrust on their part could potentially expose failings in care more quickly as well as improving outcomes more generally by engaging patients in their own care. Stimulating a constructively distrustful attitude is, however, problematic. Patients are often reluctant to complain for a wide variety of reasons. There can also be large numbers of unfounded complaints because something does not look right, whereas the real problem is that an unfamiliar procedure has not been well explained. Patients are caught in the cage of their own information asymmetry here; just because it looks right does not mean it is right, and just because it looks wrong it does not mean it is wrong (see Figure 18.1).

Looks right is right	Looks right is wrong
(patient should still be encouraged to ask questions)	*(patients encouraged to enquire even in absence of concern-invoking data; importance of constructive distrust between colleagues who may detect problems more rapidly than patient)*
Looks wrong is right	Looks wrong is wrong
(health professional needs to understand that routine procedure may appear strange to patient)	*(patient and colleagues must be supported to act quickly when they are given cause for concern)*

Figure 18.1 Encouraging patient distrust

To break out of this cage, effort is needed to help patients bring to bear a spirit of constructive distrust. Situations and procedures normal to those working in this environment are unfamiliar and possibly intimidating or frightening to those, such as patients, who are temporary visitors. Thus, to make patient distrust viable and constructive, effort is also needed to help health professionals comprehend the unfamiliarity of healthcare settings to others, 'see' how something familiar to them is so strange to their patients, and practise in a way which supports patient enquiry in a spirit of constructive distrust.

There is also, we believe in the light of these cases, an important role for regulation in protecting patients when their propensity to trust is too high or their ability to distrust is too low. Both cases led to significant regulatory reform; as is common to healthcare failures, more or different regulation was the proposed solution to repair trust through impersonal means. In recent years, however, the concept of right-touch regulation has made its way into the debate about healthcare professional regulation (Professional Standards Authority for Health and Social Care 2015). Right-touch regulation is an approach which helps policy makers to decide whether or not regulation is the right answer where risk is present. It recognizes that in situations involving risk, a number of parties will be engaged in managing it: the patient, the professional, the regulator, the employer, and the law, among others. These agents all contribute differently according to the specific situation in question and the nature of the risks involved.

As regulatory practitioners, we believe that to ensure the right level of regulation we need the right level of trust. The concept of right-touch regulation does not suggest that all risk can be removed, but rather that a proportionate approach to risk management should be taken; under 'right-touch trust' conditions, appropriate levels of trust would be balanced with appropriate levels of constructive distrust. A trustor would make a rational and timely decision on whether or not to engage with a trustee based on a reasonable level and mix of evidence of ability, benevolence, and integrity weighed against the possible risks, both positive and negative. They would neither waste time looking for exhaustive evidence nor make a too hasty decision based on too little evidence. In order to achieve such a balance, patients must be able to enquire freely of people and situations, supported to question and challenge, and better aided to satisfy themselves of professionals' and organizations' benevolence, integrity, and ability.

The further pursuit of knowledge in this area would be more than an academic exercise. The evidence shows that the existence of trust is essential for the delivery of healthcare to proceed in a rational, efficient, and compassionate way. Health professionals and organizations need to understand more about the central role of trust in the delivery of care, how their communication with patients affects the process of trust being established, and how they can support constructive and enquiring distrust. If we understood better the way that patients process information that could contribute to their decision to trust, and the information that they seek in satisfying their distrust, healthcare organizations and professionals could target their efforts accordingly. Significant benefits could be achieved for patient safety and the delivery of care.

Note

1   Professional Standards Authority (2015) *Right-touch regulation.*

References

Abbott, A., 1988. The System of Professions: An essay on the division of labor.Chicago, IL: University of Chicago Press.

Abelson, J., Miller, F.A. and Giacomini, M., 2009. What does it mean to trust a health system?: A qualitative study of Canadian health care values. *Health Policy*, 91(1), pp.63–70.

Armstrong, K., Rose, A., Peters, N., Long, J.A., McMurphy, S. and Shea, J.A., 2006. Distrust of the health care system and self-reported health in the United States. *Journal of General Internal Medicine*, 21(4), pp.292–297.

Baer and Colquitt [this publication]

Baier, A., 1986. Trust and antitrust. *Ethics*, 96(2), pp.231–260.

Baker, R. and Hurwitz, B., 2009. Intentionally harmful violations and patient safety: The example of Harold Shipman. *Journal of the Royal Society of Medicine*, 102(6), pp.223–227.

Baker, R., 2004. Patient-centred care after Shipman. *Journal of the Royal Society of Medicine*, 97(4), pp.161–165.

Baker, R., Mainous III, A.G., Gray, D.P. and Love, M.M., 2003. Exploration of the relationship between continuity, trust in regular doctors and patient satisfaction with consultations with family doctors. *Scandinavian Journal of Primary Health Care*, 21(1), pp.27–32.

Balkrishnan, R., Dugan, E., Camacho, F.T. and Hall, M.A., 2003. Trust and satisfaction with physicians, insurers, and the medical profession. *Medical Care*, 41(9), pp.1058–1064.

Barnard, D., 2016. Vulnerability and trustworthiness. *Cambridge Quarterly of Healthcare Ethics*, 25(2), pp.288–300.

Barney, J.B. and Hansen, M.H., 1994. Trustworthiness as a source of competitive advantage. *Strategic Management Journal*, 15(S1), pp.175–190.

Benkert, R., Hollie, B., Nordstrom, C.K., Wickson, B. and Bins-Emerick, L., 2009. Trust, mistrust, racial identity and patient satisfaction in urban African American primary care patients of nurse practitioners. *Journal of Nursing Scholarship*, 41(2), pp.211–219.

Birungi, H., 1998. Injections and self-help: Risk and trust in Ugandan health care. *Social Science & Medicine*, 47(10), pp.1455–1462.

Calnan, M. and Rowe, R., 2004. *Trust in health care: An agenda for future research*: Discussion paper. Nuffield Trust.

Calnan, M. and Rowe, R., 2006. Researching trust relations in health care: Conceptual and methodological challenges – an introduction. *Journal of Health Organization and Management*, 20(5), pp.349–358.

Calnan, M. and Rowe, R., 2008. Trust relations in a changing health service. *Journal of Health Services Research & Policy*, 13(suppl 3), pp.97–103.

Calnan, M.W. and Sanford, E., 2004. Public trust in health care: the system or the doctor? *Quality and Safety in Health Care*, 13(2), pp.92–97.

Checkland, K., Marshall, M. and Harrison, S., 2004. Re-thinking accountability: Trust versus confidence in medical practice. *Quality and Safety in Health Care*, 13(2), pp.130–135.

Colquitt, J.A., Scott, B.A. and LePine, J.A., 2007. Trust, trustworthiness, and trust propensity: A meta-analytic test of their unique relationships with risk taking and job performance. *Journal of Applied Psychology*, 92(4), pp.909–927.

Deutsch, M., 1973. *The resolution of conflict*. New Haven: Yale University Press.

Dibben, M.R. and Lean, M.E.J., 2003. Achieving compliance in chronic illness management: Illustrations of trust relationships between physicians and nutrition clinic patients. *Health, Risk & Society*, 5(3), pp.241–258.

Dinç, L. and Gastmans, C., 2012. Trust and trustworthiness in nursing: An argument-based literature review. *Nursing Inquiry*, 19(3), pp.223–237.

Dirks, K.T., and Ferrin, D.L., 2001. The role of trust in organisational settings. *Organization Science*, 12(4), pp.450–467.

Dwyer, D., Liu, H. and Rizzo, J.A., 2012. Does patient trust promote better care? *Applied Economics*, 44(18), pp.2283–2295.

Field, R. and Scotland, A., 2004. Medicine in the UK after Shipman: Has "all changed, changed utterly"? *The Lancet*, 364, pp.40–41.

Flores, F. and Solomon, R.C., 1998. Creating trust. *Business Ethics Quarterly*, 5(2) pp.205–232.

Frowe, I., 2005. Professional trust. *British Journal of Educational Studies*, 53(1), pp.34–53.

Fulmer, C.A. and Gelfand, M.J., 2012. At what level (and in whom) we trust: Trust across multiple organizational levels. *Journal of Management*, 38(4), pp.1167–1230.

Gambetta, D., 2000. Can we trust trust? Making and breaking cooperative relations, 13, pp.213–237.

Gargiulo, M., and Ertug, G., 2006. The dark side of trust. In *The handbook of trust research*, Bachmann, R., and Zaheer, A., (eds), Edward Elgar, Cheltenham, United Kingdom, pp.165–181.

Gilson, L., 2003. Trust and the development of health care as a social institution. *Social Science & Medicine*, 56(7), pp.1453–1468.

Gilson, L., 2006. Trust in health care: Theoretical perspectives and research needs. *Journal of Health Organization and Management*, 20(5), pp.359–375.

Gilson, L., Palmer, N. and Schneider, H., 2005. Trust and health worker performance: Exploring a conceptual framework using South African evidence. *Social Science & Medicine*, 61(7), pp.1418–1429.

Goel, S., Bell, G.G. and Pierce, J.L., 2005. The perils of Pollyanna: Development of the over-trust construct. *Journal of Business Ethics*, 58(1–3), pp.203–218.

Goold, S.D., 2001. Trust and the ethics of health care institutions. *Hastings Center Report*, 31(6), pp.26–33.

Goold, S.D., 2002. Trust, distrust and trustworthiness. *Journal of General Internal Medicine*, 17(1), pp.79–81.

Graham, J.L., Giordano, T.P., Grimes, R.M., Slomka, J., Ross, M. and Hwang, L.Y., 2010. Influence of trust on HIV diagnosis and care practices: A literature review. *Journal of the International Association of Physicians in AIDS Care (JIAPAC)*, 9(6), pp.346–352.

Graham, J.L., Shahani, L., Grimes, R.M., Hartman, C. and Giordano, T.P., 2015. The influence of trust in physicians and trust in the healthcare system on linkage, retention, and adherence to HIV care. *AIDS Patient Care and STDs*, 29(12), pp.661–667.

Hall, M.A., Dugan, E., Zheng, B. and Mishra, A.K., 2001. Trust in physicians and medical institutions: What is it, can it be measured, and does it matter? *Milbank Quarterly*, 79(4), pp.613–639.

Hardin, R. 2006. The street-level epidemiology of trust. In Organizational trust, Kramer, R. M., (ed.), Oxford University Press, Oxford, United Kingdom, pp.21–47.

Hawley, K., 2015. Trust and distrust between patient and doctor. *Journal of Evaluation in Clinical Practice*, 21(5), pp.798–801.

Hem, M.H., Heggen, K. and Ruyter, K.W., 2008. Creating trust in an acute psychiatric ward. *Nursing Ethics*, 15(6), pp.777–788.

Hillen, M.A., de Haes, H.C. and Smets, E., 2011. Cancer patients' trust in their physician – a review. *Psycho-Oncology*, 20(3), pp.227–241.

Horton, R., 2001. The real lessons from Harold Frederick Shipman. *The Lancet*, 357(9250), pp.82–83.

Howerton, A., Byng, R., Campbell, J., Hess, D., Owens, C. and Aitken, P., 2007. Understanding help seeking behaviour among male offenders: Qualitative interview study. *BMJ*, 334(7588), p.303.

Kao, A.C., Green, D.C., Davis, N.A., Koplan, J.P. and Cleary, P.D., 1998. Patients' trust in their physicians. *Journal of General Internal Medicine*, 13(10), pp.681–686.

Kaplan, R.M., Allen, Unwin, 2009. *Medical murder: Disturbing cases of doctors who kill.* Summerdale, Chichester, United Kingdom.

Keating, N.L., Gandhi, T.K., Orav, E.J., Bates, D.W. and Ayanian, J.Z., 2004. Patient characteristics and experiences associated with trust in specialist physicians. *Archives of Internal Medicine*, 164(9), pp.1015–1020.

Kramer, R.M., Brewer M.B. and Hanna, B.A., 1996. Collective trust and collective action: The decision to trust as a social decision. In *Trust in organizations*, Kramer, R. M., and Tyler T. R., (eds), Sage Publications, CA, pp.357–389.

Langfred, C.W., 2004. Too much of a good thing? Negative effects of high trust and individual autonomy in self-managing teams. *Academy of Management Journal*, 47(3), pp.385–399.

LaVeist, T.A., Isaac, L.A. and Williams, K.P., 2009. Mistrust of health care organizations is associated with underutilization of health services. *Health Services Research*, 44(6), pp.2093–2105.

Lee, Y.Y. and Lin, J.L., 2009. The effects of trust in physician on self-efficacy, adherence and diabetes outcomes. *Social Science & Medicine*, 68(6), pp.1060–1068.

Lewicki R.J. and Bunker, B.B., 1996. Developing and maintaining trust in work relationships. In *Trust in organizations*, Kramer, R. M., and Tyler T. R., (eds), Sage Publications, CA, pp.114–139.

Lewicki, R.J., McAllister, D.J. and Bies, R.J., 1998. Trust and distrust: New relationships and realities. *Academy of Management Review*, 23(3), pp.438–458.

Lien, C.H., Wu, J.J., Chen, Y.H. and Wang, C.J., 2014. Trust transfer and the effect of service quality on trust in the healthcare industry. *Managing Service Quality*, 24(4), pp.399–416.

Lord, K., Ibrahim, K., Kumar, S., Rudd, N., Mitchell, A.J. and Symonds, P., 2012. Measuring trust in healthcare professionals – A study of ethnically diverse UK cancer patients. *Clinical Oncology*, 24(1), pp.13–21.

Lumineau, F., 2014. How contracts influence trust and distrust. *Journal of Management*, pp.1516–1544.

Maarse, H., Jeurissen, P. and Ruwaard, D., 2016. Results of the market-oriented reform in the Netherlands: A review. *Health Economics, Policy and Law*, 11(02), pp.161–178.

Mainous III, A.G., Baker, R., Love, M.M., Gray, D.P. and Gill, J.M., 2001. Continuity of care and trust in one's physician: Evidence from primary care in the United States and the United Kingdom. *Family Medicine*, 33(1), pp.22–27.

Mainous III, A.G., Goodwin, M.A. and Stange, K.C., 2004a. Patient-physician shared experiences and value patients place on continuity of care. *The Annals of Family Medicine*, 2(5), pp.452–454.

Mainous III, A.G., Kern, D., Hainer, B., Kneuper-Hall, R., Stephens, J. and Geesey, M.E., 2004b. The relationship between continuity of care and trust with stage of cancer at diagnosis. *Family Medicine*, 13, p.14.

Mayer, R.C., Davis, J.H. and Schoorman, F.D., 1995. An integrative model of organizational trust. *Academy of Management Review*, 20(3), pp.709–734.

McEvily, B., Perrone, V. and Zaheer, A., 2003. Trust as an organizing principle. *Organization Science*, 14(1), pp.91–103.

McKnight, H., Cummings, L.L. and Chervany, N.L., 2006. Initial trust formation in new organizational relationships. In *Organizational trust*, Kramer, R. M., (ed.), Oxford University Press, Oxford, United Kingdom, pp.111–139.

McKnight, H. and Chervany, N.L. 2006. Reflections on an initial trust-building model. In *Handbook of trust research*, Bachmann, R., and Zaheer, A. (eds), Edward Elgar, Cheltenham, United Kingdom, pp. 29–51.

Mechanic, D., 1996. Changing medical organization and the erosion of trust. *The Milbank Quarterly*, 74(2), pp.171–189.

Mechanic, D., 1998. The functions and limitations of trust in the provision of medical care. *Journal of Health Politics, Policy and Law*, 23(4), pp.661–686.

Mechanic, D. and Meyer, S., 2000. Concepts of trust among patients with serious illness. *Social Science & Medicine*, 51(5), pp.657–668.

Meyerson, D., Weick, K.E. and Kramer, R.M., 1996. Swift trust and temporary groups. In *Trust in organizations: Frontiers of theory and research*, Kramer, R. M., and Tyler T. R., (eds), Sage Publications, CA, pp.166–195.

Meyerson, D., Weick, K.E. and Kramer, R.M., 2006. Swift trust and temporary groups. In *Organizational trust*, Kramer, R. M., (ed.), Oxford University Press, Oxford, United Kingdom, pp. 415–444.

Mohseni, M. and Lindstrom, M., 2007. Social capital, trust in the health-care system and self-rated health: The role of access to health care in a population-based study. *Social Science & Medicine*, 64(7), pp.1373–1383.

Mollering, G., 2006. Trust, institutions, agency: Towards a neoinstitutional theory of trust. In R. Bachmann and A. Zaheer (eds) *Handbook of trust research*. Cheltenham, United Kingdom: Edward Elgar Publishing. pp. 355–376.

Murray, B. and McCrone, S., 2015. An integrative review of promoting trust in the patient–primary care provider relationship. *Journal of Advanced Nursing*, 71(1), pp.3–23.

Nooteboom, B., 2002. *Trust: Forms, foundations, functions, failures and figures*. Edward Elgar Publishing.

Nooteboom, B., 2006. Forms, sources and processes of trust. In *Handbook of trust research*, R. Bachmann and A. Zaheer (eds), Cheltenham: Edward Elgar Publishing. pp. 247–263.

Ozawa, S. and Sripad, P., 2013. How do you measure trust in the health system? A systematic review of the literature. *Social Science & Medicine*, 91, pp.10–14.

Pearson, S.D. and Raeke, L.H., 2000. Patients' trust in physicians: Many theories, few measures, and little data. *Journal of General Internal Medicine*, 15(7), pp.509–513.

Peters, S., 2010. *Blind trust: Trusting to excess in the case of Nick Leeson and Harold Shipman*. Unpublished master's project, CASS Business School, London.

Pieterse, P. and Lodge, T., 2015. When free healthcare is not free. Corruption and mistrust in Sierra Leone's primary healthcare system immediately prior to the Ebola outbreak. *International health*, 7(6), pp.400–404.

Professional Standards Authority for Health and Social Care, 2015. *Right-touch regulation: revised*. Available at www.professionalstandards.org.uk/docs/default-source/publications/thought-paper/right-touch-regulation-2015.pdf?sfvrsn=12. [Accessed 28 Sept. 2016].

Rose, A., Peters, N., Shea, J.A. and Armstrong, K., 2004. Development and testing of the health care system distrust scale. *Journal of General Internal Medicine*, 19(1), pp.57–63.

Rousseau, D.M., Sitkin, S.B., Burt, R.S. and Camerer, C., 1998. Not so different after all: A cross-discipline view of trust. *Academy of Management Review*, 23(3), pp.393–404.

Rowe, R. and Calnan, M., 2006. Trust relations in health care: Developing a theoretical framework for the "new" NHS. *Journal of Health Organization and Management*, 20(5), pp.376–396.

Saarinen, A.O., Räsänen, P. and Kouvo, A., 2016. Two dimensions of trust in physicians in OECD-countries. *International Journal of Health Care Quality Assurance*, 29(1), pp.48–61.

Schoorman, F.D., Mayer, R.C. and Davis, J.H., 2007. An integrative model of organizational trust: Past, present, and future. *Academy of Management Review*, 32(2), pp.344–354.

Sellman, D., 2007. Trusting patients, trusting nurses. *Nursing Philosophy*, 8(1), pp.28–36.

Shipman Inquiry, 2002. *First Report*. Available at www.the-shipman-inquiry.org.uk/firstreport.asp. [Accessed 1 Feb. 2010].

Shipman Inquiry, 2003. *Second Report – The Police Investigation of March 1998*. London: The Stationery Office.

Shipman Inquiry, 2004. *Fifth Report – Safeguarding Patients: Lessons from the Past – Proposals for the Future*. London: The Stationery Office.

Shipman Inquiry, 2005. *Sixth Report – Shipman: The Final Report*. Available at www.the-shipman-inquiry.org.uk/finalreport.asp.[Accessed 1 Feb. 2010].

Skinner, D., Dietz, G. and Weibel, A., 2013. The dark side of trust: When trust becomes a 'poisoned chalice'. *Organization*, 21(2), pp.206–224.

Skirbekk, H., Middelthon, A.L., Hjortdahl, P. and Finset, A., 2011. Mandates of trust in the doctor–patient relationship. *Qualitative Health Research*, 21(9), pp.1182–1190.

Soothill, K. and Wilson, D., 2005. Theorising the puzzle that is Harold Shipman. *Journal of Forensic Psychiatry & Psychology*, 16(4), pp.685–698.

Susskind, R. and Susskind, D., 2015. *The future of the professions: How technology will transform the work of human experts*. Oxford University Press, USA.

Tang, L., 2011. The influences of patient's trust in medical service and attitude towards health policy on patient's overall satisfaction with medical service and sub satisfaction in China. *BMC Public Health*, 11(1), pp.1–8.

Tarrant, C., Stokes, T. and Baker, R., 2003. Factors associated with patients' trust in their general practitioner: A cross-sectional survey. *British Journal of General Practice*, 53(495), pp.798–800.

Thom, D.H., 2001. Physician behaviors that predict patient trust. *Journal of Family Practice*, 50(4), pp.323–323.

Thom, D.H., Ribisl, K.M., Stewart, A.L. and Luke, D.A., 1999. Further validation and reliability testing of the Trust in Physician Scale. *Medical Care, 37*(5), pp.510–517.

Thom, D.H., Kravitz, R.L., Bell, R.A., Krupat, E. and Azari, R., 2002. Patient trust in the physician: Relationship to patient requests. *Family Practice*, 19(5), pp.476–483.

Thom, D.H., Hall, M.A. and Pawlson, L.G., 2004. Measuring patients' trust in physicians when assessing quality of care. *Health Affairs*, 23(4), pp.124–132.

Thorne, S.E. and Robinson, C.A., 1988. Reciprocal trust in health care relationships. *Journal of Advanced Nursing*, 13(6), pp.782–789.

Thrasher, A.D., Earp, J.A.L., Golin, C.E. and Zimmer, C.R., 2008. Discrimination, distrust, and racial/ethnic disparities in antiretroviral therapy adherence among a national sample of HIV-infected patients. *JAIDS Journal of Acquired Immune Deficiency Syndromes*, 49(1), pp.84–93.

Van Der Schee, E., Braun, B., Calnan, M., Schnee, M. and Groenewegen, P.P., 2007. Public trust in health care: A comparison of Germany, the Netherlands, and England and Wales. *Health Policy*, 81(1), pp.56–67.

Walshe, K. and Shortell, S.M., 2004. When things go wrong: How health care organizations deal with major failures. *Health Affairs*, 23(3), pp.103–111.

Walton, M., 2013. Deep sleep therapy and Chelmsford Private Hospital: Have we learnt anything? *Australasian Psychiatry*, 21(3), pp.206–212.

Ward, P.R., Rokkas, P., Cenko, C., Pulvirenti, M., Dean, N., Carney, S., Brown, P., Calnan, M. and Meyer, S., 2015. A qualitative study of patient (dis) trust in public and private hospitals: The importance of choice and pragmatic acceptance for trust considerations in South Australia. *BMC Health Services Research*, 15(1), p.297.

Wensing, M., Jung, H.P., Mainz, J., Olesen, F. and Grol, R., 1998. A systematic review of the literature on patient priorities for general practice care. Part 1: Description of the research domain. *Social Science & Medicine*, 47(10), pp.1573–1588.

Whetten, K., Leserman, J., Whetten, R., Ostermann, J., Thielman, N., Swartz, M. and Stangl, D., 2006. Exploring lack of trust in care providers and the government as a barrier to health service use. *American Journal of Public Health*, 96(4), pp.716–721.

Whittle, B., and Ritchie, J., 2005. *Prescription for murder: The true story of Harold Shipman*. (3rd edn). London: Timewarner.

Williamson, O.E., 2006. Calculativeness, trust, and economic organization. In *Organizational trust: A reader*, Kramer R. M (ed.), Oxford University Press, Oxford, pp.48–81.

Yaqub, O., Castle-Clarke, S., Sevdalis, N. and Chataway, J., 2014. Attitudes to vaccination: A critical review. *Social Science & Medicine*, 112, pp.1–11.

Zhao, D.H., Rao, K.Q. and Zhang, Z.R., 2016. Patient trust in physicians: Empirical evidence from Shanghai, China. *Chinese Medical Journal*, 129(7), p.814.

19

THE PRODUCTION AND REPRODUCTION OF TRUST VIOLATIONS

An exploration of theory and practice in universal banks prior to the global financial crisis

Robert F. Hurley

Introduction

Modern economic activity involves the exchange of products or services and money. Central to economic exchange is the movement of money through banks and the larger financial system. As we saw during the global financial crisis (GFC) in 2008, money only moves when there is trust; that is, the willingness of parties to rely on one another to fulfill obligations. As the GFC began to unfold, the interbank interest rate spread versus risk free treasuries increased fivefold in the United States reflecting a lack of confidence and a need for more of a risk premium to part with money (INTOSAI, 2010). Eventually, money stopped moving altogether and the hoarding caused a freeze not just on Wall Street but also on Main Street. After trillions of dollars of savings were wiped out, and millions of jobs lost, bankers found themselves stigmatized by stakeholders who felt betrayed by a financial system that to them seemed unreasonably self-serving and reckless.

This chapter examines the loss of trust in banks during the GFC. The chapter begins with definitions of trust and trust violation and locates these concepts in bank behavior leading up to the GFC. With this in mind, research on trust in banks and financial services is reviewed and survey data on the decline of trust in banks during the GFC is summarized. Various perspectives on why and how banks violated stakeholder trust are reviewed and an argument is put forth that we have yet to adequately understand trust violations as being part of dysfunctional and unbalanced adaptive organizational behavior or drift (Mandis, 2013), on the part of banks. The chapter concludes with some prescriptions for improving research and practice in the field of trust and trust repair.

Defining trust, trust violations and banks

Trust has been defined as the willingness to be vulnerable to the actions of another, based on positive expectations of the intentions or behavior of the other, under conditions of risk and interdependence (Mayer, Davis, & Schoorman, 1995; Rousseau, Sitkin, Burt, & Camerer, 1998). Distrust conversely has been defined as 'confident negative expectations regarding another's conduct' (Lewicki, McAlister, & Bies, 1998, p. 439). Recognizing the difficulty of parsing the construct of willingness to be vulnerable, and the multi-level nature of trust, trust has also been defined as a judgment of confident reliance by a person (a trustor) on a person, group, organization, or system (a trustee) where there is uncertainty and risk (Hurley, 2006; 2012). Since the focus of this chapter is banks and the financial system, this latter multi-level definition will be used.

A perceived trust violation is defined as an incident that lowers confidence and trusting beliefs toward a trustee (Kim, Dirks, & Cooper, 2009). Such a violation disconfirms trustors' confident positive expectations (Tomlinson, Dineen, & Lewicki, 2004). This happens through a causal attribution or sense-making process where stakeholders find answers to some or all of the following questions: (1) To what degree have expectations have been violated? (2) Were the violations caused by the trustee? and (3) Which specific aspects of trustworthiness were dishonoured (Lewicki & Bunker, 1995; Tomlinson & Mayer, 2009; Kim, Dirks, & Cooper, 2009)? Trust repair involves repairing damaged expectations and returning a stakeholder relationship to a positive state after there has been some transgression (Kramer & Lewicki, 2010; Dirks, Lewicki & Zaheer, 2009). Interestingly, while scholars have recognized that trust repair is a dynamic process (Dirks, Lewicki, & Zaheer, 2009; Tomlinson & Mayer, 2009), there has been less focus on understanding the process of the building or erosion of trust over time. Exceptions to this include work by Lewicki and Bunker (1995) and Nooteboom (2003) at the interpersonal level, and Schilke and Cook (2013) at the inter-organizational level. At the organizational and system level we know more about what a major trust violation looks like after it appears than we do about how it emerges over time.

Applying these concepts to banks and the GFC, when injured stakeholders (e.g. clients and regulators) discover that a bank has paid fines for a gross failure to disclose that it was selling an instrument designed to fail (Goldman Sachs), rigging the Libor interest rate (Citigroup, J.P. Morgan, RBS, UBS, Barclays) or foreclosing on home loans without following proper procedures (Goldman Sachs, HBSC, J.P. Morgan Chase, Bank of America, Wells Fargo), they frame these events as transgressions and willful violations of reasonable standards of trust-worthiness. As a result, negative expectations and affect replace positive ones, and there is a reduction in the willingness to be vulnerable; that is, trust declines. The data that confirms this decline of trust in universal banks will be reviewed later in this chapter.

While it is true that many of the problematic bank actions can be framed as errors, aggressive sales tactics, poor business decisions or simply a failure to anticipate market changes (e.g. the decline of home prices), they are also appropriately conceptualized as violations of basic trustworthiness expectations. The most commonly cited dimensions of trustworthiness are ABI (ability, benevolence, and integrity) which suggests that when trustees seem to be incompetent, have a lack of concern for stakeholders, or say one thing but do another, it will trigger the sense making process noted earlier and result in a loss of trust (Mayer, Davis, & Schoorman, 1995). For example, fines for deception due to inadequate disclosures are violations of expectations of benevolent concern for stakeholders and a lack of integrity in communication. The reckless use of leverage and poor risk management that contributed to the GFC can be seen as a violation of ability expectations. Increasing risk to the financial system to increase bonuses can be considered a lack of benevolent concern to those who rely on the financial system to finance their businesses and who suffer when credit freezes. In examining bank behavior and the loss of trust, all of the essential trust issues are at play: vulnerability due to jobs or money at risk, opportunistic behavior by banks, damage inflicted on investor, employee, regulator, and client stakeholders by bank actions, and perceptions that the damages were caused in part because banks failed to meet reasonable trustworthiness expectations concerning ABI. What's more, banks operate in an environment where trust is essential; in fact, the word credit is derived from the Latin word credere, to believe.

Perhaps related to the lack of understanding of the breach of trust as a process, often violations are associated with shock at how such egregious behavior could have been going on in institutions that had projected such an image of respectability. In the case of Goldman Sachs, this shock was on display at Senate hearings when emails by a senior Goldman executive describing selling a 'shitty deal' to clients or joking about selling toxic instruments to 'widows and orphans' were made public (Levin & Coburn, 2011). But beneath this shock, careful reflection suggests the possibility that, while the magnitude of trust violations may be shocking, they are unfortunately rather common. Consider for example the long list of major trust violations after the circa 2001 Enron scandal: BBC faking competitions (2006), UBS assisting with tax evasion (2007), and FOXCONN abusive employment practices (2010) to name just a few of the many examples. The world of banking offers a fertile ground for exploring how certain trustors' expectations and trustee behavior grow apart over time. This exploration will start with a review of both the research on trust in financial services and the data that exists on the level of trust in banks.

Research on trust in banks and financial services

Since research shows that different kinds of banks have different business models that affect trust (Hurley, Xue, & Waqar, 2014a; 2014b), to explore the topic of trust properly it is important to define what we mean by banks. Universal banks are large diverse banking organizations that take savings deposits and also engage in lending, investment banking, underwriting of securities, trading, and market making. Notable examples of universal banks include Barclays, Société Générale, Deutsche Bank, Bank of America, Citigroup, J.P. Morgan Chase, UBS, and Credit Suisse. Some of these banks have investment banks within them, but they tend to be a rather small portion of the organization. Stand-alone investment banks historically have not taken savings deposits and engage in investment banking advisory for mergers or acquisitions, securities underwriting, asset management, and trading. Examples include Morgan Stanley and Goldman Sachs. Credit unions, regional and community banks concentrate on taking deposits and lending among a more narrowly targeted group of stakeholders that they serve. As Hurley, Xue, and Waqar (2014b) pointed out, universal banks which serve many different types of stakeholders globally, have more challenges in building and sustaining trust than do firms such as community banks that consciously constrain their business models to serve a narrower group of stakeholders. Other than presenting some overall data on trust in different kinds of banks and taking a broader financial services perspective in the literature review, most of this chapter will concentrate on the large universal and investment banks that have such a large global impact.

Research on trust in financial services generally, and banks specifically, has covered a wide swath. Studies come primarily from the domain of marketing and management and can be categorized as belonging to two basic categories: (1) narrow scope trust focused on the relationship or transactions between customer stakeholders and the firm or its personnel and (2) broad scope trust which considers factors in the larger system (e.g. firm incentives, governance and regulations) that affect relations at a more systemic level. The terms narrow and broad scope trust are borrowed from a study by Grayson, Johnson, and Chen (2008), which is reviewed in this chapter.

Narrow scope trust

At the micro level, Harrison (2003) suggested that trust was crucial for financial services because they (1) are highly intangible and therefore can be harder to understand, (2) often involve pronounced information asymmetries where there is heavy reliance on credence qualities, and (3) have high perceived risk when it involves the buyers' livelihood. Based on empirical work, we know that trust enhances various aspects of performance in financial services and that there are certain markers that stakeholders use to assess trustworthiness in this context. Table 19.1 summarizes empirical research in financial services linking trust to various dimensions of performance. Findings concerning the antecedent factors that define perceptions of trustworthiness in financial services contexts are summarized in Table 19.2.

Table 19.1 Trust promotes aspects of performance in financial services

Findings	Citations
Relationship marketing	Ndubisi, (2006)
Adoption of e-banking	Lee & Turban, (2001)
Client satisfaction	Balasubramanian, Konana, & Menon, (2003); Ndubisi, (2006)
Perceptions of reduced risk	Balasubramanian, Konana, & Menon, (2003); Dahlstrom et al., (2014)
Loyalty	Ennew, Sekhon, & Kharouf, (2011); El-Manstrly et al., (2011); Ball, Coelho, & Machas, (2004)
Opportunities for cross-selling of products and services	Liu & Wu, (2007)
Likelihood of future interactions	Johnson & Grayson, (2005)

Table 19.2 Markers of trustworthiness in financial services

Findings	Citations
Positive corporate image or reputation	Flavin, Guinaliu, & Torres, (2005); Adamson, Chan, & Handford, (2003); Liu & Wu, (2007)
Effective communication	Adamson, Chan, & Handford, (2003); Mukherjee & Nath, (2003)
Perceptions of quality, competence or expertise	Shainesh, (2012); Aurier & N'Goala, (2009); Balasubramanian, Konana, & Menon, (2003); Chiou, Droge, & Hanvanich, (2002); Eisingerich & Bell, (2008); Roy, Eshghi, & Shekhar, (2011)
Not engaging in opportunistic behavior	Deb & Chavali, (2010); Mukherjee & Nath, (2003).
Being customer focused	Adamson, Chan & Handford, (2003); Eisengerich & Bell, (2008); Roy, Eshghi & Shekhar, (2011); Sanchez-Franco, (2009)
Integrity	Roy, Eshghi & Shekhar, (2011)
Having a long-term orientation	Adamson, Chan & Handford, (2003)
Customer satisfaction with the overall firm, service or product	Aurier & N'Goala, (2009); Kantsperger & Kunz, (2010); Ndubisi, (2006)
Having shared values or other similarities with stakeholders	Deb & Chavali, (2010); Mukherjee & Nath, (2003)

Broad scope trust

While trust between customer and financial service providers at the service-agent and organization level are important, they do not capture elements operating in the larger system. In a sense, they fail to capture key aspects of the context for the decision to trust, which research has shown are important (Grayson, Johnson, & Chen, 2008). Gillespie and Hurley (2013) and Gillespie, Hurley, Dietz, and Bachmann (2012) examined trust violations during the GFC at all three levels (the financial system as a whole, banks, and individual bankers). This research suggested that properly understanding trust in banks requires examining the larger financial system as a complex, interdependent system that had grown to be untrustworthy for certain stakeholders. They argue that restoring trust requires aligning the values and incentives of the banks with stakeholders, improving governance at the board levels, and culture change within the banks and the industry to counter institutional logics that facilitated rationalizations of untrustworthy decisions.

There are two empirical studies which support the idea that macro variables beyond the transaction level are critical to trust. Grayson, Johnson, and Chen (2008) showed empirically that firm-level trust (narrow scope) fully mediated the impact of government and generalized trust (broad scope) on customer satisfaction. The implication of this research is that the highest levels of trust in a financial services firm can only come when there is a high broad scope trust context combined with high narrow scope firm level trust. They suggest that when regulatory or other mechanisms enhance broad scope trust in financial services, all firms benefit from increased customer satisfaction. More importantly, firms that are low in narrow scope trust will not be able to free ride on others' efforts to create a high broad scope context. In the other empirical paper, Nienaber, Hofeditz, and Searle's (2014) meta-analytic study concluded that trust is of great importance in the financial services sector and that the banking sector is heavily affected by two distinct forces: (1) customers' perceptions of an organization's level of compliance and conformity with laws and (2) responses to non-compliance on the part of governments and regulators. Nienaber, Hofeditz, and Searle (2014) also found empirical support for the view that elements of trustworthiness in financial services have declined over the past 20 years, and they emphasize the criticality of external regulation and customer centricity in restoring trust.

Data on trust in banks

It is not just academic research that has pointed out the decline of trust in banks. Longitudinal survey data from practitioners presents compelling evidence that confidence has declined in large banks but held fairly steady in community banks. Gallup polls in the late 1970s showed that nearly 60 percent of North Americans said they trusted big banks 'a great deal' or 'quite a lot' but by 2012 that number was down to 21 percent (Jacobe, 2012). Data from the Edelman Trust Barometer shows that the decline of trust in banks among the general public after the financial crisis was a global phenomenon (Edelman, 2015). Similar skepticism was found among institutional trustors. More than half of institutional investors surveyed did not trust how banks measure the riskiness of their assets (Partnoy & Eisinger, 2013). Post GFC, when hedge-fund managers were asked how trustworthy they found the numbers that banks use to calculate their required capital cushion, about 60 percent of those managers answered 1 or 2 on a five-point scale, with 1 being 'not trustworthy at all.' None of the respondents gave banks a 5 rating (Partnoy & Eisinger, 2013).

A review of some of the data on trust in banks can be summarized as follows:

- Trust in banks has declined significantly over time. Figure 19.1 shows Gallup poll trend data on how much confidence Americans said they had in banks. Samples comprised of a minimum of 1,000 U.S. adults aged 18 and older living in all 50 states and the District of Columbia.
- Trust in banks showed major declines after the global financial crisis and this is true on a global basis with the exception of China where the validity of data have been questioned. Figure 19.2 shows the Edelman Trust Barometer (over 20,000 respondents from the general public and informed public in 27 countries). Numbers represent the top two boxes' scores (percentage selecting 8 and 9) where people were asked to indicate how much they trust banks to do what is right using a nine-point scale where 1 means that they 'do not trust them at all' and 9 means that they 'trust them a great deal.'
- Banking is currently one of the least-trusted industries. Figure 19.3 shows the same global Edelman data as the earlier figure but reports the results across industries.

% A great deal/Quite a lot

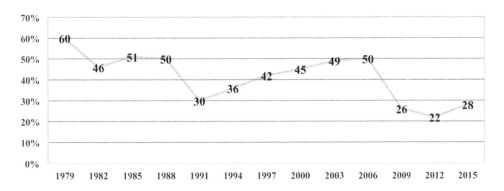

Figure 19.1 Americans' confidence in banks 1979–2015 trend.

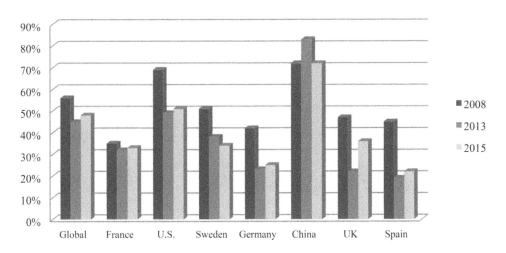

Figure 19.2 Percentage of people who trust banks to do what is right.

- Credit unions and local banks have shown generally higher trust and loyalty than larger banks. Figure 19.4 shows data on the percentage of people trusting different areas of the banking industry, based on a survey of 1,029 Americans conducted by *Social Science Research Solutions (SSRS) for the Chicago Booth/Kellogg Trust Index*. Participants were asked about the amount of trust that Americans have in the institutions in which they invest their money; based on the question on a scale from 1 to 5 where 1 means 'I do not trust them at all' and 5 means 'I trust them completely,' they were asked how much they trusted the financial institutions. All of the Booth/Kellogg surveys from 2009 to 2015 show higher trust levels for credit unions and local banks than for national banks.

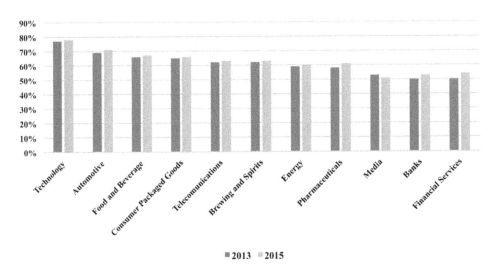

Figure 19.3 Percentage of people who trust business in different industries to do what is right.

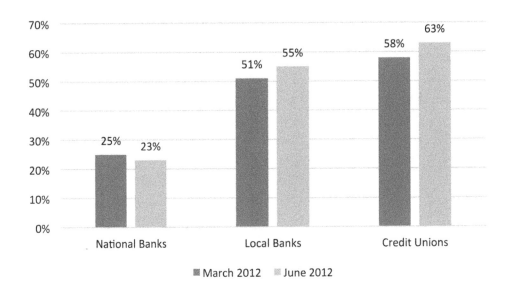

Figure 19.4 Percentage of people trusting different areas of the banking industry.

Beyond the more quantitative survey results, distrust of universal banks has even come to be part of the cultural narrative in some countries (e.g. UK and United States). For example, the July 2, 2012 cover of *The Economist* about the LIBOR scandal was titled 'Banksters,' a play on the word gangsters. Movies with villainous, greedy bankers have become popular vehicles for generating audience's emotional involvement and anger (e.g. *Rogue Trader*, *Too Big To Fail*, *The Big Short*).

Achieving a better understanding of the loss of trust in large banks

The data clearly shows that the GFC was a watershed event that affected trust in banks but policy makers and researchers have yet to achieve a full explanation for how and why this happened. While an exhaustive list of the competing narratives for the loss of trust in banks during the GFC is beyond the scope of this chapter, many of the main themes and shortfalls can be summarized by noting a few studies. In the domain of government investigations, one of the most narrow explanations suggested that the GFC was a case of Wall Street and greedy bankers who manipulated the political and financial systems to take advantage of homeowners and investors (The Financial Crisis Inquiry Report, 2011). This seems to be a common post-crisis explanatory script: flawed people (bad apples) and flawed organizations (bad barrels of apples). Other explanations (Thomas, Hennessey, & Holtz-Eakin, 2011) from a public policy perspective include bank-related variables (nontraditional mortgages, toxic financial instruments, excess use of short-term financing with inadequate long-term capital) but also note non-bank-related externalities (credit bubble, housing bubble, risk contagion, panic, and severe contraction in the real economy). Those taking a process-oriented perspective have suggested that underlying the crisis were cycles of deregulation and rapid financial innovation combined with perverse incentives that encouraged excessive risk taking (Crotty, 2009). Finally, those taking a management-oriented perspective of the GFC emphasize misaligned incentives, weak controls, poor accounting policies, weak human capital and poor cultures (Sahlman, 2010).

While much of this work has not framed these failures from the perspective of the trust literature, it is easy to make the connections. For example, banks with weak controls, poor accounting policies, toxic products, excessive use of short-term financing and underwriting that lent money into a housing bubble with inadequate collateral can all be categorized as a lack of trustworthiness due to a failure of competence or ability. Bank cultures that lacked a concern for customers, incentives that encouraged excessive risk taking, greed, and the manipulation of the financial system can be categorized as a lack of trustworthiness due to a failure of benevolent concern for damaged stakeholders. As noted earlier, to the degree that stakeholders are damaged by perceived willful failures of basic trustworthiness expectations, research suggests that it is likely to be framed as a trust violation.

Turning to the mainstream trust literature, researchers (Gillespie, Hurley, Dietz, & Bachmann 2012; Gillespie & Hurley, 2013) have summarized the erosion of trust in banks according to failures of trustworthiness: (1) *Ability failures*: Reasonable expectations for competence were not met by bank management (e.g. poor loan underwriting, failure to notice emerging signs of risk). (2) *Benevolence failures*: Basic fairness and concern for stakeholders were lacking (e.g. predatory lending practices). (3) *Integrity failures*: There was evidence of dishonesty and deception (e.g. off-balance sheet financing, misleading sales and marketing techniques and lack of full disclosure). Hurley, Gong, and Waqar (2014a) extended the examination of the failures of trustworthiness in banks to include the lack of alignment of interests, lack of value congruence, and failure of communication with stakeholders. They contrast higher trust community banks with universal banks and suggest that universal banks are overly complex, have too many conflicts of interests and have not communicated a mission and purpose that resonates with stakeholders. Nienaber, Hofeditz, and Searle (2014) suggest that weakness in compliance and regulation along with low customer centricity were partly to blame for the loss of trust during the GFC.

In explaining the GFC and the loss of trust in banks and the financial system, each analyst or researcher has examined the crisis from their own particular perspective, but all seem incomplete. None of these perspectives do a very good job explaining why major trust violations seem to reoccur even in the same industries where major failures have been studied and dissected at length. For example, a precursor financial crisis emerged in 1998 when Long Term Capital Management faced bankruptcy when its derivative trading went haywire. The government and industry bailed the firm out only to repeat the same errors years later during the GFC, only on a much greater scale. The explanations also do not provide much insight into why, post GFC, many of the interventions made to repair trust were rejected by the dominant culture or so weakened that they seemed only to serve as window dressing to appease. For example, in 2015 four major European banks that had major trust violations during the GFC removed their reform-focused CEOs due to stubbornly low stock prices (Patrick, 2015). The rejection of reforms by banks' organizational systems was also evident in the United States, prompting former Treasury Secretary Tim Geithner to publish an opinion piece entitled 'Financial Crisis Amnesia' (Geithner, 2012). It seems that we may have only scratched the surface in understanding the powerful forces inside these organizations that erode trustworthiness over time and persist after the crisis.

An argument to be proffered here is that a more robust understanding of the loss of trust in universal banks, and why needed reforms are often rejected by the system, is linked to the need to achieve a better understanding of the organizational trust erosion process. For example, we have not fully examined how the documented pressure to improve return on equity among the universal banks in the decade prior to the GFC, contributed to organizational drift and the shifting of risk to stakeholders (McGee, 2010; Mandis, 2013). Further, we have yet to fully understand the extent to which massive profit-focused innovation (e.g. deregulation, leverage, exotic financial instruments) introduced excess complexity and unmanaged risks that caused stakeholder damage (Salz, 2013; Grocer, 2010; McGee, 2010; Sorkin, 2010). Finally we have failed to explain the process whereby banks, which were supposed experts in risk management, allowed a deliberate weakening of risk management and control functions to expedite innovation (Tett, 2010; McGee, 2010; McDonald & Robinson, 2009).

Conclusion

This chapter summarizes the evidence that trust is critical in financial services and banking and that trust in universal banks has declined. More importantly, despite the many books and articles written, existing theory development is incomplete as it relates to understanding and correcting the decline in trust in these economically and socially critical institutions. Ascribing the causes of bank trust violations to failures in ethics, regulation, controls, corporate social responsibility, alignment of incentives, and bank governance, while partially true, seems to miss the underlying dynamic which explains why these types of trust violations are shocking and routine. The decline of trust in banks is much more complicated and much more interesting than the bad-apples and static-organization-failures narratives suggest. In fact, the root causes of trust violations may be more likely to be located in normal rather than abnormal organizational behaviors and routines (e.g. aggressive goal setting and an unbalanced culture of achievement).

If trust researchers are going to help solve these problems, we need a better understanding of the longer-term dynamics that lead to major trust violations. There has been a great deal of good work characterizing the nature of the trust violations perpetrated by the banks but a dearth of work concerning the underlying dynamics of how this occurred. Researchers need to go beyond depicting the post hoc description of trustworthiness failures to understand how the disease entered the organization and grew systemically. Is organizational drift a combination of conflicting goals, pressure to achieve, poorly managed growth and innovation, and a disabling of drift correction and risk management mechanisms that causes trust violations? What distinguishes situations where drift does and does not lead to trust violations? Is organizational drift inhibited because there is less pressure, more legitimate options for goal achievement or more deeply embedded ethics and controls that act as constraints in the firm's culture, routines, and processes? How does the human sense making that shapes organizational cultures and institutional logics come into play when ignoring risk, controls, and multi-stakeholder interests is rationalized or even celebrated as 'innovative management'? How are actions that bring the organization closer and closer to trust violations relegated to ethical blind spots and culturally supported rationalizations that violate trust (Bazerman & Tenbrunsel, 2011)? How much do trade-offs among conflicting goals with limited cognition form the basis of drift? To what degree is this process of drift conscious? Are the learning processes of high trust companies different from those that cross the line into reputational damage? Research is also needed to examine the suggestion made here, but in no way proven, that these processes of drift are the 'normal' ways in which most organizations function and that this is somehow connected to the reason that trust violations seem to reoccur. Is it true that more trust violations are produced by the normal rather than abnormal organizational behavior?

This theorizing would be pointless if it did not help us get closer to better managing trust. If the arguments made in this chapter are correct, they suggest that the following interventions warrant more consideration particularly as they relate to restoring trust in banks:

1   Train leaders in complex systems theories that reflect multi-stakeholder and sub-system interdependencies, include long-term feedback loops and emphasize organizational learning devices to notice unintended consequences and drift.
2   Train leaders to manage the innovation–control paradox to achieve the right balance of growth and stability in the light of the system's long-term multi-stakeholder goals. Teach innovators how to bring the compliance and control functions into the innovation process as collaborators rather than downstream obstacles.
3   Be more mindful and objective about the external and internal pressures that shape competition, metrics, organizational culture, and institutional logics. Pressure will cause culture to shift but it need not be an unspoken change.
4   Change the way ethics are taught in companies and universities. Address the organizational and systems component, the power of external and internal pressure to corrupt, culturally based rationalizations, and ethical blind spots. Focus on how leaders can create trustworthy organizational systems and not rely on biased and unreliable ethical reasoning or on the job moral philosophizing.
5   Recommit to the criticality of independent, competent, well-resourced, and powerful external governance structures and regulators to examine the pressures and forces encouraging drift and take corrective action on a timely basis. Create external and internal, non-commercially oriented counter weights to the power of market-induced drift (e.g. powerful compliance departments).
6   Invest in competent regulatory structures that can navigate the innovation–risk management tension with industry actors without stifling all progress or being financially or culturally co-opted.

The GFC and the world of banking represent a painful but fascinating laboratory in which to understand the erosion of trust. To avoid a repeat of history, we need to rethink theory and practice concerning how to build and sustain trustworthy organizations. A great place to start would be with the large banks that are so vital to our economic well-being.

Bibliography

Adamson, I., Chan, K. and Handford, D. (2003). Relationship marketing: Customer commitment and trust as a strategy for the smaller Hong Kong corporate banking sector. *International Journal of Bank Marketing*, 21(6/7), pp.347–358.

Aurier, P. and N'Goala, G. (2009). The differing and mediating roles of trust and relationship commitment in service relationship maintenance and development. *Journal of the Academy of Marketing Science*, 38(3), pp.303–325.

Balasubramanian, S., Konana, P. and Menon, N. (2003). Customer satisfaction in virtual environments: A study of online investing. *Management Science*, 49(7), pp.871–889.

Ball, D., Simões Coelho, P. and Machás, A. (2004). The role of communication and trust in explaining customer loyalty. *European Journal of Marketing*, 38(9/10), pp.1272–1293.

Bazerman, M. and Tenbrunsel, A. (2011). *Blind Spots*. Princeton, N.J.: Princeton University Press.

Chicago Booth/Kellogg School Financial Trust Index (2012) [online] Available at: www.financialtrustindex. org/resultswave16.htm [Accessed August 25, 2015].

Chiou, J., Droge, C. and Hanvanich, S. (2002). Does customer knowledge affect how loyalty is formed? *Journal of Service Research*, 5(2), pp.113–124.

Crotty, J. (2009). Structural causes of the global financial crisis: A critical assessment of the 'new financial architecture.' *Cambridge Journal of Economics*, 33(4), pp.563–580.

Deb, M. and Chavali, K. (2010). Significance of trust and loyalty during financial crisis: A study on customer behavior of Indian banks. *South Asian Journal of Management*, 17(1), pp.43.

Dirks, K.T., Lewicki, R.J. and Zaheer, A. (2009). Repairing relationships within and between organizations: Building a conceptual foundation. *Academy of Management Review*, 34(1), pp.68–84.

Edelman, (2015). *Trust and Innovation – 2015 Trust Barometer*. [online] Available at: www.edelman.com/ 2015-edelman-trust-barometer-2/trust-and-innovation-edelman-trust-barometer/ [Accessed August 24, 2015].

Eisingerich, A. and Bell, S. (2008). Perceived service quality and customer trust: Does enhancing customers' service knowledge matter? *Journal of Service Research*, 10(3), pp.256–268.

Ennew, C., Kharouf, H. and Sekhon, H. (2011). Trust in UK financial services: A longitudinal analysis. *Journal of Financial Services Marketing*, 16(1), pp.65–75.

El-Manstrly, D., Paton, R., Veloutsou, C. and Moutinho, L. (2011). An empirical investigation of the relative effect of trust and switching costs on service loyalty in the UK retail banking industry. *Journal of Financial Services Marketing*, 16(2), pp.101–110.

Flavin, C., Guinaliy, M. and Torres, E., (2005). The influence of corporate image on consumer trust: A comparative analysis in traditional versus internet banking. *Internet Research*, 15(4), pp.447–470.

Gallup Inc. (2015). *Confidence in U.S. Banks Low but Rising*. [online] Gallup.com. Available at: www. gallup.com/poll/183749/confidence-banks-low-rising.aspx [Accessed August 25, 2015].

Geithner, T. (2012). Financial Crisis Amnesia. *Wall Street Journal*, Available at: www.wsj.com/articles/ SB10001424052970203986604577253272042239982 [Accessed April 25, 2016].

Gillespie, N. and Hurley, R.F. (2013). Trust and the global financial crisis. In: R. Bachmann, and A. Zaheer, (Eds.), *Handbook of Trust Research*. Cheltenham: Edward Elgar.

Gillespie, N., Hurley, R.F., Dietz, G. and Bachmann, R. (2012). Restoring institutional trust after the global financial crisis: A systemic approach. In: R. Kramer and L. Pittinsky (Eds.), *Restoring Trust in Organizations and Leaders*. New York: Oxford University Press.

Grocer, S. (2010). *Is Goldman Just a Big Hedge Fund?* [online] WSJ. Available at: http://on.wsj.com/ 17mcRP5 [Accessed March 14, 2015].

Grayson, K., Johnson, D. and Chen, D. (2008). Is firm trust essential in a trusted environment? How trust in the business context influences customers. *Journal of Marketing Research*, 45(2), pp.241–256.

Harrison, T. (2003). Editorial: Why trust is important in customer relationships and how to achieve it. *Journal of Financial Services Marketing*, 7(3), pp.206–209.

Hurley, R.F., Gong, X. and Waqar, A. (2014a). Understanding the loss of trust in large banks. *International Journal of Bank Marketing*, 32(5), pp.348–366.

Hurley, R.F., Gong, X. and Waqar, A. (2014b). A Framework for understanding and restoring trust in universal banks. In: Harrison and Estelami (Eds.), *Companion to Financial Services Marketing*. New York: Routledge.

Hurley, R.F. (2006). The decision to trust. *Harvard Business Review*, 84(9), pp.55–62.

Hurley, R.F. (2012). *The Decision to Trust: How Leaders Create High Trust Organizations*. San Francisco, CA: Jossey-Bass.

INTOSAI (2010). *The Causes of the Global Financial Crisis and Their Implications for Supreme Audit Institutions*. (2010). [online] INTOSAI. Available at: www.intosai.org/uploads/gaohq4709242v1finalsubgroup1 paper.pdf [Accessed August 29, 2015].

Jacobe, D. (2012). *Americans' Confidence in Banks Falls to Record Low*. [online] Gallup.com. Available at: www.gallup.com/poll/155357/americans-confidence-banks-falls-record-low.aspx [Accessed August 25, 2015].

Johnson, D. and Grayson, K. (2005). Cognitive and affective trust in service relationships. *Journal of Business Research*, 58(4), pp.500–507.

Kantsperger, R. and Kunz, W.H. (2010). Consumer trust in service companies: A multiple mediating analysis. *Managing Service Quality: An International Journal*, 20(1), pp.4–25.

Kim, P.H., Dirks, K.T. and Cooper, C.D. (2009). The repair of trust: A dynamic bilateral perspective and multilevel conceptualization. *Academy of Management Review*, 34(3), pp.401–422.

Kramer, R.M. and Lewicki, R.J. (2010). Repairing and enhancing trust: Approaches to reducing organizational trust deficits. *The Academy of Management Annals*, 4(1), pp.245–277.

Lee, M.K. and Turban, E. (2001). A trust model for consumer internet shopping. *International Journal of Electronic Commerce*, 6(1), pp.75–91.

Levin, C. and Coburn, T. (2011). *Wall Street and The Financial Crisis: Anatomy of a Financial Collapse*. [online] Washington, D.C.: United States Senate Permanent Subcommittee on Investigations Committee on Homeland Security and Governmental Affairs. Available at: www.hsgac.senate.gov//imo/media/doc/Financial_Crisis/FinancialCrisisReport.pdf [Accessed March 7, 2016].

Lewicki, R.J. and Bunker, B.B. (1995). Trust in relationships: A model of development and decline. In: B.B. Bunker, J.Z. Rubin and Associates (Eds.), *Conflict, Cooperation and Justice: Essays Inspired by the Work of Morton Deutsch*: pp.133–173. San Francisco: Jossey-Bass.

Lewicki, R.J., McAllister, D.J. and Bies, R.J. (1998). Trust and distrust: New relationships and realities. *Academy of Management Review*, pp.439.

Liu, T.C. and Wu, L.W. (2007). Customer retention and cross-buying in the banking industry: An integration of service attributes, satisfaction and trust. *Journal of Financial Services Marketing*, 12(2), pp.132–145.

Mandis, S.G. (2013). *What Happened to Goldman Sachs: An Insider's Story of Organizational Drift and its Unintended Consequences*. Boston, MA: Harvard Business Review Press.

Mayer, R.C., Davis, J.H. and Schoorman, F.D. (1995). An integrative model of organizational trust. *Academy of Management Review*, 20(3), pp.709–734.

McDonald, L. and Robinson, P. (2009). *A Colossal Failure of Common Sense*. New York: Crown Business.

McGee, S. (2010). *Chasing Goldman Sachs*. New York: Crown Business.

Mukherjee, A. and Nath, P. (2003). A model of trust in online relationship banking. *International Journal of Bank Marketing*, 21(1), pp.5–15.

Nienaber, A., Hofeditz, M. and H. Searle, R. (2014). Do we bank on regulation or reputation? A meta-analysis and meta-regression of organizational trust in the financial services sector. *International Journal of Bank Marketing*, 32(5), pp.367–407.

Nooteboom, B. (2003). The trust process. In: Bart Nooteboom and Frédérique Six (Eds.), *The Trust Process in Organizations*: pp.16–36. Cheltenham, UK: Edward Elgar.

Oly Ndubisi, N. (2006). Effect of gender on customer loyalty: A relationship marketing approach. *Marketing Intelligence & Planning*, 24(1), pp.48–61.

Partnoy, F. and Eisinger, J. (2013). What's Inside America's Banks? *Atlantic Monthly*, [online] Available at: www.theatlantic.com/magazine/archive/2013/01/whats-inside-americas-banks/309196/ [Accessed January 2, 2013].

Patrick, M. (2015). Barclays Fires Chief Executive Antony Jenkins. *Wall Street Journal*, [online] Available at: www.wsj.com/articles/barclays-chief-executive-antony-jenkins-to-leave-bank-1436335989 [Accessed April 28, 2016].

Rousseau, D.M., Sitkin, S.B., Burt, R.S. and Camerer, C. (1998). Not so different after all: A cross-discipline view of trust. *Academy of Management Review*, 23(3), pp.393–404.

Roy, S.K., Eshghi, A. and Shekhar V. (2011). Dimensions of trust and trustworthiness in retail banking: Evidence from India. *The Marketing Management Journal*, 21(1), pp.97–110.

Sahlman, W. (2010). Management and the financial crisis (We have met the enemy and he is us . . .). *Economics, Management and Financial Markets*, 5(4), pp.11–53.

Salz, A. (2013) *An Independent Review of Barclays' Business Practices*. [online] The Salz Review. Available at: www.salzreview.co.uk/web/guest/home [Accessed April 3, 2013].

Sanchez-Franco, M. (2010). WebCT – The quasimoderating effect of perceived affective quality on an extending Technology Acceptance Model. *Computers & Education*, 54(1), pp.37–46.

Shainesh, G. (2012). Effects of trustworthiness and trust on loyalty intentions. *International Journal of Bank Marketing*, 30(4), pp.267–279.

Schilke, O. and Cook, K. (2013). Sources of alliance partner trustworthiness: Integrating calculative and relational perspectives. *Strategic Management Journal*, 36, pp.276–297.

Sorkin, A. (2010). *Too Big to Fail*. New York: Penguin Books.

Tett, G. (2010). *Fool's Gold*. New York: Free Press.

Thomas, B., Hennessey, K. and Holtz-Eakin, D. (2011). What Caused the Financial Crisis? [online] WSJ. Available at: www.wsj.com/articles/SB10001424052748704698004576104500524998280 [Accessed April 4, 2013].

The Financial Crisis Inquiry Commission, (2011). *The Financial Crisis Inquiry Report*. Washington, D.C.: U.S. Government Printing Office.

Tomlinson, E.C., Dineen, B.R., and Lewicki, R.J. (2004). The road to reconciliation: Antecedents of victim willingness to reconcile following a broken promise. *Journal of Management*, 30(2), pp.165–187.

Tomlinson, E.C. and Mayer, R.C. (2009). The role of causal attribtuion dimensions in trust repair. *Academy of Management Review*, 34(1), pp.85–104.

20

TRUST IN PUBLIC PROFESSIONALS AND THEIR PROFESSIONS

Frédérique Six

Trust in professions is inherently linked to the special position that professions have within our societies. This special position is based on two foundations: their unique expert knowledge and their commitment to public service and societal values (Evetts, 2006; Freidson, 2001). Professionalism as a governance mechanism (cf. Freidson, 2001) is therefore particularly appropriate for tasks and task environments that may be characterized as factually complex – there is uncertainty about what and how things work – and normatively homogeneous with no contested standards and values (Bannink, 2013; Matland, 1995; Noordegraaf & Abma, 2003). This chapter focuses on public professionals, i.e. professionals performing public tasks, like doctors, nurses, teachers or social workers. Public tasks are (partly) funded by the government, even though there may be parallel private markets such as in private education or private health care. It excludes professions that are (primarily) privately funded like consultants, lawyers or engineers.

Over the past decades, however, the values that professionals have committed to have become increasingly contested in the context of many professions, and in particular for public professionals. These value conflicts arise in two distinct ways. First, more has become known about the actual behaviour and norms of professionals; in particular, more transgressions have reached the media where personal interests trumped professional or societal interests and the societal values were not upheld. Even if the most serious transgressions were cases of occasional bad apples (e.g. general practitioner Harold Shipman in the UK or neurologist Jansen Steur in the Netherlands), this reflected on the profession as a whole and questions arose about the quality of the professional control system. In other cases it was less individual professionals but more the complex system that let citizens down, examples in child protection are the deaths of Baby P. in the UK or Savannah in the Netherlands. Second, cultural and social changes in society and changes in risk perceptions (Beck, 1992) have made it more difficult to agree on the societal or public values that should be central to professions (Evetts, 2006). As a result of all these developments, trust in professionals declined.

The response of many governments and employer organizations has been to impose more controls with the aim to restore trust in professions, but the effects are equivocal. This increase in controls coincided with the introduction of New Public Management reforms that stimulated management by measurement (Noordegraaf & Abma, 2003; Pollitt, 2003) and most of the controls imposed took the form of managerialism. Different authors see different causal relations here, which is not the focus of this chapter. This chapter focuses on trust in public professionals and their profession. It is inevitable to see this in the context of how public professionals are controlled, through self-control within the profession (professionalism) or increased output control systems such as managerialism or a combination of the two.

When talking about trust in public professionals it is important to specify whose trust in professionals we are talking about. Ultimately the main concern is client's trust in public professionals. Traditionally the pure professions (Noordegraaf, 2007) were granted the discretion to put in place systems of self-control so that clients could trust in those professional controls. These self-control systems consisted of extensive education and training, continuous retraining and socialization within professional associations where a shared work culture is developed and maintained. Malfunctioning professionals are spotted early on and sanctioned (Evetts, 2006; Freidson, 2001; Rueschemeyer, 1983). Such a system of self-control is only granted by regulators, employer organizations or managers as long as it delivers what these actors want: if the profession helps solve important social problems with its expertise and does so in line with dominant social values. So the other trustors are regulators and employer organizations. When client trust declines, regulators and employer organizations often feel the need to step in and impose controls on public professionals and their professions in order to restore and safeguard client trust in professionals. I show that over the past decades this dynamic has occurred in many public professions and review the literature on how these changes in control systems have been implemented and perceived, and with what consequences. Most of these control systems have taken the form of managerialism.

The chapter starts with a conceptual analysis of trust in public professionals and their professions, followed by a review of the challenges to trust in public professionals and their professions. After that I present the results from a semi-systematic literature review and find that there are two patterns for how the relationship between professionals and their employers and regulators has evolved over the past decades. In the first dominant pattern, the relationship between public professionals and their managers, employers and regulators is seen as an adversarial struggle: it is professional autonomy versus managerial control; while in the second, more collaborative pattern, we see practices emerging where professional autonomy is felt to still be present together with increased managerial control. This analysis shows the contingent nature of the relationship between trust and control (Sitkin, 1995). I propose that Weibel and Six's model (2013) provides the theoretical basis for identifying the conditions for trust in professional autonomy and managerial control to strengthen each other in support of professionals intrinsic motivation.

Trust in public professionals and professions

Research on professionalism and professions goes back at least a century and is quite diverse. The same is true for research on trust. The perspectives on the relationship between the two concepts has changed over time as Evetts (2006) shows in her overview.

(Public) professionalism and professionals

Historically, professionalism was a concept that was reserved for occupational systems with professional associations controlling access to the profession, organizing the educational system, setting standards and with formal powers to sanction malfunctioning members. This occupational organization for professional groups combined control of the labour market with informal cooperation and control within employing organizations, also called double closure (Ackroyd, 1996, p. 599). Freidson (2001) called professionalism the third logic, next to hierarchy and market. Professionalism is about handling knowledge and expertise that is special because it takes effort, training and time to acquire. This makes it legitimate for professionals to be sheltered from market laws and bureaucracy (Freidson, 2001).

In recent years the debate about who was seen as a professional and who was not has received more attention. The orthodox insisted that only occupations that had achieved certain privileges in terms of self-control were professions, whereas others argued that it was more relevant to focus on the requirements for the task and the ways in which these tasks could be controlled so as clients could trust the professionals performing the tasks. Evetts (2006, p. 519) rightly concludes that the debate should move on from definitional questions which are 'a time-wasting diversion'. Professions may be characterized by extensive specialized education and training to acquire the necessary knowledge and expertise; sustained by an occupational community of peers with a shared identity and values; their decision-making is based on a professional ethical code; they operate altruistically and are motivated by universalistic values (di Luzio, 2006; Evetts, 2006, 2011; Noordegraaf, 2015; Rueschemeyer, 1983). Whether they have professional courts for sanctioning malfunctioning peers, or whether they can control the entry into their profession and have a legally underpinned privilege to regulate the content of the working process, is of less relevance (Evetts, 2006). In their work with clients they have discretion and professional autonomy to decide the best course of action for that particular client situation (Hasselberg, 2013; Rueschemeyer, 1983).

In the functionalist model of professionalism, trust in professions is the answer to the central problem of social control of professional work (di Luzio, 2006; Evetts, 2006; Rueschemeyer, 1983). The problem of social control arises because the knowledge-based competence is held by experts, while this competence is accepted as relevant for societal problems which are important to those involved because of the interests involved. The work the experts perform is grounded in values that are important to many (Rueschemeyer, 1983). In this functionalist model, professions, individual professionals and their associations are seen to strike a deal with society in which they provide competence and integrity, 'commitment to a service ethos' (Rueschemeyer, 1983, p. 44) in exchange for trust of client and community.

Trust

In trust research, trust in professions is seen as a form of institutional-based trust (Zucker, 1986) and more specifically role-based trust (Kramer, 1999). It goes beyond mere interpersonal trust to also include trust in the system of professional social control that guides the behaviour of individual professional workers.

Trust has been studied in many different academic disciplines and this has resulted in many different definitions (see other chapters in this volume). Dietz (2011) provides a useful overview of the trust process distinguishing between (1) trustworthiness: the beliefs, (2) the trust decision and (3) trust-informed actions (see also Dietz & Den Hartog, 2006). '[T]here is *always* an assessment (however thorough) of the other party's trustworthiness which informs a preparedness to be vulnerable that, in genuine cases of trust, leads to a risk-taking act' (Dietz, 2011, p. 215). Variations in trust definitions can often be traced back to whether authors define trust as an attitude or belief, or as an action. Trust implies that there is uncertainty about the trustee's future behaviour. Möllering's key point regarding trust is that none of the three bases that he identifies – reasons, routines or reflexivity – can ever provide certainty about the trusted party's future actions and therefore, trust inevitably involves a leap of faith in which the 'irreducible social vulnerability and uncertainty [are suspended] *as if* they were favourably resolved' (Möllering, 2006, p. 111). When clients consult professionals they are particularly vulnerable as they are not in a position, as a lay person, to judge the trustworthiness of the professional, while their questions are usually 'of vital importance to individual lives' (di Luzio, 2006, p. 551).

Authors have proposed many different categorizations for the dimensions of trustworthiness (see other chapters in this volume) and this chapter uses the overall distinction between competence or ability on the one hand, and intentions, goodwill or value-congruence on the other (Sako, 1998; Sitkin & Roth, 1993; Weibel, 2007). This is appropriate since, as we have seen, the emphasis of professionalism is on both the special expertise of the professional and the difficulty for lay persons to assess that expertise; as well as on the normative dimension of the professional's goodwill to the client and broader society. However, clients often do not know enough about the professional as an individual to provide enough basis to take Möllering's leap of faith. But if they can trust in the system of professional control, then they may be able to take the leap. This is what Kramer's notion of role-based trust is about: it 'constitutes a form of depersonalized trust because it is predicated on knowledge that a person occupies a particular role in the organization rather than specific knowledge about the person's capabilities, dispositions, motives, and intentions' (Kramer, 1999, p. 578). Role-based trust falls in the broader category of person or firm-specific institutional-based trust which rests on being a member of a specific subculture 'within which carefully delineated specific expectations are expected to hold, at least in some cases based on prior socialization' (Zucker, 1986, p. 63). In this conceptualization, professionalism is seen as 'an alternative formal source of information about how much an individual could be trusted. Extensive socialization, emergence of licensing standards across the country, and creation of professional associations all increased the certainty of performance characteristics' (Zucker, 1986, p. 94).

Trust in public professionals is a multilevel construct (cf. Kroeger, 2012; Kroeger & Bachmann, 2013; Möllering, 2006; Sydow, 2006): trust exists at the interpersonal level, where the 'face work' (cf. Giddens, 1990) takes place and at the system level that is independent of specific individuals, in other words the institutional-based trust in the profession. In his review of the literature on trust in institutions, Möllering (2006) notes that both Simmel and Luhmann suggest that trust in systems is not much more than an assumption that a system is functioning, and a willingness to place trust in that system without placing trust in people. Luhmann (1979) adds that system trust includes the assumption that everybody else also trusts the system. In his conceptualization, experts, in our case the professionals, play the role of controlling the system to ensure its proper functioning. Giddens (1990) also gives experts a central role to play in system trust, but in his conceptualization they are the representatives of the system at the 'access points' where the trustor experiences the system, which in our case is also the professional. What is missing in these conceptualizations is attention to different perceptions of when a system is 'functioning'. This is a value-laden concept and therefore different perceptions may exist leading to value conflicts.

Challenges to trust in public professionals and professions

Professionalism as the third logic of social coordination and control seemed to have been operating satisfactorily until roughly the second half of the twentieth century. Satisfaction with professional competence has remained high, but the values and standards became increasingly contested. One dimension of this value conflict is that more became known about the actual behaviour and norms of professionals, in particular more transgressions have reached the media where personal interests trumped professional or societal interests and the societal values were not upheld. Even if the most serious transgressions were cases of occasional bad apples, this reflected on the profession as a whole and questions arose about the quality of the professional control system. And as Hardin (2002) noted, having more knowledge about how authorities actually operate is likely to lead to a decrease in trust. This may not be a problem, 'indeed, it may even be a sign that citizens are becoming increasingly sophisticated about the conditions of trust' (Warren, 1999, p. 6). So increased sophistication, partly due to better education, may have triggered the change in trust in professions, rather than a change in professional performance; we do not know.

Social and cultural changes in society have also meant that values and standards have become more diverse and contested. Trust in authorities, like professions, declined. Professions were no longer able to tell the rest of society what is good and right for it (Evetts, 2006). And when value congruence decreases distrust is more likely (Bijlsma-Frankema, Sitkin, & Weibel, 2015; Sitkin & Roth, 1993). This dynamic is particularly fierce for public professionals whose tasks have always been characterized by high goal ambiguity and value conflict. These cultural and social changes led to increased criticism on all government activities, not just those performed by public professionals (Pollitt, 2003). This led to a programme of reforms called New Public Management (NPM) of which managerialism was the one that had most impact on public professionals.

From the 1980s, NPM reforms were introduced to improve the effectiveness and efficiency of public service delivery for public professionals. Where possible the actual public service delivery was contracted out to private, third sector or public organizations with performance management targets; this was called marketization (Pollitt, 2003). Within the organizations performing the public tasks, managerialism was introduced based on the same performance targets. The idea was that those actors (organizations and professional workers) that deliver the public service should not be prescribed by policy makers *how* to do their job, but only *what* to achieve. This would stimulate innovation and efficiency (Pollitt, 2003) and ensure goal clarity (i.e. value congruence).

In theory, managerialism might have been plausible as a governance mechanism for public professionals in practice however, there were many complications. First, given the dominance of the neoliberal and market ideology in NPM reforms, efficiency and economic values were seen as dominant preferences in the performance targets that were set (Noordegraaf & Abma, 2003), which ran counter to professional values of service to clients. Second, in theory setting clear targets sounded good, but in most public services, quality was a contested concept and goal ambiguity was the norm (e.g. Bijlsma-Frankema et al., 2015; Bolton, 2004; Cooke, 2006; Flynn, 2002; Noordegraaf & Abma, 2003). And third, even where agreement could be reached about what quality entailed, it proved difficult to measure it as a performance indicator, so proxy indicators were often used. Ample research exists, though, that you get what you measure, so if you do not measure exactly what you want, you get perverse effects (see the classic Kerr, 1975).

Most research conducted on the impact of the introduction of managerialism and marketization has a binary focus on either advocating a return to professionalism or going beyond professionalism (Noordegraaf, 2011). Noordegraaf (2011) argued, however, that this is too limited a focus and misses the explanation of why managerialism and marketization were introduced. He identified three bundles of non-economic external influences: changing work preferences due to demographic conditions, calls for multi-professional work forms due to changing social realities, and the omnipresence of risks and incidents. These changes impact on what professionals have traditionally called secondary aspects of professional service – 'efficiency, communication, cooperation, safety, reputation management and so on' (Noordegraaf, 2011, p. 1365) – and make these aspects more important. Taken together these changes call for what Noordegraaf called organized professionalism, in which organizational and professional features are combined rather than opposed. De Bruijn and Noordegraaf (2010) argued that it is inevitable that managers get more influence over professional practices given the changes in society and professions' slow response to these changes. But also, some of the changes that professions need to make to adapt to their changing environment imply more collaboration between professionals and managers, in other words more organized professionalism. Introducing managerialism in the form of management by measurement based on hard data that are knowable, identifiable and comparable, however, is not appropriate for professional tasks that are characterized by high factual complexity – we do not know the issues – and simultaneously highly contested values and goal ambiguity (Noordegraaf & Abma, 2003).

In the semi-systematic literature review presented below, the studies show different reforms to the control arrangements of public professionals and their professions (variations of managerialism) and variations in the results of those reforms.

Semi-systematic literature review

Empirical research into trust relations between professional workers and their manager, employer and regulators is scattered across many different academic fields and, as a consequence, across many publication outlets. This makes it difficult to do a proper systematic review of the literature, so I cannot and do not claim to be complete or exhaustive. I searched within the Web of Science database in the Social Science Citation Index between 2000 and 2015, selecting English language journal articles. I used the search terms combinations Trust* AND profession* AND manag*; and Trust* AND profession* AND govern*. This generated more than 1000 hits. Next 16 research areas were selected that focused on public tasks, such as public administration, sociology, health care, education, social work. This generated 600–700 sources that were scanned by title and abstracts; when in doubt they were saved for the next step. The selection was based on whether the article focused on the relationship between professional workers and their manager, employer and/or regulator. Also, the term trust was often used in its legal form such as NHS trust. This selection step generated a list of 178 sources for which the PDF's were downloaded and searched in full on what was said about trust and regulation; often the reference to trust or professionals was only in passing, rather than the focus of the study. In total 27 sources found through this search process were used in the literature review. Table 20.1 provides a descriptive overview in terms of industry/sector, which method was used and which trust relationships are covered. Where relevant to the analysis, some other sources were added.

Two patterns emerged of how governance arrangements were perceived by public professionals: adversarial or collaborative relationships between professionals and their managers. A similar distinction seems to have been made by Adler and Borys (1996) who distinguished coercive from enabling controls. The studies reviewed fall roughly equally in the two patterns, but from the analysis and the broader literature, it becomes clear that the dominant pattern was the adversarial one. In this pattern, either managers 'win' and get (more) power over professionals, or professionals 'win' and have the power for discretion over how they interact with citizens in the delivery of their public task. I interpret this as managerialism with its managerial control *versus* professionalism with its professional autonomy. It also meets most of the explanatory factors that Sitkin and Roth (1993) identified for the failure of legalistic remedies for trust. In the other pattern, studies showed that more collaborative relationships between public professionals and their managers were possible. It was suggested that this collaborative pattern led to better public service quality than the adversarial pattern. When analysing those studies I found support for the conditions that Weibel and Six (2013) identified for trust and control to strengthen each other. These conditions emphasize *how* controls are developed and implemented (see Long and Weibel, this volume).

Dominant pattern: emphasis on managerial control and distrust

The dominant pattern in the governance arrangements in the literature appears to be based on the assumption that there is an inevitable power struggle between professionals and their managers, employers and regulators. It is managerialism with its managerial control *versus* professionalism with its professional autonomy. This is reminiscent of the dominant perspective in the relation between trust and control: that they are substitutes (Das & Teng, 2001; Weibel, 2007). When you trust you cannot control; and when you control you cannot trust. Controls are seen as signs of distrust. NPM reforms triggered a strong distrust discourse. For example, audit generates 'an ever-increasing spiral of distrust of professional competence' (Flynn, 2002, p. 163), or audit 'implies a culture of distrust' (Cooke, 2006, p. 976). Empirical studies showed that the introduction of managerialism has been met 'with distrust by the staff' (Bolton, 2004, p. 322). In many studies, managerialism is seen as a form of control that is based on 'organized distrust' (e.g. Avis, 2003; Cooke, 2006; Flynn, 2002; Gilbert, 2005a). Quite often the reforms were introduced after incidents in the public service delivery had hit the media, highlighting the public's vulnerability to the competence and goodwill of public professionals delivering the public service. Policy makers or organizational leadership responded to these incidents with new regulation and audits.

Empirical research into the impact of NPM reforms on public professionals and the relationship between public professionals and their managers therefore predominantly stressed the adversarial relationship (e.g. Bargagliotti, 2012; Bijlsma-Frankema, Sitkin, & Weibel, 2015; Bolton, 2004; Brown & Calnan, 2011; Gilbert, 2005b; Harrison & Smith, 2004; Hoecht, 2006; Lasky, 2005). Managerial discourses are critical of professionals and their activities and trust in professionals comes under pressure (e.g. Gilbert, 2005a). Professional opinions are criticized for representing the interests of professions rather than the interests of clients/citizens; in this way both managerial and professional discourses claim to represent the interests of clients (Gilbert, 2005b). Several studies also investigated the impact of managerialism on outcomes to clients and found no improvement or even lower outcomes (e.g. Cooke, 2006; Lasky, 2005), for example because the risk analysis system in child care social work may actually obscure risks to children (Pithouse et al., 2012).

These studies cover a wide range of fields such as social work, education and health care. In social work, Ruch (2012) emphasized the rational-cognitive foundations of managerialism – privileging 'cognition, rationality and predictability' – and contrasted these with the professional foundations of social work, 'the holistic understanding of human beings that encompasses all dimensions of behaviour' including the emotional, irrational and unpredictable (Ruch, 2012, p. 1317). In education, performance management, as part of managerialism, has been claimed to encourage 'masculinist and bullying forms of management', has led to closer surveillance and operated 'within a blame culture' (Avis, 2003, p. 324). In higher education, stricter quality-control regimes were shown to have led to loss of professional autonomy and 'rituals of verification' instead of fostering trust (Hoecht, 2006, p. 541). More importantly, these new control systems may very well be detrimental to innovative teaching and learning.

Table 20.1 Characteristics of studies found in literature search

Source	Sector	Type of study	Relationship	Type of pattern
Dixon-Woods, Yeung, and Bosk (2011)	Medical profession UK	Public debate analysis	Professionals and their managers, regulators	Adversarial
Flynn (2002)	Health care UK	Critical essay	Professionals and their regulators	Adversarial
Freeman, McWilliam, MacKinnon, DeLuca, and Rappolt (2009)	Health care Canada	Qualitative	Professionals and their managers, regulator and professional bodies	Adversarial
Friedman (2011)	Teaching Israel	Qualitative	Professionals, supervisors and school leaders	Adversarial
Gilbert (2005a)	Nursing	Qualitative	Professionals and their managers	Adversarial
Gilbert (2005b)	Nursing	Qualitative	Professionals and their managers	Adversarial
Hirvonen (2014)	Welfare	Qualitative	Professionals and their clients	Adversarial
Hoecht (2006)	Higher education	Qualitative	Professionals and their managers	Adversarial
Lasky (2005)	Education	Qualitative/ quantitative	Professionals and their clients	Adversarial
Liljegren (2012)	Social work	Qualitative	Professionals and managers, regulator and clients	Adversarial
Pithouse et al. (2012)	Social work	Qualitative	Impact of risk analysis system on child safety	Adversarial
Sellman (2006)	Nursing	Essay	Professional and clients	Adversarial
Sheaff et al. (2003)	Health care	Qualitative	Professionals and their managers	Adversarial
Anand, Chhajed, and Delfin (2012)	Health care	Quantitative	Professionals and their managers	Collaborative
Auer, Schwendimann, Koch, De Geest, and Ausserhofer (2014)	Health care	Quantitative	Professionals and their managers	Collaborative
Avis (2003)	Education	Essay	Professionals and their managers, regulators	Collaborative
Bargagliotti (2012)	Health care	Conceptual	Professionals and their managers	Collaborative
Blomeke and Klein (2013)	Education	Quantitative	Professionals and their managers	Collaborative
Bolton (2004)	Health care	Qualitative	Professionals and their managers, regulators	Collaborative
Brown and Calnan (2011)	Health care	Essay	Professionals and their managers, regulators	Collaborative
Cooke (2006)	Health care	Qualitative	Professionals and their managers	Collaborative

continued . . .

Table 20.1 Continued

Source	Sector	Type of study	Relationship	Type of pattern
Ghamrawi (2011)	Teaching Lebanon	Qualitative	Professionals and their managers	Collaborative
Harrison and Smith (2004)	Health and social care	Essay	Professionals and their managers, regulators	Collaborative
Marshall, Mannion, Nelson, and Davies (2003)	Health care	Qualitative	Professionals and their managers	Collaborative
Mastrangelo, Eddy, and Lorenzet (2014)	Education	Quantitative	Professionals and their managers	Collaborative
Nyhan (2000)	Public sector	Quantitative	Professionals and their managers	Collaborative
Paille, Grima, and Bernardeau (2013)	Public sector	Quantitative	Professionals and their managers	Collaborative

In health care, several studies concluded that trust in professionals had declined and that the controls that were introduced were based on distrust, often leading to perverse effects. Some studies pointed to the lack of moral agency in managerialism that led to a deficiency in social engagement, which was seen as central in good health care (e.g. Brown & Calnan, 2011). In nursing, the introduction of practice protocols and audit procedures had not been able to establish claims of successful control of nursing practice; quality of nursing and control of the nursing labour process remained a contested domain (Bolton, 2004). Brown and Calnan (2011) contrasted the 'checking-based' audit culture with a 'trust-based' model. They argued, in line with others, that this checking-based audit culture is fundamentally flawed in driving quality and performance, while the trust-based model would, in their eyes, be more capable of 'acknowledging the meaning, complexity and the specificities inherent to professional work' (Brown & Calnan, 2011, p. 19).

Summarizing these studies, the way in which public professionals were managed within their organizations was perceived by public professionals as managerial control based on distrust. It led to greater social distance (Sitkin & Roth, 1993). It was experienced as demotivating, driving out their (professional) intrinsic motivation to help vulnerable citizens, and often stimulated only ritualistic compliance to the controls and taking away time from client interaction to satisfy the increased administrative demands (e.g. Avis, 2003; Cooke, 2006). It sometimes even led to increased risks to clients (Pithouse et al., 2012) or reduced innovation (Hoecht, 2006). Managerial controls took away professional autonomy, often to the detriment of the quality of the public service that the professionals were providing.

More collaborative pattern: emphasis on managerial control and trust in professional autonomy

In contrast to this dominant adversarial pattern, a more collaborative pattern emerged that showed a predominantly collaborative relationship between public professionals and their managers. These studies showed that such governance arrangements led to more committed and more intrinsically motivated professionals (Anand et al., 2012; Ghamrawi, 2011; Nyhan, 2000). How may these studies be analysed to better understand their commonalities and underlying mechanisms?

Sitkin (1995) pointed to the contingent nature of the relationship between trust and control. Controls that do not match task requirements (Adler & Borys, 1996) and/or the values and identity of those controlled (Bijlsma-Frankema et al., 2015) are generally perceived as distrusting, leading to the adversarial pattern identified as dominant in professional contexts. When, on the other hand, controls match those task requirements and values and identity, trust and control are perceived as complementary to each other (Bijlsma-Frankema et al., 2015; Das & Teng, 2001; Sitkin, 1995; Weibel, 2007). Long and Weibel (this volume) emphasize that the process of design and implementation of the control system (the how) may be more important than the what. The analysis in this chapter shows how both the how and the what are important. Through a collaborative process, control systems were agreed that meet the conditions for managerial controls to strengthen trust in professional autonomy.

Weibel and Six's model (2013) helps structure the conditions found in the studies in the second more collaborative pattern. This model formulates the conditions for when and how managerial trust and control may complement each other in strengthening employees' intrinsic motivation. This model is based on self determination theory (SDT; e.g. Ryan & Deci, 2000; Stone, Deci, & Ryan, 2009). SDT's focus is on the intrinsic importance of work, which is relevant for public tasks and has been shown to be particularly relevant for tasks that are simultaneously complex and ambiguous (Stone et al., 2009). According to SDT, human beings have three core psychological needs: autonomy, competence and relatedness. Individuals feel autonomous when they experience a sense of choice and volition. Autonomy is not independence; one may feel autonomous while being (inter)-dependent on others. Individuals may feel supported in their competence development when they perceive that they can develop new skills and mental frames. Their need for relatedness is about the desire to experience satisfying and supportive social relationships; in work contexts these relationships are with colleagues and managers. Mutual understanding, trust and respect are important here (Stone et al., 2009; Weibel, 2007; Weibel & Six, 2013). Central in this theory is the notion that professionals will be more intrinsically motivated, self-determined, to do what is expected of them by their organization when they feel more autonomous, supported in their competence development and trusted by their managers and organization.

Autonomy

Weibel and Six (2013) found support for the proposition that the more control systems are designed in dialogue between professionals and their managers, the more professionals will feel self-determined and the more trust is experienced. Control is about setting standards or performance indicators; monitoring those standards and indicators; judging whether the standards or indicators have been met; and deciding interventions (sanctions and rewards) (e.g. Weibel, 2007). The more professionals and management together make sense of the monitoring results and judge and decide possible interventions, the more likely it is that professionals feel autonomously motivated and the more trust is experienced. Research into the perverse effects of performance management systems, and how to mitigate these effects, provided support for the important role of dialogue in the design and execution – including interpretation – of performance controls (De Bruijn, 2007).

In education, the studies found in the search showed the need for dialogue across a range of stakeholders, because different views need to be heard to find the creative responses needed to deal with today's radical uncertainty (Avis, 2003). And when teachers engaged in a professional dialogue in their schools with colleagues and school principals, they got the chance to build more congruence between their classroom goals and the overall goals that govern the school system (Ghamrawi, 2011). Also, teaching quality improved when teachers perceived more autonomy (e.g. Blomeke & Klein, 2013).

In health care, several studies found a 'negotiated order' or new forms of consultation as they studied the relationship between managerialism and professional autonomy (Bolton, 2004; Brown & Calnan, 2011; Thomas & Hewitt, 2011). Quality-assurance mechanisms that were developed locally by professionals were more effective and seen as more legitimate (Brown & Calnan, 2011). Autonomy was shown to have positive effects on nurses' work engagement (Bargagliotti, 2012) and on frontline worker commitment to continuous improvement (Anand et al., 2012).

Competence

In relation to the need for competence development, Weibel and Six (2013) proposed that learning-oriented and constructive feedback by managers to professionals strengthened professionals' intrinsic motivation. Several studies found in the search supported this. Teaching quality improved when teachers received more frequent appraisals (Blomeke & Klein, 2013) and more constructive feedback about failures was conducive to developing a safety culture in health care (Auer et al., 2014). More generally, constructive feedback from managers to professionals strengthened intrinsic motivation and had a positive effect on quality of public service delivery (Ghamrawi, 2011; Nyhan, 2000). Professional reflection was seen as important as it had a positive effect on how the complexity and ambiguity of the public task were dealt with (e.g. Brown & Calnan, 2011).

Relatedness

The need for relatedness is about the experience of mutual understanding, trust and respect. Weibel and Six (2013) proposed that governance focused on intrinsic work engagement and manager trust in professionals positively affected professionals' intrinsic motivation. The positive effects of manager trust in professionals was found in studies across the board (Anand et al., 2012; Blomeke & Klein, 2013; Cooke, 2006; Ghamrawi, 2011). Professionals' trust in their managers or organization also showed positive effects (e.g. Anand et al., 2012; Blomeke & Klein, 2013; Ghamrawi, 2011). Trust among professionals was also seen as having a positive effect on motivation, work engagement and quality of service delivery (Avis, 2003; Brown & Calnan, 2011; Ghamrawi, 2011). The need for a culture of trust is regularly mentioned (e.g. Ghamrawi, 2011; Harrison & Smith, 2004). Direct manager involvement in professional work helped professionals' perception of support and helped reduce manager reliance on audits, 'I can gain far more knowledge about the quality of a [hospital] ward by working on it than I could on a thousand audits' (Cooke, 2006, p. 980).

Summarizing, despite the wealth of studies that show that the implementation of managerialism in professional work has often led to adversarial relations and further decrease in trust, there is a growing body of studies across many public professions that empirically support the proposed model by Weibel and Six (2013), identifying the conditions for trust and control to complement each other. Managers and professionals need to work together to deal with the simultaneous complexity and ambiguity, developing shared understandings of the expected performance – what is quality of service? – and agreeing on ways of working and accountability.

Conclusions

Public professions are trusted to organize their own professional controls in order to safeguard their unique expert knowledge and their commitment to public service and societal values. In the second part of the twentieth century, however, these societal values were increasingly contested and trust in professionals and their professions came under pressure. Since trust in professionals and their profession is role-based trust – a form of institutional-based trust – the institutions on which it is based are important. Traditionally these were professional controls (professionalism), but in response to the (perceived) decline in trust in professionals, their managers, employers and/or regulators have introduced managerial controls (managerialism).

This chapter has analysed studies that investigated the effect of managerialism on public professionals and their work. Two distinct patterns emerged, an adversarial and a collaborative approach to improving the institutional bases for trust in public professionals. In the adversarial pattern, managerial controls were imposed on professionals in ways that were perceived as distrusting and inappropriate because the quality of public service was deemed to deteriorate. In the collaborative pattern, relationships between professionals and their managers are more collaborative and may be characterized by trust based on actual interactions, mutual understanding and respect; both 'parties' acknowledge and respect each other's role in the delivery of public services. The governance arrangements in this pattern may be conceptualized as manager trust and control complementing each other to stimulate professionals' intrinsic motivation, in line with Weibel and Six's (2013) model. Through dialogue, and other forms of constructive inter-action, managers and professionals develop shared understandings of quality of service and other facets of the expected outcomes, and agree on the design and execution of work practices and accountability procedures. Continuous professional development and organizational learning are stimulated via constructive feedback and reflection. This results in and is supported by trust: manager trust in professionals, professionals' trust in manager/organization, trust among professionals and more generally a trust culture within the organization.

The proposition to be tested in future research is that professional work in the twenty-first century is best governed by a collaborative arrangement in which manager trust and control complement each other in stimulating professionals' intrinsic motivation. The conditions identified in Weibel and Six's (2013) model were supported in a wide range of empirical studies. Further research is needed to test the proposition to its full extent.

Also, so far the focus has been on the impact of the institutions – the controls – on the quality of professional work and the motivation of professionals, but we do not know the impact of these controls on client trust in professions: the real test. Recent developments in public governance focus on co-production and co-creation of public services between public professionals and clients. If the dialogue and trust found to be important between public professionals and their managers and regulators are extended to also include clients, then values congruence is more likely, even if it becomes more localized, and this most directly influences client trust in professions.

References

Ackroyd, S. (1996). Organization contra organizations: Professions and organizational change in the United Kingdom. *Organization Studies*, 17(4), 599–621.

Adler, P. S., & Borys, B. (1996). Two types of bureaucracy: Enabling and coercive. *Administrative Science Quarterly*, 41(1), 61–89.

Anand, G., Chhajed, D., & Delfin, L. (2012). Job autonomy, trust in leadership, and continuous improvement: An empirical study in health care. *Operations Management Research*, 5(3–4), 70–80. doi: 10.1007/s12063-012-0068-8

Auer, C., Schwendimann, R., Koch, R., De Geest, S., & Ausserhofer, D. (2014). How hospital leaders contribute to patient safety through the development of trust. *Journal of Nursing Administration*, 44(1), 23–29. doi: 10.1097/nna.0000000000000017

Avis, J. (2003). Re-thinking trust in a performative culture: The case of education. *Journal of Education Policy*, 18(3), 315–332. doi: 10.1080/0268093032000081116

Bannink, D. B. D. (2013). Localized crafting. Management tools responding to a double management challenge. In D. Bannink, H. Bosselaar, & W. Trommel (Eds.), *Crafting local welfare landscapes* (pp. 79–94). The Hague, the Netherlands: Eleven.

Bargagliotti, L. A. (2012). Work engagement in nursing: A concept analysis. *Journal of Advanced Nursing*, 68(6), 1414–1428. doi: 10.1111/j.1365-2648.2011.05859.x

Beck, U. (1992). *Risk society, towards a new modernity*. Los Angeles, CA: Sage.

Bijlsma-Frankema, K., Sitkin, S. B., & Weibel, A. (2015). Distrust in the balance: The emergence and development of intergroup distrust in a court of law. *Organization Science*, 26(4), 1018–1039. doi: 10.1287/orsc.2015.0977

Blomeke, S., & Klein, P. (2013). When is a school environment perceived as supportive by beginning mathematics teachers? Effects of leadership, trust, autonomy and appraisal on teaching quality. *International Journal of Science and Mathematics Education*, 11(4), 1029–1048. doi: 10.1007/s10763-013-9424-x

Bolton, S. C. (2004). A simple matter of control? NHS hospital nurses and new management. *Journal of Management Studies*, 41(2), 317–333. doi: 10.1111/j.1467-6486.2004.00434.x

Brown, P. R., & Calnan, M. (2011). The civilizing process of trust: Developing quality mechanisms which are local, professional-led and thus legitimate. *Social Policy & Administration*, 45(1), 19–34. doi: 10.1111/j.1467-9515.2010.00751.x

Cooke, H. (2006). The surveillance of nursing standards: An organisational case study. *International Journal of Nursing Studies*, 43(8), 975–984. doi: 10.1016/j.ijnurstu.2005.11.003

Das, T. K., & Teng, B. (2001). Trust, control and risk in strategic alliances: An integrated framework. *Organization Studies special issue: Trust and Control in Organizational Relations*, 22(2), 251–284.

De Bruijn, H. (2007). *Managing performance in the public sector*. London: Routledge.

De Bruijn, H., & Noordegraaf, M. (2010). Professionals versus managers? De onvermijdelijkheid van nieuwe professionele praktijken [professionals versus managers? The inevitability of new professional practices]. *Bestuurskunde*, (3), 6–20.

di Luzio, G. (2006). A sociological concept of client trust. *Current Sociology*, 54(4), 549–564. doi: 10.1177/0011392106065087

Dietz, G. (2011). Going back to the source: Why do people trust each other? *Journal of Trust Research*, 1(2), 215–222.

Dietz, G., & Den Hartog, D. N. (2006). Measuring trust inside organisations. *Personnel Review*, 35(5), 557–588. doi: 10.1108/00483480610682299

Dixon-Woods, M., Yeung, K., & Bosk, C. L. (2011). Why is UK medicine no longer a self-regulating profession? The role of scandals involving "bad apple" doctors. *Social Science & Medicine*, 73(10), 1452–1459. doi: 10.1016/j.socscimed.2011.08.031

Evetts, J. (2006). Introduction: Trust and professionalism: Challenges and occupational changes. *Current Sociology*, 54(4), 515–531. doi: 10.1177/0011392106065083

Evetts, J. (2011). A new professionalism? Challenges and opportunities. *Current Sociology*, 59(4), 406–422. doi: 10.1177/0011392111402585

Flynn, R. (2002). Clinical governance and governmentality. *Health Risk & Society*, 4(2), 155–173. doi: 10.1080/13698570220137042

Freeman, A. R., McWilliam, C. L., MacKinnon, J. R., DeLuca, S., & Rappolt, S. G. (2009). Health professionals' enactment of their accountability obligations: Doing the best they can. *Social Science & Medicine*, 69(7), 1063–1071. doi: 10.1016/j.socscimed.2009.07.025

Freidson, E. (2001). *Professionalism, the third logic*. Cambridge, UK: Polity press.

Friedman, H. (2011). The myth behind the subject leader as a school key player. *Teachers and Teaching*, 17(3), 289–302. doi: 10.1080/13540602.2011.554701

Ghamrawi, N. (2011). Trust me: Your school can be better – A message from teachers to principals. *Educational Management Administration & Leadership*, 39(3), 333–348. doi: 10.1177/1741143210393997

Giddens, A. (1990). *The consequences of modernity*. Stanford, UK: Polity Press.

Gilbert, T. P. (2005a). Impersonal trust and professional authority: Exploring the dynamics. *Journal of Advanced Nursing*, 49(6), 568–577. doi: 10.1111/j.1365-2648.2004.03332.x

Gilbert, T. P. (2005b). Trust and managerialism: Exploring discourses of care. *Journal of Advanced Nursing,* 52(4), 454–463. doi: 10.1111/j.1365-2648.2005.03611.x

Hardin, R. (2002). *Trust and trustworthiness* (Vol. IV). New York: Russell Sage Foundation.

Harrison, S., & Smith, C. (2004). Trust and moral motivation: Redundant resources in health and social care? *Policy and Politics,* 32(3), 371–386. doi: 10.1332/0305573041223726

Hasselberg, Y. (2013). In defence of discretion. In S. Riders, Y. Hasselberg & A. Waluszewski (Eds.), *Transformations in research, higher education and the academic market* (pp. 137–144). London: Springer.

Hirvonen, H. (2014). From embodied to disembodied professionalism? Discussing the implications of medico-managerial management in welfare service work. *Social Policy & Administration,* 48(5), 576–593. doi: 10.1111/spol.12045

Hoecht, A. (2006). Quality assurance in UK higher education: Issues of trust, control, professional autonomy and accountability. *Higher Education,* 51(4), 541–563. doi: 10.1007/s10734-004-2533-2

Kerr, S. (1975). On the folly of rewarding A, while hoping for B. *The Academy of Management Journal,* 18(4), 769–783. doi: 10.2307/255378

Kramer, R. M. (1999). Trust and distrust in organizations: Emerging perspectives, enduring questions. [Review]. *Annual Review of Psychology,* 50, 569–598. doi: 10.1146/annurev.psych.50.1.569

Kroeger, F. (2012). Trusting organizations: The institutionalization of trust in interorganizational relationships. *Organization,* 19(6), 743–763. doi: 10.1177/1350508411420900

Kroeger, F., & Bachmann, R. (2013). Trusting across boundaries. In J. Langan-Fox & C. L. Cooper (Eds.), *The Routledge companion to boundary spanning in organizations* (pp. 253–284). London: Routledge.

Lasky, S. (2005). A sociocultural approach to understanding teacher identity, agency and professional vulnerability in a context of secondary school reform. *Teaching and Teacher Education,* 21(8), 899–916. doi: 10.1016/j.tate.2005.06.003

Liljegren, A. (2012). Pragmatic professionalism: Micro-level discourse in social work. *European Journal of Social Work,* 15(3), 295–312. doi: 10.1080/13691457.2010.543888

Luhmann, N. (1979). *Trust and power.* Chicester, UK: John Wiley & Sons.

Marshall, M. N., Mannion, R., Nelson, E., & Davies, H. T. O. (2003). Managing change in the culture of general practice: Qualitative case studies in primary care trusts. *British Medical Journal,* 327(7415), 599–602. doi: 10.1136/bmj.327.7415.599

Mastrangelo, A., Eddy, E. R., & Lorenzet, S. J. (2014). The relationship between enduring leadership and organizational performance. *Leadership & Organization Development Journal,* 35(7), 590–604. doi: 10.1108/lodj-08-2012-0097

Matland, R. E. (1995). Synthesizing the implementation literature: The ambiguity-conflict model of policy implementation. *Journal of Public Administration Research and Theory,* 5(2), 145–174.

Möllering, G. (2006). Trust, institutions, agency: Towards a neoinstitutional theory of trust. In R. Bachmann & A. Zaheer (Eds.), *Handbook of trust research* (pp. 355–376). Cheltenham, UK: Edward Elgar.

Möllering, G. (2006). *Trust: Reason, routine, reflexivity.* Amsterdam, the Netherlands: Elsevier.

Noordegraaf, M. (2007). From 'pure' to 'hybrid' professionalism, present-day professionalism in ambiguous public domains. *Administration & Society,* 39(6), 761–785.

Noordegraaf, M. (2011). Risky business. How professionals and professional fields (must) deal with organizational issues. *Organization Studies,* 32(10), 1349–1371.

Noordegraaf, M. (2015). Hybrid professionalism and beyond: (New) Forms of public professionalism in changing organizational and societal contexts. *Journal of Professions and Organization,* 2(2), 187–206. doi: 10.1093/jpo/jov002

Noordegraaf, M., & Abma, T. (2003). Management by measurement? Public management practices amidst ambiguity. *Public Administration,* 81(4), 853–871. doi: 10.1111/j.0033-3298.2003.00374.x

Nyhan, R. C. (2000). Changing the paradigm: Trust and its role in public sector organizations. *The American Review of Public Administration,* 30(1), 87–109. doi: 10.1177/02750740022064560

Paille, P., Grima, F., & Bernardeau, D. (2013). When subordinates feel supported by managers: Investigating the relationships between support, trust, commitment and outcomes. *International Review of Administrative Sciences,* 79(4), 681–700. doi: 10.1177/0020852313501248

Pithouse, A., Broadhurst, K., Hall, C., Peckover, S., Wastell, D., & White, S. (2012). Trust, risk and the (mis)management of contingency and discretion through new information technologies in children's services. *Journal of Social Work,* 12(2), 158–178. doi: 10.1177/1468017310382151

Pollitt, C. (2003). *The essential public manager.* Maidenhead, UK: Open University.

Ruch, G. (2012). Where have all the feelings gone? Developing reflective and relationship-based management in child-care social work. *British Journal of Social Work*, 42(7), 1315–1332. doi: 10.1093/bjsw/bcr134

Rueschemeyer, D. (1983). Professional autonomy and the social control of expertise. In R. Dingwall & P. Lewis (Eds.), *The sociology of the professions* (pp. 38–58). London: MacMillan.

Ryan, R. M., & Deci, E. L. (2000). Self-determination theory and the facilitation of intrinsic motivation, social development, and well-being. *American Psychologist*, 55(1), 68–78.

Sako, M. (1998). Does trust improve business performance? In C. Lane & R. B. (Eds.), *Trust within and between organizations*. Oxford, UK: Oxford University Press.

Sellman, D. (2006). The importance of being trustworthy. *Nursing Ethics*, 13(2), 105–115. doi: 10.1191/0969733006ne860oa

Sheaff, R., Rogers, A., Pickard, S., Marshall, M., Campbell, S., Sibbald, B., . . . & Roland, M. (2003). A subtle governance: 'Soft' medical leadership in English primary care. *Sociology of Health & Illness*, 25(5), 408–428. doi: 10.1111/1467-9566.00352

Sitkin, S. B. (1995). On the positive effects of legalization on trust. *Research on Negotiation in Organizations*, 5, 185–218.

Sitkin, S. B., & Roth, N. L. (1993). Explaining the limited effectiveness of legalistic remedies for trust distrust. *Organization Science*, 4(3), 367–392. doi: 10.1287/orsc.4.3.367

Stone, D., Deci, E. L., & Ryan, R. M. (2009). Beyond talk: Creating autonomous motivation through self-determination theory. *Journal of General Management*, 34, 75–91.

Sydow, J. (2006). How can systems trust systems? A structuration perspective on trust-building in inter-organizational relations. In R. Bachmann & A. Zaheer (Eds.), *Handbook of trust research* (pp. 377–392). Cheltenham, UK: Edward Elgar.

Thomas, P., & Hewitt, J. (2011). Managerial organization and professional autonomy: A discourse-based conceptualization. *Organization Studies*, 32(10), 1373–1393. doi: 10.1177/0170840611416739

Warren, M. E. (1999). *Democracy and trust*. Cambridge, UK: Cambridge University Press.

Weibel, A. (2007). Formal control and trustworthiness: Shall the twain never meet? *Group & Organization Management*, 32(4), 500–517.

Weibel, A., & Six, F. E. (2013). Trust and control: The role of intrinsic motivation. In R. Bachmann & A. Zaheer (Eds.), *Handbook of advances in trust research* (pp. 57–81). Cheltenham, UK: Edward Elgar.

Zucker, L. G. (1986). Production of trust: Institutional sources of economic structure, 1840 – 1920. *Research in Organizational Behavior*, 8, 53–111.

21

EMPLOYMENT RELATIONS AND TRUST

Kim Mather

Introduction

The concept of trust in employment relations is underpinned by a persistent concern with the 'problem' of low productivity that besets the UK economy (ACAS, 2015). One 'solution' is argued to rest on high-performance, high-trust workplace relations that realize employees' full potential (CIPD, 2013). There are some insightful and useful contributions about both the nature of, and the potential impact of high performance work (HPW) regimes with regard to trust as debated by Searle earlier in this text. At the same time, the UK labour market is characterized by low-autonomy work and increased reliance on 'flexible', zero-hours contracts and other casualized forms of employment (Rubery, 2015; Adams & Deakin, 2014; TUC, 2014; Van Wanrooy et al., 2013). These labour market developments hardly signify employers' commitment to high-trust relations between employers and employed. As the CIPD itself admits, 'job insecurity is associated with distrust' (CIPD, 2013:11). Wider empirical evidence of UK developments paints a bleak picture of job insecurity and work intensification for those in work and of generally low-trust workplace relations (Worrall et al., 2016). Several detailed studies also highlight work intensification and work pressure trends that are particularly apparent across the public sector: in the civil service (French, 2014); among prison governors (French, 2015); in the NHS (Mather, 2014); in further education (Mather & Seifert, 2014) and in schools (Carter & Stevenson, 2012). Perhaps unsurprisingly then, there is a reported 'crisis of trust . . . that cuts across politics and public and private sector organisations' (Royles, 2010:239).

This chapter aims to offer a critically informed contribution to this complex debate about trust in the sphere of employment relations. The discussion draws on the UK context to discuss the ways in which employers, workers, trade unions, and state policy interact and what this may all mean for how trust might then be conceptualized. It takes as its starting point the nature of the employment relationship to explain the inherently low-trust-based arrangements around which work is contractually and practically organized at the outset. There are three caveats to note. First, in line with Williams (2014) it is acknowledged that not all workers are directly employed. As noted above, the UK economy is increasingly characterized by casualized employment forms including zero-hours and (sometimes bogus) self-employed arrangements (ONS, 2015). Second, some commentators suggest that the term 'employment relations', as distinguished from 'industrial relations' more accurately depicts the field of study under discussion. The view taken here, again in line with Williams is that the terms 'can be, and are often used interchangeably' (2014:xxiv). The value of taking an industrial relations (or indeed, employment relations) perspective, following Edwards (1995a), is that it enables a discussion of trust that captures the concepts of power, control and job regulation. Third, it is not the intention here to provide an analysis of employment relations and trust in comparative context. The chapter draws on insights from the UK employment relations landscape as any serious comparative study would need to reflect the different political, historical, economic and legal trajectories that frame different countries' institutional arrangements. This is beyond the scope of this chapter.

While many mainstream HRM-style accounts of employment relations hinge on how best to cultivate 'high trust' relations between managers and managed (Albrecht & Travaglione, 2003; Tzafrir, 2005; Saunders et al., 2014) and, on occasions, along 'partnership' lines between employers and trade unions (Ackers & Payne, 1998; Dietz, 2004), less attention is afforded to (a) why employers seek out such trust and (b) the institutional and policy factors that impact on the nature of these relations between employers and employed. Nor do such accounts reflect the material circumstances of shared working experiences that give rise to the trust that may surface *between* workers. This is essentially the logic of worker solidarity that stimulates workplace trade unionism and which employers may seek to dismantle and then attempt to reconstruct in terms of 'happy teams'. The chapter seeks to develop these arguments by establishing the nature of the labour problem (Kaufman, 1993) as this explains managerial interest in cultivating 'high trust' in the employment relationship. It also highlights contradictions in the basic premise of the employment contract itself – a contract that perpetuates an assumed equality between the parties, but which effectively underwrites the subordinate position of employees in this exchange, while at the same time obscuring what is effectively an open-ended or 'indeterminate' deal.

The industrial relations perspectives offer ways of analysing all that flows from this set of relations. While the preferred managerial (unitary) view offers important ideological support to claims about the right to manage employees, it also relies on unrealistic assumptions about the employment relationship and therefore of how to cultivate trust. These same ideological underpinnings have framed various labour management interventions, HRM included, to address the productivity problem. The pluralist perspective explains the inherently conflictual nature of the employment relationship while allowing for a discussion of how workers respond to their material conditions as waged labour, especially through the logic of collectivism (Crouch, 1979). Both accounts afford little attention to the imbalance of power between the parties, and a Marxist perspective offers one way forward in this debate.

Threading through this discussion is the inherent low trust that pervades both employers' views and dominant state policy on how best to cultivate a 'productive' employment relations climate. The state provides the regulatory framework within which employers, workers and their organizations interact, as well as being a major employer in its own right (Williams, 2014). As this chapter observes, the increasingly restrictive legal framework that applies to trade union activities, particularly with regard to industrial action, casts trade unions as part of a problem to be dealt with in the UK industrial relations landscape, rather than as part of the solution. The inference is that unions (and therefore their members) interfere with the right to manage and they cannot be trusted. And here is the conundrum. As Emmott observes, 'in order to establish and maintain high-trust workplaces, the challenge for employers going forward is to develop a deeper understanding of employer engagement, conflict management, and the values and mechanisms needed to support them' (2015:667). This implies a genuine willingness on the part of employers and the state to legitimize and welcome trade unions as integral to decision-making processes. This chapter concludes that evidence of such willingness is hardly encouraging.

The employment relationship and trust: keeping it in perspective?

Central to the discussion about trust is a need to understand the employment relationship and the associated ideological assumptions that arise from how we chose to frame this. In economic terms, and regardless of the precise terms on which labour is engaged in work, the employment relationship is a 'wage-work bargain' (Flanders, 1970; 1988) wherein the employer pays a wage in return for purchasing the capacity of workers to labour (their labour power). The employment relationship is therefore a market-based transaction, that is, an economic exchange. This implies a freedom on both parties to engage in the relationship and to freely (and equally) agree its terms, although workers are seldom in the position of being able to choose between alternatives (Cohen, 1991). The terms of employment reflect the market relations between the buyer (employer) and seller (worker) of labour (Flanders, 1975) and will therefore reflect claims to a special skill, labour market shortages, or a 'going rate' for the job that may derive from extant industry/sector-based collective agreements.

The employment relationship is then underwritten by an employment contract that also assumes equality in law of both parties to the agreement. It is actually predicated on the sub-servient position of the employee at the outset, in what is an unequal contractual set of relations (Wedderburn, 1986; Cohen, 1991). The contract upholds the right to manage in what is termed 'the prerogative contract' with its historical antecedents rooted in master and servant laws and in property rights (Selznick, 1969). Among other things, this means employees are subject to an implied common law duty to obey reasonable instructions, thereby enshrining the legal principle that enables employers to command work subordinates (Davies & Freedland, 1993). This plays out in practice through claims to the rights of managers to manage unimpeded. For example Hallier and James' 1997 study in an air traffic organization (in Cullinane and Dundon) notes:

> employee compliance with management decisions was perceived to arise primarily from a legal transaction underpinned by the notion of managerial ownership and their assumed right to redirect resources. It can be argued that management, far from accepting the obligation of reciprocal promises and inducements between employer and employee, seemed more inclined to conceive of the relationship in a manner that could be regarded as owning the employees' time and effort.

(2006:120)

It is the realization of labour power that adds value in the production process (Marx, 1976 edn; Braverman, 1974) but herein is the problem. This is an indeterminate contract: 'the worker's wage buys only the capacity to work, with this capacity being translated into actual labour within the process of production' (Edwards, 1995a:9). The precise quantities of worker effort are ambiguous as the employment contract neither guarantees the quantity (productivity) or the quality (performance) of labour that will be delivered. This gives rise to the labour problem (Kaufman, 1993) that is how to maximize the productivity and performance of labour in relation to unit labour cost. Management must therefore find ways of both controlling (maximizing) labour effort, while also securing an element of worker cooperation in the production process. This is potentially problematic when considering the concept of trust as workers must on the one hand 'be trusted' to exercise their skill in the execution of their tasks (Fox, 1974), while at the same time being subjected to close supervision and, at times, close surveillance while at work (Mather & Seifert, 2014; Carter et al., 2011; Taylor & Bain, 1999).

Workers therefore find themselves in an inherently contradictory set of contractual relations – they sell their labour power – and they must, for all alternatives are worse (Cohen, 1991) in return for wages that they will rationally seek to maximize, but such wages represent a cost to employers. The wage–work exchange effectively orientates each party to the cash nexus, emphasizing the calculative basis of the relationship that cuts across notions of mutual high trust (Salamon, 2000; Rousseau et al., 1998). This plays out on a daily basis at the point of production through a contested and uncertain set of arrangements between managers and managed, so the workplace is characterized by 'the negotiation of order' (Edwards, 1995b:45). Both parties therefore observe what the other is doing to ensure the terms of engagement are met, as far as both expect at the outset, or as Fox (1974) explains, both parties guard their side of the bargain.

Once employed, the employee is subject to the rules contained within the employment contract and must subscribe to the authority of superiors. These rules are what Flanders (1970) termed the managerial relations concerned with the regulation of workers' behaviour, effort and attitudes at work. Unitary assumptions suggest that this is an unproblematic endeavour as employers and employees are presumed to coexist harmoniously on the basis of shared or 'common interests' (Fox, 1966) or perhaps, high trust. This, then, provides the bedrock of management exaltations to the common good, happy teams and, more recently, 'can-do' cultures and myriad culture change initiatives (Mather et al., 2012). From this perspective high-trust relations are therefore simply assumed into existence, with any deviance or conflict attributed to miscreants and trouble-makers.

The unitary perspective also provides an important ideological underpinning to the managerial prerogative and the right to unilaterally regulate the labour process (Storey, 1983). From this perspective, trade unions have no legitimate role to play – if there is no conflict and employees are 'on message', then there is no need for trade unions in the workplace. For example, the CIPD's (2013) prescription for addressing the low-trust employment relations rests on improved communications and building a culture that cultivates employee behaviours in line with corporate values. This and other such HRM-style accounts of trust tend to be driven by normative assumptions and unestablished causal links between management activity, employee behaviour and performance outcomes (Guest, 2011). The concept of trust is then constructed so that it accords with a top-down, managerially driven philosophy of how employment relations *should* look, rather than as a reflection of the contested nature of the employment relationship. This is not to suggest that HRM interventions are inherently problematic, but rather, that they are underpinned by unitary assumptions and, as such, they tend to assume common rather than alternate interests in the workplace (Legge, 2005). This has implications for how trust is subsequently conceptualized and managed.

The problem is that unitarism tends to 'oversimplify the intricate network of power-based relationships between employees, employers, unions, management and the state' (Mather, 2011:205). For example, workers may define their obligations rather more narrowly that their employers (Baldamus, 1961). While they may share an interest in the success of the organization (for reasons of job security, pay and so on), there are inevitable antagonisms arising from the contested, uncertain parameters of the employment relationship already outlined here. The pluralist perspective acknowledges the legitimacy of these alternate interests and thus the emphasis shifts towards a management model that incorporates mechanisms for institutionalizing conflict and the procedures for its resolution. This denotes, at least in theory, a clear shift from management by right to management by consent (Fox, 1966). The same antagonisms around workers' interests provide the material basis of trade unionism. From this perspective, trade unions are then cast as part of the solution, rather than the cause of the problem, and they therefore have a legitimate role to play in protecting workers' interests (Williams, 2014; Crouch, 1979). Embedded within the pluralist position is an acknowledgement of two key issues that can deepen our understanding of the complexities of trust in employment relations. First, the logic of solidarity that evolves *between* groups of workers around their shared material circumstances and second, the inherently low-trust relations that characterize the unequal employment relationship (Mather, 2011). Some do argue that unionized workplaces are characterized by low trust in management (Holland et al., 2012; Guest & Conway, 1999). However such accounts focus on cultivating a positive psychological contract between employers and employees and, while valuable, the psychological contract is itself a deeply ambiguous concept. For example, Cullinane and Dundon 'unpick the construct of the psychological contract as portrayed in much of the extant literature and argue that, in its present form, it symbolizes an ideologically biased formula designed for a particular managerialist interpretation of contemporary work and employment' (2006:113).

More broadly, a Marxist perspective roots its analysis in the nature of work as an exploitative activity as workers are paid less than the value of the product of their labour (Marx, 1976 edn.; Hyman, 1975). Braverman (1974) develops this analytical device, arguing that the profit imperative drives managerial efforts to control all aspects of a labour process through division of labour and task routinization, thereby deskilling and cheapening labour. Workers become alienated from the product of their labour (Hyman, 1975) and this provides the material basis for worker solidarity and the objective basis of trade unionism. This suggests a number of issues impacting on workers and for how trust is then conceived: the extent of routinization of a task; the rate of exploitation; autonomy and the limits set on workers' discretion around task performance.

Solving the labour problem: when to use the carrot and when to use the stick?

The preferred managerial view rests on unitary assumptions and this gives rise to a range of labour management approaches, notably HRM and interest in cultivating 'high-trust relations', with high trust often assumed to be the product of 'good' HRM (Ashleigh et al., 2012; Gould-Williams, 2003; Boxall & Purcell, 2011; Young & Daniel, 2003). The overarching logic is that if managers do things 'right', then the labour problem is solved. Management authority is buttressed in this respect by the legal foundations embedded in the prerogative contract, the ideological trappings of unitarism, and claims about functional expertise (Storey, 1983). Each of these is limited with regard to solving the labour problem, not least on account of the unitary assumptions on which they rest. Hence there is a need for labour management techniques to control all aspects of workplace behaviour, so 'management desires three responses from workers: (1) subordination, (2) loyalty, and (3) productivity . . . in all its relationships with workers, management is continuously confronted with the question of where to use the carrot and where to employ the stick as it goes about the task of building a subordinated, loyal and productive workforce' (Harbison & Myers 1959:48–49). These general prescriptions offer a useful lens through which to view the concept of trust in employment relations. They need to be understood in the context of labour market developments, and in particular, the precarious nature of employment for some workers that has already been outlined in this chapter (Rubery, 2015; Adams & Deakin, 2014; TUC, 2014; Van Wanrooy et al., 2013).

Labour management strategies embracing scientific management (Taylor, 1911); human relations (Rose, 1975) and more recently human resource management are all predicated on solving this same labour problem through a combination of carrot and stick approaches. Recent workplace studies bear testament to the resilience of Taylorism (Noon et al., 2013; Mather & Seifert, 2014; Carter et al., 2011; Taylor & Bain, 1999; Bain et al., 2002; Gale, 2012) and its modern day variants that aim to secure more productive, compliant labour (Mather et al., 2012). These accounts do not point to high-trust employment relations. It is the case that trust is an two way street, but much of the mainstream literature tends to focus on how to garner trust *from* employees. So,

> the characteristic top management exhortation to rank and file employees to trust the company is often received with cynicism. In the very way it structures work, authority, and rewards it excludes them from its own high discretion, high-trust fellowship, yet asks them to submit to its discretion in handling their interests and destinies. In other words: 'we do not trust you, but we ask you nevertheless to trust us.'
>
> (Fox, 1974:76)

This raises important questions about HRM practices that can dismantle any notion of trust such as presenteeism cultures (Taylor et al., 2010), appraisal and performance management regimes (Bain et al., 2002; Mather & Seifert, 2011; Winstanley & Stuart-Smith, 1996) and skill mix changes that close down task discretion (Gale, 2012; Mather & Seifert, 2014). These measures are hardly conducive to building high-trust-based relations between managers and managed.

However, there are employers who are heavily reliant on skilled labour. The more highly skilled the job, then the more discretion will need to be afforded to these workers in discharging their tasks. There is therefore a direct relationship between skill and the degree of trust that managers cede to workers in completion of their tasks, as it is the skill that will ultimately add the value in the production process. Fox's (1974) wide-ranging analysis of low discretion (low skilled) and high discretion (skilled) jobs is helpful here in highlighting the complexities of trust in relation to skill and task discretion embedded within particular jobs and their subsequent bearing on labour management strategies. While skill is a multi-valent construct, it encapsulates overlapping debates around the skill required to actually perform the task, and the means by which groups of workers may seek to control their own occupational interests, and therefore their wages (Wood, 1987; Turner, 1962). These debates also throw light on the deskilling tendencies identified by Braverman (1974) of ever more detailed division of labour arrangements that reduce task discretion, deliver more control to managers and reduce dependence on skilled (and therefore more expensive) labour. Recent studies have revealed employee resourcing strategies focussed on precisely this trajectory (Carter et al., 2011; Mather & Seifert, 2017).

Some empirical evidence reveals widespread patterns of distrust and 'broken' promises wherein downward pressure on costs impacts negatively on employees through job insecurity (Rubery, 2015) and/or downward pressure on wages and pensions (ONS 2015; Whittaker & Hurrell, 2013), work intensification and extensification and the erosion of workers' control over their own labour (Burchell et al., 2005) and declining levels of reciprocal trust (ibid.; Worrall et al., 2010). These trends have also extended to include junior management, professional and public service work (Worrall et al., 2016; Sitala, 2013). So while the notion of reciprocal trust is much vaunted, it runs counter to some important empirical evidence that points to a widening gap between the trust rhetoric and reality within organizations (ibid.) The same evidence suggests that while senior managers call for everyone to 'get on board' and 'trust us', the views and experiences of those lower down the organizational hierarchy can be sharply juxtaposed with these espoused views from the top. As employers have sought to cut costs through reorganization, restructuring and change initiatives, this has negatively impacted on employees and they are then less likely to exhibit trust, goodwill and cooperation at work (Hudson, 2005).

Furthermore, financialization and its impact on corporate regimes has led to the externalizing of employment for many workers and this means the risks get passed from employers to employees (Thompson, 2011; 2013; Vidal, 2013; Rubery, 2015). These circumstances render trust particularly difficult to create and sustain. Likewise, temporary and zero-hours contracts (ONS,

2015; TUC, 2014) represent precarious contractual arrangements that are difficult to align with proclamations of 'valuing our employees'. The key questions become, why would workers on these contracts trust their 'employer'? And why would such employers seek out high-trust behaviours? If an employer is unhappy with the commitment and engagement of these workers then one solution is to simply replace one zero-hour contract worker with another. Of note then is the observation from recent ACAS research that the problems with these insecure contracts are

> deep-rooted, and revolve around a more profound fear of raising concerns or questions about access to rights. This hints at a significant loss of trust in the employment relationship, characterized by a sense of power imbalance which makes workers fearful of asserting their employment rights.
>
> (Gee, 2015:2)

Labour utlization strategies therefore have a direct bearing on trust and how this is actually operationalized and experienced. In this sense, the ways in which work is organized shapes social relations in the workplace that are then marked by 'patterns of trust and distrust generated by men's [sic] exercise of power over others in the pursuit of their own purposes' (Fox, 1974:15). Decisions about job design, job hierarchies and organizational structures that in turn influence the distribution of rewards, status and extent to which individuals are included (or indeed excluded) in decisions that affect their working lives runs to the heart of how workers actually perceive and experience trust: 'some, as a consequence see themselves as trusted; others see themselves as distrusted' (ibid:14). Labour management decisions therefore reflect the skills (and therefore the labour market position) of certain categories of labour. As has already been argued, skilled labour may command a premium in relation to pay, job controls and autonomy, rendering deskilling tendencies potentially attractive for employers when circumstances permit. These same highly skilled workers may be employed for their expertise – and this is a mark of professional work. The implication is that such expertise does not need to be closely managed. However, there are reports of ever closer surveillance and supervision regimes that are the hallmark of low trust (Mather & Seifert, 2014). As a consequence, employees who lack trust in managers spend time 'covering their backs' while managers invest much of their time in systems for monitoring and checking employees – 'which are likely to erode trust in management further because they are visible signs of a lack of trust in employees' (CIPD, 2013:18).

This is not to suggest that employers are omnipotent in their enactment of chosen labour management approaches. Workers can and do resist both formally and informally, and via collective and individual responses to their material experiences of work. There is therefore a dialectical interplay of management efforts and workers' responses that are symptomatic of ongoing negotiated settlements and contested terrain between the two parties (Edwards, 1979). For example, 'key ways of developing trust include training, indoctrination and assimilation' (Edwards, 1995b:53). This is revealed in Beale and Mustchin's (2014) study of Royal Mail's attempt to use an employee involvement (EI) programme to secure greater control over the content and method of communication with the workforce, while undermining well-established trade union traditions. This study reveals the inherently adversarial, low-trust relations between the two parties.

Workers also engage in their own informal work rules and behaviours to best serve their own interests (Flanders, 1970:89). This provides the basis for inter-worker solidarity and the roots of collectivism that are predicated on high trust *between* workers (Mather, 2011). The point is that workers can and do resist and thus the employment relationship is characterized by this uneasy balance of conflict and accommodation (Edwards, 1995a) and the dialectics of management action-worker reaction. Trust, and low trust, needs to be understood in this context. Essentially, then, the employment relationship rests on a web of rules (again both formal and informal) that are generated, interpreted, broken and recast as part of these ongoing dialectics. Historically, any meaningful restraint on employers has emerged from trade unions and collectivism.

Trade unions and state policy: from part of the 'solution' to the cause of the 'problem'?

While trade unionism transcends national boundaries, the focus of this discussion is with the UK context, not least on account of the diffuse institutional arrangements affecting trade union activity in different countries, as well as the different historical, political and social policy trajectories underpinning each country's trade union development, organization, structure, governance and overarching legislative framework. It is beyond the scope of this chapter to debate the origins and development of UK trade unionism, but suffice to note that its roots are embedded in both the material circumstances and sectional interests of discrete worker groups and also within the UK voluntarist tradition (Davies and Freedland, 1993). The main method is collective bargaining and

> this is not just an economic process, concerned with setting conditions on which workers are hired (i.e. market relations) but it is also a political activity since it enables workers . . . to influence and thus regulate jointly with managers, workplace decision-making.
>
> (Williams, 2014:176)

Another important aspect of UK union activity is its representational role through workplace shop stewards who act as the primary source of support for workers at the point of production. Unions also have a political arm in relation to pressing the government on broader employment rights and political issues, as articulated in TUC policy and campaigning activities.

UK trade unionism is uniquely a product of the voluntarist tradition. This historical preference for voluntarism is captured in the concept of collective laissez faire (CLF) and the system of trade union immunities (Kahn-Freund, 1964). CLF was the dominant theory in the post WWII period for describing government policy towards labour law and indeed towards the trade union movement (Davies & Freedland, 1993:8). The basic policy position underpinning CLF rested on the removal of legal obstacles to override common law barriers or impediments to trade union activities. While CLF effectively cleared the way for free collective bargaining, it did this through a system of negative law that on the one hand provided immunities from the law, but did not establish positive legal rights. Importantly then, 'there is no legal right to strike in the UK. Instead unions have immunity against legal liability for actions committed in contemplation or furtherance of a trade dispute' (Lyddon, 2015:739).

So while CLF infers a form of benign state abstentionism, it has involved a unique UK state role with regard to how trade unions were initially 'accommodated', and have subsequently been dealt with in the industrial relations framework, largely reflecting the relative, or at least perceived, power imbalance between capital and labour at a particular moment in time. Regulation of the employment relationship was thus historically cast as 'not a matter for law and legal institutions, but for the social institutions of IR (Industrial Relations), especially collective bargaining . . . self-regulation rather than legal regulation' (Davies & Freedland, 1993:10). The implication of this was that the state effectively delegated regulation to the social institutions created by employers and workers and the system of immunities provided the two parties with the freedom to engage in collective bargaining. This meant that the body of labour law concerning employment protection rights was very limited – a position that prevailed until the end of the twentieth century.

The problem is that the potential effectiveness of these self-regulatory measures, at least in so far as workers themselves are concerned, is essentially predicated on the presence and involvement of strong trade unions. State policy since 1980 has been dominated by a neoliberal discourse that has followed the Hayekian logic (Hayek, 1984) in reframing trade union 'immunities' as union privileges. This policy shift, although in evidence long before 1980 (Lyddon, 2015), presaged a raft of laws throughout the 1980s and early 1990s that among other things, significantly curtailed the ability of trade unions to engage in industrial action (ibid.). This point is important in underlining the inherent lack of trust at the level of state decision-making that pervades the fabric of UK industrial relations, particularly with regard to the role, perceived legitimacy and, indeed, active engagement of trade unions in regulating the employment relationship.

Much of the political rhetoric since 2010 has been concerned with removing the 'burden of the red tape' in the sphere of employment relations – for red tape, read protective legislation and collectivism (Rubery, 2015). The Conservative government from 2015 has subsequently mounted a further 'crackdown' on trade union activity (Wintour, 2015). The 2016 Trade Union Act underlines a clear ministerial intent to curb 'the problem' of over-powerful unions. The legal changes contained within this Act were legitimized in policy terms as being in the interests of modernizing trade union law (Pyer, 2015), with the introduction of 'representative' mandates for industrial action (higher thresholds for industrial action ballots) and provisions to enable employers to more readily make contingency plans in the event of industrial action. Interestingly as Pyer himself observed in the House of Commons Briefing Paper (2015) during the passage of the Act, there has been a general decline in strike activity apart from a spike during 2013/14 across parts of the public sector.

The propositions that underpin the Act therefore seem clear with regard to both their intent and also their inherent mistrust of trade unions and collectivism. The ministerial rationale was that threshold ballots address the perceived democratic deficit inherent in current voting arrangements with regard to industrial action, but here is the rub. There are currently no planned changes to voting arrangements to accommodate on-line or workplace ballots, so de facto the legislative changes are likely to make it more difficult for unions to achieve both the desired turnouts and indeed the voting thresholds. Arguably this is the intention. The point is that the ability of trade unions to engage effectively in collective bargaining is predicated on their ability to engage in industrial action. This offers the only means by which workers may exert their power and attempt to redress the power imbalance between employers and employed. This is not about high-trust relations between the two parties but is concerned with providing the means by which workers may combine in collective action in order to counterbalance the greater power of employer (Deakin & Morris, 2012). Essentially there appears to be little trust in the unions.

There has also been a decline in both union membership and collective bargaining coverage in the UK over the last twenty-five years (Van Wanrooy et al., 2013; Williams, 2014). At face value this may indicate that the material bases on which trade unionism was initially predicated have somehow dissipated. However, the trends in casualized, deskilled and intensified work experiences of many workers hardly bear testament to any significant material improvements in working conditions that would negate the need for collectivism. Nor are such trends any indicator of high-trust relations in the workplace. There are a range of explanations for the changing fortunes of trade unions in the UK (Bain & Price, 1983; Mason & Bain, 1993), all of which highlight factors external to the trade unions. Such explanations imply that the unions have been passive bystanders in their own misfortunes, but this is not the case.

UK trade unions have pursued a range of strategies to address membership decline and these can give rise to paradoxical outcomes. For example, on the one hand, partnership (with employers) purports to cultivate high-trust industrial relations, which is then linked to positive organizational performance (or mutual gains) (Butler et al., 2013). The basis of such arrangements is the promotion of cooperative, rather than adversarial industrial relations (Terry, 2010). The stated benefits of partnership working are therefore based on 'business benefits' attaching to the potential mutual gains it offers to employers and employees. It is supposed to enable managers to more easily gain support for organizational change, while securing greater commitment from employees. For employees there is an opportunity, via the involvement of their trade union representatives, for them to gain influence over decisions affecting their working lives. From this perspective the real essence of partnership in industrial relations should be predicated on meaningful employee participation whereby employees, via their representatives are able to influence these decisions. However such arrangements remain highly variable in practice (Williams, 2014; Terry, 2010).

While high trust may therefore be the espoused outcome of partnership deals, such agreements may actually reflect trade union weakness rather than strength (Danford et al., 2002). This then infers a more circumscribed, weakened union role that may have damaging consequences for trust *between* union members and their union as 'partnership relations detach senior activists from union members and restrict member participation and mobilisation' (ibid., 2002:1). As a consequence, 'partnership' agreements may simply offer the means by which trade unions become assimilated into the managerial decision-making process. They then enhance managerial control while restricting workplace trade unionism activity – so, unions engage in 'high-trust' partnership deals and union members become disaffected (ibid.). In summary, the argument is put that partnership arrangements 'serve managerial interests' and tend to be driven by a largely unitary perspective (Williams, 2014:198).

As an alternative, unions may pursue an organizing strategy that is based on recruiting members in new areas. The aim is to mobilize workers into union membership to articulate collective grievances, thereby challenging the managerial prerogative (Heery & Simms, 2011). This marks a departure from simply recruiting new members. Rather, its focus is on galvanizing prospective members through building a sense of collective grievance as articulated by lay activists at workplace level. This may build membership numbers and cultivate high-trust relations between members and their union, but may run counter to high trust with the employer because it is predicated on contesting employers at the point of production. Prospects for organizing were initially revitalized by the statutory recognition procedure introduced in the Employment Relations Act 1999 (one relatively recent legislative intervention that moved marginally in favour of trade unions). On the one hand, one might argue that such developments should have positively promoted employee participation among hitherto unorganized workers through the focus on new areas of work, thereby securing greater employee participation and therefore the scope for higher trust. However, the key obstacles are reported to be employer opposition and, also, some barriers internal to the unions, not least the very real pressures they face in having to represent existing members, rather than diverting scarce resource into mobilizing potential new recruits (Byford, 2011).

Although trade union membership remains relatively robust in the UK public sector (Van Wanrooy et al., 2013; BIS 2015), this sector has also been the site of significant change since the 1980s in the wake of public policy interventions driven by neoliberal ideals (Seifert & Mather,

2013). The embedding of neoliberal ideals about how best to organize, deliver and manage public services has been witnessed in the general ascendancy of New Public Management (NPM) (Hood, 1995). The importing of 'business-like', unitary-framed models of financial and labour management has had a detrimental impact on the experiences of many who work in the public services, as evidenced in reports of fragmented employment relations (Martinez-Lucio, 2015), job insecurity, work intensification and low-trust relations (Sitala, 2013; Worrall et al., 2010; Worrall et al., 2016), stress and work overload (French, 2014) and low levels of morale and dissatisfaction with pay (Mather, 2014). The more recent austerity measures have been associated with spending cuts, wage restraint and attacks on pensions, job losses, reorganizations and a 'them and us culture that increases further the distance between public sector workers and their managers' (CIPD, 2013:12). More broadly, while government policy emphasizes the need for flexible, highly skilled labour markets, the current economic conditions are characterized by 'structural demand for low-autonomy work' and the displacement of any notion of decent wages delivered by strong unions and collective bargaining (Vidal, 2013:605). All of this would suggest that trust in UK employment relations is at best a deeply ambiguous state of affairs.

Concluding remarks

This chapter has sought to throw light on the contested concept of trust in the sphere of employment relations. Trust is often reified as the silver bullet that will deliver highly competitive, productive, 'high-performing' organizations and that is that. It has been suggested here that these accounts are potentially problematic for several reasons: first, they disregard the nature of the employment relationship and how this is predicated on an unequal relationship between employers and employed at the outset; second, there is a need to engage with a range of perspectives on this relationship if we are to understand why shared interests and 'high trust' cannot simply be assumed; third, the wider UK labour market evidence highlights trends of work intensification, insecurity and low trust. All of this suggests that high-trust relations are at best contestable. It is also the case that employment relations are multi-faceted, comprising relations between employers and employed, employers and trade unions, trade unions and their members, the sectional interests of different groups of workers, and the state. This chapter has sought to provide an overview of these overlapping and interlocking strands to the trust debate – it is by necessity brief, but it serves to highlight the complexity and, indeed, the scope for alternate views in the field.

The chapter began with a brief contextual discussion of rising job insecurity and work intensification in order to sketch out the territory within which to understand the complex construct of trust between employers and employees. The argument is put that while 'high performance' is a laudable aim, there needs to be some understanding of the essence of the employment relationship itself. Its basis in the wage-work exchange is based on securing maximum labour utilization in relation to unit labour cost. This provides at the outset the basis of structured antagonisms between employers and employed. The problem is twofold. First, managers must cede control to workers at the point of production in order to realize labour potential. Second, workers can and do respond to managerial efforts to manage them. It is also the case that the objective experience of work for some is characterized by short-term, insecure contracts, low pay and attacks on pensions, as well as changes in work organization that effectively intensify their work and close down their task-based discretion.

There has therefore been an attempt here to illuminate the debate on trust through a focus on the employment relationship and a concern with the lived realities of work and with the institutions and processes that have an impact. In so doing, the discussion has reflected on how trust and, indeed, low trust can be construed in a wider sense through consideration of the interaction of a range of interrelated and overlapping factors: management attempts to secure productive workers, workers' responses to these activities, and the role of the state in shaping the framework within which these two parties engage. Against the backdrop of falling union membership levels and a decline in collective bargaining coverage, this discussion has contemplated two of the unions' strategic responses, noting some of the paradoxical outcomes with regard to trust that may flow from both partnership and organizing options. There also remain deep-seated structural factors that work against the traditional institutions and mechanisms of worker voice. For example, the chapter has highlighted how the hostile legal environment contributes to difficult terrain for trade unions and for their members. Indeed the whole fabric of state policy with regard to collective labour law appears to rest on inherent low-trust – and high-blame–stakes.

Following Edwards (1995a), the argument has been put that exposition of industrial relations as a field of study makes clear that workers' experience of employment cannot be divorced from the politics of the employment relationship and its inherently contested nature. This general proposition needs therefore to underpin any analysis of trust from an industrial relations perspective. Employers and workers (and their trade unions) engage in a process of mutually reinforcing and contested relations on a daily basis. This is played out in a context of shifting expectations and 'low levels of self-interested trust' (Mather, 2011:205). The implication is that the nature of the relationship between employers and employees is essentially predicated on low trust but there is potential to cultivate productive, high-trust relations where they incorporate meaningful independent representative structures. This is hardly achievable in a context of anti-union laws that are intent on further curbing the influence of those same representative bodies. Nor do vulnerable workers in flexible labour markets on precarious contractual arrangements necessarily buy into the high-trust, high-involvement mantra.

The focus of this chapter has been with how trust may be conceptualized within the UK context. Clearly, there exist different historical, political, legal, economic and social frameworks within which employment relations are enacted and experienced, and this renders generalizability of specific UK evidence to other countries problematic. For example, the scope for trade union engagement is variable from one country to another, dependent upon extant and historical legal interventions. Likewise, both product and labour markets may be differentiated from one country to another. It is therefore beyond the scope of this chapter to provide an account of trust in employment relations outside of the confines of the political economy and the legal framework of the UK. That said, in essence the underlying debates about the structurally determined and antagonistic nature of the employment relationship still resonate outside of the UK's geographical boundaries.

References

ACAS. (2015) Workplace trends of 2015: What they mean for you. *ACAS, in conjunction with HR zone and CIPD.* Accessed at www.acas.org.uk.

Ackers, P. and Payne, J. (1998) British trade unions and social partnership: Rhetoric, reality and strategy. *International Journal of Human Resource Management,* 9(3): 529–550.

Adams, Z. and Deakin, S. (2014) *Re-regulating zero-hours contracts.* Liverpool, UK: Institute of Employment Rights.

Albrecht, S. and Travaglione, A. (2003) Trust in public sector senior management. *International Journal of Human Resource Management,* 14(1): 76–92.

Ashleigh, M.J., Higgs, M. and Dulewicz. V. (2012) Exploring the relationship between propensity to trust and individual well-being: The implications for HR policies and practices. *Human Resources Management Journal,* 21: 360–376.

Bain, G. and Price, R. (1983) Union growth: Dimensions, determinants and density In G. Bain. (ed.) *Industrial Relations in Great Britain*. Oxford, UK: Blackwell, 3–33.

Bain, P., Watson, A., Mulvey, G., Taylor, P. and Gall, G. (2002) Taylorism, targets and the pursuit of quantity and quality by call centre management. *New Technology, Work and Employment*, 17(3): 70–185.

Baldamus, W. (1961) *Efficiency and Effort*. London: Tavistock.

Beale, D. and Mustchin, S. (2014) The bitter recent history of employee involvement at Royal Mail: An aggressive management agenda versus resilient workplace unionism. *Economic and Industrial Democracy*, 35(2): 289–308.

Boxall, P. and Purcell J. (2011) *Strategy and Human Resource Management*, (3rd edn). Basingstoke, UK: Palgrave Macmillan.

Braverman, H. (1974) *Labor and Monopoly Capital: The Degradation of Work in the Twentieth Century*. New York: Monthly Review Press.

Burchell, B., Lapido, D. and Wilkinson, F. (eds) (2005) *Job Insecurity and Work Intensification*. London: Routledge.

Butler, P., Tesgaskis, O. and Glover, L. (2013) Workplace partnership and employee involvement – contradictions and synergies: Evidence from a heavy engineering case study. *Economic and Industrial Democracy*, 24(1): 5–24.

Byford, I. (2011) Union renewal and young people: Some positive indications from British supermarkets In G. Gall (ed.) *Union Organising: Current Practice, Future Prospects*. London: Macmillan, 223–238.

Carter, B., Danford, A., Howcroft, D., Richardson, M., Smith, A. and Taylor, P. (2011) 'All they lack is a chain': Lean and the new performance management in the British civil service. *New Technology, Work and Employment*, 26(2): 83–97.

Carter, B. and Stevenson, H. (2012) Teachers, workforce remodelling and the challenge to labour process analysis. *Work, Employment and Society*, 26(3): 481–496.

CIPD. (2013) *Megatrends: Are Organisations Losing the Trust of Their Workers?* London: CIPD.

Cohen, G.A. (1991) *Karl Marx's Theory of History: A Defence*. Oxford, UK: Oxford University Press.

Crouch, C. (1979) *Industrial Conflict in Modern Britain*. London: Croom Helm.

Cullinane, N. and Dundon, T. (2006) The psychological contract: A critical review. *International Journal of Management Reviews*, 8(2): 113–129.

Danford, A., Richardson, M. and Upchurch, M. (2002) 'New unionism', organising and partnership: An analysis of union renewal strategies in the public sector. *Capital and Class*, 76: 1–27.

Davies, P. and Freedland, M. (eds) (1993) *Kahn-Freund's Labour and the Law* (3rd edn). London: Stevens.

Deakin, S. and Morris, G.S. (2012) *Labour Law* (6th edn). Oxford, UK: Hart Publishing.

Department for Business Innovation and Skills. (BIS) (2016) *Trade Union Membership 2015 Statistical Bulletin*, London Deprtment for Business Innovation and Skills. Accessed at www.gov.uk/govenrment/statistics/trade–union-statitics-2015

Dietz, G. (2004) Partnership and the development of trust in British workplaces. *Human Resource Management*, 14(1): 5–24.

Edwards, R. (1979) Contested terrain: The Transformation of the workplace of the twentieth century. London: Heinemann.

Edwards, P. (1995a) *Industrial Relations: Theory and Practice in Britain*. Oxford, UK: Blackwell.

Edwards, P. (1995b) From industrial relations to the employment relationship: The development of research in Britain. *Industrial Relations*, 50(1): 39–65.

Emmott, M. (2015) Employment relations over the last 50 years: Confrontation, consensus or neglect? *Employee Relations*, 37(6): 658–669.

Gale, J. (2012) Government reforms, performance management and the labour process: The case of officers in the UK probation service. *Work, Employment and Society*, 26(5): 882–838.

Gee, S. (2015) *What Part Will Atypical Contracts Play in the Future of Working Life?* London: ACAS.

Gould-Williams, J. (2003) The importance of HR practices and workplace trust in achieving superior performance: A study of public sector organization. *International Journal of Human Resource Management*, 14(1): 28–54.

Guest, D. (2011) Human resource management and performance: Still searching for some answers. *Human Resource Management Journal*, 21(1): 3–13.

Guest, D. and Conway, N. (1999) Peeping into the black hole: The downside of the new employment relations in the UK. *British Journal of Industrial Relations*, 37(3): 367–389.

Holland, P., Cooper, B.K. and Pyman, A. (2012) Trust in management: The role of employee voice arrangements and perceived managerial opposition to unions. *Human Resource Management Journal*, 22(4): 377–391.

Flanders, A. (1970) *Management and Unions: The Theory and Reform of Industrial Relations.* London: Faber.

Flanders, A. (1975) *Management and Unions.* London: Faber and Faber.

Fox, A. (1966) *Industrial Sociology and Industrial Relations. Research Paper No.3, Royal Commission on Trade Unions and Employers' Associations.* London: HMSO.

Fox, A. (1974) *Beyond Contract: Work, Power and Trust Relations.* London: Faber and Faber.

French, S. (2014) *Public Services at Risk: The Implications of Work Intensification for the Wellbeing and Effectiveness of PCS Members. Full Report of the 2013 PCS Workload and Work-Life Survey.* London: Public and Commercial Services Union.

French, S. (2015) Fair and sustainable? The implications of work intensification for the wellbeing and effectiveness of PGA members: Report of the PGA Working Time, Workload and Work-Life Balance Survey 2015, available at prison-governors-association.org.uk.

Hayek, F. (1984) *The 1980s, Unemployment and the Unions.* London: Institute of Economic Affairs.

Harbison, F. and Myers, C. (1959) *Management in the Industrial World.* New York: McGraw-Hill.

Heery, E. and Simms, M. (2011) Seizing an opportunity? Union organizing campaigns in Britain 1998–2004. *Labor History,* 52(1): 23–47.

Hood, C. (1995) The 'New Public Management' in the 1980s: Variations on a theme. *Accounting, Organizations and Society,* 20(2/3): 93–109.

Hudson, M. (2005) Flexibility and the reorganisation of work. In Burchell et al. *op cit.* 39–60.

Hyman, R. (1975) *Industrial Relations: A Marxist Introduction.* London: Macmillan.

Kahn-Freund, O. (1964) Legal framework. In A. Flanders and H. Clegg (eds) *The System of Industrial Relations in Great Britain.* Oxford: Blackwell: 42–127.

Kaufman, B. (1993) *The Origins and Evolution of the Field of Industrial Relations in the United States.* Ithaca, NY: Cornell University Press.

Legge, K. (2005) *Human Resource Management: Rhetoric and Realities.* Basingstoke, UK: Palgrave Macmillan.

Lyddon, D. (2015) The changing pattern of UK strikes, 1964–2014. *Employee Relations,* 37(6): 733–745.

Martinez Lucio, M. (2015) Beyond consensus: The state and industrial relations in the United Kingdom from 1964 to 2014. *Employee Relations,* 37(6): 692–704.

Marx, K. (1976) *Capital: A Critique of Political Economy* (Volume 1). Harmondsworth, UK: Penguin.

Mason, B. and Bain, P. (1993) The determinants of trade union membership in Britain: A survey of the literature. *Industrial and Labour Relations Review,* 46(2): 332–355.

Mather, K. (2011) Employee relations and the illusion of trust. In R. Searle and D. Skinner (eds) *Trust and Human Resource Management.* London: Edward Elgar, 201–222.

Mather, K. and Seifert, R. (2011) Teacher, lecturer or labourer? Performance management issues in education. *Management in Education,* 25(1): 26–31.

Mather, K. (2014) *Under pressure and 'the whole umbrella's going to have to come down': Capturing the voices of NHS workers.* Submission (with UNISON) to NHS Pay Review 2015–2016: Special Remit on Seven-Day Services, available at www.unison.org.uk

Mather, K. and Seifert, R. (2014) The close supervision of further education lecturers: 'You have been weighed, measured and found wanting'. *Work Employment and Society,* 28(1): 95–111

Mather, K. and Seifert, R. (2017) Heading for disaster: Extreme work and skill mix changes in the emergency services of England. *Capital & Class,* 41(1): 3–22.

Mather, K., Worrall, L. and Mather, G. (2012) Engineering compliance and worker resistance in UK further education – The creation of the Stepford Lecturer. *Employee Relations,* 34(5): 534–554.

Office for National Statistics. (2015) Employee contracts that do not guarantee a minimum number of hours – 2015 update, September, available at www.ons.org.uk.

Noon, M., Blyton, P. and Morrell, K. (2013) *The Realities of Work: Experiencing Work and Employment in Contemporary Society.* Basingstoke, UK: Palgrave Macmillan.

Pyer, D. (2015) The Trade Union Bill. House of Commons Briefing Paper CBP 7295, September.

Rousseau, D., Sitkin, S., Burt, R. and Camerer, C. (1998) Not so different after all: A cross-discipline view of trust. *Academy of Management Review,* 23(3): 393–404.

Rose, M. (1975) Reassessing Human Relations In *Industrial Behaviour,* (1st edn). Harmondsworth, UK: Penguin,103–112.

Royles, D. (2010) A point of inflection for HR in the NHS. *Human Resource Management Journal,* 20(4): 329–331.

Rubery, J. (2015) Change at work: Feminisation, flexibilisation, fragmentation and financialisation. *Employee Relations,* 37(6): 633–644.

Salamon, M. (2000) *Industrial Relations Theory and Practice,* (4th edn). Harlow, UK: Pearson Education.

Saunders, N.K., Dietz, G. and Thornhill, A. (2014) Trust and distrust: Polar opposites, or independent but co-existing? *Human Relations*, 67(6): 639–665.

Seifert, R. and Mather, K. (2013) Neo-Liberalism at work: A case study of the reform of the emergency services in the UK. *Review of Radical Political Economics*, 45(4): 456–462.

Selznick, P. (1969) *Law, Society and Industrial Justice*. New York: Russell Sage.

Sitala, J. (2013) New public management: The evidence-based worst practice? *Administration and Society*, 46(4): 468–493

Storey, J. (1983) *Managerial Prerogative and the Question of Control*. London: Routledge.

Taylor, F.W. (1911) *Scientific Management*. New York: Harper Bros.

Taylor, P. and Bain, P. (1999) 'An assembly line in the head': Work and employee relations in the call centre. *Industrial Relations Journal*, 30(2): 101–117.

Taylor, P., Cunningham, I., Newsome, K. and Scholarios, D. (2010) 'Too scared to go sick' – reformulating the research agenda on sickness absence. *Industrial Relations Journal*, 41(4): 270–288.

Terry, M. (2010) Employee Representation In T. Colling and M. Terry (eds) *Industrial Relations: Theory and Practice*. Chichester, UK: John Wiley, 275–297.

Thompson, P. (2011) The trouble with HRM, Provocation Series Paper. *Human Resource Management Journal*, 21(4): 355–367.

Thompson, P. (2013) Financialization and the workplace: Extending and applying the disconnected capitalism thesis. *Work, Employment and Society*, 27(3): 472–488.

TUC. (2014) *Ending the Abuse of Zero-Hours Contracts*. London: TUC.

Turner, H. A. (1962) *Trade Union Growth, Structure and Policy*. London: Allen and Unwin.

Tzafrir, S. (2005) The relationship between trust, HRM practices and firm performance. *International Journal of Human Resource Management*, 16(9): 1600–1622.

Van Wanrooy, B., Bewley, H., Bryson, A., Forth, J., Freeth, S., Stokes, L. and Wood, S. (2013) *Employment Relations in the Shadow of Recession: Findings from the 2011 Workplace Employment Relations Study*. London: Palgrave.

Vidal, M. (2013) Low-autonomy work and bad jobs in postfordist capitalism. *Human Relations*, 66(4): 587–612.

Wedderburn (Lord). (1986) *The Worker and the Law*. Harmondsworth, UK: Penguin.

Whittaker, M. and Hurrell, A. (2013) *Low Pay Britain*. London: Resolution Foundation.

Williams, S. (2014) *Contemporary Employment Relations: A Critical Introduction*. Oxford, UK: Oxford University Press.

Winstanley, D. and Stuart-Smith, K. (1996) Policing performance: The ethics of performance management. *Personnel Review*, 25(6): 66–84.

Wintour, P. (2015) Biggest crackdown on trade unions for 30 years launched by conservatives. *The Guardian*, 15 July.

Wood, S. (1987) The deskilling debate: New technology and work organisations. *Acta Sociologica*, 30(1): 3–24.

Worrall, L., Mather, K. and Seifert, R. (2010) Solving the labour problem among professional workers in the UK public sector: Organisation change and performance management. *Public Organization Review*, 10: 117–137.

Worrall, L., Mather, K. and Cooper, C. (2016) The changing nature of professional and managerial work: issues and challenges from an empirical study of the UK. In A. Wilkinson, D. Hislop and C. Coupland (eds) *Perspectives on Contemporary Professional Work*. London: Edward Elgar, 60–85.

Young, L. and Daniel, K. (2003) Affectual trust in the workplace. *International Journal of Human Resource Management*, 14(1): 139–55.

22

INDIVIDUAL TRUST AND THE INTERNET

Lisa van der Werff, Colette Real and Theodore G. Lynn

Introduction

The emergence of Web 2.0 technologies and associated services heralded a second generation of the internet emphasizing collaboration and sharing among users. This resulted in a seismic shift in the relationship between individual consumers and firms but also between individual consumers and the internet as a system. Consumers, not firms, became an emerging locus of value production and through the ability to publish and connect with known and unknown others, an emerging locus of power (Berthon, Pitt, Plangger, & Shapiro, 2012). Powered by broadband telecommunications and device connectivity, the intensity of these changes was further deepened by being freed from the desktop to the mobile web. We are more connected now than ever before. The high levels of societal interconnectedness encouraged by the internet have made trust an even more vital ingredient in today's society (Hardin, 2006). The more recent development of Web 3.0 technology emphasizes ubiquitous connectivity and a machine-facilitated understanding of information that may once more change the locus of activity, value production and control. In order to keep pace with the issues of contemporary society, trust researchers must consider the how trust relationships and perceptions operate and are influenced by the online environment.

This chapter will discuss how traditional trust concepts translate to the online context and will examine empirical literature on online trust at three different levels. Interpersonal trust between individuals using the internet as a medium for communication is particularly relevant in a world where personal and professional relationships are increasingly mediated by technology. We will also discuss the role of the internet in relationships between individuals and organizations with particular attention to the provision of e-services. Finally, we discuss trust in the system of the internet itself as a distributed connected infrastructure made up of indirect system service providers which are often nameless or in the background. Our focus in the chapter is on individual trust in other individuals, organizations and the system of the internet itself. Trust from the perspective of the organization may also be of interest to trust scholars. This includes issues relating to organizational trust in individuals, inter-organizational trust and organizational trust in the system of the internet itself however these topics are outside of the scope of this chapter (see Perks & Halliday, 2003; Ratnasingam, 2005).

Traditional trust theory in an internet context

As can be seen from previous chapters, the topic of trust has attracted scholarly attention across a range of disciplines. This research attention has led to an overabundance of possible definitions for the construct. However, irrespective of the discipline, two key components are common to the majority of trust definitions: a willingness to be vulnerable and a perception of the intentions of the other party (Lewicki & Brinsfield, 2012). Reflecting these commonalities, Rousseau and colleagues (1998) propose a cross-disciplinary definition of trust as 'a psychological state comprising the intention to accept vulnerability based upon positive expectations of the intentions or behaviour of another' (Rousseau, Sitkin, Burt, & Camerer, 1998, p. 395). This is the perspective from which we will approach the discussion of trust in the internet context.

The positive expectations identified in Rousseau's definition are thought to be based predominantly on perceptions of the other party's ability, benevolence and integrity collectively known as trustworthiness (Mayer, Davis, & Schoorman, 1995). A smaller body of literature points to either predictability (Dietz & Den Hartog, 2006; McKnight, Cummings, & Chervany, 1998) or value congruence as possible fourth sub-dimensions of trustworthiness perceptions. However, the Mayer et al. trustworthiness concept incorporates a moral conceptualization of integrity that includes a value congruence between trustor and trustee as a necessary component (Tomlinson, Lewicki, & Ash, 2014). Evidence regarding these trustworthiness dimensions is collected to allow an individual to make a trust decision on the basis of which that individual may engage in trust behaviour (McEvily, Perrone, & Zaheer, 2003). The context of the internet has a number of important implications for these commonly accepted characteristics of the trust process. First, many decisions to trust online are likely to involve trust in a number of known and unknown referents. For instance, a decision to buy groceries online may be influenced by trust in the retailer (organizational trust), trust in the individuals who will select or deliver your groceries (interpersonal trust), trust in the online payment system and trust in the internet itself (system-level trust).

Second, whether each of the trustworthiness dimensions is applicable to all possible referents in an online environment is the subject of debate. At an individual and organizational level, it could be expected that the components of trustworthiness perceptions would translate relatively neatly to the internet context, although the evidence on which these perceptions are based may be quite different (see McKnight & Chervany, 2001 for discussion). In essence, the internet in many situations acts a medium through which individuals and organizations can communicate and many of the same trust cues can be perceived. However, with regards to system-level trust, such as trust in web-based software applications or in the internet itself, the applicability of ability, benevolence, integrity and predictability is not unequivocal. Consider for example judging the trustworthiness of an IT application. It may be possible to make a competence or ability judgement or an evaluation of predictability, but is it possible to make a benevolence or integrity judgement about another party that does not have agency? Some scholars have argued that these traditional trust concepts are not suitable for discussing trust in IT systems (Friedman, Khan, & Howe, 2000).

However, a number of scholars have endeavoured to apply traditional trust theory to the context of automated systems. Notable among these is the work of Harrison McKnight and colleagues along with that of Matthias Söllner. Drawing on Lee and See (2004), Söllner and colleagues propose a model of technology system trust antecedents that includes performance, purpose and process (Hoffman & Söllner, 2014; Söllner, Pavlou, & Leimeister, 2013). Within this model, performance is an indicator of ability like constructs such as competence, reliability and information accuracy. Purpose (sometimes referred to as helpfulness) represents an assessment

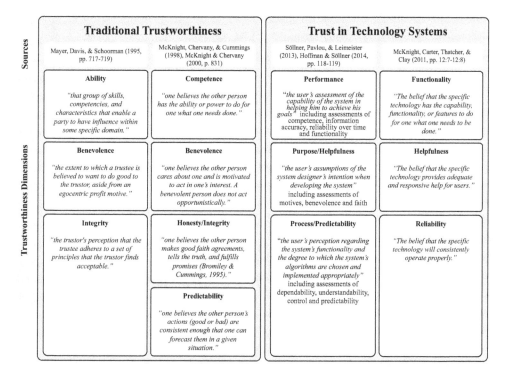

Figure 22.1 Comparing models of trustworthiness across contexts

of the motives and benevolence of developers, while process reflects user perceptions of the predictability, consistency, dependability and understandability of the system. In a similar vein, McKnight and colleagues put forward a model of attributes of information technology that contribute to trust in a technology system. Their subdimensions of functionality, helpfulness and reliability are proposed to map directly to the more traditional ability, benevolence, integrity and predictability characteristics. Thus far, the issue of value congruence remains largely unaddressed in the context of trustworthiness cues for technology systems. Figure 22.1 displays how seminal models of trustworthiness have been translated in this context.

Third, in interpersonal trust relationships trust behaviour and behavioural intentions are often portrayed as cooperation (Deutsch, 1958) or reliance and disclosure intentions (Gillespie, 2003). A common critique of the trust literature is that there is a scarcity of theoretical and empirical research exploring actual trust behaviour, as opposed to trust intentions or cooperative behaviour in a laboratory setting. This criticism has been addressed to some extent in the online environment where a more specific context has allowed researchers to explore trust behaviours in more detail. Risk taking in a relationship has been operationalized in the online context as a variety of behaviours including purchasing behaviours (Lim, Sia, Lee, & Benbasat, 2006; Pavlou & Dimoka, 2006) and interaction with technology (McKnight et al., 2011).

Vulnerability and assurance on the internet

Do perceptions of risk and vulnerability differ in an online context from those discussed in the traditional trust literature? What do individuals or organizations do to alleviate these concerns?

While many similarities exist between online and offline trust relationships (Corritore, Kracher, & Wiedenbeck, 2003), significant differences are also apparent. In line with our discussion above, trust interactions with individuals or organizations online will generally be complicated by trust in the system of the internet itself and third-party organizations that may be involved in supporting the technology (Beldad, de Jong, & Steehouder, 2010). Many online trust interactions are also characterized by a lack of face-to-face interaction, an asymmetry in the information available to each party and privacy concerns.

A lack of face to face interaction in online relationships can impede trust development through the removal of physical cues such as gestures, eye contact and facial expressions (Jarvenpaa & Leidner, 1998). At an organizational level, research suggests that trust can transfer from offline to online if there is evidence that the organization providing the web service also has physical premises (Stewart, 2003). Similarly, information asymmetry between parties interacting online is driven by physical separation between individuals and a relative lack of opportunity to monitor previous behaviour, which influences the quantity and quality of information shared between them. Typically, in e-commerce relationships, information asymmetry is thought to favour the vendor leaving the buyer with high levels of uncertainty (Pavlou, Liang, & Xue, 2006).

Online information privacy is a key concern for the digital consumer (for an overview see Grant & Waite, 2013). Information privacy describes issues relevant to access to personal information that is individually identifiable (Smith, Dinev, & Xu, 2011). Concerns regarding privacy violations can be categorized according to whether they relate to social, institutional (Brandtzaeg, Luders, & Skjetne, 2010) or malicious third-party privacy. Social privacy issues relate to the risks involved in other users sharing information you have disclosed to them, such as making private communications public. Institutional privacy refers to the unauthorized use of personal information by organizations you have disclosed information to, for instance, sharing customer data with third-party organizations for marketing purposes. In contrast, concerns related to malicious third parties cover security and privacy threats from insider misbehaviour, and externally from malevolent third parties such as cybercriminals. Consideration of privacy and security-related issues is important to understanding online trust, as empirical research demonstrates that perceptions of privacy and security are key antecedents of trust in e-commerce transactions (Pavlou & Chellappa, 2001).

In the face of these risks and vulnerabilities, there are a number of system-level cues which may be important to building trust at individual and organizational levels by providing a sense of security and a reduction in feelings of uncertainty. In their seminal paper on initial trust, McKnight et al. (1998) posit that institution- or system-based trust is composed of structural assurances and perceptions of situational normality. Structural assurance refers to the safeguards and regulations inherent in the context that are likely to govern or restrict certain behaviours. In the internet environment, cues for such structural assurances may include affiliations with a third party, seals of approval, policy or guarantee statements, firewalls, encryption mechanisms and contact details for representatives of an overseeing organization (Gefen, Karahanna, & Straub, 2003; Pavlou, 2003). Structural assurances such as these have been reported to significantly reduce system-related uncertainty and build trust (Kim & Prabhakar, 2002). In light of this, many government and industry-level organizations introduce regulations and monitoring mechanisms to govern conduct around compliance to a set of minimum standards across industries and organizations as well as mandatory rules on disclosure. However, outside of the online context, the influence of control mechanisms on trust has been the focus of a long history of debate. Empirical research has shown that control mechanisms are seldom flawless (Sitkin & Roth, 1993) and may even undermine cooperation (Fehr & Gächter, 2002).

Situational normality describes the extent to which the setting is perceived as normal, customary and in proper order (McKnight et al., 1998). In the context of the internet, feelings of familiarity are reported to be an important predictor of trust in online organizations (Bhattacherjee, 2002; Gefen, 2000). Situational normality influences trust both directly and indirectly via perceptions of how easy a technology is to use (Gefen et al., 2003). Furthermore, when experience with a technology matches expectations, users report positive attitudes towards that technology while unmet expectations lead to negative consequences (Lankton, McKnight, & Thatcher, 2014). The concept of situational normality has been applied repeatedly in the design of IT applications. For instance, many cloud-based storage services (e.g. Dropbox, Office365, Apple iCloud) offer folder solutions that are designed to integrate and look very similar to those provided by the user's chosen operating system.

Empirical research on trust and the internet

Research examining trust in an online context has been conducted across a range of disciplines including human–computer interaction, organizational behaviour, economics and marketing, and management information systems. This section of the chapter will draw together some of the research from these areas to explore the issues of individual trust in individuals, organizations and technology systems in the context of the internet.

Interpersonal trust online

Online interaction between individuals is increasing for professional and personal purposes alongside the globalization and virtualization of work and the popularity of social networks and cross-platform mobile messaging applications. Using the internet as a medium for communication, we interact with known and unknown others through channels such as email, social media, instant messaging and online video conferencing.

As a critical ingredient of positive social interaction, trust is regularly cited as a potential hurdle for effective online communication (Naquin & Paulson, 2003). Early theoretical work from Green and Gillespie (2014) suggests that online interactions are experienced as increasingly distant and abstract, and thus more difficult for trust building, depending on the extent to which they are temporally, spatially and geographically separate. Communication methods such as online teleconferencing are affected only by geographic separation while text-based, online communication is also characterized by spatial separation as no physical or non-verbal cues are available. In addition, text-based communications can also be temporally separated depending on whether the interaction happens in real time (e.g. live chat) or has potential to be time lagged (e.g. email). Effective communication in such scenarios is impacted by the challenge of communicating affective and relational information through text-based online communication (Walther, 1995). This is a problem which has arisen through an emphasis on work effectiveness and neglect of socioemotional communication in designing computer-mediated communication technology (Redfern & Naughton, 2002). Naquin and colleagues argue that psychological distance triggers different norms for appropriate behaviour and increases the likelihood of deceptive behaviour (Naquin, Kurtzberg, & Belkin, 2010). Interestingly in online avatar interactions, where visual cues are re-embedded into the online context, alterations to avatar appearance influence trust in the party represented by that avatar (Peña & Yoo, 2014). In fact, some research suggests that avatar-mediated student communications show no significant differences from video conferencing in terms of affective trust or perceptions of social closeness (Bente, Ruggenberg, Kramer, & Eschenburg, 2008).

While the majority of personal and workplace relationships now include some degree of virtual interaction, a large body of research has been dedicated to the study of virtual work including virtual teams and virtual leadership (for a full discussion see Gilson, Maynard, Young, Vartianen, & Hakonen, 2015). Virtual teams are characterized by geographical dispersion and a reliance on information technology as their primary means of coordinating work (Hertel, Geister, & Konradt, 2005). Approximately 66 percent of multinational organizations use virtual teams to organize their workforce (Society for Human Resource Management, 2012) and this number continues to rise (Gilson et al., 2015). The importance of trust for collaboration is widely acknowledged, and virtual team researchers argue that trust is even more vital for collaboration in virtual work where individuals experience a high level of self-direction and self-control (Robert, Dennis, & Hung, 2009). Robert et al. (2009) demonstrate that higher perceptions of the risk involved in interacting via the internet decrease as virtual teams gather more information about each other. Henttonen and Blomqvist (2005) argue that trust can be built in virtual teams through positive communication behaviours such as timely responding, provision of feedback and openness. For leaders of virtual teams and organizations, typically referred to as e-leaders (see Avolio, Kahai, & Dodge, 2000), appearing available and engaging in informal personal communication is important to building follower trust (Savolainen, 2014). Over time, computer-mediated teams can develop levels of trust comparable to traditional face-to-face teams, but trust starts out at a lower level and takes longer to develop in computer mediated teams, influenced by the more limited communication medium (Wilson, Straus, & McEvily, 2006).

Outside of the work environment, individuals use the internet to establish and maintain a host of personal relationships. Social media platforms are designed to allow users to create and share information with others creating a conflict between sociability, social capital and heightened visibility for shared content on one side and privacy on the other (Brandtzaeg et al., 2010). Many of these platforms present the opportunity for interaction with individuals or groups of individuals who are largely unknown and often likely to remain unknown to the user. For instance, social media platforms like Twitter involve communicating information to a wide network of followers with the potential for that information to be shared far beyond one's own social network. These new media offer interesting avenues for the study of interpersonal interaction and trust at an individual level. In particular, the internet offers individuals increased control over self-presentation and impression management (Ellison, Heino, & Gibbs, 2006) and identity misrepresentation which may have important implications for trust. Unfortunately, much of the research on trust in this context has focused on the social media platform itself as the referent rather than other users.

Individual trust in online organizations

Consumer trust relationships with organizations in the context of the internet resemble offline trust interactions with organizations in that they involve conditions of risk and vulnerability for the consumer as a result of reliance on an organization. However, as discussed above, the context of the internet brings some unique aspects of the trust relationship into consideration. For organizations providing services over the internet, consumer trust in web-based services is critical to enable three risk-taking behaviours: following advice from the website organization; sharing personal information with the organization via the website; and making purchases from the organization via the website (McKnight, Choudhury, & Kacmar, 2002). Much of the research carried out in this area has been in the context of e-commerce, with limited attention focused on other types of e-services such as e-health and e-government. This section draws on several review papers (Beldad et al., 2010; Wang & Emurian, 2005; Gräbner-Krauter & Kalusha, 2003) in discussing the empirical research on trust in online organizations. For the purposes of this section, we have organized our discussion into three categories: website characteristics, organizational characteristics and the external environment.

Website characteristics

The impression, content and interactive experience of a website can influence consumer trust perceptions of the organization it represents, in a similar manner to the influence of the physical premises of an organization and interaction with its agents. For instance, website visual design factors such as colour and graphics can influence trust beliefs. Cool pastel colour tones, symmetrical colour balance, low brightness and use of 3D dynamic graphic effects have been shown to bring about feelings of trustworthiness (Kim & Moon, 1998). However, preferences for visual factors have been found to vary across culture (Cyr, Head, & Larios, 2010) and gender (Tuch, Bargas-Avila, & Opwis, 2010), limiting the usefulness of website aesthetics to elicit trust in a universal context. Research suggests that individuals are also influenced by less aesthetic factors such as perceived ease of use and information quality. Perceived ease of use in the context of the internet consists of easy website navigation enabled by the overall structure, organization and accessibility of information, and has a key impact on the formation of trust in e-commerce (Bart, Shankar, Sultan & Urban, 2005; Flavián, Guinalíu, & Gurrea, 2006; Koufaris & Hampton-Sosa, 2004). Furthermore, quality of website information (accuracy, currency, clarity, completeness) is critical for online trust in e-organizations (Bart et al., 2005; Kim, Song, Braynov, & Rao, 2005; Liao, Palvia, & Lin, 2006).

Although, both aesthetic and practical website features are important cues for trusting an organization, researchers have yet to agree how these factors interact. Evidence suggests that a balance is needed between good website design to attract a consumer, and good website content to retain a consumer. Consumers may never reach a stage of information quality assessment if they reject the site early on because of poor website design, but once the design is acceptable to them, quality of information becomes key to building trust (Sillence, Briggs, Harris, & Fishwick, 2007). Other researchers (e.g. Li & Yeh, 2010) have suggested that the impact of design aesthetics on trust is mediated by perceptions of usefulness and ease of use. In contrast, Seckler and colleagues suggest that website design issues are more likely to influence perceptions of distrust, whereas trust is based on social factors such as reviews or recommendations by friends (Seckler, Heinz, Forde, Tuch, & Opwis, 2015).

Another theme in the website trust literature is the influence of social and relational factors on online trust. Social presence cues, such as socially rich text content, personalized greetings, human photos, audios or videos, live chats and online user numbers, can make impersonal online interactions more personal thereby increasing levels of trust (Cyr, Hassanein, Head, & Ivanov, 2007; Hassanein & Head, 2007) especially the benevolence aspects of trust (Gefen & Straub, 2004). However, reactions to the use of photographs on websites can be mixed, ranging from enthusiasm to suspicion, and they can be considered as superfluous to functionality or even manipulative (Riegelsberger & Sasse 2002, Riegelsberger, Sasse, & McCarthy, 2003), suggesting care is needed in this aspect of trust elicitation. Similarly, customization – tailoring websites, products and services to target users – and personalization – the inclusion of personal information – can improve levels of trust (Beldad et al., 2010; Koufaris & Hampton-Sosa, 2004). However, concerns for privacy in these instances can undermine trust particularly if information is collected covertly (Aguirre, Mahr, Grewal, de Ruyter, & Wetzels, 2015).

Finally, consumer perceptions of website security and privacy are vital for online trust (Kim, Ferrin, & Rao, 2008). The inclusion of strong privacy policy declarations on the website can improve levels of trust (Lauer & Deng, 2007). Indeed, the mere existence of a privacy policy may serve to build trust, regardless of the content, as many consumers ignore the actual policy and assume it is similar to others (Pan & Zinkhan, 2006). Organizations often try to communicate security and privacy through the use of independent third-party certification evidenced by the presence of seals of approval on a website. These seals communicate that the organization adheres to the seal programme's standards and principles, and can be successful trust-building mechanisms in e-commerce (Aiken & Bousch, 2006; Chang, Cheung, & Tang, 2013; Hu, Wu, Wu, & Zhang, 2010), although research findings in this area are mixed (e.g. Kim, Ferrin, & Rao, 2008). Trust seals can be classified into three categories: security seals, privacy seals and business identity seals (Hu et al., 2010, Özpolat & Jank, 2015). Security seals (e.g. VeriSign, McAfee, GoDaddy) certify that data transmission is secure through SSL technologies and that the website is protected against malware. Privacy seals (e.g. TRUSTe, VeraSafe) certify that the website retailer has a privacy policy regarding consumer data confidentiality. Business identity seals (e.g. BBB, buySAFE) certify that the website retailer is a real, trustworthy business. Trust seals have been shown to be more effective for small online retailers and new shoppers, compensating for both shopper experience and seller sales volume (Özpolat & Jank, 2015). Trust seals have been shown to have a greater effect on perceived trustworthiness than either objective third-party reviews or declarations of advertising investment by a retailer (Aiken & Boush, 2006). However, the presence of too many seals can lower the likelihood of purchase completion (Özpolat & Jank, 2015), and combined multiple function seals are not necessarily more effective than single function seals (Hu et al., 2010).

Organization characteristics

In addition to characteristics of the website, consumer trust in an organization is also influenced by more direct perceptions of the organization itself. A number of organizational characteristics have been reported to impact individual trust in online organizations. Specifically, satisfaction with previous online transactions with a particular company allows organizations to build a more long-term trusting relationship with their consumers (Casaló, Flavián, & Guinalíu, 2007; Pavlou, 2003). An offline presence has also been shown to enhance online trust (Kuan & Bock, 2007), although not when the offline and online channels are poorly integrated (Teo & Liu, 2007). Similarly, perceived size of an e-service organization may have an impact on trust, although research results in this area are mixed (Jarvenpaa, Tractinsky, & Vitale, 2000; Teo & Liu, 2007).

Consumers who do not have previous experience with an online e-service vendor often rely on the reputation of that vendor when making a trust decision (e.g. Jarvenpaa, Tractinsky, & Saarinen, 1999; McKnight et al., 2002). Similar to offline transactions, trust can result from being well-known and well-respected (e.g. Kim, Ferrin, & Rao, 2003), and from word-of-mouth within a consumer's social network (Kuan & Bock, 2007). Uniquely, the nature and scale of the internet facilitates easy provision of feedback from a wider set of previous buyers in relation to their experience of specific products or sellers, via online feedback mechanisms (Dellarocas, 2003) and reputation systems (Jøsang, Ismail, & Boyd, 2007; Resnick, Zeckhauser, Friedman, & Kuwabara, 2000). Online feedback mechanisms are primarily informal and self-regulated (e.g. Tripadvisor, Ebay), and usually there is no way of verifying the feedback, with the assumption that false or biased information will be diluted by a larger amount of accurate feedback (Sabater & Sierra 2005). Research has shown that these mechanisms engender trust, not only in the reported reputable sellers (Koehn, 2003), but also in the wider community of sellers in an online marketplace such as Amazon (Pavlou & Gefen, 2004). Some scholars have argued that high usage of third-party feedback mechanisms in supporting consumer transactions may, in fact, bring about so much certainty that conditions of risk and vulnerability are effectively eliminated (Gefen & Pavlou, 2012). In practice, however, while strong institutional structures may reduce the role of trust in the economic aspect of internet transactions, trust may continue to play a vital role in the social aspect of internet transactions (Gefen & Pavlou, 2012). For example, the comments themselves in feedback mechanisms seem to play a role above and beyond the actual numerical feedback rating, building trust by addressing the credibility and benevolence of the seller, more on a social than an economic basis (Pavlou & Dimoka, 2006).

The role of context

The system-level determinants of online trust in an organization differ according to the function and context of the website in question (Bart et al., 2005; Bansal, Zahedi, & Gefen, 2016). Privacy and order fulfilment are the strongest determinants of trust where there is high information risk and high involvement, such as travel sites. In contrast, navigation is strongest for information-intensive sites, such as sports, portal and community sites, while brand strength is strongest for high-involvement categories, such as automobile and financial services sites (Bart et al., 2005). Personal safety is emerging as a key consideration for trust in newer peer-to-peer marketplaces such as private accommodation sharing (e.g. AIRBNB) and location-based taxi hire and ridesharing services (e.g. Uber, Lyft, Hailo), where the service goes beyond buying a physical product or exchanging information, and enables the connection of strangers with each other for access-based consumption. In this sharing economy, in addition to traditional reputation feedback mechanisms, marketplace intermediary companies are prioritizing identity verification as part of their service, in order to promote trust. In fact, with the right screening and authentication mechanisms and safety policies, there is a case to be made that peer-to-peer marketplaces for access-based consumption can be safer (for both service providers and consumers) than the traditional business model it replaces (such as hailing a cab on the street) although, in many markets, there is greater or lesser regulation than traditional models. This unbalanced approach to regulation may create an uneven playing field for market participants.

The legal jurisdiction in which internet transactions are conducted is also critical for trust formation and maintenance. The inherently global nature of the internet, combined with the recent advent of cloud computing, has introduced issues of legal jurisdiction to many transactions. For example, the consumer could be in one country, the organization in another, the server provider in another, and the data held in another, all with different national laws applicable. Relatedly, beliefs about government surveillance on the internet can impact privacy concerns and intentions to disclose personal information. While some trust scholars propose that controls and monitoring are likely to undermine trust (De Jong & Dirks, 2012), this may not always be the case, particularly where the monitoring is expected and considered appropriate (Ferrin, Bligh, & Kohles, 2007). A perceived need for the government to have greater access to personal information and to monitor personal activities in order to increase security procedures and to ensure safe and reliable internet transactions, can reduce privacy concerns and encourage disclosure of personal information. On the other hand, concerns about government intrusion regarding individual internet activity and account information increases privacy concerns (Dinev, Hart, & Mullen, 2008). As our use of, and reliance on, the internet as a means for personal and professional interaction grows this is likely to become an issue of greater focus for scholars interested in trust in the internet context.

Finally, issues of temporal context play a role in which antecedents drive trust between individuals and online organizations. In new relationships with unfamiliar vendors, website quality, vendor reputation and structural assurance strongly influence consumer trust (McKnight et al., 2002). Consumers interacting with a website for the first time make strong judgements about the unknown vendor from their initial experience on the website (including technical performance, visual appeal, ease of navigation, ease of access to information, contact details). In addition, second-hand information about the reputation of the vendor and structural assurance play a role in influencing initial web-based trust in vendors (McKnight et al., 2002). In more established relationships, familiarity and prior satisfaction with e-commerce in general, influence trust in specific web vendors (Yoon, 2002). For experienced, repeat online shoppers, trust has been shown to be fostered by a typical and easy-to-use website with built-in safety mechanisms (Gefen, Karahanna, & Straub, 2003).

In any ongoing relationship, trust has the potential to be violated. The extent to which a consumer information privacy violation leads to a reduction in trust in the organization can depend on the attributed cause of the violation. General trust research has found that integrity-based violations have a greater impact on trust than competence-based violations (Kim, Dirks, Cooper, & Ferrin, 2006). Similarly, in an online context, unauthorized sharing of information by the website company (an integrity violation) may have a greater negative impact on trust than unauthorized access by external agents (a competence violation; Bansal & Zahedi, 2015). In line with offline trust violation research (Kim, Ferrin, Cooper, & Dirks, 2004), apology is an effective response in both situations (but more so for hacking), whereas denial is only effective for the externally attributed hacking violation (Bansal & Zahedi, 2015).

Individual trust in technology systems

Trust in technology is an under-explored area of research (Lankton & McKnight, 2011). Most of the trust research in online environments examines trust in the humans who use the technology or trust in the organizations that provide the technology. Research that has focused on trust in the technology system itself has occurred primarily in the computer science and information systems literature. Unfortunately, conceptualizations of trust and related constructs in the field of computer science are considerably different to those found in the business literature. Trust is often portrayed as synonymous with security, and vulnerability is associated with low levels of trust whereby trusted systems are those where all vulnerabilities have been eliminated (e.g. Abbadi & Alawneh, 2012; Takabi, Joshi, & Ahn, 2010). Contributions to understanding from the field of information studies have, however, begun to shed light on how trust, as a generalized and more specific psychological state, can be applied to understand the relationship between individuals and technology systems.

Generalized trust in information technology plays a role in shaping IT-related beliefs and behaviour (McKnight, Carter, Thatcher, & Clay, 2011). This propensity to trust technology is a form of general trust similar to dispositional trust, and distinguished from specific trust (in the merchant and the website). McKnight and colleagues (2011) differentiate between faith in general technology – a belief that IT is generally reliable, functional and helpful – and a technology trusting stance – a belief that interacting with technology is likely to lead to positive outcomes. In an internet context, Thatcher, Carter, Li, & Rong (2013) examine general trust in the internet as an IT infrastructure and report that trust in the internet (trusting beliefs in three technical attributes – capability, reliability and security) significantly influences trust in the website, but does not influence trust in the online merchant. They suggest that trust in IT infrastructure is a foundational belief for online behaviour, and that the evolving nature of the internet environment makes this a dynamic factor in trust interactions online. Empirical evidence demonstrates the impact of a lack of trust in internet technology on outcomes such as anxiety about internet use (Thatcher, Loughry, Lim, & McKnight, 2007).

Researchers have also examined trust in specific technology systems. However, as discussed above, considerable debate exists around whether trust as a psychological state can be experienced in a relationship with another party that does not possess consciousness or agency. One perspective on this maintains that trust in technology reflects beliefs about the technology's characteristics rather than its will or motives (McKnight, Carter, Thatcher, & Clay, 2011). From this perspective, uncertainty and vulnerability in trusting technology systems arise predominantly from the potential of unanticipated technical problems or lack of knowledge on the part of the trustor (Paravastu, Gefen, & Creason, 2014). However, with the increasing automation of technology systems and the advent of ubiquitous information systems, it can be argued that the systems themselves can possess attributes such as benevolence and integrity.

Much of the research in this area has thus far focused on technologies that have fewer human-like characteristics and more technology-like characteristics e.g. software. However, in many online interactions with technology, the distinction between human and technology characteristics is not all that clear. In a study of trust in relation to online recommendation agents (intelligent virtual assistant software), Wang and Benbasat (2005) found that in addition to a rational process governed by assessments of perceived usefulness and perceived ease of use (technology acceptance model; Davis et al., 1989), consumers treat online recommendation agents as social actors and form social relationships with them, which involve trust. Similar to models of interpersonal trust (Mayer et al., 1995; McKnight et al., 2002), they contend that consumers assess the competence of the recommendation software to accurately understand their needs, its benevolence demonstrated by prioritization of the needs of the consumer over those of the e-service provider, and its integrity demonstrated by the provision of unbiased recommendations. In another study of online recommendation agents, Komiak and Benbasat (2006) suggest that trust in technology consists of emotional trust as well as cognitive trust, and is influenced by the perceived personalization of the IT artefact. Similarly, in a study of social networking, Lankton & McKnight (2011) discovered that users trust Facebook as both a technology and as a quasi-person, proposing an integrated trustworthiness assessment model covering both interpersonal and technology factors (competence/functionality, integrity/reliability, benevolence/helpfulness). However, it seems that human-like trust only applies to particular internet technologies, and may depend on the characteristics of the individual technology such as intelligence and personalization (Wang & Benbasat, 2005).

Recent advances in cognitive neuroscience show promise for new insights into whether or not trust in technology is similar or different to interpersonal trust. Riedl, Mohr, Kenning, Davis and Heekeren (2014) demonstrate that people are better at making trustworthiness assessments of humans than of human-like avatars, and neurobiological analysis shows that trustworthiness assessments activate the medial frontal cortex of the brain more strongly where the trustee is a human rather than an avatar. In the context of e-commerce, Dimoka (2010) finds support for different constructs of trust and distrust, which activate different brain areas. There appears to be considerable potential for using cognitive neuroscience theories and functional brain imaging tools to enhance the understanding of trust in the broad environment of the internet.

Future developments and potential avenues for research

While a considerable body of literature has been devoted to examining online trust, the fast pace of change in the technology realm means that methods of online interaction are continually updated and new trust-related issues will continue to arise. As it stands, there are a number of key issues which deserve further attention.

The conceptualization of trustworthiness in relation to a technology system requires further consideration both theoretically and empirically. For instance, it may be that certain dimensions of trustworthiness are more applicable in particular online circumstances such as those which involve more vulnerability on behalf of the trustor or more autonomy and intelligence on behalf of the technology. Similarly, privacy debates and the extent to which our lives are now accessible online are likely to highlight the more motivational and value-laden aspects of trustworthiness in interacting online with individuals and organizations. As we continue to grapple with the appropriateness of the traditional ABI (ability, benevolence and integrity) model for the internet context, the concepts of predictability and value congruence may gain additional significance in this regard. Once we have gained further conceptual clarity around the components of trustworthiness in the online context, further research into how these characteristics are best communicated at the individual, organizational and system levels will provide an interesting avenue for researchers.

The internet context also offers a fruitful avenue for further research into the debate around trust and control. As organizations and governments strive to keep pace with technological advances and their influence on society and business, the focus has been predominantly on the introduction of control mechanisms such as regulation and contracts or service-level agreements to provide a foundation for interaction. Although often considered a costly overhead with negative trust impacts, the benefits of legal remedies as a support for trust have also been highlighted (e.g. Sitkin, 1995). However, the complexity of the impact of these mechanisms on trust requires further research. For example, in a general context, contracts are proposed to have both positive and negative influences on interorganizational trust through different control and coordination mechanisms (Lumineau, in press). The application of trust and control theory to the context of the internet offers significant potential for further theoretical development and empirical research.

One relevant issue that is gaining increasing attention in terms of media debate is online privacy. As the internet has evolved and content becomes increasingly user generated, it is not merely that corporations and governments can engage in surveillance, but that private citizens themselves will directly engage in sousveillance of their own lives and of those that they encounter on a day-to-day basis. This can be seen already with the use of social media to tag the location and activities of contacts, or ubiquitous technology in the form of wearable devices such as glasses. This data and its metadata may be stored, accessed and combined with other data sources along the chain of service provision inherent in the Future internet potentially in unintended ways and for unintended purposes. As a result, the number of unknown referents involved in any online trust relationship is likely to grow, and theory and empirical work regarding trust in unknown individuals and systems becomes increasingly relevant. Another aspect of online privacy with relevance for trust scholars is the increased prevalence of data privacy breaches and the effectiveness of trust breach responses. In the context of many trust referents within the internet service supply chain, a deeper examination of responses may be appropriate, including not only apologies and denials, but potentially other responses such as reticence (Bansal & Zahedi, 2015), social accounts or explanations (Sitkin & Bies, 1993).

The emergence, maturation and integration of new technologies such as cloud computing, social media, big data, sensor and mobile computing technologies are rapidly redefining what the internet is and might be in the future. Unsurprisingly, the 'Future Internet' or the 'Internet of Everything' remains definitionally ambiguous although it encompasses a number of common features and themes. At the core of the Future Internet is the increasing pervasiveness of highly distributed heterogeneous but interconnected technology infrastructures. The pervasiveness, interoperability and inter-dependency of these infrastructures extends how we conceive of the internet beyond networks and people to the relationship between machines, virtual constructs or other entities (including networks and people) with greater or lesser degrees of autonomy and intelligence. Furthermore, as the technology underlying these infrastructures complexifies there are significant implications for an individual's capacity to understand new technologies and make sense of their relationship with entities in the Future Internet. This raises questions for researchers around how trust can be developed in the face of high levels of uncertainty and a lack of prior experience. These contextual issues may increase the difficulty of forming systematic, logical trustworthiness judgements, leading to heuristic factors playing an increasing role in driving online trust. Such a process may also provide a central role for emotions as an important determinant of trust. Although they have been largely overlooked in the existing literature, emotions both negative (e.g. fear, anxiety, anger) and positive (e.g. enthusiasm, excitement) are likely to influence trust and risk-related behaviours online. The debate on whether we can trust technology is not a new one but is an increasingly relevant one and will be for a long time to come.

References

Abbadi, I. M., & Alawneh, M. (2012). A framework for establishing trust in the Cloud. *Computers & Electrical Engineering*, *38*(5), 1073–1087.

Aguirre, E., Mahr, D., Grewal, D., de Ruyter, K., & Wetzels, M. (2015). Unraveling the personalization paradox: The effect of information collection and trust-building strategies on online advertisement effectiveness. *Journal of Retailing*, *91*(1), 34–39.

Aiken, K. D., & Boush, D. M. (2006). Trustmarks, objective-source ratings, and implied investments in advertising: Investigating online trust and the context-specific nature of internet signals. *Journal of the Academy of Marketing Science*, *34*(3), 308–323.

Avolio, B. J., Kahai, S., & Dodge, G. E. (2001). E-leadership: Implications for theory, research, and practice. *The Leadership Quarterly*, *11*(4), 615–668.

Bansal, G., & Zahedi, F. M. (2015). Trust violation and repair: The information privacy perspective. *Decision Support Systems*, *71*, 62–77.

Bansal, G., Zahedi, F. M., & Gefen, D. (2016). Do context and personality matter? Trust and privacy concerns in disclosing private information online. *Information and Management*, *53*(1), 1–21.

Bart, Y., Shankar, V., Sultan, F., & Urban, G. L. (2005). Are the drivers and role of online trust the same for all web sites and consumers? A large-scale exploratory empirical study. *Journal of Marketing*, *69*(4), 133–152.

Beldad, A., de Jong, M., & Steehouder, M. (2010). How shall I trust the faceless and the intangible? A literature review on the antecedents of online trust. *Computers in Human Behavior*, *26*(5), 857–869.

Bente, G., Rüggenberg, S., Krämer, N. C., & Eschenburg, F. (2008). Avatar-mediated networking: Increasing social presence and interpersonal trust in net-based collaborations. *Human Communication Research*, *34*(2), 287–318.

Berthon, P. R., Pitt, L. F., Plangger, K., & Shapiro, D. (2012). Marketing meets Web 2.0, social media, and creative consumers: Implications for international marketing strategy. *Business Horizons*, *55*(3), 261–271.

Bhattacherjee, A. (2002). Individual trust in online firms: Scale development and initial test. *Journal of Management Information Systems*, *19*(1), 211–241.

Brandtzæg, P. B., Lüders, M., & Skjetne, J. H. (2010). Too many Facebook 'friends'? Content sharing and sociability versus the need for privacy in social network sites. *International Journal of Human–Computer Interaction*, *26*(11–12), 1006–1030.

Casaló, L. V., Flavián, C., & Guinalíu, M. (2007). The influence of satisfaction, perceived reputation and trust on a consumer's commitment to a website. *Journal of Marketing Communications*, *13*(1), 1–17.

Chang, M. K., Cheung, W., & Tang, M. (2013). Building trust online: Interactions among trust building mechanisms. *Information & Management*, *50*(7), 439–445.

Corritore, C. L., Kracher, B., & Wiedenbeck, S. (2003). On-line trust: Concepts, evolving themes, a model. *International Journal of Human-Computer Studies, 58*(6), 737–758.

Cyr, D., Hassanein, K., Head, M., & Ivanov, A. (2007). The role of social presence in establishing loyalty in e-service environments. *Interacting with Computers, 19*(1), 43–56.

Cyr, D., Head, M., & Larios, H. (2010). Colour appeal in website design within and across cultures: A multi-method evaluation. *International Journal of Human-Computer Studies, 68*(1), 1–21.

Davis, F. D., Bagozzi, R. P., & Warshaw, P. R. (1989). User acceptance of computer technology: A comparison of two theoretical models. *Management Science, 35*(8), 982–1003.

de Jong, B. A., & Dirks, K. T. (2012). Beyond shared perceptions of trust and monitoring in teams: Implications of asymmetry and dissensus. *Journal of Applied Psychology, 97*(2), 391–406.

Dellarocas, C. (2003). The digitization of word of mouth: Promise and challenges of online feedback mechanisms. *Management Science, 49*(10), 1407–1424.

Deutsch, M. (1958). Trust and suspicion. *Journal of Conflict Resolution, 2*(4), 265–279.

Dietz, G., & Hartog, D. N. D. (2006). Measuring trust inside organisations. *Personnel Review, 35*(5), 557–588.

Dimoka, A. (2010). What does the brain tell us about trust and distrust? Evidence from a functional neuroimaging study. *MIS Quarterly, 34*(2), 373–396.

Dinev, T., Hart, P., & Mullen, M. R. (2008). Internet privacy concerns and beliefs about government surveillance – An empirical investigation. *The Journal of Strategic Information Systems, 17*(3), 214–233.

Ellison, N., Heino, R., & Gibbs, J. (2006). Managing impressions online: Self-presentation processes in the online dating environment. *Journal of Computer-Mediated Communication, 11*(2), 415–441.

Fehr, E., & Gächter. S. (2002). Do incentive contracts undermine voluntary cooperation. Working Paper No. 34, *Institute for Empirical Research in Economics*, University of Zurich.

Ferrin, D. L., Bligh, M. C., & Kohles, J. C. (2007). Can I trust you to trust me? A theory of trust, monitoring, and cooperation in interpersonal and intergroup relationships. *Group & Organization Management, 32*(4), 465–499.

Flavián, C., Guinalíu, M., & Gurrea, R. (2006). The role played by perceived usability, satisfaction and consumer trust on website loyalty. *Information & Management, 43*(1), 1–14.

Friedman, B., Khan Jr, P. H., & Howe, D. C. (2000). Trust online. *Communications of the ACM, 43*(12), 34–40.

Gefen, D. (2000). E-commerce: The role of familiarity and trust. *Omega, 28*(6), 725–737.

Gefen, D., Karahanna, E., & Straub, D. W. (2003). Trust and TAM in online shopping: An integrated model. *MIS Quarterly, 27*(1), 51–90.

Gefen, D., & Pavlou, P. A. (2012). The boundaries of trust and risk: The quadratic moderating role of institutional structures. *Information Systems Research, 23*(2), 940–959.

Gefen, D., & Straub, D. W. (2004). Consumer trust in B2C e-Commerce and the importance of social presence: Experiments in e-products and e-services. *Omega, 32*(6), 407–424.

Gillespie, N. (2003). Measuring trust in work relationships: The Behavioural Trust Inventory. *Paper presented at the annual meeting of the Academy of Management*, Seattle, USA.

Gilson, L. L., Maynard, M. T., Young, N. C. J., Vartiainen, M., & Hakonen, M. (2015). Virtual teams research 10 years, 10 themes, and 10 opportunities. *Journal of Management, 41*(5), 1313–1337.

Green, T., & Gillespie, N. (2014). Swift trust in virtual services: A construal-level perspective. *Paper presented at the 8th First International Network on Trust Conference* (FINT), Coventry University, United Kingdom.

Grabner-Kräuter, S., & Kaluscha, E. A. (2003). Empirical research in on-line trust: A review and critical assessment. *International Journal of Human-Computer Studies, 58*(6), 783–812.

Grant, I., & Waite, K. (2013). In R. W. Belk, & R. Llamas (Eds.). *The Routledge companion to digital consumption*. (pp. 333–345). Abingdon, UK: Routledge.

Hardin, R. (2006). *Trust*. Cambridge, UK: Polity Press.

Hassanein, K., & Head, M. (2007). Manipulating perceived social presence through the web interface and its impact on attitude towards online shopping. *International Journal of Human-Computer Studies, 65*(8), 689–708.

Henttonen, K., & Blomqvist, K. (2005). Managing distance in a global virtual team: The evolution of trust through technology-mediated relational communication. *Strategic Change, 14*(2), 107–119.

Hertel, G., Geister, S., & Konradt, U. (2005). Managing virtual teams: A review of current empirical research. *Human Resource Management Review, 15*(1), 69–95.

Hoffmann, H., & Söllner, M. (2014). Incorporating behavioral trust theory into system development for ubiquitous applications. *Personal and Ubiquitous Computing, 18*(1), 117–128.

Hu, X., Wu, G., Wu, Y., & Zhang, H. (2010). The effects of Web assurance seals on consumers' initial trust in an online vendor: A functional perspective. *Decision Support Systems, 48*(2), 407–418.

Jarvenpaa, S. L., & Leidner, D. E. (1998). Communication and trust in global virtual teams. *Journal of Computer-Mediated Communication, 3*(4).

Jarvenpaa, S. L., Tractinsky, N., & Saarinen, L. (1999). Consumer trust in an internet store: A cross-cultural validation. *Journal of Computer-Mediated Communication, 5*(2).

Jarvenpaa, S. L., Tractinsky, N., & Vitalec, M. (2000). Consumer trust in an internet store. *Information Technology and Management, 1*, 45–71.

Jøsang, A., Ismail, R., & Boyd, C. (2007). A survey of trust and reputation systems for online service provision. *Decision Support Systems, 43*(2), 618–644.

Kim, P. H., Dirks, K. T., Cooper, C. D., & Ferrin, D. L. (2006). When more blame is better than less: The implications of internal vs. external attributions for the repair of trust after a competence-vs. integrity-based trust violation. *Organizational Behavior and Human Decision Processes, 99*(1), 49–65.

Kim, P. H., Ferrin, D. L., Cooper, C. D., & Dirks, K. T. (2004). Removing the shadow of suspicion: The effects of apology versus denial for repairing competence-versus integrity-based trust violations. *Journal of Applied Psychology, 89*(1), 104–118.

Kim, D. J., Ferrin, D. L., & Rao, H. R. (2008). A trust-based consumer decision-making model in electronic commerce: The role of trust, perceived risk, and their antecedents. *Decision Support Systems, 44*(2), 544–564.

Kim, D. J., Song, Y. I., Braynov, S. B., & Rao, H. R. (2005). A multidimensional trust formation model in B-to-C e-commerce: A conceptual framework and content analyses of academia/practitioner perspectives. *Decision Support Systems, 40*(2), 143–165.

Kim, J., & Moon, J. Y. (1998). Designing towards emotional usability in customer interfaces: Trustworthiness of cyber-banking system interfaces. *Interacting with Computers, 10*(1), 1–29.

Kim, K.K., & Prabhakar B. (2004). Initial trust and the adoption of B2C e-commerce: The case of internet banking. *ACM Sigmis Database, 35*(2), 50–64.

Koehn, D. (2003). The nature of and conditions for online trust. *Journal of Business Ethics, 43*(1–2), 3–19.

Komiak, S. Y., & Benbasat, I. (2006). The effects of personalization and familiarity on trust and adoption of recommendation agents. *MIS Quarterly, 30*(4), 941–960.

Koufaris, M., & Hampton-Sosa, W. (2004). The development of initial trust in an online company by new customers. *Information & Management, 41*(3), 377–397.

Kuan, H. H., & Bock, G. W. (2007). Trust transference in brick and click retailers: An investigation of the before-online-visit phase. *Information & Management, 44*(2), 175–187.

Lankton, N. K., & McKnight, D. H. (2011). What does it mean to trust Facebook?: Examining technology and interpersonal trust beliefs. *ACM SIGMIS Database, 42*(2), 32–54.

Lankton, N., McKnight, D. H., & Thatcher, J. B. (2014). Incorporating trust-in-technology into Expectation Disconfirmation Theory. *The Journal of Strategic Information Systems, 23*(2), 128–145.

Lauer, T. W., & Deng, X. (2007). Building online trust through privacy practices. *International Journal of Information Security, 6*(5), 323–331.

Lee, J. D., & See, K. A. (2004). Trust in automation: Designing for appropriate reliance. *Human Factors: The Journal of the Human Factors and Ergonomics Society, 46*(1), 50–80.

Lewicki, R. J., & Brinsfield, C. (2012). Measuring trust beliefs and behaviours. In F. Lyon, G. Mollering, M.N.K. Saunders (Eds.). *Handbook of research methods on trust.* (pp.29–39). Cheltenham, UK: Edward Elgar.

Li, Y. M., & Yeh, Y. S. (2010). Increasing trust in mobile commerce through design aesthetics. *Computers in Human Behavior, 26*(4), 673–684.

Liao, C., Palvia, P., & Lin, H. N. (2006). The roles of habit and web site quality in e-commerce. *International Journal of Information Management, 26*(6), 469–483.

Lim, K. H., Sia, C. L., Lee, M. K., & Benbasat, I. (2006). Do I trust you online, and if so, will I buy? An empirical study of two trust-building strategies. *Journal of Management Information Systems, 23*(2), 233–266.

Lumineau, F. (in press). How contracts influence trust and distrust. *Journal of Management, 43*(5), 1553–1577.

Mayer, R. C., Davis, J. H., & Schoorman, F. D. (1995). An integrative model of organizational trust. *Academy of Management Review, 20*(3), 709–734.

McEvily, B., Perrone, V., & Zaheer, A. (2003). Trust as an organizing principle. *Organization Science, 14*(1), 91–103.

McKnight, D. H., Carter, M., Thatcher, J. B., & Clay, P. F. (2011). Trust in a specific technology: An investigation of its components and measures. *ACM Transactions on Management Information Systems (TMIS), 2*(2), 12.

McKnight, D. H., & Chervany, N. L. (2001). What trust means in e-commerce customer relationships: An interdisciplinary conceptual typology. *International Journal of Electronic Commerce, 6*(2), 35–59.

McKnight, D. H., Choudhury, V., & Kacmar, C. (2002). The impact of initial consumer trust on intentions to transact with a web site: A trust building model. *The Journal of Strategic Information Systems, 11*(3), 297–323.

McKnight, D. H., Cummings, L. L., & Chervany, N. L. (1998). Initial trust formation in new organizational relationships. *Academy of Management Review, 23*(3), 473–490.

Naquin, C. E., Kurtzberg, T. R., & Belkin, L. Y. (2010). The finer points of lying online: E-mail versus pen and paper. *Journal of Applied Psychology, 95*(2), 387.

Naquin, C. E., & Paulson, G. D. (2003). Online bargaining and interpersonal trust. *Journal of Applied Psychology, 88*(1), 113–120.

Özpolat, K., & Jank, W. (2015). Getting the most out of third party trust seals: An empirical analysis. *Decision Support Systems, 73*, 47–56.

Pan, Y., & Zinkhan, G. M. (2006). Exploring the impact of online privacy disclosures on consumer trust. *Journal of Retailing, 82*(4), 331–338.

Paravastu, N., Gefen, D., & Creason, S. B. (2014). Understanding trust in IT artifacts: An evaluation of the impact of trustworthiness and trust on satisfaction with antiviral software. *ACM SIGMIS Database, 45*(4), 30–50.

Pavlou, P. A. (2003). Consumer acceptance of electronic commerce: Integrating trust and risk with the technology acceptance model. *International Journal of Electronic Commerce, 7*(3), 101–134.

Pavlou, P. A., & Chellappa, R. K. (2001). The role of perceived privacy and perceived security in the development of trust in electronic commerce transactions. Working paper. *Marshall School of Business, USC, Los Angeles.*

Pavlou, P. A., & Dimoka, A. (2006). The nature and role of feedback text comments in online marketplaces: Implications for trust building, price premiums, and seller differentiation. *Information Systems Research, 17*(4), 392–414

Pavlou, P. A., & Gefen, D. (2004). Building effective online marketplaces with institution-based trust. *Information Systems Research, 15*(1), 37–59.

Pavlou, P. A., Liang, H., & Xue, Y. (2006). Understanding and mitigating uncertainty in online environments: A principal-agent perspective. *MIS Quarterly, 31*(1), 105–136.

Peña, J., & Yoo, S. C. (2014). The effects of avatar stereotypes and cognitive load on virtual interpersonal attraction mediation effects of perceived trust and reversed perceptions under cognitive load. *Communication Research*, 1–23.

Perks, H., & Halliday, S. V. (2003). Sources, signs and signalling for fast trust creation in organisational relationships. *European Management Journal, 21*(3), 338–350.

Ratnasingam, P. (2005). Trust in inter-organizational exchanges: A case study in business to business electronic commerce. *Decision Support Systems, 39*(3), 525–544.

Redfern, S., & Naughton, N. (2002). Collaborative virtual environments to support communication and community in internet-based distance education. *Journal of Information Technology Education, 1*(3), 210–220.

Resnick, P., Kuwabara, K., Zeckhauser, R., & Friedman, E. (2000). Reputation systems. *Communications of the ACM, 43*(12), 45–48.

Riedl, R., Mohr, P. N., Kenning, P. H., Davis, F. D., & Heekeren, H. R. (2014). Trusting humans and avatars: A brain imaging study based on evolution theory. *Journal of Management Information Systems, 30*(4), 83–114.

Riegelsberger, J., & Sasse, M. A. (2002). Face it – photos don't make a web site trustworthy. In *CHI'02 Extended Abstracts on Human Factors in Computing Systems*, (pp. 742–743). ACM.

Riegelsberger, J., Sasse, M. A., & McCarthy, J. D. (2003). Shiny happy people building trust?: Photos on e-commerce websites and consumer trust. In *Proceedings of the SIGCHI conference on Human Factors in Computing Systems*, (pp. 121–128). ACM.

Robert, L. P., Denis, A. R., & Hung, Y. T. C. (2009). Individual swift trust and knowledge-based trust in face-to-face and virtual team members. *Journal of Management Information Systems, 26*(2), 241–279.

Rousseau, D. M., Sitkin, S. B., Burt, R. S., & Camerer, C. (1998). Not so different after all: A cross-discipline view of trust. *Academy of Management Review, 23*(3), 393–404.

Sabater, J., & Sierra, C. (2005). Review on computational trust and reputation models. *Artificial Intelligence Review, 24*(1), 33–60.

Savolainen, T. (2014). Trust-building in e-leadership: A case study of leaders' challenges and skills in technology-mediated interaction. *Journal of Global Business Issues, 8*(2), 45.

Seckler, M., Heinz, S., Forde, S., Tuch, A. N., & Opwis, K. (2015). Trust and distrust on the web: User experiences and website characteristics. *Computers in Human Behavior, 45*, 39–50.

Sillence, E., Briggs, P., Harris, P. R., & Fishwick, L. (2007). How do patients evaluate and make use of online health information? *Social Science & Medicine, 64*(9), 1853–1862.

Sitkin, S. B. (1995). On the positive effects of legalization on trust. In R. J. Bies, R. J. Lewicki, & B. H. Sheppard (Eds.). *Research on negotiation in organizations*, Vol. 5 (pp. 185–217). Greenwich, CT: JAI Press.

Sitkin, S. B., & Bies, R. J. (1993). Social accounts in conflict situations: Using explanations to manage conflict. *Human Relations, 46*(3), 349–370.

Sitkin, S. B., & Roth, N. L. (1993). Explaining the limited effectiveness of legalistic "remedies" for trust/distrust. *Organization Science, 4*(3), 367–392.

Smith, H. J., Dinev, T., & Xu, H. (2011). Information privacy research: An interdisciplinary review. *MIS Quarterly, 35*(4), 989–1016.

Society for Human Resource Management. (2012). Virtual teams. www.shrm.org/research/surveyfindings/articles/pages/virtualteams.aspx.

Söllner, M., Pavlou, P. A., & Leimeister, J. M. (2013). Understanding trust in IT artifacts – A new conceptual approach. *Paper presented at the annual meeting of the Academy of Management*, Florida, USA.

Stewart, K. J. (2003). Trust transfer on the world wide web. *Organization Science, 14*(1), 5–17.

Takabi, H., Joshi, J. B., & Ahn, G. J. (2010). Security and privacy challenges in cloud computing environments. *IEEE Security & Privacy, 8*(6), 24–31.

Teo, T. S., & Liu, J. (2007). Consumer trust in e-commerce in the United States, Singapore and China. *Omega, 35*(1), 22–38.

Thatcher, J. B., Carter, M., Li, X., & Rong, G. (2013). A classification and investigation of trustees in B-to-C E-commerce: General vs. specific trust. *Communications of the Association for Information Systems, 32*(1), 107–134.

Thatcher, J. B., Loughry, M. L., Lim, J., & McKnight, D. H. (2007). Internet anxiety: An empirical study of the effects of personality, beliefs, and social support. *Information & Management, 44*(4), 353–363.

Tomlinson, E. C., Lewicki, R. J., & Ash, S. R. (2014). Disentangling the moral integrity construct: Values congruence as a moderator of the behavioral integrity–citizenship relationship. *Group & Organization Management, 39*(6), 720–743.

Tuch, A. N., Bargas-Avila, J. A., & Opwis, K. (2010). Symmetry and aesthetics in website design: It's a man's business. *Computers in Human Behavior, 26*(6), 1831–1837.

Walther, J. B. (1995). Relational aspects of computer-mediated communication: Experimental observations over time. *Organization Science, 6*(2), 186–203.

Wang, W., & Benbasat, I. (2005). Trust in and adoption of online recommendation agents. *Journal of the Association for Information Systems, 6*(3), 4.

Wang, Y. D., & Emurian, H. H. (2005). An overview of online trust: Concepts, elements, and implications. *Computers in Human Behavior, 21*(1), 105–125.

Wilson, J. M., Straus, S. G., & McEvily, B. (2006). All in due time: The development of trust in computer-mediated and face-to-face teams. *Organizational Behavior and Human Decision Processes, 99*(1), 16–33.

Yoon, S. J. (2002). The antecedents and consequences of trust in online-purchase decisions. *Journal of Interactive Marketing, 16*(2), 47–63.

23

TRUST IN THE ENTREPRENEURIAL PROCESS

Trenton A. Williams and Dean A. Shepherd

Trust is a 'lubricant' that facilitates cooperative exchange, especially under conditions of uncertainty, information asymmetry, and unobservable actions . . . It enables entrepreneurs to overcame the lack of legitimacy . . . and serves as a flexible and adaptive governance structure. [However], developing trust and trustful relations . . . involves the expenditure of scarce resources (time, psychological and social energy, and perhaps even economic resources).

(Venkataraman, 1997: 127)

Introduction

Research on trust issues in the psychological, sociological and organizational sciences is an established topic of interest (Graham & Tarbell, 2006; Mayer, Davis, & Schoorman, 1995; Mayer & Gavin, 2005; Rousseau, Sitkin, Burt, & Camerer, 1998). In a recent literature review on trust, Fulmer and Gelfand (2012) highlight the importance of studying trust not only across disciplines, but also at multiple levels of an organization (i.e. organization, team and individual levels). Similarly, they recommend drawing upon various theoretical insights associated with each level to better understand how trust influences various outcomes of interest. While this research helps push us toward an understanding multi-level interactions of trust, there remain opportunities to take stock of extant research on trust at *different stages* of an organization's lifespan. In particular, theoretical insights are likely to come from theorizing on trust across stages of organizational emergence and across stages of the entrepreneurial process (opportunity recognition, exploitation of an opportunity, exiting a venture) because each stage likely alters the importance and forms of trust.

In the entrepreneurship literature on organizational emergence, researchers explore how, when, where and by whom opportunities to bring future goods and services into existence are discovered, evaluated and exploited under uncertainty (Shane & Venkataraman, 2000). Importantly, entrepreneurship scholars focus on how individuals 'pursue opportunities without regard to resources they currently control' (Stevenson & Jarillo, 1990: 23), which suggests a

408

reliance on 'non-owned' resources that can be controlled or deployed toward the pursuit of an opportunity. Given this definition, researchers have focused on informal resources accessed through social networks (Blundel & Smith, 2001; Burt, 2005). While beneficial, these studies traditionally focus on structures of networks as opposed to their content (i.e. the relationships and exchanges that occur over structural networks). Network content is important in gaining a greater understanding of how entrepreneurs mobilize resources they do not control; at the heart of network content lies trust, which is essential in 'hold[ing] networks together' (Welter & Smallbone, 2006: 466).

Trust assists in activating the *potential value* of non-owned resources (such as favourable network positions) (Zahra et al., 2006) and 'promotes adaptive organizational forms . . . reduces harmful conflict; decreases transaction costs; facilitates rapid formulation of ad hoc work groups (Meyerson, Weick, & Kramer, 1996); and promotes effective responses to crisis', all of which could be directly related to important actions within the entrepreneurial process (Rousseau et al., 1998: 394). However, as illustrated in the opening quotation, despite the potential benefits of trust, entrepreneurs must weigh the costs and potential return of investing in trust and trustful relationships as they seek to successfully navigate uncertainty with limited resources. In sum, entrepreneurs must balance investments in trusting relationships with other resource investments to facilitate venture founding, growth and (eventually) harvesting.

Given the potentially significant influence of trust at nearly every stage of entrepreneurial activity (Welter & Smallbone, 2006), researchers could benefit from a literature review on what we know about trust and entrepreneurship as a foundation for advancing theory in both entrepreneurship and organization literatures. The extant literature on trust in entrepreneurship is fragmented in terms of level of analysis (e.g. individual trust with other stakeholders, social context of venture founding) and empirical definitions of trust (i.e. possession of a social network, etc.) which limits our ability to explain what trust is and how it relates to other important constructs of interest. By taking stock of findings at different stages of the entrepreneurial process, we anticipate an enhanced perspective on the value of trust (depending on stage), as well as the role it plays in helping entrepreneurs pursue opportunities. In this paper we provide an extensive review of the literature to capture and represent the body of work on trust and entrepreneurship. In so doing, we 'question our accumulated wisdom and push ourselves to build an even more rigorous research program' (Walsh, 1995: 302) on the important topic of trust and entrepreneurship by offering a research agenda.

In the sections that follow we (1) describe our method for gathering and analysing papers for consideration, (2) discuss the thematic findings from these papers and (3) discuss potential opportunities for future contributions. We now turn to our research methods.

Method

To provide an analysis of the current state of the literature on trust and entrepreneurship we followed criterion sampling (Patton, 1990) based on keyword searches in top-tier journals in the areas where entrepreneurship research is published (similar to Grégoire, Corbett, & McMullen, 2011; Shepherd, Williams, & Patzelt, 2015). These journals include entrepreneurship-specific journals (*Entrepreneurship Theory & Practice, Journal of Business Venturing, Journal of Small Business Management* and *Strategic Entrepreneurship Journal*) as well as general management journals (*Academy of Management Journal, Academy of Management Review, Administrative Science Quarterly, Journal of Management, Journal of Management Studies, Organization Science, Management Science* and *Strategic Management Journal*).

Using Thomson Reuters' Web of Science database, we collected all articles published in the journals mentioned above up to the present date that included our keywords of interest pertaining to both entrepreneurship and trust. In developing keywords for the entrepreneurship topic we followed Grégoire and colleagues (2011) but with two substantive exceptions. First, given our focus on organizational emergence as an important stage of entrepreneurship we included the word 'founder' as this term is often affiliated with *de novo* and/or *de alio* venture creation. Second, we did not include the term 'small business' as this often refers to a specific type of venture management that (1) is not always considered entrepreneurial and (2) does not represent the broadest type of entrepreneurial activity which we seek to understand (Guth & Ginsberg, 1990; Shane & Venkataraman, 2000).

We built the list of keywords to capture 'trust' based on Rousseau and colleagues' (1998: 395) definition: 'Trust is a psychological state comprising the intention to accept vulnerability based upon positive expectations of the intentions or behavior of another.' Similarly, we considered other reviews of trust (i.e. Lewicki, Tomlinson, & Gillespie, 2006; Fulmer & Gelfand, 2012) who used the key word *trust* in conducting their literature review. Based on the above, we searched for papers containing any of the following words: (entrepreneu*) or (founder*) AND any of the following words: trust, reliance or entrust. This search generated 82 papers.

After generating the initial list of papers we then reviewed each study to remove papers that are (1) commentaries or dialogues, (2) book reviews, (3) primarily a review and/or research agenda paper, (4) research methods paper, (4) did not investigate the entrepreneur and (5) did not focus on trust as a key component of the paper. This secondary review resulted in us removing 62 papers.

After refining our search, we then inductively categorized the remaining 20 papers into five 'trust topics' as emerged from our analysis and as displayed in Figure 23.1. These topics include (1) entrepreneurial teams and trust, (2) intra-organizational trust, (3) institutions and trust, (4) entrepreneurial finance and (5) inter-organizational trust. In discussing these articles, we separated categories of articles into three primary trust relationships: internal to the entrepreneurial venture, external to the venture and at the intersection of internal and external (as shown in Figure 23.1). In the sections that follow, we discuss the key findings from the papers that fit

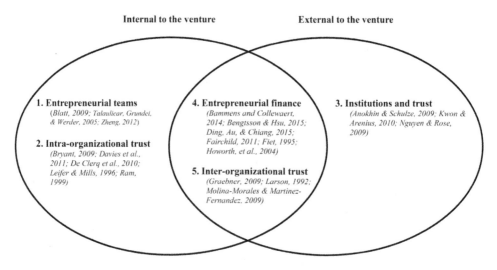

Figure 23.1 Entrepreneurship and trust research

within these categories and then discuss opportunities for future research within each section. Given the emerging nature of trust research in entrepreneurship, we anticipate considerable opportunities to explore the nature and influence of trust along the primary activities associated with entrepreneurship: (1) opportunity assessment, (2) entrepreneurial action and (3) entrepreneurial exit. As such, we discuss recommendations for future research within these three categories.

Trust internal to the entrepreneurial venture

Entrepreneurial teams and trust

Although entrepreneurial firms are often described in terms of a charismatic founder, most new ventures are founded by teams (Blatt, 2009; Harper, 2008), and the management team is critical in developing and growing the firm (Iacobucci & Rosa, 2010; Schjoedt et al., 2013). Trust between the members of an entrepreneurial team appears important in understanding progress in the entrepreneurial process. Indeed, attributes of the team have been found to influence new venture performance. For example, Zheng (2012) found that the transactive memory system of the team (i.e. the 'sum of the individual knowledge and shared understanding of the location of expertise among team members' [Zheng, 2012: 579; see also Lewis, 2003]) positively influenced new venture performance. Similarly, Zheng found that this positive relationship was magnified by intra-team trust – 'the showed perception of trust among the team members' (2012: 577). Theorizing on this moderating role Zheng (2012) highlights how intra-team trust increases awareness of the knowledge possessed by the team, facilitates task conflict to encourage the showing and discussion of information, and reduced relational conflict, which would otherwise obstruct coordination.

Perhaps this intra-team trust is important for any firms, not just entrepreneurial firms. However, Blatt (2009) noted that one aspect that makes entrepreneurial teams unique is the novelty they face. In terms of products, novelty can be a source of advantage (Tzabbar & Vestal, 2015), but in terms of teams novelty can damage trust. Specifically, Blatt (2009) highlights how novelty represents a less familiar situation such that members of the team have a more difficult time predicting and understanding others' actions, which may create relational conflict and coordination problems. To overcome the challenges of maintaining (or building) trust under high levels of novelty, Blatt (2009) proposes the development of communal schemas. Communal relationship schemas represent 'the type of relationship people desire from others' and influence how they interpret experiences and make decisions' (Blatt, 2009: 539). These schemas include a concept of the self, as well as a team member and how all parties are meant to interact. These communal schemas can be developed by attending to, and responding to others' needs (Clark, Mills, & Cororan, 1989), and by encouraging the expression and management of the negative emotions often generated by a novel situation (Clark, Fitness, & Brissette, 2001). These communal schemas then help alleviate the potential negative consequence of novelty on trust by increasing the members' knowledge of the other team members and reduce misunderstandings and conflicts that would otherwise arise from the display and expression of negative emotions (Blatt, 2009). Related directly to the entrepreneur's decision making, Talulicar, Grudei and Wader (2005) found that in top management teams of tech-based start-ups, those teams with a more communal schema are more likely to have a comprehensive strategic decision-making process.

Taken together, these papers highlight the importance of entrepreneurial teams in venture founding and highlight some of the complexity involved in how entrepreneurs interact with others, including building or enhancing trusting relationships, which then shape important outcomes.

Research opportunities: entrepreneurial teams and trust

As highlighted by the limited research on entrepreneurial teams and trust revealed by our review, there are considerable opportunities to extend research in this area that could contribute both to the entrepreneurship literature as well as general interests in trust relationships. We focus our recommendations for future contributions in three primary areas relating to the entrepreneurial process. First, future contributions are likely to come from research that explores opportunity assessment conducted by entrepreneurial teams. Is there a certain point where team diversity is more important than trusting relationships for developing novel ideas? What influence does trust have on helping team members identify and explore the most relevant business idea? Is trust less important during opportunity recognition than other stages? Could trust play a negative role in encouraging 'group think' or discouraging feedback seeking from multiple sources (or the opposite)?

Second, future contributions are likely to come from research that explores entrepreneurial action, and how trust within teams influences these decisions to act. Do high levels of trust on a team result in different levels of opportunity recognition and exploitation? Does trust make a team more risk seeking or open to exploration? How does team trust evolve as projects progress and in some cases fail? Does this have a long-term impact on entrepreneurial behavior or trust in future business relationships?

Finally, future contributions are likely to come from research that explores trust within teams and entrepreneurial exit. We anticipate considerable opportunities for research in this domain given the general lack of extant research on the role of trust in exit strategies including timing, methods, selection of advisors and so forth. Do higher levels of trust relate to certain types of exit? Does trust make it more difficult to exit a failing project (i.e. extend the period of throwing good money after bad)? How do entrepreneurial teams reassess their original exit goals and objectives as they receive performance feedback and how do these assessments influence trust, subsequent venturing and exit timing decisions? Does higher trust in an entrepreneurial team result in greater identification with the venture, and therefore create greater emotional obstacles to terminating a poorly performing venture?

Intra-organizational trust

Above, we highlighted the role of trust within the founding team, but trust is also important within the organization more broadly. For example, trust between functional managers of an organization enhances the positive relationship between the firm's entrepreneurial orientation and performance because this trust facilitates the amount and quality of information exchanged between founders necessary to engage in entrepreneurial activities (DeClercq, Dimov, and Thongpapanl, 2010). Indeed, some organizations have a 'high-trust' organizational environment that enhances entrepreneurial action and performance. Specifically, in building theory from a single case study, Ram (1999: 890) found that trust was emphasized in discussions about the 'nature and dynamics of project teams', yet these high-trust relationships can come under considerable strain with increased market uncertainty. Yet it is in these highly uncertain environments that employees need to be given greater autonomy over their tasks so that the organization can adapt to changing market conditions (Steward, Courtright, & Manz, 2011; Wall, Kemp,

Jackson, & Clegg, 1986). To provide autonomy, the organization needs to loosen control and one way to loosen control is through trust (Leifer & Mills, 1996). To gain trust, employees can engage in bonding activities as part of their self-management and in doing so demonstrate trustworthiness and reinforce employee autonomy (Leifer & Mills, 1996). This sort of employee autonomy has been associated with entrepreneurial outcomes such as opportunity recognition and/or identification (Shimizu, 2012), creativity and opportunity pursuit (Kuratko et al., 2004) and exploitation of (often) new and breakthrough ideas (Morris & Kuratko 2002).

Although not strictly within a particular business, franchising does involve relationships between the franchisers – the owner who grants a license or contractual privilege – and the franchisees – the user or receiver of a license to market a product or service under a name in accordance with the franchisor's system (Withane, 1991). The franchisors must try to achieve a delicate balance between, on the one hand, ensuring that franchisees comply with the standards detailed in the franchising agreement, and, on the other hand, not constraining the franchisees contribution and initiative (Davies, Lassar, Marolis, Prince & Winson, 2011). In their study of 135 franchisees, Davies and colleagues (2011) found that the franchisee's trust in the franchisor explained franchisee compliance, and that overall trust was positively influenced by franchisee's satisfaction and negatively influenced by relationship conflict.

Research opportunities: intra-organizational trust

There are a number of opportunities to make substantial primary contributions to entrepreneurship and trust literatures by exploring intra-organizational trust in entrepreneurial ventures. First, future contributions can be made in understanding intra-organizational trust and its influence on opportunity assessment. How do founding teams interact to identify opportunities? What is the nature of these founding teams historically (e.g. serial entrepreneur teams? Newly formed teams?) and how does that history influence trust and subsequent opportunity recognition? In a corporate entrepreneurship setting, how do inter-departmental collaborations and trusting relationships influence the identification of new ideas? This area of research is virtually untapped across a number of entrepreneurship settings (*de novo* or *de alio* venturing, social entrepreneurship, etc.) and could provide a number of substantial contributions.

Second, future contributions can be made in better understanding how intra-organizational trust influences entrepreneurial action. Are there different outcomes (e.g. first person opportunity recognition versus third person opportunity recognition [McMullen & Shepherd, 2006]) depending on intra-organizational trust dynamics? If so, what is the nature of these relationships? Do higher levels of intra-organizational trust result in unhealthy levels of risk taking? That is, can organizations become too trusting and therefore overconfident in their ability to discern between potential opportunities?

Third, future research can make a contribution by exploring the role of intra-organizational trust in entrepreneurial exit. Are there patterns of trusting relationships that result in persistence over shutting down a business? What effect (if any) does trust have on motivating an entrepreneur to delay the much-needed termination of a failing venture? Are firms with less-trusting intra-firm relationships more likely to sell quickly as opposed to await a larger payout or long-term ownership? How does trust influence the selection of advisors and partners for entrepreneurial exit? What impact does intra-firm trust have on individuals following entrepreneurial exit? Are these individuals more likely to pursue another venture together?

Finally, future research can make a contribution by exploring the role of intra-organizational trust in how organizations take entrepreneurial risks, approach learning from failure and navigate the pursuit of firm goals (Sitkin, 1992; Sitkin et al., 2011). Appropriate risk taking, learning from failure and adjusting venture goals are critical aspects of a successful new venture (Sarasvathy, 2001; Shepherd, 2003). Intra-organizational trust likely plays an important role in new venture (and corporate venture) teams that face extreme uncertainty in creating new products, services and organizations. Does increased trust lead to greater risk taking? How does trust shape a team's ability to learn from intermittent (and near certain) failures that occur during the emergence of a new venture or idea? Does trust influence a venture's goals pertaining to the scale, scope and goals of a firm (i.e. bigger and broader, more likely to take on major industry players)?

As discussed above, the opportunities for research on trust relationships internal to entrepreneurial ventures have been virtually unexplored. While contributions in this area have potential to be substantial, researchers must also consider external factors when seeking to understand entrepreneurial decision making and actions, to which we now turn.

Trust external to the entrepreneurial venture

Institutions and trust

Trust is held by entrepreneurs, and as described above, operates within teams, within organizations, franchise systems and other relationships. Trust also appears to have an institutional component relevant to entrepreneurship. For example, Anokhin and Schulze (2009) argued that corruption within a market institution undermines (potential) entrepreneurs' trust that commercial exchanges with other parties will proceed as expected. In the study of 64 nations, Anokhin and Schulze (2009) found that efforts to reduce corruption within an institution will increase confidence in the other institutional elements necessary to facilitate entrepreneurial action. However, in countries with less developed institutions, such as in a transition economy, entrepreneurs rely heavily on trust-based partnerships (rather than, e.g. the enforcement of laws). In such a situation, Nguyen and Rose (2009) found that trust was higher when the manager used his or her social network for the benefit of the partnership, used personal interactions to establish rapport, and shared information and business practices with the partner. This development of interpersonal trust was found to be positively associated with inter-firm collaboration.

Countries also differ in their generalized trust – 'placing trust in others one does not know intimately, that is, stronger' (Nguyen & Rose, 2009: 166). Consistent with the arguments that generalized trust facilitates the flow of information across diverse groups, the divulgence of unique information, and reduced inter-group conflict, Kwon and Averius (2010) proposed and found that a resident of a country higher in generalized trust was more likely to perceive entrepreneurial opportunities and invest in an entrepreneur with whom they had weak ties than was a resident of a country lower in generalized trust. This finding is consistent with a study of 191,907 individuals across 25 countries; in this study Ding, Au and Chiang (2015) found that in countries with a high level of trust there is more angel investing (i.e. investments in entrepreneurial firms). The notion is that trust is critical for (potential) business angels to invest in entrepreneurial firms.

Research opportunities: institutions and trust

Entrepreneurship scholars have long recognized the importance of contextual factors and how they influence nearly every aspect of the entrepreneurial process. However, there are considerable opportunities to provide contributions to the literature by exploring how institutional trust influences opportunity assessment, entrepreneurial action and entrepreneurial exit. First, institutional trust in communities, states and countries is likely to influence both the type and number of opportunities entrepreneurs recognize. Are certain levels of institutional trust more conducive to entrepreneurial activity than others? When extensive distrust exists, such as in 3rd world economies, does the type of entrepreneurial activity differ substantially (i.e. micro-business entrepreneurs versus high-growth entrepreneurs)?

Second, researchers could make contributions by exploring how institutional trust influences decisions to act on potential opportunities. What aspects of an institution result in mistrust and what effect (if any) do these have on entrepreneurial activity? In the United States or other developed countries, is there variance across geographies depending on tax or other incentives? What role do formal institutional policies have on trust and in turn, decisions to exploit opportunities?

Finally, in exploring institutional trust and entrepreneurial exit, scholars can explore how institutional norms, expectations and factors that uphold trusting relationships influence exit decisions. Do entrepreneurs hold on to ventures longer than needed when institutional trust is stronger? If so, what effect does this have on the venture, entrepreneur and subsequent activity? What are the consequences of a highly distrustful institutional environment on the entrepreneur's exit strategy? Are entrepreneurs less likely to grow their ventures to prepare them for public sale (and scrutiny)? Does institutional distrust toward entrepreneurs generate negative stigma for failure? How does this impact decisions to exit?

While contributions could be made in exploring the internal or external trust relationships in the entrepreneurship process, the intersection of these relationships could also be compelling in offering contributions to both the entrepreneurship and trust literatures. We now review literature that explores this topic and discuss opportunities for future research.

Trust at the intersection of internal and external

As ventures emerge, the boundaries between what is internal and external to the firm are often blurred (Vanacker, Collewaert, & Paeleman, 2013). For example, external resource providers can become major stakeholders and/or advisors as opposed to remaining on the outside (Casamatta, 2003), which alters the nature of social and business relationships. Similarly, new or emerging ventures must achieve understanding among other organizational entities that 'things will work out', earning their trust as a reliable partner, customer, or supplier (Aldrich, 2000: 218). To emerge successfully, entrepreneurs build and develop trust with various stakeholders, gaining legitimacy with outside organizations and recruiting new organizational members as resource providers and team members (Blundel & Smith, 2001; Brüderl & Preisendörfer, 1998).

Trust and entrepreneurial finance

Research on entrepreneurial finance focuses on two primary sources of capital for firm creation, development and growth – venture capitalists and business angels. Venture capitalists are professional investors that use institutional money to invest, and usually carry a portfolio of entrepreneurial investments (Sapienza, 1992). In contrast, business angels use personal funds to invest, and often seek to provide guidance or advice to entrepreneurs drawing on previous entrepreneurial experience (Mason & Harrison, 1996). In using a game theoretic model to compare these two sources of capital for entrepreneurial firms, Fairchild (2011) proposes that while venture capitalists offer entrepreneurs greater 'value added' contributions, the entrepreneur anticipates a more trusting relationship with business angels. This higher level of trust between the entrepreneur and business angel is believed to mitigate the risks the entrepreneur will shirk and the financer will try to 'steal the business' from the entrepreneur. But how is it that some entrepreneurs, and for that matter, sources of equity funding, start with more or less trust?

It appears that from whom the funder hears about the entrepreneurial venture impacts the initial nature of the relationship. Specifically, potential funders rely on the trustworthiness of the informant about the entrepreneurial firm in their decision-making process, such as the higher trustworthiness of the informant the lower the costs of due diligence (Fiet, 1995). Similarly, more trusted informants are believed to provide more reliable information for the investment decision (Fiet, 1995). This finding is critical in demonstrating the value of trust, how it can provide real advantages that translate to financial contributions, and how it can facilitate emergence at one of the most difficult stages of a venture's lifespan.

Trust between the entrepreneur and a venture capitalist also appears to be enhanced by co-ethnicity, that is, if the entrepreneur and the venture capitalist share the same ethnicity then the venture capitalist is more likely to invest in the entrepreneur's business and be actively involved in the entrepreneurial firm's board of directors (Bengtsson & Hsu, 2015). Furthermore, there is evidence that trust plays a stronger role between entrepreneurs and angels than between entrepreneurs and venture capitalists (De Clercq, Fried, Lehtoner, & Sapienza, 2006; Fairchild, 2011; Fiet, 1995). This finding suggests that resource-poor entrepreneurs might benefit from appropriately aligning their investments in trusting relationships with the specific type of resource provider (e.g. angel investor versus venture capitalist).

Beyond providing a path to resources, trust may not always be a good thing when engaging in an investment relationship in the unique context of entrepreneurship. Bammens and Collewaert (2014) found that entrepreneur's perception of intra-team trust (between the entrepreneur and the business angel) is negatively related to the business angel's assessment of venture performance. This suggests a 'potential darker side of trust' in entrepreneurs' relationships with investors (angel/venture capitalist) (Bammens & Collewaert, 2014; 2004). That is, it suggests that while trust facilitates the transaction between and entrepreneur and investor, it could also cloud the judgment of investors when they assess a firm and its potential for success.

Research opportunities: trust and entrepreneurial finance

Acquiring and maintaining financial resources during venture emergence is critical; similarly, there are important implications of these resources when investors seek to grow and eventually exit the venture. Given the importance and implication of venture financing, substantial contributions could be made by exploring trust and entrepreneurial finance. First, venture finance relationships are useful not only in providing financial resources, but also offer potentially unique perspectives on identifying opportunities. How does trust influence opportunity recognition? Are angel investors more trustworthy and does this result in more opportunities identified? Does it result in more lucrative opportunities? Does the motivation of venture capitalists (e.g. maximum return on investment) outweigh trust in influencing the identification of high-growth, high-potential opportunities or does it have other consequences? Is there a dark side to trust in terms of opportunity recognition? For example, does the inclination to trust put an investor and/or entrepreneur more at risk to be exploited? Does the inclination to trust someone of the same ethnicity cloud other important data needed to make an accurate evaluation?

Second, future contributions are likely to come from research that explores trust in entrepreneurial finance relationships and entrepreneurial action. Is the nature of trust different across types of financers (i.e. trust to achieve high growth, trust to effectively start and manage a venture long-term, etc.)? How important is trust compared to other decision criteria in deciding between alternate sources of venture funding? Do entrepreneurs more heavily weigh trust when entering into financial relationships with angels than with venture capitalists?

Finally, future contributions are likely to come from research that explores how trust in entrepreneurial finance relationships influences entrepreneurial exit. Are these exit decisions heavily reliant on trust or are they more contractual/transactional? Does trust in a relationship influence the method of exit (e.g. IPO, selling to a larger firm, liquidation, etc.) over and above other factors (e.g. goals of investors, firm performance, etc.)? How are exit decisions determined and how are those influenced by trust? Does trust influence the establishment and nature of 'stage-gates' needed to assess intermittent venture performance? How does trust influence the decision to persist in a failing venture and with what consequences (for the entrepreneur, investor and entrepreneurial firm)?

Inter-organizational trust

Beyond entrepreneurial finance relationships, entrepreneurial firms, as other firms, often engage in inter-organizational relationships. These relationships are important for new firms to gain legitimacy, grow and survive (Aldrich, 2000). Trust appears to play an important role in understanding the nature and effectiveness of these inter-organizational relationships. For example, in a field study of social control, Larson (1992) developed a process model of network formation that highlighted, among other things, the importance of trust. Indeed, before a tie was established between the two companies, a foundation of mutual trust was established – in particular, 'honesty made trust possible and was therefore essential to the formation of a successful tie' (Larson, 1992: 95).

However, high trust may not always be an unambiguous blessing. For example, after highlighting the benefits of trust for the performance of an inter-organizational relationship, Molina-Morales and Martinez-Fernandez (2009) noted that too much attention can be invested in maintaining a trusting relationship – that is, this time dedication provides less time for speaking out and interpreting alternate sources of information and less time for monitoring; both of which can adversely impact performance. Indeed, Molina-Morales and Martinez-Fernandez (2009) found an inverted U-shaped relationship between trust and firm value creation. This finding is consistent with the notion of network embeddedness (Uzzi, 1997). On the one hand, groups that have highly embedded networks know one another, draw upon informal means to self-monitor, and are more capable at coordinating actions to enhance efficiency and continuous improvement. However, these groups are less likely to challenge the status quo and gain insights through information not available within the group, which can hamper innovation and development (see Burt, 2005 for review). Therefore, trust and embeddedness are likely reinforcing the concepts, which come with both positive and negative consequences for key entrepreneurial outcomes.

The potential negative consequences of trust in inter-organizational relationships are explored further in Graebner (2009). In studying both the buyer and the seller in the process of the acquisitions of entrepreneurial firms, Graebner (2009) found that there is trust asymmetry between buyers and sellers. This asymmetry arises because in the initial stage of the acquisition process sellers 'select out' distrusted buyers, yet buyers did not 'select out' distrusted sellers. As a result, relative to sellers, buyers engaged in more due diligence about deal terms, and were more likely to behave deceptively (Graebner, 2009). Relative to buyers, sellers of entrepreneurial firms were more likely to trust but with high uncertainty this high sense of security from trust may be false. This finding again demonstrates the complex and often fluid nature of trust for entrepreneurs acting under conditions of uncertainty, and suggests that trust is (potentially) fragile, especially during early stages of venturing.

Research opportunities: inter-organizational trust

Future contributions will likely come from research that focuses on inter-organizational trust relationships and how they influence opportunity assessment, entrepreneurial action and entrepreneurial exit. First, opportunities are identified or created often through interaction with other stakeholders (Sarasvathy, 2001). How does trust in inter-organizational relationships influence opportunity recognition and assessment? Are some relationships more important than others (i.e. with suppliers, customers, investors) in terms of levels of trust to facilitate opportunity recognition? How does trust in inter-organizational relationships influence the type of opportunities entrepreneurs identify and pursue?

Second, inter-organizational trust likely influences how and when entrepreneurs decide to exploit opportunities. How does inter-organizational trust influence approaches to opportunity exploitation (e.g. result in more economic-focused outcomes, social outcomes, short-term gains, etc.)? What relationships are the most influential and/or in need of trust to accomplish the entrepreneur's objectives? Is there variance across types of ventures (i.e. social, environmental or economic venture)?

Finally, in what way does inter-organizational trust influence entrepreneurial exit? Does trust in this context make vertical integration within an industry more likely? Does enhanced trust between firms allow for more rapid growth due to merger or acquisition options? Does trust between organizations result in delayed responses to indicators of failure? If so, what effect does that have long term on learning? How do trust and exit influence broader macroeconomic outcomes in a clustered industry or geography? For example, does trust delay the release of inefficiently used resources (e.g. resources held by failing firms)?

Discussion

Entrepreneurs face unique challenges in identifying opportunities, gathering resources to pursue those opportunities and growing businesses in preparation for successful exit. The challenges are unique in that entrepreneurs must work with a number of other actors under extreme conditions of uncertainty (Sarasvathy, 2001), where the goals and objectives of the various actors are not always aligned with those of the entrepreneur (Aldrich, 2000; Arthurs & Busenitz, 2003). Emerging organizations are exposed to liabilities associated with being new, which increases the likelihood of failure and therefore the need to rely on strangers for activities critical to the successful emergence, growth and sustainability of a venture (Stinchcombe, 1965).

Given the unique situational environment faced by entrepreneurs, understanding how entrepreneurs identify, build and mobilize relationships to achieve their desired ends is a critical emphasis in entrepreneurship research (Shane, 2003; Shane & Venkataraman, 2000). In this article, we reviewed literature on trust, as it is likely an important resource in helping entrepreneurs achieve their desired outcomes in that, among other things, it 'reduces harmful conflict . . . [and] facilitates rapid formulation of ad hoc work groups' (Rousseau et al., 1998: 394). Our literature review confirmed the relevance of trust as an important construct in entrepreneurship research, in particular in understanding relationships internal to a venture, in the environmental context external to the firm, and at the intersection of internal and external environments. This finding is consistent with recent reviews on trust (e.g. Fulmer & Gelfand, 2012) that call for a better understanding of the multi-faceted nature of trust in organizational life and how these different relationships influence important outcomes. We anticipate that contributions can be made to both the literatures on trust and entrepreneurship by continuing to explore the internal, external and boundary trust-relationships associated with entrepreneurship.

Beyond contributions to the entrepreneurship literature, our review also revealed that there are considerable opportunities to extend research on trust by exploring the role of trust at different stages in the organizational lifecycle. There is much to be explored at many different levels of the organization *at each stage* to better understand how trust influences important organizational outcomes. As highlighted in our future research recommendations throughout the chapter, the nature and influence of trust likely evolves depending on the stage of entrepreneurial activity. Highlighting research in this way offers opportunities to expand research on trust, as well as management research beyond entrepreneurship. Specifically, we anticipate that research on organizational behavior can extend our understanding of the role of trust in team dynamics, leadership and individual performance at various stages of a venture. Similarly, strategic management research can explore the role of trust in new venture boards, inter-organizational relationships and potential M&A partners in exploring firm performance outcomes at various stages (growth, exit, etc.).

Conclusion

Despite the extensive body of research on trust in the organizational sciences, there are considerable opportunities to explore the different relationships associated with entrepreneurship through the lens of trust. By developing programs to systematically explore this field, researchers will likely make significant contributions to our understanding of how trust is defined and understood in different contexts, how individuals develop or build trust under uncertainty and how entrepreneurship scholars should account for trust in subsequent studies.

References

Aldrich, H. E. 2000. *Organizations evolving*, New York, NJ, Prentice-Hall.

Anokhin, S. & Schulze, W. S. 2009. Entrepreneurship, innovation, and corruption. *Journal of Business Venturing*, 24, 465–476.

Arthurs, J. D. & Busenitz, L. W. 2003. The boundaries and limitations of agency theory and stewardship theory in the venture capitalist/entrepreneur relationship. *Entrepreneurship Theory and Practice*, 28, 145–162.

Bammens, Y. & Collewaert, V. 2014. Trust between entrepreneurs and angel investors exploring positive and negative implications for venture performance assessments. *Journal of Management*, 40, 1980–2008.

Bengtsson, O. & Hsu, D. H. 2015. Ethnic matching in the US venture capital market. *Journal of Business Venturing*, 30, 338–354.

Blatt, R. 2009. Tough love: How communal schemas and contracting practices build relational capital in entrepreneurial teams. *Academy of Management Review*, 34, 533–551.

Blundel, R. & Smith, D. 2001. Business networks: SMEs and inter-firm collaboration: A review of the research literature with implications for policy. SBS Research.

Brüderl, J. & Preisendörfer, P. 1998. Network support and the success of newly founded business. *Small Business Economics*, 10, 213–225.

Burt, R. S. 2005. *Brokerage and closure: An introduction to social capital*, New York: Oxford University Press.

Casamatta, C. 2003. Financing and advising: Optimal financial contracts with venture capitalists. *The Journal of Finance*, 58, 2059–2086.

Clark, M. S., Fitness, J. & Brissette, I. 2001. Understanding people's perceptions of relationships is crucial to understanding their emotional lives. In: G. J. O. Fletcher & M. S. Clark (eds) *Blackwell handbook of social psychology: Interpersonal processes* (pp. 253–278). Malden, MA: Blackwell Publishers.

Clark, M. S., Mills, J. R. & Corcoran, D. M. 1989. Keeping track of needs and inputs of friends and strangers. *Personality and Social Psychology Bulletin*, 15, 533–542.

Davies, M. A., Lassar, W., Manolis, C., Prince, M. & Winsor, R. D. 2011. A model of trust and compliance in franchise relationships. *Journal of Business Venturing*, 26, 321–340.

De Clercq, D., Dimov, D. & Thongpapanl, N. T. 2010. The moderating impact of internal social exchange processes on the entrepreneurial orientation–performance relationship. *Journal of Business Venturing*, 25, 87–103.

De Clercq, D., Fried, V. H., Lehtonen, O. & Sapienza, H. J. 2006. An entrepreneur's guide to the venture capital galaxy. *The Academy of Management Perspectives*, 20, 90–112.

Ding, Z., AU, K. & Chiang, F. 2015. Social trust and angel investors' decisions: A multilevel analysis across nations. *Journal of Business Venturing*, 30, 307–321.

Fairchild, R. 2011. An entrepreneur's choice of venture capitalist or angel-financing: A behavioral game-theoretic approach. *Journal of Business Venturing*, 26, 359–374.

Fiet, J. O. 1995. Reliance upon informants in the venture capital industry. *Journal of Business Venturing*, 10, 195–223.

Fulmer, C. A. & Gelfand, M. J. 2012. At what level (and in whom) we trust trust across multiple organizational levels. *Journal of Management*, 38, 1167–1230.

Graebner, M. E. 2009. Caveat venditor: Trust asymmetries in acquisitions of entrepreneurial firms. *Academy of Management Journal*, 52, 435–472.

Graham, M. E. & Tarbell, L. M. 2006. The importance of the employee perspective in the competency development of human resource professionals. *Human Resource Management*, 45, 337–355.

Grégoire, D. A., Corbett, A. C. & McMullen, J. S. 2011. The cognitive perspective in entrepreneurship: An agenda for future research. *Journal of Management Studies*, 48, 1443–1477.

Guth, W. D. & Ginsberg, A. 1990. Guest editors' introduction: Corporate entrepreneurship. *Strategic Management Journal*, 11, 5–15.

Harper, D. A. 2008. Towards a theory of entrepreneurial teams. *Journal of Business Venturing*, 23, 613–626.

Iacobucci, D. & Rosa, P. 2010. The growth of business groups by habitual entrepreneurs: The role of entrepreneurial teams. *Entrepreneurship Theory and Practice*, 34, 351–377.

Kuratko, D. F., Hornsby, J. S. & Goldsby, M. G. 2004. Sustaining corporate entrepreneurship: Modelling perceived implementation and outcome comparisons at organizational and individual levels. *The International Journal of Entrepreneurship and Innovation*, 5, 77–89.

Kwon, S.-W. & Arenius, P. 2010. Nations of entrepreneurs: A social capital perspective. *Journal of Business Venturing*, 25, 315–330.

Larson, A. 1992. Network dyads in entrepreneurial settings: A study of the governance of exchange relationships. *Administrative Science Quarterly*, 37, 76–104.

Leifer, R. & Mills, P. K. 1996. An information processing approach for deciding upon control strategies and reducing control loss in emerging organizations. *Journal of Management*, 22, 113–137.

Lewicki, R. J., Tomlinson, E. C. & Gillespie, N. 2006. Models of interpersonal trust development: Theoretical approaches, empirical evidence, and future directions. *Journal of Management*, 32, 991–1022.

Lewis, K. 2003. Measuring transactive memory systems in the field: Scale development and validation. *Journal of Applied Psychology*, 88, 587–604.

Mason, C. M. & Harrison, R. T. 1996. Informal venture capital: A study of the investment process, the post-investment experience and investment performance. *Entrepreneurship & Regional Development*, 8, 105–126.

Mayer, R. C., Davis, J. H. & Schoorman, F. D. 1995. An integrative model of organizational trust. *Academy of management review*, 20, 709–734.

Mayer, R. C. & Gavin, M. B. 2005. Trust in management and performance: Who minds the shop while the employees watch the boss? *Academy of Management Journal*, 48, 874–888.

McMullen, J. S. & Shepherd, D. A. 2006. Entrepreneurial action and the role of uncertainty in the theory of the entrepreneur. *Academy of Management Review*, 31, 132–152.

Meyerson, D., Weick, K. E. & Kramer, R. M. 1996. Swift trust and temporary groups. In: R. M. Kramer & T. R. Tyler (eds) *Trust in organizations: Frontiers of theory and research* (pp. 166–195). Thousand Oaks, CA: Sage Publications.

Molina-Morales, F. X. & Martínez-Fernández, M. T. 2009. Too much love in the neighborhood can hurt: How an excess of intensity and trust in relationships may produce negative effects on firms. *Strategic Management Journal*, 30, 1013–1023.

Morris, M. H. & Kuratko, D. 2002. *Corporate entrepreneurship: Entrepreneurial development inside organisations*, Orlando, FL, Harcourt Publishers.

Nguyen, T. V. & Rose, J. 2009. Building trust—Evidence from Vietnamese entrepreneurs. *Journal of Business Venturing*, 24, 165–182.

Patton, M. Q. 1990. *Qualitative evaluation and research methods*, Newbury Park, CA, Sage.

Ram, M. 1999. Managing consultants in a small firm: A case study. *Journal of Management Studies*, 36, 853–873.

Rousseau, D. M., Sitkin, S. B., Burt, R. S. & Camerer, C. 1998. Not so different after all: A cross-discipline view of trust. *Academy of Management Review*, 23, 393–404.

Sapienza, H. J. 1992. When do venture capitalists add value? *Journal of Business Venturing*, 7, 9–27.

Sarasvathy, S. D. 2001. Causation and effectuation: Toward a theoretical shift from economic inevitability to entrepreneurial contingency. *Academy of Management Review*, 26, 243–263.

Schjoedt, L., Monsen, E., Pearson, A., Barnett, T. & Chrisman, J. J. 2013. New venture and family business teams: Understanding team formation, composition, behaviors, and performance. *Entrepreneurship Theory and Practice*, 37, 1–15.

Shane, S. 2003. *A general theory of entrepreneurship: The individual-opportunity nexus*, Northampton, MA, Edward Elgar.

Shane, S. & Venkataraman, S. 2000. The promise of entrepreneurship as a field of research. *Academy of Management Review*, 25, 217–226.

Shepherd, D. A. 2003. Learning from business failure: Propositions of grief recovery for the self-employed. *Academy of Management Review*, 282, 318–328.

Shepherd, D. A., Williams, T. A. & Patzelt, H. 2015. Thinking about entrepreneurial decision making: Review and research agenda. *Journal of Management*, 41, 11–46.

Shimizu, K. 2012. Risks of corporate entrepreneurship: Autonomy and agency issues. *Organization Science*, 23, 194–206.

Sitkin, S. B. 1992. Learning through failure: The strategy of small losses. In B. M. Staw & L. L. Cummings (eds) *Research in organizational behavior* (Vol. 14, pp. 231–266). Greenwich, CT: JAI Press.

Sitkin, S. B., See, K. E., Miller, C. C., Lawless, M. W. & Carton, A. M. 2011. The paradox of stretch goals: Organizations in pursuit of the seemingly impossible. *Academy of Management Review*, 36, 544–566.

Stewart, G. L., Courtright, S. H. & Manz, C. C. 2011. Self-leadership: A multilevel review. *Journal of Management*, 37, 185–222.

Stevenson, H. H. & Jarillo, J. C. 1990. A paradigm of entrepreneurship: Entrepreneurial management. *Strategic Management Journal*, 11, 17–27.

Stinchcombe, A. L. 1965. *Organizations and social structure*, Chicago, IL, Rand McNally.

Talaulicar, T., Grundei, J. & Werder, A. V. 2005. Strategic decision making in start-ups: The effect of top management team organization and processes on speed and comprehensiveness. *Journal of Business Venturing*, 20, 519–541.

Tzabbar, D. & Vestal, A. 2015. Bridging the social chasm in geographically distributed R&D teams: The moderating effects of relational strength and status asymmetry on the novelty of team innovation. *Organization Science*, 26(3), 811–829.

Uzzi, B. (1997). Social structure and competition in interfirm networks: The paradox of embeddedness. *Administrative Science Quarterly*, 42, 35–67.

Vanacker, T., Collewaert, V. & Paeleman, I. 2013. The relationship between slack resources and the performance of entrepreneurial firms: The role of venture capital and angel investors. *Journal of Management Studies*, 50, 1070–1096.

Venkataraman, S. (1997). The distinctive domain of entrepreneurship research. In J. Katz (ed.) *Advances in entrepreneurship, firm emergence, and growth*. Greenwich: JAI Press.

Wall, T. D., Kemp, N. J., Jackson, P. R. & Clegg, C. W. 1986. Outcomes of autonomous workgroups: A long-term field experiment. *Academy of Management Journal*, 29, 280–304.

Walsh, J. P. 1995. Managerial and organizational cognition: Notes from a trip down memory lane. *Organization Science*, 6, 280–321.

Welter, F. & Smallbone, D. 2006. Exploring the role of trust in entrepreneurial activity. *Entrepreneurship Theory and Practice*, 30, 465–475.

Withane, S. 1991. Franchising and franchisee behavior: An examination of opinions, personal characteristics, and motives of Canadian franchisee entrepreneurs. *Journal of Small Business Management*, 29, 22–29.

Zahra, S. A., Sapienza, H. J. & Davidsson, P. 2006. Entrepreneurship and dynamic capabilities: A review, model and research agenda. *Journal of Management Studies*, 43, 917–955.

Zheng, Y. 2012. Unlocking founding team prior shared experience: A transactive memory system perspective. *Journal of Business Venturing*, 27, 577–591.

24

TRUST IN SAFETY-CRITICAL CONTEXTS

Brian C. Gunia, Sharon H. Kim and Kathleen M. Sutcliffe[1]

Introduction

On the morning of March 24, 2015, Lufthansa's Germanwings Flight 9525, en route from Barcelona to Dusseldorf, fell from a clear sky, slamming into the craggy French Alps and killing all 144 passengers plus six crew members (Clark & Bilefsky, 2015a). France's aviation authority reported that, prior to the crash, air traffic control had lost contact with the pilots, yet surprisingly had received no distress call. Early reports suggested that the crash of the Airbus A320 – carrying high school students, vacationers and others – was a horrible "accident" (Clark & Bilefsky, 2015a). By early next morning, however, preliminary analyses of the cockpit voice recorder led officials to doubt this initial explanation.

Although the voice recorder data made terrorism look unlikely (Spector, 2015), other puzzling clues began to emerge. Before the plane's descent, for example, the commanding pilot had left the cockpit and was unable to re-enter. As officials described, "The guy outside is knocking lightly on the door, and there is no answer. . . . And then he hits the door stronger, and no answer . . .You can hear he is trying to smash the door down" (Clark & Bilefsky, 2015b). Investigators trying to make sense of the data were uncertain about the "condition or activity of the pilot who remained in the cockpit" (Clark & Bilefsky, 2015b). Although it often takes months or years to determine the causes of plane crashes, aviation safety experts were quick to offer alternative theories. One analyst suggested that perhaps "a pilot was incapacitated by a sudden event such as a fire or a drop in cabin pressure" (Clark & Bilefsky, 2015b). Another took a more pessimistic view, suggesting that pilot silence during the plane's descent raised the possibility of intentionality: "So far, we don't have any evidence that points clearly to a technical explanation. So we have to consider the possibility of deliberate human responsibility" (Clark & Bilefky, 2015b).

On Thursday, March 26, after more extensively analysing the plane's transponder and audio voice recording, French authorities asserted that the co-pilot had deliberately crashed the plane (Spector, 2015). The transponder showed that the co-pilot had manually reset the autopilot to take the plane from 38,000 feet to 98 feet. And in the final moments of the flight, the voice recorder captured the co-pilot's steady and calm breathing, as well as sounds from outside the cockpit door – "knocking and pleading from the commanding pilot that he be let in, then violent pounding on the door and finally passengers' screams" (Bilefsky and Clark, 2015). Taken together, the evidence left little doubt about the purposeful nature of the act. This possibility was affirmed three days after the crash when new evidence surfaced suggesting that the co-pilot suffered psychological problems that he had hidden from his employer.[2]

Trust suffuses safety-critical contexts, like commercial aviation, in myriad ways, providing a backdrop for this chapter. Although trust is a complex, multi-dimensional construct defined differently across contexts, it has generally been defined as "a psychological state comprising the intention to accept vulnerability based on positive expectations of the intentions or behavior of another" (Rousseau, Sitkin, Burt, & Camerer, 1998). In safety-critical contexts, it has been defined more specifically as "an individual's willingness to rely on another person based on expectations that he or she will act safely or intends to act safely" (Conchie, Donald, & Taylor, 2006: 1097). In the case of Germanwings Flight 9525, European regulatory agencies trusted airline policies to detect pilots who were unfit to fly, allowing European (unlike American) pilots to occupy the cockpit alone. The public trusted that the airline would hire highly skilled, competent, and mentally stable pilots who would get them safely to their destination. Lufthansa trusted that its pilots would adhere to company policies and would self-regulate by notifying the company of conditions that could affect their flying or licensure (Eddy, Bilefsky, & Clark, 2015). Passengers on this particular flight trusted that their pilots would get them to their destination without incident. The commanding pilot trusted his co-pilot's competence and, in his absence, assumed that the co-pilot would fly the plane with safety in mind.

Research examining the role of trust in safety-critical contexts is relatively nascent (Conchie & Donald, 2006: 1151), but extant research often indicates that trust is an important antecedent of safe behaviours and outcomes. Trust affects safety through various mechanisms. For example, as Conchie and Donald point out (2006: 1151), trust facilitates risk communication (e.g. open and frequent safety communication), encourages safety leadership, enables group cohesion, and appears to enhance the success of safety initiatives. Trust is also conceptualized as the bedrock on which strong "safety cultures" are built (Vogus, Sutcliffe, & Weick, 2010).

At the same time, as the Germanwings story and an emerging stream of research suggest, unconditional trust is not always beneficial. Trust sometimes can lead to overconfidence (McEvily, Perrone, & Zaheer, 2003), reductions in risk perception (Viklund, 2003), and decreased vigilance and wariness (Weick & Sutcliffe, 2007) with a variety of accompanying unintended consequences. Consequently, an emerging stream of research on this topic has considered the potential benefits of low trust (the conceptual opposite of trust) and the related, but perhaps conceptually distinct, construct of distrust, defined as "confident negative expectations regarding another's conduct" (Lewicki, McAllister, & Bies, 1998: 439). In this focus on the conceptual alternatives to trust, research on trust in safety-critical contexts mirrors the management literature. Building on the work of Luhmann (1979), Lewicki et al. (1998) presented a pioneering model indicating that trust and distrust represent separate dimensions and suggested that each deserves independent research attention. While adopting the insight that the consequences of low trust and distrust are important to study, the safety-critical literature has not (in our reading) often adopted the insight that trust and distrust are separate dimensions. As a result, it often equates concepts like "low trust" and "distrust" that Lewicki et al.'s (1998) model would differentiate. Indeed, our reading of the literature suggests that words like "low trust," "no trust," "mistrust," and "distrust" are used rather interchangeably.

This presents inherent challenges for the current chapter, which seeks to review existing research to better understand the positive and negative roles that trust and its conceptual opposites play in safety-critical contexts, as well as the mechanisms through which these effects come about. In our review of the original findings, we address this issue by preserving the terminology that the original authors used (including terms like "mistrust" that have not been widely used in the management literature). In our own interpretations of the results, however, we generally use the words "high trust" and "low trust," as we believe that these terms capture the majority of the measures reported in this literature. The rest of our review is organized as follows: We begin by defining safety-critical contexts. We then review the extant literature in order to examine the various ways that high trust and low trust influence safety behaviours and outcomes. Next, we discuss some integrative perspectives on the contributions of high trust and low trust to safety. We conclude with a set of ideas for future research and practice.

Safety-critical contexts

Like trust, safety-critical contexts are challenging to define, as safety represents a potentially critical goal of all organizations that could create harm (Zacharatos, Barling, & Iverson, 2005). That is, safety in its broadest sense simply means the state of being safe from the risk of experiencing or causing injury, danger, or loss. Thus, all organizations are concerned with safety in one form or another, in that they seek to minimize the exposure of organizational members, customers, and other stakeholders to conditions considered dangerous in some way. For example, financial institutions are presumably concerned with minimizing their risk of exposure and loss and also with minimizing risks and losses for their customers (Weick & Sutcliffe, 2015). Automobile manufacturers are concerned with the safety features of vehicles. They try to inspire confidence that some project, process, or product will not result in loss or harm (Weick & Sutcliffe, 2015). Museums are concerned with the stability of exhibits so that visitors are not at risk of danger (Christianson, Farkas, Sutcliffe, & Weick, 2009). Consequently, we view "safety-critical" as a particular *view* of organizations more than a particular *set* of organizations – or, more specifically, the view that any organization takes when primarily seeking to prevent harmful outcomes (versus promote beneficial outcomes). Since individuals in organizations routinely switch between prevention and promotion goals (Crowe & Higgins, 1997), safety-critical contexts arise in all organizations, and therefore all organizations need to manage the trust issues that surround safety.

Still, safety concerns do loom larger in some organizations than others. Given their elevated and ever-present risk of severe harm, for example, organizations in industries like healthcare, military operations, nuclear power generation, oil and gas extraction, chemical processing, and mass transportation tend to assume a safety-critical view more often than organizations in less risky industries (Rochlin, 1993). Thus, our review is grounded in research on industries facing relatively high risks (and requiring high reliability), but we wish to point out that the proposed implications may be relevant to all organizations, when focused on preventing harm.

The high trust–low trust dilemma

Scholarly interest on trust in safety-critical contexts is growing, particularly in the organizational sciences. Much of this work has taken the form of commentaries, perspectives, or conceptual articles. Many of these articles (e.g. Entwistle & Quick, 2006; Firth-Cozens, 2004; Fleming & Lardner, 2001; Mearns, Flin, Gordon & Fleming, 1997; Reason, 1997), as well as some empirical studies (e.g. Clarke, 1999; Jeffcott, Pidgeon, Weyman, & Walls, 2006; Luria, 2010; Watson, Scott, Bishop, & Turnbeaugh, 2005; Zacharatoes, Barling, & Iverson, 2005), have suggested that high trust is a positive contributor to safety. Specifically, trust enables people to share information that could avert a future error but could also get them into trouble if the organization chooses to blame them for what they share (Conchie & Donald, 2009). Additionally, trust enables people to provide and receive safety-oriented feedback, as indicated in a study of nuclear reactor employees in the UK (Cox, Jones, & Rycraft, 2004). More generally, trust may underlie the four important elements (reporting, flexibility, justice, and learning) that are necessary for building a solid safety culture (Reason, 1997). Without high levels of organizational trust, people are unlikely to assume the risks involved in reporting errors and the benefits of learning from them, in part because the organization will likely treat them unjustly for doing so (Burns, Mearns, & McGeorge, 2006; Cox, Jones, & Collinson, 2006).

Despite the logical coherence of these arguments, however, they tend to conflict with a large and growing body of theory and empirical research that suggests another path to safety (Conchie, Donald, and Taylor, 2006). In a word, this alternative view suggests that lower levels of trust, and in some cases even distrust, may contribute positively to safety. In the original work that inspired Lewicki et al.'s (1998) model, for example, Luhmann (1979) argued that highly complex systems require both trust and distrust (especially "institutionalized distrust"): the former to take highly unlikely events out of consideration and the latter to keep unlikely but possible events within consideration (Tharaldsen, Mearns, & Knudsen, 2010). Similarly, Pidgeon, Walls, Weyman, and Horlick-Jones's (2003) critical trust model suggests that 'critical trust' (a practical reliance on other people combined with a skepticism of the system) complements government risk regulations to encourage safe outcomes. This argument is also consistent with the view that distrust is particularly helpful when designing safety institutions, as it helps designers perceive latent risks (Turner & Pidgeon, 1997). Similarly, Hale (2000) influentially advocated for "creative mistrust," a stance in which employees creatively question the risks inherent in organizational systems in order to promote both constant questioning and searching for weak points in the existing culture. Finally, McEvily and colleagues (2003) argued that excessive trust creates overconfidence and reduces innovation, while Entwistle and Quick (2006) noted that in certain circumstances, unjustified trust can result in harmful or unethical patterns of behaviour.

Findings from a variety of studies support these views by identifying positive relationships between high trust and low trust, casting doubt on the unequivocal benefits of trust, identifying some unexpected benefits of low trust, and raising questions about the concepts of distrust and mistrust. For example, Burns, Mearns, and McGeorge (2006) studied explicit and implicit trust and distrust within a UK gas plant, measuring trust and distrust both explicitly (with self-report questions) and implicitly (with an implicit association task). An unexpected finding showed a positive correlation between employees' level of implicit trust and distrust in organizational colleagues, suggesting that they were implicitly trusting and distrusting colleagues at the same time, thereby indicating that implicit trust and distrust may go hand in hand. A qualitative study of UK train operators revealed a deep trust in rules and regulations ("rule-based trust"), which promoted safety during normal operations but actually undermined operators' abilities to respond to novel safety challenges (Jeffcott et al., 2006). Specifically, operators reported feeling "programmed" by the rules and unable to adjust their behaviour in such unexpected situations.

Cox, Jones, and Collinson's (2006) qualitative study of a nuclear power plant showed that a safety intervention improved safety by increasing both employees' trust and their capacity for creative mistrust (the ability to creatively question the risks in organizational systems; Hale, 2000). Specifically, the intervention provided employees with "the opportunity to develop the skills that would enable them to challenge unsafe practices in an appropriate manner" (2006: 1131). Similarly, the quantitative survey component of a mixed-method study on an offshore oil rig (Tharaldsen, Mearns, & Knudsen, 2010) revealed a positive association between trust in workmates and safety performance, suggesting that trust in workmates prevents people from being involved in safety incidents. At the same time, the qualitative focus group component of this same research revealed that employees are also acutely aware that excessive trust makes people complacent and exposes them to risk. Additionally, interviews of offshore employees revealed that excessive trust resulted in reduced personal responsibility for safety (Conchie & Donald, 2008), and a survey (also of offshore employees) showed that "attitudes of trust appear to have minimal influence on safety" (Conchie & Donald, 2006: 1157), in that distrust predicted safety incidents much more consistently than did trust. Finally, a pair of survey studies of forest harvesting (Burt, Chmiel, & Hayes, 2009) and firefighting (Burt & Stevenson, 2009) organizations showed that excessive trust in organizational onboarding and training programs led existing employees to underestimate the risks associated with new-employee mistakes and thus take fewer precautionary measures.

Collectively, this body of theoretical and empirical work suggests that the logically appealing 'trust is beneficial' perspective is incomplete. Beyond stimulating organizational safety interventions that may fall flat, this view may also contribute to conceptual confusion in the safety literature. For example, studies have identified inconsistent roles of trust in relation to leadership and safety behaviours, e.g. by identifying trust as a moderator but not a mediator (Conchie & Donald, 2009) as well as a mediator but not a moderator (Conchie, Taylor, & Donald, 2012) of the leadership-safety behaviors relationship. Specifically, Conchie and Donald (2009) examined the possibility that trust either mediates or moderates the association between safety-specific transformational leadership and safety citizenship behaviors, but only found support for moderation. Leaders influenced subordinates' citizenship behaviors under conditions of high or moderate safety-specific trust, but not under low trust. In a later study, Conchie and colleagues (2012) examined safety-specific transformational leadership and safety voice behaviors, finding that affect-based (but not cognitive-based) trust mediated the relationship between leader behaviour and voice behaviors. The authors suggested that leaders who wish to encourage safety voice among employees should cultivate affective bonds with employees. These studies differ in several ways, and the different findings may result from different conceptualizations of trust (e.g. cognition-based trust grounded in beliefs versus affect-based trust grounded in emotions; McAllister, 1995). Nevertheless, we propose that some of the discrepant findings in the literature could also relate to the latent costs of high trust or latent benefits of low trust, which have not often been measured.

By focusing on the benefits and costs of high trust and low trust in tandem and distinguishing trust from distrust, as some of the above-cited research has done, a more complete view is now beginning to emerge. This view emphasizes that high trust and low trust both hold an important place within safety-critical contexts (Conchie & Donald, 2008). This view is not without its own challenges, however, as high and low trust would seem to coexist in an uneasy balance. We call this uncomfortable coexistence the "high trust–low trust dilemma." In the next section, we discuss various perspectives on the integration of high trust and low trust, describing several ways that safety and other streams of research have allowed for their coexistence, helping to resolve this dilemma.

Under the traditional "trust is beneficial" assumption, there is no dilemma: since low trust hampers safety, it should simply be minimized in favor of high trust (Reason, 1997). A dilemma has only arisen in the wake of research identifying both high trust and low trust (and in some cases distrust) as necessary for safety, in conjunction with the fact that trusting and not trusting the same object, at the same time, seems contradictory. The dilemma comes into focus when comparing the definitions of trust and distrust. For example, consider the definitions of safety-specific trust as "a means of reducing social complexity by allowing undesirable conduct to be removed from consideration" and safety-specific distrust as "allowing undesirable conduct to be seen as likely – even certain" (Tharaldsen, Mearns, & Knudsen, 2010: 1063). Holding both conflicting beliefs about the same conduct at the same time would seem, at first blush, impossible. The next section explores the literature's several perspectives on bridging this dilemma (e.g. through emotional ambivalence).

Perspectives on the integration of high trust and low trust

Faced with the high trust–low trust dilemma, one response is to conclude that the benefits of trust must be curvilinear: that some trust is better than no trust as well as full trust. Qualitative data often highlight this idea, as employees allude to the benefits of "a little" trust but the risks of "complete" trust. (Conchie & Donald, 2008). Additionally, a study of employees engaged in total quality management suggested an "optimal" level of trust is necessary to prevent group-think (Erdem, 2003). This response begs the question of how to identify an inflection point – or the level of trust that maximizes safe outcomes. The existing empirical research on trust in the safety-critical context has yet to address this issue directly.

As noted, another response is to differentiate trust and distrust by indicating that they are two separate dimensions ranging from high to low (Lewicki et al., 1998). Lewicki and his colleagues, for example, have argued that employees often highly trust and highly distrust the same colleague at the same time; they are ambivalent. Similarly, an introduction to a special issue on safety-specific trust concluded that, in light of the articles' conclusions, trust and distrust are unlikely to lie on the same dimension (Conchie et al., 2006). One's assumptions regarding the relationship between trust and distrust may have meaningful consequences for safety-critical organizations. For example, if trust and distrust are experienced at the same time, this ambivalence may cue a particular type of decision. Emotional ambivalence has been shown to affect cognition in that it results in the ability to identify novel, unusual opportunities (Fong, 2006; Plambeck & Weber, 2009). To the extent these effects apply to the simultaneous experience of trust and distrust, ambivalence may hold some interesting, positive consequences for safety (Vogus, Rothman, Sutcliffe, & Weick, 2014). For instance, it is possible that ambivalence could improve an individual's chances of identifying something that is amiss or awry.

Other perspectives on the high trust–low trust dilemma do not necessarily study distrust; rather they study high and low trust, indicating that people can (1) trust and not trust different people at the same time, (2) trust and not trust the same person in different situations at the same time, (3) trust the person but not trust the situation at the same time, or (4) trust and not trust the same person at different times. The following sections review these perspectives, and Table 24.1 lists the relevant papers, including several from other disciplines, such as management.

The possibility that people can trust and not trust different people at the same time (#1) arises from research suggesting that real employees in safety-critical organizations do just that. Employees of a UK gas plant, for example, implicitly trusted their workmates more than their supervisors or senior managers (Burns, Mearns, & McGeorge, 2006). Other studies of offshore employees showed that one sample of employees trusted senior management but did not trust local rig management (Cox, Jones, & Collinson, 2006), whereas another sample trusted full-time employees but did not trust contractors (Conchie & Donald, 2008). Among still other samples of offshore employees, safety issues were better predicted by trust in workmates than trust in others (Tharaldsen, Mearns, & Knudsen, 2010). This perspective, differentiating trust in different individuals or groups, helps to resolve the high trust–low trust dilemma by allowing people to direct their high and low trust toward different people, but doing so is probably conducive to safety only when the trusted colleagues also happen to be engaging in safe practices. Applying this line of thinking to our Germanwings example, in an ideal world, a pilot might put more trust in her co-pilot rather than an air traffic controller because a co-pilot might have more direct experience with (and information about) the conditions the crew are facing.

Table 24.1 Papers illustrating perspectives on the integration of high trust and low trust

Perspectives on the integration of high trust and low trust	Relevant papers
(1) Trust and do not trust different people at the same time	Burns, Mearns, & McGeorge (2006)
	Conchie & Donald (2008)
	Cox, Jones, & Collinson (2006)
	Tharaldsen, Mearns, & Knudsen (2010)
(2) Trust and do not trust the same person in different situations at the same time	Conchie & Donald (2008)
	Mayer, Davis, & Schoorman (1995)
(3) Trust the person but do not trust the situation at the same time	Burt, Chmiel, & Hayes (2009)
	Burt & Stevenson (2009)
	Hale (2000)
	Jeffcott, Pidgeon, Weyman, & Walls (2006)
	Luhmann (1979)
	Turner & Pidgeon (1997)
	Yamagishi & Yamagishi (1994)
(4) Trust and do not trust the same person at different times	Burt, Chmiel, & Hayes, 2009
	Burt & Stevenson, 2009
	Conchie & Donald (2008)
	Tharaldsen, Mearns, & Knudsen (2010)

The second perspective on the high trust–low trust dilemma allows people to trust and not trust the same person in different situations. This perspective links to a basic definition of trustworthiness as a combination of ability, benevolence, and integrity (Mayer, Davis, & Schoorman, 1995). This definition implies that people are trustworthy for a wide variety of reasons ranging from their ability to complete a particular task to their general level of ethicality. Additionally, since the ability dimension involves a specific referent, the definition implies that people can trust another person's ability to do one thing but not another. As Mayer and his colleagues (1995) put it, organizational leaders would not necessarily trust a high-ability technical analyst to contact an important customer. Consistent with this line of reasoning, Conchie and Donald (2008) suggested that integrity may represent the most important, and ability the least important, dimension of safety-specific trust. If so, then employees in safety-critical contexts could trust each other's integrity but not trust their ability to guarantee safety in a particular domain. This perspective helps to resolve the high trust-low trust dilemma by allowing people to direct their high and low trust toward different attributes of the same person, but this combination of high and low trust may be difficult to sustain if the elements of trustworthiness are interrelated (as suggested in Mayer et al., 1995). For example, the pilot in the Germanwings example might have trusted Lufthansa to hire a technically competent pilot but not trusted in the airline's ability to know whether that pilot was mentally unstable at any given time, which might have increased his vigilance regarding his co-pilot's condition.

The third perspective on the dilemma allows people to trust a person but not trust the situation that they are facing. Multiple lines of research point toward this perspective. First, the cross-cultural psychology literature suggests that the members of some cultures fundamentally anchor their trust in perceptions of other people, whereas the members of different cultures anchor their trust in perceptions of other people's situations – namely, the norms and sanctions that they are facing (e.g. Cook et al., 2005; Gelfand et al., 2011; Gunia, Brett, Nadkeolyar & Kamdar, 2011; Yamagishi & Yamagishi, 1994). Specifically, people from Western cultures like

the US tend to extend interpersonal trust, trusting individuals perceived to have ability, benevolence, and integrity (Mayer et al., 1995). In other words, they trust the person rather than
the situation. Conversely, people from Eastern cultures such as Japan tend to extend institutional
trust, meaning they trust that strong situational norms and sanctions will prevent other people
from behaving badly. They trust the situation rather than the person. Evidence for this
proposition comes from investment games (Berg, Dickhaut, & McCabe, 1995), which allow
people to express trust financially but are generally devoid of norms and sanctions. When playing
these games, the otherwise "high-trust" Japanese tend to demonstrate low trust, presumably
because the absence of norms and sanctions leaves no basis for trust (Cook et al., 2005). This
research suggests, at a basic psychological level, that people can readily distinguish between trusting
the person and trusting the situation, and that their level of trust can readily change when the
person or situation changes. In the Lufthansa example, the company demonstrated such high
trust in the effectiveness of their oversight and accountability system for pilots to self-report
psychological problems that they failed to anticipate or even imagine the possibility and the
horrific consequences associated with an unstable individual locking the cockpit.

Evidence from the safety literature provides insight into the ways that differentiating the
person from the situation could help resolve the high trust–low trust dilemma. First, Jeffcott et al.
(2006) highlighted the risks of excessive rule-based trust in the railway industry, suggesting that
placing too much trust in the rules (i.e. the situation) prevented railway workers from trusting
each other when novel situations arose. This suggests that less trust in the situation and more
trust in the people may produce a healthier balance. Second, Hale (2000) suggested that people
should primarily direct their "creative mistrust" at the risk control system rather than their
colleagues, whereas Luhmann (1979) and Turner and Pidgeon (1997) suggested that people
should not trust their institution's safety culture but should trust their colleagues. Finally, two
studies examining employees' trust in the system used to onboard and train new employees (in
the forest harvesting and firefighting industries, respectively) found that employees placed too
much trust in the onboarding system (Burt et al., 2009; Burt & Stevenson, 2009). As a result,
they perceived too little risk from new employee accidents and took too few measures to prevent
them. The authors suggested that existing employees would be better served by lessening their
trust in the system of onboarding and training, even while trusting new employees themselves.
In sum, extant research suggests that trusting the people but not trusting the dangerous situations
they face holds substantial promise for resolving the high trust–low trust dilemma. That is, to
achieve collective safety (Conchie & Donald, 2008) this perspective points to an even more
profound level of interpersonal trust in which people are generally trusted, but situations are not.

A final perspective on the high trust–low trust dilemma involves allowing trust in the same
person to vary over time. The above-noted onboarding studies illustrate this perspective, as
they suggest that low trust plays an important role in risk reduction, especially during a new
employee's first few months of employment, before they gain familiarity with an organization's
norms and procedures (Burt et al, 2009; Burt & Stevenson, 2009). Similarly, Tharaldsen et al.
(2010) argued that low trust and formal control are most important in the early stages of an
employment relationship, whereas controls can loosen and trust can predominate as the
relationship deepens. Additionally, Conchie and Donald (2008) showed that offshore employees
did not trust contractors before meeting them, but quickly conditioned their trust on the
contractors' personal attributes after developing a relationship. Finally, allowing trust to vary
over time is consistent with a "tit-for-tat" approach (Axelrod & Hamilton, 1981), in which
people trust unless and until their trust is violated. With respect to our initial Germanwings
example, more experienced pilots may be wary of less experienced pilots until they demonstrate

their capabilities. Collectively, these perspectives on the high trust–low trust dilemma suggest that safety-critical organizations have various options for thoughtfully encouraging high and low trust, as a means of achieving safety. Reviewing the Germanwings disaster through the lens of these perspectives helps to illustrate the real-world relevance and importance of research that further explores these perspectives in safety-critical contexts.

Directions for future research: representing the complexities of trust and safety

Our examination of the growing literature on the role of trust in safety-critical contexts clearly reveals that the study of trust is often incomplete without some consideration of low trust and distrust. Building on this and other gaps we have identified, this section looks ahead and identifies some promising opportunities for advancing research in this important domain of inquiry. We start with the proposition that the nuances of trusting behavior in a safety-critical context should be properly recognized. By this we mean that decisions to trust, trust less, or distrust in this context are often complex. The individual decision-making process is influenced by various emotions, calculations of risk, existing normative influences, past experiences with individuals and institutions, and general ambiguity (Dunning, Anderson, Schlosser, Ehlebracht, & Fetchenhauer, 2014). However, in many studies we reviewed, trust, low trust, and distrust (if mentioned) in the safety-critical context are theorized and measured only in terms of their general absence or presence. While this perspective is useful to some degree, it also represents the variable as more static in theory than it might actually be in practice as it pertains to dynamic safety-related behaviours. Rather than continue to capture snapshots of trust in these contexts, we recommend making a shift toward representing additional, important facets of these variables that will help to further enrich the existing body of knowledge on the topic.

One particular area that warrants further research is the examination of the individual psychology of trust behaviour in safety-critical contexts. For instance, safety voice (Conchie et al., 2012) is considered to be a critical factor in the maintenance of safe organizations because it has been shown to prevent injuries and increase opportunities for organizational learning (Hofmann & Morgeson, 1999; Kath, Marks, & Ranney, 2010). Much of the literature has focused primarily on how individuals may be compelled to voice their concerns via factors of safety climate and/or leadership style (see e.g. Conchie et al., 2012; Tucker & Turner, 2015; Edmondson, 1999) with the general idea being that leaders can set a tone that encourages employees to speak up about safety concerns.

Considerably less attention has been paid to the psychology that underpins behaviours like safety voice of individual employees. The expression of voice can often be dependent on the ability of employees to think critically about safety. The decision to communicate concerns regarding a safety matter requires individuals to be able to identify potential problems and opportunities as well as overcome certain social-psychological barriers to speaking up (Asch, 1956). The challenge in executing this particular combination of behaviours is that it depends on the individual's ability to be flexible about following her instincts. Individual employees must be able to both trust and distrust their own instincts depending on the circumstances. On the one hand, the individual should trust her intuition that an action should be taken. This action could range from the acknowledgement of a doubt, discrepancy, or feeling (see Klein, 2003; Weick & Sutcliffe, 2007: 31) that something is amiss, to the actual reporting of an observed error. On the other hand, she must override a different instinct to protect her own interests. Often, we think of extreme examples such as fear of retaliation; however, an individual may be reluctant to speak due to other, more common reasons, for instance, fear of embarrassment. In other words, safety voice relies on the ability of individuals to effectively toggle between trusting and distrusting their own feelings and perceptions. Flexibility in this regard is an ability that is unlikely to be automatic or effortless. And yet, we know little about the psychological dimensions of trusting behaviour at the individual level in such safety-critical contexts. Overlooking this aspect results in an incomplete picture of the responsibilities placed on, and the challenges faced by individuals in these situations.

We also recommend examining trust, low trust, and distrust as important parts of a more holistic approach to safety. Several researchers have shown that trust is a key input to safety; however, we argue that focusing too narrowly on trust only may inadvertently obscure insights about the primacy of its role in safety-critical contexts. Expanding the focus to include other levers of safety that likely work in conjunction with trust could help create a more complete picture, one that accurately portrays the role of trust within the greater system of organizational safety. For instance, trust is a necessary scaffold for mindful organizing.

Mindful organizing is a macro-level pattern of collective daily processes and organizing practices that help people to focus attention on perceptual details that are typically lost when they coordinate their actions and share their interpretations and conceptions (Weick, Sutcliffe, & Obstfeld, 1999). Mindful organizing reduces the loss of detail by increasing the quality of attention across the organization, enhancing people's alertness and awareness so that they can detect discrepancies and subtle ways in which situations and contexts vary and call for contingent responding (Sutcliffe & Weick, 2013; Weick & Sutcliffe 2006, 2007). By increasing employees' willingness to speak up about potential problems (Blatt, Christianson, Sutcliffe, & Rosenthal, 2006; Vogus & Sutcliffe, 2007b), trust counteracts tendencies for employees under production pressure to normalize weak signals and fail to take adaptive actions (Barton & Sutcliffe, 2009). But trust does not deliver safety alone. Mindful organizing is enacted through a set of five-interrelated guiding principles and accompanying contextualized practices (Weick et al., 1999; Vogus & Sutcliffe, 2007a, 2007b; Sutcliffe & Vogus, 2014) that increase information about failures, simplifications, operations, capacities, and expertise associated with present and emerging challenges (Weick & Sutcliffe, 2007). Without these contextual inputs, awareness is more likely to be simplified into familiar categories that have been applied in the past (e.g. mindlessness).

The application of an inclusive approach to safety, like mindful organizing, captures the importance of trust without overlooking how it is inextricably linked to other behaviours that are all integral to safety management. In doing so, the representation of trust in safety research may become more faithful to the role it actually plays in this context as well as yield additional insights as to its contribution to safety outcomes. The examination of trust and distrust, (particularly of the situation, and the inadequacy of one's context-specific knowledge in new situations; see Barton & Sutcliffe, 2009) functions as a critical piece of more complex systems of safety rather than a solution in and of itself.

Additionally, we suggest that individuals contemplating both past and future research on trust, low trust, distrust, and safety should remember that a large proportion of the existing research on this topic has taken place in Western cultures, often in the US or the UK Yet, research from outside the safety domain has revealed marked effects of national culture on trust and the role it plays in influencing safety behaviours and outcomes. In particular, culture influences the trust assumptions that people bring to bear, with the members of some cultures assuming that individuals are trustworthy until they prove otherwise and the members of other cultures assuming that others are untrustworthy until they prove they are trustworthy (Gunia et al., 2011). Accordingly, in interactions with strangers, the members of the former cultures often show some immediate yet fragile trust ("swift trust"; Meyerson, Weick, & Kramer, 1996), whereas the members of the latter cultures often develop trust slowly, over longer stretches of time. Finally, as noted, some cultures (often Western) tend to ground their trust in individuals and their attributes, whereas other cultures (often Eastern) tend to ground their trust in features of the situation like the existence of norms and sanctions (Cook et al., 2005). Collectively, these insights imply that past findings from the safety literature may not automatically generalize globally, and that future research with a global purview is needed.

Finally, we suggest that it may be useful to explore alternatives to trust that might play a role in facilitating safety behaviours and outcomes. Focusing on different behaviours may even prove to be more appropriate and effective. For example, Sutcliffe (2011) suggests that self-respect is an important factor in maintaining the ability to adapt to change – an important skill in the safety-critical organizational context. Her definition describes self-respect as respecting one's own perceptions as well as the perceptions of others and valuing both in safety reporting. Although she suggests that self-respect operates in tandem with trust and honesty, it might be worth considering self-respect as a potential proxy for trust where safety voice is concerned. Unlike the challenges faced in the high trust-low trust dilemma, emphasizing self-respect places a clear value on the individual's observations, thereby removing some of the barriers to expressing safety concerns. Furthermore, the added emphasis on integrating self- and other-perceptions establishes the expectations of accountability, responsibility, and, most importantly, critical thinking regarding matters of safety. It is possible that self-respect can lead to the same outcomes as trust with fewer downsides. For example, encouraging self-respect tends to preserve a healthy amount of skepticism, which is necessary for behaviors such as dissent and safety voice (Weick et al., 1999).

Self-respect might also serve as a useful "placeholder" in instances where trust has been lost or is newly developing. Though studies of safety-critical contexts often note the presence or absence of trust, we recognize that trust behaviors can and do change depending on the situation. For instance, Jones and Jones (2011) found that participation in an interprofessional project resulted in an increase in collegial trust and overall safety. Though the study is a somewhat straightforward representation of the development of trust over time and with increased familiarity, it clearly highlights the variable nature of trust under rather ordinary circumstances. We can imagine that in this and other similar situations where trust has not yet been developed or has been diminished somehow, self-respect might help to promote safety voice or other relevant behaviors until trust reaches desired levels. It is important to note that self-respect is not the only potential alternative variable of interest. It is but one important alternative that could be investigated as a potential proxy or substitute for trust or distrust.

In sum, we suggest that greater recognition of the dynamic properties of trust, low trust, and distrust as variables and their roles in broader processes of safety, and the consideration of other variables of interest such as self-respect as potential proxies and substitutes, offer some promising directions for future research. Taken together, these opportunities may help researchers envision trusting behavior in novel and different ways and ultimately help to create a more complete picture of its role in safety management. Furthermore, approaching the study of trust and safety in alternative ways may result in a more accurate description of trust, in terms of how individuals experience it as well as how it influences organizational (and individual) safety on a larger scale. In doing so, we may successfully capture the complexities of trusting behavior in the safety-critical context.

Trust and safety: practical implications

In light of the collective knowledge above, we can also advance some practical implications about trust in safety-critical contexts. As our review has hopefully revealed, integrating trust and distrust is essential for safety, but complicated. Thus, one clear implication is that practitioners attempting to promote safety should prepare themselves for the complex and intellectually demanding task of managing the competing and sometimes conflicting imperatives of trust and distrust. Although we hope that the above perspectives offer guidance on how to integrate trust and distrust, we harbor no illusions that the integration process will be easy.

With that said, we do believe that the above research suggests some relatively straightforward 'rules of thumb' that practitioners might use to balance the competing imperatives of trust, low trust, and distrust. Recognizing that each of these rules oversimplifies the world and requires additional research, we now describe them in the hope of offering useful guidance. First, the above research suggests that practitioners should neither trust nor distrust too much, as either is likely to raise safety concerns. Thus, if practitioners find themselves consistently and fully trusting most or all individuals involved in a safety-critical activity, across most or all situations, over long stretches of time, they might interpret this as a cue to distrust more. Conversely, if they find themselves consistently and fully distrusting across situations and time, additional trust is potentially warranted.

Second, and relatedly, practitioners should expect to see neither too little nor too much dissent in their safety-critical contexts. Across the safety and other literatures, too little dissent is often a sign of complacency, and complacency is a common precursor to mistakes, accidents, and errors. Too much dissent, in turn, can signal a "blaming and shaming" culture that leads people to cover up mistakes and avoid recriminations rather than learning and growing from mistakes. Thus, in contrast to many practitioners' expectations that well-functioning organizations "feel good," practitioners in safety-critical contexts should generally expect some intermediate amount of dissent, which may not always feel particularly positive.

Finally, the above research suggests that practitioners might make greater use of "emotional markers" to determine when trust should be reduced or distrust is necessary. Specifically, when practitioners in a safety-critical context sense that something does not "feel right," they are advised to respect themselves enough to trust this feeling and use it as a cue that trust should be reassessed – whether the original object of the trust is other people or some aspect of the situation. Additionally, in some safety-critical organizations, leadership may implicitly or explicitly equate trust with feeling at ease. This emotional state may be detrimental to the preservation of healthy skepticism or distrust. For instance, it is possible that the ideal emotional state for promoting safety includes regularly living with some amount of doubt, fear, and concern. Training may be needed to help individuals manage the emotions that inherently accompany behaviors such as vigilance and safety voice, and to recognize the types of emotions that tend to cue larger problems. In sum, extant research on trust and safety suggests that integrating trust and distrust is essential but far from easy. Nevertheless, the research points toward some initial recommendations that practitioners might use to calibrate the integration process, balancing high and low trust in the hope of safer organizations.

Conclusion

The tragic events of Germanwings Flight 9525 illustrate all too clearly the importance of both trust and distrust in a safety-critical context. In this case, the various stakeholders trusted the mechanisms that were in place to keep them reasonably safe. Our review suggests that these mechanisms need to be coupled with the critical thinking that can help individuals know when to distrust a person or a situation. Moreover, fostering appropriate levels of trust and distrust, within a comprehensive approach to safety such as mindful organizing, may aid in the avoidance of incidents, like the Germanwings crash, 2015, that are almost unimaginable until they occur.

Notes

1 The authors contributed equally to this chapter.
2 Although the chief executive of Lufthansa reported that the co-pilot (Mr. Lubitz) was 100 percent flight-worthy and had passed the company's health checks with flying colours (Eddy, Bilefsky, & Clark, 2015), the case is more complicated. Evidently, early in his training, Mr. Lubitz had taken a break from his flight training because of depression. In the months leading up to the final flight, Mr. Lubitz had sought treatment for a number of physical and mental health problems. Moreover, he had a no-fly note, of which Lufthansa was completely unaware.

References

Asch, S. E. (1956). Studies of independence and conformity: I. A minority of one against a unanimous majority. *Psychological Monographs: General and Applied*, 70, 1–70.

Axelrod, R., & Hamilton, W. D. (1981). The evolution of cooperation. *Science*, 211, 1390–1396.

Barton, M., & Sutcliffe, K. M. (2009). Overcoming dysfunctional momentum. *Human Relations*, 62(9), 1327–1356.

Berg, J., Dickhaut, J., & McCabe, K. (1995). Trust, reciprocity, and social history. *Games and Economic Behaviour*, 10, 122–142.

Bilefsky, D., & Clark, N. Fatal descent of Germanwings plane was "deliberate," French authorities say. *NYTimes.com*, March 26, 2015, accessed June 1, 2015, www.nytimes.com/2015/03/27/world/europe/germanwings-crash.html.

Blatt, R., Christianson, M., Sutcliffe, K., & Rosenthal, M. (2006). A sensemaking lens on reliability. *Journal of Organizational Behaviour*, 27, 897–917.

Burns, C., Mearns, K., & McGeorge, P. (2006). Explicit and implicit trust within safety culture. *Risk Analysis*, 26, 1139–1150.

Burt, C. D. B., Chmiel, N., & Hayes, P. (2009). Implications of turnover and trust for safety attitudes and behaviour in work teams. *Safety Science*, 47, 1002–1006.

Burt, C. D. B., & Stevenson, R. J. (2009). The relationship between recruitment processes, familiarity, trust, perceived risk and safety. *Journal of Safety Research*, 40, 365–369.

Christianson, M., Farkas, M., Sutcliffe, K. M., & Weick, K. E. (2009). Learning through rare events: Significant interruptions at the Baltimore and Ohio Railroad museum. *Organization Science*, 20(5), 846–860.

Clark, N., & Bilefsky, D. (2015a). Germanwings crash in French Alps kills 150: Cockpit voice recorder is found. *NYTimes.com*, March 24, 2015, accessed June 1, 2015, www.nytimes.com/2015/03/26/world/europe/germanwings-crash.html.

Clark, N., & Bilefsky, D. (2015b). Germanwings pilot was locked out of cockpit before crash in France. *NYTimes.com*, March 25, 2015, accessed June 1, 2015, www.nytimes.com/2015/03/26/world/europe/germanwings-airbus-crash.html.

Clarke, S. (1999). Perceptions of organizational safety: Implications for the development of safety culture. *Journal of Organizational Behaviour*, 20, 185–198.

Conchie, S. M., & Donald, I. J. (2006). The role of distrust in offshore safety performance. *Risk Analysis*, 26, 1151–1160.

Conchie, S. M., & Donald, I. J. (2008). The functions and development of safety-specific trust and distrust. *Safety Science*, 46, 92–103.

Conchie, S. M., & Donald, I. J. (2009). The moderating role of safety-specific trust on the relation between safety-specific leadership and safety citizenship behaviours. *Journal of Occupational Health Psychology*, 14, 137–147.

Conchie, S. M., Donald, I. J., & Taylor, P. J. (2006). Trust: Missing pieces in the safety puzzle. *Risk Analysis*, 26, 1097–1104.

Conchie, S. M., Taylor, P. J., & Donald, I. J. (2012). Promoting safety voice with safety-specific transformational leadership: The mediating role of two dimensions of trust. *Journal of Occupational Health Psychology*, 17, 105–115.

Cook, K. S., Yamagishi, T., Cheshire, C., Cooper, R., Matsuda, M., & Mashima, R. (2005). Trust building via risk taking: A cross-societal experiment. *Social Psychology Quarterly*, 68, 121–142.

Cox, S., Jones, B., & Collinson, D. (2006). Trust relations in high-reliability organizations. *Risk Analysis*, 26, 1123–1138.

Cox, S., Jones, B., & Rycraft, H. (2004). Behavioural approaches to safety management within UK reactor plants. *Safety Science*, 42, 825–839.

Crowe, E., & Higgins, E. T. (1997). Regulatory focus and strategic inclinations: Promotion and prevention in decision-making. *Organizational Behaviour and Human Decision Processes*, 69, 117–132.

Dunning, D., Anderson, J. E., Schlösser, T., Ehlebracht, D., & Fetchenhauer, D. (2014). Trust at zero acquaintance: More a matter of respect than expectation of reward. *Journal of Personality and Social Psychology*, 107, 122–141.

Eddy, M., Bilefsky, D., & Clark, N. Co-pilot in Germanwings crash hid mental illness from employer, authorities say. *NYTimes.com*, March 27, 2015, accessed June 1, 2015, www.nytimes.com/2015/03/28/world/europe/germanwings-crash-andreas-lubitz.html.

Edmondson, A. (1999). Psychological safety and learning behaviour in work teams. *Administrative Science Quarterly*, 44(2), 350–383.

Entwistle, V. A., & Quick, O. (2006). Trust in the context of patient safety problems. *Journal of Health Organization and Management*, 20, 397–416.

Erdem, F. (2003). Optimal trust and teamwork: From groupthink to teamthink. *Work Study*, 52, 229–233.

Firth-Cozens, J. (2004). Organisational trust: The keystone to patient safety. *Quality of Safety and Health Care*, 13, 56–61.

Fleming, M., & Lardner, R. (Eds.). (2001). *Behaviour modification to improve safety: A review of the literature.* Sudbury, UK: HSE Books.

Fong, C. T. (2006). The effects of emotional ambivalence on creativity. *Academy of Management Journal*, 49, 1016–1030.

Gelfand, M. J., Raver, J. L., Nishii, L., Leslie, L. M., Lun, J., Lim, B. C., & Yamaguchi, S. (2011). Differences between tight and loose cultures: A 33-nation study. *Science*, 332, 1100–1104.

Gunia, B. C., Brett, J. M., Nandkeolyar, A., & Kamdar, D. (2011). Paying a price: Culture, trust, and negotiation consequences. *Journal of Applied Psychology*, 96, 774–789.

Hale, A. (2000). Editorial: Culture's confusions. *Safety Science*, 34, 1–14.

Hofmann, D. A., & Morgeson, F. P. (1999). Safety-related behaviour as a social exchange: The role of perceived organizational support and leader–member exchange. *Journal of Applied Psychology*, 84, 286–296.

Jeffcott, S., Pidgeon, N., Weyman, A., & Walls, J. (2006). Risk, trust, and safety culture in UK train operating companies. *Risk Analysis*, 26, 1105–1121.

Jones, A., & Jones, D. (2011). Improving teamwork, trust and safety: An ethnographic study of an interprofessional initiative. *Journal of Interprofessional Care*, 25(3), 175–181.

Kath, L. M., Marks, K. M., & Ranney, J. (2010). Safety climate dimensions, leader-member exchange, and organizational support as predictors of upward safety communication in a sample of rail industry workers. *Safety Science*, 48, 643–650.

Klein, G. (2003). *The power of intuition.* New York: Currency-Doubleday.

Lewicki, R. J., McAllister, D. J., & Bies, R. J. (1998). Trust and distrust: New relationships and realities. *Academy of Management Review*, 23, 438–458.

Luhmann, N. (1979). *Trust and power.* Chichester, UK: Wiley.

Luria, G. (2010). The social aspects of safety management: Trust and safety climate. *Accident Analysis and Prevention*, 42, 1288–1295.

Mayer, R. C., Davis, J. H., & Schoorman, D. F. (1995). An integrative model of organizational trust. *Academy of Management Review*, 20, 709–734.

McAllister, D. J. (1995). Affect and cognition-based trust as foundations for interpersonal cooperation in organizations. *Academy of Management Journal*, 38, 24–59.

McEvily, B., Perrone, V., & Zaheer, A. (2003). Trust as an organizing principle. *Organization Science*, 14, 91–103.

Mearns, K., Flin, R., Gordon, G., & Fleming, M. (1997). *Organisational and human factors in offshore safety.* OTH 543 Report. Sudbury, UK: HSE Books.

Meyerson, D., Weick, K. E., & Kramer, R. M. (1996). Swift trust and temporary groups. In R. M. Kramer & T. R. Tyler (Eds.), *Trust in organizations: Frontiers of theory and research* (pp. 166–195). Thousand Oaks, CA: Sage.

Pidgeon, N., Walls, J., Weyman, A., & Horlick-Jones, T. (2003). *Perceptions of and trust in the health and safety executive as a risk regulator.* Research Report 2003/100. Norwich, UK: HSE Books.

Plambeck, N., & Weber, K. (2009). CEO ambivalence and responses to strategic issues. *Organization Science*, 20, 993–1010.

Reason, J. T. (1997). *Managing the risks of organizational hazards.* Aldershot, UK: Ashgate.

Rochlin, G. I. (1993). Defining "high-reliability" organizations: A comparative framework: In K. H. Roberts (Ed.), *New challenges to understanding organizations.* New York: Macmillan Publishing.

Rousseau, D. M., Sitkin, S., B., Burt, R. S., & Camerer, C. (1998). Not so different after all: A cross-discipline view of trust. *Academy of Management Review,* 23, 393–404.

Spector, D. Here's a timeline of exactly what happened inside the Germanwings plane before it crashed. *Businessinsider.com,* March 26, 2015, accessed July 7, 2015, www.businessinsider.sg/timeline-of-germanwings-flight-4u9525-2015-3/.

Sutcliffe, K. M. (2011). High reliability organizations (HROs). *Best Practice & Research Clinical Anaesthesiology,* 25, 133–144.

Sutcliffe, K. M., & Vogus, T. (2014). Organizing for mindfulness. In A. Ie, T. Ngnoumen, & E. Langer (Eds.), *The Wiley-Blackwell handbook of mindfulness* Oxford, UK: Wiley-Blackwell, 407–423.

Sutcliffe, K. M., & Weick, K.E. (2013). Mindful organizing and resilient healthcare. In E. Hollnagel, J. Braithwaite, & R. L. Wears (Eds.), *Resilient healthcare* London, UK: Ashgate, 145–158.

Tharaldsen, J. E., Mearns, K. J., & Knudsen, K. (2010). Perspectives on safety: The impact of group membership, work factors and trust on safety performance in UK and Norwegian drilling company employees. *Safety Science,* 48, 1062–1072.

Tucker, S., & Turner, N. (2015). Sometimes it hurts when supervisors don't listen: The antecedents and consequences of safety voice among young workers. *Journal of Occupational Health Psychology,* 20, 72–81.

Turner, B. A., & Pidgeon, N. F. (1997). *Man-made disasters,* 2nd ed. Oxford, UK: Butterworth-Heinemann.

Viklund, M. (2003). Trust and risk perception in Western Europe: A cross-national study. *Risk Analysis,* 23, 727–738.

Vogus, T. J., Rothman, N. B., Sutcliffe, K. M., & Weick, K. E. (2014). The affective foundations of high-reliability organizing. *Journal of Organizational Behaviour,* 35, 592–596.

Vogus, T. J., & Sutcliffe K. M. (2007a). The safety organizing scale: Development and validation of a behavioural measure of safety culture in hospital nursing units. *Medical Care,* 41(1), 45–54.

Vogus, T. J., & Sutcliffe, K. M. (2007b). The impact of safety organizing, trusted leadership, and care pathways on reported medication errors in hospital nursing units. *Medical Care,* 41(10), 992–1002.

Vogus, T. J., Sutcliffe, K. M., & Weick, K. E. (2010). Doing no harm: Enabling, enacting, and elaborating a culture of safety in health care. *Academy of Management Perspectives,* 24(4), 60–78.

Watson, G. W., Scott, D., Bishop, J., & Turnbeaugh, T. (2005). Dimensions of interpersonal relationships and safety in the steel industry. *Journal of Business and Psychology,* 19, 303–318.

Weick, K. E., & Sutcliffe, K. M. (2006). Mindfulness and the quality of attention. *Organization Science,* 17(4), 514–525.

Weick, K. E., & Sutcliffe, K. M. (2007). *Managing the unexpected: Resilient performance in an age of uncertainty.* San Francisco, CA: Jossey-Bass.

Weick, K. E., & Sutcliffe, K. M. (2015). *Managing the unexpected: Sustained performance in a complex world.* San Francisco, CA: Wiley.

Weick, K. E., Sutcliffe, K. M., & Obstfeld, D. (1999). Organizing for high reliability: Processes of collective mindfulness. In B. Staw & R. Sutton (Eds.), *Research in Organizational Behaviour* Greenwich, CT: JAI, (Vol. 21, pp. 81–123).

Yamagishi, T., & Yamagishi, M. (1994). Trust and commitment in the United States and Japan. *Motivation and Emotion,* 18, 129–166.

Zacharatos, A., Barling, J., & Iverson, R. D. (2005). High-performance work systems and occupational safety. *Journal of Applied Psychology,* 90, 77–93.

25

TRUST IN FOOD

Assuring quality, sustainability, price and availability

Lovisa Näslund and Fergus Lyon

Introduction

We often take access to food for granted and only question this when there are food scares. The horse meat scandal of 2008 and various scandals of baby milk quality are examples where trust has become central to public debates. But how can we trust what we are eating and how can we trust those providing food around the world. Access to secure and adequate food is a universal human need, as is evident in the annual global retail food sales of 4 trillion USD, half of which is the result of international trade (USDA, 2016; World Trade Statistical Review, 2016). However, eating could also be seen as inherently a source of anxiety, since food also has the potential to cause discomfort, sickness and environmental degradation (Freidberg, 2003). We are therefore both dependent on, and inherently vulnerable to, food. This inherent vulnerability in our relationship to food makes trust essential in situations where we are able to choose between different foods. Buying and consuming food necessitates trust, which may be defined as 'a willingness to be vulnerable to another party' (Schoorman et al., 2007, p. 347). A fuller definition of trust adds to this, in that 'trust is a psychological state comprising the intention to accept vulnerability based upon positive expectations of the intentions or behaviour of another'(Rousseau et al., 1998, p. 395).

There is, however, often a choice, and thereby, the necessity of trust. Given that most consumers largely lack the means to oversee the production, it is not surprising that trust has a significant influence on consumers' food decisions (Hobbs & Goddard, 2015). As a result of the complexity of global trade, creating this trust involves a number of different actors and activities: consumers, farmers, producers, NGOs, governments, retailers, quality assurance schemes, regulations, standards and marketing, and information about the qualities of the food will not be symmetrically divided between them. As a consequence, studies of food production and supply have moved from seeing agriculture, food processing and retailing as separate sectors, to seeing them as part of a food commodity chain, and increasingly as global agro-food networks or systems (encompassing, e.g. governments, third party certification bodies and NGOs). This development in research mirrors the increasing complexity of food supply resulting from the globalization of trade, but also what has been termed the 'cultural turn' (the production and consumption of narratives and meaning around food) and the 'quality turn' (increased concerns and demands for quality assurance) in the food sector, which makes intermediaries increasingly important (Jackson et al., 2006; Goodman, 2004b).

A sizeable body of research has explored the significance of trust in food supply systems with regards to consumer decisions, the relations between other actors, and in regulations (Meijerink et al., 2014; Lassoued & Hobbs, 2015; Hobbs & Goddard, 2015; Murdoch et al., 2000; Lang, 2013; Kjaernes et al., 2013; Bernzen & Braun, 2014). As a consequence of the complexity of the agri-food network, this trust differs in form, depending on the nature of the trustee. Through face-to-face interaction in the supply chain, interpersonal trust may emerge, but, as a result of the increasing complexity and social and spatial distances of modern society, such interpersonal trust is often replaced by system trust: in intermediaries, systems of control and regulation for quality assurance. When the consumer finally encounters food in the marketplace or in the store, their trust will to a large degree be trust in the signs the food has been labelled with (Giddens, 1990; Shapiro, 1987; Gambetta & Bacharach, 2001; Van Loo et al., 2014). Trust in the context of food supply may thus be interpersonal trust, system trust or trust in signs.

In order to understand the role of trust and how it is created in the agri-food system, the differences between these forms of trust need to be understood. This is important not only from a consumer perspective, but also because the agricultural sector and access to the global market is seen as key to poverty reduction in developing countries, which will not be possible without creating trust for their agricultural products (Humphrey & Memedovic, 2006)

While trust issues in relation to food share many similarities to trust in other areas of life and the economy where we may encounter trust in individuals, systems or signs, there are distinct issues related to the millions of producers around the world and the billions of consumers. Furthermore, there is considerable vulnerability of people related to accessing food of a suitable quality, and the implications of mistrust on the health and security of whole populations. In periods of dramatic demographic and environmental change, trust in food supply and quality is of central importance. As we look to alternatives to provide sustainability, flourishing lives and prosperity, understanding the nature of trust in food becomes increasingly significant.

Food therefore presents a fruitful context for trust studies due to its universal importance in our lives and the complexity of the process that enables people to trust the food they eat. Furthermore, from a trust research perspective, studying trust in the context of food enables contributions to a number of trust topics which are relevant to other industries/contexts. These include the trust/control relationships, the role of intermediaries in trust creation and trust in systems or institutions, such as audits and quality-assurance schemes. The agri-food system provides empirical examples of many of the issues discussed elsewhere in this handbook, for example control and trust, interpersonal trust and systemic trust.

In the following chapter, we will begin by discussing the notion of vulnerability in relation to food, which makes trust significant in this context. We will then move on to trust creation, beginning with direct interpersonal relationships between farmer and consumer, and then to the more common situation of intermediaries, and the role they are playing. While trust has significance in all food consumption, it becomes even more significant in situations where the trustor – in this case the buyer of food – has an increased perception of uncertainty or vulnerability: for example, where the producer is distant and impossible to assess or monitor and there are uncertainties as to the content and quality of the food, which can contribute to perceptions of vulnerability. As a result, a demand for quality assurance schemes, signs and labels ensues, as intermediaries become necessary not only for logistical reasons, but also in order for producers to be able to create consumer trust in their products (Carriquiry & Babcock, 2007).

Perceptions of vulnerability

The perception of vulnerability, paired with the readiness to overlook this vulnerability, lies at the heart of trust, and, as we shall see in the following sections, vulnerability has particular significance in the context of food. Therefore it is useful to explore more closely the notion of vulnerability in the context of trust, and moreover what vulnerability means with regards to food.

In situations where uncertainty and vulnerability are combined, trust becomes essential for cooperation or interaction to be possible. The presence of vulnerability means that whoever trusts also gives the trustee the potential to harm or deceive the trustor (Luhmann, 1979; Rousseau et al., 1998). Trusting thus creates a risk, making the trustor vulnerable. The positive expectation that enables the leap of faith that is the essence of trust might even be seen as a form of self-deception. The trustor is aware of the possibility of deceit, but chooses to act as if it was not there. Not because they are unaware, but because they choose to ignore it (Möllering, 2008, 2001). That trust entails enabling deception and the willing acceptance of risk is not so much the consequence of misplaced or unwarranted trust as it is a (possibly regrettable) inherent quality of trust itself, one which can be overlooked, but never eliminated (Skinner et al., 2014).

The anticipation of risk and vulnerability may give rise to fear, which in turn will act as a deterrent to trust. Amplified by fear, the uncertainty and vulnerability may become impossible to overlook, and as a consequence, the potential trustor chooses not to make a leap of faith. Therefore, a key aspect of interpersonal trust creation is that the trustee understands the precise nature of the threat that the potential trustor perceives, and what they perceive themselves to be vulnerable to. If the trustee is aware of what the trustor fears, they may be able to put these fears to rest. Affect is a vital part of trust dynamics, which may strengthen or deter the development of trust, and emotion management will consequently be of the essence in trust creation (Williams, 2007).

In the context of food, the nature of vulnerability may seem self-evident, as eating in and of itself carries a risk, and not having food at all poses an even greater danger. However, from a trust perspective, the precise nature of vulnerability matters. In a more general sense, vulnerability can be understood as the absence of security, protection and power – in short, the potential for suffering (Webb & Harinarayan, 1999). In food research, vulnerability is often defined in relation to outcomes, such as famine, hunger or illness. In other words, we are not vulnerable to events, but to the outcomes of these events. Vulnerability may therefore be defined as the inability to cope with the outcomes of events that risk occurring. The perception of threat and the ensuing fear therefore depends on the perceived likelihood of certain events, the likelihood of certain outcomes of those events, and finally your susceptibility to those outcomes. This susceptibility will vary depending on who you are and what position you have (e.g. in social or economic terms), and as a consequence, the sense of threat and the resulting willingness to overlook vulnerability will depend on the economic, social and physical systems through which food is obtained. The vulnerability of a population is a function of how that particular population is affected by a certain event, and the characteristic magnitude of these hazards (Dilley & Bourdeau, 2001).

When it comes to food, the nature of these hazards or shocks will vary depending on context: it may be the risk of famine and inadequate food supply, it may be food that is toxic, or it may be food that does not meet the standards the buyer expected or was promised (Maxwell, 1996; Goodman, 2004a). Since the sense of vulnerability depends on the perceived susceptibility, it follows that trust dynamics will be influenced by the social, physical and institutional context of the trustor. The perception of food safety, and the ensuing willingness to trust food, is not only the result of the probability of a certain hazard, but also the result of political and cultural negotiations (Chen 2008). As a result, in Western Europe, what has been termed 'the paradox of progress' has emerged: as food supply chains become increasingly complex and difficult to overlook, stricter standards, quality controls and monitoring procedures have been applied, resulting in closer monitoring and more food safety alerts, which in turn lowers consumer trust in food suppliers (Houghton et al., 2008; Dreyer et al., 2010).

Therefore, when consumers are exposed to negative information about food quality problems, there is an increased perceived vulnerability. Consumers become aware of their susceptibility to different outcomes in relation to food, health issues and the environment, and the frequent reporting make the hazards leading to these outcomes seem more frequent. The effect of such recurrent scares might be seen as raised awareness, but also as the creation of a *risk society* (Kjaernes et al., 2013).

The increasing concern by consumers about the way their food is produced is amplified not only by news reports on scandals and deceits in food manufacturing, but also by environmental groups and NGOs, who strive towards a more socially and ecologically sustainable society. The result is a rising demand for guardians of trust and other regulations and quality assurance systems that promise to lower the likelihood of food hazards. If hazards become less frequent, then risk and the sense of threat is reduced, making it more likely that consumers would be willing to overlook vulnerability (Van Loo et al., 2014). The increased demand for expert systems is therefore not only the result of growing complexity and distance, but is also self-generating, as experts increase awareness and thereby the perceived magnitude of the problem they seek to solve.

However, the increased concern and expectations of food quality, and resulting demand for quality assurance schemes that would reduce vulnerability is not necessarily a global phenomenon – largely, it would seem representative mainly of a socially exclusive niche (Goodman, 2004a). The demand for organic food, for example, is almost solely concentrated to Europe and North America, and even there, only makes up a small proportion of total food sales (Perrini et al., 2010). Likewise, research predominantly focuses on the more wealthy parts of the world, such as Europe and North America. However, there is also a need to explore how these issues relate to the rest of the world where state institutions can be weaker and legal systems are less accessible or less trusted. In this context, people therefore rely on trust that arises from social relationships (Amoako & Lyon, 2014). Poverty shapes food consumption and accessibility and while there is inequality and food-related poverty in all countries, there is a greater concentration of poverty in less developed countries. Many developing countries are also facing dramatic demographic changes and migration to urban areas, breaking the trust-based interpersonal relationships underpinning traditional food supply systems.

In less affluent parts of the world, perceived vulnerability may have more to do with food supply and affordability, and thus assurance schemes and trust in food will require a different set of actions and controls. For example, a study of rice production in northern Vietnam shows how the rice harvest, and thereby rice supply, relies on government distribution of seed at the right time, and is thus heavily dependent on public institutions and local agricultural conditions in terms of soil and water supply (Bonnin & Turner, 2012)

Consumer trust in producers and traders: from direct sales to the commodification of food

Few people today produce all of the food they eat, which means that there will always be some uncertainty as to the exact content and circumstances through which the food was produced. The nature and characteristic of food (as perishable and with unknown potential health/

environmental impact), creates specific forms of uncertainty. In consumer research, a distinction is made between *search goods*, where the buyer can discern quality prior to purchase; *experience goods*, where quality can only be discerned after consumption; and *credence goods*, whose attributes remain unknown even after consumption. If there are no means to discern these qualities, a market for credence goods will turn into Akerlof's well-known market for lemons, where information asymmetry leads to a situation where opportunistic sellers take advantage of unknowing buyers (Perrini et al., 2010; Darby & Karni, 1973; Nelson, 1970). Food may fall into all three categories, and in each case an element of trust may be needed. In this section we examine the role of trust in different types of food markets that have evolved over time.

We start by examining the direct sales of food from producers to consumers. This is found in the earliest rural economies and continues today, for example in the form of farmers' markets. Interpersonal trust, the trust between individuals, is based on an assessment of the others' bene-volence, integrity and ability, which, taken together, make for an assessment of trustworthiness (Mayer et al., 1995). Since interpersonal trust, by necessity, is embedded in a social relationship, it also follows that it is reciprocal: trusting someone implies an endorsement of their character and capabilities, enhances their status within your mutual social network, and creates an obli-gation to reciprocate (Skinner et al., 2014). When traded in such an embedded relationship, food to some extent becomes a search good as both the product and producer are known to the buyer before purchase. However, food produced by someone else will to some extent always be an experience or credence good, as some qualities (e.g. health effects or production means) will remain unobservable.

With urbanization, more specialization and division of labour, consumers become further removed from producers and traders begin to play a role in linking the supply and demand for food. This may lead to the development of a chain of interpersonal relationships, or the replacement of interpersonal trust by trust in trade regulations or other impersonal systems. However, research on the role of traders shows that they draw on personalized trust relations with both farmers and consumers. They draw on norms of reciprocity and cultural ties to ensure that there is a continuation of quality and guaranteed supplies at times of shortages (Lyon, 2000). This is particularly important for perishable food that cannot be stored, or in countries where there is a lack of infrastructure. More specifically where there has been a lack of investment in cold storage and transportation systems, relationships of trust become more important, as the actors in the supply chain rely on each other to transport the food without it deteriorating (Lyon & Porter, 2009).

Food supply chains in many less developed countries are characterized by a large number of small-scale traders operating with limited access to banking and investment. In such cases trust between different types of traders becomes important in terms of providing the finance for food trade. For example in the Ghanaian perishable food trade, trust is evident when traders lend money to farmers to pay for labour and inputs before harvest. Farmers then pay traders back with produce and the traders then take the remainder of the harvest on credit and pay the farmer back after selling it. This is all done without legal contract. The traders then may give produce to other traders or small scale retailers on credit and they pay for the goods post sale (Lyon, 2000; Lyon & Porter, 2009). Despite little use of formal legal contracts, the traders and farmers can use parallel alternative institutions such as traders associations that act to settle disputes and ensure that each marketplace maintains a good reputation (Amoako & Lyon, 2014; Lyon, 2005).

Across the world there has been a growing role for supermarkets which are able to use their economies of scale to offer lower-priced food, and offer a degree of trust based on the brand of the business. However, these more industrialized food systems have longer supply chains, sourcing goods from different counties and offering consumers more choice, particularly when local produce is out of season. The longer supply chains, and increased focus on processed food, adds to potential hazards, and thus increases perceived vulnerability and uncertainty, as food increasingly becomes a credence good since quality is unknown even after consumption (Dreyer et al., 2010). In Europe, supermarkets faced a number of scandals and food scares in recent years, such as the use of horse meat in processed food instead of minced beef. In this case, the complex supply chains covering many countries concealed the use of horse meat, while trust in retailers, and in quality-regulation systems led consumers to assume the quality of the produce they were consuming. Increased monitoring and analysis of DNA proved the product to be false, resulting in a loss of trust and an increased demand for regulation and quality assurance. This may be seen as an illustration of the 'paradox of progress' described earlier.

With such alienation of consumers from food producers, the regulation by government and forms of systemic trust become more important. Supermarkets themselves attempt to build trust by using their own systems such as branding and selling branded goods that have reputations for quality. In *The Consequences of Modernity*, Giddens (1990) argues that one of the key changes in society as a result of modernization is that interpersonal trust is replaced by trust in systems. Trust in such systems rests not, as in the case of interpersonal trust, on the perception of benevolence or good intentions, but rather on faith in the correctness of how regulations and principles will be applied. Such system trust is based on a belief in the validity and correctness of the abstract principles and procedures of social and technical systems. These are expected to be impersonal, impartial, bureaucratic machinery that will pass judgment based solely on incoming data, not on considerations of loyalty or willingness to please (Sydow & Windeler, 2003). In contrast to interpersonal trust, system trust will not carry the same expectation of reciprocity, nor will it be dependent on the perception of benevolence. Rather than faith in the good will and benevolence of the system, system trust relies solely on the perception of competence of those that have designed the system and the integrity of those regulating the system, (in terms of intent to act on behalf of citizens or the greater good, rather than self-interest) (Sapp et al., 2009; Giddens, 1990; Grebitus et al., 2015).

The establishment of formal systems makes traders less reliant on interpersonal trust, as was shown in a study of the effects of the creation of a formalized direct market for sesame seeds in Ethiopia. Following the establishment of a formal commodity exchange, traders began trading with traders they had no relationship with, and as a consequence had lower levels of trust in their trading partners (Meijerink et al., 2014). System trust therefore undermines the need, and thereby the development of, interpersonal trust. Conversely, in the absence of such system trust, people tend to become more reliant on interpersonal relations and informal systems of obligations (Gambetta, 1988).

Institutions, in the sense of common codes of conduct and standards, provide actors with a perception of predictable patterns of behaviour that reduce uncertainty, and restrict vulnerability in relation to others. In certain circumstances they can therefore facilitate the development of interpersonal trust (Bachmann & Inkpen, 2011). Such an institutionalized context may also be described in terms of a culture of trust, which increases people's propensity to trust, an iterative development which increases the prevalence of trust in individuals and organizations (Sztompka, 1999). Sharing norms and codes of conduct therefore makes interpersonal trust development more likely. This explains why consumers that want to buy organic food are very prone to trusting ecolabels (i.e. systems), but also individual farmers, who seem to be sharing norms of sustainability and ethical production (i.e. interpersonal trust) (Näslund & Tamm Hallström, 2014).

In the food chain, the nature of relationships also shows the interaction of trust and control. The perishable nature of food accentuates the issues of control with buyers often accused of exerting undue power on producers as farmers may be in particularly weak positions when holding perishable unharvested produce in their fields. The current consolidation in retailing further exacerbates this power discrepancy. These relationships do show a mixture of institutional and personal trust with institutional trust coming from legal contracts, but the personal ties are needed to ensure that the farmers are suitably flexible to increase or decrease supply on a daily basis to ensure that there are not gluts in the supermarkets. However, supermarket buyers have been accused of using their powerful position to drive down prices and exploit the farmers. Similarly, in a developing-country context, traders buying perishable produce can exert considerable power when there is glut of produce. In such cases, trust and power are closely intertwined, with weaker parties forced to trust as there are few other alternatives. This can be seen as simply confidence rather than trust, or a form of coerced cooperation (Lyon, 2005).

Trust in alternative food systems: quality, sustainability and ethics of production

The distrust of the industrialized food chain in Europe and North America has led to a small but growing movement to find alternatives to the small number of large supermarkets that dominate the food supply. This involves a focus by consumers on food quality and its origins. The 'quality turn' described earlier in the chapter may be seen as a response or reaction to an increasingly industrialized and standardized global food industry, as quality is often linked to notions of nature, alternative agri-food networks and strategies to valorize locally produced foods (Jackson et al., 2006; Murdoch et al., 2000). The growing social and physical gap between producers in conventional, industrialized food production thus increases the need for trust in two ways: first, because it causes a reaction in the form of a focus on quality that increasingly turns food into credence goods, and second, because the distance causes a decline in consumer trust for conventional food, and an ensuing demand for quality assurance systems, regulations and monitoring of food production (Meyer et al., 2012).

One expression of this shift in consumption is the return to purchasing directly from producers, with a range of different farmers' markets emerging. In these alternative markets, personal trust relationships are perceived to be important by consumers wanting to feel closer in proximity to producers. Such farmers' markets, once almost obsolete in industrialized countries, have lately become more common, acting as counterpoints to what is often perceived as faceless industrialized systems of food production, since they provide a human connection where production and consumption of food converge. Thus, direct agricultural markets carry the promise of re-embedding food production, and of interpersonal trust rather than trust in systems and organizations (Hinrichs, 2000).

However, this can be an idealized image of a direct market. Assumptions that direct exchange is necessarily completely immersed in interpersonal trust relationships will in many cases be to fall into the trap of oversocialization. Furthermore, the reality of a farmers' market might be closer to a bazaar market, where goods are heterogeneous and information scarce, rather than an interpersonal network (Geertz, 1978; Granovetter, 1985). A study of direct agricultural markets in Germany shows that while such markets do create a context where interpersonal ties between farmers and consumers is possible, the relationship is primarily one of impersonal commodity exchange (Hinrichs, 2000). Buying your food from the small, personal corner-shop – in contrast to shopping at the supermarket – is perceived as a fundamentally different trust relation between consumer and retailer. However, it is not so much the relationship per se, but rather the perception that the supermarket is part of the modernized world, where trust relies on impersonal systems rather than interpersonal relations. Shopping at a corner store, customers in a German study describe how 'one has the illusion of them picking the apples from the trees themselves', and it is this illusion that creates the perception of an interpersonal bond, having replaced the global agri-food system with a close to direct link to the farmer (Everts & Jackson, 2009).

Studies in England also show that when consumers try to overcome uncertainty and find a 'fix' to the problem of ascertaining quality in foods, they rely on set ideas as to what 'good' food should look like, namely proxies such as that food should not look too perfect, otherwise it seems less fresh and authentic: mucky carrots seem more trustworthy than clean ones (Eden et al., 2008a, 2008b). Trustworthiness and the true qualities of the good become unobservable properties, and so consumers rely on manifest signs and cues to ascertain them (Gambetta & Bacharach, 2001). Therefore, when consumers make an assessment in the store or at the market of whether a particular foodstuff can be deemed trustworthy, it is as much a matter of trust in signs as it is trust in individuals or systems. Trust in signs becomes relevant when a sought-after quality, for example how a carrot has been grown, is unobservable. The consumer will then look for a manifest cue of that unobservable property. Hence looking for the mucky carrot – or the organic label, or any other manifest sign deemed reliable.

A Swedish study shows that in this search for cues, the mere presence of the farmer, and the framing of the farmer's market, is perceived as a signal of quality – not because an interpersonal bond of trust has been formed between consumer and farmer, but because food bought directly from the farmer is perceived as fresher, healthier and more authentic. The marketplace and the context of the commodity exchange thus becomes a signal of quality in itself (Näslund & Tamm Hallström, 2014). In direct markets, trust often still relies on institutions and conventions: in the form of set ideas and proxies related to how the sought-after qualities of naturalness and authenticity may be ascertained. These forms of cultural and moral-norm systems render the behaviour of other actors predictable as a result of the perception of shared values, and thus consumers tend to look for cues as to what system products are part of, rather than for opportunities for interpersonal trust development (Lang, 2013). In line with the semiotic nature of signs, the meaning assigned to them is largely context dependent, and perceptions of the same label vary depending on, for example, national context, or what other labels it is combined with on the product (Janssen & Hamm, 2014; Ubilava & Foster, 2009; Van Loo et al., 2014; Lang, 2013).

Supermarkets and the more industrialized forms of food production have sought to counteract this alternative food movement with attempts to produce premium quality food with branding attempting to show the direct links to the food producers (Eden et al., 2008b). These trust-building practices and reputation mechanisms cover not only the quality of the food but also the wider social, economic and environmental impact of how that food is produced. In such cases, the production and consumption of food not only concerns the good itself, but also narratives and meanings, so that food is 'sold with a story'. Food production thereby also becomes a production of meaning, and the perceived quality of a food will therefore also be influenced by the political, economic and social conditions which shape this narrative process (Freidberg, 2003). The commodification of food is thus the result of a discursive/semiotic production, as discursive fields surround, construct and politicize foods. Through organic and fair trade labels, a political ecological image is created, which educates and shapes consumers to take responsibility through choices (Goodman, 2004b). When food does become a credence good, the demand for trustworthy signals and cues as to its qualities increases, as a result of increased uncertainty, and consequently the desire for increased regulation and quality assurance systems also rises (Meyer et al., 2012).

For example, supermarket shelves across Europe and North America show links to the producers, with milk bottle labels having photos of one of the many farmers supplying that brand and a description of their farm. While this offers signals that seem trustworthy to consumers, the benefit to farmers is less clear and falling prices have forced many dairy farmers to sell below their cost of production price.

Packaging of vegetables can also be branded by particular farms, giving consumers the perception that they are buying direct from a farmer. While these businesses may be producers themselves, they have been growing by buying in produce from other producers and hence become part of the industrialized food chain, operating very similarly to conventional food processors. Investigative journalism in the UK recently found that many of these 'farm brands' were diversifying into foreign food production but still using the image of a small farm to sell produce from Spain and Morocco. The increasing significance of the semiotic/discursive aspect of food production thereby also opens up new vulnerabilities and possibilities of deceit – and possible new quality-assurance systems, and ever-increased demands for trust creation.

The role of intermediaries

The social and spatial distances that have to be overcome in a globalized food industry and increased consumer demands for quality and sustainability, there is now a plethora of intermediaries, who play an important part in the process of creating trust in food. In modern society, Giddens (1990) argues, trust in abstract systems rather than interpersonal trust forms the structure of society, and the agri-food system is no exception to this development. The consumer or the buyer has little possibility to ascertain quality – not only because they lack closeness and means, but also because they lack knowledge.

Where there is a lack of trust, people rely on experts, forming a 'chain of strangers' who they rely upon to be unflappable, and have integrity in their judgment (Luhmann, 1979). In the agri-food system, such expert systems are becoming increasingly common, in the form of third-party certification bodies and quality-assurance schemes (Hatanaka et al., 2005). Third-party certification offers a solution to the problem of trust creation not only for producers, but also for intermediaries in the food supply chain, such as retailers. Store brands are typically perceived by consumers as having lower quality and become low-trust goods.

By adding a quality or organic label from a legitimate and trustworthy certification body, consumers increase their trust in the product, and will perceive it as having higher quality (Ku et al., 2012). These certification bodies thereby act as guardians of trust, whose legitimacy and authority is founded on their perceived independence from those that they monitor, which ensures that a conflict of interests can be avoided. The faith in such guardians of trust is not primarily based on an assessment of their expertise in monitoring, as consumers most likely lack the knowledge to make such an evaluation (Shapiro, 1987).

While independence is thus key to the legitimacy and trustworthiness of an audit, the prevalent financial dependency and client relationship between the auditor and the auditee means that this independence might be called into question, as has indeed often been the case in the wake of, for example, food scandals or the financial crisis (Power, 2011). In the case of third-party certification bodies in the food sector, the question of independence is often further complicated by links to retailers (Almeida et al., 2010; Davey & Richards, 2013). A perception of independence of certification bodies and accreditation inspectors requires careful construction by the practitioners involved. If it fails, they will also fail to elicit trust in the quality-assurance scheme. When an intermediary does attain the appearance of independence, this is most likely the result of careful construction rather than an inherent quality in the organization itself (Dogui et al., 2013).

A study of three eco-labels on the Swedish market (Näslund & Tamm Hallström, 2017) shows how they strike a balance between being a trustworthy collaborator and supplier of consumer trust to the producer, and at the same time trustworthy in the role of consumer watchdog from the consumers' perspective. This requires both organizational and narrative efforts. Within the labelling organization, those that maintain the client relationship with the customer are separated from those that perform the certification. Often it will not be the labelling organization itself, but another independent auditor who performs the monitoring and decides whether the client will pass or not. Furthermore, the dialogue with the producers, where the labelling organization appears as a business partner, is shielded from the consumers. Information given to the consumers typically centres on content of the criteria, rather than on the process by which the organization decides on this content (which may be a multi-stakeholder process where producers are included) or the details of how the monitoring is performed.

The construction of independence is thus inherently problematic, and takes considerable efforts and resources to be resolved. The legitimacy and authority of such intermediaries depend on their ability to set up and follow procedural norms. However, if these were to be followed to the letter, this would leave no room for judgement, discretion, experience and innovation. This is necessary in order to ensure the mutual trust that enables compliance to the rules and criteria set up by the intermediary (Pixley, 1999). The reason for this is that, if the regulated producer perceives the intermediary as overly suspicious with no concern for their well-being, complete openness and willingness to comply is unlikely (Weibel, 2007; Six & Sorge, 2008).

In addition to the construction of independence, expert systems also instil trust by 'trust transfer' and by 'borrowing' trust (Sztompka, 1999; Mueller et al., 2015). Although expert systems may appear faceless, they are operated by people, and there might be a transfer of trust between the position and the person that holds the position. The person is given a certain trustworthiness by holding a certain position, so that trust is transferred from the system to the individual, but the transfer may also run in the opposite direction: if the individual that holds a certain position appears to do a good job and be trustworthy, this trust may transfer to the system, and increase trust in it. What seems as impersonal trust in a regulatory system may thus, as a result of interpersonal interaction in the access points to such systems, turn out to rely heavily on interpersonal trust (Giddens, 1990; Hedgecoe, 2012). Similarly, systems may 'borrow' trust from other legitimate institutions – in the case of food certification, this is commonly done by borrowing either from government or from accreditation bodies and quality assurance systems, which ascertain that the labelling organization follows rules and practices so as to be legitimate in their role (Gustafsson & Tamm Hallström, 2013; Albersmeier et al., 2009; Bartley, 2007). The EU-logo for organic food, recently introduced in the EU and mandatory for all organic goods produced within the EU with the support of EU regulations and the EU commission, may be seen as an example of such borrowed trust (Janssen & Hamm, 2014).

Future research in trust and food

With the complexity of the food systems around the world and the growing degrees of vulnerability, research on trust and food has never been more important. As mentioned before, there is growing uncertainty and asymmetry of information related to urbanization and the globalization of food chains. However, there is still a lack of understanding of the shifting consumption patterns and growing interest in the origins of food and accessing healthy food.

The issue of trust is central to understanding how alternatives to food supply that provide quality, affordable food with less impact on the environment can be developed. This leads to four areas of research for trust research.

First, as food systems and supply chains face greater uncertainty, a comprehensive understanding of the nature of distrust is required in order to understand the impact of food scares and generalized distrust in the global agri-food system on trust in food. Recent studies in research on distrust support the viewpoint that trust and distrust should be regarded as distinct concepts, and, although advances have been made, we lack a precise understanding of the dynamics between these two constructs and how distrust is created and upheld (Bijlsma-Frankema et al., 2015; Saunders et al., 2014; Lewicki et al., 1998). Defining these dynamics would allow us to fully understand how and under what circumstances distrust may function as a barrier to the development of trust, not only in food systems and supply chains but also in other contexts. This needs to go beyond the views of the affluent or discerning in society and also explore the role of distrust for those who, by choice or by the force of poverty, buy the cheapest food rather than the healthier or more ethical options. In these parts of society, there seems to be evidence of 'suspension of distrust', as distrust is either accepted or 'assumed away'. There is a need for research that explores the nature and location of such displacement of distrust, which would contribute to our understanding of trust–distrust dynamics.

Second, there is a need for research in the approaches to building trust in food chains. This is particularly important where there is rapid urbanization and a growing physical distance of production from consumption. Research into the process of building trust should focus on a wide range of contexts beyond the food supply systems in Europe and North America, and include the global agri-food system from producer to consumer, through the net of intermediaries. There is particular need to understand how to build trust in less developed countries, and also in contexts where there is a breakdown in traditional supply chains. In conflict situations and during periods of food shortage, the nature of disruption can be severe and trust-building processes particularly challenging.

Trust-building processes include a range of stakeholders including public-sector policy makers introducing legislation, civil society organizations creating additional institutional forms of trust such as ethical or sustainable branding, and businesses investing in trust-building processes to reduce the vulnerability felt by consumers. Research on the roles of each of these actors can allow greater understanding of trust-building mechanisms. The interplay between interpersonal and systemic trust has to some extent been studied, looking for example at the transfer of trust between individuals and systems (Sztompka, 1999; Mueller et al., 2015) or the role of access points, where lay individuals interact directly with representatives of abstract systems, in building trust in systems (Giddens, 1990). As such expert systems gain in numbers and significance, not only in the form of quality assurance schemes in the agri-food system, but also in the form of auditing and valuation in other parts of society, there is also an increasing need for a fuller understanding of how trust in different stakeholders interacts. Furthermore, the food sector also demonstrates that, for the public, it is not only a matter of trust in systems or individuals, but largely of trust in signs. We therefore need more research on how trust in signs, systems and individuals relate and influence each other.

Thirdly, there is a need to understand the nature of deceit and betrayal of trust in the food chain and the perceptions of the consumer. Research should explore how people make decisions when trust has been damaged. Businesses in the food system have been accused of betraying the trust of consumers during food scares or when malpractice has been unearthed. Research is needed that understands how unscrupulous businesses may be exploiting the trust of consumers, and how consumers make use of different cues in assessing foods.

Finally, there is a need to understand the processes of repairing trust in food systems after trust has been violated. As we showed at the start of this chapter, there have been food scares in the past and there are likely to be more in the future. There are particular opportunities to explore how businesses rebuild trust with both consumers and other businesses in their supply chain. There is a need to understand how trust violation in one area affects institutional trust elsewhere in the system.

References

Albersmeier, F., H. Schulze, G. Jahn, and A. Spiller. 2009. The reliability of third-party certification in the food chain: From checklists to riskoriented auditing. *Food Control* 20:927–935.

Almeida, F., H. F. Pessali, and N. Maciel de Paula. 2010. Third-party certification in food market chains: Are you being served? *Journal of Economic Issues* 44 (2):479–485.

Amoako, I., and F. Lyon. 2014. 'We don't deal with courts': Cooperation and alternative institutions shaping exporting relationships of SMEs in Ghana. *International Small Business Journal* 32 (2):117–139.

Bachmann, R., and A. C. Inkpen. 2011. Understanding institutional-based trust building processes in inter-organizational relationships. *Organization Studies* 32 (2):281–301.

Bartley, T. 2007. Institutional emergence in an era of globalization: The rise of transnational private regulation of labor and environmental conditions. *American Journal of Sociology* 113 (2):297–351.

Bernzen, A., and B. Braun. 2014. Conventions in cross-border trade coordination: The case of organic food imports to Germany and Australia. *Environment and Planning A* 46:1244–1262.

Bijlsma-Frankema, K., S. B. Sitkin, and A. Weibel. 2015. Distrust in the balance: The emergence and development of intergroup distrust in a court of law. *Organization Science* 26 (4):1018–1039.

Bonnin, C., and S. Turner. 2012. At what price rice? Food security, livelihood vulnerability, and state interventions in upland northern Vietnam. *Geoforum* 43:95–105.

Carriquiry, M., and B. A. Babcock. 2007. Reputations, market structure, and the choice of quality assurance systems in the food industry. *American Journal of Agricultural Economics* 89 (1):12–23.

Chen, M.-F. 2008. Consumer trust in food safety – A multidisciplinary approach and empirical evidence from Taiwan. *Risk Analysis* 28 (6):1553–1569.

Darby, M., and E. Karni. 1973. Free competition and the optimal amount of fraud. *The Journal of Law and Economics* 16 (1):67–88.

Davey, S. S., and C. Richards. 2013. Supermarkets and private standards: Unintended consequences of the audit ritual. *Agriculture and Human Values* 30:271–281.

Dilley, M., and T. E. Bourdeau. 2001. Coming to terms with vulnerability: A critique of the food security definition. *Food Policy* 26:229–247.

Dogui, K., O. Boiral, and Y. Gendron. 2013. ISO auditing and the construction of trust in auditor independence. *Accounting, Auditing & Accountability Journal* 26 (8):1279–1305.

Dreyer, M., O. Renn, S. Cope, and L. J. Frewer. 2010. Including social impact assessment in food safety givernance. *Food Control* 21 (12):1620–1628.

Eden, S., C. Bear, and G. Walker. 2008a. Mucky carrots and other proxies: Problematising the knowledge-fix for sustainable and ethical consumption. *Geoforum* 39:1044–1057.

Eden, S., C. Bear, and G. Walker. 2008b. Understanding and (dis)trusting food assurance schemes: Consumer confidence and the 'knowledge fix'. *Journal of Rural Studies* 24 (1):1–14.

Everts, J., and P. Jackson. 2009. Modernisation and the practices of contemporary food shopping. *Environment and Planning D: Society and Space* 27:917–935.

Freidberg, S. 2003. Not all sweetness and light: New cultural geographies of food. *Social and Cultural Geography* 4 (1):3–6.

Gambetta, D. 1988. Mafia: The Price of Distrust. In *Trust: Making and Breaking Cooperative Relations*, edited by D. Gambetta. New York, NY: Basil Blackwell.

Gambetta, D., and M. Bacharach. 2001. Trust in Signs. In *Trust in Society*, edited by K. S. Cook. New York: Russell Sage Foundation.

Geertz, C. 1978. The bazaar economy: Information and search in peasant marketing. *Supplement to the American Economic Review* 68:28–32.

Giddens, A. 1990. *The Consequences of Modernity*. Cambridge: Polity Press.

Goodman, D. 2004a. Rural Europe redux? Reflections on alternative agro-food networks and paradigm change. *Sociologia Ruralis* 44 (1):3–16.

Goodman, M. K. 2004b. Reading fair trade: Political ecological imaginary and the moral economy of fair trade foods. *Political Geography* 23:891–915.

Granovetter, M. 1985. Economic action and social structure: The problem of embeddedness. *The American Journal of Sociology* 91 (3):481–510.

Grebitus, C., B. Steiner, and M. Veeman. 2015. The roles of human values and generalized trust on stated preferences when food is labeled with environmental footprints: Insights from Germany. *Food Policy* 52:84–91.

Gustafsson, I., and K. Tamm Hallström. 2013. The Certification Paradox: Monitoring as a Solution and a Problem. In *Trust and Organizations: Confidence Across Borders*, edited by M. Reuter, F. Wijkström, and B. Kristensson Uggla. New York, NY: Palgrave.

Hatanaka, M., C. Bain, and L. Busch. 2005. Third-party certification in the global agrifood system. *Food Policy* 30:354–369.

Hedgecoe, A. 2012. Trust and regulatory organizations: The role of local knowledge and facework in research ethics review. *Social Studies of Science* 42 (5):662–683.

Hinrichs, C. C. 2000. Embeddedness and local food systems: Notes on two types of direct agricultural market. *Journal of Rural Studies* 16:295–303.

Hobbs, J. E., and E. Goddard. 2015. Consumers and trust. *Food Policy* 52 (April):71–74.

Houghton, J. R., G. Rowe, L.J. Frewer, E. Van Kleef, G. Chryssoidis, O. Kehagia, S. Korzen-Bohr, J. Lassen, U. Pfenning, and A. Strada. 2008. The quality of food risk management in Europe: Perspectives and priorities. *Food Policy* 33:13–26.

Humphrey, J., and O. Memedovic. 2006. *Global Value Chains in the Agrifood Sector*. Vienna: United Nations Industrial Development Organization.

Jackson, P., N. Ward, and P. Russell. 2006. Mobilising the commodity chain concept in the politics of food and farming. *Journal of Rural Studies* 22:129–141.

Janssen, M., and U. Hamm. 2014. Governmental and private certification labels for organic food: Consumer attitudes and preferences in Germany. *Food Policy* 49:437–448.

Kjaernes, U., M. Harvey, and A. Ward. 2013. *Trust in food: A comparative and institutional analysis*. Hampshire, UK: Palgrave Macmillan.

Ku, H.-H., P.-J. Wang, and C.-C. Kuo. 2012. Effects of product quality certification on quality perceptions of stores' own brands. *The Service Industries Journal* 32 (5):807–820.

Lang, J. T. 2013. Elements of public trust in the American food system: Experts, organizations, and genetically modified food. *Food Policy* 41:144–154.

Lassoued, R., and J. E. Hobbs. 2015. Consumer confidence in credence attributes: The role of brand trust. *Food Policy* 52:99–107.

Lewicki, R. J., D. J. McAllister, and R. J. Bies. 1998. Trust and distrust: New relationships and realities. *Academy of Management Review* 23 (3):438–458.

Luhmann, N. 1979. *Trust and Power*. Chichester: John Wiley & Sons.

Lyon, F. 2000. Trust, networks and norms: The creation of social capital in agricultural economies in Ghana. *World Development* 28 (4):663–682.

———. 2005. Managing co-operation: Trust and power in Ghanaian associations. *Organization Studies* 27 (1):31–52.

Lyon, F., and G. Porter. 2009. Market institutions, trust and norms: Exploring moral economies in Nigerian food systems. *Cambridge Journal of Economics* 33 (5):903–920.

Maxwell, S. 1996. Food security: A post-modern perspective. *Food Policy* 21 (2):155–170.

Mayer, R. C., J. H. Davis, and F. D. Schoorman. 1995. An integrative model of organizational trust. *Academy of Management Review* 20 (3):709–734.

Meijerink, G., E. Bulte, and D. Alemu. 2014. Formal insitutions and social capital in value chains: The case of the Ethiopian Commodity Exchange. *Food Policy* 49:1–12.

Meyer, S. B., J. Coveney, J. Henderson, P. R. Ward, and A. W. Taylor. 2012. Reconnecting Australian consumers and producers: Identifying problems of distrust. *Food Policy* 37:634–640.

Möllering, G. 2001. The nature of trust: From Georg Simmel to a theory of expectation, interpretation and suspension. *Sociology* 35 (2):403–420.

———. 2008. Inviting or avoiding deception through trust? Conceptual exploration of an ambivalent relationship. In *MPIfG Working Paper 08/1*. Köln: Max-Planck-Institut für Gesellschaftsforschung.

Mueller, F., C. Carter, and A. Whittle. 2015. Can audit (still) be trusted? *Organization Studies* 36 (9):1171–1203.

Murdoch, J., T. Marsden, and J. Banks. 2000. quality, nature and embeddedness: Some theoretical considerations in the context of the food sector. *Economic Geography* 76 (2):107–125.

Näslund, L., and K. Tamm Hallström. 2014. 'I trust they're checking': The role of eco-labels in reducing consumer uncertainty. In *30th EGOS Colloquium*. Rotterdam, The Netherlands.

———. 2017. Being Everybody's Accomplice: Trust and Control in Eco-labeling. In *Trust in Regulatory Regimes*, edited by F. Six and K. Verhoest. Cheltenham, UK, and Northampton, MA: Edward Elgar.

Nelson, P. 1970. Information and consumer behavior. *Journal of Political Economy* 78 (2):311–329.

Perrini, F., S. Castaldo, N. Misani, and A. Tencati. 2010. The impact of corporate social responsibility associations on trust in organic products marketed by mainstream retailers: A study of Italian customers. *Business Strategy and the Environment* 19 (8):512–526.

Pixley, J. 1999. Impersonal trust in global mediating organizations. *Sociological Perspectives* 42 (4):647–671.

Power, M. K. 2011. Assurance worlds: Consumers, experts and independence. *Accounting, Organizations and Society* 36:324–326.

Rousseau, D. M., S. B. Sitkin, R. S. Burt, and C. Camerer. 1998. Not so different after all: A cross-discipline view of trust. *Academy of Management Review* 23 (3):393–404.

Sapp, S. G., C. Arnot, J. Fallon, T. Fleck, D. Soorholz, M. Sutton-Vermeulen, and J. J. H. Wilson. 2009. Consumer trust in the U.S. food system: An examination of the recreancy theorem. *Rural Sociology* 74 (4):525–545.

Saunders, M. N. K., G. Dietz, and A. Thornhill. 2014. Trust and distrust: Polar opposites, or independent but co-existing? *Human Relations* 67 (6):639–665.

Schoorman, F. D., R. C. Mayer, and J. H. Davis. 2007. An integrative model of organizational trust: Past, present, and future. *Academy of Management Review* 32 (2):344–354.

Shapiro, S. P. 1987. The social control of impersonal trust. *The American Journal of Sociology* 93 (3):623–658.

Six, F., and A. Sorge. 2008. Creating a high-trust organization: an exploration into organizational policies that stimulate interpersonal trust building. *Journal of Management Studies* 45 (5):857–884.

Skinner, D., G. Dietz, and A. Weibel. 2014. The dark side of trust: When trust becomes a 'poisoned chalice'. *Organization* 21 (2):206–224.

Sydow, J., and A. Windeler. 2003. Knowledge, trust and control: Managing tensions and contradictions in a regional network of service firms. *International Journal of Management & Organization* 33 (2):69–99.

Sztompka, P. 1999. *Trust: A Sociological Theory*. Cambridge, UK: Cambridge University Press.

Ubilava, D., and K. Foster. 2009. Quality certification vs product traceability: Consumer preferences for informational attributes of pork in Georgia. *Food Policy* 34:305–310.

USDA. 2016. Global Food Industry. Washington, DC: United States Department of Agriculture Economic Research Service.

Van Loo, E. J., V. Caputo, R. M. Nayga Jr, and W. Verbeke. 2014. Consumer's valuation of sustainable labels on meat. *Food Policy* 49:137–150.

Webb, P., and A. Harinarayan. 1999. A measure of uncertainty: The nature of vulnerability and its relationship to malnutrition. *Disasters* 23 (4):292–305.

Weibel, A. 2007. Formal control and trustworthiness: Shall the twain never meet? *Group and Organization Management* 32 (4):500–517.

Williams, M. 2007. Building genuine trust through interpersonal emotion management: A threat regulation model of trust and collaboration across boundaries. *Academy of Management Review* 32 (2):595–621.

World Trade Organization. 2016. *World Trade Statistical Review 2016*. Geneva, Switzerland: World Trade Organization.

PART VI

Future directions

The titles of the chapters in this final part might at first surprise readers, but we have deliberately identified key topics where we see there being some important new developments or synergies with other areas that are worthy of further examination. Deanne N. Den Hartog commences this part with a reminder about the positive and significant role of leaders. Looking back to Dirk and Ferrin's (2002) important meta-analysis, reviews of Fulmer and Gelfand (2012) and Nienaber et al. (2015), she reminds us of the impact on trust of leaders. She considers the development of trust in leaders, which has obvious synergies with some of the work on fairness which Chapter 10 by Lind reviews. She identifies a useful dichotomy between character and relationship-based views of trust in the leader, and highlights how leaders' behavioural styles influence the building and eroding of their followers' trust, building on Chapter 2 by Korsgaard. There are synergies with Chapter 28 by Searle, in her attention to the roles that leaders play in developing pertinent climates and in their efforts to implement Human Resource Management practices that can help build and sustain employee trust. Den Hartog also updates our thinking to ensure that adequate attention is paid to individual difference facets for followers in understanding better trust in this nexus. She concludes by emphasizing the importance of including relevant situation factors but also making more fine-grained distinctions in terms of cognitive- and affect-based trust for and in this central organizational relationship. There are important synergies with other chapters concerning this relationship including Chapter 2 by Korsgaard, on reciprocal trust, Chapter 5 by Lyu and Ferrin, on interpersonal trust, Chapter 10 by Lind, on fairness, and Chapter 11 by Coyle-Shapiro and Diehl, on social exchange.

Chapter 27 by Raaphorst and Van de Walle examine trust in and by the public sector, looking at trust issues in and for citizens. They develop further some of the elements found in Chapter 20 by Six. They show the dichotomy between citizens' trust in the public sector, as distinct from public-sector organization's trust in citizens. This chapter distinguishes between trust and distrust, and contends that trust in the public sector is changing, identifying pertinent clues and signals both of more trust, but also of areas where trust is low and concern more the emergence of distrust. There are therefore synergies with Chapter 4 by Sitkin and Bijlsma-Frankema, on distrust. They highlight an array of projects designed to enhance trust and reduce the incidence of distrust. They make the case that the relative dearth of attention to this sector is unfortunate as this is a context in which trust and distrust are critical matters. This chapter has obvious further links with Chapter 12 by Bachmann, on institutional trust.

In Chapter 28, Rosalind H. Searle outlines the importance of trust in terms of the employee Human Resources Management cycle to draw attention to the dynamics of trust within the context of Human Resources Management, but also to how important stages of that cycle have been omitted or only partially considered. In her review of this area, she differentiates the work to date that has focused on studies of bundles of HRM practices from that which considers single policy topics. From this analysis, she highlights the fragmentation of the current bundles field, but also reveals the paucity of work in some surprising areas. She outlines an agenda not just of key topics requiring further attention, but also for the importance of better measures and methods to create a more comprehensive insight into the seminal ways trust influences Human Resources Management policies and practice. This chapter has synergies with Chapter 26 by Den Hartog, but also with others including Chapter 12 by Bachmann, on institutional trust, those looking at the relationships, including Chapter 2 by Korsgaard, on reciprocal trust, Chapter 5 by Lyu and Ferrin, on interpersonal trust, Chapter 10 by Lind, on fairness, Chapter 12 by Coyle-Shapiro and Diehl, on social exchange, and Chapter 8 by Baer and Colquitt, which gives insights into antecedents. The chapter has links to Chapter 21 by Mather, which gives insights into employment relations, and Chapter 29 by Long and Weibel, on control and trust. Further, this is a context which has underexplored emotion and relationships as Chapter 1 by van Knippenberg, usefully outlines.

Chris P. Long and Antoinette Weibel undertake a review of the dynamics of control-trust to discuss how and why control *and* trust jointly constitute important components of organizational effectiveness. They outline the contributions of trust and control towards organizations and identify the two conflicting perspectives of trust as being undermined by control, versus control being a complement of trust. Their chapter includes attention to the important contextual variables that influence this relationship. They also identify the dearth of scrutiny by trust researchers into the cognitive and behavioural processes of managers that encourage others to trust them. There are synergies with Chapter 26 by Den Hartog, Chapter 28 by Searle and Chapter 29 by Long and Weibel, regarding how trust in subordinates impacts on managers' control decisions. There are also links with Chapter 13 by Poppo and Cheng, on contracts.

Then, Shay S. Tzafrir, Guy Enosh and Laliv Egozi bring us full circle by looking more specifically at the question of affect, in particular at trust and anger. Their chapter takes a deep dive into effect in the social environment of work to examine the relationships between trust, anger and aggression. The chapter takes ideas discussed in three previous chapters – namely Chapter 6 by Nienaber, Holtgrave and Romeike, on trust and teams, Chapter 8 by Fulmer, on multilevel perspective and Chapter 1 by van Knippenberg, on affect-based relational trust – to enhance understanding of aggression and anger at work. While reviewing the current literature on anger and trust, this chapter includes concepts of microfoundation (Devinney, 2013) and multi-level effects to enhance how and why team members choose to show externally the anger they might feel. The chapter has further synergies with Chapter 5 by Lyu and Ferrin, on inter personal trust and with Chapter 2 by Korsgaard, which gives insights into reciprocal trust, Chapter 10 by Lind, on fairness, Chapter 11 by Coyle-Shapiro and Diehl, on social exchange, Chapter 9 by Baer and Colquitt, a review of antecedents and Chapter 26 by Den Hartog, on leadership.

26

LEADERSHIP AND TRUST

Deanne N. Den Hartog

Introduction

Trust forms a psychological state that involves confident positive expectations about another's motives with respect to oneself in situations entailing risk (cf. Boon & Holmes, 1991). Trust is essential to cooperation between different parties and forms an important feature in dyadic interpersonal relationships as well as in larger collectivities such as organizations. In other words, cooperation 'requires trust in the sense that the dependent parties need some degree of assurance that the other, non-dependent parties will not defect' (Williams, 1988, p. 8). In line with this, Cook and Wall (1980) view trust between individuals and groups within the organization as crucial to its long-term stability. They define trust as the extent to which one is willing to ascribe good intentions to and have confidence in the words and actions of other people.

Leaders and their behaviour often have strong effects on employee behaviours and attitudes, including trust. Especially relevant to the relationship between leadership and trust is the notion that trust occurs in a dependent relationship and involves risk and vulnerability. For example, Mayer, Davis and Schoorman (1995) emphasize that the willingness of one party to be vulnerable to the actions of another party forms a key feature of trust, and McAllister (1995) focuses on trust as the extent to which a person is confident in, and willing to act on the basis of, the words, actions and decisions, of another. In organizations, employees are often at least to some extent and often largely dependent on the words, actions and decisions of their leaders. Their leaders at different levels in the organization set both individual and collective objectives to strive for. Leaders at the top determine the course of action of the organization and thus affect the long-term results of the organization, which matter to employees. Leaders at lower levels affect employees as well. They tend to have the position power to affect important proximal outcomes for employees such as their promotions and pay. Leaders often also play an important role in determining other crucial work features, such as work content and the types of challenges and assignments employees get.

In line with this, Nienaber and colleagues (2015) note that several asymmetries characterize the supervisor–subordinate relationship and that these make trust concerns especially important for employees: the leader typically has higher status, more power and information, and the possibility to exercise more control, and thus subordinates tend to face greater uncertainty and dependency in the leader–follower relationship. For employees, it is of course both cognitively and emotionally hard to willingly follow or go the extra mile for leaders whom they do not trust, which undermines cooperation and effort. As leaders are agents of the organization, not trusting one's direct supervisor may spill over to also not trusting management or the organization as a whole, further eroding the basis for cooperative behaviour. Also, uncertainty, stress and fear are likely to arise in situations in which trust in the leader is lacking, and, in the longer run, a lack of trust in this crucial organizational relationship partner is thus also likely to affect employees' well-being.

Consequently, employees' trust in their leaders has formed an important topic of research and has been studied much more than the reverse, that is, whether and when leaders trust their followers. Yet, while there is an asymmetry in power and influence with followers typically more dependent on their leaders than vice versa, leaders too are (to an extent) dependent on their followers' cooperation and effort to be able to meet (collective) goals and realize strategic plans. Leaders too are vulnerable because if they cannot trust their employees to cooperate and deliver, this decreases their own and their unit's effectiveness. Thus, trust between leaders and followers can have important benefits for employees, leaders and the organization as a whole. However, creating trust and sustaining such trust over time can be difficult (e.g. Kramer, 1999).

This chapter focuses on the important relationship between leadership and employee trust. I review the literature on trust in the leader and also discuss work on mutual trust between leader and follower. This review is not exhaustive and several other resources that are relevant to the topic of leadership and trust include a quantitative meta-analysis on this topic of Dirks and Ferrin (2002) as well as two qualitative reviews (Fulmer & Gelfand, 2012; Nienaber et al., 2015). While the emphasis of this chapter is on reviewing the work that has been done, throughout I also outline several areas related to leadership and trust that are in need of future research.

Research shows that employee trust in their leader relates to different, generally positive outcomes. Thus, to illustrate why trust in leaders is so important for organizations, I first describe the outcomes of employees having trust in their leaders. Second, I turn to how trust in leaders develops and what forms such trust can take. I discuss both the character- and relationship-based views of trust in the leader. Third, I review the research on how specific leader behavioural styles affect employee trust. In doing so, I discuss leader behaviours that can help build stronger bonds of trust as well as leader behaviours that can erode follower trust. Fourth, I briefly outline several additional and indirect ways in which leaders affect employee trust, for example through their role in creating certain work climates or their implementation of human resource management practices. Fifth, I touch upon the need to know more about the role of follower characteristics and trust in followers. Finally, I end the chapter with some concluding remarks highlighting the need to better understand when trust between leaders and followers is more and when it is less crucial in organizations.

Leadership and the outcomes of trust in leaders

Leadership forms an important area of investigation in the social sciences and can be defined as 'the process of influencing the activities of an organized group in its efforts toward goal setting and goal achievement' (Stogdill, 1950, p. 4) or more elaborately as 'the ability of an individual to influence, motivate, and enable others to contribute toward the effectiveness and success of the organizations of which they are members' (House, Hanges, Javidan, Dorfman & Gupta, 2004, p. 15). Trust between leaders and followers is crucial in being able to exert this kind of influence efficiently and effectively without the need for coercion or constant close monitoring (e.g. Searle et al., 2011). In line with this, research suggests that in practice several trust-related qualities are universally endorsed by employees and managers alike as being important to be a good leader. The GLOBE study, which focused on cultural similarities and differences in implicit leadership theories, for example asked middle-managers as respondents to rate to which extent leaders needed to show certain characteristics to be an outstandingly effective leader. In all 60 countries involved in this study, an outstanding leader was expected to be a confidence builder who is decisive and intelligent, good at team building and communicating, as well as trustworthy, just and honest (Den Hartog, House, Hanges, Ruiz-Quintanilla & Dorfman, 1999; House et al., 2004). Thus, clearly, trust-related characteristics are universally seen as important for leaders to be able to effectively influence others.

In addition, trust in leaders is generally found to have positive correlates or outcomes in organizations. For example, Podsakoff and colleauges (1990) showed that trust in leaders related positively to employee organizational citizenship behaviour. Grant and Sumanth (2009) found in their research in mission-driven organizations that managers' perceived trustworthiness related positively to employees' experienced task significance as well as pro-social motivation and pro-social behaviour. Also, Davis, Schoorman, Mayer and Tan (2000) found that employees' trust in the general manager of their restaurant was related to higher financial performance of the restaurant (sales and profits) and to reduced employee turnover. In line with this, in their meta-analytical review of the research, Dirks and Ferrin (2002) show that overall, trust in leaders was positively related to many desirable outcomes, including enhanced job performance, organizational citizenship behaviour, satisfaction, commitment and reduced turnover intentions. Its many positive correlates and outcomes suggest that trust in leaders can form an important resource for organizations. For example, Hernandez, Long and Sitkin (2014) suggest follower trust can 'facilitate the achievement of organizational goals, the implementation of organizational changes, and the ability to guide organizations through challenging situations' (p. 1).

Gao, Janssen and Shi (2011) showed that trust in the leader is positively related to employee voice. When employees trust their leader, they are more likely to take the risk to speak up with their opinions, concerns, suggestions and recommendations about work matters. In contrast, low trust makes it less likely that they will risk voicing such matters. Employee voice can help improve organizational processes and decision-making (e.g. Morrison, 2011). However, Gao et al. (2015) also showed that the main effect of leader trust does not always hold and should be considered within boundary conditions. Specifically, they found that empowering leader behaviours moderated the relationship between leader trust and employee voice: the positive relationship between trust in leader and employee voice only existed when employees perceive their leaders to be empowering. Thus, they found that trust *only* leads to more employee voice when leaders actively encourage participation and invite and encourage such voice. When leaders do not exhibit empowering leader behaviours, leader trust remained unrelated to voice. This interactive effect held for three empowering behaviours, namely participative decision-making, informing and coaching (Gao et al., 2011). These findings suggests that trust in the leader in and of itself may not always be sufficient to produce positive outcomes, but that the (leadership) context also remains important to be able to fully benefit from the existence of such trust. More research on the boundedness of the outcomes of trust in the leader is of interest.

It is also important to note much of the theorizing around trust in leaders suggests that the directionality of causation (mostly) runs from trust in leaders to different outcomes, for example, employees will show more citizenship when they trust their leader, rather than vice versa (engaging in citizenship affects trust levels). Yet, much of the research to date is correlational in nature and cannot rule out that reversed causation also plays a role for certain outcomes; for example, it may be that having high trust affects subsequent performance positively. However, it may also be easier to trust the leaders in better-performing organizations as success of the collective may be attributed to its leader and make them seem more capable. Thus, outcomes such as success may form a trustworthiness cue for leader ability. Likely, causation between trust and performance runs both ways (trust better enabling performance as well as performance inspiring further trust). This may also hold for other outcomes; for example, high trust may make teams more cohesive over time, but cohesiveness may also form a benevolence-related trust cue in teams. Future research on this reciprocal influence between trust and outcomes as well as more generally the causal processes involved would be of interest. Below, I turn to how trust in leaders develops and what different forms such trust in leaders can take.

Different forms of trust in the leader and their development

As discussed above, trust seems to have many positive outcomes and correlates in organizations, and given that trust in leaders plays such a positive role in organizations, it is interesting to explore how such trust comes about. Or, in other words, when and why do employees decide to trust their leaders or not to do so?

Trust in organizational leaders at different levels can take different forms. For example, trust in leadership is to some extent role-based. In other words, the role or office leaders hold and their training or background in that role play a role in the trust others place in leaders and managers (see e.g. Kramer, 1999). However, person-specific knowledge about a given leader's actions, capabilities or intentions also strongly affect interpersonal trust as they impact on how trustworthy the leader is perceived to be. Behaviours and characteristics form trustworthiness cues for employees, and a leader's trustworthiness in the eyes of followers relies on the intentions that followers attribute to the leader (e.g. Searle, Weibel & Den Hartog, 2011). Is the leader's behaviour perceived to be driven by benevolence and integrity versus malevolence and dishonesty? Is the leader seen as competent and able to set the right goals and achieve them? Below I discuss the research on how leaders' characteristics affect followers' trust in more detail.

Followers thus try to judge the leader's characteristics such as integrity, predictability, dependability, fairness, competence and ability. Cognitive inferences they make on these characteristics affect whether they decide to trust the leader, and these inferences also affect whether employees show cooperative or trusting behaviours themselves (cf. Dietz & Den Hartog, 2006). This process refers to what Dirks and Ferrin (2002) label the character-based perspective of trust in leadership and it relates to what McAllister focuses on as cognitive trust. Such trustworthiness inferences seem to be universally important in relation to leadership. As noted above, in the so-called GLOBE study (see e.g. House et al., 2004) several such character-related trust qualities were universally endorsed as important for outstanding leadership (e.g. being just, honest and intelligent; see Den Hartog et al., 1999).

The character-based perspective thus focuses on the perception of the leader's character – often operationalized in terms of ability, benevolence and integrity – and how this influences a follower's sense of vulnerability in a hierarchical relationship (Mayer et al., 1995). As noted, trust-related concerns about leaders are important because the leader tends to have decision authority that can have a significant impact on employees (e.g. performance evaluations, pay, promotions, task assignments). However, the basis or nature of interpersonal trust may vary (or may over time even develop) from a shallow, calculative form of trust in which a cost-benefit analysis is central, to a more knowledge-based form of trust in which perceived reliability and dependability of the relationship partner (in this case the leader) are important to form a deeper relational bond of trust that is more affective and derived from shared experiences, identities and values (e.g. Lewicki & Bunker, 1996).

Thus, in addition to the character-based or cognitive form of trust, Dirks and Ferrin (2002) distinguish the relational perspective of trust in leadership that focuses on how followers understand the nature of the leader–follower relationship. McAllister (1995) refers to this relationship-based form of trust as affective trust. Social exchange processes are often proposed to play a central role in this form of trust (e.g. Whitener, Brodt, Korsgaard & Werner, 1998). Followers perceive a high-quality relationship and in this relationship care, consideration and reciprocation are central variables. Researchers have, for example, used this relational perspective in describing how trust in leaders can elicit citizenship behaviour (e.g. Konovsky & Pugh, 1994).

The above character-based and relational trust perspectives are clearly linked. Leader characteristics and behaviours both form cues for trustworthiness and can directly affect the relationship between leader and follower. However, while both affect clearly trust, some research suggests that the relational perspective might be most central to the development of follower trust. Hernandez and colleagues (2014) studied how leader behaviour relates to trust in leaders through three lenses: the leader (personal leadership), the leader–follower relationship (relational leadership) and the situation (contextual leadership). Personal leadership behaviours are leader-related and can be thought of leader-focused leadership behaviours that convey to followers that the leader has personal qualities that merit trust as discussed above. Relational leadership behaviours relate to the dyad relationship level. Relationship-focused leadership behaviours are those aimed to facilitate the connection between a leader and follower, build their relationship and emphasize that leaders will not take advantage of followers' trust. Contextual leadership behaviours are situation-focused leadership behaviours that help followers interpret the context and organizational dynamics.

When they were assessed independently, Hernandez and colleagues found that all three forms of leader behaviour affected follower trust. When considered jointly, relational leadership behaviours formed the most proximal source of trust and mediated the impact of personal and contextual leadership behaviour on trust. These findings suggest that leader behaviours that communicate competence and other personal characteristics (as suggested in the character-based approach) as well as broader context-focused leadership behaviours mostly 'influence follower trust through the relational features of follower treatment, such as leader behaviours that demonstrate concern, respect, and fairness' (Hernandez et al., 2014, p. 17). These findings start to point to the importance of leader behaviour for follower trust; thus, below, I discuss the research on how different (perceived) behaviours of leaders or styles of leadership affect employees' trust in the leaders positively or negatively.

Leader behaviour and trust in the leader

Many different leader behaviours have been related directly to trust in the leader and to subsequent attitudinal and behavioural outcomes (with trust often proposed to form an important mediator between leadership and such outcomes). Here, I discuss several examples of such leader behaviours and the relationships that have been shown with trust, starting with leader behaviours that relate positively to trust and then turning to behaviours that erode trust.

One of the most classic distinctions in leader behaviour arguably focuses on task- versus relationship-oriented leader behaviour, also often labelled initiating structure versus consideration (see Bass & Bass, 2008, for an overview of the classic studies in this area; and see Judge, Piccolo & Ilies, 2004, for a meta-analysis of the effectiveness of both of these classic behaviours). Relationship-oriented leader behaviour or consideration describes leader behaviours aimed to develop good relationships based on mutual trust, respect and a certain warmth between leader and followers as well as among the team as a whole. This form of leader behaviour is closely related to the aforementioned relationship-based or affective forms of trust. A leader's task orientation or initiating structure focuses on how the leader organizes, directs and defines group activities, roles and tasks and as such relates more to knowledge-based or ability-related trust elements (Searle et al., 2011).

Transformational and transactional leadership

In the last few decades, transformational, visionary and charismatic models have been very influential in the field of leadership research, albeit not without criticism (see e.g. van Knippenberg, & Sitkin, 2013, for one such critique). These models propose that both transformational and charismatic leaders articulate an attractive and inspiring vision and behave in ways that reinforce the values inherent in that vision. Followers come to share this vision of the collective future with which they can identify and become highly committed to the goals of the collective (e.g. Bass, 1985; Shamir, House & Arthur, 1993).

Charisma involves followers bestowing exceptional qualities on the leader (e.g. Shamir et al., 1993). Transformational and charismatic leadership are related, yet while attributions of charisma and the strongly related element of inspirational motivation through a communicated vision are central to both charismatic and transformational leadership, transformational leadership was originally conceptualized as being broader. Bass (1985) proposed that intellectual stimulation and individualized consideration additionally form transformational leader behaviours (Bass, 1985). Intellectual stimulation focuses on whether the leader asks followers to provide ideas and input and challenge current assumptions. Individualized consideration focuses on leaders providing support and mentoring to meet individual needs and caring about individual followers' concerns.

Conceptually, transformational forms of leadership are proposed to relate strongly to (relationship-based, affective and identification-based) trust. In line with this, both field and experimental research shows that transformational leadership relates positively to trust in the leader (e.g. Gillespie & Mann, 2004; Jung & Avolio, 2000; Pillai, Schriesheim & Williams, 1999; Podsakoff et al., 1990; see also the Dirks & Ferrin 2002 meta-analysis) and such trust in the leader related to transformational leadership seems to spill over to trust in generalized others in the collective such as management and coworkers (e.g. Den Hartog, 2003).

Research also shows that trust in the leader mediates the relationship between transformational leadership and other relevant outcomes such as organizational citizenship behaviour (e.g. Podsakoff et al., 1990). As such, enhanced follower trust seems to form one of the mechanisms through which transformational forms of leadership affect followers. Although transformational leadership thus clearly has quite a substantial relationship with trust, the exact causal process remains unclear, and Dirks and Ferrin (2002) suggest that one issue that needs to be solved is to identify which behavioural components are responsible for relationships with different trust components, for example, role modelling and charisma may be more related to character-based trust, and consideration to relationship-focused forms of trust.

Transformational leadership is usually contrasted with transactional leadership. Transactional leadership is an exchange-based form of leadership, focusing on leader–follower relations as a series of (implicitly economic) exchanges between leaders and followers where, in exchange for promised rewards, followers will perform as expected. Here too trust is important as followers will need to trust their leader to be fair, keep their word and provide them with the promised rewards in exchange for their efforts. The meta-analysis by Dirks and Ferrin (2002) indeed shows transactional leadership also relates to trust in the leader as expected, albeit somewhat less strongly than to transformational leadership.

Ethical and related forms of leadership

More recently, ethical forms of leadership have received increasing attention. Ethical leadership has been defined as 'the demonstration of normatively appropriate conduct through personal actions and interpersonal relationships and the promotion of such conduct to followers through two-way communication, reinforcement and decision-making' (Brown, Trevino & Harrison, 2005, p. 120) and is also described in terms of the socially responsible use of power (De Hoogh & Den Hartog, 2009). Ethical leadership has been proposed to enhance both followers' cognitive and affective trust and, in turn, to enhance desirable forms of follower behaviour (e.g. De Hoogh & Den Hartog, 2009; Eisenbeiss, 2012).

Ethical leaders are seen as moral people and moral managers (cf. Brown & Trevino, 2006). This implies they are honest and trustworthy (that is, they show trustworthiness cues which should relate to character-based forms of trust) and that they act fairly and supportively, create a work environment that is psychologically safe and in which ethical standards are upheld, and in doing so they build trusting relationships with followers. Both cognitive and affective trust (cf. McAllister, 1995) are likely to result and will make followers more willing to engage in potentially risky and trust-related work behaviours that can benefit the organization, such as voicing concerns and ideas, reporting errors or taking the initiative to solve problems (e.g. Den Hartog, 2015; Kalshoven et al., 2013).

Initial research supports the proposed positive relationship between ethical leadership and trust (and the mediational role of trust in the relationship between ethical leadership and subsequent outcomes such as follower citizenship). For example, positive relationships were found of ethical leadership with trust in the leader (e.g. Brown et al., 2005; Lu, 2013; Newman, Kiazad, Miao & Cooper, 2013) as well as trust in wider management (Den Hartog & De Hoogh, 2009). In addition to the unidimensional measure of overall ethical leadership that was developed by Brown and colleagues (2005) and that most of these studies used, Kalshoven, De Hoogh and Den Hartog (2011) developed a multi-dimensional measure of ethical leadership differentiating between seven related but different ethical leader behaviours. Specifically these are fairness, power sharing, people orientation, integrity, role clarification, ethical guidance and a concern for sustainability. They found that all seven of these perceived behavioural dimensions related positively and significantly to followers' trust in the leader.

In addition, Kalshoven and Den Hartog (2009) proposed and found that group prototypicality and trust sequentially mediate the relationship between ethical leadership and leader effectiveness. Building on social identity theory, leaders' group prototypicality has been shown to form an important determinant of perceived leader effectiveness (for a review, see van Knippenberg, van Knippenberg, Cremer, & Hogg, 2004). A prototype forms an ideal representation of appropriate attitudes and behaviours in the group (e.g. Hogg, 2001). A leader who is characterized as the group prototype is typically more effective in influencing the employees within the workgroup because followers identify with such a leader. Giessner and van Knippenberg (2008) showed that prototypicality influences leader effectiveness via trust, and Kalshoven and Den Hartog (2009) further extended this to show that ethical leaders who form powerful role models for employees tend to be seen as more group prototypical and, in turn, they are more trusted and more effective. While this may form one mechanism by which ethical leaders affect trust, the research to date is mainly cross-sectional and the exact causal mechanisms that occur are in need of further study.

Related forms of leadership that should relate positively to employees' trust include servant leadership (e.g. Graham, 1991; Liden et al., 2007) and authentic leadership (e.g. Gardner et al., 2011). For example, servant leadership behaviour emphasizes the leader's personal integrity and their role in serving others including employees and focuses on how leaders forgo self-interest and attend to subordinates' personal needs and help followers to develop and prosper (Graham, 1991; Chan & Mak, 2014; Liden et al., 2007). As expected, perceiving one's leader to engage in servant leadership behaviour correlates positively with trusting this leader (e.g. Chan & Mak, 2014) as does authentic leadership, a construct that focuses on leaders staying true to their values and behaving consistently, while focusing on positive psychological capacities (e.g. Clapp-Smith et al., 2009).

Also related to ethical leadership is the work on leader fairness and more specifically interactional justice that focuses on the quality of the interpersonal treatment individuals receive when procedures are implemented in the organization (e.g. Bies & Moag, 1986) as such implementation is often done by leaders. These fairness- and justice-focused types of behaviours are similarly expected and found to relate positively to trust in the leader. A meta-analysis of the justice literature by Cohen-Charash and Spector (2001) shows that justice indeed relates positively to trust. In addition, the meta-analysis by Dirks and Ferrin (2002) showed that interactional justice and transformational leadership had the largest relationships with trust in the leader, followed by transactional leadership and participative decision-making (the meta-analysis of course did not yet include more recent leadership styles such as ethical or authentic). As noted, more work on causality and how the trust process develops over time in relation to different leader behaviours is needed.

Leader behaviour that erodes trust

The work to date suggests that leader behaviour can strengthen the bond of trust, however leaders' negative or deceitful behaviours can of course also erode trust. For example, unethical leadership which can be defined as 'behaviors conducted and decisions made by organizational leaders that are illegal and/or violate moral standards, and those that impose processes and structures that promote unethical conduct by followers' (Brown & Mitchell, 2010, p. 11) should relate negatively to different forms of employee trust. Such behaviours will undermine perceptions of integrity, benevolence and ability and thus form cues that a leader is not trustworthy. Examples of such unethical or destructive forms of leadership include abusive, despotic and undermining leadership (De Hoogh & Den Hartog, 2008; Duffy et al., 2002; Tepper, 2007).

Kalshoven and Den Hartog (2013) note that many unethical leader behaviours are in direct contrast with the aforementioned forms of ethical leader behaviour and have opposing effects. For example, such leaders show a lack of consideration and care, are unfair, hostile, exploitative, self-aggrandizing and harsh as opposed to treating others fairly, supportively and respectfully (see also Den Hartog, 2015). They are not intent on acting benevolently and do not build supportive relationships with followers. Followers of destructive leaders are thus found to have negative attitudes and show resistance towards their leaders (see the meta-analysis by Schyns & Schilling, 2013). These unethical forms of leadership are therefore also likely to relate negatively to both cognitive and affective forms of trust in the leader. In addition, passive leaders are not dependable, show no care for others and show minimal effort or involvement, and thus passive leadership should also relate negatively to trust, which indeed is also found empirically (e.g. Gillespie & Mann, 2004). More research on this erosion of trust in leaders and when and how such damaged trust might be repaired is of interest to the field.

In addition, it is of interest to develop further understanding of whether and when trust breaches by one leader also affect trust in subsequent or other leaders (i.e. is there a spillover effect from one target to another?). While one would expect such 'spillover' trust in subsequent or other leaders to be less strongly affected by such breaches than trust in the focal (trust breaching) leader, organizational justice research does suggest that such spillover to other targets may occur (see, e.g. Rupp, Shao, Jones & Liao, 2014).

Another area that is in need of attention is that leader behaviour is not always consistent, and this inconsistency and lack of predictability is likely to erode trust in the leader (Den Hartog, 2015). Research on behavioural integrity focuses on the perceived alignment between leaders' words and deeds and the effects of this on followers. Whether a leader's words and deeds are aligned or misaligned strongly affects employees' trust and mistrust (e.g. Simons, 2002). Similarly, different actions can be misaligned or contradicting. Leaders can, for example show both ethical and unethical acts towards followers. For example, Duffy et al. (2002) found that being both unethical and supportive towards followers negatively affects outcomes. Showing this inconsistent mix of ethical and unethical leader behaviour was even related to lower levels of trust and higher levels of insecurity on the part of followers than when unethical leader behaviour was shown by itself.

Also, observing others being treated badly is likely to affect the feelings of the observer (Den Hartog, 2015). For example, research shows that when employees observed leader bullying of other followers, they experienced lower levels of job satisfaction and higher levels of stress and turnover (e.g. Rayner, Hoel, & Cooper, 2002). This is also likely to hold for trust, with observing bad treatment of others eroding trust in the leader. This too forms an interesting area for research.

In addition, unequal and differential treatment between followers may negatively affect trust levels. For example, Duffy, Ganster, Shaw, Johnson and Pagon (2006) argue that when leaders treat all employees badly, the impact of bad treatment is likely to be attenuated compared to leaders who treat a single employee differently. Similarly, research on justice climate level and strength shows that these interact to predict outcomes (e.g. Colquitt, Noe & Jackson 2002). For example, Buengeler and Den Hartog (2015) found high justice in the interaction with the line manager (i.e. high justice climate level) promotes the performance of diverse teams, but only when team members shared this perception (i.e. there was also high climate strength) and not when leaders treated team members differentially. This may also occur for trust. Future work thus needs to further consider what the impact of showing inconsistent leader behaviours towards some or all followers on trust is and address the role of observer effects in the trust process in more detail.

Additional and indirect effects

Leaders do not only affect trust and subsequent outcomes through their own characteristics and behaviours, but also through their contextual behaviours (Hernandez et al., 2014) as well as their key role in the implementation of broader management practices, such as control systems (Weibel et al., 2015) and HRM practices (Searle et al., 2011). For example, as Purcell and Hutchinson (2007, p. 3) suggest: 'The HR practices perceived or experienced by employees will, to a growing extent, be those delivered or enacted by line managers, especially front-line managers with direct supervisory responsibility.' Den Hartog and Boon (2013) note that leaders' HR roles typically involve the performance management process, including setting objectives, monitoring progress and appraising performance, and providing performance feedback. They also often involve selecting new employees, determining training and development needs, and they can offer more or less participation in decision-making. Procedural fairness as well as skill in execution of these crucial HR tasks as well as leader characteristics and behaviours are all likely to affect trust in the leader as well as trust in the organization as a whole.

In addition to their direct impact on employees through leader behaviour and management tasks, leaders also affect trust indirectly through creating a certain work environment and work climate. For example, leaders can help establish an ethical climate (Dickson et al., 2001), and in turn, this climate can affect mutual trust levels. Work on ethical leadership suggests that the process of influencing ethical norms and the corresponding attitudes and behaviours is likely to start at the top of organizations and cascade down via the existing middle management and supervisory levels in the organization. Top managers are the role models for managers at lower levels who in turn are the role models for the shop floor (Mayer et al., 2009). Thus, the behaviour of leaders at multiple levels is likely to directly or indirectly affect employee trust levels. Most research on trust in leaders focuses on direct supervisors and more research on the impact of more distal organizational leaders on trust is of interest. Also, Fulmer and Gelfand (2012) indicate research should clearly distinguish between trust at a given level of analysis and trust in specific different referents (such as the leader, team, organization) and it would be of interest to the field to better understand the role of leadership in trust both at different levels and towards different referents.

The role of the follower

Besides character and behaviour of the leader, individual differences as well as behaviour on the part of the follower may play a role in the development of trust between leaders and followers. For example, employees having a secure attachment style (Simmons et al., 2009) has been linked to higher levels of trust in leaders. Also, employees' propensity to trust has been proposed to facilitate the development of interpersonal trust because individuals with a high propensity to trust are willing to form new relationships and to give others a second chance when needed (e.g. Dirks & Ferrin, 2002; Fulmer & Gelfand, 2012). Indeed, Colquitt and colleagues (2007) found that individuals' propensity to trust is positively correlated with perceiving others as trustworthy (in terms of ability, benevolence and integrity; cf. Mayer et al., 1995). This should also hold for trust in leaders.

In addition, Grant and Sumanth (2009) found that perceiving managers as trustworthy strengthened the relationship between employees' prosocial motivation and their performance. Dispositional trust propensity played a role such that high trust propensity compensated for low manager trustworthiness to strengthen the relationship between employees' prosocial motivation and performance. More work on how individual differences between followers affect the bond of trust with the leader as well as outcomes would be of interest.

As noted, most work in this area to date focuses on followers' trust in leaders, rather than leaders' trust in followers or mutual trust. Interestingly, Sniezek and Van Swol (2001) found that individuals with low power trusted their counterparts with high power more than the high-power counterparts trusted them. Thus, trust in a dyad is not always equally strong for both partners. More research on when and why leaders place more or less trust in their followers and how this affects (leader) decision-making and performance would be of interest to further understand the trust between leaders and followers and its effects.

Conclusion

The above study clearly shows that trust in leaders matters for organizationally relevant outcomes and that there are many ways in which leaders can build or erode such trust. At the same time it is important to note that trust in leaders and management or trust in followers does not always have an equally large impact on outcomes and that trust is not always an equally salient concern (see e.g. Searle et al., 2011). For example, research by Brockner, Siegel, Daly, Tyler and Martin (1997) focused on whether employees' trust in authorities affects employees' support for these organizational authorities. They reasoned that issues of trust are less salient or critical in determining support for leaders when outcomes of decisions are favourable for employees than when they are unfavourable. Receiving favourable outcomes is far less likely to raise questions of trustworthiness with employees as these favourable outcomes themselves suggest that the leader can be relied upon to benefit the employee. Thus the impact of trust should be less strong under those conditions. Instead, when they receive unfavourable outcomes, employees' trust levels become more salient in determining their support in the authority, and the relationship should then be stronger. The findings of Brockner and colleagues (1997) indeed showed that trust related more strongly to support for the authority when outcomes were unfavourable. Thus, for organizations, ensuring high trust levels among employees is especially important when decisions with unfavourable outcomes for the employees may need to be taken, and it should form an especially salient concern under such conditions (see also Searle et al., 2011).

More generally speaking, there may also be other conditions under which trust is more or less salient or important, and more research on this is of interest. One more general example of such a situational factor, suggested by Dirks and Ferrin (2002), is that the greater the uncertainty or vulnerability in a context (e.g. a situation of downsizing or crisis), the more mindful individuals may be of trust, and trust is then also more likely to have a larger impact on outcomes. In addition, whether cognitive or affective trust is more relevant may also depend on the situation (Dirks & Ferrin, 2002). For example, believing that a more socially distant leader has integrity may affect outcomes more than affective trust, whereas in relation to one's daily supervisor both forms of trust in may have an impact on outcomes. Creating a better understanding of when which form of trust is more or less salient is both of scientific interest and of practical relevance for organizations as it can help direct the attention of trust-building efforts.

References

Bass, B. M. (1985). *Leadership and Performance Beyond Expectations*. New York: Free Press.

Bass, B. M., & Bass, R. (2008). *The Bass Handbook of Leadership: Theory, Research, and Managerial Applications*. New York: Simon and Schuster.

Bies, R. J. & Moag, J. S. (1986). Interactional justice: Communication criteria of fairness. In R. Lewicki, B. H. Sheppard & M. H. Bazerman (Eds.), *Research on Negotiation in Organizations* (pp. 43–55). Greenwich, CT: JAI Press.

Boon, S. D. & Holmes, J. G. (1991). The dynamics of interpersonal trust: Resolving uncertainty in the face of risk. In R. A. Hinde & J. Groebel (Eds.), *Cooperation and Prosocial Behavior* (pp. 190–211). Cambridge, UK: Cambridge University Press.

Brockner, J., Siegel, P. A., Daly, J. P., Tyler, T. & Martin, C. (1997). When trust matters: The moderating effect of outcome favorability. *Administrative Science Quarterly*, 42: 558–583.

Brown, M. E. & Mitchell, T. R. (2010). Ethical and unethical leadership: Exploring new avenues for future research. *Business Ethics Quarterly*, 20: 583–616.

Brown, M. E. & Treviño, L. K. (2006). Ethical leadership: a review and future directions. *Leadership Quarterly*, 17: 595–616

Brown, M. E., Treviño, L. K. & Harrison, D. A. (2005). Ethical leadership: a social learning perspective for construct development and testing. *Organizational Behavior and Human Decision Processes*, 97: 117–34

Buengeler, C. & Den Hartog, D. N. (2015). National diversity and team performance: The moderating role of interactional justice climate. *The International Journal of Human Resource Management*, 26(6): 831–855.

Chan, S. & Mak, W. M. (2014). The impact of servant leadership and subordinates' organizational tenure on trust in leader and attitudes. *Personnel Review*, 43(2): 272–287.

Clapp-Smith, R., Vogelgesang, G. R. & Avey, J. B. (2009). Authentic leadership and positive psychological capital: The mediating role of trust at the group level of analysis. *Journal of Leadership and Organizational Studies*, 15: 227–240.

Cohen-Charash, Y. & Spector, P. E. (2001). The role of justice in organizations: A meta-analysis. *Organizational Behavior and Human Decision Processes*, 86(2): 278–321.

Colquitt, J. A., Noe, R. A. & Jackson, C. L. (2002). Justice in teams: Antecedents and consequences of procedural justice climate. *Personnel Psychology*, 55(1): 83–109.

Colquitt, J. A., Scott, B. A. & LePine, J. A. (2007). Trust, trustworthiness, and trust propensity: a meta-analytic test of their unique relationships with risk taking and job performance. *Journal of Applied Psychology*, 92(4): 909–927.

Cook, J. & Wall, T. (1980). New work attitude measures of trust, organizational commitment and personal need non-fulfilment. *Journal of Occupational Psychology*, 53(1): 39–52.

Davis, J. H., Schoorman, F. D., Mayer, R. C. & Tan, H. H. (2000). The trusted general manager and business unit performance: Empirical evidence of a competitive advantage. *Strategic Management Journal*, 21(5): 563–576.

De Hoogh, A. H. B. & Den Hartog, D. N. (2008). Ethical and despotic leadership, relationships with leader's social responsibility, top management team effectiveness and subordinates' optimism: A multi-method study. *The Leadership Quarterly*, 19: 297–311.

De Hoogh, A.H.B. & Den Hartog, D.N. (2009). Ethical leadership: The socially responsible use of power. In D. Tjosvold & B.M. Wisse (Eds.), *Power and Interdependence in Organizations* (pp. 338–354). Cambridge, UK: Cambridge University Press.

Den Hartog, D. N. (2003). Trusting others in organizations: Leaders, management and co-workers. In B. Nooteboom & F. Six (Eds.), *The Trust Process in Organizations* (pp. 125–146). London: Edward Elgar.

Den Hartog, D. N. (2015). Ethical leadership. *Annual Review of Organizational Psychology and Organizational Behavior*, 2: 409–434.

Den Hartog, D. N. & Boon, C. (2013). HRM and leadership. In S. Bach & M. Edwards (Eds.), *Managing Human Resources* (5th ed.) (pp. 198–217). Chichester, UK: Wiley.

Den Hartog, D. N. & De Hoogh A. H. B. (2009). Empowerment and leader fairness and integrity: Studying ethical leader behavior. *European Journal of Work and Organizational Psychology*, 18: 199–230.

Den Hartog, D. N., House, R. J., Hanges, P. J., Ruiz-Quintanilla, S. A., Dorfman, P. W. & GLOBE Associates. (1999). Culture specific and cross culturally generalizable implicit leadership theories: Are attributes of charismatic/transformational leadership universally endorsed? *The Leadership Quarterly*, 10: 219–256.

Dickson, M. W., Smith, D. B., Grojean, M. W. & Ehrhart, M. (2001). An organizational climate regarding ethics: The outcome of leader values and the practices that reflect them. *The Leadership Quarterly*, 12(2): 197–217.

Dietz, G. & Den Hartog, D. (2006). Measuring trust inside organisations. *Personnel Review*, 35: 557–588.

Dirks, K. T. & Ferrin, D. L. (2001). The role of trust in organizational settings. *Organization Science*, 12: 450–467.

Dirks, K. T., & Ferrin, D. (2002). Trust in leadership: Meta-analytic findings and implications for research and practice. *Journal of Applied Psychology*, 87: 611–628.

Duffy, M. K., Ganster, D. C. & Pagon, M. (2002). Social undermining in the workplace. *Academy of Management Journal*, 45: 331–351.

Duffy, M. K., Ganster, D. C., Shaw, J. D., Johnson, J. L. & Pagon, M. (2006). The social context of undermining behavior at work. *Organizational Behavior and Human Decision Processes*, 101: 105–126.

Eisenbeiss, S. A. (2012). Re-thinking ethical leadership: An interdisciplinary integrative approach. *The Leadership Quarterly*, 23: 791–808.

Fulmer, C. A. & Gelfand, M. J. (2012). At what level (and in whom) we trust: Trust across multiple organizational levels. *Journal of Management*, 38(4): 1167–1230.

Gao, L., Janssen, O., & Shi, K. (2011). Leader trust and employee voice: The moderating role of empowering leader behaviors. *The Leadership Quarterly*, 22(4): 787–798.

Gardner, W. L., Cogliser, C. C., Davis, K. M. & Dickens, M. P. (2011). Authentic leadership: A review of the literature and research agenda. *The Leadership Quarterly*, 22(6): 1120–1145.

Giessner, S. R., & Van Knippenberg, D. (2008). 'License to fail': Goal definition, leader group prototypicality and perceptions of leadership effectiveness after leader failure. *Organizational Behavior and Human Decision Processes*, 105: 14–35.

Gillespie, N. A. & Mann, L. (2004). Transformational leadership and shared values: The building blocks of trust. *Journal of Managerial Psychology*, 19(6): 588–607.

Graham, J. W. (1991). Servant-leadership in organizations: Inspirational and moral. *The Leadership Quarterly*, 2: 105–119.

Grant, A. M. & Sumanth, J. J. (2009). Mission possible? The performance of pro-socially motivated employees depends on manager trustworthiness. *Journal of Applied Psychology*, 94: 927–944.

Hernandez, M., Long, C. P. & Sitkin, S. B. (2014). Cultivating follower trust: Are all leader behaviors equally Influential? *Organization Studies*, 35(12): 1867–1892.

Hogg, M. A. (2001). A social identity theory of leadership. *Personality and Social Psychology Review*, 5: 184–200.

House, R. J., Hanges, P. J., Javidan, M., Dorfman, P. & Gupta, V. (2004). *Culture, Leadership, and Organizations: The GLOBE Study of 62 Societies*. Thousand Oaks, CA: Sage.

Judge, T. A., Piccolo, R. F. & Ilies, R. (2004). The forgotten ones? The validity of consideration and initiating structure in leadership research. *Journal of Applied Psychology*, 89(1): 36–51.

Jung, D. I. & Avolio, B. J. (2000). Opening the black box: An experimental investigation of the mediating effects of trust and value congruence on transformational and transactional leadership. *Journal of Organizational Behavior*, 21(8): 949–964.

Kalshoven, K. & Den Hartog, D. N. (2009). Ethical leader behavior and leader effectiveness: The role of prototypicality and trust. *International Journal of Leadership Studies*, 5: 102–119.

Kalshoven, K. & Den Hartog, D. N. (2013). Ethical and unethical leader behaviors and their impact on individual well-being. In R. A. Giacalone & M. D. Promislo (Eds.) *Handbook of Unethical Work Behavior: Implications for Well-being* (pp.140–154). Armonk, NY: M. E. Sharpe.

Kalshoven, K., Den Hartog, D. N. & De Hoogh, A. H. (2011). Ethical leadership at work questionnaire: Development and validation of a multidimensional measure. *Leadership Quarterly*, 22: 51–69.

Kalshoven, K., Den Hartog, D. N. & De Hoogh, A. H. B. (2013). Ethical leadership and followers' helping and initiative: The role of demonstrated responsibility and job autonomy. *European Journal of Work and Organizational Psychology*, 22(2): 165–81

Konovsky, M. A. & Pugh, S. D. (1994). Citizenship behavior and social exchange. *Academy of Management Journal*, 37: 656–669.

Kramer, R. M. (1999). Trust and distrust in organizations: Emerging perspectives, enduring questions. *Annual Review of Psychology*, 50(1): 569–598.

Lewicki, R. & Bunker, B. (1996). Developing and maintaining trust in work relationships. In R. Kramer & T. Tyler (Eds.) *Trust in Organizations: Frontiers of Theory and Research* (pp. 114–139). Thousand Oaks, CA: Sage.

Liden, R. C., Wayne, S. J., Zhao, H. & Henderson, D. (2008), Servant leadership: Development of a multi-dimensional measure and multi-level assessment. *The Leadership Quarterly*, 19(2): 161–177.

Lu, X. (2014). Ethical leadership and organizational citizenship behavior: The mediating roles of cognitive and affective trust. *Social Behavior and Personality: An International Journal*, 42(3): 379–389.

Mayer, D. M, Kuenzi, M., Greenbaum, R., Bardes, M. & Salvador, R. (2009). How low does ethical leadership flow? Test of a trickle-down model. *Organizational Behavior and Human Decision Processes*, 108: 1–13.

Mayer, R. C., Davis, J. H. & Schoorman, F. D. (1995). An integrative model of organizational trust. *Academy of Management Review*, 20(3): 709–734.

McAllister, D. J. (1995). Affect-and cognition-based trust as foundations for interpersonal cooperation in organizations. *Academy of Management Journal*, 38(1): 24–59.

Morrison, E. W. (2011). Employee voice behavior: Integration and directions for future research. *The Academy of Management Annals*, 5(1): 373–412.

Newman, A., Kiazad, K., Miao, Q. & Cooper, B. (2014). Examining the cognitive and affective trust-based mechanisms underlying the relationship between ethical leadership and organisational citizenship: A case of the head leading the heart? *Journal of Business Ethics*, 123(1): 113–123.

Nienaber, A. M., Romeike, P. D., Searle, R. & Schewe, G. (2015). A qualitative meta-analysis of trust in supervisor-subordinate relationships. *Journal of Managerial Psychology*, 30(5): 507–534.

Pillai, R., Schriesheim, C. A. & Williams, E. S. (1999). Fairness perceptions and trust as mediators for transformational and transactional leadership: A two-sample study. *Journal of Management*, 25(6): 897–933.

Podsakoff, P. M., MacKenzie, S. B., Moorman, R. H. & Fetter, R. (1990). Transformational leader behaviors and their effects on followers' trust in leader, satisfaction, and organizational citizenship behaviors. *The Leadership Quarterly*, 1(2): 107–142.

Purcell, J. & Hutchinson, S. (2007). Front-line managers as agents in the HRM-performance causal chain: Theory, analysis and evidence. *Human Resource Management Journal*, 17(1): 3–20.

Rayner, C., Hoel, H. & Cooper, C. L. (2002). *Workplace Bullying: What We Know, Who is to Blame, and What Can We Do?* London: Taylor and Francis.

Rupp, D. E., Shao, R., Jones, K. S. & Liao, H. (2014). The utility of a multifoci approach to the study of organizational justice: A meta-analytic investigation into the consideration of normative rules, moral accountability, bandwidth-fidelity, and social exchange. *Organizational Behavior and Human Decision Processes*, 123(2): 159–185.

Schyns B, & Schilling J. (2013). How bad are the effects of bad leaders? A meta-analysis of destructive leadership and its outcomes. *The Leadership Quarterly*, 24(1): 138–158.

Searle, R., Den Hartog, D. N., Weibel, A., Gillespie, N., Six, F., Hatzakis, T. & Skinner, D. (2011). Trust in the employer: The role of high-involvement work practices and procedural justice in European organizations. *The International Journal of Human Resource Management*, 22(5): 1069–1092.

Searle, R., Weibel, A. & Den Hartog, D. N. (2011). Employee trust in organizational contexts. *International Review of Industrial and Organizational Psychology*, 26: 143–191.

Shamir, B., House, R. J. & Arthur, M. B. (1993). The motivational effects of charismatic leadership: A self-concept based theory. *Organization Science*, 4(4): 577–594.

Simons, T. (2002). Behavioral Integrity: The perceived alignment between managers' words and deeds as a research focus. *Organization Science*, 13(1): 18–35.

Sniezek, J. A. & Van Swol, L. M. (2001). Trust, confidence, and expertise in a judge-advisor system. *Organizational Behavior and Human Decision Processes*, 84(2): 288–307.

Stogdill, R. M. (1950). Leadership, membership and organization. *Psychological Bulletin*, 47(1): 1–14.

Tepper, B. J. (2007). Abusive supervision in work organizations: Review, synthesis, and research agenda. *Journal of Management*, 33: 261–89.

van Knippenberg, D., van Knippenberg, B., Cremer, D. & Hogg, M. A. (2004). Leadership, self and identity: A review and research agenda. *The Leadership Quarterly*, 15: 825–856.

van Knippenberg, D. & Sitkin, S. B. (2013). A critical assessment of charismatic–transformational leadership research: Back to the drawing board? *The Academy of Management Annals*, 7(1): 1–60.

Weibel, A., Den Hartog, D. N., Gillespie, N., Searle, R., Six, F. & Skinner, D. (2015). How do controls impact employee trust in the employer? *Human Resource Management*, 55(3): 437–462.

Whitener, E. M., Brodt, S. E., Korsgaard, M. A. & Werner, J. M. (1998). Managers as initiators of trust: An exchange relationship framework for understanding managerial trustworthy behavior. *Academy of Management Review*, 23(3): 513–530.

Williams, B. (1988). Formal structures and social reality. In D. Gambetta (Ed.), *Trust: Making and Breaking Cooperative Relations* (pp. 3–13). New York: Blackwell.

27

TRUST IN AND BY THE PUBLIC SECTOR

Nadine Raaphorst and Steven Van de Walle

Introduction: a trust gap between citizens and the public sector?

Declining trust between citizens and the public sector has been high on the public agenda for quite a while now. Such declining trust and sometimes even increasing distrust has been related to issues such as the emergence of new political parties running on an anti-government sentiment, aggression of citizens towards civil servants, a low attractiveness of public employment, public organizations' desire to demand ever more proof from citizens when taking decisions, or increased government surveillance. Such evidence of declining trust can be complemented by an almost equally substantial body of evidence of stable or increasing levels of trust. Examples are a desire to involve citizens in public decision-making, an absence of large-scale visible challenging of government decisions, and a move towards less coercive and more collaborative relations between the public sector and citizens.

We take Möllering's (2006: 111) definition of trust as our starting point: 'trust is an ongoing process of building on reason, routine and reflexivity, suspending irreducible social vulnerability and uncertainty *as if* they were favourably resolved, and maintaining thereby a state of favourable expectation toward the actions and intentions of more or less specific others'. We thus assume that knowledge about specific others alone does not warrant trust; it also involves some sort of faith that is not explained by knowledge. Distrust also reduces uncertainty, but in a different way: it does not involve a leap of faith, since it involves negative expectations toward people's intentions and intentions (Van de Walle & Six, 2014).

In this chapter, we distinguish between two trust relationships. One is that of citizens in the public sector. The other is that of the public sector in citizens. The focus will thus be on relationships between citizens and the public sector. Trust relationships between public organizations themselves will not be discussed in this chapter. We will first look at signals and evidence that trust is changing – both in the direction of more trust, and in the direction of less trust and more distrust. Then, we discuss initiatives aimed at increasing trust and reducing distrust between citizens and the public sector, both at the institutional level, and at the level of specific encounters between citizens and public services or public servants. We end by formulating a research agenda to study trust and distrust in and by the public sector, to counter the current scarcity of empirical literature on trust in and by the public sector.

Citizen trust in the public sector – signals and evidence

Public sector reforms have often been motivated by a presumed lack of public trust in public services (Bok, 2001; Van de Walle & Bouckaert, 2007). Public services are said to be either inefficient, wasteful and ineffective, or power-hungry with little eye for citizens' needs and desires. Political rhetoric in itself is however insufficient to get a coherent picture of the extent to which citizens actually trust the public sector, public services and individual public servants. To construct such a picture, one needs to look at various pieces of evidence. In this section we look at several pieces of evidence. First, we discuss attitudes as measured in polls. Then we look at citizen voice, or the ways in which citizens express their discontent. This can range from mere complaining, to going to court, or to becoming outright aggressive during interaction with the public sector. Finally, one can look at exit behaviours, whereby citizens decide to end their relation with the public sector. While trust in the public sector has been at the core of reform debates, the academic literature on trust in the public sector is remarkably scarce.

Attitudes

Citizen trust in the public sector is traditionally measured through opinion surveys that contain a number of items on the public sector. Changes in political trust have been well documented, yet for trust in public administration, far fewer indicators are available. Established surveys such as the World Values surveys, the American National Election Studies, the European Social Survey, or various barometers (Eurobarometer, Latinobarómetro, Asia and Asian Barometer) have collected information about attitudes towards a number of specific public services, as well as more general attitudes toward the public sector, bureaucracy or government. Many of these measurements are fairly recent. Where such data is available, there is no apparent trend of decreasing trust in the public sector (Van de Walle et al., 2008), although there is wide variation across institutions and countries. More specific evidence regarding citizens' attitudes to public services can be found in the literature on satisfaction with services, but this material tends not to use the concept 'trust'. Seminal works in this respect have been written by Goodsell (1983, *The case for bureaucracy*) or Katz et al. (1977).

Many public services are among the most trusted institutions. Examples are schools, the health system or the fire services. Individuals within these services enjoy even more trust, especially when it concerns teachers, doctors or firefighters. Opinions on the army and defence personnel are more mixed – very positive in some countries, but negative in others. At the same time, citizens tend to have low trust in more abstract institutions of functions, such as public administration, civil servants or bureaucrats (Van de Walle & Van Ryzin, 2011). They also tend to place high trust in their own local school, hospital and so on, yet tend to be more critical about the school system or health system as a whole (Cowell et al., 2012). Trust in public services also to a large extent depends on the process through which services are delivered, and not just on the actual outcomes of interactions with the public sector (Van Ryzin, 2011). Finally, trust can be based on actual experiences and interactions, but also on generalized attitudes towards others and towards government (Houston & Howard Harding, 2013; Marlowe, 2004).

While information on attitudes is fairly easy to collect, and measurement practice is improving (see e.g. Grimmelikhuijsen & Knies, 2017), attitudes do not tell us all there is to know about trust in the public sector. For governments themselves, attitudes become important when they are associated with behaviours. Researchers have also started paying closer attention to behaviours rather than to attitudes.

Voice

A first type of behaviour to look at when assessing whether citizens trust the public sector, is by looking at what Hirschman (1970) has called 'voice'. Voice is a response to a perceived decline in a (public) organization. When citizens use voice, they signal a problem in the organization, a signal that can then be used by the organization to repair. Such voice can consist of formal and informal complaints or of complaints through ombudsmen, or it can become more public and political when citizens take their compliant to social media or to a political forum. Voting for an anti-system party or a party that promises to do away with wasteful government is another example. Voice can also be organized collectively, and then becomes visible in organized interest groups, consumer committees or more ad-hoc protests against public sector organizations. Examples include, for instance, protests against discriminatory police practices, the planned implantation of an asylum-seekers centre etc. Voice can be a powerful signal and often confrontational, and is especially important to monitor in a public-sector context where citizens do not always have the option to stop interacting with a public service (Dowding & John, 2012).

Aggression against public servants

Another type of behaviour is citizen aggression against public servants. This could be considered an extreme type of voice, or even beyond, and clearly signals discontent or frustration. Aggression towards public servants is receiving increasing attention, both in academia and among policy makers. Such aggression can take a fairly low-key appearance, such as shouting, but could also be more serious, in the form of stalking, stabbing or even murdering public employees (Tummers et al., 2016). One such event, the 1995 Oklahoma City bombing, in which a US government building was targeted, served as the inspiration for Nye et al.'s 1997 book *Why People Don't Trust Government* (Nye et al., 1997)

Legalization of interactions

A less extreme signal of potentially low levels of citizen trust in the public sector is a legalization of interactions, as is apparent in strong rule following and the use of extensive contractual arrangements to regulate interactions. This is a specific expression of a trend towards legalistic organizations (Sitkin & Bies, 1993). While it is true that contract-like arrangements make trust between parties possible, the extensive use of contracts may also mean that that trust was absent in the first place (see e.g. Klein Woolthuis et al., 2005). Sitkin and Bies suggested such legalization does little to restore trust (Sitkin & Roth, 1993). Such legalization makes delivering public services increasingly expensive with transaction costs spiralling. Where voice is a first line of defence against public services that do not live up to expectation, citizens going to court is a second. A lack of trust then becomes visible in the number of lawsuits citizens wage against government, or the number of appeals through various appeal boards. Examples can be found throughout the public sectors, ranging from students appealing against their grades, or citizens suing their local government for defective infrastructure, to companies appealing against procurement decisions. It remains unclear though whether such an increase is due to declining trust, or the result of previously silent citizens now knowing what their rights are. The opposite trend also appears to exist, with relations between government and citizens or between government and other public and private actors becoming increasingly based on informal norms and new steering mechanisms not governed by law or contracts, but by long-term established relations of trust (see Groeneveld & Van de Walle, 2011, for an overview).

Exit

A final signal one can use to assess the state of citizen trust in the public sector is what Hirschman (1970) called exit, or citizens turning their back on the public sector and moving elsewhere. Exit is a response to failing public service (Dowding & John, 2008). Exit can take many different forms, for instance when parents decide to start home-schooling their children or to set up their own care-initiative for a disabled child (Gofen, 2015), or when communities start using their own dispute settlement mechanism or set up their own security services. It can also mean moving from a public to a private provider in health care or education, or even moving to alternative providers such as homeopaths or natural healers when trust in the public health system is low. Exit can also take the form of total exit, when citizens decide to end their relationship with a public service altogether. Extreme forms of exit are visible in, for example, anti-vaccination movements or communities of off-gridders.

Non-entry is an alternative approach. Non-entry means that citizens do not even make the decision to start using public service (Rokkan, 1974). Other scholars have used the term 'non-take-up' of public services referring to citizens who are entitled to use a service but who have decided not to make use of it (Warin, 2008). Distrust is an important explanation for such non-take-up. It occurs especially in relation to welfare services when citizens are for instance distrustful of the motives of a social service or youth affairs department, when they suspect the education system of brainwashing their children, or when immigrants decide not to register with immigration departments.

Public sector trust in citizens – signals and evidence

When trust in the public sector is discussed or studied, attention mainly goes to citizens' trust in the public sector. The other side of the trust relationship generally receives less attention: the public sector's trust in citizens. The public sector and the people working therein also make decisions about the trustworthiness of citizens when interacting with them. This is important, because making an incorrect judgement may mean that disproportionate burdens are inflicted on citizens to prove their case, or that citizens get away with benefits they are not entitled to. Some citizens are considered trustworthy, and hence not subject to elaborate surveillance or coercion, whereas other citizens are seen as untrustworthy and therefore to be monitored. Meeting with citizens who are untrustworthy is quite common for public servants, and many public organizations exist precisely because of this assumption – think for instance about police forces, tax inspections, or parking wardens. Again, one can look at various signals and evidence to establish whether or not public servants trust the citizens they are supposed to serve, and whether distrust also plays a role in this. These signals are located both at the level of delivery and at the level of policymaking.

Surveillance, monitoring and control

When governments use an elaborate array of monitoring and surveillance tools, this may tell us something about the public sector's trust in citizens. It is not entirely clear though what it tells us (Van de Walle, 2016). Monitoring and surveillance tools have become ever more omnipresent, and the public sector's capacity to control has increased (Power, 1999). The public sector combines datasets and constructs profiles of citizens and citizen groups. On the one hand, one could see the presence of such surveillance as an indication that government and public servants distrust citizens and deploy monitoring tools to punish untrustworthy behaviours. Monitoring tools are then substitutes for trust. On the other hand, having more information about the trustee makes it easier to decide whether or not to extend trust. Monitoring tools are then complements to trust.

The dominant reasoning in the literature, however, appears to be that the increase in monitoring tools reflects an increasing distrust in citizens. Indeed, a move to new public management-style steering arrangements brought with it a strong rhetoric about citizen empowerment (Osborne & Gaebler, 1992), but did in fact institutionalize a range of distrust-based instruments. (Van de Walle, 2010). More recently, one can also observe a gradual trend towards transferring the burden of proof away from the public sector to the citizen, as was already the case in taxation issues.

Public involvement in decision-making

Whether or not public servants trust citizens can also be deduced form their general willingness to involve citizens in policy making. This is a quite contentious topic, because public servants are often quite reluctant to involve citizens, who are sometime seen as untrustworthy (Yang, 2006). The main reasons for such an attitude are perceived lack of ability on the part of citizens to understand complex policy issues, and fear that citizens will mainly try to further their own self-interest rather than the common good (Moyson et al., 2016). The extent to which citizens are involved in actual decision making, within but also beyond legal involvement requirements, gives a good indication of their perceived trustworthiness.

Closing the trust gap

Distrust is an essential building block of the relation between citizens and the public sector. Dysfunctional effects of such distrust, such as the need for documentation, control-mechanisms and high transaction costs, are at the core of how governments function, which is seen as a way to protect citizens against illegal government actions or too strong concentration of power. Low citizen trust in the public sector can be seen as a healthy attitude leading to proper oversight, and low public sector trust in citizens as a necessity to avoid abuse of public means (see also Möllering, 2006; Hardin, 2002). Still, a desire to build more trust is at the centre of many public-sector modernization initiatives, with an aim to lower transaction costs and to become more effective in service delivery. Such measures to build trust and reduce distrust operate at different levels: the institutional level and the interpersonal level. A number of measures have received a fair degree of attention in the public administration literature and are discussed below.

At the institutional level we see a strong focus on increasing transparency as a means of increasing trust. We also see a tendency away from command-and-control-based ways of working to trust-based working. At the level of the actual encounter between citizens and the public sector, we see for example that frontline tax officials have more leeway to look at the specificity of each case, and to reach agreements with taxpayers when the latter have proven to be trustworthy. When we look at social services, we see a trend in which public officials do not take professional responsibility for citizens' situations, but in which professionals stress citizens' own responsibility or in which the latter's wishes are uncritically met (Eikenaar et al., 2015). In these instances, professionals do not adopt the role of 'omniscient expert', but both trust citizens' capacity to indicate what they need, and their intentions as to why they need a service.

Creating trust and reducing distrust – institutional solutions

Transparency

One way of attempting to increase trust between citizens and the public sector consists of improving transparency. Prominent examples are the widespread adoption of freedom of information laws and publicly available indicators and rankings about the performance of public institutions (Van de Walle & Roberts, 2008). But it is not just government that is made more transparent. Government is also obtaining ever more information about citizens, making citizens more transparent. These two types of transparency can be seen as attempts to make knowledge- or information-based trust possible. Despite transparency's prominent place on the agenda of many political movements, the contribution of transparency to trust is not entirely convincing. Making the public sector or citizens transparent may also give rise to more reasons to distrust each other (see e.g. Etzioni, 2010). Good examples are the publication of politicians' and public servants' expense accounts or Wikileaks.

Experimental research by Grimmelikhuijsen (2012) found that the effect of increased transparency of government organizations on citizen trust is limited. Indeed, many decision-making bodies operate behind closed doors, because transparency is expected to decrease the quality of decision-making, or may undermine institutional trust when it would become visible that public decision-making is not always rational or when it would appear that decisions are not always based on generalizable principles (Chambers, 2004). Examples are decisions of judges, some appeals boards, juries, peace negotiations, recruitment committees or talks between a monarch and his or her ministers. Full transparency could also undermine the effectiveness of measures, such as when a decision would lead to higher property prices, or when a bank or currency is to be saved.

Trust-based working

Dissatisfaction with the enormous transaction costs as a result of relying on distrust-based mechanisms and extensive control and surveillance mechanisms has stimulated a gradual move towards trust-based working within the public sector. This is visible in a number of areas (see also Groeneveld & Van de Walle, 2011). One example is the area of public and public-private partnerships, where scholars focus on the need for trust between partners to make policy and delivery networks function (Agranoff & McGuire, 2001; Huxham & Vangen, 2005). A similar evolution is visible in contracting and commissioning relationships where partners commit to each other for the long term, rather than having a short-term antagonistic relationship governed by extensive contracts and dispute-settlement mechanisms (Greve, 2008). A final example comes from the literature on inspections and regulators where initiatives such as self-regulation or responsive regulation are replacing more punitive regulation styles (see Six, 2013, for an overview).

Creating trust and reducing distrust in bureaucratic encounters

Institutional solutions are emphasized in the public administration literature, giving more room to frontline public officials to involve citizens and establish trust. However, whether and how trust is or is not established in official–citizen interactions is often neglected. While not explicitly addressed, the street-level bureaucracy literature (based on Lipsky, 1980) suggests that trustworthiness judgments are part and parcel of frontline public service work. For social workers, for example, it has always been problematic to determine disability of a citizen, 'because physical and mental incapacity are conditions that can be feigned for secondary gain' (Stone, 1984: 23). Since it is assumed that people have incentives to escape the labour market, 'the concept of disability has always been based on a perceived need to detect deception' (ibid.: 23). The traditional top-down bureaucracies, then, are based on distrust encounters with citizens.

Nowadays, however, there appears to be the assumption among public administration scholars and policy makers alike, that citizens' trust in government is related to the trust governments have in citizens: 'citizens will not trust public administrators if they know or feel that public officials do not trust them' (Yang, 2005: 273). Hence, the interaction between public officials and citizens has come to the forefront and is increasingly seen as a valuable phenomenon for study in itself (Bartels, 2013). The public encounter, the place where officials and citizens meet, is seen as a crucial aspect in fostering trust, commitment and collaboration between public officials and citizens (Bartels, 2013), which in turn could help to democratize and legitimate the state (Peters, 2004). This is not only discernable in social welfare agencies, but also in organizations engaged in the more traditional regulation and law enforcement functions of the government, such as inspection agencies and tax administrations (e.g. Burgemeestre et al., 2010; Leviner, 2009; Mascini & Van Wijk, 2009; Sakurai, 2002). This trend in (street-level) bureaucracies towards more horizontal relationships with citizens, then, shifts attention from detecting deception and untrustworthiness to establishing trust relationships.

The street-level bureaucracy literature suggests that officials' trustworthiness judgments are affected by different factors: citizens' characteristics, officials' mind-sets and working routines, and their work context.

Goodwill and competence

Frontline work is essentially about categorizing citizens: who is trustworthy and who isn't, based on both organizational classification systems and rules, such as cultural schemes, moral beliefs and stereotypes (Dubois, 2013; Hasenfeld, 2000; Kingfisher, 1998; Lipsky, 1980; Maynard-Moody & Musheno, 2003; Mennerick, 1974; Prottas, 1979). The specific categories a public official looks at depends on the specific policy fields s/he is working in (e.g. disability benefits, work reintegration, horizontal inspection), but also on the type of work he/she is doing (service provision or regulation), and the organizational norms and culture (stringent or more room for discretion). The street-level bureaucracy literature points out that public service workers are generally concerned with distinguishing the deserving from undeserving citizens (Maynard-Moody & Musheno, 2003). Besides assessing whether there is a 'real need', frontline public officials also look at the moral deservingness of citizens (Maynard-Moody & Musheno, 2003; Møller & Stone, 2013).

Deserving citizens are believed to be benevolent towards the government and individual officials: 'morally worthy citizens do not try to con or scam workers or the system' (Maynard-Moody & Musheno, 2003: 104). It is held that citizens, even with genuine needs, 'who try to manipulate the system for undue advantage are labelled troublemakers' (ibid.: 104). Although these citizens are not withheld the services, workers do not go out of their way to help the manipulative and over-demanding citizens. Such citizens are viewed with suspicion, since they might be driven by other reasons, beyond a 'real disability', to apply for a service. Moreover, worthy clients are considered good investments in the long run: 'if citizens have genuine needs, are of good character, and are motivated to respond to treatment, then they are likely to repay society for street-level workers' investments of time, effort and money' (ibid.: 106). In this sense, they trust those citizens that make workers' investment worth the effort.

The literature on regulatory encounters theorizes about how regulators' enforcement styles influence citizens' compliance with rules and regulation, and about the latter's motivations for complying or not complying (e.g. Ayres & Braithwaite, 1992; Bardach & Kagan, 1982/ 2002; Mascini & Van Wijk, 2009). Much research has been done on how regulatees can be classified in terms of their compliance. Kagan and Scholz (1984) distinguish three types of regulatees: the amoral calculator who justifies non-compliance by economic opportunity and profit; the political citizen who generally complies with legislation but is prepared to disobey in case of principled disagreement; and the organizational incompetent regulatee whose violations are unintended. This suggests that the category of compliance encompasses two aspects of trust-worthiness: a regulatee must be *competent and willing* to abide by the law.

Public officials' mind-sets and working routines

Besides citizen characteristics, also officials' mind-sets and working routines affect whether trust is established and distrust minimalized within the public encounter. Officials who are in public service for over 30 years probably have a different outlook on their work and clientele than their less seasoned colleagues (e.g. Blau, 1960; Engbersen, 2006). In this vein, Blau (1960: 349) talks about the reality shock newcomers experience when they first enter public welfare agencies:

> Finding out that people one has trusted have lied is a threatening experience. It implies that one has been made a fool of and that others are laughing behind his back at his naiveté. To protect his ego against these threats, a case worker is under pressure to change his orientation toward clients. If he anticipates deception by distrusting the statements of recipients, their lies no longer pose a threat to his ego.

Moreover, more tenured and newly hired employees likely differ in their mindsets not only because of years of experience in working with citizens, but also because they are differently trained. Where distrust-based encounters were commonplace in the traditional machine-like bureaucracies, nowadays public organizations also want their employees to be open and trusting toward citizens. New institutional solutions such as trust-based working give more room for interpretation to frontline workers, and mean officials also need to be willing to trust citizens. Moreover, since there is more room for interpretation, there will likely be differences in judgments between frontline officials, leading to different decisions. When trust or distrust serves as an attitude in itself, positive or negative expectations 'colour all aspects of interaction, and influence even the most basic perceptions of the other' (Van de Walle & Six, 2014: 162). The same situation, then, could be differently judged by people who have different dispositions (ibid.).

Digitalization is another trend that affects how citizens are classified, and that supports the making of judgments on trustworthiness. The public encounter increasingly proceeds indirectly via telephone or email (screen-level bureaucracy), or is even totally automated and pre-programmed involving no contact with a 'real official' (system-level bureaucracy) (Bovens & Zouridis, 2002). On the one hand, this could make the bureaucratic process more transparent, enabling citizens to access more information in a codified manner (Margetts, 2006). Moreover, since interactions are codified, this leads to more consistency in how cases are treated. On the other hand, formalized digital interactions also take away or diminish officials' discretion at the frontline, making it harder to be responsive towards citizens' particular circumstances. It might be easier to be responsive to a citizen when encountering him/her in person, than when only knowing him/her 'on paper'. The street-level bureaucracy literature shows that frontline officials look at citizens' attitude and behaviour in the interaction in order to judge their deservingness (e.g. Maynard-Moody & Musheno, 2003; Erickson, 1975). What characteristics do officials look at when they only have indirect contact with citizens? Is there still room for responsiveness (could be trust and distrust) when officials need to fill out fixed templates on a computer? How does this impersonal contact affect citizens' trust in the government?

Moreover, when bureaucracies do not employ street-level bureaucrats who handle individual cases, but mainly employees involved in data and system management, we need to extend our focus to the discretionary powers of system designers, legal policy staff and IT experts (Bovens & Zouridis, 2002). What consequences do algorithms employed by information systems, for instance, have for how citizens are classified? Is a generalized trust and distrust in certain social groupings, then, translated in these algorithms? The notion of responsiveness, then, shifts from being interpersonal, between officials and citizens, to being impersonal; 'the system' is responsive to certain social groupings with specific characteristics that are believed to deserve a different treatment.

This also relates to the role of paper forms in bureaucracies, mediating the relationship between officials and citizens (See Hull, 2012, for an overview). Weber (1921/1968) viewed the use of documents in bureaucracy as the perpetuation of norms and as a means to establish organizational control. By using forms, interactions between people can be (pre)structured, according to what is deemed important within the bureaucratic organization. If frontline officials are urged and trained to use documents to 'process citizens', but also to guide them in conversing with citizens, how does this influence their relationship with citizens? Do these documents perpetuate the unequal power balance between officials and citizens? Or do they enable officials to be more open towards citizens? When documents are intended to curtail officials' discretion and steer officials' actions within an interaction, this logically hampers a trust-based interpersonal relationship.

Signals as shortcuts

A final aspect affecting street-level judgment and decision-making is the pervasive uncertainty frontline officials deal with in interactions with citizens (Maynard-Moody & Musheno, 2003). It has been suggested that they look for signals or cues that are believed to be linked to citizens' unobserved properties (i.e. trustworthiness) to reduce this uncertainty (Gambetta & Hamill, 2005; Mennerick, 1974; Raaphorst & Groeneveld, forthcoming). Social workers, for instance, look at citizens co-cooperativeness in the interaction to know something more about his/her deservingness. Employers look at job applicants' educational level to gain insight in that person's competences. The sorting of cues, it is held, is based on social typologies of citizens (Mennerick, 1974). These typologies are held to provide strategic information, where formal categories are lacking.

Although this matching of cues to social typologies reduces uncertainty, there is always the danger of classifying citizens wrongly as 'good' or 'bad', or as trustworthy or untrustworthy. Initial encounters between frontline workers and citizens may be pervaded by uncertainty and fear on the part of workers, and within this context 'workers are likely to employ stigmatizing social identities to get a fix on a person and in so doing put themselves on the defensive, keenly attuned to their own safety' (Maynard-Moody & Musheno, 2003: 91). The use of social typologies could thus reinforce existing stereotypes regarding citizens, which could be difficult for the latter to break through.

This interpretation of signals is not only affected by the uncertainty in interaction, but also by officials' mind-sets. If officials have a tendency to distrust or trust (certain groups of) citizens, they will probably primarily discern the signals and cues confirming this view (Van de Walle & Six, 2014). How cues and signals are interpreted is not a purely individual matter, but affected by the organizational culture and social typologies shared by society at large (Raaphorst & Groeneveld, 2015).

Although the 'selective perception' of cues is inevitable, since people cannot go beyond their own perspective, the question for practitioners is whether officials' interpretation, fed by cultural beliefs, is reconcilable with democratic notions of equality and fairness. When societal or organizational cultural beliefs regarding citizens' trustworthiness or untrustworthiness 'leak' into the public encounter, what does this mean for equal treatment of citizens? When frontline officials have more room to establish trust-based encounters with citizens, do governments then also allow more room for individual differences between public officials' judgments? This demonstrates that the public sector's move to trust-based working also comes with important caveats.

Trust in the public sector: emerging topics and research agenda

We end this chapter by formulating a brief research agenda outlining a number of emerging issues in the field of public administration.

Citizen behaviour

Signals and scholarly work on the alleged trust gap between the public sector and citizens point in different directions. Where data is available, there is no apparent trend of decreasing citizen trust in the government (Van de Walle, 2008). Citizens tend to trust specific institutions such as schools, health systems or fire services, whereas they have low trust in more abstract notions such as public administration, civil servants or bureaucrats (Van de Walle & Van Ryzin, 2011). However, to know more about whether citizens trust the government, scholars should not only look at their attitudes, but also study their behaviour. Future studies should more closely examine citizen behaviour that seems to stem from a distrusting or low-trusting stance toward the government, such as complaining, aggressiveness toward frontline officials, lawsuits and exit behaviour.

The effects of trust-based working

Whereas citizens' trust in the public sector receives scholarly attention, the other side of the trust gap – government's trust in citizens – is barely studied (but see Keulemans, 2015; Moyson et al., 2016; Raaphorst & Groeneveld, forthcoming; Yang, 2005). Whereas there is a trend towards trust-based collaboration with citizens, the scholarly attention to whether officials do, indeed, trust citizens is lagging behind. Future research could study whether and how trust is created in institutions as well as in interpersonal interactions. The trend towards trust-based working is moreover based on expectations about the alleged positive effects of more trust, such as a reduction in red tape and transaction costs. Public administration scholars should focus on what the effects of trust-based working actually are, also looking more broadly and non-normatively at the consequences for citizens.

Socialization of public officials

Studies have suggested that frontline officials become more cynical the longer they are in service and experience more disappointing interactions with citizens (Blau, 1960; Engbersen, 2006). This could imply that more tenured officials have a different attitude towards citizens than new-comers. This raises questions as to how newcomers are socialized in the public organization; what do they learn, and how do their attitudes evolve over time? What is the role of interactions with citizens in how public officials' attitudes are shaped? And also important: how do public organizations deal with differences in attitudes between employees? Public administration scholars should focus more on how newcomers in public organizations 'learn the ropes' and how they learn to interact with citizens (see Oberfield, 2014, for a good example). The street-level bureaucracy literature suggests that officials' mind-sets are important in how citizens are judged and classified. This raises issues for practitioners working with newcomers in the public sector, since officials' dispositions are probably acquired through organizational socialization, but also through socialization earlier in life. Does the public sector want officials with a low-trust attitude or high-trust attitude? And is there also room for distrust? These are all questions that arise when public sectors promote trust and collaboration, and that need not to be addressed by scholars, but by policy makers and public managers.

Consequences for public values

The classical Weberian perspective on bureaucracy conceives of it as an apparatus serving the larger powers that is characterized by a clear and hierarchical 'sphere of competence' (Weber, 1921/1968), in which bureaucrats ideally work according to rules, procedures and policies so as to safeguard 'expertise, equality, and reliability over arbitrariness, power abuse, and personal whims' (Bartels, 2013: 470). In this ideal typical model, 'bureaucracy develops the more perfectly, the more it is "dehumanized", the more completely it succeeds in eliminating from official business love, hatred, and all purely personal, irrational and emotional elements which escape calculation' (Weber, 1921/1968: 973). Clearly, within this ideal typical view of bureau-cracy there is no room for trust between officials and citizens. As an interpersonal notion, trust brings in human judgment. Whereas trust is considered a valuable thing within today's collaborative forms of governance, from a more traditional view of bureaucracy all interactions between officials and citizens should be neutral and guided by rules and procedures. Our main task as scholars is not to take stances in this debate, but to closely follow the developments in the public sector and critically analyse them against the notions on which democracy is based, and the consequences these developments have for how the government carries out its tasks and how citizens are treated.

References

Agranoff, R. & McGuire, M. (2001). Big questions in public network management research. *Journal of Public Administration Research and Theory, 11*(3): 295–326.

Ayres, I. & Braithwaite, J. (1992). *Responsive regulation: Transcending the deregulation debate.* New York: Oxford University Press.

Bardach, E. & Kagan, R.A. (1982/2002). *Going by the book: The problem of regulatory unreasonableness.* New Brunswick. NJ: Transaction Publishers.

Bartels, K.P.R. (2013). Public encounters: The history and future of face-to-face contact between public professionals and citizens. *Public Administration, 19*(2): 469–483.

Blau, P.M. (1960). Orientation toward clients in a public welfare agency. *Administrative Science Quarterly, 5*(3): 341–361.

Bok, D. (2001). *The trouble with government.* Cambridge, MA: Harvard University Press.

Bovens, M. & Zouridis, S. (2002). From street-level to system-level bureaucracies: How information and communication technology is transforming administrative discretion and constitutional control. *Public Administration Review, 62*(2): 174–184.

Burgemeestre, B., Hulstijn, J. & Tan, Y.H. (2010). The role of trust in government control of business. In H.D. Zimmermann (Ed.), *Proceedings of 23rd Bled eConference: eTust, implications for the individual, enterprizes and society* (pp. 301–313). Bled, Solvenia: eBled.

Chambers, S. (2004). Behind closed doors: Publicity, secrecy, and the quality of deliberation. *Journal of Political Philosophy*, *12*(4): 389–410.

Cowell, R., Downe, J., Martin, S. & Chen, A. (2012). Public confidence and public services: It matters what you measure. *Policy & Politics*, *40*(1): 120–140.

Dowding, K. & John, P. (2008). The three exit, three voice and loyalty framework: A test with survey data on local services. *Political Studies*, *56*(2): 288–311.

Dowding, K. & John, P. (2012). *Exits, voices and social investment: Citizens' reactions to public services*. Cambridge, UK: Cambridge University Press.

Dubois, V. (2013). The functions of bureaucratic routines in a changing welfare state: On interactions with recipients in French welfare offices. In P. Sandermann (Ed.), *The end of welfare as we know it? Continuity and change in western welfare practices*. Opladen, Berlin & Toronto: Barbara Budrich Publishers.

Eikenaar, T., De Rijk, A.E. & Meershoek, A. (2015). What's in a frame? How professionals assess clients in Dutch work reintegration practice. *Social Policy & Administration*. *50*(7): 767–786.

Engbersen, G. (2006). *Publieke bijstandsgeheimen: Het ontstaan van een onderklasse in Nederland*. Amsterdam, the Netherlands: Amsterdam University Press.

Erickson, F. (1975). Gatekeeping and the melting pot: Interaction in counseling encounters. *Harvard Educational Review*, *45*(1): 44–70.

Etzioni, A. (2010). Is transparency the best disinfectant? *Journal of Political Philosophy 18*(4): 389–404.

Gambetta, D. & Hamill, H. (2005). *Streetwise: How taxi drivers establish their customers' trustworthiness*. New York: Russell Sage Foundation.

Gofen, A. (2015). Citizens' entrepreneurial role in public service provision. *Public Management Review*, *17*(3): 404–425.

Goodsell, C.T. (1983). *The case for bureaucracy: a public administration polemic*. Chatham, UK: Chatham House Publishers Inc.

Greve, C. (2008). *Contracting for public services*. Abingdon, UK: Routledge.

Grimmelikhuijsen, S. (2012). Linking transparency, knowledge and citizen trust in government: An experiment. *International Review of Administrative Sciences*, *78*(1): 50–73.

Grimmelikhuijsen, S. & Knies, E. (2017). Validating a scale for citizen trust in government organizations. *International Review of Administrative Sciences*, *83*(3): 583–601. DOI: 10.1177/0020852315585950.

Groeneveld, S. & Van de Walle, S. (Eds.) (2011). *New steering concepts in public management*. Research in public policy analysis and management series, Vol. 21. Bingley, UK: Emerald Group Publishing.

Hardin, R. (2002). *Trust and trustworthiness*. New York: Russell Sage Foundation.

Hasenfeld, Y. (2000). Organizational forms as moral practices: The case of welfare departments. *Social Service Review*, *74*(3): 329–351.

Hirschman, A.O. (1970). *Exit, voice, and loyalty: Responses to decline in firms, organizations, and states*. Cambridge, MA: Harvard University Press.

Houston, D.J. & Howard Harding, L. (2013). Public trust in government administrators. *Public Integrity*, *16*(1): 53–76.

Hull, M.S. (2012). Documents and bureaucracy. *Annual Review of Anthropology*, *41*: 251–267.

Huxham, C. & Vangen, S.E. (2005). *Managing to collaborate: The theory and practice of collaborative advantage*. Abingdon, UK: Routledge.

Kagan, R. & Scholz, J. (1984). The "Criminology of the Corporation" and regulatory enforcement strategies. In K. Hawkins and J.M. Thom (Eds.), *Enforcing regulation*. Boston, MA: Kluwer-Nijhoff.

Katz, D., Gutek, B.A., Kahn, R.L. & Barton, E. (1977). *Bureaucratic encounters: A pilot study in the evaluation of government services*. Ann Arbor, MI: Institute for Social Research.

Keulemans, S. (2015, August). *Official-client relations in the bureaucratic encounter: Development and validation of a multicomponent measurement instrument for the public official's attitude toward citizens*. Paper presented at the EGPA Conference, Toulouse, France.

Kingfisher, C.P. (1998). How providers make policy: An analysis of everyday conversation in a welfare office. *Journal of Community and Applied Social Psychology*, *8*(2): 119–136.

Klein Woolthuis, R., Hillebrand, B. & Nooteboom, B. (2005). Trust, contract and relationship development. *Organization Studies*, *26*(6): 813–840.

Leviner, S. (2009). A new era of tax enforcement: From 'big stick' to responsive regulation. *University of Michigan Journal of Law Reform*, *42*(2): 381–429.

Lipsky, M. (1980). *Street-level bureaucracy: Dilemmas of the individual in public services*. New York: Russell Sage Foundation.

Margetts, H. (2006). Transparency and digital government. In C. Hood and D. Heald (Eds.), *Transparency: The key to better governance?* Oxford, UK: Oxford University Press.

Marlowe, J. (2004). Part of the solution or cogs in the system? The origins and consequences of trust in public administrators. *Public Integrity, 6*(2): 93–113.

Mascini, P. & Van Wijk, E. (2009). Responsive regulation at the Dutch food and consumer product safety authority: An empirical assessment of assumptions underlying the theory. *Regulation & Governance, 3*(1): 27–47.

Maynard-Moody, S. & Musheno, M. (2003). *Cops, teachers, counselors: Stories from the front lines of public service.* Ann Arbor, MI: The University of Michigan Press.

Mennerick, L.A. (1974). Client typologies: A method of coping with conflict in the service worker-client relationship. *Work and Occupations, 1*(4): 396–418.

Moyson, S., Van de Walle, S. & Groeneveld, S. (2016). What do public officials think about citizens? The role of public officials' trust and their perceptions of citizens' trustworthiness in interactive governance. In J. Edelenbos and I.van Meerkerk, (Eds.), *Critical Reflections on Interactive Governance.* Cheltenham, UK: Edward Elgar Publishing.

Möllering, G. (2006). *Trust: Reason, routine, reflexivity.* Bingley, UK: Emerald Group Publishing.

Møller, M. & Stone, D. (2013). Disciplining disability under Danish active labour market policy. *Social Policy & Administration, 47*(5): 586–604.

Nye, J.S. jr., Zelikow, P.D. & King, D.C. (Eds.). (1997). *Why people don't trust government.* Cambridge, MA: Harvard University Press.

Oberfield, Z.W. (2014). *Becoming bureaucrats: Socialization at the front lines of government service.* Philadelphia, PA: University of Pennsylvania Press.

Osborne, D. & Gaebler, T. (1992). *Reinventing government: How the entrepreneurial spirit is transforming the public sector.* Reading, MA: Addison-Wesley.

Peters, G.P. (2004). Governance and public bureaucracy: New forms of democracy or new forms of control? *Asia Pacific Journal of Public Administration, 26*(1): 3–15.

Power, M. (1999). *The audit society: Rituals of verification.* Oxford, UK: Oxford University Press.

Prottas, J.M. (1979). *People-processing: The street-level bureaucrat in public service bureaucracies.* Lexington, MA & Toronto, ON: Lexington Books.

Raaphorst, N. & Groeneveld, S. (forthcoming). Double standards in frontline decision making: A theoretical and empirical exploration. *Administration & Society.*

Rokkan, S. (1974). Entries, voices, exits: Towards a possible generalization of the Hirschman Model. *Social Science Information, 13*(1): 39–53.

Sakurai, Y. (2002). Comparing cross-cultural regulatory styles and processes in dealing with transfer pricing. *International Journal of the Sociology of Law, 30*(3): 173–199.

Sitkin, S.B. & Bies, R.J. (1993). The legalistic organization: Definitions, dimensions and dilemmas. *Organization Science, 4*(3): 345–351.

Sitkin, S.B. & Roth, N.L. (1993). Explaining the limited effectiveness of legalistic 'remedies' for trust/distrust. *Organization Science, 4*(3): 367–392.

Six, F. (2013). Trust in regulatory relations. *Public Management Review, 15*(2): 163–185.

Stone, D. (1984). *The disabled state.* Philadelphia, PA: Temple University Press.

Tummers, L., Brunetto, Y. & Teo, S.T. (2016). Workplace aggression: Introduction to the special issue and future research directions for scholars. *International Journal of Public Sector Management, 29*(1): 2–10.

Van de Walle, S. (2010). New public management: Restoring the public trust through creating distrust? In T. Christensen and P. Lægreid (Eds.), *The Ashgate Research Companion to New Public Management.* Aldershot, UK: Ashgate.

Van de Walle, S. (2016). Trust in public administration and public services. In European Commission (Ed.), *Trust at risk? Implications for and responses of research and innovation policies in a medium-term perspective.* Brussels, Belgium: Directorate-General for Research and Innovation.

Van de Walle, S. & Bouckaert, G. (2007). Perceptions of productivity and performance in Europe and the USA. *International Journal of Public Administration, 30*(11): 1–18.

Van de Walle, S. & Roberts, A. (2008). Publishing performance information: An illusion of control? In W. van Dooren and S. van de Walle (Eds.), *Performance information in the public sector: How it is used.* Houndmills, UK: Palgrave Macmillan.

Van de Walle, S. & Six, F. (2014). Trust and distrust as distinct concepts: Why studying distrust in institutions is important. *Journal of Comparative Policy Analysis: Research and Practice, 16*(2): 158–174.

Van de Walle, S., Van Roosbroek, S. & Bouckaert, G. (2008). Trust in the public sector: Is there any evidence for a long-term decline? *International Review of Administrative Sciences*, 74(1): 45–62.

Van de Walle, S. & Van Ryzin, G. (2011). The order of questions in a survey on citizen satisfaction with public services: Lessons from a split-ballot experiment. *Public Administration*, 89(4): 1436–1450.

Van Ryzin, G. (2011). Outcomes, process, and trust of civil servants. *Journal of Public Administration Research and Theory*, 21(4): 745–760.

Warin, P. (2008). Le non-recours par désintérêt: la possibilité d'un 'vivre hors droits'. *Vie Sociale*, 1(1): 9–19.

Weber, M. (1921/1968). *Economy and society*, 3 Vols. Edited by G. Roth & C. Wittich. Totowa, NJ: Bedminster Press.

Yang, K. (2005). Public administrators' trust in citizens: A missing link in citizen involvement efforts. *Public Administration Review*, 65(3): 273–285.

Yang, K. (2006). Trust and citizen involvement decisions: Trust in citizens, trust in institutions, and propensity to trust. *Administration & Society*, 38(5): 573–95.

28

TRUST AND HRM

Rosalind H. Searle

Introduction

Human resource management (HRM) is one of the most influential areas of an organization's policy and practice. HRM involves the operationalization of strategic interventions focused on human capital, designed to identify and develop resourceful employees. Trust is a form of psychological attachment to an employing organization and so is central in the gaining of employees' commitment and co-operation in delivering the organization's objectives (Ng 2015). It can be a multi-faceted topic, concerning the expectations and vulnerabilities of both employees and employer, with growing interest in the salience of trust within the employment context, and its significance to people's experiences of work and employment. It is a rich context for study, featuring elements of both the interpersonal and organizational.

Trust implicitly permeates HRM in three key ways; first, the strategic policy choices offer clues and signals about the organization's trustworthiness towards both employees and external stakeholders. These range from decisions about the type of work contracts (Reilly 1998) to the approach taken to recognize and reward different groups and levels of employee. Second, trust emerges in how these policies are implemented not only by HR professionals, but increasingly by line managers with devolved responsibility for their day-to-day implementation (Searle 2013). This creates the possibility of trust breaching through to intra-organizational variations (Gould-Williams & Davies 2005). In addition, some organizations' outsourcing of key HR systems (Cooke, et al. 2005), such as payroll or recruitment, can result in a third party's actions having a bearing on employees' experiences. However, such multi-level concerns have yet to be explored by trust and HR scholars.

This chapter is organized into four sections, commencing with a review of policy "bundles" research, before using the employee HR cycle (Searle & Skinner 2011: 6) as a means of exploring the uneven interest in trust in ten HR policy areas, most notably performance management (Mayer & Davis 1999) and downsizing (Spreitzer & Mishra 2002; Pugh, et al. 2003). In these sections, I consider how trust has been conceptualized and the main theoretical approaches used, but also note the use of novel non-survey-based research designs. In the third section, I explore briefly trust and the HR profession itself, reflecting on its role in creating, maintaining, breaching and repairing trust for organizations, before closing with an agenda for future research.

Bundles of HR

One of the most significant areas of research has been studies of groups, or bundles, of HR policies. Arising from debate about which are the "best" HR practices (Marchington & Grugulis 2000; Ichniowski & Shaw 2003), this inherent divergence reflects the lack of consensus of any "coherent set" of policies (Wright & Boswell 2002; Boselie, et al. 2005). Instead, three policy groupings are evident (see Table 28.1). The first approach "high commitment practices" (e.g. Whitener 2001), typically incorporates Snell and Dean's (1992) emphasis on policies designed to influence employee motivation and commitment, and includes selection, developmental appraisal, externally competitive and internally fair compensation, and training and development practices. The second is derived from Pfeffer and Veiga's (1999) seven policy areas, comprising selection, employment security, teamwork, performance-related pay, training and development, information sharing and egalitarianism. The final approach explores "high performance systems" (Appelbaum, et al. 2001) and contains policies directed towards improving employees' skills and their involvement. Here selection is removed, and promotions, decision-making, autonomy, work–life balance and more broad communications added, with training extended to include informal elements (e.g. Searle, et al. 2011).

Summarized in Table 28.1, the dominance of training and compensation policies is evident (see Table 28.1, row 1) with far less attention given to those concerning employment security, teamwork, promotions and career development, and work–life balance initiatives.

Relatively few scholars have considered conceptually how HR bundles might be connected to trust (e.g. Whitener 1997; Kim & Wright 2011). Those that have, highlight the particular significance of "goodwill" trust, which concerns benevolence and the assurance of non-harmful behaviour (Sako 1998; Dekker 2004) (see Chapter 9 by Baer and Colquitt, on antecedents). The dominant theoretical approach remains social exchange (Homans 1961; Emerson 1962; Blau 1964; Emerson 1972), with only one study using the allied procedural justice theory (Leventhal, Karuza, et al. 1980). Half of these studies include fairness perceptions with procedural justice dominating (e.g. Pearce, et al. 2000; Chen, et al. 2004; Tzafrir, et al. 2004; Tremblay, et al. 2010; Farndale, et al. 2011; Searle, et al. 2011; Cho & Poister 2013) (for more detailed discussion on fairness and trust see Lind's chapter). The inclusion of justice allows insight into trust in terms of the effects of policy choice on trust perceptions, but also its implementation.

The positioning of trust and HRM policies in these studies also varies (see Table 28.1 – columns relating to trust and HRM dimensions). Some examine trust as an antecedent important in shaping employers' choice of HR policy (Gould-Williams & Davies 2005; Tzafrir 2005; Brown, et al. 2015), but more typically trust is included as an outcome of HR policies, either at the organizational level (Searle, et al. 2011; Cho & Poister 2013), or in relation to key referents – management (Gould-Williams 2003; Chen, et al. 2004; Tzafrir, et al. 2004), or co-workers (Pearce, et al. 2000). More recently, research has shifted to examine the "black box" in organizations, looking at HR's influence on a range of metrics including performance, well-being, commitment. This work has included trust as a moderator on outcomes including turn-over, well-being or performance (Farndale, et al. 2011; Innocenti, et al. 2011; Alfes, et al. 2012; Ertürk 2014), or as a mediator (Whitener 2001; Tzafrir and Gur 2007; Tremblay, et al. 2010).

Major differences are evident in the quality of the operationalization of the key elements of HRM and trust (see Table 28.1 for details). Some studies have a relatively simplistic approach towards HRM and created a summative index of HRM systems based simply on whether the HR policy is used by the organization (e.g. Gould-Williams 2003). In contrast, others have retained each HR area to allow examination of how policies influence employee outcomes (e.g. Whitener 2001; Cho & Poister 2013). The latter are more valuable in isolating how and

Table 28.1 HR elements included in trust and HR policy bundles research

Author	Components used														Trust conceptualisation	HR conceptualisation
	Job security	Selection	Communication–information	Pay & reward/compensation	Decision-making participation	Performance mangement	Training	Team work	Promotion	Career	Feedback	Home–work balance	Trade union density	Output control		
No. of studies found in	4	6	8	14	9	8	13	3	3	3	3	1	1	1		
Farndale, Hope–Hailey, et al. (2011)				X	X		X								Moderator Trust in org	Antecedent HCMP
Whitener (2001)		X		X		X	X								Mediators Trust in mang	Moderator HCHRM
Brown, Gray, et al. (2015)				X	X	X	X						X		Outcome Trust in mang	Antecedent
Ertürk (2014)			X	X	X										Moderator Org trust Trust in line mang	Outcome HIWP
Tremblay, Cloutier, et al. (2010)			X	X			X				X				Mediating org trust	Antecedent
Cho and Poister (2013)			X	X		X	X			X				X	Outcome Org trust Top team trust Sup trust	Antecedent
Pearce, Branyiczki, et al. (2000)			X	X		X		X							Outcome Trust in co-worker	Mediator
Searle, Den Hartog, et al. 2011	X		X	X	X	X	X					X			Outcome Trust in Org Mediator Org trustworthiness	Antecedent HIWP

continued . . .

Table 28.1 Continued

Author	Components used														Trust conceptualisation	HR conceptualisation
	Job security	Selection	Communication–information	Pay & reward/compensation	Decision-making participation	Performance management	Training	Team work	Promotion	Career	Feedback	Home–work balance	Trade union density	Output control		
No. of studies found in	4	6	8	14	9	8	13	3	3	3	3	1	1	1		
Chen, Chen, et al. (2004)	X	X		X		X			X						Outcome Trust in mang	Antecedent Summative measure
Alfes, Shantz, et al. (2012)	X	X		X		X	X		X	X	X				Moderator Trust in employer	Antecedent Summative measure
Tzafrir (2005)		X		X	X		X								Antecedent org trust	Mediator HR
Tzafrir, Harel, et al. (2004)			X		X	X	X								Outcome Trust in mang	Antecedents
Gould–Williams and Davies (2005)	X	X	X	X	X	X	X	X		X					Antecedent Trust in mang	Antecedent
Tzafrir and Gur (2007)				X			X		X		X				Mediator Trust in mang	Antecedent
Gould–Williams (2003)	X	X	X	X	X		X	X							Outcome Trust in mang	Antecedent Summative measure of HR activity
Innocenti, Pilati, et al. (2011)			X	XX			X								Moderator Trust in mang	Antecedent Summative measure of HR activity

why trust might matter in organizations. For example, HR policies relating to teamwork are found to influence levels of employee commitment and motivation, while those aimed at improving empowerment and involvement, fair rewards and job security are significant to employee motivation (e.g. Gould-Williams & Davies 2005). Whitener's (2001) cross-level research on five policies reveals the importance of equitable rewards and developmental appraisals for trust, but found only appraisal enhanced trust in management. Differences also arise in the sophistication of trust measures, ranging from the use of a simple single item (e.g. Cho & Poister 2013), through to inclusion of multi-dimensional trustworthiness measures (e.g. Searle, et al. 2011).

Cross-sectional designs dominate this type of research, typically using surveys to collect perceptions of either employees or management about an array of HR policies and other measures. Only one study combined surveys with an experimental design (Chen, et al. 2004). Typically, research focuses on trust and HR policies within a single organization, with western contexts dominating, including the United States (Whitener 2001), UK (Farndale, et al. 2011), Canada (Tremblay, et al. 2010) and Israel[1] (Tzafrir, et al. 2004). Few have involved multiple organizations in similar contexts such as Europe (e.g. Searle, et al. 2011). Some attention has looked at different cultures, including Turkey (Ertürk 2014), and China, the latter focusing particularly on understanding trust and the impact of *guanxi HRM* (e.g. Chen, et al. 2004). Pearce, Branyiczki and Bigley's (2000) study makes an interesting comparison, comparing employees' attitudes in a collective context, Hungary, and the more individualistic United States. This work showed differences in HR practices mediated by the relationships between political system and the trust employers had in each other, their perceptions of co-worker "social loafing", and the commitment of their employing organization. In increasingly globalized organizations HR policies are often imposed across multiple geographical locations, regardless of some important differences regarding trust (Ferrin & Gillespie 2010). An interesting counter to study of more progressive organizations has been exploration of "black hole" organizations, where HRM practices are not progressive, nor trade unions recognized (Guest & Conway 1999). Significantly for this field, their research highlighted the importance of HRM practices above trade union membership in the attitudes and experiences of employees.

To summarize, while study of HRM bundles has been a productive seam for research, gaps are evident in the coverage of HRM systems, the variations in the sophistication of design and operationalization of key measures. Perhaps more significantly, it is an area ripe for development to explore within-workforce differences in relationships between HRM and trust for a range of referents. For example, are there perceptual differences on dimensions such as gender, ethnicity, religious belief or tribal affiliation? Relatively few studies even control for evident gender differences (e.g. exception Searle, et al. 2011). While Tzafrir (2005) revealed how trust influenced HR managers' decisions about employees' training and promotion, little consideration has been extended towards understanding the differences in perceptions of trust and fairness among traditionally more marginalized groups within organizations. What are the significant policy areas for them? What are their implementation concerns? Certainly more nuanced attention is required to explore members of groups who, evidence shows, fail to rise to the top of organizations. We now consider research on single HRM policies.

Distinct areas

A review of research into distinct HR policies and practices reveals the dominance of three areas: early socialization, performance management and downsizing (see Table 28.2). This next section is organized in terms of the HR employee cycle (Searle & Skinner 2011) (see Figure 28.1)

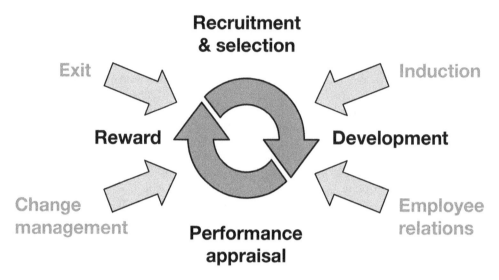

**Recruitment
& selection**

Exit

Induction

Reward

Development

Change
management

**Performance
appraisal**

Employee
relations

Figure 28.1 HR employee cycle

to deliberately call attention to areas of omission and also towards more dynamic consideration of HR in terms of the formation and maintenance of trust. It is reported in Table 28.2 by showing how trust has been conceptualized in such work. Due to the close relationship between trust and justice, I have also shown whether fairness has been a dimension in such study (see Chapter 10 by Lind, for more discussion).

Given that trust concerns confidence and vulnerability, there are key points in the employment relationship where HR policies and practices are likely to be more significant in setting expectations about the organization (Searle & Skinner 2011). These include the start, periods of pronounced change, and those involving exposure to others' critique and appraisal. The choice of policies selected by an organization sends clues and signals about their values, and insight as to what an employee might expect.

Pre-entry and selection

Prior to the start of an employment relationship is a phase of very high risk for individuals who want to join an organization (Searle & Billsberry 2011). Pre-entry is a period of potentially scarce information about the organization, save from the HR policies and practices themselves, and so trust is likely to be critical (McKnight, et al. 1998). Extant research shows that early employment experiences are a particularly important phase to study, setting initial expectations which form the basis of employees' subsequent trust and enduring affective, cognitive and behavioural response to employers (Pugh, et al. 2003). The creation of the psychological contract is more than simple expectations, rather it is concerned with "mutual obligations" that are key to a successful employment relationships (Robinson & Rousseau 1994: 246). Subjective perceptions of promises between the distinct parties emerge that will be central to the mutual and ongoing exchanges, and to perceptions of breach and violation (Robinson & Morrison 2000). Yet, despite the centrality of these experiences for the future, it is somewhat surprising that so little attention has been paid by researchers to trust and pre-entry.

Table 28.2 Trust in HR studies

Trust as a Key issue	Antecedent	Consequence	Mediator	Moderator	Justice included	Conceptual development
	Shaping the HR policy choices of employers	*HR policy influencing trust levels inside an organisation*	*Trust as a 'black box' candidate for HRM's impact on performance and well-being metrics*	*A trusting work climate enhancing/diminishing HRM's impact on performance*		
Meta analysis	Jiang, Lepak, et al. (2012)					
Multi-HR	Tzafir (2005)	Brown, Gray, et al. (2015); Cho and Poister (2013); Pearce, Branyiczki, et al. (2000); Searle, et al., (2011a); Chen, Chen, et al. (2004); Tzafir, Harel, et al. (2004); Gould-Williams and Davies (2005); Gould-Williams (2003); Robinson (1996); Robinson and Rousseau (1994)	Tremblay, Cloutier, et al. (2010); Tzafir and Gur (2007); Katou (2013); Whitener (2001)	Ertürk (2014); Alfes, Shantz, et al. (2012); Innocenti, Pilati, et al. (2011); Farndale, Hope-Hailey, et al. (2011)		Kim and Wright (2011); Whitener (1997)
Psychological contract						
Selection						Searle and Billsberry (2011); Klotz, Motta Veiga, et al. (2013); Celani, Deutsch-Salamon, et al. (2008); Ashleigh and Prichard (2011)
Learning and development	Guinot, Chiva, et al. (2013);		Lapointe, Vandenberghe, et al. (2014)			
Newcomer socialisation	Schaubroeck, Peng, et al. (2013); van der Werff and Buckley (2014)					

continued . . .

Table 28.2 Continued

Trust as a Key issue	Antecedent Shaping the HR policy choices of employers	Consequence HR policy influencing trust levels inside an organisation	Mediator Trust as a 'black box' candidate for HRM's impact on performance and well-being metrics	Moderator A trusting work climate enhancing/diminishing HRM's impact on performance	Justice included	Conceptual development
Careers & promotion			Crawshaw and Brodbeck (2011)		Crawshaw and Brodbeck (2011);	Brodt and Dionisi (2011)
Arbitration		Bernardin, Richey, et al. (2011);			Bernardin, Richey, et al. (2011)	
Bullying		Harrington, Rayner, et al. (2012);				
Industrial relations		Blunsdon and Reed (2003); Guest and Conway (1999)				Fox (1974); Mather (2011)
Worker arrangement – contractual staff		Pearce (1993)				
Performance management		Mayer and Davis (1999)	Earley (1986); Fulk, Brief, et al. (1985); Mayer and Davis (1999); Maley and Moeller (2014)	Cho and Lee (2012); Farndale and Kelliher (2013)		Searle and Skinner (2011); Bragger, Kutcher, et al. (2014)
Pay		Lee and Farh (1999); Folger and	Zhang, Long, et al. (2015)		Lee and Farh (1999)	

Change	Konovsky (1989); Chenhall and Langfield-Smith (2003)	Morgan and Zeffane (2003)	Albrecht and Travaglione (2003)	Saunders and Thornhill (2003); Smollan (2013)	
Downsizing	Spreitzer and Mishra (1997); Mishra and Spreitzer (1998); Spreitzer and Mishra (1999); Spreitzer and Mishra (2002)	Lo and Aryee (2003); Pugh, Skarlicki, et al. (2003)	Lo and Aryee (2003)	Parzefall (2012)	Buckley (2011); Spreitzer and Mishra (2002); Hope-Hailey, Searle, et al. (2012)
Retention & turnover	Wong (2012)		Tzafir and Enosh (2011); Clinton and Guest (2014); Tzafir, Gur et al. (2015)		Mishra and Spreitzer (1998)
Trust repair					Gillespie and Dietz (2009)
HR manager role	Tzafir (2005)		Chang and Chi (2007)		Harrington, Rayner, et al. (2012); Buckley (2011)
HR values	Tzafir, Gur, et al. (2015)				

While early scholars of psychological contract do explore trust at the start of the employment relationship (Robinson & Rousseau 1994; Robinson 1996) this research commences following employment. Therefore, despite some conceptual work (Celani, et al. 2008; Searle & Billsberry 2011; Klotz, et al. 2013), this pre-employment recruitment domain remains one of a real scholastic dearth. This omission is particularly noteworthy due to its stark contrast with the plethora of attention in this area from the closely aligned field of justice scholarship (e.g. Bauer, et al. 2004; Bauer, et al. 2011).

Socialization

In contrast to pre-entry, far greater attention has been paid to trust and early employment experiences. Robinson and colleagues' (Robinson, et al. 1994; Robinson & Rousseau 1994; Robinson 1996) seminal work identifies the significance of these initial trust levels in producing a substantial and multi-faceted impact; insulating against subsequent psychological contract breach, mediating between contract violation and later behaviours including job performance, citizenship and intention to quit, and moderating the impact of contract violation on subsequent trust levels. Thus, the underlying psychological mechanisms of critical confirmatory bias are exposed. Low initial employer trust is associated with lower trust and increased likelihood of psychological contract breach, while high trust buffers against subsequent breach, reducing the rate of employees' trust decline. Qualitative evidence reveals differences in the attributions made by these two distinct groups (see Chapter 14 by Tomlinson, for more details). Developing from Robinson's work, trust is often positioned as a mediator in situations where psychological contract may be threatened. In addition, it draws attention to fairness as a further mediator to better understand trust.

More recent work has looked at trust and socialization, offering insights into how trust is built, using more dynamic longitudinal designs and techniques of analysis such as latent growth modelling (van der Werff and Buckley 2014), logistic regression (Lapointe, et al. 2014) and cross-lagged structural equation modelling (Schaubroeck, et al. 2011). This research has identified the significant role of relationships, with leaders (Schaubroeck, et al. 2011; Lapointe, et al. 2014) and also co-workers (van der Werff & Buckley 2014) in new employee trust. These studies have used trust as an antecedent important in new employees' subsequent role performance and identification (Schaubroeck, et al. 2011), through trust cues in subsequent trust intentions, including reliance and disclosure (van der Werff & Buckley 2014), or as a mediator between the early socialization tactics and subsequent organizational commitment (Lapointe, et al. 2014) (see Table 28.2). They have also included more fine-grained elements of trust, specifically affect-based (Lapointe, et al. 2014) and both cognitive- and affect-based trust (Schaubroeck, et al. 2011). Such work reveals some of the dynamics in the progression of intention to trust and the types of cues being utilized (van der Werff & Buckley 2014). It is an area important in advancing not only understanding of social exchange processes, but also the formation of social identity. Studies have either examined a variety of contexts (Lapointe, et al. 2014) or distinct organizations, such as accountancy and consultancy (van der Werff & Buckley 2014) or the military (Schaubroeck, et al. 2011).

Development

Learning and training

While included in bundles, scant distinct attention has explored learning and development (for exceptions see Ashleigh & Prichard 2011; Guinot, et al. 2013) (see Table 28.2). This is somewhat surprising as it is a context in which employees might feel vulnerable. Empirical work has included trust as an antecedent for a wider mediating role of organizational learning in a Spanish context (Guinot, et al. 2013) or conceptually in team training (Ashleigh and Prichard 2011). Importantly, in the latter, both trust and over-trusting are considered. It is evidently an area for further scholarly attention.

Careers and promotion

Careers and promotions are more specific aspects of development in which trust might be an important issue, and yet here too scholars have failed to explore in depth (see Table 28.2). This is striking as it is a domain where expectations and aspects of the psychological contract are central, and could be extended into multi-level considerations, such as trust between co-workers. The limited empirical work that there has been has adopted social exchange theory to explore trust as a mediator in employees' perceptions of procedural justice and their subsequent orientation towards managing their career (Crawshaw & Brodbeck 2011). Fairness, specifically distributive justice, has been included as a moderator between trust and subsequent career orientation to reveal how individuals become more self-managing in their careers.

With regard to promotion, this has only been explored conceptually (Brodt & Dionisi 2011) but raises interesting questions about trust dynamics by suggesting that trusted peers become less trusted new leaders as they rise within the organization. It is an area where progress in the dynamics of trust maintenance and repair might emerge.

Performance management

In contrast to many other HR policies, performance appraisal is one of the most developed research areas (see Table 28.2). These annual processes are easily examined, with scholarly interest including both employees' relationships with their appraisers (usually their line manager) and trust in these systems (Skinner & Searle 2011). The supervisor is the most frequent focus for trust interest. Early work looked at telecoms engineers revealing how perceived fairness and accuracy of the assessment were important to trust levels in critical leader–follower relationships, as well as to trust emanating from the characteristics of this HR policy (Fulk, et al. 1985). Another study compared the impact of feedback on English and US workers, to show how workers' responses to feedback type (praise vs criticism) varied by country (Earley 1986). A subsequent 14-month quasi-experimental design study examined both the consequence of trust in top management from performance management systems (Mayer & Davis 1999) and the mediating role of trustworthiness, based on the ABI dimensions (see Chapter 9 by Baer and Colquitt). Mayer and Davis's (1999) paper is unusual in conceptualizing trust as an outcome.

More recent research has explored the moderating role of trust (see Table 28.2). For example, a large US public sector study considered the role of performance management in the performance at both work-unit and organizational level (Cho & Lee 2012). Examining more closely the trust scale used here, however, reveals a conflation between fairness and trust items. A second study confirmed trust's moderating effect for employee commitment, and showed how those business units with a climate of trust in senior management had not only greater levels of organizational commitment, but also a stronger relationship at the individual level between perceived line manager fairness of treatment in the performance management process and enhanced levels of commitment (Farndale & Kelliher 2013). An Australian qualitative study has explored further line managers' roles looking at multinational country managers and confirming the importance of this key relationship for employees' trust (Maley & Moeller 2014);

They found the level of trust between the country manager and their boss played a critical role in maximizing the benefits of appraisal systems.

This domain has received conceptual attention too. For example, there is conjecture as to different long- and short-term trust consequences, with weak line management being ameliorated by a good appraisal system, but eroding in the long run organizational-level trust if ineffective management endures (Searle & Skinner 2011). Another study considered distinct formal components of appraisal systems, including goal setting, evidence collection, ongoing feedback and performance review (Bragger, et al. 2014). These aspects are argued to be particularly helpful for trust by reducing employees' uncertainty (De Cremer, et al. 2010), and outline why relational-trust dimension might be far more significant for successful performance management systems.

As with many of the preceding areas, social exchange remains the core theoretical lens through which trust is explored, with many studies omitting any mention of an underlying theory. Mayer et al.'s (1995) three trustworthiness framework is also popular. There have, however, been some novel theoretical departures, to include expectancy theory (found in Cho & Lee 2012), and signalling theory (Farndale and Kelliher 2013).

Contracts, pay and rewards

A related HR area of study is trust and contracts, which can include the start of the employment relationship or rewards. Pearce's (1993) empirical research compared contractors and full-time engineers, to reveal that the presence of contractors within a workplace was associated with depressed levels of organizational trustworthiness. Strikingly, while she found the type of tasks allocated to staff did vary as a result of their contractual status, with full employees being more likely to be allocated interdependent jobs, there was no significant difference in the quasi-moral involvement between these two groups; they suggest little suppression of contract workers trust levels. A further policy is pay and reward (see Table 28.2). Here too, the quality of the line-manager and subordinate relationship, as well as the fairness of processes, appears to be critical. An early study showed procedural fairness as an important antecedent for the resultant trust in supervision following a pay raise (Folger & Konovsky 1989). Further distributive fairness has been shown to be of significance here, but only for women (Lee & Farh 1999): gender was a moderating influence in the relationship between distributive justice and supervisor trust. Despite the topicality of gender pay inequality debates, little further attention has been given to gender by trust researchers.

Another study of pay for performance (PfP) looked at the impact of this policy on creativity, using a sample from mainland China and Taiwan to explore guanxi HRM practices (Zhang, Long et al. 2015). As with results from other psychological contract-based studies, the use of guanxi HRM practices reduced trust in management, and had a mediated moderating influence on PfP effect on creativity. A 15-year qualitative case study exploring gain-sharing reward systems highlighted the positive impact of such reward systems on the development of organizational and personal trust (Chenhall & Langfield-Smith 2003).

Looking at such studies reveals that trust is often not the main focus, yet emerges as an important matter influencing either the resultant trust levels (trust as an outcome) or enhancing the effectiveness of this HR policy.

Industrial and employee relations and conflict resolution

Fox's (1974) seminal book identified the important imbalance of power to contend that trust is a feature not only of the existing social processes, but was also is embedded in the policy choices made. He therefore reflected the potential for both cooperation and conflict in the workplace, and identified this as a context in which trust might be developed but also breached. Mather (2011) continues to explore collaborative, trust-based working relationships and suggests they need to constituted in a way that more realistically reflects the complexities and realities of the employment relationship. She has discussed trust for employee and industrial relations in an earlier chapter (see Chapter 21, this volume).

Two empirical examinations have looked at these complex interactions, using trust as an outcome (see Table 28.2). The first, Blunsdon and Reed's (2003) Australian study, built on Fox (1974) to differentiate between social and technical systems. Their results corroborate earlier work showing how experiences of arbitrary particularistic processes can undermine trust (Pearce, et al. 2000). Using a simple single-item measure of trust in management ("Management at this workplace can be trusted to tell things the way they are" (ibid: 19)), they found trust levels in management declined with the age of a workplace and, more surprisingly and contrary to expectations, with the presence of formal systems, including joint consultative committees, task forces and formal policies. Further, somewhat contrary to expectations, they showed devolved first-line supervisors' responsibility depressed management trust rates for overtime decisions, and the opposite effect in dismissing employees. Thus trust in supervisions is more dependent on punitive matters, rather than arbitrary reward. Recent related study of trust and control correlated the importance of both transparent and non-arbitrary processes and sanctions for trust (Weibel, et al. 2016). Blunsdon and Reed's (2003) study considered some organizational features, such as whether the number of professional staff independently affect trust in management. On closer inspection, however, their results are from the health-care sector and so might arise due to tension between employees' vocationally derived notions of patient care and managers' financial and resources-focused organizational goals. A second UK survey-based study compared the impact of trade union membership with progressive HR practices for trust in management, to confirm the greater influence of HR practices (Guest & Conway 1999). Differences in values and objectives for distinct hierarchical levels are rarely considered in HR research. Nor is comparison made of differences in the levels of trust for trade union officials, HR and line management. Certainly, Searle and Ball's (2004) study of mergers in confectionery manufacturing showed how the huge power differentiation between the trade union and management, could be cynically exploited by management who deliberately promoted trade union leaders into management, positions.

Research into conflict resolution processes and trust has been sparse. Bernardin, et al.'s (2011) study of dispute resolution programmes compared mandatory mediation with mandatory and binding arbitration (MMBA), and explored their impact on trust. Other HR conflict-focused research areas have considered bullying and harassment (Harrington & Rayner 2011; Harrington, et al. 2012). These qualitative studies draw attention to the key triadic relationship at the heart of dealing effectively with allegations of workplace bullying, HR professionals, employees and managers (the role of HR professions will be considered briefly in the next section).

Organizational change

There are two distinct types of policy in this area: one concerned with programmes designed to develop an organization, and the other aimed at reducing its headcount. They are therefore distinct in terms of employees' vulnerability, with a significant skew in scholarly activity towards exploring the latter.

Organizational development

Although the twin trust dimensions of expectation and uncertainty are critical for change management, as Morgan and Zaffane (2003) lament, little attention has been paid to trust and distrust in this context (see Table 28.2). Their Australian survey-based exploration of over 2,000 organizations examined three forms of major organizational change: technological, structural, and work role, to reveal that trust decline varied depending on the type of change and the level of employee participation. They found structural change was the most corrosive, with senior management playing a critical role, but direct consultation and involvement of staff in major transitions could reduce the impact. Another study in the same special issue used trust as a mediator to explore the antecedents and consequences of public sector employees' trust in top management (Albrecht & Travaglione 2003). Using data from two public sector organizations, they confirmed again the importance of procedural fairness, but also organizational support, effective communication and job security in the retention of trust. Trust in top management was found to be a partial, rather than full, mediator. Senior management had influence in two forms of employee commitment – affective and continuance, but also could ameliorate the pernicious impact of employee cynicism towards the change.

In contrast to the typical dominance of interview or survey-based research methods, some novel methodologies are found here. Of note is the use of card-sort technique to explore employees' reactions to change (Saunders & Thornhill 2003; Saunders & Thornhill 2004). Another small-scale New Zealand-based qualitative study has examined cognitive antecedents and behavioural responses to change (Smollan 2013), confirming fairness as central to both the creation and decline of management trust. (See Chapter 10 by Lind, on trust and fairness).

Unsurprisingly in this policy area, social exchange theory (Blau 1964) remains the dominant theoretical lens, but psychological contract (Robinson & Rousseau 1994), justice concerns (Colquitt 2001) and fairness heuristic theory (Lind 2001; van den Bos 2001) have also been used. More critically, despite much mention of trustworthiness, it remains a neglected dimension in studies of change. This is a context where more dynamic study designs and analysis is under-utilized; instead retrospective recall dominates. It is disappointing to see that no attention has really been paid to understanding how trust processes unfurl in the context of change either through collection of baselines of trust or from individual difference factors, such as propensity to trust, which might influence how change processes are received. This area could also profit from comparative study of systems and relational trust, critically those examining the roles of distinct organizational agents, including senior management, line management and HR professions, in preserving and undermining trust, and in the production of mistrust and distrust. An aligned paper on distrust shows the merit of case studies in examining these interrelationships (Bijlsma-Frankema, et al. 2015). Strikingly, to date, most of the studies here have been public sector. While clearly a turbulent sector for change, private or not-for-profit contexts also have involved in transitions that might be worth scholarly exploration.

Downsizing

Change in order to reduce the headcount of an organization has been a long-standing area for trust study (see Table 28.2). This conspicuously negative HR policy in which vulnerabilities come to the fore is important for both interpersonal and organizational trust, especially perceived fairness of both processes and practice (Brockner & Siegel 1996). Studies show the enduring and pernicious impact of organizational mistreatment on people's lives, regardless of whether they stay or remain (Pugh, et al. 2003). However, well-managed downsizing processes include transparent communications, and fairly applied procedures can actually enhance trust in an employer (Hope-Hailey, et al. 2012).

Seminal work confirms trust as an important antecedent in managing downsizing (Spreitzer & Mishra 1997; Mishra & Spreitzer 1998; Spreitzer & Mishra 1999; Spreitzer & Mishra 2002). US samples reveal it is not just to those leaving the organization, but also to the retention of survivors in the new leaner organization that it is critical. Research shows all three forms of fairness – distributive, procedural and interactional – are important, and also trustworthy top management, in the retention of surviving staff (Spreitzer & Mishra 2002). This work reveals how retaining trust results in more constructive responses to staff-reduction programmes, and could help reduce stress-threat responses.

Another important contribution from Pugh, Skarlick and Passell (2003) has revealed the enduring impact of downsizing experiences on subsequent employment relationships. They show how earlier trust breaches suppress trust in the new employer and increase employees' levels of cynicism. Contrasting outcomes for trust and cynicism, they identified the impact on other work-related behaviours, including organizational citizenship and employee cooperation (Dean, et al. 1998). Their research found that employees' concerns about subsequent similar mistreatment mediated the relationship between psychological contract violation, and both their levels of trust and cynicism in their new employers. This work attests to the value of including emotions, especially negative affect, in studies. They identified how responses to an initial downsizing experience could shape both subsequent attitudes and behaviours towards new employers. Other work has looked at the meditating role of trust in a Hong Kong Chinese context (Lo & Aryee 2003). They found levels of trust in the employer fully mediated the impact of this psychological contract breach, and two key work outcomes – psychological withdrawal and civic virtue – partially mediated the impact on intention to quit.

Qualitatitive research of this policy area offers some alternative perspectives. For example, Parzefall (2012) considered different HR practices to downsizing, showing that decisions which allowed downsized employees to be retained helped to avoid the aforementioned negative consequences. Further, a series of case studies has revealed how trust might be preserved, rather than simply executing a policy of trust breach and repair (Hope-Hailey, et al. 2012). Their examples found trust could be sustained, if not even enhanced, through attention towards fairness and the emotions of staff in downsizing processes; in other cases, trust breach was unnecessarily exacerbated. A more unusual perspective is provided by Buckley (2011) who considered downsizing in term of HR professionals. He outlined that while downsizing could increase the power HR at board level, there was a personal cost to HR managers at the forefront of implementing this organizational strategy.

In reviewing this aspect of policy, an important theoretical lens that has been used is psychological contract (Robinson & Rousseau 1994) and attention towards the type of breach. Additional richness has been added through frameworks including Lazarus and Folkman's (1984) theory of stress to distinguish cognition and affect dimensions, justice concerns (Aquino, et al. 1997) and also identity and organizational attachment dimensions (Brockner, et al. 1990).

Studies in this area have examined trust as both an antecedent and consequence, and also as a mediator (see Table 28.2). More attention, however, should be given to exploring the dynamics and mechanisms that shape employees and also HR managers' responses. Further research should consider alternative policy responses rather than downsizing to offer greater insight into how to better manage this deeply traumatizing experience. Work might consider trust levels for different actors, such as HR professionals involved in the process to reveal the breadth of those affected by downsizing.

Exit

The final stage of the employee cycle includes voluntary and involuntary exit, such as for retirement. It is an area where some research has been done (see Table 28.2), and includes discernible differences in the theories and approaches used. For example, Wong's (2012) Chinese-based study of international joint ventures revealed the different impact on retention of trust in the line manager compared to trust in management. He showed how higher-level trust perceptions affected turnover intentions, while trust in a more immediate line manager influenced organizational citizenship. This research used social exchange as the main theory and included two antecedents of trust – fairness and job security.

In contrast, Tzafrir, et al. (2015) adopted the theory of reasoned action (Fishbein & Ajzen 1975) for their exploration of employees' attitudes and intention to quit, testing and confirming the impact of "leaving scripts" (Tzafrir & Enosh 2011). This research built on Fox's (1974) work by considering how HR might be important in transmitting the underlying values of the organization. It explored how the wider social environment might play a role in the mediating the relationship between HR values and staff's intentions to leave. They operationalized the social environment through three elements: employees' well-being, trust in term members and abusive supervision. Their results confirm the importance of team-level trust and its mediating role between HR values and retention.

A further large UK-based armed forces study used psychological contract theory to consider the impact of a breach on subsequent retention and found two clear mediational pathways – regarding fairness and trust (Clinton & Guest 2014). Their results affirm the importance of psychological expectations in maintaining staff, with trustworthy employers able to fulfil and not violate their employees' expectations.

Research in this area is important in revealing the pathways that precipitate employees' decisions to leave. Although many consider separation between intention and behaviour, it is striking that most use recall rather than a more dynamic means of exploring trust. Again this is an area where longitudinal study could be invaluable. It is also a context in which multi-foci relational trust might be used to produce more fine-grained differentiation of the roles of trust in co-worker, line manager, HR professional and top team in retention and leaving decisions (see Chapter 8 by Fulmer). An unanswered question is whether staff leave because of low trust or distrust.

HR value, professionals and managers

This penultimate section briefly directs attention towards the uniqueness of this context in accessing inclusion of the role of the HR profession in organizational trust. In the preceding sections, I have explicitly drawn attention to those few studies that have included this profession; they have explored the role of trust in HR managers' decisions (Tzafrir 2005), the experiences of HR professionals in bullying and harassment (Harrington & Rayner 2011; Harrington, et al. 2012) and downsizing (Buckley 2011). More recently, a study has looked at the role of trust at three levels (line manager, HR professional and organization) in employees' decisions to divulge sensitive informational about their sexual orientation (Capell, et al. 2016). Although elsewhere in HR, scholars have considered differences in the intentions, enactment and experiences of HR policies (Nishii & Wright 2008; Guest & Conway 2011), they have not included trust. Some trust scholars have commented on HR professionals as caught in a distinct role as agents of the organization (Dietz, et al. 2011). The relationships between HR professionals and managers can automatically make them distrusted by employees, rendering HR policy ineffectual, inconsistent and potentially more harmful to victims (Ferris 2004). The contextual complexities of trust in this area really remain largely unexplored, making it a fertile ground for multi-level trust scholarship.

Future research agendas

In each section, I have identified areas for further exploration of trust regarding specific HR policies and practices. Future study might take different approaches and I outline five advances needed here. Most critical, in terms of study design, is the lack of longitudinal focus to better illuminate the developments of trust in both the organization and the different referents (Searle & Skinner 2011). The dynamics *between* HR policies, especially the potential spillovers and interrelationships that might exist over the course of an employee cycle, remain under-examined. Thus, the triggers and trajectories for employees' trust developments over time remain largely unchartered. However, given the recent development in conceptualization of time, it is important that future researchers pay attention to transitions and the way time may play a role (see Shipp & Fried 2014; Shipp & Cole 2015 for more detailed discussions of temporal aspects).

Second, as noted earlier, there are many neglected areas. Specifically, little attention has been paid to pre-employment interactions which may be central to the early formation of unrealistic psychological contracts and the decline of trust in the organization. Also, little direct work has examined the conceptual arguments of importance of HR in trust repair (Gillespie & Dietz 2009). Given the parallel scholarly attention to post-violation for psychological contracts (Tomprou, et al. 2015), there are obvious connections between these two areas that could be productively explored.

Third, going forward, in studying HR, trust studies must consider interpersonal and systems-based trust. Interpersonal trust conceptualizations could draw on the multi-foci approach as Fulmer outlines in her chapter. Fourth, the range of conceptual lenses could be expanded. While justice is an important factor to include in studies, and I have specifically noted those that have, this related field has new concepts, such as anticipated justice (Guo, et al. 2011), which may be important for trust scholars to include in their studies. While social exchange theory dominates, other conceptual lenses might be important in teasing out the distinctions between confidence and vulnerability, as Colquitt and colleagues (2011) have done. To this end, fairness heuristic theory and uncertainty management theory (Lind & Van den Bos 2002; Van den Bos & Lind 2002) offer considerable potential (see Chapter 10 by Lind, for more details). Similarly this is a context where emotion-based trust could also be productive (see Chapter 1 by van Knippenberg). Work that uses theories to explore the relationship between attitudes and subsequent behaviours, such as reasoned action theory (Ajzen & Fishbein 1973; Fishbein & Ajzen 1975; Ajzen & Fishbein 1977), may also be fruitful choices for scholars studying employees' retention (Tzafrir & Enosh 2011).

Finally, individual differences factors, particularly propensity to trust, remain omitted in much of the research. They are found to enhance perceptions of trust (Searle, et al. 2011), but may have a role in shaping perceptions of fairness too (Bianchi & Brockner 2012). Such measures may be of value in understanding why the impact of the same experience may vary between individuals. It is striking that dimensions, including gender, remain neglected (for exceptions see Lee & Farh 1999; Searle, et al. 2011). Diversity is another fertile area, with evidence suggesting policies may be perceived in different ways by those from minority groups (Wyatt & Silvester 2015). We know little of the clues and signals used by different genders and minority groups, yet there are debates in HR on how members of minority groups favour colour-blind

(Apfelbaum, et al. 2012) HR approaches, while "sex aware" (Koenig & Richeson 2010) policies are attended to more by women. What happens to trust levels of these different groups of employee? Similarly, little attention has been paid to considering trust in HR practices where employee experiences might vary due to their religious beliefs, sexual orientation or tribal affiliation. We need to understand these nuances between employees better to discern whether trust is best served by having a "one size fits all" approach.

HR is an important crucible in which to explore trust. It comprises many germane issues and there are many remaining lacunas that require empirical attention. It is a very promising context in which to understand individual differences, relationship, and systems that might build, sustain and cause breaches of trust.

Note

1 Israel is typically found to be more aligned in its policies with more Western countries, such as Germany.

References

Ajzen, I. and M. Fishbein (1973). "Attitudinal and normative variables as predictors of specific behavior." *Journal of Personality and Social Psychology* 27(1): 41–57.

Ajzen, I. and M. Fishbein (1977). "Attitude-behavior relations: A theoretical analysis and review of empirical research." *Psychological bulletin* 84(5): 888 – 918.

Albrecht, S. and A. Travaglione (2003). "Trust in public-sector senior management." *International Journal of Human Resource Management* 14(1): 76–92.

Alfes, K., A. Shantz and C. Truss (2012). "The link between perceived HRM practices, performance and well-being: The moderating effect of trust in the employer." *Human Resource Management Journal* 22(4): 409–427.

Apfelbaum, E. P., M. I. Norton and S. R. Sommers (2012). "Racial color blindness: Emergence, practice, and implications." *Current Directions in Psychological Science* 21(3): 205–209.

Appelbaum, E., T. Bailey, P. Berg and A. L. Kalleberg (2001). Do high performance work systems pay off? In S. Valles (ed.) *Research in the sociology of work series, Vol. 10*. Bingley, UK: Emerald Group Publishing. pp.85–107.

Aquino, K., R. W. Griffeth, D. G. Allen and P. W. Hom (1997). "Integrating justice constructs into the turnover process: A test of a referent cognitions model." *Academy of Management Journal* 40(5): 1208–1227.

Ashleigh, M. and J. Prichard (2011). Enhancing trust through training. In R. H. Searle and D. Skinner (eds) *Trust and Human Resource Management*. Cheltenham, UK: Edward Elgar Publishing. pp.125–138.

Bauer, T. N., D. M. Truxillo, K. Mack and A. B. Costa (2011). Applicant reactions to technology-based selection: What we know so far. In N. T. Tippins, S. Adler and A. I. Kraut (eds) *Technology-Enhanced Assessment of Talent*, San Francisco, CA: Jossey-Bass. pp.190–223.

Bauer, T. N., D. M. Truxillo, M. E. Paronto, J. A. Weekley and M. A. Campio (2004). "Applicant reactions to different selection technology: Face-to-face, interactive voice response, and computer-assisted telephone screening interviews." *International Journal of Selection & Assessment* 12(1/2): 135–148.

Bernardin, H. J., B. E. Richey and S. L. Castro (2011). "Mandatory and binding arbitration: Effects on employee attitudes and recruiting results." *Human Resource Management* 50(2): 175–200.

Bianchi, E. C. and J. Brockner (2012). "In the eyes of the beholder? The role of dispositional trust in judgments of procedural and interactional fairness." *Organizational Behavior and Human Decision Processes* 118(1): 46–59.

Bijlsma-Frankema, K., S. B. Sitkin and A. Weibel (2015). "Distrust in the balance: The emergence and development of intergroup distrust in a court of law." *Organization Science* 26(4): 1018–1039

Blau, P. M. (1964). *Exchange and Power in Social Life*. New York and London: John Wiley & Sons.

Blunsdon, B. and K. Reed (2003). "The effects of technical and social conditions on workplace trust." *International Journal of Human Resource Management* 14(1): 12–27.

Boselie, P., G. Dietz and C. Boon (2005). "Commonalities and contradictions in HRM and performance research." *Human Resource Management Journal* 15(3): 67–94.

Bragger, J. D., E. J. Kutcher, A. Menier, V. I. Sessa and K. Sumner (2014). "Giving nonselective downsizing a performance review." *Human Resource Development Review* 13(1): 58–78.

Brockner, J., R. L. Dewitt, S. Grover and T. Reed (1990). "When it is especially important to explain why: Factors affecting the relationship between managers explanations of a layoff and survivors reactions to the layoff." *Journal of Experimental Social Psychology* 26(5): 389–407.

Brockner, J. and P. A. Siegel (1996). Understanding the interaction between procedural and distributive justice: The role of trust. In R. Kramer and T. Tyler *Trust in Organisations: Frontiers of Theory and Research*. Thousand Oaks, CA: SAGE. pp.390–413.

Brodt, S. E. and A. Dionisi (2011). When peers become leaders: The effects of internal promotion on workgroup dynamics. In R. H. Searle and D. Skinner (eds) *Trust and Human Resource Management*. Cheltenham, UK: Edward Elgar Publishing. pp.247–267.

Brown, S., D. Gray, J. McHardy and K. Taylor (2015). "Employee trust and workplace performance." *Journal of Economic Behavior & Organization* 116(C): 361–378.

Buckley, F. (2011). Trust and engagement in a downsizing context: The impact on human resource managers. In R. H. Searle and D. Skinner (eds) *Trust and Human Resource Management*. Cheltenham, UK: Edward Elgar Publishing. pp.309–329.

Capell, B., S. S. Tzafrir and S. L. Dolan (2016). "The disclosure of concealable stigmas: Analysis anchored in trust." *Cogent Psychology* 3(1): 1121066.

Celani, A., S. Deutsch-Salamon and P. Singh (2008). "In justice we trust: A model of the role of trust in the organization in applicant reactions to the selection process." *Human Resource Management Review* 18(2): 63–76.

Chen, C. C., Y.-R. Chen and K. Xin (2004). "Guanxi practices and trust in management: A procedural justice perspective." *Organization Science* 15(2): 200–209.

Chenhall, R. H. and K. Langfield-Smith (2003). "Performance measurement and reward systems, trust, and strategic change." *Journal of Management Accounting Research* 15(1): 117–143.

Cho, Y. J. and J. W. Lee (2012). "Performance management and trust in supervisors." *Review of Public Personnel Administration* 32(3): 236–259.

Cho, Y. J. and T. H. Poister (2013). "Human resource management practices and trust in public organizations." *Public Management Review* 15(6): 816–838.

Clinton, M. E. and D. E. Guest (2014). "Psychological contract breach and voluntary turnover: Testing a multiple mediation model." *Journal of Occupational and Organizational Psychology* 87(1): 200–207.

Colquitt, J. A. (2001). "On the dimensionality of organizational justice: A construct validation of a measure." *Journal of Applied Psychology* 86(3): 386–400.

Colquitt, J. A., J. A. LePine, R. F. Piccolo, C. P. Zapata and B. L. Rich (2011). "Explaining the justice-performance relationship: Trust as exchange deepener or trust as uncertainty reducer?" *Journal of Applied Psychology* 97(1): 1–15.

Cooke, F. L., J. Shen and A. McBride (2005). "Outsourcing HR as a competitive strategy? A literature review and an assessment of implications." *Human Resource Management* 44(4): 413–432.

Crawshaw, J. R. and F. C. Brodbeck (2011). "Justice and trust as antecedents of careerist orientation." *Personnel Review* 40(1): 106–125.

De Cremer, D., J. Brockner, A. Fishman, M. van Dijke, W. van Olffen and D. M. Mayer (2010). "When do procedural fairness and outcome fairness interact to influence employees' work attitudes and behaviors? The moderating effect of uncertainty." *Journal of Applied Psychology* 95(2): 291–304.

Dean, J. W., P. Brandes and R. Dharwadkar (1998). "Organizational cynicism." *Academy of Management Review* 23(2): 341–352.

Dekker, H. C. (2004). "Control of inter-organizational relationships: Evidence on appropriation concerns and coordination requirements." *Accounting, Organizations and Society* 29(1): 27–49.

Dietz, G., A. Martins and R. H. Searle (2011). Trust, HRM and the Employment relationship. In A. Wilkinson and K. Townsend *The Future of Employment Relations: New Paradigms, New Developments*. Basingstoke, UK: Palgrave MacMillian. pp.141–164.

Earley, P. C. (1986). "Trust, perceived importance of praise and criticism, and work performance: An examination of feedback in the United States and England." *Journal of Management* 12(4): 457–473.

Emerson, R. M. (1962). "Power-dependence relations." *American Sociological Review.* 27(1): 31–41.

Emerson, R. M. (1972). Exchange theory, part II: Exchange relations and networks. In J. Berger, M. Zelditch and B. Anderson (eds) *Sociological Theories in Progress, Volume 2*. Boston, MA: Houghton Mifflin. pp.58–87.

Ertürk, A. (2014). "Influences of HR practices, social exchange, and trust on turnover intentions of public IT Professionals." *Public Personnel Management* 43(1): 140–175.

Farndale, E., V. Hope-Hailey and C. Kelliher (2011). "High commitment performance management: The roles of justice and trust." *Personnel Review* 40(1): 5–23.

Farndale, E. and C. Kelliher (2013). "Implementing performance appraisal: Exploring the employee experience." *Human Resource Management* 52(6): 879–897.

Ferrin, D. L. and N. Gillespie (2010). Trust differences across national-societal cultures: Much to do, or much ado about nothing. In M. N. Saunders, D. Skinner, G. Dietz, N. Gillespie and R. J. Lewicki (eds) *Organisational Trust: A Cultural Perspective*. New York: Cambridge University Press. pp.42–86.

Ferris, P. (2004). "A preliminary typology of organisational response to allegations of workplace bullying: see no evil, hear no evil, speak no evil." *British Journal of Guidance & Counselling* 32(3): 389–395.

Fishbein, M. and I. Ajzen (1975). *Belief, Attitude, Intention and Behavior: An Introduction to Theory and Research*. Reading, MA: Addison-Wesley.

Folger, R. and M. Konovsky (1989). "Effects of procedural and distributive justice on reactions to pay raise decisions." *Academy of Management Journal* 32(1): 115–130.

Fox, A. (1974). *Beyond Contract: Work, Power and Trust Relations*. London: Faber and Faber.

Fulk, J., A. P. Brief and S. H. Barr (1985). "Trust-in-supervisor and perceived fairness and accuracy of performance evaluations." *Journal of Business Research* 13(4): 301–313.

Gillespie, N. and G. Dietz (2009). "Trust repair after an organization-level failure." *Academy of Management Review* 34(1): 127–145.

Gould-Williams, J. (2003). "The importance of HR practices and workplace trust in achieving superior performance: A study of public-sector organizations." *International Journal of Human Resource Management* 14(1): 28–54.

Gould-Williams, J. and F. Davies (2005). "Using social exchange theory to predict the effects of HRM practice on employee outcomes: An analysis of public sector workers." *Public Management Review* 7(1): 1–24.

Guest, D. and N. Conway (1999). "Peering into the black hole: The downside of the new employment relations in the UK." *British Journal of Industrial Relations* 37(3): 367–389.

Guest, D. and N. Conway (2011). "The impact of HR practices, HR effectiveness and a 'strong HR system' on organisational outcomes: A stakeholder perspective." *The International Journal of Human Resource Management* 22(8): 1686–1702.

Guinot, J., R. Chiva and F. Mallén (2013). "Organizational trust and performance: Is organizational learning capability a missing link?" *Journal of Management & Organization* 19(5): 559–582.

Guo, J., D. E. Rupp, H. Weiss and J. Trougakos (2011). Organizational justice: A person-centric approach. In S. Gilliland, D. Steiner and D. Skarlicki (eds) *Research in Social Issues in Management, Volume 7*. Charlotte, NC: Information Age Publishing. pp.3–32.

Harrington, S. and C. Rayner (2011). Whose side are you on? Trust and HR in workplace bullying. In R. H. Searle and D. Skinner (eds) *Trust and Human Resource Management*. Cheltenham, UK: Edward Elgar Publishing. pp.223–245.

Harrington, S., C. Rayner and S. Warren (2012). "Too hot to handle? Trust and human resource practitioners' implementation of anti-bullying policy." *Human Resource Management Journal* 22(4): 392–408.

Homans, G. C. (1961). *Social Behaviour: Its Elementary Forms*. London: Routledge & Kegan Paul.

Hope-Hailey, V., R. Searle and G. Dietz (2012). *Where Has All the trust Gone?* London: CIPD.

Ichniowski, C. and K. Shaw (2003). "Beyond incentive pay: Insiders' estimates of the value of complementary human resource management practices." *The Journal of Economic Perspectives* 17(1): 155–180.

Innocenti, L., M. Pilati and A. M. Peluso (2011). "Trust as moderator in the relationship between HRM practices and employee attitudes." *Human Resource Management Journal* 21(3): 303–317.

Kim, S. and P. M. Wright (2011). "Putting strategic human resource management in context: A context-ualized model of high commitment work systems and its implications in China." *Management and Organization Review* 7(1): 153–174.

Klotz, A. C., S. P. Motta Veiga, M. R. Buckley and M. B. Gavin (2013). "The role of trustworthiness in recruitment and selection: A review and guide for future research." *Journal of Organizational Behavior* 34(S1): S104-S119.

Koenig, A. M. and J. A. Richeson (2010). "The contextual endorsement of sexblind versus sexaware ideologies." *Social Psychology* 41(3): 186–191.

Lapointe, É., C. Vandenberghe and J.-S. Boudrias (2014). "Organizational socialization tactics and newcomer adjustment: The mediating role of role clarity and affect-based trust relationships." *Journal of Occupational and Organizational Psychology* 87(3): 599–624.

Lazarus, R. S. and S. Folkman (1984). *Stress, Appraisal, and Coping.* New York: Springer.

Lee, C. and J.-L. L. Farh (1999). "The effects of gender in organizational justice perception." *Journal of Organizational Behavior* 20(1): 133–143.

Leventhal, G. S., J. Karuza and W. R. Fry (1980). "Beyond fairness: A theory of allocation preferences." *Justice and social interaction* 3: 167–218.

Lind, E. A. (2001). Fairness heuristic theory: Justice judgments as pivotal cognitions in organizational relations. In J. Greenberg and R. Cropanzano *Advances in Organizational Justice.* Stanford, CA: Stanford University Press. pp.56–88.

Lind, E. A. and K. Van den Bos (2002). "When fairness works: Toward a general theory of uncertainty management." *Research in Organizational Behavior* 24: 181–224.

Lo, S. and S. Aryee (2003). "Psychological contract breach in a Chinese context: An integrative approach." *Journal of Management Studies* 40(4): 1005–1020.

Maley, J. F. and M. Moeller (2014). "Global performance management systems: The role of trust as perceived by country managers." *Journal of Business Research* 67(1): 2803–2810.

Marchington, M. and I. Grugulis (2000). " 'Best practice' human resource management: Perfect opportunity or dangerous illusion?" *The International Journal of Human Resource Management* 11(6): 1104–1124.

Mather, K. (2011). Employee relations and the illusiveness of trust. In R. H. Searle and D. Skinner (eds) *Trust and Human Resource Management.* Cheltenham, UK: Edward Elgar Publishing. pp.201–222.

Mayer, R. C., Davis, J. H. and Schoorman, F. D. (1995). "An Integrative Model of Organizational Trust." *Academy of Management Review* 20(3): 709–734.

Mayer, R. C. and J. H. Davis (1999). "The effect of the performance appraisal system on trust for management: A field quasi-experiment." *Journal of Applied Psychology* 84(1): 123–136.

McKnight, D. H., L. L. Cummings and N. L. Chervany (1998). "Initial trust formation in new organizational relationships." *Academy of Management Review* 23(3): 473–491.

Mishra, A. and G. M. Spreitzer (1998). "Explaining how survivors respond to downsizing: The roles of trust, empowerment, justice, and work redesign." *Academy of Management Review* 23(3): 567–588.

Morgan, D. E. and R. Zeffane (2003). "Employee involvement, organizational change and trust in management." *The International Journal of Human Resource Management* 14(1): 55–75.

Ng, T. W. H. (2015). "The incremental validity of organizational commitment, organizational trust, and organizational identification." *Journal of Vocational Behavior* 88: 154–163.

Nishii, L. H. and P. Wright (2008). Variability within organizations: Implications for strategic human resource management. In D. B. Smith. Mahwah *The People Make the Place.* NJ: Lawrence Erlbaum Associates pp.225–248.

Parzefall, M. R. (2012). "A close call: Perceptions of alternative HR arrangements to layoffs." *Journal of Managerial Psychology* 27(8): 799–813.

Pearce, J. L. (1993). "Toward an organizational-behavior of contract laborers: Their psychological involvement and effects on employee coworkers." *Academy of Management Journal* 36(5): 1082–1096.

Pearce, J. L., I. Branyiczki and G. A. Bigley (2000). "Insufficient bureaucracy: Trust and commitment in particularistic rganizations." *Organization Science* 11(2): 148–162.

Pfeffer, J. and J. F. Veiga (1999). "Putting people first for organizational success." *Academy of Management Executive* 13(2): 37–48.

Pugh, S. D., D. P. Skarlicki and B. S. Passell (2003). "After the fall: Layoff victims' trust and cynicism in re-employment." *Journal of Occupational & Organizational Psychology* 76(2): 201–212.

Reilly, P. A. (1998). "Balancing flexibility—Meeting the interests of employer and employee." *European Journal of Work and Organizational Psychology* 7(1): 7–22.

Robinson, S. (1996). "Trust and breach of the psychological contract." *Administrative Science Quarterly* 41(4): 574–599.

Robinson, S., M. Kraatz and D. Rousseau (1994). "Changing obligations and the psychological contract: A longitudinal study." *Academy of Management Journal* 37(1): 137–152.

Robinson, S. L. and E. W. Morrison (2000). "The development of psychological contract breach and violation: A longitudinal study." *Journal of Organizational Behavior* 21(5): 525–546.

Robinson, S. L. and D. M. Rousseau (1994). "Violating the psychological contract: Not the exception but the norm." *Journal of Organizational Behavior* 15(3): 245–259.

Sako, M. (1998). Does trust improve business performance? In C. Lane and R. Bachmann *Trust Within and Between Organizations*. Oxford, UK: Oxford University Press. pp.31–63.

Saunders, M. N. K. and A. Thornhill (2003). "Organisational justice, trust and the management of change: An exploration." *Personnel Review* 32(3): 360–375.

Saunders, M. and A. Thornhill (2004). "Trust and mistrust in organizations: An exploration using an organizational justice framework." *European Journal of Work and Organizational Psychology* 13(4): 493–515.

Schaubroeck, J., S. S. K. Lam and A. C. Peng (2011). "Cognition-based and affect-based trust as mediators of leader behavior influences on team performance." *Journal of Applied Psychology* 96(4): 863–871.

Searle, R. H. (2013). HRM and trust, or trust and HRM? An underdeveloped context for trust research. In R. Bachmann and A. Zaheer *Advances in Trust Research*. Cheltenham, UK: Edward Elgar Publishing. pp.9–28.

Searle, R. H. and K. S. Ball (2004). "The development of trust and distrust in a merger." *Journal of Managerial Psychology* 19(7): 708–721.

Searle, R. H. and J. Billsberry (2011). The development and destruction of organizational trust during recruitment and selection. In R. H. Searle and D. Skinner (eds) *Trust and Human Resource Management*. Cheltenham, UK: Edward Elgar Publishing. pp.67–86.

Searle, R. H., D. Den Hartog, A. Weibel, N. Gillespie, F. Six, T. Hatzakis and D. Skinner (2011). "Trust in the employer: The role of high involvement work practices and procedural justice in European organizations." *International Journal of Human Resource Management*. 22(5): 1068–1091.

Searle, R. H. and Skinner, D. (2011). Introduction. In R. H. Searle and D. Skinner (eds) *Trust and Human Resource Management*. Cheltenham, UK: Edward Elgar Publishing. pp.3–17.

Searle, R. H. and D. Skinner (2011). Organisational trust in the context of performance appraisal: An empirical study. *European Group of Organization Studies (EGOS) Track Organizational Trust*. Gothenburg, Sweden: Edward Elgar Publishing.

Searle, R. H. and D. Skinner (eds), (2011). *Trust and Human Resources Management*. Cheltenahm, UK: Edward Elgar Publishing.

Shipp, A. J. and M. S. Cole (2015). "Time in individual-level organizational studies: What is it, how is it used, and why isn't it exploited more often?" *Annual Review of Organizational Psychology and Organizational Behavior* 2(1): 237–260.

Shipp, A. J. and Y. Fried (2014). *Time and Work, Volume 1: How Time Impacts Individuals*, Hove, UK: Psychology Press.

Skinner, D. and R. H. Searle (2011). Trust in the context of performance appraisal. In R. H. Searle and D. Skinner (eds) *Trust and Human Resource Management*. Cheltenham, UK: Edward Elgar Publishing. pp.177–197.

Smollan, R. K. (2013). "Trust in change managers: The role of affect." *Journal of Organizational Change Management* 26(4): 725–747.

Snell, S. A. and J. W. Dean (1992). "Integrated manufacturing and human resource management: A human capital perspective." *Academy of Management Journal* 35(3): 467–504.

Spreitzer, G. M. and A. K. Mishra (1997). *Survivor Responses to Downsizing: The Mitigating Effects of Trust and Empowerment*. Southern California Studies Center, Los Angeles, CA: University of California.

Spreitzer, G. M. and A. K. Mishra (1999). "Giving up control without losing control: Trust and its substitutes' effects on managers' involving employees in decision making." *Group & Organization Management* 24(2): 155–187.

Spreitzer, G. M. and A. K. Mishra (2002). "To stay or to go: Voluntary survivor turnover following an organizational downsizing." *Journal of Organizational Behavior* 23(6): 707–729.

Tomprou, M., D. M. Rousseau and S. D. Hansen (2015). "The psychological contracts of violation victims: A post-violation model." *Journal of Organizational Behavior* 36(4): 561–581.

Tremblay, M., J. Cloutier, G. Simard, D. Chênevert and C. Vandenberghe (2010). "The role of HRM practices, procedural justice, organizational support and trust in organizational commitment and in-role and extra-role performance." *The International Journal of Human Resource Management* 21(3): 405–433.

Tzafrir, S. S. (2005). "The relationship between trust, HRM practices and firm performance." *International Journal of Human Resource Management* 16(9): 1600–1622.

Tzafrir, S. and G. Enosh (2011). Beyond attitudes and norms: trust commitment and HR values as triggers of intention to leave. In R. H. Searle and D. Skinner (eds) *Trust and Human Resource Management*. Cheltenham, UK: Edward Elgar Publishing pp.289–308.

Tzafrir, S. S. and A. B.-A. Gur (2007). "HRM practices and perceived service quality: The role of trust as a mediator." *Research and Practice in Human Resource Management* 15(2): 1–20.

Tzafrir, S. S., A. B.-A. Gur and O. Blumen (2015). "Employee social environment (ESE) as a tool to decrease intention to leave." *Scandinavian Journal of Management* 31(1): 136–146.

Tzafrir, S., G. H. Harel, Y. Baruch and S. Dolan (2004). "The consequences of emerging HRM practices for employees' trust in their managers." *Personnel Review* 33(5–6): 628–647.

van den Bos, K. (2001). Fairness heuristic theory. Assessing the information to which people are reacting has a pivotal role in understanding organizational justice. In S. Gilliland, S. D. and D. Skarlicki *Theoretical and Cultural Perspectives on Organizational Justice*. Greenwich, CT: Information Age. pp.63–84.

van den Bos, K. and E. A. Lind (2002). "Uncertainty management by means of fairness judgments." *Advances in Experimental Social Psychology* 34: 1–60.

van der Werff, L. and F. Buckley (2014). "Getting to know you: A longitudinal examination of trust cues and trust development during socialization." *Journal of Management* 43(3): 742–770.

Weibel, A., D. N. Den Hartog, N. Gillespie, R. Searle, F. Six and D. Skinner (2016). "How do controls impact employee trust in the employer?" *Human Resource Management* 55(3): 437–462.

Whitener, E. M. (1997). "The impact of human resources activities on employees trust." *Human Resource Management Review* 7(4): 389–404.

Whitener, E. M. (2001). "Do 'high commitment' human resource practices affect employee commitment? A cross-level analysis using hierarchical linear modeling." *Journal of Management* 27(5): 515–535.

Wong, Y.-T. (2012). "Job security and justice: Predicting employees' trust in Chinese international joint ventures." *The International Journal of Human Resource Management* 23(19): 4129–4144.

Wright, P. M. and W. R. Boswell (2002). "Desegregating HRM: a review and synthesis of micro and macro human resource management research." *Journal of Management* 28(3): 247 – 276.

Wyatt, M. and J. Silvester (2015). "Reflections on the labyrinth: Investigating black and minority ethnic leaders' career experiences." *Human Relations* 68(8): 1243–1269.

Zhang, Y., L. Long, T.-y. Wu and X. Huang (2015). "When is pay for performance related to employee creativity in the Chinese context? The role of guanxi HRM practice, trust in management, and intrinsic motivation." *Journal of Organizational Behavior* 36(5): 698–719.

29

TWO SIDES OF AN IMPORTANT COIN

Outlining the general parameters of control-trust research

Chris P. Long and Antoinette Weibel

Introduction

This chapter reviews research on control-trust dynamics by outlining how and why control *and* trust jointly constitute vital components of organizational effectiveness (Adler, 2001; Bradach & Eccles, 1989; Emsley & Kidon, 2007; Long, 2010; Ross, 1994). Controls describe the actions that individuals and organizations take to direct others to achieve objectives by specifying, channelling attention and effort as well as measuring, monitoring and incentivizing/sanctioning work (Dekker, 2004; Fayol, 1949; Ouchi, 1979). When individuals foster trust they generate a level of confidence in them that encourages others to have positive expectations about their intentions and behaviours (Rousseau, Sitkin, Burt, & Camerer, 1998).

Scholars have focused their attention on control-trust dynamics for two primary reasons. First, because research indicates that, to the extent that trustees (e.g. managers, leaders decision-makers) generate appropriate levels of control and trust among their trustors (e.g. subordinates, followers, decision-recipients) in work environments, they are able to foster high levels of goal commitment, compliance and cooperation (Christ, 2013; Dirks & Ferrin, 2002; Eisenhardt, 1989; Ouchi, 1977, 1979; Williamson, 1975), an increased willingness to communicate and exchange information (Sitkin & Bies 1994; Coletti, et al., 2005), enhance the perceived legitimacy of their own and their organization's actions (Blau, 1964), and increase levels of organizational performance (Cao & Lumineau, 2015).

The second reason that scholars have focused attention on control-trust dynamics is because control and trust direct, motivate and coordinate interdependent actors through distinctly different and often opposing psychological mechanisms such as the desire to increase intimacy and the desire to avoid vulnerability (Anderson, Christ, Dekker, & Sedatole, 2013; Coletti, Sedatole, & Towry, 2005; Emsley & Kidon, 2007; Ross, 1994; Vosselman & van der Meer-Kooistra, 2009; Weibel, 2007). The key tension that exists is this: when managers rely too much on controls, they may compromise their subordinates' desires for self-determination that are necessary to effectively foster their trust (Blau, 1964; Christ, Sedatole, Towry, & Thomas, 2008; Coletti, et al., 2005; Fox, 1974; Long & Sitkin, 2006; Shapiro, 1987: Weibel, 2007; Weibel &

Six, 2013). Conversely, if managers focus too much on building trust by providing their sub-ordinates autonomy and addressing their personal needs, they may fail to effectively control their subordinates in ways that motivate them to accomplish desired objectives (Dekker, 2004; Emsley & Kidon, 2007; Long, 2010; Shapiro, 1987; Spreitzer & Mishra, 1999). Thus, while important, it is often hard for managers and organizations who operate in complex and uncertain environments to establish and maintain the optimal balance between control and trust (Blau, 1964; Christ, 2013; Long, 2010; Long & Sitkin, 2006; Sitkin, 1995; Ouchi, 1979, 1980; Weibel, Wildhaber, et al., 2016).

Scholarly work examining these issues addresses a range of interpersonal and organizational/institutional issues from a variety of disciplinary perspectives. By reviewing these viewpoints, this chapter aims to achieve three primary objectives. First, existing work on control-trust relationships is organized and reviewed in ways that distil and highlight its central contributions. Second, this review also draws attention to persistent and ongoing theoretical and empirical debates in this topical area. Third, an agenda for future research is presented towards the end of the chapter that charts a way forward and provides some suggestions for addressing persistent, theoretical dilemmas. By examining important scholarship in this area, a practical objective motivating this review is to provide managers and organizations with ways to more critically evaluate their own decisions regarding how they direct their subordinates and, at the same time, develop quality work relationships with them.

Conceptualizing control and trust

A distinctive feature about current control-trust research is that scholars have used a relatively wide variety of control, trustworthiness and trust concepts and measures in their theoretical and empirical work (Ferrin, Bligh, & Kohles, 2007). The control, trust and trustworthiness concepts most commonly used in this literature are summarized below.

Control

Controls generally describe desired standards that managers use to direct employees' work activities and apply rewards or sanctions according to their employees' achieved performances on the dimensions they specify (Ouchi, 1979; Weibel, Den Hartog et al., 2016). Scholars in the control-trust domain have traditionally adopted broad definitions of controls that include a variety of mechanisms managers can use to ensure that individuals and organizational units 'act in a coordinated and cooperative fashion, so that resources will be obtained and optimally allocated in order to achieve the organization's goals' (Lebas & Weigenstein, 1986: 259).

For example, differences in the content and effects produced by formal and informal controls comprise a key set of issues on which scholars have focused (Ouchi, 1977; Mintzberg, 1979; Roth, Sitkin & House, 1994; Sitkin & Roth, 1993). *Formal controls* describe mechanisms that are institutionally sanctioned and generally manifest in codified rules and directives. These mechanisms include written contract parameters, hiring criteria, goal specifications, formal performance management HR practices or standard operating procedures. In contrast, *informal control mechanisms* describe a range of often unwritten but collectively understood values, norms and beliefs that guide employees' decisions and actions. Examples of informal control mechanisms include culturally accepted norms for communicating, exchanging information, managing performance and enforcing contract agreements (Cao & Lumineau, 2015; Cardinal, Sitkin, & Long, 2010; Kirsch, 2004). Using the formal–informal distinction, scholars utilize a wide variety of control mechanisms, policies and procedures, control systems, as well as singular and multiple contract-based specifications in their work. As is described below, researchers have repeatedly demonstrated how controls that are applied using formal and informal means often generate distinctly different reactions from control recipients.

Another key distinction between types of controls used in this research describes the target of the control. A common distinction differentiates whether controls are targeted to the input (e.g. personnel, selection, training, values), process (e.g. action, behaviours, procedures, routines, practices) or output (e.g. outcome, results) portion of the production process (Merchant, 1985; Snell, 1992; Cardinal, et al., 2004, 2010; Long, Burton & Cardinal, 2002; Ouchi, 1977: 1979). *Output controls* (e.g. incentives, targets, goal-based standards) are applied to ensure the attainment of desired performance standards by comparing achieved outputs against results-based standards (Ouchi, 1977, 1979; Mintzberg, 1979). *Process controls* (rules, norms, SOPs) are applied to individuals performing organizational tasks to ensure that they employ prescribed methods in doing their work. *Input controls* in the form of selection, training and socialization mechanisms are applied to choose and ready human and material resources for their roles in production (Arvey, 1979; Van Maanen & Schein, 1979; Wanous, 1980).

While Cardinal, Sitkin and Long (2010) argue that input, process and output controls can each be applied in either formal or informal ways, significant portions of the literature have yet to fully adopt this conceptualization. Instead, several scholars tend to combine control form and target by arguing that output and process controls constitute formal controls because they tend to be applied in ways that restrict subordinate autonomy (Das & Teng, 1998, 2001; Inkpen & Currall, 2004). They contrast these controls with clan or social controls which scholars suggest comprise informal, normatively focused input control mechanisms that foster collegiality by placing fewer restrictions on individual autonomy and facilitate the development of shared norms and values (Ouchi, 1980; Van Maanen & Schein, 1979; Weibel, Den Hartog, et al., 2016).

Recently, control-trust researchers have begun to distinguish controls by the function they serve in monitoring or coordinating production activities (Cao & Lumineau, 2015; Das & Teng, 2001; Malhotra & Lumineau, 2011; Mallewigt, et al., 2007; Velez et al., 2008). When controls are used to 'monitor' work, they are applied in ways that facilitate the supervision, measuring and rewarding (i.e. or pushing) of work performances. Research to date has focused on how managers use the monitoring function of controls to reduce subordinate opportunism by providing managers with key indicators of aberrant performance and providing them with mechanisms to align superior-subordinate incentives. Alternatively, scholars suggest that controls can also be used to coordinate the work of interdependent actors in uncertain environments. In coordinating, managers use controls to enhance planning and decision-making by directing attention and transferring important information between distributed employees performing specialized tasks to enhance their learning, expertise and overall productive capacities.

Trust

Conceptualizations of trust vary in control-trust research with psychologists focusing on attributional processes that generate trust perceptions and attitudes, economists focusing on trustors' calculations of the level of confidence they maintain in trustees, and sociologists focusing on trust as a product of social embeddedness. In addition, forms of trust have been identified at various levels of analysis with referents ranging from individuals to organizations and institutions (Fulmer and Gelfand, 2012; Weibel, Den Hartog, et al., 2016).

Much research in the control-trust domain examines the development of a psychological state akin to interpersonal trust where individuals experience 'the intention to accept vulnerability based upon positive expectations of the intentions or behavior of another' (Rousseau, Sitkin,

Burt and Camerer, 1998: 395). Generally, this research attempts to identify if, how and to what extent trustors (those who trust/don't trust) think, feel and act towards trustees (those who are trusted/not trusted) and how those factors influence various outcomes (e.g. performance, relationship quality, job satisfaction, employee commitment).

Research to date has tended to focus on how individuals generate these trust-based assessments from the attributions developed from observing their trustees' words and actions. Much of this work has focused on the distinction between competence and goodwill trust because how controls are applied will differentially affect these forms of trust (Das and Teng, 1998, 2001; Mayer, et al., 1995; Sako, 1992). Competence trust develops when trustees are perceived to exhibit expertise and developed abilities to effectively perform important cognitive or technical tasks. Goodwill trust, on the other hand, is based on positive assessments of trustees' manifest values, moral character, authenticity, credibility and consideration of others' interests. Some control-trust research has further separated goodwill trust into two sub-dimensions of managerial trustworthiness that are consistent with the dimensions described by Mayer Davis and Schoorman (1995): their *benevolence* or interest in accommodating a trustor's specific needs and their *integrity* or their willingness to fulfil promises and obligations made to trustors.

A growing amount of research has begun to more closely examine the target of trustors' attributions. While much research already evaluates trust directed towards managers or exchange partners, researchers have recently begun to focus on the level trust that individual actors exhibit towards organizations, employers and other institutions (Weibel, Den Hartog, et al., 2016). This work builds from previous research by scholars such as Giddens (1990) who emphasizes how organizational policies and procedures that comprise abstract systems influence whether individuals develop trust in organizations and institutions (Cook and Wall 1980; Butler 1991; Tyler and Lind, 1992). Scholars suggest that this form of trust is based on aggregated assessments from multiple sources of evidence operating at various organizational levels (Rousseau et al. 1998; Zaheer, McEvily and Perrone 1998). Often, what is crucial in determining organizational/institutional trust are the decisions and performance management systems that a top management team or higher level organizational authorities put into place (Whitley 1999).

Control and trust as distinct concepts

Conceptualizations of control and trust extend past basic definitional issues and continue to examine interrelationships between these two conceptual mechanisms. Some scholars conceptualize trust as a form of control (Bradach and Eccles, 1989; Lebas and Weigenstein, 1986; Pennings and Woichesyn, 1987) and focus on how individuals make decisions to preserve forms of trust that develop around mutually beneficial, collegial and usually informal exchange relationships. More recent research has emphasized the distinctiveness of control and trust with various authors (e.g. Das and Teng, 2001; Long and Sitkin, 2006; McEvily, Perrone, and Zaheer, 2003; Nooteboom, 1996) arguing that control and trust constitute fundamentally different ways of managing interdependencies and uncertainties in organizations. These issues, however, remain unresolved with scholars such as Tomkins (2001) and Leifer and Mills (1996) suggesting that the existence of trust connotes the absence of control while others such as Möllering (2005) argue that control and trust comprise a 'duality' of omnipresent mechanisms that assume, create and refer (explicitly and implicitly) the existence of each other.

Critical theorists provide a related but distinct view on these matters by suggesting that the presence of both control and trust in organizations does not just happen but results from conscious efforts by authorities to subjugate their subordinates. For example, Jermier (1998), Reed (2001) and Roberts (2001) cite critical analyses describing how authorities force subordinate accountability using control and trust mechanisms embedded within complex organizational forms. Roberts (2001) discusses how higher authorities hold individuals accountable for complying with intricate networks of controls that foster forms of trust that are beneficial for them (Shapiro, 1987; Sydow and Windeler, 2003). They argue that when the inability or unwillingness of actors to exhibit desired forms of trust compromises performance within these systems, authorities assert their power by developing and implementing various forms of control that subjugate workers by overtly or covertly restraining their personal freedoms (Skinner and Spira, 2003; Walgenbach, 2001). Observations like these have given rise to a rather new branch of research that analyses the dark side of trust. This work specifies how trust can lead to unwanted (moral) obligations that force employees to think and act against their own interests and values (Skinner, Dietz, and Weibel, 2014).

Research on control-trust relations

An essential factor in control-trust dynamics is that controllees (those being controlled) cede at least some of their capacity for self-determination to their controllers (those trying to control) who specify their objectives, evaluate their performance, and provide them with both resources and remuneration in exchange for their work. This basic dynamic has been identified in relationships at various levels of analysis (i.e. in superior-subordinate, peer, or interorganizational relationships (IORs)). As controllees in these conditions feel more vulnerable to and dependent on their controllers, they are motivated to actively assess their controllers' motivations and intentions towards them (Weber, Malhotra, & Murnighan 2004). These assessments manifest in attributional processes that controllees use to evaluate if and how they can trust their controllers to promote their values and interests if they comply with the controls that are being used to direct them in their work.

Complements or substitutes?

The fundamental tension between control and trust that these relationships describe has given rise to one of the most enduring questions in the trust literature: whether control and trust are substitutes or complements (Costa and Biljsma-Frankema, 2007; McEvily et al. 2003; Poppo and Zenger, 2002; Weibel, Wildhaber et al., 2016). It is important to note that researchers who examine the 'nexus' of control and trust (Bijlsma-Frankema and Costa, 2005) have used the complementarity/substitution question to motivate two related but distinct streams of research. The first stream examines relationships between control and trust mechanisms to assess whether these factors are synergistically (i.e. are complements) or antithetically (i.e. are substitutes) related in the actions of controllers and the perceptions of controllees (Bijlsma-Frankema & Costa, 2005; Cao & Lumineau, 2015; Long & Sitkin, 2006; Sitkin, 1995) The second stream examines whether control and trust independently (i.e. are substitutes) or jointly (i.e. are complements) affect key performance outcomes (Cao & Lumineau, 2015; Costa and Bijlsma-Frankema, 2007; Ferrin, Bligh, and Kohles, 2007). Each of these streams is discussed separately below.

Relationships between control and trust

How forms of control affect trust

Research to date on relationships between control and trust has primarily modelled if and how managers' control applications influence various forms of trust. One theoretical maxim guiding much of this research is that when managers apply formal controls they discourage subordinate trust (Das and Teng 1998, 2001; Fox, 1974; Shapiro, 1987; Sitkin and Roth 2004). Scholars who examine both interpersonal and interorganizational relationships suggest that by prescribing and closely monitoring subordinates' goals or behaviours, managers who apply more formal controls (i.e. usually output or process controls) express distrust in their subordinates' reliability or competence. This leads subordinates to exhibit less confidence in managers who appear to be challenging their desires for autonomy, threatening their self-determination, and exhibiting an unwillingness to protect their personal or professional interests (Bijlsma-Frankema and Costa, 2005; Christ, Sedatole, Towry, and Thomas, 2008; Das and Teng 1998, 2001; Falk and Kosfeld, 2006; Ghoshal and Moran, 1996; Inkpen and Currall, 2004; Jagd, 2010; Kruglanski, 1970).

While this relationship appears robust, other researchers highlight how the negative association between formal controls and trust looks different when the details of these relationships are closely examined. For example, Sitkin (1995) emphasizes that formal controls can foster trust when they reduce perceived levels of risk and uncertainty, or prevent authorities from encroaching on their personal freedoms. Consistent with this, Emsley and Kidon (2004) and Malhotra and Lumineau (2011) both observe that while formal controls tend to compromise goodwill trust, managers who astutely apply formal controls to codify key coordination mechanisms can help to foster competence trust between exchange partners. Malhotra and Murnighan (2002) and Lumineau (2015) suggest that this may be particularly important early in relationships where formal controls can help exchange partners coordinate their activities to foster knowledge-based or more calculative forms of trust and cooperation. Finally, McKnight and colleagues (1998) argue that formal control allows trusting relationships to grow even in difficult situations when those controls are perceived as important institutional safeguards.

Research within this stream also suggests that informal controls (e.g. social controls) encourage individuals to forge more positive, trusting relationships that foster mutually acceptable goals, norms and values. This is because individuals who encounter informal controls feel subjected to lower levels of explicit monitoring and, as a result, feel less scrutinized, more autonomous and more respected by authorities (Christ et al. 2008). In addition, because they see authorities affirming their values and protecting their sense of self-determination, these individuals have high confidence that their interests will be protected (Bradach and Eccles 1989; Das and Teng 2001; Inkpen and Currall 2004; Malhotra and Murnighan 2002).

It is important to note that descriptions of dynamics related to informal controls often describe how these forms of control emerge as asset specificity, uncertainty and interdependence render more formal mechanisms of control, obsolete, unnecessary or counterproductive (Bijlsma and Costa, 2005). In these situations, informal controls help facilitate useful exchanges between partners who develop common sets of norms and values that can encourage the development of mutual relational, identification-based, or goodwill trust (Cao & Lumineau, 2015; Emsley & Kidon, 2004; Şengün & Wasti, 2007).

Control implementation and trust

As research on relationships between forms (i.e. formal or informal) of controls and trust continues, a growing amount of scholarly work is examining how subordinate trust is affected by the ways managers apply controls (Christ, 2013; Christ, Sedatole, & Towry, 2012). Colletti and colleagues (2005), for example, suggest that controls stimulate trust when they are implemented in ways that attenuate employees' relational risk perceptions and highlight the benefits of superior–subordinate cooperation. This can happen when managers apply controls in ways that affirm their subordinates' interests for self-determination, communicate that they share their values, care about them and want to foster positive relationships with them (Chenhall, Hall, & Smith, 2010; Christ, 2013; Christ et al., 2012; Vosselman & van der Meer-Kooristra, 2009).

Whitener and colleagues' (1998) work on managerial trustworthiness suggests that when managers apply controls in ways that are considerate of their needs, are consistent and effectively foster collaboration, they increase employee perceptions of trust (see also Dineen, Lewicki, & Tomlinson, 2007). Weibel (2007) argues that this happens when managers recognize their employees' desires for self-determination by including them in the development and implementation of controls, by increasing their knowledge and expertise through training and feedback, and by helping them understand the importance of their work (Burke, Sims, Lazzara, & Salas, 2007; Connell, Ferres, & Travaglione, 2003; Dineen, Lewicki, & Tomlinson, 2006).

Several authors emphasize the importance of transparency and fairness in fostering trust through control (Aryee, Budhwar, & Chen, 2002; De Cremer & Tyler, 2007; Whitener, 2001). Weibel and colleagues (2015), for example, demonstrate how controls elicit trust when they are applied fairly and consistently and that controls that are applied inconsistently or in opaque ways elicit subordinate distrust. Searle, et al. (2011), Korsgaard and colleagues (1995), and Bijlsma-Frankema and van de Bunt (2003) emphasize procedural fairness in observing how trust can be fostered through high involvement work practices that afford employees decision and process control. Lastly, Hartmann and Slapnicar (2009) and Mislin, Compagna and Bottom (2011) highlight the importance of interactional justice in control applications by outlining how managers should provide employees with relevant and timely performance feedback through formal and informal interpersonal interactions.

Control, trust and performance

An alternative perspective on the complementarity/substitution debate seeks to understand the joint impact of control and trust on key performance outcomes. Arguably, the most vibrant research in this area has examined IORs and has largely determined that issues of asset specificity, difficulties in measuring performance and uncertainties about a variety of exchange contingencies increase both the complexity of contracts and the use of relational governance mechanisms (i.e. informal controls and trust) (Poppo & Zenger, 2002; Woolthius, HIllebrand, & Nooteboom, 2005; Zhou, Poppo, & Yang, 2008; Chapter 13 by Poppo & Zheng, this volume). Cao and Lumineau's (2015) review and meta-analysis of contracting in interorganizational relationships finds support for a complementary relationship between formal controls, informal controls, trust and performance. Specifically, they observe that these factors together reduce opportunism between exchange partners while increasing their partners' perceptions of performance and relational satisfaction.

It is important to note, however, that while supporting the idea that formal and informal control produce complementary effects on performance, research also suggests that if characteristics of exchanges (e.g. one-sided contracts) lead individuals to engage in self-interested behaviour, relational contracts become less effective (Poppo et al., 2008; Woolthius, et al., 2005). These concerns can, however, attenuate, and returns to trust through relational ties can increase if partners view their mutual relationship as strategically important or if asset specificity and low levels of uncertainty lead exchange partners to maintain both a positive track record as well as a desire to foster cooperation and continuity (Emsley & Kidon, 2004; Mellewigt, Madhok, & Weibel, 2007).

Individual studies continue to provide evidence that it is important to understand the exact nature of control and trust dynamics in IORs because they substantially influence the effects that are generated. Lui and Ngo (2004), for example, suggest that in non-equity alliances, competence trust and contractual safeguards produce complementary effects on project satisfaction and completion time while goodwill trust and contractual safeguards (formal controls) act as substitutes and produce independent and equivalent effects on these outcomes. Velez and colleagues (2008) observe, however, that when formal controls are used to coordinate actions between exchange partners, cooperation and the potential to foster both competence and goodwill trust over time increases (Cao & Lumineau, 2015).

Research on relationships between control, trust and performance within organizations has also afforded researchers with a close-up, more micro-level view of factors influencing partner cooperation and performance. Ferrin, Bligh and Kohles' (2007) review highlights how monitoring and the extent to which one feels that one is trusted generates equivocal levels of cooperation. However, when partners apply controls in ways that are perceived as trustworthy, partners are more willing to cooperate with and commit to each other (Dirks, 1999; Ferrin et al., 2007; Neves & Caetano, 2006; Tyler, 2003).

Contextual influences

A growing amount of research is now examining how control, trust and performance are influenced by a variety of contextual factors. In a recent paper, Mishra and Mishra (2013) use a case study to examine how particular actions do or do not foster interpersonal or institutional trust depending on the context within which they are enacted. Their findings align with other scholars who argue that the context surrounding organizations will significantly influence how control and trust manifest and influence key outcomes (Bijlsma-Frankema, Sitkin, & Weibel, 2015; Mayer & Davis, 1999; Mayer et al., 1995; Mishra & Mishra, 2013; Sitkin, 1995).

For example, over the span of the last 20 years, researchers have identified relationship length as an important contextual factor influencing control and trust dynamics (Nooteboom, Berger, & Noorderhaven, 1997). O'Leary and colleagues (2002) undertake one of the most ambitious investigations of this factor in their case study of the Hudson Bay Company where they examine how this organization grew their use of informal control mechanisms over a 150-year period to establish effective levels of control and trust over the operations of a global organization. Fryxell et al. (2002) observed a similar trajectory with modern international joint ventures (IJVs) where organizations rely more on formal controls early before increasing their reliance on social control mechanisms as goodwill trust between exchange partners increase. Regarding these relationships, both Vlaar et al. (2007) and Cao and Lumineau (2015) highlight the path dependence of control-trust dynamics by accounting how levels of trust or distrust that occur early in the development of IORs influence the attributions that managers make about their exchange partners as relationships evolve and develop.

Research also highlights how various cultural and geo-political factors influence conceptualizations of control and trust manifest within and across organizations (Bachmann, 2001; Cao & Lumineau, 2015; Mizrachi, et al., 2007; Reed, 2001; Roberts, 2001). For example, Rus and Iglic (2005) show how Slovenian entrepreneurs base business agreements on trust because they trust the institutions that govern their economic activities; while, Bosnian entrepreneurs who do not trust their governing institutions do more business through formal contracts. Alternatively, Grey and Garsten (2001) describe how the uncertainty and institutional complexity surrounding modern organizations have increased the importance of using trust to manage employees while Pearce and colleagues (2000) argue that the universalistic control practices adopted by modern organizations have led to greater levels of employee trust and organizational commitment (Bijlsma & Costa, 2005).

Issues for future research

What becomes clear from examining research on control-trust dynamics is that while scholars have identified some of the basic parameters of these relationships, many important questions remain to be investigated in this topical area. Emsley and Kidon (2007: 829), for example, suggest that 'we are, however, a long way from understanding how trust and control coexist, and many basic issues remain unresolved.' Several noted organizational scholars have made similar statements over the past two decades (Bachmann, 2001; Coletti, et al., 2005; Bijlsma-Frankema & Costa, 2005, 2010; Das & Teng, 1998; 2001; Langfield-Smith & Smith, 2003; Long & Sitkin, 2006; Weibel, 2007).

The following section presents ways to address these issues by outlining an agenda for future research and highlighting a variety of topics that require further study. Notably, Grabner and Moers recently (2013) expressed concerns that organizational research evaluating control and trust as complements or substitutes is seriously deficient because trust researchers have largely ignored evaluating how managers (trustees) think and act to encourage others to trust them (Long & Sitkin, 2006; Vosselman & van der Meer-Kooistra, 2009). As a result, scholars cannot currently explain how managers attempt to effectively balance and integrate their control and trust-building activities in ways that accurately describe subordinate reactions to the intentions and behaviours that managers actually exhibit (Dekker, 2004; Langfield-Smith & Smith, 2003; Long, 2010; Vosselman & van der Meer-Kooistra, 2009).

A managerial perspective on trust-building

This acknowledgement should lead scholars to more directly examine how managers concurrently apply controls *and* take actions that are designed to foster subordinate trust (Chenhall, Hall, & Smith, 2013; Long, 2010; 2015; Long & Sitkin, 2006; Sitkin & George, 2005). Grabner and Moers (2013) encourage scholars to examine whether and how these activities constitute sets of 'internally consistent' control practices that managers use concurrently to motivate the achievement of a variety of performance objectives (Grabner & Moers, 2013; Merchant, Van der Stede, & Zheng, 2003; Merchant & Van der Stede, 2007). Future research could, for example, examine both the composition of managers' trust-building activities as well as how and why they manifest within various organizational environments. In addition, scholars could more actively examine how performance concerns stimulate managers to use control and trust-building initiatives independently and jointly to encourage their subordinates to work with them and accomplish key strategic and operational goals (Long & Sitkin, 2006; Long, 2010; Sitkin & George, 2005; Whitener, Brodt, Korsgaard, & Werner, 1998).

Trust influencing control decisions

A key issue that should be addressed by this research is how a manager's trust in their subordinates influences their control decisions. Several authors have highlighted the importance of this issue and provided initial ideas about these relationships. For example, Woolthius and colleagues' (2005) four-company qualitative study demonstrates how evaluations of trust between exchange partners in IORs often preceded the development of formal contracts. Gulati and Nickerson (2008) outline how these choices influence both the relationships between control and trust activities and the levels of performance that were achieved through formal and relational contracts. While other scholars have also observed similar phenomena of perceived trust influencing control decisions (Langfred, 2004; McAllister, 1995; Pearce, et al., 2002), what may be needed now is to develop a more fine-grained understanding of how managers' perceptions of specific forms of trust and distrust influence their control-based actions and how those actions together influence subordinate cooperation, managerial legitimacy and organizational performance. Here the emerging literature on implicit followership theories could enlighten the control-trust research nexus by providing the means to map the general attitude of leaders towards their followers. Mapping these attitudes may show how managers classify certain employees as trustworthy – 'prototypical' and others as non-trustworthy – 'anti-prototypical' with the former perception leading to more positive control-trust dynamics (Sy, 2010).

Investigating control perceptions

Future research should also more closely examine the content and implications of trustors' control perceptions as previous research has highlighted that this concern is important and significantly affects their subsequent actions (Ouchi, 1978). For example, Christ, Sedatole and Towry (2012) argue that how agents frame work contracts impacts their perceptions of how much trust principals have in them. Ferrin and Dirks (2003) show why this is important by demonstrating how whether subordinates perceive themselves to be in a competitive or a cooperative environment influences their subsequent motivations and perceptions.

To address this issue, control-trust scholars may draw on the extensive research examining perceived control in the psychological literature which examines the cognitive, emotional and motivational implications of individuals' perceptions that they possess agency and maintain discretion over aspects of their environments (Bandura, 1977, 1982; Skinner, 1996; Thompson, 1981). While not generally utilized to examine subordinate perceptions in control-trust research, it has been applied in other contexts to predict the extent to which individuals adhere to norms, engage in impression management behaviours, as well as exhibit job satisfaction, work motivation and organizational commitment (Burger, 1987, 1989; Lee Ashford & Bobko, 1990).

A close look at issues related to perceived control could potentially assist scholars in understanding how subordinates formulate their perceptions of personal control through observations both of the controls their managers apply and the ways their managers demonstrate (i.e. or do not demonstrate) that they are trustworthy in applying those controls (Chapter 14 by Tomlinson, this volume). Alternatively, personal control theory could be used to evaluate managers' reactions to factors in their operational environments. For example, perceptions of personal control may be found to be strong predictors of managers' subsequent control and trust-building activities. Investigations that are directed in this way can begin to illuminate key issues surrounding why and how managers take actions to assert greater levels of control, significantly increase subordinate trust, combine certain control and trust-building activities, as well as foster the achievement of other performance goals.

Studying control under extreme conditions

Another way to further our understanding on how control, trust and possibly performance relate is to analyse new, and much more pervasive forms of controls. Of particular interest is the effect of electronic and growingly big-data-based formal controls on employee trust and performance. These types of controls differ from traditional controls in important ways as they can invade privacy through mechanisms that allow low-cost on-and-off-the-job tracking of employee behaviour (Ball, 2010). Alternatively, big-data-based controls can also be used to predict and govern future behaviour and performance through fraud-predicting computer programs that prominent financial institutions use to forecast the emergence of 'rogue traders' (Son, 2015).

Increasingly, these programs that rely on elaborate algorithms to generate and monitor standards against goals are challenging human managers as controllers (Hongo, 2015).

These controls challenge trust research in a number of ways that highlight the need for new referents of trust to be included in our research. Here, it is becoming increasingly important to understand whether the ways that these controls are selected and implemented influence trust and performance in organizations. For instance, the effectiveness of increasingly popular electronic controls might depend on the extent to which algorithms, machines and organizations are trusted by those being monitored. Complexity researchers argue that highly refined technological systems may be prone to more and more dramatic breakdowns that impact how big-data-based controls impact performance and overall trust perceptions (Perrow, 2011). Specifically, because the reliability and overall performance of these systems relies on the willingness of authorities to prevent, identify and remediate possible breakdowns, researchers need to recognize that employees in these highly controlled environments are impacted by the extent to which they trust the parameters of the systems of which they are a part. (Weick, Sutcliffe, and Obstfeld, 2008).

Examining contextual factors

Previous research suggests that configurations of control mechanisms and systems are dynamic in that they affect and are affected by factors within organizational environments (Cardinal et al., 2004). Observations presented in previous research provide clear evidence that this dynamism extends to trust and trust-building activities and that researchers in this topical area should seek to understand how control-trust dynamics change and develop over time (Weber, Malhotra, & Murnighan, 2004; Vlaar, et al., 2007). Using a co-evolutionary perspective, scholars could begin to chart how a variety of factors surrounding managers both within and outside of their organizations directly influence the decisions that they make about how to manage through control and trust-building initiatives. These models could then show how the decisions that managers make about controlling and developing relationships with their employees influence and are influenced by relationships between managers and their environments (Lewin, Long, & Carroll, 1999).

Doing this effectively will require scholars to conduct much more finely tuned analyses of the key contextual factors surrounding managers, employees and their organizations. While research has begun to catalogue some broad institutionally based factors influencing control-trust dynamics (Cao & Lumineau, 2015), much more needs to be done in this area. Because the dynamics surrounding how control and trust manifest in organizations will vary with geo-political conditions (Creed & Miles, 1996; Pearce et al., 2000; Rus & Iglič, 2005), scholars should take a close look at what those conditions are, how they are evaluated by managers and subordinates, how they influence individuals' actions and perceptions, and how those responses evolve in dynamic environments.

Directed research in this area can help scholars begin to understand how managers determine the appropriate levels of control and trust in given work environments. This is important because managers do appear to carefully consider whether the actions they take are appropriate for a given organizational/institutional context and because managers are concerned with developing appropriate levels of trust (Chenhall, Hall, & Smith, 2013; Long, 2010, 2015; Long & Sitkin, 2006; Sitkin & George, 2005). Understanding how they do this effectively by navigating through complex and uncertain environments will help us understand what is needed to capitalize on opportunities to build cooperative relationships that can be empowerment-producing, personally enriching and value-enhancing (Wicks, Berman & Jones, 1999).

References

Adler, P. S. (2001). Market, hierarchy, and trust: The knowledge economy and the future of capitalism. *Organization Science, 12*(2), 215–234.

Anderson, S. W., Christ, M. H., Dekker, H. C., & Sedatole, K. L. (2013). The use of management controls to mitigate risk in strategic alliances: Field and survey evidence. *Journal of Management Accounting Research, 26*(1), 1–32.

Arvey, R. D. (1979). Unfair discrimination in the employment interview: Legal and psychological aspects. *Psychological Bulletin, 86*(4), 736.

Bachmann, R. (2001). Trust, power and control in trans-organizational relations. *Organization Studies, 22*(2), 337–365.

Ball, K. (2010). Workplace surveillance: An overview. *Labor History, 51*(1), 87–106.

Bandura, A. (1977). Self-efficacy: toward a unifying theory of behavioral change. *Psychological Review, 84*(2), 191.

Bandura, A. (1982). Self-efficacy mechanism in human agency. *American Psychologist, 37*(2), 122.

Bijlsma-Frankema, K., & Costa, A. C. (2005). Understanding the trust-control nexus. *International Sociology, 20*(3), 259–282.

Bijlsma-Frankema, K, Sitkin, S. B. & Weibel, A. (2015). Distrust in the balance: The emergence and development of intergroup distrust in a court of law. *Organization Science, 26*(4), 1018–1039.

Bijlsma, K. M., & Van De Bunt, G. G. (2003). Antecedents of trust in managers: a 'bottom up' approach. *Personnel Review, 32*(5), 638–664.

Blau, P. M. (1964). *Exchange and power in social life*. Transaction Publishers.

Bradach, J. L., & Eccles, R. G. (1989). Price, authority, and trust: From ideal types to plural forms. *Annual review of sociology*, 97–118.

Cummings, L. L., & Bromiley, P. (1996). The organizational trust inventory (OTI). In *Trust in organizations: Frontiers of theory and research*, (pp.302–330).

Burger, J. M. (1987). Increased performance with increased personal control: A self-presentation interpretation. *Journal of Experimental Social Psychology, 23*(4), 350–360.

Burger, J. M. (1989). Negative reactions to increases in perceived personal control. *Journal of Personality and Social Psychology, 56*(2), 246.

Burke, C. S., Sims, D. E., Lazzara, E. H., & Salas, E. (2007). Trust in leadership: A multi-level review and integration. *The Leadership Quarterly, 18*(6), 606–632.

Butler, J. K. (1991). Toward understanding and measuring conditions of trust: Evolution of a conditions of trust inventory. *Journal of Management, 17*(3), 643–663.

Cao, Z., & Lumineau, F. (2015). Revisiting the interplay between contractual and relational governance: A qualitative and meta-analytic investigation. *Journal of Operations Management, 33*, 15–42.

Cardinal, L. B., Sitkin, S. B., & Long, C. P. (2004). Balancing and rebalancing in the creation and evolution of organizational control. *Organization Science, 15*(4), 411–431.

Cardinal, L. B., Sitkin, S., & Long, C. (2010). A configurational theory of control. In *Control in organizations: New directions in theory and research*, edited by S. Sitkin, L. B. Cardinal and K. Bijlsma-Frankema. Cambridge, UK: Cambridge University Press (pp. 51–79).

Chenhall, R. H., Hall, M., & Smith, D. (2010). Social capital and management control systems: A study of a non-government organization. *Accounting, Organizations and Society, 35*(8), 737–756.

Christ, M. H. (2013). An experimental investigation of the interactions among intentions, reciprocity, and control. *Journal of Management Accounting Research, 25*(1), 169–197.

Christ, M. H., Sedatole, K. L., & Towry, K. L. (2012). Sticks and carrots: The effect of contract frame on effort in incomplete contracts. *The Accounting Review, 87*(6), 1913–1938.

Christ, M. H., Sedatole, K. L., Towry, K. L., & Thomas, M. A. (2008). When formal controls undermine trust and cooperation. *Strategic Finance, 89*(7), 39.

Coletti, A. L., Sedatole, K. L., & Towry, K. L. (2005). The effect of control systems on trust and cooperation in collaborative environments. *The Accounting Review, 80*(2), 477–500.

Connell, J., Ferres, N., & Travaglione, T. (2003). Engendering trust in manager–subordinate relationships: Predictors and outcomes. *Personnel Review, 32*(5), 569–587.

Cook, J., & Wall, T. (1980). New work attitude measures of trust, organizational commitment and personal need non-fulfilment. *Journal of occupational psychology, 53*(1), 39–52.

Costa, A. C., & Bijlsma-Frankema, K. (2007). Trust and control interrelations new perspectives on the trust—control nexus. *Group & Organization Management, 32*(4), 392–406.

Creed, W. D., Miles, R. E. (1996). Trust in organizations. In *Trust in organizations: Frontiers of theory and research*, edited by R. Kramer and T. Tyler. Thousand Oaks, CA: Sage (pp. 16–38).

Das, T. K., & Teng, B. S. (1998). Between trust and control: Developing confidence in partner cooperation in alliances. *Academy of Management Review, 23*(3), 491–512.

Das, T. K., & Teng, B. S. (2001). Trust, control, and risk in strategic alliances: An integrated framework. *Organization Studies, 22*(2), 251–283.

De Cremer, D., & Tyler, T. R. (2007). The effects of trust in authority and procedural fairness on cooperation. *Journal of Applied Psychology, 92*(3), 639.

Dekker, H. C. (2004). Control of inter-organizational relationships: evidence on appropriation concerns and coordination requirements. *Accounting, Organizations and Society, 29*(1), 27–49.

Dineen, B. R., Lewicki, R. J., & Tomlinson, E. C. (2006). Supervisory guidance and behavioral integrity: relationships with employee citizenship and deviant behavior. *Journal of Applied Psychology, 91*(3), 622.

Dirks, K. T. (1999). The effects of interpersonal trust on work group performance. *Journal of Applied Psychology, 84*(3), 445.

Dirks, K. T., & Ferrin, D. L. (2002). Trust in leadership: meta-analytic findings and implications for research and practice. *Journal of Applied Psychology, 87*(4), 611.

Eisenhardt, K. M. (1989). Agency theory: An assessment and review. *Academy of Management Review, 14*(1), 57–74.

Emsley, D., & Kidon, F. (2007). The relationship between trust and control in international joint ventures: Evidence from the airline industry. *Contemporary Accounting Research, 24*(3), 829–858.

Falk, A., & Kosfeld, M. (2006). The hidden costs of control. *The American Economic Review, 96*(5), 1611–1630.

Fayol, H. (1949). *General and industrial administration*. New York: Pitman.

Ferrin, D. L., Bligh, M. C., & Kohles, J. C. (2007). Can I trust you to trust me? A theory of trust, monitoring, and cooperation in interpersonal and intergroup relationships. *Group & Organization Management, 32*(4), 465–499.

Ferrin, D. L., & Dirks, K. T. (2003). The use of rewards to increase and decrease trust: Mediating processes and differential effects. *Organization Science, 14*(1), 18–31.

Fryxell, G. E., Dooley, R. S., & Vryza, M. (2002). After the ink dries: The interaction of trust and control in US-based international joint ventures. *Journal of Management Studies, 39*(6), 865–886.

Fox, A. (1974). *Beyond contract: Work power and trust relations*. London: Faber.

Fulmer, C. A., & Gelfand, M. J. (2012). At what level (and in whom) we trust. *Journal of Management, 38*, 1167–1230.

Ghoshal, S., & Moran, P. (1996). Bad for practice: A critique of the transaction cost theory. *Academy of Management Review, 21*(1), 13–47.

Giddens, A. (1990). Structuration theory and sociological analysis. In *Anthony Giddens: consensus and controversy*, edited by J. Clark, C. Modgil and S. Modgil. London, New York, Philadelpia, PA: The Falmer Press (pp. 297–315).

Grabner, I., & Moers, F. (2013). Management control as a system or a package? Conceptual and empirical issues. *Accounting, Organizations and Society, 38*(6), 407–419.

Grey, C., & Garsten, C. (2001). Trust, control and post-bureaucracy. *Organization Studies, 22*(2), 229–250.

Gulati, R., & Nickerson, J. A. (2008). Interorganizational trust, governance choice, and exchange performance. *Organization Science, 19*(5), 688–708.

Hartmann, F., & Slapničar, S. (2009). How formal performance evaluation affects trust between superior and subordinate managers. *Accounting, Organizations and Society, 34*(6), 722–737.

Hongo, J. (2015). Who's the boss? Hitachi looks to promote artificial intelligence. *The Wall Street Journal*. Retrieved from http://blogs.wsj.com/japanrealtime/2015/09/08/whos-the-boss-hitachi-looks-to-promote-artificial-intelligence/

Inkpen, A. C., & Currall, S. C. (2004). The coevolution of trust, control, and learning in joint ventures. *Organization Science, 15*(5), 586–599.

Jagd, S. (2010). Balancing Trust and Control. *Society and Business Review, 5*(3), 259–269.

Jermier, J. M. (1998). Introduction: critical perspective on organizational control. *Administrative Science Quarterly, 43*(2), 235–256.

Kirsch, L. J. (2004). Deploying common systems globally: The dynamics of control. *Information Systems Research, 15*(4), 374–395.

Korsgaard, M. A., Schweiger, D. M., & Sapienza, H. J. (1995). Building commitment, attachment, and trust in strategic decision-making teams: The role of procedural justice. *Academy of Management Journal, 38*(1), 60–84.

Kruglanski, A. W. (1970). Attributing trustworthiness in supervisor-worker relations. *Journal of Experimental Social Psychology, 6*(2), 214–232.

Langfield-Smith, K., & Smith, D. (2003). Management control systems and trust in outsourcing relationships. *Management Accounting Research, 14*(3), 281–307.

Langfred, C. W. (2004). Too much of a good thing? Negative effects of high trust and individual autonomy in self-managing teams. *Academy of Management Journal, 47*(3), 385–399.

Lebas, M., & Weigenstein, J. (1986). Management control: The role of rules, market and culture. *Journal of Management Studies, 23*(3), 259–272.

Lee, C., Ashford, S. J., & Bobko, P. (1990). Interactive effects of 'Type A' behavior and perceived control on worker performance, job satisfaction, and somatic complaints. *Academy of Management Journal, 33*(4), 870–881.

Leifer, R., & Mills, P. K. (1996). An information processing approach for deciding upon control strategies and reducing control loss in emerging organizations. *Journal of Management, 22*(1), 113–137.

Lewin, A. Y., Long, C. P., & Carroll, T. N. (1999). The coevolution of new organizational forms. *Organization Science, 10*(5), 535–550.

Lui, S. S., & Ngo, H. Y. (2004). The role of trust and contractual safeguards on cooperation in non-equity alliances. *Journal of Management, 30*(4), 471–485.

Long, C. P. (2010). Control to cooperation: Examining the role of managerial authority in portfolios of managerial action. *Organizational Control*, 365–395.

Long, C. P. (2015). How managers direct subordinates through applications of controls and demonstrations of their trustworthiness. *Journal of Applied Business Research, 31*(5), 1645–1666.

Long, C. P., Burton, R. M., & Cardinal, L. B. (2002). Three controls are better than one: a computational model of complex control systems. *Computational & Mathematical Organization Theory, 8*(3), 197–220.

Long, C. P., & Sitkin, S. B. (2006). Trust in the balance: How managers integrate trust-building and task control. *Handbook of trust research*, edited by R. Bachmann and A. Zaheer. Cheltenham, UK and Northampton, MA: Edward Elgar (pp. 87–106).

Malhotra, D., & Lumineau, F. (2011). Trust and collaboration in the aftermath of conflict: The effects of contract structure. *Academy of Management Journal, 54*(5), 981–998.

Malhotra, D., & Murnighan, J. K. (2002). The effects of contracts on interpersonal trust. *Administrative Science Quarterly, 47*(3), 534–559.

Mayer, R. C., & Davis, J. H. (1999). The effect of the performance appraisal system on trust for management: A field quasi-experiment. *Journal of Applied Psychology, 84*(1), 123.

Mayer, R. C., Davis, J. H., & Schoorman, F. D. (1995). An integrative model of organizational trust. *Academy of Management Review, 20*(3), 709–734.

McAllister, D. J. (1995). Affect-and cognition-based trust as foundations for interpersonal cooperation in organizations. *Academy of Management Journal, 38*(1), 24–59.

McEvily, B., Perrone, V., & Zaheer, A. (2003). Trust as an organizing principle. *Organization Science, 14*(1), 91–103.

McKnight, D. H., Cummings, L. L., Chervany, N. L. (1998). Initial trust formation in new organizational relationships. *Academy of Management Review, 23*(3), 473–490.

Mellewigt, T., Madhok, A., & Weibel, A. (2007). Trust and formal contracts in interorganizational relationships: Substitutes and complements. *Managerial and Decision Economics, 28*(8), 833–847.

Merchant, K. A. (1985). *Control in business organization*. New York: Prentice Hall.

Merchant, K. A., & Van der Stede, W. A. (2007). *Management control systems: performance measurement, evaluation and incentives*. Pearson Education.

Merchant, K. A., Van der Stede, W. A., & Zheng, L. (2003). Disciplinary constraints on the advancement of knowledge: the case of organizational incentive systems. *Accounting, Organizations and Society, 28*(2), 251–286.

Mintzberg, H. (1979). *The structuring of organizations: A synthesis of the research*. Englewood Cliffs, NJ: Prentice-Hall.

Mishra, A. K., & Mishra, K. E. (2013). The research on trust in leadership: The need for context. *Journal of Trust Research, 3*(1), 59–69.

Mislin, A. A., Campagna, R. L., & Bottom, W. P. (2011). After the deal: Talk, trust building and the implementation of negotiated agreements. *Organizational Behavior and Human Decision Processes, 115*(1), 55–68.

Mizrachi, N., Drori, I., & Anspach, R. R. (2007). Repertoires of trust: The practice of trust in a multinational organization amid political conflict. *American Sociological Review, 72*(1), 143–165.

Möllering, G. (2005). The trust/control duality an integrative perspective on positive expectations of others. *International Sociology, 20*(3), 283–305.

Nooteboom, B. (1996). Trust, opportunism and governance: A process and control model. *Organization Studies, 17*(6), 985–1010.

Nooteboom, B., Berger, H., & Noorderhaven, N. G. (1997). Effects of trust and governance on relational risk. *Academy of Management Journal, 40*(2), 308–338.

O'Leary, M., Orlikowski, W., & Yates, J. (2002). Distributed work over the centuries: Trust and control in the Hudson's Bay Company, 1670–1826. In *Distributed Work*, edited by S. Kiesler nd P. Hinds. Cambridge, MA: MIT Press (pp. 27–54).

Ouchi, W. G. (1977). The relationship between organizational structure and organizational control. *Administrative Science Quarterly*, 95–113.

Ouchi, W. G. (1978). The transmission of control through organizational hierarchy. *Academy of Management Journal, 21*(2), 173–192.

Ouchi, W. G. (1979). A conceptual framework for the design of organizational control mechanisms. In *Readings in accounting for management control,* edited by C. Emmanuel, D. Otley and K. Merchant. Boston, MA: Springer (pp. 63–82).

Ouchi, W. G. (1980). Markets, bureaucracies, and clans. *Administrative Science Quarterly, 25*(1), 129–141.

Pearce, J. L., Branyiczki, I., & Bigley, G. A. (2000). Insufficient bureaucracy: Trust and commitment in particularistic organizations. *Organization Science, 11*(2), 148–162.

Pennings, J. M., & Woiceshyn, J. (1987). A typology of organizational control and its metaphors. *Research in the Sociology of Organizations, 5*, 75–104.

Perrow, C. (2011). *Normal accidents: Living with high risk technologies.* Princeton, NJ: Princeton University Press.

Poppo, L., & Zenger, T. (2002). Do formal contracts and relational governance function as substitutes or complements? *Strategic Management Journal, 23*(8), 707–725.

Reed, M. I. (2001). Organization, trust and control: a realist analysis. *Organization Studies, 22*(2), 201–228.

Roberts, J. (2001). Trust and control in Anglo-American systems of corporate governance: The individualizing and socializing effects of processes of accountability. *Human Relations, 54*(12), 1547–1572.

Ross, A. (1994). Trust as a moderator of the effect of performance evaluation style on job-related tension: A research note. *Accounting, Organizations and Society, 19*(7), 629–635.

Roth, N. L., Sitkin, S. B., & House, A. (1994). Stigma as a determinant of legalization. *The legalistic organization*, edited by S. B. Sitkin and R. J. Bies. Thousand Oaks, CA: Sage (pp. 137–168).

Rousseau, D. M., Sitkin, S. B., Burt, R. S., & Camerer, C. (1998). Not so different after all: A cross-discipline view of trust. *Academy of Management Review, 23*(3), 393–404.

Rus, A., & Iglič, H. (2005). Trust, governance and performance the role of institutional and interpersonal trust in SME development. *International Sociology, 20*(3), 371–391.

Sako, M. (1992). *Price, quality and trust: Inter-firm relations in Britain and Japan* (No. 18). Cambridge, UK: Cambridge University Press.

Searle, R., Den Hartog, D. N., Weibel, A., Gillespie, N., Six, F., Hatzakis, T., & Skinner, D. (2011). Trust in the employer: The role of high-involvement work practices and procedural justice in European organizations. *The International Journal of Human Resource Management, 22*(5), 1069–1092.

Şengün, A. E., & Wasti, S. N. (2007). Trust, control, and risk a test of Das and Teng's conceptual framework for pharmaceutical buyer-supplier relationships. *Group & Organization Management, 32*(4), 430–464.

Shapiro, S. P. (1987). The social control of impersonal trust. *American Journal of Sociology*, 623–658.

Skinner, D., & Spira, L. F. (2003). Trust and control-a symbiotic relationship? *Corporate Governance: The International Journal of Business in Society, 3*(4), 28–35.

Sitkin, S. B., & Bies, R. J. (1994). *The legalistic organization.* Thousand Oaks, CA: Sage.

Sitkin, S. B., & George, E. (2005). Managerial trust-building through the use of legitimating formal and informal control mechanisms. *International Sociology, 20*(3), 307–338.

Sitkin, S. B., & Roth, N. L. (1993). Explaining the limited effectiveness of legalistic 'remedies' for trust/distrust. *Organization Science, 4*(3), 367–392.

Skinner, E. A. (1996). A guide to constructs of control. *Journal of Personality and Social Psychology, 71*(3), 549.

Skinner, D., Dietz, G., & Weibel, A. (2014). The dark side of trust: When trust becomes a poisoned chalice. *Organization, 21*, 206–224.

Snell, S. A. (1992). Control theory in strategic human resource management: The mediating effect of administrative information. *Academy of Management Journal, 35*(2), 292–327.

Son, H. (2015). JPMorgan algorithm knows you're a rogue employee before you do. Retrieved from http://bloomberg.com/news/articles/2015–04–08/jpmorgan-algorithmknows-you-re-a-rogue-employee-before-you-do

Spreitzer, G. M., & Mishra, A. K. (1999). Giving up control without losing control trust and its substitutes' effects on managers' involving employees in decision making. *Group & Organization Management, 24*(2), 155–187.

Sy, T. (2010). What do you think of followers? Examining the content, structure, and consequences of implicit followership theories. *Organizational Behavior and Human Decision Processes, 113*(2), 73–84.

Sydow, J., Windeler, A. (2003). Knowledge, trust, and control: Managing tensions and contradictions in a regional network of service firms. *International Studies of Management & Organization, 33*(2), 69–100.

Thompson, S. C. (1981). Will it hurt less if i can control it? A complex answer to a simple question. *Psychological Bulletin, 90*(1), 89.

Tomkins, C. (2001). Interdependencies, trust and information in relationships, alliances and networks. *Accounting, Organizations and Society, 26*(2), 161–191.

Tyler, T. R., & Lind, E. A. (1992). A relational model of authority in groups. *Advances in Experimental Social Psychology, 25*, 115–191.

Van Maanen, J., & Schein, E. H. (1979). Toward a theory of organizational socialization. *Research in Organizational Behavior, 1*, 209–264.

Vélez, M. L., Sánchez, J. M., & Álvarez-Dardet, C. (2008). Management control systems as inter-organizational trust builders in evolving relationships: Evidence from a longitudinal case study. *Accounting, Organizations and Society, 33*(7), 968–994.

Vlaar, P. W., Van den Bosch, F. A., & Volberda, H. W. (2007). On the evolution of trust, distrust, and formal coordination and control in interorganizational relationships toward an integrative framework. *Group & Organization Management, 32*(4), 407–428.

Vosselman, E., & van der Meer-Kooistra, J. (2009). Accounting for control and trust building in interfirm transactional relationships. *Accounting, Organizations and Society, 34*(2), 267–283.

Walgenbach, P. (2001). The production of distrust by means of producing trust. *Organization Studies, 22*(4), 693–714.

Wanous, J. P. (1980). *Organizational entry: Recruitment, selection and socialization of newcomers.* Reading, MA: Addison Wesley.

Weber, J. M., Malhotra, D., & Murnighan, J. K. (2004). Normal acts of irrational trust: Motivated attributions and the trust development process. *Research in Organizational Behavior, 26*, 75–101.

Weibel, A. (2007). Formal control and trustworthiness shall the twain never meet? *Group & Organization Management, 32*(4), 500–517.

Weibel, A., Den Hartog, D. N., Gillespie, N., Searle, R., Six, F., & Skinner, D. (2016). How do controls impact employee trust in the employer? *Human Resource Management, 55*(3), 437–462.

Weibel, A. & Six, F. (2013). Trust and control: the role of intrinsic motivation. *Handbook of advances in trust,* edited by R. Bachmann and A. Zaheer. Cheltenham, UK and Northampton, MA: Edward Elgar (pp. 57–81).

Weibel, A., Busch, T., Leicht-Deobald, U., Schank, C., & Wildhaber, I. (2016). 'Big Brother' in Swiss companies? Trust, data and personal privacy of employees. Grant proposal (and granted) for National Research Programme 75 'Big Data'. Berne, Switzerland: Swiss National Science Foundation.

Weick, K. E., Sutcliffe, K. M., & Obstfeld, D. (2008). Organizing for high reliability: Processes of collective mindfulness. *Crisis Management, 3*(1), 81–123.

Whitener, E. M. (2001). Do 'high commitment' human resource practices affect employee commitment? A cross-level analysis using hierarchical linear modeling. *Journal of Management, 27*(5), 515–535.

Whitener, E. M., Brodt, S. E., Korsgaard, M. A., & Werner, J. M. (1998). Managers as initiators of trust: An exchange relationship framework for understanding managerial trustworthy behavior. *Academy of Management Review, 23*(3), 513–530.

Whitley, R. (1999). *Divergent capitalisms: The social structuring and change of business systems.* Oxford, UK: Oxford University Press.

Williamson, O. E. (1975). *Markets and hierarchies.* New York: Free Press.

Woolthuis, R. K., Hillebrand, B., & Nooteboom, B. (2005). Trust, contract and relationship development. *Organization Studies, 26*(6), 813–840.

Zaheer, A., McEvily, B., & Perrone, V. (1998). Does trust matter? Exploring the effects of inter-organizational and interpersonal trust on performance. *Organization Science, 9*(2), 141–159.

Zhou, K. Z., Poppo, L., & Yang, Z. (2008). Relational ties or customized contracts? An examination of alternative governance choices in China. *Journal of International Business Studies, 39*(3), 526–534.

30

THE INTER-RELATIONSHIP OF TRUST, ANGER AND AGGRESSION

A two-level perspective[1]

Shay S. Tzafrir, Guy Enosh and Laliv Egozi

Introduction

The relationship between trust, anger and aggression in an Employment Social Environment (ESE) (Tzafrir, Gur & Blumen, 2015) is the topic of this chapter. We will explore these three constructs on the interplay between individual and team levels within the Emotional Social ENvironment (ESEN). ESEN is a microfoundation (Barney & Felin, 2013; Devinney, 2013) representing a team's emotional characteristics, various forms of social interactions, and the process dynamics involved. This environment is a systematic and iterative process between individuals, which creates a team-level modus operandi that consequently affects the individuals and vice versa. In this context, trust serves as a cognitive-emotional mechanism that infuses certainty into uncertain situations (Colquitt, et al., 2012; see Chapter 1 by van Knippenberg, this volume and Chapter 9 by Baer and Colquitt, this volume). Also, the interactive and iterative process of trust dynamics at the team level can be asymmetric and may differ between team members (De Jong & Dirks, 2012; Korsgaard, Brower & Lester, 2015; see Chapter 2 by Korsgaard, this volume). Understanding how the iterative process is influenced at the higher-order level and at the individual level can help predict employee behaviour, such as aggressive behaviour.

Employees in an organization may face different kinds of aggressive behaviours from different perpetrators. On the interpersonal level, an individual can be the target of aggressive behaviour from his/her supervisor, from a colleague, or from a customer (Einarsen, Hoel, Zapf & Cooper, 2003; Mitchell & Ambrose, 2007; Shih, Lie, Klein & Jiang, 2014). All of the above may lead to decreased levels of trust in the direct supervisor as well as in the organization that is perceived by the employees as responsible for their wellbeing and secure working environment (Shoss, Eisenberger, Restubog & Zagenczyk, 2013; Yang, 2015). The consequent reduced/increased trust depends on the organization's reaction to misbehaviour or various aggressive behaviours (Kramer & Lewicki, 2010). On the team level, an employee may face bullying from the team (Einersen, 1999), and a team may face destructive behaviour by a team member (Xia, Yuan & Gay, 2009), as well as aggressive behaviour from management (Beale & Hoel, 2010). Taken together, the level of team trust serves as an important mechanism for determinants of team behaviour (Mach, Dolan & Tzafrir, 2010). Our chapter is derived from the integrative theoretical model of individual and team motivation by Chen and Kanfer (2006) that discussed the interplay between these levels.

Integrating the concepts of microfoundation (Devinney, 2013) and multilevel effect (Chen et al., 2009; Klein & Kozlowski, 2000; see also Chapter 8 by Fulmer, this volume) in order to explain the pattern of relationship among trust, anger and aggressiveness – attribution and exchange theories will be utilized. There are many studies on trust, anger and aggression at the individual level (e.g. Enosh, Tzafrir & Gur, 2013; Shih, Lie, Klein & Jiang, 2014), which do not take into account the importance of the team level of analysis and diffusion between levels and vice versa (Tzafrir, Enosh, Parry & Stone, 2013). Starting at the individual-social level, trust acts as a moderating factor of the relationship between anger and aggression. When anger and aggression at the individual level aggregate and become more of the social norm, an ESEN of hostile attribution develops. Trust at the team level is then affected, serving as a mediating factor between the hostile-attributive ESEN and the organizational aggressive culture. This, in turn, affects an individual employee's aggressive behaviour.

This chapter focuses on the inter-relationship between the individual and team levels (Chen et al., 2009) within employment social environment (Tzafrir et al., 2015). More specifically, we explore the double meaning of trust at the individual level and at the team level as an intervening factor that decreases or increases aggression.

Social environment, trust and aggression

ESE is a microfoundation (Barney & Felin, 2013) representing individuals' characteristics, various forms of social interactions and the process dynamics (Ferris et al., 1998) at different levels of organizational analysis. Growing evidence supports the view that the ESE is an important and useful predictor of people's health (Goh, Pfeffer & Zenios, 2015; Norstrand, Glicksman, Lubben & Kleban, 2012), prosaic behaviour (Linardi, & McConnell, 2011) and workplace mistreatment (Sliter, Jex & Grubb, 2013). Geurts, Schaufeli and De Jonge (1998) assert that burnout and intention to leave the workplace stem from the social context; hence, in order to properly specify factors associated with individual aggressive behaviour,[2] it is necessary to understand individual and team level processess, as well as the interaction between them. Goh and colleagues (2015) recommended that in order to improve employees' health, organizations should attain comprehensive knowledge of the work environment. They emphasized the role of workplace stressors including emotional components of the environment.

While a single case of aggression towards a worker is specific, at the team level such cases become generalized and create a team or even an organizational attitude towards the generalized individual behaviour. More specifically, personal emotion can become a team-level aggregated tendency towards attributing hostility to others in general and in situations of uncertainty and ambiguity in particular. In such situations trust becomes a critical element (Kong, Dirks & Ferrin, 2014). As McEvily, Perrone and Zaheer, (2003) mentioned, 'relying on others is difficult when there is uncertainty about their intentions, motives, and competencies' (p. 92). Thus, trust becomes a key factor in the relation between anger and aggression, as it is a concept that involves cognitive, affective and behavioural dimensions. It develops over time and requires reciprocity between the trustors and the trustees (Lewicki, Tomlinson & Gillespie, 2006). Trust can potentially prevent or reduce undesirable behaviours, such as aggressiveness. More specifically, the moderating role of trust can affect the behavioural outcome. Also, Schaubroeck, Peng and Hannah (2013) argued that '[T]rust is seen to reduce individuals' uncertainty in relationships and thus to enhance the

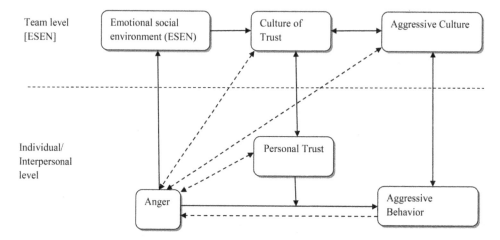

Figure 30.1 Hypothetical model – The moderating role of trust on aggressive behaviour on interplay between individual and team levels

Note: Dotted arrows indicate possible relationships that are not part of the focus of this review.

quality of social exchanges in ways that better enable workers to acquire information, support, and other resources.' (p. 1149). Therefore, trust serves as a cognitive-emotional mechanism that infuses certainty into uncertain situations (Colquitt, et al., 2012). The ESEN impacts team culture of trust, and socialization of newcomers (see Chapter 28 by Searle, this volume). In order to understand the ecological relationship between various organizational levels, we need to begin with the pattern of relationship at the individual level. Figure 30.1[3] summarizes the individual–social environment inter-influence.

Aggression stems from the interaction between individual characteristics, the situation and the organizational factors, such as culture and leadership. According to *Social Learning Theory* (Bandura, 1978), people learn aggressive behaviour either from personal experience or from observing other employees behaving aggressively. *Social Interaction Theory* (Tedeschi & Felson, 1994) adds that the motive for aggressive behaviour is to obtain something, such as resource, reputation, power or self-esteem (Bushman & Baumeister, 1998). When combining the knowledge accumulated from both theories, it becomes clear how team culture and leadership influence aggressive behaviour of individuals in the team. If an aggressive behaviour is a common practice in a team or unit, a new employee that joins the team will learn this behaviour (Bandura, 1978). For instance, if the norm in the team is that an employee is expected to be aggressive or manipulative to receive resources or a promotion, a new employee will have to adapt to the norm in order to succeed. In keeping with this assertion, Glomb and Liao (2003) found that team aggression significantly predicted individual aggressive behaviour beyond reciprocal and individual factors. Some of the team factors that were found to influence employees' aggressive behaviour are presented in Hershcovis and colleagues' (2007) meta-analysis and are elaborated on below.

Aggressive behaviour: individual, situational and team factors

Aggressive behaviour can be instrumental or reactive. Instrumental aggression is motivated by the drive to gain some benefits, such as power, control, reputation, goods and resources. Reactive aggression (hostile aggression) is driven by anger resulting from interpersonal conflict, insult, or sense of injustice (see Pinto's Taxonomy, 2014). A hostile attitude may be a generalized stance towards interpersonal relationships stemming from past experiences[4] and social learning. Aggressive behaviour can also be a mix of the two types of aggression (Anderson & Bushman, 2002). Anger arises when an individual feels disrespect, ego threat, ego depletion or other frustration that can lead to aggressive behaviour (Ainsworth, Baumeister, Ariely & Vohs, 2014; Baumeister, Smart & Boden, 1996; Berkowitz, 2014; DeBono & Muraven, 2014). The anger can arise due to a real action or due to a misunderstanding attributed to harmful intentions (Bies, 2001; Tripp, Bies, & Aquino, 2007). Also, individuals become more likely to seek redress because either no alternative situational explanation applies and no apology is provided or only internal attributions, either of selfishness or malevolence, are possible. In this way they argue revenge, contrary to popular opinion, becomes a rational and deliberate act (Bies & Tripp 1996).

Attribution refers to the perception or inference of cause (see Chapter 14 by Tomlinson, this volume). The common ideas are that people interpret others' behaviour in terms of its causes, and these interpretations play an important role in determining reactions to this behaviour (Kelley & Michela, 1980). If the behaviour causes offense, but the offended individual deems the offender to have good intentions rather than to have sought to deliberately insult and upset them, then they are less likely to behave aggressively (Bies, 2001; Tripp, Bies & Aquino, 2007). This is partially due to the *attribution of unintentionality* that leads offended individuals to control their aggressive behavioural intention (Berkowitz, 2014, Krieglmeyer, Wittstadt & Strack, 2009). Yet, in situations of ego-depletion (lack of mental energy leading to less self-control) the level of behavioural trust is decreased (Ainsworth, Baumeister, Ariely and Vohs, 2014). Thus, one may suggest that aggressive behaviour will increase (Stucke & Baumeister, 2006).

A good example of this assertion can be found in interactions with customers in service organizations such as health, tourism or social work (Enosh & Tzafrir, 2015; Tzafrir, Enosh & Gur, 2015). Such interactions are a potential source of aggressive behaviour from both the customer and the employee (Enosh, Tzafrir & Gur, 2013; Shih, Lie, Klein & Jiang, 2014). For instance, at the individual level, when a social worker is angry at a specific client, her level of trust in that client decreases (Dunn & Schweitzer, 2005; Gino & Schweitzer, 2008), resulting in higher likelihood of aggressive behaviour. Simultaneously, on the team level, accumulation of anger of individual social workers shapes the ESEN to create an environment of hostile attribution, decreasing the culture of trust, which in turn diffuses (Tzafrir, Enosh, Parry & Stone, 2013) to the entire team, and decreases each individual team member's trust. This further-reduced trust increases the likelihood that anger will result in an aggressive behaviour.

Overall, aggression directed at other employees may be a reaction to stressful situations or a stressful work environment, such as interpersonal conflicts, role ambiguity, work–home conflict and organizational changes (Baron & Neuman, 1996; Hauge, Skogsta & Einarsen, 2009; Liu, et al., 2015), as well as to a team culture in which this behaviour is the norm (see Ehrhart & Raver, 2014 for review; Laschinger, Wong, Cummings & Grau, 2014).

Team culture and norms

A negative social environment in the workplace decreases employees' organizational citizenship behaviour, well-being and ability to deliver advanced services, as well as cooperation between individuals and teams within organizations (Tzafrir, et al. 2014; Nixon & Spector, 2015). Knowing that teams develop shared perceptions and climate (Rupp & Paddock, 2010), a team's hostile attribution affects the aggressive behaviour of its members. Therefore, no matter who or what the target of the aggressive behaviour is, the social environment is negatively influenced (Dupré,

Dawe & Barling, 2014). As indicated by the microfoundation literature (Barney & Felin, 2013), team trust is a possible factor mediating the intentionality attribution, and consequently, the aggressive behaviour. For instance, when an employee feels anger, the more he/she attributes the cause to an intended deed (Bies, 2001; Tripp, Bies & Aquino, 2007), the higher the chance he/she will react aggressively. The attribution is mediated by the team's trust – the higher the trust in the team, the lower the intentionality attributions.

Job characteristics and situational factors

Stressful and insecure situations were found to be correlated with aggressive behaviour. Extant research proposes two probable causes. The first explanation is 'instrumental opportunity utilization'. When individuals are faced with changing situations and contexts, they may try to get as much as one can in the face of change and insecurity (e.g. in times of management replacement, downsizing, reconstruction), therefore behaving aggressively. The second possible explanation is that increased insecurity leads to decrease in situational trust and increased perceived injustice, thus leading to aggressive behaviour (Ambrose, Seabright & Schminke, 2002; Hoel & Salin, 2011; Neuman & Baron, 2011).

Individual characteristics

In studying aggressive behaviour against social workers, Enosh and his colleagues (2013) found emotional and behavioural aspects related to aggressive behaviour at the individual level. In keeping with Liu and colleagues (2015), it was found that individual stress and exhaustion are factors contributing to anger, leading in turn to aggressive behaviour. Aggressive behaviour increases in specific organizational, social and individual conditions that increase perceived threat, such as job insecurity and personal insecurity – physical or emotional (Chernyak-Hai & Tziner, 2014; Neuman & Baron, 2011). This leads to the attribution of hostility (Lyu, Zhu, Zhong & Hu, 2016) and an increase in emotional reactions, such as anger (Oh & Farh, 2017). Threatening conditions increase the potential for feelings of anger (Baumeister, Smart & Boden, 1996, Berkowitz, 2014; DeBono & Muraven, 2014). Based on studies demonstrating that the attribution of unintentionality moderates aggressive behaviour but does not reduce anger (Berkowitz, 2014; Klackl, Pfundmair, Agroskin & Jonas, 2013; Krieglmeyer, Wittstadt & Strack, 2009), we maintain that the attribution of unintentionality is facilitated by trust. In other words, when one individual trusts another, although an emotional response such as anger may arise, it will not lead to aggressive behaviour, and vice versa – when there is a feeling of distrust, the anger will be translated into aggression.

Integrative model

While a single case of individual aggression towards a worker is specific, at the team level, such cases become generalized and create a team or attitude towards the generalized individual behaviour. More specifically, personal emotion can become a team-aggregated tendency towards attributing hostility to others in general. This ESEN impacts the team culture of trust, and socializes newcomers, and vice versa. Extant literature presents the role of trust and lack of trust at the individual and team levels in shaping the relationship between anger and aggressiveness (Baumeister, Smart & Boden, 1996; Berkowitz, 2014; Bies & Tripp, 1996; Neuman & Baron, 2011; Tripp, Bies & Aquino, 2007; Tzafrir, et al., 2013). Figure 30.1 describes the diffusion process from individual to team and vice versa, and focuses on the moderating role of trust on aggressive behaviour. The figure presents the two parallel yet highly interrelated processes – at the individual level and the team level. The figure is divided by a dashed line, separating the team level in the upper part from the individual level in the lower part. It should be noted that every model attempting to describe interactions in linear terms is punctuating a circular and iterative process (Watzlawick, Weakland & Fisch, 2011) and therefore diminishes it to some degree. Therefore, some potential paths may seem to be missing. Otherwise presenting every potential link would create an incoherent cobweb mesh.

Aggressive behaviour increases under specific social, group (team) and personal conditions that increase perceived threat to employees (Chernyak-Hai & Tziner, 2014; Hoel & Salin, 2011; Neuman & Baron, 2011). At the individual level (lower part), anger arises when one's goals or expectations are thwarted, and the individual feels disrespect, ego threats or other frustration (Berkowitz, 2014); for instance, unmet social expectations, attack on one's social identity or reputation, rule violations, honor violations and abusive authority (Bies & Tripp, 1996). Also, anger can arise due to friction (Tzafrir et al., 2013), real action or a misunderstanding attributed to harmful intentions (Bies, 2001; Kramer, 1996; Tripp, et al., 2007).[5] Anger may consequently lead to aggressive behaviour (Baumeister, et al., 1996). Based on all of the above, we considered as a truism that individual anger impacts individual aggressive behaviour. According to attribution theory, people are likely to rely on their trust level as a basis for their presumptions (Ferrin & Dirks, 2003; Kelley & Michela, 1980), actions and plans for the future. When the offended trusts the offender's good intentions, sincere concern and unintended misbehaviour, he/she is less likely to behave aggressively, since attribution of un-intentionality (Weiner, 1985) leads to control of aggressive behaviour, though not to reduced anger (Berkowitz, 2014; Krieglmeyer, Wittstadt & Strack, 2009).

The upper part of the figure deals with processes at the team level. The dashed line signifies the permeable border between the two levels. According to Rogers (2010), the diffusion process is the spread of an idea from its source to further actors and stakeholders. Teams develop shared perceptions and climate (Rupp & Paddock, 2010). Von Scheve and Ismer (2013) described three ways in which team emotion develops: emotional contagion depends on physical proximity; similar meanings are assigned to events based on shared knowledge; and culture and team membership and social identity elicit specific emotions in response to events affecting the team (see also Chapter 1 by van Knippenberg, this volume). Our review describes the impact of individual emotional processes – dealing with anger and trust – on the team's ESEN. Based on extant literature, we integrate current knowledge into a model of interactive influence between team and individual employees (Fulmer, & Gelfand, 2012; Kozlowski, & Klein, 2000).

Kozlowski and Klein (2000) suggested that 'a phenomenon is emergent when it originates in the cognition, affect, behaviours, or other characteristics of individuals, is amplified by their interactions, and manifests as a higher-level, collective phenomenon' (p. 55). Therefore, diffusion of attitudes and emotions between team and individual are presented in the next propositions. When referring to the aggression cycle, it is crucial to keep in mind that the literature describes interactive and cyclical processes. For the sake of clarity we begin our review with individual anger, although each stage may serve as a starting point (Lewis, Lange & Gillis, 2005). For instance, a team that develops a hostile attribution mood towards its customers may lead individual's feelings of anger towards a specific customer that represent the distrusted population. The aggressive-anger cycle may start as well from instrumental-opportunistic aggressive behaviour where there is no initial anger, as often happens at times of organizational change, for instance (Hershcovis, et al., 2007; Neuman & Baron, 2011), or organizational political culture (Javor & Jancsics, 2013).

Team level hostile attribution, operating through various mechanisms of communication, diffusion, interaction and even subverted yearning (Tzafrir, et al., 2013), affects the team culture of trust. Lack of trust may be rooted in the tendency of the team members to interpret situations in negative or even paranoid ways[6] (Kramer, 2001). Combining emergent phenomena (Kozlowski & Klein, 2000) with van der Werff and Buckley's (2014) trust development dynamic, we suggest that this dynamic is also influenced by team level.

A low level of cultural trust affects team aggressive culture and results in a team culture that ignores or even condones aggressive behaviour among employees, or between employees and customers (see Ehrhart & Raver, 2014 for review; Laschinger, Wong, Cummings & Grau, 2014). Also, simultaneously, a team's aggressive culture may affect the team's culture of trust (De Dreu, Giebels, & Van de Vliet, 1998), as people use social cues to base their initial trust in the team member on and gradually establish trust (or distrust) through repeated personal interactions (van der Werff & Buckley, 2014). Therefore, the two constructs interdependently create a holistic social environment (Tzafrir et al., 2013).

Furthermore, Costa (2003) measured team level of trust by aggregating individuals within teams and found a relationship between trust at the team level and several social aspects within the teams. Also, as Kozlowski and Klein (2000) suggested, a phenomenon at the individual level can emerge at the team level and vice versa (Tzafrir, et al., 2013). For instance, van der Werff and Buckley (2014) explored how socialization impacts newcomers' trust.

When members of the team work in a stressful work environment or experience interpersonal conflicts, ambiguity, work–home conflict and organizational changes (Baron & Neuman, 1996; Hauge, Skogstad & Einarsen, 2009; Liu, et al., 2015), they are likely to experience aggressive culture. Such culture is permitted by a norm of aggressive behaviour (see Ehrhart & Raver, 2014 for review; Laschinger, Wong, Cummings & Grau, 2014). According to the social learning theory (Bandura, 1978), people learn aggressive behaviour either from personal experience or from observation. Relying on Glomb and Liao (2003), who found that team aggression significantly predicted individual aggressive behaviour beyond reciprocal and individual factors, we propose that an atmosphere of aggression and mistrust within the team will affect individuals in the team beyond their actual anger at a specific time, creating an escalatory loop of anger and aggression.

Trust as glue: future research and implications

The major role trust plays in the nexus between social emotional environment and individual behaviour has to be taken into account when managers considered the future of the team's achievements (Ben Sasson & Somech, 2015). In order to cope with various stakeholders, team leaders should bear in mind the culture of trust as a cognitive and emotional tool for shaping stakeholders' behaviours such as aggression. As the vast organizational literature concerning aggressive behaviour shows, aggressive behaviour has various consequences affecting the employees, and the team's wellbeing, attitudes and performance. Thus, organizations have high interest in preventing aggression and improving employment social environment (Enosh, et al., 2013; Tzafrir, et al., 2015).

From a theoretical point of view, our review contributes to both the trust literature and aggressive behaviour literature by demonstrating the moderating impact of attribution and trust at the individual level, while emphasizing the role of diffusion (Tzafrir, et al., 2013) of trust and attribution from the team level to the individual level, and vice versa. That said, the question remains – what are the future research and practical implications of such a model for real-life individuals and teams in organizations? In order to consider these implications, we should think about the role of symmetric and asymmetric trust and their impact on re-active and pro-active behaviour. In order to do so, future research should build and develop tools to allow this to occur. This is in line with Goe and colleagues' (2015) recommendation for organizational evidence-based and measurable interventions. For ESEN and trust to be used to cope with aggressive behaviour, evidence-based research should look at possible preventive interventions in three stages – primary, secondary and tertiary preventions.

While organizations can and should react to phenomena of aggression within the organization (re-action), one may expect that organizations should take a more pro-active approach. Enhancing the culture of trust will increase sense of belonging and reduce feelings of uncertainty, thus, preventing and decreasing aggressive culture in advance, before it escalates. Primary prevention aims to prevent such phenomena, even before they occur. This may be achieved by creating a just and positive emotional social environment as well as preventing injustice (Bies, 2001; Kramer, 1996; Tripp, Bies & Aquino, 2007) and encouraging transparency within the organization, thus building and developing a trustful relationship between the organization and its stakeholders.

Further research should focus also on secondary prevention, which aims to increase dyadic trust and thus reduce the impact of hostile attribution and aggression that has already occurred. Such research may focus on processes of detecting and simultaneously treating hostile attribution and aggression at both individual and team levels, as soon as possible, to avoid escalation. Moreover, research should look for positive strategies on all levels to prevent recurrence and social learning processes (Bandura, 1978); and finally, it should examine evidence-based action programmes aimed at returning homeostasis and coping with long-term problems. For instance, let's consider an employee who faced aggressive behaviour from a customer, another employee or his/her supervisor, and expects recognition, remedy and protection from further aggression. Such situations are part of the psychological contract (Robinson & Rousseau, 1994; Rousseau, 1989; see also Chapter 11 by Coyle-Shapiro & Diehl, this volume, on social exchange theory; as well as Chapter 28 by Searle, this volume, on psychological contract). Research into secondary prevention should examine the organizational reaction to aggressive behaviour and how it affects the offended party, and in turn, the employment social environment, the offender, and other potential stakeholders (Chernyak-Hai & Tziner, 2014, Morken, Johansen & Alsker, 2015). Current research has demonstrated that when an organization, team and manager supports employees faced with customer aggression, it moderates the negative influence on job satisfaction and leaving intentions (Shih, Lie, Klein & Jiang, 2014). On the other hand, when managers do not actively react to aggressive behaviour, such reticence to act or failure to provide leadership altogether (DeRue, Nahrgang, Wellman & Humphrey, 2011) may lead to team hostile attribution, and may increase workplace incivility within the organization (Harold & Holtz, 2015; see also Chapter 8 by Fulmer, this volume, for a review on the multi-level link).

Can the consequences of aggressive behaviour be fixed? This question may be part of the issue of tertiary prevention. In some organizations, the impact of an ongoing lack of trust, hostile attribution and aggression may have lasting effects. To deal with chronic organizational problems (such as team hostile attribution), managers should employ a gradual, long-term strategy through human resources that aims to build and develop a culture of justice and trust (Dolan, Garcia & Richley, 2006). In a similar line, Pate, Morgan-Thomas and Beaumont (2012) described a case study of an organization that was faced with an increasing ESEN of chronic bullying and norms of harassment, while trust in top management was declining. In order to change the course of deterioration, top management offered an apology, invested in learning and understanding the problem of bullying in organizations, and initiated an organization-wide intervention (see Part IV Trust repair, this volume). Nevertheless, trust in top management has only partially improved.

The overall trust was found to correlate with bullying – reduction in bullying environment perception correlated with trust increase. Pate and colleagues (2012) described an implementation of Gillespie and Dietz's (2009) trust repair framework which used both emotional and cognitive aspects as well as focusing simultaneously on individuals and macro-level facet (see Chapter 16 by Gillespie and Siebert, this volume). For instance, the organization initiated a new policy titled 'Dignity at Work' as well as trying to 'reverse the negative trend in trust' (p. 157). Pate and colleagues' (2012) study demonstrated the need for a multidimensional approach when using trust as a pro-active tool for increasing or decreasing organizational behaviour phenomena.

Another current example is the organization development programme called Civility, Respect and Engagement at the Workplace (CREW), conducted within the Department of Veterans Affairs (Leiter, 2013; Osatuke, Leiter, Belton, Dyrenforth & Ramsel, 2013). CREW is a new programme to support a culture of civil and respectful exchanges on the job within the agency; it included a dual approach tackling bullying and harassment, even to the extent of dismissals of senior staff. It was combined with employee training programs emphasizing the organization's policy. Follow up evaluation research two years after the initiation, shows employee attitude regarding bullying has undergone a significant change.

Building on Gillespie and Dietz's (2009) seminal work regarding preventive and constructive measures at various components of intervention, we suggest that a comprehensive approach should focus on the interplay between levels, processes and assets. In the context of this review, we may relate to the individual and team levels; internal and external processes; and intangible and tangible assets. On recognizing that ongoing interpersonal conflicts escalate at a team level, a pro-active approach should be immediately taken. For instance, human resource staff may want to organize formal meetings and workshops focused on understanding possible value gaps between team, managers, employees, customers and other stakeholders, combining such formal activities and assets with intangible assets such leaderships (Bies, Tripp & Shapiro, 2016) within the team, facilitating a positive ESEN.

Describing and understanding the process of ESEN within teams and organizations is the first step towards its modification and transformation. To achieve this, it is necessary for management to support and assist individuals and teams, and deal with problems that arise in or to 'combat' aggressive culture. In addition, managers need to take into account the micro, meso and macro levels while trying to confront the issue for the sake of the health and wellbeing of the team and entire organization. Thus, organization, team and individual levels should be integrated and coordinated simultaneously, conveying clear and unequivocal support. Following the integration of organization, team and individual levels and the analysis of Fulmer and Gelfand (2012) on the interaction between various levels of trust in the organization, we suggested that future research will focus on the contextual level (Johns, 2006) as well as on the effect of organizational culture of trust on individual trust, and vice versa. Also, as Tzafrir and colleagues (2013) recommended, future research should take into account how aggressive culture diffuses to individual members of the team, enhancing aggressive behaviour.

We began our journey by explaining the team, situational and individual antecedents of anger, which leads to aggressive behaviour. Moving forward, we elaborated the individual process leading from the antecedents of anger to aggressive and non-aggressive behaviour, focusing on the moderating role of trust both at the individual and team-culture levels. Finally, we elevated the ecological level back from the individual to the team levels. Therefore, our review may have major implications for research on interventions at the team level, which could lead to a long-term process for primary prevention. Finally, we believe the same framework might apply at other organizational and societal levels.

Notes

1 Equal contribution, names appear in a random order.
2 Anger is an emotion defined by Berkowitz (1962) in terms of the tendency to become aggressive following frustration. Aggressive behaviour at the workplace can be defined as 'a general term encompassing all forms of behaviour by which individuals attempt to harm others at work or their organizations' (Neuman & Baron, 1998, p. 393). Nevertheless, there are many definitions for each construct with no clear agreement. Also, as Berkowitz (1993) explained, people used these terms with different meanings in various contexts (Johns, 2006).
3 As every dynamic model is characterized by multi-factorial feedback, it seems plausible that individual anger can be the cause as well as the outcome of contextual factors such as culture of trust and aggressive culture, as well as personal trust. Accordingly, given the specific focus of the current review, we used dotted arrows to indicate possible relationships that are not part of the focus of this review.
4 Those experiences don't have to be related directly to the current interaction.
5 When considering the possible effects of personal trust on anger, and vice versa, we may realize that in certain contexts, personal trust may reduce anger, while at other times personal trust may increase anger, for example, when feeling 'betrayed' by a trusted person (Tripp, Bies & Aquino, 2007). Furthermore, following such a feeling of betrayal, sense of personal trust may be drastically reduced. Since the focus of our paper is on the interaction between individual and team levels, rather than on micro-level interpersonal interactions, we present such possible relationships in our model using a double ended arrow; however, we do not specify any related hypotheses.
6 Based on Kramer's (2001) seminal work on workplace paranoid ideation at the individual level, we suggest that 'distrust that encompasses an array of beliefs, including organizational members' perceptions of being threatened, harmed, persecuted, mistreated, disparaged, and so on, by malevolent others within the organization' (2001, p. 6) can also exists at a collective team level.

References

Ainsworth, S. E., Baumeister, R. F., Ariely, D., & Vohs, K. D. (2014). Ego depletion decreases trust in economic decision making. *Journal of Experimental Social Psychology, 54*, 40–49.

Ambrose, M. L., Seabright, M. A., & Schminke, M. (2002). Sabotage in the workplace: The role of organizational injustice. *Organizational Behavior and Human Decision Processes, 89*(1), 947–965.

Anderson, C. A., & Bushman, B. J. (2002). Human aggression. *Annual Review of Psychology, 53*(1), 27–51.

Bandura, A. (1978). Social learning theory of aggression. *Journal of Communication, 28*(3), 12–29.

Barney, J., & Felin, T. (2013). What are microfoundations? *Academy of Management Perspectives, 27*(2), 138–155.

Baron, R. A., & Neuman, J. H. (1996). Workplace violence and workplace aggression: Evidence on their relative frequency and potential causes. *Aggressive Behavior, 22*(3), 161–173.

Baumeister, R. F., Smart, L., & Boden, J. M. (1996). Relation of threatened egotism to violence and aggression: the dark side of high self-esteem. *Psychological Review, 103*(1), 5–33.

Beale, D., & Hoel, H. (2010). Workplace bullying, industrial relations and the challenge for management in Britain and Sweden. *European Journal of Industrial Relations, 16*(2), 101–118.

Ben Sasson, D., & Somech, A. (2015). Do teachers misbehave? Aggression in school teams. *Journal of Educational Administration, 53*(6), 755–772.

Berkowitz, L. (1962). *Aggression: A social psychological analysis.* New York: McGraw-Hill.

Berkowitz, L. (1993). *Aggression: Its causes, consequences, and control.* New York: McGraw-Hill.

Berkowitz, L. (2014). Towards a general theory of anger and emotional aggression: implications. In R. S. Wyer Jr. & T. K. Srull (eds.), *Perspectives on Anger and Emotion: Advances in Social Cognition, 6* (pp. 1–46). NY and London: Psychology Press, Taylor & Francis Group.

Bies, R. J., & Tripp, T. M. 1996. Beyond distrust: Getting even and the need for revenge. In R. M. Kramer & T. Tyler (eds.), *Trust in organizations* (pp. 246–260). Thousand Oaks, CA: Sage.

Bies, R. J. (2001). Interactional (in)justice: The sacred and the profane. In J. Greenberg & R. Cropanzano (eds.), *Advances in Organizational Justice* (pp. 89–118). Stanford, CA: Stanford University Press.

Bies, R. J., Tripp, T. M., & Shapiro, D. L. (2016). Abusive leaders or master motivators? "Abusive is in the eye of the beholder. In N. Ashkanasy, R. B. Bennett, & M. J. Martinko (eds), *Understanding the High Performance Workplace: The line between motivation and abuse* (pp. 252–276). New York: Routledge.

Bushman, B. J., & Baumeister, R. F. (1998). Threatened egotism, narcissism, self-esteem, and direct and displaced aggression: Does self-love or self-hate lead to violence? *Journal of Personality and Social Psychology, 75*(1), 219–229.

Chen, G., & Kanfer, R. (2006). Toward a systems theory of motivated behavior in work teams. *Research in Organizational Behavior, 27*, 223–267.

Chen, G., Kanfer, R., DeShon, R. P., Mathieu, J. E., & Kozlowski, S. W. J. (2009). The motivating potential of teams: A test and extension of model. *Organizational Behavior and Human Decision Processes, 110*, 45–55.

Chernyak-Hai, L., & Tziner, A. (2014). Relationships between counterproductive work behavior, perceived justice and climate, occupational status, and leader-member exchange. *Journal of Work and Organizational Psychology, 30*, 1–12.

Colquitt, J. A., LePine, J. A., Piccolo, R. F., Zapata, C. P., & Rich, B. L. (2012). Explaining the justice–performance relationship: Trust as exchange deepener or trust as uncertainty reducer? *Journal of Applied Psychology, 97*(1), 1–15.

Costa, A. C. (2003). Work team trust and effectiveness. *Personnel Review, 32*(5), 605–622.

DeBono, A., & Muraven, M. (2014). Rejection perceptions: Feeling disrespected leads to greater aggression than feeling disliked. *Journal of Experimental Social Psychology, 55*, 43–52.

De Dreu, C. K., Giebels, E., & Van de Vliet, E. (1998). Social motives and trust in integrative negotiation: The disruptive effects of punitive capability. *Journal of Applied Psychology, 83*(3), 408–422.

De Jong, J. P., Curşeu, P. L., & Leenders, R. T. A. (2014). When do bad apples not spoil the barrel? Negative relationships in teams, team performance, and buffering mechanisms. *Journal of Applied Psychology, 99*(3), 514–522.

De Jong, B. A., & Dirks, K. T. (2012). Beyond shared perceptions of trust and monitoring in teams: implications of asymmetry and dissensus. *Journal of Applied Psychology, 97*(2), 391–406.

DeRue, D. S., Nahrgang, J. D., Wellman, N., & Humphrey, S. E. (2011). Trait and behavioral theories of leadership: A meta-analytic test of their relative validity. *Personnel Psychology, 64*, 7–52.

Devinney, T. M. (2013). Is microfoundational thinking critical to management thought and practice? *The Academy of Management Perspectives, 27*(2), 81–84.

Dolan, S. L., Garcia, S., & Richley, B. (2006). *Managing by Values: A corporate guide to living, being alive, and making a living in the 21st Century.* New York: Palgrave Macmillan.

Dunn, J. R., & Schweitzer, M. E. (2005). Feeling and believing: the influence of emotion on trust. *Journal of Personality and Social Psychology, 88*(5), 736–748.

Dupré, K. E., Dawe, K. A. & Barling, J. (2014). Harm to those who serve effects of direct and vicarious customer-initiated workplace aggression. *Journal of Interpersonal Violence, 29*(13), 2355–2377.

Einarsen, S., Hoel, H., Zapf, D. & Cooper, C. (eds). (2003). *Bullying and emotional abuse in the workplace: International perspectives in research and practice.* CRC Press. http://rosskirilov.com/cjue/wp-content/uploads/2015/04/Bullying-and-Emotional-Abuse-in-the-Workplace.pdf

Enosh, G., Tzafrir, S., & Gur, A. (2013). Client aggression towards social workers and social services in Israel – a qualitative analysis. *Journal of Interpersonal Violence, 28*(6), 1123–1142.

Enosh, G., & Tzafrir, S. S. (2015). The scope of client aggression toward social workers in Israel. *Journal of Aggression, Maltreatment & Trauma, 24*(9), 971–985.

Ehrhart, M. G., & Raver, J. L. (2014). The effects of organizational climate and culture on productive and counterproductive behavior. In B. Scheider and K. Barbera (eds), *The Oxford Handbook of Organizational Climate and Culture,* (pp. 153–176). Electronic version New York: Oxford University Press.

Ferrin, D. L., & Dirks, K. T. (2003). The use of rewards to increase and decrease trust: Mediating processes and differential effects. *Organization Science, 14*(1), 18–31.

Ferris, G. R., Arthur, M. M., Berkson, H. M., Kaplan, D. M., Harrell-Cook, G., & Frink, D. D. (1998). Toward a social context theory of the human resource management-organization effectiveness relationship. *Human Resource Management Review, 8*(3), 235–264.

Fukuyama, F. (1996). *Trust: The social virtues and the creation of prosperity.* Vol. 457. New York: Free Press.

Fulmer, C. A., & Gelfand, M. J. (2012). At what level (and in whom) we trust: Trust across multiple organizational levels. *Journal of Management, 38*(4), 1167–1230.

Geurts, S., Schaufeli, W., & De Jonge, J. (1998). Burnout and intention to leave among mental health-care professionals: A social psychological approach. *Journal of Social and Clinical Psychology, 17*(3), 341–362.

Goh, J., Pfeffer, J., & Zenios, S. A. (2015). Workplace stressors & health outcomes: health policy for the workplace. *Behavioral Science & Policy, 1*(1), 43–52.

Gino, F., & Schweitzer, M. E. (2008). Blinded by anger or feeling the love: how emotions influence advice taking. *Journal of Applied Psychology, 93*(5), 1165–1173.

Glomb, T. M., & Liao, H. (2003). Interpersonal aggression in work groups: Social influence, reciprocal, and individual effects. *Academy of Management Journal, 46*(4), 486–496.

Harold, C. M., & Holtz, B. C. (2015). The effects of passive leadership on workplace incivility. *Journal of Organizational Behavior, 36*(1), 16–38.

Hauge, L. J., Skogstad, A., & Einarsen, S. (2009). Individual and situational predictors of workplace bullying: Why do perpetrators engage in the bullying of others? *Work & Stress, 23*(4), 349–358.

Hershcovis, M. S., Turner, N., Barling, J., Arnold, K. A., Dupré, K. E., Inness, M. & Sivanathan, N. (2007). Predicting workplace aggression: a meta-analysis. *Journal of Applied Psychology, 92*(1), 228.

Hoel, H., & Salin, D. (2011). Organisational antecedents of workplace bullying. In J. H. Neuman, R. A. Baron, S. Einarsen, H. Hoel, D. Zapf, & C. Cooper (eds.), *Bullying and Harassment in the Workplace: Developments in theory, research, and practice*, E-reader version (pp. 205–214). London: CRC Press.

Jávor, I., & Jancsics, D. (2013). The role of power in organizational corruption: an empirical study. *Administration & Society*, 1–33. Published online 0095399713514845.

Johns, G. (2006). The essential impact of context on organizational behavior. *Academy of Management Review, 31*(2), 386–408.

Kelley, H. H., & Michela, J. L. (1980). Attribution theory and research. *Annual Review of Psychology, 31*(1), 457–501.

Klackl, J., Pfundmair, M., Agroskin, D., & Jonas, E. (2013). Who is to blame? Oxytocin promotes nonpersonalistic attributions in response to a trust betrayal. *Biological Psychology, 92*(2), 387–394.

Kong, D. T., Dirks, K. T., & Ferrin, D. L. (2014). Interpersonal trust within negotiations: Meta-analytic evidence, critical contingencies, and directions for future research. *Academy of Management Journal, 57*(5), 1235–1255.

Korsgaard, M. A., Brower, H. H., & Lester, S. W. (2015). It isn't always mutual: A critical review of dyadic trust. *Journal of Management, 41*(1), 47–70.

Kozlowski, S. W. J., & Klein, K. J. (2000). A multilevel approach to theory and research in organizations – Contextual, temporal and emergent processes. In K. J. Klein & S. W. J. Kozlowski (eds), *Multilevel theory, research and methods in organizations* (pp. 3–90). San Francisco, CA: Jossey-Bass.

Kramer, R. M. (1999). Trust and distrust in organizations: Emerging perspectives, enduring questions. *Annual Review of Psychology, 50*(1), 569–598.

Kramer, R. M. (2001). Organizational paranoia: Origins and dynamics. *Research in Organizational Behavior, 23*, 1–42.

Kramer, R. M., & Lewicki, R. J. (2010). Repairing and enhancing trust: Approaches to reducing organizational trust deficits. *Academy of Management Annals, 4*(1), 245–277.

Krieglmeyer, R., Wittstadt, D., & Strack, F. (2009). How attribution influences aggression: answers to an old question by using an implicit measure of anger. *Journal of Experimental Social Psychology, 45*(2), 379–385.

Laschinger, H. K. S., Wong, C. A., Cummings, G. G., & Grau, A. L. (2014). Resonant leadership and workplace empowerment: the value of positive organizational cultures in reducing workplace incivility. *Nursing Economics, 32*(1), 5–15.

Leiter, M. (2013). *Analyzing and theorizing the dynamics of the workplace incivility crisis.* Amsterdam: Springer.

Lewicki, R. J., Tomlinson, E. C., & Gillespie, N. (2006). Models of interpersonal trust development: Theoretical approaches, empirical evidence, and future directions. *Journal of Management, 32*(6), 991–1022.

Lewis, K., Lange, D., & Gillis, L. (2005). Transactive memory systems, learning, and learning transfer. *Organization Science, 16*(6), 581–598.

Linardi, A., & McConnell, M. A. (2011). No excuses for good behavior: Volunteering and the social environment. *Journal of Public Economics, 95*, 445–454.

Liu, Y., Wang, M., Chang, C. H., Shi, J., Zhou, L., & Shao, R. (2015). Work–family conflict, emotional exhaustion, and displaced aggression toward others: The moderating roles of workplace interpersonal conflict and perceived managerial family support. *Journal of Applied Psychology, 100*(3), 793.

Lyu, Y., Zhu, H., Zhong, H. J., & Hu, L. (2016). Abusive supervision and customer-oriented organizational citizenship behavior: The roles of hostile attribution bias and work engagement. *International Journal of Hospitality Management, 53*, 69–80.

McEvily, B., Perrone, V., & Zaheer, A. (2003). Trust as an organizing principle. *Organization Science, 14*(1), 91–103.

Mitchell, M. S., & Ambrose, M. L. (2007). Abusive supervision and workplace deviance and the moderating effects of negative reciprocity beliefs. *Journal of Applied Psychology, 92*(4), 1159–1168.

Morken, T., Johansen, I. H., & Alsaker, K. (2015). Dealing with workplace violence in emergency primary health care: a focus group study. *BMC Family Practice, 16*(1), 1–7. Electronic version http://biomed central.com/content/pdf/s12875-015-0276-z.pdf

Neuman, J. H., & Baron, R. A. (1998). Workplace violence and workplace aggression: Evidence concerning specific forms, potential causes, and preferred targets. *Journal of Management, 24*(3), 391–419.

Neuman, J. H., & Baron, R. A. (2011). Social antecedents of bullying: A social interactionist perspective. In J. H. Neuman, R. A. Baron, S. Einarsen, H. Hoel, D. Zapf, & C. Cooper (eds), *Bullying and Harassment in the Workplace: Developments in theory, research, and practice*, E-reader version (pp. 176–204). London: CRC Press.

Nixon, A. E., & Spector, P. E. (2015). Seeking clarity in a linguistic fog: Moderators of the workplace aggression-strain relationship. *Human Performance, 28*(2), 137–164.

Norstrand, J. A., Glicksman, A., Lubben, J., & Kleban, M. (2012). The role of the social environment on physical and mental health of older adults, *Journal of Housing for the Elderly, 26*, 290–307.

Oh, K. J., & Farh, C. (2017). An emotional process theory of how subordinates appraise, experience, and respond to abusive supervision over time. *Academy of Management Review, 42*(2), 207–232.

Osatuke, K., Leiter, M., Belton, L., Dyrenforth, S., & Ramsel, D. (2013). Civility, Respect and Engagement at the Workplace (CREW): A national organization development program at the department of veterans affairs. *Journal of Management Policies Practices, 1*, 25–34.

Pate, J., Morgan-Thomas, A., & Beaumont, P. (2012). Trust restoration: an examination of senior managers' attempt to rebuild employee trust. *Human Resource Management Journal, 22*(2), 148–164.

Pinto, J. (2014). Expanding the content domain of workplace aggression: A three level aggressor–target taxonomy. *International Journal of Management Reviews, 16*(3), 290–313.

Robinson, S. L., & Rousseau, D. M. (1994). Violating the psychological contract: Not the exception but the norm. *Journal of Organizational Behavior, 15*(3), 245–259.

Rogers, E. M. (2010). *Diffusion of Innovations*. New York: Simon and Schuster.

Rousseau, D. M. (1989). Psychological and implied contracts in organizations. *Employee Responsibilities and Rights Journal, 2*(2), 121–139.

Rupp, D. E., & Paddock, E. L. (2010). From justice events to justice climate: A multi-level temporal model of information aggregation and judgment. *Research on Managing Groups and Teams, 13*, 245–273.

Schaubroeck, J. M., Peng, A. C., & Hannah, S. T. (2013). Developing trust with peers and leaders: Impacts on organizational identification and performance during entry. *Academy of Management Journal, 56*(4), 1148–1168.

Shih, S. P., Lie, T., Klein, G., & Jiang, J. J. (2014). Information technology customer aggression: The importance of an organizational climate of support. *Information & Management, 51*(6), 670–678.

Shoss, M. K., Eisenberger, R., Restubog, S. L. D., & Zagenczyk, T. J. (2013). Blaming the organization for abusive supervision: The roles of perceived organizational support and supervisor's organizational embodiment. *Journal of Applied Psychology, 98*(1), 158–168.

Sliter, M. T., Jex, S., & Grubb, P. (2013). The relationship between the social environment of work and workplace mistreatment. *Journal of Behavioral Health, 2*(2), 120–126.

Stucke, T. S., & Baumeister, R. F. (2006). Ego depletion and aggressive behavior: Is the inhibition of aggression a limited resource? *European Journal of Social Psychology, 36*, 1–13.

Tedeschi, J. T., & Felson, R. B. (1994). *Violence, Aggression, and Coercive Actions*. Washington, DC: American Psychological Association.

Tripp, T. M., Bies, R. J., & Aquino, K. (2007). A vigilante model of justice: Revenge, reconciliation, forgiveness, and avoidance. *Social Justice Research, 20*(1), 10–34.

Tzafrir, S. S., Enosh, G., Parry, E., & Stone, D. L. (2013). CODIFYing Social issues in organizations – Scope and perspectives. *Global Business Perspective, 1*(1), 39–47.

Tzafrir, S. S. Gur, A., and Blumen, O. (2015) Employee social environment as a tool to decrease intention to leave. *Scandinavian Journal of Management, 30*(1), 136–146. http://sciencedirect.com/science/article/pii/S0956522114000906

Von Scheve, C., & Ismer, S. (2013). Towards a theory of collective emotions. *Emotion Review, 5*(4), 406–413.

Weiner, B. (1985). An attributional theory of achievement motivation and emotion. *Psychological Review, 92*(4), 548–573.

Yang, I. (2015). Perceived conflict avoidance by managers and its consequences on subordinates' attitudes. *Business Ethics: A European Review*. http://mfa.gov.il/MFA/AboutIsrael/State/Law/Pages/Prevention_of_Sexual_Harassment_Law_5758-1998.aspx

Xia, L., Yuan, Y. C., & Gay, G. (2009). Exploring negative group dynamics adversarial network, personality, and performance in project groups. *Management Communication Quarterly, 23*, 32–62.

van der Werff, L., & Buckley, F. (2014). Getting to know you: A longitudinal examination of trust cues and trust development during socialization. *Journal of Management, 43*(3), 742–770.

Watzlawick, P., Weakland, J. H., & Fisch, R. (2011). *Change: Principles of problem formulation and problem resolution* (Rev. edn). New York, NY: Norton.

31

IMPLICATIONS FOR FUTURE DIRECTIONS IN TRUST RESEARCH

Rosalind H. Searle, Ann-Marie I. Nienaber and Sim B. Sitkin

This book's 31 chapters reflect trust as an important and vibrant field of study, both in terms of what has already been done, but more significantly in the fruitful future research agendas our contributing authors have outlined. The chapters that comprise the book's six parts highlight some of the foundational approaches and building blocks in this field. In this last chapter, we do not merely repeat what our contributors have identified, but instead offer a meta-level perspective that identifies eight challenges and future directions for study.

Affect

A consistent theme that many of our authors raise is the importance of rebalancing current conceptual and empirical attention in this field to incorporate more affective elements. Many of our contributors outline the necessity and value of trust research shifting away from the dominance of cognitive considerations, to include the relatively neglected topic of affect as a fundamental feature of trust. Many chapters have identified the value and importance of incorporating the role of emotions into the study of trust (see Chapter 1 by van Knippenberg, but also Chapter 9 by Baer & Colquitt) and ensuring emotion in studies of distrust (see Chapter 4 by Sitkin & Bijlsma-Frankema). Indeed, affect is maybe one of the defining elements that not only distinguishes trust from distrust, but that is also central in detecting transitions of trust into distrust (Nienaber, et al., 2016).

Dynamic models

Insight into the triggers, patterns and effects of trust and distrust (see Chapter 2 by Korsgaard) can benefit from more systematic exploration of the dynamics of trust and distrust (see Chapter 4 by Sitkin & Bijlsma-Frankema; Chapter 15 by Kim; Chapter 16 by Gillespie & Siebert; Chapter 28 by Searle). In promoting more dynamic perspectives, attention would be given to how processes may be interrelated, such as prior experiences being seminal to shaping future trajectories as Robinson's (1996) work has identified. This directs attention to emergent and ongoing processes of trusting (Möllering, 2013). These are matters likely to require far more sophisticated thought if trust researchers are to meet the challenges that accompany greater use of dynamic and longitudinal study and so devise far more rigourous designs.

Biological basis of trust

Another broad area of concern raised by many of our authors is the impact of the ability to analyse the neurological foundations of trust in today's society. Trust studies are at a crossroads, with technological advances offering the possibility of significant shifts in the field through permitting far greater illumination of previously hidden biological dimensions of human experiences. Critically, important contributions have highlighted the biological bases of trust and distrust, including Zak and colleagues (2005) on trustworthiness and oxytocin, and Dimoka's (2010) identification of the biological differences between trust and distrust. This research has heralded new directions for further empirical study. Such work is, however, likely to produce interesting debates regarding the objective assessment of levels of trust and distrust and individuals' subsequent subjective decisions and actions which Bies and colleagues explore (see Chapter 17, this volume). Thus, while biological measures might register distrust, if there are few options but to remain in a situation, observable behaviours might signal trust due to situational constraints that mask underlying psychological preferences.

Technology

Developments in technology have revolutionized both the convenience and the level of intrusion of data gathering. New applications, such as apps on a mobile phone, but also miniaturization of technology, are likely to ease dynamic biographical and attitudinal measurement, and so enable significant inroads into the study of dynamics. As well as affecting our ability to observe and measure indicators of trust, changes in technology have implications for what is the object of trust. For example, trust in technical systems and trust in the privacy measures put in place by technology organizations will continue to grow in prominence. The ability of governments and corporations to monitor and record the actions of individuals and groups has grown faster than our ability as individuals or as scientists to keep up with its implications. Undoubtedly, this will continue to grow as a significant focus of future research on trust (see Bernstein, 2012, for an illustration). Further, alongside these fresh insights for the field, new developments will create opportunities to revisit and compare results using more cross-sectional recall-based methods.

Time

Related to our use of more dynamic models, noted above, is scholars' ability to extend conceptual and methodological attention regarding time. While advances in statistical techniques have kept pace with developments in dynamics, there has certainly not been the same level of sophistication applied to our conceptualization of whether and how temporality might impact trust. Little attention has been paid to growing insight into time and its impact on organizational life (Roe, Waller, & Clegg, 2008; Shipp & Fried, 2014a, 2014b). Further, the question of time and both its subjective and objective impact are all too often afterthoughts to the development of trust study designs. Yet, temporality is a pressing concern that demands far more rigourous thinking, especially if our longitudinal and dynamic studies are really to capture phenomena. For example, earlier studies of teams (Gersick, 1988, 1991, 1994) have much to offer in terms of showing how time, pace and temporal aspects shape behaviours. Such work reveals how beginnings, middles and ends of work processes exhibit predictable patterns in terms of the pace and types of decisions and behaviours. Scholars who gather multiple assessment points, could extend their insights by examining differences across starting, middle and end phases of events. For example, in the study of trust repair, temporal considerations might include questions about whether the object of interest concerns the onset or closure of a phenomenon (such as capturing the tipping points that occur in the transitions of trust to distrust), or include the types and frequency of measurement necessary to ensure adequate capture of the flows and waves of activity and change. Studies might seek to focus on temporal location (e.g. what day in the week or what time of the day data are collected) (see Shipp & Cole, 2015; Shipp, Edwards, & Lambert, 2009; Shipp & Fried, 2014a, 2014b), duration (e.g., length of distinct stages) or intensities (e.g., extremes of highs and lows in different stages or processes for repair) of phenomena (Roe, 2008). Further, we need more attention paid to *when* assessments are collected – for example, might it matter whether they are gathered on the same day, as we know experiences at the start of the week (Monday blues or manic Mondays) are different from those captured at the end (start of the weekend Friday).

Levels of analysis

Historically, most trust research focused on an individual trustor and an individual trustee. Over recent years, trust research has broadened to conceptualize trust beyond dyads of individuals (Chapter 5 by Lyu & Ferrin) to include multi-level models (see Chapter 8 by Fulmer) that include the group (Chapter 6 by Nienaber et al.) and organization (Chapter 7 by Brattström & Bachmann). These broader perspectives facilitate novel insights into a variety of interrelationships and spillovers that affect trust. Adopting more multi-level perspectives might necessitate revisiting less sophisticated use of simple aggregation by researchers, and demand more attention on the value of focusing on asymmetries and outliers, or trust reciprocations (De Jong & Dirks, 2012; Korsgaard, Brower, & Lester, 2015). Attention and assessment to identify the distinct curvilinear patterns of trust and distrust will be a potentially important future opportunity.

Context

This book includes a whole part that reflects how trust may function differently in diverse contexts and how different situations may raise various determinants and effects, making context central to enhancing our understanding of trust. While scholars have long attested to the centrality of context to enhancing the study of organizational phenomena (Griffin, 2007; Johns, 2006; Rousseau & Fried, 2001), there remains greater insight required regarding the specific ways that context may be critical to studies of trust. Through the increased scrutiny of trust matters in different locations, there has been greater illumination of the distinct types and severity of risks, and in revealing the asymmetries of information and power. It clearly remains important that further studies also pay attention to the influence and impact of context to allow more fine-grained distinctions to be made of important trust antecedents or to shape distinctive processes and major outputs (Griffin, 2007). Context may also be significant in attending to the subtleties required to adequately capture the dynamics of interpersonal and organizational relations (Shipp & Cole, 2015). In this book, scholarly attention has explored trust in the safety-critical domain in Chapter 24 by Gunia and colleagues and indicated some key omissions to our knowledge. Dichotomising trust further into the dual concerns of vulnerability and confidence could allow focus on the tones and shades in other high-stakes contexts, such as those involving the military, police, and oil and gas. Likewise, perspectives of different stakeholders may offer important dimensionality to future impactful study.

A further important domain that is captured in at least two chapters is the cyber world (see Chapter 3 by Blomqvist and Cook and Chapter 22 by van der Werff and colleagues. The speed of current developments makes this remain an ongoing domain for further research. The scale and scope of its influence is high for individuals, teams, organizations and more globally. It is one in which to explore institutional trustworthiness (see Chapter 12 by Bachmann), such as found in the encroachments and tensions between the state and private corporations regarding individuals' privacy, in the fidelity and robustness of systems, or in understanding better the motives involved in the protection of individual citizens or users. It offers an important fresh domain to explore perceptions and triggers for vulnerability and trust breach as both individuals and organizations seek to mitigate against system breaches from either their own distrusting employees, such as demonstrated by Snowdon, or external nefarious sources, such as unsympathetic states or movements (e.g. ISIS/DAESH), competitors, criminals or loose configurations of hackers. Trust is, therefore, inherently susceptible to breach, courtesy both of its novelty and lack of knowledge by users, and of system weaknesses. It is important to consider whether the potential for malignance from criminals and overarching institutions makes this simply a new domain in which to study old trust questions; or might it offer something to advance exploration of the dynamics of trust and distrust. Does context matter more in cyber domains than in others, or is it merely a different backdrop for the same concerns?

Conceptualizing trust

A concern raised in many of the chapters, concurrently with the wider field is the adequacy and application of measures (McEvily & Tortoriello, 2011) and the degree to which those measures are grounded in clear and consensual conceptualizations of trust. For example, questions of what generalized trust means in both a conceptual and methodological sense have broad implications (Freitag & Traunmüller, 2009; Kong, 2016). Debates are ongoing about whether the willingness to trust is something stable within individuals, derived from early experiences, or something that might change related to key experiences, or by virtue of aging processes (Kong, 2016). Might measures be robust and able to transcend contexts, or distinct to a particular context or culture (Ferrin & Gillespie, 2010)? Or is trust something more specific, and so varying with the referent and thus a particular relationship? In contrast, might measurement be better focused on conceptualizing processes of trusting (Möllering, 2013) and identifying particular thresholds or optimal levels for trust? Can we gain consensus on what constitutes excessive levels of trust or distrust? What are the differences between such levels or the dynamics between trust and distrust, or can these two coexist (Buckwalter, 2008; Cho, 2006; Dimoka, 2010; Gill & Butler, 2003; Kramer & Cook, 2004; Kramer & Isen, 1994; Saunders, Dietz, & Thornhill, 2014; Searle & Ball, 2004)? Should greater attention be given to feeling trusted, rather than to trusting others (Brower, Lester, Korsgaard, & Dineen, 2009) or to feeling distrusted? Finally, many of our authors identify the need for greater attention to the relationships between trust and other phenomena, either to develop greater insight into the nominological network of trust and dimensions such as commitment and identification (Ng, 2015), justice (see Chapter 10 by Lind), or to understanding better trust's antecedents (see Chapter 9 by Baer & Colquitt) and consequences (see Chapter 5 by Lyu & Ferrin).

In conclusion, this volume has included chapters that address a wide range of issues in how we theorize about trust, measure it, test our models and apply it to a wide range of social phenomena. Trust has been one of the most rapidly growing areas of social science research because it is first so broadly relevant and second our understanding of the phenomenon has increased so substantially. Yet, our authors have also identified many unresolved issues that require further study and application. Trust remains a vibrant field of study and one which has wide-ranging applications. The eight issues we have identified in this chapter show clearly there remain many perplexing and emergent topics that require further study. Thus, we expect trust to remain a vibrant and compelling area of study for the foreseeable future, and one that invites scholars to continue to vigourously pursue these important and engaging issues.

References

Bernstein, E. S. (2012). The Transparency Paradox: A role for privacy in organizational learning and operational control. *Administrative Science Quarterly, 57*(2), 181–216.

Brower, H. H., Lester, S. W., Korsgaard, M. A., & Dineen, B. R. (2009). A closer look at trust between managers and subordinates: Understanding the effects of both trusting and being trusted on subordinate outcomes. *Journal of Management, 35*(2), 327–347.

Buckwalter, R. L. (2008). Trust and distrust in organizations: Dilemmas and approaches. *Knowledge Management Research & Practice, 6*(2), 166–168.

Cho, J. (2006). The mechanism of trust and distrust formation and their relational outcomes. *Journal of Retailing, 82*(1), 25–35.

De Jong, B. A., & Dirks, K. T. (2012). Beyond shared perceptions of trust and monitoring in teams: Implications of asymmetry and dissensus. *Journal of Applied Psychology, 97*(2), 391–406.

Dimoka, A. (2010). What does the brain tell us about trust and distrust? Evidence from a functional neuroimaging study. *MIS Quarterly, 34*(2), 373–396.

Ferrin, D. L., & Gillespie, N. (2010). Trust differences across national-societal cultures much to do or much ado about nothing. In M. N. Saunders, D. Skinner, G. Dietz, N. Gillespie & R. J. Lewicki (eds), *Organisational trust: A cultural perspective* (pp. 42–86). New York: Cambridge University Press.

Freitag, M., & Traunmüller, R. (2009). Spheres of trust: An empirical analysis of the foundations of particularised and generalised trust. *European Journal of Political Research, 48*(6), 782–803.

Gersick, C. (1988). Time and transition in work teams: Toward a new model of group development. *Academy of Management Journal, 31*(1), 9–41.

Gersick, C. (1991). Revolutionary change theories: A multilevel exploration of the punctuated equilibrium paradigm. *Academy of Management Review, 16*(1), 10–36.

Gersick, C. (1994). Pacing strategic change: The case of a new venture. *Academy of Management Journal, 37*(1), 9–45.

Gill, J., & Butler, R. (2003). Cycles of trust and distrust in joint-ventures. *European Management Journal, 14*(4), 81–89.

Griffin, M. A. (2007). Specifying organizational contexts: systematic links between contexts and processes in organizational behavior. *Journal of Organizational Behavior, 28*(7), 859–863.

Johns, G. (2006). The essential impact of context on organizational behavior. *Academy of Management Review, 31*(2), 386–408.

Kong, D. T. (2016). Exploring democracy and ethnic diversity as sociopolitical moderators for the relation-ship between age and generalized trust. *Personality and Individual Differences, 96*, 28–30.

Korsgaard, M. A., Brower, H. H., & Lester, S. W. (2015). It isn't always mutual: A critical review of dyadic trust. *Journal of Management 41*(1), 47–70.

Kramer, R. M., & Cook, K. S. (2004). *Trust and distrust in organizations: dilemmas and approaches.* New York: Russell Sage Foundation.

Kramer, R. M., & Isen, A. M. (1994). Trust and distrust – Its psychological and social dimensions. *Motivation and Emotion, 18*(2), 105–107.

McEvily, B., & Tortoriello, M. (2011). Measuring trust in organisational research: Review and recommendations. *Journal of Trust Research, 1*, 23–63.

Möllering, G. (2013). Process views of trusting and crises. In R. Bachmann and A. Zaheer (eds), *Handbook of Advances in Trust Research* (pp. 285–305). Cheltenham, UK: Edward Elgar.

Ng, T. W. H. (2015). The incremental validity of organizational commitment, organizational trust, and organizational identification. *Journal of Vocational Behavior, 88*, 154–163.

Robinson, S. (1996). Trust and breach of the psychological contract. *Administrative Science Quarterly, 41*(4), 574–599

Roe, R. A. (2008). Time in applied psychology. *European Psychologist, 13*(1), 37–52.

Roe, R. A., Waller, M. J., & Clegg, S. R. (2008). *Time in organizational research.* New York: Routledge.

Rousseau, D. M., & Fried, Y. (2001). Location, location, location: contextualizing organizational research. *Journal of Organizational Behavior, 22*(1), 1–13.

Saunders, M. N. K., Dietz, G., & Thornhill, A. (2014). Trust and distrust: Polar opposites, or independent but co-existing? *Human Relations, 67,* 639–665.

Searle, R. H., & Ball, K. S. (2004). The development of trust and distrust in a merger. *Journal of Managerial Psychology, 19*(7), 708–721.

Shipp, A. J., & Cole, M. S. (2015). Time in individual-level organizational studies: What is it, how is it used, and why isn't it exploited more often? *Annual Review of Organizational Psychology and Organizational Behavior, 2*(1), 237–260.

Shipp, A. J., & Fried, Y. (2014a). *How time impacts groups, organizations and methological choices.* Vol. 2. London: Psychology Press.

Shipp, A. J., & Fried, Y. (2014b). *How Time Impacts Individuals.* Vol. 1. London: Psychology Press.

Zak, P., Kurzban, R., & Matzner, W. (2005). Oxytocin is associated with human trustworthiness. *Hormones and Behavior, 48*(5), 522–527.

POSTWORD

Four research-based approaches to teaching trust

Michele Williams

With organizations and their executives frequently in the news for violating the trust of their customers and shareholders, U.S. business schools who train many of these executive decision makers have begun to require courses in business ethics. While ethics is a subject area that can be taught, instilling ethical behaviour and trustworthiness may be more complicated. The chapters in this book have shed light on the importance of trustworthiness not just for preventing un-ethical behaviour but for leader–follower relationships (e.g. Chapter 26 by Den Hartog, this volume; Chapter 5 by Lyu & Ferrin, this volume), entrepreneurs (Chapter 23 by Williams and Shepherd, this volume), teams (Chapter 6 by Nienaber, Holtgrave and Romeike, this volume) and inter-organizational relationships (Chapter 7 by Brattström and Bachmann, this volume; see also Fulmer & Gelfand, 2012 for a review).

Business schools and executive education centres have taken four distinct approaches to helping students and executives understand the importance of trust and fortify their own trustworthiness. In this chapter, I introduce and describe the core characteristics of these four approaches: (1) the bounded rationality approach, (2) the behavioural approach, (3) the social construction approach and (4) the relational approach. Each approach focuses on a different challenge to developing and maintaining trust. *The Bounded rationality approach*, for example, focuses both on the components of trustworthiness and on the attributions and biases associated with trust judgments. According to this approach, trustworthy behaviour is impeded both by a lack of understanding of what trustworthy behaviour entails and by specific cognitive processes that bias our ability to objectively evaluate our own trustworthiness and that of others (Kramer & Lewicki, 2010; Mayer & Norman, 2004). *The behavioural approach* focuses on behaviours associated with demonstrating trustworthiness. From the behavioural perspective, individuals need to align their actions with their trustworthy intentions (e.g. Simons, 2008). The focus here is on identifying the discrepancy between intentions, statements and actions. Although psychological biases may influence one's ability to perceive these discrepancies, the focus of this approach is on accurately measuring and decreasing discrepancies rather than on the psychological influences on our ability to perceive these discrepancies. The third approach, *the social construction approach* views characteristics of trustworthiness as interpretive acts that are co-constructed by interaction partners rather than as static traits that one can aspire to attain independent of one's specific interaction partners (Williams, 2007). The challenges to trust building and maintenance, from this approach, stem both from a lack of open communication of expectations and from an unwillingness to explore assumptions and create a shared perspective on trustworthy behaviour within a relationship (Williams, 2012). Fourth, *the relational approach* views trust as integral to high-quality connections (Dutton, 2003) and thus, an inextricable part of broader relationship building. From the relational perspective, people often allocate an inadequate amount of time, emotional energy and attention to their interpersonal relationships, and this lack of investment can either prevent initial trust development or undermine the trust within an existing relationship.

Teaching trust

All approaches to teaching trust are likely to start with research, cases and/or video clips that give students and executives a feel for the personal, professional and legal ramifications of untrustworthy behaviour as well as the organizational and financial costs of such behaviour. Stories of large auto manufacturers engaging in emissions fraud, others failing to recall life-threatening defects when first noticed and banking fraud perpetrated on low- and mid-income consumers are just a few of the current examples available for use in the classroom. These shocking but true narratives about trust abuses are often followed with classroom exercises. I argue that there are not merely a wide-variety of exercises from which faculty, consultants and trainers choose, but that these various exercises often have different underlying assumptions about the nature of trust building, trust maintenance and trust repair. This chapter seeks to clarify the relationship among (1) different approaches to teaching trust, (2) the assumptions and challenges to trustworthy behaviour that are identified by those approaches and (3) the smorgasbord of trust-related instructional exercises that we see on executive retreats and in the MBA classroom.

Bounded rationality approach

The bounded rationality approach is character-based. It posits that one of the main obstacles to building trust is understanding the core components that others use to assess one's trustworthiness. This lack of understanding stems both from not knowing the core elements of trustworthiness and not understanding the emotional and psychological biases that may influence the attributions that individuals make when evaluating their own and others' trustworthiness.

Understanding trustworthiness

Teaching the core components of trustworthiness is the foundation of this approach. This often entails instruction in Mayer, Davis and Schoorman's (1995) Ability, Benevolence, Integrity (ABI) model, which has received wide spread validation (Colquitt et al., 2007; Schoorman et al. 2007). Students, professionals and executives are taught the definition and importance of these characteristics and then engage in activities that make the experience 'real' for them. For example, Mayer and Norman (2004) have developed a scenario-based activity that involves gauging your trust in individuals who are low on one of the three attributes of trustworthiness. This activity not only opens up a discussion of trust, but also promotes a deeper understanding of its ABI antecedents.

Trust repair can also be approached from a bounded rationality perspective (Lewicki & Brinsfield, 2017 for review). For example, Kim and colleagues (2004; 2006; 2009) have linked strategies such as apology, reparations and denial to the ability to repair violations of different dimensions of trustworthiness (e.g. ability-based violations versus integrity-based violations, see also Dirks, Kim, Ferrin & Cooper, 2011; Kim, this volume). Understanding the dimensions of trustworthiness may be central to identifying the type of violation one has perpetrated and choosing an effective repair strategy.

Psychological biases

Psychological biases are the second aspect of the bounded rationality approach. Based on an attribution-bases model of trust (e.g. Tomlinson & Mayer, 2009), psychological biases, including self-serving biases and the sinister attribution error, influence the types of attributions others make for our behaviour. Jones and Shah (2015), for instance, found that initial trust in team members was primarily actor-centred. In other words, when relationships are new, it is our own past experiences, trust propensity, sinister attribution biases etc. that drive most of the variance in how trustworthy others appear to us.

Perceptions of trustworthiness are influenced by a variety of self-serving biases that people enact to maintain their self-esteem: egocentrism (overestimates of the extent to which our own behaviour is widely accepted, appropriate and, in our case, trustworthy); the self-serving attribution bias (the increased likelihood of noticing extenuating circumstances for our own questionable behaviour, while attributing others' questionable behaviour to their dispositional lack of trustworthiness); and self-confirmation bias (seeking out and attending to information that supports our perceptions of our own trustworthiness and that of others, while ignoring disconfirming information, See Bazerman & Moore, 2013).

Exercises that highlight self-serving biases often involve perspective-taking exercises that have students practise imagining a scenario from another person's point of view in addition to thinking about how contextual factors have influenced the behaviour of others. Perspective-taking exercises include hands-on exercises (see Lego® Serious Play activities, 2016) as well as cases for which each half of the class or a few individuals receive case materials with information that provides a different perspective from that in the material given to the other members of the class (e.g. Williams & Stumpf, 2008, teaching note). Contextual-mapping exercises such as described by Gittell (2016) can involve mapping the demands and interdependencies across organizational roles or departments to demonstrate how structural aspects of role interactions can contribute to difference in perspectives on trustworthy behaviour in a situation.

Kramer (1994) found that status and uncertainty can lead to paranoid or hostile attribution biases (i.e. the 'sinister attribution error') that also influence how trust is evaluated during uncertain times such as organizational changes. Exercises designed to uncover these sinister attributions often strive to demonstrate how easy it is to create unwarranted suspicion. Sitkin (2014) developed a disruptor exercise that creates suspicion and hypervigilance by first providing teams with a challenging but fun block-building task, and then indicating that there may be a team member on some of the teams who has received secret directions to try to interfere with the team's ability to reach its goal. Given this set of instructions, students experience bias first hand because they often identify honest mistakes as sinister actions and identify disruptive intent in well-meaning team members (see Table P.1 for summary and teaching exercises).

Behavioural approach

The behavioural approach is based on the assumption that there are clear-cut expectations for trustworthy behaviour that you can follow to ensure that you are building trust, such as aligning one's words with one's actions (e.g. Simons, 2002; Whitener et al., 2008). The challenge people face is that behavioural consistency is not always easy. In their paper on managerial trustworthiness, Whitener et al. (1998) identified a set of behaviours that managers can use to demonstrate benevolence and integrity and thereby build trust. Simon's (2002) introduced the concept of behavioural integrity, defined as the alignment between one's words and deeds. Behavioural integrity has been linked to follower commitment and performance (Leroy, Palanski, & Simons,

Table P.1 The four approaches to teaching trust

Teaching trust	Challenge	Key take aways	Sample exercise
Bounded rationality approach	A lack of understanding of the psychological biases that can undermine trust development.	Learn to define and recognize the core components of trustworthiness; Identify and address biases in accessing the trustworthiness of others; Identify and address biases others are likely to have in assessing your trustworthiness.	Trustworthiness scenarios (Mayer & Norman, 2004); Disruptor exercise (Sitkin, 2014); Perspective taking Lego® Serious Play (2016) (www.lego.com/en-us/seriousplay); (Role Play Case Study (Williams & Stumpf, 2008) RC Survey (Gittell, 2016); http://rcrc.brandeis.edu/survey/RC%20Survey.html
Behavioural approach	Acting in ways that are inconsistent with espoused values and trustworthiness.	Practise refraining from making promises that you are unlikely to be able to keep; Practice kindness; Reflect on gap between what you value and what you do. Try to reduce that gap.	The Integrity Interview (Simons, 2008: 132–133).
Social con-structionist approach	Lack of interpersonal understanding; Self-esteem threat sensitivity.	Perspective taking and testing is critical; Creating a third story about trustworthy interactions that builds on the two parties' perspectives.	Perspective taking (see bounded rationality exercises); Dialogue: www.pearceassociates.com/essays/comm_perspective.htm; Third story (Stone, Patton & Heen, 2010).
Relational approach	Not investing appropriate time, attention and relational energy to interpersonal relationships.	Practise relationship building with guidance; Mindfully interact with others and reflect on how you attempt to build relationships; Focus on connecting with others.	Building High Quality Connections at Lightning Speed (Dutton, 2012); Gratitude letters (Toepfer, Cichy & Peters, 2012).

2012). Teaching exercises from this approach focus on helping students identify the gap between their intended trustworthiness and their behaviour. For example, Simons (2008) provided a self-relevant, behavioural integrity interview protocol that students and executives can use as interviewers to gain insight into the gaps that others see between the interviewers' words and behaviour. Another activity has individuals compare what they say they value with the time they actually spend on activities relevant to their values in order to identify integrity gaps for themselves (Simons, 2008) (see Table P.1).

Social constructionist approach

Social constructionism posits that knowledge is not the direct result of sensory data, but rather shaped and filtered by the language and beliefs of communities (Berger & Luckmann, 1966). The social constructionist approach to teaching about trust views trust and trustworthiness as actively co-constructed between individuals (Williams, 2007; 2012). From this perspective, ability, benevolence and integrity are not individual traits that are revealed by watching how other people behave, but rather attributes based on the interpersonal understanding of another's expectations for trustworthy behaviour (Williams, 2007; Williams and Belkin, 2016). According to this approach, perspective taking, perspective testing and dialogue are critical for helping people undercover their hidden assumptions and beliefs about trustworthiness. While the need for perspective taking overlaps with the bounded rationality approach, when using the social construction approach, perspective taking is not used to uncover or correct bias but rather to provide a starting point for dialogue. Dialogue is then used to come up with a 'third story' (Stone, Patton & Heen, 2010) or a mutual understanding of what trustworthiness means within the context of a specific relationship. This co-created understanding may overlap with interaction partners' original views or may reflect a new way of seeing the relationship that could only be arrived at through dialogue. From the social constructionist perspective, the main challenges to trust are self-esteem threat and defensive behaviour that impede the open communication and respectful engagement necessary to undertake a meaningful dialogue. For instance, a study in the UK found that major obstacles to bias-changing dialogues about racial stereotypes and race relations come from majority-group members' fears about having this type of discussion (DiAngelo, 2011). Exercises to teach trust from a social construction approach not only include exercises in perspective taking but also exercises in generative listening, open communication and dialogue (see Table P.1).

Relational approach

The relational approach takes a holistic approach to trust-filled relationships, one that focuses on the emotional, cognitive and behavioural components of a relationship. The relational approach addresses both cognitive and affective aspects of trust (see van Knippenberg, this volume, for review) as components of a relationship that develop through mindful interrelating. Dutton and colleagues, for instance, have developed the concept of high-quality connections between individuals (Dutton, 2003). High-quality connection reflects 'short-term, dyadic, interactions that are positive in terms of the subjective experience of the connected individuals and the structural features of the connection' (Stephens, Heaphy & Dutton, 2012). Interactions that foster high-quality connection can build trust, but require time, emotional energy and attention. The challenge to trust development from this perspective is the lack of mindful engagement with others and the limited relational work that people are often willing to put into their interpersonal interactions, in part because they do not know this work is necessary for high-quality connections and strong trusting relationships. Teaching exercises include those that have students practise and reflect on their relationship building as well as develop practices related to gratitude, mindfulness and forgiveness – practices which have been found to strengthen interpersonal relationships (see Table P.1).

Conclusion

Over the past 20 years, researchers have contributed to an impressive stock of knowledge about the importance of trust for leaders, teams and organizations (e.g. Fulmer & Gelfand, 2012; Kramer

& Lewicki, 2010; chapters in this volume, for reviews). However, during the same period, news about executives and teams who have betrayed the trust of their employees, customers and/ or regulatory agencies has also proliferated. The next frontier may not only involve teaching ethics in business schools but also teaching about trust development – building, repairing and maintaining trust – in a systematic way that has an impact on the current and future leaders of corporate, family and non-profit businesses. This chapter identifies four approaches to teaching trust: (1) the bounded rationality approach, (2) the behavioural approach, (3) the social construction approach and (4) the relational approach. It is not meant to be a teaching handbook, it does not present a comprehensive review of all of the experiential exercises used to teach trust, but rather provides an overarching framework of the approaches to teaching trust and sample exercises that I hope can broaden the teaching of trust by allowing instructors to select from a wider variety of perspectives and by providing students and executives with more insight into the factors which affect their ability to develop the trust that they need to achieve sustainable and productive relationships within their own organizations and in collaborations with other organizations.

References

Bazerman, M. H., & Moore, D. A. (2013). *Judgment in managerial decision making.* 8th ed. New York: Wiley.

Berger, P. L., & Luckmann, T. T. (1966). *The social construction of reality: A treatise in the sociology of knowledge.* New York: Double and Company.

DiAngelo, R. (2011). *White Fragility.* Downloaded November 6, 2016: http://libjournal.uncg.edu/ijcp/article/viewFile/249/116

Dirks, K. T., Kim, P. H., Ferrin, D. L., & Cooper, C. D. (2011). Understanding the effects of substantive responses on trust following a transgression. *Organizational Behavior and Human Decision Processes, 114*(2), 87–103.

Dutton, J. E. (2003). *Energize your workplace: How to create and sustain high-quality connections at work.* Vol. 50. San Francisco, CA: John Wiley & Sons.

Dutton, J. E. (2012). Building high quality connections at lightening speed. 2012 Annual Academy of Management Meetings. First downloaded November 1, 2016. http://positiveorgs.bus.umich.edu/wp-content/uploads/Dutton-BuildingHQC-AOM2012-TeachingPOS-handout.pdf

Fulmer, C. A., & Gelfand, M. J. (2012). At what level (and in whom) we trust trust across multiple organizational levels. *Journal of Management, 38*(4), 1167–1230.

Gittell, J. H. (2016). *Transforming relationships for high performance: The power of relational coordination.* Stanford, CA: Stanford University Press.

Jones, S. L., & Shah, P. P. (2015). Diagnosing the locus of trust: A temporal perspective for trustor, trustee, and dyadic influences on perceived trustworthiness. *Journal of Applied Psychology, 101*(3), 392–414.

Kim, P. H., Dirks, K. T., & Cooper, C. D. (2009). The repair of trust: A dynamic bilateral perspective and multilevel conceptualization. *Academy of Management Review, 34*(3), 401–422.

Kim, P. H., Dirks, K. T., Cooper, C. D., & Ferrin, D. L. (2006). When more blame is better than less: The implications of internal vs. external attributions for the repair of trust after a competence- vs. integrity-based trust violation. *Organizational Behavior and Human Decision Processes, 99*(1), 49–65.

Kim, P. H., Ferrin, D. L., Cooper, C. D., & Dirks, K. T. (2004). Removing the shadow of suspicion: The effects of apology vs. denial for repairing ability vs. integrity-based trust violations. *Journal of Applied Psychology, 89*(1), 104–118.

Kramer, R. M. (1994). The sinister attribution error: Paranoid cognition and collective distrust in organizations. *Motivation and Emotion, 18*(2), 199–230.

Kramer, R. M., & Lewicki, R. J. (2010). Repairing and enhancing trust: Approaches to reducing organizational trust deficits. *The Academy of Management Annals, 4*(1), 245–277.

Lego® Serious Play (2016). *Professional development workshop.* Anaheim, CA: Academy of Management Meeting.

Leroy, H., Palanski, M. E., & Simons, T. (2012). Authentic leadership and behavioral integrity as drivers of follower commitment and performance. *Journal of Business Ethics, 107*(3), 255–264.

Lewicki, R. J., & Brinsfield, C. (2017). Trust Repair. *Annual Review of Organizational Psychology and Organizational Behavior, 4*, 287–313.

Mayer, R. C., & Norman, P. M. (2004). Exploring attributes of trustworthiness: A classroom exercise. *Journal of Management Education, 28*(2), 224–249.

Simons, T. (2002). Behavioral integrity: The perceived alignment between managers' words and deeds as a research focus. *Organization Science, 13*(1), 18–35.

Simons, T. (2008). *The Integrity Dividend: Leading by the Power of Your Word*. Hoboken, NJ: John Wiley & Sons.

Sitkin, S. (2014) Trust disruptor exercise. Workshop Presented at First International Network on Trust (FINT) 2014 Conference, Coventry, UK.

Stephens, J. P., Heaphy, E. & Dutton, J. E. (2012). High-quality connections. In K. Cameron & G. Spreitzer (eds.), *Oxford handbook of positive organizational scholarship* (pp. 385–399). New York: Oxford University Press.

Stone, D., Patton, B., & Heen, S. (2010). *Difficult conversations: How to discuss what matters most*. New York: Penguin.

Toepfer, S. M., Cichy, K., & Peters, P. (2012). Letters of gratitude: Further evidence for author benefits. *Journal of Happiness Studies, 13*(1), 187–201.

Williams, M. (2007). Building genuine trust through interpersonal emotion management: A threat regulation model of trust and cooperation across boundaries. *Academy of Management Review, 32*(2), 595–621.

Williams, M. (2012). Building and re-building trust: Why perspective taking matters. In R. Kramer, & T. L. Pittinsky (eds.), *Restoring trust: Enduring challenges and emerging answers*. New York: Oxford University Press.

Williams, M., & Belkin L. (2016). Trust maintenance: The role of interpersonal meaning construction. *Academy of Management Proceedings*. Vol. 2016. Academy of Management.

Williams, M., & Stumpf, S. A. (2008). Peter Vosek. *Journal of the International Academy for Case Studies, 14*(7), 105, case; *14*(8), 99, teaching note.

SUBJECT INDEX

Note: Page numbers in *italic* refer to Figures; page numbers in **bold** refer to Tables

549

AUTHOR INDEX

Note: Page numbers in *italic* refer to Figures; page numbers in **bold** refer to Tables

557